Drugs and Drug Policy

Drugs and Drug Policy

The Control of Consciousness Alteration

Second Edition

Clayton J. Mosher

Washington State University—Vancouver

Scott M. Akins

Oregon State University

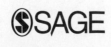

Los Angeles | London | New Delhi
Singapore | Washington DC

Los Angeles | London | New Delhi
Singapore | Washington DC

FOR INFORMATION:

SAGE Publications, Inc.
2455 Teller Road
Thousand Oaks, California 91320
E-mail: order@sagepub.com

SAGE Publications Ltd.
1 Oliver's Yard
55 City Road
London EC1Y 1SP
United Kingdom

SAGE Publications India Pvt. Ltd.
B 1/I 1 Mohan Cooperative Industrial Area
Mathura Road, New Delhi 110 044
India

SAGE Publications Asia-Pacific Pte. Ltd.
3 Church Street
#10-04 Samsung Hub
Singapore 049483

Acquisitions Editor: Jerry Westby
Editorial Assistant: MaryAnn Vail
Production Editor: Laura Barrett
Typesetter: C&M Digitals (P) Ltd.
Proofreader: Theresa Kay
Indexer: Kathy Paparchontis
Cover Designer: Scott Van Atta
Marketing Manager: Terra Schultz
Permissions Editor: Jennifer Barron

Copyright © 2014 by SAGE Publications, Inc.

Image Credits
Wikimedia Commons: 82, 99, 100, 103, 104, 110, 121, 137, 139, 142, 145
Drug Enforcement Agency: 155
Office of National Drug Control Policy: 267, 278, 281

Printed in the United States of America

Library of Congress Cataloging-in-Publication Data

Mosher, Clayton James.

Drugs and drug policy : the control of consciousness alternation / Clatyon J. Mosher, Washington State University-Vancouver; Scott M. Akins, Oregon State University.—Second edition.

pages cm
Includes bibliographical references and index.

ISBN 978-1-4522-4239-2 (pbk.: alk. paper)

1. Drug abuse—United States. 2. Drug control—United States. 3. Substance abuse—United States. I. Akins, Scott. II. Title.

HV5825.M69 2014
362.290973—dc23   2013002601

This book is printed on acid-free paper.

SUSTAINABLE FORESTRY INITIATIVE
Certified Chain of Custody
Promoting Sustainable Forestry
www.sfiprogram.org
SFI-01268
SFI label applies to text stock

13 14 15 16 17 10 9 8 7 6 5 4 3 2 1

Contents

Preface   xi

Acknowledgments   xxiv

1. Drug Controversies and Demonization   1
   Demonizing (Illegal) Drugs: The Social Construction of
      Drug "Epidemics"   3
   Glue Sniffing   5
   Marijuana   7
    The Portrayal of Marijuana: 1800s to 1960   7
    The Portrayal of Marijuana: 1960s to 1980s   12
    The Portrayal of Marijuana: 1980 and Beyond   15
   Crack Cocaine   24
   Heroin   25
   Ecstasy (MDMA)   26
   Methamphetamine   31
   Drug "Epidemics" of the 2000s and 2010s   39
   Salvia Divinorum   39
   Spice/K2   40
   Bath Salts   41
   Prescription Drugs (Synthetic Opiates)   42
   Conclusion   43
   Review Questions   44
   Internet Exercises   44

2. Theories of Drug Use   45
   Nature Theories   46
   Genetic/Biological Theories   47
   Disease Theory   51
   Psychological Theories   56
   Sociological Theories   58
    Differential Association, Social Learning, and
      Subcultural Learning Theories   58

Subcultural Learning Theories 62
Social Control/Bonding Theory 65
Lifecourse/Age-Graded Theory 67
Anomie/Strain Theories 69
Social Conflict Theory 73
Conclusion 76
Review Questions 78
Internet Exercises 78
Web Resources 79

3. The Effects of Drugs: Part I 80
U.S. Legal Drug Schedules 89
Stimulants 90
Caffeine 90
"Energy" Drinks 92
Tobacco 94
Cocaine 97
Amphetamines 103
Bath Salts 107
Ritalin, Adderall, and Other ADD Prescription Drugs 108
Ecstasy 109
Depressants 112
Alcohol 112
Barbiturates 115
Benzodiazepines 117
GHB 118
Inhalants 119
Opiates 121
Morphine 123
Heroin 124
Codeine 127
Oxycodone 128
Nonopiate Analgesics 130
Review Questions 131
Internet Exercises 132

4. The Effects of Drugs: Part II 133
Hallucinogens/Psychedelics 133
LSD 135
Psilocybin 139
Peyote and Mescaline 141
Salvia 144
DMT and Bufotenine 145
PCP and Ketamine 147
Marijuana 149
Spice/Synthetic Marijuana 155

Antidepressant Drugs 157
Aphrodisiacs/Erectile Dysfunction Drugs 160
Steroids and Other Performance-Enhancing Drugs 165
Conclusion 173
Review Questions 175
Internet Exercise 176

5. Patterns of Illegal Drug Use 177
   Self-Report Surveys 178
      Monitoring the Future 180
      Other Surveys on Adolescent Drug Use 183
      The National Survey on Drug Use and Health 184
   International Data on Adult Drug Use 185
   World Drug Report 187
   Data on Substance Use by Adult Offenders—ADAM and I-ADAM 188
      Drug Abuse Warning Network Statistics 190
   Correlates of Illegal Drug Use 194
      Age 194
      Gender/Sex 199
      Race/Ethnicity 203
      Social Class 218
      Rural/Urban Location 220
   Conclusion 223
   Review Questions 224
   Internet Exercise 224

6. Patterns of Legal Drug Use 225
   Age 225
      Use of Drugs by the Elderly 234
   Gender/Sex 237
   Race/Ethnicity 242
      African Americans 245
      Hispanics 247
      American Indians/Native Americans 249
      Asians and Pacific Islanders 251
   Social Class 253
   Geography and Rural/Urban Location 258
   Conclusion 262
   Review Questions 263
   Internet Exercises 263

7. Drug Prevention Programs 265
   Drug Education Programs 265
      D.A.R.E. 266
      Alternative Drug Education Programs 273
   Antidrug Advertising Campaigns 276
   Zero-Tolerance Policies 283

Drug Testing Policies   286
   Schools   286
   Drug Testing of Workers   291
Conclusion   297
Review Questions   299
Internet Exercises   300

8. **Drug Treatment**   301
Pharmacological Treatment Approaches   303
   Drug Agonists   305
   Drug Antagonists   312
Residential Drug Treatment Programs   317
   Therapeutic Communities   318
Compulsory Treatment Programs   322
Alcoholics Anonymous   332
   The 12 Steps of Alcoholics Anonymous   338
Outpatient Drug Treatment   343
Conclusion   346
Review Questions   348
Internet Exercises   349

9. **Policies Regulating Legal Drugs, Part I: Alcohol and Tobacco**   350
Tobacco   351
   A Brief History of Tobacco Regulation   351
   Bans on Smoking in Public Places   352
   Restrictions on Advertising and Marketing of Tobacco Products   356
   Taxes on Tobacco Products   357
   The 1998 Tobacco Settlement and Antismoking Programs   361
   International Tobacco Legislation   362
   The Future of Tobacco Regulation   363
Alcohol   365
   Temperance Movements and Prohibition in
      American History   365
   Alcohol Regulation in the Current Era   369
   Minimum Legal Drinking Age   371
   Regulating Drinking on College Campuses   374
   Drunk Driving Laws   377
Conclusion   386
Review Questions   389
Internet Exercise   390

10. **Policies Regulating Legal Drugs, Part II: Prescription and
Performance-Enhancing Drugs and Herbal Supplements**   391
Regulation of Pharmaceutical Products   392
   Early Legislation   392
   FDA Approval of Pharmaceutical Products   393

Regulating the Sale and Advertising of Prescription Drugs   401
    Restricting the Sale of Canadian Pharmaceutical Products   401
    Advertising Pharmaceutical Products   404
    The Criminal Practices of Pharmaceutical Companies   408
The Political Economy of the
    Pharmaceutical Business   410
The Future of Prescription Drug Regulation?   412
The Regulation of Performance-Enhancing Drugs   415
    The Rationale for Regulation   415
    National Collegiate Athletic Association   417
    International Olympic Committee   418
    Professional Sports   425
    Federal Government Regulation of Herbal and
      Dietary Supplements   434
Conclusion   435
Review Questions   438
Internet and Media Exercises   439

11. Policies Regulating Illegal Drugs   440
Trends in Arrests and Incarceration   441
Racial and Class-Based Inequality in
    the Application of Drug Laws   446
    "Crack Babies"   450
    "C.R.A.C.K."   453
Mandatory Minimum Sentences   453
"School Zone" Policies   458
Public Housing Evictions   459
Denial of Welfare   460
Denial of Student Aid   461
Asset Forfeiture   462
Ecstasy and the RAVE Act   466
Methamphetamine Legislation   468
Marijuana Laws   470
    Hemp   470
    Medical Marijuana   471
    The Recent War on Medical Marijuana   476
    Marijuana Legalization Measures   477
Signs of Change? Recent Changes in State Drug Laws and
    Developments at the Federal Level   480
Conclusion   484
Review Questions   486
Internet Exercises   486

12. Drug Policies in Other Countries and U.S. Influence   487
International Treaties   488

Countries With Severe Drug Policies   490
   Russia   490
   Asian and Middle Eastern Countries   491
Drug Policies in Western Countries   492
   Australia   492
   Sweden   494
   Germany   494
   Portugal   495
   Spain   497
   The Netherlands   497
   Britain   499
   Canada   503
American Influence and Intervention in Drug-Producing Countries   514
   Certification Policies   517
   Mexico and Other Central American Countries   518
   Afghanistan   520
Conclusion   521
Review Questions   523
Internet Exercise   524

Glossary   525

Bibliography   531

Index   625

About the Authors   662

Preface

The pursuit of consciousness alternation through the use of both legal and illegal psychoactive substances is a pervasive feature of humans; some scholars have even argued that the pursuit of intoxication is a basic human drive (R. Siegel 1989) and that absolute sobriety is not a natural or primary human state (Davenport-Hines 2001). In fact, there are only a few recorded instances of societies anywhere in history that have lived without the use of psychoactive substances. And while substance use and abuse have been a concern of researchers and policy makers in the United States and other countries since at least the early 1900s, a number of significant developments in the last few decades suggest that the dynamics of drug use and policies to deal with drug use are at a critical juncture.

In considering issues related to drug use and drug policy in the United States, it is useful to begin by noting some rather strange paradoxes. To take just one example, it is estimated that several million Americans use antidepressant drugs. These drugs are widely advertised and marketed, and the individuals who consume them generally experience no legal penalties for their consumption of these substances. At the same time, approximately half a million individuals, the majority of whom are members of minority groups, languish in American jails and prisons for possession and trafficking in consciousness-altering substances that the United States has deemed to be illegal. In fact, the increasing stringency of drug laws has been one of the primary factors associated with unprecedented levels of incarceration in the United States over the past 30 years (Austin & Irwin 2012). As Sullum (2003a) comments, "if an unhappy person takes heroin, he is committing a crime. If he takes Prozac, he is treating his depression" (p.284). Similarly, in questioning the distinction between legal and illegal drugs in the United States, Pollan (1999) notes,

> "You would be hard pressed to explain the taxonomy of chemicals underpinning the drug war to an extraterrestrial. Is it, for example, addictiveness that causes this society to condemn a drug? (No; nicotine is legal, and millions of Americans have battled addictions to prescription drugs.) So, then, our inquisitive alien might ask, is safety the decisive factor? (Not really; over the counter and prescription drugs kill more than 45,000 Americans every year, while there is no risk of death from smoking marijuana.) Is it drugs associated with violent

behavior that your society condemns? (If so, alcohol would be illegal). Perhaps then it is the promise of pleasure that puts a drug beyond the pale? (That would rule out alcohol as well as Viagra)."

It is also important to note that the traffic in drugs—both legal and illegal—is big business. It is estimated that the international illicit drug business generates hundreds of billions of dollars in trade annually, representing about eight percent of all international trade—about the same percentage as tourism and the oil industry (Davenport-Hines 2001). At the same time, consumer spending on prescription drugs was estimated at $319 billion in 2011 (IMS Health 2012). In this context, it is notable that while the United States government enacts policies and devotes considerable monetary resources to punishing those who use mind-altering drugs produced in countries such as Colombia, Mexico, and Afghanistan, it has also enacted policies that serve to expand domestic and international markets for mind-altering substances manufactured by companies such as Anheuser-Busch, RJ, Reynolds, and large pharmaceutical companies, among others.

The United States has achieved this through the promotion and dissemination of Drug War propaganda, which, as Bruce Alexander (1990) has noted, creates a "systematic reduction in people's ability to think intelligently about drugs" (p. 71). Part of our goal in this book then, is to deconstruct this drug war propaganda, to assist readers in thinking intelligently about drugs, and to critically assess our current drug policies with respect to both legal and illegal drugs.

MISINFORMATION AND DISTORTION—A NOTE ON SOURCES USED IN THIS BOOK

In discussing drugs, their effects, who uses them, and policies regulating them, it is obviously important to review the scientific literature; this book includes extensive coverage of research published in medical, scientific, social-scientific, and other academic journals. However, unlike most authors writing on the topic of drugs, we also draw extensively from print and Internet media discussions of drugs. We adopt this strategy because we believe, based on our teaching experience and participation in conferences and public forums on these issues, that most of the general public derive their (often mis-) information about drugs, their effects, and drug policies from these sources. While a considerable proportion of the discussion of drugs in print media sources, is, in fact, derived from scientific literature, reporters and journalists, either through ignorance or design, often misinterpret the scientific information in ways that may serve to mislead the general public. It is thus necessary to include, and critically review, media materials on drugs.

We also draw on materials from organizations such as the National Organization for the Reform of Marijuana Laws (NORML), the Marijuana Policy Project (MPP), the Drug Police Alliance (DPA), and Common Sense for Drug Policy, all of which have been critical of U.S. drug policies and have called for reform. We are aware that some will view these organizations as "advocacy groups" in the drug policy context, and we would tend to agree. However, we find many of the arguments made by these organizations to be compelling; as will be demonstrated, unlike several "official government " publications and commentaries on drugs and drug policies from bureaucracies such as the federal government's Office of National Drug Control Policy (ONDCP), to support their arguments for drug law reform, these so-called advocacy groups typically refer to actual scientific studies in their publications. In contrast, much of the information on drugs published by official government organizations is blatantly misleading, and in some cases, simply false. It is thus important to critically review the information disseminated by these government sources because, as will be discussed, this information has had a direct impact on policies regulating both licit and illicit drugs.

Over the last few decades, much of the misinformation on drugs has been presented by "drug czars" appointed by U.S. presidents. For example, in criticizing the more relaxed approach to drugs in the Netherlands, General Barry McCaffrey (drug czar under President Clinton) commented, "The Dutch experience is not something we want to model. It's an unmitigated disaster" (as quoted in J. Gray 2001). McCaffrey claimed that all youth in Amsterdam's Vondel Park were "stoned zombies" and stated that "the murder rate in Holland is double that of the United States. . . . that's drugs" (as quoted in Reinarman 2002, p.127). In justifying this claim, the drug czar noted that there were 17.58 murders per 100,000 population in the Netherlands, compared to 8.22 per 100,000 in the United States. However, the Dutch homicide rate cited by McCaffrey combined homicides and attempted homicides in the same category: the actual Dutch homicide rate was 1.8 per 100,000 or less than one-quarter the U.S. rate (Reinarman 2002). When an official from the Dutch embassy questioned McCaffrey's deputy drug czar about these misleading statistics, the deputy's response was, "Let's say that's right. What you're left with is that they [the Dutch] are a much more violent society and more inept [at murder] and that's not much to brag about" (as quoted in Reinarman 2002, p.129).

In another example of distortion and misinformation propagated by federal government officials, John Walters, the drug czar under President George W. Bush, pointed to data from the Monitoring the Future Study (a study that measures drug use among young people in the United States) and claimed that "this survey confirms that our drug prevention efforts are working" (as quoted in J. Cole 2005). But as Cole points out, a comparison of the 1991 and 2002 Monitoring the Future data indicated that over this period, marijuana use increased by 30% for 12th-grade students, 128% for 10th- grade students, and 188% for 8th-grade students. These data prompted Cole to ask, "How can John Walters say this study shows our drug prevention efforts are working? Could the drug warriors possibly be lying to us?" Throughout this book we will critically assess the contentions of government officials in their support of the United States' continuing war on drugs.

THE NEED FOR DRUG LAW REFORM

It is important to note that in addition to the groups mentioned above who have advocated for drug policy reform, several prominent Americans and international figures, including leading conservatives, politicians, judges, and law enforcement officials have called for drug law reform. Former CBS news anchor Walter Cronkite (2006) noted that the casualties of the war on drugs "are the wasted lives of our citizens," and commented that "amid the clichés of the drug war, our country has lost sight of scientific facts. Amid the rhetoric of our leaders, we've become blind to reality. The war on drugs, as it is currently fought, is too expensive, and too inhumane." Earlier, Nobel-Prize winning economist Milton Friedman argued in a 1998 *New York Times* editorial,

"Can any policy however high-minded, be moral if it leads to widespread corruption, imprisons so many, has so racist an effect, destroys our inner cities, wreaks havoc on misguided and vulnerable individuals, and brings death and destruction to foreign countries?" (cited in Drug Policy Alliance 2006c).

Similarly, in the introduction to a series of articles about American drug policy published in 1996, the editors of the conservative magazine *National Review* commented,

"it is our judgment that the war on drugs has failed, that it is diverting intelligent energy away from how to deal with the problem of addiction, that it is wasting our resources, and that it is encouraging civil, judicial, and penal procedures associated with police states" ("Introduction 1996).

Among the contributors to this edition of *National Review* was William F. Buckley, Jr. (founder of the magazine) who lamented the tremendous costs (both monetary and social) of the war on drugs and recommended legalization of the sale of most currently illegal drugs, except to minors (Buckley et al. 1996). In the same edition of *National Review* , Kurt Schmoke, then mayor of Baltimore, Maryland, referred to the United States' war on drugs as a "domestic Vietnam" and called for medicalization or regulated distribution of drugs (Buckley et al. 1996). Under this system, the government would set up a scheme to place drug addicts in the public health care system, and would control the price, distribution, and purity of addictive substances.

An increasing number of current and former law enforcement officials have also called for drug law reform. Former Kansas City and San Jose police chief Joseph McNamara referred to the extensive corruption in law enforcement created by the drug war, and commented,

"We are familiar with the perception that the first casualty in any war is truth. Eighty years of drug war propaganda has so influenced public opinion that most politicians believe they will lose their jobs if opponents can claim they are soft on drugs and crime" (Buckley et al. 1996).

Norm Stamper, who served as chief of the Seattle police department for six years, wrote a book (Stamper 2005a) and an op-ed article that appeared in the *Los Angeles Times* and several other newspapers, in which he argued "it's time to accept drug use as a right of adult Americans, treat drug abuse as a public health problem, and end the madness of this unwinnable war" (2005b). Stamper further commented,

"It's not a stretch to conclude that our draconian approach to drug use is the most injurious domestic policy since slavery" and called for the legalization of *all* drugs (not just marijuana) including heroin, cocaine, methamphetamine, psychotropics, mushrooms, and LSD (Stamper 2005b).

While it is certainly true that they do not represent the views of all—or even a majority of—criminal justice system officials, perhaps the most prominent example of law enforcement officials' critique of the drug war is represented by a group known as Law Enforcement Against Prohibition (LEAP). This organization was formed in 2002 and consists of more than 13,000 former and current criminal justice system officials (police officers, judges, prosecutors, prison wardens and others) (Mendoza 2010) who

"believe the existing drug policies have failed in their intended goals of addressing the problems of crime, drug abuse, addiction, juvenile drug use, stopping the flow of illegal drugs into this country, and the internal sale and use of illegal drugs" (LEAP n.d.).

LEAP's mission is to reduce the harmful consequences created by the war on drugs and to "lessen the incidence of death, disease, crime, and addiction by ultimately ending drug prohibition." Jack Cole (2005) a member of LEAP, echoing some of the comments above, referred to the war on drugs as a "total and abject failure. . . . a war on our people—our own people—our children, our parents, ourselves" and recommended the legalization of all drugs "so we can regulate and control them and keep them out of the hands of our children."

In addition to the myriad of domestic problems created by the war on drugs, internationally, the drug wars have contributed to increases in the number of people with HIV/AIDs. An estimated 33 million people worldwide are HIV positive, and nearly 20% of injection drug users are HIV-positive (Global Commission on Drug Policy, 2011; Ludwig 2012). Drug laws that treat these individuals as criminals prevent them from seeking treatment for their condition, and can lead to higher HIV rates in prisons and jails.

In 2011, former U.S. president Jimmy Carter (who in a 1977 message to Congress recommended decriminalization of marijuana possession) wrote an editorial in the *New York Times* in which he argued "To make drug policies more humane and more effective, the American government should support and enact the reforms of the Global Commission on Drug Policy" (Carter 2011).

While we realize that many reading this book will have considerable difficulty accepting arguments in favor of the legalization of drugs, and we are not necessarily advocating outright legalization of all drugs, these arguments must be placed in the context of an evaluation of the successes and failures of current drug policies. The apparent goal of drug policy is to reduce, if not eliminate, drug abuse and the social harms associated with drug abuse. However, as the commentaries above indicate, and as will be further demonstrated in this book, not only have these goals not been realized, but current drug policy has resulted in tremendous social and economic costs and significant ancillary harms. As such, serious consideration must be given to drug policy reform.

CHAPTER OUTLINES

In Chapter 1, we address the widespread use of psychoactive substances across time and societies. The ubiquity of drug use is particularly interesting given that the use of *all* forms of drugs—both legal and illegal—involves some level of risk. The substantial level of harm posed by the use of legal drugs contrasts with the typical view of some drugs as "good" and others as "bad." Accordingly, this chapter demonstrates how legal and illegal drugs are similar and different and addresses the way certain drugs have been demonized in order to justify their illegal status.

A variety of strategies have been employed to emphasize the dangers of (illegal) drugs over the past century. Common tactics include claims that illegal drug use is responsible for the majority of crime that occurs in society; that illegal drugs possess unique powers that encourage otherwise normal people to engage in bizarre and often violent behaviors while under the influence of these drugs; that minorities, immigrants, and foreign nationals are the primary users and traffickers in illegal drugs; and that illegal drugs (in contrast to legal drugs) pose a unique threat to the health of children. Finally, illegal drugs have been demonized through a misrepresentation of the scientific evidence on the effects of these drugs, particularly by government agencies.

The intent of Chapter 1 is not to ignore or minimize the substantial harm caused by the use of drugs in society, but rather to properly assess the threat posed by the use of particular drugs and to demonstrate that both legal and illegal drugs pose significant risks. Socially constructed drug epidemics tend to exaggerate and distort the nature and magnitude of drug problems, making appropriate prevention, treatment, and drug control responses more difficult.

In Chapter 2, we address a variety of theoretical explanations for substance use and dependency. Theories of substance use are designed to explain why drug use and abuse occurs and why it varies across different circumstances and social conditions. We summarize nature, genetic/biological, psychological, and sociological theories of substance use and examine the scientific evidence with respect to the validity of these theories.

The nature perspective contends that people have a universal and innate drive to alter their consciousness and that substance use is simply one way in which humans express this drive. Genetic/biological explanations of substance use emphasize that inherited predispositions to substance use largely determine whether an individual will use, and especially abuse, psychoactive drugs. The disease model of addiction is often confused with the genetic model, but there are important differences between these two explanations. Like the genetic model, most versions of the disease theory assert that substance use and addiction are related to genetic predispositions; however, the disease model makes several ideological assumptions (e.g., that abstinence is the only remedy for alcoholics and that alcoholism invariably grows worse, ultimately resulting in death) that are not supported by scientific research.

Psychological perspectives on substance use include the self-derogation perspective, which contends that people use psychoactive substances as a result of a lack of self-esteem. According to this perspective, individuals engage in substance use and abuse in the pursuit of positive affirmation from others—affirmation that they have not received from more conventional sources. Another predominantly psychological perspective is "problem behavior" theory, which asserts that substance use is just one type of behavior that is typical of a "problem behavior personality." The traits that characterize this personality (e.g., risk taking, rebellion, pleasure seeking) are not necessarily pathological in and of themselves; however, they encourage behaviors that often conflict with social and legal norms.

Sociological perspectives on drug use addressed in Chapter 2 include social learning theory, social bonding theory, anomie or "strain" theories, social development theories, and conflict theories. Social learning theory emphasizes how interactions with others, especially intimate others, may contribute to substance use when people learn positive messages that encourage substance use. Social bonding theory contends that substance use results when a person is not sufficiently integrated into conventional society in terms of his or her relationships to family, spouses, children, conventional friends, employment, education, religion, school, community organizations, and other institutions in society. Anomie or strain theories of substance use emphasize the importance of economic and emotional stressors in the etiology of substance use and abuse, while developmental theories focus on changes in substance use across the life course. Finally, conflict perspectives of substance use emphasize the importance of power differentials in society in influencing substance use and drug policies and pay particular attention to differential outcomes across social class and race/ethnicity in criminal justice system responses to illegal drug use and trafficking.

In Chapters 3 and 4, we discuss several categories of drugs based on their physiological, psychological, and behavioral effects. Based on these effects, psychoactive substances—which include herbal supplements, over-the-counter medications, prescription drugs, and other legal and illegal substances—are grouped into the following categories: stimulants, depressants, opiates, hallucinogens, PCP and ketamine, inhalants, marijuana, antidepressants, aphrodisiacs, and steroids and other performance-enhancing drugs.

As noted above, the illegal status of certain drugs is often based on rhetoric that illegal substances are distinct in terms of the harms they pose to society and the user. To assess the potential of a drug to cause harm to the individual and society, multiple dimensions of risk must be considered simultaneously. In addition to their psychoactive effects, drugs can be assessed in terms of their ability to generate physical dependence, psychological dependence, and both short- and long-term adverse health effects in users. When substances are evaluated across all these dimensions of harm, it is clear that there are few differences between legal and illegal drugs.

Chapters 5 and 6 examine patterns of legal and illegal drug use in society. Information on the use and abuse of illegal drugs is derived primarily from several large-scale surveys and selected compilations of criminal justice and health statistics, as well as observational studies and interviews with drug users and officials in drug-related fields. These data have enabled researchers to demonstrate that drug use is more common in some populations than others.

The key demographic factors that influence legal and illegal drug use are age, gender, race/ethnicity, social class and urbanity. Drug use is more common in late adolescence and early adulthood than at any other point in the lifecourse. Gender is another important predictor of illegal drug use because males are more likely than females to use illegal drugs. Drug use also varies by race/ethnicity, but in contrast to what is commonly believed, Whites are among the most likely to use both illegal and legal drugs. Where data allow, in Chapters 5 and 6 we examine the divergent patterns of drug use that exist within certain racial/ethnic subgroups (e.g., Hispanics and Asians), illustrating that drug use varies both within as well as across race/ethnicity. We also note that racial differences in drug use are linked to social class and review the relationship between social class and substance use and abuse. Finally, residence characteristics, such as whether one lives in an urban area as opposed to a small town or rural area, are important for understanding drug use.

In Chapter 7, (Chapter 8 in the first edition) we examine issues related to drug use prevention, which involves a wide variety of strategies intended to limit the use and abuse of psychoactive drugs. While research indicates that prevention programs focused on reducing drug risk factors and enhancing drug protective factors can be effective, current prevention expenditures and efforts are primarily invested in programs that are based on narrow and misguided conceptions of the reality of drug use. Among these programs are select drug education programs (e.g., D.A.R.E.), anti-drug advertising campaigns primarily directed at youth, zero tolerance drug policies in schools, and drug testing (as applied in schools and the workplace).

Although several jurisdictions in the United States have discontinued this program, D.A.R.E. was the largest school-based drug education program in the country for two decades. Nearly every scientific study of D.A.R.E. found the program to be ineffective in reducing drug use. This is largely because D.A.R.E. (similar to many other drug education programs) is based on a number of problematic assumptions about drug use, including that (1) experimentation with drugs is not a common aspect of youth culture; (2) any drug use is either equivalent to, or will eventually lead to, drug *abuse*; (3) marijuana is the gateway to hard drugs such as heroin and cocaine; and (4) exaggerating the risks associated with drug use will deter young people from experimenting with drugs. While the D.A.R.E program has undergone changes in recent years, the fundamental "just say no" to drugs message of the program has persisted.

Anti-drug advertising campaigns are another form of drug prevention efforts that have been found to be ineffective at reducing drug use by youth. These advertising campaigns often present false and sometimes ridiculous information about illegal drug use, and they typically pay little attention to the dangers of tobacco, alcohol, and prescription drug use. Like the ineffectiveness of D.A.R.E., the ineffectiveness of these campaigns is tied to how young people respond to the messages promoted. The campaigns may have a counterproductive effect on youth drug use because young people tend to reject all anti-drug messages when they identify some as being false, or because they encourage young people to desire and seek out something that is forbidden (known as "reactance").

School-based "zero tolerance" policies typically involve the suspension or expulsion of students who are in possession of or under the influence of drugs on school property. Advocates of these policies believe that they are beneficial because they send a clear message that drug use will not be tolerated and they supposedly keep drug-using youth away from the rest of the student body. Part of this strategy involves drug testing students who want to participate in athletics or other extracurricular activities. These policies have little preventative effect on drug use among students who remain in school, and they may, in fact, encourage drug use by those young people who are most at risk.

Drug testing in the workplace is another widely implemented prevention strategy in the United States. We do not dispute that there are occupations for which drug testing is appropriate in the interest of public safety, but workplace drug testing outside such contexts is increasingly widespread and is typically justified as being an effective deterrent to drug use that will increase worker productivity and company profits. However, scientific research does not identify a preventive effect of drug testing for employee drug use, and there is little evidence to suggest that these programs increase worker productivity. In part, this is because the drug that is most likely to be identified in drug tests (by far) is marijuana, due to the fact that it remains detectable in the urine for weeks after use. Marijuana is far less likely to limit productivity than is alcohol, and the illegal drugs that would be more likely to negatively influence worker productivity (e.g., heroin, cocaine, amphetamines) become undetectable in the urine within days and are thus rarely identified by drug tests. Drug testing may also limit productivity because it creates a negative work environment that alienates workers from their employers.

Chapter 8 (Chapter 9 in the first edition) provides an overview of the five broad categories of drug treatment currently available and reviews the evidence on their effectiveness. Pharmacological drug treatment involves the use of drugs or medications to treat substance abuse. This form of treatment can be temporary, long term, or permanent in nature. Temporary forms of pharmacological treatment involve using one drug to relieve withdrawal symptoms or otherwise facilitate the goal of abstinence or reduced use of another drug. Long-term or permanent pharmacological treatment involves use of a drug in the belief that the new drug will reduce or eliminate the use of a more problematic drug (e.g., methadone maintenance for heroin addicts).

Long-term residential drug treatment programs, the most notable being therapeutic communities, involve treatment provided to patients who live in a treatment facility for periods of up to two years. The therapeutic community model typically views drug abuse as only one symptom of a broader problem that afflicts the individual. Because of this, the re-socialization of the individual is thought to be necessary to achieve positive post-treatment outcomes.

Compulsory drug treatment involves treatment that is mandated in some way by the criminal justice system. While the specific strategies are diverse, this can involve treatment in prison or in the larger community. Among the most popular forms of compulsory treatment are drug courts, which allow individuals to participate in drug treatment in lieu of prison, with the understanding that sanctions (including the possibility of incarceration) may result if the individual does not comply with the requirements of the treatment program as agreed upon in court.

Alcoholics Anonymous, 12-step, and related "peer support" programs involve treatment in which individuals identified as alcoholics or addicts attend meetings in their community with other people identified as alcoholics or addicts, enabling them to draw on each other for support and understanding in their struggle with addiction. Alcoholics Anonymous (A.A.) represents by far the largest drug treatment "program" in the world. While the central tenets of the A.A. model—including that alcoholics are afflicted with an incurable disease characterized by a loss of control over alcohol and that total abstinence is the only effective means of treatment—are not supported by scientific research, these groups have helped many individuals with their problem drinking, largely because of the peer-support network and structure provided by the program.

The need for drug treatment from both a humanitarian and economic standpoint is clear. Studies of treatment efficacy find that many programs are useful in terms of reducing drug use, reducing criminal activity, and increasing levels of employment. As such, treatment is far more cost effective and humanitarian than dealing with drug problems exclusively through the criminal justice system.

Chapters 9 and 10 address the regulation of legal drugs. Chapter 9 (Chapter 10 in the first edition) focuses on the regulation of tobacco and alcohol while Chapter 10 (Chapter 11 in the first edition) examines policies regulating prescription drugs, performance-enhancing substances, and herbal supplements. Many of the legal substances whose regulation we cover in these chapters are, in fact, more harmful, both in terms of their effects on individual users and the larger society, than drugs that are currently categorized as illegal in the United States.

The apparent goals of policies designed to regulate legal and illegal drugs are the same: to prevent drug misuse and abuse and minimize the harms to society. However, the nature of regulation for legal and illegal drugs is fundamentally different. The regulation of illegal drugs relies heavily on punitive criminal justice system responses, while the regulation of legal drugs involves controlling access to them, taxing them, and in some cases, dealing with the harmful consequences associated with the use of these drugs.

Another fundamental difference between policies regulating illegal and legal drugs is that the companies who produce legal drugs have an advantage in marketing and selling their respective products that is not enjoyed by those who sell illegal substances. The profits associated with the sale of legal drugs, including tobacco, alcohol, and prescription drugs, are tremendous, and the companies manufacturing these products have substantial political and economic power, which they use to influence legislators who create policies to regulate these substances. While current laws allow companies to sell their legal drug products, it is also important to consider how they are dealt with by government authorities when they are found to be in violation of the (already comparatively weak) laws designed to regulate them.

The pronounced lack of regulation for alcohol and tobacco is particularly notable when placed in the context of the levels of harm associated with use of these substances. As one indication of their level of harm, in the United States, the annual number of deaths attributable to the use of tobacco and alcohol is roughly 30 times the annual number of deaths attributable to the use of all illicit drugs combined. While modern alcohol and tobacco policies have been enacted with the laudable goal of reducing alcohol- and tobacco-related harm, in practice, some of these policies are relatively effective, but some are totally ineffective and serve to exacerbate problems.

Chapter 9 thus examines attempts to regulate the consumption of tobacco through bans on public smoking, restrictions on the advertising and marketing of tobacco products, and taxes on the sale of these products. The chapter also addresses age limits for the purchase and consumption of alcohol, alcohol interventions targeted at college populations, and policies designed to reduce drunk driving.

The regulation of prescription drugs is addressed in Chapter 10. We recognize that millions of people benefit from the products manufactured by pharmaceutical companies, but note that the motivation of these companies to increase their profits often takes precedence over more general public health concerns. Several unsafe drugs have been aggressively marketed by these companies and used by consumers, resulting in significant numbers of injuries and deaths. Perhaps more disturbingly, pharmaceutical companies have used their considerable political and monetary power to influence the Food and Drug Administration and to shape legislation regulating their products.

Chapter 10 also examines the regulation of performance-enhancing drugs and herbal supplements. In our discussion of performance-enhancing drugs, we discuss the rationale for the regulation of drugs in sport and note that until fairly recently, federal and state governments allowed various sports organizations to create their own policies to regulate these substances. We also examine the regulation of these drugs across a variety of sports, noting the considerable variation that exists in terms of the stringency of these policies. Our discussion of the regulation of dietary/herbal supplements points out that these substances are associated with tens of thousands of adverse health outcomes in users in any given year. Despite this considerable level of harm, the regulation of dietary/herbal supplements is even more lax than the regulation of pharmaceutical products.

Chapter 11 (chapter 7 in the first edition) presents a critical examination of current policies dealing with illegal drugs in the United States, focusing on issues of effectiveness in achieving their stated goals, economic and social costs, and unintended consequences resulting from these policies. Several Western countries treat drug use and dependency primarily as public health issues, but the United States has a long history of addressing drug problems through the criminal justice system. Our review of U.S. policies suggests that criminal justice responses to drug use do little or nothing to reduce drug use in the general population, while they simultaneously create a number of social and economic problems. The most problematic consequences of these policies are that they substantially increase prison populations and justice system expenditures, with a disproportionately negative impact on members of minority groups and the lower social cases.

While "wars on drugs" have been virtually continuous throughout the 20th century and into the 21st century in the United States, the most recent war on drugs, which began in the mid-1980s, has resulted in an intensification of the criminal justice system response to drug use. Annual arrests for drug use have increased substantially since the mid-1980s, average sentences for drug crimes are considerably longer, and the number of people incarcerated for drug offenses has increased exponentially. These policies have also had a disparate impact on the lower class and members of minority groups. Despite the fact that African-Americans and Hispanics use illegal drugs less frequently or in approximately the same proportion as Whites, the consequences of drug policies fall disproportionately on minorities in terms of arrests, prosecutions, incarcerations, and a host of additional social and monetary costs.

While the United States' policies toward illegal drugs were apparently implemented with the goal of preventing and reducing drug use and drug-related harm, after thirty years and billions of dollars in criminal justice system and other expenditures, it is clear that these policies have failed to achieve these goals, and they have also created substantial ancillary harms in the process. Although there are some signs of a softening of drug policies, particularly at the level of individual states, fundamental change seems unlikely to occur.

In Chapter 12, we compare and contrast the drug policies of a sample of countries with those of the United States, and also critically examine the U.S. government's efforts to influence drug policies in some of these countries, particularly in Canada and Latin America. We consider countries that have adopted very severe penalties for the use, sale, and production of drugs (e.g., China and Indonesia) as well as countries that place more emphasis on the principles of harm minimization or harm reduction (e.g., Canada, Portugal, the Netherlands, and most Western European countries).

For many countries, the shift to drug policies based on harm reduction transpired in recognition of the substantial challenges and costs, both human and financial, that accompany drug criminalization and the rigorous enforcement of drug laws. Drug laws that are disproportionately based on criminalization and enforcement tend to do little or nothing to reduce the level of drug use in the general population, while at the same time creating a vast array of additional problems. In large part, this is because the policies do nothing to reduce the demand for psychoactive substances. Such policies are least defensible when they target "soft" drugs such as marijuana because they tend to cost society a great deal and result in considerable harm to users in their attempt to prevent the use of a drug that, in many cases, is no worse than available legal drugs.

Advocates of harm-reduction policies in many countries have emphasized that the damage done by the response to drug use must be weighed against the harms posed by drug use itself. Harm-reduction efforts aimed at "hard" drug use are more controversial than those aimed at marijuana. Some have nothing to do with the legal status of a drug (e.g., needle exchange programs) and simply attempt to minimize the negative consequences associated with heroin and other intravenous drug use. Other harm reduction approaches, such as heroin maintenance programs are much more controversial because they provide users with illegal drugs. Advocates of these programs remind us that these approaches in no way "approve" of heroin use, but consistent with the harm reduction approach, they attempt to minimize severe drug problems (c.g., high rates of overdose and HIV infection) that have not been effectively managed under existing drug policies.

Several countries—in particular the United States—have attempted to prevent domestic drug use by eliminating the production of drugs in other countries. These "supply side" efforts to reduce drug use (e.g., crop eradication) face many challenges. Such policies do nothing to reduce the substantial demand for drugs in Western countries. In addition, the generally impoverished residents of underdeveloped countries have a strong incentive to produce illegal drugs, so eliminating one source of drugs does not reduce supply to Western markets; it simply relocates drug growth and production to some other area.

Future drug policies should consider the empirical evidence on the harms posed by particular drugs and enact laws that do more good than harm. The shift of most developed countries (and a growing number of underdeveloped countries) to approaches that are based on harm minimization, and the lack of substantial increases in drug use following such policy changes, suggests that the United States needs to reconsider its strict criminal justice system approach to regulating currently illegal drugs.

PREFACE TO THE 2ND EDITION

As noted above, we have reconfigured the chapters for the second edition and several chapters have been restructured and substantially re-written. We have also attempted to make the second edition more "student friendly" with the addition of several more exhibits, "boxed material," graphs and charts, and additional questions and internet exercises at the end of each chapter. Data on patterns and trends in substance use have been revised to reflect the most current information available on these issues, and recent policy changes in drug laws in both the United States and other countries are included.

This edition of the book includes more than 500 additional references. However we include much of the material from the first edition, because in several of the domains covered, changes have not been been particularly significant.

In the fall 2012 elections, voters in the states of Washington and Colorado passed initiatives to legalize marijuana. In addition, the state of Massachusetts became the 18th state to legalize marijuana for medicinal purposes. While it remains to be seen how the federal government will respond to the legalization measures in Washington and Colorado, these developments in the United States and in several other countries suggest that the prospects for progressive drug law reform are promising.

Acknowledgments

We would like to acknowledge the contributions of Chad Smith, Franci Benson, Laurie Drapela, and Janet Westendorf, who read and commented on earlier versions of chapters of the first edition of the book and made suggestions for the inclusion of additional materials.

Although some of these reviewers did not agree with some (much?) of what we write here, their suggestions served to improve this manuscript. These reviewers include David Allen of the University of New Orleans; Tammy Anderson of the University of Delaware; Don Barrett, California State University, San Marcos; Deborah Baskin, California State University, Los Angeles; Joseph Bebo, University of Massachusetts, Boston; Michelle Brown, Ohio University; Jennifer Butters, Centre for Addiction and Mental Health, Toronto; Gini Deibert, Texas State University, San Marcos; Peter Fenton, Kennesaw State University; Anne Hatcher, Metropolitan State College, Denver; James Hawdon, Virginia Polytechnic and State University; Jerry Himmelstein, Amherst College; Darrell Irwin, University of North Carolina at Wilmington; Barbara Kail, Fordham University Graduate School of Social Sciences; Sheila Katz, Sonoma State University; Robert O. Keel, University of Missouri, St. Louis; David N. Khey, University of Florida; Tina Livingston, St. Cloud State University; Mathai Vairamon Mathew, Texas Southern University; Scott Maggard, Old Dominion University; Carl Maida, California State University, Northridge; Sylvia Mignon, University of Massachusetts, Boston; Leah Moore, University of Central Florida; Kelly Mosel-Talavera, Texas State University, San Marcos; Bryan Payne, Old Dominion University; Aaron Peeks, University of Nebraska, Lincoln; Adam Rafalovich, Texas Tech University; Gregory Rosenboom, University of Nebraska, Lincoln; Ronnie Swartz, Humbold State University; Bobby Sykes, University of New Mexico; Ken Szymkowiak, Chaminade University of Honolulu; Alex Thomas, SUNY Oneonta; Shelly Watkins Fichtenkort, Modesto Junior College; and Lisa Anne Zilney, Montclair State University. Taj Mahon-Haft contributed to portions of this book.

We are also indebted to several scholars whose work has shaped our approach to thinking about drugs and drug policies: Bruce Alexander, Neil Boyd, Edward Brecher, Ethan Nadelmann, and Andrew Weil, to name just a few.

Finally, we would like to thank the staff at SAGE Publications, including MaryAnn Vail, Scott Van Atta, Jennifer Barron, and Laura Barrett. We are particularly indebted to our editor Jerry Westby, whose patience and sense of humor (and tolerance of our attempts at humor) throughout the various stages of preparation of this manuscript have been invaluable.

CHAPTER 1

Drug Controversies and Demonization

"Drugs appeal to us because they deliver a variety of moods and states not immediately available from our surrounding realities. These may take in complete relaxation, ecstatic happiness, the negation of suffering, radically transformed perceptions, or just a sense of being alert and full of potential energy" (Walton, 2002).

Drug use is ubiquitous in American society and throughout the world. The U.S. Substance Abuse and Mental Health Services Administration's National Survey on Drug Use and Health estimated that in 2010, 22.6 million Americans aged 12 or older, or 8.9% of the population in that age group, used an illegal drug during the month prior to the survey (Substance Abuse and Mental Health Services Administration [SAMHSA], 2011). The same survey indicated that 131.3 million people (51.8% of the population aged 12 or older) were current (past month) users of alcohol, while 69.6 million reported current use of a tobacco product in 2010. The use of prescription drugs is also widespread—almost half (47.9%) of the population takes at least one prescription medicine, and one in five (21.4%) used at least three in 2010 (SAMHSA, 2011). In 2010, more than 3.7 billion prescriptions were filled at retail pharmacies in the United States (this figure does not include mail, Internet, and other types of prescription purchases; Kaiser Family Foundation, 2011), and the $234.1 billion spent on prescriptions in 2008 was nearly six times higher than the amount spent in 1990. And in 2010, an estimated seven million Americans (2.7% of the population) reported use of prescription drugs for nonmedical purposes (SAMHSA, 2011).

The widespread use of drugs, both legal and illegal, is by no means restricted to the United States. The United Nations Office on Drugs and Crime (UNODC) estimates that approximately 210 million people (roughly 5% of the world's population aged 15 to 64) used illegal drugs at least once in the past month (2011), and the retail value of the world trade in illicit drugs is at least $322 billion (United Nations World Drug Report, 2007). Although the estimates vary widely, globally,

> Elephants, like many of us, enjoy a good malted beverage when they can get it. At least twice in the past ten years, herds in India have stumbled upon barrels of rice beer, drained them with their trunks, and gone on drunken rampages. . . . Howler monkeys, too, have a taste for things fermented. In Panama, they've been seen consuming overripe palm fruit at the rate of ten stiff drinks in twenty minutes. Even flies have a nose for alcohol. They home in on its scent to lay their eggs in ripening fruit, ensuring their larvae a pleasant buzz. Fruitfly brains, much like ours, are wired for inebriation. (Bilger, 2008)

between 125 and 203 million people use marijuana, 14 to 56 million use amphetamines, 12 to 21 million use opioids, 14 to 21 million use cocaine, and 11 to 21 million inject drugs (UNODC, 2011). Data such as these have led some commentators on drug use to assert that intoxication is not unnatural or deviant; instead, absolute sobriety is not a natural or primary human state. As Andrew Weil (1986) suggests, "the ubiquity of drug use is so striking that it must represent a basic human appetite" (p. 17).

While drugs—both those that are currently illegal in the United States and those that are legal—provide a number of benefits to those who use them, all drugs are also associated with certain harms. For example, it is estimated that more than 440,000 deaths in the United States in the year 2010 were related to tobacco (Centers for Disease Control, 2011), more than 24,000 to alcohol (excluding accidents and homicides), and more than 27,000 to prescription drug overdoses. It is important to note that all of these drugs are currently legal in the United States. In contrast, there were fewer than 20,000 deaths related to all illicit drugs combined in 2010, and there were no deaths related to the use of marijuana; in fact, marijuana alone has never been shown to cause an overdose death. If we consider deaths associated with the use of particular substances to be at least one acceptable measure of their harmfulness, we may question why alcohol and tobacco are legal substances, while marijuana and drugs such as cocaine, ecstasy, heroin, and methamphetamine are currently illegal.

We may also question why the most noteworthy response to the alleged *illegal* drug problem in the United States has been the incarceration of massive numbers of people. In fact, there are more people imprisoned for the commission of drug offenses in the United States—close to 500,000—than are incarcerated in England, France, Germany, and Japan, for all crimes combined. Examined in another way, the United States has 100,000 more people incarcerated for nonviolent drug offenses than all the countries of the European Union have for all crimes combined, despite the fact that the European Union has 100 million more citizens (Wood et al., 2003).

These paradoxes require us to consider the distinction between legal and illegal drugs, and, more directly, to examine how certain drugs have been demonized in order to justify their illegal status.

DEMONIZING (ILLEGAL) DRUGS: THE SOCIAL CONSTRUCTION OF DRUG "EPIDEMICS"

The data presented above indicate that the use of psychoactive substances—both legal and illegal—is widespread throughout the United States and the rest of the world. It appears that people need to ingest an increasingly diverse array of substances in order to alter their consciousness. But this need for psychoactive substances extends to other constituencies, including government and criminal justice system officials and the popular media. As O'Grady (2010) notes, "the drug warrior industry, which includes both the private sector and a massive government bureaucracy devoted to 'enforcement' has an enormous economic incentive to keep the war raging." Government officials need drugs in order to create heroes and villains and, in many cases, to divert attention from policies that have led to drug use in the first place. Criminal justice system officials need psychoactive substances in order to justify increases in financial and other resources devoted to their organizations, and the popular media need drugs in order to create moral panics and sell newspapers and advertising time.

> Government officials, the media, and other authorities have found that drug addiction, abuse, and even use can be blamed by almost anyone for long-standing problems and the worsening of almost anything. Theft, robbery, rape, malingering, fraud, corruption, physical violence, shoplifting, juvenile delinquency, sloth, sloppiness, sexual promiscuity, low productivity, and all around irresponsibility—nearly any social problem can be said to be made worse by drugs. (Levine, 2001)

As a result of these needs, throughout the 20th century and into the 21st century, government and criminal justice system officials in the United States, frequently assisted by the popular media, have engaged in a concerted campaign to demonize *certain* drugs in order to justify their prohibition. A number of tactics have been used in this endeavor. One strategy used in emphasizing the dangers of (illegal) drugs is to claim, often without any sound empirical data, that the use of these substances is responsible for a significant proportion of the crime that occurs in society. For example, when President Nixon was attempting to justify his administration's war on drugs in the early 1970s, which he referred to as the United States' "second civil war," he claimed that heroin users were responsible for $2 billion in property crime annually. This was a rather strange calculation, given that the total amount of property crime in 1971 amounted to only $1.3 billion (Davenport-Hines, 2001).

A second frequently used strategy is to attribute unique powers to (illegal) drugs that allegedly induce users to commit bizarre acts (including sexually deviant acts) while under their influence. Sullum (2003a) refers to this tendency as "voodoo pharmacology"—the idea that (illegal) drugs are incredibly powerful substances that can take control of people's behavior, turning them into "chemical zombies." Zimring

> The news media can always be relied upon to come up with somebody who had a six-day session on the stuff and ended up by killing and eating the neighbor's dog, later claiming that they remember nothing of what had happened, and another devastating crime wave. The last arises because each new substance has to be described as being more rapaciously, instantaneously addictive than anything else previously heard of. (Walton, 2002, p. 171)

and Hawkins (1992) emphasize a similar theme in their discussion of the metaphysical notion of the unique psychoactive drug that leads to a situation whereby each new substance identified as being problematic is viewed as chemically, physiologically, and psychologically both novel and unique.

Illegal drugs have also been demonized over the past 100 years by claims that they are consumed primarily by members of minority groups and that the substances are distributed primarily by evil foreign traffickers. As Musto (1999) suggests, "the projection of blame on foreign nations for domestic evils harmonized with the ascription of drug use to ethnic minorities. Both the external cause and the internal locus could be dismissed as un-American" (p. 298). A definitive example of the attribution of drug problems to members of minority groups and foreigners appeared in a 2003 U.S. Drug Enforcement Administration (DEA) publication, titled *Drug Trafficking in the United States*:

> Cocaine and heroin come through Mexico. Ecstasy has increased at an alarming rate; Israeli and Russian drug trafficking syndicates are the principal traffickers of MDMA worldwide. Finally, groups based in southeast and southwest Asia smuggle heroin into the United States. Street gangs such as Crips and Bloods, and groups of Dominicans, Puerto Ricans, and Jamaicans dominate the retail market for crack cocaine. (p. 3)

More recently, and consistent with this theme, Arizona governor Jan Brewer commented, "I believe today, under the circumstances we're facing, that the majority of the illegal trespassers that are coming into the state of Arizona are under the direction and control of organized drug cartels and they are bringing drugs in" (as quoted in Davenport, 2010).

Government and criminal justice system officials and media sources have also demonized drugs through assertions that their use results in death and references to the threat they supposedly pose to children. Finally, government, criminal justice system officials, and media sources have demonized drugs through the misrepresentation, distortion, or, in some cases, suppression of scientific studies on the effects of these drugs.

In order to preface our discussion in later chapters on the effects of and policies to deal with both legal and illegal drugs, this chapter addresses the demonization of drugs and the social construction of drug epidemics in the United States over the last 100 years. It is important to state at the outset that in critically examining these issues, we are not suggesting that drug "epidemics" are constructed without any foundation whatsoever; obviously, at least some use of the substance in question has to occur in order for a particular drug to be a candidate for "epidemic" status. But in this context, it is important to consider the meaning of the term *epidemic*. In the 1300s, the bubonic plague claimed the lives of 25 million people, one-third of the world's population ("Past Pandemics," 2005); the Irish famine of 1846 to 1850 resulted in the death of as many as one million people out of a population of eight million (Bloy, n.d.); tens of millions of people around the world had died of HIV/AIDS–related causes by 2010 (including 1.8 million in 2010 alone), and at least 34 million people are currently HIV positive (United Nations, 2011). Most of us could agree that these are examples of epidemics. However, to use the term *epidemic* in the context of statistics that 1.4% of Americans report ever using heroin in their lifetime, 2.8% report ever using crack cocaine, 3.6% report ever using ecstasy, and 4.3% report ever using methamphetamine is alarmist and misleading (SAMHSA, 2001). This is not simply a matter of semantics, but rather it points to the misapplication of scientific terminology, which, in the context of drug use and with respect to its implications for policies, is inappropriate.

In addressing the demonization of drugs and the social construction of drug epidemics in this chapter, we are also not suggesting that the substances in question are harmless—as will be discussed in Chapters 3 and 4, no drugs are. However, as will be seen, government and media accounts have created myths about certain substances through the exaggeration of harms associated with them; it is necessary to deconstruct these myths.

We will provide several examples of the social construction of drug epidemics, focusing on different substances over different historical periods, including crack cocaine in the 1980s, heroin in the 1990s to 2000s, ecstasy in the 1990s to 2000s, methamphetamine in the 1990s to 2000s, as well as "spice/K2" and "bath salts" in the 2000s to 2010s. We devote considerably more attention to marijuana, given that this substance continues to dominate the United States' drug war in terms of number of arrests and larger criminal justice system activity. In order to set the stage for the discussion of constructed drug epidemics, we begin with a discussion of the "glue-sniffing epidemic" that emerged in the United States in the late 1950s and early 1960s. The principles outlined by Brecher (1972) in his discussion of this particular epidemic are strikingly similar to those that have been applied in constructing drug epidemics in both earlier and later time periods and also for other substances.

GLUE-SNIFFING

Glue sniffing, while likely engaged in (perhaps inadvertently) by a significant proportion of young people, was virtually unheard of in the United States before 1959. The media first mentioned this issue in that year after children were arrested in Tucson, Arizona, and Pueblo, Colorado, for glue-sniffing (Brecher, 1972). The phenomenon then apparently surfaced in Denver, where a juvenile court judge said he viewed glue sniffing as "the number one problem in the metropolitan area" (p. 324). At least partially as a result of considerable media attention to the practice, 130 youth were arrested for glue sniffing in Denver over a 2-year period, and in October

1961, the *New York Times* published an article describing a similar problem with glue-sniffing in New York City. Within 5 months, police in New York had arrested 778 individuals for glue sniffing.

Similar to the pattern we will see for other substances addressed in this chapter, media sources began to recount bizarre acts and behaviors that were allegedly caused by glue inhalation. In a 1962 *Newsweek* article, for example, it was noted that "a 12-year-old boy, discovered sniffing airplane glue by his father, snatched up a knife and threatened to kill him." The same article quoted a Miami police officer who asserted, "It's common for boys who sniff glue to become belligerent. They are willing to take on policemen twice their size" (as cited in Brecher, 1972, p. 329). Federal government officials also began to weigh in on the problem, emphasizing another consistent theme used to demonize drugs: the idea that glue sniffing led to involvement in sexual (and homosexual) activities (see box).

An FBI Bulletin (1965) on the topic of glue-sniffing noted, "Glue-sniffers have described how a number of children, boys and girls, meet in unoccupied houses where they will sniff glue together and later have sexual relations, both homosexual and heterosexual.... Recently, while conversing with deputy probation officers, I have been informed that several episodes of homosexual relations have occurred between adults and children under the influence of glue. Some of these sexual perverts are encouraging the children to sniff glue with the intentions of having homosexual relations with them. (cited in Brecher, 1972, p. 330)

Brecher (1972) further notes that an additional strategy in constructing the glue-sniffing epidemic was to report on deaths allegedly caused by the activity; a number of popular magazines and newspapers contained reports that nine deaths had been caused by glue sniffing. However, when these deaths were subject to further investigation, it turned out that at least six (and possibly seven) of them were the result of asphyxiation caused by the glue-sniffer's head being covered by an airtight plastic bag. Another of the deaths attributed to glue sniffing involved a young person who was suffering from other ailments and had sniffed gasoline fumes, but not glue. Attributing the ninth death to glue sniffing was also problematic because the individual in question had not even been sniffing glue before his death.

Brecher (1972) concludes that this glue-sniffing "epidemic" was constructed by the media and government, and that the distortions with respect to the dangers associated with glue sniffing may have inadvertently contributed to an increase in drug use among youth.

It seems highly likely, in retrospect, that the exaggerated warnings against glue sniffing were among the factors desensitizing some young people to drug warnings in general. Most teenagers knew of others in their own neighborhoods who had sniffed glue repeatedly, and who did not drop dead or go to the hospital with brain damage, kidney damage, or liver damage. (p. 332)

A related "epidemic" associated with the use of solvents emerged in 2001. Referring to alleged increases in the use of solvents by young people, Dr. Jo Ellen Dyer of the California Poison Control System commented, "I would say we're at epidemic proportions. This is the new major drug of abuse out there" (as quoted in Pena, 2001). Evidence for this particular epidemic was that there were six deaths nationwide associated with solvent use over a one-and-a-half-year period.

MARIJUANA

As discussed above, one of the prominent strategies used to justify prohibition of a particular substance is to emphasize a wide range of negative effects associated with its use. Although most would agree that marijuana is the most benign of currently illegal drugs, an examination of the history of its portrayal by government officials and in media sources reveals a number of recurrent themes that served to demonize the substance and rationalize its prohibition. At various points in history, marijuana has been portrayed as a substance that is primarily used by members of minority groups, as a substance that causes violence and "aberrant" sexual behaviors, as a substance that causes amotivational syndrome, and as a substance that is a "gateway" to the use of harder drugs.

The Portrayal of Marijuana: 1800s to 1960

Marijuana has a long, rich, and fascinating history, both in the United States and globally. Hemp was used for shipbuilding around 470 B.C., and the cannabis plant was cultivated for its psychoactive properties throughout Asia and the Far East as early as the first century B.C. (Davenport-Hines, 2001). Although the exact date when the substance was introduced to Western Europe is not known, an archeological investigation at two Bronze Age (roughly 6,000 B.C. to 2,500 B.C.) sites uncovered the remains of marijuana seeds and pipes that were apparently made specifically for smoking the substance (Walton, 2002). In Britain, a law passed in the 1500s required that farmers set aside part of their land for the cultivation of hemp (Walton, 2002), and similar laws were passed in the United States, where hemp was also used as money from 1631 until the early 1800s (J. Gray, 2001). Medicinal use of marijuana was also fairly common in earlier eras: George Washington grew the substance for this purpose, and Queen Victoria used it for relief from menstrual cramps.

Early reports on the effects of marijuana indicated that it was a relatively benign substance, especially when compared with alcohol. For example, the 1893 Indian Hemp Drugs Commission, which had been appointed by the British government to examine cannabis use in India, concluded, "On the whole, the weight of the evidence is to the effect that the moderate use of hemp drugs produces no injurious effects on the mind. . . . The temptation to excess is not as great as with alcohol" (Indian Hemp Drugs Commission, 1893, pp. 264, 286).

Similarly, in an article published in the *Journal of Mental Science*, Walsh (1894) wrote,

> It would seem that the moderate use of hemp drugs may be beneficial under
> certain conditions; at any rate such moderate use cannot be harmful. . . .
> [T]here is not, in my opinion, any specific property in hemp drugs which incites
> to violence or crime. (p. 27)

An editorial in the same journal noted, "apparently it is much less liable than alcohol to induce men to commit violent actions" ("Editorial," 1894, p. 107).

Despite a lack of scientific evidence identifying any significant deleterious effects of marijuana, when the U.S. federal government decided to create marijuana legislation in the 1930s, the Federal Bureau of Narcotics (FBN) initiated a vigorous anti-marijuana propaganda campaign. The Bureau and its director, Harry Anslinger, provided media sources with "information" on the effects of marijuana that was widely reported and served to demonize the substance. Mosher's (1985) content analysis of articles addressing the topic of marijuana published in popular magazines and newspapers identified a number of themes that were emphasized in order to justify legislation banning marijuana. From 1900 to 1934 (just prior to the passage of the Marijuana Tax Act in 1937), most articles on the topic asserted that the primary users of marijuana were members of minority groups—in particular, Mexicans. For example, one commentator from Sacramento, California, noted, "marijuana, perhaps now the most insidious of narcotics, is a direct by-product of Mexican immigration. . . . Mexican peddlers have been caught distributing sample marijuana cigarettes to schoolchildren" (cited in Musto, 1999, p. 220). The purported effects of the drug ranged from "temporary elation" ("Facts and Fancies," 1936, p. 7) to "the most violent of all sexual stimulants . . . reason dethroning and causing its users to enter into criminal life" (Simon, 1921, p. 14).

An article published in the *St. Louis Dispatch* in 1934, titled "Drug Menace at the University of Kansas—How a Number of Students Became Addicts of the Strangely Intoxicating Weed," noted,

> The physical attack upon the body is rapid and devastating. In the initial stages
> the skin turns a peculiar yellow color, the lips become discolored, dried, and
> cracked. Soon the mouth is affected, the gums are inflamed and softened. Then
> the teeth are loosened and eventually, if the habit is persisted in, they fall out.
> Like all other drugs, marijuana also has a serious effect on the moral character
> of the individual, destroying his will power and reducing his stamina. (cited in
> J. Gray, 2001 p. 24)

Between 1935 and 1939, a number of articles suggested that cannabis posed a specific threat to young people; for example, a *Scientific American* article referred to the substance as the "assassin of youth" ("Marijuana Menaces," 1936, p. 150). Other articles emphasized that the use of marijuana led to violent crime, sexual immorality, and a variety of adverse psychological effects. For example, an article appearing in the popular magazine *Survey Graphic* reported "Victor Lacata, while under the influence of marijuana, murdered his mother, father, sister, and two

brothers with an axe." The same article recounted the case of "Lewis Harris, 26, arrested for the rape of a nine-year-old girl while under the influence of marijuana" ("Danger," 1938, p. 221). At a meeting of the American Psychiatric Association in 1934, Dr. Walter Bromberg similarly emphasized marijuana's effect on involvement

in sexual activity, albeit with a different focus: Marijuana "releases inhibitions and restraints imposed by society and allows individuals to act out their drives openly [and] acts as a sexual stimulant [particularly to] overt homosexuals" (as quoted in Musto, 1999, p. 220). With respect to the adverse psychological effects allegedly associated with marijuana, an article in *Scientific American* listed, among others, "the weakening of power to direct thoughts, emotional disturbances" and "irresistible impulses which may result in suicide" ("Marijuana More Dangerous," 1938, p. 293).

In addition to antimarijuana propaganda appearing in popular magazines and newspapers, there were a number of movies produced in the 1930s and 1940s that further served to demonize the substance.

Reefer Madness (1935), produced largely in collaboration with the Federal Bureau of Narcotics, was the best known of these movies. The film depicted marijuana as a "demon weed" that was capable of altering the personalities of young people who, after smoking the drug, went insane, immersed themselves in "evil" jazz music, and committed suicide or went on murder sprees (Talvi, 2003b). Perhaps less well-known are other antimarijuana films produced in this era, including *Weed With Roots in Hell* (1936), *The Devil's Harvest* (1942), and *She Shoulda Said No (Wild Weed)* (1948) (Schlosser, 2003).

In the 1940s, research conducted under the auspices of New York Mayor LaGuardia's Commission refuted some of the earlier reports of marijuana's allegedly negative effects. Allentuck and Bowman (1942) studied 77 marijuana users and concluded, "while exerting no permanent deleterious effects, marijuana gives rise to pleasurable sensations, calmness, and relaxation and increases the appetite" (p. 249). These authors also suggested that the substance had valuable therapeutic applications.

In response to this and another 1942 publication on the topic of marijuana that had stated "unqualifiedly that the use of marijuana does not lead to physical, mental, or moral degeneration and that no permanent deleterious effects from its continuous use were observed" (as cited in Davenport-Hines, 2001, p. 278), the head of the FBN, Harry Anslinger (1943), wrote an editorial in the *Journal of the American Medical Association* stating that "unsavory persons" who were engaged in the marijuana trade would "make use of the statement in pushing their dangerous traffic" (p. 212). The editorial also stated that a boy had read an account of the LaGuardia Commission report and that this had led him to initiate the use of marijuana.

In addition to attempting to discredit the findings of scientific studies indicating that marijuana was not as dangerous a substance as had previously been reported, the FBN and the popular media began to emphasize new themes in order to justify prohibition of the substance. The most prominent and enduring of these themes was the notion that marijuana was a stepping-stone or gateway drug. This theme was illustrated in an article in the *New Yorker*, which noted, "most drug addicts begin on marijuana, which though rarely habit-forming, is very apt to lure users of it on to the deadlier drugs" ("Saw-toothed," 1951, p. 18). Similarly, an article in *Newsweek* asserted, "marijuana may not be more habit-forming than alcohol, but it makes the switch to heroin easy" ("Reefers," 1954, p. 17).

Interestingly, despite FBN Commissioner Anslinger's efforts to demonize marijuana and to have legislation passed prohibiting use of the substance, he initially rejected the idea that marijuana was a gateway drug. In the course of legislative hearings on the substance in the 1930s, Anslinger was asked whether "the marijuana addict graduates into a heroin, an opium, or cocaine user." Anslinger responded, "No sir, I have not heard of a case of that kind. The marijuana addict does not go in that direction" (as quoted in Brecher, 1972, p. 416). Later, Anslinger would change his views on this issue, asserting, without providing any scientific evidence to support it, that "over 50% of heroin users started on marijuana smoking . . . and they graduated to heroin; they took to the needle when the thrill of marijuana was gone" (as quoted in Davenport-Hines, 2001, p. 285). Such assertions were, of course, useful in justifying federal legislation banning marijuana.

Popular conceptions of the dangers of marijuana use and the legitimacy of employing criminal sanctions against the substance did not really come into question again until the 1960s. In what Himmelstein (1983) refers to as the "embourgeoisement" of marijuana, the consensus over the dangers of the drug that had been established in the 1930s and largely survived into the 1950s began to disintegrate when use became associated with middle-class youth in the 1960s (p. 98). But it is also important to note that the identification of marijuana use with middle-class youth provides only a partial explanation of changes in portrayals of the substance and the relaxation of criminal penalties associated with it in the 1970s (see Chapter 11). Marijuana itself, regardless of propaganda to the contrary, is simply not an extremely dangerous substance. If marijuana was actually a significant contributor to violent crime, as several commentators have alleged, it is probable that there would have been calls for more severe penalties for users and traffickers in the drug rather than the reverse. In addition, a considerable number of scientific experts, primarily from the medical profession, were willing to argue that marijuana was a relatively safe substance.

The Portrayal of Marijuana: 1960s to 1980s

"If an enemy nation were to plan to undermine America's fortune, they could not think of a more effective strategy of poisoning our youth. Marijuana is such a poison" ("Putting a Match," 1980, p. 12).

This statement by Robert L. Dupont, the former director of the National Institute on Drug Abuse, is reflective of the fact that marijuana had still not received full social acceptability in the United States as of 1980. It is also reflective of the confusion and controversy surrounding the regulation of the substance. Only 4 years earlier, Dupont had recommended decriminalization of marijuana ("Marijuana: A Conversation," 1976).

As mentioned above, several portrayals of marijuana in popular magazines prior to the 1960s emphasized that it caused violence and crime; however, in the debate over the drug that occurred in the 1960s through the 1980s, these themes were largely ignored or denied. This is not to suggest, however, that popular literature and government sources universally portrayed the substance as benign. One of the most blatant examples of distortion and misinformation regarding the effects of marijuana was published in the prestigious *Journal of the American Medical Association* in 1971. Psychiatrists Kolansky and Moore studied 38 individuals, most of whom smoked marijuana once or more per week, and reported that "these patients consistently showed very poor social judgment, poor attention span, poor concentration, confusion, anxiety, depression, apathy, indifference, and often slow and slurred speech." A 20-year-old male subject "developed delusions of grandeur six months after starting to smoke marijuana—[he] believed he was in charge of the Mafia." An 18-year-old boy who smoked marijuana and hashish for a 3-year period "became a vegetarian and practiced yoga. He had the delusion that he was a guru and eventually believed that he was the son of God who was placed on the earth to save all people from violence and destruction." A 19-year-old boy who smoked marijuana for 4 months "[believed] he had superhuman powers; he felt he was able to communicate with and control the minds and actions of animals, especially dogs and cats" (Kolansky & Moore, 1971, p. 489).

But perhaps most bizarre in the Kolansky and Moore (1971) article was their assertion that the use of marijuana led to involvement in aberrant sexual behaviors. They noted, for example, that 13 females aged 13 to 22 exhibited

> an unusual degree of sexual promiscuity, which ranged from sexual relations with individuals of the opposite sex to relations with individuals of both sexes, and sometimes, individuals of both sexes on the same evening. In the histories of these individuals, we were struck by the loss of sexual inhibitions after short periods of marijuana smoking. (pp. 490–491)

Further,

> A 17-year-old boy was seduced homosexually after an older man gradually introduced him to marijuana smoking over a period of one year. . . . He continued to smoke marijuana and gradually withdrew from reality, developing an interest in occult matters which culminated in the delusion that he was to be the messiah returned to earth. (p. 488)

Finally,

> Shortly after a 14-year-old boy began to smoke marijuana, he began to demonstrate indolence, apathy, and depression. Over a period of eight months, his condition worsened until he began to develop paranoid ideas. Simultaneously, he became actively homosexual. (p. 488)

The contention of a relationship between marijuana use and homosexuality was echoed at a political convention in Vancouver, British Columbia, in 1979. Delegates to this convention were informed that cannabis contained female estrogen that was affecting male users of the substance. "The growing gay population is largely due to cannabis. . . . Unless the data we have is soon transmitted to the public, we will probably witness the decline of Western civilization as we have known it." ("Socreds Told," 1979, p. 3)

While one hopes it is obvious that many of Kolansky and Moore's assertions regarding the effects of marijuana are inaccurate, it is also important to address some of the methodological problems with this study. It is notable that Kolansky and Moore only studied subjects who volunteered for the study, which may indicate that these individuals had prior psychological problems not directly attributable to their use of marijuana; unfortunately, the authors provided very little background information on their research subjects. Furthermore, Kolansky and Moore made no effort to explain the specific mechanisms through which marijuana supposedly caused the effects they identified. Their definition of sexual promiscuity is also questionable because they did not delineate how many times a particular individual would need to engage in sexual relations to be labeled sexually promiscuous. One would expect single males and females of the age of the subjects in this study to be sexually active, so the attribution of this activity to marijuana use seems highly questionable.

Despite these methodological problems and the rather outlandish claims regarding the effects of marijuana, it is notable that Kolansky and Moore's findings were widely cited in popular magazines in the early 1970s (Mosher, 1985). Carlton Turner, who served as drug czar under President Ronald Reagan, linked the smoking of marijuana to anti-authority behavior, and, echoing Kolansky and Moore, argued that use of the drug could turn young men into homosexuals (Busse, 2003). And as late as 1999, the head of the United States Public Health Service suggested that marijuana should not be prescribed as medicine for AIDS patients because such individuals would become "crazed" by the high and would be more likely to practice unsafe sex as a result (Manderson, 1999).

A more common theme regarding the effects of marijuana that emerged in the 1960s and that continues to be emphasized in the current period is the notion that its use leads to indolence, or what is sometimes referred to as "amotivational syndrome." Thus, an article in *Life* magazine suggested, "potheads tend to be irresponsible and uninterested in things like keeping a job or supporting a family" ("Marijuana: Millions," 1967, p. 18). Similarly, quoting the director of the Bureau of Narcotics and Dangerous Drugs, an article in *Time* magazine noted, "pot can be psychologically habituating, often resulting in amotivational syndrome in which the user is more likely to contemplate a flower pot than try to solve his problem" ("New Views," 1971, p. 65). However, as Weil and Rosen (1998) suggest, the assertion that marijuana causes amotivational syndrome is also of questionable scientific validity. While it is true that some people who lack motivation tend to engage in marijuana smoking, it is unlikely that marijuana consumption is the cause of their lack of motivation. "Heavy pot smoking is more likely to be a symptom of amotivation than a cause of it, and those same young people would probably be wasting their time in other ways if pot were not available" (p. 119).

Considered in its totality, however, the portrayal of marijuana in popular media sources from 1960 to 1980 stressed that the earlier information on the substance had overemphasized its dangers (Mosher, 1985). As will be discussed in further detail in Chapter 11, this led to a general relaxation of penalties for marijuana possession in a number of states and decriminalization of marijuana in 11 states. However, between 1980 and 2010, several million people were arrested for marijuana offenses in the United States, the overwhelming majority for simple possession of the substance. For example, in 2009, of 858,408 arrests for marijuana in the United States, 88.4% were for simple possession (FBI, 2011). And given that, in the same year, marijuana arrests accounted for 51.6% of the 1,663,482 drug arrests in the United States, statistically speaking, the war on drugs is, in essence, a war on marijuana use and possession. As such, it is important to examine the official rationalizations for this continued war on marijuana in the context of scientific evidence on the effects of the drug.

The Portrayal of Marijuana: 1980 and Beyond

It is ironic that Drug Czar John Walters cites the movie *Reefer Madness* in his opinion/editorial "The Myth of Harmless Marijuana." Indeed, many of Mr. Walters' more egregious claims about cannabis appear to have been lifted straight from the 1936 propaganda film. (Stroup & Armentano, 2002, p. 223)

The Office of National Drug Control Policy (ONDCP) and President George W. Bush's drug czar, John Walters, justified the continuing war on marijuana and the arrest of hundreds of thousands of people for possession of the substance by invoking a number of old, and some new, themes regarding the dangers associated with the substance. These themes have been emphasized in both official ONDCP reports and in an opinion-editorial article written by Walters and published in the *Washington Post* titled "The Myth of Harmless Marijuana" (Walters, 2002).

The first of these themes is one we discussed earlier—the notion that marijuana leads to violence. A 2002 ONDCP report suggested "the truth is that ~~~~ and violence are linked" (ONDCP, 2002a). Similar allegations have been law enforcement officials in some jurisdictions. For instance, the c Bronx, New York Narcotics Division claimed,

Some people may think the drug [marijuana] is benign, but network certainly is not. For some of our policy makers .. only connection to marijuana was watching the Grateful De

East. Times have changed. None of the dealers in the Bronx are smoking joints and discussing Nietzsche. (Flynn, 2001)

But as is typically the case, despite claims that police in New York were witnessing increasing violence among those involved in marijuana distribution, "it is unclear how much the number of violent incidents has grown . . . [because] New York City does not keep statistics on marijuana-related violence" (Flynn, 2001).

It is worth considering the alleged connection between marijuana and violence in the context of reports from non–U.S. government agencies and scholarly research on the issue. The Canadian Senate's 2002 report on cannabis noted, "cannabis does not induce users to commit other forms of crime. Cannabis use does not increase aggressiveness or anti-social behavior" (Government of Canada, 2002, p. 4). Similarly, the British Advisory Council on the Misuse of Drugs concluded in its 2002 report,

> Cannabis differs from alcohol . . . in one major respect. It does not seem to increase risk-taking behavior. . . . This means that cannabis rarely contributes to violence either to others or to oneself, whereas alcohol is a major factor, in deliberate self-harm, domestic accidents, and violence. (Advisory Council on the Misuse of Drugs, 2002)

The key difference between the claims in the ONDCP report and those of other sources appears to be related to the former's apparent confusion over the effects of marijuana versus the effects of marijuana's status as an illegal drug. While there is virtually no scientific evidence indicating that marijuana induces psychopharmacological changes causing an individual to be violent (Weil & Rosen, 1998), because the substance is distributed in illegal markets where individuals and organizations may compete for domination, violence may ensue. If marijuana were a legal substance that could be purchased in legal contexts, such potentially violent turf battles would not occur.

The 2002 ONDCP report also claimed that "60 percent of teenagers in [drug] treatment have a primary marijuana diagnosis. That means that addiction to marijuana by our youth exceeds their addiction rates for alcohol, cocaine, heroin, methamphetamine, ecstasy and all other drugs combined" (ONDCP, 2002a). Leaving aside the fact that marijuana is not a physically addicting substance (see Chapter 4), it is important to note that the increase in marijuana treatment admissions is almost exclusively the result of an increase in teenagers referred to drug treatment by the criminal and juvenile justice systems. This, in turn, is at least partially the result of the tremendous increase in marijuana arrests of juveniles over the last decade or so. According to the federal Drug and Alcohol Services Information System, 54% of all adolescent admissions for marijuana treatment are through the criminal justice system (cited in National Organization for the Reform of Marijuana Laws [NORML], 2002).

In further emphasizing the alleged dangers of marijuana, the 2002 ONDCP report, referring to Drug Abuse Warning Network (DAWN) data, claimed that "as ＿tor in emergency room admissions, marijuana has risen 176% since 1994, and now surpasses heroin" (ONDCP, 2002a). This statement is also misleading, in that it implies that marijuana use is a *causal* factor in emergency room admissions. As will be discussed further in Chapter 5, for every emergency room visit related to drug use, hospital staff can list up to five drugs the individual reports having used recently, regardless of whether the particular drug was the cause of the visit. Because a far greater proportion of the population uses marijuana than uses other illegal drugs, it is far more likely to be reported by patients. Marijuana is infrequently mentioned independently of other drugs in these DAWN data; in fact, mentions of marijuana alone accounted for less than 4% of all drug-related emergency room visits (NORML, 2002).

The ONDCP has also justified the continued prohibition of marijuana on the grounds that the THC (the main psychoactive ingredient) content of marijuana in circulation in the current period is much higher than in the past, allegedly making it a more dangerous substance. In the 2002 ONDCP report, it was noted that the average THC levels of marijuana in samples seized by the Drug Enforcement Administration had increased from less than 1% in the late 1970s to more than 7% in 2001. It was also asserted that the potency of more powerful sinsemilla strains of the substance had increased from 6% to 13%, and reached as high as 33%. Based on these data, drug czar John Walters was widely quoted in the media claiming that the potency of marijuana had increased as much as 30 times its previous potency, and commented, "It's not your father's marijuana" (as quoted in Forbes, 2002). As Forbes (2002) revealed, however, Walters's claims were tremendously misleading. First, the figures provided for "today's sinsemilla" were, in fact, based on data from 1999. Walters conveniently ignored data from 2000 and 2001, probably because the potency of sinsemilla strains of marijuana peaked at 13.38% THC content in 1999. In addition, high-grade marijuana such as sinsemilla tends to be prohibitively expensive for most users and constitutes only a small percentage of the overall marijuana market. It is thus highly unlikely that a majority or even a significant minority of users were consuming this high-THC-content marijuana.

Walters's distortions with respect to the THC content of marijuana samples went even further. According to a study published in the *Journal of Forensic Sciences* (and based on data from the federal government's own marijuana potency monitoring project housed at the University of Mississippi), the THC content of marijuana samples increased threefold over the 1980–1997 period, from approximately 1.5% in 1980 to 4.5% in 1997 (ElSohly et al., 2000). We therefore must question where Walters obtained the previously mentioned figure of 7%. As Zimmer and Morgan (1997) further point out, a small number of low-THC-content (approximately 1% THC) samples seized by the Drug Enforcement Administration in the 1970s are typically used to calculate the dramatic increases in the potency of the drug (p. 137). However, these samples were not representative of the marijuana that was available to most users, and very few people smoke marijuana with such low THC content (Forbes, 2002).

The discussion above emphasizes how the ONDCP and drug czar Walters presented misleading information with respect to increases in the THC content of marijuana; however, we do not deny that marijuana at the high end of the THC continuum is probably more widely available than in previous years. It does not necessarily follow, however, that marijuana is now more dangerous to users.

Research suggests that consumers of hard liquor typically consume fewer drinks than those who drink beer and wine, which have a lower alcohol content, in order to experience the psychoactive effects of alcohol (Weil & Rosen, 1998). Similarly, consumers of high-potency marijuana will generally smoke less of the substance; studies have shown that most users smoke until they experience a high (Wanjek, 2002). This is further confirmed from data derived from Monitoring the Future surveys on drug use, which indicate that the average size of marijuana cigarettes that users consume has declined over time (Forbes, 2002; Wanjek, 2002). This would imply that marijuana smokers are aware of the fact that they are consuming a higher-potency substance and are regulating their intake accordingly. In addition, marijuana poses no risk of fatal overdose, regardless of THC content; as noted earlier, there has never been a documented death from marijuana consumption (Zimmer & Morgan, 1997). In fact, one estimate suggests that a person would have to consume approximately 100 pounds of marijuana a minute for 15 minutes in order to induce a lethal response (Schlosser, 2003). Furthermore, since the substance's most serious potential hazard is related to consumers' intake of potentially carcinogenic smoke, it could be argued that higher-potency marijuana is actually less harmful because it permits users to achieve the desired psychoactive effects while inhaling less burning material (NORML, 2002; Sullum, 2003a).

Perhaps the most prominent argument used by the ONDCP to justify the continued prohibition of marijuana is one that, as noted above, first appeared in the 1950s: the notion that marijuana is a gateway drug.

> The truth is that marijuana is a gateway drug. . . . People who use marijuana are eight times more likely to have used cocaine, fifteen times more likely to have used heroin, and five times more likely to develop a need for treatment of abuse or dependence of any drug. (ONDCP, 2002a)

Before examining the empirical support (or lack thereof) for the gateway drug hypothesis, it is important to examine its theoretical logic.

As Kandel (2003) explains, the gateway drug hypothesis is based on three interrelated propositions. First, the notion of "sequencing" implies that there is a fixed relationship between two drugs, such that the use of one substance is regularly initiated before the other. Second, "association" implies that the initiation of one drug increases the probability that use of the second drug will be initiated. Finally, the notion of "causation" suggests that the use of one substance actually causes use of the second substance. These facts are generally marshaled in support of the gateway effect: (1) Marijuana users are more likely than nonusers to progress to the use of harder drugs such as cocaine and heroin; (2) more individuals who have used hard drugs tried marijuana first; and (3) the greater the frequency of marijuana use, the greater the likelihood of hard drug use.

A 1994 report by the Center on Addiction and Substance Abuse was one of the first to present statistical evidence in support of the gateway drug hypothesis (cited in Zimmer & Morgan, 1997). This report claimed that marijuana users were 85 times more likely than non-marijuana users to have used cocaine; this figure was derived from respondents' reports of lifetime use of marijuana and cocaine in the 1991 National Household Survey on Drug Abuse. However, in an interesting twist on mathematical logic, in order to obtain this factor of 85, the report divided the proportion of marijuana users who admitted they had ever tried cocaine (17%) by the percentage of cocaine users who had never tried marijuana (.02%). In other words, the risk factor is large not because a substantial proportion of marijuana users try cocaine, but because very few people try cocaine without trying marijuana first. As Zimmer and Morgan (1997) point out, a similar relationship exists between other kinds of common and uncommon activities that tend to be related to one another. For example, most people who ride motorcycles, which is a relatively rare activity, have also ridden a bicycle, which is a fairly common activity. It is also likely that the prevalence of motorcycle riding among individuals who have never ridden a bicycle is quite low. Sullum (2003a) offers a similar analogy, noting that people who engage in bungee jumping are probably more likely to try parachuting than people who don't engage in bungee jumping. It would stretch logic, however, to claim that bicycle riding *causes* motorcycle riding or that bungee jumping *causes* skydiving. Similarly, it is misleading to suggest that marijuana use causes cocaine use.

Having said that it is necessary to question the logic of the gateway drug hypothesis, it is also important to review recent research on this issue. A longitudinal study based on a sample of 311 monozygotic (identical) twins in Australia found that individuals who had used marijuana by the age of 18 had odds of other illegal drug use and/or clinical diagnoses of alcohol dependence and drug abuse that were 2.1 to 5.2 times higher than their twin who did not use marijuana before the age of 18 (Lynskey et al., 2003). While this study would appear to provide evidence in support of the gateway drug hypothesis, the authors did not claim that they had presented incontrovertible proof. They noted that if the association between early use of cannabis and the use of other illegal drugs is causal, the particular mechanisms through which this association operates are not completely clear. Lynskey and colleagues outline three possible mechanisms that might explain the association: (1) Early experiences with marijuana, which often produce pleasurable psychoactive effects, may encourage the continued use of marijuana and experimentation with other drugs; (2) experiences with marijuana that do not result in short-term harm to the user may serve to reduce the perceived risks associated with the use of harder drugs; and/or (3) experience with and access to marijuana may provide users with access to other illegal drugs via contact with individuals who deal in such substances (pp. 430–431).

Research conducted by Morral, McCaffrey, and Paddock (2002) based on analyses of data from the U.S. National Household Surveys on Drug Abuse found that associations between marijuana and hard drug use would be uncovered even if marijuana has no gateway effect. Instead, the well-documented associations between marijuana and hard drug use likely result from differences in the age at which young people have opportunities to use marijuana and hard drugs and differences in individuals' willingness to try any type of drugs. In simple terms, marijuana is typically the first illegal drug used by young people because it is more widely available than other illicit substances. It is important to note that the Morral and colleagues study did not disprove the gateway theory; instead, it shows that an alternative explanation for the association between marijuana and hard drug use is possible.

| Table 1.1 | Percentage of Illegal Drug Use in the United States and the Netherlands: Lifetime Use Among People Aged 12 and Older in 2001 |

	United States[a]	The Netherlands[b]
Marijuana	36.9	17.0
Cocaine	12.3	2.9
Ecstasy	3.6	2.9
LSD	9.0	1.0
Heroin	1.4	0.4

SOURCE: European Monitoring Centre for Drugs and Drug Addiction (EMCDDA, 2002b).

a. Data obtained from the 2001 National Household Survey on Drug Abuse.
b. Data obtained from EMCDDA (2002a).

Considering the scientific research assessing the gateway drug hypothesis as a whole, it is safe to say that there is no pharmacological basis for this theory. However, as noted above, there may be a relationship between marijuana use and the use of other drugs that is due to the fact that marijuana must be purchased in illicit markets. Here, it is worth considering the situation in the Netherlands. As will be discussed in more detail in Chapter 12, the Dutch decriminalized cannabis possession and retail sale of the drug in 1976, which, among other things, allowed for sale and use of marijuana in coffee shops. In the United States, 36.9% of respondents in the 2001 U.S. National Household Survey on Drug Abuse reported using cannabis at least once in their lifetime; in the Netherlands, the comparable figure was 17.0%. With respect to use of marijuana in the previous year, approximately 3% of people in the Netherlands, compared to 8.6% in the United States, reported such use (Dilanian, 2006). In addition, an earlier survey conducted in the city of Amsterdam found that the average age at which young people began use of cannabis was 20, compared to an average age of initiation of approximately 16 in the United States (Zimmer & Morgan, 1997, p. 52). But more relevant to the gateway drug hypothesis are data on the use of other drugs by people in the Netherlands compared to the United States. As Table 1.1 reveals (the data are the most recent comparable data available), only 2.9% of people in the Netherlands reported ever using cocaine, compared to 12.3% in the United States. Similarly, while 1.4% of respondents in the 2001 U.S. National Household Survey on Drug Abuse reported lifetime use of heroin, only 0.4% of respondents in a similar survey in the Netherlands reported such use. The fact that the Netherlands is a small, relatively homogeneous country with comparatively low rates of poverty and homelessness and with a superior health care system may contribute to lower rates of hard drug use in that country. However, these data raise the possibility that the lower rate of drug use in the Netherlands may be partially attributable to the success of the Dutch in separating the cannabis and hard drug markets (see box).

A government report from the Netherlands noted, "If young adults wish to use soft drugs—and evidence has shown that they do—they should...not be exposed to the criminal subculture surrounding hard drugs. Tolerating relatively easy access to quantities of soft drugs for personal use is intended to keep the consumer markets for soft and hard drugs separate, thus creating a social barrier to the transition from soft to hard drugs." (as quoted in Zimmer & Morgan, 1997, p. 53)

Perhaps the most convincing evidence refuting the gateway drug hypothesis is that by the early 2000s, approximately 83 million people in the United States had tried marijuana at some point in their lives but had never used heroin. Data from the U.S. National Household Survey on Drug Abuse reveal that if individuals had ever tried marijuana in their lifetime, their chance of using other illegal drugs in the previous month was 1 in 7 for marijuana, 1 in 12 for any other illegal drug, 1 in 50 for cocaine, and 1 in 677 for heroin (Earleywine, 2003). As NORML (2002) noted, given such statistics on the prevalence of marijuana use and the use of other illegal drugs, for the majority of marijuana users, the substance is a "terminus" rather than a gateway. A National Academy of Sciences report (1999) observed, "there is no evidence that marijuana serves as a stepping stone on the basis of its particular drug effect." A Canadian Senate Committee report similarly concluded, "cannabis itself is not a cause of other drug use; in this sense, we reject the gateway theory" (Government of Canada, 2002). In short, the claims of the ONDCP, drug czar John Walters, and others that marijuana is a gateway drug and therefore should retain its status as a Schedule I drug in the United States are not based on sound scientific evidence.

In his editorial in the *Washington Post,* John Walters also claimed, without providing any source, that "each year, marijuana is linked to tens of thousands of serious traffic accidents" (Walters, 2002). He also linked marijuana to brain damage in asserting, "the THC in marijuana attaches itself to receptors in the hippocampal region of the brain, weakening short-term memory and interfering with the mechanisms of long-term memory. Do our struggling schools really need another obstacle to student achievement?"

In this statement, Walters may have been referring to a study conducted by Solowij and colleagues (2002). This study compared 33 nonusers with 102 cannabis users who had smoked an average of two marijuana cigarettes a day for an average of 24 years and found that the latter experienced more problems related to impaired learning and retention and retrieval of information. The authors concluded, "These results confirm that long-term heavy cannabis users show impairments in memory and attention that endure beyond the period of intoxication and worsen with increasing years of regular cannabis use" (p. 1132). However, the authors of this study were careful to note that their research did not indicate that marijuana causes brain damage, and also that they had not been able to take into account a number of additional factors that may have affected the marijuana users' memory impairment. In fact, a meta-analysis of 15 previously published studies examining the impact of long-term marijuana consumption on the cognitive functioning of adults found that recreational marijuana use had only minor negative effects on learning and memory. There were no effects of marijuana on other cognitive functions, such as reaction time, attention, language, reasoning ability, and perceptual motor skills. This study suggested that the problems with respect to memory and learning indicate that long-term marijuana use may result in selective memory problems, but that the impact is relatively small (Drug Policy Alliance, 2003l).

Related to the allegations that marijuana affects cognitive functioning are assertions that it can be a causal factor in users developing psychiatric illnesses. Thus, a 2003 ONDCP report claimed that marijuana use was linked to mental illnesses such as schizophrenia and depression (ONDCP, 2003b). This particular conclusion may have been based on two studies published in the *British Medical Journal* in 2002. In the first of these studies, Rey (2002) asserted that frequent cannabis use could increase the risk of suffering from depression or schizophrenia later in life. However, in a critique of this study, Iversen (2003) suggested that the existence of a causal relationship between cannabis use and psychiatric illness has not been proven. Referring to aggregate-level data, Iversen notes that if cannabis use causes schizophrenia, there would have been a substantial increase in the number of people diagnosed with schizophrenia when cannabis use increased substantially over the 1960 to 1990 period. However, the number of individuals diagnosed with schizophrenia did not increase over this period.

The second study published in the *British Medical Journal* followed a cohort of 1,947 14- and 15-year-old Australians for 7 years and found that daily consumption of cannabis resulted in more than a fivefold increase in anxiety or depression (Patton et al., 2002). The authors of this study did note, however, that "because the risks seem confined to daily users, the question about a direct pharmacological effect remains" (p. 1197). More generally, the question in this type of research, similar to what we discussed with respect to "amotivational syndrome," is related to causal ordering. That is, does cannabis use lead to anxiety and/or depression, or do people suffering from these conditions self-medicate with cannabis?

Although not a point emphasized specifically by ONDCP in its discussion of marijuana, some commentators justify the continued prohibition of marijuana on the basis of its alleged carcinogenic effects. Leaving aside the fact that the substance causing by far the most cancer deaths (tobacco) remains legal in the United States, the scientific evidence does not indicate a strong relationship between marijuana consumption and cancer.

Researchers in Britain asserted that cannabis use was linked to cancer and claimed that there were as many as 30,000 deaths per year in that country caused by marijuana smoking (Henry, Oldfield, & Kon, 2003). Although these researchers did not have access to actual cannabis-related mortality data, they asserted that because the percentage of British citizens who smoked marijuana was approximately one-quarter of the percentage of British who smoked cigarettes, the number of deaths attributable to marijuana smoking would be about one-quarter the number attributed to cigarettes (p. 943). As Sidney (2003) pointed out, however, there are several differences between marijuana and tobacco smokers that have implications for the estimates of Henry and colleagues. Compared to tobacco smokers, most individuals who use marijuana stop using the substance fairly early in their adult lives, and the typical marijuana smoker consumes about one marijuana cigarette per day, while tobacco users usually consume 20 or more cigarettes per day (p. 636). While it is true that marijuana smokers typically inhale more deeply and retain smoke in their lungs for a longer period of time each time they smoke (Zimmer & Morgan, 1997), the key issue with respect to the potential relationship to cancer is the total volume of toxic material accumulated over time, not the amount inhaled per individual cigarette. Sidney (2003) concluded, "Although the use of cannabis is not harmless, the current knowledge base does not support the assertion that it has any notable adverse public health impact in relation to mortality" (p. 636). The United States National Academy of Sciences Institute of Medicine affirmed this conclusion, noting, "there is no conclusive evidence that marijuana causes cancer in humans, including cancers usually related to tobacco use" (National Academy of Sciences, 1999).

Almost paradoxically, while claiming that marijuana is a dangerous substance, drug czar John Walters has also tried to silence critics of laws against marijuana through assertions that it is a myth that large numbers of Americans have been incarcerated for marijuana offenses. However, calculations based on Bureau of Justice Statistics revealed that 59,300 prisoners (3.3% of the total incarcerated population) in 1999 were convicted of violations of marijuana laws. In the same year, offenders charged with crimes related to marijuana comprised close to 12% of the total federal prison population and approximately 2.7% of the state prison population (C. Thomas, 1999). Schlosser (2003) further notes that the number of marijuana offenders sent to federal prisons in 1999 was greater than the number of offenders sent to such prisons for methamphetamine, crack, or cocaine powder, which are supposedly more dangerous drugs. Marijuana offenders were given life sentences under federal laws in 1992, 1993, and 1994, and over the 16-year period of 1984 to 1999, 16 people were sentenced to life in federal prison as a result of a conviction for a marijuana offense. Zimmer and Morgan (1997) note that 22% of those sentenced for the violation of marijuana statutes in Michigan in 1995 were sent to prison, as were 34% of those in Texas and New York. Similarly, under California's "Three Strikes and You're Out" law, more people had been sent to prison for marijuana than for all violent offenses combined. Schlosser (2003) also provides specific examples of the severe penalties imposed on individuals for marijuana offenses. In Oklahoma, a paraplegic who smoked marijuana to relieve muscle spasms was sentenced to life imprisonment plus 16 years for possession of marijuana with intent to distribute (two ounces) of marijuana, possession of drug paraphernalia, unlawful possession of a weapon, and maintaining a place resorted to by users of controlled substances. Another individual in the same state was found in possession of 0.16 of an ounce of marijuana and was sentenced to life imprisonment.

Finally, in one of the most egregious examples of government attempts to manipulate science to unveil the negative effects of marijuana, researchers at the Nati Institute on Drug Abuse, in an attempt to demonstrate that the subs physically addicting, conducted experiments in which they tried to induce monkeys to self-administer THC. As the Lindesmith Center (2001b) reported, when these attempts were not successful, the researchers taught the monkeys to self-administer cocaine, and "after strapping the monkeys into chairs and turning them into cocaine addicts, NIDA found that previously disinterested monkeys would willingly self-administer the THC when forced into cocaine withdrawal."

To conclude this section, from the time marijuana was first prohibited at the federal level in the United States in 1937 to the present, the government, and at times certain media sources, have engaged in a concerted campaign to demonize it and thereby justify its continued prohibition. However, it is important to note that a number of government commissions, both in the United States and in other countries, have concluded that the possession and consumption of marijuana should not be subject to criminal penalties. The 1975 U.S. Shafer Commission report recommended that possession of cannabis should not be a criminal offense (Trebach, 1988). The 1973 Canadian LeDain Commission report concluded that the prohibition of cannabis was an excessive, ineffective, and costly tool for controlling marijuana use (Government of Canada, 1973). These conclusions were consistent with the Wooton report in Britain (1968); reports in the Netherlands (1971–1972); and the Baume Commission in Australia (1977) (cited in Fischer et al., 2003). And in 1995, the World Health Organization's (WHO) Program on Substance Abuse, commenting on the effects of cannabis, noted, "on existing patterns of use, cannabis poses a much less serious public health problem than is currently posed by alcohol and tobacco in Western societies" (as cited in Jelsma, 2003, p. 190). However, in the final WHO report, the comparison to alcohol was deleted, likely in response to U.S. officials' concerns. In Chapter 11, we address recent developments in marijuana policies in the United States.

CRACK COCAINE

The crack cocaine "epidemic" was constructed by media, government, and law enforcement officials in the mid- to late-1980s (Brownstein, 1996). Reinarman and Levine (1997) note that in July of 1986 alone, the three major television networks in the United States presented 74 evening news segments on drug-related topics, half of which focused on crack. Between October 1998 and October 1999, the Washington Post alone featured 1,563 stories about the drug crisis. Many of the alleged that its use led to the commission of violent crime and that cocaine was more addictive than cocaine administered nasally; of the justifications for treating the former substance more in drug legislation passed in the 1980s (see Chapter 11). 1990) and others have noted, there is no difference in the crack cocaine and cocaine hydrochloride. Furthermore, it for a relatively short period of time. the image that crack was primarily a drug used by to demonize it in the eyes of many whites.

However, a study published in the *Journal of the American Medical Association* found that given similar social and environmental conditions, crack use was not strongly related to race-specific individual factors. Once respondents in this study were grouped into neighborhood clusters, the relative odds of crack use were not significantly different for African Americans or Hispanics compared with whites (Lillie-Blanton, Anthony, & Schuster, 1993, p. 996).

More generally, several authors have noted that crack cocaine use never did constitute an epidemic in the United States (Akers, 1992; Reinarman & Levine, 1997). As Alexander (1990) comments, "one could argue that there is an epidemic of having used cocaine at least once, if about 10% of the American population . . . can be taken as constituting epidemic proportions" (p. 187). However, the crack cocaine "epidemic" allowed legislators to shift the blame for many of the social problems of the 1980s, including relatively high rates of unemployment and crime, from the actions (or nonactions) of government to the drug taking and trafficking of individuals. "Crack was a godsend to the Right. They used it and the drug issue as an ideological fig leaf to place over the unsightly urban ills that had increased markedly under the Reagan administration's social and economic policies" (Reinarman & Levine, 1997, p. 16). We address recent developments in the legislation dealing with crack cocaine in Chapter 11.

HEROIN

When the crack cocaine "epidemic" subsided in the early 1990s, government officials and media sources were apparently in search of another drug to demonize. Although heroin never received the same amount of attention as ecstasy and methamphetamine (discussed below), there were several reports in the 1990s and 2000s of an emerging heroin "epidemic." In 1996, for example, it was asserted that "heroin, once considered the poisonous habit of pathetic junkies, is being reborn as the hip drug of choice among the trend setters of Generation X" ("Ads Show Reality," 1996). General Barry McCaffrey, drug czar under President Clinton, also weighed in, noting, "heroin is back, and it's cheaper, more potent, and deadlier than ever" (as quoted in Fields, 1999). Richard Bonnette, President of the Partnership for a Drug-Free America (PFDFA), said heroin was becoming "the drug of the 90s"; another PFDFA spokesperson claimed, "heroin looks like a thermonuclear disaster waiting to happen" (as quoted in J. Gray, 2001).

Employing the tactic of marshaling misleading statistics to indicate the emergence of a heroin epidemic, the media and politicians claimed that heroin use had doubled between 1995 and 1996. The basis for this claim was a National Institute on Drug Abuse survey of 4,500 youth that revealed that 32 admitted to using heroin in 1996; in the previous year, only 14 in a similar survey had acknowledged the use of heroin (J. Gray, 2001). In early 2003, a law enforcement official in Maine was quoted as saying, "Through the state, heroin use is an epidemic, no question" (as quoted in Ferdinand, 2003). In the same year, heroin was also apparently spreading to the Midwest region of the United States, with one article referring to "the rising tide of small town heroin abuse in the Midwest, occurring in little tidy communities with town squares, bicycles on front lawns, and American flags" (C. Jones, 2003).

As mentioned above, socially constructed drug epidemics can be made to appear even more threatening when they involve children. Writing about an allegedly emerging "heroin epidemic" in New England, Cambanis (2003) noted, "Heroin dealers who target children as young as 12 with free samples and drug packets decorated with cartoon characters have spawned an epidemic of illicit heroin use in Massachusetts and New England."

The heroin "epidemic" has also been attributed to foreign drug traffickers. A *Chicago Tribune* article, alleging an increasing problem with heroin in that city, noted, "in 1985, federal agents dismantled much of the Mexican heroin supply that dominated the Chicago market. Nigerians quickly filled the void, then were replaced by Colombians after another federal investigation in the late 1990s" (Bebow, 2004).

ECSTASY (MDMA)

Ecstasy is a drug invented by German psychiatrists in 1912. It was tested as a "truth drug" by the U.S. Central Intelligence Agency in the 1940s (Davenport-Hines, 2001) and has also been used to facilitate psychotherapy (ONDCP, 2002a). In fact, in the 1950s and 1960s, treatment with hallucinogenic drugs such as ecstasy was seen to be the cutting edge of psychotherapy (Ehrman, 2003).

As the use of ecstasy allegedly increased in the United States in the late 1990s and early 2000s, especially at dance parties ("raves") and similar events, government officials deemed it necessary to inform the public of the dangers associated with the substance. During this period, thousands of articles on the topic of ecstasy appeared in popular magazines, newspapers, and on the Internet. A police officer in Richmond, Virginia, told a reporter, "it appears that the ecstasy problem will eclipse the crack cocaine problem we experienced in the 1980s" (as quoted in Cloud, 2000). An editorial written by former drug czar William Bennett claimed, "while the crack cocaine epidemic of the 1990s has passed, methamphetamine and ecstasy are growing in popularity, especially among the young" (Bennett, 2001). Although Bennett did not provide statistics to support his assertion of an increase in ecstasy use, a survey conducted under the auspices of the Partnership for a Drug Free America found that the percentage of teenagers reporting use of ecstasy had doubled between 1995 and 2000, from 5% to 10% (PFDFA, 2000).

In order to provide evidence of an "alarming explosion" (Rashbaum, 2000) in ecstasy use, media sources relied on statistics on seizures of ecstasy tablets, reports of law enforcement officials, and emergency room admission (DAWN) data. The commissioner of the U.S. Customs Service claimed that seizures of ecstasy by his agency had increased from 350,000 in 1997 to 3.5 million in 1999, then to 2.9 million in just the first 2 months of 2000. He also predicted that ecstasy seizures would increase to seven or eight million by the end of 2000 (Wedge, 2000). Hays (2000) indicated that "seizures of the tablets . . . have multiplied like rabbits." Gullo (2001) noted, "ecstasy, a drug once used primarily at night clubs, has expanded beyond the club scene and is being sold at high schools, on the street, and even at coffee shops in some cities." The source of the claims that ecstasy was being used in contexts in which it had not previously been used was an informal survey of officials in 20 cities in the United States.

> A similar pattern of constructing an ecstasy epidemic through reference to seizures of the substance occurred in Canada. In May 2000, several Canadian newspapers announced that the largest seizure of ecstasy in the country's history had occurred at the Toronto airport. Police reported that they had seized 170,000 ecstasy tablets, valued at $5 million. However, it turned out that the police had made a mathematical error in their calculations, weighing the quantity of pills per pound instead of per kilogram. Thus, the actual seizure was 61,000 tablets, valued at $1.8 million. A spokesperson for the Royal Canadian Mounted Police noted, "It's one of those unfortunate situations. It was an error that we made and we're only human. So I apologize for that." (as quoted in Alphonso, 2000)

An additional indicator of the alleged increase in ecstasy use was derived from Federal Drug Abuse Warning (DAWN) data: Mentions of the drug as a factor in hospital emergency room admissions increased from 68 in 1993 to 637 in 1997 (Rashbaum, 2000). However, as we discussed with respect to mentions of marijuana in DAWN data, it is likely the case that the majority of ecstasy users consumed ecstasy along with other drugs, as opposed to ecstasy alone.

Although the popular press and government officials emphasized that ecstasy was a dangerous substance because of claims that it was the cause of several deaths, the causal relationship between ecstasy consumption and death has not been well established. For example, in New York, a study of 20 deaths that had been attributed to ecstasy found that only three were caused by ecstasy alone (Gill et al., 2002). This phenomenon also occurred in Britain, where it was found that 19 of 27 individuals whose death had originally been attributed to ecstasy had other drugs in their system (Boseley, 2002), and Canada, where an inquest into 13 deaths said to be caused by the drug revealed that seven of the individuals has also used heroin, cocaine, and/or methadone (Prittie, 2000).

Consistent with the theme of demonizing drugs by attributing their distribution to foreigners, several media and government sources indicated that the main traffickers in ecstasy were Israelis. One report on ecstasy asserted that "Hasidic Jews" were couriers and that "Israeli organized crime dominates the global trade [in ecstasy]" (Cloud, 2000). This connection was confirmed in another article: "For the most part, Israeli-organized crime syndicates have been implicated as the main source of distribution of the drug in the United States" (Hernandez, 2000). Further, Leinwand and Fields (2000) noted, "The international crime agency Interpol, the U.S. Customs Service, and the Drug Enforcement Administration have tracked Israeli crime groups and Russian mobsters trading in ecstasy." Even the "official" federal government source of information on ecstasy, an ONDCP (2002a) Fact Sheet, noted "the majority of MDMA comes from Europe and is thought to be trafficked by Israeli organized crime syndicates."

One of the most prominent themes in government and popular media sources on the topic of ecstasy was assertions that use of the substance causes brain damage. As we have discussed already, and as will be discussed in more detail later in this book, there have been numerous instances of "scientific" studies on the effects of drugs that present misleading and, in some cases, fraudulent information that is then used to justify stringent drug policies. A particularly disturbing example of this phenomenon is seen in research on the effects of ecstasy by George Ricaurte and his colleagues at Johns Hopkins University. One of Ricaurte's studies, sponsored by the National Institute of Drug Abuse and published in the prestigious journal *Science*, claimed that ecstasy could cause permanent brain damage in human users of the substance: "Even one night's indulgence [in ecstasy] may increase the odds of contracting Parkinson's disease" (Ricaurte et al., 2002).

In this study, Ricaurte and his colleagues administered three consecutive doses of what they claimed to be ecstasy to monkeys at 3-hour intervals. When these monkeys were tested after 6 weeks, their dopamine levels had decreased by approximately 65%. Ricaurte and colleagues (2002) concluded,

> These findings suggest that humans who use repeated doses of MDMA over several hours are at risk of incurring severe dopaminergic neural injury. . . . This injury, together with a decline in dopaminergic function known to occur with age, may put these individuals at increased risk for developing Parkinsonism and other neuropsychiatric diseases involving brain dopaminergic/serotonin deficiency, either as young adults or later in life. (p. 2263)

The Ricaurte and colleagues (2002) study was widely reported in the popular media and led to calls for tougher laws to deal with ecstasy. Dr. Alan Leshner, former director of the Drug Abuse Institute, claimed that using the substance "is like playing Russian roulette with your brain" (as quoted in Ehrman, 2003). Perhaps coincidentally, the Ricaurte and colleagues study was published around the same time that Congress was considering a bill designed to control ecstasy (the RAVE Act; see Chapter 11).

However, it turned out that rather than administering MDMA to the monkeys in his lab, Ricaurte and his colleagues, apparently unbeknownst to them, had been administering methamphetamine. The mistake was blamed on a labeling problem; apparently the labels attached to drug containers supplied to Ricaurte's lab were incorrect. Ricaurte claims he realized his mistake when he could not replicate his own results by administering MDMA to the monkeys orally (McNeil, 2003). Ricaurte further asserted that his laboratory had made a "simple human error. We're scientists, not politicians." When asked why the vials of drugs were not checked by those conducting the research, he responded, "We're not chemists. We've got hundreds of chemicals here. It's not customary to check them" (as quoted in McNeil, 2003). This response seems rather bizarre when we consider that Ricaurte's research laboratory's primary activity is to examine the effects of chemical substance on animals (see box).

As one critic noted in response to Ricaurte's comments, "OK. Slow down. Read that again. We get hundreds of chemicals in here, in this scientific laboratory where we analyze the effects of chemicals on primate subjects, and we do not bother to check the chemicals. Nope, we just read the labels, get out the syringe, and hello monkey want some whatever-it-is?" (McNeil, 2003)

Once this mistake was revealed, a retraction of the article was published in *Science* (Ricaurte et al., 2003). However, in issuing this retraction, Ricaurte and his colleagues added, "The apparent labeling error does not call into question multiple previous studies demonstrating the serotonin neurotoxic potential of MDMA in various animal species" (p. 1479). Although Ricaurte and colleagues thus claimed that the wrong chemical (methamphetamine instead of MDMA) had been used only in the study published in *Science*, of the other journals that published research on the effects of ecstasy written by Ricaurte and his colleagues, including the *European Journal of Pharmacology*, the *Journal of Pharmacology*, and *Experimental Therapeutics*, the only other article retracted was the one appearing in the *Journal of Pharmacology*. However, Ricaurte was only able to account for 2.25 grams of the 10 grams of methamphetamine that were in the original container that had been labeled as MDMA, suggesting the possibility that other published studies by his research team should also be retracted (Doblin, 2003).

While Ricaurte and his colleagues should be commended for issuing the retraction of the *Science* article, it is important to keep in mind that their findings of a relationship between ecstasy use and brain damage had already been widely cited in print and other forms of media as evidence of the dangers of ecstasy. It is also possible that scientists and/or journalists conducting research on the effects of ecstasy will continue to cite this study.

Even before the revelations that Ricaurte and his research team had been administering methamphetamine rather than MDMA to the monkeys, other researchers had criticized the study. One commentator noted, "The multiple-dose regimen of injected MDMA administered by Dr. Ricaurte does not simulate human exposure, does not cause cell death, and does not predict anything as a result of MDMA" (as quoted in Drug Policy Alliance, 2002d). Similarly, Colin Blakemore, chair of the British Association for the Advancement of Science, and Leslie Iversen, a British pharmacologist, had communicated with the editor of *Science* and suggested that Ricaurte's article should not have been published due to several methodological problems. Interestingly, the very title of Ricaurte's (2002) article published in *Science* was misleading, in that it used the phrase *common recreational dose regimen*. As Blakemore and Iversen pointed out, Ricaurte had administered the drug to monkeys subcutaneously, which would deliver a much higher dose to the brain than the normal amount of ecstasy consumed by humans (Walgate, 2003). An additional issue was the extreme effect on the dopamine system reported by Ricaurte; such effects had not been previously associated with MDMA but were known to occur with methamphetamine (Walgate, 2003). In fact, well before Ricaurte discovered the mistake, Iversen had suggested that the reported results appeared to be more characteristic of amphetamine than of MDMA ("Retracted Ecstasy Paper," 2003). This possibility had also been raised in another *Science* article published some 9 months after the Ricaurte and colleagues (2002) publication. Mithofer, Jerome, and Doblin (2003) had noted, "the dopamine changes produced by MDMA [in the Ricaurte et al. study] have long been known as potential effects of d-amphetamine and d-methamphetamine" (p. 1504).

> In addition to the alarmist media reports emanating from the findings of the Ricaurte et al. (2002) study, the claim that ecstasy causes brain damage was reinforced through disturbing images showing holes in the brain of an alleged MDMA user—these images were shown on a MTV special documentary about the substance, as well as on the popular *Oprah Winfrey* show. However, these brain images had in fact been graphically manipulated to represent areas of lower brain blood flow as holes and were completely fraudulent. (Doblin, 2003)

Ricaurte's laboratory has received millions of dollars in funding from the National Institute on Drug Abuse and has produced several studies concluding that ecstasy is a dangerous substance (McNeil, 2003). His earlier studies were cited as evidence of the dangers of ecstasy in the previously mentioned ONDCP (2002a) Fact Sheet on MDMA, which noted, "A recent study sponsored by the National Institute on Drug Abuse showed that monkeys that were given doses of MDMA for four days suffered damage to the brain six or seven years later." Although, as we will discuss in Chapter 7, federal government agencies that provide financial support for drug research have discontinued the funding of researchers who produce results that do not support the continuation of the drug war, apparently this does not apply to researchers who produce findings such as those of Ricaurte. Despite the documented problems associated with Ricaurte's research, to the best of our knowledge, the National Institute on Drug Abuse has not discontinued funding his research. As the British pharmacologist Iversen suggested,

It's another example of a certain breed of scientist who appear to do research on illegal drugs mainly to show what the government wants them to show. They extract large amounts of money from the government to do this sort of biased work. ("Retracted Ecstasy Paper," 2003)

The above discussion is not intended to suggest that there are no harms associated with the use of ecstasy. As will be discussed in Chapter 3, ecstasy exerts its effects by stimulating the brain to produce serotonin. Given that the brain can only produce a finite amount of serotonin over a lifetime, long-term heavy use of ecstasy could lead to the depletion of the brain's serotonin supply, possibly resulting in a higher risk for depression among long-term users (Richburg, 2001). But the most serious short-term risks associated with ecstasy are related to the fact that many pills are adulterated with other chemicals (Stafford, 2012), several of which are more dangerous to users than pure ecstasy. A study of the composition of seized ecstasy pills conducted by the Royal Canadian Mounted Police found that many contained methamphetamine, MDA, ketamine, and PCP (Leinwand, 2002). Other adulterants included caffeine, cocaine, and a number of over-the-counter drugs. One of the most dangerous adulterants is dexotromethorphan (DXM), a cough suppressant that can produce hallucinations if it is taken in concentrated form (McColl, 2001). And because DXM also inhibits sweating, it can easily cause heatstroke (Cloud, 2000). The problems resulting from unknown and often dangerous adulterants in ecstasy could be alleviated under a system of government regulation of the substance, although we are not necessarily advocating regulation here. But it is also important to note that recent studies indicate that MDMA does not impair cognitive functioning (Halpern et al., 2011), and the Multi-disciplinary Association for Psychedelic Studies has administered the drug to at least 500 people in various clinical trials, with no reports of any adverse events associated with its use (Stafford, 2012).

METHAMPHETAMINE

After the crack cocaine "epidemic" subsided, arguably the most prominent candidate for the "drug of the 1990s" was methamphetamine. Brecher's (1972) comments in the context of declining rates of methamphetamine use in the late 1960s and early 1970s seem especially prescient in the context of recent developments with respect to the substance:

> If these trends continue, the speed freak may in the not too distant future be merely a historical oddity. Unless, of course, a new wave of anti-speed propaganda campaigns serve to encourage a shift from less dangerous to more dangerous drugs. (p. 3)

Once again, it is important to emphasize that in our discussion of methamphetamine, we are by no means trying to minimize its often devastating effects. Our purpose, instead, is to critically examine the extant information on this drug and to focus on how, as has been the case with other illegal drugs, official government, criminal justice system, and media sources have grossly exaggerated the extent of the methamphetamine problem.

Numerous government, media, and Internet sources in the late 1990s claimed that methamphetamine use in the United States constituted an "epidemic" (a Google Internet search using the words *methamphetamine epidemic* on December 29, 2005, resulted in more than 246,000 hits). President Clinton referred to methamphetamine as "the crack of the 90s," and in February 1998, drug czar Barry McCaffrey asserted, "Methamphetamine has exploded from a west coast biker drug into America's heartland and could replace cocaine as the nation's primary drug threat" (as quoted in Pennell et al., 1999).

The title "crack of the 90s" had earlier been given to gambling and heroin. As Sullum (2003a) notes, "Since heroin was perceived as the chief drug menace in the 1970s, crack could be described as the heroin of the 80s. Then meth was the crack of the 90s, and it looked like heroin could become the meth of the next decade." (p. 238)

McCaffrey also referred to methamphetamine as "the worst drug that has ever hit America" (as quoted in Nieves, 2001). Some years later, representative Tom Osborne of Nebraska called methamphetamine "the biggest threat to the United States, maybe even including Al Qaida" (as quoted in "My Mistress Methamphetamine," 2005). In a 1996 publication, the National Institute of Justice asserted that statistics from the Drug Use Forecasting (DUF) program (a program that administers drug tests to jail inmates; see Chapter 5) "may signal an impending methamphetamine pandemic." The publication noted that approximately 6% of all adult and juvenile arrestees at DUF sites tested positive for methamphetamine in 1996. And while it is certainly true that rates of methamphetamine-positive drug tests for arrestees were significantly higher in cities such as San Diego and Phoenix, the DUF system was developed to examine drug use trends among arrestees and variations in these trends across cities; it was not designed to be a measure of drug use in the general population. We should thus treat these statistics alleging an emerging methamphetamine "pandemic" with skepticism.

In addition to government claims of a methamphetamine "epidemic," a number of popular media sources made similar assertions. Thus a 1996 article in the Spokane, Washington, *Spokesman-Review* with the headline "Meth Turning Kids Into Monsters" claimed that methamphetamine was "exploding through the Inland Northwest and the nation." An official from the city of Spokane claimed that half of the young people booked into the juvenile detention center in the city had used the drug (Sitamariah, 1996). Methamphetamine was also said to have "ravaged the state [of Missouri] for more than a decade, ensnaring young and old, businessmen, housewives, and entire families" (Pierre, 2003). A detective in Franklin County, Missouri, argued, "it used to be big news to find a meth cook. Now *everybody* is cooking meth" (as quoted in Pierre, 2003; italics added). An official from the Bureau of Alcohol, Tobacco, and Firearms stated "[meth] has literally spread like dermatitis. . . . It's like trying to fight a water balloon. You fight it and it goes somewhere else" (as quoted in Pierre, 2003).

A 2005 *Newsweek* article ("America's Most Dangerous Drug") made questionable use of the U.S. National Household Survey on Drug Use and Health statistics to bolster claims of a methamphetamine epidemic. The article claimed that in 2004, there were 1.5 million "regular users" (equivalent to approximately 0.6% of the population aged 12 and older) of meth in the United States (Jefferson, 2005); however, it is important to note that this figure was based on survey respondents who reported that they had used methamphetamine at least once in the previous year. Gillespie (2005) questions whether use of methamphetamine in the past year is equivalent to "regular use"; "Are you a regular user of liquor if you've had one drink in the past year?"

The same 2005 *Newsweek* article also included data from a July 2005 telephone survey of 500 law enforcement agencies conducted by the National Association of Counties; 58% of those responding to the survey said methamphetamine was their "biggest drug problem." However, as Gillespie (2005) notes, the law enforcement officials' responses to the survey may have been influenced by the preface to the survey, which stated, "As you may know, methamphetamine use has risen dramatically in counties across the nation." In addition, there are questions surrounding the methodology of the National Association of Counties' survey because it provided no information regarding response rates or how representative the sample of 500 counties was of all counties in the United States (Gillespie, 2005; see also Shafer, 2006).

Newspaper reports documenting the methamphetamine phenomenon often made rather questionable statistical comparisons in order to underline the extent of the alleged problem. An article in the *Spokesman-Review* noted that the number of methamphetamine addicts in Spokane County treated in publicly funded clinics rose "nearly 2,200 percent" between 1993 and 1999 (Martin, Rourke, & Gaddy, 2002). While this may appear to be an alarming increase, it is perhaps less so when we realize that in terms of actual numbers, there was an increase from 22 individuals being treated for methamphetamine in 1993 to 503 in 2000 (the population of Spokane County in the year 2000 was 417,939). A related media strategy is to report on large percentage increases in methamphetamine cases and/or methamphetamine-related crime without providing the raw figures on which the percentage increases were calculated. For example, an article on the topic of methamphetamine in *Newsweek* magazine noted, "In North Dakota, where meth cases have quadrupled since 1994, a Northeastern University study estimates that the teen murder rate jumped by 320 percent. Across the river, in Clay County, Minnesota, crime is up 500 percent over five years" (Bai, 1997). However, the actual numbers of murders and crimes were not provided in this article. A *USA Today* article reported that there was a "144 percent rise in meth-related deaths from 1992–1994—deaths were up 222 percent in Los Angeles and 510 percent in Phoenix" (Davis, 1995). Again, no raw data were provided.

There have also been allegations that in comparison to other substances, methamphetamine has properties that make users more susceptible to addiction. Several sources emphasized that the "high" from methamphetamine lasts longer than the psychoactive effects of other drugs, although the actual length of time the high is alleged to last varies widely depending on which source is consulted. Thus Durbin (2003a) asserts that a methamphetamine high can last 14 hours or more; Brandon (2001) suggest that it lasts 12 hours, while a National Institute of Justice Report claimed that "the high can last up to 24 hours" (Pennell et al., 1999). Apparently, these longer highs are partial contributors to meth users being more susceptible to addiction. A sheriff's lieutenant in Spokane, Washington, claimed that "nearly 95% of all meth users are addicted to the drug six months after using it" (as quoted in Blocker, 2001a), and an *Associated Press* article asserted, "smoking it provides a high so intense and long-lasting that addiction can be instant, withdrawal is excruciating, and brain damage is often permanent" ("Meth Threatens Hawaii's," 2003).

Another article suggested "just one hit, and meth can take over a life" and that "even two binges scorch the pleasure center of the brain, causing lifelong depression" (Martin et al., 2002).

The Drug Enforcement Administration's website (www.justthinktwice.com) included a link to "Meth is Death," a site sponsored by the Tennessee District Attorneys General Conference, which claimed that "one in seven high school students will try meth"; "99 percent of first-time users are hooked after the first try"; "only five percent of meth addicts are able to kick it and stay away"; and "the life expectancy of a habitual meth user is only five years." Sullum (2005) encourages a critical consideration of these statistics:

> Do the math . . . and you will see that 13.4% of Americans die as a result of methamphetamine abuse within five years of graduating from high school. According to the U.S. Census Bureau, there are more than 20 million 15- to 19-year olds in the U.S., so we are talking about hundreds of thousands of deaths a year, and that's not even counting people who start using meth *after* high school.

Clearly, there have been nowhere close to this number of deaths caused by methamphetamine, which underlines the absurdity of the "information" contained on the Tennessee District Attorneys General website.

Linked to the idea that methamphetamine is more addicting than other psychoactive substances is the assertion that users of the substance are less amenable to treatment. However, scientific research suggests that methamphetamine addicts are not necessarily more difficult to treat. A study conducted by the California Department of Alcohol and Drug Programs reported that treatment of individuals addicted to the major stimulant drugs, including methamphetamine, was just as effective as treatment for alcohol problems and somewhat more effective than treatment for individuals who had heroin as their primary drug of addiction (cited in Pennell et al., 1999). Similarly, a study in Washington State found that methamphetamine addicts were just as amenable to treatment as individuals addicted to alcohol or other drugs, and that methamphetamine addicts who completed treatment had a reduced likelihood of involvement in criminal activity (Washington State Department of Social and Health Services, 2003). More generally, outcome measures of treatment programs in 15 states indicate that methamphetamine users are amenable to treatment (King, 2006).

Media sources discussing methamphetamine also claimed that the substance was related to increases in the commission of property and other crimes. An attorney in Butler County, Missouri, claimed that criminal cases accounted for 75% of his practice, and that 75% of those cases were meth related. The same attorney also claimed that one in four of the divorce cases he handled involved situations in which the husband or wife used methamphetamine (Pierre, 2003). Similarly, a prosecutor in Spokane, Washington, claimed that "most property crimes are committed by people addicted to meth" (as quoted in Blocker, 2001b). Going even further, a detective in the Spokane County Sheriff's office asserted, "in *all* the stolen property cases, meth has been at the center" (as quoted in Martin et al., 2002; italics added). In Oregon, the Governor's Public Safety Advisor asserted that methamphetamine was the "driving force in 80 to 90 percent of the property crimes committed" (as quoted in Esteve, 2003).

Even "environmental crime" has been attributed to methamphetamine addicts. For example, in the Olympic National Forest in Washington State, it was alleged that methamphetamine addicts were funding their daily drug habits by chopping down trees and selling the wood. ("Addicts Blamed," 2001)

An analysis of the Portland *Oregonian*'s coverage of methamphetamine noted that the newspaper had published at least 261 stories on methamphetamine over the one-and-a-half-year period ending in March 2006, and that the statistic that the drug "fuels" 85% of the property crime in Oregon had appeared in at least 14 articles between 2002 and 2006, without any attribution (Valdez, 2006). However, as Scott Moore (2006) pointed out, if methamphetamine was responsible for 85% of the crimes, one would expect that the property crime rate in Oregon in the early 2000s would be close to double the rates in the "pre-epidemic" years. However, in 1990, the property crime rate in Oregon was 521 per 10,000 population; it decreased to 478 per 10,000 population in 2003. Further evidence that estimates of the relationship between methamphetamine use and involvement in crime are inflated is provided by data from the Arrestee Drug Abuse Monitoring (ADAM) Program (see Chapter 5). In 2003, 25.4% of arrestees subject to drug tests in Portland, Oregon, tested positive for methamphetamine use (ADAM, 2003). While this is by no means an insignificant figure, it is a far cry from the 85% figure cited by law enforcement and government officials. In short, while scientific research generally confirms that users of some illicit drugs are more likely to be involved in property crimes than those who do not use drugs, we need to ask if methamphetamine (or any other illegal drug, for that matter) were eliminated, would all property crime also be eliminated?

As discussed above with respect to other drugs, a useful rhetorical device used to demonize a substance is to report anecdotal cases of bizarre acts committed by individuals allegedly under its influence. Several media sources recounted the story of a man (Eric Smith) in New Mexico who was high on methamphetamine and beheaded his 14-year-old son and "tossed the head from his van window onto a busy highway" (D. Johnson, 1996). This particular incident was also recounted in a *USA Today* article, which added, "Smith's grisly act last July was just another bizarre outburst blamed on methamphetamine, a powerful stimulant known on the street as 'crank' or 'ice' that's fast becoming the top choice of Americans buzzing in life's fast lane" (Davis, 1995). Quoting UCLA pharmacologist Ron Siegel, the article further noted, "[the Smith case] is pretty mild compared to the kind of case we're seeing in California. . . . We're seeing everything from serial killing to necrophilia." This article also noted that abusers of methamphetamine included Adolf Hitler and recounted another incident to emphasize the dangers associated with the substance:

A California woman, who fueled her long days cleaning houses with meth, sat down to watch the *Ten Commandments* [movie] with her kids after work. By the end of the movie, she'd killed her first born child in a ritual way that was a copycat of the movie. (Davis, 1995)

In Oregon, it was reported that

Jeffrey Cooper was high on meth when he helped kidnap Elizabeth Gumm at an ATM machine and then watched as his friends beat her and threw her down a hill to die. How did he go so wrong? The answer is methamphetamine, a highly addictive powder with a jolt more powerful and longer-lasting than cocaine. (N. McCarthy, 1995)

This article also quoted a drug treatment center caseworker, who said,

I guess the thing that alarms me about this drug is that it literally turns people into animals. They don't eat, they don't bathe. They don't take care of their children. The live in filth, and they just become subhuman. (N. McCarthy, 1995)

In Fargo, North Dakota, a "meth addict who burned his house down while hallucinating, killing his own mother, pleaded guilty to manslaughter" (Bai, 1997). A report on methamphetamine use in Washington State even went so far as to attribute animal abuse to the effects of the drug, noting "there were tweakers [methamphetamine users] who clubbed to death 17 newborn calves" (Solotaroff, 2003). Apparently, the connection between methamphetamine use and killing animals is not a uniquely American phenomenon. When a 37-year-old businessman in Sydney, Australia, killed 17 rabbits and a guinea pig in 2005, he claimed to be in a "drug-induced psychosis caused by ice." A forensic scientist's report on this individual noted that meth use caused him to have hallucinations and to "communicate" with rabbits (C. Munro, 2006). While we are not denying that the incidents described above occurred, does it make sense to attribute them to methamphetamine alone, or could other factors be involved?

Accounts of bizarre acts engaged in by individuals allegedly under the influence of methamphetamine have not been restricted to the popular media. A 1999 National Institute of Justice report on methamphetamine recounted the case of "[an individual] in San Diego who commandeered an army tank and wreaked havoc on people before being shot down by the police. . . . The individual was an acknowledged meth user." The same report noted, "In Riverside, California, a 40-year-old mother killed her children, ages one, two, and three, when she was using her kitchen to cook meth, and an explosion occurred" (Pennell et al., 1999).

In the previous example, we also see another consistent theme in drug demonization: an emphasis on how drugs threaten children. In an example of this theme, Swetlow (2003) noted,

Hazardous living conditions and filth are common in meth lab homes. Loaded guns and other weapons are usually present and often found in easy-to-reach locations. Living and play areas may be infested with rodents and insects, including cockroaches, fleas, ticks, and lice. Ashtrays and drug paraphernalia are often scattered within a child's reach, sometimes even in cribs.

Swetlow (2003) further commented,

> Dangerous animals trained to protect illegal meth labs pose added physical hazards, and their feces contribute to filth in areas where children play, sleep, and eat. Many children who live in meth homes are also exposed to pornographic materials or overt sexual activity.

While all of these assertions may, in fact, be true, is it logical to imply that the *drug* is the *cause* of the children's exposure to danger in general, and pornography and sexual activity in particular?

In 2005, two additional issues surrounding the alleged negative consequences of methamphetamine use surfaced: "meth-mouth" and "meth-addicted babies." Pictures of methamphetamine users "whose gums are pus-streaked and whose rotting teeth . . . are blackened and broken" (Shafer, 2005) appeared in several popular media articles in 2005. These articles implied that methamphetamine was the sole cause of tooth decay and loss and gum disease. However, as Shafer (2005) notes, it is by no means clear that methamphetamine is the only cause of these conditions. Methamphetamine users suffer from dry mouth, which is associated with tooth decay and gum disease, and many users try to refresh their dry mouths with soda that contains sugar, which further contributes to tooth decay. Perhaps even more importantly, many methamphetamine users neglect proper dental care, including brushing, flossing, and visiting dentists on a regular basis.

> Hungry children sat quietly in a darkened room, terrified of their abusive father. In the kitchen, maggots and rotting food filled the fridge. With the electricity out, cooking was done on a propane stove. The furniture was repossessed. The welfare check was already spent. The family was being evicted. None of this mattered to Wayne and Dina Tamura. As long as the couple from the tiny town of Kau was high on crystal methamphetamine, they were happy. ("Meth Threatens Hawaii's," 2003)

Several popular media articles on the topic of "meth babies" also appeared in 2004 and 2005. Similar to the portrayal of crack babies (see Chapter 11), these articles alleged that there were numerous negative outcomes for children whose mothers used methamphetamine while pregnant. For example, an article in the *Minneapolis Star Tribune* stated "[meth] babies can be born with missing and misplaced body parts. [She] heard of a meth baby born with an arm growing out of the neck and another who was missing a femur" (McCann, 2004). A commentary signed by several prominent medical and psychological researchers in response to these portrayals noted that there was no scientific evidence for the alleged connection between mothers' methamphetamine use and negative outcomes in their children.

We are deeply disappointed that American and international media as well as some policy makers continue to use stigmatizing terms and unfounded assumptions that not only lack any scientific basis but also endanger and disenfranchise the children to whom these labels are applied. Similarly, we are concerned that policies based on false assumptions will result in punitive civil and child welfare interventions that are harmful to women, children, and their families. (D. Lewis, 2005)

> A deputy sheriff in Scott County, Tennessee, attributed an increase in methamphetamine lab arrests in his county to prayers by residents. "We have seen a 600% increase in drug arrests, specifically with meth, since we have had the prayer vigil. . . . We have used every tool that we could to slow down the drug problem that we have here and prayers have been the answer." (as quoted in Lake, 2011)

Finally, as has been demonstrated with the other illegal drugs discussed in this chapter, methamphetamine has been demonized through assertions that in recent years, trafficking in the substance is primarily engaged in by members of minority groups. Prior to the late 1990s, most reports indicated that biker gangs (who also constitute a pariah group) were the main traffickers in methamphetamine. However, in the late 1990s and early 2000s, several articles on the substance asserted that Mexican organized crime groups were becoming involved in the methamphetamine trade (Nieves, 2001). Thus Swetlow (2003) referred to the "expansion of Mexico-based traffickers," and a report on the arrests of nine individuals for methamphetamine trafficking in the central region of Washington State noted, "most of the accused smugglers were illegal aliens" (Morlin, 2003). Similarly, a newspaper report on the situation in Oregon examined the surnames of those appearing in federal court on what were described as "major methamphetamine cases" in order to demonstrate a Hispanic connection. Despite the obvious problems with respect to the reliability of measuring ethnicity in this manner, the report noted, "in 1990, of the 34 persons charged with methamphetamine cases in federal court, none had a Hispanic surname. In the first 7 months of 1995, 56%—41 out of 73—have Hispanic surnames" (Ortiz, 1995). Illicit imports of pseudoephedrine, a main precursor substance used in the manufacture of methamphetamine, have also been attributed to foreigners. Thus, one article attributed these imports to a "loose network of people of Middle Eastern origin" who may have had ties to "terrorist groups in the Asian world" (Eisler & Leinwand, 2002).

In an opinion/editorial published in the *Los Angeles Times*, Kleiman and Satel (1996) make the important point that "in the case of methamphetamine, there is no need for the exaggeration that has created a credibility problem for other drug campaigns." It is certainly important that we not underestimate the very real problems substance abuse in general, and the use of methamphetamine in particular, cause in society. At the same time, our ability to effectively deal with these problems is not helped through overstatement and misrepresentation of facts.

DRUG "EPIDEMICS" OF THE 2000s AND 2010s

Not surprisingly, several socially constructed drug "epidemics" have emerged in recent years. Although we focus on salvia divinorum, K2/Spice, bath salts, and prescription drugs below, several other drug scares, focusing on a variety of consciousness-altering substances, have emerged. For example, in the spring of 2012, it was reported that the California Poison Control Center had received 60 reports of teenagers drinking hand sanitizer, and public health officials said the cases could "signal a dangerous trend" (Knox, 2012). Also in 2010, it was reported that in the first 3 months of 2012, Poison Control Centers in the United States had received 139 calls seeking help and information about the "intentional misuse of cinnamon" (Healy, 2012). In 2010, newspapers and television broadcasters reported that youth were consuming nutmeg to achieve highs, that the substance was (obviously) cheap and readily available, and "hence the end of the world has come" (Shafer, 2010; see also Curtis, 2012). There were also reports of teenagers inhaling air from mothball bags in order to achieve a high ("Teenagers 'Bagging,'" 2009). In Britain and Australia, there were allegations of a "mephedrone" (also known as "meow meow," an ecstasy-like drug and an analogue of methcathinone, related to bath salts in the United States—see below) epidemic (Laurance, 2010a; Travis & Weaver, 2010). Similar to what has happened with several other drugs, this drug was further demonized after allegations that it caused the death of two British teenagers. After toxicology tests revealed that the youths did not take the drug, David Nutt, former chair of the British Advisory Council on the Misuse of Drugs (see also Chapter 12), commented, "This news demonstrates why it is so important to base drug classification on the evidence, not fear, and why the police, media, and politicians should only make public pronouncements once the facts are clear" (as quoted in Laurance, 2010).

SALVIA DIVINORUM

Another emerging drug in the 2000s was salvia divinorum (known on the streets as "Sally D" and "Magic Mint"), which is regarded as the world's most potent hallucinogenic herb (Sack & McDonald, 2008)—among the "prominent" alleged users of this substance were Miley Cyrus (Hall, 2011). The federal government estimated that approximately 1.8 million people had tried salvia in their lifetime, and similar to what we have seen with other drugs, stories of atrocious acts committed by those allegedly under the influence of this substance proliferated in the media. For example, it was reported that a 42-year-old restaurant manager in Yonkers, New York, shot himself in the face 10 minutes after smoking salvia. Another 17-year-old boy committed suicide in Delaware at a time when he was apparently smoking the drug several times a week (Sack & McDonald, 2008). It was also alleged that Jared Loughner, who killed six people and injured 14 others (including U.S. Representative Gabrielle Giffords) in Tucson, Arizona, in January of 2011, was under the influence of salvia when he committed these acts. A *New York Times* article noted,

No one has suggested that the use of a hallucinogenic herb or any other drugs contributed to Jared Lee Loughner's apparent mental unraveling. . . . Yet it is striking how closely the typical effects of smoking the herb, salvia divinorum . . . matched Loughner's comments about how he saw the world, his oft-repeated assertion that he spent most of his waking hours in a dream world that he had learned to control. (Sulzberger & Medina, 2011)

SPICE/K2

Spice/K2 (synthetic cannabis) also emerged in the 2000s and was similarly connected to the commission of deviant and/or bizarre acts by its users. This drug, whose active ingredients are synthetic cannibinoids, was developed by Clemson University chemist John Hoffman (Gay, 2010) and, up until 2011, could be purchased in head shops in several jurisdictions in the United States. Similar to the construction of other drug epidemics, one strategy is to present data on adverse events connected to the use of a substance. Thus it was noted that in 2009, Poison Control Centers in the United States had 13 reports of K2/Spice poisonings, but in the first 6 months of 2010, there were 766 such reports (Havrelly, 2010). K2 was also demonized through reports of the commission of deviant acts by users of the substance: For example, 18-year-old "athlete and band standout" David Rozga "got high on fake pot" and "though he had never suffered from depression . . . went home, found a shotgun, and killed himself" (Salter & Suhr, 2011). Detective Sergeant Brian Sher of the Indianola police department, who led the investigation into Rozga's death, commented, "I've seen it all. I don't know what else to attribute it [Rozga's suicide] to. It has to be K2" (as quoted in Gay, 2010). Similarly, "Charlie Davel, 19, was killed after he fled police and went the wrong way on a highway in Mukwonago, Wisconsin. Friends told authorities he had smoked K2 several hours before the crash" (Blum, 2011). In Seattle, it was reported that an individual who crashed his vehicle into several pedestrians had been smoking K2 before driving (Sullivan, 2010). This substance was also apparently being widely used by individuals in the Armed Forces (at least partially because it cannot be detected in routine drug tests), with 113 members of the Navy and 260 Air Force personnel being disciplined for use or possession of the substance in 2011 (deVise, 2011). K2 is also apparently popular with individuals who must submit to drug tests, such as firefighters, police officers, and individuals on probation (Zagier, 2010), again, because it cannot be detected in routine drug tests.

Of course, as anecdotal accounts of the use of Spice proliferated, it was alleged that this drug too was a candidate for epidemic status. Ward Franz, the state representative who sponsored legislation in Missouri to ban Spice, stated, "it's like a tidal wave. It's almost an epidemic. We're seeing middle school kids walking into stores and buying it" (as quoted in Gay, 2010). In 2010, bans on Spice were implemented by legislators or public health officials in Alabama, Arkansas, Georgia, Hawaii, Iowa, Illinois, Kansas, Kentucky, Louisiana, Mississippi, Missouri, North Dakota, and Tennessee (Leinwand, 2010; Zagier, 2010). Several other states followed suit, and in 2012, the Drug Enforcement Administration placed K2/Spice under a Schedule I classification (Cohen et al., 2012). However, in the proverbial game of the dog chasing its tail, such bans have little effect, as manufacturers of psychoactive substances circumvent the bans by making slight changes to the chemical formula. Dr. Nora Volkow, director of the National Institute on Drug Abuse, commented, "the moment you start to regulate one of them, they'll come out with a variant that is even more potent" (as quoted in "Bath Salts Ban," 2012). Similarly, an owner of a shop who sold K2 commented, "You can't prohibit something that hasn't been invented yet" (as quoted in Zagier, 2010). Interestingly, some have argued that laws criminalizing cannabis have been partially responsible for driving people to the use of Spice/K2 (Savage, 2010).

BATH SALTS

Perhaps the most prominent emerging drug "epidemic" of the 2010s was related to "bath salts." "These are not the Epsom salts that aunt Ethel used to sprinkle in a warm tub, nor are they soothing, fragrant bottles you pick up at the aromatherapy store" (T. Wilson, 2011). Instead, this is a stimulant drug whose active ingredient is methylenedioxpyrovalernoe (mdpv), which, similar to K2/Spice, could be purchased at smoke and head shops and even some convenience stores. Users of this substance (which also goes by the names ivory wave, red dove, vanilla sky, super coke, cloud 9, pevee, ivory snow, ocean magic, white dove, white knight, and white lightning, among others), typically snort it, similar to cocaine, but it can also be injected, smoked, or even eaten. It was reported that during the January to June 2011 period Poison Control Centers in the United States received 3,470 calls about bath salts, compared to 303 such calls in all of 2010 (Goodnough & Zezima, 2011a). An emergency room physician in Virginia, in reference to the "epidemic" surrounding this drug commented, "If cocaine and methamphetamine were tropical storms, bath salts was a hurricane" (as quoted in Fischer, 2012).

> Despite widespread coverage of bath salts drugs in the media, apparently there is still some confusion in the general public regarding the nature of these drugs. For example, in Toronto, Ontario, it was reported that a teenage boy attempted to purchase bath salt drugs at a beauty/bath shop. When the proprietor showed him a section of Epsom and dead sea bath salts, the youth indicated that he didn't want these, but instead wanted "the kind that can get you high" (Donkin, 2012). It was also reported that "truckloads" of (actual) products such as bubble bath and shower gel were being intercepted at the border after investigations found boxes that were labeled as bath salts.

As is typical of the characterization of almost all emerging drug "epidemics," the popular media are fed stories from law enforcement officials regarding the bizarre behaviors of individuals consuming these drugs. For example, Indiana state police claimed that a 42-year-old woman who was high on bath salts

> trashed a hotel room. Police said when they arrived . . . Tammy Winter was sitting on a bed, rambling about evil spirits and needing to write on the walls of the room to protect her from the spirits. A relative who was present told police that Winter was an abuser of bath salts. (T. Wilson, 2011)

In Kentucky, a young woman driving on a highway after consuming bath salts "became convinced her 2-year-old was a demon. She allegedly stopped the car and dropped the child on his head" (Salter & Suhr, 2011). In Mississippi, "a man who hallucinated after taking bath salts used a hunting knife to slit his face and stomach" (Salter & Suhr, 2011). A sheriff in Mississippi reported, "we had a deputy injured a week ago. They were fighting with a guy who thought they were two devils. That's what makes this drug so dangerous" (as quoted in Byrd, 2011). In Washington State, the drug was linked to the death of an army sergeant, his 5-year-old son, and the boy's mother. "[Stewart] raced past a trooper on I-5, refused to pull over, shot his wife, and then shot himself. Bath salts were found on his person, in one of his pockets, inside the interior of his car, and in his house" (Estaban, 2011). One of the most widely recounted cases involving this drug was that of a man in Florida who chewed off the face of another man in May of 2012 in a "zombie-like cannibal attack" (Martinez, 2012) and was initially alleged to have tested positive for bath salts. However, subsequent drug tests revealed that this individual had used marijuana, not bath salts.

Given the anecdotal cases surrounding the use of bath salts recounted above, it is perhaps not surprising that this drug was nominated as the worst drug ever. For example, a spokesperson for the Carolinas Poison Control Center described bath salts as "like being on cocaine, but ten times worse" (as quoted in Salter & Suhr, 2011). Similarly, Mark Ryan, Director of the Louisiana Poison Control Center, commented, "if you take the worst characteristics of LSD, PCP, ecstasy, cocaine, and methamphetamine and put all those together, you've got one big, bad thing" (as quoted in Halladay, 2011; see also Goodnough & Zezima, 2011b). And, in further revealing displacement effects, a sheriff from a county in Northern Mississippi noted that the problem with bath salts in his rural area grew after a law restricting sales of pseudoephedrine was passed in Mississippi (Byrd, 2011).

PRESCRIPTION DRUGS (SYNTHETIC OPIATES)

Prescription drug abuse has also been labeled an "epidemic" (including by Obama's drug czar Gil Kerlikowske; Nano, 2011) and, arguably, the supporting data on this problem are more reflective of a serious problem than data on the use of the illegal substances presented above. Nationally, emergency room visits related to prescription drug overdoses doubled over the 2004–2009 period (to 1.2 million), and between 2000 and 2007, overdose deaths from painkillers increased from fewer than 4,000 per year to more than 11,000 (Fagan, 2010); it was also estimated that 80% of Americans between the ages of 12 and 20 had used a controlled drug that was prescribed for someone else at least once (Holmes, 2012). One of the more prominent deaths related to prescription painkillers was that of actor Heath Ledger (Nano, 2011). In reference to the trafficking in oxycodone, the Staten Island New York District Attorney commented, "we are equating this now to the epidemic we saw when crack cocaine was first introduced to New York City" (as quoted in Eligon, 2011). This quest for prescription opiates has led to increases in robberies of vehicles transporting drugs, drugstores and pharmacies (Goodnough, 2010), and also warehouses—in 2010, $75 million in pharmaceutical products was stolen from an Eli Lilly warehouse in Connecticut (Perrone, 2010), and an estimated 686 pharmacies were held up in 2010 (Colliver, 2011).

Although some reports have made reference to an increase in newborn babies being dependent on painkillers (Goodnough & Zezima, 2011a; Leinwand-Leger, 2011; Patrick et al., 2012; Ungar, 2012), what is conspicuously absent from media reporting on this alleged prescription drug epidemic is accounts of bizarre behaviors committed by individuals under the influence of these substances that we have seen for illegal drugs.

It is also notable that, due to the higher cost of prescription painkillers, a significant proportion of individuals who became addicted to these drugs apparently shifted to heroin. For example, referring to a "tidal wave" of heroin use in Oregon, the state medical examiner noted that in 2011, 143 people had died of heroin overdoses in that state (Tomlinson, 2012).

CONCLUSION

This chapter has addressed how, over the past 100 years, government and criminal justice system officials, with the assistance of media sources, have used a number of tactics to demonize certain drugs and to socially construct drug epidemics. While we have not claimed that drug problems do not exist in the United States, socially constructed epidemics tend to exaggerate and distort the nature and magnitude of drug problems, making appropriate prevention, treatment, and drug control responses more difficult.

Psychoactive drug use is ubiquitous across time and cultures/societies, and this has led some to assert that intoxication is not unnatural or deviant, but, rather, that absolute sobriety is not a natural or primary human state (Davenport-Hines, 2001; Weil, 1986). Drug use remains widespread in society despite the fact that the use of *all* forms of drugs—legal and illegal—involves some level of risk. As we will discuss in more detail in Chapters 3 and 4, the risks associated with drug use are diverse, but fatalities associated with use are one important measure of harm. Data on drug-related mortality indicate that the number of deaths annually caused by the use of alcohol, tobacco, and prescription drugs is roughly 30 times the number of deaths attributed to all illegal drugs combined (Mokdad et al., 2004). Given the substantial level of harm posed by the use of legal drugs, we find it interesting that psychoactive drugs are typically dichotomized into those that are considered to be "good" and those that are considered to be "bad." We consider how legal and illegal drugs are similar and different and how certain drugs have been demonized in order to justify their illegal status.

Drug use is not only widespread in society; it fills an important role for a number of constituencies. Government officials and politicians create "heroes" and "villains" that resonate with voters, and drugs provide a common "enemy" that can unite an otherwise divided public. In many cases, the attention directed to drugs acts to divert attention from policies that may have contributed to drug use in the first place. Similarly, criminal justice system officials need psychoactive substances as drug problems because "epidemics" justify increases in financial and other resources devoted to their organizations. Finally, the media emphasize and exaggerate the negative consequences of drug use because moral panics sell newspapers and advertising.

A variety of strategies have been employed to emphasize the dangers of (illegal) drugs over the past century. These include claims that illegal drug use is responsible for the majority of crime that occurs in society and that drugs possess unique powers that encourage otherwise normal people to engage in bizarre and often violent behavior. Illegal drug use has also been demonized through claims that minorities, immigrants, and foreign nationals are the primary users and traffickers of illegal drugs. Through this strategy, both the external cause and internal problems associated with drug use can be attributed to something that is foreign and clearly "un-American" (Musto, 1999). Finally, illegal drugs are demonized by claims that they pose a unique threat to the health of children, often through a misrepresentation of the scientific evidence on the effects of these drugs.

REVIEW QUESTIONS

1. In terms of the annual number of deaths in the United States related to drug use, how do legal and illegal drugs compare?

2. How does the United States compare to other Western countries in terms of incarcerations for drug violations?

3. What techniques have been employed to demonize particular drugs? What themes have been emphasized in this demonization?

4. What are the propositions of the "gateway drug" theory as it applies to marijuana? Of those who have ever tried marijuana, what is the probability that they will become regular users of heroin or cocaine?

5. What alternative explanations have been provided to account for the fact that hard drug users are likely to have tried marijuana?

INTERNET EXERCISES

1. Every year, the United States Bureau of Justice Statistics and Federal Bureau of Investigation provide information on the number of arrests for a variety of offenses. Access data on drug arrests for the current year (for example, 2010 arrests are available at http://www.fbi.gov/about-us/cjis/ucr/crime-in-the-u.s/ 2010/crime-in-the-u.s.-2010/persons-arrested) and discuss the reasons for regional variation and differences in arrests for various substances.

2. Using an Internet search engine, type in one of the following terms: *methamphetamine epidemic, ecstasy epidemic, Oxycontin epidemic, bath salts epidemic.* Note how many "hits" are obtained, and examine the content of five of the sources you identify. What themes are emphasized in referring to the issue as an epidemic?

CHAPTER 2

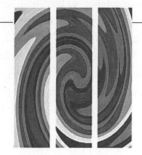

Theories of Drug Use

In this chapter, we discuss several theoretical explanations for drug use and abuse in society, with particular emphasis on sociological explanations. A theory is simply an explanation for some phenomenon that has the flexibility to be applied across a variety of circumstances and conditions. Accordingly, the theories discussed in this chapter provide explanations for why people use and abuse drugs across a variety of different conditions and circumstances.

There are several dozen theories of substance use and abuse. Some theories are applicable to all forms of drugs and patterns of use, while others are extremely focused, addressing only a particular drug or a particular pattern of use. A very broad theory of substance use is able to provide an explanation for the experimental, occasional, and heavy use of a number of different drugs, both legal and illegal. In this chapter, we focus on a number of relatively broad theories, and we assess the accuracy of these theories by considering the empirical support (research findings) for them. Research provides the evidence that tells us whether the explanations offered by these theories are correct—but what is typically found is that a particular theory may be empirically valid ("right") under some circumstances and not under others. For example, one theory may be good at explaining the use of marijuana by adolescents, but a different theory may be better at explaining why middle-aged adults abuse prescription drugs. Thus, these theories should not necessarily be viewed as if they are in competition with one another, but rather as complimentary explanations for substance use that often overlap (Goode, 1999).

In this chapter, we review several distinct theories of substance use and abuse. The first of these is commonly called the "nature perspective," and proponents of this approach assert that substance use is one way that people express a universal and innate drive to alter their consciousness. This drive to alter one's consciousness is argued to be present at birth and is expressed in a variety of nondrug ways. Drug use is a very common way for the drive to be expressed because drugs are among the most convenient and widely available means to alter consciousness.

Genetic/biological explanations are another category of theories that is discussed in this chapter. With their focus on heredity, these perspectives may seem, on their

45

face, to be similar to nature explanations. However, genetic explanations are actually quite distinct from the nature model because they contend that genetic *differences* in people account for different substance use and abuse patterns. In contrast, nature theories argue that the tendency to use and abuse substances is *universal*, although different people manifest this tendency in different ways.

We also examine the disease model of substance use. Versions of the disease model differ in terms of what they contend causes substance dependency, but these perspectives all tend to phrase their discussion of drug use in medical terms and to view alcoholics and addicts as suffering from an illness that is largely beyond their control.

Psychological perspectives of drug use are also addressed in this chapter. These include the self-derogation model, which views substance use as pathological and the result of a lack of self-esteem, and the "problem behavior" perspective, which regards substance use as symptomatic of an underlying problem behavior condition characterized by risk taking and unconventionality. Several other psychological explanations for substance use exist as well, and most notable are those that focus on behaviorism and the role that reinforcement and punishment play in substance use and abuse. However, we examine these perspectives in the context of social learning theory, a sociological perspective that incorporates the principles of operant conditioning (positive/negative reinforcement and punishment; Skinner, 1953) as well as imitation (Bandura, 1973, 1977), but that also acknowledges the role of social variables in substance use and abuse.

Sociological theories of substance use and abuse are then examined with a particular focus on learning and subcultural learning theories, social bonding theory, interactional theory, age-graded theory, and perspectives addressing the importance of economic and emotional strain and social conflict perspectives. This chapter places particular emphasis on sociological explanations of substance use because, as compared to psychological and especially genetic theories of substance use, sociological theories acknowledge the importance of environmental factors for an understanding of substance use, abuse, and problems.

NATURE THEORIES

Nature theories contend that the desire to use psychoactive substances is an innate and universal drive in human beings analogous to the hunger or sex drive (Weil, 1986; Weil & Rosen, 1998). The foremost proponent of the contemporary nature perspective of substance use is Andrew Weil, a medical doctor and well-known expert on alternative medicine. Regarding the innate human drive toward consciousness alteration, this perspective recognizes that, from infancy, humans engage in behaviors that produce alterations in their consciousness. Weil claims that early in life, this desire for consciousness alteration is manifested in behaviors such as infants rocking themselves into calm, blissful states and children "spinning" themselves or purposefully hyperventilating to produce dizzying mental states. However, as people grow older, "they find that certain available substances put them in similar states" (Weil & Rosen, 1998, p. 15). Drugs become a commonly used mechanism for achieving the goal of consciousness alteration not because they are distinct in their capacity to alter consciousness, but because they offer a quick and convenient means to achieve this goal (Weil & Rosen, 1998).

Supporting Weil's position is the ubiquity of psychoactive substance use in human societies (discussed in Chapter 1) and the fact that drugs have been used to alter consciousness for thousands of years despite their potential harms. Supporters also point to the fact that altered consciousness is pursued by people in many nondrug ways, including the behavior of children discussed above; meditation; intense physical activity (e.g., runners report being "addicted" to the high associated with exercise); risk-taking behaviors such as skydiving or dangerous driving; fasting from food or water; and even through self-inflicted pain (see box). Research on the theory is limited as it is not amenable to conventional empirical testing.

> Self-inflicted pain is one method by which people alter consciousness. One example is the traditional American Indian Sun Dance ceremony, historically practiced by a number of tribes. The Sun Dance ceremony involved a process in which warriors would skewer their chests with bone or wood, attach the skewers to a pole, and dance until the skewers pulled free. This process of self-torture often lasted many days and the pain and sacrifice of the flesh was deeply spiritual, prompting visions and signifying rebirth and a desire to return something of themselves to nature (Atwood Lawrence, 2004).

Because the drive to alter consciousness is argued to be present in all humans, this perspective contends that drug use should not necessarily be viewed as bad or pathological. However, it also recognizes that drug use has the potential to be manifested in ways that are harmful to users or those around them. Weil thus emphasizes the importance of nonbiased drug education to inform people of the dangers associated with drugs should they choose to use them (Weil & Rosen, 1998).

GENETIC/BIOLOGICAL THEORIES

Genetic or biological theories of substance use suggest that the individuals who are most likely to use and (especially) to become addicted to drugs are characterized by genetically inherited predispositions to these problems. Although some genetic theories focus almost entirely on the role of heredity for explanations of substance use and abuse, most argue, more reasonably, that genetics are one of many factors that may predispose individuals to use substances and to abuse them once they have used.

Genetic theories of substance abuse and addiction typically propose that inherited characteristics affect how people metabolize substances and/or experience the effects of a substance. Via genetics, an individual's biological makeup is proposed to affect "the experience of substance use" in a variety of ways, including whether an individual feels unpleasant rather than good upon ingesting a particular drug, whether the consumption of a drug causes illness at low rather than high doses, and whether the consumption of a drug increases as opposed to reduces feelings of anxiety. As an example, research has documented the "flushing response" that some people experience as a result of alcohol consumption (see also Chapter 6). The flushing response is thought to be primarily genetic in origin and is more likely among certain racial/ethnic groups than others, particularly people of Asian ancestry (Eng, Luczak, & Wall, 2007). Symptoms of the flushing response include facial flushing, sweating, nausea, and sometimes tachycardia, and this unpleasant reaction to alcohol is predominantly due to an inherited deficiency in the enzyme aldehyde dehydrogenase (Eng et al., 2007). This represents a biological explanation for substance use because, due to an inherited condition, afflicted individuals will respond to alcohol consumption by feeling anxious and nauseous as opposed to relaxed and will therefore be less likely to drink, all other things being equal.

Recent work in the area of biology and addiction suggests that people may also develop biological predispositions to substance abuse and addiction as a neurological consequence of their previous drug use. Referred to as sensitization theory, this perspective suggests that the chronic administration of certain psychoactive drugs generates alterations in the brain that increase vulnerability to continued drug use, relapse, and craving (concepts discussed in Chapter 3; Cami & Farre, 2003). Sensitization theory is similar in ways to genetic theories of addiction but distinct in the sense that *a behavioral pattern*, chronic substance use, places the individual at elevated risk for drug use, relapse, and craving *via a biological process*.

Sensitization theory can be summarized with the following principles (technical jargon is minimized as much as is possible): (1) Drugs that have the potential to be addictive have the ability to alter brain organization; (2) the brain systems that are altered include those involved in incentive, motivation, and reward; (3) the neurological changes pertaining to addiction render these brain systems hypersensitive or "sensitized" to drugs and drug-associated stimuli; and (4) the brain systems that are sensitized do not affect how the individual perceives the pleasurable or euphoric effects of drugs (called drug "liking") but instead affect the "incentive value" of the drug, or how much the individual wants the drug (called drug "wanting"; Robinson & Berridge, 2001, p. 103; see also Robinson & Berridge, 1993). Put more simply, the theory suggests that chronic drug use makes the brain system involved in reward especially sensitive (hypersensitized) to both the direct effects of the drug and the other cues or stimuli that are not directly related to but are associated with the drug. Hypersensitization affects levels of drug wanting, and when wanting reaches a pathological level, it is considered drug craving, which is an intense desire to re-experience the effects of a drug (Cami & Farre, 2003). The process of hypersensitization, drug wanting, and ultimately craving can occur independent of any physical withdrawal symptoms (Robinson & Berridge, 2001).

While a behavioral process, chronic substance use initiates the process described above, and there is individual variation in susceptibility to the sensitization (Robinson & Berridge, 2001). Therefore, some people may abuse drugs and never experience wanting, craving, and addiction, while others may abuse drugs and experience chronic problems with wanting, craving, and addiction. The reasons for the variation in susceptibility to sensitization and supposedly addiction remain generally unknown, but it is likely that genetic, hormonal, and environmental factors all play important roles. This illustrates the overlap of the biological theories discussed in this chapter and the intersection of biological risk factors with the environmental risk factors proposed by the sociological theories discussed later in this chapter.

The vast majority of research on biological or quasibiological theories of drug use have focused on alcohol as the drug at issue, with much less attention directed to other substances. Although this remains (very) debated, some research goes so far as to suggest that a link to alcoholism may even be traced to a specific gene (e.g., Dick et al., 2004). Despite the fairly extensive research that has been conducted on genetics and alcoholism, it is important to recognize that "no genetic physiological or biochemical marker has been found that strongly predicts alcoholism or any other addiction" (Ray & Ksir, 2004, p. 53). Regardless, research continues to direct a great deal of attention to the potential link between genetics and alcoholism. At least in part, this is because numerous studies have demonstrated that alcoholism tends to run in families, with individuals who have a close relative who is an alcoholic being more likely to become alcoholics themselves (Cadoret, 1995; Johnson & Leff, 1999; Schuckit, 1985, 1995). The question remains whether alcoholism runs in families because the child learned to become an alcoholic from his or her parents and environment or because the child inherited a gene or genes that predispose him or her to alcoholism. In actuality, it is likely that both of these explanations have some merit, and much of the research that has tried to assess the relative contribution of genetics and environment in patterns of alcoholism is based on studies of twins or adopted siblings.

Twins studies are based on the logic that because twins are born to the same parents at the same time, they are likely to experience very similar circumstances in terms of their family and upbringing, thus controlling for environmental effects to some degree. However, because identical twins originate from one egg and possess 100% genetic concordance, it is hypothesized that they should be more similar in terms of later alcoholism (and other behaviors) than should fraternal twins (who, like regular siblings, share 50% of the same genes). Most of the research examining these issues has found identical twins to be more similar than fraternal twins in terms of patterns of alcoholism and alcohol-related behaviors such as binge drinking, and this is particularly the case among males (Kendler, Heath, Neale, Kessler, & Eaves, 1992; Partanen, Bruun, & Markkanen, 1966; Pickens et al., 1991; Sher, 1991).

A Genetic Cause for Political Views?

Twin studies have been employed to study the possibility that genetics influence one's political views. An article published in *The American Political Science Review* used survey data obtained from more than 8,000 sets of twins to examine the possibility that political orientation is linked to heredity. The study examined questions pertaining to politically charged issues such as taxes, unions, capitalism, and pornography and found that while most respondents had a mixture of conservative and liberal views, identical twins were slightly more likely than fraternal twins to share a particular political orientation. (Alford, Hibbing, & Funk, 2005)

Adoption studies of alcoholism are similar. Although adoption studies involve many different types of research design, most examine people who were born to alcoholic parents but were adopted by nonalcoholic parents soon after their birth. These individuals are then compared with persons who were born to nonalcoholic parents and then adopted by nonalcoholic parents in terms of later alcohol-related behaviors. As individuals from both groups are raised by nonalcoholic parents, arguably, the main difference between them is that one group involves persons with at least one biological parent who was an alcoholic and who may have passed on some predisposition to alcoholism. As with the twin studies, adoption studies have generally found support for the hypothesis that a predisposition to alcoholism may be inherited, with several studies finding adoptees whose biological parents were alcoholics more likely to demonstrate alcoholism later in life than other adoptees (Cloninger, Bohman, & Sigvardsson, 1981; Goodwin, Schulsinger, Hermansen, Guze, & Winokur, 1973; Schuckit, 1985; Sher, 1991).

Although the twin and adoption studies are generally supportive of some genetic association to alcoholism and should not be ignored, caution must be used when interpreting these findings. What these studies show is that there may be certain inherited characteristics that can put some individuals at a higher risk of alcoholism. However, genetic theories cannot explain why the vast majority of drinkers experience no serious problems or why the majority of people with this "genetic susceptibility" to alcoholism do not go on to become alcoholics. Thus, as Fingarette (1990) comments on the applicability of genetic studies:

> These studies provide no evidence of a genetic factor in the largest group of heavy drinkers—those who have significant associated problems but are not diagnosable as alcoholics. Even among the minority who can be so diagnosed, the data suggest that only a minority have the permanent genetic background. And even in this category, a minority of the minority, studies report that the majority do not become alcoholics. (p. 50)

Several factors other than genetics may be responsible for the findings evidenced in the twin and adoption studies. Potential confounding factors include the role of peer influence, systematic differences in those selected to participate in the research, and the inability of the twin studies to fully control for environmental factors. Peer influence is a particularly important factor in twin studies, as identical twins may be more likely than fraternal twins to spend extensive time together and to share peers, and peer influence is among the strongest predictors of substance use and abuse (Prescott & Kendler, 1995). The selection of research subjects may also be important to consider, as the twins and other siblings who are included in these studies may not be representative of those in the general population. For example, research subjects in studies such as these are often recruited from substance treatment centers, and twin/sibling pairs in which both individuals are alcoholics may be more likely to participate in treatment, attract the attention of researchers, and thus be included in studies on abuse (Prescott & Kendler, 1995). Perhaps the most important qualification for studies in this area is that that despite their efforts, researchers have been unable to control for the influence of environmental differences between groups (whether identical twins, fraternal twins, regular siblings, or single adoptees). Thus, differences in substance use between groups, to the extent that they exist, cannot be traced directly to the role of genetics. For example, taking a study in which identical twins were separated and then raised apart, Smyer, Gatz, Simi, and Pedersen (1998) found that the twin who was raised by his or her biological parent(s) was more likely to drink excessively. However, they concluded that the effect of economics and education likely explained these differences, as people who give children up for adoption and people who adopt children are different in many ways, most notably age, income, and educational level, and these factors are likely to influence substance use by the parents and also their children.

Research into the genetic causes and correlates of drug use is important for a complete understanding of drug use and drug dependence, but it is important to recognize that genetics play a relatively limited role in explaining human behavior. The causes of drug use and dependence are complex, yet it is all too common for people to place a great deal of faith in genetic explanations of drug use and dependence because of their concise and unequivocal nature. Reinarman comments on this tendency by pointing to a cartoon published in *New Yorker* magazine "in which a genetic scientist, replete with lab coat, clipboard, and genome chart, rushes into the lab and announces to his colleagues 'I've found it! I've found the gene that makes us think everything is determined by a gene!'" (2004, p. 32). As Reinarman (2004) points out, genetically determinist explanations of drug use will always be lacking insofar as they neglect the importance of environmental influences.

DISEASE THEORY

The disease model has a very long history (records of substance abuse/addiction being regarded as a "disease" date back more than 2,000 years; White, 2000a) and is perhaps most easily described alongside its counterpoint, the moral model of addiction. The moral model of addiction views drug use and excessive drinking as evidence of weak moral character. Advocates of the moral model regarded the disease theory as nothing more than a groundless excuse for bad behavior—they would tell people with substance problems that their problems are "all their fault." Conversely, advocates of the disease model would tell the people, "none of this is your fault." The truth of the matter likely falls somewhere in between.

Disease perspectives of drug use are somewhat similar to the genetic theories described above. Some versions of disease theory emphasize genetic/inherited factors in the etiology of addiction, while others emphasize more psychological processes and use the term *disease* metaphorically. Most significantly, all disease perspectives tend to phrase their discussion of drug use in medical terms and to contend that alcoholism and addiction should be viewed in the same way as traditional medical problems. Indeed, the disease perspective is often referred to as the medical model of substance use, particularly the version of disease theory advocated by Alcoholics Anonymous. This model does not view the *use* of substances as necessarily pathological, but it does argue that for some people, use will inevitably result in abuse and addiction. The disease model is supposedly applicable to all psychoactive substances (and numerous other addictions as well, discussed below), but it has been applied mostly to alcoholism. According to this model, alcoholism is an incurable, degenerative disease that is often fatal if left untreated.

The view that alcoholism is a disease is not new. Evidence from ancient Greece and Egypt indicates that drunkenness was seen as a sickness of the body and soul and caretakers were recommended to help those suffering from "drink madness" (White, 2000a). The development of the disease model in America dates back to at least 1784, when noted American physician Benjamin Rush published a pamphlet titled *Inquiry Into the Effects of Ardent Spirits on the Human Body and Mind*, which referred to alcoholism in medical terms and proposed treatments for this "odious disease." However, through the 19th and part of the 20th century, the disease model was largely ignored while a moral model of addiction dominated. In contrast to the disease model, the moral model viewed drug use and excessive drinking as evidence of weak moral character and regarded the medical model as simply providing an excuse for bad behavior (White, 2000a). One of the most vociferous early critics of the disease concept of addiction was Dr. C. W. Earle, who noted in *The Chicago Medical Review* in 1880:

It is becoming altogether too customary in these days to speak of vice as disease. . . .That is the responsibility of taking the opium or whisky . . . it is to be excused and called a disease, I am not willing for one moment to admit, and I propose to fight this pernicious doctrine as long as is necessary. (as quoted in White, 2000a)

The puritanical sentiment regarding substance use reflected in the moral model was perhaps at its highest point in the United States early in the 20th century. In the first two decades of the 20th century, many states banned alcohol consumption, and eventually this spread to entire nation with the Eighteenth Amendment to the Constitution that prohibited the production, sale, and consumption of alcohol (see also Chapter 9). Prohibition lasted from 1920 to 1933, and its repeal signified an ideological shift in the country back to the disease model of addiction. In part, the resurgence of popularity for the disease model is due to the formation of Alcoholics Anonymous (AA) in 1935. AA was formed by two alcoholics, stockbroker Bill Wilson and physician Robert Smith, who proposed that alcoholism was an "allergy to alcohol" that could only be "treated" with total abstinence.

Although Wilson and Smith regarded alcoholism as a disease and insinuated that the origin of this "allergy to alcohol" was genetic, when pressed, they acknowledged that the use of the term *disease* was somewhat metaphoric. For example, as Wilson commented on AA's use of the term *disease* with regard to alcoholism in 1960:

We have never called alcoholism a disease because, technically speaking, it is not a disease entity. For example, there is no such thing as heart disease.

Instead, there are many separate heart ailments, or combinations of them. It is something like that with alcoholism. Therefore we did not wish to get in wrong with the medical professional by pronouncing alcoholism a disease entity. Therefore we always call it an illness, or a malady—a far safer term for us to use. (as quoted in White, 2000b)

According to Smith, the disease metaphor was necessary, as it was the only term that conveyed the enormity of the challenge that alcoholism presented for alcoholics in all phases of life. Smith once wrote a short note to Wilson arguing that "Have to use disease—sick—only way to get across hopelessness" (quoted in White, 2000b, the final word written in large letters and double underlined in original).

Around the time that AA was created, scientists at the Research Council on Problems of Alcohol (RCPA) were also advocating the disease model of alcoholism. Shortly after its formation at Yale University in 1938, the RCPA released a research report that argued for the validity of the disease model of alcoholism and noted that, "An alcoholic should be regarded as a sick person, just as one who is suffering from tuberculosis, cancer, heart disease, or other serious chronic disorders" (as cited in Kurtz, 2002).

Video Gaming as a Disease?

A government study in South Korea found that 8% of the country's population suffers from an Internet or (video) gaming addiction. In an attempt to address what is perceived as a significant problem, the country passed a new "shutdown law" that blocks those under the age of 16 from accessing online gaming sites after midnight (Lee, 2011). In the United States, the *Diagnostic and Statistical Manual of Mental Disorders* (*DSM*) does not currently recognize gaming or the Internet as possible sources of addiction, but a revision to the *DSM* is pending, and "Internet use disorder" may be recognized in the new edition (see Chapter 3 on *DSM* revisions). A leading researcher in this area, Dr. Han Dou-hyun from Chung-Ang University Hospital in Seoul, has proposed five warning signs of gaming or Internet addiction:

1. Disrupted regular life pattern. If a person plays games all night long and sleeps in the daytime, that can be a warning he or she should seek professional help.

2. If the potential gaming or Internet addict loses his or her job or stops going to school in order to be online or to play a digital game.

3. Need for a bigger fix. Does the gamer have to play for longer and longer periods in order to get the same level of enjoyment from the game?

4. Withdrawal. Some Internet and gaming addicts become irritable or anxious when they disconnect or when they are forced to do so.

5. Cravings. Some Internet and gaming addicts experience cravings, or the need to play the game or be online when they are away from the digital world. (Sutter, 2012)

The most influential researcher at the RCPA was medical doctor Elvin Jellinek, who over a number of years developed and refined the disease model of alcoholism based on his surveys of AA members. This culminated in the publication of his *The Disease Concept of Alcoholism* in 1960, which remains among the most widely cited pieces of research on the disease model. However, it is important to recognize that the paths of AA and Jellinek were heavily intertwined. AA emerged under Wilson and Smith, who believed alcoholism was a disease because of their experience with it and the scientific "evidence" for the disease model is mostly attributed to Jellinek, who tested the propositions of the disease model (and, not surprisingly, found support for it), based on questionnaires he gave to AA members who had been told by AA that alcoholism was a disease! As Jung (2001) notes:

> It should hardly be surprising, then, if the self-reports of self-labeled alcoholics fit the primary model proposed by AA and Jellinek very closely. Interestingly it also may be noted that none of the interview responses of females were included because they often differed with those provided by males. (p. 405)

The disease theory of addiction and alcoholism is typically credited to Elvin Jellinek. Following the publication of Jellinek's influential *The Disease Concept of Alcoholism* in 1960, the American Psychological Association began the use of disease terminology for alcoholism in 1965, and the American Medical Association followed suit in 1966. However, the survey data Jellinek used in his work were seriously problematic—even Jellinek himself acknowledged that little scientifically valid information could be obtained from these data. The surveys were distributed to approximately 1,600 AA members through the AA newsletter, but Jellinek's analysis was based on the 98 surveys that were returned and determined to be valid, none of which involved responses from women. (Fingarette, 1990)

Despite the lack of rigorous scientific evidence for the disease concept of alcoholism, in 1956, the American Medical Association declared alcoholism to be a treatable illness, and by 1966, partly because of Jellinek's work, both the American Psychiatric Association and the American Medical Association were referring to alcoholism as a disease.

As might be expected, there is considerable criticism of the disease model of addiction. Perhaps most fundamental is the fact that the disease model, particularly as it is advocated by AA, considers alcoholism a disease, but this classification is not based on any measurable physical effects on the body (as with physical diseases) or with measured thoughts, feelings, and behaviors (as is the case with mental illnesses; Peele, 1989). Rather, alcoholism is considered a disease *because it was called a disease* in the writings of Jellinek and others, who arrived at this conclusion based on a number of scientifically baseless propositions. As noted by Fingarette, these assumptions include the following:

1. Heavy problem drinkers show a single distinct pattern of ever greater alcohol use leading to greater bodily, mental, and social deterioration.

2. The condition, once it appears, persists involuntarily: The craving is irresistible and the drinking is uncontrollable once it has begun.

3. Medical expertise is needed to understand and relieve the condition ("cure the disease") or at least ameliorate its symptoms. (1990)

The view that addiction requires medical treatment has become increasingly pervasive over the years, and in part this is because of the tremendous profits associated with treating disease. Although people suffering from substance dependency may benefit from medical assistance, the list of addictions now includes a vast array of non–drug-related patterns of behavior including eating, child abuse, surfing the Web, exercise, shopping, gambling, sleeping, and sex (see box, "Addicted to Tanning?"). According to Peele (1989), this reflects an increasing tendency to medicalize behavior that previously was not viewed in a medical context (see also material on *DSM* revisions to "addiction" diagnostics in Chapter 3). Peele notes that this is done "by elevating the unhealthy side of normal functioning to the status of disease state," and in doing so, medical health practitioners and others "who claim this mantle of science now *guarantee* the preeminence, pervasiveness, and persistence of sickness in everyday life" (1989, p. 143).

Addicted to Tanning?

A study titled "UV Light Tanning as a Type of Substance-Related Disorder" published in the *Archives of Dermatology* concluded that a significant percentage of beachgoers may be "addicted" to tanning. The study surveyed 145 beachgoers using questions similar to those used to screen for substance abuse and dependency including:

- Do you ever try to cut down on the time you spend in the sun but find yourself still suntanning?
- Do you ever get annoyed when people tell you not to tan?
- Do you ever feel guilty that you are in the sun too much?
- Do you think you need to spend more and more time in the sun to maintain your perfect tan?

Researchers found that more than one-quarter of respondents showed signs of addiction to tanning by one standard, and using another measure, more than half of the survey participants were considered addicted. Like drug use, exposure to ultraviolent light may cause the body to release endorphins, chemicals that improve mood. (Warthan, Uchida, & Wagner, 2005)

PSYCHOLOGICAL THEORIES

Psychological perspectives of substance use tend to emphasize either the importance of reinforcement and punishment (which, as mentioned, will be discussed in the context of social learning theory) or the importance of a dysfunctional personality characteristic or type. Regarding the latter, we discuss self-derogation theory, which views substance use as one result of a personality defect or inadequacy, and problem behavior theory, which does not view substance use as necessarily pathological but as one symptom of a problem behavior pattern that is apt to cause the individual difficulties in terms of functioning in society.

The self-derogation model, advocated most notably by Kaplan (1975), views substance use, particularly illegal drug use and the abuse of legal drugs, as pathological and the result of self-rejection and a lack of self-esteem (Kaplan, 1980). As Kaplan notes on this perspective, "The theoretical model is based upon the postulate of the self-esteem motive, whereby, universally and characteristically, a person is said to behave so as to maximize the experience of positive self-attitudes, and to minimize the experience of negative ones" (1980, p. 129).

Thus, the theory contends that all social behavior, including drug use, is engaged in to maximize experiences that are positive to self-esteem and minimize experiences that are damaging to self-esteem. Deviant behaviors such as drug use are most likely to develop in individuals who are unable to develop a positive self-image from their interaction with family, school, and conventional peers. According to the theory, the more negative a person's experience with conventional others, the more likely deviant behavior such as drug use becomes because all people seek responses from others that are positive and rewarding for their self-image. When positive affirmation is not provided for conventional behavior, the theory contends that individuals will pursue other identities and engage in deviant forms of behavior (e.g., drug use) as they continually seek positive affirmation and self-esteem.

Critics of self-derogation theory have pointed out that the emphasis the theory places on self-rejection is difficult to reconcile with the fact that illicit drug users tend to have *more* close friends than nondrug users (Goode, 1999; Kandel & Davies, 1991). Subcultural perspectives may be informative here. For example, classic research on youth subcultures (Cohen, 1955; Miller, 1958) has pointed out that youth who have failed to "measure up" to societal expectations will often seek out deviant subcultures. As discussed in detail below, subcultures are groups that have adopted alternative values, and many "rejected" youth identify with these groups as the values prized in the subcultures (e.g., fighting ability, street smarts) are ones that they are more able to meet. Self-derogation theorists might similarly argue that youth who are negatively received, particularly by their peers, may suffer in terms of their self-esteem and thus adopt a deviant persona characterized by drug use, which they are then rewarded for by a deviant peer group or subculture. Among these deviant peers, bonding and intimacy may be particularly high, which would facilitate long-term friendships and reconcile findings that drug use may be motivated by feelings of self-rejection but that users often tend to have more intimate friends.

Scientific research has provided some support for this, including that by Hussong and Hicks (2003), who concluded on the relationship between self-esteem and delinquent-peer associations that

> adolescents who experience negative feelings toward themselves may seek out a non-normative peer context that more easily offers a sense of acceptance and, subsequently, self-worth. Often, these peer contexts also offer greater access to substance-using friends who may be more likely to model, provide, encourage, and reinforce the adolescent's own involvement with alcohol and drugs. (p. 413)

Thus, to some degree, the self-derogation perspective may overlap with social learning theory (discussed below). This is particularly the case as more emphasis is placed on the importance of nonconventional peers, which are emphasized by learning theory, rather than self-rejecting feelings for understanding substance use and abuse.

Distinct from the self-derogation perspective but also psychological in nature is problem behavior theory, advocated most notably by Jessor and Jessor (Jessor, Graves, Hanson, & Jessor, 1968; Jessor & Jessor, 1975, 1977, 1980). This perspective regards substance use as just one of a number of problem behaviors that are symptomatic of a broader underlying condition. This problem behavior condition is evidenced by a set of distinct personality traits and attitudes that include, most importantly, a willingness to take risks and a commitment to unconventionality. Other traits that commonly characterize this personality type include a desire for independence, a tolerance of differences and deviant behavior, a tendency toward rebellion and pleasure seeking, and a susceptibility to peer influence (Jessor & Jessor, 1977). Problem behavior theory contends that some proportion of youth will develop these personality traits, and these traits tend to encourage behavior that conflicts with some of the social (and often legal) norms of society. As Donovan (1996) notes, conduct such as substance use and abuse that typically accompanies the problem-behavior personality traits, "It is behavior that is socially disapproved by the institutions of authority and that tends to elicit some form of social control response, whether mild reproof, social rejection, or even incarceration" (p. 380).

Thus, it is important to recognize that this "problem behavior" condition is not necessarily negative or pathological, it simply refers to a tendency to engage in behaviors that society has deemed unacceptable to varying degrees.

It is also interesting to note that this is consistent with the propositions of the more sociologically oriented labeling theory. Labeling theorists have argued that victimless behaviors such as substance use are only considered "bad" because certain groups in society have defined or labeled the behavior as morally inappropriate. As Becker (1963) comments: "From this point of view, deviance is not a quality of the act the person commits, but rather a consequence of the applicaby others of rules and sanctions" (p. 9; emphasis original).

Similarly, problem behavior theory does not view individuals characterized by "problem behavior" traits as necessarily "bad" or dysfunctional, only more likely

to engage in a variety of behaviors that may get them into trouble. It is also important to recognize that the same qualities that may cause problems for an individual, such as a proclivity toward risk taking and unconventionality, are also related
to imagination, independent and critical thinking, ingenuity, creativity, important
talents and abilities that may benefit both the individual and the broader society
(Goode, 1999). Indeed, as Goode (1999) notes, whether these behaviors are problematic "has no meaning outside a specific social and cultural context, and a
society that provides a place for eccentrics may also profit from their often considerable contributions—just as it often punishes for their unconventional behavior" (1999, p. 98).

Thus, the same risk-taking tendencies that may encourage the individual to
engage in potentially dangerous or illegal behaviors like substance use can also benefit society immeasurably in terms of the art, music, literature, science, and other
advances produced by these individuals (Goode, 1999). Some of the most successful,
creative, and amazing people in society have been characterized by this willingness
to take risks, and this tendency may have even been *necessary* for their success,
without which their contributions to society may never have been realized.
Accordingly, whether these "problem behavior" traits are beneficial or problematic
for the individual, and to what degree, is likely to vary. This will depend on the
intensity or degree to which these traits are expressed, the nature of the society, and,
perhaps most importantly, the social status of the individual (e.g., race, social class,
gender), as these factors will influence how this problem behavior is perceived and
reacted to by the broader society.

SOCIOLOGICAL THEORIES

In contrast to the perspectives discussed above, sociological theories of substance
use and abuse place more emphasis on the role of social structure as opposed to
individual or psychological factors. However, the extent to which individual factors
are emphasized varies in sociological theory.

Differential Association, Social Learning, and
Subcultural Learning Theories

An important sociological explanation for substance use is offered by the learning
theories. Learning theories propose that all people are *tabula rasa* or "blank slates"
and that all forms of behavior, including deviant behaviors like drug use, are
learned. All sociological learning theories draw from Edwin Sutherland's theory of
differential association. Differential association theory proposes that when people
"differentially associate" with people who value deviant behaviors, those people will
learn prodeviant values and be more likely to engage in deviance themselves.
Sutherland also recognized that some relationships are more important than others,
and the importance of messages received varies accordingly. According to Sutherland,

learning is most influential when it is derived from associations that occur early in life (what Sutherland calls "priority"), last longer ("duration"), take place most often ("frequency"), and involve individuals with whom one is most closely attached ("intensity"; Sutherland, 1939).

Social Learning Theory

In the late 1960s, Sutherland's classic differential association theory was substantially expanded upon by Ronald Akers (initially with Robert Burgess) to develop social learning theory (Akers, 1973, 1998; Burgess & Akers, 1968). In addition to drawing heavily on the principles of differential association theory, social learning theory addresses the importance of social-psychological processes such as imitation (Bandura, 1973, 1977) and operant conditioning (Skinner, 1953), making it more applicable for understanding substance use and abuse. Akers's recognition of the roles that reinforcement and punishment (i.e., operant conditioning) play in the learning process is important with regard to substance use since, unlike most other forms of behavior, drug use can be reinforced both socially and physiologically. Substance use may be reinforced socially, as in the case of positive feedback from one's friends for getting high, but it can also be reinforced in a nonsocial, physiological sense based on the effects of the drug. This physiological reinforcement can be negative, as in the case of drugs that can produce physical withdrawal symptoms, prompting another dose of the drug to alleviate the discomfort, or the reinforcement can be positive, as illustrated by the effects of the drug on the body to the extent that they are perceived to be pleasurable (Winfree & Bernat, 1998).

Social learning theory also recognizes that whether the effects of a drug are viewed as enjoyable is at least partially dependent upon the learning process. This is illustrated by Becker's classic study on marijuana use *Outsiders* (1963). Becker noted that upon smoking marijuana, users did not automatically feel high, as they first needed to learn how to perceive the effects of the drug. For example, in an interview, Becker asked one marijuana user if he got high the first time he "turned on" (or smoked marijuana), to which the user replied, "Yeah, sure. Although come to think of it, I guess I really didn't. . . . It was only after the second time I got high that I realized I was high the first time. Then I knew something different was happening" (as quoted in Becker, 1963, p. 51). Further, Becker noted that even among those users who learn to perceive the effects of marijuana and to recognize these feelings as being high, the user must identify the effects as pleasurable for use to continue. As Becker notes:

> Marihuana-produced sensations are not automatically or necessarily pleasurable. The taste for such an experience is a socially acquired one, not different from acquired tastes for oysters or dry martinis. The user feels dizzy, thirsty; his scalp tingles; he misjudges time and distances. Are these things pleasurable? He isn't sure. If he is to continue marihuana use, he must decide that they are. (1963, p. 53)

Learning theory acknowledges that the messages that inform a person's attitudes about the effects and desirability of drugs come from a variety of sources. Accordingly, whether substance use comes to be defined by an individual as desirable or justified depends a great deal on the behavior of those whom the individual values and most commonly interacts with. As Akers and colleagues note, "The principal behavioral effects come from interaction in or under the influence of those *groups which control individuals' major sources of reinforcement and punishment and expose them to behavioral models of normative definitions*" (Akers, Krohn, Lanza-Kaduce, & Radosevich,1979, p. 838, italics original).

Although the groups responsible for providing messages, reinforcement (both positive and negative), and punishment about drug use include extended family members, neighbors, religious and church groups, teachers, authority figures, and other influences in the community and mass media, it is parents and peers that have the most pronounced effect in this regard (Akers, 1998; Akers & Lee, 1996). Thus, social learning theory recognizes that some people are much more important to us than others and are therefore much more influential in the learning process.

However, whether it is parents or peers that exert the strongest effect on learning typically varies with age and the type of behavior in question (Warr, 1993). With respect to drug use, "the most important of the primary groups in the initiation and continuation of substance use among adolescents are peers, particularly close friends" (Akers, 1998, p. 172). This may be due in part to the fact that substance use is typically initiated during adolescence, a period of the lifecourse in which a large portion of one's time is spent with peers. However, parents also play a key role in the learning process, and this is particularly the case prior to adolescence. Social learning theory acknowledges that the influence of parents is likely to be especially important for learning that occurs relatively early in the lifecourse. The core tenets of differential association posit that experiences and associations that occur earliest in life and involve individuals with whom one is most closely attached are apt to be the most significant in the learning process (Sutherland, 1939). Thus, substance use and abuse by one's parents that is witnessed very early in the lifecourse and involves someone with which the individual is (likely) closer than any other is regarded by the theory as very important for understanding subsequent substance use by the individual. Further, social learning theory acknowledges that it is not necessary for parents to *directly* encourage substance use for the behavior to be learned and valued. Indeed, it is likely that such behaviors are more commonly learned through an informal process of observation and mimicry. As Akers notes:

> Although parents may deliberately and directly socialize their children into deviant substance use, such direct tutelage is not necessary. It is more likely that family-fostered deviant use of alcohol, tobacco, marijuana or other drugs grows out of inadequately socializing the children into conventional definitions and abstinent behavior. (1992, p. 172)

Numerous studies have found adolescent substance use to be associated with substance use and abuse by the adolescents' parents (Adler & Lotecka, 1973;

Hawkins, Lishner, & Catalano, 1990; Herd, 1994; Kandel, 1974, 1980). One example of this is a limited body of research that examines intergenerational drinking patterns. Among the earliest work in this area was Cahalan, Cisin, and Crossley's (1969) study on American drinking practices. Using national survey data, Cahalan and colleagues found that parental drinking attitudes and drinking frequency were strongly associated with the subsequent drinking patterns of their adult children (1969). Similar findings were identified by Fillmore, Bacon, and Hyman (1979), who concluded that adults' drinking patterns were to some degree predicted by their parents' frequency of drinking and attitudes about drinking.

More comprehensive studies on parental influences on drinking patterns were completed several years later with a series of longitudinal studies based on 420 sets of father, mother, and adult offspring from Tecumseh, Michigan (Gleiberman, Harburg, Di Franceisco, & Schork, 1991; Webster, Harburg, Gleiberman, Schork, & Di Franceisco, 1989). Studies using these data identified a positive association between parental drinking practices and the adult drinking patterns of their offspring. The studies also indicated that the drinking patterns of the parents and their adult children converged over time, so that children who initially drank more than their parents came to drink less in later life, and those that drank less than their parents early on came to drink more. Research on these subjects also found abstaining parents to be more likely to have children who were abstainers both during their early adult years and also during later life (Gleiberman et al., 1991; Webster et al., 1989). However, studies conducted by this group also found what they referred to as a "fall-off effect." Specifically, although there was a positive association between parental drinking and drinking by their adult offspring, adult offspring tended to moderate their drinking if they had parents who drank frequently, in high volume, and/or exhibited problems associated with their drinking, ostensibly in reaction to their parents' experience (Harburg, Di Franceisco, Webster, Gleiberman, & Schork, 1990).

It is important to recognize that although learning undoubtedly plays some role in these similar patterns of intergenerational substance use, this relationship may be due to many factors other than those directly attributable to learning from one's parents. For example, heavy parental substance use may encourage substance use in childhood by impairing the ability of the parents to supervise and monitor children, which may facilitate substance use directly or indirectly by allowing children to more readily associate with delinquent peers (Johnson & Leff, 1999; Kumpfer, 1999; Lewis & Irwanto, 2001). Parental substance abuse has also been found to block parent–child communication and increase parent–child conflict, and it may facilitate child abuse. Each of these factors may be to some degree responsible for the similarity in substance use patterns by parents and their children (Barnes, 1990; Johnson & Leff, 1999).

It is also important to note that there is substantial variation in the influence of parents on their child's substance use across social groups. Examining intergenerational substance use by race, Herd (1994) analyzed data on 1,947 black and 1,777 white adults and identified important differences in the significance of parental drinking behavior for later drinking patterns. Her analyses found that parental drinking attitudes were not associated with the later drinking patterns of black men, although they were highly correlated with the drinking behavior of white men (Herd, 1994).

As discussed above, social learning theory recognizes that parental behavior is important for understanding patterns of substance use, but during adolescence and early adulthood, it is one's peers that are likely to exert the most prominent influence on substance use (Akers, 1998). In part, this may be because substance-using behavior typically begins in adolescence, and this is a time when increasing amounts of time are spent with peers. Indeed, the most consistent finding in research on adolescent substance use is the relationship between an individual's substance use and substance use by that person's peers (Duan et al., 2009; Elliott, Huizinga, & Ageton, 1985; Johnson, Marcos, & Bahr, 1987; Kandel, 1974, 1980; Warr, 2002). Further illustrating the importance of peers for early substance use is the fact that the use of alcohol and marijuana by youth occurs largely in a group context (Warr, 1996) and the fact that peer use of drugs appears to contribute to substance use via a number of mechanisms. For example, drug use among adolescents is strongly associated with the extent of perceived drug use by peers, self-reported drug use by peers, and tolerant attitudes about drug use among peers (Kandel, 1980; Warr & Stafford, 1991).

With respect to these findings, a common critique of the learning model addresses the causal ordering of the relationship between delinquent peers and delinquency. Critics of the learning approach to substance use point out that substance users are likely to seek out and identify with other substance users. Thus, in opposition to the propositions of learning theory that people learn to use drugs once they come into contact and associate with drug-using peers, it may be that drug use actually comes first. Although social learning theorists recognize that "birds of a feather flock together," the theory proposes, "The sequence of events in which deviant associations precede the onset of delinquent behavior will occur more frequently than the sequence of events in which the onset of delinquency precedes the beginning of delinquent associations" (Akers & Lee, 1996, pp. 321–322).

Thus, the emphasis of learning theory is on associations with delinquent peers, and this relationship has been more empirically supported than the alternative argument (Chilcoat, Dishion, & Anthony, 1995; Menard, Elliott, & Wofford, 1993; Oxford, Harachi, Catalano, & Abbott, 2001). However, evidence demonstrates that substance users are likely to seek out others like them as well, possibly due to a lack of attachments to family, school, and other conventional institutions (principles elaborated on by control theory). Thus, it may be best to consider learning theory as a partial explanation for substance use and one that is complimentary to control theory rather than as seeing these theories as rival explanations of drug use (discussed in more detail below).

Subcultural Learning Theories

Subcultural learning theories are very similar to the learning theories discussed above, but the key difference is that in the learning process, the primary reference group, or the group that the individual learns from and models more than any other, is the members of the subculture. Subcultures are groups of people that hold patterns of norms and values that are in some way distinct from the norms and values held by the broader society (e.g., favorable versus unfavorable attitudes toward drug use). Unlike countercultures, subcultures also hold many of the same values of the larger society in which they reside, and because of this subculture, members often feel pressure to conform more completely to the norms and values of the broader society (Hebdige, 1979). However, subculture members tend to interpret the world according to the unique norms and values present in their subcultures (Short, 1968), and because of this, the behaviors that are learned, valued, and respected in a subculture (e.g., drug use) are often not approved of in broader society.

Field studies provide tremendous insight on drug subcultures. For example, Goode's *The Marijuana Smokers* (1970) documents the ways in which subculture members maintain their shared values and bonds in the face of resistance from the broader society. Goode found several themes to characterize marijuana-using subcultures, including: that drug use typically occurred in a group setting; that drug use generally occurred in the presence of intimates or friends but not with strangers; that group members viewed drug use as a legitimate basis for identity; and that social bonds among members were maintained and reaffirmed through drug use. Goode also noted that there was a high degree of value consensus in the subculture and that value convergence increased with continued subculture involvement (1970).

Similar studies have been conducted on the heroin subculture, which is one of the most notable and enduring drug subcultures in the United States. Research on chronic heroin users has noted that most are able to quickly identify others like them and that the trait of being a heroin user is often sufficient to encourage companionship as users seek allies in a world where they are typically despised by the broader society (Waldorf, 1973). Based on interviews with chronic heroin addicts (who referred to themselves as "dope fiends"), Waldorf (1973) concluded that:

> As with other outcast or persecuted groups, both criminal and noncriminal, dope fiends band together . . . dope fiends claim they can spot another dope fiend with only the most superficial contact, in many instances without talking to the other person. . . . Most of us gravitate towards persons like ourselves— persons who share age, attitudes, interest, or occupations—because we find them easy to communicate with. Dope fiends find similar comfort among other dope fiends. (p. 21)

Another interesting examination of the heroin-using subculture is provided by Faupel's (1991) field study of chronic heroin users in Wilmington, Delaware. Among other things, Faupel examined the criminal behavior of heroin users, concluding that members of a heroin subculture often develop skills in a wide variety of criminal offenses designed to generate the money necessary to support their heroin habit (e.g., robbery, burglary, shoplifting, forgery). Subculture members were often found to pass on these criminal skills to other members of the subculture. However, Faupel also concluded that the common view of this group as completely without ethics was inappropriate despite their criminal involvement. For example, Faupel noted that criminal exploitation, which was regarded in the subculture as "taking care of business," was considered acceptable only if certain rules are followed. Most important was the rule that the victim be someone outside the heroin-using world, as those who were "in the life," or part of a heroin-using subculture, were considered off limits for criminal victimization by other heroin users (1991).

The ethical code of the heroin subculture also extended to the "proper" use of heroin. For example, Faupel found that heroin users had strong rules regarding where and when it was appropriate to use heroin. As noted by Faupel (1991):

> There is perhaps no normative prescription as pervasive in the heroin-using subculture as that against turning young children onto drugs . . . the normative proscription extends beyond selling or sharing drugs with children, however. The study participants were nearly unanimous in their contention that turning anyone on who had not used drugs before, regardless of the person's age, constituted a violation of their code of ethics. (pp. 86–87)

As with the norms surrounding the selection of criminal victims, these unique norms surrounding drug use illustrate the point that rather than being *without* values or norms, drugs subcultures clearly have a normative code, even though it is one that would be considered deviant and inappropriate in broader society.

The Use of Slang in Drug Subcultures

A trait common to most drug subculture is *argot,* a specialized vocabulary involving slang terms with meanings that are not commonly known outside the subculture (Goode, 1970). Illustrating this is Inciardi's (1993) ethnographic study titled "Kingrats, Chicken Heads, Slow Necks, Freaks, and Blood Suckers: A Glimpse at the Miami Sex-for-Crack," which examines the prostitution-for-drugs trade.

Documenting the argot present in this subculture, Inciardi notes that women who will trade sex for crack are commonly called *freaks, gut buckets, rock monsters,* or *skeezers*. Defining the terms used in the title of his article, Inciardi explains that *kingrats* are crack house owners; *chicken heads* and *slow necks* are prostitutes who perform oral sex for crack; and *blood suckers* are prostitutes who will engage in oral sex with another woman who is menstruating. (Inciardi, 1993)

Some subcultural theories propose that individuals learn deviant behavior such as illegal drug use once they come into contact with the subcultural group (consistent with learning theory), while others are more flexible with respect to this point. For example, the "selective interaction/socialization" model of substance use proposed by researchers such as Goode (1970) and others assert that drug users are "attracted to particular individuals and circles—subcultural groups—because their own values are compatible with those of current users" (Goode, 1999, p. 107). This model suggests that the link between substance use by peers and substance use by an individual is not a unidirectional or either-or type of relationship but rather that drug users tend to associate with other drug users, and once these associations develop, messages and behaviors encouraging substance use are learned in this distinct subcultural setting (Goode, 1999).

Social Control/Bonding Theory

Social control or social bonding theories are different from the perspectives described above, as they explain deviance and, by extension, substance use and abuse as a natural tendency of humans that will be realized if the individual is not adequately socialized into conformity. The most widely applied and recognized control theory is Hirschi's (1969) social bonding theory, which argues that people will engage in deviance such as drug use and abuse to the extent that their "bond to society is weak or broken" (Hirschi, 1969, p. 16). This bond reflects a person's integration into conventional society and includes relationships to family, spouses, children, conventional friends, employment, education, religion, community organizations, and other institutions in society. According to social bonding theory, the greater the number and strength of the ties that bind the individual to conventional society, the less likely it is that the individual will engage in deviance such as illegal substance use and abuse.

The theory proposes that four principal elements constitute the social bond—attachment, commitment, involvement, and belief. Attachment refers to feelings of sentiment and affection for others and is said to be important for understanding drug use because it affects how much a person cares about others' opinions of him or her and thus how constraining these opinions are. When attachment is low, the opinions of others are much less effective at preventing people from engaging in behavior such as drug use. The second element of the bond, commitment, refers to the extent to which a person is invested in society in terms of educational attainment, occupational advancement, wealth, and the like. Social bonding theory recognizes that as commitment increases, a person has more to lose from engaging in deviant acts, particularly those acts that might bring the attention of law enforcement, such as the use of illegal drugs. The third element of the bond, involvement, refers to the amount of time a person spends engaged in conventional activities (e.g., after-school sports). The more time that is spent engaged in conventional activities, the less time there is available for engaging in unconventional activities such as drug use. The final element of the social bond, belief, involves the extent to which a person holds and endorses conventional rules and norms in society. Each of these elements of the social bond is related to the other, so it is probable that the strengthening of one bond (e.g., commitment in the form of a new job) will result in strengthening of the other (e.g., involvement in the form of more time spent in work as a result of the new job) and vice versa.

There is extensive research that examines the relationship between drug use and the conventional institutions described by social bonding theory (e.g., school, work, family, religion), but there is less research that directly tests the ability of social bonding theory to predict substance use and abuse. Of those studies that have been conducted on substance use, few have provided support for social bonding theory (see, for example, Arnett, 1998; Burkett & Warren, 1987; Cochran & Akers, 1989), and this contrasts sharply with the relative abundance of support for the theory with respect to crime and deviance more generally (Akers & Sellers, 2009). The lack of support for social bonding theory in the area of substance use appears to be due, in large part, to the fact that this theory deemphasizes the importance of peer associations for substance use (as peers are central to learning theory), and peer associations have proven to be one of the strongest predictors of drug use (Duan et al., 2009; Elliott et al., 1985; Johnson et al., 1987; Kandel, 1974, 1980; Warr, 2002). Accordingly, when social bonding variables such as family attachment are included alongside peer variables in studies of substance use, they are often dominated and obscured by the more powerful peer-related influences.

While family factors may be less salient for an understanding of substance use than peer influence, some studies have found family-related social bonding variables to remain a relevant, if weaker, predictor of substance use (Chilcoat, Dishion, & Anthony, 1995; Menard, Elliott, & Wofford, 1993; Oxford, Harachi, Catalano, & Abbott, 2001). In part, the effect of these social bonding variables is important for understanding substance use because of the influence they have on peer selection. That is, attachment to parents and also to conventional societal institutions such as school and religion tends to strongly influence people's choices of friends, and these peer groups, once chosen, are central for understanding subsequent drug use patterns by the individual (Faupel et al., 2004).

With respect to these relationships, it seems reasonable that the bonds to conventional institutions such as family and work may be more important for understanding substance use and abuse than is suggested by many studies. The vast majority of studies on substance use examine adolescents and young adults, particularly those in their high school and college years (Beauvais, 1998), with much less research examining substance use by subjects who are in their early adolescent years (e.g., 11–13) or at ages beyond early adulthood (e.g., the late 20s and older). This is important because both early adolescence and later adulthood represent periods of life when peer influence on drug use is comparatively less salient (Akers, 1998; Warr, 1996).

Integrated theories such as Thornberry's interactional theory and the social development model of Hawkins, Catalano, and colleagues are especially useful for understanding the interdependency of peer influence and traditional social bonds. To account for delinquent behaviors including drug use, each of these perspectives incorporates key structural and individual risk factors (sex, race, class, neighborhood characteristics) and variables from differential association, social learning, and social control theories and emphasizes the interdependency of learning and control variables (i.e., peer influence versus attachment to parents, family, and work) in delinquent/drug abuse outcomes (Catalano & Hawkins, 1996; Catalano, Oesterle, Flemin, & Hawkins, 2009; Thornberry, 1987). Interactional theory proposes that youth who are not adequately bonded to their parents are more likely to experience weakened bonds to school (and vice versa), which might facilitate association with delinquent peers and the learning of antisocial attitudes and behaviors. Accordingly, the association with delinquent peers in youth and/or adolescence will increase the likelihood of weak conventional attachments later in life, thus facilitating deviant behaviors such as illegal drug use and crime.

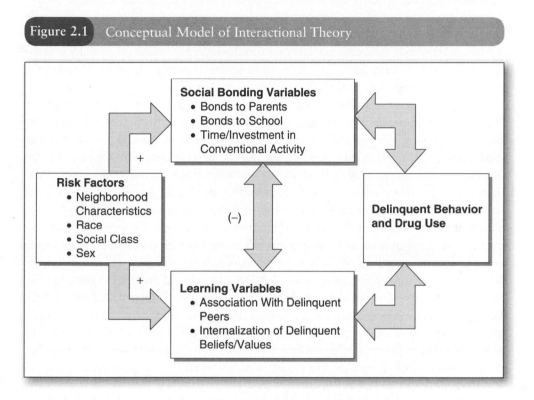

Figure 2.1   Conceptual Model of Interactional Theory

Interactional theory is important for an understanding of the etiology of substance use and abuse because it reconciles differences in the social control and learning approaches and incorporate them into a single theoretical model (see Figure 2.1). When social control variables are regarded alongside learning variables, research has found social control theory relevant to substance use and abuse. For example, Oxford and colleagues (2001) found that the strongest predictor of initiation into substance use in early adolescence was delinquent peers, but also that family variables such as parent–child attachment played an important role in substance use, both directly by preventing the initiation of substance use and indirectly by limiting involvement with antisocial peers. Findings such as these suggest that future work on control theory and substance use may be best directed at examining how control variables such as family attachment interact with peer-related variables to predict substance use.

Lifecourse/Age-Graded Theory

Lifecourse theories (sometimes called developmental theories) of deviance are designed to explain "pathways through the age differentiated life span" (Elder, 1985, p. 17). When applied to substance use, lifecourse theories are most suited to explaining the stability and change in the occurrence of this type of behavior over the lifecourse.

Put simply, a substantial percentage of people engage in deviant behavior such as illegal drug use during adolescence and early adulthood but "age out" of this behavior. This represents the change in the likelihood of deviance over the lifecourse, because people age into and then out of this form of behavior. Conversely, a small portion of people who engage in illegal drug use during adolescence *never* age out of this type of behavior but instead continue their drug use late into adulthood, representing the stability in deviance over the lifecourse. So lifecourse theories of deviance provide an explanation for why most people age into and then out of deviance, but some people never do.

An important lifecourse theory of deviance is Sampson and Laub's age-graded theory. As with most lifecourse theories, age-graded theory proposes that there are important life trajectories (or "pathways"), transitions, and turning points that occur over the lifecourse (Elder, 1985). A *trajectory* is a pathway of development over the lifespan that involves a consistent pattern of behavior, such as a marriage, parenthood, or a criminal or drug using career (Sampson & Laub, 2003). Trajectories are characterized by a series of *transitions*, which are periods of a trajectory that are marked by key life events such as getting married or entering college. Many (not all) transitions are age graded, meaning that they tend to occur at relatively predictable times in the lifecourse. For example, entering college or the labor force most often occurs immediately after adolescence. Much life-course research focuses on the duration, timing, and ordering of these key life events and the implications that this has for the lifecourse (Sampson & Laub, 1993). When a transition occurs, the way in which an individual adapts to it can lead to different trajectories, and a *turning point* occurs when the adaptation to a transition leads to a very different trajectory (or life pathway). As an example, an important transition that occurs for most people in their 20s or 30s is parenthood. If, after making the decision along with his spouse to have children, a new father embraces his role as a parent, it would facilitate stability in his marriage and life trajectory. Conversely, if he rejected his duties as a father, it would likely represent a turning point, as his relationship with his spouse would likely deteriorate and potentially collapse, and he may not develop any relationship with his child. This is a turning point because the rejection of parenthood sent him down a new life pathway (trajectory).

Age-graded theory is heavily influenced by social control theory, particularly for predictions of deviance after adolescence, but it also addresses the importance of learning theory, social structural factors, and early lifecourse temperament variables. As is illustrated in Figure 2.2, there are roughly five stages of development important for understanding patterns of deviance such as drug use (after age 45, it is less common for a person to alter their trajectory). The first of these lifecourse stages is *childhood*, roughly ages 0 to 10, and during this period, the most important variables are a number of structural and individual risk factors that predispose children to getting into trouble, particularly with their parents and teachers. These risk factors are things that a child is born into, whether environmental—like poverty, being from a single-parent family, or living in a neighborhood characterized by criminogenic circumstances—or individual characteristics like temperament problems, impulsivity, and conduct disorders. Upon reaching *adolescence*, roughly ages 10 to 18, the aforementioned environmental and individual conditions predispose adolescents to delinquent peer attachment and weak social bonds, particularly to family and school. As described earlier in our discussion of interactional theory, a reciprocal process can occur in which weakened conventional bonds put the adolescent at high risk for delinquent influence (e.g., drug use, criminal behavior), and the delinquent behavior, particularly if identified and resulting in a formal sanction like incarceration, can further weaken the bonds to family and school, intensifying the cycle of deviance.

In the late teens and early 20s, people typically enter the *transition to young adulthood,* and social bonds—particularly bonds to education, the labor force, marriage, and parenthood—are the primary factors influencing criminal and deviant behavior such as drug use. As noted in our discussion of social control theory earlier, individuals who have these bonds, like a college education, a good job, or a family, are protected from deviance in part *because they have much more to lose* than those who don't have these bonds. These bonds are most often formed in young adulthood (roughly ages 17–32), and if not present by this point, their formation become less likely as one ages into middle and later adulthood. Incarceration at any point makes it less likely that people will be able to develop bonds in adulthood (like maintain a marriage or a career-track job), so incarceration is associated with an increased likelihood of continued drug use/offending (Sampson & Laub, 1993). Finally, note that no matter how many "strikes" a person has against him or her, the person can become bonded or rebonded to conventional society, and this is typically the case when someone "turns it all around." Common examples include a young person who has been in trouble with the law prior to joining the military, which brought stability to this person's life, or someone who has had drug problems getting married and having a family and leaving drugs behind. For these individuals, joining the military and marriage/parenthood represent turning points in their pathway as they became bonded to conventional society.

Anomie/Strain Theories

Anomie or strain theories propose that when societies are characterized by an imbalance in their social order, it creates conditions favorable to crime and deviance such as substance use. Robert Merton's theory of anomie (1938, 1957) is the most well known of these theories, and it has had tremendous influence on the study of deviance. According to anomie theory, there is a discrepancy between the valued goals in American society, such as monetary success, and the legitimate means to achieve these goals, such as high-paying jobs. Not everyone can succeed in his or her pursuit of the American Dream, but everyone wants to succeed (at least initially), and this discrepancy between goals and means will generate strain (hence, strain theory). People seek to alleviate this strain by adapting to it in a variety of ways. According to Merton, one way people could alleviate strain was to use and abuse illegal drugs and alcohol, an adaptation Merton regarded as a form of "retreatism" (1957, p. 153). Subsequent research, including that based on Cloward and Ohlin's (1960) subcultural version of Merton's theory, has found little support for Merton's anomie theory when applied to drug use and abuse (this is not the case for other forms of deviance), and this is largely due to the fact that the theory relies almost exclusively on poverty or failure in economic terms as the key explanatory variable. As will be discussed in more detail in Chapter 5, "Patterns of Illegal Drug Use," social class is, at best, a weak predictor of substance use (legal and illegal), meaning

Figure 2.2 Sampson and Laub's Age-Graded Theory

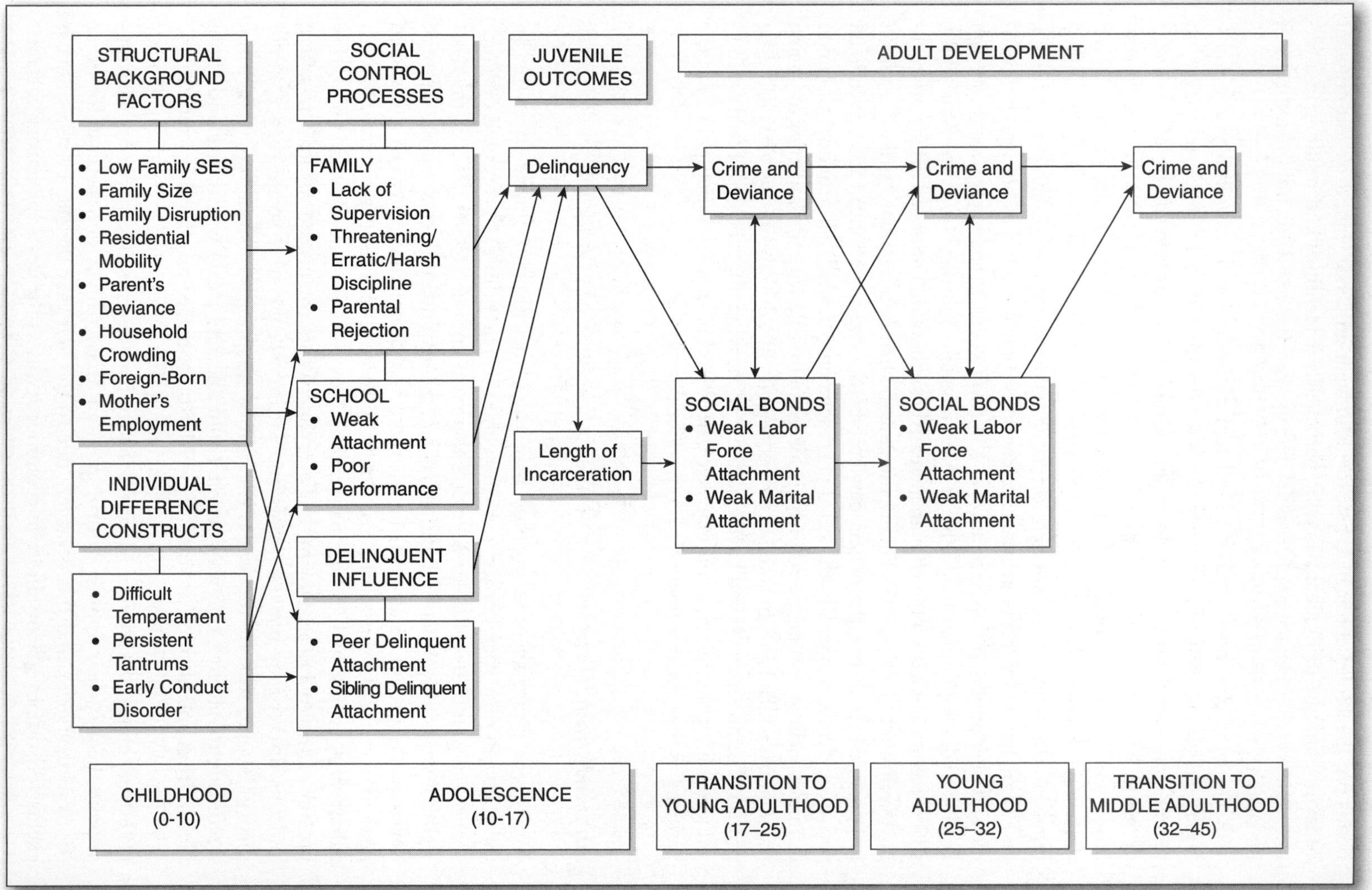

SOURCE: Samson & Laub, 1993. © Harvard University Press.

that the rich, middle class, and poor use drugs at very similar rates. Because of this, anomie theory is not a robust explanation for substance use and abuse.

Although the almost complete reliance on economics as the primary source of strain in society likely makes anomie theory inappropriate for understanding broad patterns of substance use and abuse, recent theoretical work by Agnew (1992) has significantly expanded upon strain theory, making it more applicable to drug use. Agnew's general strain theory is much broader than Merton's original theory in that it addresses strains other than those generated by a disjuncture between goals and means. That is, in addition to addressing the importance of monetary strain in what Agnew refers to as a *failure to achieve positively valued goals* (of which economic success is only one), Agnew also addresses strain resulting from the *removal of positively valued stimuli* (e.g., the loss of a family member) and from *the confrontation with negative stimuli* (e.g., repeated academic failure; Agnew, 1992). Agnew notes that each source of strain "increases the likelihood that individuals will experience one or more of a range of negative emotions," including "disappointment, depression, fear, and anger" (1992, p. 59). According to the theory, the strained individual must adapt in order to deal with the strain, and Agnew (1992) notes that many elect to manage their negative emotional states through drug use.

According to general strain theory, the use of substances is particularly effective at managing strain, as it functions to minimize strain-related distress, alleviate depression and despair, and produce positive emotions (Agnew, 1992; Brezina, 1996). This is consistent with more psychologically oriented perspectives such as the stress-coping model (Wills & Shiffman, 1985), the tension-reduction hypothesis (Sher & Levenson, 1982), and the self-medication hypothesis (Khantzian, 1985), which all recognize that people frequently use psychoactive substances to relieve tension and distress or to improve their mood. Empirical research also supports the efficacy of this practice, including that by Kaplan, Tolle, and Yoshida (2001), which found that substance use was negatively related to later violent acts as people used substances to "assuage distressful self-feelings" (p. 205). However, general strain theory also acknowledges the potential of substance use to exacerbate existing psychological strain, as alcohol and illicit drug use may create new problems and aggravate existing ones as substance use is increasingly relied upon to cope with stress. To the extent that substance use is effective (or thought to be effective) at managing strain, it may be perceived by the individual as a temporary or immediate solution to problems (Agnew, 1992).

It is also likely that the economic component of general strain theory (again, derived largely from Merton's anomie theory) is useful for understanding substance use (and especially substance *abuse*) among *certain* segments of the population, despite the inability of research to identify empirical support for the theory in the past. Research has found that the relationship between economics and substance use may not be the same across racial/ethnic groups, in part because there are important interactions between race/ethnicity, income/poverty, and substance use (Barr, Farrell, Barnes, & Welte, 1993). For example, Herd (1990) found that for white men, the prevalence of alcohol use increased with income, but for black men, the prevalence of alcohol use decreased with income. Barr and colleagues (1993) reached similar conclusions, finding increased income to substantially decrease alcohol consumption, alcohol-related problems, and illicit drug use for adult black males but to have little or no effect on alcohol consumption, alcohol-related problems, and illegal drug use for adult white males. Examining only alcohol-related problems, Jones-Webb, Hsiao, and Hannan (1995) found that lower-class blacks were much more likely to report alcohol-related problems than were lower-class whites and that the magnitude of these problems had increased over time. However, similar findings were not identified for middle-class blacks and whites (Jones-Webb et al., 1995). Finally, research conducted by Jones-Webb and colleagues (1997) examined alcohol problems experienced by Hispanic, black, and white men and concluded that neighborhood poverty was much more harmful for blacks as compared to Hispanics and whites once alcohol consumption was controlled for. The study concluded that the social isolation, employment, and marital characteristics of lower-class blacks distinguished them from comparably poor Hispanics and whites, resulting in greater substance related problems for blacks. Each of the studies discussed here illustrates the importance of economic strain for substance use and abuse when race is taken into account.

Research on class polarization and social isolation by William Julius Wilson (1987, 1996) may be particularly useful for understanding the disparate patterns of drug use and abuse by race. According to Wilson, as a result of economic transformation and other macrostructural processes in the United States, middle- and lower-class minority-group members may be gradually growing more isolated from one another. Indeed, research has noted that while the portion of the middle class comprising minority-group members has grown in recent years, due in part to an increasing commitment to civil rights and as a result of programs like affirmative action, inner-city minority communities have become more isolated and impoverished (Massey & Denton, 1993; Wilson, 1987). The cumulative disadvantage present in these communities also clearly distinguishes minority poverty from white poverty. As Wilson has noted regarding the difference between poor whites and poor blacks, poor whites live "in areas which are ecologically and economically very different from poor Blacks . . . with respect to jobs, marriage opportunities, and exposure to conventional role models" (Wilson, 1987, pp. 59–60). In addition to these factors, substance use and abuse by lower-class minorities may be exacerbated due to the absence of conventional social institutions and coping resources in impoverished communities. For example, as one poor resident of inner-city Chicago says about youth drug use in his or her community:

> They're in an environment where if you don't get high you're square . . . I watched kids, I saw their fathers ruined, and I seen 'em grow up and do the very same thing. . . . The children, they don't have any means of recreation whatsoever out here, other than their backyards, the streets, nothing . . . The only way it can be intervened if (*sic*) the child has something outside the house to go to, because it is—just go by the environment of the house, he's destined to be an alcoholic or drug addict. (in Wilson, 1996, pp. 56–57)

The availability of conventional recreation, entertainment, and stress-coping resources is essential for limiting substance use and abuse. General strain theory recognizes that only some of those people who are strained will resort to substance use and abuse to alleviate their strain. The obvious reason for this is that people can elect to adopt a variety of alternative, nondrug coping strategies to deal with their strain. However, these conventional coping resources are not equally accessible to all. As class and race are inexorably linked in American society, minorities are not only more likely to encounter many key sources of strain, but they are also less likely to have access to the resources that enable or facilitate conventional coping. This includes access to conventional recreation and entertainment options (e.g., shopping malls, rec centers, sports clubs, movie theaters, and libraries); coping and treatment resources (e.g., medical care, professional counseling, and substance treatment centers); and access to institutions that make psychological coping more easy (e.g., work and education; Peterson, Krivo, & Harris, 2000; Wallace, 1999a; Wallace & Bachman, 1991; Williams & Collins, 1995). Thus, there is substantial evidence to suggest that economic strain is useful for understanding patterns of substance use and especially substance abuse, but it is predominately or only applicable to the most disadvantaged in society.

Social Conflict Theory

As compared to strain theory, social conflict theory is even more structural or macro in nature. Most research in the area of drug use and abuse that is grounded in a conflict perspective examines the creation, enforcement, and consequences of laws designed to regulate drug use. Because of this, conflict theory as applied to drug issues might be better seen as a conflict theory of law formulation and enforcement as opposed to theory that attempts to explain the drug-using behavior of individuals, as do the other theories described in this chapter.

Although there are many forms of conflict theory, at base they all assume that the existing social order is not a product of consensus and mutual benefit but rather a function of power differentials in society. These perspectives recognize that societal resources are limited and contend that opposing groups are in a constant struggle for a greater share of the resources and the power that comes with them. As groups struggle to gain a greater share of the limited societal resources, some groups in society are inevitably marginalized, and these are the groups that will suffer the most in the existing social order in terms of living conditions, wealth, education, employment opportunity, health, criminal victimization, and almost every other indicator of social well-being. Additionally, because the most powerful in society control the law and many sources of influence (e.g., television, newspapers, political lobbyists, etc.), many of the laws and values in society tend to reflect the interests of these groups and benefit them. While conflict theory recognizes that laws against crimes such as murder and assault tend to be beneficial to all, and that some laws will be passed "which reflect the interests of the general population and which are antithetical to the interests of those in power" (Chambliss, 1969, p. 10), they also recognize that some laws and policies may benefit those in power to the detriment of the powerless. It is in this regard that conflict theory may be most applicable for an understanding of substance use and the consequences that are often associated with it.

As discussed in Chapter 1, psychoactive substance use is universal across time and society, and as will be discussed in later chapters, punitive policies designed to control substance use are generally counterproductive if their intent is harm minimization. Why then do punitive policies surrounding drug use and abuse exist? Conflict theorists would argue that laws against morally prohibited and victimless crimes such as substance use provide those in power with the necessarily latitude to enforce the law when and how they see fit. That is, although substance use is ubiquitous in society, with even illegal substances being used broadly across all social and economic groups (see Chapter 3), the illegal status of certain drugs enables coercive force to be brought to bear against the poor and powerless when those in power see it as beneficial or necessary. To support this, conflict theorists point to the vastly disproportionate manner in which laws against substance use are enforced. Policies that prohibit and regulate certain drugs are particularly detrimental to poor minorities (Tonry, 1995), which is ironic given that, as discussed in Chapter 3, minorities have comparatively modest use patterns for legal and illegal drugs.

Research examining drug issues from a conflict perspective includes that by Chambliss (1994) and Mosher (2001), who note that policing practices, particularly those focused on drug offenses, have been exceptionally harmful to poor minority communities. As Chambliss (1994) notes:

> The intensive surveillance of black neighborhoods . . . has the general consequence of institutionalizing racism by defining the problem of crime generally, and drug use in particular, as a problem of young black men . . . Young African-American and Latino men are defined as a criminal group, arrested for minor offenses over and over again, and given criminal records which justify long prison sentences. (p. 183)

So, despite the fact that the use of illegal drugs (including cocaine—the drug targeted by many of these proactive policing efforts) is not more likely among minorities, the consequences of drug policies fall much more heavily on the minority population. As conflict theorists point out, one of the reasons for this inequity is that drug arrests are commonly carried out in poor, minority communities because such practices are socially and politically palatable *only so long as the person arrested is relatively powerless*. As Chambliss (1994) comments on this, in contrast to drug arrests among the lower class, "Arrests of white male middle class offenders (on college campuses for example) are guaranteed to cause the organization and the arresting officer strain, as people with political influence and money hire attorneys for their defense" (p. 192 , see also Alexander, 2010).

Accordingly, affluent groups are not targeted for drugs arrests despite their comparable use patterns, with the end result being that even though there are many times more white illegal drug users than black illegal drug users, those incarcerated for drug offenses are disproportionately black. According to the annual report of the Bureau of Justice Statistics, *Prisoners in 2010*, of the more than 255,000 people serving time in state prisons for drug offenses, 130,300 (50.9%) were black while only 76,900 (30.0%) were white, despite the fact that blacks comprise just over 13% of the population (Bureau of Justice Statistics, 2011).

An additional element of conflict theory is that it argues that the nonlegal consequences associated with drug use are felt most acutely by the lower class because
of their impoverished status. Most notably, conflict theorists would argue that the
hoarding of resources in society has left large portions of the lower class
concentrated into socially isolated and disadvantaged ghettos where drug abuse/
dependence, drug-related violence, and drug dealing proliferate (Anderson, 1990,
1999; Wallace, 1999a; Wilson, 1996). On this point, the arguments of conflict
theorists and anomie/strain theorists (discussed above) overlap, but conflict theorists typically place more emphasis on the culpability of the upper class in society
for generating these adverse conditions. According to this form of conflict theory,
structural conditions with their origins in politics and economics have generated
extreme poverty and isolation among the lower class, resulting in feelings of
alienation, frustration, and hopelessness for many. Rates of drug and alcohol use
are exceedingly high in these communities as people seek escape and relief from
these adverse life conditions. Research by Lillie-Blanton, Anthony, and Schuster
(1993) supports these arguments by examining the importance of community
structure for crack cocaine use. Noting how adversely crack has affected the black
community in particular, Lillie-Blanton and colleagues (1993) analyzed differences
in crack-cocaine use for whites, blacks, and Hispanics and found that the higher
rates of crack use by blacks and Hispanics were the result of economic and environmental conditions—and once these factors were controlled for, the differences
in crack use disappeared.

In addition to the escapism that frequent drug use may provide extremely disadvantaged individuals, the severe poverty and almost total lack of decent employment
opportunity characterizing these communities has made drug dealing among the
most lucrative and attractive, if locally despised, sources of employment. Despite the
fact that the vast majority of all lower-class residents resist this temptation, drug
selling is a form of employment in an otherwise extremely poor and opportunity-
deprived environment that can provide the symbols of success so valued in society.
As Anderson (1999) has noted on these issues,

> Where the wider economy is not receptive to these dislocated people, the under-
> ground economy is. That does not mean that anyone without a job is suddenly
> going to become a drug dealer; the process is not that simple. But the facts of
> race relations, unemployment, dislocation and destitution create alienation, and
> alienation allows for a certain receptivity to overtures made by people seeking
> youthful new recruits for the drug trade. (p. 120)

Conflict theorists would argue that as the opportunities provided to the lower
class remain extremely limited, the wealth promised by drug sales becomes a source
of competition and conflict among the lower class. Violence is the predominant
form of mediation in these relationships, and consequently, great harm is done to
residents of these communities, both those involved directly in the drug trade and
those caught in the crossfire. Consistent with the propositions of conflict theory, the
relative lack of power and political representation held by the residents of these

extremely poor communities hampers their ability to address the problem. Consequently, the drug trade may become entrenched in the area, and the community disruption, drug dependence, and violence associated with it further serves to limit the opportunities of these residents.

CONCLUSION

Theories of substance use are designed to explain why drug use and abuse occurs and why it varies across a variety of different circumstances and social conditions. Although there are several dozen theories of drug use, we have focused on a number of theoretically distinct and broad perspectives and examined what research has to say about their validity.

The nature perspective, advocated most notably by Weil, contends that substance use and abuse is simply one way in which people express a universal and innate drive to alter their consciousness. Although empirical research on this perspective is limited, Weil points to the fact that substance use is historically ubiquitous in human societies and that from birth, children the world over engage in behaviors designed to alter their consciousness (e.g., rocking, spinning) and that people engage in a number of nondrug behaviors that also alter consciousness (e.g., meditation, exercise, risk taking).

Genetic/biological explanations of substance use were also addressed. Focusing largely on alcoholism, genetic perspectives emphasize that inherited predispositions toward substance use largely determine whether an individual will use and especially abuse psychoactive drugs. Although there is evidence that substance dependency runs in families, the genetic perspectives have been unable to eliminate environmental influences, and evidence suggests that genetic perspectives will be lacking as long as they ignore personal and environmental influences on substance use. Sensitization perspectives view the chronic administration of certain psychoactive drugs as capable of altering brain chemistry, increasing the individual's vulnerability to continued drug use. Sensitization is distinct from many biological perspectives in the sense that a behavioral pattern, chronic substance use, places the individual at elevated risk for drug use via a biological process.

The disease model of addiction is often confused with the genetic model, but there are important differences. Like the genetic model, most versions of the disease model argue that substance use and addiction are related to genetic predispositions—but the disease model makes several ideologically based assumptions (e.g., that abstinence is the only remedy for alcoholics; that alcoholism invariably grows worse) that are not supported by research.

Psychological perspectives of substance use include the self-derogation perspective, which contends that substance use is the result of lacking self-esteem. According to this perspective, individuals engage in substance use and abuse in the pursuit of positive affirmation from others, affirmation they have not received from more conventional sources. This perspective has been criticized in part because its emphasis on self-rejection as the cause of substance use is difficult to reconcile with the fact that illicit drug users tend to have *more* close friends than nondrug users, not fewer (Goode, 1999; Kandel & Davies, 1991).

The problem-behavior perspective contends that substance use is just one pattern of behavior that is typical of a problem-behavior personality. The traits that characterize this personality (e.g., risk taking, rebellion, pleasure seeking) are not necessarily negative or pathological, but they encourage behavior that conflicts with social and sometimes legal norms. Whether these traits are beneficial or problematic for the individual will likely depend on the intensity or degree to which they are expressed, the particular society or social group they are part of, and, perhaps most importantly, the social status of the individual.

Our examination of sociological theories includes differential association theory and social learning theory, theories that represent some of the most empirically supported explanations for substance use. Social learning theory emphasizes how interactions with others, especially intimate others, may contribute to substance use as people learn messages about substance use. More recent versions of the theory proposed by Akers also recognize the importance that reinforcement, both social and physiological, can have in drug use. Empirical support for the theory is substantial, particularly research that addresses the importance of parents and peers in predictions of substance use and abuse.

Social bonding theory contends that substance use results when an individual's bond to society is weak or broken (Hirschi, 1969). The bond reflects a person's integration into conventional society in terms of his or her relationships to family, spouses, children, conventional friends, employment, education, religion, community organizations, and other institutions in society. Social bonding theory has been widely supported when it has been used to explain crime and deviance more generally, but there has been relatively little support for the theory with respect to substance use, as the theory places too little emphasis on peer associations. Future work on control theory and substance use may be best directed at examining how control variables such as family attachment interact with peer-related variables to predict substance use at different points in the lifecourse, as is proposed by Thornberry's interactional theory (Thornberry, 1987) and the social development model (Catalano et al., 1996).

Age-graded theory is a developmental or lifecourse theory that integrates concepts from many theoretical perspectives, illustrating how these theoretical processes contribute to deviant behavior, including drug use, at several stages over the lifecourse. Developmental theories are among the best at explaining the stability and change evident in data on drug use, or why most people who use illegal drugs do so for a time (typically adolescence and young adulthood) and then "age out" of this behavior, but others use drugs during adolescence and continue using late into adulthood.

Anomie or strain theories of substance use emphasize the importance of economic (Merton, 1938, 1957) and emotional stressors (Agnew, 1992) in the etiology of substance use and abuse. Despite a lack of empirical support for classical strain explanations of substance use, recent findings indicate that the relationship between economic factors and substance use may not be the same across racial/ethnic groups, in part because there are important interactions between race/ethnicity, income/poverty, and substance use (Barr et al., 1990; Herd, 1990; Jones-Webb, Hsiao, & Hannan, 1995; Jones-Webb et al., 1997). Thus, economic strain explanations may be ineffective for explaining substance use and abuse among whites and the middle class, but these explanations appear to be more effective at explaining patterns of substance use among minorities and particularly among the most disadvantaged in society.

Finally, conflict perspectives of substance use emphasize the importance of power differentials in society for substance use and especially *outcomes* associated with substance use and abuse. Conflict perspectives focus on the differential application of the law, noting that illegal drugs are used broadly across all social and economic groups, but the consequences of these drug policies fall much more heavily on minorities and the lower class.

REVIEW QUESTIONS

1. What does current research reveal about the strength of the relationship between genetics and alcoholism?

2. How does the disease model of addiction differ from the moral model of addiction?

3. According to the self-derogation perspective, what causes drug use and abuse?

4. Discuss the similarities and differences between social learning theory and subcultural learning theory.

5. Why is there less empirical support for the propositions of social control theory than for social learning theory?

6. How did Agnew's general strain theory expand and improve upon earlier versions of strain theory?

7. Discuss this statement: Conflict theory is most concerned with outcomes of drug use, not drug use per se.

INTERNET EXERCISES

1. Using a search engine available at your college/university's library (JSTOR; Proquest), type in "social control theory drugs" and "social learning theory drugs." Compare the number of articles identified through each search, and access two articles from each category. Review the articles and compare and contrast their findings.

2. Access current data on illegal drug use provided by the Monitoring the Future Study at http://www.monitoringthefuture.org/ and National Survey on Drug Use and Health (NSDUH) at https://nsduhweb.rti.org/.

Find data on racial/ethnic differences in illegal drug use. Keep these windows open.

Now access UCR data on arrests for illegal drug use at http://www.fbi.gov/about-us/cjis/ucr/crime-in-the-u.s/2010/crime-in-the-u.s.-2010/tables/table-43/10tbl43a.xls.

Compare the data on use by race with data on arrests by race. According to the data provided by the Monitoring the Future study, are blacks more or less likely to use illegal drugs than whites? How about NSDUH? According to the data provided by the UCR, are blacks more or less likely than whites to be arrested for drug offenses (remember to account for the fact that blacks comprise approximately 13% of the U.S. population)?

How would a conflict theorist interpret these findings?

WEB RESOURCES

National Institute of Drug Abuse: "Drugs, Brains, and Behavior—The Science of Addiction"

http://www.nida.nih.gov/scienceofaddiction/

Stanton Peele Critiques the Disease Model

http://www.peele.net/lib/faithhealers.html

Alcoholics Anonymous

http://www.aa.org/?Media=PlayFlash

National Institute of Drug Abuse: Protective Factors in Drug Abuse Prevention

http://www.drugabuse.gov/publications/preventing-drug-abuse-among-children-adolescents/chapter-1-risk-factors-protective-factors

CHAPTER 3

The Effects of Drugs: Part I

As noted in Chapter 1, the use of substances for their conscious-altering effects is ubiquitous in human history. There is evidence that psychoactive plants such as ephedra were used by Neanderthal man as far back as 50,000 years ago (Merlin, 2003), and all civilizations that have had access to these substances have significant numbers of individuals who choose to use them. The tendency to alter consciousness is not even unique to humans, as animals, both domesticated and wild, have been shown to seek out intoxicating substances such as fermenting fruit or psychoactive plants (Siegel, 1989). Drugs are often viewed as possessing an almost mystical quality in terms of their ability to generate psychoactive effects, but it is important to recognize that these substances do not "create" these effects—they simply stimulate a natural function of the brain. Or, as Gahlinger comments, *"All drug sensations, feelings, awareness or hallucinations can also be achieved without drugs"* and *"all* effects of psychoactive drugs can be produced naturally and spontaneously"* (Gahlinger, 2001, p. 159, italics original).

In the following two chapters, we discuss several categories of drugs based on their subjective psychoactive effects as well as their effects on the body. This chapter will focus on the stimulants, depressants, inhalants, and opiates, and the following chapter will address the hallucinogens, PCP and ketamine, marijuana, antidepressants, aphrodisiacs, and steroids and other performance-enhancing drugs. Significant differences exist between these drug types, and as compared to the other drugs we address, the antidepressants, aphrodisiacs, and steroids and other performance-enhancing drugs stand apart. However, it is important to recognize that the antidepressants, aphrodisiacs, and performance-enhancing drugs share many characteristics with more "traditional" psychoactive drugs, as all of these substances have potential benefits and drawbacks, all may be abused, and each represents a means by which people may alter their consciousness or reality.

Although it is true that antidepressants will not get users "high" in the fashion of other psychoactive drugs, they do have the ability to alter perception and mood—indeed, this is why they are useful in a medical context. We do not question that these drugs have been very helpful for countless individuals suffering from mental illnesses such as depression. But the fact remains that these substances alter consciousness, and this illustrates our point that consciousness alteration should not be seen as negative *per se*; it is only when this tendency is manifested in ways that are harmful to others that it becomes problematic.

Similarly, aphrodisiacs are clearly a unique form of drug in that their sole purpose is to allow for sexual pleasure (Shenk, 1999). As discussed below, these drugs may allow for or assist in the attainment of sexual pleasure for those who have lost the ability to achieve erection/orgasm, but they are also widely used recreationally by those who seek to enhance their sex lives despite the absence of any problems with them. Although we do not see the use of these substances as directly analogous to the use of more traditional psychoactive drugs, aphrodisiacs are similar to the others discussed in the sense that they are designed to assist in the achievement of a state of overpowering emotion and feeling—in this case, sexual ecstasy.

Finally, we recognize that steroids and (certain) other performance-enhancing drugs are in many respects different from the other substances discussed. These substances are used primarily to enhance athletic performance and/or to improve physique. Thus, while the primary motivation for using performance-enhancing drugs is to some degree unique, the use of these substances also represents "an expression of a basic human drive to stimulate the human organism beyond its normal metabolic state" (Hoberman, 1992, p. 105). In this sense, then, these drugs are similar to others that will be discussed. It is also important to recognize that steroids and similar substances have also been shown to possess mood-altering effects. Of these, aggression is the most well known, but more desirable effects associated with steroid use include euphoria, increased sexual desire, friendliness, and stimulant-like properties including alertness, decreased fatigue, increased energy and vitality, and improved memory and concentration (Bahrke et al., 1996; Pope et al., 2000; Rubinow & Schmidt, 1996; Yates, 2000). Although we are not making the claim that steroids and similar substances are initially taken in pursuit of these effects, the effects may come to be important reasons that people continue to use these drugs.

> The only known societies that had no access to psychoactive substances were the Inuit, who traditionally lived near the Arctic Circle, and some people of the Pacific Islands. These groups shared the trait of being extremely isolated from other civilizations, and when these people were eventually exposed to psychoactive substances, especially alcohol, they exhibited catastrophic rates of addiction and abuse (Gahlinger, 2001).

It is interesting to note that the effects of drugs are often seen as either "good" or "bad" depending on the context of their use. However, it is important to recognize that drugs are just substances, and regardless of their reputation and legal status, they affect the functioning of the brain and corresponding mood states in very similar ways. This is because psychoactive drugs either act on or resemble various neurotransmitters, which are messenger chemicals that carry messages within the brain and from the brain to the rest of the body. Neurotransmitters are produced by nerve cells, called neurons. Neurons produce all thoughts, sensations, and stimulations of the body, and they produce neurotransmitters as needed to carry messages across the synapse, which is a tiny gap separating neurons. At the end of each neuron are receptors, which neurotransmitters may fit in or "bind to" like a key fits into a lock, allowing the "message" to jump from neuron to neuron (Gahlinger, 2001).

Commonly known neurotransmitters include serotonin, dopamine, and adrenaline, and as Gahlinger (2001) notes, "psychoactive drugs either act on or resemble certain neurotransmitters" (p. 138), and the effects of a drug often depend on which neurotransmitters it resembles and how close the resemblance is. Drugs such as the amphetamines mimic adrenaline (also called epinephrine) and, as a consequence, the amphetamines produce feelings and physiological responses similar to those of adrenaline, namely those associated with the "fight or flight" response: accelerated heart rate, increased respiration, and increased attention and alertness. Some psychoactive drugs do not resemble neurotransmitters closely enough to bind to the associated receptors but prevent the reuptake or reabsorption of natural neurotransmitters, causing the neurotransmitters to linger in the synapse longer than they normally would and produce a more intense effect. For example, cocaine prevents the natural reuptake of adrenaline, norepinephrine, dopamine, and serotonin from the synapse, generating the effects associated with the drug (Gahlinger, 2001).

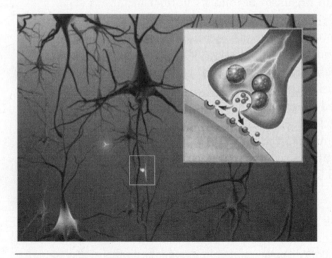

Neurotransmitters travelling across a synapse.

Because of their psychoactive effects, all drugs have the potential to cause harm in society, as drug users may harm people, either intentionally or accidentally, while under the influence. Some have referred to this as a drug's "behavioral toxicity" (Ray & Ksir, 2004). Although this is difficult to assess (is it the drug or the person using the drug that creates the problem?) and varies with the potency and amount of the drug that is taken, we discuss the subjective mental effects of various drugs and consider their potential behavioral toxicity.

Aside from their subjective psychoactive effects, drugs are also assessed in terms of the physical and psychological risks they pose to users. The risks presented by various drugs are commonly assessed in terms of their toxicity, or ability to generate negative health consequences in users, and their potential to result in dependency (often used interchangeably with *addiction*). Toxicity can be both acute and chronic. Acute toxicity refers to problems that come on immediately or very quickly, as in the case of a drug overdose, while chronic toxicity refers to effects that result from long-term exposure to the drug, such as emphysema associated with smoking or cirrhosis caused by alcohol consumption (Ray & Ksir, 2004).

Although issues of acute toxicity are often provided as justification for policies against certain illegal drugs, it is important to recognize that many legal drugs have among the highest levels of acute toxicity. For example, prescription opiate-based painkillers have fatal overdose rates that far exceed those of illicit drugs (see Table 3.1). Drug overdose deaths generally now rival deaths from motor vehicle crashes as the leading causes of accidental death in the United States (36,450 to 39,973 in 2008, respectively), and partially due to their widespread use, prescription drugs are responsible for the majority of drug overdose deaths. For example, in 2008, 20,044 of the 36,450, or 55%, of fatal drug overdoses were the result of prescription drugs (CDC, 2011b).

Table 3.1 Drug Overdose Death Rates per 100,000 People by Selected Characteristics—National Vital Statistics System, United States, 2008

Characteristic	All drugs[†]	Prescription drugs[§]	Opioid pain relievers[¶]	Illicit drugs[**]
			Age-adjusted rate[*]	
Overall	11.9	6.5	4.8	2.8
Sex				
Men	14.8	7.7	5.9	4.3
Women	9.0	5.3	3.7	1.4
Race/Ethnicity				
White	13.2	7.4	5.6	2.8
Hispanic[††]	6.1	3.0	2.1	2.5
Non-Hispanic	14.7	8.4	6.3	2.9
Black	8.3	3.0	1.9	4.0
Asian/Native Hawaiian or Pacific Islander	1.8	1.0	0.5	0.6
American Indian/ Alaska Native	13.0	8.4	6.2	2.7
Age group (yrs)				
0–14	0.2	0.2	0.1	—[§§]
15–24	8.2	4.5	3.7	2.2
25–34	16.5	8.8	7.1	4.4
35–44	20.9	11.0	8.3	5.3
45–54	25.3	13.8	10.4	6.0
55–64	13.0	7.3	5.0	2.5
≥65	4.1	3.0	1.0	0.3
Intent				
Unintentional	9.2	4.8	3.9	2.6
Undetermined	1.1	0.6	0.5	0.2
Suicide	1.6	1.1	0.5	0.1

SOURCE: CDC, 2011b.

* Rate per 100,000 population age-adjusted to tghe 2000 U.S. standard population using the vintage 2008 population. Because deaths might involve both prescription and illicit drugs, some deaths are included in both categories.
† Deaths with underlying causes of unintentional drug poisoning (X40–44), suicide drug poisoning (X60–64), homicide drug poisoning (X85), or drug poisoning of undetermined intent (Y10–Y14), as coded in the *international Classification of Diseases, 10th Revision.*
§ Drug overdose deaths, as defined, that have prescription drugs (T36–T39), T40.2–T40.4, T41–T43.5, and T43.7–T50.8) as contribution causes.
¶ Drug overdose deaths, as defined, that had other opioids (T40.2), methadone (T40.3), and other synthetic narcotics (T40.4) as contributing causes.
** Drug overdose deaths, as defined, that have heroin (T40.1), cocaine (T40.5), hallucinogens (T40.7–T40.9), or stimulants (T43.6) as contributing causes.
†† Non-White Hispanics are included in the other racial groups.
§§ Rate is not presented when the estimate is unstable because the number of deaths is less than 20.

Despite the attention paid to acute toxicity, it is a drug's chronic toxicity that is, by far, most harmful in terms of illness and loss of life. For example, tobacco is estimated to be involved in the deaths of more than 530,000 Americans every year, almost entirely as a result of the chronic toxicity of the drug (CDC, 2008, 2010). Although the measurement of alcohol and tobacco mortality figures is confounded by other factors, estimates indicate that tobacco and alcohol kill between 50 and 100 times the number of people annually as all illegal drugs combined (Gahlinger, 2001). Figure 3.1 summarizes data on the relative mortality figures in the United Kingdom, associated with the use of tobacco, alcohol, and an assortment of illegal, prescription, and over-the-counter drugs. These mortality data include deaths not directly attributed to the acute or chronic toxicity of the drug (e.g., a car crash while under the influence).

Figure 3.1   Drug-Related Mortality in England, 2010

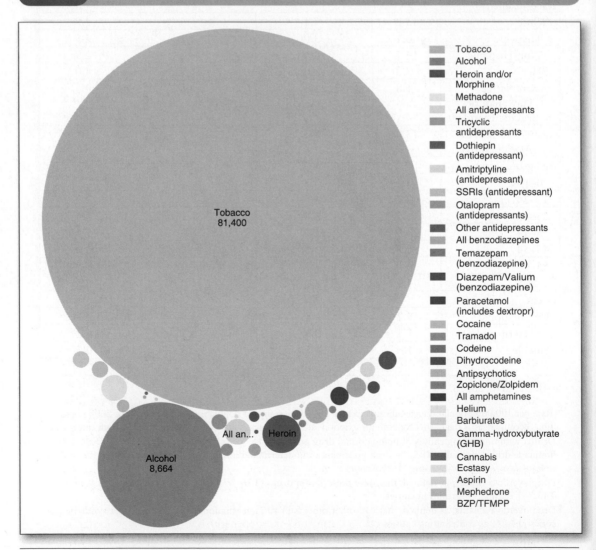

SOURCE: Neurobonkers (2012), http://neurobonkers.com/2011/12/22/the-year-in-drug-deaths-and-data-fraud/.

Drugs can also be evaluated in terms of their ability to generate dependence, sometimes called addiction. In layman's terms, these conditions collectively refer to people's inability to stop using a drug when its use is causing them problems (Weil & Rosen, 1998). The terms *dependence* and *addiction* are very loosely used in society, and many health professionals now avoid using the term *addiction*. In part, this is because *addiction* is commonly used to refer to many behaviors that have nothing to do with drugs or anything able to generate physical dependence (e.g., sex, gambling, exercise, TV, shopping), suggesting that addiction or dependence "has more to do with human beings than with drugs" (Weil & Rosen, 1998, p. 171).

Referring to substance use, there are two distinct forms of dependence. The first is physical (or physiological) dependence, which refers to the potential of a drug to generate a withdrawal syndrome, or a predictable set of symptoms that affect the user when the use of a drug is discontinued after some period of use. Thus, drugs that are not accompanied by a withdrawal syndrome when long-term or heavy use is stopped are not regarded as physically addicting. Physical dependence arises in part because users develop **tolerance** to some forms of drugs, meaning that the body adapts to repeated drug use so that the same dose of a drug produces less of the desired effect. In order to overcome increased tolerance, users often increase their dose of the drug to the point that they may be taking an amount that would kill a novice user (Ray & Ksir, 2004). For some drugs, such as alcohol and heroin, the body comes to depend on the presence of some amount of the drug in the system, and when drug use is rapidly discontinued, users experience physical withdrawal.

In addition to physical dependence, drugs may also result in psychological (or behavioral) dependence. Behavioral psychologists have pointed out that repetitive and positively reinforced behaviors such as drug use are often accompanied by a desire (i.e., "craving") and tendency to be repeated (Hart & Ksir, 2013).

Accordingly, a drug that cannot cause a user to become physically dependent may still be able to produce psychological dependence. Although this is more difficult to assess, psychological dependence is typically determined according to the criteria set forth in the *Diagnostic and Statistical Manual of Mental Disorders (DSM-IV-TR)* produced by the American Psychiatric Association (2000; see box). The *DSM*, which is the primary arbiter of mental illness classifications, is currently being revised, and the pending changes to the diagnostic criteria for addiction are expected to substantially increase the number of people who would be diagnosed as addicts. Under the change, there would be one classification for addiction, but it would vary in severity from mild to moderate to severe. As many as 20 million additional people will be classified as addicts under the revised standard for addiction (Urbina, 2012). The new criteria would classify people who "crave alcohol" or "who drink more than intended" as mild alcohol addicts, a standard that would apply to roughly 40% of American college students (Szalavitz, 2012). The expected changes have been heavily criticized as "medicalizing" everyday behavior and broadening clinical criteria to the point they become meaningless (Urbina, 2012).

Routes of administration, meaning the ways in which a drug is taken into the body, also substantially affect the experience of taking a drug and, potentially, the reward and likelihood of repetitive dosing. There are five primary routes of administration, discussed below in the order in which the drug affects the brain and exerts its psychoactive effect. Smoking is the most time-efficient route of administration in terms of generating a psychoactive effect. Smoke results when a material is vaporized under heat, generating a gas. When the gas is inhaled, the effect quickly (within 7 to 10 seconds) reaches the brain due to the high density of blood vessels in the lungs (Gahlinger, 2001). Not all drugs can be smoked, as the combustion involved may destroy the psychoactive properties of the drug (e.g., powder cocaine). Intravenous (IV) injection is the most direct method of taking a drug, as it puts the substance directly into the bloodstream, but the effect is not as fast because the blood containing the drug is diluted once it enters the heart with blood that does not contain the drug. Drugs can also be injected under the skin (subcutaneous injection) or into a muscle (intramuscular injection), but neither method approximates the efficiency of intravenous injection, which affects the brain in 15 to 30 seconds (Gahlinger, 2001). A drug must be water soluble to allow it to be injected and many are not (e.g., marijuana). Snorting or intranasal administration causes the drug to be absorbed by the mucous membranes in the nasal passages and then carried to the heart and then the brain. Effects are felt in 3 to 5 minutes. Contact involves the administration of a drug through the skin or mucous membranes in the eyes, mouth, vagina, or anus (via suppositories). Nicotine replacement therapy ("the patch") is often taken this way, and LSD is also commonly absorbed through the eye or skin. Depending on the area of the body the drug makes contact with, effects will be felt in 3 to 30 minutes (Gahlinger, 2001). Finally, drugs may be administered via **ingestion,** whether eaten, drunk, or consumed in pill form. The drug moves to the stomach, where it is combined with gastric juices. Drugs are then typically taken into the bloodstream through the stomach wall or via the small intestine, with the timing and potency of the effect being affected by any food, drink, or other drugs present. When psychoactive drugs are ingested, the effects typically are felt within 20 to 30 minutes. Not all psychoactive drugs can be administered via ingestion, as the psychoactive effect is "deactivated" via the digestive process before it can be absorbed from the digestive tract (e.g., DMT).

Previously, we have discussed several different forms of risks that drugs pose. Specifically, we discussed the potential behavioral toxicity of drugs due to their psychoactive effects; we addressed the potential for a drug to generate physical and psychological dependence; and we have noted that the use of *all* drugs, both legal and illegal, poses some level of physical and/or psychological risk that can be both acute and chronic. Thus, it is essential to keep in mind that the risks legal and illegal drugs pose are multifaceted, and all these risks must be considered in order to accurately interpret how harmful or beneficial a particular drug is.

The *DSM-IV-TR* distinguishes between substance abuse and substance dependence. According to these criteria, an individual is an *abuser* of a substance if he or she meets one of the four following criteria:

1. Recurrent use of the substance resulting in a failure to fulfill major role obligations

2. Recurrent use of the substance in physically hazardous situations

3. Recurring drug use related legal problems

4. Continued use of the substance despite having persistent or recurrent problems caused by or exacerbated by use of the substance

Also under the *DSM-IV-TR*, an individual is *dependent* on a substance if he or she meets at least three criteria from the following list:

1. Tolerance, as defined by a need for increased amounts of the drug to achieve the desired effect or a markedly diminished effect with continued use of the same amount of the substance

2. Withdrawal, as manifested by the characteristic withdrawal syndrome for the substance or that the same substance is taken to relieve or avoid withdrawal symptoms

3. Using the substance in larger amounts over a longer period of time than intended

4. A persistent desire or unsuccessful efforts to cut down or reduce use of the drug

5. A considerable amount of time spent obtaining, using, or recovering from the effects of the drug

6. Giving up or reducing important social, occupational, or recreational activities in favor of consuming the substance

7. Continued use of the drug despite persistent or recurrent physical or psychological problems caused or exacerbated by use of the drug

Reprinted with permission from the *Diagnostic and Statistical Manual of Mental Disorders*, Copyright © 2000 American Psychiatric Association.

In the following two chapters, we discuss several categories of substances based on their primary effects on the mind and the body, considering their legal classification and the indicators of harm discussed above. The most significant piece of legislation regarding the legal status of psychoactive drugs in the United States is the Comprehensive Drug Abuse Prevention and Control Act, passed in 1970. Title II of this act is known as the Controlled Substances Act, which classifies drugs into five

Figure 3.2   Do Our Drug Laws Focus on the Truly Dangerous Drugs?

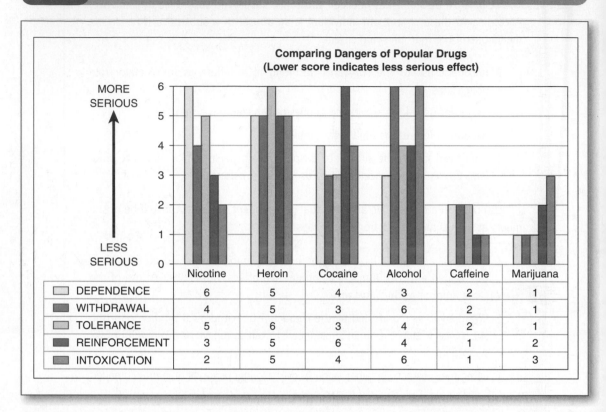

Comparing Dangers of Popular Drugs
(Lower score indicates less serious effect)

	Nicotine	Heroin	Cocaine	Alcohol	Caffeine	Marijuana
DEPENDENCE	6	5	4	3	2	1
WITHDRAWAL	4	5	3	6	2	1
TOLERANCE	5	6	3	4	2	1
REINFORCEMENT	3	5	6	4	1	2
INTOXICATION	2	5	4	6	1	3

Dependence: How difficult it is for the user to quit, the relapse rate, the percentage of people who eventually become dependent, the rating users give their own need for the substance, and the degree to which the substance will be used in the face of evidence that it causes harm. **Withdrawal:** Presence and severity of characteristic withdrawal symptoms. **Tolerance:** How much of the substance is needed to satisfy increasing cravings for it and the level of stable need that is eventually reached. **Reinforcement:** A measure of the substance's ability, in human and animal tests, to get users to take it again and again and in preference to other substances. **Intoxication:** Though not usually counted as a measure of addiction in itself, the level of intoxication is associated with addiction and increases the personal and social damage a substance may do.

NOTE: This advertisement appeared in *New Republic*, the *National Review*, *NewsMax*, the *American Prospect*, *Reason*, the *Progressive*, and *The Nation* in winter 2005.

SOURCE: Dr. Jack E. Henningfield, Ph.D., for NIDA, Reported by: Philip J. Hilts, *New York Times*, Aug. 2, 1994, "Is Nicotine Addictive? It Depends on Whose Criteria You Use."

legal "schedules." The legal classification of a drug is allegedly based on (1) the potential for abuse of the drug; (2) whether the drug has medical applications; and (3) the potential of the drug to generate psychological and physical dependence (see box below). As will be demonstrated, when substances are compared in terms of their psychoactive effects and potential to generate harm, distinctions between legal and illegal drugs are very difficult to make.

U.S. LEGAL DRUG SCHEDULES

The Controlled Substances Act, passed as part of the Comprehensive Drug Abuse Prevention and Control Act of 1970, places all regulated psychoactive drugs into one of five schedules. Below are the schedules and well-known drugs included in each schedule.

Schedule I: Substance has a high potential for abuse, has no medical use in the United States, and has a lack of accepted safety for use under medical supervision.

Heroin	Psilocybin	PCP
LSD	Peyote	MDMA (ecstasy)
Marijuana	Rohypnol	Methadone
Methaqualone	Bufotenine	Gamma Hydroxybutyrate
Mescaline	Hashish and oil	(GHB)

Schedule II: Substance has a high potential for abuse, has a currently accepted medical use in the United States with severe restrictions, and abuse may lead to severe psychological or physical dependence.

Cocaine	Phencyclidine (PCP)	Ritalin	Oxycodone
Codeine	Amobarbital	Percodan	THC
Hydrocodone	Secobarbital	Demerol	Dexedrine
Morphine	Pentobarbital	Opium	
Methamphetamine	Percocet		

Schedule III: Substance has a potential for abuse (less than Schedule I or II), has currently accepted medical use in the United States, and may lead to moderate or low physical dependence or high psychological dependence.

Codeine with aspirin	Vicodin	Nandrolone
Hydrocodone with aspirin	Anabolic steroids	Testosterone
		Marinol

Schedule IV: Substance has a low potential for abuse as compared to Schedule III, has currently accepted medical use in the United States, and abuse may lead to limited physical and psychological dependence.

Valium/Diazepam	Darvon/Propoxyphene	Chloral Hydrate
Phenobarbital	Triazolam/Halcion	Restoril/Temazepam
Diazepam	Fenfluramine	Chlordiazepoxide/Librium
Xanax/Alprazolam	Phentermine	

Schedule V: Substance has a low potential for abuse as compared to Schedule IV, has currently accepted medical use in the United States, and abuse has a narrow scope for physical and psychological dependence.

Cough medicines with codeine

SOURCE: Drug Enforcement Agency. (2005). *Drugs of Abuse*. Washington, DC: U.S. Department of Justice.

STIMULANTS

Stimulants are drugs that often make users feel more alert and energetic. They exert these effects by causing nerve fibers in the brain to release adrenaline and other neurotransmitters (Weil & Rosen, 1998). Like many types of drugs, some stimulants are found in nature, present in various plant species, while others are chemicals made in laboratories (because it is often cheaper and easier to make drugs synthetically than to harvest them from plants). Although stimulants can make users feel more alert and energetic for a time, as is true with most things, you don't get "something for nothing" (Weil & Rosen, 1998). That is, stimulants don't "create" energy out of nothing; they simply force the body to use up some of its reserves of chemical energy, energy that must be replenished later (Weil & Rosen, 1998). Because of this, stimulants can be useful when energy or alertness is needed to complete an important task or obligation, and such use is apt to have few consequences provided the body is given time to recharge itself. As noted by Weil and Rosen (1998), problems arising from the use of stimulants generally occur because users don't want to allow for this "down time," they want to feel good again right away, and they keep taking stimulants in order to obtain this effect.

Caffeine

Caffeine occurs naturally in plants used to produce coffee, tea, and chocolate and has long been the most widely used drug in the world. In the United States, 90% of the population reports annual use (Frary, Johnson, & Wang, 2005). Coffee beans have been chewed for their stimulating effects at least as far back as 600 AD, and grinding the beans to make a hot-water drink then known as "the wine of Islam" (Gahlinger, 2001) dates back more than 1,000 years, when groups of Muslims would meet once a week to have all-night prayer and chanting sessions with the help of large amounts of coffee (Weil & Rosen, 1998). By 1674, coffee was being widely used in Europe, and an English women's group protested the use of coffee in its pamphlet "The Women's Petition Against Coffee," which noted the

> grand inconveniences accruing to their sex from the excessive use of the drying and enfeebling liquor . . . Our countrymens pallates are becoming as Fanatical as their brain . . . to run a Whoreing after such variety of destructive Foreign Liquors, to trifle away their time, scald their Chops, and spend their Money, all for a little base, black, thick nasty bitter stinking, nauseous Puddle water . . . (as cited in Ray & Ksir, 2004, p. 330, as original)

Charles II of England briefly outlawed coffeehouses at the end of the 17th century, and in the 18th century, coffeehouses became "penny universities," when for a penny a cup, patrons could sit and listen to literary, political, and scholarly figures (Ray & Ksir, 2004). Until the end of the 18th century, users bought the green coffee beans and then roasted them just before use, but in 1790, commercial roasting began in New York City, and by 1900, vacuum-packed ground coffee was being marketed (Ray & Ksir, 2004). In 1902, Crothers claimed that coffee drinkers often became less satisfied with the psychoactive effects of coffee and moved to the consumption of other drugs, making coffee one of the first substances purported to be a gateway drug (as cited in Brecher, 1972; Faupel, Horowitz, & Weaver, 2004).

The other main source of caffeine, tea, was first reported being used medically in China around 350 AD, and reports dating to 780 AD suggest that tea was being widely cultivated and used nonmedically by this time (Ray & Ksir, 2004). By the early 17th century, tea had made its way to Europe, being imported by the East India Company along with spices and other riches from Asia and Africa. Being partial to the substance and loyal to the crown, early American colonists bought large amounts of tea from England, but heavy taxes on tea led to the Boston Tea Party in 1773, speeding the outbreak of the American Revolutionary War. Despite its wide use in these years, tea came to be condemned by many, with one critic claiming in the early 20th century that tea produced "a strange and extreme degree of physical depression . . . a grievous shrinking may seize upon a sufferer . . . the speech may become vague and weak" and that "By miseries such as these, the best years of life may be spoilt" (Crothers, 1902, as cited in Brecher, 1972, p. 198).

> Howard Schultz, the inventor of Starbucks, deemphasizes the importance of caffeine to his company's success, commenting, "I don't think it is the caffeine. I think the ritual, the romance of the thing, is really more important." (as quoted in Reid, 2005, p. 31)

While caffeine is a very safe drug compared to other stimulants when consumed "normally," like many drugs, the excessive use of caffeine is associated with a number of negative side effects. The drug is irritating to the stomach, and caffeine can produce physical dependence, sometimes from consumption levels as low as 100 milligrams a day (1–2 cups of coffee; Weil & Rosen, 1998). Withdrawal symptoms are likely to occur if regular users suddenly stop consuming caffeinated coffee, and these symptoms include lethargy, irritability, a severe headache, and potentially nausea and vomiting for 36 to 72 hours (Sigmon et al., 2009; Weil & Rosen, 1998). Heavy caffeine use will produce restlessness, insomnia, rapid heartbeat, and muscle twitching, and although it is not widely known, caffeine can be a potent poison if taken in large enough doses. Like many drugs, caffeine can cause death by overdose. Ten grams of caffeine (roughly 100 cups of coffee) is sufficient to cause convulsions, respiratory failure, and death (Gahlinger, 2001), and in 2002, a university student in Wales committed suicide by purposely ingesting caffeine pills equivalent to 100 cups of coffee (Reid, 2005, pp. 24–25). It is also believed that health problems can occur in individuals who consume more than 300 milligrams of caffeine per day, including an increased risk of heart disease and an increased risk of stillbirth among pregnant women (Ray & Ksir, 2004; Wisborg, Hedegaard, & Henriksen, 2003).

As noted by Charles Czeisler, a neuroscientist and sleep expert at Harvard Medical School, "The principal reason that caffeine is used around the world is to promote wakefulness. But the principal reason that people need that crutch is inadequate sleep. Think about that: We use caffeine to make up for a sleep deficit that is largely the result of using caffeine." (as quoted in Reid, 2005, p. 36)

Caffeine has many positive uses as well. In addition to its well-known and valued stimulating effects, caffeine is a vasoconstrictor (i.e., it constricts blood vessels), making it useful for treating headaches, particularly migraines (e.g., caffeine is a key ingredient in Excedrin, which markets itself as "the headache medicine"). Coffee use may also lower the risk of diabetes. For example, a longitudinal study published in the *Annals of Internal Medicine* of more than 120,000 healthy men and women found that, as compared to those who did not drink coffee, men who drank more than six cups of caffeinated coffee per day reduced their risk of diabetes by more than 50%, while women's risk of diabetes declined by 30% (Salazar-Martinez et al., 2004).

As compared to coffee, tea (especially green tea) contains less caffeine. As a consequence, tea drinkers are less likely than coffee drinkers to develop a dependence on the substance (Weil & Rosen, 1998). Tea (again, particularly green tea) is also thought to have a number of health benefits. The positive health benefits of green tea are associated with the polyphenols it contains. Polyphenols are powerful antioxidants that can eliminate cell-damaging free radicals and reduce abnormal cell growth and inflammation and are related to what makes eating certain fruits and vegetables so good for the body (Roan, 2003). Recent studies have found that the use of green tea is associated with a reduced risk for conditions such as cancer—including stomach, colon, lung, pancreas, breast, and skin cancer—as well as a reduced risk for heart disease and high cholesterol (Briffa, 2004). For example, in one study, it was found that women drinking approximately half a cup of green tea per day had a 47% reduced risk of breast cancer, and research has also found that men consuming three cups of green tea per day had approximately one-quarter the risk of contracting prostrate cancer (Briffa, 2004).

"Energy" Drinks

A more recent development with respect to substances containing caffeine is the boom in the marketing and sales of high-caffeine "energy drinks." Although Red Bull is the best known of these products, countless copycat products such as Monster, RockStar, Full Throttle, V, SoBE Adrenaline Rush, No Fear, Amp, and Nos are now widely sold. The target audience for these products is largely adolescents and young adults looking for a boost (Reid, 2005).

Although these products are marketed partly on the basis of the supplements they contain (e.g., taurine, ginseng, guarana, yerba mate), the stimulating effects of energy drinks result primarily from their high caffeine content (e.g., 80 mg in a 8.3-ounce can of Red Bull, roughly equivalent to 2½ cans of Coke or two one-ounce shots of espresso; Reid, 2005; Rowley, 2001).

> The prevalence of caffeine use in the form of energy drinks is particularly high among adolescents and young adults. For example, the manager of the London dance club Egg comments, "actually, we see a revival at about half four or so in the morning. That's when we get the real rush at the bar for Red Bull. And the kids say 'I've had eight Red Bulls—I'm flying!'" Says nurse and club-goer Lee Murphy, "By four or five in the morning you're totally blotto. That's when the Red Bull comes in. I drink these two tins, it's like drinking a pint of speed." (as quoted in Reid, 2005, pp. 5–6)

Teens and young adults are the primary consumers of energy drinks. Prevalence studies have found roughly a third of all teenagers and young adults (Simon & Mosher, 2007) and more than half of college students (Malinauskas et al., 2007) to report regular use of energy drinks, with the latter group regularly consuming three or more at a time when studying or partying. Because of their heavy use among the "party crowd," Red Bull and similar beverages are sometimes labeled as "clubbers' drinks" or "party drinks" (see box).

As well as being consumed on their own, energy drinks are frequently combined with alcohol. A recent study of university students found 76% of energy drink consumers reported having mixed alcohol and energy drinks, with 19% reporting this behavior in the past week (Price et al., 2010). Common "energy cocktail" concoctions involving Red Bull include the Vodka Bull (Red Bull and vodka), Chambull (Red Bull and champagne), Bullgarita (Red Bull and tequila), and Bull Meister (Red Bull and Jagermeister; Reid, 2005). With respect to this practice, Red Bull has provided party-goers with the assurance that "adding alcohol does not change Red Bull's properties" (as quoted in Reid, 2005, pp. 20–21).

Like caffeine in other forms, consumption of energy drinks is associated with a number of positive and negative effects. Energy drinks have been found to increase motivation and performance in athletes (Duncan et al., 2011; Ivy et al., 2009), but evidence of cognitive benefits remains lacking, notable given that these products are commonly used while studying. Negative physical symptoms reported by energy drink users are similar to those reported due to caffeine use generally and include extreme "caffeine crashes," headaches, and heart palpitations (Malinauskas et al., 2007). Given the heavy marketing of energy products to adolescents and children and the high use patterns by youth, it is important to note that caffeine use has been found to be linked to increased depressive symptoms among children and adolescents (Luebbe & Bell, 2009), though whether the association is causal remains debated.

In 2012, the FDA opened an investigation into the potential link between Monster energy drink and six heart attacks, five of them fatal. The investigation commenced following a wrongful death suit filed by the parents of a 14-year-old Maryland girl who died after drinking two 24-ounce Monster energy drinks in 24 hours. The autopsy concluded the girl died of cardiac arrhythmia due to caffeine toxicity, though the girl had an inherited disorder that can weaken blood vessels. (Disheau & Perrone, 2012)

Combining alcohol and energy drinks has been found to result in a higher incidence of risky behavior, problematic drinking, and alcohol-related problems. For example, Thombs and colleagues (2009) found that bar patrons who drank energy drinks were three times as likely to leave legally intoxicated and four times as likely to intend to drive. Additional research indicates that those who combine alcohol and energy drinks have increased desire for alcohol consumption (Marczinski et al., 2011) and are more likely to underestimate their intoxication level (Ferreira et al., 2006). Research has also found alcohol consumers who mixed energy drinks with alcohol to report much higher levels of heavy drinking and drunkenness as well as increased rates of sexual victimization, physical injuries, and risky behavior (O'Brien et al., 2008). In response to these substantially increased risks associated with combining caffeine/energy drinks and alcohol, the FDA announced that caffeine is an unsafe food additive to alcoholic beverages on November 17, 2010, issuing warning letters to four manufacturers of high-alcohol malt beverages that unless they changed their recipes, they would be guilty of illegal marketing (Arria & O'Brien, 2011). However, the warning was limited to the companies making Four Loko, Joose, Core Spike, and El Jefe, products more commonly associated with low-income, minority consumers. Four Loko was subsequently banned by many states and at the federal level, behind a push by Senator Chuck Schumer (D/NY) that "we must protect our children from the severe and deadly consequences of drinks like Four Loko" (Detrick, 2012).

Tobacco

Tobacco, or *Nicotiana tabacum*, has been cultivated in South America since the early Neolithic period, up to 8,000 years ago (Meyer, 2003). Christopher Columbus reported in his journals that the native inhabitants of San Salvador presented him with a gift of tobacco leaves on his birthday in 1492, and a member of Columbus' party, Rodrigo de Jerez, was possibly the first European to smoke tobacco (Ray & Ksir, 2004). de Jerez was introduced to smoking by the aboriginal Americans, and when he continued the practice upon his return to Portugal, his friends were "convinced the Devil had possessed him as they saw the smoke coming out of his mouth and nose" (Ray & Ksir, 1993, p. 231). Holy inquisitors agreed with this assessment, and de Jerez was jailed for 7 years, only to discover upon his release that people everywhere were now smoking tobacco!

Despite claims that tobacco was useful as a medicine, some early commentaries on the substance were quite negative. For example, in 1604, King James I of England produced a pamphlet titled "A Counterblast to Tobacco" in which he wrote, "[tobacco use] a custome (custom) lathsome (loathsome) to the eye, hateful to the nose, harmeful (harmful) to the brain, dangerous to the lungs, and the blacke (black) stinking fume thereof, resembling the horrible stigian some of the pit that is bottomless" (as cited in Walton, 2002, p. 133). In 1617, Dr. William Vaugh claimed tobacco would, among other things, make women barren, writing, "Tobacco that outlandish weede, It spends the braine and spoiles the seede, It dulls the spirite, it dims the site, It robs a woman of her right" (as quoted in Ray & Ksir, 2004, p. 302, as original). Similarly, in 1650, Johann Michael Moscherosch wrote of tobacco

> They who smoke can be compared only to men possessed, who are in need of exorcising. While their throats belch forth with the stinking, poisonous fumes, they remain nonetheless thralls to the tobacco fiend to whom they cling with an idolatrous devotion, exalting him as their God above all others, and striving to entice all they meet to imitate their folly. (as cited in Sullum, 1998, p. 15)

In the late 1800s and early 1900s, tobacco became increasingly seen as potentially harmful rather than medically useful. Though still commonly recommended for the treatment of bronchitis and asthma, the excessive use of tobacco was said to cause sterility and birth defects and to lead to insanity (Troyer & Markle, 1983). The famous inventor Thomas Edison even claimed that tobacco had "a violent action on the nerve centers, producing degeneration of the cells of the brain, which is . . . permanent and uncontrollable" (as quoted in Shenk, 2003).

Although Edison may have exaggerated the damage of tobacco on the brain, tobacco smoke does contain about 4,000 distinct chemicals, 400 of which are toxic and 43 that are known carcinogens (Gahlinger, 2001). Modern commercially marketed cigarettes have about 700 *additional* ingredients, including 13 that are considered too toxic to be allowed in food and 5 that are classified as "hazardous," such as Freon, ethyl 2-furoate, ammonia, and various pesticides (Gahlinger, 2001). In raw plant form, tobacco is one of the most powerful stimulants known, and its primary active ingredient, nicotine, is one of the most toxic of all known drugs (Weil & Rosen, 1998). Although most of the nicotine in tobacco is destroyed when it is burnt, an average cigar, if soaked in water and consumed, contains a sufficient amount of nicotine to kill several people (Weil & Rosen, 1998), and a small child who eats a cigarette is in serious danger (Goldberg, 2003).

Nicotine was isolated from tobacco in 1828 and comprises about 5% of raw tobacco by weight. Because nicotine is so toxic, the body rapidly develops tolerance to it to protect itself. Tolerance to nicotine may develop in a matter of hours, as compared to days or weeks for heroin and months for alcohol (Weil & Rosen, 1998). Ironically, because of this rapid tolerance, it is only the occasional users who experience a high from nicotine, with most addicted smokers feeling no alteration of consciousness at all when they ingest the drug (Weil & Rosen, 1998).

Nicotine exerts its effects on the body by mimicking the neurotransmitter acetylcholine, a chemical that, among other things, assists the brain in communicating with the muscles and in processing information (Goldberg, 2003). Although the primary effects of nicotine are stimulatory, including increasing the heart rate and blood pressure, it is important to note that nicotine first stimulates and then depresses the nervous system (Schilit & Lisansky-Gomberg, 1991) so it can also act as tranquilizer (Brecher, 1972).

Tobacco can be consumed in a variety of forms, and in addition to cigarettes, cigars, pipe tobacco, snuff, and "chew," several other variations exist. Globally, tobacco consumption has steadily increased, but roughly 80% of the world's approximately 1 billion smokers now live in poor or middle-income countries (World Health Organization, 2012). In the United States, tobacco consumption via smoking has decreased significantly over the last few decades (see Figure 3.3). Since 2000, per-capita consumption of cigarettes is down by more than a third, but a portion of this drop is attributed to smokers switching from cigarettes to pipes/cigars as a result of the 2009 federal tobacco excise tax, which resulted in tax disparities between tobacco products (CDC, 2012a).

| Figure 3.3 | Estimated Percentage of Adults Who Were Current Smokers by Year and Sex, U.S., 1965–2006* |

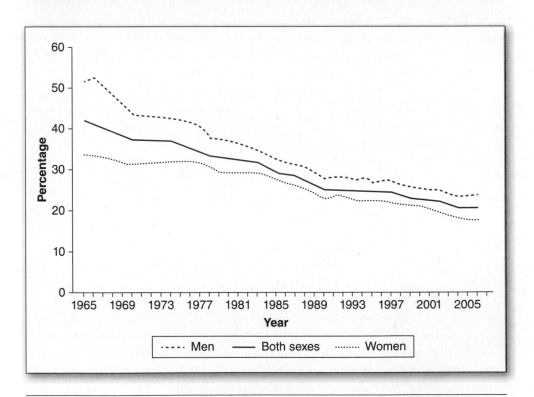

SOURCE: Centers for Disease Control and Prevention. Cigarette Smoking Among Adults—United States, 2006. *Morbidity and Mortality Weekly Report.* November 9, 2007: 56(44):1 157–61.

NOTE: *Due to the redesign of the NHIS survey in 1997, comparisons with data from prior years must be conducted with caution.

In 1798, Dr. Benjamin Rush wrote an essay in which he purported that tobacco was a gateway drug to alcohol, noting:
   One of the usual effects of smoking and chewing is thirst. This thirst cannot be allayed by water, for no sedative or even insipid liquor will be relished after the mouth and throat have been exposed to the stimulus of the smoke, or juice of tobacco. A desire of course is excited for strong drinks, and these when taken between meals soon lead to intemperance and drunkenness. One of the greatest sots I ever knew, acquired a love for ardent spirit by swallowing ends of tobacco, which he hid, to escape the detection of the use of it. (as quoted in Robert, 1949, p. 106)

In its most commonly used form of cigarettes, tobacco is one of if not the most addictive drugs known—rivaling alcohol, heroin, and cocaine (Gahlinger, 2001; Weil & Rosen, 1998). There is also no question that tobacco consumption is associated with many negative health outcomes and higher mortality rates. Globally, it is estimated that more than six million people die from smoking-related diseases annually, and the World Health Organization estimates that the number of annual tobacco-related deaths will reach eight million by the year 2030 (World Health Organization, 2012). Although there is no question that smoking poses a substantial health risk, as Sullum (1998) notes, smoking mortality rates should be examined critically. These rates are based on epidemiological research using samples that are typically not representative of the general population, and they often do not take into account other variables that may be related to the high mortality rates of smokers. For example, smokers tend to have higher levels of alcohol consumption, have poorer diets, be less likely to engage in physical exercise, have lower incomes, and be employed in more hazardous occupations than nonsmokers (Sullum, 1998). Accordingly, a 1992 British study concluded that between 10 and 20% of the deaths attributed to smoking were in fact due to confounding variables such as those listed above (as cited in Sullum, 1998).

While the effects of tobacco are mostly negative and it has become a pariah substance in the United States (and several other, primarily Western countries), like any other drug, it has its benefits. For example, it has been demonstrated that tobacco smoking actually has a facilitating effect on learning and memory in animals and humans (Schilit & Lisansky-Gomberg, 1991; Sullum, 1998), and studies suggest that it may help people with brain disorders such as Alzheimer's disease and schizophrenia (Goldberg, 2003). Research also suggests that current smokers have a 60% reduction in the risk of contracting Parkinson's disease compared to those who have never smoked (Martin & Gale, 2003). Similarly, in a study conducted on teenagers diagnosed with attention deficit disorder, it was found that nicotine (administered through a skin patch) was effective in helping them with some mental functions (Goldberg, 2003).

Cocaine

Coca is a shrub native to the Andes Mountains in South America that has been cultivated by native peoples in that region for thousands of years. Archaeological evidence from Ecuador and Chile indicates that the practice of chewing coca leaves for their psychoactive effects has occurred for at least 2,000 years and perhaps much longer (Davenport-Hines, 2001). Today, millions of Indians still chew coca leaves every day as a medicine and stimulant, which has an effect similar in intensity to coffee, although it soothes rather than irritates the stomach and doesn't produce the jitteriness of coffee (Weil & Rosen, 1998).

According to Incan legend, the first Incan Emperor, Manco Capac, son of the Sun God, brought coca from heaven (Gahlinger, 2001). Coca was said to be "a gift from the gods to satisfy the hungry, fortify the weary, and make the unfortunate forget their sorrows" (Bugliosi, 1991, as cited in Gahlinger, 2001, p. 38). It is easy to see why the natives viewed these leaves as a gift from God. In addition to being a stimulant, coca leaves are rich in B vitamins, stabilize body blood-sugar levels, and contain more iron and calcium than any of the food crops grown in the Andes and, as noted by Gahlinger, "it is likely that without coca the Indians would not have even been able to survive on their potato diet" (2001, p. 38). When the Spanish Conquistadors invaded the Americas in the 16th century, they initially attempted to ban coca chewing but quickly relented when they discovered that the natives could not bear the labor involved in extracting silver (to be sent to Spain) from the high-altitude mines without the use of the drug (Gahlinger, 2001).

Coca leaves were exported to Europe once their value was discovered by the Conquistadors, but Europeans remained largely uninterested in the substance until the mid-19th century because the leaves lost much of their potency on the long sea voyage (Gahlinger, 2001). The change came when French chemist Angelo Mariani developed an extract of the leaves for use in lozenges, tea, and, most popularly, wine (Ray & Ksir, 2004). Mariani wine was a Bordeaux that was combined with the coca leaf extract, and it came to be used by many, including inventor Thomas Edison, Civil War general and U.S. President Ulysses S. Grant, and Pope Leo XIII, who had a special Vatican medal issued in praise of coca wine (Gahlinger, 2001). In fact, Pope Leo carried Vin Mariani in a "personal hipflask to fortify himself in those moments when prayer was insufficient" (Vallely, 2006), and Robert Louis Stephenson wrote the book *The Strange Case of Dr. Jekyll and Mr. Hyde* during a "six day cocaine binge" (Vallely, 2006).

Although coca contains 14 different drugs, cocaine is the most important in terms of its psychoactive effects (Weil & Rosen, 1998). What is called "cocaine" is actually cocaine hydrochloride, which is roughly 90% cocaine and 10% hydrochloric acid. The exact year that cocaine was isolated from coca is debated, but this had certainly occurred by 1860. In the 1880s, physicians began experimenting with cocaine as an anesthetic, including Dr. W. S. Halstead, who later became known as "the father of modern surgery." Cocaine was found to be especially useful for eye operations, which had previously been very difficult and excruciatingly painful (cocaine is still used today in ear, eye, nose, and throat operations; Ray & Ksir, 2004; Weil & Rosen, 1998). In 1884, purified cocaine became commercially available in the United States, and in 1885, Parke-Davis marketed a coca cigarette (Gahlinger, 2001). Cocaine was used for many different recreational and medicinal purposes at this time, including as a topical ointment to numb the vagina and prevent masturbation in women (Alexander, 1990). At the end of the 19th century, pharmaceutical companies even sold "cocaine kits," which contained everything needed to take the drug including syringes (Gahlinger, 2001). In 1887, cocaine was declared the official remedy of the Hay Fever Association, with products such as Ryno's Hay Fever and Catarrh (which was 99.9% cocaine) recommended for use "whenever the nose is stuffed up, red, and sore" (Davenport-Hines, 2001).

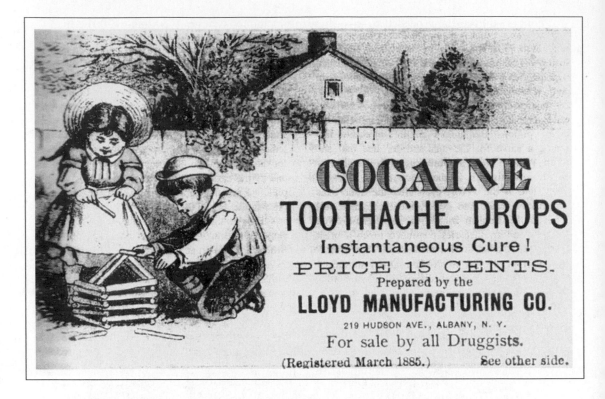

Coca-Cola was invented by a pharmacist in 1886 and contained significant amounts of cocaine until 1902. As an early ad for Coca-Cola proclaimed:

> The "INTELLECTUAL BEVERAGE" and "TEMPERANCE DRINK" contains the valuable TONIC and NERVE STIMULANT properties of the Coca plant and Cola (or Kola) nuts, and makes not only a delicious, exhilarating, refreshing and invigorating Beverage but a valuable Brain Tonic, and a cure for all nervous afflictions—SICK HEADACHE, NEURALGIA, HYSTERIA, MELANCHOLY, &c. (as cited in Ray & Ksir, 2004, p. 338, as original)

Early 20th-century legislation resulted in the Coca-Cola Company removing coca from the Coca-Cola recipe, but the soft drink still contains a decocanized extract of coca leaves.

Among the prominent early users of cocaine were Queen Victoria of England, U.S. President William McKinley, and the psychologist Sigmund Freud, who injected the drug periodically over a 3-year period in the 1880s to alleviate his depression and chronic fatigue (Brecher, 1972; Kunitz, 2001). Freud published an article titled "On Coca" in 1884, which promoted cocaine as a cure for morphine addiction and argued that while excessive consumption of the substance could lead to physical problems and "moral depravity," its benefits outweighed the risks associated with it (Walton, 2002). At least partially as a result of Freud's promotion of the substance, the Merck pharmaceutical company's production of cocaine increased from less than one kilogram in 1883 to more than 80,000 kilograms in 1885 (Davenport-Hines, 2001). Freud later retracted his statements regarding the substance's utility as a medical treatment, but he continued to use small quantities of cocaine without developing an addiction to it (Alexander, 1990).

The fact that cocaine became widely illegal in the late 19th and early 20th centuries may seem surprising given the vast number of commercial products that contained the drug (Ray & Ksir, 1993). However, the circumstances that had come to surround cocaine by the turn of the century included everything necessary to demonize the drug. As noted by Ashley (1975),

"All the elements needed to insure cocaine's outlaw status were present by the first years of the twentieth century: it had become widely used as a pleasure drug, and doctors warned of the dangers attendant on indiscriminate sale and use; it had become identified with despised or poorly regarded groups—blacks, lower-class whites, and criminals; it had not been long enough established in the culture to insure its survival; and it had not, though used by them, become identified with the elite, thus losing what little chance it had of weathering the storm of criticism." (as quoted in Ray & Ksir, 2004, p. 171)

The effects of cocaine are both euphoric and stimulating. Users typically report feelings of excitement, alertness, well-being, and increased confidence, pulse rate and blood pressure increase, appetite is suppressed, and users often experience insomnia (Gahlinger, 2001). As noted earlier in this chapter, route of drug administration can substantially affect the experience of taking a drug, and this point is particularly salient with respect to cocaine due to the variation in legal penalties in the United States for crack cocaine (which is smoked) and powder cocaine (which is snorted or injected or used to make crack). Snorted cocaine reaches the brain in 1 to 3 minutes, providing a high that lasts roughly half an hour. Conversely, the intravenous injection of cocaine produces an effect in 15 to 30 seconds, with the high peaking in 3 to 5 minutes and lasting 15 to 20 minutes. Smoking cocaine produces an effect in 10 seconds, with the high peaking in 3 to 5 minutes and lasting for approximately 15 minutes (Gahlinger, 2001). Powder cocaine cannot be smoked because the combustion destroys the drug, so in order to be smoked, cocaine hydrochloride must be modified, which was first done by making freebase cocaine and later crack cocaine. Crack is made by dissolving cocaine hydrochloride in water and adding baking soda to make a solution that is then boiled or put in a microwave and finally cooled, often in ice or a freezer. The result is a yellowish-white substance that looks like soap, and small chunks (often called "rocks") are broken off and smoked, making "cracking" sounds when burned—hence the name "crack" (Gahlinger, 2001). Regardless of the method of ingestion, the high associated with cocaine is typically followed by a "dysphoric crash—a disagreeable feeling of fatigue, depression and anxiety" (Gahlinger, 2001, p. 253), and another dose of cocaine is often taken to remedy this.

There is no evidence that the occasional use of small amounts of cocaine is a threat to the health of users (Jelsma, 2003; Ray & Ksir, 2004; Weil & Rosen, 1998). As noted by the World Health Organization's Program on Substance Abuse, "most participating countries agree that occasional cocaine use does not typically lead to severe or even minor physical or social problems" (1995; as cited in Jelsma, 2003). However, both the extended and short-term heavy use of cocaine can produce effects such as hallucinations, paranoia, repetitive behaviors, and depression after use. The drug is also among the most likely to generate psychological dependence and craving and thus repetitive use and subsequent problems. In addition, because cocaine is a vasoconstrictor, meaning it shrinks blood vessels and slows bleeding, excessive use of the substance can cause physical damage to tissues by starving them of blood (Gahlinger, 2001). For example, heavy snorting of cocaine often gives people a "cocaine nose" in which there are ulcers and perhaps a perforated septum, and those who put it inside of the penis (done in the belief that it will enhance sexual performance) may have their penis tissue damaged, possibly necessitating amputation (Gahlinger, 2001).

The use of both powder and crack cocaine will increase the heartbeat and may cause irregular heart activity, but deaths due to cocaine use alone are relatively rare (Weil & Rosen, 1998). Unfortunately, the physical dangers associated with cocaine are increased many times over when it is used in combination with alcohol. A study published in the *Journal of the American Medical Association* reported that in studies of both animals and humans, when cocaine was combined with alcohol, a new drug, cocaethylene, was produced in the body. Cocaethylene produces a different, more euphoric high than cocaine, is likely more addictive than either cocaine or alcohol, and is many times more likely to cause sudden death than is the use of cocaine alone (Randall, 1992).

One of the common problems associated with cocaine use is addiction—however, it is important to note that physical dependence, in the traditional sense, does not occur with cocaine. For example, a cocaine user who is deprived of the substance will not suffer physical withdrawal symptoms similar to those experienced by opiate or alcohol users (Schilit & Lisansky-Gomberg, 1991). The user may, however, experience a cluster of symptoms, including irritability, depression, agitation, insomnia, and fatigue, that some believe may represent mild physical withdrawal (Cami & Farre, 2003; Hart & Ksir, 2013). Several studies have also shown that individuals can maintain patterns of moderate use of cocaine for several years without becoming psychologically dependent on the substance (Sullum, 2003a). On the other hand, there is clear evidence that, like other powerful stimulants, the potential for psychological dependence on cocaine is very high if the drug is used more than occasionally (Weil & Rosen, 1998).

With the emergence of the crack "epidemic" in the United States in the mid-1980s, it was widely reported that crack cocaine was much more addictive than powder cocaine, and this served as one of the justifications for treating crack cocaine more severely than powder cocaine in drug legislation. But as Alexander (1990) and others have pointed out, there is no pharmacological difference in the addictive liability of crack and cocaine hydrochloride. The only distinction between crack and powder cocaine in terms of addiction arises due to its route of administration. Because smoking crack cocaine and injecting powder cocaine results in a more immediate high, and because the high is shorter in duration, encouraging more frequent use, both of these routes of administration may be more psychologically addicting than snorting cocaine (Gahlinger, 2001).

Crack Cocaine

Amphetamines

Very similar to cocaine are the amphetamines, a group of powerful stimulants that are synthesized from adrenaline and ephedrine (discussed below). As compared to cocaine, amphetamines are more toxic and more difficult to metabolize, and their effects last longer—but as a consequence of their longer duration of effect, users are less likely to dose repeatedly in a short period of time in order to maintain their high (as many do with cocaine; Weil & Rosen, 1998). The first amphetamine, Benzedrine (levoamphetamine), was synthesized in Germany in 1887. Other forms of amphetamines include Dexedrine (dexamphetamine), which is twice as strong as Benzedrine, and methamphetamine, developed by a Japanese chemist in 1919, which is twice as strong as Dexedrine (Davenport-Hines, 2001). The effects of the various amphetamines are very similar but may vary in intensity and duration. The variation is due to the differences in the potency of the amphetamine and also to the typical method of ingestion (i.e., oral, smoking, injecting).

Following its discovery in 1887, Benzedrine remained relatively obscure until the 1930s, when it was marketed as an over-the-counter nasal spray to treat asthma and low blood pressure. Soon after, amphetamines were used to treat narcolepsy—a condition that causes victims to suddenly fall asleep—and also a behavioral syndrome called minimal brain dysfunction (MBD), what we would now call attention deficit hyperactivity disorder (ADHD; Gahlinger, 2001).

Because the effects of amphetamines include the relief of mental fatigue, increased attention and endurance, appetite suppression, and potentially an increase in feelings of aggression, these drugs have been widely used in various war efforts (Gahlinger, 2001). During World War II, German, Japanese, and Allied troops were widely using amphetamines. American soldiers actually received amphetamines in their ration kits, and by the end of the war, the number of amphetamine tablets dispensed equated to one pill per soldier per day (Eisner, 1993; Gahlinger, 2001).

1940s Ad for Benzedrine

The use of amphetamines to treat various medical conditions soon led to the realization that they were strong appetite suppressants. Their application as a weight-control aid resulted in unprecedented levels of amphetamine use to the point that in the United States during the 1950s, 50 doses of amphetamine were produced for every American man, woman, and child, with amphetamines accounting for 20% of all written prescriptions (Gahlinger, 2001). The 1960s and 1970s saw amphetamines further marketed for dieting and for the treatment of depression, and in 1971, 12 billion amphetamine tablets were legally produced in United States (Gahlinger, 2001). Today, pharmaceutical companies continue to cater to the dieting and weight-control market, often with serious or disastrous consequences when the side effects of these substances are not clearly understood. For example, one of the most popular diet drugs ever, Fen-Phen (a combination of fenfluramine and phentermine), was used by millions of people in the 1990s. Although the drug was clearly effective at reducing weight, users typically gained the weight back very quickly once they stopped using Fen-Phen. This prompted many to use the drug long term, potentially putting them at a greater risk for heart disease. A study conducted by researchers at the Mayo Clinic found the use of Fen-Phen to increase users' risk for pulmonary hypertension and valvular heart disease (Connolly et al., 1997). Although subsequent studies debated whether Fen-Phen was medically harmful, American Home Products Corporation, the makers of Fen-Phen, later agreed to pay $3.75 billion in compensation to the thousands of people who used the diet drugs before they were removed from the market in 1997 ("Fen-Phen Maker Agrees to $3.75 Billion Settlement," 1999).

Modafinil (trade name Provigil) is also commonly used for its amphetamine-like properties. As with certain amphetamines, modafinil is intended for the treatment of narcolepsy, but numerous reports indicate that it is primarily being used to abstain from sleep. For example, an article in the *New York Times* titled "Wakefulness Finds a Powerful Ally" claimed that modafinil "has quietly altered the lives of millions of people" as it "revs up" the central nervous system, supposedly without the jitteriness of caffeine or the addiction of amphetamines (O'Connor, 2004). As with other stimulants, modafinil can have serious side effects, which, according to Provigil's website, include nervousness, mania, "sensing things that are not there," suicidality (suicidal thoughts), aggression, difficulty falling or staying asleep, dizziness, depression, chest pain, shortness of breath, and a fast, pounding, or irregular heart beat ("Welcome to Provigil.com," 2012).

In part due to the increased illicit use of this and similar drugs since the late 1990s, many have raised concerns about the use of such drugs "to get ahead" or accomplish tasks, particularly among young people. For example, as Dr. Farah at the Center for Cognitive Neuroscience notes with respect to modafinil in particular,

> It would be a shame for a generation of young adults to come of age believing that the only way they can take on a challenging project is with some kind of pharmacological help. It is quite possible that modafinil will be the next Ritalin on campus, something that kids go off to college with. If it is used widely for A.D.H.D., then it will probably end up being readily available to the under-graduate masses. (as quoted in O'Connor, 2004)

The type of amphetamine of most concern in recent years has been metham-phetamine. Methamphetamine is the most potent and fast acting of the amphet-amines, and as it is available in a powder form, it is rarely taken orally (as Benzedrine and Dexedrine typically are), but rather snorted, smoked, or injected, which intensifies its effects (Faupel et al., 2004). Methamphetamine, in its vari-ous forms, is often called meth, crank, speed, ice, glass, crystal, and crystal meth, and the drug is commonly diluted or "cut" with substances such as baking soda, lactose, ether, insecticides, photo developer, and strychnine (Gahlinger, 2001). As with other amphetamines, both the rush and the high associated with metham-phetamine result from the release of dopamine into the areas of the brain that regulate pleasure. As compared to cocaine, it is metabolized quite slowly, result-ing in a larger amount of the drug remaining unchanged in the user's body (Pennell et al., 1999).

The use of methamphetamine results in increased energy, alertness, and stamina, as well as decreased appetite and sleeplessness (ONDCP, 2003b). Although these effects are similar to all amphetamines, the effects of methamphetamine are typically more intense due to the greater potency of methamphetamine and because metham-phetamine is typically snorted, smoked, or injected rather than taken orally in pill form. The side effects are often worse as well because methamphetamine causes the user to expend a great deal of energy over an extended period of time. Additionally, although methamphetamine can be prescribed (under rare circumstances), the drug as consumed in street form includes methamphetamine (probably) as well as an unknown assortment of other chemicals, many more harmful to the body than pure methamphetamine, and some that may have psychoactive properties. Frequent and high-dose users of the substance display increased nervousness, paranoia, irritability, confusion, insomnia, schizophrenia-like symptoms, and possibly hallucinations or delusional symptoms, including scratching at the "crank bugs" methamphetamine abusers sometimes believe are crawling under their skin (this tactile hallucination is referred to as "formication"; Liska, 2000; ONDCP, 2003b). Some of the most erratic and violent behaviors resulting from methamphetamine use may result when users binge or "run" on methamphetamine, using it heavily and repeatedly over a period of days, typically foregoing sleep during this time, which further compounds the problem (Swetlow, 2003).

In 2005, an open letter to the media regarding methamphetamine was drafted by medical doctor David C. Lewis and signed by nearly 100 other medical doctors and health professionals. The letter requested that the media coverage of methamphetamine avoid making sensationalistic and scientifically baseless claims and instead base their reports about methamphetamine "on science, not presumption or prejudice." The letter criticized the use of the scientifically baseless term *meth-addicted baby*, noting that "By definition, babies cannot be 'addicted to methamphetamines'" and criticized the common media portrayal of methamphetamine addiction as being especially difficult to treat when scientific data have not found this. (Lewis, 2005)

Although the amphetamines and especially methamphetamine have attracted a great deal of negative attention recently, it is important to recognize that several legal herbal products and cold remedies, sold widely in health food and grocery stores, act in a similar fashion to the amphetamines. For example, many herbal products contain ephedrine, which, along with adrenaline, was used to create the amphetamines. Accordingly, if herbal products containing ephedrine are taken in sufficient quantities, they will generate effects similar to amphetamines (Gahlinger, 2001).

Ephedra Plant

Ephedrine is naturally found in several species of the ephedra plant, which are leafless bushes somewhat similar to pine trees that grow in arid regions throughout the world (Weil & Rosen, 1998). As noted at the beginning of this chapter, ephedra was one of the first psychoactive substances used by humans. The Chinese have used the ephedra plant in traditional medicines (e.g., ma huang) for the treatment of asthma and other respiratory problems for thousands of years (Gahlinger, 2001). Ephedra was similarly used for its stimulant properties by American Indians of the Southwest, and it is also sometimes called "Mormon tea" because the Mormons began using it as a substitute for coffee and tea, which were prohibited by their religion (Weil & Rosen, 1998). Ephedrine was isolated from the ephedra plant in 1892 by Chinese and Japanese scientists, and by the 1920s, the pharmaceutical company Eli Lilly was mass producing it for the treatment of asthma (Gahlinger, 2001). Soon after this, a synthetic version of ephedrine, pseudoephedrine, was developed, which remains a common ingredient in many cough and cold medications. The similarity of these substances to amphetamines is further illustrated by the fact that methamphetamine can be synthesized from ephedrine or pseudoephedrine with common household products (e.g., drain cleaner and table salt). As noted in Chapter 1, this has prompted many states as well as the federal government to pass laws regulating pseudoephedrine.

Bath Salts

The term *bath salts* has been generically applied by media and government sources to the broad category of synthetic stimulants that are often variants of banned substances but have recently gained popularity as legally obtainable recreational drugs available online or at some local convenience stores and head shops. These drugs have been broadly dubbed bath salts because that was the type of product officially marketed by a small number of manufacturers of these drugs when media attention first began. More accurately, they are a variety of products that contain one or more of three chemicals: mephedrone, methylone, or MDPV (methylenedioxypyrovalerone), or derivatives of these chemicals (Martinez, 2012).

These drugs have stimulant and hallucinogenic properties, with users reporting effects that are similar to cocaine, methamphetamine, LSD, and ecstasy (Martinez, 2012). Street chemists are continually making new derivatives of the primary chemicals associated with bath salts, and until these new drugs are identified, it is impossible to test for and difficult to legislate against them. Many of the chemicals used to create bath salts have been banned and the products are illegal in many states, but as of this writing bath salt products remain technically legal in other states. This is because a substance not specifically listed in Title 21 of the U.S. Code governing food and drugs is difficult to prosecute. However, the Controlled Substances Act does allow for the prosecution of analogs—or derivatives of a banned substance, as is the case with bath salts—and the DEA has successfully prosecuted some of these analog cases (NPR, 2012). So as of this writing, many bath salts products still skirt the letter of the law and remain legally sold in some states and over the Internet under product names like Ivory Wave, Eclipse, White Lightning, Purple Wave, Vanilla Sky, or Bliss.

There have been many accounts of extreme side effects due to bath salt use in recent media exposés (see Chapter 1), many of which are not scientifically based, but researchers have demonstrated numerous negative consequences associated with the abuse of these chemicals. For instance, side effects of use may include neurological, cardiovascular, and psychopathological side effects as well as psychomotor agitation, delusions, hallucinations, psychosis, hypertension, palpitation, chest pain, seizures, and headaches (Wood et al., 2010), and at least a few deaths have been linked to the use of these drugs in combination with other factors (James et al., 2010).

Most commonly, users entering hospitals experience agitation and tachycardia (highly elevated heart rate; CDC, 2010). At the same time, highly publicized accounts have sensationalized the risks associated with these synthetic stimulants. In one such instance, a disturbed individual was shot when he attempted to eat the face of a homeless man after reportedly consuming bath salts, an incident that led to "zombie bath salt" headlines (Haggin, 2012). However, a toxicology report later found that the attacker had no synthetic drugs in his system (Szalavitz, 2012).

> Despite the broad scope of empowerment granted to the DEA by the Synthetic Drug Abuse Act, variant drugs continue to emerge, complicating enforcement of laws banning synthetic drugs. Following the original temporary ban of MDPV (methylenedioxypyrovalerone), the active ingredient in the "Charley Sheen Bath Powder," researchers at the Michigan State Police Forensics Lab tested a new version of the same product and found that it contained alpha-PVP (alpha-Pyrrolidinovalerophenone), a stimulant not included in any current legislation. This has led to concern from many officials that the current ban is not broad enough, leading to calls for even broader legislative and enforcement empowerment (Deveraux, 2012).
>
> However, there have also been concerns raised by some lawmakers and researchers over the potential pitfalls of such measures, including the increased social and economic costs associated with punishing users and the potential loss of medical applications associated with some of these research chemicals (Haggin, 2012). Fifteen other stimulants flagged for banning by the DEA were included in a stand-alone bill approved by the House in December of 2011, but they did not make it into the FDA bill.

Ritalin, Adderall, and Other ADD Prescription Drugs

Methylphenidate, more commonly known by its trade name Ritalin, is a chemical relative of the amphetamines used predominately in the treatment of attention deficit hyperactivity disorder (ADHD) or attention deficit disorder (ADD; Gahlinger, 2001). ADHD and ADD typically involve children who have difficulty learning despite average or even above-average IQ scores (Ray & Ksir, 2004). The utility of amphetamines for treating these conditions was discovered accidentally when a doctor in Rhode Island administered Benzedrine to children who had undergone spinal taps in an effort to reduce the headaches commonly experienced after this procedure. While the substance was not effective in reducing the children's headaches, it did result in an increase in their activity level and also improved their academic performance, so amphetamines then came to be used for this purpose (Diller, 1998). It was during the 1950s that the Swiss pharmaceutical company Ciba began selling Ritalin to treat these conditions, and the FDA approved the drug for sale in the United States in 1961 (Davenport-Hines, 2001; Diller, 1998).

Ritalin is often called Vitamin R or R-Ball on the street, and it is common for users to crush and snort Ritalin pills in order to obtain a speed-like high.

Despite the fact that Ritalin is often regarded as different from other stimulants, likely because it is a widely prescribed medical drug, it is important to stress that there is little difference between Ritalin, cocaine, and methamphetamine if one considers the effects of the substance rather than the motivation for taking it. For example, the *Journal of the American Medical Association* noted in 2001 that Ritalin "acts much like cocaine" (Vastag, 2001), and others have noted that the effects of Ritalin when abused "are similar to those produced by methamphetamine" (Gahlinger, 2001, p. 209). This should come as no surprise, as Ritalin and other drugs prescribed for the treatment of ADHD such as Adderall and Dexedrine all operate on the same neurotransmitters as cocaine and are classified, along with cocaine, as Schedule II controlled substances under U.S. law. As with cocaine, Ritalin can have serious side effects, particularly when misused. Negative side effects of Ritalin include a racing heart, nausea, headaches, and insomnia, and prolonged or heavy abuse may result in a state of "paranoid psychosis identical to that of chronic methamphetamine abuse" (Gahlinger, 2001, p. 209).   *symptoms*

In part because it is so widely prescribed, illicit access to the drug (especially among students) is high. Data from the Monitoring the Future survey indicate that among 12th graders in 2011, 6.5% reported the use of Adderall and 2.6% used Ritalin (Johnston, O'Malley, Bachman, & Schulenberg, 2012c).

Ecstasy

The drug commonly known as ecstasy (3-4 methylenedioxymethamphetamine or MDMA) was invented by German psychiatrists in 1912 in the mistaken belief that it might be an effective appetite suppressant (Gahlinger, 2001). In the early 1950s, ecstasy was also tested and rejected as a possible "truth drug" by the U.S. Army Office of Strategic Services (which later became the CIA). Later (and currently on a limited basis), ecstasy was used by psychiatrists and other doctors in order to facilitate psychotherapy (Davenport-Hines, 2001). An early advocate of the healing properties of the drug, Dr. George Greer, noted that ecstasy "enabled people to communicate ideas, beliefs, opinions, and memories that may have long been repressed in them" (as cited in Gahlinger, 2001, p. 340). At a scientific conference in 1983, Ralph Metzner, Dean of the California Institute of Integral Studies, proposed the name "empathogen" for MDMA, reflecting the ability of the drug to stimulate empathy and feelings of closeness, but by then it had come to be known as ADAM (rearranging the letters of MDMA) on the street (Gahlinger, 2001). The boom in the use and sale of the drug reportedly occurred when it was dubbed ecstasy in the apparently accurate belief that this would sell better than calling the drug empathy (Eisner, 1993).

The effects of ecstasy are distinct from those produced by other stimulants, and some have referred to the drug as a "hallucinogenic amphetamine" (Valentine,

2002). This is because ecstasy has effects that are similar to both mescaline and amphetamines (the "MA" in MDMA stands for methamphetamine), although it does not have as strong a stimulatory effect as other amphetamines (Valentine, 2002). Partly because of this strange combination of effects, a clear grouping of this drug into one category or another is difficult, which is illustrated by the fact that in laboratory studies, animals trained to recognize amphetamines recognized ecstasy, but animals trained to recognize hallucinogens also recognized ecstasy (Gahlinger, 2001). The reason for the distinct effects of ecstasy is that like all amphetamines, its use increases levels of serotonin, dopamine, and adrenaline in the brain, but as compared to other amphetamines, ecstasy results in a much greater release of serotonin (which causes perceptual and mood effects; Gahlinger, 2001).

As in therapeutic trials of the drug, recreational users of ecstasy report feeling much more empathy and closeness to others, as well as feelings of compassion, openness, and caring while on the drug (Valentine, 2002). Ecstasy also induces heightened mood, increased self-confidence, extroversion, and emotional excitability (Valentine, 2002). Heightened physical sensations, especially tactile, are also typically associated with the use of ecstasy, causing ecstasy to sometimes be regarded as an aphrodisiac or sexual aid. While it is true that many people report feeling sexually aroused and close to others while on the drug, ecstasy may also interfere with the ability of males to achieve an erection, and it may cause both men and women to have difficulty reaching orgasm (Weil & Rosen, 1998).

Currently, many in the mental health community remain convinced that MDMA is an invaluable therapeutic resource and struggle to have its experimental use permitted for medical research purposes. Some have proposed that MDMA be considered the prototype for a new group of drugs referred to as "enactogens," which are substances thought to have the ability to help mental patients to access painful and heavily guarded emotions (Valentine, 2002). MDMA has also been found to be useful in treating depression, addiction, anxiety, eating disorders, and other mental problems, but research on these connections has been limited due to MDMA's status as a Schedule I controlled substance. In spite of this, research continues to investigate whether MDMA can relieve anxiety and pain in end-stage cancer patients (Adam, 2005) and as a treatment for posttraumatic stress disorder. Only two clinical trials have occurred thus far (in the United States and Switzerland), but positive short- and long-term effects of MDMA therapy were identified in both, (as reported in Buchen, 2010).

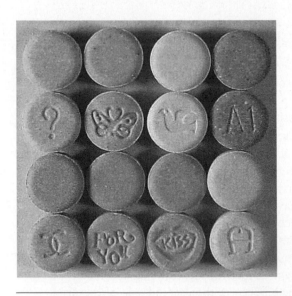

Ecstasy Capsules and Tablets

In the U.S. study, 20 to 30 therapy sessions with ecstasy resulted in 85% of patients no longer meeting the criteria for posttraumatic stress disorder, a benefit maintained by 13 of 16 participants in follow-up studies after 3 years.

Evidence continues to mount, suggesting that ecstasy's legal classification as a Schedule I substance (most restricted) is inappropriate relative to its potential risks. When measuring dependence, social costs, and individual harm from various substances, MDMA was found to be among the safest commonly used recreational drugs (Nutt et al., 2007; van Amsterdam et al., 2010).

In the UK, where ecstasy is classified as a Class A drug (most dangerous), there is a similar push to loosen restrictions. As early as 2000, the Police Foundation in the UK made this recommendation following an independent review, and more recently, both the House of Commons Science and Technology Committee (2006) and Advisory Council on the Misuse of Drugs (2009) released government reports by top UK scientists strongly recommending the rescheduling of ecstasy to a Class B drug. However, changes have not been made in Britain, and the lead scientist in the British Advisory Council, David Nutt, lost his post over his commitment to the proposed change in the scheduling of ecstasy.

Along with the potentially beneficial therapeutic effects and the desired recreational effects of ecstasy, the drug may have a number of negative consequences. According to the Office of National Drug Control Policy (ONDCP) Fact Sheet on ecstasy, the psychological effects associated with use of the substance include confusion, depression, anxiety, sleeplessness, and paranoia (2002b). Among the physical effects are muscle tension, involuntary teeth clenching, nausea, blurred vision, feeling faint, tremors, rapid eye movement, sweating, and dehydration (particularly when combined with intense exertion, such as at dance raves; Weil & Rosen, 1998). The negative side effects of ecstasy can be exacerbated when alcohol and other drugs are used in combination with it, and many of these symptoms may occur due to withdrawal from ecstasy. For example, because tolerance to ecstasy develops quickly, the drug is often used in increasing quantities to get the same high, and some users refer to the negative, depressed moods often experienced after a weekend ecstasy binge as the "Terrible Tuesdays" (Gahlinger, 2001). It appears that the greatest risks associated with ecstasy result from the fact that pills sold as ecstasy are often contaminated with other drugs, including ephedrine, amphetamine, methamphetamine, dextromethorphan, ketamine, PCP, and analogous synthetics such as MDA, MDEA, and 2C-B, many of which are more dangerous than pure ecstasy (Valentine, 2002).

"Smiles," or 2C-L, is another synthetic drug that is commonly used in the club scene. The drug is used for its hallucinogenic and euphoric properties. Similar to ecstasy, the drug may generate feelings of relaxation and empathy. Chemically similar to 2C-B, smiles may be taken in tablet or capsule form, snorted, or consumed on blotter paper and is sometimes sold as or combined with ecstasy and LSD. 2C-L has no approved medical uses and has been implicated in the deaths of at least two people (Drug Enforcement Administration, 2011; Pappas, 2012).

DEPRESSANTS

Depressants are substances that reduce the energy level of the nervous system, dampen sensitivity to external stimulation, and, in high enough doses, induce sleep. These drugs are also called sedative-hypnotics because they sedate users at low doses and can induce sleep (i.e., hypnotize) at high doses. Although it is not commonly known, depressants are more dangerous than stimulants due to the fact that the use of such drugs can kill people by interfering with vital centers in the brain (Weil & Rosen, 1998). Many depressants, including alcohol, are also characterized by severe physical withdrawal symptoms and, unlike other forms of drugs—including narcotics such as heroin—there is a real possibility of death due to withdrawal when quitting depressants after a period of long and extensive use (Weil & Rosen, 1998).

Alcohol

Alcohol is an intoxicant that is more widely used than any other, at least partially due to the fact that all types of plant species, from cereal grains to fruits and others, can be turned into it (Walton, 2002). Mead may date back as far as 8000 BC; beer and berry wine were used by Neolithic man as far back as 6400 BC, and grape wine dates to 300 to 400 BC (Ray & Ksir, 2004). Distillation, which is necessary to produce beverages with alcohol concentrations above 12 to 15% (because when alcohol reaches this point, it kills the yeasts that act to produce alcohol), probably originated in the Arabic world around 800 AD (Gahlinger, 2001). Distilled spirits came to medieval Europe around 1250 AD and arrived in America with the colonial explorers. Europeans and early American settlers used alcohol in a wide variety of ways—it served as "a social beverage, a before meals aperitif, a thirst-quenching beverage, during meals, an after dinner drink, an evening drink, a nightcap, a tranquilizer, a sedative, a religious offering, a deliriant, and as a means of getting drunk" (Brecher, 1972). Alcohol was widely consumed historically in part because it kills bacteria, so alcoholic beverages were safer to drink during times when a large portion of all deaths were due to infectious disease. Many early Europeans and Americans even viewed alcoholic beverages as especially healthy and beneficial to the user (Ray & Ksir, 2004). For example, the early Puritans viewed alcohol as "the Good Creature of God" despite their strict and austere ways of living (as cited in Ray & Ksir, 2004, p. 272).

Attitudes toward alcohol, especially in the United States, can best be described as ambivalent, if not schizophrenic. Sullum (2003a) recounts how this ambivalence is reflected in a passage from the Hebrew Bible:

> Seeing Noah plant his vineyard, Satan offers to help. He slaughters a lamb, a lion, a pig, and an ape, pouring their blood into the soil. "This signifies," says the legend, that before a man drinks wine he is simple like a lamb, who doesn't know anything. ... When a man drinks as is customary, he is bold like a lion,

saying there is no one like him in the world; when a man drinks too much, he becomes like a swine, peeing on himself; and when he is drunk, he becomes like a monkey, standing and dancing and acting foolishly, and says inappropriate things in front of everyone, for he does not know what he is doing. (p. 61)

As is reflected in this passage, most people are aware of the fact that individuals react to alcohol consumption in different ways. In addition to the amount consumed, individual reactions to alcohol may vary across individual personalities, the mood of the user at the time of consumption, and the social setting in which one consumes alcohol.

The effects of alcohol are also influenced by individuals' expectations, as several experimental studies have demonstrated. For example, Lang, Goeckner, Adesso, and Marlatt (1975; as cited in Bushman & Cooper, 1990) found that in an experimental situation, subjects were more likely to administer electric shocks when they *believed* they had consumed alcohol, regardless of whether they really had. Other research on the effects of alcohol, expectations, and behavior includes that by Hull and Bond (1986), which noted that alcohol expectancies, rather than consumption per se, had the greatest impact on involvement in socially deviant behaviors. Thus, it is important to recognize that the behavioral effects of alcohol (and many other drugs) are in part due to their ability to lower social inhibitions and allow individuals to "cut loose" or misbehave with the knowledge that, if necessary, they can always excuse this behavior later as a result of their drinking.

> Debate surrounds the production and marketing of flavored malt beverages, as many feel these products target underage drinkers. One of these beverages is Tilt, a raspberry-flavored malt beverage, advertised in brightly colored cans, that is spiked with energy-drink ingredients such as caffeine, guarana, and ginseng. To improve the public image of the products, Anheuser-Buch recently reduced the alcohol content in its 24-ounce offering of Tilt from 12%, roughly the potency of wine, to 8%, which is stronger than almost all beer available. (Korn, 2011)

Because alcohol is a widely used psychoactive drug with a relatively high level of toxicity, the number of deaths due to alcohol is roughly 25 times the number attributed to all illegal drugs combined (Gahlinger, 2001). According to the Centers for Disease Control, roughly 38 million American adults (1 in 6) are binge drinkers, measured as five or more drinks for men, four or more for women, in a short period of time (CDC, 2012b). Alcohol results in approximately 80,000 U.S. deaths each year (CDC, 2012b) and globally, it is the cause of roughly 2.5 million deaths annually (WHO, 2011). Although exact figures and estimates vary and are subject to debate, there is no question that both globally and in the United States, alcohol is responsible for far more fatalities than all illegal drugs combined.

Deaths resulting from alcohol consumption occur in a variety of ways. As with other depressants, alcohol can kill by overdose, as it depresses the respiratory function of the brain. Thus, if intoxication is severe enough, this can shut down respiration, causing death (this is more likely to occur when alcohol is combined with other depressants, such as sleeping pills). Alcohol can also cause death via overdose when individuals regurgitate but are so sedated that they don't awake and thus asphyxiate on their own vomit. Indirectly, alcohol is related to tens of thousands of deaths resulting from accidents; it is also a contributor to a significant number of traffic deaths in the United States (National Highway Traffic and Safety Administration, 2002), and it is involved in a large portion of all assaults, homicides, and suicides.

Although the short-term consequences of alcohol use are substantial, it is the long-term effects of alcohol that are most damaging. The prolonged use of alcohol can cause considerable physical damage, including cirrhosis of the liver, heart disease, cancer, and brain damage, particularly at high levels of consumption. Cirrhosis is an irreversible disease associated with alcohol abuse that involves normal liver cells being replaced by useless tissue and is one of the leading causes of death in the United States, particularly among men between the ages of 25 and 65 (CDC, 2012b).

Although limited alcohol consumption can be good for cardiovascular health (discussed below), alcohol abuse can damage the heart muscle itself (cardiomyopathy) as well as cause cardiovascular disease (CDC, 2011). Additionally, because alcohol exerts effects on the brain and peripheral nervous system, individuals who are dependent on the substance develop the shakes, amnesia, and even problems with intellectual functioning (Weil & Rosen, 1998). As with the physical withdrawal, negative mental effects may be especially pronounced when one stops consuming alcohol after long-term heavy use. For example, upon quitting, alcoholics may develop *delirium tremens*, which involve hallucinations, delusions, disorientation, and severe shaking. The pronounced physical dependence associated with alcoholism is further illustrated by the fact that withdrawal from such a state is medically difficult and, in severe cases, can result in death (Ray & Ksir, 2004).

Another major public health problem associated with alcohol abuse is fetal alcohol syndrome (FAS), a condition in which some babies born to alcoholic mothers display neurological problems, low birth weight, mental retardation, and facial malformations (Carroll, 2003). Although he was unable to identify the physiological mechanisms that produce FAS, Howard (1918) was one of the first to mention this condition, noting, "The child of the female drunkard is not born with a direct alcoholic tendency, but is probably born with ill-nourished tissues, and especially with a badly developed brain and nervous system" (p. 75).

Prior to the formal discovery of FAS in the 1970s, some doctors assumed that alcohol was such a harmless substance that it was administered intravenously to women who were thought to be at risk of losing their pregnancies (Carroll, 2003). However, since 1989, all beer, wine, and liquor products sold in the United States must have Surgeon General's warnings advising that "women should not drink alcoholic beverages during pregnancy because of the risk of birth defects."

It is important to recognize that it is by no means inevitable that women who drink alcohol when pregnant will give birth to babies with FAS. As the former director of the National Institute on Alcoholism and Alcohol Abuse, Morris Chafetz, notes, "Recent studies reaffirm the finding that fetal alcohol syndrome is a danger only to women who are chronic excessive drinkers" (as quoted in Sullum, 2003a, p. 90). In most cases, even when their mothers drink heavily during pregnancy, children do not develop FAS (Carroll, 2003), with only 23 to 29 out of 1,000 births to women who are "problem drinkers" resulting in FAS babies (Ray & Ksir, 2004). There is also very little scientific evidence to suggest that the light consumption of alcohol during pregnancy will cause harm to the fetus (Ray & Ksir, 2004).

The myriad health problems associated with alcohol illustrate the fact that if our current substance policies are intended to minimize public harm, then perhaps they are directed at the wrong drugs. In fact, as Ross (1992, p. 80) suggests, "Were alcohol to be introduced as a new drug, it would very likely fail to be approved by the FDA on the grounds that its side effects are too damaging to warrant its benefits." However, while it is true that serious health problems are associated with the heavy use of alcohol, as with all drugs, there are also health benefits associated with alcohol consumption. For example, a study of Vancouver, Washington, and Portland, Oregon–area residents conducted by the Kaiser Permanente Health Care company found that 25% of the 3,803 people surveyed were abstainers from alcohol, but these individuals had both worse health and worse health habits than light to moderate drinkers (as cited in Olsen, 2001). Research has also shown that moderate daily consumption of alcohol may prevent Alzheimer's disease and other forms of dementia (Ross, 2002). The authors of this study suggested that the blood-thinning and cholesterol-lowering properties of the ethanol contained in alcohol may reduce the probability of dementia, which is frequently caused by blood vessel problems. It is also possible that low levels of alcohol in the bloodstream stimulate the release of acetylcholine, which is believed to facilitate learning and memory (Ross, 2002).

As mentioned above, perhaps the most well-known health benefit of light to moderate alcohol consumption is its role in the prevention of heart attacks. Red wine was the first alcoholic beverage identified as having positive health benefits when, in 1979, researchers reported that the higher a country's average per-capita wine consumption, the lower its rate of coronary heart disease (Zuger, 2002). France was at one end of the spectrum with very low rates of heart disease, while Finland, Scotland, and the United States, countries where far less wine is consumed, had rates of heart disease almost four times higher. It has been suggested that the pattern of drinking rather than the type of alcohol consumed is the primary reason for the relationship between wine consumption and protection from heart disease. This is because most wine consumers drink in small amounts, several days per week, rather than in larger amounts on only one or two days per week (National Institute on Alcohol Abuse and Alcoholism, 2000).

Barbiturates

Sometimes called downers, tranquilizers, sedatives, or sleeping pills, barbiturates have been used for more than 100 years. All barbiturates are based on barbituric acid, first discovered in 1864, with the first barbiturate sleeping pill, barbital, appearing in 1903 (Weil & Rosen, 1998). Since this time, more than 2,500 different types of barbiturates have been synthesized, but even during their heyday in the 1950s, only about 50 were marketed for human use, and today, this figure is only about a dozen (Gahlinger, 2001).

Barbiturates are loosely grouped into either the long-acting or the slow-acting category. Long-acting barbiturates such as Phenobarbital are slowly metabolized and eliminated by the kidneys, producing effects that last 12 to 24 hours (Weil & Rosen, 1998). These barbiturates are used as daytime sedatives and for the treatment of anxiety disorders or seizures. Because their psychoactive effects are more diffuse than those of the fast-acting variety, long-acting barbiturates are rarely abused. Conversely, fast-acting barbiturates produce effects that are very similar to alcohol. Lasting 6 to 7 hours, barbiturates such as amobarbital (Amytal) and secobarbital (Seconal) produce pleasant, euphoric feelings at low to moderate doses and, at high doses, produce a heavy, drunken stupor (Weil & Rosen, 1998).

As the famous writer William Burroughs described the "drunkenness" associated with barbiturate use in a letter to the *British Journal of Addiction* in 1956 and later in his book *The Naked Lunch* (1959):

The barbiturate addict presents a shocking spectacle. He cannot coordinate, he staggers, falls off bar stools, goes to sleep in the middle of a sentence, drops food out of his mouth. He is confused, quarrelsome, and stupid. Barbiturate users are looked down upon in addict society: "Goofball bums. They got no class to them." The next step down is coal gas and milk or sniffing ammonia in a bucket.

The effects of barbiturates are similar to those of alcohol because, like alcohol, barbiturates depress the brain by interfering with oxygen consumption and producing a reduction in central nervous system activity, leading to drowsiness and a lack of muscular coordination (Schilit & Lisansky-Gomberg, 1991). Also like alcohol, the use of barbiturates results in hangovers, and when taken in excess, barbiturates can kill the user by severely depressing the respiratory center of the brain (Weil & Rosen, 1998). In fact, the potential lethality of barbiturates is perhaps what they are best known for (countless celebrities have died from barbiturate overdose, including Marilyn Monroe and Elvis Presley), as, by far, barbiturates represent the greatest threat of death by overdose of any class of drugs (Gahlinger, 2001). This is because barbiturates have a very narrow therapeutic ratio, meaning that the amount of the drug needed get a desired or therapeutic effect is close to the amount that is dangerous or even lethal to the user (Ray & Ksir, 2004). This is compounded by the fact that when barbiturates are combined with alcohol or another depressant such as Valium, the effects are additive—meaning that if one simultaneously drinks an amount that he is used to (and has no problems with) and also takes a dose of barbiturates that would be fine on its own, together, this combination can kill the person (Weil & Rosen, 1998). Barbiturates are involved in an estimated 3,000 deaths each year, half of which are determined to be suicides, usually also involving alcohol (Young, 2010), and there were more than 16,000 emergency department visits attributed to barbiturates in 2009 (SAMHSA, 2011c).

Although effective as sleeping aids and sedatives, the very high potential for overdose presented by barbiturates has caused them to be replaced, both therapeutically and recreationally, with other depressants. Initially, nonbarbiturate downers such as methaqualone, known better by its trade name, Quaalude, filled this role, as the effects of these drugs are very similar to barbiturates, but the drugs were thought to be less likely to result in abuse and overdose (Weil & Rosen, 1998). Unfortunately, methaqualone turned out to be very similar to the barbiturates in terms of abuse and overdose potential, and all medical use of the drug was banned in 1984. Although some nonbarbiturate depressants are still used medically and recreationally, another class of depressants, the benzodiazepines, are now the most widely used recreational downers and are some of the most widely medically prescribed drugs in the world.

Benzodiazepines

more difficult to overdose

Like the barbiturates, the benzodiazepines are commonly referred to as sedatives, tranquilizers, or downers. The first benzodiazepines were developed in the 1950s to offer a safer alternative to the barbiturates. These drugs *are* much safer than barbiturates because their wider therapeutic ratio makes death by overdose much less likely (Ray & Ksir, 2004). The first benzodiazepine was chlolradiazepoxide, patented by the Hoffman-LaRoche pharmaceutical company in 1957 and given the trade name Librium, perhaps with the thought that it could "liberate one from anxieties" (Ray & Ksir, 2004). Librium was the top-selling pharmaceutical drug for several years when, in the early 1960s, Hoffman-LaRoche identified and marketed a new benzodiazepine, Valium (diazepam). Five times stronger than Librium, Valium quickly became the best-selling psychoactive pharmaceutical drug ever. The use of Valium in the United States is reflected in domestic sales of the drug that increased from $27 million in 1963 to $200 million in 1970 (Davenport-Hines, 2001). From 1972 until 1978, Valium dominated the psychoactive pharmaceutical market, leading sales for all medical drugs in those years.

At least part of the reason the benzodiazepines became so widely used was that pharmaceutical companies aggressively marketed these products as cures for the stresses associated with everyday life. For example, advertisements in medical journals for Librium stressed that the drug would assist college girls whose "newly stimulated intellectual curiosity may make her more sensitive to and apprehensive about national and world conditions" (as cited in Weil & Rosen, 1998, p. 76). Other advertisements encouraged the use of tranquilizers by mothers and housewives, from the "woman who cannot get along with her new daughter-in-law" to the "newcomer in town who can't make friends" (as quoted in Weil & Rosen, 1998, p. 76). Valium was even referred to as "mother's little helper" by the Rolling Stones in their song of the same name on their 1966 album *Aftermath*.

The most widely used tranquilizer in the present day is Xanax (alprazolam), a drug for which tens of millions of prescriptions are written annually (Kotaluk, 2002). Xanax, and similar drugs such as Halcion (triazolam), Ativan (lorazepam), and Restoril (tempazepam), work by triggering the release of dopamine in the brain (drugs with names ending in "am" indicate they are benzodiazepines). Initially developed and marketed as a less addicting substitute for Valium, research now indicates that Xanax and similar drugs may have an even stronger addiction potential, and along with Valium and certain narcotic-based painkillers, Xanax is one of the most widely prescribed and abused pharmaceutical drugs (Wartell & La Vigne, 2004).

Another widely used benzodiazepine is flunitrazepam, better known by the trade name Rohypnol. Made by Hoffman-La Roche, Rohypnol (also called roofies) is not approved for medical use in the United States, but it is marketed (and even sold over the counter) in many countries in Europe and Central and South America for the treatment of anxiety, sleep disorders, and alcohol withdrawal (Gahlinger, 2001). Rohypnol, which is roughly 10 times as strong as Valium, has also been called a rape drug, because people may spike others' drinks with the substance. Especially when combined with alcohol (they are both depressants and their effects interact), Rohypnol can cause paralysis, extreme sedation, unconsciousness, and anterograde amnesia, meaning that users may not recall what happened in the hours following the ingestion of the drug. Although it may be used in order to facilitate rape, Rohypnol has also been used by people deliberately and recreationally (particularly in the club or rave scene), as it can produce a drunken state and heavy sedation, cheaply and without the hangover of alcohol. However, Rohypnol can also cause visual disturbances, dizziness, confusion, and difficulty urinating, and when taken at high doses, especially when combined with alcohol or other depressants, the use of Rohypnol may result in coma and death (Gahlinger, 2001).

It is important to note that all benzodiazepines (including those that are medically prescribed) are addictive. Although drugs such as Valium and Xanax may be medically useful as short-term tranquilizers, when people use them for weeks or months at a time, it is likely to generate anxiety, depression, and insomnia and to make the user dependent on the drug (Weil & Rosen, 1998). Benzodiazepine withdrawal is similar to the withdrawal associated with alcohol, and individuals who rapidly stop using these drugs after a period of use are likely to experience shakiness, a loss of appetite, muscle cramps, memory and concentration problems, insomnia, agitation, and anxiety (Ray & Ksir, 2004).

GHB

Another depressant of recent note is gamma-hydroxy-butyric acid, commonly known as GHB. First synthesized in 1960 by a French researcher seeking a better anesthetic, GHB was sold by U.S. health food stores and gyms and through the mail and Internet as a natural sleep aide and as a nutritional supplement (Gahlinger,

2001). Bodybuilders began to use GHB in the 1980s in the belief that it would facilitate muscle growth and reduce body fat, a claim that has never been supported by research. The drug grew in popularity in the early 1990s (soon after being banned by the FDA in 1990) when clubbers or ravers began to use it recreationally because of its euphoric effects. The drug is generally dissolved in water, where it is odorless, colorless, and looks just like water (it is also called salty water, as well as liquid ecstasy). Like Rohypnol, GHB can be used as a rape drug, because in addition to causing euphoria and reduced inhibitions, at high doses, the drug can cause heavy sedation and sometimes sleep. As with alcohol and methaqualone (drugs with similar effects), an overdose of GHB, especially if combined with alcohol or other drugs, can depress the respiration to the point that coma or death results (Gahlinger, 2001).

In one of the first criminal trials involving GHB, four Detroit men were charged with manslaughter after spiking 15-year-old Samantha Reid's soft drink with GHB in January of 1999. Reid went into a coma and died the next day, and three of the men were subsequently convicted of manslaughter, with the fourth convicted of being an accessory to manslaughter and other charges. ("Four Guilty in GHB Death," 2000)

Complications arise in the regulation of GHB as, like many other drugs including methamphetamine, it is easily produced out of legal and widely available products. Although the recreational use of GHB and related drugs such as GBL (gama-butrolactone) and BD (1,4-butanediol) is illegal in the United States, they remain widely available, as they are contained in paint strippers, industrial solvents, fish tank cleaners, and similar products (Gahlinger, 2001).

Inhalants

Inhalants are a broad class of drugs that are grouped together due to their route of administration—they include a wide variety of household products that induce psychoactive effects when inhaled. The effects of many inhalants are similar to those of alcohol and include disorientation and the impairment of judgment and coordination (Weil & Rosen, 1998), but because the inhalants involve so many different chemicals with many distinct effects, they do not fit neatly into any drug category. However, these substances perhaps best illustrate the point that people will consume virtually any substance that acts to alter their consciousness.

The inhalants can be grouped into four general categories of products. The first category is the volatile solvents. These are liquids that vaporize at room temperature and include paint thinners and removers, dry-cleaning fluids, gasoline, glues, and felt-tip markers. A second form of inhalants are the aerosols, which are sprays that contain propellants and solvents and include products such as spray paint, deodorant and hair sprays, vegetable oils used for cooking, and fabric-protector sprays. The use of aerosols is more difficult than the use of other forms of inhalants because the aerosol propellants come out of the can mixed with other substances, which must often be separated from the gas (e.g., by spraying into a balloon) before the propellant can be inhaled (Weil & Rosen, 1998). A third category of inhalants is the **gases**, which are found in many household products, including butane lighters, propane tanks, whipped cream dispensers, and refrigerants. Finally, the **nitrites** are a group of inhalants that have effects somewhat similar to anesthetics and are primarily used as sexual enhancers (National Institute on Drug Abuse, 2000). Although amyl nitrite (also called amys, poppers) is only available via prescription (as a heart medicine), butyl nitrite and isobutyl nitrite produce the same effects and are legally available in "herbal high" stores or head shops. Although butyl nitrite and isobutyl nitrite are typically sold as liquid incense or something similar, those who buy these products generally do so for their psychoactive effects (Weil & Rosen, 1998).

Because of their wide availability as solvents, fuels, and the like, these products have been used for their psychoactive effects since at least the 1800s, and scares about their use have periodically erupted. One of the first inhalants to be widely used is ether, which was also the first anesthetic to be used in surgical procedures. Prior to the use of ether as an anesthetic, surgery was a horrible and painful process, in which "patients had to be tied down, and their screams could be heard far from the operating rooms" (Weil & Rosen, 1998, pp. 78–79). Once its role in surgery and medicine became well known, the recreational use of ether spread to the general public. Ether parties were common through the 1800s, with people gathering for the purpose of sniffing ether fumes and becoming intoxicated, and many users who abstained from alcohol chose to use ether as an alternative drug (Walton, 2002; Weil & Rosen, 1998).

Another inhalant of note is nitrous oxide or laughing gas. Because nitrous oxide is much weaker than ether and cannot produce unconsciousness, nitrous oxide is not useful as major anesthetic, but is still used to relax patients during dental work or minor surgery (Weil & Rosen, 1998). Discovered in 1776 by Joseph Priestly (who also discovered oxygen), the effects of nitrous oxide come on almost immediately when inhaled and disappear almost immediately when the use is stopped (Weil & Rosen, 1998). Nitrous oxide has been claimed to lead to revelations, and among those who used this substance were the poets Coleridge and Southey, Roget of *Roget's Thesaurus*, and Dr. Oliver Wendell Holmes of the Harvard Medical School (Brecher, 1972). Other effects of nitrous oxide include silliness and laughing, which is why it is called laughing gas. Historically, traveling medicine shows and carnivals allowed members of the public to pay a small fee to consume a minute's worth of nitrous oxide, after which the crowds were often said to erupt in uncontrollable laughter that quickly and awkwardly stopped once the effect of the drug wore off (Weil & Rosen, 1998).

In more recent times, it has been estimated that more than 1,000 common household products are inhaled for their psychoactive effects (Fackelmann, 2002). Although inhalants are used by adults, this is much less frequent, as "Grownups tend to regard glue, gasoline, paint thinner, and the rest as cheap highs—easy to obtain and not very good" (Weil & Rosen, 1998, p. 128). Conversely, inhalants are widely used by the young because they are often the only intoxicating substances available at this age. This is particularly concerning because many inhalants are acutely toxic. Because they are such a wide group of drugs, it is impossible to make generalizations about their harms, but some substances, especially solvents and gases such as toluene, benzene, gasoline, butane, and propane, are extremely dangerous and can potentially result in death from even one use. Conversely, the nitrites, if used occasionally, are unlikely to result in ill effects (Weil & Rosen, 1998).

OPIATES

The opiates are all products and derivatives of opium, a milky extract contained in the seedpod of certain poppy plants that grow in regions throughout the world. Raw opium contains more than 40 pharmacologically active alkaloids, but the two most important of these are morphine (which constitutes 4 to 20% of dried opium) and codeine (1 to 5% of dried opium; Gahlinger, 2001). Other opiates, such as heroin, are semisynthetic, and finally, some (called opioids) are purely synthetic, created entirely in the lab (Weil & Rosen, 1998).

The opiates were among the first drugs ever to be used by humans, with records of their use dating back at least as far as 5000 BC. Early Egyptian texts suggest that opium was used to alleviate the pain of wounds, and an Ebers papyrus scroll dating to 1500 BC mentions opium as useful "to prevent the excessive crying of children" (Ray & Ksir, 2004). Homer's *Odyssey*, published in approximately 1000 BC, also makes reference to a drug believed to be opium, and Hippocrates, after whom the Hippocratic oath of physicians is named, wrote of opium's ability to relieve pain (Gahlinger, 2001). Similarly, Galen, the last of the great Greek physicians, lauded opium as the cure to all that ills, as it

Opium Poppy

resists poison and venomous bites, cures chronic headache, vertigo, deafness, epilepsy, apoplexy, dimness of sight, loss of voice, asthma, coughs of all kinds, spitting of blood, tightness of breath, colic, the iliac poison, jaundice, hardness of the spleen, stone, urinary complaints, fevers, dropsies, leprosies, the troubles to which women are subject, melancholy and all pestilences. (as quoted in Ray & Ksir, 2004, p. 379)

Although Galen might have been accused of overprescribing today, opium was widely used in the Arab world for thousands of years as well. This was mostly for its psychoactive rather than medicinal properties, and at least in part because the Koran forbade the use of alcohol in any form (Ray & Ksir, 2004). The arrival of the drug in Western Europe occurred in 1524 when the Swiss physician Paracelsus, often called the father of scientific medicine, brought a tincture of opium in alcohol from Constantinople that he called laudanum (Gahlinger, 2001). Later, the famed Dr. Thomas Sydenham would refine laudanum by combining this mixture with substances such as saffron, cinnamon, cloves, and wine to remove the bitter taste (Ray & Ksir, 2004). Sydenham, often called the English Hippocrates for his great contributions to the field of medicine, claimed that "without opium the healing art would cease to exist" (as cited in Ray & Ksir, 2004, p. 379). Among the early users of laudanum were Benjamin Franklin, who reportedly consumed it to deal with gout and respiratory failure (Davenport-Hines, 2001), and Thomas De Quincey, who wrote the book *Confessions of an English Opium Eater* in 1821. De Quincey initially used laudanum to relieve a toothache, then came to take up to 8,000 drops of laudanum per day (a dose that would easily kill a person who had not developed De Quincey's tolerance level; Weil & Rosen, 1998). Upon first taking laudanum, De Quincey proclaimed,

> What a resurrection, from its lowest depths, of the inner spirit! What an apocalypse of the world within me! That my pains had vanished was now a trifle before my eyes. . . . Here was a panacea . . . for all human woes; here was the secret of happiness, about which philosophers had disputed for so many ages, at once discovered; happiness might now be bought for a penny, and carried in the waistcoat pocket; portable ecstasies might be had corked up in a pint-bottle; and peace of mind could be sent down by the mail. (De Quincey, 1971, p. 1)

De Quincey continued to regularly use laudanum for over 50 years, the rest of his life, dying at the age of 74 (Weil & Rosen, 1998).

Opiates are often considered a subclass of the depressants, because one of their effects is to depress the central nervous system. These drugs cause constricted pupils, slurred speech, drowsiness, and a release of histamine in the body, and they also suppress cough, which is why codeine remains one of the most prescribed medicines in the world. The opiates also affect the nausea center of the brain, which often causes people to vomit once they have ingested opiates, and some heroin users are even pleased when vomiting occurs in this context, seeing it as evidence that they have taken "good stuff" (Gahlinger, 2001, p. 377). A small amount of these drugs generates a short-lived feeling of intense euphoria, which some have described "as a whole body orgasm that persists up to 5 or more minutes" (in Ray & Ksir, 2004, p. 399), followed by several hours of mental and physical relaxation (Gahlinger, 2001). People under the influence of opiates often display an unusual head-nodding behavior, which is why using these drugs is sometimes referred to as being "on the nod." The opiates are also among the best analgesics, or pain-killers, known to man, which is why they are carried by all hospitals, in virtually every ambulance, on the battlefield, and by emergency medical technicians.

One of the greatest fears associated with the opiates is the physical dependence that can result from their use. As noted earlier, although tolerance and physical dependence are definitely cause for concern with these drugs, despite media images to the contrary, the physical withdrawal from opiates is less problematic than withdrawal from sedative-hypnotic drugs such as alcohol. However, the ability of the opiates to generate psychological dependence is high and is likely the most difficult part of recovery from opiate addiction (O'Brien, 1997; Ray & Ksir, 2004). Although opiate use and addiction, particularly the intravenous use of opiates, may be accompanied by a number of indirect health risks (e.g., HIV, hepatitis, overdose due to unpredictable potency of the drug, etc.), the *direct* physical consequences of long-term opiate use are, in fact, relatively minor compared to alcohol and other depressants, with the worst chronic medical effect of regular narcotic drug use being severe and chronic constipation (Weil & Rosen, 1998). As Brecher (1972, p. 27) comments, "There is thus general agreement throughout the medical and psychiatric literature that the overall effects of opium, morphine, and heroin on the addict's mind and body under conditions of low price and ready availability are on the whole amazingly bland."

Morphine

Morphine was extracted from opium in 1806 by Frederich Serturner, and even today, morphine remains one of the most effective drugs for the relief of severe pain. Upon its discovery in 1806, Serturner named morphine after Morpheus, the Greek god of dreams. The widespread use of morphine resulted from several factors. One of these was the invention of the hypodermic syringe by Dr. Alexander Wood in 1853. The development of the syringe allowed morphine to be injected, which not only generated a much stronger effect than ingestion, but it also allowed the drug to take effect much faster. Probably because of the "medical context" of injection, this was also thought to be less likely to result in addiction, although this proved not to be the case (Ray & Ksir, 2004).

The other major factor involved in the increased use of morphine was several large military conflicts in the second half of the 19th century, including the American Civil War (1861 to 1865), the Prussian-Austrian War (1866), and the Franco-Prussian War (1870). The countless severe injuries generated by these conflicts led to the widespread use of morphine as a painkiller, and so many soldiers returned from these wars addicted to morphine that morphine addiction came to be called "soldier's disease" or "army disease" (Ray & Ksir, 2004).

The above-mentioned factors contributed to the widespread recreational use of morphine. However, during the late 1800s and early 1900s, most users of narcotic drugs were women, primarily because the drugs were prescribed for menstrual disorders and advertised for "female troubles" (Brecher, 1972). For example, a 1902 report in the *British Medical Journal* referred to morphine being used by women at tea parties, noting "After the service [of tea] the ladies would be invited to draw up their sleeves and receive an adorably divine injection of morphine from their hostess" (as cited in Walton, 2002, p. 157). Although morphine continued to be widely used and remains in use today, in 1874, morphine was slightly altered to produce a new drug in the hopes that it would be less addicting than morphine and codeine. The drug was heroin.

Heroin

Heroin, or diacetylmorphine, was first marketed for public use by Bayer Laboratories (of Bayer aspirin) in 1898. The name by which we know the drug today was invented by Bayer, who marketed the drug under the trade name Heroin (Davenport-Hines, 2001).

At this time, tuberculosis and pneumonia were leading causes of death in the United States, and heroin was widely sold in patent medicines designed to help with coughs. As an article in the *Boston Medical and Surgical Journal* noted on the advantages of heroin in 1900, "It possesses many advantages over morphine. It's not hypnotic, and there's no danger of acquiring a habit" (as cited in Askwith, 1998). Clearly this proved not to be the case, but although heroin is often regarded as the most evil of all drugs, it is important to recognize that it is extremely similar to morphine, which remains widely used in the United States for medical purposes. The only distinction between these drugs is that there are two acetyl groups added to the morphine molecule, and this increases the drug's lipid solubility and thus allows it to enter the brain more rapidly (Ray & Ksir, 2004). This makes heroin able to produce the same effects as morphine, but more quickly and at smaller doses, but once the drug is in the body, it is quickly converted back to morphine (a positive drug test for heroin comes up morphine positive; Weil & Rosen, 1998). Although heroin is illegal and without any approved medical uses in the United States, doctors in England use it for extreme pain because it can be given in smaller doses than morphine, making it preferable for some patients who are sensitive to the nauseating effects of opiates (Weil & Rosen, 1998).

One of the major concerns with heroin (and morphine as well) and a rationale often provided for the illegal status of heroin is that it has a high potential for overdose. Although the overdose potential for heroin is high, this is largely a function of its illegal status. As noted by Ray and Ksir (2004), "Heroin was once sold in small doses in tablet form. If it were still available in that form as a prescription drug, many more people would be taking it but almost none would die from it" (p. 26). The high overdose rate associated with heroin results from the wide disparity in the purity of the drug available to users. Heroin is often cut with various additives such as starch, sugar, talcum powder, baking powder, and powdered milk, as well as other drugs such as methamphetamine, PCP, and cocaine (Gahlinger, 2001). Because there is significant variation in the purity of the drug, and because heroin is a powerful central nervous system (CNS) depressant, overdoses are likely when there are changes in the supply or availability of the drug on the street (e.g., if a dealer is arrested, forcing users to get heroin from unknown sources). One tragic example of this occurred in 1979, when an illegal lab in California produced a variant of the synthetic narcotic fentanyl, which is about 30 times more potent than heroin, and marketed it as China White heroin. Batches of this substance varied in potency as much as 300-fold, and as a consequence, there were more than 100 overdose deaths from the drug in a short period of time (Henderson, Harkey, & Jones, 1990). Similar events have occurred since that time, with the most recent in 2005 when a mixture of heroin and fentanyl distributed mainly in Chicago and several cities on the east coast produced more than two dozen overdose deaths and more than 300 hospitalizations in only 3 weeks (Leinwand, 2006a). Similar "overdose outbreaks" will occur in the future barring major changes in drug policy.

Heroin is far from the strongest opiate. For example, entorphine is approximately *10,000 times* as strong as morphine, and a scratch from a needle contaminated with the drug may be sufficient to kill a person (Gahlinger, 2001). The only practical application of entorphine is as a dart-gun anesthetic to sedate elephants and rhinoceroses. The drug was accidentally discovered in Edinburgh in 1960 when the scientists' morning tea was inadvertently stirred with a glass rod used in an experiment. All the scientists involved were put into a coma due to their ingestion of trace elements of the drug but subsequently recovered. (Gahlinger, 2001)

As noted earlier, the direct effects of heroin on the body are surprisingly mild. There is no scientific evidence that indicates any long-term consequences of heroin to any tissue or organ system (although, as mentioned, there are indirect risks associated with injecting these drugs; Ray & Ksir, 2004). Conversely, a serious concern with heroin, and opiates more generally, is the risk of addiction. The claim that "try it once and you're addicted" is an exaggeration, but the risk of psychological dependence for heroin is substantial. Because the effects of heroin are less intense and immediate if the drug is not administered intravenously (such as by snorting, smoking, or even subcutaneous injection, known as "skin popping"), these forms of heroin use are less likely to result in psychological dependence. For example, as Weil and Rosen (1998) comment, "people who snort heroin can do so on and off for long periods of time without becoming strongly addicted" (p. 88). Even some intravenous heroin users may be able to use the drug only occasionally (known as "chipping") and not become dependent, but a high percentage of these users do eventually become addicted to the drug (Weil & Rosen, 1998). Interestingly, although heroin can result in physical dependence, many intravenous users report being as addicted to the process of using the drug as to the drug itself (leading to the term *needle freaks*; Weil & Rosen, 1998). For example, Powell (1973, cited in Ray & Ksir, 2004) reports one user as saying,

Once you decide to get off it is really exciting. It really is. Getting some friends together and some money, copping, deciding where you're going to do it, getting the needles out and sterilizing them, cooking up the stuff, tying off, the whole thing with the needle, booting, and the rush, that's all part of it. Sometimes I think that if I just shot water I'd enjoy it as much. (p. 396)

Physical dependence on heroin can result in withdrawal that may begin, for chronic users, as soon as the effects of the drug begin to wear off. Heroin withdrawal has been compared by some to "having a good case of the flu," including nausea, vomiting, diarrhea, cramps, chills, hot flashes, and shakes, which grow progressively worse with the time elapsed since the last dose (peaking in 24 to 72 hours and then subsiding; Gahlinger, 2001). However, as noted earlier, it is a common misconception that the physical withdrawal from heroin alone can be fatal.

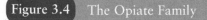
Figure 3.4   The Opiate Family

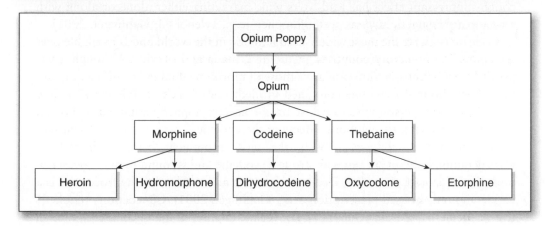

SOURCE: Gahlinger, 2001.

In order to treat heroin addiction, a synthetic narcotic known as methadone is often used to wean users off heroin or to keep them off the drug over time (this is known as methadone maintenance). It was first invented by German researchers during World War II in order to provide a synthetic substitute for morphine, which was in short supply due to wartime demand (Gahlinger, 2001). Although it is still used for pain relief (e.g., chronic back pain), methadone is most well-known for its drug treatment application. It is usually taken orally (with juice) for purposes of methadone maintenance and while it can provide users with the pleasant euphoric feeling typical of narcotics, the effect is last much longer (up to 24 hours) and does not provide the intense rush associated with the injection of heroin or morphine (Gahlinger, 2001). Methadone is thought to be less addicting than heroin, but it does pose a substantial risk of addiction and can causes severe physical withdrawal symptoms. Methadone is also risky in terms of acute toxicity. The CDC estimates that roughly 30% of lethal overdoses from prescription painkillers are due to methadone, despite the fact that it is not among the most commonly prescribed narcotics (CDC, 2012). We discuss methadone maintenance therapy in detail in our discussion of drug treatment in Chapter 8.

Codeine

Along with morphine, codeine is the primary psychoactive element in opium. Isolated from opium shortly after morphine in 1832, codeine is weaker than morphine in terms of its psychoactive and physical effects, but it is absorbed well if taken orally (unlike morphine). Codeine is often prescribed to treat moderate levels of pain, such as those originating from back injuries, surgical recovery, migraine headaches, or broken bones. The analgesic effect of the drug along with its strong cough-suppressant effect has lead to its wide marketing either alone or along with a nonopiate analgesic such as acetaminophen (e.g., Tylenol #3; Gahlinger, 2001).

Codeine is by far the most widely used narcotic in the world and is available over the counter in numerous countries, including Canada and Mexico. Although it has psychoactive effects that are similar to those of morphine if taken in sufficient quantities, the amount of codeine contained in medications such as Tylenol #3 is low enough that the person may overdose on the acetaminophen contained in Tylenol #3 before achieving the euphoric effects of the codeine. There are several semisynthetic versions of codeine as well, the most prominent being hydrocodone. Hydrocodone is about six times as strong as codeine and is found in many prescription painkillers (e.g., Vicodin). Due to its strength and availability, hydrocodone is a very commonly abused prescription drug (Gahlinger, 2001). Concoctions "cooked" from codeine-based pain relievers (sold over the counter in many countries, though not in the United States) are also widely abused. This includes crocodile (or krokodil), an injectable substitute for heroin cooked using desomorphine (synthetic opiate from codeine-based painkillers), iodine, and other household chemicals that is widely used as a heroin replacement in Russia (Walker, 2011).

> Vicodin and its generic equivalents are now the most prescribed drugs in the United States, with 131.2 million prescriptions dispensed in 2010 alone, almost 40 million more than its closest challenger (IMS Institute for Healthcare Informatics, 2011). The majority of the approximately 400 deaths linked to acetaminophen each year also involve hydrocodone, leading the FDA to recommend banning Vicodin in June 2009. (Herper, 2010)

Oxycodone

Oxycodone is another semisynthetic opiate that is synthesized from thebaine. Like morphine and codeine, thebaine is present in raw opium, but it does not have psychoactive properties in its natural form. Oxycodone is contained in products such as Percodan (oxycodone and aspirin) and Percocet (oxycodone and acetaminophen), but most recently it has been used to make OxyContin. Manufactured by Purdue Pharma, OxyContin is a sustained-release formula of oxycodone used to treat serious and chronic pain. Prescriptions for OxyContin have essentially doubled every year since its release in 1996, and in 2000, doctors wrote more than 6.5 million prescriptions for this drug, making it the 18th best-selling prescription drug in the United States at that time (Tough, 2001).

The drug is at least equivalent to morphine in its analgesic effect, and it is potentially as strong as or even stronger than morphine in terms of its psychoactive effect (Tough, 2001). This is particularly the case when users engage in the common

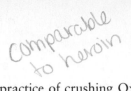 Comparable to heroin

practice of crushing OxyContin pills into a powder and snorting or injecting them. When this is done, the effects of OxyContin, designed to be released over a 12-hour period, are felt immediately and the associated high is claimed to be "as strong as that of heroin" (Gahlinger, 2001, p. 366; also Martin, 2002). The formula of the pills was changed by Purdue Pharma in 2010 in order to make it more difficult to crush and dissolve, limiting somewhat the ability to abuse OxyContin in this way. This change was found to be linked to an increase in heroin use as people addicted to the synthetic narcotic sought alternatives (Cicero, Ellis, & Surratt, 2012).

Drug "Take-Back" Programs

In an effort to control access to prescription pharmaceuticals, "take-back" programs collect unused prescription drugs and properly dispose of them. The amount of unused medication is staggering. The National Community Pharmacists Association estimates 200 million pounds of unused prescription drugs are collecting dust in American medicine cabinets (CNN, 2012).

As one example of the volume of drugs involved in such efforts, a take-back collection program in Vancouver, Washington, collected 819 pounds of medications in a single day. (Clark County PREVENT!, 2012)

OxyContin abuse is relatively prevalent throughout the United States (less so since the anticrush change), but the highest rates of abuse are typically found in rural areas and those characterized by high unemployment rates and fairly large populations of disabled and chronically ill people who require pain relief (Collins et al., 2011; Levine & Coupey, 2009; SAMHSA, 2012a).

In areas that are more geographically remote and thus separated from major illegal drug trafficking routes on interstate highways, OxyContin use tends to be higher, sometimes rivaling marijuana and cocaine as the most commonly used illicit drug (Collins et al., 2011).

The widespread use of OxyContin combined with its narrow therapeutic ratio has resulted in numerous oxycodone-related emergency department (ED) visits and deaths over the last decade. There were approximately 175,000 oxycodone-related ED visits in 2009, a 242% increase since 2004 (SAMHSA, 2010a), and fatalities associated with oxycodone and other opiate-based painkillers have continued to rise over the last decade (see Figure 3.5 below), albeit tapering off in the last few years.

With the increased use and demand for OxyContin, there have been reports of increased pharmacy robberies in several jurisdictions in the United States, ostensibly linked to the drug (Butterfield, 2001a).

Individuals have even attempted to illegally obtain OxyContin by posing as potential homebuyers, building inspectors, and law enforcement officers in order to obtain access to houses and subsequently look for OxyContin and related substances in medicine cabinets. There have also been reports of addicts scanning newspaper obituaries for people who died of cancer or other conditions associated with

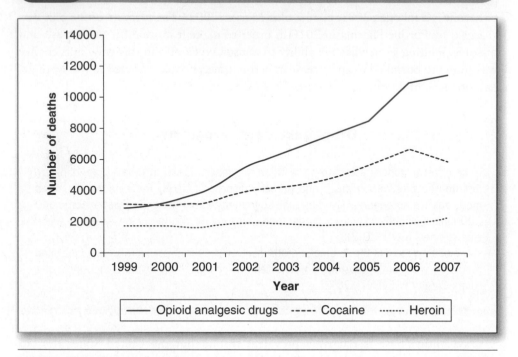

Figure 3.5 Unintentional Deaths From Opioid Analgesic Drugs, Cocaine, and Heroin Overdose in the United States, 1999–2007

SOURCE: CDC, 2011.

considerable pain, so that when the family of the deceased attends the funeral, the thieves are able to break into their homes and search for any leftover painkillers (Leinwand, 2003b).

Regarding the addictive potential of prescription pain killers, a study of more than 300,000 worker compensation claim recipients in 21 states found that nearly one in 12 injured workers who were prescribed narcotic pain killers were still taking the drugs three to six months later (Fauber, 2012).

NONOPIATE ANALGESICS

The nonopiate analgesics have no psychoactive effects and thus will be discussed only briefly. Like the opiates, the nonopiate analgesics have a pain-killing effect (although they are much weaker than the opiates), they can be misused, and they also result in a significant number of overdoses and deaths every year. This class of drug includes acetylsalicylic acid (patented and marketed as Aspirin by Bayer in 1899), acetaminophen, and ibuprofen. Aspirin has an antipyretic effect, meaning it reduces body temperature when elevated by fever, and it also has an anti-inflammatory effect, as it

Over the counter

reduces swelling and inflammation (Ray & Ksir, 2004). Acetaminophen does not provide the anti-inflammatory effect of aspirin, but it may be the best option for pain relief, and ibuprofen provides only a very limited antipyretic effect, but it is an effective anti-inflammatory and may be the best choice for this (Ray & Ksir, 2004).

All of these drugs can cause serious health complications—particularly those relating to the liver and even death via overdose if abused. In the event of a serious overdose, symptoms are generally not realized for 24 to 48 hours, when the individual's impaired liver function becomes evident, but at this point it is often too late to help the individual (Ray & Ksir, 2004).

The toxicity of nonopiate analgesics when abused combined with their extremely wide use generates significant public health problems. As Alexander (1990) notes, "because of the risk of gastric, liver, and kidney damage, it seems likely that regular, heavy use of ASA [acetylsalicylic acid]-like drugs is more physically harmful than the use of many other drugs, including the opiates" (p. 223). Despite this, a large portion of users takes these drugs in ways that place them at increased risk for adverse effects. For example, research on the patterns and effects of over-the-counter analgesics such as ibuprofen (called nonsteroidal anti-inflammatory drugs—NSAIDs) presented at the annual meeting of the American Gastroenterological Association (AGA) in 2004 found that in 2003, 44% of respondents said they took more than the recommended dose of these medications. This was a significant increase from the 26% who reported misuse in 1997, according to Dr. Byron Cryer, lead author of the study.

> Each day, more than 30 million Americans take an NSAID for quick, easy pain relief from common ailments like headaches and arthritis. Because these drugs are easily accessible and can be very effective, there is a misperception out there that they have no risks. In reality, there are serious side effects associated with inappropriate use that patients need to recognize. (AGA, 2004)

Available data indicate that NSAIDs are involved in roughly 128,000 ED visits annually, with incidence of ED visits associated with NSAIDs use increasing more than 50% since 2004 (SAMHSA, 2011c).

The following chapter will continue our discussion on the effects of drugs, focusing on hallucinogens, PCP and ketamine, marijuana, antidepressants, aphrodisiacs, and steroids and other performance-enhancing drugs.

REVIEW QUESTIONS

1. What criteria are used to group drugs into the schedules established by the Controlled Substances Act? What supposedly distinguishes Schedule I drugs from Schedule II drugs?

2. Distinguish between acute and chronic toxicity and provide an example of these effects for a particular drug or group of drugs.

3. What is a therapeutic ratio and how does it relate to acute toxicity?

4. How do we know if a drug can cause physical dependence?

5. What is tolerance? How does tolerance relate to physical dependence?

6. What is reinforcement and how is it related to psychological dependence?

7. Ritalin is similar in its effect to what drugs?

8. In terms of withdrawal, how do the depressants compare to other categories of drugs?

9. How are opium, morphine, and heroin related?

10. How does drug purity affect the potential for overdose associated with the use of "street" opiates such as heroin?

11. What are inhalants and in what ways are they problematic?

12. How many hospitalizations and deaths result from the misuse of aspirin, acetaminophen, and ibuprofen?

INTERNET EXERCISES

1. Want to determine how much caffeine it would take to kill you if you were able to consume the caffeine all at once? Access the link below, enter your beverage, and find out.

   http://www.energyfiend.com/death-by-caffeine

2. Access data from the Drug Abuse Warning Network (DAWN) at http://www
   .samhsa.gov/data/DAWN.aspx and compare the number of emergency department visits resulting from illicit drug use. How does the number of ED visits prompted by cocaine use compare to ED visits prompted by methamphetamine use? Examine ED visits caused by misuse of pharmaceutical drugs (referred to as "overmedication" by DAWN). How do these patterns compare to the visits related to the use of various illegal drugs?

CHAPTER 4

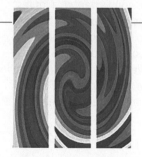

The Effects of Drugs: Part II

Continuing with our discussion from last chapter, we address several categories of drugs based on their effects. Recall that in addition to their psychoactive effects, drugs can be assessed in terms of their ability to generate physical dependence, psychological dependence, and both short- and long-term adverse health effects in users (referred to as acute and chronic toxicity, respectively). As we discussed in the previous chapter, it is important to recognize that all drugs—legal and illegal—pose some level of risk to users, and the many dimensions of risk must be considered simultaneously in order to accurately interpret how harmful or beneficial a particular drug is.

Following our discussion of the stimulants, depressants, inhalants, and opiates in the previous chapter, we now cover several remaining categories of drugs. This chapter will address the hallucinogens, PCP and ketamine, marijuana, antidepressants, aphrodisiacs, and steroids and other performance-enhancing drugs. As noted previously, there are important differences between these categories of drugs and the antidepressants, aphrodisiacs, and steroids and other performance-enhancing drugs are particularly distinct. Despite their differences, each of these forms of drugs is similar to the others discussed in that each has potential benefits and drawbacks, each may be abused, and each represents a means by which people may alter their consciousness.

HALLUCINOGENS/PSYCHEDELICS

In 1931, this unusual class of drugs was called "phantastica," but they are now commonly referred to as hallucinogens (from the Latin word *alucinare*, meaning "to wander in mind") or psychedelics (rooted in Greek with the meaning "mind manifesting" or "mind vision"). As with others, we have chosen to use these terms interchangeably (Weil & Rosen, 1998).

The legal status of a drug often does not accurately reflect the level of harm posed by the substance, either to the user or to society in general. In the previous chapter, Figures 3.1 and 3.2 compared the risks posed by a variety of drugs across several indicators of harm, illustrating that to objectively assess risk, you must consider all indicators of harm simultaneously. In Figure 4.1, an evaluation of collective drug risk obtained from a panel of experts is overlaid with the legal regulation standards employed in England (Under England's Misuse of Drugs Act, Class A is considered highest risk and legal penalty, C lowest). Similar to the situation in the United States, there are many inconsistencies between the level of harm posed by a drug and its legal status.

Figure 4.1   British Legal Code and Experts Rating of Harmful Drugs

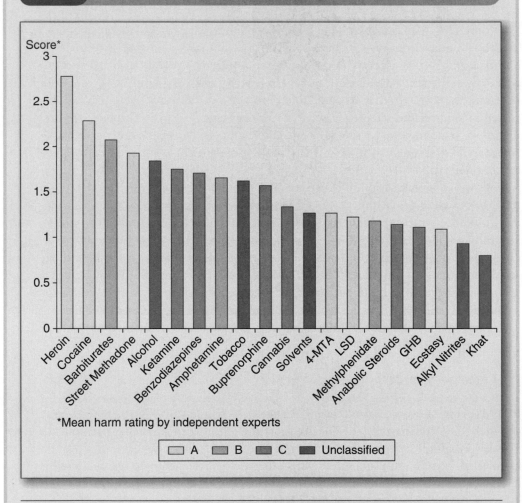

*Mean harm rating by independent experts

Legend: A   B   C   Unclassified

SOURCE: Nutt et al., 2007.

Psychedelics are defined by Grinspoon and Bakalar (1979, p. 9) as drugs that without causing physical addiction, craving, major psychological disturbances, delirium, disorientation, or amnesia, more or less reliably produce thought, mood, and perceptual changes otherwise rarely experienced except in dreams, contemplative or religious exaltation, flashes of involuntary memory, and acute psychoses.

Physiologically, hallucinogenic drugs are some of the safest known drugs—they have no physical dependence potential, no long-term physical health consequences, and these drugs are either very difficult or impossible to fatally overdose on (Ray & Ksir, 2004; Weil & Rosen, 1998). Many argue that hallucinogens are also important for the treatment of severe pain and vital for our understanding of mental illness, as they can be used to treat alcoholism, depression, anxiety disorders, and obsessive-compulsive disorder. However, because of their powerful psychoactive effects, hallucinogens also have the potential, particularly at high doses, to "cause the most frightening experiences imaginable, leaving long-lasting psychological scars" (Weil & Rosen, 1998, p. 94).

LSD

Lysergic acid diethylamide or LSD was first discovered in 1938 by Swiss chemist Albert Hoffman, who produced it from lysergic acid, a chemical in ergot (Weil & Rosen, 1998).

Ergot is a naturally occurring fungus that grows on wheat, rye, and other grasses, and Hoffman was studying the ergot fungus in an attempt to develop medically useful drugs from it. The psychoactive effects of LSD were not known until Hoffman accidentally ingested it in 1943 when he spilled some of the substance on his hands (Davenport-Hines, 2001). As Hoffman noted on his experience in a report to the head of his department:

Last Friday, April 16, 1943, I was forced to stop my work in the laboratory in the middle of the afternoon to go home, as I was seized by a peculiar restlessness associated with a sensation of mild dizziness. Having reached home, I lay down and sank in a kind of drunkenness which was not unpleasant and which was characterized by extreme activity of imagination. As I lay in a dazed condition with my eyes closed (I experienced daylight as disagreeably bright) there surged upon me an uninterrupted stream of fantastic images of extraordinary plasticity and vividness and accompanied by an intense, kaleidoscope-like play of colors. This condition gradually passed off after about 2 hours. (Hofmann, 1970, p. 91)

In 1947, LSD was marketed by Sandoz Laboratories (under the trade name Delysid) with claims that the drug was "a cure for everything from schizophrenia to criminal behavior, sexual perversions, and alcoholism" (Henderson & Glass, 1994, p. 3). Sandoz also suggested that psychiatrists should take LSD in order to "gain an understanding of the subjective experiences of the schizophrenic" (Henderson & Glass, 1994, p. 3). In the 1950s, LSD became widely used in psychiatric treatment as, along with mescaline, it proved useful for recovering repressed memories and emotions during psychoanalysis. By 1965, between 30,000 and 40,000 psychiatric patients had taken LSD for therapeutic purposes, and there were few reports of problematic outcomes (Gahlinger, 2001).

LSD was used to treat alcoholics at a number of rehabilitation centers in the United States prior to its strict regulation (Brecher, 1972) and the practice is currently under study in experimental work (Krebs & Johansen, 2012). LSD has also been used as a painkiller for terminal cancer patients who were nonresponsive to traditional pain medications (Gahlinger, 2001). For example, a study of 128 terminal cancer patients found LSD to completely relieve pain for 12 hours and to reduce it for another 2 to 3 weeks without other adverse effects. The study determined that rather than just numbing the symptoms of pain, LSD actually altered how patients perceived their pain and that it also reduced their fear of death (Kast, 1966). Exploratory research on this has continued recently, including studies conducted at the psychiatry department at Harvard University that are examining whether LSD may provide relief to the pain and depression experienced by terminally ill patients (Eisner, 2001).

In the late 1940s, LSD was also thought to have several military applications. The U.S. military experimented with the use of LSD as a debriefing drug or brainwashing agent (Walton, 2002), and the drug was thought to be potentially useful as a chemical weapon because it could produce temporary mental instability. In the 1950s, the Central Intelligence Agency (CIA) authorized the Eli Lilly pharmaceutical company to produce large quantities of LSD, operating on the false belief that Sandoz Laboratories had sent 50 million doses of LSD to the Soviets (Gahlinger, 2001). The CIA's subsequent LSD research program, code-named MK-ULTRA, involved administering the drug to subjects, often unbeknownst to them, and spying on their activities (some of which involved sexual activities; Davenport-Hines, 2001). As one of the directors of this CIA project commented, "We tested these drugs in bars, in restaurants, in so-called massage parlors—any place where there was a drink and people were eating and drinking" (as quoted in Egelko, 2002). Investigations into the U.S. government's activities involving LSD have revealed that at least 585 soldiers and 900 civilians were given LSD in Army-sponsored experiments between 1956 and 1967, most unwillingly or unknowingly (Ray & Ksir, 2004).

Investigations into the CIA's use of LSD on civilians revealed the case of Frank Olson. Olson was a 43-year-old biochemist who committed suicide on November 28, 1953, less than 2 weeks after CIA agents had secretly slipped LSD into his drink. As a result of being drugged, Olson experienced a severe panic attack, which is not surprising given that he was unaware he had ingested LSD. He was then taken to New York City for treatment, where he apparently jumped or fell from his 10th-story hotel room in Manhattan. In 1975, the involvement of the CIA in Olson's death was revealed in a report to the government by the Rockefeller Commission, and President Ford apologized to the Olson family at the White House, saying the incident was "inexcusable and unforgivable." Eventually, Frank Olson's family was awarded $750,000 in compensation for his death. (Ray & Ksir, 2004)

The recreational use of LSD spread rapidly during the 1960s. As the popularity of the drug increased, people from all walks of life used the substance, not just hippies, looking for a new high. The founder of *TIME* magazine, Henry Luce, took LSD many times and also introduced it to several friends, including actor Carey Grant, who took the drug more than 100 times and noted "it has completely changed me" (as cited in Gahlinger, 2001, p. 48). One of the most famous advocates of LSD was Timothy Leary, who commented in a 1966 interview with *Playboy* magazine, "There is no question that LSD is the most powerful aphrodisiac ever discovered by man. Compared with sex under LSD, the way you have been making love—no matter how ecstatic the pleasure you think you get from it—is like making love to a department store window dummy" (as quoted in Sullum, 2003a, p. 145).

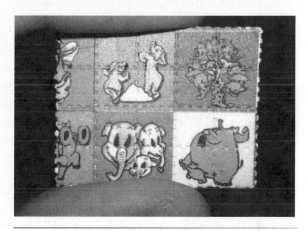

LSD on Blotter Paper

LSD can be taken in many forms but is often consumed on tabs of "blotter paper" (see image). The effects of LSD are typically felt between 20 and 60 minutes after ingestion, and users' experiences differ according to the expectations and mood of the individual, the setting in which the substance is consumed, and other nonchemical factors (Brecher, 1972). Typical LSD experiences often involve perceptual distortions, such as colors being perceived as very vivid and sounds being perceived as louder than they are; an altered sense of time; and "synesthesia" or a condition of "mixing senses" in which one sensation is converted into another such as sounds appearing as visual images (Gahlinger, 2001). Enhanced emotionality is also typical of LSD, such as regarding images as especially beautiful or perceiving ordinary events as awe inspiring (Ray & Ksir, 2004).

Another effect of the psychedelics is that they tend to enhance or intensify users' moods or feelings. As Weil and Rosen (1998) comment:

> Psychedelics do not necessarily produce any particular mood or state of mind. They act as intensifiers of experience. If you take them when you are elated, they make you superelated. If you take them when depressed, they make you superdepressed. If you take them with a friend you feel totally comfortable with, they may deepen your friendship. If you take them with someone you feel uncomfortable with, they may intensify that discomfort to an unbearable degree. (p. 110)

In terms of LSD's effects on the body, there have been many sensationalistic reports suggesting that LSD use can result in serious health consequences, including chromosome damage, birth defects, brain damage, and cancer. The vast majority of the evidence indicates that these reports are totally baseless (Ray & Ksir, 2004; Weil & Rosen, 1998). However, as noted earlier, LSD use may produce adverse psychological effects for some users. Among the more common adverse reactions linked to LSD are panic attacks. Drug-related panic attacks are often thought of as "bad trips," and while these reactions are not unique to LSD, the experience may be especially unsettling while under the influence of LSD (Ray & Ksir, 2004).

Statistical data connecting LSD to serious psychological reactions are lacking, but the most severe effect anecdotally linked to LSD use is a prolonged psychotic reaction, which some have termed hallucinogen persisting perceptual disorder (HPPD) in the *DSM-IV.* Those who report being afflicted with HPPD describe it as like "living in a bubble under water" with a continuous struggle for perceptual control, and constant anxiety, depression, and phobias (Gahlinger, 2001, p. 316). Experimental studies involving LSD users have found only 0.8 in 1,000 regular subjects and 1.8 in 1,000 subjects undergoing psychotherapy to experience any form of psychotic reaction lasting more than 48 hours (Ray & Ksir, 2004). It may be that the drug stimulates an existing mental condition or problem, but at this point, these issues remain unknown and under study. A review of studies of the phenomenon from 1955 to 2001 found the research filled with methodological problems and inconsistencies but concluded that HPPD is a genuine though rarely occurring disorder far more common following illicit LSD use than in clinical or controlled settings (Halpern & Pope, 2003).

In terms of potency, LSD may be the most powerful psychoactive substance known, having psychoactive effects at doses as small as 25 micrograms (a microgram is one-millionth of a gram, and an average postage stamp weighs approximately 60,000 micrograms; Weil & Rosen, 1998). Given that LSD is 100 times stronger than psilocybin and 2,000 times more potent than mescaline, roughly 2 gallons of LSD would be sufficient to have the entire population of the United States "tripping." (Gahlinger, 2001)

"Flashbacks" are another reported consequence of LSD use. Flashbacks involve brief episodes in which former (i.e., not currently under the influence) LSD users supposedly experience perceptual distortions similar to those experienced while under the influence of LSD. A review of the research literature on flashbacks found this term to be "defined in so many ways that it is essentially valueless" (Halpern & Pope, 2003, p. 109) and, in many cases, to refer to behavior that some would classify as symptoms of the aforementioned HPPD, so at present it is not known if these are distinct conditions. It is likely that some flashbacks may actually be intense memories or unusual mental episodes also experienced by non-LSD users such as *deja-vu* (Ray & Ksir, 2004).

Since 1970, all psychedelic drugs including LSD have been classified as Schedule I controlled substances, classifying them as having no medical value and a high potential for abuse. This classification persists despite the findings of a 1973 report of the U.S. National Commission on Marijuana and Drug Abuse that concluded that LSD had "a low dependence liability," that its use "tends to be age-specific and transitory," and that those under the influence of the substance "do not generally act in ways qualitatively different from their normal patterns of behavior" (Shafer, 1973; as cited in Davenport-Hines, 2001, p. 269). There are no withdrawal symptoms associated with the use of LSD, indicating that individuals do not become physically dependent on the substance, and there have been no recorded human fatalities (directly) resulting from the use of LSD (Brecher, 1972). However, LSD use can result in frightening experiences that can cause long-term psychological trauma (Weil & Rosen, 1998).

Psilocybin

Psilocybin is the psychoactive agent in three different genera and about 100 species of mushrooms, the most powerful of which is *Psilocybe mexicana* (Gahlinger, 2001). Although psilocybin was identified in 1958 by Albert Hoffman (who also discovered LSD 20 years earlier), these mushrooms had been used by Native Americans and Mexicans for hundreds and perhaps even thousands of years. Referred to as "teunamacatlth" or "God's flesh" by the Aztecs, there is recorded evidence of psilocybin-containing mushrooms being consumed at the coronation of the Aztec ruler Montezuma in 1502 (Gahlinger, 2001). The conquering Spaniards viewed the Aztec reference to "God's flesh" as blasphemous and attempted to prevent the use of the substance. As Spanish priests wrote of the use of psilocybin by the indigenous peoples:

Psilocybe mexicana

> They possessed another method of intoxication, which sharpened their cruelty; for if they used certain small toadstools . . . they would see a thousand visions and especially snakes. . . . They called these mushrooms in their language teunamacatlth, which means "God's flesh," or of the Devil whom they worshipped, and in this wise with that bitter victual by their cruel God were they houseled. (in Schultes, Hoffman, & Ratsch, 2001)

Because of the Spanish condemnation of psilocybin-containing mushrooms, the use of the drug in spiritual and religious ceremonies became increasingly secretive over the years, and it was not until the 1930s that proof emerged of the continued use of psilocybin by Mexican natives.

The recreational use of psilocybin in the United States is traced to 1955, when Gordon

Wasson, an ethnobotanist, participated in a religious ceremony of the Mazatec Indians that involved psilocybin (Harvard University Press Herbaria, 2002). As Wasson describes his experience with psilocybin:

> It permits you to see . . . vistas beyond the horizons of this life, to travel backwards and forwards in time, to enter other planes of existence, even (as the Indians say), to know God. . . . Not unnaturally what is happening to you seems freighted with significance, beside which the humdrum of everyday life seems trivial. All these things you see with an immediacy of vision that leads you to say to yourself, "Now I am seeing for the first time, seeing direct, without the intervention of mortal eyes." (Wasson, Hofman & Ruck, 2008)

From Wasson's reports, Albert Hoffman became interested in the mushrooms and extracted their chemical properties. His employer, the pharmaceutical company Sandoz, then manufactured and marketed a synthetic form of psilocybin (called Indocybin) for psychiatric purposes until it became illegal in 1965.

Psilocybin: The Headache Medicine?

A 2006 study examined the therapeutic effects of LSD and psilocybin in the treatment of chronic cluster headaches, a condition in which people experience multiple intense headaches for extended periods of time. The study found both LSD and psilocybin to reduce future headache episodes more than mainstream medicine (Frood, 2006).

In fact, "magic mushrooms" aborted attacks in 85% of users as well, an astounding rate for this often "untreatable" condition.

The headache-treating benefits of mushrooms are thought to be due to the calming effect that the drug has on certain brain areas. MRI mapping of users during a "trip" has revealed reduced activity in the medial prefrontal cortex (mPFC) as well as anterior and posterior cingulate cortices, which is consistent with the subjectively reported calming aftereffects of the drug (Carhart-Harris et al., 2012a). This neurological soothing may indicate substantial therapeutic potential for the treatment of posttrauma disorders, stress, and depression, all of which are associated with hyperactivity in the mPFC. (Carhart-Harris et al., 2012b)

The effects of psilocybin are relatively similar to those of LSD, although the intensity of the effects may be weaker and the duration of effect is shorter, lasting roughly 4 to 6 hours (Weil & Rosen, 1998). Lower doses of psilocybin "yield a pleasant experience, relaxation, and some body sensations," while higher doses "cause considerable perceptual and body image changes with hallucinations in some individuals" (Ray & Ksir, 1993, p. 336). Although many regard psilocybin as a "natural, harmless, nonaddictive drug that does not require paraphernalia such as pipes or needles" (Gahlinger, 2001, p. 272), what is sold on the street as psilocybin is often something else, such as store-bought mushrooms laced with LSD or PCP. For example, one study analyzed 886 samples of substances sold as psilocybin and found 35% to contain other drugs, mostly PCP and LSD, 37% to have no psychoactive properties, and 28% to be authentic (Renfroe & Messinger, 1985), and recent qualitative evidence suggests that a considerable portion do not contain psilocybin today (McCaughan, Carlson, Falck, & Harvey, 2005).

Mushrooms containing psilocybin are common in the wild in North America, particularly on the west coast from California to British Columbia (Gahlinger, 2001). However, no one should attempt to pick mushrooms for consumption without extensive knowledge and experience, as there are many species of wild mushrooms, many that look quite similar, and some are so toxic that they can cause death or permanent organ damage within hours of ingestion (Gahlinger, 2001; Weil & Rosen, 1998).

As with many of the drugs we have discussed, there is interest in the value of psilocybin for medicinal purposes. Research on the drug has examined whether it may be useful for the treatment of mental illness, with some positive results. For example, as Dr. David Nichols notes, "It remains unclear how these drugs exert their action in the brain, but anecdotal evidence and some earlier studies indicate they may help a variety of psychiatric conditions" (as quoted in Eisner, 2001). Relatedly, psilocybin has also been used in the treatment of posttraumatic stress disorder and similar conditions arising from severe trauma. Research has found that the use of psilocybin just once can produce long-term psychological benefits in those suffering from extreme stress or trauma; nearly all research subjects in the study reported sustained life improvements 2 months later, long after the drug left their systems (Griffiths et al., 2006). A long-term follow-up with those patients found that the majority considered the experiences to be among the most important and positive in their lives, with many reporting increased spirituality, while none reported any side effects or psychological changes (Griffiths et al., 2011). This has led many medical experts to call for greater research opportunities on the therapeutic applications of psilocybin through a rescheduling of the substance.

Peyote and Mescaline

Peyote refers to a small, spineless cactus that grows in Texas and northern Mexico, and mescaline is the most powerful (although not only) psychoactive compound present in peyote. Although the entire peyote cactus is psychoactive, it is the top of the plant that is harvested for its psychoactive properties, being sliced into thin sections and then dried to make peyote or mescal "buttons." Although the consumption of peyote is illegal in the United States (excepting members of the Native American Church, discussed below), there are numerous hallucinogenic cacti in the Americas whose consumption is not prohibited by law. These include the Doña Ana (or Doñana) and San Pedro cacti of the American Southwest (also sighted in gardening stores), which have effects that are relatively comparable to peyote (Gahlinger, 2001).

Similar to psilocybin, peyote has been used by the indigenous peoples of North America for thousands of years. Europeans were exposed to peyote when Cortés conquered the Aztec civilizations of central Mexico in 1519, and despite the subsequent attempts of the Spaniards to destroy the historical record of the Aztecs, some documents remain. These include the writings of Bernardino de Sahagún, a holy man and naturalist who accompanied the conquistadors and worked with Aztec physicians to chronicle the medical practices of the Aztecs. His records include a discussion of the Aztec use of peyote, "which they called *péyotl*, and those who drank it took it in place of wine" (de Sahagún, 1938, as cited in Gahlinger, 2001, p. 397).

As they had been with psilocybin, the conquering Spaniards were fearful and suspicious of peyote, declaring the drug "the work of the Devil" and prohibiting its use in 1620 (Leonard, 1942, as cited in Gahlinger, 2001, p. 398). Despite this, like psilocybin, the use of peyote continued and was eventually adopted by various Native American tribes in the United States. Today, the drug is consumed by a limited number of recreational users, but the vast majority of peyote use is confined to the religious ceremonies of the Native American Church (Ray & Ksir, 2004).

The Native American Church (NAC) emerged near the end of the 19th century among the Kiowa tribe and under the leadership of John Wilson, also known as Big Moon. By this time, the American Indian populations in the United States had been almost completely annihilated, concluding with the Wounded Knee massacre in 1890. In response to these events, John Wilson and other leaders began preaching nonviolence and accommodation as the only way for Indians to survive the colonization of America. Combining traditional Native beliefs with some elements of Christianity, the teachings of the NAC became known as the Peyote Road. In these teachings, peyote was seen as a holy sacrament, to be consumed like the body of Christ, and the drug was thought to be able to connect the user to God and to help cure physical and spiritual disease (Gahlinger, 2001).

The organization of the NAC as an official institution is traced to a Smithsonian anthropologist, James Mooney, who was sent to the Oklahoma Territory in 1891 to study Indian culture. In the course of his work, Mooney participated in peyote ceremonies and became convinced that peyote could provide a source of spiritual salvation for Indians. Mooney organized a meeting of Indian leaders and proposed that they unite to form the NAC, which now numbers roughly 300,000 members (Gahlinger, 2001). The organization of a formal (i.e., government-recognized) church was important, as it meant that the religious practices of this group, including the sacramental use of peyote, would be protected under the Constitution's First and Fourteenth Amendments regarding religious freedom.

Critics have condemned the religious use of peyote by American Indians, often arguing that

Peyote Buttons

it is simply an "excuse to use drugs." However, it is important to recognize that unlike the recreational use of psychoactive drugs, which often occurs in a very loose and unregulated fashion, the use of peyote by members of the NAC occurs in a very formal and respected ceremonial process. As Beauvais (1998) notes with respect to this:

> The ceremony itself has a prescribed structure, and the leader, called a "road-man," makes certain that the rules and forms are precisely followed. Peyote is used to facilitate communication and is not ingested to produce hallucinations. The roadman will use a variety of sensory stimuli (e.g., cedar smoke and sprinkled water) to prevent participants from drifting off into a disconnected state of consciousness. Clearly, the powerful and ritualized experience of a peyote ceremony cannot be likened to out-of-control drunkenness. (p. 253)

It is also important to note that the use of peyote in this context tends to discourage the use of other mind-altering drugs (including alcohol) for recreational purposes (Beauvais, 1998).

Since 1965, the religious use of peyote by American Indians has been protected by U.S. federal law. Although many states enacted laws that were consistent with this federal regulation, many other states did not, and the constitutionality of prohibiting religious peyote use by Indians at the state level was challenged in the 1990 case of *Employment Division of Oregon v. Smith*, 494 U.S. 872. The case involved two followers of the NAC who lost their jobs as a result of peyote use and were seeking employment compensation. The Supreme Court decided in *Smith* that the use of peyote was not protected by the First Amendment, but this decision was in effect overturned with a 1994 amendment to the American Indian Religious Freedom Act. This amendment prevents both federal and state governments from prohibiting "the use, possession, or transportation of peyote by an Indian for bona fide traditional ceremonial purposes in connection with the practice of a traditional Indian religion . . ." (American Indian Religious Freedom Act Amendments of 1994).

Mescaline and peyote are often discussed interchangeably despite the fact that these are distinct drugs. As noted, mescaline is the component of peyote that is primarily responsible for the hallucinogenic effects of the cactus, but there are actually more than 30 different psychoactive alkaloids in the peyote cactus (Ray & Ksir, 2004). Mescaline was isolated from peyote in 1896 by Arthur Heffter and later synthesized in 1918, but it only reached any widespread degree of use during the 1960s and remains relatively rare today (most drugs sold on the street as mescaline are actually LSD or LSD mixed with PCP; Gahlinger, 2001).

The effects of peyote and mescaline are similar to those of LSD and psilocybin and typically involve feelings of euphoria at lower doses and hallucinations at higher doses, along with physical effects including pupil dilation and increased body temperature, pulse rate, and blood pressure (Ray & Ksir, 2004). However, one distinct feature of mescaline, and particularly peyote, is that it often produces nausea and vomiting. Although some claim that with repeated use, vomiting becomes less frequent (Weil & Rosen, 1998), others note that vomiting remains common and is even encouraged in ceremonial settings as an important part of the religious ritual (Gahlinger, 2001). For example, Gahlinger comments that "throwing up, rather than attempting to hold it in, is encouraged as a purging of both physical and psychological ills" (Gahlinger, 2001, p. 410).

There is little or no evidence of physical problems, dependence, or serious adverse reactions to peyote. However, the drug has been argued to have several medicinal applications, the most notable being as a treatment for alcoholism, particularly in the context of the NAC (Albaugh & Anderson, 1974; Blum, Futterman, & Pascarosa, 1977). Although the nature of this effect is not well understood, the renowned psychiatrist Dr. Karl Menninger has commented that peyote "is a better antidote to alcohol than anything [the] American Medical Association, and the public health services have come up with" (as cited in Gahlinger, 2001, p. 411). Research on the potential efficacy of peyote as a treatment for alcoholism continues today, including in a study conducted by Dr. Harrison Pope of Harvard Medical School (Eisner, 2001).

Salvia

Salvia, short for *Salvia divinorum*, is a member of the mint family and is a powerful naturally occurring hallucinogen (Johnson et al., 2011). The plant's fresh leaves have been ingested by Mazatec shamans in the Oaxaca region of present-day Mexico to inspire spiritual visions for centuries (Siebert, 1994).

Mainstream recreational use of salvia, also known as Magic Mint, Ska Maria Pastora, and Sally D, generally involves smoking dried leaves. Use has increased in recent years. As of this writing, salvia remains legal in many states and is widely available in tobacco and head shops in those states and also online. Data from recent Monitoring the Future surveys indicate salvia is most popular among teenagers and young adults, with about 6% of high school seniors and about 3% of college students and young adults reporting past year use (Johnston et al., 2011).

The active ingredient, salvinorin A, yields effects similar to those of psilocybin, PCP, and ketamine. Specifically, users report a range of hallucinogenic effects, particularly spatial disorientation, dream-like visions, excited laughter, and strong visual perception alteration (Johnson et al., 2011 Siebert, 1994;). For most, salvia acts quickly (producing effects within a minute that peak after 2 minutes), with effects that are very intense, though the experience tends to end within an hour and produces no negative physiological reactions during the high (Johnston et al., 2011a). Double-blind, placebo-controlled experimental work has confirmed previous self-reports of widely positive subjective experiences as well as negative reactions to the disorienting effects of the drug in a small portion of subjects (Baggott et al., 2010; Johnson et al., 2011).

As a selective kappa opioid agonist, salvia acts upon pain centers differently from other hallucinogens or opioids, leading some researchers to conclude that it is nonaddictive and offers medical potential as a pain reliever or mood stabilizer. (Hooker et al., 2008; Johnston et al., 2011a)

DMT and Bufotenine

DMT and its close chemical relative bufotenine are hallucinogenic compounds similar to psilocybin and LSD. These drugs have been used by indigenous peoples of South and Central America for centuries. First synthesized in 1931, DMT is naturally present in numerous plant and animal species, including toads, moth larvae, grubs, fish, mushrooms, trees, vines, and grasses (as well as being found naturally in the body; Gahlinger, 2001). DMT will have no effect if orally ingested because it is broken down quickly by stomach acid, but if injected or smoked, DMT has a powerful hallucinogenic effect. For example,

Salvia divinorum

experienced users of hallucinogens such as Allen Ginsberg and Richard Alpert (who popularized LSD) found DMT to be "too powerful and uncontrollable for enjoyment" (as quoted in Gahlinger, 2001, p. 265). DMT can be consumed in yage, a drink made from an Amazonian vine, and yopo, a snuff used by certain South American Indian tribes, but the most well-known way to consume DMT is toad licking and toad smoking (Weil & Rosen, 1998). Bufotenine is the form of DMT contained in the venom secreted by many species of *Bufo* toads and has led to the interesting and comic (though probably not to users) practice of toad licking. Toad licking can be traced to 1935, when one species of *Bufo* toad, *Bufo marinus* (indigenous to North and South America and commonly known as the cane toad), was introduced to Australia in an attempt to kill greyback beetles, which were destroying the sugarcane crop (Gahlinger, 2001). Until this point, Australia had no toad species, and the introduction of the cane toad has turned out to be an ecological disaster. Not only are cane toads totally ineffective at controlling the greyback beetle population (they cannot jump very high, and the beetles are rarely on the ground), they reproduce prodigiously (up to 35,000 eggs per clutch) and have almost no natural predators (Queensland Department of Natural Resources, 2004). As a consequence, their numbers have massively increased, creating substantial problems for Australia's indigenous species. The venom contained in their skin has minimized their predation by Australia's extensive reptile species, as when caught (e.g., by a snake), the venom of the toad often kills the predator (Queensland Department of Natural Resources, 2004).

Although smoking toad is a rare phenomenon, arrests for possession of DMT are not unheard of. One arrestee was 41-year-old schoolteacher and Boy Scout troop leader Robert Shephard, who was apprehended in California in 1994 for possessing bufotenine (in the form of his toads). Shephard was charged with "possessing a toad for illicit purposes," and his four toads—Brian, Peter, Hans, and Franz—were confiscated by the police (Richards, 1994). According to Gahlinger (2001), this charge of "possessing a toad for illicit purposes" was the first since 1579, when a British woman was similarly charged, declared a witch, and then executed.

The practice of licking these toads began in Australia in 1960 when a newspaper jokingly reported that the slime of the toad was hallucinogenic and youth began to try to consume it by licking the skin of the toads (Gahlinger, 2001). Not only is the taste reported to be exceedingly disgusting, but, as mentioned, orally consumed DMT is not psychoactive—so the people who engaged in toad licking not only failed to get high, but the venom typically made them very sick (Carillo, 1990; Horgan, 1990). As Dr. Andrew Weil, an ethnopharmacologist and respected authority on drugs, has noted on this misguided practice, "I would think you could poison yourself pretty badly before you got high licking toads" (as quoted in Richards, 1994).

Conversely, smoking the venom of certain *Bufo* toads can provide a powerful psychoactive effect, although this practice is rare. A species commonly used in order to smoke toad is the Sonoran Desert Toad (*Bufo alvarius*), which, as the name indicates, is found in the Sonoran Desert regions of California, Arizona, and northern Mexico. The venom of the toad can be harvested off the skin and smoked, which provides an intense hallucinogenic high. This experience is described in a 1994 article published in the *Journal of Ethnopharmacology*, which relates the personal experiences of Wade Davis and Dr. Andrew Weil (mentioned above) with smoking toad. As Davis notes:

> Shortly after inhalation I experienced warm flushing sensations, a sense of wonder and well-being, strong auditory hallucinations, which included an insect-cicada sound that ran across my mind and seemed to link my body to the earth. Though I was indoors, there was a sense of the feel of the earth, the dry desert soil passing through my fingers, the stars at midday, the scent of cactus and sage, the feel of dry leaves through hands. Strong visual hallucinations in orblike brilliance, diamond patterns that undulated across my visual field. The experience was in every sense pleasant, with no disturbing physical symptoms, no nausea, perhaps a slight sense of increased heart rate. Warm waves coursed up and down my body. The effects lasted only a few minutes but a pleasant afterglow continued for almost an hour. (as quoted in Richards, 1994)

Others have described the experience as more powerful and less pleasant, with Dr. Weil noting that "I've seen people take one deep puff and fall over backward as they exhale" (as quoted in Richards, 1994).

PCP AND KETAMINE

PCP and ketamine are often grouped with the hallucinogens, but these substances are distinct from those discussed above. PCP and ketamine are synthetic compounds that have numerous effects, including effects that are typical of the depressants, stimulants, and hallucinogens. Medically, PCP and ketamine have been used as anesthetics, and ketamine (marketed as Ketalar) remains in use as a surgical anesthetic for humans because it allows major surgery without paralyzing the muscles used for breathing (Gahlinger, 2001). PCP was first synthesized in 1926, but it was not until 1957 that Parke-Davis marketed it as a surgical anesthetic under the trade name Sernyl (Gahlinger, 2001). PCP was used to anesthetize humans during surgery, and early trials of the drug yielded good results—patients felt no pain and remembered nothing of their surgical procedure despite remaining conscious during the surgery (Ray & Ksir, 2004). However, the use of PCP as a surgical anesthetic in humans was short lived. After surgery, many patients complained of delirium, visual disturbances, and delusions, and roughly 15% demonstrated a "prolonged confusional psychosis," characterized by depersonalization, depression, intense anxiety, and feelings of unreality, which lasted up to 4 days after the administration of the drug (Ray & Ksir, 2004). As a consequence, the use of the drug on humans was discontinued in 1965, but it was reintroduced in 1967 as Sernylan, a veterinary anesthetic. As Weil and Rosen (1998) have commented, perhaps this was because animals were less likely to report the negative side effects of the drug to their doctors.

The use of PCP by veterinarians was discontinued in 1978 (U.S. Department of Justice, 2005), but as the drug became available as a veterinary anesthetic, it also became widely available on the black market and experienced its greatest use historically. It has been marketed under names such as peace pill, angel dust, hog, and trank, and many users of PCP have consumed it unknowingly. Because it is inexpensive, easy to make, and possesses powerful psychoactive effects, PCP has been sold to buyers as synthetic THC, psilocybin (supermarket mushrooms treated with PCP), and mescaline. It is also sprinkled on marijuana or herbs such as oregano or parsley and sold as "killer joints" or "sherms"—so called because they "hit the user like a Sherman tank" (Ray & Ksir, 2004, p. 437).

The effects of PCP include a decreased sensitivity to pain and tactile feeling; impaired coordination; dizziness and nausea; feelings of being disconnected from one's body; distorted perceptions of time and space; apathy; and difficulty in concentrating and thinking (Weil & Rosen, 1998). Although its dependence potential is low, PCP overdose can result in convulsions, coma, and potentially death (Weil & Rosen, 1998). The effects of PCP have received a great deal of attention, particularly as users have supposedly engaged in violent, criminal behavior of an almost superhuman nature while under the influence of the drug. For example, as noted by Ray and Ksir (2004),

> Every cop knows for a fact the story about the PCP user who was so violent, had such superhuman strength, and was so insensitive to pain that he was shot twenty-eight times (or a similar large number of times) before he fell. Although everyone "knows" that this happened no one can tell you exactly when or where. (p. 438)

With respect to this, it is important to recognize that there is nothing in the chemical properties of PCP that makes otherwise normal people turn into violent criminals or lunatics (although this has been the rationale behind banning many drugs). As noted by Weil and Rosen (1998), "tendencies to criminal violence are inherent in certain people, not in certain drugs" (p. 138). Further, as noted by Ray and Ksir (2004), while on PCP, "Most users do not report feeling violent and feel so uncoordinated that they can't imagine starting a fight" (p. 438).

What it is important to remember with respect to the supposed connection of PCP and violence is that PCP is a powerful anesthetic, which was previously used to perform serious surgery on people while they remained conscious. This level of dis-association from reality, combined with the fact that PCP provides a high degree of insensitivity to pain, is likely why the drug has such a negative reputation. Specifically, many of the problems between law enforcement and PCP users likely result from the fact that an individual under the influence of PCP may have no idea what he is doing (recall that surgical patients had no recollection of their surgery or talking to the doctors while anesthetized with PCP), and these individuals may be so insensitive to pain that typical police restraint methods are rendered ineffective. However, as Ray and Ksir (2004) comment, "one might question how different this is from arresting a violent drunk who is 'feeling no pain'" (p. 438).

"Robo-Dosing"

Further illustrating the importance of public perception for the legal status of a drug is the case of dextromethorphan, also called DXM or DM. DXM has effects similar to those of PCP and ketamine when consumed in sufficient doses, and the drug is present in many popular brands of cough medicine such as Robitussin. Although the labeling of cold products containing DXM indicates that "no more than 120 mg should be taken in a 24-hour period," when a single dose of 300 mg or more is taken, it may cause "dissociative-type hallucinations similar to those produced by PCP" (Ray & Ksir, 2004, p. 437). This practice is sometimes called "Robo-dosing," and despite the fact that this generates the same effects as PCP (often portrayed as the "most dangerous drug known"), products containing DXM are available over the counter, to anybody, in almost any supermarket.

Ketamine has effects that are very similar to those of PCP, but the drug is less potent than PCP—100 milligrams of ketamine produces an effect roughly equivalent to 25 milligrams of PCP (Gahlinger, 2001). Discovered by American pharmacist Calvin Stevens in 1961, ketamine remains a surgical anesthetic and is also employed in veterinary medicine (marketed as Ketajet, Ketaset, and Vetelar; Gahlinger, 2001). Exploratory research has found ketamine to be useful in the treatment of PTSD and depression (see box). However, outside of its role as an anesthetic, the medical use of ketamine on humans remains limited because of its psychoactive effects, which, like those of PCP, include feelings of disassociation from the body and reality (Weil & Rosen, 1998). The fact that ketamine and PCP have almost identical effects is interesting, because the drugs are viewed very differently by the public. This is likely due to the fact that the recreational use of ketamine is primarily among clubbers and young professionals and, as a consequence, the drug is not viewed with nearly the same concern and alarm as PCP (Weil & Rosen, 1998).

Ketamine and Depression

Recent research has found ketamine to be effective in the treatment of depression. Traditional antidepressant medications (e.g., Prozac) are designed to affect the reuptake of serotonin in the brain. Ketamine works in a completely different manner, activating the glutamine system in the brain. The belief is that ketamine increases communication among existing neurons by creating new neural connections, which has a much faster effect on depression than existing antidepressant medication. (Hamilton, 2012)

MARIJUANA

Marijuana is the most widely used illegal drug in the world, and we discuss it separately due to its numerous and distinct effects. It has some properties of the stimulants and depressants, but it is neither of these, and although it has been called a narcotic, mostly for political purposes, it is very distinct from these drugs as well. Marijuana has also been called a hallucinogen, although whether it is capable of producing hallucinations is debated, and if this occurs, it is only at extremely high doses (Earleywine, 2002). In sum, marijuana is a distinct drug and belongs in a category by itself.

There is some debate about whether there are one, two, three, or more species of the *Cannabis* plant, which is interesting, as laws mention only *Cannabis sativa* (Ray & Ksir, 2004). Botanists including Richard Shultes and Richard Anderson have concluded there are actually three distinct species of the cannabis plant, the commonly known *Cannabis sativa*, which is taller with narrow leaves; *Cannabis indica*, which is shorter and has wider leaves; and *Cannabis ruderalis*, which is short and branchless. (Anderson, 1980; Schultes, Klein, Plowman, & Lockwood, 1974)

The term *marijuana* (or *marihuana*) actually refers to a preparation of the leafy material of *Cannabis* plants for smoking, although technically the entire plant is psychoactive (*cannabis* and *marijuana* are used interchangeably). The primary psychoactive agent in cannabis is delta 9-tetrahydrocannabinol (THC), which is concentrated in the resin of the cannabis plant. Because the resin (and thus THC) concentration is highest in the flowering tops or buds of the plant, it is this part of the plant that has the strongest psychoactive effect and is most commonly smoked.

There is less THC on the leaves of the plant (sometimes called "shake"), and there is so little THC on the fibrous stalks of the cannabis plant that it is useless for psychoactive purposes (Ray & Ksir, 2004).

Although it has no psychoactive effects, this fibrous material of the cannabis plant, called hemp, has many other uses. Hemp fibers were likely the first to be used by humans. Archeological evidence indicates that hemp fibers were used to decorate clay pots dating to 8000 BC, and by comparison, linen dates to roughly 3500 BC and cotton to 2500 BC (Earleywine, 2002). Hemp has many practical applications, including its use in the production of cloth, paper, food, oils, soap, and shampoo (Earleywine, 2002).

The earliest written record of using cannabis for its medicinal effects is found in a pharmacy book written by the Chinese emperor Shen Nung in 2737 BC, who called cannabis "the Liberator of Sin" (Ray & Ksir, 2004). Other early writings on the drug can be found in the *Atharvaveda*, a holy text written in India in approximately 1400 BC, which noted that the god Shiva took pity on humans and brought marijuana down from the Himalayas to relieve stress and provide pleasure and good health (Earleywine, 2002; Gahlinger, 2001). By 1000 AD, the use of marijuana had spread to North Africa and the Muslim world, and an Arabic text entitled *On Poisons* written about this time warned that hashish "renders one blind and mute, eventually leading to continuous wretching (*sic*) and death" (as cited in Earleywine, 2002, p. 11). In 1484, Pope Innocent VIII condemned the use of cannabis as "a tool of the Satanic Mass" (Gahlinger, 2001), and when Napoleon invaded Egypt in the early 19th century, he forbade his troops to engage in the use of hashish. By the 1830s and 1840s, hashish was being widely used in France and other parts of continental Europe.

Clinical trials have demonstrated that alternative methods of marijuana consumption can eliminate virtually all smoke-related risks posed by marijuana. Many medical patients are now receiving THC by ingesting it within other foods or vaporizing the buds instead of smoking them. Results from a clinical trial showed that respiratory ailments previously linked to marijuana became almost nil when switching to a vaporized delivery of the drug (Earleywine & Barnwell, 2007).

The benefits of vaporization are created by heating the marijuana to a temperature high enough to break apart the cannabinoids (180–190 degrees Celsius), but not high enough to produce the toxins that come from combustion (about 230 degrees Celsius), thus suppressing most toxins.

The Pilgrims took cannabis with them to New England in 1632, and in 1639, in order to meet the need for hemp in England, Virginia colonists were required by law to plant and harvest a certain number of cannabis plants each year (Gahlinger, 2001). The production of cannabis as a source of fiber and cloth gradually increased in the colonies so that by the time America declared its independence in 1776, roughly 90% of all clothing in the United States was made from cannabis (Gahlinger, 2001).

Recreational use of marijuana in the United States began in the early 1900s, with the drug being introduced largely by Mexican immigrants and migrant workers and by soldiers returning from World War I (Weil & Rosen, 1998). Early on, marijuana use was especially popular among jazz musicians and those who frequented jazz clubs, being referred to as "tea" by this group. In the years that followed, the use of marijuana spread across diverse populations, but the perceived association between marijuana and jazz persisted over time. For example, in 1948, the Senate asked Federal Bureau of Narcotics Director Harry Anslinger who the current users of marijuana were and Anslinger replied, "Musicians. And I'm not speaking about good musicians, but the jazz type" (as quoted in Gahlinger, 2001, p. 36). The fact that most people believed marijuana to be used almost entirely by stigmatized groups such as jazz musicians and minorities was instrumental in the establishment of policies directed to criminalize marijuana use in the years that followed.

As noted earlier, the effects of marijuana are diverse. There is general consensus that users of cannabis experience changes in perception and an intensification of all the senses. Common perceptual sensations and behaviors associated with the drug include a sense of well-being, feelings of relaxation, a distorted sense of time and distance, laughter, talkativeness, and increased sociability when it is consumed in a social setting (SAMHSA, 1997). The drug may also result in paranoia, impaired memory for recent events, difficulty concentrating, impaired motor coordination, slowed reaction time, and altered peripheral vision (SAMHSA, 1997).

While the abovementioned effects certainly occur, it is important to note that they are not consistent across users of the substance. Weil (1986) goes as far as to suggest that marijuana is simply an "active placebo," contending that cannabis itself does not create but simply triggers the mental state that individual users define as being high. As noted in our discussion of Becker's *Outsiders* in Chapter 2, most first-time marijuana users do not feel high or stoned, at least partly because they have yet to identify and label the effects. Pollan (2001) provides further support for this by noting that the psychological experiences associated with marijuana use are far too varied, not only from individual to individual but also from occasion to occasion, to be explained purely in terms of the chemical effects of the substance.

There are few acute, physical effects of marijuana, although users of the substance will experience a moderate increase in their heart rate and typically a reddening of the eyes and drying of the mouth and eyes (Weil, 1986). Although physical withdrawal symptoms are not associated with the cessation of marijuana use (even for long-term heavy use), tolerance to the substance can occur (Weil & Rosen, 1998). The specific action of marijuana on the brain is still under study, but it is pleasurable at least partially because its active ingredient, THC, mimics "a natural substance produced in the body that has marijuana-like effects when administered to animals" (Ray & Ksir, 2004, p. 462). This cannabis-like substance in the body, or endocannabinoid, was named anandamide (after *ananda*, a Sanskrit word meaning bliss), and subsequent research continues to investigate how THC is related to this substance. Already connections have been found linking the cannabinoid system with everything from the "runner's high" (Platforma, 2012) to impulsive behavior (Knight, 2012).

Much of the debate surrounding marijuana regards the claim that it is a gateway drug or a substance that will cause its users to go on to harder drugs such as cocaine and heroin. We discussed the gateway argument in more detail in Chapter 1, but briefly, there is no evidence that marijuana use pharmacologically causes people to go on to use heavier drugs. The very small association between marijuana use and hard drug use has to do with the populations under consideration and the current legal status of marijuana, which requires users to purchase it in illicit markets where they may also be offered other drugs. As Weil and Rosen (1998) note of the myth of the gateway effect:

> Even in heaviest usage marijuana does not lead to heroin or any other drug. Many junkies smoked marijuana before they tried opiates, but few marijuana users take narcotics. Many junkies also drank alcohol heavily before they discovered heroin, sometimes at very young ages, yet no one argues that alcohol leads to heroin. The reason, of course, is that alcohol enjoys general social approval, while marijuana is a "bad" drug and so invites false attributes of causality. (p. 120)

The argument has also been made that marijuana is very harmful to the health of users, and thus the drug should remain illegal and not be used for any medical purpose. Again, this argument is problematic when considering the risks posed by alternative medications. In terms of acute toxicity, there has never been a fatal overdose attributed to marijuana despite its extremely widespread use, and the reason for this is that it is virtually impossible to fatally overdose on marijuana. While the therapeutic ratio of barbiturates is about 3 to 1 and heroin about 5 to 1 depending on potency, experiments on animals indicate the therapeutic ratio of marijuana is about *40,000 to 1* (Gahlinger, 2001). In practical terms, at the very minimum, a 160-pound person would require all the THC in 900 1-gram joints in a relatively short period of time to reach a fatal dose (Earleywine, 2002).

The primary chronic health concern associated with marijuana use is the potential for lung cancer and emphysema. Some of the toxins in marijuana smoke are known to be carcinogenic in other contexts (e.g., ammonia), though THC itself is not carcinogenic, and at present there is only limited or equivocal evidence regarding an increased risk for various smoking-related illnesses due to marijuana (Bowles et al., 2012). A related issue is whether there is an elevated potential for lung cancer among marijuana smokers because marijuana users tend to hold marijuana smoke in for longer periods of time than they do tobacco smoke. Thus, the lungs may be exposed to carcinogenic chemicals such as ammonia, hydrogen cyanide, and nitric oxide for longer periods of time, enhancing risk (Moir et al., 2007). However, it is important to recognize that very few people, even heavy users, smoke marijuana in the way that tobacco is typically consumed (e.g., consuming 20 or more cigarettes per day; Earleywine, 2002). Although subject to ongoing debate, the available research in this area suggests that marijuana smokers are at an elevated risk for lung

Research on a potential link between marijuana use and cancer includes a growing number of large scale studies, like that from Hashibe and colleagues (2006), who studied the association of marijuana and cancer in a population of more than 1,000 control subjects and more than 1,200 cancer cases. The study found that subjects who used marijuana for more than 30 years experienced an increased risk of lung and digestive tract cancers, but this difference disappeared when controlling for other risk factors like cigarette smoking and lifestyle. More importantly, when examining only those marijuana users that had never used tobacco, the odds of getting pharyngeal, laryngeal, esophageal, and lung cancer were all significantly lower among marijuana users of any level, while there was an increase only in the odds of getting oral cancer and only with lengthy use. (Hashibe et al., 2006)

cancer and smoking-related illnesses, but their level of risk does not approximate that experienced by cigarette smokers.

Another concern raised regarding marijuana use is a potential connection to serious mental illness, including schizophrenia. There has been extensive research on this topic, and while an association exists, it remains debated whether the link is causal. It has been speculated that marijuana use may be associated with schizophrenia in one of more of the following ways: Marijuana use may (1) cause schizophrenia use in some patients, (2) trigger schizophrenia, but only among those already predisposed to the disease, (3) exacerbate the symptoms of schizophrenia in those that have the disease, or (4) be more common among those with the disease, consistent with the self-medication hypothesis (Bostwick, 2012).

Any association between marijuana use and schizophrenia that may exist is clearly not strong. This is illustrated most clearly with basic trend data: When rates of marijuana use skyrocketed in the 1960s and 1970s in countries such as the United States and England, the rates of schizophrenia were either stable or dropping (Lindsay, 2010; Szalavitz, 2010). When considering research in this area, it is important to note that schizophrenia is quite rare, affecting roughly 1% of the population (or less; Hickman, Vickerman, Macleod, Lewis, Zammit, Kirkbride, & Jones, 2009; Szalavitz, 2010). It may be that any connection between marijuana use and schizophrenia is limited to or much more likely to be present among those who use marijuana heavily at young ages (Manrique-Garcia, Zammit, & Dalman, 2012). Recent research by Hickman and colleagues put the risk into perspective by considering the number of marijuana users in the British population, the likelihood of developing schizophrenia (in England, at or below 0.080% early in adulthood, declining thereafter), and the risk that marijuana use causes schizophrenia based on available research. The study concluded that in order prevent a single case of schizophrenia, it would be necessary to stop 2,800 heavy cannabis users in young men and more than 5,000 heavy cannabis users in young women. Among light cannabis users, the authors concluded it was necessary to stop more than 10,000 young men and

Medical Applications of Marijuana

There are myriad medical applications for marijuana including for the treatment of glaucoma; migraine and chronic headaches; relieving the pain, nausea, vomiting, and weight loss associated with surgery, cancer, and AIDS; Tourette's syndrome; autoimmune disorders including multiple sclerosis, rheumatoid arthritis, and inflammatory bowel disease; and to provide relief to those suffering from seizures, depression, and insomnia, among other conditions (Bostwick, 2012; Cohen, 2010; Grotenhermen & Muller-Vahl, 2012; Haney et al., 2007; Lucas, 2012; Molina et al., 2011; Parolaro & Massi, 2008). Importantly, research has found marijuana to produce these outcomes with less severe side effects than current pharmaceuticals used to treat such conditions. (Wang, Collet, Shap & Ware, 2008).

almost 30,000 young women to prevent one case of schizophrenia (Hickman, Vickerman, Macleod, Lewis, Zammit, Kirkbride, & Jones, 2009). So, based on the available research on the topic, it appears that a relationship between marijuana use and schizophrenia may in fact exist, but it is a very weak relationship.

The vast medical applications and the comparative safety of the drug when compared to alternative treatments has prompted many physicians, medical practitioners, and policy makers to argue that marijuana should be reclassified as a Schedule II controlled drug (indicating a substance has medical value and is acceptable for medical prescription). Recently, the American Medical Association followed suit, adopting a resolution requesting the government review its classification of marijuana, as research on the medical applications of the drug can only be fully realized in the United States if the Schedule I status of marijuana is downgraded. This seems unlikely to occur in the near future. In fact, the federal government's classification of marijuana has instead been reinforced in recent years, as the DEA officially reproclaimed its stance claiming no medicinal value and high risk. DEA Administrator Michele M. Leonhart's letter announcing the decision claimed it was due to a lack of clinical research evidence, stating that "the known risks of marijuana use have not been shown to be outweighed by specific benefits in well-controlled clinical trials that scientifically evaluate safety and efficacy" (as quoted in Hoeffel, 2011). All of this has worked to tie researchers' hands, further reinforcing a 2005 report by the FDA announcing that it had established definitively that marijuana lacks medicinal value (FDA, 2006). Not only did the report contradict research evidence, it also relied upon antiquated and inaccurate arguments, including the gateway drug theory (as reported in Spiesel, 2006).

In shoring up these decisions, the federal government also recently threatened cultivation operations legally permitted in some states with federal prosecution should they continue operating, in the process offering veiled threats to city officials in support of these tax-generating farms (Hoeffel, 2009). Perhaps most notably, the meddling by federal authorities in states' regulation of medicinal marijuana prompted officials from several states to write President Obama, chastising him for breaking his promise to avoid federal enforcement that tramples states' rights (Graves, 2012). The letter was signed by legislators from California, Washington, New Mexico, Maine, and Colorado, and it followed a related request to change marijuana's legal status to Schedule II by two state governors. In December 2011, following threats from federal authorities to prosecute Washington state employees with legal medicinal prescriptions, Governor Gregoire was joined by Rhode Island's Lincoln Chaffee in officially requesting the legal downgrading of marijuana. Gregoire explained, "[W]e have patients who really either feel like they're criminals or may be engaged in some criminal activity, and really are legitimate patients who want medicinal marijuana." She was echoed by Chaffee, a former Republican turned Independent whose involvement marked this as a bipartisan effort, who explained, "It is time to show compassion and time to show common sense" (as quoted in Cooper, 2011).

At the conclusion of a 2-year public hearing on the efficacy and safety of medical marijuana in 1988, the Drug Enforcement Agency's chief administrative law judge, Judge Francis Young, reached the conclusion that marijuana was safe and medically useful. Judge Young declared, "Marijuana is one of the safest therapeutically active substances known to man. (T)he provisions of the (Controlled Substances) Act permit and require the transfer of marijuana from Schedule I to Schedule II" (U.S. Drug Enforcement Administration, 1988, p. 57).

Despite this, Judge Young's order that marijuana be moved to Schedule II was subsequently overruled by the Drug Enforcement Agency. Today, marijuana remains classified a Schedule I drug in the United States—a classification that declares a drug to have no medical value and a high potential for abuse.

Spice/Synthetic Marijuana

K2 and Spice

"Spice" refers to a wide variety of herbal mixtures that produce experiences similar to marijuana (NIDA, 2012). The drug is sold under many names, including K2, Spice, Black Mamba, Gorrilaz, and fake weed among others, typically including a warning noting that the product is "not for human consumption" (often the products are sold as "incense"; NIDA, 2012). The products sold as spice contain dried, shredded plant material from one or more psychoactive plants and/or nonpsychoactive plant material that has been sprayed with psychoactive chemicals (thus "synthetic marijuana"), typically from the cannabinoid family. Upon analysis, many of the ingredients and chemicals found in various preparations of spice have not been reported on the packaging, and some of the ingredients listed on the packaging have been found to be absent (EMCDDA, 2012).

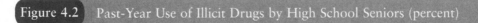

Figure 4.2 Past-Year Use of Illicit Drugs by High School Seniors (percent)

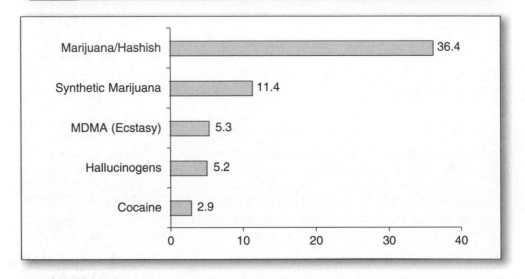

SOURCE: University of Michigan, 2011, Monitoring the Future Study.

"Spice" is Schedule I at the federal level and illegal under most state laws. Although the diversity of substances sold as "herbal highs" makes them more difficult to regulate (similar to bath salts, discussed in Chapter 3), in 2012 the Controlled Substance Act was amended to ban any "cannabimimetic agents" enabling easier prosecution of spice cases. Many of the plants used in preparations of spice have been used as marijuana substitutes, and the effects of the drug typically approximate the effects of marijuana, though this can vary (EMCDDA, 2011a). Symptoms reported by those having adverse reactions to the drug include rapid heart rate, vomiting, and confusion (AAPCC, 2012). Because the preparations sold as spice vary so widely, it is impossible to know exactly what substances might be responsible for these adverse reactions or how likely one is to experience such a reaction. Some of the psychoactive plants sold as spice are listed in Table 4.1 below.

The prevalence of spice use has increased since the introduction of the products. In 2011, the American Association of Poison Control Centers (AAPCC) reported just fewer than 7,000 cases of people reporting adverse reactions related to spice, more than double the number from 2010 (AAPCC, 2012). Data from the 2011 Monitoring the Future survey indicate 11.4% of high school seniors reported using the drug in the previous year, so it is used at a rate roughly one-third that of marijuana (see Figure 4.2).

Table 4.1	Herbal Components of "Spice" (a non-exhaustive list)	
Common name	**Species**	**Family**
Beach bean	*Canavalia maritima; syn. C. rosea*	Fabaceae
White and blue water lily	*Nymphaea alba and N. caerulea*	Nymphaeaceae
Dwarf skullcap	*Scutellaria nana*	Lamiacae
Indian warrior	*Pedicularis densiflora*	Orobanchaceae
Lion's ear/tail, Wild dagga	*Leonotis leonuru*	Lamiacae
"Maconha brava"	*Zornia latifolia or Z. diphylla*	Fabaceae
Blue/Sacred lotus	*Nelumbo nucifera*	Nelumbonaceae
Honeyweed/Siberian motherwort	*Leonurus sibiricus*	Lamiaceae
Marshmallow	*Althaea officinalis*	Malvaceae
Dog rose/Rosehip	*Rosa canina*	Roseceae

SOURCE: EMCDDA 2011. © EMCDDA, 1995–2012.

ANTIDEPRESSANT DRUGS

Antidepressants are generally considered to be completely different from other types of drugs, but these substances share many features of the drugs discussed throughout this chapter and the last. For example, both ecstasy and commonly prescribed antidepressants such as Prozac, Zoloft, and Paxil serve to enhance serotonin, albeit through slightly different biochemical mechanisms (Carey, 2003). It is true that antidepressants will not get users high in the fashion of other psychoactive drugs, but they do have the ability to alter perception and mood (indeed, this is why they are regarded as therapeutically useful). Like stimulants, antidepressants may make people agitated and anxious, and like depressants, they can also have sedative effects.

It is important to note that "normal" people who take these drugs are likely to experience only the negative side effects associated with them and none of the mood-elevating effects (Weil & Rosen, 1998). Another interesting characteristic of antidepressants is that many of the side effects associated with these drugs arise soon after ingesting them, but unlike the other drugs we have discussed, the desired mood-altering effect of antidepressants may require days or even weeks to occur (Weil & Rosen, 1998).

The treatment of depression has become a multibillion-dollar industry, but early medical efforts to treat the condition date to the 1920s, when doctors administered depressed males a serum of ground-up animal testicles in the belief that boosted testosterone would improve their mood (Barry, 2003). The primary antidepressant agents used today can be traced to the early 1950s and an accidental discovery that occurred during an experiment on the treatment of tuberculosis. At this time, anti-microbial drugs such as isoniazid were instrumental in emptying the hospitals of tuberculosis patients, and at one point, a new drug, iproniazid, was combined with isoniazid as a treatment for tuberculosis (Ray & Ksir, 2004). Although this combi-nation of drugs was soon discontinued because the withdrawal symptoms were too harsh, doctors discovered that many patients who had taken iproniazid were found to demonstrate improvements in mood and activity levels (Schulz & Macher, 2002). This discovery lead to further research on the mood-elevating effects of iproniazid, which belongs to what we now regard as the first major class of antidepressants, the monoamine oxidase (MAO) inhibitors.

MAO inhibitors are not widely used today, partly because they interact with stimulant drugs (including those in cold medications, diet pills, etc.) and partly because they alter the normal metabolism of tyramine, an amino acid, which is con-tained in foods such as cheese, Chianti wine, and pickled fish (Ray & Ksir, 2004). Individuals who consume these foods while on MAO inhibitors can become very sick and even die as a result of this interaction (which is sometimes called a "cheese reaction" because of the tyramine in cheese; Ray & Ksir, 2004).

Another group of antidepressants is the tricyclics (also discovered accidentally during research on antihistamines), but these drugs have been increasingly replaced by the selective serotonin reuptake inhibitors (SSRIs) in recent years. Tricyclics and SSRIs have been found to be about equally effective for the treatment of depression, but SSRIs are more commonly prescribed because they have fewer side effects and are less effective as a means to commit suicide (Boyce & Judd, 1999). Today, SSRIs such as Prozac, Zoloft, Paxil, Effexor, Serzone, and Celexa are some of the most widely used drugs in the world.

As noted earlier, the process by which antidepressants work is quite similar to other psychoactive drugs, and whether a drug is used for a legitimate medical pur-pose or for recreational purposes is irrelevant in terms of the effect of the drug on the body—these are just substances, and they affect the functioning of the brain and the associated mood states in similar ways. Recall that psychoactive drugs either act on or resemble various neurotransmitters (e.g., serotonin, dopamine, etc.), and because neurotransmitters affect mood, taking psychoactive drugs produces changes in mood (Gahlinger, 2001). The key distinction between antidepressants and other psychoactive drugs is that antidepressants primarily affect mood by *hampering or slowing the removal of various neurotransmitters* that naturally occur in the body (Jung, 2001). For example, the MAO inhibitors prevent the body from breaking down and removing mood-affecting monoamine neurotransmitters such as dopa-mine (which is why they are called MAO *inhibitors*). By preventing the breakdown of these neurotransmitters, the drugs in effect prolong the "good mood" effects produced by the neurotransmitter (Jung, 2001). SSRIs such as Prozac work in a similar fashion, as they block the reuptake (or removal) of one specific neurotrans-mitter, serotonin, and thus prolong the improved mood states associated with the release of serotonin (Jung, 2001).

It is important to note that depression is a very serious and pervasive disease, with studies suggesting that it affects approximately 10% of adults and 8% of adolescents in the United States (National Institute of Mental Health, 2000). Similar trends exist in other countries, and there is no question that antidepressant drugs have improved and even saved the lives of countless people who experience severe depression. However, it is also important to note that the effectiveness of SSRIs in treating depression remains debated in the scientific literature. For example, in more than half of the 47 trials used by the FDA to approve the six leading antidepressant drugs, these substances did not prove to be more effective than placebos, and in the trials indicating greater success of SSRIs, the advantages over placebos were slight (Greenberg, 2003). Related to this, Kirsch and colleagues (2002) found that the effects of antidepressant drugs *and placebos* on reducing symptoms of depression have steadily increased over time. In fact, the best predictor of whether research shows positive results for both placebos and SSRIs is the year the particular study was published. Kirsch speculates that this result is explainable in the context of widespread publicity and advertising of antidepressant drugs in the past few years, which has served to create expectations that SSRIs will be effective in treating depression (an expectation that would also apply to individuals administered placebos in clinical trials).

Acute Toxicity of Antidepressants

In the United States in 2009 there were more than 224,000 ED visits related to antidepressants (SAMHSA, 2011c). Antidepressants are thus responsible for about one-fourth as many ER visits as all illicit drugs combined. In the UK during 2010, there were 157 deaths caused by antidepressants, more than were caused by any substance other than heroin/morphine or methadone. (Office of National Statis 2011)

In addition to the debate over their effectiveness, antidepressants have many side effects, including sexual dysfunction, emotional numbing, insomnia, weight gain, restlessness, and memory lapses, as well as sedation, dry mouth, blurred vision, constipation, and difficulty in urinating (Weil & Rosen, 1998). There are also indications that, similar to use of alcohol, the use of antidepressant drugs during pregnancy can cause complications. For example, doctors at the Hospital for Sick Children in Toronto found that babies suffered from withdrawal symptoms if their mothers used certain antidepressant drugs during the last 3 months of their pregnancy (Vallis, 2002).

These drugs also produce withdrawal symptoms, although interestingly, pharmaceutical company officials prefer to label this "discontinuation syndrome" (Crister, 2004). Paxil appears to be the drug most likely to cause this condition. A review of SSRI discontinuation syndrome noted that a meta-analysis of discontinuation syndrome studies found nearly two-thirds of all cases to be attributed to Paxil, with

Prozac being least likely to generate discontinuation symptoms (Tamam & Ozproyaz, 2002).

Patients that have stopped using these drugs report effects that were similar to electric shocks in their heads, dizziness, mood swings, upset stomachs, myoclonic jerks ("sleep starts"), and unpleasant vivid dreams. Advertising for Seroxat claims, "These tablets are not addictive," but these symptoms only disappeared after patients began taking the drug again (Boseley, 2002b).

Another area of concern is the association of antidepressant use and suicidal thought and actions (sometimes called suicidality). Many studies have found an association between suicidality and antidepressant use. Although depressed people are more likely than nondepressed people to attempt suicide (and to be taking anti-depressants), research in this area typically involves experimental studies that compare depressed people taking these drug with depressed people taking placebos or no drugs.

A meta-analysis of 372 double-blind, placebo-controlled experiments involving almost 10,000 subjects by Stone and colleagues (2009) found that the use of this class of drug increased the odds of suicide by 62% in those under 25 years of age. At the same time, the drugs appeared to exert an overall protective effect on older patients, whose risk of suicide was reduced. The connection remains under study, but the potential link between antidepressant use and suicidality concerned the U.S. Food and Drug Administration (FDA) to the point that it required manufacturers of numerous antidepressant drugs to include a warning statement (similar to the one on cigarettes and alcohol) on their labels. This warning recommended the close observation of patients treated with these drugs for worsening depression or the emergence of suicidality (Vedantam, 2004).

Finally, it is important to note that although there are many documented negative short-term effects associated with antidepressants, many of these drugs have only been in circulation for a relatively short period of time. As a consequence, very little is known about the long-term effects of antidepressant drugs.

APHRODISIACS/ERECTILE DYSFUNCTION DRUGS

As with antidepressant drugs, we discuss aphrodisiacs and erectile dysfunction drugs in a separate section due to the fact that they are distinct from the other substances addressed in this book. As noted earlier, these drugs are unique in that their sole purpose is to allow for or assist in the attainment of sexual pleasure (Shenk, 1999). In this capacity, they are medically prescribed to those who are experiencing problems with normal sexual functioning, but they are also widely used recreationally by those who want to enhance their otherwise normal sex lives. Again, we do not see the use of these substances as directly analogous to the use of more traditional psychoactive drugs, but aphrodisiacs are similar in the sense that they are designed to assist in the achievement of sexual ecstasy, which is clearly an altered mental state.

You can imagine an alternative history in which Viagra wound up on the other side of the line—had it, say, been cooked up in an uptown drug lab and sold first on the street under the name "Hardy Boy."

—Pollan (1999)

According to Pfizer's website, about 25 million men have taken Viagra since it was introduced. Although Viagra (certified for use by the U.S. FDA in 1998) is the most well known of these drugs, there are several other substances being marketed to address erectile dysfunction in men and sexual problems in women. Similar to other substances discussed in this chapter, the ability of Viagra to address erectile dysfunction problems was discovered serendipitously, as the drug was originally developed to treat angina (Swidey, 2002).

While there has been a proliferation of erectile dysfunction drugs since the 1990s, aphrodisiacs have been used throughout human history. In the late 1800s, users of amyl nitrate found that the rush of blood created through inhalation of the substance increased the sexual excitement of men "and in many cases agreeably postponed but ultimately enhanced their orgasms. Perhaps rather later some men also found that it relaxed their sphincters, apparently enabling them to be more comfortably sodomized" (Davenport-Hines, 2001, p. 102). Another popular substance used during this period to enhance the sexual drive or performance of males was arsenic, which was listed, along with cannabis, strychnine, and phosphorous, as an aphrodisiac in the 1882 *Dictionary of Medicine* (Davenport-Hines, 2001).

Levitra became the sponsor of professional golf's popular Skins game, prompting one commentator to suggest, "Maybe it's me, but I don't think I'm going to hear the phrase 'he's got about an 18 footer...' the same way ever again." (Scheft, 2003)

It is important to recognize that although these drugs have been promoted to treat the physical condition of erectile dysfunction in males, the recreational use of these substances is considerable. For example, a study published in the *International Journal of Impotence Research* found that from 1998 to 2002, the use of Viagra in men under 45 tripled, with the authors commenting that "what this study indicates is that Viagra is being used as a recreational drug, not as a drug to treat a medical condition" (Delate, Simmons, & Motheral, 2004, p. 318).

The major erectile dysfunction (ED) drugs on the market include Viagra; Levitra, manufactured by Bayer and GlaxoSmithKline; and Cialis, produced by Eli Lilly (Howard, 2003). As competitors in the lucrative market for erectile dysfunction drugs, the manufacturers of these products have engaged in aggressive advertising and marketing campaigns that emphasize how they are different from Viagra. As compared to Viagra, which takes effect in approximately 1 hour and lasts up to 5 hours, Cialis takes effect in about 30 minutes and can last up to 36 hours (Howard,

2003). This has lead commentators to refer to it as "the weekender" (Gupta, 2003). Levitra (notice the similarity between the words *Levitra* and *elevate*) is relatively similar to Viagra in the amount of time it lasts, so it is marketed as being less influenced by the consumption of food.

Nasal Spray Ergogenic Aids

Nastech has recently initiated Phase II clinical trials for a nasal spray designed to boost libido in both males and females. The drug is already approved for treatment of male sexual dysfunction and works to increase arousal neurochemically, making it potentially effective for both sexes. The estimated market for a nasal spray that acts quickly is estimated to be more than $850 million in its first year. (Nastech Pharmaceutical Company, 2012)

Unlike many of the other substances discussed in this chapter, there have been few scientific studies of Viagra's effects. However, there are reports of individuals taking the drug recreationally, often in combination with illegal party drugs such as ecstasy and methamphetamine, who experience prolonged, painful erections (Kingston, 2003). More seriously, Viagra may be linked to sudden blindness. The FDA investigated approximately 50 cases in which men have experienced partial or complete sight loss shortly after taking Viagra or Cialis. These drugs, which affect blood circulation, may affect sight by influencing the circulation of blood to the optic nerve (Kaufman, 2005b). The three main impotence drugs, Viagra, Cialis, and Levitra, already include warnings that the drug can cause vision problems including blurring and sensitivity to light, and the makers of Cialis added a notice about the risk of sudden blindness to their label (Kaufman, 2005b).

It is also notable that some anecdotal evidence suggests that Viagra may be associated with negative social consequences. Experts say that the biggest problem is that men take the drug without talking with their partners, resulting in "Viagra wives" who apparently are "not excited to be asked once again for sex" (Peterson, 2001).

It has also been suggested that some older men, "spurred on by their new sense of manhood" as a result of using erectile dysfunction drugs, are more likely to cheat on their wives (Smyth, 2003). There are also indications that these drugs may be contributing to an increase in the incidence of venereal diseases among elderly men in Florida, who, perhaps as a result of their use of these substances, are seeking out prostitutes (Smyth, 2003).

While the market for erectile dysfunction drugs has been extremely lucrative for pharmaceutical companies, it is believed that the market for a prescription sex drug for women is potentially even more lucrative. Female sexual dysfunction is defined as decreased sexual desire, decreased sexual arousal, pain during intercourse, or inability to climax (Shah, 2001), and estimates indicate that 43% of all women suffer sexual dysfunction as compared to 31% of men (Lauman, Paik, & Rosen, 1999). The widespread pharmaceutical treatment of female sexual dysfunction (FSD) in the

United States remains an elusive goal for the drug manufacturers. Repeated failures to receive FDA approval have haunted many companies' attempts, with 12 previous attempts for drug approvals having failed in that goal (Miller, 2010). Most recently, an online marketing campaign had already begun when Flibanserin (a substance proposed to treat FSD) was dismissed by the FDA advisory panel, who voted 10 to 1 that it did not perform significantly better than a placebo.

Estrogen replacement therapy has demonstrated success in improving sexual response and is FDA approved, but it is usually only prescribed for FSD related to vaginal dysfunction due to serious side effects (Barma, Patel, & Patel, 2008). Approximately 50% of postmenopausal women have used hormone replacement therapy at some point despite the fact that research has shown this treatment to increase the risk of breast cancer, heart attacks, strokes, and blood clots (Groopman, 2002). As early as 1975, the FDA had also identified links between estrogen and higher rates of uterine cancer, but companies such as Wyeth (whose hormone replacement therapy product was known as Prempro) continued to advertise the benefits of hormone replacement therapy despite the fact that they had never conducted a large enough study to determine the effects of this treatment (Woodman, 2002). A vacuum-like device that stimulates blood flow to the clitoris has been approved by the FDA for the treatment of female sexual dysfunction, but it is not a pharmaceutical treatment and has not been well received because patients report limited comfort with a mechanical aid (Barma, Patel, & Patel, 2008), being described by some as a "glorified vibrator" (Shah, 2001).

Closely associated with substances designed to improve sexual function are drugs marketed for treating menopause and the emerging condition of male menopause. Also called andropause or viropause (the end of virility), this condition is purported to be related to low levels of testosterone in aging males. Advertisements for these products have depicted a car's gas gauge pointing to empty with the caption "Fatigued? Depressed mood? Low sex drive? Could be your testosterone is running on empty" (Groopman, 2002). In recent years, an advertising campaign has encouraged middle-aged men to take the "Low T" quiz in commercials, suggesting that any loss of sex drive or energy is likely due to a medical condition involving decreased testosterone.

As a result, testosterone prescriptions have increased 400% in the United States, though not elsewhere, since 1999 (*Science News*, 2010). This is despite the fact that evidence suggests that they are not effective in producing the advertised effects, such as increased machismo, motivation, and metabolism (Institute of Medicine, 2004). In fact, starting at age 40, a slight but gradual decline in testosterone levels is normal. A large study of men in Europe by Wu and associates (2010) found that only 9 of the 32 purported symptoms associated with low testosterone were actually associated with the condition and that the symptoms highlighted by the manufacturer were not necessarily associated with any changes in testosterone. Additionally, the risks associated with such hormone replacement therapy are severe and include elevated risk of cancer and heart disease (Fernández-Balsells et al., 2010).

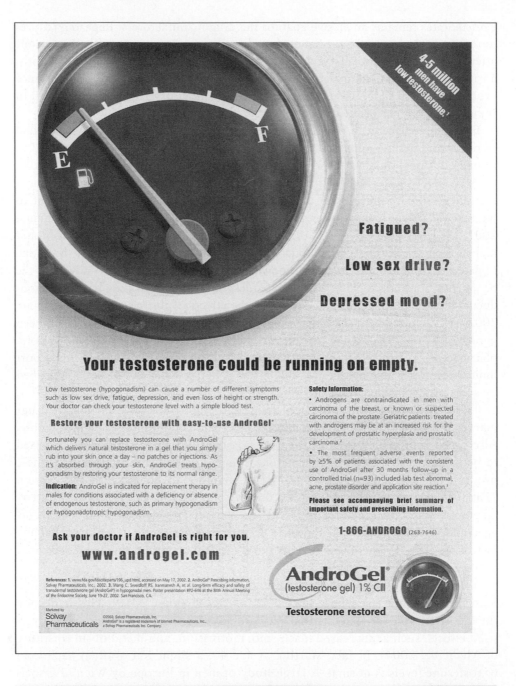

AndroGel is a colorless jelly that is rubbed on the body approximately once per day to deliver testosterone. AndroGel was approved by the FDA in 2000, but the FDA's Director of the Division of Reproductive and Urological Drug Products claimed that the FDA had not approved AndroGel for the treatment of andropause with the reasoning that "we're not sure what andropause is." (as quoted in Groopman, 2002)

STEROIDS AND OTHER PERFORMANCE-ENHANCING DRUGS

The use of steroids and other performance-enhancing substances is typically viewed as being completely different from other forms of drug use. While we recognize that the use of drugs to enhance physical performance is to some degree unique, it is important to note that this type of drug use is similar to other forms of drug use in many ways. As with other forms of drugs use, and as noted in our introduction to Chapter 3, the use of drugs in sport can be seen as "an expression of a basic human drive to stimulate the human organism beyond its normal metabolic state" (Hoberman, 1992, p. 105). Steroids and other performance-enhancing drugs have been shown to be capable of influencing mood and emotion in ways typical of other psychoactive drugs (e.g., generating euphoria, friendliness, alertness, increased energy and vitality, etc.). Thus, while users of these substances may initially seek them out for their performance-enhancing properties, the psychoactive effects of the substances may also be important for understanding why users continue to take these drugs over time.

> "The use of artificial means [to improve performance] has long been considered wholly incompatible with the spirit of sport and has therefore been condemned. Nevertheless, we all know that this rule is continually being broken, and that sportive competitions are often more a matter of doping than of training."
> —Otto Reisser, Director of a German Pharmacological Institute, at the 1933 annual meeting of the German Swimming Federation (as quoted in Hoberman, 1992, p. 131)

There are many forms of performance-enhancing drugs, but the anabolic steroids are the most well known, and our discussion of these substances will focus largely on them. Anabolic steroids are similar in many ways to the testosterone therapies discussed above, because steroids are synthetic derivatives of testosterone—the naturally occurring male sex hormone that is present in men and (to a lesser extent) women. Like testosterone, steroids possess anabolic effects—meaning they promote muscle growth, protein synthesis, the production of red blood cells, and the stimulation or inhibition of skeletal growth—and it is for this reason that they are commonly used to enhance performance. However, steroids also have androgenic effects, meaning they encourage the development of male sexual characteristics, such as hair growth and a deepening of the voice in both men and women. The androgenic effects always accompany steroid use, as efforts to isolate the anabolic properties of these drugs from their androgenic properties have only been partially successful (Haupt & Rovere, 1984). Because the use of all anabolic steroids produces both anabolic and androgenic effects, the more appropriate term for these substances is *anabolic-androgenic steroids* (AAS), although we will refer to these drugs using the more commonly used terms of *anabolic steroids* or *steroids* for convenience of expression.

To date, hundreds of steroids have been synthesized, and these drugs are generally taken orally or via intramuscular or subcutaneous injection (but not intravenous injection; Browder, 2001). Steroids may also be administered in the form of nasal spray, skin patches, or creams that are rubbed on the skin. The most commonly used form of steroids are those that can be taken orally, but orally consumed steroids are also more harmful to the liver and more negatively affect cholesterol levels (Browder, 2001). Conversely, injected forms of steroids are less toxic to the liver and less likely to cause cholesterol problems, but they are less convenient to use, result in greater estrogen increases, and also come with the risks associated with using contaminated needles (Browder, 2001).

> The use of crushed testicles as performance enhancers appears to be related to the "research" of the French physiologist Charles-Edouard Brown-Seguard. At a conference in 1889, the 72-year-old Brown-Seguard reported that he had been able to reverse the effects of his physical decline by injecting himself with a liquid extract derived from the testicles of a dog and a guinea pig. Apparently, these injections had increased his physical strength and intellectual energy, relieved his constipation, and even lengthened the arc of his urine. (Hoberman, 1992)

Steroids are the most well known of the performance-enhancing drugs, but numerous substances have been taken throughout history in the belief that they will increase strength or speed or in some way enhance athletic performance. For example, dating back to the third century BC, Greek athletes were known to ingest mushrooms, sesame seeds, dried figs, and herbs in the belief that these substances provided precompetition energy boosts (Sokolove, 2004). The ancient Egyptians consumed the ground rear hooves of Abyssinian mules for their purported performance-enhancing qualities (National Center on Addiction and Substance Abuse [CASA], 2000), and gladiators were known to use stimulants to overcome fatigue and injury in the Roman Coliseum (Yesalis, 2000).

The use of performance-enhancing substances by athletes expanded considerably in the late 1800s, at least partially due to advances made in the scientific study of athletic potential (Hoberman, 1992). In England, the breeding, systematic training, and timing of racehorses began as early as the 17th century, and by the end of the 19th century, the doping of racehorses and jockeys was becoming commonplace as competitors sought an edge on their competition. The historical prevalence of performance-enhancing drug use in sport is evident in a paper titled "Doping" published in the *Bulletin of the Health Organization of the League of Nations* in 1939. Reflecting how little things have changed since this time, Ove Boje commented,

There can be no doubt that stimulants are to-day (*sic*) widely used by athletes participating in competitions; the record-breaking craze and the desire to satisfy an exacting public play a more and more prominent role, and take higher rank than the health of the competitors itself. (as cited in Yesalis, 2000, p. 5)

It is clear that athletes have used performance-enhancing drugs throughout history. The development of anabolic steroids (and similar substances) and their use in competitive sports is only the most recent example of this long-standing phenomenon.

Currently, low doses of steroids are used to treat several medical conditions. For example, steroids are used in the treatment of testosterone deficiency, a condition in which the sex glands do not produce sufficient testosterone, causing abnormal growth and development; angioedema, a painful and dangerous skin disease involving intense swelling; and anemia, a condition in which affected individuals produce insufficient amounts of red blood cells (Browder, 2001). Steroids are also used to treat advanced breast cancer; to counteract the symptoms associated with menopause; to assist patients recovering from surgery, burns, or trauma; and to treat those suffering from the wasting effects of AIDS (Bahrke, Yesalis, & Wright, 1996; Browder, 2001).

Experimentally, steroids have been used to treat osteoporosis, impotency in men, and low sexual desire in both sexes, and they have also been used as a male contraceptive (quite safely and effectively; Yesalis, 2000). Despite the many therapeutic applications of steroids, the medical use of these drugs is relatively uncommon, either because the conditions for which steroids are prescribed are rare or because alternative treatments are preferred (Browder, 2001).

In the late 1800s, cyclists in racing competitions used strychnine, cocaine, morphine, bull's blood, and the crushed testicles of wild animals in attempts to enhance their performance (Barnes, 2000). Cycling participants in competitions including the Tour de France also smoked cigarettes while racing, as it was thought to improve performance by "opening up the lungs." (Brunel, Lovett, & Sport, 1996)

Although certain patterns of steroid use can result in serious health problems, it remains unknown whether significant adverse health effects can be attributed to all forms of steroid use (Friedl, 2000). For example, research has concluded that the adverse health effects associated with steroids may be dependent on several factors, including the characteristics of the individual, the specific steroid or combination of steroids taken, the duration of use, and the dosage level (Petersen & Goldberg, 1996). Dosage and duration of use may be particularly important for predicting negative health outcomes associated with steroid use. As compared to the therapeutic use of steroids, illicit steroid users often take these substances at extremely high doses and over long periods of time. For example, research has documented power lifters using very high doses of steroids continuously for periods of 7 years or more (Cohen, Noakes, & Benande, 1988).

Steroid Dosing—How Much Should I Take?

A number of companies based in foreign countries sell steroids over the Internet, and their web pages provide suggested dosage levels for their customers. Websites for companies such shopsteroids.net suggests that the "optimal dosage" of Deca-Durabo a commonly used steroid, is "in the range of 200-500 mg per week." As the maximum recommended therapeutic dose for Deca-Durabolin is 100 mg in a month, the dosages suggested by many of these sites are between 8 and 60 times the recommended therapeutic dosage! (Boyadjiev et al., 2000)

It is also important to recognize that there is no established or recommended dose of steroids provided for the goal of weight gain or strength development (Friedl, 2000). Illicit steroid users often determine what steroids to take, how much to take, and in what combinations based on anecdotal experience or "what works for their friends" (Friedl, 2000). With medical guidance either unsolicited or unavailable, some illicit steroid users have even reported equating the same dose of different types of steroids as analogous, regardless of differences in drug potency or effect. Other users have reported basing their dosing upon a specified number of tablets, regardless of which steroid or steroids they are taking (Friedl, 2000). Although this haphazard pattern of use is certainly not universal, with many athletes and body-builders being extremely knowledgeable about the specific substances they take and the health risks posed by them (Monaghan, 2001), the fact remains that for many, whether the drugs are working is often determined by noticeable gains in size and strength. This often leads to a "more is better" approach, with users taking extremely high doses of steroids despite the general lack of information on whether and to what extent taking more also involves greater health risks (Browder, 2001; Kerr, 1982; Wright, 1982; Yesalis, 2000).

In addition to their effects on the body, steroids can influence the mental state of users. In terms of their psychoactive potential, steroids are distinct from many of the drugs we have discussed, in part because they are generally taken for their anabolic rather than psychoactive properties. Despite this, extensive research has demonstrated that steroids do have psychoactive effects (see, for example, Bahrke, 2000; Browder, 2000; Pope, Kouri, & Hudson, 2000). The most well-known of these is aggression, but more pleasurable psychoactive effects associated with steroid use include euphoria, elevated mood, friendliness, increased sexual desire, and stimulant-like properties including alertness, decreased fatigue, increased energy, and improved memory and concentration (Bahrke, Yesalis, & Wright, 1996; Rubinow & Schmidt, 1996; Yates, 2000). Research has also indicated that as many as 43% of steroid users report feeling great pleasure or feeling high from extended steroid use (Browder, 2000; Browder, Blow, Young, & Hill, 1991), and studies have found that some steroid users may eventually come to take these drugs at least partially for these psychoactive effects (Browder, 2000).

The most well-known psychoactive effect linked to steroid use is aggression, which involves feelings of suppressed or overt hostility. Particularly in the popular media, reports that steroid users will experience "roid rage," or violent outbursts associated with steroid use, have been common. Extensive research has examined the association of steroid use and aggression, and although the exact nature of the relationship remains unclear, numerous studies have concluded that steroid use may contribute to aggressive behavior in some people (see Bahrke, 2000; Bahrke, Yesalis, & Wright, 1990, for reviews). However, it is important to emphasize that the effect of steroids on aggression is quite variable, depending on factors such as dose, the specific steroid or combination of steroids taken, and numerous characteristics of the individual (Bahrke, 2000; Bahrke, Yesalis, & Wright, 1996). Aside from existing characteristics of users (i.e., was the person prone to aggression before he began taking steroids?), dosage may be the most important factor in predicting aggressive feeling and behavior in steroid users. Illicit steroid users often take these substances at 10 to 100 times suggested therapeutic doses (Browder, 2001; Kerr, 1982; Wright, 1982; Yesalis, 2000) and, as with all drugs, there are likely to be very different consequences when the amount of a drug ingested is increased 10 times or more.

In terms of their negative health effects, the known and suspected consequences of steroid use can be grouped into seven categories:

- Cosmetic effects
- Liver disease
- Cardiovascular disease
- Dependence
- Infertility and testicular atrophy
- Musculoskeletal effects
- Indirect effects associated with purity and sharing needles

Ironically, despite the fact that they are relatively innocuous by comparison, the cosmetic effects of steroid use are some of the best known and most feared problems associated with these drugs, particularly among appearance-conscious users such as bodybuilders (Friedl, 2000). Relatively minor cosmetic problems associated with steroid use include a coarsening of the skin, acne, and a marked change in body hair production. Scalp hair loss in both men and women is common, as is abnormal hair production and distribution over the body (Browder, 2001).

One of the more serious cosmetic effects associated with steroid use is gynecomastia. Gynecomastia (or "gyno") afflicts only men and involves the abnormal development of mammary breast tissue in males (Friedl, 2000; Mottram & George, 2000). Sometimes pejoratively referred to as "bitch-tits" by weight lifters, gynecomastia is the result of abnormal estrogen production by the body that accompanies steroid use. Steroid users often attempt to counteract this effect by taking estrogen blockers along with steroids, or steroids less likely to convert to estrogen, but gynecomastia may develop despite these efforts. In the more serious cases of gynecomastia, surgery is often necessary to remedy the condition.

Similar to gynecomastia in men, steroid use can have a masculinizing effect on women's bodies. Women steroid users are likely to experience more developed muscularity and a decrease in body fat, irregular or absent menstrual cycles, shrinkage of the breasts, acne, and sterility. All of these effects typically disappear after steroid use is discontinued, but potentially irreversible effects include a deepening of the voice, increased body and facial hair growth, and an enlargement of the clitoris (Strauss & Yesalis, 1993).

The appearance of many female Olympians from East Germany and other Eastern Bloc countries in the 1960s, 1970s, and 1980s illustrates the masculinizing effect of steroids on women. These athletes were the product of state-sponsored doping programs that particularly targeted women and adolescent girls. Because females have a relatively minute level of natural testosterone production, steroid use is thought to be particularly effective for enhancing athletic performance among females. Officials in the East German program frequently administered steroids to female athletes in doses of up to 35 milligrams per day, and since an average teenage girl naturally produces approximately half a milligram of testosterone a day, the doses administered to these athletes represented approximately 70 times their natural levels of testosterone (Gladwell, 2001). The resulting masculine appearance of these competitors prompted speculation that the female athletes were either hermaphrodites or men disguised as women and prompted chromosome testing to verify sex at international competitions (Yesalis, Courson, & Wright, 1993).

One former East German athlete, Heidi Krieger, is now known as Andreas Krieger, having undergone a sex-change operation in 1997. Heidi Krieger was the 1986 European women's shot put champion, and Andreas now claims that the extensive regime of steroids and other performance-enhancing drugs that he underwent while a world-class female athlete contributed significantly to the confusion he experienced over his sexual identity and influenced his decision to have a sex change. Andreas currently reports numerous serious health problems as well and attributes these to his use of steroids and other performance-enhancing drugs. Another 500 to 2,000 former East German athletes are also believed to be experiencing serious health problems related to steroid use, including liver, breast, and testicular cancer; heart disease; gynecological problems; infertility; depression; and eating disorders. (Longman, 2004)

The liver is the principle organ by which steroids are cleared from the body, and liver problems are among the most serious health threat posed by these substances (Friedl, 2000). Liver problems associated with steroid use include jaundice, liver tumor development, and peliosis hepatis, a life-threatening form of hepatitis (Browder, 2001; Haupt & Rovere, 1984).

High-dose steroid use is also associated with cardiovascular disease. As with liver disease, the orally consumed form of steroids seems to be more problematic for the cardiovascular health of users (Browder, 2001). There is a well-established association between the use of certain steroids and reduced levels of "good cholesterol" or high-density lipoprotein cholesterol (HDL; Mottram & George, 2000). Because HDL binds to cholesterol and renders it inert, pathologically low levels of HDL are associated with atherosclerosis, a condition in which deposits of cholesterol and other substances build up in the inner lining of an artery. As this waste accumulates, it can significantly reduce the ability of blood to flow through an artery (causing high blood pressure), and these waste blockages can also "break off" and block a blood vessel leading to the heart (causing a heart attack) or block a blood vessel leading to the brain (causing a stroke; American Heart Association, 2004). The use of estrogen blockers can also aggravate this situation. As noted above, estrogen blockers are often taken by steroid users in an attempt to prevent gynecomastia, but these substances also reduce levels of HDL, which further increases the risk of cardiovascular disease (Friedl, 2000). Given these risks, the fact that more steroid users do not experience serious cardiovascular problems is likely due to the fact that steroid users are also frequently on low-fat diets and intense exercise programs, both of which are key factors in combating heart disease.

Dependence on steroids may also result from their use. Studies indicate that 14 to 57% of users become dependent on these substances, depending largely on use patterns (Yesalis, Bahrke, Kopstein, & Barsukiewicz, 2000). Research has also demonstrated that users develop tolerance to steroids over time (Browder, 2001; Copeland, Peters, & Dillon, 2000), but whether tolerance develops to the psychoactive effects of steroids is not known (Browder, 2001).

Sexual and hormonal side effects are also associated with steroid use. Common side effects include infertility, a reduced sperm count, and testicular atrophy, a condition characterized by shrinking of the testicles. Additionally, because sex hormone levels affect skeletal growth, steroid use by adolescents may signal bones to stop growing earlier than they would otherwise, resulting in short stature (Browder, 2001).

Prior to his unexpected death at the age of 41 in 2004, former Major League Baseball player Ken Caminiti told *Sports Illustrated* that he used steroids when he won the National League Most Valuable Player Award in 1996 and claimed that at least half of major league baseball players also used steroids. Noting that he would not discourage other players from using steroids, Caminiti told *Sports Illustrated,* "Look at the money in the game. A kid got $252 million. So I can't say 'Don't do it,' not when a guy next to you is as big as a house and he's going to take your job and make the money." (Verducci, 2002, 2004)

Other risks associated with steroid use are musculoskeletal in nature. Problems such as tendon rupture have also been reported in association with steroid use because steroids may produce gains in muscle strength that outpace gains in tendon strength and/or because steroids inhibit the production of collagen, a protein that promotes tendon and ligament strength (Mottram & George, 2000).

Lastly, there are indirect effects associated with steroid use. These risks mainly deal with mislabeling or impurities present in black-market steroids and also risks associated with intravenous drug use. Studies have repeatedly found that between 50 and 80% of all steroids are obtained from black-market sources (Bahrke, 2000; Gale, 2009; United States Drug Enforcement Agency, 1994), and many of these products do not report the dose or ingredients on the label (Bahrke et al., 1996; Gale, 2009). For example, Walters, Ayers, and Brown (1990) conducted an analysis of seized steroids and found 26% of the products to contain no steroids, 53% to contain steroids other than those indicated on the label, and 85% to contain dosages different from those reported on the label. More recently, Gale (2009) reported on a study that found 30% did not contain any of the listed substances, 44% contained inaccurate labeling, and 20% were contaminated with potentially hazardous metals. The risks associated with the injection of steroids are the same as those that accompany the injection of drugs such as heroin or cocaine—namely, the use of dirty needles may transmit diseases such as hepatitis and HIV among steroid users.

Steroids are the most well-known of the performance-enhancing drugs, but a variety of other substances can be used to enhance athletic performance. Among these are powerful nonsteroidal hormones such as human growth hormone (hGH), insulinlike growth factor (IGF-1), and human chorionic gonadotropin (HCG). These substances are very similar in effect to the anabolic steroids because, like steroids, they stimulate the production of testosterone in the body (Bamberger & Yeager, 1997). hGH is the most commonly used of these. Produced by the pituitary gland, hGH spurs growth in children and adolescents and, like steroids, spurs muscle and bone growth. However, it remains debated whether the increase in muscle mass generated by hGH translates to an increase in strength (Mayo Clinic, 2012). Like testosterone, hGH production decreases in middle age, and people often supplement with hGH in the belief it will stave off the effects of aging. Although the side effects of hGH use in healthy adults are not well understood due to a relative scarcity of studies, many of the side effects of hGH appear to mimic those of illicit steroid use, including gynecomastia and joint pain (Mayo Clinic, 2012).

Steroids and similar ergogenic aids are thought to be of less use to athletes in endurance sports such as cycling or running (aside from recovery from rigorous workouts). This does not mean that endurance sports are free from performance-enhancing substances—far from it. Erythropoietin (EPO) is a hormone that is naturally produced by the kidneys and is often prescribed for dialysis and chemotherapy patients (Barnes, 2000). EPO has been widely used by endurance athletes, as it increases red blood cell production, and through this, the amount of fatigue-delaying oxygen that the blood can carry to the muscles (Gladwell, 2001). It is believed that athletes who inject EPO can improve their performance in a 20-minute run by as much as 30 seconds and in a marathon by as much as 4 minutes (Sullivan & Song, 2000).

The injection of EPO is a new twist on the long-standing practice of "blood doping"—a process in which athletes remove a unit of blood weeks prior to an event and then transfuse the blood back into their body just prior to a competition. As the body will naturally replace a unit of blood in approximately 3 weeks, blood doping gives an athlete an extra unit of blood (and that many more red blood cells), which increases the body's oxygen carrying capacity (Lawson, 2003).

Blood doping is unquestionably effective at enhancing performance, but this practice, and the use of EPO, can be very dangerous, especially to athletes engaged in rigorous exercise. This is because blood is composed largely of red blood cells and plasma, and plasma is mostly water. As doped blood is already "thickened" with the red blood cells added through the doping process, the water loss that accompanies intense exertion will cause the blood to become even thicker—and if the blood becomes thick enough, it can clog, causing a stroke or heart attack. EPO is suspected in the heart attack deaths of many elite cyclists and runners (Henderson, 2004). As one European Olympic distance runner who used EPO himself commented, "you have guys who will go to the funeral of a friend who died from this stuff, come home and inject it again" (as cited in Bamberger & Yeager, 1997).

Although over 6000 blood and urine tests samples were collected at the Olympic Games in London these tests identified only one PED user, Nadzeya Ostapchuk, a female shot putter from Belarus.   There was an HGH test used during the 2004 Olympic Games in Athens, but it caught exactly no one despite the fact that the Games was so rife with HGH users they were dubbed "the HGH games." The commissioner of the NFL has been pushing its players union to implement the new HGH test for all NFL players and this is expected to occur in the near future. (Assael, 2012)

The prevalence and variety of performance-enhancing drug use over time reflects the desire of competitors to gain an edge on their competition. As the rewards associated with success in sports can be substantial, many athletes may feel compelled to use these drugs. The knowledge that other athletes are almost certainly using performance-enhancing substances is also a very compelling motivation, as those that choose to stay clean are likely placing themselves at a competitive disadvantage. Balanced against these pressures are the efforts of governing sports bodies to prevent the use of performance-enhancing drugs. The ongoing effort to regulate and prevent performance-enhancing drug use in sports is discussed in detail in Chapter 10.

CONCLUSION

Chapters 3 and 4 have reviewed the effects of several categories of drugs. Although psychoactive drugs can be classified in a number of ways, taxonomies often group substances based on their primary effects on the body and behavior. We have followed this practice throughout the previous two chapters, examining illegal drugs alongside prescription medications, over-the-counter medications, and other legal drugs such as alcohol. What has been apparent is that there is little difference between these substances when they are considered in terms of their effects alone. It is important to note that all drugs, regardless of their legal status, have potentially beneficial as well as potentially harmful effects. However, the illegal status of certain drugs is often based on rhetoric claiming that illegal substances are distinct in terms of the harms they pose to society and the user.

The potential harm associated with a drug is often assessed in terms of its psychoactive potential, physical toxicity, and potential to generate dependence. The psychoactive potential of a drug, although not necessarily negative, is important to consider, as people under the influence of a drug may intentionally or accidentally hurt others or damage property (sometimes referred to as behavioral toxicity). Reports in the popular media and those released by regulatory agencies often sensationalize these effects with claims that a particular drug possesses an almost mystical ability to change normal people into mindless zombies or that some new drug is "more dangerous, more threatening, more harmful than any substance that has preceded it" (Akers, 1992, p. 35). However, what is clear is that differences in the behavioral toxicity of drugs are overstated (particularly between legal and illegal drugs), and violent or threatening behavior that occurs while under the influence of drugs has much more to do with the characteristics of particular drug *users* rather than with the pharmacological properties of the drugs.

In addition to their subjective psychoactive effects and potential for behavioral toxicity, drugs are commonly assessed in terms of the physical and psychological risks they pose to users. *Toxicity* refers to the negative health consequences associated with ingesting a drug, and it can be both acute and chronic. Acute toxicity refers to problems that come on very soon after a drug is taken, as in the case of an overdose, while chronic toxicity addresses the long-term health consequences associated with the use of a drug, such as emphysema or cirrhosis. The acute toxicity of certain drugs is often invoked as a justification for their illegal status. This rationale is problematic, as many legal drugs (e.g., alcohol, prescription pharmaceuticals, acetaminophen, and ibuprofen) have among the highest levels of acute toxicity, while some illegal drugs (e.g., marijuana) have very low levels of acute toxicity. It is also important to recognize that, for many drugs, the chronic health effects associated with use pose a much greater risk to users than do the acute effects. As a result of this, and partly due to the way in which certain drugs are used, deaths and illnesses attributed to legal drugs such as alcohol and tobacco far exceed those attributed to all illegal drugs combined.

The potential of a drug to produce dependence is also a serious concern associated with drug use. *Addiction* and *dependence* are terms widely used in society, but in the context of substance use, these conditions collectively refer to a person's inability to stop using a drug when it is causing them problems. Physical dependence on certain types of drugs can occur because the body has come to depend on the presence of some amount of the drug in the system, and when drug use is rapidly discontinued, users experience physical withdrawal symptoms. Drugs that are not accompanied by a predictable set of physical symptoms when long-term or heavy use is stopped are not regarded as physically addicting. In terms of their ability to generate physiological dependence, the opiates and depressants are of most concern, although the depressants (including alcohol) are the only class of drugs that can cause death due to withdrawal. Psychological dependence on drugs may also occur. Psychological dependence arises through the psychological process of reinforcement. Specifically, drug use is typically followed by good feelings or a high and/or the removal of bad feelings, and this causes the person to want to repeat the behavior. Accordingly, a drug that cannot cause a user to become physically dependent may still be able to produce psychological dependence.

A number of drugs are said to be psychologically addicting, particularly those that involve a short, intense duration of effect, as this encourages repeated dosing and repeated reinforcement. However, it is important to recognize that psychological dependence is more difficult to assess than physical dependence (which produces actual physical symptoms) and is based on a variety of behavioral indicators. When assessed using these behavioral indicators, *addiction* can apply to a number of non-drug behaviors as well, including shopping, sex, and gambling, and this has prompted some to suggest that "dependence has more to do with human beings than with drugs" (Weil & Rosen, 1998, p. 171). Thus, what is important to recognize is that all drugs can be harmful and all drugs can be beneficial, and when we categorize substances according to their psychoactive effects and potential to generate harm rather than by their legal status, clear distinctions between legal and illegal drugs are impossible to make.

REVIEW QUESTIONS

1. Prior to being declared illegal in the United States, in what ways was LSD used? What is known about the physical and psychological dependence potential of LSD?

2. In what ways is the use of peyote by members of the Native American Church distinguished from recreational drug use?

3. What medical application does PCP have? Regarding the effects of PCP, why might individuals under the influence of this substance be difficult for authorities to control?

4. What is "robo-dosing"?

5. In terms of their mood-altering effects, how do SSRIs differ from other psychoactive drugs?

6. What are the anabolic and androgenic effects of steroids?

7. Compared to the medical use of steroids, how do illicit steroid users often take these substances?

8. What are the known and suspected negative health consequences associated with steroid use?

INTERNET EXERCISE

States in the United States have very different laws regarding the regulation of marijuana. These laws can be accessed via the link below. Access the link and select five states that have substantially different regulatory laws for marijuana. Summarize these differences in a table and make sure to consider the weight allowed for possession by the state; any differences in the penalty assigned for first, second, and third violations of the possession statute; and any mandatory penalties or elevated penalties associated with possession or sale in proximity to a school zone and the like.

   http://norml.org/laws

CHAPTER 5

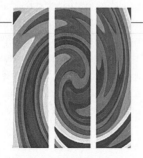

Patterns of Illegal Drug Use

What is known about the use and abuse of illegal drugs, drug treatment, and consequences associated with drug use is derived primarily from several large-scale surveys and selected compilations of justice and health statistics. Although information on drug use in the United States, Canada, and many European countries is plentiful, data on substance use in other regions of the world, particularly third-world countries, are much scarcer. Available data have enabled researchers to demonstrate that drug use varies significantly in the population and that it is more common in some populations than in others (i.e., drug use is *correlated* with certain populations and statuses).

Among the correlates of illegal drug use is age, as the use of drugs is much more common in late adolescence and early adulthood than at any other point in the lifecourse. Gender is another important predictor of illegal drug use, as males are more likely than females to use illegal drugs. Drug use also varies by race/ethnicity, but in contrast to what is commonly believed or portrayed in the media, research consistently demonstrates that whites use illegal drugs at rates that are comparable to or exceed the use patterns of racial/ethnic minorities. In part, racial and ethnic differences in substance use are a function of differences in social class. Social class is a measure that captures differences in economic prosperity and educational attainment and is another important correlate of drug use. Finally, residential location is an important factor impacting rates of drug use, with most drugs used more frequently in the West and in urban areas.

The correlates of illegal drug use are the primary focus of this chapter and are discussed in depth below. However, in order to understand research on the correlates of drug use, it is necessary to have a basic understanding of the methods and sources of data used to generate this information. The two most widely used and perhaps the best sources of information on substance use and abuse are the Monitoring the Future Study and the National Survey on Drug Use and Health. Both are large, ongoing surveys based in the United States that have collected data on substance use and abuse for decades. The former is predominately focused on substance use by adolescents, although it also provides information on adults, while the latter is a household survey focusing mainly on adults, although data on youth aged 12 to 17 are also included.

Similar surveys on drug use have been conducted in many other nations, particularly throughout Europe, providing data that allow an examination of the trends and correlates of international illegal drug use. Sources commonly used include the European School Survey Project on Alcohol and Drugs and the British Crime Survey. Other key sources of information on substance use and abuse focus on specific populations of interest, such as those seeking treatment or individuals accused of crimes. One very useful data source for data on offenders' drug use is the Arrestee Drug Abuse Monitoring (ADAM) study. Various health, social service, and justice agencies also compile data on drug use and health, including the Drug Abuse Warning Network (DAWN), which tracks drug-related visits to hospital emergency departments.

Criminal justice data also provide important information on drug use, drug sales, and the consequences of these behaviors. Data on arrests and incarcerations for drug offenses are available from organizations such as the Bureau of Justice Statistics, but these data are more focused on the response to drug use than drug use per se. Therefore, we limit our discussion of these data sources. Finally, ethnographic studies of drug use that rely on direct observation and/or interviews of drug users and people in drug-related fields provide invaluable data on drug use and abuse. These data are particularly useful for examining drug use by populations that may be excluded from the data sources mentioned above. There are many individual studies of drug use that employ ethnographic data, and we draw on these throughout the book. We now turn our attention to a discussion of the primary sources of data on drug use, followed by a discussion of the key correlates of illegal drug use.

SELF-REPORT SURVEYS

The application of the self-report survey method to the study of deviant behavior began in the 1940s and 1950s, and these early surveys included measures of substance use (Porterfield, 1946; Short & Nye, 1957; Straus & Bacon, 1953). Survey research allowed the study of deviance by going "straight to the source" or by asking people about their illegal and deviant behavior. This was an important breakthrough in the study of crime and deviance and was especially significant for the study of the most common, often victimless crimes like drug use.

One of the major advantages of the self-report method is that it enables inferences to be made about a general population based on a relatively small sample of subjects, provided that every person in the population has an equal chance of being selected for the sample. With a properly drawn sample, we can examine numerous issues related to drug use with a relatively high degree of accuracy, including whether the use of a particular substance is increasing or decreasing, demographic differences in use and abuse patterns, how available and expensive the drug is on the street, if treatment resources are available and adequate for those wanting help, attitudes about drugs and drug policy in the general population, and what the consequences of use and abuse are.

The flexibility of surveys also allows them to be used to examine substance use and abuse by those who may be most likely to have experience with drugs or drug-related problems, such as people in substance treatment centers or prison. Self-report surveys also provide a great deal of flexibility in terms of the issues covered and questions asked. For example, major national surveys have added questions on the use and availability of drugs such as methamphetamine and ecstasy when it became clear that these drugs were an issue of growing concern to the public, and questions on the cost of particular drugs have also been added to surveys in the past as one measure of examining the success of interdiction efforts. In sum, the broad flexibility of surveys and the fact that they allow us to study large populations relatively cheaply and accurately makes them an extremely useful tool for social research in general and research on substance use in particular.

Despite the numerous benefits of the self-report method, a number of issues and limitations to survey research must be considered when interpreting findings. One major concern with survey research on substance use is that some of the people who are most likely to use and abuse illegal drugs are also among the most difficult to contact. This problem is commonly referred to as *coverage error,* and it can hamper the ability of a survey to yield findings that are generalizable to the entire population (Dillman, 2000). For example, the most widely used sources of information on substance use by adolescents are based on middle and high school student populations. Although student-based drug surveys provide valuable data, because they are based on student populations, they exclude high-school dropouts and are less likely to capture students with high rates of absenteeism. This is important, as the U.S. Department of Education estimates that 10 to 15% of students permanently drop out of school, and dropouts are more likely than enrolled students to use illegal drugs and alcohol (Johnston, O'Malley, Bachman, & Schulenberg, 2012b). Dropouts are also more likely to use more serious drugs such as cocaine and heroin and to use substances in more harmful ways (e.g., "daily" use) than are students who remain in school.

Because of these factors, surveys of student populations are likely to underreport the overall level of substance use and abuse by young people (Johnston et al., 2012a). Further complicating the interpretation of student-based data on drug use is the fact that dropout and absenteeism rates may also vary according to other sociodemographic characteristics. For example, Hispanics have been found to have significantly higher dropout rates at every age and social class, and because this affects their survey participation, it also affects the reported levels of substance use and abuse for this group (Johnston et al., 2012a; USDHHS, 2003).

Like surveys on students, general population surveys are also likely to underestimate levels of drug use and dependency as a result of coverage error. For example, household surveys will disproportionately miss people who use drugs, especially those who use "hard" drugs or are addicted to drugs, as these individuals are more likely to be homeless or to be living in various institutions, meaning they will be missed in samples of households (Ramsay & Partridge, 1999).

Another issue of concern in survey research on drug use is *underreporting* by respondents. Underreporting involves the tendency of survey respondents to lie, minimize, or fail to answer questions that are perceived to be threatening to the respondent (Aquilino & LoSciuto, 1990). Related to underreporting is the issue of *social desirability*, which is the tendency of respondents to reply to sensitive questions in ways that are believed to be more socially appropriate. For example, research has found people to be less likely to report sensitive and illegal behavior, particularly as respondent anonymity decreases (e.g., answering the question in person rather than in an anonymous written survey) or as the respondent feels less in control of the interview process (Fendrich & Vaughn, 1994). These issues are further complicated by the fact that the underreporting of drug use is likely to vary not only by the survey mode but by a number of sociodemographic variables and the type of substance as well. For example, underreporting may be he higher when questions ask about "harder" drugs such as heroin, cocaine, and methamphetamine, ostensibly because the additional stigma (and legal consequences) associated with these drugs increases the pressure to respond in socially desirable ways (Fendrich & Vaughn, 1994). Similarly, research has indicated that members of racial/ethnic minority groups, members of the lower class, and those with lower levels of education may be more likely to underreport substance use even when controlling for other relevant variables (Mensch & Kandel, 1988). Rather than a tendency toward dishonesty, this pattern is generally explained as resulting from distrust of predominantly white authority figures in regard to anything potentially construed as criminal behavior, which has resulted from ongoing criminal justice discrimination against these groups.

Although survey data on drug use therefore should be regarded with caution, most researchers believe these data are reasonably valid indicators of substance use and abuse and that response validity can be held to a reasonably high level provided the survey is properly conducted. An example of the relatively high validity potential in drug surveys is provided by the drugs component of the British Crime Survey (BCS), which has previously inserted a fictitious drug called Semeron into its measures of drug use as a validity check. In 1998, 9,988 people responded to the BCS and of these 4% claimed to have ever heard of Semeron, but only 4 respondents claimed to have used it in their lifetime and only one respondent claimed to have used it in the previous month (Home Office, 2001). In sum, there are limitations to the use of survey data for the study of drug use and abuse, but these data can be extremely valuable provided that they are used cautiously and with their limitations in mind.

Monitoring the Future

The Monitoring the Future (MTF) study is perhaps the most commonly used source of information on legal and illegal drug use by American adolescents and young adults (Johnston et al., 2012a). With approximately 100 questions on substance use, MTF surveys address respondents' use of a variety of illegal drugs, alcohol, tobacco, psychoactive pharmaceuticals (nonmedical use), and inhalants during the last 30 days (both "daily" use and ever used in last 30 days), the last year, and in their lifetime. In addition to this, MTF includes questions regarding the age at first use for various drugs, the frequency and quantity of use, perceived availability of drugs, peer norms regarding drug use, beliefs about the health and social risks associated with drug use, and expected future use of drugs, among other things (Johnston et al., 2012a).

First implemented in 1975, MTF began as a cross-sectional survey of high school seniors alone but quickly developed into a longitudinal project that has also expanded to include additional age groups. Beginning in 1991, MTF extended the study to include 8th and 10th graders, and now about 17,000 8th graders from 150 schools and 16,000 10th graders from 130 schools are surveyed annually (Johnston et al., 2012b). In all, each year, the high school sample involves approximately 45,000 students from about 400 public and private secondary schools in the United States. Surveys of 8th and 10th graders are conducted anonymously, but 12th-grade respondents are asked to confidentially provide their names, enabling follow-up surveys of a random sample of graduating seniors for a number of years after their graduation (Johnston et al., 2012a).

Figure 5.1 Annual Illegal Drug Use by 12th Graders, 1975–2011

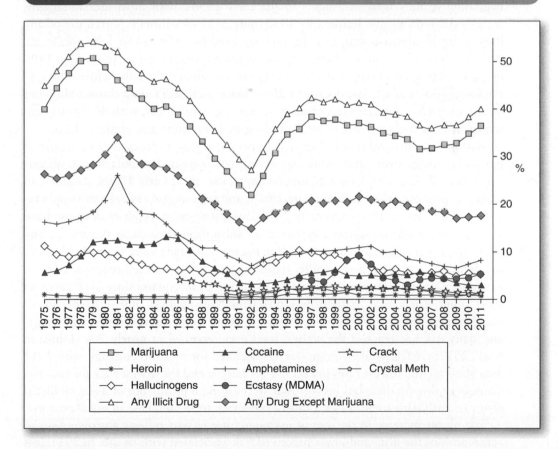

SOURCE: Johnston et al., 2012b. *Monitoring the Future national survey results on drug use, 1975–2011. Volume I: Secondary school students.* Ann Arbor: Institute for Social Research, The University of Michigan, p. 751.

Longitudinal information collected by the MTF project began with the graduating class of 1976. Today, from the original 15,000 to 17,000 senior respondents that participate in the survey each year, a representative sample of 2,400 persons is drawn, and these individuals are then followed and surveyed by mail. The longitudinal data collected by the MTF allow researchers to examine the association of adolescent substance use with a number of outcomes in later life, including college enrollment and completion, marriage, parenthood, employment, and the use and abuse of substances in adulthood. The examination of adult substance use and abuse by MTF is also facilitated by oversampling procedures designed to include adequate numbers of frequent marijuana users (i.e., daily users) and serious drug users in the sample (Johnston et al., 2011). Although the MTF study suffers from the limitations of school-based surveys discussed earlier, it is an excellent source of information on the prevalence and incidence of substance use by American adolescents.

Due to the study's longitudinal design, MTF data are especially adept at monitoring change in substance use over time. As illustrated in Figure 5.1, findings from the MTF survey demonstrate that the annual use of illicit drugs by American adolescents decreased significantly from the late 1970s (i.e., several years prior to the beginning of the "war on drugs") to the early 1990s, with most individual substances showing steady declines. By 1992, only 27% of seniors reported use of any illicit drug in the past year, half the rate reported in 1979 (54%; Johnston et al., 2012b). After 1992, annual illicit drug use increased steadily before peaking in 1999 (42% of 12th graders reported annual use), then leveling off briefly before falling to the lowest point of the last decade in 2007. Since then, MTF data show a slow but steady increase in annual rates of drug use among adolescents, with 40.0% of high school seniors reporting use of an illicit drug in 2011 (Johnston et al., 2012a).

Within these general trends, Figure 5.1 also illustrates several spikes in the use of particular drugs over time, reflecting periods of increased popularity of various substances. This can be seen with amphetamine use in the early 1980s, cocaine and crack cocaine use in the mid- and late 1980s, and ecstasy and crystal methamphetamine use in the late 1990s and early 2000s. Still, long-term trends in drug use have shown remarkable consistency across most substances. Trends in the use of any illicit drug, marijuana, and any illicit drug except marijuana were virtually identical for decades. However, these parallel trends appear to have ended recently, as there has been a slow but continuous increase in the use of marijuana since 2007, even as most other drugs have become less prevalent. During that time, current use of marijuana (within the past 30 days) has increased to its highest level in a decade, and daily use has reached the highest level ever recorded at nearly 7% (Johnston et al., 2012b). Meanwhile, current use has declined for most other drugs, with 2011 data showing the lowest rates since 1991 for heroin and the lowest ever for cocaine. Thus, even though there has been growth in the annual prevalence of using all illegal drugs recently, this trend is due almost exclusively to the increase in marijuana use.

The recent increase in the rate of marijuana use in part reflects a growing social acceptance of the drug and lower perceived risk associated with its use. In 2011, less than half of respondents perceived great risk in occasional marijuana use, and even regular use was perceived as representing great risk by only roughly 60% of high school students (Johnston et al., 2012b). The increasing acceptance of marijuana has not extended to perceptions about more dangerous drugs. Ongoing disapproval and perceived risk remain above 80% for cocaine and above 90% for heroin (Johnston et al., 2012b).

Other Surveys on Adolescent Drug Use

Another useful source of information on adolescent substance use is the *Youth Risk Behavior Survey* (YRBS). Similar in many ways to the MTF study, the YRBS is a school-based study that is representative of American students enrolled in the 9th through 12th grades. The YRBS is implemented biennially by the Centers for Disease Control (CDC), which developed the survey in order to monitor serious health risks posed to American adolescents and young adults (DHHS, 2003a). Substance use is one of six categories of high-risk behavior targeted by the survey and is addressed by 14 questions on illegal drug use and 16 questions on alcohol and tobacco use in the 2003 survey. Because the YRBS has a particular focus on issues of risk and health, it examines some things that the MTF study does not (DHHS, 2003b). For example, questions included on substance use and risk in the YRBS address respondents' frequency of driving while intoxicated or riding in a car with an intoxicated driver and whether substance use had occurred during previous sexual encounters. Measures such as these have enabled researchers to link forms of drug use with a variety of negative health outcomes including accidental death, suicide, unwanted pregnancy, and the transmission of disease, including HIV (Manski, Pepper, & Petrie, 2001).

An important source of data on substance use and abuse by adolescents outside the United States is the *European School Survey Project on Alcohol and Drugs* (*ESPAD*; Hibell et al., 2012).

Having expanded to include more than 100,000 10th-grade students in 39 participating countries in 2011, the ESPAD is modeled after the MTF survey to enable comparisons between European countries and the United States. Recent ESPAD findings indicate that, as compared to American youth of the same age, European youth are more likely to be current users of tobacco and alcohol but less likely to be current users of illegal drugs. In fact, only 18% of 10th graders in the ESPAD study reported lifetime use of any illicit drug, a rate that is less than half the 37.7% observed in the United States (Hibell et al., 2012; Johnston et al., 2012b).

Comparisons of ESPAD and U.S. survey data also indicate higher rates of lifetime use among U.S. students than those in Europe for marijuana (34% vs. 17%), illicit drugs other than marijuana (16.1% vs. 6%), and all other individual substances tracked (Hibell et al., 2012; Johnston et al., 2012b). There are great variations between European nations, though, and for the first time since the inception of the ESPAD, lifetime rates of using any illegal drug in select countries are actually comparable to or slightly higher than rates in the United States. This includes rates in

France, Monaco, and the Czech Republic. Additionally, the popularity of certain drugs varies between European nations, and a few nations' students report usage rates for ecstasy, heroin, and amphetamines comparable to or slightly above rates in the United States. However, students in the United States report the use of any drug besides marijuana nearly 50% more often than the highest rate observed in the ESPAD study. Furthermore, no European nations reported rates even approaching those indicated by American students for cocaine (Hibell et al., 2012), which remains one of the most commonly used illegal drugs in the United States (Johnston et al., 2012b).

The National Survey on Drug Use and Health

Another key source of information on substance use in the United States is the National Survey on Drug Use and Health (NSDUH). Formerly called the National Household Survey of Drug Abuse (NHSDA), the NSDUH is clearly the most representative source of data on drug use in the United States, as it samples from the general United States civilian population aged 12 and above. Only 2% of this population is not represented by the NSDUH, and this mostly involves persons who are in the military, correctional facilities, or residential treatment programs or persons who are homeless but not in shelters (National Research Council, 2001). Drawing an annual sample of roughly 70,000 people, the NSDUH includes measures examining the lifetime, past-year, and past-month use of tobacco, alcohol, marijuana, cocaine, crack cocaine, hallucinogens (with separate measures included for PCP and LSD), heroin, and inhalants and the nonmedical use of prescription drugs (with separate measures included for stimulants, sedatives, tranquilizers, and analgesics; SAMHSA, 2011a).

Summary measures are also provided examining the use of any illicit drug and the use of any illicit drug excluding marijuana (SAMHSA, 2011a). Respondents are asked about the age at which they were first exposed to and used a particular drug, when they last used a particular drug, and their perceptions of the availability of drugs, the risks associated with drug use, and the behavioral and health consequences associated with use. Finally, the NSDUH also collects sociodemographic data on respondents, including age, gender, race, educational level, job status, income, and housing situation (SAMHSA, 2011a).

In general, data generated by the NSDUH are excellent for examining the prevalence of drug use in the general population. As noted, however, one limitation of these data is that they likely underreport the use of more serious drugs, such as heroin and cocaine, and the negative consequences due to drug abuse. This is partially because severe drug abusers tend to lack the social support, resources, and social capital to help them overcome their dependency and often end up without permanent shelter and are not included in household surveys. Despite its shortcomings, the NSDUH is a well-designed study, and the data are widely used to examine drug use and abuse in America.

Underreporting is always a concern in survey research on drug use, but alternative methods of measuring drug use may be even more problematic. An example of this can be seen in two studies attempting to estimate cocaine use by testing local water and sewage treatment samples to measure the amount of benzoylecgonine, a urinary byproduct of metabolized cocaine. Using water samples collected from Italy's Po River and England's Thames River, researchers first estimated that cocaine was used on a daily basis by about 2.7% of the population in Northern Italy (Zuccatoet al., 2005), then followed with an even higher estimate of daily use by 3.8% of the London population (Orr & Goswami, 2005).

These projections dwarfed all previous official estimates of heavy cocaine use, including a 15-fold increase over findings from the most recent national study. Additionally, they found levels of cocaine that remained in the water after treatment, claiming that this alone projected to 80,000 lines of cocaine contaminating the water supply each day.

However, these elevated estimates of cocaine use were likely a by-product of untested methods and unrealistic projections. While technologically plausible, these estimates involved extrapolating data from a nonrepresentative set of water samples contaminated by countless chemical compounds to the scale of entire rivers and from there to the entire urban populations, amplifying even minor errors and estimates. Notably, no evidence of the health complications that would result from such widespread cocaine exposure ever emerged.

NSDUH data are particularly useful for their (relatively) consistent measurement and nearly representative coverage, therefore placing this survey as the primary source for measuring nationwide and long-term trends in adult drug use and dependency. Even when data are slightly skewed by methodological limits, changes over time likely reflect accurately the direction and magnitude of actual trends. For this reason, it is notable that 2010 NSDUH data suggest that drug use by much of the adult population is exhibiting similar divergence to that observed among high school students in the MTF. Specifically, reported annual and monthly use of any illicit drug has been increasing incrementally since the early 2000s for all adults (SAMHSA, 2011a). As was the case for adolescents in the MTF survey, this trend also reflects almost precisely the same growth in marijuana use during that time, having reached the highest ever estimate of 4.6 million daily marijuana users (15.7% of past-year marijuana users) in 2010. Also mirroring MTF trends, the slight increase in drug use overall masks what has been a slow but steady decline in past-year and past-30-day use of, as well as dependence upon, most other drugs except for prescription painkillers and opioids (SAMHSA, 2011a).

INTERNATIONAL DATA ON ADULT DRUG USE

A key source of international data on adult substance use is the self-reported drug use component of the *British Crime Survey* (BCS). The BCS is a large-scale household survey that provides information on experiences with crime, victimization, and drug use in England and Wales. First implemented in 1982, the BCS now interviews approximately 10,000 respondents between the ages of 16 and 59 annually. The drug-use component of the BCS includes measures of the lifetime, previous-year, and previous-month use of cannabis, cocaine, crack cocaine, amphetamines, ecstasy, LSD, "magic mushrooms," heroin, methadone (not prescribed by a doctor), tranquilizers, amyl nitrite, steroids, inhalants, and two catch-all questions for drug use (Home Office, 2001). The BCS is the primary source of information on drug use in the United Kingdom, and these data have yielded some very interesting findings. For example, data indicate that one-third of respondents acknowledged having ever used an illicit drug, but only 11% had used in the past year and only 6% had used in the past month (Home Office, 2001). Other findings, which reflect patterns seen in the United States, indicate that unemployment is strongly associated with drug use by young people, with 40% of unemployed young people reporting use in the past year as compared to 25% for those with jobs (Home Office, 2001).

The BCS contributes data to another key source of international data on drug use, the European Monitoring Centre for Drugs and Drug Addiction (EMCDDA). The EMCDDA developed as many countries in the European Union agreed that it made little sense to focus solely on drug use and policy in their own country to the neglect of those around them. According to the EMCDDA, "the multifaceted and changing nature of illicit drug use, and its intercontinental and European character, imply that it transcends political, economic and geographical boundaries" (1997, p. 3). In recognition of this, the EMCDDA examines drug use and problems across several countries by collecting existing national survey data and comparing cross nationally where possible (EMCDDA, 2002b). In the latest annual report (EMCDDA, 2011), drug use data were collected from 39 nations based on independent national studies. While this creates potential comparability issues that cannot be completely avoided, the EMCDDA has worked extensively with the European Union and individual member states to ensure quality data. Through the creation of the European Model Questionnaire (EMQ), upon which national survey questions for each nation are now modeled, any potential limitations have been minimized as much as possible. Among the cross-national analyses released by the EMCDDA is a comparison of cannabis use by birth cohorts in Germany, Greece, and Spain from 1938 to 1982 (Kraus & Augustin, 2002). Results of this study indicated that the percentage of people who report ever using cannabis has increased substantially over time, but that the pattern of increase has varied by country. For example, sharp increases in use were seen in Spain in the 1970s, and similar increases were seen in the 1990s for Germany. In the most recent report, widespread growth in cannabis use during the 1990s and early 2000s appears to have stabilized, and rates have even decreased in some nations in which use is most common, such as the Netherlands and the United Kingdom (EMCDDA, 2011). The average age for first use of cannabis also varied, being 18 in Germany and Spain but 20 in Greece. Across all three countries, age was found to be a key protective factor, as after the age of 25, very few people will initiate the use of cannabis (Kraus & Augustin, 2002). While polydrug use has been found to be increasingly common, especially when one or more of the drugs used is a prescription drug, overall consumption levels of opiates have decreased considerably in recent years in those nations in which use was most common, and the drug-related spread of HIV/AIDS by users has been largely contained and, in Portugal, Spain, and a few other cases, virtually eliminated (EMCDDA, 2012).

Another interesting study that employed EMCDDA data examined cannabis use in the general populations of England and Wales, Germany, Spain, and Greece. Korf and Benschop (2002) found cannabis use patterns to have increased substantially in each of these countries in the last four decades, with the most pronounced change occurring in the new federal states of Germany, where cannabis use rapidly increased with the fall of the Berlin Wall.

WORLD DRUG REPORT

A somewhat distinct source for international data on drug use is the World Drug Report, an extensive annual publication meant to serve as a source for global and international data on drug use and drug markets (UNODC, 2012). A primary strength of this annual publication is the breadth of data collected, as it is the only single data source that can feasibly provide estimates of drug use on a global scale or offer data necessary for assessing international patterns that are often invisible at the national level. The most recent data (UNODC, 2012) were collected in 2010, at which time around 5% of the world's population (about 230 million people) had used illegal substances in the past year, while approximately 0.6% of the population (27 million people) qualify as problem drug users (UNODC, 2012). Additionally, these data have shown that global drug use has leveled off in recent years, increasing slowly but regularly for many years, an encouraging finding that is offset somewhat by the associated estimate that problem drug use and the associated health risks have continued to spread in economically developing nations during this time, particularly in China.

These data come primarily from a survey of nations and territories within the United Nations, each of which expected to provide its best available national data in the Annual Report Questionnaire. This extensive survey also requests information on drug cultivation, trafficking, seizures, markets, and enforcement from each nation, which is then supplemented by data from law enforcement agencies and international organizations extensively involved in monitoring drug trafficking, including INTERPOL, Europol, and the World Customs Organization. Collectively, this also allows for deeper analysis of patterns in drug use by examining them contextually within the scheme of production and enforcement patterns. For example, the most recent World Drug Report (UNODC, 2012) notes substantial reductions in global cultivation of both opium—down 20% from 2007 levels—and coca plants—down 18% since 2007 and 33% since 2000—before noting that this market share is being replaced by growing production of and demand for synthetic drugs.

At the same time, the data collected in the World Drug Report are burdened by major methodological limitations, including a response rate below 50% over-all that leads to uncertainty about the accuracy of global estimates. Additionally, nonresponses are concentrated among nations that are less affluent and there-fore likely to hold very different roles in the global drug market than do affluent nations with high response rates. Regional differences in response rates are also a concern. Excellent response rates, consistently above 80%, are typical of European nations, and rates above 60% in Asian nations and nearly 60% in the Americas are at acceptable levels. In contrast, the most recent survey was only returned by 20% of African nations and about 15% of nations in Oceania (the South Pacific region that includes Australia and New Zealand; UNODC, 2012).

In fact, much of the World Drug Report's potential value may be lost, as these limitations are often further exacerbated by political and economic pressures related to drug market estimates. This led Thoumi (2005) to offer a harsh assess-ment of past UNODC estimates of the total value of the global market. In some instances, nations lacking the resources necessary for major national studies have manufactured instant estimates (rather than scientifically collecting data) in an attempt to maximize political and financial support from other nations. Rigorous scientific examination of UNODC estimates has concluded that this widespread exaggeration has inflated the overall global estimate considerably, meaning that an accurate total is only between 10% and 50% of published esti-mates (Thoumi, 2005).

DATA ON SUBSTANCE USE BY ADULT OFFENDERS—ADAM AND I-ADAM

The data sources described above are designed to examine substance use in the general population, and as a consequence, they miss certain high-risk populations. This is important, as data on high-risk populations (e.g., criminal offenders) are essential for a complete understanding of drug use and its consequences. A particu-larly valuable source of information for examining these issues is the *Arrestee Drug Abuse Monitoring* (ADAM-II) program, which collects self-reported information on drug use by recent arrestees at urban sites across the country, a population often missed in household or school-based surveys. ADAM-II has been run by the Office of National Drug Control Policy (ONDCP) since 2007. Developed to provide infor-mation about illegal drug use among persons who have been arrested, the data col-lected at each stage have been valuable despite the sporadic disruptions because they are "virtually the only source of continuous information on drug use within an offender population"; serious problems with its sampling procedures resulted in the restructuring of the DUF program into the ADAM program in 1997 (National Research Council, 2001, p. 84).

Since 2007, ADAM-II has collected data from a representative sample of adult males arrested at each location across 10 sites that were also part of the original program. As with the DUF program that preceded it, both ADAM programs have employed trained interviewers to administer a structured questionnaire to arrestees within 48 hours of the individual arriving in a booking facility, which also collects a voluntary urine specimen to enable verification of self-reported drug use. In 2011, 5,051 interviews were conducted, representing a sample of more than 35,000 arrestees at those locations and providing particularly valuable information due to the high rate at which those eligible agreed to be interviewed (87%; ADAM, 2012). Numerous topics are addressed during the interviews, with arrestees asked which drugs they used and how often they used them, their age at first use of each substance, what their housing situation was in the previous year, how they supported themselves, whether they had health insurance, and how and where they purchased their drugs. There are also measures addressing the respondents' mental health and any heavy use of alcohol and drugs, which might be useful in developing treatment programs. Basic demographic data on the subjects are also collected.

A distinguishing component of the ADAM data is that following the interview stage, subjects are asked to voluntarily provide a urine sample, which can then be used to verify self-reported substance use and estimate levels of over- or underreporting. The ADAM urinalysis can detect 10 different drugs but focuses on the so-called NIDA-5, or the five most commonly used illegal drugs as identified by the National Institute of Drug Abuse: marijuana, cocaine, methamphetamine, opiates, and phencyclidine (PCP; ADAM, 2012). ADAM protocol requires that arrestees be interviewed and tested within 48 hours of their booking because all of the NIDA-5 drugs that ADAM tests for, with the exception of marijuana, remain detectable in the urine for no more than 3 days following ingestion (marijuana remains detectable for up to 30 days). The validity of ADAM data is bolstered by the fact that the vast majority of arrestees who agree to be interviewed also agree to provide a urine sample, including 87% of the most recent sample (ADAM, 2012).

In addition to their ability to assess the validity of self-reported drug use through urinalysis, ADAM data provide valuable information on the extent of substance use by known offenders. A key finding from ADAM-II data is that more than 60% of male arrestees used at least one of the NIDA-5 drugs shortly before their arrest, with figures ranging from 63% in Atlanta to 81% in Sacramento (ADAM, 2012). These data have also been used to examine changes in drug use patterns over time and to demonstrate differences in the use of particular substances by region. One example of this is the extreme regional variation in methamphetamine use, as 5 of the 10 sites had less than 1% of arrestees test positive, but the two Western sites, Portland and Sacramento, had 23% and 43% (respectively) test positive (ADAM, 2012). Rates of methamphetamine usage among arrestees are also considerably lower in Portland now than they were at the end of the original ADAM program, as well as slightly lower in all other sites. Thus, contrary to many media reports, the "meth epidemic" never occurred in many places, though in select areas (especially in the West and certain rural areas), it was a major problem. Additionally, cocaine use by arrestees also appears to be exhibiting the steady downward trend seen in the MTF and NSDUH surveys of the general public. Since the end of the first ADAM program, all 10 testing locations have seen a significant decline in positive cocaine tests, with particularly large drops in New York and Chicago, where rates went from above 50% to below 25% in just a decade (ADAM, 2012).

In recognition of the increasingly global nature of the drug trade, the National Institute of Justice launched the *International Arrestee Drug Abuse Monitoring* (I-ADAM) program in 1998 (ADAM, 2002). Efforts at understanding substance use across national borders are often confounded by the fact that laws, penalties, and recording procedures varied greatly depending upon the country in question. I-ADAM attempted to address this problem by implementing a common survey, similar to the ADAM survey used in the United States, in a number of different countries. Australia, Chile, England, Malaysia, Scotland, South Africa, the Netherlands, Taiwan, and the United States all participated in the I-ADAM program at some point, and these data have enabled international comparisons of substance use among arrestees, though not as widely as had been intended due to the interruption of the first ADAM program, which ended the international effort as well. One study that occurred compared arrestee drug use in England and the United States, finding that opiates and amphetamines were more common among British arrestees, U.S. arrestees more often tested positive for cocaine, and marijuana use was about equivalent across nations (Taylor & Bennett, 1999). Matching patterns of use in the general population, the portion testing positive for any drug in the United States (68%) was higher than in the UK (59%), yet arrestees in England had higher rates of spending on drugs and received more income illegally.

Drug Abuse Warning Network Statistics

Another valuable source of official information on substance use and abuse is the Drug Abuse Warning Network (DAWN). DAWN provides data on drug-related emergency department visits and deaths that are related to substance use by collecting data from hospitals and coroners/medical examiners. So, unlike the data sources described above, DAWN data are aimed at investigating negative health *outcomes* associated with drug use.

The DAWN program recently revised its data-collection procedures, and as a result DAWN data collected in 2003 and after are not comparable with data obtained prior to 2003 (SAMHSA, 2005a). Currently, DAWN collects data on emergency department (ED) visits for all persons who have received emergency care in a hospital sampled by DAWN for a problem that the hospital medical staff determined was related to drug use. Information is also provided on the specific condition that prompted the drug-related visit, such as whether the individual came to the ED as the result of a drug overdose, suicide attempt, or an adverse reaction to pharmaceuticals (SAMHSA, 2003c).

Drug-related incidents are reported by DAWN as the result of one or more of the following drug categories:

- Illicit drugs
- Prescription and over-the-counter medications
- Dietary supplements
- Nonpharmaceutical inhalants
- Alcohol in combination with any of the drugs mentioned above
- Alcohol alone for patients age 21 and older

ED data reported by DAWN are also grouped into *drug episodes* and *drug mentions*, due to the fact that alcohol and up to six other drugs can be included on the report corresponding to a single emergency room visit. A drug episode is defined as "an ED visit that was induced by or related to the use of an illegal drug(s) or the nonmedical use of a legal drug," while a drug mention "refers to a substance that was recorded ('mentioned') during a drug-related episode" (SAMHSA, 2003a, p. 25). For that reason, even SAMHSA reports note that "[t]he relationship between the ED visit and the drug use need not be causal. That is, an implicated drug may or may not have directly caused the condition generating the ED visit; the ER staff simply named it as being involved" (SAMHSA, 2011c, p. 15).

As a result of these recording procedures, findings reported by DAWN include many more mentions than episodes, and this tends to artificially inflate the level of drug-related health problems reported.

> Recent findings from DAWN indicate that illegal drugs are now involved in far fewer ED visits than legal drugs. As can be seen in Figure 5.2, during 2009, painkillers, psychotherapeutic drugs (e.g., antidepressants), alcohol in combination with some other substance, and painkillers represented three of the five substances most often mentioned during emergency hospitalizations as well as the top two. Painkillers were easily the most common, with nonmedical use alone involved in 978,758 visits, nearly twice as many as alcohol (519,650) and 2.5 times as often as the most commonly involved illicit drug, cocaine (422,896). In fact, pain relievers resulted in more emergency room visits than all illicit drugs combined (973,591).

In addition to data on drug-related emergency room visits, data on deaths that are either directly or indirectly related to substance use are collected by DAWN from participating medical examiners and coroners across the country (SAMHSA, 2005b). Using the same drug categories employed for the collection of ED data (mentioned above), drug-related deaths are tabulated by DAWN under the following categories:

- Suicide
- Homicide by drugs
- Adverse reaction to medication
- Overmedication
- Accidental ingestion
- All other accidental
- Could not be determined

Mortality and ED visit data from DAWN and accidental death data from the National Centers for Health Statistics both showed alarming growth in the number of acute traumatic events related to drug use in recent years. The tremendous growth in drug-related traumatic events led to the 2011 announcement that deaths due to drug overdoses had become the leading cause of accidental death for the first time in U.S. history following a six-fold increase in such fatalities between 1980 and 2008 (White et al., 2011).

Figure 5.2 Drug-Related Emergency Department Visits, 2009

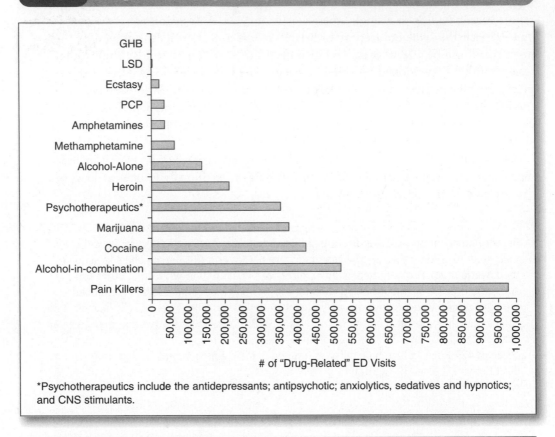

of "Drug-Related" ED Visits

*Psychotherapeutics include the antidepressants; antipsychotic; anxiolytics, sedatives and hypnotics; and CNS stimulants.

SOURCE: Drug Abuse Warning Network, 2009: National Estimates of Drug-Related Emergency Department Visits, (SAMHSA, 2011b).

According to DAWN, more than 4.5 million drug-related ED visits occurred in 2009, an 80% increase since 2004, coinciding with a 70% increase in the fatality rate during drug-related ED visits. An independent analysis of hospital admission records for young adults (18 to 24 years old) echoed these official data sources, showing a 57% growth in overdose admissions between 1999 and 2008 and producing an estimated $737 million in direct costs (White et al., 2011).

However, closer inspection of the DAWN data suggests that alarming increases in deaths and ED visits were largely the result of prescription drugs, not illegal drugs. In fact, deaths induced by illegal drugs alone (not involving alcohol or prescription medications) actually declined more than 30% since 2004, as well as a 13% drop in deaths involving "major substances of abuse," which include illegal drugs, alcohol, or the combination of both, but not pharmaceuticals (SAMHSA, 2011d). Cocaine-related visits have declined more than 20% since 2007, and cocaine-induced deaths were substantially reduced, occurring only 105 times nationwide in 2009. In fact, since 2004, rates of ED visits have dropped for heroin, all stimulants, and inhalants (SAMHSA, 2011d).

A crucial factor to consider when using DAWN data is that they examine one key consequence of drug use and abuse: health-related problems that result in an ED visit and/or death. Thus, DAWN data measure "events" (ED incidents and deaths), which can tell us about drug-related problems such as overdose (particularly among high-risk populations) but not about drug use in the general population. Only a small fraction of drug users ever wind up in an emergency department for a drug-related problem, so these data are in no way representative of drug use in the general population. Further, a single individual may wind up in an ED several times in a year for a drug-related problem, a situation that is probably most likely among certain (again, nonrepresentative) populations such as drug addicts. As each of these ED visits would be recorded without any mention that the visits involved the same person, they can only be used to estimate the incidence of drug-related ED episodes, not the prevalence of such events.

An additional issue to consider is that DAWN data focus on acute drug-related problems (e.g., overdose) and not the chronic types of drug-related medical problems (e.g., cancer, cirrhosis) that are more likely to be generated by legal drugs such as alcohol and tobacco (Faupel et al., 2004). Finally, there are several factors likely to influence whether a person who is experiencing a drug-related health problem seeks medical help at an ED, including insurance coverage, educational attainment, and proximity to a hospital. Thus, it is important for those who use DAWN data to interpret these data cautiously and with an awareness of these limitations.

There are numerous reasons that data from ED visits should be cautiously applied as an indicator of the scale of problematic drug use, not the least of which is widespread evidence from other sources suggesting contradictory trends. The recent spike in marijuana- and alcohol-related ED visits deserves particular caution, as national NSDUH and MTF studies have consistently shown only incremental increases in cannabis use and an overall decline in alcohol consumption (see, for instance, Johnston et al., 2012a; SAMHSA, 2012b).

Data-collection techniques and policy strategies may also play a part in this, producing the elevated totals of ED visits linked to alcohol and marijuana in recent years (SAMHSA, 2012b). This designation is often obtained from a few questions asked by employees with varying degrees of motivation and ability to assess the link between the substances consumed in the allotted 48-hour window and the ED visit. In that context, the likelihood that marijuana or alcohol will be mentioned is inherently high, as they are the two most commonly used substances.

Quick increases in acute trauma incidents from relatively innocuous and widely used substances can also be partially attributed to increased focus on tracking and treatment by authorities. Recent federal drug policy focus on treatment has included the rapid expansion of the "screening, brief interventions, referral to treatment (SBIRT) for illicit drug and alcohol use" program. This entails standardized training for hospital employees, in which they learn to automatically ask a full series of semistructured drug-consumption questions, regardless of the context or patient. Not only can this lead to elevated drug-related ED visits, but anyone who has consumed any amount of alcohol or marijuana during the past 48 hours is automatically referred to treatment and becomes another indicator of escalating substance abuse.

The data sources discussed above enable us to examine both legal and illegal substance use. It is important to note that there are significant differences between these data sources that must be considered in order to properly interpret findings from studies using these sources. For example, some sources of data focus on adults while others target high school students, and some data sources don't examine drug use in the general population at all but focus on drug-related incidents such as arrests or health problems resulting from drug use. Each of these data sources is valuable and provides a unique contribution to our knowledge of substance use, but data must be interpreted carefully, as the specific focus and methodology behind each data source has a great deal to do with the findings reported. This caution should be kept in mind as we use these data to examine the patterns and correlates of illegal drug use.

CORRELATES OF ILLEGAL DRUG USE

The data sources discussed above enable research on several sociodemographic factors that are associated with illegal drug use. Important correlates of drug use include age, gender, race/ethnicity, social class, and residence characteristics such as urbanity. In our discussion of the correlates of drug use, we will predominately rely on information provided by general population drug surveys (MTF, NSDUH), although we include findings from ADAM, DAWN, and other sources where appropriate. Research findings on the correlates of drug use illustrate that there is significant variation in the use of both legal and illegal drugs, with some populations being much more likely to use drugs and to experience negative consequences associated with use.

Age

Extensive data indicate that patterns of drug use increase rapidly during adolescence, peak with early adulthood, and then decline precipitously as people age into middle and late adulthood. Historically, as people reach middle age, drug use has rapidly declined fairly steadily through the lifecourse. As seen in Figure 5.3, rates of annual and past-30-day use both reflect the ongoing continuation of this pattern. Tables 5.1 and 5.2 also reflect this pattern within data obtained from the MTF survey (Johnston et al., 2012b), further demonstrating the consistency of this pattern across numerous substances.

There are exceptions and nuances to these steady historic patterns, often due to the use of alternate data sources or consideration of a particular subpopulation, such as the later onset that has been observed for some substances, including heroin and cocaine, and earlier onset for others, such as prescription drug misuse (Lopez, Krueger, & Walters, 2010). While variations are important to understand, the underlying correlation between age and drug use remains powerful and important.

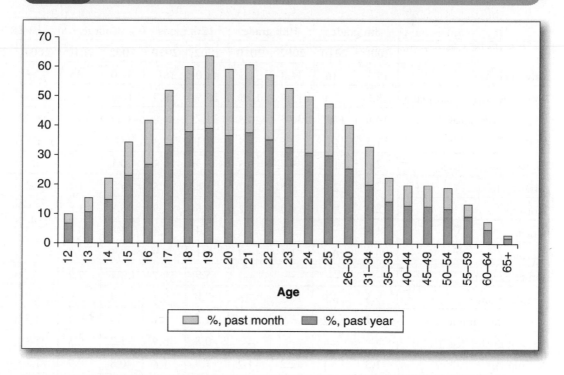

Figure 5.3   Any Illicit Drug Use in the Past Year and Month by Age, 2010

SOURCE: SAMSHA, 2011a.

As can be seen in Tables 5.1 and 5.2, adolescence represents a time during which illicit drug use increases rapidly, but it is during early adulthood that illegal drug use is at its highest. In our discussion of the theoretical explanations for substance use, we examine some of the reasons for this. However, one key reason for these relatively high use patterns during adolescence and early adulthood is the independence of users during this time period. During this period of the lifecourse, people are relatively free from the constraints and responsibilities that inhibit drug use. For adolescents, this is a period during which there is typically less and less time being spent with family, which generally acts as a protective factor against substance use, and an increasing amount of time spent with peers, which is generally a risk factor for substance use (Hoffman, 1994). This general lack of attachments and responsibilities, which serve to occupy time, may also be predictive of substance use due to the boredom that may potentially result. Research from Columbia University's National Center on Addiction and Substance Use indicates that boredom plays a key role in substance use among adolescents, with those who reported being "frequently bored" 50% more likely to get drunk and use illegal drugs (CASA, 2004).

| Table 5.1 | Past-Year Use of Various Drugs by Age, 2002 and 2010 | | | | | | | | | |

	8th grade		10th grade		12th grade		College		19–28 Yrs	
	2002	2010	2002	2010	2002	2010	2002	2010	2002	2010
Any illicit drug	17.7	16	34.8	31.1	41.0	38.3	37.0	35	32.4	33.2
Any drug except marijuana	8.8	7.1	15.7	12.1	20.9	17.3	16.6	17.1	16.3	18.5
Marijuana/hashish	14.6	13.7	30.3	27.5	34.7	34.8	34.7	32.7	29.3	28.7
LSD	1.5	1.2	2.6	1.9	2.1	2.6	34.7	4.9	1.8	1.5
Other hallucinogens	2.6	1.8	4.7	3.5	6.3	4.8	2.1	2.1	4.7	3.7
MDMA (ecstacy)	2.9	2.4	4.9	4.7	6.8	4.5	6.3	4.3	6.2	3.5
Cocaine	2.3	1.6	4.0	2.2	4.8	2.9	6.8	3.5	5.9	4.7
Crack	1.6	1	2.3	1	0.4	1.4	4.8	0.4	1.0	0.5
Heroin	0.9	0.8	1.1	0.8	0.1	0.9	0.4	0.2	0.2	0.5
Other narcotics	—	—	—	—	5.9	8.7	0.1	7.2	5.1	9
Amphetamines	5.5	3.9	10.7	7.6	7.0	8.2	5.9	9	5.9	7.1
Methamphetamine	2.2	1.2	3.9	1.6	1.2	1	7.0	0.4	2.5	0.7
Crystal meth ("ice")	—	—	—	—	0.8	0.9	1.2	0.5	1.4	0.5
Ketamine	1.3	1	2.2	1.2	1.3	1.6	0.8	0.7	1.2	0.8
GHB	0.3	0.6	0.7	0.6	—	1.4	1.3	0.1	0.8	0.3
Rohypnol ("roofies")	0.8	0.5	1.4	0.6	0.6	1.5	—	0.7	—	—
Been drunk	15.0	11.5	35.4	29.9	66.0	44	66.0	78.6	61.8	64.8
Cigarettes	—	—	—	—	38.3	—	38.3	28.1	39.1	33.0
Steroids	1.5	0.5	2.2	1.0	0.5	1.5	0.5	0.3	0.4	0.8

— indicates data not available

SOURCE: Adapted from Johnston, L. D., O'Malley, P. M., Bachman, J. G., & Schulenberg, J. E. (2012b). *Monitoring the Future national survey results on drug use, 1975–2011. Volume I: Secondary school students*. Ann Arbor: Institute for Social Research, University of Michigan, p. 751.

Similarly, for young adults, many of whom are enrolled in college, this age typically represents a time of independence from parental authority and a relative lack of serious commitments such as a family or career. A relative abundance of free time, living on one's own, meeting new people through education or work, and generally experiencing life as an adult for the first time tends to encourage experimentation with a variety of things, including the use of illegal drugs (Schulenberg, O'Malley, Bachman, Johnston, & Laetz, 2004). The experimental use of substances among young people is very common, and perhaps experimentation, at this point in the lifecourse, should not be viewed as necessarily or inevitably bad or harmful. Although research has concluded that the abuse of psychoactive substances, both legal and illegal, may pose serious risks to health and well-being, limited experimental use may also serve some positive functions. For example, research has concluded that experimental substance use during late adolescence may be constructive in the developmental process, particularly in relation to peer bonding, independence, and identity experimentation (Schulenberg et al., 2004).

Table 5.2 Past-30-Day Use of Various Drugs by Age, 2002 and 2010

	8th grade		10th grade		12th grade		College		19–28 Yrs	
	2002	2010	2002	2010	2002	2010	2002	2010	2002	2010
Any illicit drug	10.4	9.5	20.8	18.5	25.4	23.8	21.5	19.2	18.9	18.9
Any drug except marjuana	4.7	3.5	8.1	5.8	11.3	8.6	7.8	8.1	7.7	8.6
Marijuana/hashish	8.3	8	17.8	16.7	21.5	21.4	19.7	17.5	16.9	16.1
LSD	0.7	0.6	0.7	0.7	0.7	0.8	0.2	0.7	0.3	0.4
Other hallucinogens	1.2	0.8	1.6	1.2	2.3	1.5	1.2	1.2	0.9	0.8
MDMA (ecstacy)	1.4	1.1	1.8	1.9	2.4	1.4	0.7	1.0	1.3	0.8
Cocaine	1.1	0.6	1.6	0.9	2.3	1.3	1.6	1.0	2.2	1.4
Crack	0.8	0.4	1.0	0.5	1.2	0.7	0.3	0.1	0.3	0.1
Heroin	0.5	0.4	0.5	0.4	0.5	0.4	0.0	*	*	0.1
Other narcotics	—	—	—	—	3.1	3.6	1.6	2.3	1.7	3.4
Amphetamines	2.8	1.8	5.2	3.3	5.5	3.3	3.0	4.1	2.5	2.9
Methamphetamine	1.1	0.7	1.8	0.7	1.7	0.5	0.2	*	1.0	0.2
Crystal Meth ("ice")	—	—	—	—	1.2	0.6	0.0	0.2	0.5	0.2
Ketamine	—	—	—	—	—	—	—	—	—	—
GHB	—	—	—	—	—	—	—	—	—	—
Rohypnol ("roofies")	0.2	0.2	0.4	0.3	—	—	—	—	—	—
Been drunk	6.7	5	18.3	14.7	30.3	26.8	44.4	43.6	37.1	39.4
Cigarettes	10.7	7.1	17.7	13.6	26.7	19.2	26.7	16.4	29.2	22.4
Steroids	0.8	0.3	1.0	0.5	1.4	1.1	*	*	0.1	—

— indicates data not available

* indicates less than .05% but greater than 0%

SOURCE: Adapted from Johnston, L. D., O'Malley, P. M., Bachman, J. G., & Schulenberg, J. E. (2012b). *Monitoring the Future national survey results on drug use, 1975–2011. Volume I: Secondary school students.* Ann Arbor: Institute for Social Research, University of Michigan, p. 751.

Regardless, the use of legal and illegal drugs is most prevalent during early adulthood, but use declines as people age into their middle and late 20s and constraints on time and behavior become increasingly prevalent. In the mid- and late 20s, people often graduate from college, move on to more serious career-track jobs, get married, have children, and spend less time socializing with friends. All of these factors have a preventative effect on substance use (Hirschi, 1969; Kandel, 1980) and are important in understanding the relatively low and declining patterns of illegal drug use through middle adulthood and the later lifecourse.

Emerging research on individual drug-use "pathways" provides a more nuanced understanding of drug use patterns over the lifecourse. While most people who try illegal drugs in their lifetimes quit using them after a period of experimentation, certain substances are more likely to lead to persistent use. Though many hard drugs have low rates of long-term use, for some hard drugs, once a "threshold" representing steady and/or heavy use has been reached, it often leads to persistent and ongoing addiction battles. This has been found by some researchers with respect to cocaine, heroin, and methamphetamine, with early use of these drugs an important factor heightening risk for long-term problems (DeWit, Offord, & Wong, 1997; Lopez, Krueger, & Walters, 2010). Still, the overall pattern for illegal drug use remains one of rapid increase in the likelihood of use during adolescence and early adulthood followed by a steady decline in the likelihood of use after the early to mid -20s.

An interesting paradox regarding age and drug use is that while adolescents and young adults are much more likely to use illegal drugs, they are far less likely than older users to experience serious health-related *problems* with drug use. For example, data collected by the Drug Abuse Warning Network (DAWN) on the more than 670,000 drug-related visits to hospital emergency departments (ED) in 2009 indicate that only 26.1% of drug-related ED intakes were for persons age 25 and younger (SAMHSA, 2011c). Deaths due to drug use are even more disproportionately concentrated among those that are older, even though this age group represents a considerably smaller population of drug users. The drug-induced mortality rate is actually highest among 45- to 54-year-olds (25.3 per 100,000 population; Warner et al., 2010), making this group three times as likely to die from drugs as 15- to 24-year-olds and twice as likely as individuals between 25 and 34 years old (Murphy, Xu, & Kochanek, 2011). Meanwhile, even as adolescent use rates have remained fairly stable, there has been a slight decrease in the portion qualifying as dependent (SAMHSA, 2011a).

Another interesting finding on age and substance use is that there has been an increase in substance use and abuse among the elderly. From 2002 to 2010, as annual and past-30-day use of any illicit drug was declining slightly among adolescents and young adults, the rate of current illicit drug use by those in the 50-to-54 age group more than doubled, and the rate for those between 55 and 59 years old more than tripled (SAMHSA, 2011a). This primarily represents the aging of the baby boomers, a group that has significantly higher likelihood of using drugs than earlier cohorts, into these age groups. Substance use problems among the elderly are somewhat distinct in that, until very recently, they almost universally involved the abuse of alcohol and/or prescription drugs, with illegal drug use being very rare. However, a notable increase in marijuana use has also been observed among older populations, where it has replaced prescription drugs as the most commonly used illicit substance (SAMHSA, 2011a, 2011d). The expectation is that there will be continued growth of drug dependence in this population, leading some experts to refer to this trend as the "invisible epidemic" (Levin & Kruger, 2000). In fact, recent projections estimate that by 2020, there will be 5.8 million individuals over 50 who are battling substance dependency (Han, Gfroerer, Colliver, & Penne, 2009).

Increased substance use and abuse in old age is consistent with many of the explanations for substance use discussed above. Similar to the young, senior citizens typically have a great deal of free time, as retirement has often relieved them of employment commitments. For most, their children have grown up and left the house, and if individuals then suffer an illness or the loss of a spouse, this may further isolate them in terms of time spent alone and detachment from society in general. Significant life changes in late adulthood, particularly those that are traumatic, may encourage substance use and abuse in a variety of ways. For example, research has indicated that following retirement or the loss of a spouse, individuals may abuse substances because of the despair they feel over the unwanted life change, their inability to manage unstructured free time, or some combination of these factors (Benshoff, Harrawood, & Koch, 2003).

As noted, substance use by geriatric populations is expected to increase substantially in the future as members of the baby boomer generation move into their senior years. In the 20 years following World War II, more than 77 million babies were born in the United States and, consequently, record numbers of people have begun to age into their geriatric years. This has important implications in terms of substance use and treatment, as this cohort came of age in the 1960s, when illegal drug use was more common and attitudes toward drug use were more lenient. Research has found that baby boomers have maintained a comparatively liberal attitude toward drug use as they have aged (particularly when compared to cohorts who came of age in the 1950s), and this more liberal attitude is likely to result in higher levels of substance use by this group in their senior years (Patterson, Lacro, & Jeste, 1999). Unfortunately, those risk factors that parallel those of adolescents do not come with many of the same protective factors that youth can rely on, like peer support networks and family resources, so the elderly drug-using population is particularly vulnerable to associated problems with depression, isolation, and a number of other psychological effects that will require entirely new screening and treatment modes (Han, Gfoerer, & Colliver, 2010).

Gender/Sex

In general, males are more likely to use and abuse illegal drugs than are females, although the magnitude of the gender gap varies over time, by substance, and at different turning points in the lifecourse (Kandel, 1980; Teruya & Hser, 2010). As can be seen in Figures 5.4 and 5.5, patterns of use for marijuana and other illegal drugs are very similar over time for both genders, indicating that many of the same factors influence drug use by adolescent males and females.

Though the observed gender gap is consistent through much of life, early patterns of drug use do not display quite the same disparity between males and females. While boys are more likely to report first drug use at particularly young ages, through much of adolescence, most substances are used at relatively similar rates across sex (DHHS, 2003b; Johnston et al., 2012a; Shannon et al., 2011). In fact, Table 5.3 shows that throughout middle and high school, many drugs are used equally often by males and females and, in some cases, even more often by young women (SAMHSA, 2011b). Perhaps because girls tend to mature physically and psychologically before males, this is also evident in MTF data on 8th-grade students, among whom females display slightly higher rates of annual initiation into drug use. Likewise, 8th-grade females report using many substances as often as males and sometimes even more often, including inhalants, methamphetamine, intravenous heroin, and the broad category of any drug besides marijuana, as well as numerous psychotherapeutic substances to be discussed further in the next chapter (Johnston et al., 2012b).

The similar patterns of use across genders observed during early adolescence quickly change as people age into adulthood, as seen in Table 5.3. Cocaine use offers a particularly stark example of this pattern, as nearly identical usage during

Figure 5.4   Annual Marijuana Use Among 12th Graders by Gender, 1975–2010

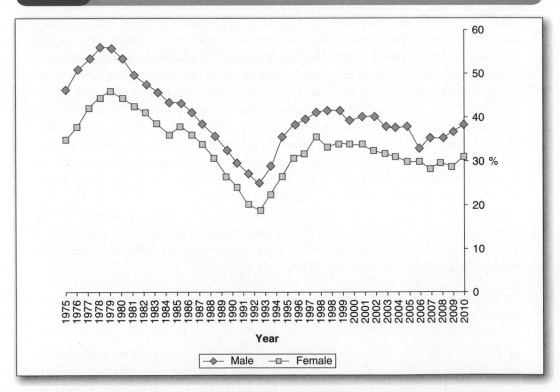

SOURCE: Adapted from Johnston, L. D., O'Malley, P. M., Bachman, J. G., & Schulenberg, J. E. (2012b). *Monitoring the Future national survey results on drug use, 1975–2011. Volume I: Secondary school students.* Ann Arbor: Institute for Social Research, The University of Michigan, 751 pp. http://www.monitoringthefuture.org/pubs.html

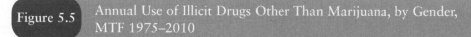

Figure 5.5 Annual Use of Illicit Drugs Other Than Marijuana, by Gender, MTF 1975–2010

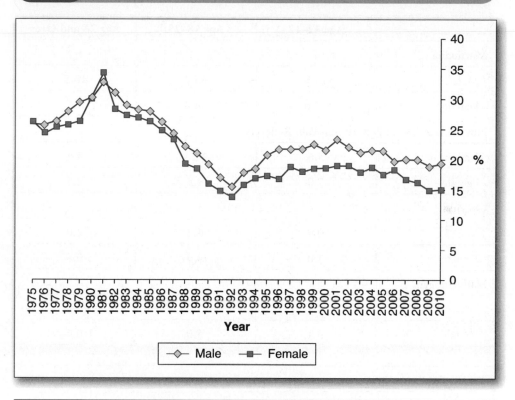

SOURCE: Adapted from Johnston, L. D., O'Malley, P. M., Bachman, J. G., & Schulenberg, J. E. (2012b). *Monitoring the Future national survey results on drug use, 1975–2011. Volume I: Secondary school students.* Ann Arbor: Institute for Social Research, University of Michigan, p. 751.

adolescence becomes a two-to-one gender gap among those 18 and over (SAMHSA, 2011b). When considering everyone over the age of 12, the disparity stands out, and males are at least about two times as likely to be current (past-30-day) users of marijuana, cocaine, and all illegal drugs together (SAMHSA, 2011a).

The fact that the gender gap in illegal drug use becomes increasingly pronounced with age may be, in part, because the social stigma and perceived consequences associated with substance use become more salient for women than men as age increases. Indeed, women generally view substance use and abuse more negatively, seeing it as more risky, and report being less tolerant of it as compared to men (Kauffman, Silver, & Poulin, 1997). This is not surprising given the distinctly different ways in which males and females are typically socialized. Specifically, men are expected to be more self-reliant, risk taking, and assertive, while women have traditionally been expected to be more nurturing and deferential. Societal institutions such as the family, education, the economy, and religion, as well as everyday interpersonal interaction, reinforce these social norms and influence gender differences in virtually all forms of social behavior, including substance use (Ensminger & Everett, 2001).

Table 5.3	Past-Year Use of Various Drugs by Age, Category, and Gender, NSDUH 2010

	Age 12–17	Age 18–25	Age 26 and Over
Marijuana			
Male	14.9	35.2	10.5
Female	13.0	24.3	5.7
Nonmedical Use of Prescription Pain Relievers			
Male	5.6	12.5	4.4
Female	7.0	9.5	2.8
Cocaine			
Male	0.9	6.2	2.0
Female	1.0	3.0	0.8
Hallucinogens			
Male	3.1	9.2	1.0
Female	3.1	5.0	0.4

SOURCE: SAMSHA, 2011a.

The use of psychoactive substances for pleasure or recreational purposes seems especially contrary to the traditional female role, particularly as it relates to motherhood. Because of this, substance use is less likely to be tolerated for women than for men (Ensminger & Everett, 1999; Lemle & Mishkind, 1989), especially during adulthood. Conversely, substance use and even abuse by males is more likely to be excused as "boys being boys," and research has found men to be more likely to report using drugs for recreational purposes (Ensminger & Everett, 1999). Thus, the fact that drug-using behavior is much more similar for males and females in adolescence than later in the lifecourse is perhaps due to the fact that, for females, the perceived and actual consequences of drug use are relatively minor during adolescence as compared to adulthood.

However, it is important to note that, even during adolescence, boys are much more likely than girls to engage in problematic drug use. This includes the heavy or daily use of alcohol and illegal drugs, the use of certain hard drugs, and the use or sale of alcohol and illegal drugs on school property (DHHS, 2003b; Robbins, 1989). Substance abuse rates are estimated to be almost twice as high nationally for men as for women (11.3% vs. 6.5% in 2010; SAMHSA, 2011b). Even studies of current problem drug users reflect this pattern, as men typically score higher on the Addiction Severity Index scores (Shannon et al., 2011). These measures may reflect the general tendency of women to be more conservative about substance use even during adolescence, when gender differences are smallest. As age increases, the social consequences of drug use increase for both men and women, but consequences become more severe for women, and thus the gender gap in *illegal* drug use becomes more pronounced. Broad gender differences in drug use, overall, can be misleading if substance use is only considered in terms of illegal drugs. Numerous studies have found that women are more likely to use and abuse legal, medically prescribed psychoactive drugs, often ostensibly explaining this use as having therapeutic purposes and relieving mental distress (Canetto, 1991; Ensminger & Everett, 1999; Green, Serrano, Licari, Budman, & Butler, 2009; Merline, O'Malley, Schulenberg, Bachman, & Johnston, 2004). These gendered motivations for drug use may be important, as perhaps the only difference between taking Valium to relieve mental distress and having some drinks with the guys after work to blow off steam is that the behaviors are thought to be more or less socially appropriate for one gender or the other. Perhaps women, particularly later in the lifecourse, are more likely to abuse pharmaceuticals as compared to other drugs because placing their substance use/abuse in a medical context provides it with a degree of legitimacy and thus enables them to conform more closely to societal expectations of femininity. Accordingly, gender differences in substance use may be more likely to affect the type and pattern of substance use rather than the general tendency to use conscious-altering substances per se.

Race/Ethnicity

Similar to the variation in illegal drug use across age and gender, there are substantial differences in patterns of illegal drug use between different racial/ethnic groups. Our focus in this section is on the five major ethnic groups in the United States (whites, African Americans, Hispanics, Native Americans/American Indians, and Asian and Pacific Islanders). However, we understand that significant heterogeneity exists within each of these groups and that this diversity has important implications. Accordingly, where available data allow, we discuss within group differences in drug use as well.

A common misperception is that African Americans and Hispanics are more likely to use illegal drugs than are whites, but extensive research has demonstrated that this is not the case. Indeed, the most striking finding identified regarding racial/ethnic differences in drug use involves the consistently low rates of use reported by African Americans through adolescence and young adulthood. Figure 5.6 shows annual illicit drug use reported by seniors in the MTF survey from 1977 to 2010, providing one measure of this phenomenon. In fact, numerous studies have repeatedly shown that nearly all forms of drug use across all time periods are less common among African American adolescents and young adults than any other group except for Asian Americans (Bachman et al., 1991; Johnston et al., 2011; Wallace & Bachman, 1991). Perhaps most notably countering stereotypes, current cocaine use is statistically nil among African American high school seniors, and the only major exception to this pattern involves current use of marijuana, for which use is equal between African

American and white students and young adults (Johnston et al., 2011). When controlling for sociodemographic factors, more nuanced analyses have also produced similar findings. For instance, Lee and colleagues' (2010) longitudinal analysis of young adult males indicated that whites were more likely than African Americans to use hard drugs, drink alcohol, and drink heavily, even after controlling for parental SES.

| Figure 5.6 | Annual Reported Use of Any Illicit Drugs Among 12th Graders, by Race, 1977–2010 |

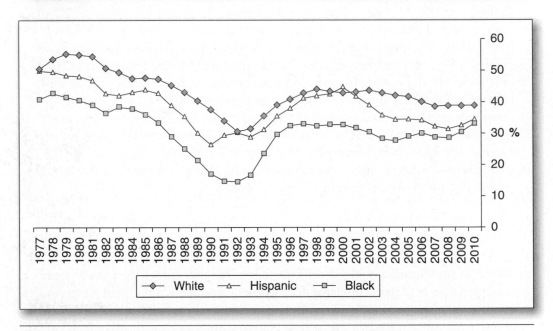

SOURCE: Adapted from Johnston, O'Malley, Bachman, & Schulenberg, 2012b.

In fact, most measures of drug use show that, besides Native Americans, whites use virtually all substances more often than any other racial/ethnic group. According to both the NSDUH and the MTF survey, lifetime, annual, and past-30-day use of virtually all substances is more common among white youth than African Americans, Hispanics, or Asian Americans (Johnston et al., 2012b), a finding that has been repeatedly confirmed when controlling for other potential factors (Lee et al., 2010; McCabe et al., 2007).

When examining racial/ethnic differences in drug use among adults, many of those racial and ethnic differences diminish or disappear, and similar rates of annual use are observed for whites, African Americans, and Hispanics. Even among adults, however, Asian Americans consistently report the lowest levels of drug use, while American Indians typically report the highest levels of use (see Table 5.4). Thus, patterns of substance use tend to vary substantially by racial/ethnic group and by age within each racial/ethnic group. We provide specific theoretical explanations for these different patterns of substance use and abuse by racial/ethnic group below.

First, however, we must note important methodological concerns that may influ-ence reported drug use by race/ethnic group. One of these concerns is specific to school surveys (such as the MTF and YRBS) and the differential dropout rates that are evidenced by racial/ethnic groups. Some have suggested that the higher levels of drug use reported by white adolescents may be accounted for by the fact that disad-vantaged minority students who become heavily involved with both legal and illegal drugs may be more likely than comparable white students to drop out of school or display high rates of truancy. Hispanics have considerably higher dropout rates than African Americans or whites, and this is likely to influence reported use by Hispanics in later grades (especially 12th grade). Consequently, actual drug use by Hispanic adolescents is likely higher than revealed in school-based surveys (Johnston et al., 2011). However, the fact that African Americans demonstrate a lower prevalence of substance use beginning with 8th-grade students is significant, as truancy and drop-outs are quite modest at this point and are thus unlikely to substantially affect survey response (Johnston et al., 2011).

Another issue of concern is that both adolescent and adult minorities may be more likely to underreport sensitive behaviors such as substance use (Fendrich & Vaughn, 1994), perhaps because they perceive the survey process to be more threat-ening than whites (Aquilino & LoSciuto, 1990). For example, Mensch and Kandel (1988) compared responses to drug use questions over two response periods and found that African Americans, Hispanics, and those with less than a high school education were more likely to deny previously reported substance abuse. However, Mensch and Kandel (1988) also noted that underreporting occurred at only the lowest levels of use, and others have found few differences in underreporting by race/ethnicity and social class (Bachman et al., 1991; Tittle, Villemez, & Smith, 1978). Regardless, there is reason to treat findings of racial/ethnic differences in substance use with a healthy degree of skepticism.

In contrast to the tendency for whites to have equal or higher rates of drug use, the consequences of substance use and abuse are felt most acutely by disadvantaged minorities. Indeed, as noted by Wallace, "the cost that substance use exacts from Americans is not distributed equally across the population; rather, its impact is experienced disproportionately by black and Hispanic adults, families, and chil-dren" (Wallace, 1999b). The extremely high costs associated with minority sub-stance use, coupled with relatively modest use patterns, have prompted researchers to suggest that there are two worlds of minority substance use—a relatively large population practicing temperance or abstinence and a smaller population that uses drugs and alcohol much more heavily (Wallace, 1999b). As will be discussed in depth below, although motivations for substance use and abuse vary to some degree across the groups, issues of social and economic disadvantage appear to be very important for understanding why these two worlds of minority substance use exist.

African Americans

Despite the rhetoric and media attention to the contrary, African Americans report comparatively low patterns of illegal drug use. Conservative patterns of use are particularly evident among adolescent subjects, with black adults reporting substance use patterns that are more similar to those of whites. Notably, a larger portion of African Americans (4.1% in 2010) was estimated to have substance abuse disorders than among any other racial/ethnic group (SAMHSA, 2011b). While other studies have contradicted this finding by suggesting that higher rates of use and abuse are present in white, upper-class environments (e.g., Cronley et al., 2012), the fact remains that NSDUH data consistently find higher rates of drug use and abuse among African Americans adults than among African American youth and slightly higher rates than white adults (SAMHSA, 2011a, 2011b).

Research examining these distinct patterns over the lifecourse has focused on the unique set of environmental and social circumstances affecting many black youth. This includes studies on racial segregation and urban poverty, which have demonstrated that, regardless of social class, African Americans are much more likely to live in areas characterized by a variety of social problems, including a greater visibility and access to both licit and illicit drugs (Anderson, 1990, 1999; Massey & Denton, 1993; Wilson, 1987). As a result, Lillie-Blanton, Anthony, and Schuster's (1993) study of racial differences in crack cocaine use found that once environmental conditions including drug availability were controlled for, even the use of crack cocaine did not differ significantly by race/ethnicity. More recent studies have also found neighborhood disadvantage to be a significant risk factor in predicting substance use and abuse independent of individual characteristics (Brook, Lee, Brown, Finch, & Brook, 2012; Fox & Rodriguez, 2012). Similarly, a longitudinal study of intravenous drug users in Baltimore found that those residing in areas characterized by extreme poverty were 29% less likely to stop using during the 20-year study, while those who moved away from such neighborhoods had a significantly higher likelihood of quitting intravenous drug use (Genberg et al., 2011).

> Other research on African American substance use has examined the hyperavailability of both legal and illegal drugs in predominately black communities. For example, Wallace points to existing research that has found black youth, as compared to white youth, to be more likely (1) to perceive that marijuana, cocaine, and heroin are fairly easy or very easy to obtain in their community, (2) to have seen someone selling drugs in their community occasionally or often, and (3) to report seeing someone drunk or high in their community occasionally or often (DHHS, 2003).

Paradoxically, the hyperavailability of drugs in minority communities may have both a negative and positive effect on levels of African American substance use. Although exposure and availability will increase access and the probability of substance use for some, this hyperavailability also means that black youth are apt to witness or experience the worst-case scenarios associated with substance abuse (Wallace, 1999b). Ironically, these problems may actually serve an indirect protective function for some African American youth, as the threat posed by illegal drugs is likely to be more immediate and less likely viewed as an abstraction, as it may be

| Table 5.4 | Past-Year Use of Various Drugs by Race and Age Category (%), 2010 National Household Survey on Drug Use and Health |

	Any Illicit Drug	Any Illicit Drug Other Than Marijuana*	Marijuana	Cocaine	Hallucinogens	Nonprescription Pain Relievers
ADOLESCENTS— age 12 to 17						
Total	19.4	12.3	13.6	1.0	3.0	6.6
Whites	19.0	13.2	12.1	1.1	3.4	6.7
African Americans	19.5	9.9	13.2	0.1	1.2	6.1
Hispanics	22.3	12.7	15.2	0.4	3.4	6.9
Asians	9.4	5.2	4.9	1.5	0.7	4.1
Native Americans	28.3	20.1	19.8	2.2	6.0	9.5
Two or more races	22.9	14.7	15.2	1.1	3.4	5.6
ADULTS— age 18 to 25						
Total	35.0	19.9	30.6	5.3	7.2	11.9
Whites	39.0	24.2	33.9	6.8	9.1	14.6
African Americans	30.2	9.6	29.9	1.2	3.4	6.3
Hispanics	29.2	16.0	23.4	4.3	4.6	8.9
Asians	18.1	7.0	14.2	1.5	2.9	4.6
Native Americans	43.4	17.6	32.5	6.5	11.4	19.5
Two or more races	42.7	25.5	40.0	5.3	10.3	11.0
ADULTS— age 26 and older						
Total	11.3	5.7	7.7	1.4	0.7	3.5
Whites	11.4	5.8	5.4	1.5	0.6	3.8
African Americans	13.3	5.4	8.7	1.8	1.0	2.5
Hispanics	10.3	5.7	6.6	1.3	0.7	3.2
Asians	7.1	3.2	2.4	0.3	0.4	1.6
Native Americans	17.5	2.2	12.9	0.3	—	—
Two or more races	17.0	6.8	15.3	2.8	1.2	5.1

— Low precision; no estimate reported

* 2005 data, most recent available

SOURCE: Adapted from SAMHSA, 2011b.

for many white youth. Thus, researchers have concluded that partly *because* of this hyperavailability, some African American teenagers may actually be deterred from substance use (Wallace, 1999b).

Perhaps due in part to the more deleterious environmental conditions facing many black youth, the relationship between black parents and adolescents has been found to be particularly strong (Giordano, Cernkovich, & DeMaris, 1993). In regard to substance use, research on adolescents has found African American teens to be more concerned about parental disapproval, while whites report being more concerned about peer disapproval (Warheit, Vega, Khoury, Gil, & Elfenbein, 1996). Possibly due in part to this fact, young African Americans are typically less peer oriented than are whites, scoring lower in terms of peer intimacy, need for peer approval, experiences with peer pressure, and perceived importance of social group membership (Giordano et al., 1993; Wallace 1999b). As prior research has found parental bonds to be among the most important protective factors and peer relationships to be among the most important risk factors for substance use (Wallace & Bachman, 1991), these differences may have important implications for understanding racial/ethnic differences in substance use.

As noted above, although substance use by African American adolescents is relatively modest, rates of illegal drug use among African American adults rival and occasionally exceed those of whites, depending on the substance (SAMHSA, 2011a). As Wallace (1999a) summarizes these different patterns of use by race and age:

> Among adolescents, black youth are no more likely, and in many instances have been found to be less likely, than White youth to be past, present, or heavy users of licit or illicit drugs. As black and white young people make the transition into young adulthood, however, there is evidence that drug use declines significantly among white young adults while it continues to increase among black young adults. (pp. 21–22)

Research examining these contrasting patterns of substance use has found socioeconomic status to be especially salient. For example, Barr, Farrell, Barnes, and Welte (1993) examined the effects of race and class on substance use and found poverty and educational level to be central to explaining differences in substance use among African Americans. When analyses examined illicit drug use by white and black males making more than $25,000 per year (a relatively modest figure), the drug use patterns were very much the same, with African Americans slightly less likely to use illicit drugs than whites. However, differences in drug use increased as income declined to the point that for those making less than $7,000 per year, African Americans used illicit drugs at five times the rate for comparably impoverished whites (Barr et al., 1993). Considering adolescents, research has identified similar findings, specifically that when socioeconomic characteristics are controlled for, levels of drug use and drug abuse are actually much lower among African Americans than among whites (Cronley et al., 2012; McCabe et al., 2007) and young adults (Lee et al., 2007).

When social class differences in drug use by race are examined using education rather than income as the measure of social class, the findings remain consistent. Among college-educated black and white males, there were few differences, with

African Americans slightly less likely to use illicit drugs than whites. However, as educational attainment declined, racial differences in drug use increased to the point that African American males with less than a high school degree used drugs at more than three times the rate of comparable whites (Barr et al., 1993).

Findings such as these suggest that poverty, joblessness, and a lack of educational opportunity may be more likely to result in illicit drug use and abuse by African Americans than comparably disadvantaged whites. Perhaps this is because African Americans experiencing these conditions are very likely to be among the "truly disadvantaged," and this is not the case for whites. Research on the truly disadvantaged by Wilson (1987, 1996) and others has noted that while the number of middle-class African Americans has increased in recent years, due in part to an increasing commitment to civil rights and programs like affirmative action, inner-city minority communities have grown more isolated and impoverished as they have lost the most successful members of their communities to the suburbs (Massey & Denton, 1993; Wilson, 1987). The cumulative disadvantage present in these communities clearly distinguishes minority poverty from white poverty. As Wilson (1987) has noted regarding the difference between poor whites and poor African Americans, poor whites live "in areas which are ecologically and economically very different from poor Blacks . . . with respect to jobs, marriage opportunities, and exposure to conventional role models" (pp. 59–60). Accordingly, drug use and abuse may be among the many negative consequences these social conditions have for impoverished minorities.

Other research examining the comparatively high rate of substance use by African Americans in early adulthood as compared to adolescence has suggested that this change may in part "reflect their response to the harshness of the racialized social system from which their parents had previously shielded them" (Wallace, 1999b, p. 30). That is, racism, poverty, and limited opportunities for employment, education, and advancement may increasingly act as stressors and sources of emotional strain on minorities once they have left the relatively sheltered environment provided by their parents. Recent research has demonstrated that young African American males are much more likely to use drugs when living in environments in which they face more racism and discrimination (Cronley et al., 2012). Presumably for this reason, neighborhood disadvantage has a greater impact on substance abuse rates for African Americans than whites (Karriker-Jaffe, Zemore, Mulia, Jones-Webb, Bond, & Greenfield, 2012).

Additionally, because class and race are inexorably linked in American society, minorities in underprivileged neighborhoods also have less access to social institutions and coping resources that help people manage these stressors (Peterson, Krivo, & Harris, 2000). For example, protective factors such as employment (especially professional), educational participation and success, and stable communities and families are all less prevalent in impoverished minority communities (Anderson, 1990; Wilson, 1987). Likewise, disadvantaged neighborhoods also provide fewer prosocial coping resources such as medical care, mental health services, substance abuse treatment centers, and outlets for conventional leisure such as shopping malls, recreation centers, and libraries (Peterson et al., 2000; Wallace, 1999b; Wallace & Bachman, 1991; Williams & Collins, 1995). Accordingly, substance use may be one outlet for people who self-medicate to cope with the stress and problems these impoverished conditions generate in their lives, which potentially explains why African Americans have the highest rate of needing but not receiving treatment (SAMHSA, 2011a) and why psychological trauma and stress have been found to act as mitigating factors for substance abuse among minorities living in disadvantaged neighborhoods (Stockdale, Wells, et al., 2007).

Hispanics

As compared to African Americans, Hispanics tend to report patterns of illegal drug use that are similar to those reported by whites. Currently, the Hispanic population in the United States is rapidly growing, and Hispanics now constitute the second largest racial/ethnic group in America (U.S. Census Bureau, 2010). Many sources of information on substance use, as well as the U.S. Census, use the term *Hispanic* to refer to a diverse group of Americans who have either immigrated to the United States themselves or whose ancestors immigrated from Mexico (approximately 60% of all Hispanics), Puerto Rico, Cuba, or Central and South America. Although this is a very heterogeneous group, "the Spanish language and certain cultural customs and traditions that are based on Catholicism and old Spanish culture bind many Hispanics with a sense of common culture" (Castro, Proescholdbell, Abeita, & Rodriguez, 1999). However, because of the diversity present in this group, many of those who are identified as Hispanic prefer to be called Spanish Americans or Latinos, as the term *Hispanic* refers to the colonizing nation of Spain. As Castro and colleagues (1999) point out with regard to this, Americans would likely resent being referred to as English people simply because they speak English and reside in areas that were once colonized by Great Britain. While acknowledging the validity of this view and the cultural diversity within the broad Hispanic population, we are forced to use the overly inclusive term *Hispanics* here, both for brevity and for consistency with the language of many past studies.

The diversity in these Hispanic subgroups is reflected in their relatively distinct patterns of substance use. Accordingly, we follow our initial examination of illegal drug use by Hispanics as a group by examining patterns of illegal drug use specific to Mexican Americans, Puerto Rican Americans, Cuban Americans, and Hispanic Americans identifying with various countries in Central and South America (see Tables 5.5 and 5.6).

Patterns of illegal substance use evidenced by Hispanics are quite similar to the patterns among whites and African Americans, with rates of annual and lifetime use slightly lower than those for whites over the entire lifecourse but slightly higher among adolescents for certain drugs (SAMHSA, 2011b). Although dropout rates likely influence findings on adolescent substance use by Hispanics, this population has long exhibited a tendency toward early initiation, with 8th- and 10th-grade Hispanic Americans reporting hard drug use in the past 30 days more than other groups, particularly cocaine and heroin, followed by similar or lower rates during 12th grade (Johnston et al., 2012b). Recently, though, elevated drug use early in adolescence appears to have extended later into life for many Hispanics. Recent MTF data show that current use of heroin, cocaine, and methamphetamine now remain higher than the national average for Hispanic high school seniors, making this also the case for the overall adolescent age group (SAMHSA, 2011a). A similarly rapid rise in annual and current use of a variety of drugs has also occurred among Hispanic young adults, leading to above-average rates of current cocaine and methamphetamine use and rates of marijuana use matching the average (Johnston et al., 2012b).

Exposure and access to drugs are important factors for understanding Hispanic substance use, particularly among adolescents. As with African Americans, Hispanics are more likely than whites to reside in areas in which illegal drug use is frequently witnessed and in which drugs are more easily obtained (Wallace, 1999b). Data also indicate that Hispanic adolescents are significantly more likely than whites to be offered, sold, or given illegal drugs on school property in the last year (DHHS, 2003b). In part, these factors may account for the finding that Hispanics are more likely to report drug use at young ages (Johnston et al., 2011). Despite the greater exposure of Hispanic adolescents to drugs, research has concluded that drug use by this group is predicted largely by the same risk factors that influence drug use among other adolescents: things such as family disruption, low school commitment or achievement, and delinquent peers (Moore, 2001).

Hispanic patterns of drug use are likely to vary with a number of cultural, environmental, and economic factors. Indeed, some Hispanic populations have been much more adversely affected by illegal drug use than others have, and a drug that has been particularly harmful to certain Hispanic communities is heroin. For example, the highest drug mortality rates in the nation are not found in Los Angeles or New York but in the heavily Hispanic Rio Arriba County in northern New Mexico. This extremely poor county is located along the drug-smuggling route from Mexico to Denver and has been characterized by exceptionally high rates of black-tar heroin use.

Partially in response to the situation in Arriba County and similarly affected areas, former New Mexico Governor Gary Johnson instituted more progressive drug policies on substance use, focusing on treatment and harm reduction rather than punishment. This has included giving families of heroin addicts overdose kits that include the drug Narcan, which is used to keep victims of heroin overdose alive. In Española, a city in Arriba County, the police chief at the time, Wayne Salazar, even argued that his officers should carry Narcan while on duty, noting, "It would be no different than if we responded to the scene of a bad accident where we had to perform CPR or first aid. We're trying to save a life" (*Nightline*, 2001).

Reflecting the considerable diversity within the Hispanic population, there is significant variation in the use of illegal substances among Hispanic subgroups. Perhaps the best ongoing source of data on these trends is the NSDUH, which provides information on substance use by Mexican Americans, Puerto Rican Americans, Cuban Americans, Dominican Americans, Spanish Americans, Hispanic Americans identifying with various countries in Central and South America, and those of two or more national origins (see Tables 5.5 and 5.6). Although the 2002 NSDUH did not report findings on Cuban respondents out of concerns with data precision, there were significant differences in the use of marijuana among the other subgroups.

Table 5.5	Drug Use by Hispanic Subgroup: Persons 12 to 17 Years Old, NSDUH 2004–2009

	Alcohol	Marijuana	Nonmedical Use of Prescription Drugs
Spanish (Spain)	21.6%	9.6%	4.6%
Cuban	19.2%	7.7%	3.2%
Two or more	17.7%	8.0%	2.5%
Puerto Rican	13.8%	8.4%	3.3%
Mexican	15.7%	6.2%	2.9%
Central or South American	14.9%	5.2%	2.4%
Dominican	16.1%	3.2%	2.1%

SOURCE: SAMHSA. (2011). *The NSDUH Report: Substance Use Among Hispanic Adolescents.* Rockville, MD: Substance Abuse and Mental Health Services Administration, Center for Behavioral Health Statistics and Quality (October 4).

Table 5.6	Substance Use and Treatment Needs by Hispanic Subgroup: Persons 18 and Older, 2009

	Binge Alcohol Use	Need for Alcohol Treatment	Any Illicit Drug Use	Need for Drug Treatment
Spanish (Spain)	26.6%	*	13.1%	*
Cuban	22.4%	5.2%	6.2%	3.6%
Two or more	25.8%	*	10.7%	*
Puerto Rican	28.7%	7.7%	9.8%	6.1%
Mexican	27.6%	9.2%	6.0%	3.3%
Central or South American	20.8%	6.8%	4.7%	2.2%
Dominican	23.8%	*	3.9%	*
Other Hispanic	*	6.4%	*	2.6%

* NOT REPORTED

SOURCE: SAMHSA. (2010). *The NSDUH Report: Substance Use Among Hispanic Adults.* Rockville, MD: Substance Abuse and Mental Health Services Administration, Office of Applied Studies (May 27).

Similar findings were identified by Zayas and colleagues (1998), who examined various Hispanic populations (Columbian, Puerto Rican, Dominican) and found Puerto Ricans to be more likely to use illegal drugs than other Hispanic men. However, these findings are not universal and are likely to vary with a number of other factors. For example, a study by Warheit and colleagues (1996) examined 5,370 adolescents in Dade County, Florida, of which more than 3,400 were Hispanic, and found Colombians to be more likely than Cubans, Nicaraguans, and Puerto Ricans to use illegal drugs. The authors concluded the differences in substance use evidenced by these groups were mostly due to differences in levels of acculturation (Warheit et al., 1996).

Acculturation involves the adoption of new cultural information and social skills by an immigrant group, which often replace traditional cultural beliefs, practices, and interaction patterns to some degree (Vega, Alderete, Kolody, & Aguilar-Gaxiola, 1998; Vega & Gil, 1998). Acculturation is typically measured with indicators such as language use and preference, ethnic identification, and nativity of both the respondent and the respondent's parents (Randolf, Stroup-Benham, Black, & Markides, 1998). Acculturation has a particularly strong impact on patterns of drug use for Hispanic groups with a relatively high percentage of recent immigrants, making it a factor unique to certain minority groups, most notably Hispanic Americans and Asian Americans as well.

Although low acculturation can be stressful due to the social isolation brought on by factors such as communication difficulties, it can also serve a protective function (Vega, Gill, & Wagner, 1998). This is the case with the use and abuse of drugs and alcohol, as many Hispanic groups are traditionally more conservative in terms of substance use than American society more generally. For example, surveys on drug use in Latin American countries have consistently identified very low patterns of illegal drug use, even in countries that are key producers and exporters of illegal drugs (Vega, Alderete, et al., 1998; Vega et al., 1998). This includes research on Mexico, the country from which most Hispanic Americans have originated, which has lower rates of use for alcohol and other drugs than does the United States (Caetano & Medina-Mora, 1989; Vega et al., 1998).

Much of the effect of acculturation has focused on alcohol use and abuse (discussed in detail in Chapter 6), but numerous studies have also identified an association between acculturation and illegal drug use (Amaro, Whitaker, Coffman, & Heeren, 1990; Vega, Alderete, et al., 1998; Vega et al., 1998; Warheit et al., 1996). This includes research that has found crack cocaine smoking to be higher among more acculturated Hispanics (e.g., those who choose to speak English rather than Spanish; Wagner-Etchegaray, Schultz, Chilcoat, & Anthony, 1994). Likewise, levels of acculturation were found to have a very strong association with all indicators of substance use, including illicit drug use, hard drug use, binge drinking, and bender drinking (Akins, Mosher, Smith, & Gauthier, 2008). In fact, that study of Hispanics in Washington State found that acculturated Hispanics exhibited rates of drug use very similar to those of whites, while nonacculturated Hispanics were only about one-fourth as likely to use illegal drugs and about half as likely to have engaged in binge drinking. Other research on the effect of acculturation on drug use has con-cluded that Hispanics are often frustrated with their social acceptance and unmet expectations of success and achievement, especially Hispanic men born in the United States (Vega et al., 1998). Additional research has found that acculturated Hispanics, particularly Hispanic females, are exposed to values that tend to encour-age or be more tolerant of drug use and abuse than are their traditional values (Vega, Alderete, et al., 1998; Vega et al., 1998).

Numerous studies indicate that, contrary to commonly held stereotypes and political rhetoric, residents without legal documentation (aka "illegal immigrants") are actually less likely to use and abuse drugs than are legal citizens. According to arrestee data in 36 major cities between 2000 and 2002, noncitizens were 55% less likely than citizens to test positive for illicit substances and 14% less likely to be arrested on drug charges (Kposowa, Adams, & Tsunokai, 2010). Similar patterns for both registered (legal) and unregistered (illegal) immigrants emerged among arrest-ees in Maricopa County (CA) between 2007 and 2009, during which time registered immigrants were at least 50% less likely and unregistered immigrants were at least 60% less likely to test positive for all substances except cocaine, even when control-ling for other factors (Katz, Fox, & White, 2011). As Vega, Gil, and Wagner (1998) note with respect to findings such as these, "there is something about American society that engenders experimentation and addiction at a much higher rate than experienced in other nations" (p. 125).

American Indians

Similar to Hispanics, American Indians are a tremendously diverse population. Although many people believe American Indians to be a relatively homogeneous group, the more than two million Aboriginal North Americans living in the conti-nental United States, Alaska, and Canada are dispersed into more than 500 tribes with more than 200 distinct languages (Caetano, Clark, & Tam, 1998). Though somewhat sporadic, past research has found American Indians to demonstrate among the highest patterns of substance use and abuse, particularly among adoles-cents and young adults, as compared to all other racial/ethnic groups (Beauvais, 1998; Beauvais et al., 1985; Mail & Johnson, 1993; Oetting et al., 1980; Plunkett & Mitchell, 2000; Young, 1988). The most recent NSDUH data, which can be seen in Table 5.4, found that Native Americans reported much higher levels of lifetime, yearly, and recent use for marijuana and illicit drugs overall (SAMHSA, 2011a). American Indians are also the only racial/ethnic group to evidence few if any gender differences in the use of certain substances. Research on American Indian females has found them to be as or even more likely than American Indian males to use a number of legal and illegal drugs (Bachman et al., 1991; Beauvais et al., 1989; Wallace & Bachman, 1991).

High patterns of substance use among American Indians can be attributed largely to the fact that, as a group, American Indians experience extreme levels of social and economic disadvantage (Akins, Mosher, Rotolo, & Griffin, 2003; Wallace & Bachman, 1991). Data from the Indian Health Service (2001) indicate that American

Indians fare much worse than the general population across key economic, social, and health indicators, and this disadvantage results, at least in part, from the nature and quality of reservation lands allotted Indians by the federal government. Although only one-third of all American Indians currently live on reservations, the conditions of disadvantage characterizing many American Indians are due, at least in part, to this legacy (Beauvais, 1998). Reservation lands are often socially and geographically isolated, and although unemployment and poverty rates for Indians are extremely high in general, this is particularly the case on reservations (Beauvais, 1998). The high levels of unemployment experienced by Indians are important for understanding their patterns of substance use and abuse, as research has linked substance abuse with unemployment in the general population (Kandel & Davies, 1991; Kandel & Yamaguchi, 1987; Wilson, 1996).

Another consequence of life on reservations is limited access to health care. For example, a report by former Surgeon General Dr. David Satcher indicated that American Indians and indigenous Alaskans living in isolated, rural communities have severely limited mental health treatment options (CNN, 2001). This may be particularly important for American Indian substance use, as a lack of access to mental health resources may encourage substance use and abuse as a form of coping and may inhibit recovery should addiction result. Perhaps partly due to these factors, American Indians who live on reservations have higher rates of alcohol and drug use than those who live off reservations (Beauvais et al., 1985).

The extreme socioeconomic disadvantage experienced by American Indians has been found to be crucial for understanding their patterns of substance use and abuse. For example, research by Wallace and Bachman (1991) concluded that the effect of socioeconomic status was central in accounting for higher levels of substance use by American Indian adolescents, noting that "Once background differences are adjusted, the white versus American Indian differences in drug use are virtually eliminated" (p. 343). Research examining American Indian adults has reached similar conclusions, finding that the higher rates of substance use among American Indians were "at least partially explained by the disadvantaged situation of American Indians, particularly with respect to socio-demographic and individual risk/protective factors" (Akins et al., 2003, pp. 64–65), as were measures of more risky drug-related behaviors like the use of hard drugs and bender drinking (Akins et al., 2012). Accordingly, when interpreting findings on substance use and abuse by American Indians, it is important to take into account the unique economic and social circumstances characterizing this group.

Asians

Similar to Hispanics and American Indians, those who are classified as Asian and Pacific Islanders (API) are extremely diverse. In the 2010 U.S. Census, the term *Asian* was used to refer to people identifying origins with any of the original peoples of the Far East, Southeast Asia, or the Indian Subcontinent, including Cambodia, China, India, Japan, Korea, Malaysia, Pakistan, the Philippine Islands, Thailand, and Vietnam (Hoeffel, Rastogi, Kim, & Shahid, 2012). At the time of the 2010 census, the API population in the United States was 14.7 million people or 4.8% of the total population, and there were 2.6 million more people who reported Asian descent as one of multiple racial/ethnic categories. Among those reporting Asian descent alone, Chinese ancestry was most common at roughly 23% of all Asians, followed by Asian Indians (19%), Filipinos (17%), and Korean and Vietnamese (roughly 10% each) (Hoeffel et al., 2012).

Asians typically report the lowest use patterns for virtually all forms of legal and illegal drugs. For example, research examining illegal drug use by high school seniors from 1976 to 2000 found Asian youth to report the lowest levels of marijuana use across this entire time period (Wallace et al., 2003). These trends of low use by Asian adolescents have been found across other substances as well, and for both males and females (Bachman, Wallace, O'Malley, Johnston, Kurth, & Neighbors, 1991; Wallace & Bachman, 1991). Similar patterns have been identified in household surveys of adults (see Table 5.4), with Asian adults reporting the lowest levels of illegal drug use, whether measured as past month, past year, or lifetime use (SAMHSA, 2010b, 2011a, 2011b).

Although there is some concern regarding the representativeness of the Asian population captured by drug surveys (Castro et al., 1999), with more affluent and acculturated Asian populations (e.g., Japanese) potentially overrepresented, other data support the conclusion that Asians are the group least likely to use illegal drugs. For example, data from the Drug Abuse Warning Network on emergency department visits involving drugs and alcohol found that in the year 2009, there were more than 2.9 million reports for whites, 667,000 for African Americans, and 353,000 for Hispanics, but only 7,829 for Asians (SAMHSA, 2011c). Although Asians constitute just under 5% of the U.S. population, this figure still represents very low levels of substance use problems given their national population figures.

In part, the relatively modest substance use evidenced by Asians may reflect their relatively high social standing in the United States. As a group, Asians report income and educational levels that are very similar to those of whites and dissimilar to other minority groups. For example, U.S. Census data indicate that the per-capita income for Asians was $22,352 in the year 2000, as compared to $25,278 for whites, $15,197 for African Americans, and $12,306 for Hispanics. The relatively high income levels reported by Asians reflect their high educational attainment and relative overrepresentation in high-paying professional/managerial occupations (Bauman & Graf, 2003). Some have speculated that the commitment to education among Asian families may also result in lower levels of adolescent and young adult substance use as Asian youth, devoting more time to their studies, spend less time in peer-oriented activities that facilitate substance use (Wallace & Bachman, 1991). As noted earlier, this tendency to spend less time with peers during adolescence is also demonstrated by African Americans, who similarly report low levels of adolescent substance use.

Despite the low levels of substance use reported by Asians as a group, it is important to note that there is significant variation in substance use among Asian subgroups. These distinct patterns of drug use are indicative of the marked differences in income, education, and culture evidenced by the distinct peoples classified as Asian. As Yu and Whitted have noted on the complexities of measuring differences in Asian subgroups, "lumping diverse ethnic groups which do not even share a common history, linguistic roots, or religious belief" causes important differences in health patterns to be glossed over (p. 105, as cited in Castro et al., 1999). So while many have labeled Asians a "model minority" in terms of their success and integration in American society, this label is overly simplistic, as it refers to only some Asian groups while ignoring the many disadvantaged Asian populations in America (Niedzwiecki & Duong, 2004; Yin, 2000).

The limited data available on Asian subgroup differences in illegal substance use makes broad conclusions difficult, but within the broader Asian American population, rates of current drug use vary with native ancestry. For instance, from 2004 to 2008, people of Japanese descent had the highest rates of drug use in the past 30 days (6.2%), while Chinese and Indian descendants reported the lowest rates at only 2.1% (SAMHSA, 2010b). Notably, even the highest rates among these subpopulations are still below those of all other major racial/ethnic groups, with annual use of marijuana reported by only 4% of Asian Americans, less than half the national average (SAMHSA, 2010b).

Variation in income, education, and especially acculturation may be important for understanding substance use differences across Asian subgroups. Specifically, in addition to their comparatively high substance use, Japanese, Filipinos, and Asian Indians are also among the most affluent and socially integrated of Asian subgroups, particularly in comparison to Southeast Asian groups. While 12.4% of the U.S. population lived in poverty in 2000, poverty rates for Japanese, Filipino, and Indian Americans were 9.2%, 7.0%, and 10.4%, respectively. Conversely, these figures were 19.1% for Laotians, 29.3% for Cambodians, and 37.6% for Hmong (Niedzwiecki & Duong, 2004). Similar findings are identified with education, as more than 60% of Asian Indians and 40% of Japanese and Filipinos had obtained a bachelor's degree or higher in 2000, while only 7% of Hmong, 8% of Laotians, 9% of Cambodians, and 20% of Vietnamese had reached this educational level (Niedzwiecki & Duong, 2004).

To account for the pronounced differences in income and educational attainment among Asian subgroups, it is important to understand the historical context of Asian immigration to the United States. Some Asian populations have constituted a significant portion of the U.S. population for more than a century (as is the case with the Chinese, Japanese, and Filipinos). As a consequence, these groups are considerably more assimilated and acculturated to mainstream American life and the relatively high prevalence of substance use that accompanies this. Conversely, groups originating from Southeast Asia primarily immigrated to the United States following the Vietnam War and corresponding unrest in Southeast Asia generally (Makimoto, 1998). Unlike other Asian groups, most notably the Japanese, the more recent immigrants were largely illiterate in both their native language and in English and were extremely poor as well. These factors have slowed the assimilation of Southeast Asian immigrants into mainstream America, and this has impacted their patterns of substance use (Makimoto, 1998).

Data on linguistic isolation support this, finding that although 4.1% of the general U.S. population may have difficulty communicating in English, this figure is roughly 24% for Asians in general, 32% for Cambodians and Laotians, 35% for Hmong, and 45% for Vietnamese (Niedzwiecki & Duong, 2004). Conversely, linguistic isolation is relatively low for Japanese, Chinese, and Asian Indians, in part due to their high average educational attainment (Makimoto, 1998).

The linguistic and social isolation of certain Asian groups has implications for our understanding of their substance use. First, this isolation is likely to mean that these groups will be more apt to use substances in a manner consistent with their native culture (which, although quite high for alcohol, is less so for illegal drugs; Makimoto, 1998). As noted in our discussion of Hispanic differences above, foreign cultural groups are typically more conservative in terms of substance use than American society in general (Castro et al., 1999). As the Asian groups with some of the highest use patterns are also some of the most affluent and educated, perhaps it is their level of acculturation that accounts for these use patterns. Indeed, among immigrant groups, higher levels of income and education typically accompany acculturation (Castro et al., 1999), and it may be that the influence of acculturation on substance use outweighs the protective effect of high income and education experienced by some minorities.

Social Class

As noted in our discussion of racial/ethnic differences in illegal drug use, social class is an important factor in understanding substance use and abuse, and it might be misunderstood even more often than race/ethnicity. For example, common measures of social class such as income and educational level do not reveal, as many assume, that members of the lower class are more likely to use illegal drugs. As can be seen in Figure 5.7, data from the Monitoring the Future Study show that measuring parents' educational attainment as a measure of socioeconomic status fails to consistently predict substance use. Although adolescents with parents reporting the lowest levels of education were more likely than any other group to report the use of methamphetamine and cocaine, middle- and upper-class adolescents were most likely to report the use of a variety of other drugs (Johnston et al., 2012b).

Interestingly, many studies find that drug use tends to occur in patterns entirely contrary to class-based common stereotypes, in that white people from more privileged backgrounds are far more likely to consume illicit substances. Using the National Longitudinal Survey of Adolescent Health (AddHealth), Humensky (2010) found that whites from higher social classes (as measured by both parental income and education) were more likely to report binge drinking, cocaine use, and marijuana use. This was the case even after controlling for early substance use and other demographic factors but was not the case among minority populations, further suggesting an interactive effect.

Similarly complicated findings on drug use and social class have been identified for adults. When using personal educational attainment as the measure of social class, 2010 NSDUH results indicate that those with the second-highest level of schooling (some college) are most likely to report using cannabis in their lifetime, annually, and in the past month, but the next highest rate is those with the least education (SAMHSA, 2011b). Meanwhile, using current employment status as an indicator of social class indicates that the greatest likelihood of marijuana use is found in those who are unemployed but that the greatest likelihood of cocaine use occurs in those with college degrees.

Similarly, poverty, in and of itself, is not strongly related to variations in rates of drug use in the general U.S. population (Jacobson, Ensminger, & Ohlenroth, 2001) or for international populations. Regarding the latter, data obtained by the British Crime Survey (BCS), which includes numerous measures of substance use, has found drug use by young people from the "poorest and richest of households" to vary only slightly, with yearly use rates being 33% and 26%, respectively (Home Office, 2001).

Despite the fact that poverty and low educational attainment do not appear to be related to higher levels of drug use in the general population, there are important qualifications to this finding. First, particularly severe poverty has been found to be associated with substance use and, especially, substance abuse, possibly due to the limited availability of coping and treatment resources in very poor communities (Wallace, 1999a). Extreme poverty has also been found to result in greater levels of substance use related problems (Fox & Rodriguez, 2010; Karriker-Jaffe et al., 2012). Additionally, the effect of social class on drug use does not appear to be consistent across racial/ethnic groups. Because samples of the general U.S. population (like the population itself) are disproportionately white, research findings based on such data tend to reflect relationships that are specific to whites. This is important because research has found that although social class is largely irrelevant for understanding white patterns of substance use and abuse (i.e., among whites, rates of use are relatively high across all social classes), this is not the case for other racial/ethnic groups. For example, as noted earlier, Barr and colleagues (1993) demonstrated the importance of income and educational level for illegal drug use by African Americans but found these variables to be largely irrelevant for understanding drug use by whites. In part, these findings may be because poverty, especially extreme poverty, typically involves exposure to numerous sources of disadvantage, and this cumulative or extreme poverty is most commonly seen in predominately minority communities (Anderson, 1990; Massey & Denton, 1993; Stockdale et al., 2007; Wilson, 1987). This is important, as research on drug use often studies poverty by examining only one critical feature of poverty in isolation (e.g., income or educational level) rather than examining it in its cumulative context (Barr et al., 1993). However, when poverty is considered along with the many other social disadvantages that typically accompany it, such as unemployment or underemployment, welfare dependency, low educational attainment or success, family disruption, and isolation and alienation from the broader society, it has been found to be an important predictor of illegal drug use (Boardman, Finch, Ellison, Williams, & Jackson, 2001; Fox & Rodriguez, 2012; Stockdale et al., 2007). Examining the effects of social class at both the individual and neighborhood levels terms, Winstanley and colleagues (2007) utilized NSDUH data and found that social disorganization greatly impacted rates of adolescent drug use. In this study, individuals with medium or high social capital were less likely to use or become dependent upon alcohol or drugs, but when neighborhoods lack social organization or social capital, residents were more likely to use and develop substance dependency.

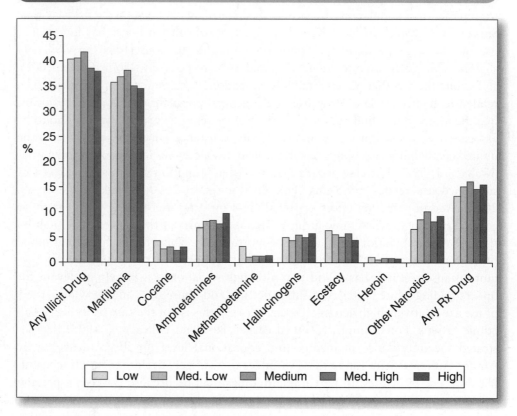

Figure 5.7   Past Year Drug Use of 12th Graders by Parents' Education, 2011

SOURCE: 2011 Monitoring the Future. Johnston et al., 2011b, 2011c.

Rural/Urban Location

The size of the place in which one resides has been found to be associated with illegal substance use, and although there are many exceptions to this based on age and type of substance, larger places typically have higher rates of illegal drug use, especially when comparing large metropolitan areas to very small towns or rural areas (see Table 5.7). One reason for this general trend is that access to particular drugs may be limited for those living in rural areas. In part this is because small towns may not have sufficient numbers of people interested in certain drugs (e.g., those less commonly used)

Table 5.7	Lifetime Prevalence of Use of Various Illegal Drugs (%) by Size of Residential Setting Among Individuals Aged 19 to 30				

	Farm/Country	Small Town	Medium City	Large City	Very Large City
Any illicit drug	51.1	57.1	59.3	63.7	64.9
Any drug other than marijuana	28.6	32.5	35.4	36.1	37.9
Marijuana	48.8	55.8	56.1	60.8	62.3
All hallucinogens	11.8	14.2	15.2	15.8	17.8
LSD	6.9	8.3	8.6	8	8.8
PCP	2.5	1.5	2.3	2.2	1
MDMA (ecstasy)	13.6	11.4	12.9	15.5	15.5
Cocaine	13	13.9	14.1	15.3	17
Crack cocaine	3.9	3.9	4.4	3.4	3.2
Heroin	2.1	1.8	1.9	2.2	1.8
Other narcotics	17.9	19	19.9	20.1	21
Amphetamines	12.8	14.8	16.9	16.8	19.8
Crystal methamphetamine	6.4	4.7	6	4.4	6.1
Steroids	0.9	1.7	1.0	2.1	1.9

SOURCE: Adapted from Johnston et al. (2011). *Monitoring the Future national survey results on drug use, 1975–2010. Volume II: College students and adults ages 19–50.* Ann Arbor: Institute for Social Research, University of Michigan, p. 312.

NOTE: A small town is defined as having fewer than 50,000 inhabitants, a medium city as 50,000 to 100,000, a large city as 100,000 to 500,000, and a very large city as having more than 500,000 residents. Within each level of population density, suburban and urban respondents are combined.

for drug sales to occur there. This may make it more difficult for rural residents to obtain illegal drugs, thereby affecting their use of these substances.

As will be discussed in more detail in the next chapter, the use of psychoactive substances in rural areas is more similar to use in urban areas than would appear to be the case if only illegal drug use is considered. This is because drug use in small towns and rural areas disproportionately involves the abuse and misuse of legal substances such as alcohol, prescription drugs, or inhalants. National surveys have found the illicit use of prescription drugs and inhalants to be very similar among rural areas, small towns, and larger metropolitan areas despite the more common use of other drugs in larger areas (Johnston, O'Malley, & Bachman, 2003b). Similar findings were identified by Cronk and Sarvela (1997), who found cocaine and marijuana to be more commonly used in urban than rural areas but that the use and especially abuse of legal drugs (e.g., binge-drinking) in rural areas exceeded that in urban areas.

Another reason illegal drug use is less common in rural areas is the more prominent role of social institutions such as religion and family. Being raised in a conventional family and participation in religious activities have both been found to act as protective factors for illegal drug use in some studies (Hawkins, Jenson, Catalano, & Lishner, 1988; Jang & Johnson, 2001; Thomas, Farrell, & Barnes, 1996), though the religion factor has often been rejected by other studies that instead suggest it is social ties to community members and organizations in general that truly matter. Either way, these protective factors more commonly characterize those living in rural areas, and research has found them to be important for understanding lower levels of substance use by rural residents (Albrecht, Amery, & Miller, 1996; Bachman, Wallace, O'Malley, Johnston, Kurth, & Neighbors, 1991).

In general, the use of any illegal drug as well as the use of specific substances, including marijuana, ecstasy, and heroin, becomes more likely as city size increases (Johnston et al., 2011, 2012a). However, there are exceptions. Data provided by the MTF study (Table 5.7) indicate that young adult rates of use for certain substances (e.g., crack cocaine, crystal methamphetamine, PCP) in smaller areas may rival or even surpass those found in large cities (Johnston et al., 2011). There are also regional variations involving pockets of high drug use in certain rural areas. For example, research investigating the use and production of methamphetamine in rural Nebraska used ADAM data to conclude that arrestees in some rural Nebraska counties were more likely to test positive for methamphetamine use than in the neighboring metropolitan area of Omaha (Herz, 2000). In part, this may be due to the relatively inexpensive cost of the drug and the fact that methamphetamine is often produced in isolated rural locations, both for distribution and personal use (U.S. Department of Justice, 2003).

The physical and social isolation of rural communities may also influence both legal and illegal substance use, and especially abuse patterns. Although spatial isolation may make access to certain illegal drugs more difficult, analogous to the isolation of minorities in disadvantaged urban communities, substance abuse treatment resources are likely to be more limited for rural residents should they need them. For example, research by Warner and Leukfeld (2001) indicates that rural residents often find themselves forced to travel large distances in order to obtain health-related services. Rural people may also be more likely to be characterized by cultural traits that make seeking treatment for substance abuse more difficult or less likely, most notably conservatism and a strong belief in self-reliance (Warner & Leukfeld, 2001).

Thus, although the isolation and more conservative nature of most small/rural areas may serve a protective function against some forms of illegal drug use, this effect appears to be decreasing over time, and differences in illegal drug use patterns may simply indicate that rural residents are more likely to use and abuse legally available substances (Cronk & Sarvela, 1997).

CONCLUSION

This chapter has discussed several correlates of illegal drug use as well as provided an overview of the primary sources of information available on substance use and abuse. The two most widely used and perhaps the best sources of information on substance use and abuse are the Monitoring the Future Study and the National Survey on Drug Use and Health, which have collected data on substance use and abuse in the United States for decades. Similar data sources provide us with information on substance use in nations abroad. Other key sources of information on substance use and abuse target populations that may be of specific interest, such as those accused of criminal offenses (ADAM) or those seeking help at hospital emergency departments for drug-related problems (DAWN). Finally, ethnographic and interview data can provide an in-depth look at drug-using populations and issues sometimes missed by other sources of data. All of these data sources are extremely valuable for an understanding of substance use and abuse, but every one also has methodological limitations that must be considered when interpreting findings on drug use.

These data sources have enabled researchers to document and examine why drug use is more common among some populations than others. One correlate of illegal drug use is age, as the use of drugs is much more common in late adolescence and early adulthood than at any other point in the lifecourse. Research has found that the amount of free time and relative lack of constraints (e.g., career, spouse, children) during this period of life may be important for understanding these patterns of high use. Gender is another predictor of illegal drug use, with males being more likely than females to use illegal drugs. However, gender differences in drug use vary significantly with age. During adolescence, differences are minimal, although males may be more likely to use drugs in harmful ways. At the stage of late adulthood, gender differences in illegal drug use also increase, although this may, at least partially, reflect a tendency of women to use more socially accepted drugs, such as psychoactive pharmaceuticals. It is possible that this is because the social condemnation of illegal drug use becomes greater for females as compared to males with age, possibly due to an association with motherhood.

Drug use also varies significantly by race/ethnicity, and in contrast to what is portrayed by the media and believed by many in the general population, whites are among the most likely to use illegal drugs. Several factors are important for understanding these race/ethnic differences in drug use, including poverty, education, employment, access to societal resources and opportunities, alienation, stress, and acculturation. Social class is also an important factor for understanding drug use and problems associated with use, although the importance of social class varies across race/ethnicity and age.

Finally, whether one lives in an urban as opposed to a more rural area or small town is an important predictor of illegal drug use. However, rates of drug use and abuse in urban, semi-urban, and rural areas may be quite similar if one considers all psychoactive substances rather than just illegal drugs.

REVIEW QUESTIONS

1. What are the two most useful surveys on drug use in the United States? What are the strengths and limitations of these surveys?

2. Aside from surveys, what other sources of data on drug use in the United States are available? What are the advantages and disadvantages of these sources, compared to surveys?

3. At what point in the lifecourse does illegal drug use peak and why is this the case?

4. What is known about gender differences in the use of illegal drugs? How does the gender gap in illegal drug use differ over the lifecourse?

5. Which racial/ethnic groups are most likely to use illegal drugs during adolescence? Do these patterns change when considering adult populations?

6. What is hyperavailability and how does it help explain racial/ethnic differences in drug use?

7. What factors account for the modest levels of illegal drug use by black adolescents as compared to white adolescents?

8. What is the relationship between social class and substance use? Are there instances in which poverty is strongly related to drug use and abuse? What are the implications of this for understanding racial differences in illegal drug use?

9. What is acculturation and what effect does it have on levels of illegal drug use among Hispanics?

10. What factors are associated with the comparative high levels of illegal drug use reported by American Indians?

11. What factors account for differences in patterns of drug use across Asian subgroups?

12. What is the relationship between rural/urban location and drug use?

INTERNET EXERCISE

Access data on patterns of adolescent drug use provided by the current Monitoring the Future study at http://www.monitoringthefuture.org/. Find the tables reporting drug use. What percentage of 12th graders used marijuana during the past year? What percentage used cocaine? Do these trends surprise you?

CHAPTER 6

Patterns of
Legal Drug Use

The following chapter examines patterns of legal drug use across key sociodemographic correlates. Our examination of legal drug use by age, gender, race, social class, and urbanity reveals that some groups of people are more likely to use and abuse legal drugs than are others, and some populations are particularly likely to experience problems associated with the use of these substances. In this chapter, we examine the use of a variety of legal drugs, with a particular focus on patterns of alcohol and prescription drug use. We also examine the use of caffeine, tobacco, inhalants, and performance-enhancing drugs. As will be demonstrated, the factors that encourage and hamper legal and illegal drug use are largely the same—further underlining the similarity of psychoactive substances regardless of their legal status.

AGE

The relationship between age and the use of legal drugs varies somewhat depending on the substance in question and the type of use (e.g., use in moderation versus heavy use/abuse), but legal drug use is typically highest during late adolescence and early adulthood with patterns of use declining steadily thereafter. As illustrated in Figures 6.1 through 6.3, the prevalence of alcohol use is greater than the prevalence of illicit drug use or marijuana use, and the dropoff in use after the early 20s is more gradual for alcohol than for the illicit drug and marijuana measures.

As might be expected given the legal drinking age, alcohol use peaks at age 21, while illicit drug use and marijuana use peak slightly earlier (between 18 and 20 years of age). However, these slightly different peaks in use patterns may arise in part *because* of the legality of alcohol at age 21. Specifically, when alcohol becomes legal for users at age 21, and thus a more convenient and easily accessible means of consciousness alteration, people may tend to moderate their illegal drug use and consume alcohol more frequently.

Aside from the minor differences mentioned above, general patterns of use for legal and illegal drugs are largely the same over the lifecourse. This is particularly the case when we compare binge drinking and the heavy use of alcohol with illicit drug use and marijuana use. For example, as seen in Figures 6.1 to 6.3, data on patterns of binge drinking, heavy alcohol use, illicit drug use, and marijuana use reveal almost *identical patterns of use by age*. These common patterns demonstrate that the tendency toward intoxication is manifested very similarly over the lifecourse, although intoxication is most commonly achieved with the heavy use of alcohol.

Data on binge drinking and heavy alcohol use demonstrate that alcohol is routinely used by a significant portion of the population to alter consciousness. As demonstrated in Figure 6.1, nearly half the population aged 21 to 25 reports binge drinking, and by age 50, binge drinking is still reported by roughly 25% of the population (SAMHSA, 2011a). Thus, using alcohol to the point of intoxication, a practice that makes distinctions between alcohol and illegal drugs increasingly difficult, is a very common practice throughout the lifecourse. Data also reveal that a large percentage of Americans drink, and drink heavily, before they are legally able to do so (Figure 6.1).

Figure 6.1   Current (30-Day), Binge, and Heavy Alcohol Use*, by Age, 2010

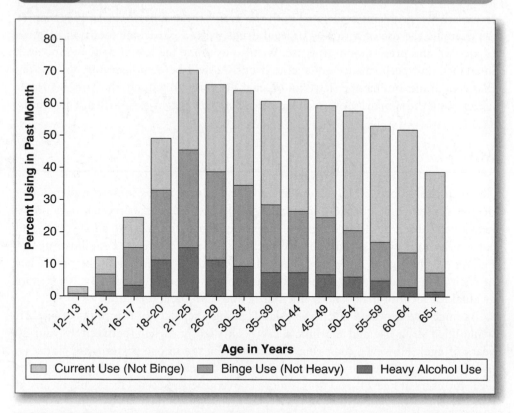

*Binge drinking is defined as five or more drinks on the same occasion at least once in the past 30 days for males, and four or more drinks on the same occasion at least once in the past 30 days for females. Heavy alcohol use involves at least five binge-drinking episodes in the last 30 days.

SOURCE: SAMHSA, 2011a.

Figure 6.2 Illicit Drug Use in the Past Year and Month by Age, 2009

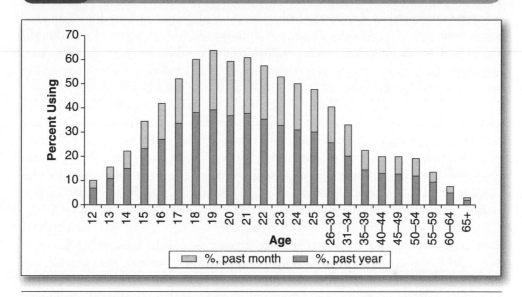

*Illicit drug use includes marijuana/hashish, cocaine (including crack), heroin, hallucinogens, inhalants, and any nonmedical prescription drug use. Percentage data for some of the age categories are not reported by the NSDUH and were calculated from the raw data.

SOURCE: SAMHSA, 2011a.

Figure 6.3 Marijuana Use in the Past Month by Age, 2010

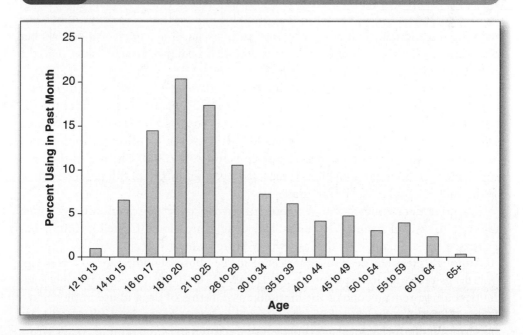

*Percentage data for some of the age categories are not reported by the NSDUH and were calculated from raw data.

SOURCES: SAMHSA, 2004, 2011a.

As noted, substance use is typically highest in late adolescence and early adulthood. Longitudinal data on alcohol and tobacco use by high school seniors indicate that these substances are used at a relatively high rate and that patterns of use have remained stable over time. For example, Figure 6.4 summarizes data from the Monitoring the Future Study indicating that patterns of drinking and drinking to the point of intoxication have decreased in recent years. Smoking by 12th graders has also decreased in recent years, although the use of "chew" or smokeless tobacco has increased slightly.

The use of legal (and illegal) drugs tends to increase rapidly between early and late adolescence. Data from the Monitoring the Future Study (summarized in Table 6.1) demonstrate that 12th graders are more than five times as likely to have been drunk in the past month as 8th graders and are roughly two to three times more likely than 8th graders to have abused some form of prescription drug. The use of inhalants represents one exception to this trend. Data in Table 6.1 also indicate that the use of inhalants is much higher among young populations, and this is for one simple reason—access.

As discussed in Chapter 3, inhalants include a wide variety of legal products that are consumed for their psychoactive properties. Unlike most other forms of legal and illegal drugs, inhalants can be found virtually anywhere. For example, it is estimated that more than 1,000 common household products can be inhaled to obtain a psychoactive effect somewhat similar to alcohol intoxication (Fackelmann, 2002; Partnership for a Drug Free America, 2005a).

Thus, inhalants are readily available to youth at a time when alcohol, marijuana, and/or psychoactive pharmaceuticals may still be difficult for youth to obtain. When youth move into middle and late adolescence, other psychoactive drugs become more widely accessible to them and the use of inhalants rapidly declines as these substances take their place. Overall, this change in the primary substance of use can be viewed as positive in the sense that although the replacement drugs may come with significant risk, common inhalants such as gasoline, paint thinner, rubber cement, and glue are extremely toxic to users and on balance are far riskier than the typical alternatives (Weil & Rosen, 1998).

Surveys on adolescent drug use also provide data on the use of performance-enhancing drugs and supplements. Data presented in Table 6.1 indicate that the use of steroids (1.2%) and androstenedione (0.7%) is reported by roughly 1% of high school seniors, down significantly since 2003 (perhaps not surprising with the latter, as "andro" had only recently been federally banned in 2003). The use of the legal supplement creatine monohydrate is reported by roughly 2% of 8th graders, 7% of 10th graders, and 8.5% of 12th graders.

Extensive data indicate that the abuse of psychoactive prescription drugs, often referred to as "pharming" by users and drug counselors (Costello, 2005), has increased substantially over the last twenty years (Johnston et al., 2011).

Although there has been a slight decline in the abuse of some forms of prescription drugs recently (Johnston et al., 2011; SAMHSA, 2011a), prescription pharmaceutical abuse remains one of the most common forms of drug abuse in the United States. As seen in Figure 6.5, 8 of the top 14 drugs abused by 12th graders are prescription pharmaceuticals, including 5 of the top 8 (6 of 8 counting cough syrup, which may or may not be prescribed).

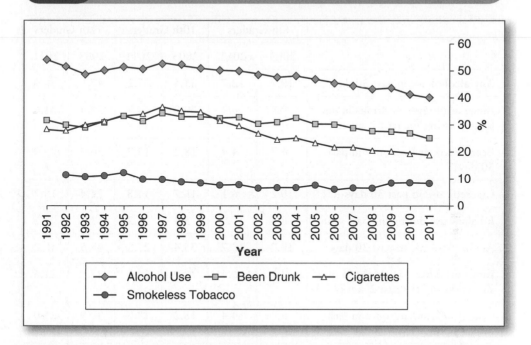

Figure 6.4   Use of Alcohol and Tobacco in the Past Month by 12th Graders, 1991–2011

NOTE: Data not available on smokeless tobacco for 1991.

SOURCE: Johnston, O'Malley, Bachman, & Schulenberg, 2012b.

Substance Abuse in the Military

Substance abuse and problems arising from substance abuse among current and former members of the military have substantially increased according to a 2012 report by the Institute of Medicine. The report found heavy drinking to be reported by about 20% of active-duty military personnel, and binge drinking was up from 35% in 1998 to 47% a decade later. Prescription drug abuse was also found to have increased substantially, from 2% in 2002 to 11% in 2008. As with the historical spikes in morphine use following 19th-century wars, many soldiers have found their need for pain medication following injury to lead to opiate addiction. The report found that adequate care for substance problems experienced by military service members and their families was hampered by inadequate prevention strategies, staffing shortages, lack of medical coverage for services known to be effective at preventing or treating drug use, and stigma associated with substance disorders. (NIH, 2012)

| Table 6.1 | Rates of Selected Drug Use by Age |

	8th Graders		10th Graders		12th Graders	
	2003	2011	2003	2011	2003	2011
Any alcohol use in past 30 days	19.7	12.7	35.4	27.2	47.5	40.0
Binge drinking—5+ drinks in one sitting during the past 2 weeks	9.8	6.4	20.0	14.7	27.9	21.6
Been drunk at least once in past 30 days	6.7	4.4	18.2	13.7	30.9	25.0
Cigarette use in past 30 days	10.2	6.1	16.7	11.8	24.4	18.7
Inhalant use during the past year	8.7	7.9	5.4	7.2	3.9	3.2
Any alcohol use in past 30 days	19.7	12.7	35.4	27.2	47.5	40.0
Binge drinking—5+ drinks in one sitting during the past 2 weeks	9.8	6.4	20.0	14.7	27.9	21.6
Been drunk at least once in past 30 days	6.7	4.4	18.2	13.7	30.9	25.0
Cigarette use in past 30 days	10.2	6.1	16.7	11.8	24.4	18.7
Inhalant use during the past year	8.7	7.9	5.4	7.2	3.9	3.2
Sedative (barbiturate) use in past year	—	—	—	—	6.0	4.4
Tranquilizer use in the past year	2.7	2.0	5.3	4.5	6.7	5.6
Vicodin* use in the past year	2.8	2.1	7.2	5.9	10.5	8.1
OxyContin* use in the past year	1.7	1.8	3.6	3.9	4.5	4.9
Ritalin* use in the past year	2.6	1.3	4.1	2.6	4.0	2.6
Steroid use in the past year	1.4	0.7	1.7	0.9	2.1	1.2
Androstenedione* use, past year	2.0	0.6	1.7	0.8	2.5	0.7
Creatine* use in the past year	2.3	1.9	5.8	7.1	8.3	8.6

*Refers to use that is not under a doctor's orders

— Data unavailable

SOURCE: Johnston, L. D., O'Malley, P. M., Bachman, J. G., & Schulenberg, J. E. (2012c). *Monitoring the Future national survey results on drug use, 1975-2011. Volume II: College students and adults ages 19-50*. Ann Arbor: Institute for Social Research, The University of Michigan, 314 pp.

Figure 6.5 A Comparison of Pharmaceutical Abuse and the Use of Common Illegal Drugs by Teens

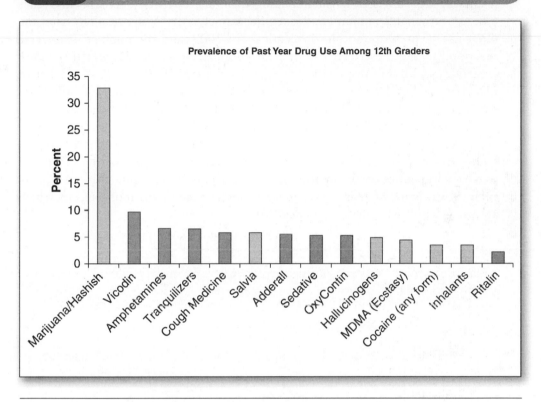

Prevalence of Past Year Drug Use Among 12th Graders

SOURCE: The Monitoring the Future study, University of Michigan.

Purple Jelly: The Abuse of Prescription Cough Syrup

The abuse of cough syrup for its psychoactive effect is common (Figure 6.5). Over-the-counter cough syrups, such as Robitussin, are abused for the dextromethorphan (DXM) they contain, but prescription cough syrups containing codeine and the sedative promethazine are also commonly abused. Some cities report greater problems with syrup abuse than others. For example, a survey of Houston teenagers found at least 30% to report the abuse of cough syrup, and the city is known in rap culture as "the City of Syrup" (Rice, 2005). On the street, prescription cough syrup is sometimes called "lean," "purple," "purple jelly," and "syzurp." Houston record producer D.J. Screw, who died of a drug overdose in 2000, was among those who popularized syrup abuse with song lyrics such as "I keep that purple stuff in my cup." (Rice, 2005)

The widespread illicit use of psychoactive pharmaceuticals, combined with the high level of risk posed by some of these drugs (particularly the narcotics), results in high levels of harm stemming from acute toxicity. As seen in Figure 6.6, more than 1.2 million emergency department (ED) visits resulted from the illicit use of prescription pharmaceuticals in 2009, and the number of adverse reactions to the prescribed use of pharmaceuticals almost doubles this figure (nearly 2.3 million). Also evident in Figure 6.6, since 2007, the total number of ED visits caused by illicit prescription drug use has exceeded total ED visits stemming from all illegal drugs combined, and the disparity between these figures is growing. Abuse and dependence figures also point to the substantial dependence problems posed by psychoactive pharmaceuticals. As can be seen in Figure 6.7, in 2010, nearly 2.5 million people reported the abuse of all forms of psychotherapeutics, with roughly 1.8 million people reporting dependence on such drugs. Most of these cases involve opiate-based pain relievers, on which almost 1.5 million people are dependent.

Figure 6.6   Drug-Related Emergency Department (ED) Visits by Type of Visit, 2004–2009*

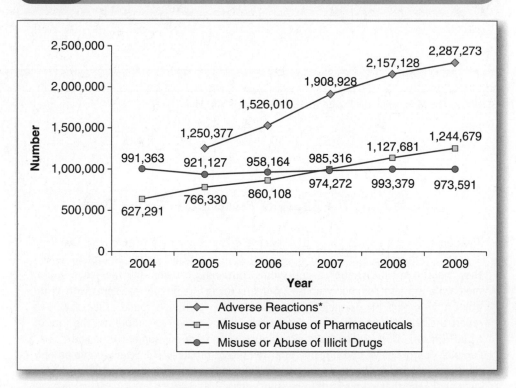

*Data for ED visits involving adverse reactions of pharmaceuticals are not available for 2004.

SOURCE: 2004 to 2009 SAMHSA Drug Abuse Warning Network (DAWN).

Figure 6.7   Estimated Persons Exhibiting Dependence and Abuse on/of Illicit Prescription Drugs and Other Illicit Drugs, 2002–2010

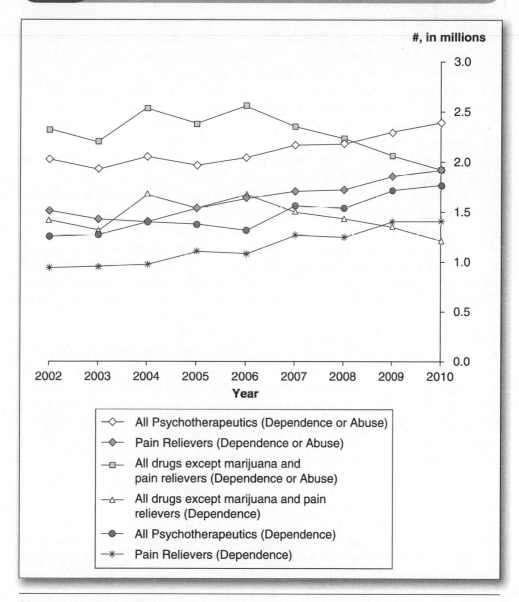

SOURCE: SAMHSA, 2011a.

The substantial increase in the abuse of prescription drugs in recent years is due to a number of factors. One of these is the perception among adolescents that these drugs are different than other drugs of abuse. For example, surveys have found that nearly half of teens believe abusing psychoactive pharmaceuticals to be much safer than using street drugs and that prescription painkillers were not addictive (Partnership for a Drug-Free America, 2005b).

Drug counselors report that young users sometimes take a handful of different prescription drugs at the same time, partly because these drugs are seen as less risky and "cleaner" than illegal drugs (Costello, 2005).

Perhaps the most significant factor contributing to the increased abuse of prescription pharmaceuticals over the last two decades is that the drugs have become so widely prescribed in society. Since 1991, the number of prescriptions written for legal stimulant drugs has risen seven-fold, and the number of prescriptions for the two most common opiate painkillers has more than quadrupled (Figure 6.9). As a consequence of their widespread prescribed availability, the illicit access to and use of these drugs has increased substantially. Many adolescents who are prescribed these drugs report they abuse them to achieve psychoactive effects (e.g., crushing and snorting Ritalin; purposely exceeding prescribed dosage) or they sell them to others (SAMHSA, 2011a; Zernike & Petersen, 2006).

In addition to peers, parents represent a major source for adolescents seeking to obtain these drugs. Adolescents often steal prescription stimulants (and other prescription drugs) from their parents' supply (SAMHSA, 2011a) with the intention of either using the drugs themselves or selling the drugs to others (Poulin, 2001). Adolescents' access to prescription drugs is further facilitated by the fact that few adults take preventative steps to keep their prescription drugs from being abused by their children (Costello, 2005). Adolescents who report the misuse of prescription drugs indicate that obtaining the drugs "free from relatives or friends" was the most common path of access, and "purchasing the drugs from friends or relatives" was the second most common (SAMHSA, 2011a). Despite growing efforts to curtail teens' psychoactive pharmaceutical access through their family and friends, these sources have become *more* common since 2007 (Johnston et al., 2012b). Reflecting this trend, more than half of high school seniors (50.7%) reported prescription narcotics were fairly easy or very easy to obtain in 2011, up from 38% in 1994 (Johnston et al., 2011).

Use of Drugs by the Elderly

As noted above, legal drug use tends to peak in late adolescence or early adulthood, declining steadily thereafter. However, one exception to this trend is a resurgence of legal drug use and abuse, particularly of alcohol and prescription drugs, late in the lifecourse. As noted in the previous chapter, illegal drug use is less common among the elderly, though this form of drug use is increasingly prevalent among older Americans as the baby boomers (persons born between 1946 and 1964) are aging into their geriatric years. As compared to the age cohorts before them, baby boomers tend to have more tolerant attitudes toward drug use and use drugs at higher rates late in the lifecourse (Wu & Blazer, 2011). As one consequence of this, the number of Americans over the age of 50 with a substance use disorder is projected to double by 2020, reaching 5.7 million people (Wu & Blazer, 2011). With respect to pharmaceutical drugs, high patterns of abuse among geriatric populations should not come

American Consumption of Prescription Narcotics in a Global Context

Although America has a population of slightly more than 300 million people, Americans received about 4 billion prescriptions in 2010, with 478 million of these prescriptions written for controlled substances and more than 120 million for opioids (Kerlikowske, 2012). Americans represent less than 5% of the global population but consume more than 80% of the global opioid supply and 99% of the global hydrocodone supply. (Manchikanti et al., 2010)

Figure 6.8 Prescriptions Written for Stimulants and Select Opiates, 1991–2007

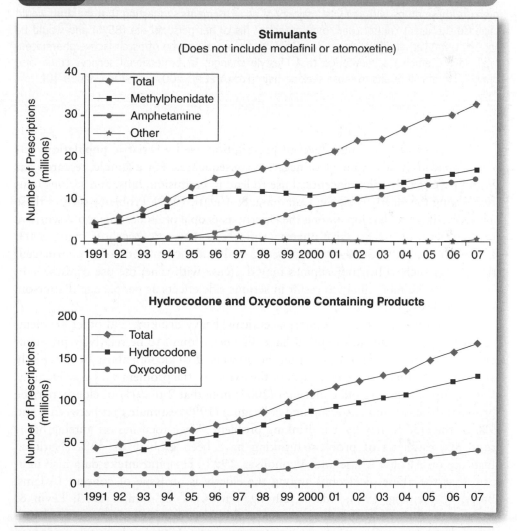

SOURCE: Verispan (VONA), extracted January 2008.

These data were provided to NIDA under a third party data access agreement between Verispan, LLC., and the FDA's Office of Surveillance and Epedemiology.

as a surprise because the elderly are two to three times more likely to be prescribed psychoactive drugs (particularly benzodiazepines) than the general population (Benshoff, Harwood, & Kosh, 2003; Levin & Kruger, 2000). Because of the frequent dosing schedules recommended for most prescription drugs, the elderly are also among the most likely to regularly (e.g., daily) consume drugs that have the "potential for misuse, abuse and addiction" (Benshoff et al., 2003, p. 43).

The advertisement of psychoactive pharmaceuticals contributes to the widespread abuse of these drugs in society. According to a content analysis by Frosch and associates (2007), prescription drug advertisements almost always (95% of the time) utilize emotional appeals to promote these drugs, with the vast majority of advertisements suggesting that the drug would increase the user's control over some aspect of his or her personal life (85%) and would be socially approved of (78%). Meanwhile, only a very small portion of psychoactive pharmaceutical advertisements acknowledge that lifestyle changes or professional services could also provide beneficial results to those seeking help (Frosch et al., 2007; see also Chapter 10).

Not surprisingly, the high level of prescription use by geriatric populations has been found to have a number of negative consequences. For example, research has found psychoactive pharmaceutical use to lead to confusion, falls, and serious injuries among the elderly (Leipzig, Cumming, & Tinetti, 1999). Problems such as these are more likely to develop among the elderly, as people often become more sensitive to the effects of psychoactive pharmaceuticals as they age (Benshoff et al., 2003; Leipzig et al., 1999). Similarly, because the body's ability to metabolize pharmaceutical drugs such as benzodiazepines may decrease with time, the use of these substances may be more likely to result in serious side effects as people age (Patterson, Lacro, & Jeste, 1999).

In addition to the abuse of pharmaceuticals, heavy drinking and other problematic forms of alcohol consumption have also been found to be relatively prevalent among geriatric populations. Data on the prevalence of alcohol abuse by the elderly are somewhat limited, and estimates of the extent of the problem vary considerably. For example, Benshoff and colleagues (2003) note that 2 to 20% of elderly may be problem drinkers, and Patterson and colleagues (1999) estimate that between 3 and 9% of the elderly may have a drinking problem. When focusing on nursing home residents, estimates of problem drinking have been as high as 49% (National Institute on Alcohol Abuse and Alcoholism, 1998). Hospital intake data also indicate that the abuse of alcohol among the elderly is an issue of concern (Adams, Barry, & Fleming, 1996; Adams, Zhong, Barboriak, & Rimm, 1993; Levin & Kruger, 2000). For example, a report released by the American Medical Association noted that between 6 and 11% of geriatric patients admitted to hospitals evidenced symptoms of alcoholism, and this figure rose to 14% when considering elderly patients who were admitted to emergency rooms (Adams et al., 1996). As was discussed in Chapter 5, the extent of this problem remains unclear, as substance abuse among the elderly tends to be minimized, ignored, or mistaken for other symptoms of aging (e.g., depression, dementia) (Levin & Kruger, 2000).

In our discussion of theories of drug use in Chapter 2, we noted that developmental theories of drug use are particularly useful for understanding patterns of substance use and abuse over the lifecourse. Developmental theories of drug use explain high rates of substance use in adolescence as the result of high levels of independence, peer association (as opposed to parental/family association), and unstructured time during this point in the lifecourse. The theory accounts for the declining patterns of substance use in middle adulthood by acknowledging the increasing commitments and responsibilities (e.g., career-track jobs, marriage, parenthood) that most people assume as they age into and through adulthood and that tend to decrease drug use (Catalano & Hawkins, 1996; Garnier & Stein, 2002; Oxford, Harachi, Catalano, & Abbott, 2001; Thornberry, 1987).

These same factors can be applied to account for the resurgence in substance abuse among the elderly. Like adolescents, geriatric populations are exposed to several key risk factors for substance use and abuse. Often, the elderly have considerable amounts of free, unstructured time on their hands, as they have been relieved of many of the responsibilities (e.g., employment, childcare) that might otherwise prevent or limit substance use (Benshoff, Harrawood, & Koch, 2003). Additionally, and as noted in the previous chapter, traumatic events such as the loss of a spouse are more likely to occur late in the lifecourse, and these events both disrupt social bonds and provide additional stress that may serve to encourage substance use and abuse (Benshoff et al., 2003).

GENDER/SEX

As with illegal drugs, males are more likely than females to use and abuse most forms of legal drugs. However, the magnitude of the gender gap varies by substance type and also by the point in the lifecourse. As Tables 6.2 and 6.3 illustrate, gender differences in drug use are relatively small during adolescence but become pronounced (for most drugs) in adulthood. With respect to alcohol, data on high school seniors obtained from the Monitoring the Future study (Table 6.2) demonstrate that adolescent boys are only slightly more likely than girls to be current alcohol users, a measure that captures any use (e.g., one beer at a party) in the past month.

Conversely, when looking at binge drinking and drinking to the point of drunkenness, data reveal boys to be significantly more likely to report these behaviors. Data on prescription pharmaceutical abuse indicate roughly similar patterns of abuse by sex, though patterns vary by type of substance, age, and other factors.

When considering patterns of alcohol consumption among adults (Table 6.3), the data reveal a significant gender gap. Again, men are a bit more likely to report any alcohol use in the past 30 days, but they are more than twice as likely as women to report binge drinking and roughly three times as likely to report heavy alcohol use. As noted in our discussion of illegal drugs, these findings are consistent with previous research that suggests that at all points in the lifecourse, men are more likely than women to use substances in ways that are likely to generate problems (Robbins, 1989; U.S. Department of Health and Human Services, 2003a).

| Table 6.2 | Legal Drug and Supplement Use by Gender Among High School Seniors, 2003 and 2010 | | | |

	Males		Females	
	2003	2010	2003	2010
Any Alcohol Use in the Past 30 Days	51.7	42.1	43.8	37.5
Binge Drinking—5+ drinks in a row in last 2 weeks	34.2	25.5	22.1	17.6
Been Drunk in the Past 30 Days	34.9	27.5	26.9	22.0
Cigarette Use in the Past 30 Days	26.2	21.5	22.1	15.1
Misuse of Any Rx Drug in Past Year	18.2	15.9	15.7	14.0
Inhalant Use in the Past Year	5.2	3.3	2.9	3.0
Illicit* Sedative Use in the Past Year	6.7	4.2	5.4	4.4
Illicit* Tranquilizer Use in the Past Year	6.9	5.4	6.3	5.6
Illicit* Vicodin Use in the Past Year	13.0	9	8.1	7.1
Illicit* OxyContin Use in the Past Year	6.2	5.9	2.8	3.8
Illicit Ritalin Use in the Past Year	5.5	2.7	2.6	2.3
Illicit Adderall Use in the Past Year	5.5	7.4	2.6	5.5
Steroid Use in the Past Year	3.2	1.0	1.1	0.3
Androstenedione Use in the Past Year	4.6	1.3	0.2	0.1
Creatine Use in the Past Year	15.9	16.1	1.4	1.0
Over-the-Counter Cough Medicines in the Past Year	7.9	5.6	5.9	4.7

*Refers to use that is without medical advice

SOURCE: Johnston, et al. (2004b, 2012a).

Data in Table 6.2 also demonstrate that males are much more likely to use muscle-building drugs and supplements, including steroids, androstenedione, and creatine. When considering gender differences in the use of these substances, it is important to recognize that physique development is a key motivation for the use of performance-enhancing drugs among both men and women. Research focused on high school and college aged populations estimates that 30 to 45% of steroid users do not engage in any competitive sports and use steroids and related substances solely to enhance their appearance and self-confidence (Buckley, Yesalis, Friedl, Anderson, Streit, & Wright, 1988). A recent review of research on this topic focused exclusively on adolescents goes even farther, finding that majority of PED use is not habitual and is motivated by a syndrome of problem behaviors (see problem behavior theory, Chapter 2) as opposed to the desire to increase athletic performance. This review concluded that organized sports participation may actually serve as a protective factor for PED use among

Table 6.3	Legal Drug Use Among Adults by Gender			
	Males		Females	
	2003	2010	2003	2010
Any Alcohol Use in the Past 30 Days	62.4	62.9	47.9	49.8
Binge Drinking—5+ drinks in a row in last 2 weeks	33.7	33.5	15.7	16.5
Heavy Drinking—Binge Drinking at least 5 days in the last month	11.7	11.0	3.1	3.6
Inhalant Use During Past Year	0.7	0.7	0.3	0.3
Nonmedical Use of Prescription Psychotherapeutic During Past Month**	2.6	3.1	2.4	2.4
Nonmedical Use of Prescription Pain Relievers During Past Month***	2.6	2.4	2.4	1.6

*For Alcohol-Related Measures, Persons 21 and Above; for Other Measures, 18 and Above.

**Refers to the nonmedical use of any prescription-type psychotherapeutics, including pain-relievers, tranquilizers, stimulants, or sedatives; does not include any over-the-counter medications.

***Refers to the nonmedical use of the pain reliever subclass of psychopharmaceuticals.

SOURCE: SAMHSA (2004, 2011a).

adolescent-aged populations (Harmer, 2010). All these findings echo the conclusions of Dr. Harrison Pope of Harvard Medical School who has commented that "A large number of teen- agers and young adult men who use steroids are taking them purely for personal appearance" (as quoted in *CBS News*, 2003).

With respect to gender differences in the use of these substances, recognize that the higher patterns of use for steroids, andro, creatine, and similar substances by men may be analogous to the abuse of diet pills and various fat burners by women. Women are two to three times as likely to take diet pills or similar substances in order to control their weight, and the use of these physique-altering substances may represent gender-specific attempts by users to conform to a societal body image ideal. For men, this ideal body image involves a trim, muscular build, particularly in the upper body, and for women involves a slim figure, particularly from the waist down, coupled with large breasts (Wichstrom & Pedersen, 2001).

Data on the use of tobacco indicate relatively similar patterns of use by men and women. As illustrated in Figure 6.7, smoking declined substantially for both men and women between 1965 and 2009, but the data also reveal convergence in patterns of smoking over time. In 1965, men were much more likely than women to report smoking, but since the 1990s, men have been only slightly more likely to report smoking. As we will discuss in more detail below, this convergence in patterns of smoking may reflect change in attitudes about acceptable female behavior over time.

Figure 6.9 Current Cigarette Smokers by Gender, 1965–2009

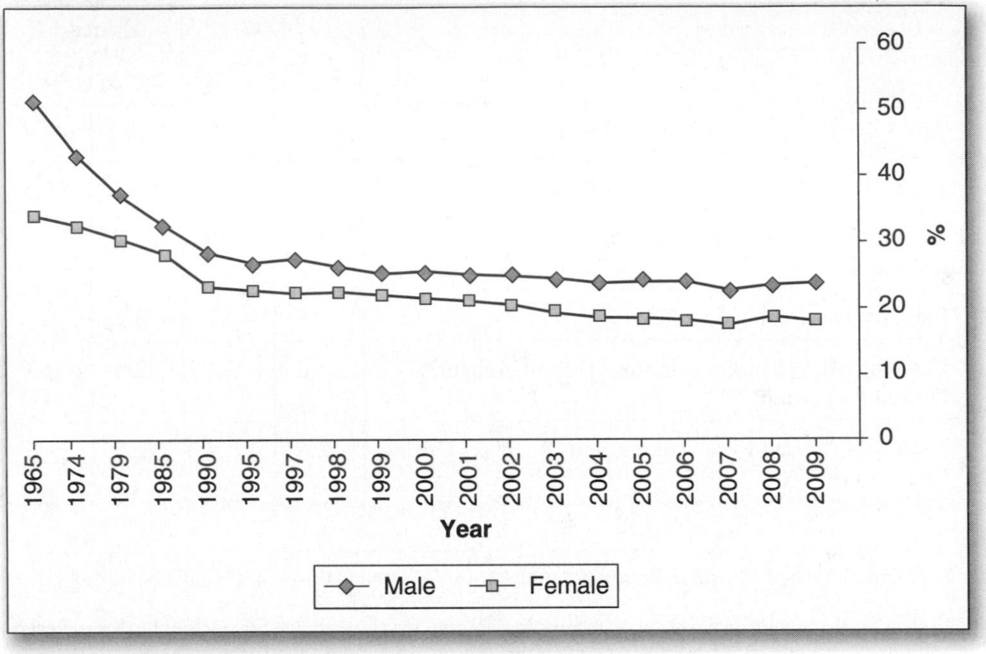

SOURCE: National Center for Health Statistics, 2011.

As noted above, research indicates that men and women have similar patterns of pharmaceutical abuse, though patterns vary somewhat across substance type, point in the lifecourse, and other factors (Canetto, 1991; Esminger & Everett, 1999). For example, data from the National Survey on Drug Use and Health (Figure 6.8) illustrate that females are more likely than males to abuse pharmaceuticals during adolescence but slightly less likely to use these drugs in adulthood. Considering substance type, findings released by the National Institute of Drug Abuse indicate that women are more likely than men to become addicted to or develop a dependence on sedatives and other drugs designed to treat anxiety (Zickler, 2001), though research has also found that the gender gap in pharmaceutical abuse is only significant for prescription opioids after important health and demographic factors are controlled for (Tetrault et al., 2007).

Considering all forms of drug use, the gender gap is probably most narrow for prescription pharmaceutical abuse (Johnston et al., 2012). In part, this may reflect gendered norms in drug use. Some research has concluded that the abuse of medical drugs, as compared to other psychoactive substances, may allow women to conform more closely to societal expectations of femininity and, particularly, motherhood (Kauffman, Silver, & Poulin, 1997). That is, while the drive to alter consciousness may be relatively similar for men and women, social norms regarding drug use are more constraining for women than men (Ensminger & Everett, 1999; Kaufman et al.,

Figure 6.10   Non-medical Use of Prescription-Type Psychotherapeutics* by Gender and Age, 2010

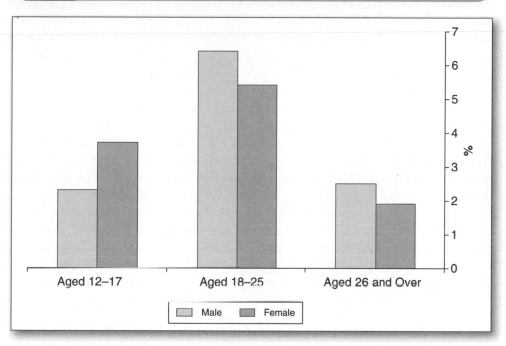

*Includes prescription pain relievers, tranquilizers, stimulants, and sedatives.

SOURCE: SAMHSA, 2011a.

1999; Lemle & Mishkind, 1989). As a result of this, women may be more likely to use psychoactive drugs in an ostensibly medical as opposed to recreational context.

With respect to gendered patterns of pharmaceutical abuse, it is important to acknowledge that women are more likely to seek treatment for mood disorders (Kauffman et al., 1999; Schwartz & Schwartz, 1993). One consequence of this willingness to seek treatment is that women are more commonly prescribed pharmaceuticals (Canetto, 1991; Esminger & Everett, 1999). However, it is also important to point out that the fact that women are more likely to seek treatment for mood disorders, and thus come to use and abuse prescription drugs, might again be attributed to differences in social role expectations. Specifically, men may be more resistant to seeking help for mental problems, perhaps seeing it as an indication of weakness. Rather than using pharmaceuticals to address their mental or emotional problems, men may self-medicate through the use of alcohol or illegal drugs (Winerman, 2005). Thus, as noted in our previous discussion of drug use by gender, the factors motivating drug use by men and women may be very similar in nature but manifested in ways that are considered more or less socially appropriate for each gender.

RACE/ETHNICITY

As with our discussion of illegal drugs, we focus on the five major ethnic groups in the United States (whites, blacks, Hispanics, Native Americans, and Asian and Pacific Islanders). Due to the significant heterogeneity that exists within each of these groups, we first examine patterns of legal drug use across these key racial/ethic categories prior to examining differences within groups where data allow.

The relationship between race and legal drug use is similar in form and magnitude to the relationship between race and the use of illegal drugs. As is the case with illegal drug use, there is a common misperception that minorities, and particularly African Americans, are much more likely to use and abuse legally available drugs, particularly alcohol. Again, available data do not support this contention. Although there are exceptions on various measures, examining data from the National Survey on Drug Use and Health and the Monitoring the Future study (Tables 6.4 and 6.5), we see that whites, Hispanics, and American Indians typically report the highest use of alcohol, followed by African Americans, with Asians Americans typically reporting the lowest levels of use. These patterns have been fairly stable over time as well. Considering rates of binge drinking among high school seniors from 1977 to the present (Figure 6.9), we can see that adolescent blacks are consistently far less likely than Hispanics or whites to report this type of drinking behavior and that whites are more likely than the other groups to binge drink.

Figure 6.11   Binge Drinking by Race/Ethnicity

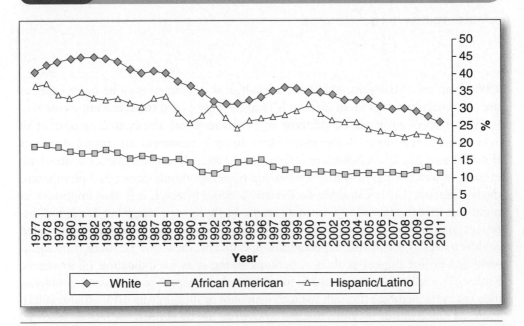

*Binge drinking is defined by the Monitoring the Future Study as five or more drinks in a row at least once within the last 2 weeks.

SOURCE: Johnston, O'Malley, Bachman, & Schulenberg (2011). *Monitoring the Future National Survey Results on Drug Use, 1975–2011. Volume I: Secondary school students* (NIH Publication No. 04-5507).

| Table 6.4 | Past Month Use of Legal Substances Among Youth (12–17), by Race |

	White		African American		Hispanic/ Latino		American Indian/ Alaska Native		Asian	
	2003	2010	2003	2010	2003	2010	2003	2010	2003	2010
Any alcohol use	20.1	14.9	10.9	10.8	16.6	13.9	22.6	11.1	7.4	4.8
Binge drinking (5+ drinks in a row at least once in past month)	12.5	8.9	4.9	4.2	10.5	8.4	18.2	8.7	3.2	2.5
Heavy drinking (binge drinking episodes on 5 or more day in past month	3.2	1.9	0.6	0.5	2.2	2	2.9	1.1	0.1	0.5
Nonmedical use of psychotherapeutics*	4.4	2.9	3.0	2.6	3.9	3.4	4.4	3.4	2.2	1.8
Any inhalant use	1.3	1	0.7	1.2	1.3	1.4	1.9	2.9	0.8	0.3
Any tobacco use	18.2	12.7	9.1	6.6	11.6	8.9	30.6	19.8	3.8	4.1

*Refers to the nonmedical use of any prescription-type psychotherapeutics, including pain-relievers, tranquilizers, stimulants, or sedatives. Does not include any over-the-counter medications or prescription stimulants.

SOURCE: SAMHSA, 2011a.

Data reported in Table 6.4 indicate that the use of tobacco by children and adolescents is far higher among American Indians (19.8%) than any other group. Whites report the second-highest rates of tobacco use (12.7%), albeit at a rate far lower than that of American Indians. Similarly, inhalant use is highest among Native American adolescents (2.9%), followed by Hispanics (1.4%), African Americans (1.2%), and whites (1.0%). Finally, with respect to prescription drug use among children and adolescents, whites, African Americans, Hispanics, and American Indians report fairly similar patterns of use (roughly 3%), with Asians less likely to report use.

Similar to the relationship with illegal drug use, patterns of legal drug use by race shift somewhat when considering adult as opposed to adolescent populations. Looking at the "any alcohol use" measure in Table 6.5, we see that whites are much more likely than any other group, and notably American Indians (least likely of all groups), to report the current use of alcohol. The change in alcohol use by American Indians from adolescence to adulthood reflects the increasing rate of abstinence among American Indians with age and is partly due to the number of alcohol-related problems experienced by American Indian populations (Beauvais, 1998; Beauvais & LaBoueff, 1985). Illustrating this are data in Table 6.5 that indicate that American Indians report the highest level of heavy drinking (9.1%) in the past month. Whites also report high levels of heavy drinking in adulthood, but patterns of heavy

| Table 6.5 | Legal Drug Use in the Past Month Among Adults (18+) by Race |

	White		African American		Hispanic/ Latino		American Indian/ Alaska Native		Asian	
	2003	2010	2003	2010	2003	2010	2003	2010	2003	2010
Any Alcohol Use	58.7	60.5	44.5	47.3	46.9	45.8	47.9	40.1	40.8	40.7
Binge brinking (5+ drinks in a row at least once in past month)	24.5	26.2	23.5	21.9	27.0	27.4	29.3	23.7	13.5	11.9
Heavy drinking (binge drinking at least 5 days in past month)	7.9	8.4	5.0	5.1	6.5	5.7	9.5	9.1	2.9	1.6
Nonmedical use of psychotherapeutics*	2.6	3	1.8	1.9	2.7	2.4	3.0	4.7	0.5	0.9
Any inhalant use	0.1	0.2	0.0	0.1	0.1	0.3	0.1	0.2	0.3	0.0
Any tobacco use	33.4	31	31.9	30.1	27.4	23.9	46.3	37.8	20.5	13.4

*Refers to the nonmedical use of any prescription-type psychotherapeutics, including pain-relievers, tranquilizers, stimulants, or sedatives. Does not include any over-the-counter medications or prescription stimulants.

SOURCE: SAMHSA, 2011a.

drinking among white, black, and Hispanic adults are quite similar, much more similar than the patterns of drinking evidenced by adolescents in these racial/ethnic categories. As will be discussed in detail below, these changing drinking patterns with age largely reflect the increased exposure of Hispanics and blacks to a number of factors that encourage substance use as they age.

In the sections below, we address patterns of legal substance use by race/ethnicity, with a particular focus on alcohol and illicit pharmaceutical use, and provide theoretical explanations for these patterns. Theoretical explanations employed to explain patterns of substance use across and within racial categories draw on a number of variables. As noted in our discussion of racial/ethnic differences in the use of illegal drugs, some factors are important for understanding variation *within* groups (e.g., acculturation in Hispanic and Asian populations), while others are important for understanding differences *across* groups.

With respect to racial/ethnic patterns of legal drug use, the vast majority of research has focused on alcohol, and many of the explanations used to account for racial/ethic differences in alcohol use are the same as those employed to understand patterns of illegal drug use. For example, Caetano, Clark, and Tam (1998) point to three factors crucial for understanding alcohol abuse among racial/ethnic minorities— acculturation, socioeconomic stress, and the strains minorities encounter as a result of their minority status (e.g., racism). Recall from the previous chapter that these factors were also found to be essential for understanding patterns of illegal drug use by race.

Racial Differences in the Use of Antidepressants

The use of antidepressant medication has increased significantly in the United States over time, with prevalence of use increasing from 5.8% in 1996 to 10.1% in 2005 (Olfson & Marcus, 2009). With increasing use has come increasing disparity in the use of these drugs across race/ethnicity—antidepressant use is much greater among whites than among blacks or Hispanics, and the racial gap in use patterns has increased over time (NCHS, 2005; Olfson & Marcus, 2009). For the years 1988 and 1994, whites were about one and a half times as likely to use antidepressant drugs as were blacks or Hispanics, but by 1999 to 2000, the use of antidepressants by whites was approximately three times that of blacks and Hispanics (NCHS, 2005). Data indicate significant increases in the use of antidepressants by all race/ethnic groups excepting African Americans in the last decade, and although Hispanics have seen significant increases in antidepressant use, their patterns of use remain low compared to those of whites (Olfson & Marcus, 2009). Race/ethnic differences in the use of these drugs have been traced to differential access to healthcare (NCHS, 2005) and differential likelihood of receiving a diagnosis of depression following treatment by a health care provider for symptoms consistent with depression (Trinh et al., 2011), as well as race/ethnic differences in the perceived stigma associated with admitting a depressive condition and the use of antidepressants to treat it. (Menke & Flynn, 2009)

African Americans

Extensive available data indicate that African American youth report low patterns of legal (and illegal) drug use (Figure 6.9; Table 6.4), which is particularly notable given the environmental conditions that many black youth are exposed to. However, African American adults report patterns of drinking and heavy drinking that are similar to those reported by whites. This is particularly the case when comparisons of white and black adults are made later in the lifecourse. The changing patterns of heavy alcohol consumption by race over the lifecourse are illustrated in Figure 6.10. Consistent with many studies in this area, the data reveal whites to consume alcohol at relatively high levels early in life and to demonstrate increased drinking patterns until the mid- to late 20s, when use typically begins to gradually decrease. Conversely, African Americans tend to drink much less than whites early in life but exhibit increased drinking patterns in later life that eventually approach and in some cases exceed whites' levels of use (Caetano & Kaskutas, 1995; Jones-Webb, 1998). Research on these issues includes that by Caetano and Clark (1998), who note that rates of heavy drinking among blacks have been found to be highest in the 40s and 50s, while whites display their highest rates of heavy drinking during their 20s (Caetano & Clark, 1998).

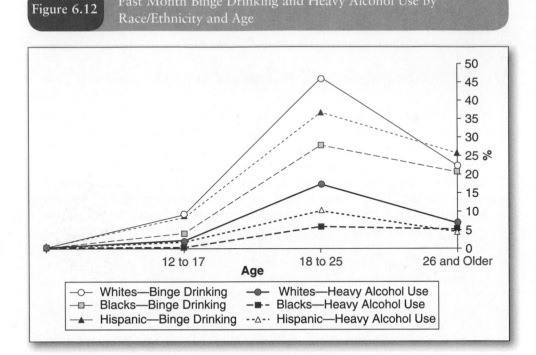

Figure 6.12 — Past Month Binge Drinking and Heavy Alcohol Use by Race/Ethnicity and Age

SOURCE: U.S. Department of Health and Human Services.

Despite the relatively high levels of abstinence practiced by African Americans (Jones-Webb, 1998), research has found that the *consequences* associated with drinking are more severe for disadvantaged minorities than for whites (Wallace, 1999b). To understand this seemingly paradoxical situation in which blacks report high levels of abstinence/temperance and also high levels of alcohol-related problems, research has pointed to the importance of social class. For example, focusing on alcohol-related problems, Jones-Webb, Hsiao, and Hannan (1995) found that social class was a key factor in predicting negative outcomes associated with alcohol consumption for blacks but not for whites. Jones-Webb and colleagues (1995) concluded that lower-class blacks were far more likely to report alcohol-related problems than were lower-class whites, and that the magnitude of these problems increased over time. However, they did not identify similar findings for middle-class blacks and whites (Jones-Webb, Hsiao, & Hannan, 1995; see also Jones-Webb, Snowden, Herd, Short, & Hannan, 1997).

Barr, Farrell, Barnes, and Welte (1993) identified similar conclusions regarding the effect of social class on alcohol-related problems among whites and blacks. Barr and colleagues (1993) found that when looking only at people making more than $25,000 per year (a relatively modest sum), black males were less likely than white males to report alcohol-related problems. Conversely, when considering those who made less than $15,000 per year, black men were "three to four times more likely to experience drinking-related problems than comparable Whites" (p. 325). As noted in our discussion of illegal drug use, these distinct patterns of use have prompted some to suggest that there are two worlds of minority substance use—a relatively large population that practices temperance or abstinence and a smaller, disproportionately lower-class population that drinks and drinks heavily at a much higher rate (Wallace, 1999b).

Research examining the high rates of substance use and problems among poor minorities has concluded that environmental influences related to poverty are vital to consider. These influences include family disruption and single parenthood, segregation and the associated social isolation, unemployment, and joblessness (Caetano et al., 1998; Wilson, 1987, 1996). With respect to drug use and abuse, these environmental conditions tend to minimize the presence of drug protective factors and increase the presence of drug risk factors (e.g., availability of conventional recreational opportunities, presence/absence of parental supervision, time spent in conventional activities, availability of treatment resources, exposure/access to drugs and alcohol; Wallace, 1999b).

Focusing on the issue of exposure and access to drugs and alcohol, studies examining racial segregation and urban poverty have demonstrated that, regardless of social class, blacks are much more likely to live in areas characterized by a greater visibility of and access to both licit and illicit drugs (see also Chapter 5; Alaniz, 1998; Anderson, 1990, 1999; Massey & Denton, 1993; USDHHS, 2003; Wallace, 1999b; Wilson, 1987). This increased access and exposure to drugs and alcohol is sometimes referred to as hyperavailability. Research on the hyperavailability of alcohol in predominately black communities has noted the high concentration of alcohol outlets (e.g., bars, liquor stores), as well as the heavy advertising of alcohol in these communities, concluding that these factors contribute to higher levels of alcohol use and abuse (Caetano & Clark, 1998; Wallace, 1999b).

Another consequence of the hyperavailability of drugs and alcohol in poor minority communities is that parents of black children are often extremely vigilant about substance use and abuse by their children (USDHHS, 2003; Wallace, 1999b). Blacks also report attitudes that are less tolerant of drinking and drunkenness (Caetano & Clark, 1998), and because the relationship between black parents and adolescents has been found to be particularly strong and also more authoritarian (Giordano, Cernkovich, & DeMaris, 1993), many black youth are prevented from using alcohol. While these factors tend to reduce levels of alcohol and other drug use during adolescence, these protective factors disappear as young blacks enter adulthood, and these changes are partly responsible for the converging patterns of alcohol use and abuse by whites and blacks in adulthood (Wallace, 1999b).

Hispanics

As compared to other racial/ethnic groups, Hispanics tend to report moderate to high levels of substance use in both adolescence and adulthood. However, there is substantial variation in patterns of legal drug use across Hispanic groups due to the differential exposure of Hispanic subpopulations to drug risk factors and to the cultural differences between these groups.

With respect to substance use and abuse among Hispanics generally, it is important to recognize that Hispanics are disproportionately exposed to many of the same risk factors affecting blacks (discussed above). For example, a report by the National Institute on Drug Abuse titled *Drug Use Among Racial/Ethnic Minorities* concluded that

> Stresses associated with what are often more constrained economic conditions, combined with lower educational attainment, a generally higher degree of drug availability, and the possible impact of racism on self-esteem are believed to make Hispanics particularly vulnerable to alcohol and other drug use and problems. (USDHHS, 2003; see also Delgado, 1995)

Because of their disproportionate exposure to these risk factors, Hispanics (like blacks) are more likely to suffer serious problems associated with their substance use than are whites. This is despite the fact that Hispanic patterns of use are comparable to or less than those reported by whites. As Wallace (1999a) of the Monitoring the Future project comments with respect to these issues, "analyses of racial/ethnic disparities in alcohol-related problems suggest that relative to Whites, the experience of problems is more chronic among Blacks and Hispanics" (p. 1124), and Wallace (1999a) further notes the racial disparity in problems is growing worse over time.

Although many of the same environmental risk factors affect blacks and Hispanics, as compared to blacks, Hispanic populations are characterized by a number of protective factors that serve to attenuate their levels of substance use and substance-related problems. Research on these issues includes that by Jones-Webb and colleagues (1997), who focused on alcohol-related problems that were experienced by Hispanic, black, and white men. The study found that alcohol-related problems were greater for blacks as compared to Hispanics and whites once alcohol consumption was controlled for. Jones-Webb and colleagues (1997) concluded that although Hispanics suffer from many of the same disadvantages as blacks, they were more likely to be employed, be married, and have access to resources outside of their communities (i.e., they are less socially and spatially segregated). All of these factors were thought to counter the disadvantages associated with Hispanics' minority status.

Similar to variation in illegal drug use across Hispanic subpopulations, extensive research has found that the use of legal drugs varies significantly across Hispanic subpopulations (see, for example, Bachman, Wallace, O'Malley, Johnston, Kurth, & Neighbors, 1991; Caetano et al.,1998; Randolf, Stroup-Benham, Black, & Markides, 1998; Warheit, Vega, Khoury, Gil, & Elfenbein, 1996). For example, across Hispanic subgroups, women tend to drink less than their male counterparts, particularly among recent immigrants (Aguirre-Molina & Caetano, 1994; Caetano, 1984). Other research has found Mexican American men to be more likely than other Hispanics to report patterns of heavy and binge drinking and to report more problems associated with use (Bachman et al., 1991; Caetano, 1988; Gilbert & Cervantes, 1986). In a pattern sometimes referred to as "fiesta drinking," Mexican American men tend to abstain from alcohol at a greater rate than other Hispanic men, but they also report the highest rates of binge drinking (Caetano, 1988; Caetano et al., 1998).

Research attempting to explain variation in alcohol consumption across Hispanic populations has pointed to a number of important factors. In addition to the risk factors related to minority status mentioned above, acculturation has been found to be essential for understanding differences in legal drug use and abuse among Hispanic subgroups (Caetano et al., 1998; Randolf, Stroup-Benham, Black, & Markides, 1998; Warheit, Vega, Khoury, Gil, & Elfenbein, 1996). As noted in the previous chapter, acculturation is the process by which an immigrant group adopts the cultural information and social skills of the new culture, often replacing their traditional cultural beliefs and practices (Vega et al., 1998).

Research that has examined the effect of acculturation on the drinking practices of Hispanic groups includes that by Warheit and colleagues (1996), who examined a large sample of Cuban, Nicaraguan, Colombian, and Puerto Rican adolescents from Dade County, Florida. This study found substantial differences in patterns of drug use across groups, with Colombians being the most likely to use cigarettes and alcohol (and also illegal drugs) and Puerto Ricans reporting the lowest patterns of legal drug use. These differences were attributed to the distinct patterns of acculturation among the groups (measured as length of time in the United States). Similar conclusions were reached by Black and Markides (1993) in their examination of Cuban American drinking patterns. They found Cuban Americans to drink more frequently than many other Hispanic groups but also to drink more moderately, somewhat similar to non–Hispanic whites. Conversely, when examining only Cubans who had recently immigrated, Black and Markides (1993) found the recent immigrants to display drinking patterns that were similar to those of Mexican Americans (less frequent, though in greater volume).

In sum, although the effects of acculturation on alcohol consumption are not totally unequivocal (Randolf et al., 1998), traditional Hispanic norms tend to discourage heavy alcohol use, especially for women due to the strongly delineated gender roles, but the emphasis on machismo may also encourage binge drinking among men (Castro, Proescholbell, Abeita, & Rodriguez, 1999).

American Indians/Native Americans

Similar to the findings on illegal drug use discussed in the previous chapter, numerous studies and several ongoing drug surveys have found American Indians to display among the highest patterns of legal drug use, particularly forms of substance use most likely to cause harm (Johnston et al., 2011; SAMHSA, 2011a). For example, American Indians adults report the lowest rates of current alcohol use but high rates of binge drinking and the highest rates of heavy drinking (see Table 6.5). Attempts to explain these patterns have considered a wide range of potentially influential factors, and for many years, in part due to early (problematic) findings of an enhanced susceptibility to alcohol abuse among Native American populations (e.g., Fenna, Mix, Schaefer, & Gilbert, 1971), the dominant belief was that Native Americans were one of a few populations whose unique genetic lineages led greater levels of alcohol related problems. Genetic explanations are invoked almost exclusively with respect to alcohol as opposed to other substances, with the contention being that the higher rates of alcohol consumption and alcohol related problems by American Indians might be attributed to a "firewater gene" that supposedly makes individuals of Indian ancestry especially vulnerable to alcoholism and extreme behavior when under the influence (Caetano et al.,

1998; Leland, 1976; Mail & Johnson, 1993). While many believe that Indians are naturally predisposed to drunkenness and that binge drinking is the "Indian way" of drinking (Caetano et al., 1998), the majority of research does not support the contention that higher rates of heavy drinking among American Indians result from an increased physiological or psychological reactivity to alcohol (Garcia-Andrade, Wall, & Ehlers, 1997; May, 1982).

Juxtaposed against this body of work are extensive biomedical studies that conclude genetics is a moderate to strong predictor of problem drinking, alcoholism, and "responsiveness" to alcohol in the general (i.e. not race-specific) population (Mayfield, Harris, & Schukit, 2008; Prescott & Kendler, 1999; Schuckit et al., 2001). Considering race, recent biomedical research suggests that although genetic and environmental factors are important to the development of addictive disorders, their relative importance may vary across groups. Specifically referring to colonized aboriginal populations, some biomedical research suggests that the experience of historical trauma likely far outweighs any genetic influence on alcoholism or other forms of addiction. This includes work by Enoch (2011) who notes, "in populations exposed to severe current and historical trauma such as some Native American tribes and Australian aboriginal groups, environmental stressors can swamp genetic influences" (p. 17). With no clear research findings indicating that genetics play any greater a role in American Indian substance use as compared with other groups, other research in the area focuses on work grounded in the legacy of colonization/forced assimilation and consequent social and economic deprivation.

There is substantial evidence that suggests the high patterns of substance use among American Indians can be attributed to the fact that, as a group, American Indians experience extremely high levels of social and economic disadvantage (Akins, Mosher, Rotolo, & Griffin, 2003; Akins, Lanfear, Cline & Mosher, 2013; Wallace & Bachman, 1991). Median income levels for employed American Indians are substantially lower than comparable earnings in the general population, and American Indian rates of poverty are more than double those for the general population, with poverty rates being exceptionally high for American Indians living on reservations (DeVoe & Darling-Churchill, 2008). Similar to work discussed earlier regarding poverty thresholds and substance problems among African Americans and whites, research has identified race–poverty interaction effects when considering substance use by American Indians (Akins et al., 2013). Essentially, such research suggests that structural factors such as poverty and employment status are more important for understanding substance abuse by impoverished minorities such as American Indians than they are for understanding substance abuse by whites. The effect of economic disadvantage on drug use was explored in detail in our discussion of illegal drug use by American Indians (Chapter 5), and research has used these same explanations to understand the use and abuse of legal drugs.

Conversely, there is substantial evidence that suggests the high patterns of substance use among American Indians can be attributed to the fact that, as a group, American Indians experience extremely high levels of social and economic disadvantage (Akins, Mosher, Rotolo, & Griffin, 2003; Wallace & Bachman, 1991). Median income levels for employed American Indians are substantially lower than comparable earnings in the general population, and American Indian rates of poverty are more than double those for the general population, with poverty rates being exceptionally high for American Indians living on reservations (DeVoe & Darling-Churchill, 2008). Similar to work discussed earlier regarding poverty thresholds and substance problems among African Americans and whites, research has identified race–poverty and race–employment interaction effects when considering substance use by American Indians (Akins, Cline, Lanfear, & Mosher, 2012). Essentially, the results suggest that poverty and employment status are more important for understanding substance abuse by American Indians than they are for understanding substance abuse by whites (Akins et al., 2012). The effect of economic disadvantage on drug use was explored in detail in our discussion of illegal drug use by American Indians (Chapter 5), and research has used these same explanations to understand the use and abuse of legal drugs.

Often drawing on these disadvantage/poverty explanations, others have proposed that high patterns of alcohol abuse and problems among American Indians are evidence of Indians attempting to cope with negative emotions such as frustration, alienation, low self-esteem, and hopelessness (Caetano et al., 1998). These explanations are often cultural in nature and point to the history of colonialism and the subsequent decimation of the indigenous populations in North America (Beauvais, 1998). These perspectives often emphasize the legacy of colonialism and the destruction of the traditional Indian culture, noting how this has influenced, to a greater or lesser degree, nearly every aspect of Indian life. Research has conceptualized this experience as historical trauma, which is defined as "cumulative emotional and psychological wounding across generations, including the lifespan, which emanates from massive group trauma" (Brave Heart, Chase, Elkins, & Altschul, 2011, p. 283). Historical trauma is thought to originate primarily from the genocide, forced relocation, and forced assimilation practices (e.g., boarding schools) associated with colonialization. It manifests itself in the present day through disrupted (or eliminated) economic and sustenance practices, spiritual practices, kinship networks, and family ties that limit or eliminate cultural identity and, through this, American Indians' sense of self-worth, support systems, and coping mechanisms (Wiechelt, Gryczynski, Johnson, & Caldwell, 2012). Many American Indians believe these processes to be responsible for most of the problems they face, particularly those relating to substance abuse (Beauvais, 1998).

Asians and Pacific Islanders

In contrast to the patterns of substance use evidenced by American Indians, research consistently finds Asians to report the lowest patterns of use for legal (and illegal) drugs (Bachman et al., 1991; Barnes, Welte, & Hoffman, 2002; Johnston, O'Malley, Bachman, & Schulenberg, 2011; SAMHSA, 2011a). For example, as can be seen in Tables 6.4 and 6.5, Asians demonstrate the lowest patterns of use for all substances with the exception of "any alcohol use" for adult respondents.

Although a number of factors likely contribute to the modest levels of legal drug use reported by Asians, these patterns are partly accounted for by the fact that Asians fare well on most of the key risk/protective factors related to substance use. Specifically, Asian youth place comparatively more importance on family as opposed to peer influence and devote more time to scholastics than do other racial/ethnic groups (Wallace &

Bachman, 1991). Similarly, as compared to other groups, Asian adults are relatively affluent, well educated, and disproportionately employed in professional/managerial professions (Bauman & Graf, 2003; U.S. Census Bureau, 2002; see also Chapter 5).

The Flushing Response

Numerous data sources indicate that Asians report very low levels of alcohol consumption. One explanation for this is physiological in nature. Known as the "flushing response," researchers have found some Asian populations to have an increased physiological susceptibility to alcohol in which consumption results in "flushing of the skin, especially the head and torso … nausea, dizziness, headache, fast heartbeat and anxiety." (Caetano et al., 1998, p. 236)

However, as discussed in the previous chapter, there is substantial social, cultural, and economic variation present in populations that are aggregated under the Asian category. Asians represent one of if not the most diverse American ethnic group (Castro et al., 1999), and the pronounced cultural, social, and economic differences characterizing Asian subgroups are reflected in their distinct patterns of legal drug use. For example, while most Asian populations report modest alcohol use, recent immigrants from Southeast Asia have been found to binge drink and drink heavily at very high rates (Amodeo, Robb, Peou, & Tran, 1997). National prevalence data indicate that Korean Americans are the Asian subgroup that is most likely (by far) to be current drinkers and binge drinkers, with rates above the national average, while Asians of Indian descent are least likely to consume alcohol and those of Chinese descent are least likely to binge drink (SAMHSA, 2010c). Japanese Americans report rates of current alcohol consumption and binge drinking that are near the national average, and the binge drinking rates reported by Filipino-American and Vietnamese-American populations are also close to the national average (SAMHSA, 2010c).

The variation in alcohol consumption among Asian subgroups is due to a number of factors, including the availability of alcohol in the United States as compared to Southeast Asia, the perception (consistent with the view of many Southeast Asian cultures) that alcohol is not harmful and may have healing properties, and the use of alcohol by certain immigrant populations to self-medicate the symptoms of post-traumatic stress disorder (Amodeo et al., 1997).

Like other forms of legal drug use, tobacco consumption varies substantially across Asian subgroups. For example, research has also found very high rates of smoking among recent immigrants from Southeast Asia, further distinguishing these groups from long-established Asian-American populations such as the Japanese (Myers et al. 1995).

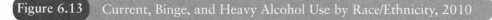

Figure 6.13   Current, Binge, and Heavy Alcohol Use by Race/Ethnicity, 2010

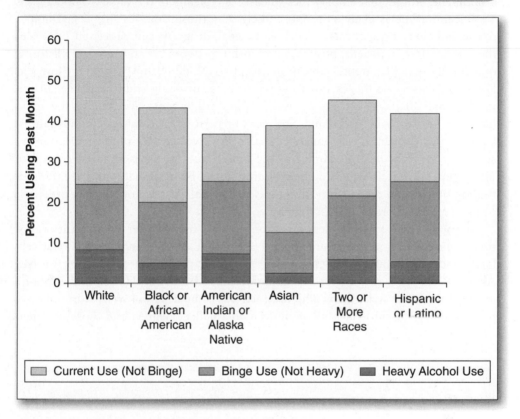

Data include only persons 12 years and older.

SOURCE: SAMHSA, 2011a.

SOCIAL CLASS

Similar to the situation with illegal drugs, the use of legal drugs varies somewhat by social class. Perhaps the most important finding is that it is a commonly held misconception that the poor are most likely to use drugs—rates of use for many legal (and illegal) drugs are highest among the middle and upper classes. As discussed above, it is important to recognize that there are important racial-specific effects of social class on legal drug use. That is, although whites are among the most likely to use legal (and illegal) drugs across economic and educational categories (so there is little effect of social class on *white* patterns of use), minorities are more adversely affected by poverty/low educational attainment in terms of substance use and problems related to use (see, for example, Barr et al., 1993). Having focused on the race-specific effects of social class on legal drug use earlier, we now turn our attention to patterns of drug use by social class in the general (predominately white) population.

Social class is typically assessed using measures of income and/or educational attainment. Studies that employ these measures typically find middle- to upper-class adolescents to be as likely as or more likely than those from less privileged homes to use and abuse many forms of legal (and illegal) drugs. As can be seen in Table 6.6, there is a fairly consistent, positive relationship between social class and all forms of alcohol use (high parental education excepted). Notably, those from very low and low social classes are the least likely to report binge drinking and having been drunk in the past 30 days. Lower- to middle-class adolescents are among the most likely to use tobacco, inhalants, and certain performance-enhancing substances. Considering the abuse of pharmaceutical drugs, we see substantial variation by substance type. As illustrated in Figure 6.12 (and Table 6.6), it is impossible to make many generalizations regarding prescription abuse by class. The most meaningful finding that can be taken from the data is that social class is not a strong predictor of most forms of prescription drug abuse.

Although there has been less attention to class-based differences in the use of tobacco, inhalants, pharmaceuticals, and performance-enhancing drugs, a relatively large body of literature has examined class-based differences in alcohol use (see Akers, 1992, for a review). For example, research by Crum, Helzer, and Anthony (1993) found that individuals who dropped out of high school were more than six times as likely to abuse alcohol as those with a college degree; and those who had

Table 6.6	Past Month Substance Use by Parents' Educational Attainment, 12th Graders, 2011				
	PARENTAL EDUCATION LEVEL				
	Very Low	**Low**	**Moderate**	**High**	**Very High**
Any alcohol use	36.7	38.8	41.2	40.1	41.9
Previously been drunk	19.1	22.9	26.3	25.6	27.5
Binge drinking	17.9	21.1	23.2	21.4	22.1
Any illicit Rx drug use	7.2	7	8	6	7.9
Cigarettes	18.2	22.4	19.6	15.9	14.3
Inhalants	2.3	1.1	1.2	0.4	0.8
Steroids*	1.6	0.6	0.9	0.5	0.5

*Without a doctor's prescription

SOURCE: Johnston, L. D., O'Malley, P. M., Bachman, J. G., & Schulenberg, J. E. (b. *Monitoring the Future national survey results on drug use, 1975–2011. Volume I: Secondary school students.* Ann Arbor: Institute for Social Research, University of Michigan, p. 751.

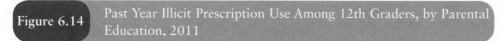

Figure 6.14   Past Year Illicit Prescription Use Among 12th Graders, by Parental Education, 2011

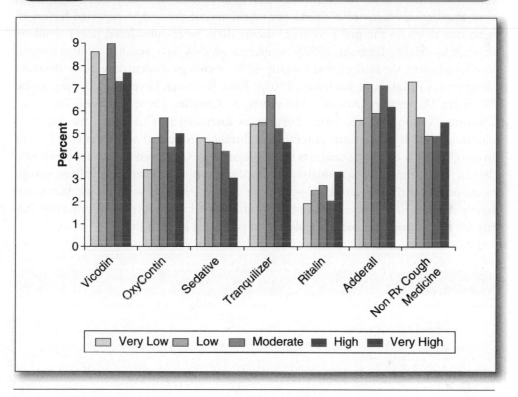

SOURCE: Johnston, O'Malley, Bachman, & Schulenberg (2011).

some college education but who had not completed a degree were three times as likely to abuse alcohol as college graduates.

The relationship between educational attainment and alcohol use is complicated by the fact that the relationship varies over the lifecourse. Specifically, when considering people in later adulthood, alcohol abuse is lower for those who have completed college, ostensibly because a college degree tends to enable people to obtain better jobs, income levels, and the like (U.S. Census Bureau, 2004). However, when looking at alcohol use and abuse for adults *who are enrolled in college*, there are significantly higher levels of binge drinking and heavy alcohol use (SAMHSA, 2011a). For example, looking at Figure 6.13, we see that for those aged 18 to 22, full-time college students are considerably more likely to report heavy drinking than are similarly aged young adults who are not enrolled in college. Conversely, adults aged 26 and older who have graduated from college are about one third less likely to report heavy drinking as compared to similarly aged people who have not graduated from college.

Similar findings were identified by Engs and colleagues (1996), who examined more than 12,000 university students from across the United States. The study found that more than 70% of collegians were current drinkers, that respondents consumed an average of 9.6 drinks per week, and of those who reported having at least one drink in the previous year, almost 30% were considered heavy drinkers (Engs, Hanson, & Diebold, 1996). Numerous studies have reached similar conclusions, including the finding that roughly 40% of college students are binge drinkers (Johnston, O'Malley, & Bachman, 2003a; Kuo, Wechsler, Greenberg, & Lee, 2003; Wechsler, Davenport, Dowdall, Moeykens, & Castillo, 1994; Wechsler, Lee, Kuo, Seibring, Nelson, & Lee, 2002). Further, as discussed in Chapter 3, the expected changes to *DSM*'s diagnostic criteria for substance abuse and addiction could result in roughly 40% of college students being diagnosed as addicted to alcohol (Szalavitz, 2012). Thus, there is a seemingly paradoxical relationship between college enrollment and binge/heavy drinking—full-time college enrollment is a risk factor for heavy drinking in young adulthood, but graduation from college is a protective factor for heavy drinking and alcohol-related problems later in life.

| Figure 6.15 | Heavy Alcohol Use by College Attendance and Age |

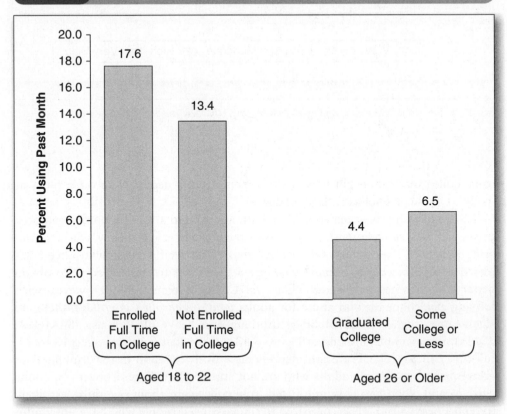

SOURCE: SAMHSA, 2011a.

In attempting to explain the prevalence of heavy drinking in college, many studies have noted the importance of the party subculture that is present on college campuses. College campuses are generally surrounded by numerous businesses that cater to student populations—and this typically includes a high concentration of bars, restaurants, and liquor stores that provide students with easy access to alcohol (Kuo et al., 2003; Weitzman, Folkman, Folkman, & Wechsler, 2003). College bars often include a variety of strategies designed to sell alcohol and promote consumption as well. These include happy hours, drink specials, and drink theme nights, which have the general effect of encouraging binge drinking and intoxication among college students (Kuo et al., 2003). Thus, there is a hyperavailability of alcohol on and around college campuses, in much the same way that there is a hyperavailability of alcohol in poor, predominately minority neighborhoods. As noted earlier, the hyper-availability of alcohol and other drugs in minority communities is linked to a variety of negative outcomes (Wallace, 1999b), and this is the case for college campuses as well (Weitzman, Nelson, Lee, & Wechsler, 2004). However, college campuses are clearly distinguished from poor, urban environments in a number of ways, and this includes the availability of resources for addressing/minimizing the impact of drug and alcohol-related problems. For example, college campuses typically provide a wide variety of conventional recreational opportunities, health care facilities, and counseling and drug-treatment resources (often at no additional charge to students)—resources that are scarce in poor, predominately minority neighborhoods (Wallace, 1999b). Thus, while the heavy use of alcohol may be relatively similar across social class, the *consequences* associated with these use patterns are felt more acutely by members of the lower class.

Research on the differential consequences associated with heavy drinking includes that by Hagan (1991). Hagan examined the effects of participating in a party subculture in late adolescence and early adulthood on professional outcomes later in life. His results indicated that participation in a party subculture resulted in lower educational achievement for the vast majority of adolescents. However, most interesting was his finding that once the effect of educational attainment was controlled for, participation in the party subculture resulted in *positive* occupational outcomes later in life among middle- and upper-class respondents but *negative* occupational outcomes later in life among working-class respondents (Hagan, 1991). Hagan (1991) concluded that adolescents form distinct subculture preferences during this period of life that have "class-specific effects on their trajectories towards adult occupational prestige" (p. 580). Hagan's work seems to account well for the finding that although many college students engage in very high patterns of alcohol use during college, often belonging to groups in which heavy alcohol consumption is the norm (e.g., fraternities and sororities), these individuals often experience few negative consequences from their substance abuse. Conversely, substance abuse among working- and lower-class individuals during adolescence and adulthood may be far more harmful in terms of outcomes later in life, in part because the societal response to the abuse of alcohol and other drugs is more likely to be punitive for members of the lower classes.

GEOGRAPHY AND RURAL/URBAN LOCATION

It is difficult to make broad generalizations with respect to legal drug use patterns by population size. Because use patterns vary depending on the substance in question, it is easiest to contrast drug use in large places and small ones. Data on adolescent populations are presented in Table 6.7 and Figure 6.14 and reveal that as compared to large cities, rural areas tend to have higher rates of drinking of all types, tobacco use, and inhalant use. When considering the abuse of prescription drugs, generally rural areas and large places have roughly comparable patterns of use (Table 6.7). But considering size of place across substance type, more nuanced findings emerge. For example, nonmetro areas report the highest levels of use for the prescription opiate OxyContin and metro areas the lowest, but this pattern is reversed when considering the prescription opiate Vicodin (Figure 6.14).

Table 6.7   Past Month Legal Drug Use by Size of Place, Adolescents Aged 12 to 17

	Completely Rural	Nonmetro*	Metro (Under 250K)	Metro (250K–1M)	Large Metro (>1M)
Any Alcohol Use	15.9	13.4	12.7	13.9	13.7
Binge Drinking	11.9	8.5	7.2	7.9	7.8
Heavy Alcohol Use	2.3	2.0	1.2	1.9	1.6
Tobacco Use (any form)	17.1	14.2	11.1	11.0	9.4
Inhalant Use	1.5	0.9	1.3	1.1	1.1
Illicit Use of Prescription Psychotherapeutics**	2.9	3	3.4	3.4	2.8
Illicit Use of Prescription Painkillers	2.5	2.5	2.6	3.1	2.3

*The Nonmetro category includes individuals living in completely rural areas, as well as those living in nonmetro less urbanized and nonmetro urbanized areas.

**Prescription-type therapeutics includes the nonmedical use of any prescription pain reliever, tranquilizer, stimulant, or sedative and does not include over-the-counter drugs.

SOURCE: SAMHSA, 2011a.

Adult patterns of legal drug use by population size are presented in Table 6.8. Although adults in large cities are much more likely to report any drinking than rural or small-town residents, they are only slightly more likely to report binge drinking, and there is not much variation in reported heavy drinking across population size. Reported tobacco use among adults is highest in nonmetro and rural areas, respectively, and tobacco use becomes increasingly less common as population size increases. Table 6.8 also presents data on the abuse of prescription psychotherapeutics (e.g., Xanax, Valium) and painkillers (e.g., Vicodin, OxyContin). These data reveal that patterns of

| Figure 6.16 | Psychoactive Pharmaceutical and Steroids Use by 12th Graders in Non-, Small-, and Large Metropolitan Areas |

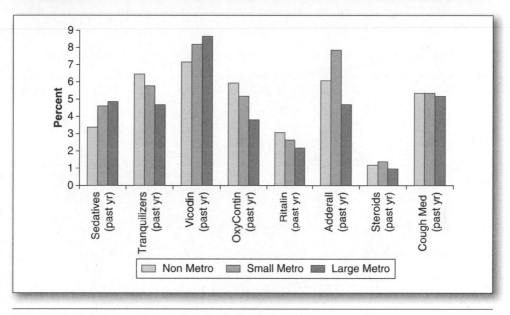

SOURCE: Johnston, O'Malley, Bachman, & Schulenberg (2011).

| Table 6.8 | Past Month Legal Drug Use by Size of Place, Adults Aged 18 or Older |

	Completely Rural	Non-metro**	Small Metro (Under 250K)	Metro (250K–1M)	Large Metro (>1M)
Any Alcohol Use	45.2	49.6	54.6	55.2	58.4
Binge Drinking	20.4	23.5	24.4	23.9	25.2
Heavy Alcohol Use	7.8	7.3	7.8	7.5	6.9
Tobacco Use (any form)	32.8	34.1	31.3	29.1	27.4
Inhalant Use*	0.2	0.1	0.2	0.3	0.3
Illicit Use of Prescription Psychotherapeutics***	0.9	2.6	2.6	2.9	2.7
Illicit Use of Prescription Painkillers	0.9	2.1	1.8	2.1	1.9

*Due to unavailability of data on persons 18 and over, inhalant use reports on all persons, 12 and over.

**The Nonmetro category includes individuals living in completely rural areas, as well as those living in nonmetro less urbanized and nonmetro urbanized areas.

***Prescription-type therapeutics includes the nonmedical use of any prescription pain reliever, tranquilizer, stimulant, or sedative and does not include over-the-counter drugs.

SOURCE: SAMHSA, 2011a.

Figure 6.17   Binge Alcohol Use in Past Month among Persons Aged 12 or Older, by State: Percentages, Annual Averages Based on 2006 and 2007 NSDUH

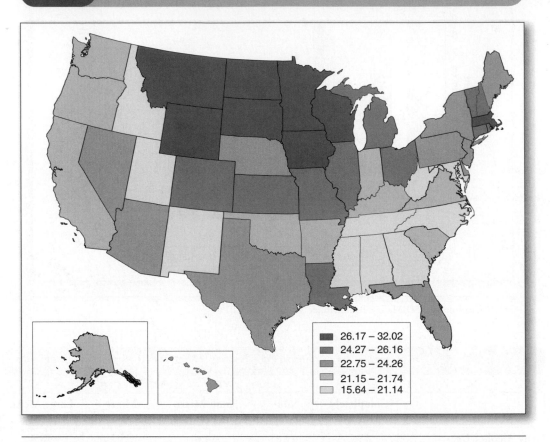

26.17 – 32.02
24.27 – 26.16
22.75 – 24.26
21.15 – 21.74
15.64 – 21.14

SOURCE: SAMHSA, Office of Applied Studies, National Survey on Drug Use and Health, 2006 and 2007.

State Variation in Alcohol Use

There is substantial variation in the use of legal drugs in the United States. State-level data on alcohol consumption reveal Utah residents to report the lowest levels of binge drinking in the country, with approximately 15% of the population admitting to binge drinking during the previous month. The highest rates of binge drinking in the country are reported in the Midwest, with nearly 30% of the population of Wisconsin and North Dakota reporting binge drinking during the previous month.

prescription drug abuse are fairly similar across cities of varying size, with the exception of completely rural residents, who are less likely to report prescription drug abuse.

Perhaps the most interesting finding with respect to population size and drug use is that, unlike the other correlates, we see significant differences in the use of legal as opposed to illegal drugs by population size. Specifically, as noted above, patterns

Figure 6.18	States With Highest and Lowest Portion of Binge Drinking Among Residents (12+ yrs.)

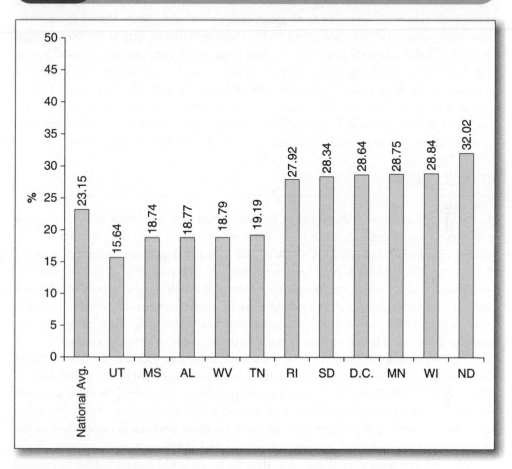

SOURCE: SAMHSA, 2004b.

of legal and illegal drug use are very similar across age, gender, race, and social class. Conversely, we see dissimilar patterns of legal and illegal drug use by population size. As noted in Chapter 5, larger places typically have significantly higher rates of illegal drug use, and this is due to a number of factors. Among these is the fact that small towns may lack the "critical mass" of people interested in a particular drug (inhibiting drug sales and access). Illegal drug use may also be more socially disapproved in small-town and rural areas, given the stronger emphasis on political and religious conservatism (Warner & Leukfeld, 2001).

Recall from our discussion of these issues in the context of illegal drug use that social institutions such as religion and the family are more salient influences on individual behavior in rural as opposed to urban areas. Research has found these factors to be important for understanding the low patterns of illegal drug use in rural as opposed to urban areas (Albrecht, Amery, & Miller, 1996; Bachman, Wallace, O'Malley, Johnston,

Kurth, & Neighbors, 1991), and these same factors are important for understanding legal drug use and abuse. While rural populations may be less likely to approve of the use or abuse of certain legal drugs than are urban populations, the abuse of legal drugs is likely to meet with lower levels of social disapproval (e.g., binge drinking) or to be more easily concealed (e.g., prescription pharmaceutical abuse) than is the use of illegal drugs. Thus, the relatively high rates of legal drug use in rural areas and small towns (e.g., binge/heavy drinking, tobacco use, pharmaceutical abuse, inhalant abuse) are to be expected if the drive toward consciousness alteration is universal and access to and approval of illegal drugs is more limited. That is, the differences in legal and illegal drug use by population size may largely reflect variation in the *type* of drug used rather than of the tendency to use psychoactive drugs in general (Cronk & Sarvela, 1997).

CONCLUSION

As with our discussion of illegal drugs, we have noted how legal drug use varies across a variety of sociodemographic factors. We have examined legal drug use across age, gender, race, social class, and size of place and found that patterns of legal and illegal drug use are very similar across these correlates, with the exception of size of place. As with illegal drugs, the use and abuse of legal drugs is much more common in late adolescence and early adulthood. For example, we examined patterns of intoxication using three distinct measures of drug use—binge and heavy drinking, illicit drug use, and marijuana use—and found almost identical patterns of use over the lifecourse.

Gender is another important factor influencing the use of legal drugs. As with illegal drugs, males are more likely to use and abuse most forms of legal drugs, particularly in adulthood. Exceptions to this pattern include the abuse of some forms of prescription pharmaceuticals, particularly during adolescence, which women were as or even more likely to report using than were men. We interpret these findings in the context of the distinct social roles adopted by men and women. For example, women are more likely to seek help for mental problems and thus to be prescribed certain pharmaceutical drugs, and women may also be less likely than men to view other forms of legal drug use (e.g., binge drinking) as acceptable behavior. Thus, the motivation to use and abuse substances may be somewhat similar but manifested in ways that are considered more or less socially appropriate for each gender.

Drug use also varies significantly by race/ethnicity, but similar to the situation with illegal drugs, whites are among the most likely to use and abuse legal drugs. Among adolescents and young adults, extensive research has typically found Asians to demonstrate the lowest patterns of substance use, followed by blacks, with whites, Hispanics, and Native Americans demonstrating the highest patterns of use. However, as with illegal drug use, age is an important factor to consider when interpreting race-specific patterns of legal drug use. Additionally, the effects of social class, peer versus family influence, and acculturation are more salient predictors of legal drug use for some racial/ethnic groups than for others. As might be expected, there is also significant variation in legal drug use by social class. Social class and race are highly correlated, and while the use and abuse of legal drugs does not vary substantially across social class categories, the *problems* associated with legal drug use and abuse often do.

Finally, we examined the relationship of legal drug use by size of place. This correlate was the only one that demonstrated a significantly different relationship with legal as opposed to illegal drugs. Illegal drug use is more likely among urban populations, but rural populations and small towns were as or nearly as likely to report the use of most legal drugs (exceptions include certain forms of pharmaceuticals). With respect to this, and in the context of the greater political and religious conservatism among rural residents, it may be that the abuse of legal drugs is likely to meet with lower levels of disapproval (e.g., binge drinking) or to be more easily concealed than illegal forms of consciousness alteration (e.g., marijuana use). Thus, the relatively high rates of legal drug use in rural areas may largely reflect variation in the type of drug used rather than the general tendency to alter consciousness with substances.

REVIEW QUESTIONS

1. Compare the patterns of legal and illegal drug use by age. Are these patterns similar or different? What factors account for the similarities and differences?

2. What types of over-the-counter and prescription medications are commonly abused by adolescents? Compared to illegal drugs, how prevalent is the abuse of prescription medications?

3. Why does legal drug abuse tend to resurge late in the lifecourse?

4. Compared to males, what types of drugs are females as or even more likely to report abusing?

5. How do patterns of alcohol abuse among whites and blacks vary over the lifecourse? What accounts for these distinct patterns of alcohol abuse?

6. What factors have been found to be important for explaining variation in alcohol consumption across Hispanic subpopulations?

7. What explains the high rates of alcohol use and abuse among American Indians? What has research concluded about the validity of these explanations?

8. In terms of social class, which groups are most likely to report binge drinking or being drunk?

9. What effect does college enrollment and graduation have on heavy alcohol use?

INTERNET EXERCISES

1. The Drug Abuse Warning Network (DAWN) collects extensive data on any emergency department visit that is reported as being "drug-related." The longitudinal data produced provide a unique, detailed instrument for measuring the acute health impact produced by drug use, both legal and illegal. For this Internet exercise, you will be examining data from 2010. To access that data set, already organized into relevant subcategories, start by going to http://www.samhsa.gov/data/dawn.aspx.

2. Click on the link for DAWN 2010 Emergency Department Excel Files— National Tables, located at the top of the page. Familiarize yourself with how to find the number of ED visits associated with different demographic subsets of the population or with particular substances. Next , select the three illicit substances you believe are the most dangerous to users, along with the three most dangerous prescription drugs and over-the-counter medicines. Using the data from every year from 2006 through 2010, make a chart tracking drug-related ED visits associated with each substance.

   • Which one has been associated with the most drug-related ED visits overall?
   • What trends did you observe, and were they what you would have predicted?
   • Which of three different subclasses of drugs (OTC, Rx, or illegal) caused the most harm in 2010? Which directions were the trends for each class, collectively?

3. Next, expand your list by adding two additional drugs within each level of regu-lation, this time picking ones that you believe are among the more commonly used. Find the drug-related ED visit data for each of the new substances and input them on your chart. Next, find the raw number of times each substance was in the system of emergency room patients, whether it was deemed drug-related officially or not. This may require a few moments spent examining the data definitions on the website, but a clue to the difference involves whether the substances were taken according to medical advice.

   • When you look at the total number of people experiencing acute side effects from the drugs you chose, regardless of whether they were taken as suggested, what individual substances on your list caused the most harm? The least harm?
   • What about for the three regulatory levels of drugs, collectively? Were those what you would have expected for trends?
   • When combined with the data from Exercise 1, what does it suggest about the objectivity of the official claims regarding the harmfulness of illegal drugs? What does it suggest about pharmaceutical companies' claims about safety?
   • Why do you think there is such an inaccurate portrayal of the relative scope of harm caused by these different drugs, from cough medicine to heroin, provided even today by the government and media, overall?

4. Access data on drug use provided by the Monitoring the Future study at: http://www .monitoringthefuture.org/pubs/monographs/vol1_2004.pdf. Scroll down to Table 3 (p. 52) and find the measure of past month intoxication ("been drunk"). What per-centage of 12th graders reported "being drunk in the last 30 days" in 1991? What percentage reported being drunk in 2000? What percentage reported being drunk last year? What do these tends suggest about the underage drinking "epidemic"?

5. Access data on prescription abuse provided by the 2004 NSDUH at http://oas .samhsa.gov/NSDUH/2k4NSDUH/2k4results/2k4results.htm#ch2. Scroll down to Figure 2.5, which summarizes patterns of abuse for opiate-based pharmaceu-ticals by young adults from 2002 to 2004. What do the data indicate about use patterns from 2002 to 2004? Which opiate-based medications are commonly abused? Referring to the coverage of these substances in Chapter 3, what types of effects do these drugs have? What risks accompany the use of these drugs?

CHAPTER 7

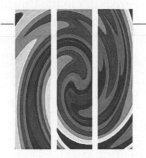

Drug Prevention Programs

It is important to note that although we address them here in a separate chapter, programs focused on the prevention of illicit drug use in the United States are important components of larger drug policy in this country. As our review of these prevention policies demonstrates, the programs are consistent with and founded on many of the same misguided themes as the policies reviewed elsewhere in this book. Relative to the funds devoted to law enforcement, corrections, and even treatment in the war on drugs, prevention programs are grossly underfunded and characterized by the neglect and, in some cases, suppression of scientific information that should be used to inform them, by the dominance of vested bureaucratic interests in shaping and maintaining them, and, above all, by their almost universal failure to achieve their stated goals of preventing or reducing drug use. In this chapter, we critically review drug education programs, antidrug advertising campaigns aimed primarily at youth, zero-tolerance policies in schools, and drug testing (as applied in schools and the workplace).

DRUG EDUCATION PROGRAMS

> Children may be ignorant, but they are not stupid. When the evidence of their own experience contradicts adult propaganda, they (like sensible adults) rely on their own experience—and tend to distrust in the future a source of information which they had found unreliable in the past. (Brecher, 1972, p. 332)

While there is no evidence to indicate that drug education programs in the United States are not well-intentioned, a critical examination of their features and the outcomes associated with them leads to the inescapable conclusion that they have almost universally failed to achieve their stated goals while at the same time wasting billions of dollars of taxpayer money.

265

The drug education programs in place today, in particular Drug Abuse Resistance Education (D.A.R.E.), are remarkably consistent with the scare tactics and misinformation about drugs promoted in the earliest drug education programs in the United States. In the late 1800s when alcohol was a drug of major concern, health lessons in schools promoted by the Women's Christian Temperance Union (WCTU) and its Department of Scientific Instruction depicted the substance as an evil poison that inevitably created an uncontrollable appetite in its users. One WCTU treatise, appearing in an 1887 schoolbook *The House I Live In*, asserted,

> Many persons who at first take only a little beer, cider, or wine form a great desire for them. . . . The appetite for alcoholic liquors usually grows rapidly, and men who use but little at first often become drunkards in a short time. (as quoted in Moilanen, 2004)

It is worth comparing the WCTU admonitions regarding the addictive properties of alcohol to a 1999 drug education pamphlet titled "Making Life Choices":"Attachment to the drug becomes almost like a great love relationship with another person. The only way to escape drug addiction is to never experiment with taking the drugs that produce it" (as quoted in Moilanen, 2004).

Current education about marijuana generally emphasizes the dual themes that its use results in amotivational syndrome and a progression to the use of harder drugs (the gateway hypothesis), both of which, as noted in Chapter 1, were found to be scientifically questionable assertions. As Moilanen (2004) notes, more than 100 years ago, young people were exposed to essentially identical warnings about the dangers associated with tobacco use. A 1904 book titled *Our Bodies and How We Live* claimed that "the mind of the habitual tobacco user is apt to lose its capacity for study or successful effort."Similarly, according to the 1924 *Primer of Hygiene*, a tobacco user "forgets the importance of the work he has to do and idles away his time instead of going earnestly to finish the task."An 1892 publication, *Essentials of Health,* alleged that the use of tobacco would eventually lead to the consumption of harder drugs:"It is to be feared that if our young men continue the use of cigarettes we shall see, as a legitimate result, a large number of young adults addicted to the opium habit" (as quoted in Moilanen, 2004).

D.A.R.E.

The Drug Abuse Resistance Education program was developed by the Los Angeles Police Department in 1983 and quickly became the most prominent school-based drug education program in the United States. As will be discussed further below, the number of schools using the program has declined substantially in recent years, but as of 2001, more than 50,000 law enforcement officers were acting as D.A.R.E. representatives, and approximately 80% of schools in the United States had adopted D.A.R.E. (Wright, 2001). The program was also adopted in more than 40 other countries. The original D.A.R.E. program sent trained police officers to teach

5th- and 6th-grade students about drugs, self-esteem, peer resistance, stress management, assertiveness, and healthful alternatives to the use of drugs; the underlying message of the program was that young people should "Just Say No" to drugs. With training costs of more than $2,000 per officer and program costs as high as $90,600 per year for each full-time officer involved in the program, D.A.R.E. was very expensive to implement and maintain. In 1993, for example, total national expenditures for the program were estimated at more than $700 million (Wysong, Aniskiewicz, & Wright, 1994). Shepard (2001) later estimated that in total, D.A.R.E. was costing between $1 and $1.3 billion per year.

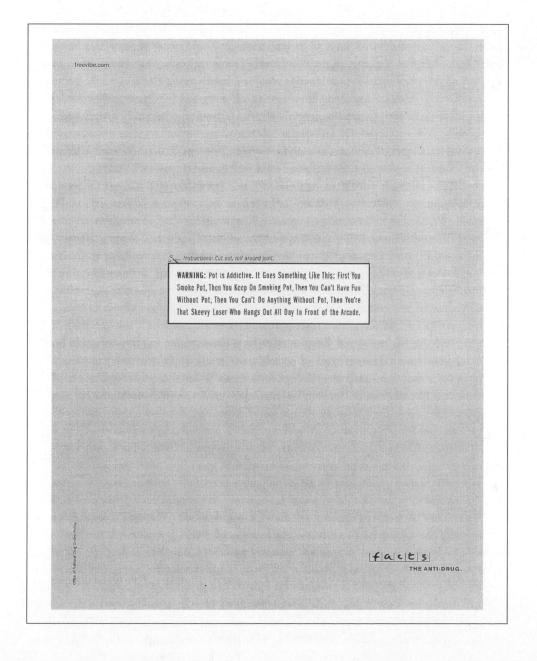

The initial, largely nonscientific evaluations of D.A.R.E. (typically conducted by D.A.R.E. officials themselves) showed that the program was popular with parents, D.A.R.E. officers, teachers, and school administrators, and that the program improved student knowledge about the risks associated with drug use. However, virtually every subsequent scientific study of the program has found that it has either no effect or, in some cases, a counterproductive effect on youth drug use. In 1999, the American Psychological Association published a study that found "no reliable, short-term, long-term, early adolescent, or young adult positive outcomes associated with D.A.R.E. intervention" (cited in Wright, 2001). In another evaluation of D.A.R.E., Wysong and colleagues (2003) collected data from 1987 through 1992 as part of a multiyear assessment of a D.A.R.E. program in Indiana and also found it to be ineffective in reducing youth substance use. Rosenbaum and Hanson (1998) conducted an evaluation of D.A.R.E. programs in the state of Illinois and found that 5 years after they had been exposed to the program, D.A.R.E. students, in comparison to those in a control group who had not experienced the program, actually reported significantly higher scores on scales measuring total drug and alcohol use, as well as with respect to the severity of their alcohol consumption. In 2003, a study released by the U.S. General Accounting Office concluded, "the six long-term evaluations of the D.A.R.E. elementary school curriculum that we reviewed found no significant differences in illicit drug use between students who received D.A.R.E. and those who did not" (U.S. General Accounting Office, 2003a). Similarly, Des Jarlais and colleagues (2006) note, "To our knowledge, there has been no review of research studies on D.A.R.E. that has concluded that the curricula are effective in reducing illicit drug use among school-aged children and youth" (p. 1355). In addition, both the Surgeon General's Office and the National Academy of Sciences issued reports indicating that D.A.R.E. was ineffective in reducing youth drug use (Wright, 2001).

The "Just Say No" approach to drug education is sadly consistent with other public education campaigns in the United States, particularly with respect to teenage sex. For example, many schools do not allow access to condoms, alleging that they will encourage young people to become involved in sexual activities. However, a study of high schools in Massachusetts published in the *American Journal of Public Health* found that teenagers at high schools where condoms were accessible were no more likely to engage in sex than teenagers at schools where condoms were not available (Blake et al., 2003). Obviously, if youth are engaging in unprotected sex, the risks of sexually transmitted diseases and unwanted pregnancies are significantly increased.

D.A.R.E. Officials' Reactions

Not surprisingly, D.A.R.E. officials and supporters, as part of the "drug industrial complex" (Gray, 2001), did not react positively to the results of these studies. In some cases, D.A.R.E. officials attempted to suppress the studies, in others they dismissed the findings, and in still others engaged in active intimidation of those who criticized the program. When a 1995 study conducted by the California Department of Education concluded that D.A.R.E. was ineffective and might actually have been counterproductive with respect to reducing youth drug use, the findings were suppressed by the state education agency and not made public until 1997 (Wright, 2001). In response to another negative evaluation of D.A.R.E., Executive Director Glen Levant argued, "Scientists will tell you bumblebees can't fly, but we know better" (as quoted in Dineen, 2001) and also referred to studies critical of D.A.R.E. as "voodoo science" (as quoted in Kaufman, 1999). Similarly, in response to the previously mentioned findings of Wysong and colleagues (2003), a D.A.R.E. official in Indiana commented to community groups, "They must not know how to measure things. . . . If they could just see the kids' faces they'd know how much good it's doing" (as quoted in Wysong et al., 2003, p. 109). Glen Levant further indicated that D.A.R.E. officers constantly provide anecdotal evidence that the program works, and that if the program had resulted in positive changes for only one young person, it was worth the effort. But as one commentator pointed out, it is not clear why the standard of success for D.A.R.E. programs should be set so low. It is highly unlikely that we would deem a math curriculum to be successful if only one child learned to add as a result of exposure to the curriculum (Glass, 1997).

D.A.R.E. officials have also attempted to counter the negative evaluations of the program through claims, for example, that 97% of teachers rate D.A.R.E. as good to excellent, 93% of parents of children who experience D.A.R.E. believe the program teaches children to avoid drugs, and 86% of school principals believe students would be less likely to use drugs after participating in the program (Moilanen, 2004). However, we must question whether such measures should be accepted as valid indicators of the success of drug education programs because they do not speak at all to the issue of actual drug use by students.

There have also been several cases of intimidation directed at critics of D.A.R.E. Glass (1997) recounts the case of an assistant professor at a college in Illinois who performed a study of college freshmen and, similar to several other evaluations of D.A.R.E., found no differences in drug use by students who had been exposed to the program and those who had not. This professor shared his data with a colleague in a different department at his institution and was soon contacted by local D.A.R.E. officials. He later received a phone call from the chair of his department, who informed him that a D.A.R.E. official had alleged that he had been offering his study participants marijuana as an incentive to participate in the research. Another researcher who published a study critical of D.A.R.E. had the words "Kid Killer" and "Drug Pusher" painted on his car (Glass, 1997). It appears that, as Lloyd Johnston, lead researcher for the Monitoring the Future youth drug surveys, commented, "criticizing D.A.R.E. is like going after motherhood or apple pie" (as quoted in Seltz, 2000).

Andrew Weil (1986) cites an example of "information" presented in a (pre–D.A.R.E.) drug education program that purported to "give unbiased facts so that students can decide for themselves whether or not they will try marijuana."Part of the curriculum in the program included the following example:"Some people when they smoke a joint and eat a cheeseburger think the cheeseburger tastes better. Actually, this is not so. What happened is that the marijuana has interfered with the immediate memory so that they do not remember what the last cheeseburger they ate tasted like." (p. 84)

The almost universally negative findings from evaluations of D.A.R.E. lead to two important questions. First, why does the program not work, and second, why, until fairly recently, did it maintain its popularity?

National surveys on drug use, reviewed in Chapter 5, indicate that more than half of teenagers in the United States admit to trying an illegal drug before finishing high school, thus suggesting that the majority of young people have basically rejected the "Just Say No to Drugs" message. In the context of these high levels of use, it is important to realize that most drug use by young people is essentially experimental, "a rite of passage that most children pass through unscathed" (Weil & Rosen, 1998, p. 5). Newcomb and Bentler (1988) concluded that the experimental use of drugs, both licit and illicit, "may be considered a normative behavior among United States teenagers in terms of prevalence and (also) from a developmental task perspective" (p. 214). Similarly, Shedler and Block's (1990) longitudinal study of drug users concluded that adolescents who engaged in some drug experimentation were the best socially adjusted in their sample, while those who had completely abstained from drug use were more socially isolated. What these and other studies imply, then, is that drug use among young people *is* going to occur, and that a "Just Say No" approach is not likely to be effective in drug education.

As Marsha Rosenbaum (2002) notes, D.A.R.E. programs are characterized by a number of problematic myths about drugs, which she lists as follows: (1) experimentation with drugs is not a common aspect of youth culture; (2) any drug use is either equivalent to or will eventually lead to drug *abuse*; (3) marijuana is the gateway to hard drugs such as heroin and cocaine; and(4) exaggerating the risks associated with drug use will deter young people from experimenting with drugs. This type of misinformation can have counterproductive effects, in many cases leading youth to reject all of the antidrug messages they are exposed to.

Particularly important here is the misinformation presented on marijuana, because it is the illicit drug that students are most likely to have exposure to and experience with. The early D.A.R.E. curriculum's statement on marijuana suggested that

> someone who uses marijuana has slow reflexes, poor memory, a short attention span, an inability to think, and changes in the sense of time and space. Students who use marijuana may have difficulty in remembering what they have learned, are slow, dull, have little ambition, and may become dependent on the drug. (D.A.R.E., 1996)

As discussed in Chapter 4, most of this "information" about the effects of marijuana is simply not true and is inconsistent with young people's own observations and experiences with the substance. Rosenbaum (2002) recounts the case of a 17-year-old girl she interviewed who said, "They told my little sister that you'd get addicted to marijuana the first time, and it's not like that. You hear that and then you do it, and you say 'ah, they lied to me.'"As the director of the Addiction

Research Foundation in Toronto, Canada, has argued, it is important that young people not be given misleading or blatantly inaccurate information about drugs:

> Kids should be given truthful information about drugs, in particular, marijuana, just as they generally are about alcohol. . . . We give our kids some understanding, knowing they're going to encounter alcohol. We encourage them to hire limousines for the grad parties, knowing they'll be drinking even though they're underage. It is a more pragmatic approach—it doesn't mean we're encouraging them to drink. A young person who finds out that marijuana does not cause the "reefer madness" he's been warned about is going to wonder if adults lie about every drug. If he gets offered cocaine at a party, he is apt to say "Gee, they lied to me about marijuana, maybe they're lying to me about this too." (as quoted in Carey, 1998)

MacCoun and Reuter (2001) raise the additional possibility that D.A.R.E.—in particular, its "Just Say No" message—may be ineffective because it promotes a "forbidden fruit" effect. Under this principle, also known as reactance, restrictions on freedom of choice can serve to increase the attractiveness of a particular object or activity. While there is very little systematic empirical research on this phenomenon with respect to drugs, MacCoun and Reuter note that scientific research in other domains may be relevant. For instance, researchers have found that young children are more interested in playing with toys when those toys are placed behind a barrier restricting their access, and people become significantly more interested in information when it is being censored by authorities. In addition, "restricted" labels on television programs and movies apparently make them more attractive to males in the 10–14 age group. In a similar sense, young people who are told that drugs are evil and that they must abstain from them may be encouraged to try them. Weil and Rosen (1998) also emphasize the possibility that the "Just Say No" message may actually increase drug use: "More often than not, lectures, pamphlets, and film strips that [exaggerate the dangers of drugs] stimulate curiosity, make the prohibited substances look more attractive to young audiences, and make authorities appear ridiculous" (p. 3).

An additional explanation for the ineffectiveness of the D.A.R.E. program is related to the fact that its curriculum is delivered by police officers. While it is important to note that such officers are likely to be well-intentioned, their scientific knowledge of the realities of drugs and drug use may well be limited. Although not necessarily representative of the information provided in all D.A.R.E. programs, Marsha Rosenbaum (2001), who has written extensively on alternative drug education programs, reports that her 5th-grade daughter informed her that the D.A.R.E. officer had told students, "when a person smokes marijuana, half of their brain cells are erased forever" (p. 26). There is also evidence to suggest that in some individual D.A.R.E. programs, the misinformation provided by police officers goes well beyond myths about the effects of psychoactive substances. Wysong and colleagues (1994) note that in interviews they conducted with D.A.R.E. participants in Indiana, students recalled that the officer teaching the class had insisted that listening to rock music led to Satan worship.

There are indications that law enforcement officials have used information that students submit to the "D.A.R.E. Box" (an aspect of the program that encourages students to inform D.A.R.E. officers if they see anyone, including their parents, using drugs) to arrest parents (Glass, 1997). This is despite the fact that students are given assurances that the information they provide will not be used for such purposes.

With respect to the long-term popularity of D.A.R.E. in the United States, Wysong and colleagues (2003) suggest that D.A.R.E. programs have resulted in substantial symbolic benefits for several stakeholders in the drug area, including politicians, corporate sponsors, school officials, and law enforcement agencies who have gained legitimacy and public support through the promotion of D.A.R.E. It may also be true that D.A.R.E. allows legislators and school officials to simply "wash their hands" of the drug problem (Eyle, 2002). Or, as one commentator put it, "D.A.R.E. is the world's biggest pet rock. If it makes us feel good to do nothing, that's okay, but everybody should know that D.A.R.E. does nothing" (Glass, 1997). Yet another detrimental aspect of the D.A.R.E. program is that both the tremendous monetary resources and classroom time devoted to it cannot be used for other, potentially more effective educational purposes. As Lloyd Johnston suggests, "the real cost is opportunity lost. Parents and school boards think they are doing something when they're not, so a lot of kids pass under the bridge of adolescence and are never touched by an effective prevention program" (as quoted in Seltz, 2000).

In the late 1990s and early 2000s, several jurisdictions in the United States discontinued their D.A.R.E. programs. In an interview with a reporter, Salt Lake City Mayor Rocky Anderson, who decided to end all D.A.R.E. programs in his jurisdiction in 2000, noted that "D.A.R.E. has built up their infrastructure through a huge fraud on the American people. Now, they've completely lost their credibility, but instead of letting them use 37,000 more of our school kids as guinea pigs as they revamp their program, we ought to be replacing them with programs that have integrity and are effective." (as quoted in Eyle, 2001)

At least partially due to its demonstrated ineffectiveness, federal government funding for D.A.R.E. programs was eliminated in 2001, and the curriculum was redeveloped. Initial changes involved shortening the curriculum from 17 weeks in the 5th grade to 10 weeks in the 7th grade and providing follow-up programs with the ostensible goal of creating long-term reductions in drug use (Wright, 2001). However, the program maintained its fundamental "Just Say No" message, and these changes did little to address additional risk factors associated with drug use.

In order to address the continued criticisms, D.A.R.E. has since developed specialized sub-programs intended to, among other things, address other risk factors. To provide drug-free social activities, D.A.R.E. P.L.U.S. (Play and Learn Under Supervision) provides on-campus after-school activities for middle school students, while D.A.R.E. Dance involves competitive dance activities. The D.A.R.E. Community Education program has also recently been introduced to provide resources for parents and community members to complement the in-school curriculum (http://www .dare.org). To their credit, D.A.R.E. officials have also responded to the emerging problem of prescription drug abuse by young people through the Prescription and Over-the-Counter Drug curriculum.

More recently, in 2009, the national movement toward evidence-based practices in substance abuse prevention and treatment led to the development of the D.A.R.E. Keepin' It Real program, which has been promoted as a scientifically based revision to the D.A.R.E. curriculum. Allegedly founded on cognitive behavioral therapy and motivational enhancement therapy techniques, both of which have received considerable scientific support, the new approach is designed to more directly engage students in the learning process. As an alternative to lectures by D.A.R.E. officers, the strategy is intended to provide students with social skills to employ when saying no to drugs—as described by its acronym, R.E.A.L.—"Refuse, Explain, Avoid and Leave." The new curriculum is designed to promote risk assessment and general life skills in a multiculturally sensitive manner and is to be taught by officers who have received more extensive training in diversity and therapeutic strategies.

Clearly, a number of changes have been made to the traditional D.A.R.E. program since 2001, and the recent focus on more engaged preventive learning strategies reflects attention to evidence-based practices. At the same time, the fundamental program has not changed, as police officers still deliver classroom-based drug prevention education, and the drug myths perpetuated by D.A.R.E. remain largely intact. For example, despite emerging scientific evidence to the contrary, the official D.A.R.E. website still refers to marijuana as a substance without medical value and refers to doctors who prescribe the substance as "bad doctors." In addition, D.A.R.E. literature still credits the program with having been instrumental in reducing drug use among young people since its inception.

Interestingly, it also appears that President Obama was unaware of the demonstrated ineffectiveness of D.A.R.E. programs, as he declared April 8, 2009, "National D.A.R.E. Day." He stated, "The D.A.R.E. program has worked to educate students about drugs, gangs, and violence for more than 25 years. Placing law enforcement personnel in the classroom, D.A.R.E. provides students with important lessons from experts and seeks to prepare them for the difficult encounters and choices they may face. . . . The efforts of D.A.R.E.'s instructors and supporters benefit our nation's children and are deserving of praise and appreciation." (D.A.R.E., 2009)

Alternative Drug Education Programs

The federal government's Substance Abuse and Mental Health Services Administration (SAMHSA) has identified a number of substance abuse prevention programs that the agency claims are evidence based and effective (see http://nrepp.samhsa.gov/find.asp).

While these lists of evidence-based prevention practices may be useful for school officials seeking alternative drug education programs, a review of the criteria used to
determine that a program is evidence-based identified a number of concerns. Gandhi
and colleagues (2007) note that the lists require only one or two evaluations to classify
a program as effective, that the developers of programs often served as evaluators of
their own programs, that outcome measures used in evaluations were often not comparable, that the lists do not stipulate the specific conditions under which programs
are effective, and that few studies examined outcomes more than 2 years after the end
of project implementation. Gandhi and colleagues conclude,

> The findings from our review cause us to wonder if the programs cited across
> the best-practice lists are any more effective than D.A.R.E. We find it plausible
> that some of these programs may seem more effective than D.A.R.E. simply
> because they have been studied less, or over a shorter length of time, and by the
> developers of the programs themselves. (p. 66)

There are also issues with respect to adoption and implementation of these
evidence-based policies. For example, Ringwalt and colleagues (2008) collected data
from nearly 1,400 school district drug prevention coordinators in 2005 and found
that of the six programs considered by SAMHSA to be effective, only 10.3% of the
districts administered one such program.

Some have suggested that a more appropriate model for drug education would
be based on the themes that form the basis of some of the more progressive sex
education programs currently used in U.S. schools. These programs essentially
accept the fact that some young people will engage in sexual activities but attempt
to ensure that if they do so, they will do so responsibly and in ways that do not
result in the spread of sexually transmitted diseases or the occurrence of unwanted
pregnancies. As Braiker (2003) suggests,

> The message should be: Don't use drugs. Second message: Don't use drugs. But
> then the third message needs to be something like: If you do, even though we've
> told you not to and even though we strongly recommend that you do not, there
> are certain things you need to know.

In other words, drug education should provide young people with at least some
information on the relative risks of different drugs, different doses, different routes
of administration, different patterns of use (Zimmer & Morgan, 1997), and how to
minimize the risks associated with drugs if they do begin to use them.

As G. Munro (1998) notes, "our major responsibility is to learn to manage drug
use rather than pretend we can eliminate it, to limit the damage and the harms drugs
cause to individuals and the broader society." Young people should be taught about
the pharmacology of *both* illegal and legal drugs (especially given the increasing
number of young people who are taking legal stimulant drugs such as Ritalin) and
should be educated with respect to how they can use drugs in a manner that is calculated to induce the least risk of harm.

Invest in [prevention] activities that can both prevent young people from taking drugs in the first place and also prevent those who do use drugs from developing more serious problems. Eschew simple "just say no" messages and "zero tolerance" policies in favor of educational efforts grounded in credible information and prevention programs that focus on social skills and peer influences. (Global Commission on Drug Policy, 2011)

Marsha Rosenbaum's (2002) booklet *Safety First: A Reality Based Approach to Teens, Drugs, and Drug Education* emphasizes that while drug education programs may not be able to prevent drug use, it might be realistic for them to have the goal of preventing drug *abuse*. She suggests integrating the subject of drugs into physiology, biology, chemistry, psychology, political science, and history courses, and that while abstinence values should not be completely abandoned, avoiding problems with drugs should be stressed. Extracurricular and after-school programs that serve to divert young people from involvement with drugs should also be expanded.

Skager (2001) similarly suggests that we can begin to improve drug education in the United States by setting more realistic goals, such as delaying the age of first use of substances, reducing (as opposed to eliminating) overall drug use, and reducing more problematic forms of use such as bingeing and mixing drugs and using unknown or impure substances. He calls for interactional and nonjudgmental—as opposed to "top down"—teaching, because the former approach encourages young people's active participation in the learning process. Unfortunately, as Skager (2001) and others have noted, a major barrier to the implementation of such programs is that federal government guidelines only allow funding for abstinence-based programs.

While D.A.R.E. and similar "Just Say No" approaches have been dominant in drug education programs in the United States, other countries have adopted more progressive and rational programs. For example, an advertising campaign in Great Britain in 2003 made jokes about heroin and actually acknowledged that the effects of ecstasy could be pleasurable (Carvel, 2003). This program also targeted parents and urged them to "Talk to Frank" (an Internet service) for information on substance use and drug addiction. In contrast to the D.A.R.E. program, this British campaign provides "accurate, confidential, and unbiased" information about drugs ("Government Launches," 2003). Another drug education program in Britain, known as the D:side Project, adopts a nonjudgmental approach to drugs, providing accurate information about the effects of drugs and alcohol without "glamorization or demonization." The coordinator of the program commented, "We don't use scare tactics. You lose credibility if you tell kids 'you'll die if you take this drug,' when they all know people who are taking it and haven't died" (as quoted in Vallely, 2005). Similarly, in the Netherlands, children begin receiving drug education at the age of 10. This education presents the facts about drugs in a manner that removes the glamour frequently associated with their use but leaves the decision to consume drugs up to the individual. A Dutch official commented, "We say it's your responsibility, this is what drugs will do. We don't tell kids simply 'no,' we say 'know'" (as quoted in Rose, 2002).

ANTIDRUG ADVERTISING CAMPAIGNS

Does anyone seriously believe that stenciling the words "Just Say No to Drugs" on a strainer in restroom urinals actually accomplishes anything? We must remember the lesson learned by the school board that furnished 4th graders with pencils that said "It's not cool to do drugs. "The children quickly saw that when you sharpened the pencils they soon read "cool to do drugs" and eventually "do drugs." (Gray, 2001, p. 232)

An additional drug prevention strategy that has been prominent in the last three decades, and to which a considerable amount of financial resources have been devoted, is antidrug advertisements sponsored by the Partnership for a Drug Free America (PFDFA) and the federal government's Office of National Drug Control Policy (ONDCP). Over the 1986 to 2001 period, the PFDFA received more than $3 billion in donated media from a variety of sources (Block et al., 2002), and between 1998 and 2007, the federal government spent more than $1.4 billion on the anti-drug advertising campaign. In the late 1990s, in relative terms, the PFDFA was the second-largest advertiser in the United States, trailing only McDonald's (Buchanan & Wallack, 1998). The antidrug ads produced by PFDFA and ONDCP are pervasive, having appeared on television, in newspapers and magazines, on shopping bags, in comic books, on home videos, restaurant place mats, candy wrappers, bumper stickers, bookmarks, billboards, the sides of buses, and even urinal covers (Zimmer & Morgan, 1997).

The PFDFA was formerly headed by James Burke, the former chief executive officer of Johnson and Johnson, manufacturers of psychoactive substances such as Tylenol, Nicotrol (a nicotine delivery device), and numerous prescription medications. As Shenk (1999) argued, "Burke embodies a contradiction so common that few people even notice it—the idea that altering the body and mind is morally wrong with some substances and salutary when done with others."Prior to 2005, when the PFDFA stopped accepting funding from manufacturers of alcohol and tobacco products (PFDFA, 2005b), the major financial contributors to the PFDFA were the leading pharmaceutical, alcohol, and tobacco companies in the United States, including DuPont, Procter & Gamble, Bristol Meyers Squibb, SmithKlineBeecham, the Merck Foundation, Hoffman-LaRoche, Philip Morris, Anheuser Busch, RJ Reynolds, and American Brands (Buchanan & Wallack, 1998). (The names of several of these companies have changed as the result of corporate mergers and buyouts.) Cotts (2002) estimated that the PFDFA accepted more than $5 million in contributions from these and other legal drug manufacturers while producing advertisements that paid virtually no attention to the dangers of tobacco, alcohol, and prescription drugs.

Collectively, the ads produced by the PFDFA and the Office of National Drug Control Policy served to reinforce a number of the myths and stereotypes about drugs that were outlined in Chapter 1, for example, the notion that the use of (illegal) drugs inevitably causes brain damage, that marijuana is a gateway drug and that its consumption leads to involvement in violent acts, that the use of (illegal) drugs leads to involvement in sexual activities, including homosexual activities, and that traffickers in (illegal) drugs are dangerous foreigners. Sullum (2002) argues that the PFDFA and ONDCP advertisements should be viewed as propaganda, given that they "aim not to educate people but to shape their behavior by presenting a distorted, one-sided interpretation of reality that ignores important information as well as contrary perspectives."

One of the first and most notorious advertisements in the PFDFA campaign allegedly showed the brain of a 14-year-old marijuana user; the copy to the ad stated, "If you use marijuana, you are not using your brain."This ad, of course, implied that marijuana consumption leads to brain damage; in reality, and as discussed in Chapter 1, scientific studies indicate that there are no detectable differences in the brain wave patterns of individuals under the influence of marijuana and those who are not. It is also disturbing to note that the brain wave pattern used in this PFDFA marijuana advertisement was actually that of an individual who was in a coma (Buchanan & Wallack, 1998).

Another series of full-page ads sponsored by ONDCP and PFDFA appearing in the *New York Times* in 1998 further promoted mythologies about marijuana that have no basis in scientific fact. One of these ads, under the headline "How a Marijuana Habit Forced Bob Payne Onto the Street," featured a photograph of a father and his daughter. The ad gave the impression that, among other things, as a result of his daughter's marijuana use, Bob was forced onto the street to look for her. The caption to the ad stated,

> We refer to that day as dark Thursday, because that's when Lindsay finally understood her marijuana problem was out of control. Sure, I saw a change in Lindsay. She was always involved in sports, but lost interest. She dropped out of choir, but always had a reason. Eventually, marijuana led to other drugs. Acid. Mushrooms. ("How a Habit," 1998)

Clearly, this ad sends the message that marijuana causes amotivational syndrome and is a gateway drug, two claims that are not supported in the scientific literature.

PFDFA/ONDCP ads appearing in 2003 included televised images of a teenager being molested and another girl ending up with an unwanted pregnancy, apparently because they smoked marijuana (Talvi, 2003b). This ad promotes the notion that marijuana use leads to involvement in sexual behavior. Yet another advertisement aired in 2003 depicted two teenagers smoking marijuana in their father's study. One of them eventually pulled out a gun from a drawer, while the other asked if it was loaded; he was then shot (Talvi, 2003b). This ad perpetuates the myth that the use of marijuana leads to the commission of violent acts. Drug Czar John Walters defended this particular ad, asserting, "the suggestion is not to say too many children are being shot in their dens who are marijuana users, it's meant to show that marijuana alters your ability to use judgment" (as quoted in Stein, 2002). Yet another disturbing ad featured a young male drug addict describing how, after losing his job, he had to "have sex with men for money to support his habit" (Buchanan freevibe.com

✂ _Instructions: Cut out, roll around joint._

WARNING: Smoking Marijuana Can Cause Neurological Impairments. Meaning What? Meaning It Messes With Your Motor Skills, Judgment, Perception, and Attention Span. No Biggie, Right? Until You Blow Through A Stop Sign and Hit A Kid. That Might Qualify As A Biggie.

Office of National Drug Control Policy

|f|a|c|t|s|
THE ANTI-DRUG.

& Wallack, 1998), echoing the (false) theme discussed in Chapter 1 that drug use causes homosexuality.

A series of PFDFA/ONDCP ads that appeared in 2002 promoted the idea that drug problems are attributable to foreigners in order to exploit Americans' fears after the September 11, 2001, tragedies and attempt to link drug use to terrorism. Two of these ads were aired during the 2002 Super Bowl, at a total cost of approximately $3.4 million (Sullum, 2002). One of the ads asked, "Where do terrorists get their money? If you buy drugs, it might come from you." While we are not denying that such connections may exist—for example, opium was the major cash crop during the rule of the Taliban in Afghanistan—such links have been grossly overstated in the PFDFA/ONDCP advertisements.

In defending these ads and asserting a link between terrorism and drug trafficking, Drug Czar John Walters was quoted in a 2002 ONDCP publication as follows:

> Drug use hurts our families and communities. It also finances our enemies. To fight the terror inflicted by killers, thugs, and terrorists around the world who depend on American drug purchases to fund their violence, we must stop paying for our own destruction and the destruction of others. As the President has said, "When you quit using drugs, you join the fight against terror in America." (ONDCP, 2002c)

This ONDCP publication further claimed that the ads would "help make Americans aware of the link between drugs and terrorism, and, we believe, discourage drug use. . . . It doesn't matter whether people like or don't like these ads" (ONDCP, 2002c). The publication claimed that approximately half of the international terrorist organizations identified by the State Department had links to illicit drug activities; however, the report only specifically listed the Revolutionary Armed Forces of Colombia and the United Self Defense Forces of Colombia.

In the context of these advertisements, it is important to remain aware of the fact that the overwhelming majority of money generated by drug trafficking is not even remotely connected with terrorism. Marijuana, which as we have discussed is the substance consumed by the overwhelming majority of illegal drug users, is grown primarily in the United States, Mexico, and Canada, and would seem to have little if any connection to terrorism. In fact, as Ethan Nadelmann of the Drug Policy Alliance has pointed out, the War on Drugs itself is responsible for creating the illegal markets that generate profits for traffickers, regardless of whether those traffickers are members of terrorist organizations. As Nadelmann comments, "It's hard to believe that any American teenager smoking homegrown marijuana is going to believe she's subsidizing Bin Laden's terror campaign. They're going to spoof these ads just the way they spoofed the 'fried egg' ads a decade ago" (Drug Policy Alliance, 2002a). Aside from misleadingly implying that casual drug use is related to terrorism, these ads serve to further demonize illegal drug users at a time when there is at least some recognition in the United States that drug treatment can be effective. Suggesting that such users are aiding and abetting terrorists sends the message that they are unworthy of compassion and must be dealt with harshly (Bendavid, 2002). In the spring of 2003, "in a tacit admission that the tens of millions of dollars spent on a sensationalistic ad campaign were being wasted," the ONDCP terminated the drug and terror advertising campaign (Drug Policy Alliance, 2003j).

Similar to the findings of scientific studies on the effectiveness of D.A.R.E. as a drug prevention program, research on the effectiveness of the PFDFA/ONDCP advertising campaign in reducing youth drug use have generally found these advertisements to be ineffective. Although one evaluation of the PFDFA campaign, focusing on the years 1987 to 1990, found that antidrug advertisements reduced the probability of marijuana and cocaine/crack use among adolescents, the study also found that recall of the antidrug advertising was not associated with young people's decisions regarding how much marijuana or cocaine/crack to consume among those who were already using these drugs (Block et al., 2002). Another study of 30 public service announcements (PSAs) on drugs produced by PFDFA and ONDCP found mixed results. While most of the ads made adolescents think they and their friends would be less likely to use drugs, there were several that had little or no effect and six that actually had negative effects (Fishbein et al., 2002). This study also found that the most effective PSAs were those dealing with heroin and methamphetamine and suggested "PSAs that focus primarily on 'saying no' to marijuana should be aired with caution" (p. 245).

An evaluation of the effectiveness of the PFDFA/ONDCP ad campaign conducted for the National Institute on Drug Abuse by researchers at the University of Pennsylvania, which focused on ads produced between September of 1999 and June of 2002, concluded that the ads had not reduced drug use among youth and may also have led to the counterproductive effect of increasing marijuana use in the future. The study concluded,

> There is little evidence supporting a favorable effect of the Campaign on youth, either directly or through their parents' exposure to the campaign. While there is some evidence consistent with a favorable effect on parent outcomes, it does not translate into evidence of an effect on their children. (Hornik et al., 2002)

According to this study, the advertisements may have served to give young people the perception that drug use is more common among their peers than was actually the case and, similar to what we discussed above with respect to D.A.R.E. programs, may contribute to reactance on the part of youth (Drug Policy Alliance, 2003c). However, when the results of this study were released, the Office of National Drug Control Policy announced that the researchers from the University of Pennsylvania who conducted it would not have their contract renewed (Talvi, 2003b). As a *Los Angeles Times* editorial noted, "turning a blind eye to unwelcome facts is no way to run an effective antidrug campaign" ("Anti-Drug Pitch," 2003).

Apparently undaunted by the widespread criticism of their advertising campaigns and the scientific evidence that these were generally ineffective with respect to achieving their alleged goals of reducing youth drug use, in 2003, PFDFA and ONDCP placed ads in *The Nation* and other popular magazines with a picture of young boy and the caption "Is it scare tactics to tell your kids the *truth* about drug money? Drug money defends terrible things. Murder, terrorism, corruption, the infection of neighborhoods, and the destruction of indigenous cultures" ("Partnership," 2003). Reacting specifically to the previous criticism of the drug and terror advertisements, this ad also contained the following copy:

> Just calling attention to this simple truth has been labeled "scare tactics" by some. But aren't kids entitled to know the truth? . . . That the things they do for self-gratification may have horrible repercussions for other kids, families, neighborhoods and cultures? Isn't it scarier to keep them in the dark? ("Partnership," 2003)

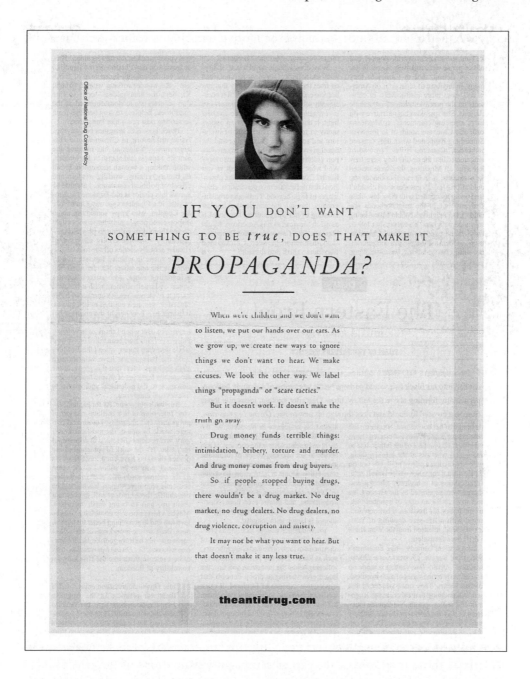

IF YOU DON'T WANT
SOMETHING TO BE *true*, DOES THAT MAKE IT

PROPAGANDA?

When we're children and we don't want
to listen, we put our hands over our ears. As
we grow up, we create new ways to ignore
things we don't want to hear. We make
excuses. We look the other way. We label
things "propaganda" or "scare tactics."

But it doesn't work. It doesn't make the
truth go away.

Drug money funds terrible things:
intimidation, bribery, torture and murder.
And drug money comes from drug buyers.

So if people stopped buying drugs,
there wouldn't be a drug market. No drug
market, no drug dealers. No drug dealers, no
drug violence, corruption and misery.

It may not be what you want to hear. But
that doesn't make it any less true.

theantidrug.com

However, as a result of the University of Pennsylvania evaluation, in 2003, the
White House Office of Management and Budget referred to the antidrug advertising
campaign as "nonperforming" and suggested that it had not demonstrated positive
results (Leinwand 2006b). And in 2004, the Senate Appropriations Committee concluded that youth drug use was increasing in spite of the campaign (Government
Accountability Office, 2005a). Drug Czar John Walters responded to these critiques
by claiming that the findings of the evaluation study were "deeply flawed" (as

quoted in Leinwand, 2006b). Perhaps even more interestingly, Walters attributed the counterintuitive findings to the design of the evaluation study itself. He argued,

> The evaluation, by conducting an extensive interview of youth (and their parents) in their homes, including showing them ads being studied on as many as four separate occasions over the life of the evaluation, could stimulate interest in drugs where none previously existed, increase beliefs that drugs are important to youth and that more teens are using drugs, thus stimulating interest in and causing intent to use drugs and eventual drug experimentation. (Leinwand, 2006b, p. 4)

Later, a 2006 Government Accountability Office (GAO) report on the antidrug advertising campaign found that "greater exposure to the campaign was associated with weaker antidrug norms," and also that, in some demographic categories such as 14- to 16-year-olds and among (all) white teenagers, greater exposure to the ads actually led to higher rates of first-time drug use. The ONDCP was not pleased with the conclusions of the GAO report—the former director of Budget and Planning for the ONDCP commented to a newspaper reporter that the office "did not like the report's conclusions and chose to sit on it" (as quoted in Grim, 2007). Another ONDCP spokesperson commented, "[the report] is irrelevant to us. It's based on data from two-and-a-half years ago, and they [the ads] were effective too. Drug use has been going down dramatically. Cutting the program would imperil [its] progress" (as quoted in Leinwand, 2006b). Despite the demonstrated lack of success of the antidrug advertising campaign, in 2007, then President Bush requested a 31% increase in funding for the campaign, which would increase the program's budget to $130 million.

In 2005, the Office of National Drug Control Policy implemented the "Above the Influence" antidrug advertising campaign, with the goal of

> helping teens to live above the influence. The more aware they are of the influences around them, the better prepared they will be to stand up to them, including the pressure to use drugs and alcohol. It's not about telling teens how to live their lives, but rather giving them another perspective and the latest facts so they can make smart decisions. (http://www.abovetheinfluence.com)

While the advertisements associated with this program are perhaps not as problematic as those produced in the earlier campaigns, evaluations of the effectiveness of the program have been mixed. For example, Fortier (2011) found that the anti-marijuana messages associated with this campaign were not effectively conveyed to youth exposed to the ads, nor did they have any impact on drug use. Similarly, examining more general public service announcements on drugs, Kang and colleagues (2009) found that high-risk adolescents' evaluations of 60 PSAs were highly negative with respect to anti-cannabis message, leading to less consideration of the messages provided.

Overall, the federal government has devoted nearly twice as much funding to antidrug advertising campaigns as to after-school programs for youth, despite the fact that the former have been demonstrated to be ineffective in preventing youth drug use, while the latter have proven to be the most effective in achieving this objective (Huffington, 2000).

ZERO-TOLERANCE POLICIES

Zero-tolerance policies for weapons have also resulted in some rather absurd outcomes. For example, in Louisiana, an 8-year-old girl was suspended when she brought her grandfather's pocket watch to show her second-grade class. The watch had a one-inch pocket-knife attached to it. In Colorado, a 10-year-old girl was suspended because her mother had put a small knife in her lunchbox for her to cut an apple. When this girl realized that the knife might violate the school's zero-tolerance policy, she turned it in to a teacher and was suspended as a result. Students have also been suspended for wearing Halloween costumes that included paper swords and fake spiked knuckles, as well as for possessing rubber bands, slingshots, water pistols, and toy guns (Skiba & Peterson, 1999). And in Albuquerque, New Mexico, a 13-year-old boy was handcuffed and taken to juvenile detention for " burping audibly" in a physical education class. (Clausing, 2011)

Additional examples of policies implemented with the apparent purpose of preventing youth drug use are zero-tolerance policies, which result in the suspension, or in some cases expulsion, of students who possess or consume drugs on school property. The first zero-tolerance policies emerged in school districts in California, New York, and Kentucky in 1989—these policies mandated expulsion of students who engaged in drug possession, fighting, and gang-related activity (Skiba & Rausch, 2006). Zero-tolerance policies were expanded with the passage of the 1994 Gun Free Schools Act and the Safe and Drug Free Schools Act, and as of 1999, 87% of schools in the United States had adopted zero-tolerance policies for alcohol, and 88% had zero-tolerance policies for illicit drugs (Cauchon, 1999).

The passage and enforcement of these policies have led to a number of negative outcomes that can be considered at both the individual and aggregate levels. In Colorado Springs, Colorado, in 1997, a 6-year-old boy was suspended for sharing a lemon drop with a friend. In this case, the school also apparently called an ambulance to assist the friend who received and ingested the lemon drop (Foldvary, n.d.). In Kingswood, Texas, a 13-year-old girl was suspended for carrying a bottle of Advil in her backpack. In Fairborn, Ohio, a 13-year-old girl caught with Midol was suspended for 9 days. Her 14-year-old friend who had given her the Midol was suspended for 2 weeks because school officials deemed that she was distributing the drug (Skiba & Peterson, 1999). In September of 2003, a teenager in Montgomery County, Texas, was suspended and eventually arrested for loaning an inhaler to a classmate who was experiencing an asthma attack ("Discipline Decided," 2003). In Portland, Oregon, a 13-year-old boy was suspended for violating the school's alcohol policy—he had taken a swig of mouthwash after lunch and swallowed it because there was no place to spit it out (Skiba & Peterson, 1999). In Virginia, eight students were suspended from school for 1 week after they were caught sniffing Kool-Aid. These students were charged with "possession of contraband," apparently because they were using Kool-Aid in a way that imitated the use of illegal drugs (Libertarian Party, 2001). In Ohio, a 7th-grade student was suspended for allegedly sniffing Wite-out. Although Wite-out is not a drug, the student's school records indicate that she was suspended for drug use (Advancement Project, 2000). In addition to these cases, students have been suspended for possession of Tylenol and Alka-Seltzer (Cauchon, 1999) and Certs (Skiba & Peterson, 1999). As the Advancement Project (2000) notes, "The stories about suspension and expulsions for sharing Midol, asthma medication, and cough drops with classmates, and bringing toy guys, nail clippers, and scissors to school are not anomalies; these incidents happen every day" (p. 6).

In a recent zero-tolerance case that eventually resulted in a Supreme Court decision, 13-year-old 8th-grade student Savana Redding, who an assistant principal suspected had brought Ibuprofen to school, was forced to strip to her underwear and then was asked to pull out her bra and move it from side to side, and then to open her legs and pull out her underwear (Liptak, 2009). In an eight-to-one Supreme Court decision, it was ruled that Arizona school officials had violated Redding's Fourth Amendment rights by conducting the search, with Justice David Souter noting, "the content of the suspicion failed to match the degree of intrusion" (as quoted in Doyle, 2009). The National Association of Social Workers, the National Education Association, the National Association of School Psychologists, the American Society for Adolescent Psychiatry, and the American Professional Society on the Abuse of Children all condemned the search of Redding and commented on searches of students more generally, noting that "social science research demonstrates that strip searches can traumatize children and result in serious emotional damage." (as quoted in Biskupic, 2009)

While these individual cases are certainly striking, it is important to consider the larger consequences of zero-tolerance policies. Skiba and Rausch (2006) note that, despite popular belief to the contrary, studies of zero-tolerance policies have generally found that school suspensions and/or expulsions tend *not* to be applied only for serious or dangerous behaviors. According to data from the U.S. Department of Education, more than three million public school students (1 in 15) were suspended in the 2000 school year, although not all of these suspensions were the result of involvement with drugs (National Center for Education Statistics, 2003). Data from specific jurisdictions are even more concerning. For example, in Baltimore, Maryland, approximately 10,000 students (12% of the total student population) were suspended during the 2006 to 2007 school year. In Milwaukee, Wisconsin, school officials reported that fully 40% of 9th-grade students had been suspended at least once during the 2006–2007 school year (Urbina, 2009). Studies of these policies have also consistently documented social class and racial disproportionality in their application, with students of lower socioeconomic status being more likely to be suspended or expelled and students of color being expelled at rates two to three times that of other students (Skiba & Raush, 2006; see also Advancement Project, 2000). In Montgomery County, Virginia, 71% of the student suspensions in 2011 for insubordination were of black students, who comprised only 21% of the student population (St. George, 2011). National statistics from the year 2006 indicated that overall, 5% of white students, 15% of blacks, 7% of Hispanics, and 3% of Asians were suspended (St. George, 2011). There is no evidence that African American over representation in suspensions and expulsions is due to higher rates of misbehavior among students from this group, and Skiba and Rausch (2006) assert that "it may be that African-American students are suspended and punished for behavior that is less serious than other students" (p. 1074). These racial disproportionalities in suspensions and expulsions are consistent with arrests and incarcerations that result from the drug war (see Chapter 11).

While the media have reported claims by school districts with zero-tolerance policies have led to reductions in problematic behaviors among students (including violence and drug use), a 1998 National Center for Education Statistics study found that schools that enforce zero-tolerance policies are, in fact, less safe with respect to experiencing crime incidents (Skiba & Peterson, 1999). And if, as research suggests, youth who are suspended or expelled are more likely to drop out of school (Skiba & Peterson, 1999), and dropouts are more likely to use drugs (Wallace & Bachman, 1991), these policies may actually result in overall increases in drug use among young people. Enforcement of these policies results in youth being put on the streets or in other places where their behavior will likely worsen. As the Advancement Project (2000) concludes, "efforts to address guns, drugs, and other truly dangerous school situations have spun totally out of control, sweeping up millions of schoolchildren who pose no threat to safety into a net of exclusion from educational opportunities and into criminal prosecution" (p. 1).

It is also important to note that school-based policies often go well beyond suspension and expulsion. For example, in 2010, police in Texas issued more than 300,000 Class C misdemeanor tickets to children as young as 6 (more than 1,000 were issued to primary school students between 2004 and 2010) for offenses such as "swearing, misbehaving on the school bus, or getting into a punch-up on the playground" (McReal, 2012). These tickets can result in fines, community service, or even serving time in juvenile detention centers, jails, or prisons.

Closely related to zero-tolerance policies are actions taken by school and law enforcement officials at particular schools with the apparent goal of intercepting drugs. There have been numerous cases involving the use of drug-sniffing dogs and unannounced searches of students at a number of schools over the last several years (American Civil Liberties Union, 2003). In a specific example of such practices, police released drug-sniffing dogs at a parking lot at a high school in Coeur D'Alene, Idaho; a total of one-third of an ounce of marijuana was found in six of the cars as a result of the search (Floyd, 1996; see box). Another example comes from Goose Creek, South Carolina, where, in an effort to deal with an alleged drug problem, police officers rounded up students, pointed guns at them, and searched their lockers. In this case, no drugs were discovered (Rosenbaum, 2003). In an even more egregious example of the lengths officials will go to in their attempts to address drug problems, an assistant principal at South Haven High School in Michigan who suspected a boy was a drug dealer and wanted him expelled placed marijuana in the boy's locker ("Principal Plants Drugs," 2004). Teachers who disagree with the practice of searching for drugs in schools have also experienced negative outcomes. For example, a high school biology teacher in Virginia was fired for objecting when school administrators entered her class unannounced and searched students for drugs and weapons ("Constitutional Literacy," 2001).

> Inside Coeur D'Alene high schools, young people learn about the rights and responsibilities that go along with citizenship. They learn, for example, that Americans needn't fear searches of themselves and their property unless authorities have a good reason to suspect them of wrongdoing.... Out on the parking lot a week ago, it was a different story. There they found that just being a teenager who drove to school on Friday was enough to bring you under suspicion. (Floyd, 1996)

DRUG TESTING POLICIES

Another example of a misguided and ineffective drug prevention policy that has gained prominence in the last three decades is drug testing. In our discussion of this policy, we examine two separate aspects for which the issues and implications are somewhat different: drug testing in schools and drug testing in employment situations or workplaces.

Schools

> In my budget, I have proposed new funding to continue our aggressive, community-based drug strategy to reduce demand for illegal drugs. Drug testing in our schools has proven to be an effective part of this effort. So tonight, I propose an additional $23 million for schools that want to use drug testing as a tool to save children's lives. The aim here is not to punish children, but to send them this message: We love you, and we don't want to lose you.—President George W. Bush (State of the Union Address, 2004, as quoted in "State of the Union," 2004)

Drug Czar John Walters referred to drug testing as the "silver bullet" (as quoted in Rosenbaum, 2004b), and he and other government officials have typically justified student drug testing on the basis of its alleged deterrent effects. For instance, Robert Dupont, President of the Institute for Behavior and Health and first director of the National Institute on Drug Abuse, defended school drug tests by asserting that "most of the middle of the road kids are looking for a reason to say no [to drugs] and still maintain their coolness . . . drug testing gives them an out" (as quoted in Luna, 2002). Similarly, in its National Drug Control Strategy, the federal government suggests that drug testing

> gives young people an "out" to say no to drugs. If they want to play on the volleyball team and know that they will be tested as members of the team, they can cite their desire to play as a reason not to use drugs when pressured by a peer. (The White House, 2006, p. 8)

While some government and school officials have supported school drug testing, many health and education groups, including the National Education Association and the American Academy of Pediatrics, have publicly opposed them (Lewin, 2002).

The right of schools to drug-test students has been upheld in some court decisions at the federal level but has been rejected in at least one state-level decision. The first of these decisions was a 1995 case known as *Vernonia School District v Acton*, in which the United States Supreme Court upheld the random testing of student athletes (Conlon, 2003). In this case, in response to an alleged increase in drug use in schools in Vernonia, Oregon, much of it connected to student athletes, the school board implemented a drug testing policy in the fall of 1989. Under this policy, athletes were tested at the beginning of the season for their particular sport, and once each week of the season 10% were selected for random drug testing. If a student's urine sample was positive for drugs, a second test was administered; if it was also positive, the student's parents were notified and a meeting between the principal, the student, and his or her parents was convened. Students testing positive for drugs were given the option of (1) participating in a 6-week program that included weekly urinalysis, or (2) suspension from participation in athletics for the remainder of the current season (*Vernonia School District v. Acton*, 1995).

In 1991, 7th-grade student James Acton signed up to play football at one of the schools in the Vernonia School District. However, because he and his parents refused to consent to drug testing, he was not allowed to participate. Acton's parents sued the school district on the grounds that the drug testing policy violated the Fourth and Fourteenth Amendments to the Constitution. At first, the District Court dismissed the action, but that decision was overturned by the United States Court of Appeal for the Ninth Circuit, which held that Vernonia School District's drug testing policy violated both the Fourth and Fourteenth Amendments to the Constitution. Upon appeal to the United States Supreme Court, the Ninth Circuit Court decision was overturned, with the Supreme Court holding that the policy was constitutional. However, in their decision, delivered by Justice Scalia, the Supreme Court noted,

We caution against the assumption that suspicionless drug testing will pass constitutional muster in other contexts. The most significant element in this case is . . . that the policy was undertaken in furtherance of the government's responsibilities, under a public school system, as guardian and tutor of children entrusted to its care. (*Vernonia School District v Acton*, 1995)

In 2002, the Supreme Court extended this authority to suspicionless drug testing of middle and high school students involved in any competitive extracurricular activity (including band, debate team, choir, and athletic activities) in the Oklahoma case of *Board of Education v Earls et al.* (2002). Lindsay Earls, an honor student at Tecumseh High School and a member of the band and choir, along with Daniel James, who wanted to join the school's academic team, challenged the school's drug testing policy, arguing it violated the Fourth Amendment to the Constitution. In this case, the Supreme Court's 5–4 decision held that the drug testing policy was a reasonable means of supporting the school district's interest in preventing and deterring drug use among students and therefore did not constitute a violation of the Fourth Amendment.

An interesting aspect of the drug testing policy in the Pottawatomie school district provided that any student who refused to submit to the urine test that was required for participation in the school choir also would not be allowed to enroll in a music course, which provided a credit for graduation. The American Civil Liberties Union issued a challenge to this policy, arguing that it effectively violated students' rights to a public education. (Steinberg, 1999)

In response to the negative reaction to the *Earls* decision, Justice Anthony M. Kennedy stated that if parents did not like the drug testing policy, they could "send their child to a druggie school" (as quoted in "It's School," 2002). However, in expressing their displeasure with the drug testing policy, the four dissenting Supreme Court justices in this case referenced studies indicating that students involved in extracurricular activities are less likely to use drugs than those who are not so involved. The dissenting justices concluded,

[The school district's] policy thus falls doubly short if deterrence is its aim. It invades the privacy of students who need deterrence least, and risks steering students at greatest risk from substance abuse away from extracurricular involvement that potentially may palliate drug problems.

While the two U.S. Supreme Court cases discussed above thus confirmed the right of schools to drug test students in certain circumstances, a 2003 case heard by the Pennsylvania Supreme Court struck down the random, suspicionless testing of students participating in extracurricular activities or applying for parking permits, holding that the program violated privacy rights protected by Pennsylvania's constitution (Drug Policy Alliance, 2003k). But school drug testing policies have proliferated in the United States and have even been applied to children in grades as low as middle school who must provide a urine sample to participate in any extra-curricular activities (states with such testing include Alabama, Arkansas, Florida, Missouri, New Jersey, Ohio, Texas, and West Virginia; Pilon, 2012).

> In addition to general drug testing, at least three states—New Jersey, Texas, and Illinois—require mandatory testing of high school athletes for steroids. Somewhat amazingly, during the 2007–2008 school year, of approximately 10,000 high school athletes who were tested in the state of Texas, only two positive results for steroids were reported. Gary Wadler of the World Anti-Doping Agency was skeptical of these results, noting that Texas is a state where high school football is very popular, and which shares a border with Mexico, from which a large percentage of steroids enter the United States. (Longman, 2008)

An important question to consider with respect to student drug testing is whether these policies achieve their stated goal of reducing drug use by young people. A study of the effectiveness of drug testing in an Oregon jurisdiction found that student athletes subjected to random testing were almost four times less likely to use illegal drugs than student athletes at a school who were not subject to testing (Silverman, 2002). However, the methodology used in this evaluation was questionable: Of the 135 student athletes who were subject to drug testing, 5.3% *self-reported* drug use (i.e., there was no objective measure of their use of drugs) compared to 19.4% who self-reported drug use at the comparison school. While the principal at the drug-testing high school claimed that the program had achieved its goal of reducing student illegal drug use, she also noted that testing had led some students to switch to substances that were more difficult to detect, such as beer.

A large-scale evaluation of the effectiveness of school drug testing programs, focusing on 76,000 students for the 1998 to 2001 period, found that drug use was just as frequent in schools that implement drug-testing programs as in schools that had not implemented such programs (Yamaguchi, Johnston, & O'Malley, 2003). The study found that 37% of 12th-grade students in schools that tested for drugs reported use of marijuana in the previous year, compared to 37% reporting marijuana use in schools with no drug testing program. Similarly, 21% of seniors in schools with drug testing reported past-year use of other illegal drugs such as heroin or cocaine, compared to 19% of seniors in non-drug-testing schools. More generally, the authors of this study concluded, "drug testing of any kind and drug testing for cause and suspicion were not significant predictors for use of marijuana or any other drug use among students in grades 8, 10, and 12" (Yamaguchi et al., 2003, p. 163). While it is of course possible that schools that implemented drug-testing programs had higher rates of drug use prior to initiating such programs, Yamaguchi and colleagues asserted that this was unlikely because the study statistically controlled for factors normally associated with substance use, such as truancy and parental absence.

In his 2004 Presidential State of the Union Address cited above, George W. Bush also referred to an 11% decline in drug use by high school students in the previous 2 years and indirectly attributed this decline to drug testing. It is important to stress, however, that the Yamaguchi and colleagues (2003) study found no difference between schools that implemented drug testing programs and those that had not. Perhaps even more importantly in this context, Yamaguchi and colleagues found that only about 5% of schools in the United States had random drug-testing programs in place (this had increased to 11.4% of middle schools and 19.5% of high schools by 2006 (Centers for Disease Control, 2007), making it highly unlikely that drug testing could have anything but a very minor effect on the reductions in youth drug use cited by President Bush (Rorvig, 2004).

We can also question the larger impact of these policies on schools and individual students. Some schools have seen significant reductions in student participation in extracurricular activities after the implementation of drug testing policies (Gunja et al., 2003). Further, as Marsha Rosenbaum (2004b) points out, in the method by which drug testing is practiced in schools in the United States, students must be observed by a teacher or other adult while they urinate to ensure that the sample is their own. The collection of the urine specimen can thus constitute a humiliating, invasive violation of privacy for students. A student in Tulia, Texas, interviewed by Rosenbaum (2004b) summarized the problems associated with drug testing:

I know lots of kids who don't want to get into sports . . . because they don't want to get drug tested. That's one of the reasons I'm not into any [activity]. I'm on medication, so I would always test positive, and then they would have to ask me about my medication, and I would be embarrassed. And what if I'm on my period? I would be too embarrassed.

There are also indications that in some schools, a new subculture of students who make a mockery of drug testing programs may be emerging. For example, in one school district in Louisiana, students who were going to be subjected to a hair test for drugs shaved their heads and all their body hair (Gunja et al., 2003).

Even the ONDCP (2003c) has acknowledged the potential problems associated with student drug testing: "If drug-using students are suspended or expelled without any attempt to change their ways, the community will be faced with drug-using dropouts, an even bigger problem in the long run" (p. 16). A final issue relates to the costs of these programs. Although national data are not available, M. Rosenbaum (2004b) notes that school administrators in Dublin, Ohio, spent $35,000 in a single year to test 1,473 students, 11 of whom tested positive for drugs. This translates to a cost of $3,200 per student testing positive. Is drug testing worth the costs?

> Random student drug testing tarnishes the relationships of trust between teachers and students, violates student privacy, may lead students to more dangerous drugs, does not address the needs of students who have a substance abuse problem, and wastes a school's scarce financial resources. (Drug Policy Alliance, 2003k)

One further disturbing development with respect to drug testing of young people is the marketing of home drug test kits on the Internet and in stores. The first home drug testing kit was approved by the Food and Drug Administration in 1998, and by 2001, more than 200 such products were on the market, including hair, breath, saliva, and urine tests (Levy, Van Hook, & Knight, 2004). Among these products is HairConfirmkit, which sells for $89.99 and tests for seven illicit and five prescription drugs. Raymond Kubacki, president of the company Psychmedics, which sells these products, has defended these tests for their ability to induce young people to resist peer pressure to use drugs: "They can say, man, I'd like to try it, but my parents are testing and I'm going to get nailed" (as quoted in Eaton, 2004). But as Levy, Van Hook, and Knight (2004) note, using these products is not even the best way to determine if an adolescent is using drugs. False positives for amphetamines can occur if the youth is using caffeine products or cold medications, and poppy seeds contained in bagels and other foods can result in a false positive for morphine. Parents may also be reassured by a false negative if the concentration of drugs in the urine is too low, and some drugs, such as ecstasy and alcohol, disappear from the system within hours. More generally, coerced home drug testing can serve to damage the parent–child relationship. Levy and colleagues (2004) conclude, "We believe that parents would be better served by a professional assessment for any young person who is suspected of using drugs" (p. 726).

Knight and Levy (2007) note that in their own personal experience in administering a drug testing program for youth identified with substance abuse problems, some youth switched from the use of marijuana, which is easily detectable in urine and relatively less harmful, to the use of inhalants, which are more harmful but not detectable in urine. Knight and Levy (2007) further note that "high quality drug testing . . . is expensive, and resources might be better spent on evidence-based prevention programs or on establishing drug treatment programs that are developmentally appropriate for adolescents" (p. 726).

Drug Testing of Workers

> Today it's the corporate class that seems transfixed by the predictive powers of piss. Eighty percent of large employers insist on testing job applicants' urine—or occasionally hair and blood—for damning traces of illegal substances. You can be the best-qualified applicant in all other ways, but if your urine speaks against you, you're out. Experience, skills, enthusiasm, and energy—pee trumps them all. (Ehrenreich, 2000)

Drug testing of workers in the United States has a fairly long history, but prior to 1980, it was limited primarily to individuals in the military and to a relatively small number of large companies that used it to screen job applicants. However, the move toward greater numbers of government agencies and companies drug testing job applicants and employees began in 1986, when President Reagan signed Executive Order 12564 establishing the goal of a federal drug-free workplace. As part of this policy, federal government agencies were required to institute urine testing programs. As of 2003, it was estimated that 98% of Fortune 500 companies had drug testing policies (Schlosser, 2003). As part of the "drugs-industrial complex" (Gray, 2001), drug testing itself has become a major industry in the United States, with annual revenues of drug testing companies estimated at $737 million in 2001 (Hawkins, 2002).

Similar to the rationale for student drug testing, workplace drug testing policies have been justified on the basis of their alleged deterrent value, as was underlined in the 1989 National Drug Control Strategy:

> Because anyone using drugs stands a very good chance of being discovered [as a result of workplace drug testing], with disqualification from employment as a possible consequence, many will decide that the price of using drugs is just too high. (The White House, 1989, p. 57)

Drug testing was also promoted to employers on the basis of claims that drug use was associated with productivity losses. In the 1980s, productivity losses associated with drug use were estimated at $33 billion per year; this figure was raised to $60 billion in the 1990s and eventually to $100 million in the early 2000s (Sullum, 2003a). However, it is important to note that these figures are not based on actual analyses of productivity. In fact, the original $33 billion estimate was derived from a 1984 federal government report that compared the annual income of households in which one person was a daily marijuana user to the annual income of households that did not include a daily marijuana user. Finding that the former households earned less than the latter, the difference was multiplied by the estimated number of marijuana users in the population to derive the $33 billion estimate. Almost magically, this wage differential became "lost productivity," and subsequent upward adjustments to the amount were made to control for inflation (American Civil Liberties Union, 1999).

In another example of the alleged association between productivity and drug use, Akers (1992) went so far as to suggest,

> The effect of active drug and alcohol use on worker and managerial productivity is so evident that it must be considered as a significant factor, on top of whatever other trade and political factors are involved, in the shrinking industrial leadership and competitiveness [of the United States] in the world economy in the past two decades. (p. 54)

While this particular argument conveniently ignores the fact that drug use was also increasing in a number of other countries (MacCoun & Reuter, 2001) and thus cannot be a causal factor in explaining the relative decline of the United States, such arguments have been predominant in justifying workplace drug testing.

There is little doubt that consumption of alcohol and other drugs can alter a person's motor skills, reaction time, sensory and perceptual ability, attention, motivation, and learning and thereby affect his or her job performance (Jardine-Tweedie

& Wright, 1998). There is also little doubt that drug testing serves an important protective function in occupations in which safety is a major concern, such as the transportation industry. However, as we have done with other aspects of drug policy, we need to critically examine the outcomes associated with widespread application of workplace drug testing policies in the United States.

> Barbara Ehrenreich (2001) notes that in 1990, the federal government spent $11.7 million to drug test 29,000 federal employees. Of these, 153 tested positive; thus, the cost of detecting a single drug user was $77,000.

Interestingly, the substance most likely to be detected through drug testing—marijuana, which can be detected weeks after its consumption—is also the least harmful of all illegal drugs both with respect to its psychoactive effects (see Chapter 4) and its effects on worker productivity. A 1999 meta-analysis of more than 200 studies of marijuana use and the workplace found that "marijuana use has no direct, negative effect on workers' productivity" (Schwenk & Rhodes, 1999, p. 177). In contrast, heroin, cocaine, and amphetamines, which should be of greater concern, are typically not detectable 3 days after consumption (Ehrenreich, 2001). At a more fundamental level, it is vitally important to consider what drug testing does and does not measure. Drug testing as currently conducted is capable of measuring—although certainly with some error—drug use, but not the level of impairment of an individual as a result of such use.

Studies of the effectiveness of drug testing policies have not been favorable for advocates of such policies. Subcommittees of the National Research Council and the Institute of Medicine estimated that in 1995, at least $1.2 billion per year was being spent in the United States on drug testing (24 million tests at approximately $50 each), despite the fact that "the preventive effects of drug testing programs have never been adequately demonstrated" ("Fed Panel Says," 1995). One study focusing on workers in 63 high-tech firms found that drug testing reduced rather than increased productivity. The authors of this study concluded,

> Companies that relate to employees with a high degree of trust are able to obtain more effort and loyalty in return. Drug testing, particularly without probable cause, seems to imply a lack of trust, and presumably could backfire if it leads to negative perceptions about the company. (Shepard & Clifton, 1998, p. 76)

More generally, it is possible that deterioration of the work environment can be a result of drug testing, which can create a climate of fear and mistrust and polarization between management and workers. As Jardine-Tweedie and Wright (1998) conclude, "managers should not test their employees for drugs. Drug testing runs counter to everything we know about good management practice. Testing is a negative input that destroys any pretense of creating a productive work environment" (p. 542). Aside from the fact that drug testing policies apparently do not achieve their stated goals, they are problematic at a more fundamental level in that they are intrusive and constitute a violation of privacy.

> I was not informed of the test until I was walking down the hall towards the bathroom with the attendant. I thought no problem. I have had urine tests before and I do not take any type of drugs besides occasional aspirins. I was led into a very small room with a toilet, a sink, and a desk. I was given a container into which to urinate by the attendant. I waited for her to turn her back before pulling down my pants, but she told me she had to watch everything that I did. I pulled down my pants, put the container in place—as she bent down to watch—gave her a sample, and even then she did not look away. I had to use the toilet paper as she watched and then pulled up my pants. This may sound vulgar and that is exactly what it is. . . . I am a forty-year-old mother of three and nothing I have ever done in my life deserves the humiliation, degradation, and mortification I felt. (as quoted in Davies, n.d.)

An additional recent development in the drug testing arena involves testing of individuals who receive welfare and/or other forms of public assistance. In 2011, Senator David Vitter of Louisiana introduced the Drug Free Families Act, which would have required all 50 states to conduct drug tests of welfare recipients (Cohen, 2011). The state of Indiana adopted drug tests for participants in their state job training program in July of 2011 (Cohen, 2011), and in Mississippi, proposed legislation even included testing for nicotine (Neary & Moreno, 2012). Such policies seem to ignore the fact that most studies find no significant differences in the rate of illegal drug use by welfare recipients and others and that United States Courts have banned such policies, ruling that they amount to an unconstitutional search of people who have done nothing wrong (Neary & Moreno, 2012). Interestingly, the drug testing law in Missouri "touched off attempts at political one upmanship as a statehouse Republican introduced a bill . . . that would require his colleagues in the state capitol to take and pass the same test" (Neary & Moreno, 2012). Similarly, although this part of the legislation was ultimately not passed into law, in Florida, an amendment to legislation requiring state agencies to randomly test up to 10% of their employees once every 3 months also included a provision requiring tests for legislators, including the governor (Delaney, 2012).

Frequently ignored in the debate over drug testing is that a high proportion of such tests are inaccurate (a concern that also applies to the debate on drug testing of students). For example, a study of 13 urine testing laboratories conducted by the federal government's Centers for Disease Control found that the average correct response rate on urine samples that were positive for drugs ranged from 31% to 88%, depending on the type of drug that was present in the urine (Staudenmeier, 1989). Research also suggests that given the increased sensitivity of drug tests for marijuana, individuals can test positive for this substance as a result of being in a room where it was smoked, even if they were not consuming it themselves. It is also known that over-the-counter drugs such as

Advil and Nuprin (Staudenmeier, 1989) and Ibuprofen (Shahandeh & Caborn, 2003) can register as equivalent to marijuana in drug tests. Similarly, use of over-the-counter decongestants can produce positive results for amphetamines, codeine can produce a positive result for heroin, and the consumption of food products containing opium poppy seeds, such as bagels, can result in a positive test for opiates (Gunja et al., 2003). It is also important to consider positive tests for prescription opiate drugs. Quest Diagnostics, one of the largest providers of workplace drug tests, reported that the number of employees testing positive for prescription opiates increased by more than 40% from 2005 to 2009. But creating rules about prescription drug use in the workplace is complicated, because it is difficult to prove employees are impaired by the use of such drugs. In addition, through the creation of such rules, employers might be violating the Americans with Disabilities Act, which prohibits asking employees about their prescription drug use unless workers are seen acting in a way that may compromise workplace safety (Zezima & Goodnough, 2010).

Given the fact that individuals who test positive for drugs face the prospect of losing their current job or not securing one in the first place, it should perhaps come as no surprise that the drug-testing industry has spawned a counter-industry that manufactures products that potentially allow drug-using individuals to beat drug tests. A search on the Internet using the phrase "passing a drug test" will result in several thousand hits, providing links to websites advertising drug-free replacement urine, herbal detoxifiers, hair follicle shampoo, and other products designed to thwart drug tests. Among the products advertised is Urine Luck (http://www.drug-testing-solutions.net). The ad copy for this product suggests,

> A urine additive is an efficient and easy way to break down your urine sample into it's [sic] natural components so foreign substances cannot be detected. The results appear completely natural. This is a safe, dependable, and fast way to get the "negative" urine analysis results you need.

There is also a product known as the Whizzinator, which resembles an athletic supporter/jockstrap with a prosthesis and a bag capable of holding drug-free urine. This product, manufactured by Puck Technology of California, is available for purchase over the Internet at a cost of approximately $150 and even comes with a sample of dehydrated toxin-free urine (Cadrain, 2003). One of the more prominent users of this product was former Minnesota Vikings running back Onterrio Smith, who was caught at the Minneapolis airport in 2005 with a Whizzinator device and several vials of dried urine (Wood, 2005). Individuals wanting to beat drug tests can also use oxidizing agents and soaps such as Mary Jane's Super Clean 13, which, when added directly to a urine sample, can serve to disrupt the tests (Cadrain, 2003), or UrinAid, Jamaican Me Clean (Sokolove, 2004), or Dr. John's Famous Pee Pee (Dworkin, 2010). There are even reports of individuals trying to pass samples of elk urine as their own (Dworkin, 2010).

In one of the more humorous examples of the "cat and mouse" game between drug testers and those trying to thwart them, an individual in Texas created a company that provided clients with clean urine for a fee of $19.95—the slogan of this company was "Pee for Pleasure, Not for Employment."Lusane (1991) reports that the proprietor of this company had originally obtained urine from church-going senior citizens but had to discontinue this practice when it was found that high levels of prescription drug use by these seniors were resulting in positive drug tests.

In reaction to individuals using various products in attempts to beat drug tests, several states, including Alabama, Idaho, Louisiana, Nebraska, North Carolina, Oregon, and Pennsylvania, have passed laws making it a criminal offense to engage in drug test fraud (Cadrain, 2003).The state of Arkansas even passed legislation prohibiting the sale of urine—individuals found guilty of trafficking in urine could be subject to 3 months' imprisonment and a fine of up to $500 (Josefson, 2003).

In response to the marketing and use of products that allow individuals to beat drug tests and also to concerns that urine testing is only capable of detecting relatively short-term drug use, we have also seen the emergence of sweat patch and hair tests for drugs. Sweat patch tests, first used in 1997 and marketed by the Texas-based company Pharmachem, involve the placement of bandage-like patches, typically on the upper arm, that work by trapping sweat excreted from the body. Since these patches can stay on the skin for as long as 2 weeks, they provide continuous monitoring through retention of all drugs used by an individual over the period they are worn. The apparent advantage of sweat patch testing over urine testing, then, is that the former tests are capable of detecting drug users who attempt to beat a urine test by flushing drugs out of their system or using some of the alternative products referred to above (Bazelon, 2003). However, studies conducted by the United States Naval Research Laboratory and Pharmachem itself have revealed that drug molecules from external sources, such as clothing, upholstery, money, or other people can penetrate the patch and trigger a false positive drug test result (Beiser, 2000; Hawkins, 2002). More generally, the amount of a substance that must be present in the sweat patch for it to indicate a positive test for drug use is quite low, thus increasing the risk of individuals falsely testing positive for drugs (Bazelon, 2003).

Hair tests have also emerged as an alternative to urine samples. Due to the fact that human hair can reveal drug use that occurred up to 3 months previously, some have argued that hair testing is more effective than urine sampling. Similar to sweat patch tests, hair tests can result in a positive drug test due to exposure to drugs from external sources. An additional problem with hair tests is that there is evidence to suggest they can result in racial bias. A 2001 study by the Center for Human Toxicology at the University of Utah found that drugs can accumulate in higher concentrations in hair by binding to the melanin pigment (Latour, 2002). Similarly, a 1995 study by the National Institute on Drug Abuse concluded that dark hair absorbs residue from the air more readily; this could potentially result in false positive tests, particularly for African Americans. This potential bias was underlined in the results of hair tests conducted on officers in the Boston Police Department; nearly twice as many minority officers tested positive for drugs as did white officers (Latour, 2002). In short, sweat patch and hair testing for drugs may be even more problematic than urine testing.

Finally, with respect to an important issue that will be addressed in more detail in Chapter 12, drug testing appears to represent an example of American exceptionalism in the drug policy arena. Although workers in certain industries, particularly the transportation industry, are subject to drug tests in Canada, the Canadian Human Rights Commission issued a policy statement on alcohol and drug testing indicating that employee drug tests are an abuse of human rights under virtually all circumstances. A spokesperson for the Commission noted,

> Positive results of drug tests do not suggest a person is impaired. . . . What I do outside work hours does not have to have an impact on what I do during work hours. That's a violation of my privacy rights and human rights. (Scoffield, 2002)

While this particular policy statement does not have the force of law in Canada, it still represents a notable contrast to the situation in the United States. Drug testing is also far less common and far more restricted in European countries. While drug testing policies in Britain and Sweden are somewhat similar to those in the United States, in France, Norway, and the Netherlands, only workers in safety-sensitive positions are drug tested, and in the Netherlands, pre-employment testing is illegal (Shahandeh & Caborn, 2003). The United States is also the only country that has adopted relatively widespread drug testing of students. In fact, in November of 2002, a rural high school in the Canadian province of Manitoba became the first in that country to randomly test its athletes for drug and alcohol use (Foss, 2002b).

As we have seen with other drug prevention policies discussed in this chapter, there is little evidence to suggest that drug testing policies are effective in reducing drug use, either among students or workers. In addition, they have sparked a booming business in products designed to allow individuals to beat them while also violating rights to privacy.

CONCLUSION

Drug prevention involves a variety of strategies intended to eliminate or limit the use and abuse of psychoactive drugs. These strategies are aimed at a variety of populations and vary considerably in terms of their effectiveness. Specific drug prevention strategies discussed in this chapter included drug education, antidrug advertising campaigns, zero-tolerance school policies, and drug testing, all of which have been implemented with the laudable goal of reducing drug use in the United States. However, as our review of these policies suggests, they have not been successful in achieving their stated goals and collectively may result in more harm than good.

The Drug Abuse Resistance Education (D.A.R.E.) program, although declining in popularity in recent years, was the largest school-based drug education program in the United States. In addition to being extremely expensive to implement and maintain, nearly every scientific study of D.A.R.E. found that it either failed to reduce drug use or that it encouraged drug use by students. In part, this is because D.A.R.E. is based on a number of problematic and misleading assumptions about drug use, including that (1) experimentation with drugs is not a common aspect of youth culture; (2) any drug use is either equivalent to or will eventually lead to drug *abuse*; (3) marijuana is the gateway drug to hard drugs such as heroin and cocaine; and (4) exaggerating the risks associated with drug use will deter young people from experimenting with drugs (Rosenbaum, 2002). Despite D.A.R.E.'s ineffectiveness, the program persists because many parents, teachers, principals, and law enforcement officials believe the program works and because it makes people feel better to believe they are taking steps to "deal with the drug problem."

Alternative drug education programs have been proposed that avoid the problematic assumptions of D.A.R.E. These programs are more likely to be effective because they set more realistic goals, such as attempting to (1) reduce (rather than eliminate) drug use; (2) delay the age of first drug use; and (3) limit more dangerous forms of drug use, such as mixing drugs or taking unknown substances. Unfortunately, the implementation of such programs is hampered by federal guidelines that allow funding for abstinence-based programs only.

Antidrug advertising campaigns are another misguided and ineffective drug prevention effort. Drug advertising campaigns often present false and sometimes ridiculous information about illegal drug use and typically pay little attention to the dangers of tobacco, alcohol, and prescription drug use. Like D.A.R.E., these programs may have a counterproductive effect on youth drug use, either because youth tend to reject all antidrug messages when they identify some as being false or because the programs encourage youth to desire and seek out something that is forbidden (known as reactance).

School-based zero-tolerance policies result in the suspension or expulsion of students who are in possession of or under the influence of drugs on school property. Advocates of zero-tolerance policies believe that these policies are beneficial because they send a clear message that drug use is not to be tolerated. As part of a zero-tolerance policy, many schools drug-test students who want to participate in after-school activities or athletics. There is little evidence that zero-tolerance and drug-testing policies prevent drug use among students who remain in school, and these policies clearly encourage drug use by students who are most at risk. Suspending or expelling drug-using students from school or preventing students from engaging in extracurricular activities by drug testing alienates the youth most likely to use drugs from the protective factors that might eventually reduce or prevent their drug use. Further, once schools have "washed their hands" of these students, the youth are likely to experience a variety of problems that must then be dealt with by the broader community.

Drug testing in the workplace is another widely implemented prevention strategy. We do not dispute that there are occupations in which drug testing is appropriate in the interests of public safety, particularly occupations in public transportation, such as bus drivers or airline pilots. However, workplace drug testing outside this context is increasingly widespread and is typically justified as being an effective deterrent to drug use that will increase worker productivity and company profits. Scientific research generally does not identify a protective effect of drug testing for employee drug use, and these programs do not appear to increase worker productivity. This is partly explained by the pharmacology of various drugs. The substance that is most likely to be identified in drug tests (by far) is marijuana, in part because it can be detected in the urine weeks after its consumption. Extensive research has found no negative effect of marijuana on worker productivity, and the drug is far less likely to limit productivity than alcohol (which is seldom tested for), in part because of the hangover associated with excessive alcohol use. Additionally, illegal drugs that would be more likely to negatively influence worker productivity (heroin, cocaine, amphetamines) also become undetectable in the urine within days and thus are less likely to be identified by drug tests. Drug testing may also limit productivity because it creates a negative working environment that alienates workers from their employers, making them disinclined to "give their all."

Consistent with our discussion of policies addressing illegal drugs (see Chapter 11), it appears that at least part of the reason for the general failure of the prevention policies discussed in this chapter is that they are based on narrow and misguided conceptions of the realities of drug use. Unfortunately, government officials have also been reluctant to significantly alter these drug prevention programs in light of scientific evidence demonstrating their ineffectiveness. A more rational approach to drug prevention would focus on reducing or eliminating the risk factors that lead to substance use and enhancing the protective factors that serve to reduce such use (Hawkins et al., 2002). Although given the current climate it appears unlikely to occur in the United States, social structural approaches to drug prevention that attempt to change the social environment to make it less conducive to drug use should also be considered as alternatives to our current prevention policies.

REVIEW QUESTIONS

1. What factors account for the almost total failure of D.A.R.E. to reduce youth drug use?

2. Alternative forms of drug education have been found to have some success in reducing youth drug use and drug-related problems. In what ways do these education programs differ from D.A.R.E.? Despite their comparative success, what challenges do these alternative programs face?

3. What has research concluded about the effectiveness of school drug testing policies? What problems are created by suspending and/or expelling youth who test positive for drugs?

4. What is the rationale behind workplace drug testing?

5. In what industries is workplace drug testing most appropriate?

6. What type of drug user is typically identified by a positive drug test? Why is this?

INTERNET EXERCISES

1. The Substance Abuse and Mental Health Services Administration (SAMHSA) maintains a website listing evidence-based drug prevention programs, which have been scientifically tested for their effectiveness in preventing and/or reducing substance use (see http://www.nrepp.samhsa.gov). Access the website, type "drug prevention programs" in the search engine, and examine the content of at least two of these programs. In what ways do these programs differ from D.A.R.E.?

2. Access the Partnership for a Drug-Free America website (http://www.drugfree .org) and click on the "drug guide" box. Enter "marijuana" in the search engine, outline the effects listed, and compare them to the effects listed in Chapter 4 of this book.

CHAPTER 8

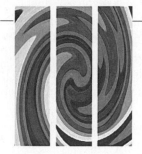

Drug Treatment

This chapter provides an overview of the numerous approaches to drug treatment that are currently in use. We address the theoretical foundations of each of these treatment approaches and assess the available empirical evidence with respect to their effectiveness. Five broad categories of drug treatment are addressed here: (1) *pharmacological drug treatment*, which involves the use of drugs or medications to treat substance abuse; (2) *residential drug treatment programs* in which patients live in a treatment facility for periods of from 1 month to 2 years; (3) *compulsory drug treatment*, which is treatment that is mandated in some way by the criminal justice system; (4) *Alcoholics Anonymous* and related peer-support and 12-step programs; and (5) *outpatient drug treatment*, which involves a diverse range of treatment options that individuals can receive while they reside in the community. It is important to recognize that these programs are not mutually exclusive; there is considerable overlap among them. For example, treatment mandated by the criminal justice system can involve elements of pharmacological treatment, residential drug treatment, and 12-step models.

Before discussing specific drug treatment programs and research on their effectiveness, it is important to address a number of issues. First, as noted in Chapter 5, the vast majority of substance users never become substance abusers, meaning most people who have used drugs are never compelled to seek treatment (Weil & Rosen, 1998). Of the small portion of users who do escalate to substance abuse, this is usually temporary, and most will eventually quit or regain control of their use without any formal treatment program (Faupel et al., 2004). For many people who become addicts, drug abuse is but one of numerous problems they face, and it is often not the most imposing (e.g., mental illness, homelessness, unemployment, poverty). Thus, successfully treating drug abuse often requires remedying broader challenges (United Nations Office on Drugs and Crime [UNODC], 2003).

Another central issue in drug treatment is that the motivation of the individual to change is likely the most important factor in predicting successful treatment outcomes (Jung, 2001). This fact is important to keep in mind when assessing the effectiveness of drug treatment programs because addicts who are motivated to quit using alcohol and other drugs are also more likely than other substance abusers to enter drug treatment in the first place (McCaul & Furst, 1994). Thus, many treatment programs (with the exception of compulsory programs) involve individuals who, despite their inability to quit using drugs on their own, generally *want* to quit. This complicates the interpretation of findings on treatment effectiveness, because those voluntarily participating are likely more motivated to change than those not in treatment, making it impossible to completely separate benefits of particular treatment services from improvements spurred by individual motivation when positive outcomes are achieved (Faupel et al., 2004).

Additionally, treatment success is difficult to define because complete abstinence from all substances for the rest of one's life is almost never achieved, nor is it necessarily a precursor for living a positive, productive life thereafter. In fact, even addicts who completely transition back to mainstream, prosperous lifestyles usually fail to stay sober when first seeking treatment. Though many treatment recipients are motivated to change, if any form of relapse to drug use following treatment is considered evidence of failure, then virtually no drug treatment program can be considered successful. Even the most "successful" programs consistently "fail" more than they "succeed" by that measure, particularly among those entering treatment for the first time (Akers, 1992; Anglin, Longshore, & Turner, 1999; Hubbard, Marsden, Rachal, Harwood, Cavanaugh, & Ginzburg, 1989). As will be discussed in more detail later in this chapter, studies measuring success this way generally find most drug treatment programs to produce only modest or moderate improvements, and often none at all (Akers, 1992; Anglin et al., 1999; Hubbard et al., 1989).

However, most researchers consider it pointless to assess treatment effectiveness solely upon relapse figures. Instead they typically use health and social functioning indicators, such as (1) eliminating or reducing drug use; (2) eliminating or reducing criminal offending; (3) reducing risky sexual behavior, needle sharing, and other forms of behavior that are likely to increase the risk of HIV and other infectious diseases (Hubbard, Cradock, & Anderson, 2003); and (4) increasing rates of conventional employment. It is important to note that even though no program always keeps clients completely sober, many do improve lives. If success is measured in terms of reduced levels of substance use, lessened criminal activity, and improved employment outcomes, then most drug treatment can be regarded as effective (Hubbard et al., 2003).

One final and particularly important issue must be considered in any discussion of the effectiveness of drug treatment programs. Although treatment success rates measured by reductions in drug use and criminal activity can be relatively modest, they still represent outcomes far superior to those that typically result when drug problems are dealt with exclusively through criminal justice system sanctions. Research has consistently demonstrated that drug offenders who are incarcerated and denied treatment have extremely high rates of subsequent drug use and offending (UNDCP, 2003). In addition, nearly all drug prisoners will eventually return to society, so not receiving treatment in prison greatly increases the likelihood that they will return to society with the same problems that originally contributed to their substance abuse. Thus, mandatory minimum sentences and other harsh criminal punishments very often reproduce and extend the harms caused by addiction. Such counterproductive outcomes benefit neither society nor the addict, which is why virtually all drug treatment scholars and professionals today consider it inhumane to respond to drug abuse with only criminal justice sanctions.

Although treatment and incarceration costs vary considerably across programs and locations, treatment has been consistently found to be the most cost-effective response to substance abuse (e.g., McCollister & French, 2002; NIDA, 1999; Roebuck, French, & McClellan, 2003; UNDCP, 2003). A recent meta-analysis examined more than 500 treatment programs nationwide, reinforcing and extending previous findings by using the most specific cost measures available (Drake, Aos, & Miller, 2009). More specifically, any dollar spent on a drug treatment program reduced future costs by at least $2 (a 200% return on the investment), with savings as high as $18 per treatment dollar observed in the most successful treatment settings. Related, a study of drug treatment programs in California found a seven-fold return on treatment spending (Ettner, Huang, Evans, et al., 2005).

> Although addictions are chronic disorders, there is a tendency for most physicians and for the general public to perceive them as being acute conditions such as a broken leg . . . when relapse occurs, as it usually does, the "treatment" is inappropriately considered a failure. Treatments for addiction, therefore, should be regarded as being long term, and a "cure" is unlikely from a single course of treatment. (O'Brien & McClellan, 1996, p. 237)

The large cost differential between drug treatment and criminal sanctions is due primarily to the extreme costs associated with building and maintaining prisons, as each cell costs about $35,000 to build and $27,000 per year to maintain at minimum security levels (UNODC, 2003). Those figures have inevitably risen since last being reliably gauged 10 years ago, further elevating the potential value of treatment-based approaches, in both tangible and symbolic terms. Not coincidentally, numerous public officials and state agencies have recently proclaimed increased commitment to drug treatment. This includes the Obama administration, whose representatives have repeatedly and vigorously promised that greater investment in treatment is and will continue to be the primary strategy used to supplant the now-defunct War on Drugs approach (ONDCP, 2012; see also Chapter 11). While the degree to which federal resources have reflected that promise thus far is debatable, treatment expansion is nonetheless ongoing and inevitable, so we now turn to consideration of the various treatment modes available today.

PHARMACOLOGICAL TREATMENT APPROACHES

Pharmacotherapy involves the use of drugs and medications in the treatment of substance abuse and dependency. Somewhat ironically, then, this form of treatment involves using one drug in order to prevent the use of another. Substances in this form of treatment are typically used in one of two ways: on a temporary basis as the individual attempts to quit the use of another drug (detoxification therapy) or on an indefinite basis (maintenance therapy) in the belief that taking the new drug will minimize use of more problematic substances and other associated criminal behavior (O'Brien, 1997).

While less commonly part of the public dialogue in the United States., pharmacological approaches have been readily available since the Industrial Revolution. For example, in the late 1800s and early 1900s, a wide variety of proprietary medicines was sold as "cures" for alcoholism. These included products such as Parker's Tonic, Schneck's Seaweed Tonic, and Boker's stomach bitters. Interestingly, several of these products contained significant proportions of alcohol: Parker's Tonic, which was advertised as "pure vegetable extract" that "gave stimulus to the body without intoxicating," was found to contain 41.6% alcohol (Trice & Staudenmeier, 1989). Similarly, prior to the passage of the 1914 Harrison Narcotics Act in the United States, physicians often treated opiate addicts with other types of opiates, including heroin. As noted in Chapter 3, when Bayer laboratories introduced heroin in 1898, it was marketed as a nonaddictive cure for morphine addiction (Askwith, 1998). Currently, a wide variety of nonpsychoactive and psychoactive drugs—referred to as "medications" in the treatment context—are available to help individuals with substance abuse problems.

Although pharmacotherapy can be used in isolation to treat substance dependency (e.g., using a nicotine patch to quit smoking), more often it coincides with other treatment techniques like psychological counseling or behavior modification (O'Brien, 1997). There is also no typical length of time associated with pharmacotherapy, which can last less than a day or for several years, and occasionally lasts indefinitely. Treatment goals generally guide treatment length, with brief drug interventions employed to facilitate and deintensify opiate detoxification and withdrawal, which ends within 3 days. Conversely, methadone maintenance therapy for heroin addicts often continues uninterrupted for several years and has been used to improve life quality indicators indefinitely in numerous cases in Europe (DHHS-CDC, 2002).

Chemically speaking, drugs used in pharmacological treatments can be classified as either *drug agonists* or *drug antagonists* (though some medications combine the properties of both). Drug agonists are also psychoactive (although their effects may only be noticeable for nonusers) and capable of generating dependency or abuse, but these substitute drugs are viewed as safer, or otherwise preferable, to the generally unregulated drugs they are meant to replace (NIDA, 1999).

Conversely, drug antagonists lack psychoactive effects or addictive potential, instead working in various ways to eliminate the positive effects users feel upon ingesting mind-altering substances. Antagonists usually work by one of two mechanisms: (1) by inhibiting the potential pleasure produced by other drugs by chemically blocking necessary receptors or (2) by directly creating physical discomfort for patients who consume a particular recreational drug, triggering a chemical side effect.

The Dovzhenko Method

Alcoholism is a very serious problem in Russia. Estimates indicate that more than 50,000 people die from alcohol poisoning each year in Russia, compared to only 400 in the United States. Over the past 20 years, one method used to treat alcoholism has been the Dovzhenko Method. Dating to the former Soviet Union, this method involves "coding" alcoholics so that they believe if they drink again, they will die. One of the ways that this is carried out is as follows: Physicians induce hypnosis in patients and then administer a drug that reacts to alcohol and affects the respiratory system. Patients are then encouraged to taste a small amount of alcohol, which prompts a reaction. Patients are even required to sign a release form that relieves the doctor of liability should they drink and die from it. The popularity of the Dovzhenko Method has waned in recent years as information about the true nature of the treatment has spread. (Finn, 2005)

Drug Agonists

Whether on a temporary or long-term basis, treatment involving agonists is based upon the belief that their consumption will reduce or eliminate the use of another substance. However, the ultimate goal in employing drug agonists with similar addictive potential is to avoid the negative outcomes and risks linked to the use of a particular street drug, and only secondary attention is given to actually curbing consumption (NIDA, 1999).

Nicotine replacement therapy (NRT) is the most commonly used drug agonist, and numerous NRT products are currently marketed to people attempting to quit smoking or using other tobacco products. Many of these products are available over the counter, and although "the patch" is the most well-known form of NRT, there are other forms: nicotine-based nasal sprays, lozenges, gum, tablets, and inhalers that can be "puffed on" like cigarettes (Campbell, 2003). Although research has generally found NRT to be effective at helping people to quit smoking, these effects are generally quite modest (Hughes, Goldstein, Hurt, & Shiffman, 1999). Moore and colleagues' (2009) recent meta-analysis of all previous double-blind experiments showed that only 6.75% of those receiving NRT maintained abstinence for 6 months. Some improvement has been consistently noted, though, as the 6-month abstinence threshold was achieved twice as often with NRT as with placebos, motivational support, or other pharmacological therapies. Rather than complete abstinence, the most common benefit of NRT therapy is reduced cigarette consumption, with 21.8% of subjects cutting their daily intake in half (compared with 16.3% for the placebo) and 6% of subjects maintaining a 50% reduction for one year (Moore et al., 2009). Thus, NRT is reliably more likely to curb and occasionally eliminate cigarette smoking than any other method, but it still does not work for the vast majority of people.

A new nicotine agonist is currently being tested, however, with initial results showing notable improvements over past NRT drugs. Clinical trials are still underway for Baclofen, which relies on GABA B agonists to quiet dopaminergic afferents and, thus, to reduce negative sensations associated with quitting smoking. Though still far from a panacea, initial double-blind experiments found that Baclofen reduced average cigarette consumption about 33% more than a placebo, with lower craving scores reported by patients (Franklin et al., 2009).

The primary concern with NRT is that, like smoking, it involves the ingestion of a highly addictive substance, meaning that relying on NRT to quit smoking may simply amount to trading one form of nicotine addiction for another, albeit one that is likely less harmful. A *New York Times* article during the height of the nicotine gum boom in 2004 noted that more than one-third of Nicorette chewers reported no longer being addicted to cigarettes, yet most had become addicted to Nicorette instead. One respondent who averaged 12 pieces each day reported, "I felt almost like a drug addict" (Bartosiewicz, 2004, cited in Center for Cognitive Liberty and Ethics [CCLE], 2004, p. 11). Still, the long-term health benefits motivate many to undergo NRT, which effectively eliminates the well-known dangers of tobacco, substituting an increased rate of nausea as the sole common side effect (Moore et al., 2009).

Among the agonists used to treat illegal drug addictions, methadone is the most familiar and often the most common. As noted in Chapter 3, methadone is a synthetic narcotic that is used predominantly in the treatment of heroin (and other opiate) addiction. First used in World War II as a pain reliever during morphine shortages, methadone has been employed as a maintenance therapy drug for heroin addicts since the mid-1960s. In the ensuing years, hundreds of thousands have been treated with methadone replacement therapy while seeking to overcome heroin habits, including between 115,000 and 160,000 Americans, about one-fifth of the nation's heroin addicts. While substantial, this figure also reflects a lost treatment opportunity for the majority of all heroin addicts, a population estimated to be between 600,000 and 900,000 strong (Firoz & Carlson, 2004).

Methadone maintenance therapy is simple and effective by tangible measures, but conceptually this approach is inevitably complex and multi-layered, offering ample pros and cons on practical, moral, and philosophical grounds, along with opportunity for extreme success and failure for the patient. As a substitution therapy, methadone maintenance involves replacing a patient's existing dependency, usually for heroin or another opiate, with regular doses of methadone that is provided by medical personnel, usually in liquid form. Itself a synthetic opiate, methadone maintenance may not lead to total abstinence, nor is that the primary goal. The cravings and withdrawal from not getting a habitual dose are the reason opiate addictions are often so consuming and tough to overcome, so methadone maintenance deprioritizes curing users' dependence. By substituting a synthetic opiate for street drugs, methadone maintenance therapy provides a "fix" that is safer, longer lasting, and cheaper (O'Brien, 1997).

It is precisely because methadone is a synthetic opiate that this treatment is possible, but it is important to recognize that the dependence generated by methadone maintenance is vastly different than addiction to heroin with respect to life outcomes and the ability of individuals to manage their day-to-day activities (DHHS-CDC, 2002; see box). As Brecher (1972) notes, the reasons for the relative success of methadone maintenance programs in treating opiate addiction are obvious. First, because methadone is a legal substance, the addict who enters a methadone maintenance program is able to relinquish the role of "hated and hunted criminal" (p. 159). Second, methadone is cheap, which means that addicts generally do not have to become involved in crime to support their drug habit. Additionally, even though the dependency remains, it is satisfied for much longer with orally administered methadone (between 12 and 24 hours) than from heroin (3 hours or less), providing much larger stretches for normative social functioning (Gahlinger, 2001). Thus, regulated dependence is maintained in a less problematic manner, allowing patients to avoid withdrawal's discomforts while they focus on avoiding direct sources of harm by living otherwise normal lifestyles. Over time, they can then gradually reduce their dependency with little discomfort and with the support offered by friendships, family, and social services.

Individual dosage depends upon patients' previous heroin use and tolerance, with typical maintenance doses of methadone ranging from 30 mg to 120 mg per day. While larger doses are associated with more successful treatment outcomes (Leshner, 1999; Marsch, 1998; NIH, 1998; UNDCP, 2002), stable oral methadone consumption does not produce any euphoria or high, and cognition, alertness, and mental functioning are unimpaired (DHHS-CDC, 2002; Nadelmann, 1996; O'Brien, 1997; Rothenberg, Schottenfeld, Meyer, Krauss, & Gross, 1977). Accordingly, opiate addicts engaged in methadone maintenance are less likely to experience the intense cravings commonly associated with opiate addiction, and if they "slip up" and inject heroin, their tolerance to methadone will largely prevent the reward or euphoria associated with heroin.

> "Addiction" to methadone looks far more similar to a diabetic's "addiction" to insulin than a stereotypical view of a heroin addict's dependence upon street drugs. Many methadone patients hold good jobs and are responsible parents. They can safely drive motor vehicles and operate heavy machinery. They are, when prescribed adequate doses of methadone, practically indistinguishable from Americans who have never used heroin or methadone. (Nadelmann, 1996, p. 84)

Research on the efficacy of methadone maintenance programs has shown this treatment strategy to be useful in the treatment of addiction to heroin and other opiates across a variety of outcome measures (Hubbard et al., 2003; Hubbard et al., 1989; Leshner, 1999; Marsch, 1998; NIH, 1998; UNDCP, 2002). Support for methadone maintenance treatments first developed in Europe, after Switzerland initiated a nationwide trial program in 1994. It was so successful in reducing HIV transmission and drug-related property crime that a skeptical Swiss populace was quickly convinced (Csete & Grob, 2011), leading to the adoption of similar programs in most EU nations (Hedrich, Pirona, & Wiessing, 2008).

More recently, Veilleux and colleagues' (2010) review of past meta-analyses and subsequent experimental studies demonstrated that across decades of research methadone maintenance therapy has consistently produced better outcomes than abstinence alone ("going cold turkey"). That pattern holds true across numerous measures of success, including rates of subsequent illicit drug use, HIV-risk behavior, and other criminal offending. An added benefit of methadone substitution is methadone maintenance is cost-effective, and every dollar spent on methadone maintenance saves from $2 to $4 in corrections costs (Flynn, Porto, Rounds-Bryant, & Kristiansen, 2003).

Even amid the overall evidence supporting the use of methadone maintenance therapy, it is important to recognize that "methadone maintenance is not a cure-all" (Rounsaville & Kosten, 2000, p. 1338). Returning to the issue of how success is defined in evaluating treatment programs, we must recognize that although methadone is clearly beneficial in reducing illicit opiate use, crime, and risky behaviors, a large portion of those who undergo methadone maintenance therapy experience relapses and/or ongoing problems related to their substance use. Further, while participating in methadone maintenance programs, many individuals still use heroin and other drugs, continue to engage in high-risk behavior, and experience problems within their personal and professional lives (Rounsaville & Kosten, 2000).

These concerns and the ongoing moral controversy aside, the relative stability experienced by methadone maintenance patients and general evidence indicating its treatment benefits have led to support from a growing number of organizations in the United States. Included on that list are major national institutions, such as the National Institutes of Health, Centers for Disease Control, and Office of National Drug Control Policy (DHHS-CDC, 2002; NIH, 1998; ONDCP, 2000b). As early as 1997, a U.S. government report that noted that methadone maintenance participants showed significant reductions in criminal activity and improved employment outcomes (Nadelmann, 2002b). As noted in the *Journal of the American Medical Association* (see box), NIH support was announced in the report produced following a special meeting of top scientists in the field, with their decisive approval evident in their conclusions.

> Society must make a commitment to order effective treatment for opiate dependency for all who need it. All persons dependent on opiates should have access to methadone hydrochloride maintenance therapy under legal supervision, and the U.S. Office of National Drug Control Policy and the U.S. Department of Justice should take the necessary steps to implement this recommendation. (NIH, 1998, p. 1936)

Despite ample evidence of its treatment benefits, methadone substitution treatment remains controversial. Some critics disapprove of the tacit approval and direct maintenance of dependency involved in administering methadone. Others object to the fact that large doses or injection of maintenance doses can produce psychoactive effects, leading a small number of patients to maintain treatment solely for that purpose alone (Blendon & Young, 1998). Andrew Weil (1986) is critical of methadone maintenance because rather than showing addicts how to achieve highs without drugs, it is a "method of giving them drugs without highs"—exactly the wrong direction in which to change things (p. 190). In large part, most criticism revolves around the ongoing physical addiction of methadone patients, which tends to be viewed as a moral shortcoming from this perspective. Interestingly, however, the same fundamental approach is not regularly seen as a moral shortcoming when applied to nicotine replacement therapy in the form of chewing gum.

Contradicting the scientific and medical evidence, moralistic judgment and one-sided media scrutiny have amplified this controversy in the United States, producing an overall attitude of intolerance in many areas. As a result, methadone maintenance remains completely unavailable in some states and severely limited in others. Even where legally permitted, methadone can be accessed exclusively through dedicated centers rather than traditional physicians. Even in those centers, methadone replacement therapy in the United States is limited to smaller doses and shorter durations than those recommended in protocol published by the the British Association of Pharmacology's guide to evidence-based practices in treating substance abuse (Lingford-Hughes et al., 2012).

Methadone maintenance programs are known to benefit a substantial proportion of opiate addicts (DHHS-CDC, 2002; NIH, 1998; UNODC, 2009), suggesting the need for greater availability (especially in the United States). Perhaps offering hope of wider support or even larger treatment gains, a slow-release oral morphine (SROM) tablet was recently released. The lengthier delivery of the drug intended to reduce the opportunity for abuse and create longer opportunities between patient visits, both goals intended to simultaneously improve treatment efficacy and increase the social acceptance of this treatment strategy. Additionally, early trials have produced encouraging results, including fewer cravings, gentler withdrawal symptoms, and lessened impacts on cognitive functioning (Kastelic, Dubajic, & Strbad, 2008).

Similar to methadone or slow release oral morphine, buprenorphine (trade name Subutex) is an increasingly popular drug in maintenance therapy for opiate addicts (SAMHSA, 2005a). Buprenorphine is a partial opioid agonist, however, meaning that although it has the effects of an opioid, these effects are significantly weaker than those of full agonists such as methadone or heroin (SAMHSA, 2005a). As a result of this difference, compared to methadone, buprenorphine arguably offers less potential for abuse, less severe withdrawal, and a reduced likelihood of overdose (Franques & Tignol, 2001; Vastag, 2003). Buprenorphine was approved by the FDA for treatment of opiate addicts in 2002, but it was not widely prescribed at first (Vastag, 2003). In part, this is because many doctors are skeptical about the ability of drugs to treat narcotics addiction (Mitka, 2003) and because physicians were originally limited to carrying a maximum of 30 buprenorphine patients, a figure many doctors have referred to as "absurd" (Vastag, 2003, p. 731).

In contrast, buprenorphine has been widely used in France since the mid-1990s, and as of 2003, France had an estimated 72,000 high-dose buprenorphine patients, far exceeding the approximately 17,000 high-dose methadone patients in the United States (French Monitoring Center for Drugs and Drug Addiction, 2004). This has begun to change, however, as Soeffing and colleagues' (2009) study of buprenorphine treatment provided by everyday doctors demonstrated positive outcomes in Baltimore, where 57% of patients remained in treatment and 65% remained opioid free after 1 year.

Expectations and some evidence of increased safety are behind buprenorphine's increasing popularity as a maintenance drug in the United States in recent years. Likewise, it has gained increasing approval from various professionals and organizations on those grounds, leading to expanded patient limits. In fact, largely because it is argued to have a lower abuse potential, buprenorphine can now be prescribed to opiate addicts at a doctor's office (Mitka, 2003) by any physician who has completed a required 8-hour training course and registers with both the Substance Abuse and Mental Health Services Administration (SAMHSA) and the Drug Enforcement Administration (Vastag, 2003).

At the same time, other studies suggest claims of increased safety are largely hype. In fact, Roux and associates (2008) found that buprenorphine was actually being abused at almost an identical rate to methadone, with approximately one-third of patients snorting or injecting the tablets for a more powerful psychoactive effect. At the same time, the potential for abuse has been reduced (but never entirely eliminated) when buprenorphine injections are coupled with oral naloxone, another partial agonist used only rarely as a stand-alone opiate substitute (Mammen & Bell, 2009).

The relatively limited regulation of buprenorphine as compared to methadone is interesting and in part reflects the need to deliver opiate treatment "outside traditional settings such as methadone clinics" (Mitka, 2003, p. 735). Specifically, buprenorphine treatment appears to be aimed more exclusively at the increasing number of middle-class opiate addicts, while methadone maintenance is predominately accessed by poor inner-city residents (Mitka, 2003). While this is justified on the grounds of increasing availability, it also reflects a greater prioritization of patient comfort now that the patient is more likely to be affluent and white. Both good intentions and differential consideration across demographic groups are evident in the comments of John Schneider, former president of the Illinois State Medical Society.

> While heroin has traditionally been associated with inner city drug addicts, today's user is more and more likely to be an employed young professional living in the suburbs . . . we need to use primary care physicians more effectively to treat these patients [who] want to be treated in private settings. (Mitka, 2003, p. 735)

Overall, research on the risks associated with buprenorphine show that it is safer than methadone in meaningful ways, but those improvements often reduced treatment success. Milder side effects are a genuine difference, as one study found that the death rate from methadone is at least three times greater than for buprenorphine (Auriacombe et al., 2001). In some studies, it has also shown excellent treatment success, such as a recent meta-analysis that found buprenorphine improved rates of total abstinence, especially in concert with psychosocial therapy modalities (Bahr, et al., 2012). Such strong evidence of buprenorphine's treatment potential and safety collectively led to its endorsement as a primary treatment method for opiate addiction by the British Association of Pharmacology (Lingford-Hughes et al., 2012). Dosage is important, however, as flexible and high-quantity prescriptions have been found to produce equivalent results to methadone maintenance, but the often limited or tapering dosages available in the United States have been found less effective (Veilleux et al., 2010). It also appears to be less effective than methadone for the treatment of more heavily dependent opiate addicts (SAMHSA, 2005a).

An even more controversial pharmacological program for treating opiate addicts involves heroin maintenance. Sometimes referred to as the "British model" due to its origin in Britain in the 1960s, heroin maintenance involves prescribing doses of heroin to individuals identified as "hardcore junkies" who inject the drug at special injection sites. Given mainstream American attitudes toward drugs, such programs are unlikely to be widely adopted in the United States in the near future. Still, the observed benefits have made heroin maintenance a routine treatment for otherwise untreatable addicts in the Netherlands, Germany, England, Denmark, and Switzerland (Uchtenhagen, 2011).

While quite limited in its application, heroin maintenance therapy also appears to produce more treatment success than any other approach in certain contexts. For those with a history of failed treatment, multiple studies have shown that heroin maintenance increases treatment retention while reducing heroin use and other illegal activities (Veilleux et al., 2009). In the Netherlands, it was more effective than methadone in terms of improving the physical and mental condition and social functioning of heroin addicts (van den Brink, Hendricks, Blanken, Koeter, van Zwieten, & van Ree, 2003). Similarly, after 31% of participants in a Swiss program dropped out in the first 18 months, those who stayed in the program experienced several positive outcomes. For example, the proportion of participants with unstable housing fell from 43% on admission to 21%; the rate of employment more than doubled, from 14% to 32%; and there was a reduction of more than 50% in criminal offenses committed by those in the treatment group (Wood et al., 2003).

Perhaps even more controversial than heroin maintenance therapy are supervised injection facilities (SIF), which simultaneously serve treatment and prevention functions by providing intravenous drug users with accessible drug therapy opportunities and medical attention while offering clean needles, a safe environment, and nonjudgmental drug education material. Particularly in the United States, some people view these facilities as morally improper, dangerous, and encouraging drug use, so SIFs were banned federally for decades until 2008. In that year, the Obama administration began the first federal funding for SIFs before quickly reversing course again and reinstituting the ban in 2010. Despite universally inspiring objections, the evidence in favor of providing SIFs is ample, so they continue to become more established in countries such as Canada, Australia, and New Zealand, as well as several European countries. Further discussion of the policy debates and implications surrounding SIFs can be found in Chapter 12.

Regardless of political or moral controversy they stir up, Safe Injection Facilities unequivocally support their own existence through the research evidence linking each new SIF with public health benefits. In a study of an Australian SIF, staff intervened in 329 overdoses over a 1-year period and saved at least four lives (Wright & Tompkins, 2004). When offered in conjunction with opioid substitution, supervised injection facilities in New Zealand prisons led to a reduction of more than 50% in intravenous drug use and needle sharing (Larney, 2010).

When offered outside institutional settings, SIFs have been found successful according to nearly all indicators, with the Insite facility in Vancouver (B.C.) having been evaluated from numerous perspectives and by a variety of disciplines, garnering strong support in almost every instance. Even the most minor indicators reflect the many ways that this approach has yielded a better overall quality of life, like the large reduction in littering in formerly dilapidated parks, especially in regards to publicly discarded syringes (Wood, Tyndall, Montaner, & Kerr, 2006). Insite's benefits were amplified by the fact that the facility attracted users with the most risky habits as well (Hayashi, Wood, Wiebe, Qi, & Kerr, 2010; Wood, Tyndall, Stoltz, Small, Lloyd-Smith, et al., 2005). Perhaps more importantly, this study found that clients of the injection center were more likely than other injecting drug users to seek treatment for their drug use (Tyndall, Kerr, et al., 2006; Wood et al., 2006).

In addition to scientific support, injection facilities have almost universally managed to stay open despite protests and political pressures (not to mention direct government pressure on Insite), often expanding their services. Quality of life gains extend to non–drug-using residents, who have consistently reported fewer sightings of public injection and syringes being discarded in public places (Wood et al., 2006; Wright & Tompkins, 2004), public disorder (Kerr et al., 2006), and drug dealing and overall crime (Hayashi et al., 2010; Wood et al., 2006). Notably, there is no evidence supporting the primary rationale used in objecting to SIFs, as no increase in drug use has been found, nor have there been increases in drug in public or discarded drug paraphernalia litter (Wood et al., 2006). For these reasons, Wright and Tompkins (2004) conclude, "[the] argument that medically supervised injecting centers promote drug use and related harm is not supported by the evidence" (p. 102).

Drug Antagonists

As noted earlier, in addition to drug agonists, drug antagonists constitute the other class of medication commonly used in the treatment of substance dependency. These drugs prevent substance abuse in one of two ways: They either make ill patients who supplement treatment with recreational drug use (e.g., alcohol), or they block the psychoactive effects of a particular drug (CCLE, 2004). With respect to the former, one of the most commonly used drugs in this category is disulfiram (or sulfiram), which is also known by its trade name, Antabuse. Disulfiram is used in the treatment of alcoholism, and although the substance is not toxic itself, it inhibits the body's ability to metabolize alcohol (O'Brien, 1997). Interestingly, the treatment effects of disulfiram were discovered serendipitously in the 1930s when workers at rubber manufacturing plants who were regularly exposed to the chemical became violently ill whenever they consumed alcohol (CCLE, 2004). Similarly, alcoholics patients become very ill when they drink after taking disulfiram, a combination that leads to symptoms including nausea, vomiting, headache, facial flushing, and high blood pressure ("Drug Treatments," 2002). These symptoms, which have been said to be analogous to those experienced in a bad hangover, typically last between 30 and 180 minutes.

The effectiveness of Antabuse/disulfiram in treating alcoholism is mixed. Jorgensen and colleagues' meta-analysis (2011) concluded that there is modest evidence indicating that disulfiram reduces the frequency of drinking and improves slightly the time before relapse, though this was only supported in six of nine individual studies and the difference became insignificant after the first year. Another meta-analysis found that disulfiram is primarily beneficial among patients who have lengthier histories of alcohol abuse and those who are highly compliant or supervised by treatment providers (Johnson et al., 2007).

Such findings are not surprising, given that the drug does nothing to reduce the initial craving for alcohol, and the effects of disulfiram typically wear off within 24 to 48 hours (Doweiko, 1999). Thus, people who have been prescribed disulfiram can plan their drinking episodes and simply quit taking the medication a day or two in advance. Additionally, because the negative effects that result from combining disulfiram and alcohol are usually of short duration, it is possible to "drink through" disulfiram (Doweiko, 1999).

An additional problem with disulfiram is that the drug cannot identify the source of the alcohol that is ingested. Thus, if an individual taking disulfiram inadvertently consumes or absorbs alcohol—which is present in commonly used products such as cough syrup, mouthwash, aftershave, and perfume—he or she becomes susceptible to a variety of serious reactions that can result from combining disulfiram and alcohol, such as liver inflammation, heart-related problems, and potentially death (CCLE, 2004). Thus, the relatively modest benefits and high potential costs keep Antabuse/disulfiram from being widely prescribed, and even then it is recommended only to be administered under direct physician supervision, according to the British Association of Psychopharmacology's (BAP) evidence-based policy suggestions (Lingford-Hughes et al., 2012). Interestingly, though, disulfiram does actually receive the BAP's recommendation as the most efficacious pharmacological treatment for co-occurring cocaine and alcohol dependence (Kenna et al., 2007).

Most commonly used for substance abuse treatment today are pharmaceuticals from the subclass of antagonists that block or reduce the psychoactive effects of recreational drugs. This occurs in one of two broad ways: (1) They bind to a drug molecule, making it too large to pass through the blood–brain barrier (thereby preventing any effect on the brain); or (2) they occupy receptor sites on brain cells or neurons, preventing the drug molecules from "docking" to these receptor sites and thus having an effect on the brain (CCLE, 2004; O'Brien, 1997).

A number of pharmaceuticals used in treating alcoholism employ antagonists to inhibit alcohol's effects. Most notable among these drugs are Acamprosate, already in use for several years in Europe, and Topirimate, a drug traditionally used to control seizures in epilepsy patients but undergoing clinical tests for alcohol treatment as well. Acamprosate is a glutamatergic modulator that depresses NMDA (N-methyl-D-aspartate) receptor activation, reducing physical and psychological withdrawal from alcohol. Comprehensive reviews of the literature show that Acamprosate improves the likelihood and length of abstinence after detoxification, but only in studies involving only heavy drinkers (Lingford-Hughes et al., 2012). Thus, current evidence led the authors of this study to conclude that Acamprosate should only be used for increasing abstinence among heavy drinkers (Lingford-Hughes et al., 2012). Although Topirimate has not yet been approved by the Food and Drug Administration for alcohol abuse treatment in the United States, European clinical trials suggest that it subdues the brain's ability to experience the pleasure of drinking and can therefore reduce the craving for alcohol without requiring abstinence to begin treatment (Vedantam, 2003). In some studies, Topirimate actually performed better than the leading contemporary brands in terms of reducing heavy drinking, alcohol-related consequences, and improving overall quality of life. However, its applicability is limited because it has also been associated with elevated risks for a variety of serious side effects, including anorexia, difficulty concentrating, taste perversion, and paraesthesia (Johnson et al., 2007).

Although there are several medications used to treat substance abuse in this fashion, among the most interesting is naltrexone, an opioid antagonist that was released in 1985 as a prescription drug for the treatment of narcotics addiction. This substance is effective in the treatment of opiate addiction because it prevents addicts from experiencing any psychoactive effects if they "slip up" and can provide an "'insurance policy' in situations where the patient is likely to be confronted with relapse risks" (McClellan et al., 2000, p. 1693).

Studies have found that orally administered naltrexone can effectively block both the physiological and subjective psychoactive effects of heroin and morphine for up to 3 days (Tai & Blaine, 1997), as well as heroin's euphoric effects for up to 6 weeks (Comer, Collins, Kleber, Nuwayser, Kerrigan, & Fischman, 2002). Naltrexone's ability to block opiates' psychoactive effects initially led many to believe that it would be ideal for the treatment of heroin addiction (McClellan et al., 2000). However, opiate dependency is often linked strongly to the ritual of "tuning out" (getting high) such that the loss of that ritual can lead to particularly intense cravings. Thus, with the exception of white-collar opiate addicts like doctors and nurses, the vast majority of addicts prefer methadone treatment to naltrexone therapy.

In fact, despite its initial promise, naltrexone has not been nearly as effective as originally expected, and naltrexone is not commonly prescribed for the singular treatment of opiate dependence today as a result (O'Brien, 1997). Anecdotal reports of patient dissatisfaction have been repeatedly confirmed by research findings, including a review of past meta-analyses that accounted for hundreds of studies, finding consistently that intense cravings often cause high treatment dropout rates. As a result, naltrexone has failed to reduce relapse rates more than nonpharmaceutical treatments, even in conjunction with psychosocial therapy, and has been linked to more severe relapses (Veilleux et al., 2010).

Still, research has demonstrated that naltrexone can produce limited benefits in certain contexts, such as reduced criminal behavior and heroin use for those who adhere completely to treatment guidelines and patients with strong existing social bonds (Minozzi et al., 2006). Additionally, naltrexone therapy reduces attrition rates (from treatment) and increases efficacy when combined with buprenorphine (Gerra, Fantoma, & Zaimovic, 2006) as well as when it is taken in a new, long-lasting form (which is implanted rather than orally ingested) in conjunction with psychosocial support therapy (Reece, 2007).

New genetics research suggests potentially strong benefits when naltrexone is directed at patients possessing certain genetic markers (Mann & Hermann, 2010). A meta-analysis conducted by Bahr, Masters, and Taylor (2012) also indicated that naltrexone led to lower relapse rates, reduced alcohol consumption, and lengthier abstinence before relapse than nonpharmacological treatments, though larger improvements have generally been found when combined with other substances. Recently, naltrexone was promoted by the British Association for Pharmacology, which proclaimed it the ideal evidence-based treatment for reducing the risk that a lapse becomes a relapse (Lingford-Hughes et al., 2012), making it effective in moderation-based approaches as well.

Substances have also been developed that are designed to prevent individuals from becoming addicted to tobacco products. For example, a drug made by the British company Xenova works by stimulating the immune system to make antibodies against nicotine. Once the antibody binds to nicotine, the resulting complex is too large to penetrate molecules in the brain, thus preventing the brain from activating the pleasure receptors that are involved in generating the pleasurable effects associated with tobacco use (Coghlan, 2002). A National Institute on Drug Abuse newsletter noted that this "nicotine vaccine . . . may even prove useful as an inoculation against nicotine addiction, much like those that protect children from tetanus, measles, and polio" (Shrine, 2000).

Until recently, antagonist substances were only available for the treatment of abuse of substances that generated physiological dependence—notably alcohol, nicotine, and the opiates. For other drugs, most notably the stimulants, hallucinogens, and marijuana, the only available treatments were behavioral in nature (O'Brien, 1997). However, as research in this area continues to advance, products are being developed that may be useful in the treatment of drug abuse involving substances whose addictive potential is purely psychological. One such drug is TA-CD (also developed by the British pharmaceutical company Xenova); the substance is being promoted as a "therapeutic vaccine" designed to treat cocaine addiction (Xenova, 2004). The company's website claims that two separate clinical trials of TA-CD have found the drug to be effective at reducing the euphoric effects of cocaine.

Despite mounting evidence that SR141716, a marijuana antagonist, reliably decreases cannabis cravings in animals during laboratory tests, a recent study involving rats hints at two important caveats. First, researchers found that single doses of SR141716 often increased physical withdrawal symptoms, such as severe paw tremors, creating discomfort and limiting the animals' dexterity (Wilson, Varvel, Harloe, Martin, & Lichtman, 2006). Projected to humans, these results suggest a risk for disorientation and pain that would greatly hinder social functioning. They also call into question the wisdom of replacing relatively innocuous drugs with those known to cause such strong side effects.

The broader implications of these results stretch far beyond this study and even the potential value or safety of synthetic marijuana agonists in general. The greatest significance of this research is likely the secondary (and, presumably, accidental) discoveries differentiating the effects of THC on the rats according to the delivery method. Injections left the animals with more THC in their systems than was found in rats who received equal doses through inhalation. Injections also produced the only severe physical side effects and sole evidence of dependence, and the withdrawal symptoms that resulted were unrelieved by marijuana smoke alone (Wilson et al., 2006).

The first clinical trials of TA-CD showed it to be successful in decreasing the pleasure users associated with cocaine within 4 minutes of smoking it in a lab setting, suggesting it would also reduce cravings in a natural setting (Haney et al., 2010). This initial success led to a considerable fanfare given the lack of consistent treatment success among stimulant-dependent patients, prompting the development of a large clinical trial that is currently ongoing (Shen & Kosten, 2011).

However, at this stage there are too many limitations and drawbacks to consider TA-CD a potential panacea in this area of treatment. In the initial clinical study, significant benefits were only observed among those whose bloodstreams showed high antibody levels following the vaccine, as was the case for reductions in self-reported use during subsequent months of outpatient therapy (Haney et al., 2011). Additionally, the magnitude of antibody production was not predicted by the dosages administered and varied widely (Haney et al., 2011), calling into serious question the ability to reliably produce such benefits. Higher antibody levels were also associated with significant increases in cardiac tachycardia (Haney et al., 2011), a potentially deadly side effect that would be made even more likely in a real-world setting because the pleasure-limiting effects can be overcome by elevated consumption (Sivagnanam, 2011).

Collectively, these findings severely devalue TA-CD's potential as a harm reduction strategy given that cocaine is very unlikely to independently cause fatal overdoses. The range of substances that can be treated with antagonists continues to expand and now even includes marijuana. For example, the marijuana antagonist SR141716 (see box) has been found to reduce both the subjective psychoactive and physiological effects of marijuana by occupying particular receptors in the brain (Huestis et al., 2001; LeFoll & Goldberg, 2005). However, research on its effects still involves only non-human species, making any report of its medical efficacy premature. Furthermore, the expansion of pharmacotherapy to include marijuana could be construed as troubling, especially given that, as discussed in Chapter 4, marijuana is a relatively innocuous substance that does not cause dependence, and very little is known about the long- or short-term effects of SR141716. As a publication of the Center for Cognitive Liberty and Ethics noted, "marijuana has been safely used for centuries, while the anti-marijuana drug SR141716 has no history of human use. One cannot help but question whether 'the cure' might be worse than 'the illness'" (CCLE, 2004, p. 14).

What is clear is that the U.S. government remains committed to reducing and ultimately eliminating particular forms of drug use and continues to look for methods to achieve this goal. Given the general failure of interdiction and criminal justice system policies in reducing drug use, perhaps the increasing emphasis on pharmacotherapy reflects another "front" in the War on Drugs or the "American government's hope . . . that the demand for drugs can be reduced, in part, by chemically eliminating the very *desire* to use an illegal drug" (CCLE, 2004, p. 6).

RESIDENTIAL DRUG TREATMENT PROGRAMS

Residential treatment programs were among the first forms of organized drug treatment available in the United States. Dating back to the 19th century, residential treatment was provided in the homes, hospitals, and sanitariums that were primarily designed to treat alcoholism and opiate addiction (Faupel et al., 2004). However, over time, two distinct models of residential drug treatment have emerged. The first model is the more "medicalized" approach and typically involves doctor-monitored and often medication-assisted drug treatment (as discussed above) that usually takes place in a hospital or similar medical facility (Ray & Ksir, 2004). The other model, which is primarily behavioral in nature, attempts to treat substance abuse by changing the patterns of behavior and/or characteristics of the individual that lead him or her to abuse drugs. This "resocialization" process involves long-term, round-the-clock, in-patient care lasting from as little as 1 month to 2 years or more (DeLeon, 1995).

Although there are many distinct residential treatment programs, the most notable are relatively short-term (28-day) in-patient programs that are based on the Minnesota Model (e.g., Hazelden, the Betty Ford Center) and the longer-term residential programs known as therapeutic communities. Most of these short-term residential programs are based on the 12-step program of Alcoholics Anonymous (A.A.); we therefore discuss the rationale behind them in the section on A.A. below. One notable difference between exclusive A.A. programs and residential programs, however, is that residential programs provide patients with a month or so "in residence" while they dry out in a drug-free environment (Faupel et al., 2004). Conversely, therapeutic communities (TCs) typically involve recommended stays of between 1 and 2 years. Although TCs are by no means the only form of long-term residential treatment, they have served as the model upon which most residential treatment approaches have been based, and they have also been implemented in a number of jail and prison settings.

Therapeutic Communities

The roots of the TC can be traced to Synanon, a drug treatment program that advocated the complete separation of the addict from the broader society for a long period of time. Synanon was founded in 1958 by Charles Dederich, a former alcoholic and member of Alcoholics Anonymous who, in promoting Synanon, coined the phrase "Today is the first day of the rest of your life" (Clark, 1999). In the late 1950s, A.A. had not yet begun to provide significant treatment resources for those addicted to substances other than alcohol, prompting Dederich to create Synanon. Although it was developed to treat addiction to drugs other than alcohol, Dederich drew on some of the principles of A.A. in creating Synanon, including the view that an addict was never truly cured of his addiction (Ray & Ksir, 2004). Accordingly, Dederich initially envisaged "recovery" from addiction as requiring 2 years of residence in the Synanon program before an individual was able to "graduate" back into the larger society.

Similar to modern TC approaches, a key part of treatment in Synanon involved encouraging patients to work, pursue their academic education (within the program), and generally better themselves. However, perhaps the most distinctive feature of Synanon was "the Game," a form of group therapy in which aggressive verbal confrontation between members was encouraged and even required to break down the person's built-up defenses, excuses, and rationalizations regarding drug use (Akers, 1992). Part of this included what has been referred to as the "Synanon encounter," a process in which the whole group would turn on a particular member and make that person the focus of the verbal attack in order to facilitate his or her "growth" (Rowan, 2001). As will be discussed in more detail below, this confrontational style of group therapy and the rationale underlying it are key features of most TCs in existence today.

As noted above, Synanon began as a treatment program that aimed to graduate drug users back into the larger society in roughly 2 years. However, Dederich later came to conclude that Synanon members could never graduate, claiming that because addiction was incurable, people with this "fatal disease" would be forced to remain in the program for the rest of their lives (Ofshe, 1980). Although Synanon was initially praised by the national media as a success story, not long after its inception, Synanon began to move away from its initial focus on drug treatment and toward an overall approach to life (Clark, 1999). An increasing number of Synanon members were nondrug users who joined the organization because of the rigidly structured way of living it offered. The story of Synanon grew increasingly bizarre in the late 1960s and 1970s as it began to progressively morph into more of a cult-like organization in which Dederich exercised tremendous control over the members (Clark, 1999; Dougherty, 1996). Although the earlier version of Synanon actually graduated only 26 members in its first 5 years of existence (Lemanski, 1999), in Synanon II, as it was called, Dederich began to increasingly resist the practice of sending "patients" back into the larger society. These members became the workforce for what eventually became a multimillion-dollar corporation (Clark, 1999; Dougherty, 1996).

As part of his attempt to further increase his control over Synanon, and ostensibly due to the importance of the "community family," Dederich ordered married couples in the group to split up and instructed each person to take on a new partner (Clark, 1999). He also separated parents from their children, with the children being cared for in dorms by Synanon teachers. In 1977, shortly before the collapse of the group, all male Synanon members who had been in the group for at least 5 years were ordered to have vasectomies (excepting Dederich), and in 1975, Synanon declared itself a religion (Lemanski, 1999). The disintegration of the group was hastened when Dederich and other Synanon members were involved in the attempted murder of several people, including a situation in which Synanon members beat a former member (a "splittee") so severely that he went into a coma. In another incident, Dederich himself pleaded no contest to a conspiracy to commit murder charge, and although he was able to avoid prison as a result of his plea, he was forced to relinquish control of Synanon. Ironically, in his 1982 plea, Dederich admitted, "I don't know how to cure a dope fiend. I never did" (as quoted in Dougherty, 1996).

Despite Synanon's problems, several components of its philosophy have been adopted by most residential treatment programs and remain widely used today. Consistent with the Synanon model, TCs advocate long-term residential stays, frequently as long as 2 years, although funding shortages have reduced the length of stay offered by many programs to only a year (NIDA, 2005). Although there are numerous distinct TC programs (e.g., Walden House, Gateway House, Daytop Village, Marathon House), they can all be distinguished from other approaches to drug treatment in two fundamental ways. As noted by DeLeon (1994), TCs are distinct because "first, the TC offers a systematic approach that is guided by an explicit perspective on the *drug use disorder, the person, recovery, and right living*. Second, the primary therapist and teacher in the TC is the *community* itself" (p. 18).

In practice, several elements or principles are emphasized in TC drug treatment programs. These include community separateness; fostering of a community environment; the participation of members in community activities; peers and staff as community members; a highly structured workday; work as therapy and education; and, most distinguishing, purposive use of the peer community to facilitate social and psychological change in individuals (DeLeon, 1995). As part of this, abstinence from drugs is a central norm espoused in the TC, so these programs are typically completely drug free (although the use of caffeine and nicotine are sometimes exceptions to this rule; DeLeon, 1994). Importantly, the emphasis placed on complete abstinence means that recovering opiate addicts who are being treated with methadone cannot simultaneously be treated in a TC.

An additional central trait of TCs is that they typically do not view drug abuse as the main problem in need of treatment but rather as one *symptom* of broader problems that afflict the individual (DeLeon, 1994). As DeLeon notes:

> Drug abuse is regarded as a disorder of the whole person. . . . Although individuals differ in their choice of substances, abuse involves some or all of the areas of functioning. Cognitive, behavioral, and mood disturbances appear, as do medical problems; thinking may be unrealistic or disorganized; and values are confused, non-existent, or antisocial. . . . Finally, whether couched in existential or psychological terms, moral issues are apparent. (p. 18)

Thus, TCs are based on the assumption that the person seeking treatment is in some way deficient; as a result, treatment "may be characterized as an organized effort to resocialize the client" (Tims, Jainchill, & DeLeon, 1994, p. 2). Resocialization is termed either habilitation or rehabilitation, depending on whether the particular client has ever adopted values that are believed to be "associated with socialized living" (NIDA, 2005), and this socialization process emphasizes the importance of "right living" (DeLeon, 1994). According to the TC model, "right living" means adhering to specific values that include "truth and honesty (in work and deed), work ethic, learning to learn, personal accountability, economic self-reliance, responsible concern for peers, family responsibility, community involvement, and good citizenry" (DeLeon, 1994, p. 20).

As noted, the process of resocializing individuals toward right living involves the use of the peer community; thus, other members of the TC are seen as central in achieving social and psychological change in the particular person (DeLeon, 1994). In practice, this involves the use of confrontation therapy, developed in the Synanon model, in which "authentic" and brutally honest responses are considered the responsibility of all members of the group (DeLeon, 1994). The objective of this process of confrontation is believed to be important as it serves to "heighten individual awareness of specific attitudes or behavioral patterns that should be modified" (DeLeon, 1994, p. 26). It is thought that when forced to confront unpleasant issues, a member will eventually correct the "deficiencies in his/her character" that have caused him/her problems throughout their life, including substance dependency (Tims et al., 1994).

As individuals increasingly adopt the values and norms of the community—honesty, responsibility, personal accountability, and the like—they assume more independence and begin the "re-entry" process to the broader society (DeLeon, 1994). Re-entry into society typically requires the person to be enrolled in school or to be employed, and once leaving the TC, the individual generally remains involved in "post-residence aftercare services" (such as counseling) through the TC (NIDA, 2005). Additionally, TC members are also often encouraged to attend self-help support groups, such as Alcoholics or Narcotics Anonymous, upon returning to the broader society.

As might be expected, due to the long-term, round-the-clock care associated with treatment in a TC, the cost of this approach is substantially higher than the cost of other forms of drug treatment (Hubbard et al., 1989; Roebuck et al., 2003). However, TCs have been found to be effective in treating many substance abusers. Although the efficacy of TCs in terms of their self-prescribed goals to resocialize the client into total abstinence, good citizenry, and similar outcomes are difficult to empirically assess and unlikely to occur in even the best cases, we can assess the effectiveness of TCs in terms of more traditional measures. As noted earlier, these measures of treatment efficacy include reduced drug use, reduced criminal activity, and increased steady employment. Condelli and Hubbard (1994) examined these issues, concluding that TCs were effective in producing moderate reductions in drug use, criminal activity, and unemployment in the months following treatment, but that length of stay was important for positive outcomes, particularly among the most disadvantaged clients.

More recently, a comprehensive review of dozens of previous studies examining a broad spectrum of TCs confirmed that, overall, drug offenders treated in TCs had lower rates of recidivism and future drug use than those not receiving treatment but also specifically noted that those benefits were far from universal and were often relatively small (Bahr et al., 2012). Another meta-analysis focusing on evaluations employing rigorous methods produced similar findings (Welsh, 2010). However, the improved precision also led to stronger evidence that benefits of TCs are more often reaped by high risk or high motivation prisoners, while those with either low risk (such as many marijuana offenders) or low motivation are considerably less likely to benefit (Welsh, 2010). Furthermore, individuals treated at TCs have also been found to have a pattern of gradually diminishing motivation followed by subsequently diminishing gains in psychosocial functioning, a trend linked to the common requirement that participants must publically acknowledge their own inability to control their drug use (Welsh, 2010). At the same time, research also suggests potential solutions to these shortcomings, as effective motivational interviews can offset this pattern and keep many participants engaged (McMurran, 2009).

Broadly speaking, research by Hubbard and associates (2003) found that long-term residential drug treatment (including but not limited to TCs) is associated with positive outcomes, even after treatment ends. At both 1- and 5-year junctures after leaving treatment, in-patient program participants were less likely to report a variety of problematic behaviors and outcomes, including drug use, predatory criminal behavior, risky sexual behavior, and unemployment. As seen in Table 8.1, rates of cocaine and heroin use did increase substantially between the 1- and 5-year follow-ups, even for residential treatment recipients, but those who had residential treatment still had much lower rates of drug use after 5 years than upon admission to treatment (Hubbard et al., 2003).

Even as numerous studies suggest a degree of overall treatment efficacy produced by residential programs and especially TCs, it is important to note that many of these studies did not include outcome measures for patients who dropped out of treatment in the early stages of the program. As such, treatment "success" figures apply only to a subset of the drug treatment population and likely exclude some of the hardest to treat (Hubbard et al., 2003).

COMPULSORY TREATMENT PROGRAMS

The term *compulsory treatment* refers to a wide variety of legally coerced drug treatment strategies. As Faupel and colleagues (2004) note, compulsory treatment is based on the philosophy that certain populations of drug users will not seek treatment themselves or will not remain in treatment once they have entered it. Some believe these individuals must be forced to enter drug treatment "for their own benefit but especially for the benefit of the community" (p. 396). Although broad in its application, the term *compulsory treatment* is used to refer to:

> [R]equired drug treatment and also a variety of legal and quasi-legal incentives for such treatment. It might refer to a probation officer's recommendation to enter treatment; a judge's order to enter treatment as a condition of probation; the option provided by a judge of entering treatment as an alternative to prison; or a mandatory treatment program while in prison. (Faupel et al., 2004, p. 395)

Among the earliest forms of compulsory treatment were the federal narcotics hospitals or "narcotics farms" that opened in Lexington, Kentucky, in 1935 and Fort Worth, Texas, in 1938. Following the passage of the Harrison Act in 1914 (and similar to the present situation), federal prisons had become increasingly overcrowded with drug offenders, and the facilities in Lexington and Fort Worth offered the government an alternative for dealing with such offenders (Musto, 1999). Because the narcotics hospitals were intended primarily for convicted drug offenders, they functioned like minimum-security prisons, yet at any given time, about half the individuals in these facilities were voluntary patients (Musto, 1999). Treatment in these facilities "consisted primarily of gradually weaning patients from heroin with decreasing dosages of morphine" and later, methadone (Faupel et al., 2004, p. 377), and research on their effectiveness found exceptionally high relapse/failure rates, with 6-month relapse rates often exceeding 90% (for reviews, see Musto, 1999; Task Force on Narcotics and Drug Abuse, 1967, 2002). As state and local drug treatment alternatives became more widely available, the facilities in Fort Worth and Lexington were eventually closed and transformed into formal prisons in 1971 and 1974, respectively (Kosten & Gorelick, 2002).

Compulsory treatment strategies have become increasingly popular in recent years due in part to the tremendous economic strain placed on federal and state governments by the War on Drugs and the resulting need to find more economically feasible options for addressing societal drug problems (NIDA, 1999). Although it is essential to discuss compulsory drug treatment strategies in any comprehensive discussion of drug treatment, it is also important to recognize legally coerced treatment is inherently incomparable to the other treatment modalities discussed in this chapter. Compulsory treatment is controversial for a variety of reasons, including the ethical and legal questions it raises with respect to whether it is appropriate to force someone to accept treatment for drug use (Gomart, 2002). In addition, it is difficult to determine whether compulsory treatment is effective (Faupel et al., 2004; Hubbard et al., 1989) because its coercive nature both hampers and encourages treatment success (Hubbard et al., 1989; Lipton, 1995).

As noted earlier, an individual's motivation to change is one of the most important predictors of treatment success. Since individuals participating in compulsory treatment are almost always under criminal justice supervision, "they may not be willing participants in the treatment process" (Hubbard et al., 1989, p. 130). Accordingly, the effect that coercion has on individuals' willingness to engage in treatment is likely to influence treatment outcomes—particularly long-term outcomes—among some patients. However, length of time spent in treatment is one of the most important factors in terms of treatment outcomes, and in this respect, the coercive element can be seen as beneficial because "clients under legal coercion generally stay in treatment longer than those who are not" (Lipton, 1995, p. 46).

Although the efficacy of compulsory treatment is to some degree debated (as discussed in more detail below), the economic benefits (and, to a certain degree, the social control effects) of this approach when compared to incarceration alone have prompted an increasing emphasis on compulsory treatment in recent years (Lipton, 1995; NIDA, 1999). Despite this, many researchers still report a large discrepancy between the number of individuals in the criminal justice system who need treatment and the number of treatment slots available (Chandler, Fletcher, & Volkow, 2009; Mosher & Phillips, 2006; Taxman, 2008; Wormer & Persson, 2010).

The recent expansion of pharmacotherapeutic approaches to drug treatment (discussed earlier in this chapter) has led some to question whether these drugs might be forced upon the substantial number of individuals in jail or prison who have substance abuse problems. There is little doubt that these populations are at particular risk of being forced to take these drugs as an "alternative" to incarceration. A similar approach has been selectively used in the treatment of sex offenders with medications designed to regulate hormones (CCLE, 2004).

The many distinct forms of compulsory treatment can be broadly categorized into those that are prison based and those that are community based. Prison-based programs obviously take place within prisons, but their specific approach to drug treatment might involve drug education classes, self-help programs, treatment based on the therapeutic community model, or some combination of these (NIDA, 1999). One of the more notable prison-based programs is Stay'N Out, a prison-based therapeutic community that isolates prisoners enrolled in the program from the general prison population (Lipton, 1995; NIDA, 1999). Research has found Stay'N Out and similar prison-based therapeutic communities to be effective in reducing rates of recidivism among released prisoners (Knight, Simpson, & Hiller, 1999; Mosher & Phillips, 2006; Wexler, Falkin, Lipton, & Rosenbaum, 1992; Wexler, Melnick, Lowe, & Peters, 1999; Wexler & Williams, 1986). It has also become evident that aftercare that reinforces cognitive and behavioral changes is imperative to maintaining treatment success for those re-entering society after prison. In a natural experiment comparing traditional release and community-treated ex-offenders, those receiving aftercare were more often employed and had 5-year abstinence rates three times higher than those who did not receive aftercare services (Butzin, Martin, & Inciardi, 2005).

Table 8.1   Effectiveness of Drug Treatment: Behaviors and Outcomes 1 and 5 Years After Treatment

Behavior or Outcome	Outpatient Methadone (n=432)			Long-Term Residential (n = 331)			Short-Term Inpatient (n = 266)			Outpatient Drug Free (n = 364)		
	Pre-admission (%)	1-year follow-up (%)	5-year follow-up (%)	Pre-admission (%)	1-year follow-up (%)	5-year follow-up (%)	Pre-admission (%)	1-year follow-up (%)	5-year follow-up (%)	Pre-admission (%)	1-year follow-up (%)	5-year follow-up (%)
Heroin use	91.0	24.1	31.1	17.3	2.5	9.7**	9.0	3.8	4.2	7.7	3.9	5.5
Cocaine use	45.1	21.7	20.9	65.4	18.2	26.0**	61.7	18.2	16.2	37.4	13.8	17.3
Marijuana use	15.8	13.1	13.9	24.5	11.9	16.3	34.2	12.6	14.0	27.0	11.6	18.7*
Problem alcohol use	16.4	15.9	10.2	36.3	14.4	14.2	51.3	21.1	16.5	32.5	14.9	13.2
Suicidal thought/attempt	14.6	12.3	14.8	22.7	10.2	10.3	30.8	15.4	16.9	21.7	11.3	15.4
Predatory illegal acts	31.2	14.3	12.7	40.1	15.3	15.7	16.3	7.7	5.6	24.3	9.8	8.5
Sexual risk behavior	27.3	12.7	17.6	48.5	26.7	26.7	37.0	20.2	20.8	33.3	25.4	17.9*
Full-time work	14.9	19.1	25.1*	10.6	25.5	36.4**	51.4	43.9	54.3**	18.0	33.2	42.3*
Health limitations	37.5	32.6	34.7*	29.3	21.8	13.3*	30.5	22.6	13.2**	31.6	19.0	19.2

SOURCE: From Hubbard, R., Craddock, S. G., & Anderson, J. (2003). Overview of 5-Year Follow-Up Outcomes in the Drug Abuse Treatment Outcome Studies (DATOS). *Journal of Substance Abuse Treatment, 25,* 125–134, A9 2003. Reprinted with permission of Elsevier.

* $p < .05$; ** $p < .01$—Differences between 1-year and 5-year follow-up percentages tested using paired *t*-tests.

In contrast to prison-based programs that largely involve the application of traditional treatment strategies to incarcerated populations, community-based treatment strategies are diversionary programs designed to allow substance-abusing offenders to avoid incarceration. Among the most popular and widespread of these diversionary programs are drug courts. The first drug court was created in Miami (FL) in 1989, providing the inspiration for more than 2,600 drug courts in every state by the end of 2011. Among them are many spin-off specialty courts, including 458 juvenile drug courts, 329 for families, 192 DUI courts, 95 for veterans, as well as dozens each serving Native American tribes, re-entry, mental health service recipients, and even college campuses (National Drug Court Resource Center; www.ndcrc.org).

Estimates can be found claiming that two-thirds of inmates are drug "abusers" who "need treatment" (Bureau of Justice Statistics, 2003), but such figures should be interpreted carefully. Often, loose definitions and measurements inflate these estimates, particularly those involving official government data. For instance, the National Institute of Drug Abuse defines "drug abuse" as "any illicit use of a substance" (NIDA, 2011).

Especially loose are official definitions related to drug treatment, as central concepts like dependence and treatment need are measured using brief survey questions that supposedly represent the hypothetical clinical observations of symptoms described for use by clinical psychiatrists in the *DSM-IV*. It is likely that inaccurate estimates result from the application of such terms, particularly with the application of even broader definitions when marijuana and alcohol are involved. Abuse of those substances officially is defined as any use on 6 or more days in a month, a situation that also indicates a need for treatment (SAMHSA, 2011a). Additionally, binge drinking includes anyone having five or more alcoholic drinks on one occasion even once in a month, a designation further indicating alcohol abuse, and drinking five such beverages in a sitting only five times officially qualifies one for the most serious designations of heavy drinking, dependence, and being in need of treatment. (SAMHSA, 2011a)

Although there is considerable variation across programs with respect to who is eligible to participate, drug courts typically deal with "offenders with a long history of drug use and criminal justice system contacts, previous treatment failures, and high rates of health and social problems" (Belenko, 2001, p. 1). In comparison to the traditional legal model, drug courts are based on more of a "restorative justice" or "therapeutic jurisprudence" paradigm, meaning that the legal process in these courts is less about assigning blame and punishment and more about achieving positive change in the life of the offender (Jensen & Mosher, 2006; Turner et al., 2002). Offenders are expected to participate in drug treatment as a condition of avoiding prison, with the understanding that sanctions (including the possibility of incarceration) may result if they do not comply with the requirements of the treatment program as agreed upon in court (Turner et al., 2002). Drug courts use this threat of sanctions in combination with rewards for successfully meeting various treatment goals to help keep the offender motivated to participate in treatment.

Generally, offenders in such programs appear more frequently in front of judges and are required to enter into an intensive treatment program; undergo frequent, random urinalysis; undergo sanctions for failure to comply with program requirements; are encouraged to become drug-free; and are encouraged to develop vocational and other skills to promote re-entry into the community. Most studies assessing the effectiveness of drug courts have found them to be reasonably effective at reducing drug use and recidivism among treated populations, at least in the short term (Bahr et al., 2012; Belenko, 2001; Shaffer, 2011; U.S. Government Accountability Office, 2005a, 2005c, 2011).

Perhaps more importantly, many studies have lauded drug courts for producing significant cost savings when compared to incarceration (Downey & Roman, 2010; Washington State Institute for Public Policy, 2002). For example, the California Department of Alcohol and Drug Programs reported in 2002 that the $15 million annual investment in drug courts saved taxpayers at least $43 million. In New York, processing 18,000 offenders in drug courts reportedly saved an estimated $254 million in prison-related expenses (von Zielbauer, 2003a). Such financial benefits are derived through incarceration costs avoided, familial and job stability created by treatment, and health costs not incurred. As a result of evidence showing success early in their history, drug courts became institutionalized by the Department of Justice (DOJ) as a primary component of the national drug control strategy, which officially occurred via a 1997 publication outlining the 10 key components of these courts. This push has continued, as drug courts are highlighted as exemplars in the move toward evidence-based practice, while the drug court model continues to spread via funding support directly backed by the Office of National Drug Control Policy under the Obama administration (ONDCP, 2012).

Despite ongoing support from many authorities and researchers, drug courts have also come under increased criticism recently, including public denouncements from the National Association of Criminal Defense Lawyers (2009), the Justice Policy Institute (2011), and Drug Policy Alliance (2011). While few doubt that drug courts represent great improvement over strictly punitive responses to drug law violations, criticisms have mounted challenging the strength of supporting evidence, their perpetuation of racial and ethnic inequities in the criminal justice system, and the societal costs accrued during the intensive and lengthy programs.

While still less financially and socially costly than imprisonment, recent research evidence increasingly suggests that early proclamations describing immense success in drug courts were exaggerated and that they are not as exemplary of evidence-based practice as originally believed. Early studies demonstrating such success appear to have inflated the magnitude to which recidivism and drug use were reduced for various reasons, such as failing to include proper comparison groups, disqualifying more problematic offenders, and creating selection bias by disregarding during analysis those who failed to complete the program (Drug Policy Alliance, 2011). Two separate meta-analyses relying only on methodologically sound studies still found reductions in recidivism, but they were only 9% (Shaffer, 2011) and 12% (Mitchell et al., 2012). Clearly, this is much less than the 75% reduction claimed by the National Association of Drug Court Professionals (NADCP.org). Other studies have called into question the long-term benefits, such as an evaluation of a Florida drug court that found benefits were not evident until 1 year after program inception and were no longer significant after 18 months (Krebs, Lindquist, Koetse, & Lattimore, 2007).

There is also great variation in drug court programs' format and efficacy, thus limiting the positive impact of this model in some settings and for some groups. Overall, juvenile drug courts consistently fail to improve future offending or drug use outcomes, likely because many juvenile clients often do not have substance abuse issues but are forced to participate following minor charges (often marijuana possession). Likewise, DUI-oriented courts generally fail to reduce drunk driving among chronic offenders (Bouffard et al., 2010).

Ultimately, drug courts do not appear to be as reliant upon scientific evidence as many proponents claim, and research often finds that they may not represent the most efficient or effective of the available treatment strategies. Examination of a wide range of drug court programs by Shaffer (2011) found that only about one-third actually qualified as evidence-based practices, perhaps the fundamental characteristic of the model. Additionally, there were considerable shortcomings in the application of practices known to improve program success, as the majority (55%) lacked inpatient treatment facilities entirely, nearly half (45%) lacked post-treatment support, and only 30% used formal reward systems to promote behavioral change. Other treatment modalities have more overall impact because drug courts often pass over the clients with the most to gain and many have high rates of non-completion, leaving numerous clients without anything to show for their efforts (Justice Policy Institute, 2011). An independent meta-analysis of 545 treatment programs by the Washington State Institute for Public Policy (including 57 drug courts) demonstrated that recidivism was reduced virtually equally by community-based treatment programs (9%) and twice as much by community programs with intensive supervision (18%) compared to drug courts (Drake, Aos, & Miller, 2009). The accompanying cost-benefit analysis also found that community treatment options yielded approximately 10 times as much in savings per dollar spent and that drug courts were more expensive than any strategy besides incarceration (Drake, Aos, & Miller, 2009). Considering the central place of economic value in the promotion of drug courts, this is especially strong evidence that drug courts may not deserve all of the claims crediting them as a utopian solution.

Additionally, there is mounting evidence of class, gender, and racial/ethnic biases being further institutionalized as a result of inequities found in drug courts. Research suggests that these programs may reproduce class stratification, as those who are unemployed or undereducated are less likely to complete drug court programs (Brown, 2010), and individuals with already limited financial resources and employment opportunities are further burdened by the intensive reporting and transportation requirements (Drug Policy Alliance, 2011). This is especially true for single mothers, as the majority of programs do not offer childcare services or female-oriented counseling (Justice Policy Institute, 2011).

Racial and ethnic disparities are also commonplace. African Americans also appear to be less likely to complete drug court programs (Brown, Zuelsdorff, & Gassman, 2009; McKean & Warren-Gordon, 2011), and nonwhite graduates of juvenile drug courts do not experience the same recidivism benefits as whites (Carter & Barker, 2011). A shortage of culturally sensitive programming for people of color has been noted (Justice Policy Institute, 2011), as well as a reduced likelihood of program inclusion and evidence of harsher sanctioning of minorities for rule violations (McKean & Warren-Gordon, 2011).

The harshest criticisms of drug courts have focused upon the broader social impacts created by forcing so many nonviolent, first-time offenders into coerced treatment and lengthy court programs. This process is increasingly seen as contributing to heightened social control by the court system via two mechanisms: "net widening" and "mesh tightening." Net widening refers to the broadening of criminal justice influence as an increasing number of citizens are brought into the system, a pattern that some researchers suggest is partially due to the public's presumptions about the benefits associated with a policy aimed at treatment rather than incarceration. The benevolent intentions attached to the belief that all drug users need treatment has, according to some researchers, contributed to an observed growth in drug arrests and drug prosecutions (Gardiner, 2008; Hoffman, 1999). Further evidence of net widening can be seen in an increasing focus by law enforcement on marijuana possession, as the marijuana arrests nearly doubled between 1990 and 2007, despite an overall decline in arrests for all offenses (Gettman, 2009). In fact, there were 853,838 arrests just for marijuana in 2010, a total that represents 52% of all drug arrests, and 88% of the resulting charges were for misdemeanor possession (FBI, 2011).

A mesh-tightening effect has occurred due to the increased formality and intensive monitoring used in drug courts, making it harder to exit the system's net once enrolled in a drug court program. Drug court clients receive greater scrutiny than traditional prisoners, probationers, or average citizens, so officials tend to discover and sanction minor offenses that previously went unnoticed or were ignored. This stems largely from the drug court movement's focus on altering behavior patterns via a system of punishments and rewards that is widely considered to be one of the greatest strengths of this model. However, it has been recklessly applied and now often involves almost daily reporting, urinalyses up to four times per week, and formal sanctions for even minor violations of program rules like failing to complete written essays. Thus, a few relatively insignificant mistakes, such as a misdemeanor marijuana charge followed by a positive marijuana screening, an incomplete assignment, and a missed check-in appointment, may lead to mandatory treatment, an addict label, and years in a drug court program.

Research on referrals, treatment admissions, and sentencing appear to confirm this mesh tightening, reflecting both elevated scrutiny of minor offenders and harsher, more formal responses to minor offenses. In a nationwide survey of prosecutors, marijuana charges were found to lead to treatment most often, especially for juveniles, while cocaine charges are more likely to lead to punitive sanctions

(Terry-McElrath & McBride, 2004). This trend represents an inappropriate application of harm-reduction principles, because marijuana is associated with very little risk (Guastaferro, 2012) and intensive treatment for low-risk offenders often increases recidivism (Andrews et al., 1990). Further evidence of increasingly strict enforcement by drug courts is visible in recent treatment admission trends. Between 1992 and 2007, court-mandated referrals to drug treatment grew from 33% to 37% of all admissions and from 38% to 47% of admissions involving juveniles. Much of this growth has also been for clients whose most dangerous drug use involves marijuana, as court-ordered treatment was due to "marijuana dependence" 56% of the time and cannabis was deemed the primary substance of abuse more than twice as often for treatment mandated by drug courts as it was for all other admissions (SAMHSA, 2009).

Greater difficulty has been experienced by many clients attempting to complete drug court programs as a result of more formally sanctioning minor violations, a trend evident in two studies finding harsher sentences were ultimately received by clients who entered drug courts but failed to complete the program than by offenders who initially pled guilty (Bowers, 2008; Gottfredson, Najaka, & Kearly, 2003).

Due to net widening and mesh tightening, some describe drug courts as mechanisms of increased social control that lessen the freedom and independence of otherwise law-abiding individuals without a history or any indicator of substance abuse. Though extreme, scholars have noted the similarly intensified social control effects due to drug courts' use of high-tech urinalysis tests that recognize the byproducts of alcohol metabolism from up to three days earlier. Other tests involve digital ankle monitors that sense alcohol in clients' perspiration, relaying a signal immediately if triggered by a positive reading or tampering, providing no opportunity for client communication in the process (Franceschina, 2005). These tests are applied indiscriminately to clients above 21 years old without any alcohol related charges or any evidence of alcohol abuse, often sanctioning adults for drinking legally in the process. While some testing is certainly necessary, such intensive monitoring drives up program costs without improving outcomes (Holloway, Bennett, & Farrington, 2005).

The incorporation in drug courts of the medical model of addiction that treats substance use as a disease amplifies these social control effects by institutionalizing a medicalized view of substance abuse, automatically labeling clients addicts, and justifying coerced treatment. Often, individuals charged with misdemeanor drug possession alone enroll in drug courts while seeking to avoid the stigma of a conviction but instead receive the stigma of an addict label (Murphy, 2011). Consequently, scientific credibility is sometimes enforced and engrained without merit, legitimizing what is otherwise seen as overly invasive monitoring by deeming it a necessary mechanism to avoid relapse (Murphy, 2011). The widespread application of components from A.A. is also complicit in controlling clients, as most participants are required by drug court programs to acknowledge personal helplessness over their addictions. Shaffer (2011) suggests that this mandate can often limit the potential benefits of treatment by limiting clients' sense of agency.

> [A] shift from moral judgment to therapeutic sympathy is particularly unlikely for the fast-growing mass of criminal offenders whose diagnosis is spearheaded by the state in the form of the … drug court. For this group, the emphasis on the need for comprehensive resocialization and the close cooperation between the intimacies of therapeutic "rehab" and the strong arm of criminal justice "backup" not only maintains, but intensifies, moral tutelage and stigmatization. The convergence of drug treatment and criminal justice tends to produce yet another stigmatizing biologization of poverty and race, lending scientific validity to new forms of criminalizing and medicalizing social hardship. (Whetstone & Gowan, 2011, pp. 309–310)

As with drug courts, a belief that alternatives to incarceration can provide more cost-effective sanctions for substance-abusing offenders provided the motivation behind California's Proposition 36 (the Substance Abuse and Crime Prevention Act [SACPA]), which was enacted in 2000 with support from 61% of voters. This legislation offers drug treatment in lieu of incarceration for individuals convicted of nonviolent drug offenses or drug-related violations of parole and probation, but it does not permit diversion for those charged with drug-trafficking, violent, or other felony offenses (Uelmen et al., 2002).

Proposition 36's impacts have been both negative and positive according to subsequent research, but the law became increasingly controversial among citizens, who often focused upon the undesirable consequences and shortcomings. For instance, initial confusion about the requirements during the first month of the law's implementation led to bench warrants for 30% of those pleading guilty and agreeing to treatment after they failed to report to treatment centers or return to court for progress reviews (Butterfield, 2001a). Analysis of subsequent offending in 13 counties also found that those receiving diversionary sentences had higher re-arrest rates for drug crimes than non-participants (Farabee, Hser, Anglin, & Huang, 2005).

Some of the blame for these negative outcomes can be attributed to systemwide institutional failures, as criminal justice authorities inhibited the potential benefits of this law by actively circumventing the legislative spirit in favor of maintaining punitive traditions, a troubling pattern exaggerated by a lack of resources for effective treatment and aftercare (Gardiner, 2008). As a result, numerous eligible defendants opted out of Proposition 36 and instead chose to plead guilty under previous statutes providing relatively brief prison or even just probationary sentences for simple drug possession convictions. This was often preferential to the blanket requirements of the law, which required treatment that usually lasted several months or more and mandated elevated monitoring and considerably longer prison sentences for re-arrest or probation violations than had previously been the norm (Butterfield, 2001a).

At the same time, as was noted by Appel and colleagues (2005), increased recidivism does not necessarily indicate program failure, and Proposition 36 also produced numerous benefits. More than 60,000 people who previously would have been subject to incarceration received drug treatment in just the first 2 years of implementation of Proposition 36 (Longshore et al., 2004), saving the state of California approximately $275 million during the first year of operation (Drug Policy Alliance, 2006c). Additionally, the most commonly used drug among SACPA clients was methamphetamine, leading Appel and associates (2005) to suggest that higher recidivism among diversion clients may have been partially due to resource and training shortages and the subsequent difficulties in treating a population with elevated needs and risks.

Despite the growing criticism regarding drug courts and other alternative-to-incarceration models, a number of other compulsory treatment programs have shown considerable promise in recent years. For instance, the Engaging Moms Program has been found to produce better outcomes than family drug courts in terms of program completion and positive child welfare dispositions (Dakof et al., 2010). This approach appears to improve voluntary treatment retention and family functioning as well, all due to an increased personalized focus and in-home counseling for individuals and families (Dakof et al., 2010).

Also showing considerable promise is Project HOPE (Hawaii's Opportunity Probation with Enforcement), a less intensive diversion program tailored to individual clients' needs. Rather than mandating treatment and indiscriminately labeling all participants as addicts requiring treatment, Project HOPE requires probationers to appear in court only after instances of noncompliance and mandates treatment only after a third or fourth "dirty" drug screening. This allows limited financial resources to be focused on intensive treatment and supervision for those clients demonstrating genuine need. Despite enacting considerably fewer punitive sanctions, failure to comply with program requirements was not a problem for HOPE, with the efficient use of resources instead extending the impact of those funds. An independent evaluation involving randomized, controlled trials found that HOPE was much more effective than traditional sentencing by various measures, with participants experiencing 55% fewer re-arrests, 72% fewer failed drug tests, 61% fewer missed check-ins, and a 53% reduction in the number of parole revocations (Hawken & Kleiman, 2009). Though not compared directly to a drug court, the outcomes observed in this evaluation amount to much larger gains relative to traditional sentencing than are found in even the most successful drug courts. HOPE also improves upon the drug court model by inspiring the support of court professionals from every position. HOPE's follow-up survey found that the program was rated as effective and desirable by the vast majority of judges and public defenders (Hawken & Kleiman, 2009).

Providing clients with even greater flexibility and freedom than Project HOPE without sacrificing outcomes, a community-based treatment program known as the Community Reinforcement Approach (CRA) has led to improved client retention during mandatory opioid detoxification, a period known for high attrition rates. By reinforcing in-patient treatment gains through community groups, the early success appears to stem from the opportunity to maintain daily routines and relationships that HOPE offers clients (Abbott, 2009). By improving outcomes through community-based treatment, CRA's success echoes the results of Shaffer's (2011) meta-analysis and provides further evidence of the potential improvements to outcomes and cost efficiency locally oriented approaches can offer.

Although programs such as drug courts, California's SACPA, and Arizona's Drug Medicalization, Prevention and Control Act (Proposition 200, passed by Arizona voters in 1996) remain controversial, coercive drug treatment continues to grow more common in these and other forms. Beyond the strengths and weaknesses of each strategy, it should be remembered that compulsory drug treatment programs are inherently unique and cannot be compared directly to voluntary treatment programs precisely because treatment recipients are required to undergo treatment. The coercive nature of these programs may discourage positive outcomes among many clients while producing numerous broader social consequences. However, their compulsory nature also increases the amount of time typically spent in treatment, potentially leading to improved outcomes for some clients who might otherwise resist treatment. These programs are diverse, and their efficacy varies between treatment strategies, but compulsory treatment is generally more effective and less costly than addressing drug problems with only punitive criminal justice responses (ONDCP, 2001). Because of the financial advantages they offer over incarceration, even growing concerns are unlikely to hinder the ongoing expansion of drug courts in the foreseeable future, potentially accompanied and influenced by even more promising applications of the harm reduction philosophy described above.

ALCOHOLICS ANONYMOUS

Alcoholics Anonymous (A.A.) represents by far the largest voluntary drug treatment program in the world, often serving as the model for other peer-based treatment options. Approximately 1 in 10 adults in the United States have attended an A.A. meeting (for themselves or on behalf of another; Doweiko, 1999). Although A.A. does not keep formal membership files or attendance records, the organization has estimated its current membership at more than two million members, dispersed across more than 150 countries and more than 100,000 separate support groups (A.A., 2005). Although we are aware that A.A. has helped many individuals deal with their problem drinking, it is important to engage in a critical discussion of the central philosophies and tenets of the A.A. model and to examine scientific research on the effectiveness of A.A. in treating those identified as alcoholics.

> Despite the strong abstinence norm of A.A., founder Bill Wilson was an enthusiastic LSD user, believing that the drug could eliminate the "barriers that stood in the way of direct contact with the cosmos and God" (Lemanski, 1999, p. 60). When his use of the drug became public, he claimed that since he had stepped down as the leader of A.A. he should be allowed to live as he chose, but under pressure from A.A. members he eventually quit the use of LSD. (Cheever, 2004)

As discussed in Chapter 2, A.A. was founded in 1935 by Bill Wilson and Robert Smith, alcoholics who had been unable to quit drinking on their own but succeeded with the help and support of each other. Accordingly, A.A. and related groups such as Narcotics Anonymous (N.A.) are peer-based self-help groups in which individuals identified as alcoholics/addicts can attend meetings in their community with other individuals identified as alcoholics/addicts, enabling them to draw on each other for support and understanding in their struggle with addiction. As A.A. members are informed on the utility of this practice in the "Big Book" (the official "manual" of A.A.), "nothing will so much insure immunity from drinking as intensive work with other alcoholics" (A.A., 2005, p. 89).

Based on this philosophy, A.A. meetings are led by recovering alcoholics who have been in the program for some time but (typically) have no formal training in counseling or therapy (McCaul & Furst, 1994). New A.A. members are expected to attend 90 meetings in their first 90 days as part of their "early recovery" phase, with the more experienced members expected to act as "sponsors" who advise and mentor members who have recently joined (McCaul & Furst, 1994). A.A. meetings can be conducted in either an open or closed format. The former are open to nonalcoholic as well as alcoholics and typically involve talks by one or more speakers who share their experiences with alcoholism and their recovery through A.A. (A.A., 2005). Conversely, closed meetings are only for those identified as alcoholics, and to emphasize their anonymous nature, these meetings are typically concluded with the motto "Who you see here, what you hear here, when you leave here, let it stay here" (Faupel et al., 2004).

As noted in Chapter 2, A.A. is based on the disease model of addiction, which considers addiction to be an incurable, degenerative disease (perhaps genetic in origin) that is often fatal if left untreated (Jellinek, 1960). However, critics of the disease model note that the classification of alcoholism/addiction as a disease is problematic because this classification is not based on any measurable physical effects on the body, as is the case with physical illness, or with measured thoughts, feelings, and behaviors, as is the case with mental illness (Peele, 1998).

Because the A.A. philosophy views the alcoholic as being afflicted with an incurable disease that is characterized by a loss of control over alcohol, total abstinence from the drug is seen as the only effective means of treatment (A.A., 2005). This constitutes one of the most controversial aspects of the A.A. model, and a considerable amount of research has concluded that individuals who have been identified as alcoholics are capable of controlling their drinking and leading normal lives without having to resort to complete abstinence from the drug.

One of the first researchers to challenge the abstinence-only philosophy of A.A. was Davies (1962), who found that 7 of 93 male alcoholics who were followed for a period of from 7 to 11 years following treatment reported being able to control their drinking and function normally in society. According to Davies, these individuals had never been drunk over the follow-up period and demonstrated improved human functioning in the domains of employment and family relationships. Subsequent to Davies's study, two studies conducted under the auspices of the Rand

Corporation provided further support for this treatment strategy, known as controlled drinking. The first Rand study involved an 18-month follow-up of alcoholics treated at 44 treatment centers across the United States. It ultimately concluded that "the majority of improved clients are either drinking moderate amounts of alcohol—but at levels far below what could be described as alcoholic drinking— or engaging in alternating periods of drinking and abstention" (Armor, Polich, & Stambul, 1976, p. v). A further 4-year follow-up of these same individuals also found that substantial proportions were still engaged in nonproblem drinking. The findings of this study were seen as a threat to A.A. and its focus on abstinence. Without even reading the full report, the National Council on Alcoholism denounced the report on the morning it was released, describing it as "dangerous" (Peele, 1983).

> In the United States, we hold out the hope that all alcoholics will stop drinking entirely. So far, this has not occurred. But as with sex education aimed at having all children remain virgins, we are committed to the ideal. (Peele, 2000)

Also in the 1970s, Mark and Linda Sobell conducted research on alternative treatments for alcoholism, which generally involved moderation-based treatment wherein subjects identified as alcohol dependent were taught how to drink in a controlled fashion. Individuals trained to engage in controlled drinking had significantly more "days functioning well" during a 2-year follow-up period than those who had experienced abstinence-based treatment (Sobell & Sobell, 1973, 1978). These researchers were criticized by another group, headed by the psychologist Mary Pendery, who conducted a 10-year follow-up of subjects in the Sobells' original study. In an article published in the prestigious journal *Science* in 1982, Pendery, Maltzman, and West essentially accused the Sobells of engaging in fraudulent research and concluded, "a review of the evidence, including official records and new interviews, reveals that most subjects trained to do controlled drinking failed from the outset" (p. 169). The popular CBS show *60 Minutes* also featured a segment that was extremely critical of the Sobells' research. At one point in the program, the narrator (Harry Reasoner) was shown at the grave of one of the patients who had been placed in the original controlled-drinking treatment condition, the implication, of course, being that the controlled-drinking option for those identified as alcoholics results in death. However, as Marlatt (1983) notes, "why didn't [Mr. Reasoner] also visit the graves of patients in the control group who received the abstinence-oriented treatment?" (p. 1106). Although the Pendery and colleagues article noted that 4 of the original 20 subjects in the controlled-drinking condition eventually died from alcohol-related causes, they neglected to note that 6 out of the 20 control (abstinence) subjects also died within the same period. But, as Miller (1986, p. 117) notes, "American professionals who advocate any alternative to abstinence are likely to be (and have been) attacked as naive fools, unwitting murderers, or perhaps themselves alcoholics denying their own disease."

The issue of whether individuals identified as alcoholics can engage in controlled drinking continues to be a controversial one, and at least part of the reason for this controversy is that some of the research on controlled drinking has been misinterpreted as suggesting that all alcohol treatment should allow for moderate consumption as a goal. In fact, advocates of this strategy actually suggest that it be recognized as a legitimate measure of success and offered as a goal for certain individuals. As Marlatt (1983) explains, the Rand studies essentially suggested that (a) controlled drinking may be a more appropriate goal than abstinence for individuals who are not severely dependent on alcohol; but, (b) for those who are older and show signs of chronic physical dependence, abstinence may be the treatment goal of choice. Similarly, Sobell and Sobell (1995) suggest that research on controlled drinking can be summarized by the following statements: (1) Recoveries of individuals who have been severely dependent on alcohol primarily involve abstinence; and (2) recoveries of individuals who have not been severely dependent on alcohol predominately involve reduced drinking. Marlatt (1983) effectively sums up the central paradox in the disease model of alcoholism in commenting:

> Patients in treatment are first told that alcoholism is a disease characterized by an inability to exercise voluntary control over drinking. Once they have accepted the diagnosis they are then told that the only way to arrest the development of this progressive disease is to stop drinking—to assert control by abstaining. (p. 1105)

Alternatively, the harm-minimization philosophy (described in detail in Chapters 11 and 12) provides the rationale that supports inclusion of controlled drinking as a treatment goal and indicator of success, which supporters believe capable of expanding treatment benefits and eliminating more of the social and individual consequences of alcohol abuse. This perspective suggests that since not all problematic drinking involves alcohol dependence and different people experience problems with alcohol in a variety of ways, greater benefits can come from greater inclusion in treatment, therefore necessitating broader treatment options. In fact, studies suggest that fewer than 25% of those with drinking problems ever seek formal help (Dawson et al., 2005), and between two-thirds and three-quarters of those resolving such problems do so without treatment.

Meanwhile, the focus on abstinence-only alcohol treatment appears to exclude many problem drinkers, particularly those who fear the social stigma associated with being labeled an alcoholic, youth, males, and those with less-severe drinking problems or who maintain daily functioning (Cohen, Feinn, Arias, & Kranzler, 2007). In another survey of treatment-seeking clients, nearly half (47%) preferred nonabstinence goals, a desire particularly common among those who were male, employed, experienced fewer alcohol-related problems, and were not alcohol dependent (Heather, Adamson, Raistrick, & Slegg, 2010). A preference for seeking assistance in the anonymous but often less effective realm of online support groups and treatment programs has been found to result from fears of associated stigma, lack of financial resources, and the risk of being coerced into in-patient treatment (Townsend, Gearing, & Polyanskaya, 2012).

In other cases, those who might benefit much sooner respond to this fear by avoiding treatment until forced to participate by courts, family, employers, health, or social consequences (Parhar et al., 2008). Thus, offering treatment options not exclusively aimed at abstinence may attract more individuals to treatment (Hersey, 2001). As Marlatt, Larimer, Baer, and Quigley (1993) comment, "offering controlled drinking alternatives to the general public may act as a motivating push to get people 'in the door,' a low threshold strategy that is consistent with the principles of harm reduction" (p. 483).

A handful of recent studies have examined the effects of controlled drinking treatments, and the results collectively suggest that this goal is attainable for a substantial minority of problem drinkers. Additionally, reduced consumption offers social and health benefits, making it an example of harm minimization, but it is less often maintained and more difficult to achieve for alcohol-dependent individuals. In a study examining long-term outcomes among severely alcohol-dependent patients, a small portion (3.9%) of even severe cases were able to maintain reduced drinking for 10 years and experienced lower mortality rates, better psychosocial functioning, and fewer alcohol-related problems than those who continued to be heavy drinkers (Gual, Bravo, Lligona, & Colom, 2009). Another long-term study of problem drinkers reported even greater controlled-drinking success among subjects who previously sought treatment, finding that 16% to 21% reported drinking without problems at 1-, 8-, and 16-year follow-ups (Ilgen, Wilbourne, Moos, & Moos, 2008).

Additionally, though this was somewhat less stable than those reporting abstinence initially, about half of those who reported controlled drinking after 1 year maintained that success thereafter. Similar success has been found in conjunction with pharmacotherapy treatment, as a meta-analysis of 16 studies involving Acamprosate showed that 39.1% of those receiving treatment were able to subsequently engage in controlled drinking (Lehert & Vanden Brink, 2011).

Successful controlled drinking appears particularly viable as a goal for subjects with less-severe alcohol problems. Among clients with mild to moderate alcohol dependency, Adamson and Sellman (2001) found that more than one-third of those setting controlled-drinking goals within the guidelines of the Alcohol Advisory Council of New Zealand were able to reach those goals. This was only moderately less than the 51.1% who achieved those levels of drinking with abstinence as a goal, and controlled drinking was actually the most common outcome even for those aiming for abstinence. In a study examining the application of reduced drinking strategies by 140 women following an initial 10-week intervention, Mendoza, Walitzer, and Connors (2012) found that controlled-drinking goals predicted reductions in drinking and, although such strategies often became less frequently used during the subsequent 18-month period, booster sessions were able to maintain commitment. Providing the strongest evidence to date, Dawson and colleagues (2007) found that when including all individuals who qualified as having alcohol disorders in a nationally representative sample, the majority of those reporting low-risk drinking goals were able to either maintain moderate consumption (48%) or begin abstinence (18%) after 3 years.

While not suited for all situations, enough evidence exists indicating that controlled drinking can be a successful approach that it led Sobell and Sobell (2011) to explain, "when one considers the full spectrum of alcohol disorders and includes people who were not in treatment (i.e., self-change recoveries) low-risk drinking outcomes occur and are common" (p. 1715).

Applying this approach has led to the development of Moderation Management, a support group that has grown since its 1994 inception, offering clients a free, peer-led support group aimed at successful moderation and "restoration of balance" through four principles: self-management, balance, moderation, and personal responsibility (Kelly & White, 2012; Lembke & Humphreys, 2012).

Like many abstinence-only programs, self-reflection, quality-of-life enhancement, and social reinforcement are central tenets of Moderation Management, and a 1-month abstinence period is expected upon joining to provide sober consideration of how alcohol has impacted one's life. However, Moderation Management is the only organization to officially permit subsequent drinking in moderation, though this must occur according to a predeveloped personal plan, does not permit daily drinking, and must remain within a set of daily and weekly limits that are below levels defined as problem drinking by the U.S. National Institute on Alcohol Abuse and Alcoholism (Kelly & White, 2012). Though no randomized experiments have tested the efficacy of this program compared to abstinence-only treatment, one experiment comparing outcomes for participants with and without the aid of online support found that both groups were able to reduce drinking consequences and consumption levels considerably at each follow-up over a year and that the online support program led to slightly greater gains (Hester, Delaney, & Campbell, 2011).

The fact that controlled-drinking programs have not been widely promoted in the United States is yet another example of American exceptionalism with respect to psychoactive substances. In Canada, 43% of treatment programs allow for moderate drinking for some clients (Shute, 1997). In many European countries, there is less emphasis on alcoholism as a problem associated with sick individuals and more emphasis on the drinking culture at large and limiting the availability of alcohol (Duckert, 1995). In the context of an increasing commitment to harm-reduction strategies in general, this has led to the acceptance and application of controlled-drinking–oriented strategies by many treatment centers and medical professionals in other parts of the world. For instance, a survey of alcohol treatment centers in Norway found that 90% of them allowed residential treatment clients to choose between abstinence and reduced consumption, and 59% did so for outpatient treatment (Duckert, 1995). Likewise, a survey of Swiss programs indicated that a strong majority approved of controlled-drinking goals for patients with lower severity dependence and higher social stability (Klingemann & Rosenberg, 2009).

Measuring treatment success also increasingly involves indicators other than abstinence now that the scientific community generally recognizes the value of reduced drinking as an indicator of treatment success. This ongoing transition has even led to a small but growing level of acceptance in the United States, such as the NIAAA's recognition that reduced heavy drinking, not just abstinence, is beneficial. As Gastfriend, Garbott, Pettinati, and Forman (2007) noted:

Although the goal of total abstinence remains important, reduction in heavy drinking offers numerous benefits, both as an intermediate clinical goal and as a research metric. Given the significant public health consequences associated with heavy drinking and the benefits associated with its reduction, it is proposed that researchers, public health professionals, and clinicians consider reduction in heavy drinking as a meaningful measure of treatment effectiveness. (p. 78)

We now return to a more detailed consideration of the Alcoholics Anonymous model.

The 12 Steps of Alcoholics Anonymous

The 12 steps that supposedly guide recovery from alcoholism under A.A. are as follows:

1. We admitted that we were powerless over alcohol—that our lives had become unmanageable.

2. Came to believe that a Power greater than ourselves could restore us to sanity.

3. Made a decision to turn our will and our lives over to the care of God *as we understood Him.*

4. Made a searching and fearless moral inventory of ourselves.

5. Admitted to God, to ourselves, and to another human being the exact nature of our wrongs.

6. Were entirely ready to have God remove all these defects of character.

7. Humbly asked Him to remove our shortcomings.

8. Made a list of all persons we had harmed, and became willing to make amends to them all.

9. Made direct amends to such people wherever possible, except when to do so would injure them or others.

10. Continued to take personal inventory and when we were wrong promptly admitted it.

11. Sought through prayer and meditation to improve our conscious contact with God, *as we understood Him*, praying only for knowledge of His will for us and the power to carry that out.

12. Having had a spiritual awakening as the result of these steps, we tried to carry this message to alcoholics, and to practice these principles in all our affairs. (A.A., 2005, pp. 59–60)

NOTE: The Twelve Steps and a brief excerpt from the pamphlet *A Newcomer Asks* are reprinted with permission of Alcoholics Anonymous World Services, Inc. (A.A.WS). Permission to reprint a brief excerpt from the pamphlet *A Newcomer Asks* and the Twelve Steps does not mean that A.A.WS has reviewed or approved the contents of this publication or that A.A.WS necessarily agrees with the views expressed herein. A.A. is a program of recovery from alcoholism *only*—use of the Twelve Steps in connection with programs and activities which are patterned after A.A. but which address other problems, or in any other non–A.A. context, does not imply otherwise.

As is evident in these 12 steps, treatment in A.A. is deeply spiritual in nature; half of the steps explicitly mention "God," "a power greater than ourselves," or "Him," and Bill Wilson apparently believed he was acting under divine guidance when he wrote the 12 steps (Ragge, 1992). Clearly, then, the central tenet of A.A. philosophy is that for an alcoholic to be effectively treated, he or she must give up control of his or her life to "a power greater than one's self." This has been one of the central critiques of A.A., but despite the heavy spiritual influence present in A.A., efforts have been made to make the organization more accessible to individuals who have no belief in God. As the A.A. homepage comments on the role of spirituality in treatment:

The majority of A.A. members believe that we have found the solution to our drinking problem not through individual willpower, but through a power greater than ourselves. However, everyone defines this power as he or she wishes. Many people call it God, others think it is the A.A. group, still others don't believe in it at all. There is room in A.A. for people of all shades of belief and nonbelief. (A.A., 2005)

As a result, critiques of A.A. have characterized it as being analogous to a "fanatical religious cult" (Trice & Staudenmeier, 1989). As Marc Galanter comments, "from the start, A.A. displayed characteristics of a charismatic sect: strongly felt shared beliefs, intense cohesiveness, experiences of altered consciousness, and a potent influence on members' behavior" (as quoted in Ragels, 2000). Similarly, George E. Vaillant, a prominent researcher and supporter of A.A., even acknowledged that "A.A. certainly functions as a cult and systematically indoctrinates its members in ways common to cults the world over" (as quoted in Ragels, 2000). This religious fervor is particularly impactful as an increasing number of individuals in the United States are being coerced into A.A. treatment, primarily as a result of DUI convictions and employee-assistance programs. As Brodsky and Peele (1991) suggest, "A.A. and the alcoholism as disease movement it inspired translated American evangelism into a medical world view. . . . We have given government support to group indoctrination, coerced confessions, and massive invasions of privacy" (p. 36). To a certain extent, A.A. members recognize and confirm this in one of the group's clichés, which states, "if A.A. uses brainwashing, then our brains must need to be washed" (Ragels, 2000). While many will not agree with the characterization of A.A. as a cult, it is notable that in every court case initiated by individuals challenging their mandatory A.A. attendance—in Wisconsin, Colorado, Alaska, and Maryland—the courts have ruled that A.A. is equivalent to a religion for First Amendment purposes (Brodsky & Peele, 1991).

> Balanced placebo-design studies conducted by Alan Marlatt and colleagues involved subjects who were identified as alcoholics being deceived about whether they were drinking an alcoholic beverage. Marlatt asked individuals to "taste-rate" three different brands of the same beverage. Unknown to the subjects, they had been assigned to one of four groups. One group was told that the beverage was tonic water, which was true. Individuals in the second group were told that the beverage was vodka and tonic, although it was actually pure tonic water. Those in the third group were told that the beverage was vodka and tonic, which it was; finally, those in the fourth group were told it was tonic water only, when in fact it was vodka and tonic. Importantly, in the context of the central tenet of disease theory and its notion of loss of control, *none* of the alcoholic subjects drank all of the beverage, even though, according to disease theory, those who were drinking vodka ought to have proceeded to drink uncontrollably. (Fingarette, 1990)

The adherence to religious authority central to A.A. also contributes to some logical inconsistencies within the group's indoctrinated 12 steps. The first step involves conceding personal power over addiction, followed by the second step's commitment to a higher power in order to restore sanity. Inconsistent with those two is the third step, requiring that decisions be turned over to the will of said higher power, as this begs the question of how one could turn over power to a higher power when already powerless and dependent upon that higher power for change. Ultimately, A.A.'s key principles effectively reason that members are responsible for some behaviors but not others.

Not only does the quasifanatical commitment to a higher power create a logical inconsistency, for many people it appears detrimental to treatment success. This is supported by evidence that A.A. produced better outcomes when spirituality was downplayed but peer-group networks were emphasized (Litt, Kadden, & Kabela-Cormier, 2007). Additionally, the number of alcoholics seeking treatment is likely reduced by this spiritual commitment, as more than 60% of respondents in a national poll preferred alternative treatments and would be unlikely to attend A.A. even if concerned about their drinking (Dillworth, 2005). Meta-analysis of four controlled experiments involving Community Reinforcement and Family Training (CRAFT), an alternative peer-based treatment method committed to peer support (like A.A.) and self-efficacy (unlike A.A.), found that the additional focus on self-efficacy doubled attendance levels and tripled participants' engagement (Roozen, de Waart, & van der Kroft, 2010).

Furthermore, the disavowal of self-efficacy inherent in this spiritual commitment is likely counter-productive as a treatment strategy. In considering the 12 steps in their entirety, Ragge (1992) argues, "the 12 steps are not a road to recovery, let alone *the* road to recovery. They are, instead, a road to substitute dependency—a dependency upon A.A. rather than upon alcohol." William White (White & Kurtz, 2006), of the North East Addiction Technology Center, elaborated, explaining that the reliance on deities "undermines personal responsibility and development of internal strengths," making A.A.'s "religious language" a barrier. In addition, Bogenschutz, Tonigan, and Miller (2006) examined the impacts that A.A. participants' personal characteristics had on their outcomes during a 15-month period, finding that attendance had no impact on abstinence but that self-efficacy was highly impactful. Thus, research evidence in recent years collectively suggests that the tenets of Alcoholics Anonymous are likely ineffectual or even counterproductive, particularly program devotion and avowal of personal inadequacy regarding alcohol, and that the benefits for some participants may be produced more widely using a more self-empowering strategy.

The 12-step model popularized by Alcoholics Anonymous has inspired countless offshoots that have also expanded rapidly, like the growth of Narcotics Anonymous from 200 to 20,000 chapters in just 25 years (Garfield, 2003). Many more 12-step groups will likely develop in the near future, following the recent recognition of behavioral compulsions (i.e., sex addiction) as distinct psychiatric conditions in the *DSM-V* (2013). An accurate total cannot be estimated, but there at least 200 fully developed "treatment programs" that apply all 12 steps, while hundreds more do so to varying degrees.

These A.A. spinoffs often assist members with similar issues involving addiction (Narcotics Anonymous, Cocaine Anonymous, etc.), but this model has also been applied to many other problems. Onlinerecovery.org lists more than 150 separate programs, including 22 engaging substance abuse and 12 involving sex (such as New Life Partners, "a Christian group for women whose husbands are caught in the web of sexual addiction"). The list of 54 "official" 12-step programs available at 12-step.com includes eight for eating concerns, nine for emotional issues, and 13 for psychiatric disorders.

Less recognizable groups focus on concerns ranging from the mundane (On Line Gamers Anonymous and Lip Balm Anonymous, offering knowledge about "the Chap Stick conspiracy") to the obscure (Pagan Paths 12 Step Recovery). Some are light-hearted (Assholes Anonymous, who note that "meetings are for assholes"), some are perplexing (Homosexuals Anonymous, "serving the recovery needs of men and women who struggle with unwanted same sex attraction"), and some are even taboo (Molesters Anonymous, which "provides support with anonymity and confidentiality for men who molest children"). Such broad applicability may be why de Miranda (2011) noted that a Google search for "12-step treatment" yields more than 429 million links in less than a second.

Many treatment practitioners strongly support the use of A.A.; however, there is only limited and equivocal scientific evidence on the program's efficacy in treating alcoholism. Although the preface to the Big Book states that "inquiry by scientific, medical, and religious societies will be welcomed" (A.A., 2005, p. xiv), rigorous empirical research on the efficacy of A.A. is relatively limited considering the number of individuals who participate in A.A. programs. This is at least partially due to the emphasis placed on anonymity and the A.A. norm that members should "utilize, not analyze." In addition, most research supporting A.A.'s effectiveness has compared outcomes between participants and nonparticipants, finding an association between voluntary A.A. participation and abstinence (Fuller & Hiller-Sturmhofel, 1999).

It is important to note that because subjects are not assigned randomly to A.A., some factor other than simply participating could be responsible for positive outcomes, such as motivation (further discussed above). A limited number of studies have found ongoing participation in A.A. to be effective in reducing alcohol-related problems (Bond, Kaskutas, & Weisner, 2003; Cross, Morgan, Mooney, Martin, & Rafter, 1990), particularly for A.A. sponsors (Pagano, Friend, Tonigan, & Stout, 2004; Zemore, Kaskutas, & Ammon, 2004). However, it is important to note that the "failure" rate of first-time A.A. members is extremely high. Research has found that at least half of new A.A. members quit attending meetings within 3 months of joining, and this figure increases to 95% by the end of the first year (Dorsman, 1996). In Brazil, Terra and colleagues (2008) also found that A.A. adherence to be low, with retention levels below 20% after only 6 months, even among a sample of individuals previously committed to hospital care for alcohol dependency.

Recent assessments of A.A.'s impacts on alcohol consumption clarify the evidence somewhat, collectively suggesting that beneficial outcomes are achieved by those who benefit from involvement in peer networking but that that the overall impact on drinking behavior is minimal. A systematic review of eight studies of A.A. and other twelve-step facilitation (TSF) programs involving randomized control trials concluded that "no experimental studies unequivocally demonstrated the effectiveness of A.A. or TSF approaches for reducing alcohol dependence or problem drinking" (Ferri, Amato, & Davoli, 2006). A longitudinal, 16-year comparison of A.A.–only, medical-only, and A.A./medical combined treatments found that those from the A.A.–only group that maintained participation after 1 year showed lower remission rates than those in the non–A.A. group after 1, 3, 5, 8, and 16 years. However, the groups showed no overall differences in remission because of the high discontinuance rate of A.A.–only recipients (Moos & Moos, 2006), suggesting that the social bonds associated with continued participation are beneficial but that the program's dogma drives away many seeking treatment.

A few studies have demonstrated that peer-support networks are a central component of A.A. that clearly offers treatment benefits, though networking and group-therapy treatment strategies lead to improved drinking outcomes in conjunction with elevated self-efficacy, not the disavowal of agency required by A.A. Majer and colleagues (2011) studied those living in residential treatment homes that utilized peer-oriented practices and also attended A.A., finding that involvement in those elements predicted abstinence and self-efficacy for abstinence but that A.A. involvement had no effect. Similarly, Gossop and associates (2008) found that participation in N.A./A.A. was not related to postresidential drug abstinence overall. However, continued involvement did predict opiate, cocaine, and alcohol abstinence rates at annual follow-ups, suggesting that the peer support provided can be useful during aftercare.

As a result, peer network-oriented treatment alternatives are beginning to gain ground, such as the SMART (Self-Management And Recovery Training) Recovery group, which was officially sanctioned by the Colorado Veterans Administration as an alternative to A.A./N.A. in response to patient complaints. SMART Recovery is a network of mutual aid groups that teach tools and techniques for self-directed change focused on self-empowerment and self-management reinforced with positive peer support. Alan Meyers, founder of Alternative Treatment International, agrees, explaining that more than 70% of those seeking alternatives have tried and been displeased with A.A. because "the perceived negativity of the 12-step approach creates a fear-based life, and most people don't want to live that way . . . We have to stop blaming the patient for our treatment failures. It is we who have to adapt" (as quoted in de Miranda, 2011).

Similar adaptation has come from offshoot groups founded by those who have found the spiritual/religious element incompatible with their personal beliefs, especially those forced to attend A.A. meetings because of court sanctions for drinking-and-driving offenses. As a result, a separate but related organization developed: Alcoholics Anonymous for Atheists and Agnostics (called Quad A), which employs principles that generally adhere to the 12-step model but de-emphasize the "power greater than ourselves" element, instead focusing upon support in participants' lives. Secular Organizations for Sobriety is another alternative to A.A. serving the same goals but geared specifically for those uncomfortable with A.A.'s religious commitment. Founded by James Christopher in 1985, this organization maintains that sobriety is a separate issue from religion or spirituality and also credits the individual for achieving and/or maintaining sobriety (Secular Organizations for Sobriety, 2003).

As noted in the introduction to this section, we are aware of the fact that A.A. has assisted many people in dealing with their dependence on alcohol. But given the critiques of A.A. discussed above, it is interesting to consider why this form of treatment for alcoholism retains its popularity and, in fact, many of A.A.'s steps continue to grow more common in the United States via their adoption by many compulsory treatment programs. Perhaps, as Gusfield (2003) asserts, A.A.'s continued popularity is related to the growth in the larger drug treatment industry, an industry that includes hundreds of thousands of individuals whose livelihoods are dependent on the continuance of this treatment model.

OUTPATIENT DRUG TREATMENT

Outpatient drug treatment refers to a broad and diverse category of substance abuse treatment strategies that enable the patient to receive treatment while remaining in the larger community (Hubbard et al., 1989). Also referred to as community-based treatment, this model developed in the 1960s in the form of "crisis clinics" and community mental health centers that provided what Ray and Ksir (2004) refer to as:

Alternatives to the emergency room for a person who was frightened and needed someone to talk to until the drug wore off. These facilities ranged from telephone hotlines, to emergency room–assisted clinics with medical support available, to "crash pads" where people could sleep off a drug's effects and receive some nonjudgmental advice and counseling. (p. 62)

From these foundations, the outpatient model developed into a diverse and flexible form of drug treatment that might involve the use of one or more distinct therapeutic philosophies and techniques. The programs usually entail some form of mental health counseling or psychotherapy, but they can range from "drop-in rap" centers to highly structured programs (Hubbard et al., 1989). Partly as a function of this, the intensity of the outpatient model also varies substantially from program to program, with some facilities "offering little more than drug education and admonition," while others, such as intensive day treatment, are "comparable to residential programs in service and effectiveness" (NIDA, 1999, p. 27).

The diverse range of treatment options and potential convenience of the outpatient model make this broad approach among the most widely supported and enacted rubrics (Ray & Ksir, 2004). This model is particularly popular with and well-suited to those individuals who are in need of drug treatment but also have stable employment, which might be disrupted by having to participate in inpatient treatment (NIDA, 1999). However, despite their popularity, there is not much research on the effectiveness of outpatient programs (Fiorentine, 1997; Hubbard et al., 1989). In large part, this lack of research is due to the substantial diversity that exists among outpatient programs; because the programs involve so many distinct approaches and treatment modalities, it is difficult to assess them collectively (Fiorentine, 1997). Additionally, the ongoing advancement of treatment research has led to the incorporation of outpatient components within other approaches, as incorporation of community aftercare has been consistently found to improve long-term outcomes for pharmacological, residential, and coercive treatment. Hubbard and colleagues (2003; see Table 8.1) do provide some information on the effectiveness of outpatient treatment in their comparison of the major (noncompulsory) treatment modalities currently employed. Their comparison found outpatient treatment alone to be among the least effective of the major treatment modalities in terms of later drug use (comparing preadmission figures to 1- and 5-year outcomes), but they did produce a small but consistent positive effect. In contrast, outpatient programs were among the most effective at outcomes not specifically related to drug use, such as rates of employment, quality of life, and criminal behavior.

However, as with other findings regarding treatment effectiveness discussed in this chapter, it is important to place such findings in their proper context. Each treatment modality is likely to serve a particular population of substance abusers, and the outpatient program is one of the more informal modes of treatment, particularly in comparison to methadone maintenance and long-term residential programs (Hubbard et al., 1989). As such, in comparison to those programs, outpatient treatment clients are likely to have fewer and less severe problems with substance abuse and fewer problems in general (e.g., employment, mental illness, social adjustment), and these characteristics are likely to have an impact on later substance use and levels of social functioning. Additionally, outpatient treatment inherently improves the likelihood of success when measured according to indicators of social functioning (e.g., employment, interpersonal relationships, etc.). It is clearly easier to maintain employment, gain education, and develop positive interpersonal relationships when residing in one's own community than when hindered by the stigma, emotional trauma, and deviant peer networks that regularly accompany incarceration, residential, and even coercive diversionary treatment. Finally, given the enormous diversity of program philosophies, expectations, and goals, it is very difficult to accurately assess programs' collective efficacy beneath the broad outpatient umbrella. Still, outpatient treatment plays an increasingly important role in the collective drug treatment mission. A number of specific treatment modalities have been studied and found to produce beneficial results, leading the British Association of Pharmacology to recommend that psychosocial therapy approaches accompany nearly all pharmacological treatment strategies (Lingford-Hughes et al., 2012).

Though most will be not be discussed in detail here, a more nuanced examination of the various forms of outpatient treatment does demonstrate the increasing prominence of cognitive behavioral therapy (CBT), which has demonstrated the most consistent success across treatment settings, populations, and drugs of abuse. Fundamentally, CBT is based on the assumption that participants possess maladaptive beliefs and understandings, which various formats of therapy seek to restructure by employing nonjudgmental self-reflection and personal growth exercises. Through client- and context-tailored combinations of introspective thinking, homework assignments, and group-therapy exercises, CBT aims to help addicts develop beneficial thought processes, interpersonal skills, and behaviors. In reviews of past research, CBT has been shown to be a predictor of reduced drug use for prisoners, parolees, and probationers in the United States (Bahr et al., 2012), within therapeutic communities (Welsh, 2010), and among incarcerated offenders in England (McMurran, 2009). Likewise, it produces stronger and quicker benefits than any other type of treatment during couples' therapy (Powers, Vedel, & Emmelkamp, 2008) and among juveniles with substance abuse issues (Deas & Clark, 2009). Likewise for those struggling with stimulant addictions, for which many types of therapy are ineffective, as CBT has repeatedly been associated with reduced use for cocaine- and methamphetamine-dependent individuals (Lee & Rawson, 2008; Penberthy, Alt-Daoud, Vaughan, & Fanning, 2010). CBT has even been found to reduce recidivism from 46% to 27% when implemented as part of a 30-day jail-based program (Bahr, Harris, Strobell, & Taylor, 2012).

Often used in conjunction with CBT, contingency management (CM) has also gained favor in recent years and demonstrated beneficial effects. CM is based on commitment to a system of accessible rewards and punishments intended to alter behavior by reinforcing beneficial and detrimental actions regularly with minor rewards and sanctions. Recent examination of the collective research evidence has indicated consistent association between CM strategies and improved drug and social outcomes, further noting that utilizing both CM and CBT regularly improves outcomes even further (Bahr et al., 2012). For that reason, both CBT and CM are included among the 10 key components of drug courts, as outlined by the National Association of Drug Court Professionals and the Drug Courts Program Office, a new division of the U.S. Department of Justice (1997).

However, evidentiary support for the effectiveness of CM alone is more limited, as a few studies have shown mixed results regarding the reinforcement systems employed in drug courts. For instance, harsher sanctions have been found not to impact drug court completion rates (Hepburn & Harvey, 2007), and contingency-based rewards have failed to improve compliance (Marlowe, Festinger, Dugosh, Arabia, & Kirby, 2008), increase retention, or reduce drug use in various settings (Hall, Prendergast, Roll, & Warda, 2009). In fact, multiple studies suggest that some applications of CM may be counterproductive, including an extensive meta-analysis of various treatment modes by Bahr and colleagues (2012), in which abstinence and compliance have suffered as soon as rewards cease in various studies. This trend has been specifically associated with outpatient settings employing CM systems intended to maintain abstinence among juveniles (Kileen et al., 2012) and among opiate and cocaine users (Bahr et al., 2012; Petry, Alessi, & Ledgerwood, 2012).

The use of negative sanctions, in general, has been found unsuccessful for improving motivation and outcomes in numerous studies, with some evidence suggesting the punishments may even be detrimental to some and might reduce program success. For instance, Shaffer's (2011) meta-analysis of drug courts found that programs with more rigid and harsh systems of sanctions were less successful, and threats associated with failing a urinalysis screening have been found ineffectual in altering the duration of program adherence among probationers (Hepburn & Albonetti, 1994) and drug court clients (Vakili, Currie, & el-Guebaly, 2009).

CONCLUSION

As we have discussed, economic and humanitarian needs clearly compel that all societies, particularly the United States, expand and improve opportunities for drug treatment, a broad realm for which the above assessment has described the dominant approaches and the current state of public and scientific support for each. Specifically, this chapter examined each of five primary treatment delivery modes: (1) pharmacological treatment, a strategy that employs the use of drugs or medications to treat substance abuse; (2) residential drug treatment, involving constant care during lengthy residence within a treatment facility; (3) compulsory drug treatment, whereby individuals officially designated as dependent undergo mandatory treatment, often in lieu of incarceration; (4) peer-support treatment, focusing on group support based primarily on the 12-step model of A.A.; and (5) outpatient drug treatment, which includes a diverse array of strategies employed within a community setting to facilitate re-entry or ongoing social functioning. Although evidence promoting each of these treatment rubrics is limited by various factors, all have reliably demonstrated some degree of utility in contributing (at least in certain contexts) to reductions in drug use and criminal activity and to improvements in employment and social functioning.

In his 2003 State of the Union address, President George W. Bush signaled that his administration would devote more funds to drug treatment. While this message could be construed as encouraging, in a move consistent with the Bush administration's approach to other social issues, the Office of National Drug Control Policy then promoted and funded faith-based treatment programs. Drug Czar John Walters claimed, "youth often turn to their faith communities to seek spiritual guidance about issues such as peer pressure and drugs. Faith communities can help parents instill antidrug values and shape teens' decisions not to use marijuana and other drugs" (as quoted in ONDCP, 2003b). One example of a faith-based drug treatment program is the in-prison program known as Inner Change, where addiction is presented as a sin that can be permanently cured through a connection with Jesus. As Shapiro (2003) notes, this program is typical of faith-based substance abuse programs supported by the Bush administration, as it relies upon principles with numerous limitations and very limited evidence of success, similar to those of Alcoholics Anonymous. When he was governor of Texas, Bush previously defended another faith-based program, Teen Challenge, against charges that it violated state and health department codes, saying, "I believe that conversion to religion, in this case Christianity, by its very nature promotes sobriety" (as quoted in Shapiro, 2003).

The Obama administration came to power thereafter, proudly vowing a commitment to employing real evidence-based policies and to investing heavily in treatment instead of incarceration. In 2010, the new drug czar, Gil Kerlikowske, unveiled what was hyped as the beginning of this revolutionary shift that would produce an entirely new federal drug control strategy. This strategy specifically announced that "[a]ll those who have a substance use disorder should receive evidence-based treatment services . . . through an expansion of community addiction centers and the development of new medications and evidence-based treatments for addiction" (ONDCP, 2010). Shortly thereafter, the White House boasted of "Relying on Science and Research to Support Our Nation's Drug Control Strategies" as one of the administration's key accomplishments to date (ONDCP, 2011, p. 1).

However, such claims of fundamental shifts in drug policy and the prioritization of treatment run afoul of the evidence in many ways. During the 2012 World Federation Against Drugs forum, the Obama administration made statements fully contradicting its purported commitment to evidence-based practices (EBP). During opening statements, Kerlikowske instead proclaimed opposition for exactly such practices by stating that "[p]olicies and programs such as injection rooms, drug distribution efforts, and drug legalization should be opposed because they tolerate drug use and allow the debilitating disease of addiction to continue untreated" (U.S. Government, 2012).

Instead, he reiterated past commitments to "providing treatment services in correctional facilities, providing alternatives to incarceration such as drug courts for nonviolent drug-involved offenders, and using monitoring, drug testing" (U.S. Government, 2012). Despite the new rhetoric, these strategies directly contradict the nonjudgmental, nonpunitive, and noncoercive tactics, as well as the healthcare and patient-first priorities fundamental to genuine harm reduction and minimization policies.

There are certainly numerous moral, political, and rhetorical justifications for the continued focus on coercive substance abuse treatment, and the current political climate condones this as the preferred approach within the national drug control strategy. Research clearly confirms that the shift to drug courts and the accompanying treatment mandate has unequivocally been an improvement over strictly punitive policies of the past. Perfectly applied, many of drug courts' key components are undeniably useful, and ample research has even demonstrated that in certain contexts they have been enacted within genuine evidence-based policy. In conjunction with recent presidential proclamations ending the "War on Drugs" and replacing it with greater focus on treatment and prevention, a long-overdue step in the right direction has occurred, for which recent policymakers deserve our applause.

Still, even practical and rhetorical reorganization has left substance abuse treatment far from realizing its potential benefits for those struggling with addiction and for the society burdened by those struggles. Rhetorical declarations of peace aside, treatment services (especially voluntary services) remain severely underfunded, with relative allotments failing to reflect the stated treatment mission (to be discussed further in Chapter 11). Even amid progress, treatment efforts remain limited in scope and efficiency, hindered by a blanket dismissal of many effective harm reduction tactics and the channeling of most resources through drug courts. While improved, the drug court model maintains a punitive and reactionary orientation because services are provided mostly through the same legal system, staffed largely by the same personnel, and offered almost entirely upon legal mandate. Thus, even as we congratulate recent progress, it seems remiss not to also question the sensibility of drug treatment policies that still ultimately prioritize the approval of lobbyists, politicians, and radio hosts above the healthcare needs of citizens struggling with substance abuse and the knowledge produced by decades of scientific research.

REVIEW QUESTIONS

1. What is likely the most important factor in predicting successful drug treatment outcomes?

2. How is success measured with respect to drug treatment?

3. What are the key benefits of drug treatment as compared to addressing drug problems predominantly through the criminal justice system?

4. What are the five broad categories of drug treatment?

5. What is the difference between drug agonists and drug antagonists?

6. What is methadone maintenance? Which government and health organizations have issued statements of support for this mode of drug treatment? In what ways does methadone maintenance differ from heroin maintenance?

7. What do therapeutic communities propose is necessary to cure someone of drug addiction?

8. What has research concluded on the abstinence mandate of Alcoholics Anonymous?

INTERNET EXERCISES

1. Access the Bureau of Justice Statistics report titled *Drugs & Crime Facts* (http:// bjs.ojp.usdoj.gov/content/pub/pdf/dcf.pdf) and read over the sections on "Drug Use & Crime" and "Correctional populations and facilities." Data elsewhere in this report indicate that in 2005, more than 250,000 prisoners were incarcerated in state and federal prisons for drug offenses, and that drug offenders constituted 20% of state prisoners and more than 53% of federal prisoners. Now examine the subsection titled "Perspectives of probationers, prisoners, and jail inmates" (p. 9). What percentage of inmates reported being under the influence of alcohol or drugs at the time of their offense? What types of crimes most often and least often involved offenders on drugs when the offense was committed?

2. Now examine data on state and federal prisons in the section on "Drug treatment under correctional supervision" (p. 44). What percentage of state and federal inmates who were recent drug users when convicted took part in treatment in 2004? Explain any inconsistencies you observe.

3. Begin by accessing the Substance Abuse Treatment Facility Locator on the SAMHSA website (http://findtreatment.samhsa.gov/TreatmentLocator/faces/ quickSearch.jspx). Once you have familiarized yourself with the controls, search your state and another state of your choosing for treatment services that would be useful and feasibly accessed for the hypothetical individuals described below. For each character, describe the degree of availability in each state and attempt to explain any differences you observe between states.

   • A 16-year-old young lady addicted to heroin who is homeless in a new city after running away
   • A single father of three young kids who makes ends meet with a small business but cannot afford health insurance so only has what Medicaid pays for, and he has developed an addiction to Oxycodone tablets he began taking to ease pain
   • A Mexican man without insurance who is 27 and wants to overcome a cocaine addiction after he began using the drug to stay awake while working three jobs to send enough money to his sick mother that she can rest

CHAPTER 9

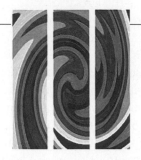

*Policies Regulating
Legal Drugs*

Part I: Alcohol and Tobacco

The issues with respect to the regulation of legal drugs are fundamentally different than those associated with the regulation of illegal drugs. While the apparent goals of policies to regulate legal drugs are similar to the goals associated with policies to regulate illegal drugs—that is, to prevent their misuse and abuse and negative individual and public health effects—these goals are not attempted through punitive criminal justice system policies. Instead, attempts to achieve these goals focus on policies designed to control access to the drugs, tax them, and in some cases, such as drunk driving legislation, deal with the harmful consequences associated with the use of these drugs.

An additional fundamental difference between policies regulating illegal and legal drugs is that the companies who produce the latter have an advantage in marketing and selling their respective products that is not enjoyed by those who market and sell illegal products. As will be discussed in Chapter 10, the profits associated with the sales of legal drugs, including tobacco, alcohol, and prescription drugs, are tremendous, and the companies selling these products have an incredible reservoir of political and economic power that they use to influence the legislators who create policies to regulate these substances. For example, one commentator referred to the tobacco industry as "the world's most powerful drug cartel" ("Editorial: Tobacco," 1992). While it is true that current laws allow companies to sell their legal drug products, it is also important to consider how they are dealt with by government authorities when they are found to be in violation of the (already comparatively weak) laws designed to regulate them.

While we focus here on policies designed to regulate the marketing and consumption of legal drugs, Chapters 9 and 10 are as much about a *lack* of regulation as they are about regulation. Although many of the practices engaged in by tobacco, alcohol, and pharmaceutical companies to promote their products and generate profits are technically legal in the United States, we will see that many of these practices are morally and ethically questionable. In light of the discussion of the effects of legal drugs in Chapters 3 and 4, it is necessary to examine the inconsistencies, if not hypocrisy, in the policies regulating legal drugs. Many of the legal substances whose regulation we cover in these chapters are, in fact, far more harmful, both in terms of their effects on individual users and on the larger society, than drugs that are currently categorized as illegal in the United States.

It is also important to note that policies regulating legal drugs in the contemporary United States are unique when considered both historically and cross-nationally. For example, in the early 1500s in Mecca, individuals who were found consuming coffee were tied to the back of a mule with their faces to its rear end, paraded in the streets, and whipped (Walton, 2002). Several states prohibited tobacco consumption in the late 1800s and early 1900s, and as is more commonly known, alcohol was prohibited in the United States from 1918 to 1932.

TOBACCO

As discussed in Chapter 3, social attitudes toward tobacco have oscillated between acceptance and demonization, and legislation regulating the substance has reflected such views. In this section, we briefly discuss the early history of tobacco legislation in the United States and follow it with an examination of current policies designed to regulate consumption of tobacco products. More specifically, we examine bans on smoking in public places, restrictions on the advertising of tobacco products, the taxation of and regulations on the marketing and advertising of tobacco products, and the 1988 settlement between tobacco companies and the governments of 46 states. A critical examination of these policies, which have typically been enacted with the goal of reducing tobacco use and thereby the negative health effects associated with its use, reveals that in the current period, tobacco has become the pariah of legal drugs. And as is the case with all policies regulating drugs—legal or illegal—there have been a number of unintended negative consequences associated with these policies.

A Brief History of Tobacco Regulation

While tobacco is one of the most widely used legal drugs in the United States and in other countries, consumption of this drug has not always been legal. Although southern states such as Virginia and North Carolina, whose economies were reliant on tobacco, did not attempt to restrict consumption, a number of northern states enacted antitobacco legislation in the 1600s. The first of these was Massachusetts, which enacted legislation forbidding smoking in public in 1632 (Werner, 1922). A law passed in 1638 in Plymouth colony similarly banned smoking on the streets; a law passed in the same jurisdiction in 1669 required that anyone found smoking on the Sabbath within 2 miles of a rooming house would be subject to a fine of 12 pence (Werner, 1922). Laws restricting tobacco use were even more severe in other countries. In 1634, Czar Mikhail Feodorovich of Russia created laws that provided for whipping, slitting of the nose, transportation to Siberia, and even castration for those who smoked (Busch, 2005); a second offense would result in execution. Similarly, in China, a regulation passed in 1638 provided that users or distributors of tobacco would be punished by decapitation (Borio, 2003).

At least partially prompted by organizations such as the national Anti-Cigarette League, between 1893 and 1909, 14 states enacted laws banning the sale, and in some cases possession, of cigarettes (Sullum, 1998). Even in states where tobacco remained legal, some businesses offered their support to the anticigarette movement by refusing to hire individuals who smoked. Most prominent among these businesses was the Ford Motor Company, whose founder Henry Ford published and distributed a book titled *The Case Against the Little White Slaver* (Troyer & Markle, 1983) and who refused to hire smokers. Some legislation to regulate tobacco consumption in the early 1900s distinguished between particular groups of users; for example, in 1908, the New York Board of Aldermen passed an ordinance (eventually vetoed by the mayor) that banned women from smoking in public (Troyer & Markle, 1983). In contrast, a law in Idaho set the minimum age for smoking cigarettes at 21 for males but 18 for females (Brecher, 1972). The demonization of tobacco in the early part of the 20th century is further revealed when we consider that in 1904, a judge in New York sentenced a woman to 30 days in jail for smoking in front of her children. A few years after this, a Seattle woman was allowed to divorce her husband on the grounds that he was a "cigarette fiend" (Tate, 2003). By the 1930s, however, cigarettes were again legal in every state.

Currently, tobacco is a legal product, with only age-related restrictions on purchase and consumption. In 1992, Congress directed states to establish 18 as the minimum legal age for purchasing cigarettes, and while most states imposed 18 as the minimum age, Alabama, Alaska, and Utah subsequently raised their minimum ages for purchase to 19, and a bill to raise the minimum smoking age to 21 was approved by a senate committee in California in 2002 (Coleman, 2002).

Bans on Smoking in Public Places

Turning to the contemporary period, primarily in respect to scientific evidence regarding the negative health effects associated with exposure to secondhand smoke, a number of jurisdictions have enacted legislation banning smoking in public venues such as restaurants and bars, parks, and other public areas. In addition to the fact that these laws will prevent nonsmokers from being exposed to secondhand smoke, they are also believed to have positive public health effects because they will make it more inconvenient for smokers to light up, thereby reducing their consumption and possibly eventually leading them to quit.

Several jurisdictions in the United States, and even entire countries, have passed legislation banning smoking in public places. On January 1, 2004, Ireland became the first European country to ban smoking in pubs, and three other countries— Norway, the Netherlands, and Malta—approved laws prohibiting smoking in bars and pubs that came into effect in the spring of 2004 and early 2005, respectively (Alvarez, 2003; Houston, 2004).

In 1973, Arizona became the first state to limit smoking in public places, and as of June 2003, more than 1,600 antismoking laws were in effect in the United States. Numerous cities have banned smoking in public parks on the grounds that tobacco is a dangerous pollutant and that young people should be protected from the sight of people smoking (Tate, 2003). In Timnath, Colorado, smoking was banned in bars and restaurants, even though the town did not have any bars and restaurants at the time the legislation was passed (Will, 2005). In Washington State, a law passed in 2005 banned smoking in all public places and workplaces, as well as within 25 feet of doorways (Eskenazi, 2005). Clark College in the same state even banned all tobacco products (including chewing tobacco) from its premises, including parking lots (Buck, 2005).

As just one specific example of these regulations, under New York City's antismoking law, establishments that allow smoking on their premises are fined $200 for a first offense, $500 to $1,000 for a second, and $2,000 for a third offense. In addition, on the third violation, the owner's license to conduct business can be revoked (Brick, 2003). Similar to laws passed in other jurisdictions, however, the New York City law did not result in a complete ban on smoking in public establishments. It allowed smoking in "cigar bars" in which tobacco accounted for at least 10% of the revenue of the establishment, in establishments that build separately ventilated rooms for smokers, and in bars/restaurants that had three or fewer owners and no employees. The law also allowed for one-quarter of a bar or restaurant's outdoor seating to be designated for smokers (von Zielbauer, 2003b). In other cities, individuals who wanted to smoke were able to do so in hookah bars (Quenqua, 2011).

> Despite the repeated attempts to classify secondhand smoke as a weapon of mass destruction, nobody has yet identified it as a cause of death. [The regulators'] zeal is more impressive because of its absurdity. Prophets bearing witness to the day of judgment while standing in a haze of carbon monoxide emitted by the passing truck traffic, the sewers below their feet emptying streams of mercury and lead into the unrepentant seas. (Lapham, 2003)

Bans on smoking have also spread to other contexts. For example, in 2009, the federal government's Department of Housing and Urban Development strongly encouraged public housing agencies to ban smoking in some or all of their units—on January 1, 2012, Maine became the first state in the country in which all public housing units were to be smoke free (Seelye, 2011).

There have also been efforts across the United States to prohibit smoking on golf courses (Geranios, 2009), and as of July, 2012, 774 college campuses banned smoking, including 562 that banned tobacco use (including chewing tobacco) altogether (Daneman, 2012). As of 2011, it was estimated that there were more than 450 municipalities in the United States that banned smoking in parks and more than 200 that prohibited smoking on beaches (Salazar, 2011). Even the top two tobacco-producing states in the United States., Virginia and South Carolina, passed bans on smoking in bars and restaurants in 2009 (Brown, 2012).

In discussing bans on smoking in public places and their impact, it is important to note that while many commentators have argued strongly that exposure to second-hand smoke is associated with negative health effects, the scientific evidence regarding the role of secondhand smoke in causing cancer, heart disease, and other chronic diseases is somewhat equivocal (Sullum, 1998; Tate, 2003). Even the American Cancer Society has noted that "there is no research in the medical litera-ture as yet that shows smoking outdoors causes cancer in people" (as quoted in Forgione, 2011). Perhaps the largest study of the effects of secondhand smoke, involving 118,094 adults in California, concluded,

> The results do not support a causal relationship between tobacco smoke and tobacco-related mortality, although they do not rule out a small effect. The association between exposure to environmental tobacco smoke and coronary heart disease and lung cancer may be considerably weaker than generally believed. (Enstrom & Kabat, 2003, p. 1057)

Critics have also questioned the intent of these laws in the context of the regula-tion of other threats to public health (see box).

In a similar vein, in reference to the ban on smoking in public places in New York City, Williams (2003) noted,

> There is one threat posed to health in America that is greater than smoking, and that's obesity. It's fair to wonder whether the city might be better served by banning fatty foods in restaurants, while it is in the business of putting its citi-zens' health above the citizenry's choice.

Or, as an editorial in the *Los Angeles Times* noted,

> Society could move forward with local ordinances that ban cookies from enclosed public places where others might be exposed to secondhand sugar, and of course, at parks, where children might see them. Vending machine sales of Ritz crackers would be banned. ("Move Over," 2005)

Similar to all laws regulating drugs, there are also certain unintended negative con-sequences associated with banning smoking in public places. For example, following the passage of the legislation in New York City, community representatives reported that noise complaints had increased as a result of restaurant and bar patrons being forced to smoke outside. There have also been reports of increased litter from smokers putting their cigarettes out on sidewalks and complaints about air pollution created by smokers ("Bouncer Fatally Stabbed," 2003). In Seattle, following Washington State's statewide ban on public smoking, it was reported that "thousands of white and tan little nubs are scattered over the sidewalks, clustered at the base of trees and clogging up gutters"; this was referred to as "the new urban scourge" (Ellison, 2006). There have also been complaints by business owners in jurisdictions where smoking bans have been implemented that their sales have decreased (Graman, 2006). And although it is obviously important to be cautious in accepting such a causal explanation, the killing of a bouncer at a Manhattan nightclub in the spring of 2003 was attributed to the fact that he was attempting to enforce the smoking ban and was subsequently stabbed by a patron. His brother was quoted as saying, "I'm very bitter. It's a senseless murder because of this stupid cigarette law. That's the only reason this guy was killed" (as quoted in "Bouncer Fatally Stabbed," 2003).

An additional unintended negative consequence of public smoking bans is that they may displace smoking activity to homes or vehicles, putting children at higher risk of exposure to secondhand smoke. A study by economist Jerome Adda found that levels of the tobacco chemical cotinine in children ages 4 to 8 were significantly higher in jurisdictions that had total bans on public smoking (cited in Revill, Doward, & Hinsliff, 2005).

In addition to bans on public smoking, and similar to the practices of the Ford Motor Company mentioned above, a number of businesses and jurisdictions have attempted to restrict smoking by their workers. For example, the city of Spokane, Washington, proposed a policy requiring its employees to be nonsmokers. The city's human resources director defended the policy, noting, "the statistics are there to show that people who use tobacco are generally sick more days a year, and they increase the cost of your medical based on the complications caused by a smoking lifestyle" (as quoted in Ellis, 2004). Under Spokane's policy, employees who break the rules and smoke, even when they are not on the job, can have their employment terminated. Other employers in Washington State who refuse to hire smokers include Seattle-based Alaska Airlines (which requires job applicants to submit to a urine test) and the Spokane-based utility company Avista (Vogel, 2005). Although there are no data on how many companies or government agencies do not hire smokers, the trend appears to be particularly strong in hospitals (Koch, 2012). The World Health Organization implemented similar policies in 2005, automatically banning people who smoke from employment in the organization (Frith, 2005). But as Chapman (2005) notes, the basis of justification for these policies—that smokers are less productive and incur higher health care costs—must be considered in the context of other behaviors of employees:

> By the same logic, employers might just as well refuse to hire younger women because they might get pregnant and take maternity leave.... By the same paternalistic precepts, employers might consult their insurance companies about dangerous leisure activities and interrogate employees as to whether they engage in risky sports.

In addition to these policies, a growing number of employers require smokers to pay extra premiums for their health care coverage—for example, Macy's (department store chain) charges workers who admit to smoking an extra $35 a month, and PepsiCo requires smokers to pay an annual $600 insurance surcharge (Ellis & Wechsler, 2011).

Restrictions on Advertising and Marketing of Tobacco Products

While tobacco companies have generally claimed that advertising of their products encourages smokers to purchase particular brands, critics assert that such advertising actually increases the number of smokers, thereby justifying government-imposed restrictions on advertising. Of particular concern are advertising campaigns targeted at young people, who may take up the practice of smoking as a result of exposure to tobacco advertisements.

> Among the prominent athletes endorsing tobacco products prior to the 1963 Surgeon General's Report were professional golfer Arnold Palmer and baseball players Babe Ruth, Joe DiMaggio, and Ted Williams. In contrast, another famous baseball player, Honus Wagner, forced the Piedmont Tobacco Company to stop inserting his baseball card into cigarette packages because he felt it would encourage children to use tobacco products. (Ditore, 2003)

After the Surgeon General's Report of 1963 indicating that tobacco use caused cancer, the tobacco companies announced they would adopt a voluntary advertising code, banning "virility" themes, unsubstantiated claims regarding the health effects of tobacco, endorsements of tobacco products by professional athletes and entertainers, and advertisements aimed primarily at people under the age of 21 (Sullum, 1998). Congress eventually prohibited all television advertising of cigarettes in 1971, but undaunted, the tobacco companies began to devote their advertising dollars to other sources, including billboards (primarily in minority communities), magazines and newspapers, and the sponsorship of cultural and sporting events—most notably, car racing.

Despite the earlier voluntary ban on targeting tobacco advertising to young people, it is notable that in the 1970s through the 1990s, tobacco companies used cartoon characters and rock stars to promote their products, leaving "little doubt that young people are the primary target" (Lewis, 1992). Although not common in the current period in the United States, the tobacco company RJ Reynolds has sponsored several rock concerts, including the Salem Madonna Concert in Hong Kong (Lewis, 1992). There has also been the practice of selling cigarettes in packages that contain fewer cigarettes, and in some cases singly, which makes them more affordable and hence more accessible to young people (Lewis, 1992).

In November of 1998, the major tobacco companies agreed to pay approximately $206 billion over a 20-year period to 46 states and 5 territories to settle lawsuits that had been initiated by a number of states to recoup smoking-related health care costs (Healton, 2001). Among the provisions of this agreement were restrictions on the marketing of tobacco products, particularly to youth. However, between the time of the settlement and 2002, promotional spending by tobacco companies actually increased from $6.7 billion to $12.5 billion (Levin, 2004), and it was estimated that in the first year of the postsettlement period, the industry increased tobacco advertising by 33% in magazines with high (15% or greater) youth readership (Daynard et al., 2001). In response to this continued targeting of youth in their advertising, a judge in California fined RJ Reynolds $20 million for placing ads for Camel and other cigarettes in magazines such as *InStyle, Spin, Hot Rod,* and *Rolling Stone,* all of which have significant youth readership (Girion & Levin, 2002). There is also evidence to suggest that tobacco companies use subliminal advertising (Aguirre, 2003), and the marketing of products such as vanilla- and citrus-flavored cigarettes (Lavelle, 2000; Wilson, 2010a) and mini-cigars with ice-cream flavors such as strawberry, watermelon, vanilla, and chocolate (Sun, 2011)—products the industry has long believed would appeal to young smokers—belies tobacco industry claims that they do not target young people. A study of 1,036 adolescents found that (RJ Reynolds) advertisements for Camel No. 9 cigarettes, which ran in magazines such as *Vogue, Cosmopolitan,* and *Glamour,* were popular with girls ages 12 to 16 (Pierce et al., 2010). Promotional giveaways associated with these advertisements included berry-flavored lip balm, cellphone jewelry, purses, and wristbands. A spokesman for RJ Reynolds denied that the ads targeted young people, noting that 85% of the readership of the magazines in which the ads appeared were over 18 years of age (Szabo, 2010).

In addition to the practices outlined above, tobacco companies have engaged in the practice of distributing free packages of cigarettes at certain establishments and events, including, in some cases, events where underage people were present. For example, in Washington State, 80 permits were issued to tobacco companies to pass out free samples in 1999, while in 2002, the state issued more than 2,000 such permits (Olsen, 2002). Tobacco companies have also given out free samples of chewing tobacco to college students in Washington State (and, presumably, other states), and during a 15-day period at the Gorge Amphitheater (a venue in which rock concerts are held), more than 15,000 packs of cigarettes were given away (Johnson & Sudermann, 2002). In 2002, a court in California imposed a $14.8 million fine on RJ Reynolds for giving away free packages of cigarettes at events where children were present. The company had distributed more than 100,000 packages of cigarettes at public events during 1999 and 2000 (Hammann, 2002). And although the practice was discontinued in December of 2005, RJ Reynolds was promoting its Camel brand cigarettes by sending drink coasters providing recipes for special cocktails to people in their 20s. Critics suggested that this practice was part of a marketing campaign to associate Camels with trendy cocktails and encourage young people to smoke and drink (Selvin & Hoffman, 2005).

Taxes on Tobacco Products

The first taxes on tobacco products (in this case snuff) were enacted in 1794 in the United States, and by 1880, tobacco taxes accounted for fully 31% of all tax dollars collected by the federal government (Heimann, 1960). Iowa became the first state to enact a tobacco tax in 1921, and by 1969, when North Carolina became the last state to do so, all 50 states and the District of Columbia imposed taxes on tobacco (Shafer Commission, 1973). In the more recent era, Sullum (1998) asserts that the single most effective antismoking measure ever enacted in the United States was not intended to reduce smoking per se, but instead was passed with the intention of reducing the federal government's deficit. Thus the 1982 Tax Equity and Fiscal Responsibility Act doubled the federal excise tax on cigarettes from 8 to 16 cents a package. Since that time, state and even local governments have increased the taxes on tobacco products several times. Part of the reason for the apparent ability of higher taxes to reduce smoking is that smokers, especially those from lower-income groups, are price sensitive. Studies indicate that the price elasticity of demand for cigarettes is somewhere between –.4 and –1.0; that is, for every 10% increase in the price of cigarettes, consumption declines by 4% to 10% (Sullum, 1998). The Centers for Disease Control and Prevention also found that lower-income smokers quit in higher proportions than upper-income smokers when the price of cigarettes increases, and that the effect of price was even greater for young members of minority groups.

> Even after analyses control for income and other variables, it is estimated that about one-quarter of 18- to 24-year-old black smokers would quit smoking altogether in response to a 10 percent price increase, whereas only about one percent of white smokers of the same age would. (as quoted in Hertzberg, 2002)

Research also suggests that increases in the price of cigarettes lead to reductions in consumption primarily by reducing the total number of smokers rather than reducing the amount consumed per smoker (Sullum, 1998).

Nationally, the average retail price of cigarettes increased by 70% from December 1997 to May 2001, largely as a result of increases in state taxes. As of 2010, state taxes ranged from 30 cents a pack in the tobacco-producing state of Virginia to a high of $4.35 in New York State (Campaign for Tobacco-Free Kids, 2012). In 2002, the city of New York raised its cigarette taxes from 8 cents to $1.50 per pack (Hertzberg, 2002), and by 2010, the price of a package of cigarettes in some New York City stores reached $14.50 (Sutherland, Fasick, & Fermiro, 2010). A study by the New York City Health Department indicated that as a result of the higher taxes on cigarettes (combined with the previously mentioned ban on smoking in public establishments), the number of smokers in New York City declined by 11% between 2003 and 2004 (Perez-Pena, 2004).

While increases in taxes are thus viewed as a logical way to reduce tobacco consumption, critics have noted that these taxes are highly regressive, both because people with lower incomes are disproportionately likely to smoke and because they also spend a higher proportion of their income on cigarettes (Sullum, 2002). Walton (2002) goes so far as to suggest that the increases in cigarette taxes "are not, despite the protestations of all governments, intended to discourage use, but represent a particularly efficacious way of exploiting dependency" (p. 132). Critics have also suggested that one of the primary justifications for increasing cigarette taxes—the notion that tobacco smokers incur increased health care costs—is without scientific foundation. Because smokers tend to die earlier than nonsmokers, they may, in fact, incur fewer health care costs than the latter, and they also receive less money out of Social Security and pension funds (Sullum, 1998; see also Zorn, 2005).

As tobacco taxes have increased in the past few decades, smokers have attempted to avoid paying them. In addition to purchasing cigarettes in states that have lower taxes than their own state, smokers seeking cheaper cigarettes have benefited from the emergence of several Internet companies selling cigarettes. A report by Prudential Securities estimated that approximately 2% of the 20 billion packages of cigarettes sold in the United States in 2002 were purchased over the Internet, and there were more than 700 websites selling cigarettes as of January 2004 (Porter, 2004).

> We do not sell the cigarettes ourselves; however, we will show you where you can purchase them for only $14.95 per carton. (Plus, you also get FREE SHIPPING!). Click the link below and see the list of CARTONS available for only $14.95! Marlboros, Camels, Winstons, Rothmans, Kent, and MORE! (email cigarette advertisement, May 2003)

Thus, an unintended consequence of higher cigarette taxes is that states are losing revenues as a result of Internet sales; one estimate suggested that consumers purchasing cigarettes over the Internet resulted in states losing more than $1.5 billion annually in cigarette taxes (Mohl, 2004). Some states have taken measures to prevent the evasion of these taxes. In late 2003, for instance, Washington State attempted to force a company known as Dirtcheapcig.com to provide a list of its Washington customers, with the state planning to send tax bills to all individuals who had purchased cigarettes from this company. State officials argued that they were authorized to engage in this practice as a result of the 1955 federal Jenkins Act, which was intended to prevent individuals from avoiding local tobacco taxes by purchasing mail-order cigarettes from states with lower tobacco taxes. As of 2005, Washington State estimated it was losing $140 million each year as a result of unpaid taxes on contraband cigarette sales (Roesler, 2005). Similarly, in 2004, the Massachusetts Department of Revenue announced it would begin asking Internet cigarette companies for the names of individuals purchasing cigarettes from their websites and also threatened to sue the companies (Mohl, 2004). In early 2005, faced with the loss of an estimated $40 million per year in untaxed cigarettes, New York City's Department of Finance sent out thousands of letters to residents who had purchased cigarettes over the Internet demanding payment of taxes; some individuals apparently owed as much as $10,000. These letters gave violators 30 days to pay the fines; if they did not comply, they would face interest on the fines and penalties of up to $200 a carton (Farley, 2005). In Illinois, in the first 8 months of

2005, the state Department of Revenue sent notices to nearly 5,000 residents who purchased cigarettes over the Internet, informing them that they collectively owed more than $2.1 million in back taxes, penalties, and interest (Chase, 2005).

An additional unintended negative consequence associated with higher cigarette prices and the emergence of Internet cigarette companies is easier access to tobacco for individuals who are not of legal age to smoke. Studies indicate that 2 to 3% of adolescents report purchasing cigarettes over the Internet (Ribisil, Williams, & Kim, 2003), a finding that is not surprising given that most Internet cigarette vendors do not have adequate age-verification methods for consumers. The most common method of age verification is self-reporting, whereby buyers click a box stating that they are of legal age to purchase cigarettes; only about 7% of Internet cigarette companies indicate that they would require purchasers to provide photographic proof of their age when the product was delivered.

Perhaps even more problematic than the emergence of Internet cigarette vendors in response to higher tobacco taxes has been the involvement of organized crime and the tobacco companies themselves in smuggling cigarettes across state and national borders. For example, when the government of Canada increased cigarette taxes in 1989 and 1991, a carton of cigarettes could be purchased for approximately $45 in the province of Ontario (compared to between $15 and $20 a carton in the United States). Because of this significant variation in prices, the smuggling of cigarettes by individuals and groups, in particular Mohawk Indians operating from reservations along the Canada–United States border in the St. Lawrence River area, increased substantially. One estimate suggested that approximately one-third of the cigarettes sold in the province of Ontario and two-thirds of those in Quebec were contraband (Sullum, 1998).

Although the tobacco companies claimed that this smuggling was solely the result of excessive taxes on cigarettes in Canada, there is strong evidence to suggest that executives of at least one major tobacco company, British American Tobacco, knowingly participated in and facilitated this smuggling. A memo sent from the chairman of Imperial Tobacco, Canada's largest cigarette manufacturer, to the managing director of its parent company, British American Tobacco, stated,

> Subsequently, we have decided to remove the limits on our exports to regain our share of Canadian smokers. . . . Until the smuggling issue is resolved, an increasing volume of our domestic sales in Canada will be exported, then smuggled back for sale here. (as quoted in Levin, 2002)

It was estimated that as a result of their involvement in smuggling, the tobacco companies realized more than $100 million in profit from contraband sales (Levin, 2002). As one commentator noted, "this activity may have been the largest and most destructive corporate misconduct in the history of Canadian business or public health" (Malarek, 2003). The Canadian government eventually sued RJ Reynolds to recover an estimated $1 billion in forfeited taxes and law enforcement costs as a result of the smuggling. It is also important to note that the involvement of tobacco companies in the illegal smuggling of cigarettes has not been restricted to Canada.

In 2002, RJ Reynolds was also sued by the European Union for selling black market cigarettes in EU countries (Weinstein & Levin, 2002). Similarly, memos from the British American Tobacco Company uncovered in 2003 included transcripts of high-ranking executives discussing the importance of illegal cigarettes in maintaining and/or expanding their market share in developing countries such as Argentina and China (Levin, 2003).

The 1998 Tobacco Settlement and Antismoking Programs

The 1998 settlement between the tobacco companies and states was at least partially in response to revelations that the companies deliberately manipulated nicotine levels to promote addiction in tobacco users (Kessler, 2001). A significant proportion of the $206 billion 1998 tobacco settlement funds were to be devoted to antismoking programs in individual states. However, when we examine how the money from the tobacco settlement has been spent by various states, it is not completely clear that governments are committed to reducing smoking. Nationally, it is estimated that only about 8% of the settlement dollars have been used for antismoking programs, and one study found that states with the highest rates of smoking were actually devoting the lowest proportion of funds to antitobacco programs (Gross et al., 2002). Most states fund tobacco prevention programs at less than half of the recommended level, and a report by a coalition of public health organizations estimated that tobacco companies spend $23 marketing tobacco products for every dollar states spend on antismoking programs (Broadwater, 2004). More specifically, Washington State spends approximately $30 million per year on tobacco prevention and control programs, while the tobacco companies spend $230 million on marketing their products in the state ("Cigarette Marketing," 2004). Olsen (2003) suggests that a major disincentive for states considering targeting tobacco settlement funds to effective antismoking programs is that under the terms of the agreement, the amount of money each state receives actually decreases as cigarette sales decline.

Some of the specific programs that have received funding from tobacco settlement money appear to be directly antithetical to the goal of reducing smoking. For example, in the fall of 2001, LEAF (Long Term Economic Advancement Foundation), a nonprofit organization established by the North Carolina legislature to distribute part of the state's tobacco settlement revenues, allotted $15,000 for a video production on the history of tobacco, and perhaps even more amazingly, granted a rural county $400,000 for the development of water facilities and sewers to improve the county's chances of attracting a tobacco processing plant (Gregory, 2002). In total, it was estimated that North Carolina used approximately three-quarters of its tobacco settlement revenue to improve the production and marketing of tobacco (Hampson, 2003). As newspaper columnist Dave Barry remarked, this was analogous to "using war on terrorism funds to buy flying lessons for Al Qaeda" (as quoted in Hampson, 2003). The state of New York used $700,000 of its tobacco settlement money to purchase golf carts and an irrigation sprinkler for a public golf course in Niagara County (Markel, 2005). The state of Virginia gave $2 million in marketing incentives from its settlement money to the cigarette company Star Scientific, which subsequently used the money to sue the state to overturn the tobacco settlement itself (Scherer, 2002). Seven states actually invested the funds obtained from the settlement in stocks of the tobacco companies they sued in the first place (Scherer, 2002). Other states facing severe budget shortfalls have issued bonds backed by future tobacco settlement payments in a process known as securitization. More generally, a 2007 report by the Government Accountability Office found that only one-third of the tobacco settlement money paid out between 2000 and 2005 was devoted to health care or tobacco control (Cave, 2009). And in 2012, it was estimated that states would spend only 2% of their settlement funds on programs to prevent smoking or to help people quit—between 2008 and 2012, state spending on tobacco prevention and cessation declined by 37% to $457 million (Andrews, 2012; see also Simmons, 2010). Only one state (North Dakota) funds its tobacco prevention programs at the Centers for Disease Control recommended level, and it was estimated that the tobacco companies spend $20 to market tobacco products for every $1 the states spend to prevent young people from smoking and helping current smokers quit (Campaign for Tobacco-Free Kids, 2009). As Christine Gregoire, one of the key negotiators in the tobacco settlement noted, "The money in the tobacco settlement is as addictive to states as the nicotine in cigarettes is to smokers" (as quoted in Hampson, 2003).

In addition to the state-level lawsuit and subsequent settlement with the tobacco companies, the federal Justice Department initiated a civil racketeering lawsuit in the late 1990s, charging tobacco companies with fraud and deception with respect to minimizing smoking's health risks and addictive potential. While the Justice Department had initially determined that the sum of $130 billion would be required, they subsequently agreed to settle for $10 billion. As a *New York Times* editorial commented, "it was an egregious example of favoritism toward a big politically connected industry by an administration that is making such favors a hallmark of its governing style" ("Torpedoing," 2005).

International Tobacco Legislation

While the material in the previous section indicates a reluctance on the part of government officials to reduce tobacco consumption in their respective states, there are also indications that the U.S. federal government, influenced by powerful multinational tobacco companies, has thwarted efforts to reduce tobacco consumption globally. President Ronald Reagan sent a memorandum to the RJ Reynolds Company promising the tobacco industry "freedom from any trouble on his watch" ("Censored," 1996). Reagan also ordered U.S. trade representatives to "declare war on government-run tobacco monopolies in Asia" by threatening to impose large tariffs on any countries that were believed to be discriminating against American tobacco companies by restricting imports of their products ("Censored," 1996). More recently, in the context of a proposed international treaty on tobacco (the Framework on Tobacco Control) in 2003, the George W. Bush administration announced it was opposed to provisions that would have prohibited the advertising of cigarettes, claiming that such restrictions would violate freedom-of-speech provisions (Yeoman, 2003). This stance may have been at least partially influenced by a 32-page letter by the Philip Morris tobacco company, which contributed approximately $58,000 to the Republican Party in 2002, expressing opposition to the proposed international treaty (Yeoman, 2003).

The Future of Tobacco Regulation

Even though tobacco has more additives than virtually any other legal drug, it was excluded from regulation in the 1906 Pure Food and Drug Act. Kaplan (1996) asserts that this was partially due to the efforts of the founder of the American Tobacco Company, Buck Duke, who hired several lobbyists to ensure tobacco's exclusion from the Act on the grounds that it was not used to cure or prevent diseases and therefore was not a drug. However, in the mid-1990s, President Clinton attempted to create legislation to allow the Food and Drug Administration to regulate the tobacco industry and treat cigarettes as drug delivery devices. Threatened by this proposed legislation, the tobacco companies engaged in an expensive advertising campaign attacking the intentions of the federal government. One of these advertisements, a full-page ad that appeared in the *New York Times* (October 17, 1995), depicted a man being handcuffed by police with the caption "federal anti-smoking police . . . has the government got its priorities right?" The ad attempted to place problems associated with smoking "in perspective" by noting,

> When it comes to national problems, Americans have a long list of urgent priorities. Crime, unemployment, the deficit, welfare and drugs. Unfortunately, the government has a different perspective. It seems that high on the administration's list is a war against smoking. While the President calls attention to his latest crusade, other problems facing Americans remain unanswered. ("Tobacco Advertisement," 1995)

While President Clinton was ultimately unsuccessful in his attempts to achieve FDA regulation of tobacco products, there were indications in 2003 that the FDA would be given the authority to regulate tobacco. Interestingly, the primary impetus for FDA regulation at that time did not come from public health advocates, but from Philip Morris, the largest tobacco company in the United States. Kaufman (2003) suggests that Philip Morris's motivation in seeking FDA regulation was not completely altruistic. Instead, he argues, the company wanted FDA regulation because it was attempting to design and market safer cigarettes and was concerned that confusion over regulation would limit the health claims it could make in marketing and advertising these products. In other words, Philip Morris viewed FDA regulation as an opportunity to increase sales and profits. In 2003, U.S. Surgeon General Richard Carmona stated that he saw "no need for any tobacco products in society" (as quoted in Kaufman, 2003) and indicated that he supported a complete ban on such products.

In a somewhat sarcastic commentary on the debate over graphic images on cigarette packages, one commentator proposed labeling bags of potato chips and/or soda cans. "With obesity now linked to almost 17% of health care costs, something must be done. Perhaps images of bulging stomachs or dimpled thighs? Or limbs amputated because of diabetes?" (Dennis, 2011)

In 2009, the federal government passed the Family Smoking Prevention and Tobacco Control Act, which, among other things, allowed the Food and Drug Administration to forbid tobacco advertising that was directed at children and to prohibit labels such as "light" and "low tar," which tobacco companies sometimes use to imply that such products are safer (Wilson, 2010b; Zeleny, 2009). The law also proposed a ban on outdoor advertising of tobacco products within 1,000 feet of schools and playgrounds, allowed only black-and-white advertising of tobacco products for print ads except in publications that had an adult readership of 95% or more, and prohibited tobacco companies from sponsoring sports or cultural events or giving away t-shirts or caps (Wilson, 2009). The law also stipulated that tobacco companies cover 50% of the front and rear panels of cigarette packages with graphic images showing the possible health consequences of smoking (including, for example, color images of a man exhaling cigarette smoke through a tracheotomy hole in his throat), and bold, specific labels such as "Warning: Cigarettes cause fatal lung disease: Smoking can kill you" (Mishori, 2009). The major tobacco companies, including RJ Reynolds and Lorillard (but not Philip Morris), sued the federal government in response to this legislation, arguing that the warnings violated their free speech rights: "Never before in the United States have producers of a legal product been required to use their own packaging and advertising to convey an emotionally-charged government message urging adult consumers to shun their products" (as quoted in Collins, 2011). Although at least 43 other countries require large, graphic labels on cigarette packages (Esterl & Corbett-Dooren, 2011), and Australia requires cigarettes to be sold in completely plain packages with no logos (Weeks, 2012), in a two-to-one decision in 2012, a United States Court of Appeals affirmed a lower court ruling that the warnings were in violation of the free speech protections under the First Amendment of the Constitution. The decision noted that the Food and Drug Administration had "not provided a shred of evidence" showing that the warnings would "directly advance" the government's goal of reducing the number of Americans who smoke (Felberbaum, 2012a).

While there has been controversy over antismoking advertisements in the United States, other countries have created even more graphic ads. For example, in France, where smoking is apparently increasing among youth, an antitobacco organization created ads with the slogan "To smoke is to be a slave to tobacco." The ads included a photo of an older man, his torso seen from the side, pushing down the head of a teenage girl who had a cigarette in her mouth—a cigarette appears to emerge from the man's pants. Two other anticigarette ads depicted young men in the same position as the girl. (Erlanger, 2010)

An interesting development in the debates over smoking is related to "e-cigarettes"—electric inhalers that vaporize a nicotine-based liquid solution into an aerosol mist, simulating the act of smoking. These products first appeared on the market in the United States in 2004 (among the users of e-cigarettes were Leonardo DiCaprio and Lindsay Lohan; Chammas, 2011) and were used by close to 3 million people in 2011 (Tierney, 2011). Some researchers have asserted that these devices may addict young people to nicotine or irritate bystanders who are exposed to the vapor (Koch, 2012), and the Food and Drug Administration, after finding trace amounts of carcinogens in samples, tried to regulate e-cigarettes as drug delivery devices (Felberbaum, 2011). However, in 2010, a federal judge ruled that the FDA lacked authority to regulate these devices, and the FDA moved to regulate e-cigarettes as tobacco products. Studies have suggested that e-cigarettes may be an effective smoking cessation method (Pearson et al., 2012) and may constitute a harm-reduction strategy for smokers—one study found that two-thirds of smokers who used this product had reduced smoking after using e-cigarettes for 6 months, and 31% had quit smoking altogether (Siegel et al., 2011). However, several U.S. cities have banned use of these products in smoke-free places, Amtrak prohibits use of them on trains, and the U.S. Department of Transportation proposed banning e-cigarettes on airplanes. (Koch, 2012; Sherman, 2011)

ALCOHOL

Temperance Movements and Prohibition in American History

As noted in Chapter 3, alcohol is the most widely used legal psychoactive substance in the United States and also the drug—legal or illegal—that is associated with the most harm in our society. Of course, alcohol has not always been legal in this country, and temperance and prohibition movements have occurred throughout America's history. In the Colonial period, high levels of alcohol consumption and the attendant social problems related to such consumption led to a number of proposals to regulate the drug. One of the advocates for the temperance movement, Dr. Benjamin Rush, published a book in 1784 titled *An Inquiry Into the Effects of Ardent Spirits Upon the Human Body and Mind*. In this book, Rush recommended the imposition of high taxes on distilled spirits and limits on the number of establishments that could sell liquor as methods of reducing consumption. Interestingly, Rush distinguished between distilled spirits and beer; he did not view the latter as alcohol and hence his proposals only applied to distilled spirits. Presaging the approach of Alcoholics Anonymous, Rush also suggested that the "cure" for alcoholism was for individuals who were addicted to the substance to abstain completely from using it (Sullum, 2003a).

Temperance movements in the United States led to the passage of prohibition legislation in a number of cities and states in the 1800s and, eventually, prohibition at the national level in 1919 (Okrent, 2010).

Although alcohol prohibition is often seen as a uniquely American phenomenon, in Canada, legislation in the 1860s allowed individual cities and counties to enact local prohibition ordinances if the majority of voters in the locale approved. In 1888, there was a national plebiscite on alcohol prohibition that ultimately did not pass, but at one point in time all Canadian provinces had prohibition laws. (Alexander, 1990)

In 1841, Portland, Maine, became the first city to adopt prohibition, and the entire state of Maine became dry in 1851. Oregon was the first "state" (it was a territory at the time) to enact prohibition in 1843, and by 1855, prohibition statutes had been enacted in New Hampshire, Vermont, Delaware, Michigan, Indiana, Iowa, Minnesota, Nebraska, Connecticut, Rhode Island, Massachusetts, and New York (McWilliams, 1996). Also during this era, entire towns, such as Harvey, Illinois, were established on temperance principles. A clause in the land title in this town stated,

> If the purchaser uses any part of property for the purpose of permitting any intoxicating drink to be manufactured, sold, or given away upon said premises, or permits gambling to be carried on therein . . . he, his heirs, executors, administrators and his assigns shall be divested of the entire estate. (as quoted in Walton, 2002, p. 109)

Although most states that enacted prohibition laws in the 1800s eventually repealed them, temperance movements, spearheaded in particular by organizations such as the Women's Christian Temperance Union (founded in 1874) and the Anti-Saloon League (founded in 1895), continued to lobby for the prohibition of alcohol throughout the late 1800s and early 1900s. Their social reform efforts culminated in the prohibition of alcohol at the national level with the Eighteenth Amendment to the Constitution and the passage of the Volstead Act (over President Woodrow Wilson's veto), which came into effect in 1920 (McWilliams, 1996).

While much has been written about the prohibition era in the United States, there is considerable confusion regarding what the Volstead Act actually prohibited and how the legislation was enforced. It is also clear that, similar to other legislation enacted to prohibit the consumption of products for which there is considerable demand, the act did not result in the cessation of alcohol consumption in the United States. The Volstead Act did not provide criminal penalties for individuals possessing (as compared to purchasing) alcohol, and home brewing of alcohol products or wine making was actually legal, as long as none of the product was sold. For example, grape growers in California created a grape juice product known as Vine-Go, suggestively informing purchasers of the product that they should *not* add water to the product and let it ferment because if they did, they would have wine within 60 days (McWilliams, 1996; Walton, 2002). In addition, in the first few years of the prohibition era, doctors were allowed to prescribe alcohol to patients, and in the first 6 months after prohibition was enacted, 15,000 physicians applied for permits (Okrent, 2010); this provision was altered in 1921 so that prescriptions were limited to one pint of alcohol every 10 days (MacCoun & Reuter, 2001). Statistics indicate that the amount of alcoholic liquors sold by physicians and hospitals doubled between 1923 and 1931, and over the same period, the amount of medicinal alcohol (95% alcohol in content) sold increased by 400% (Thornton, 1991a). The Volstead Act also allowed for the use of wine for "sacramental purposes," which increased from 2,139,000 gallons in 1922 to 2,944,970 gallons in 1924. As one commentator suggested, "there is no way of knowing what the legitimate consumption of sacramental wine is, but it is clear that the legitimate demand does not increase 800,000 gallons in two years" (Dobyns, 1940, cited in Shafer Commission, 1973).

More problematic than home brewing operations, physician-prescribed alcohol, and sacramental wines was the emergence of a large-scale bootleg alcohol trade and speakeasies to cater to the tastes of those who wished to consume alcohol. In 1921, 95,993 illicit distilleries, stills, still works, and fermenters were seized by law enforcement authorities; by 1925, the total was 173,537, and by 1930, 281,122 (Shafer Commission, 1973). Prohibition also resulted in increased consumption of stronger alcoholic beverages, such as whiskey, than of weaker beverages, such as beer and wine, in accordance with what James Gray (2001) refers to as a "cardinal rule of prohibition" or what Cowan (1986) labels "the Iron Law of Prohibition." These principles suggest that the more intense law enforcement efforts to eliminate a drug become, the more potent the prohibited substance becomes, and those distributing the illegal product realize that "there is always more money to be made in pushing the more concentrated substances" (Gray, 2001, p. 23). Due to government regulations requiring that industrial alcohol be poisoned with methanol to prevent it from being used for human consumption, thousands of individuals who consumed this product experienced blindness, paralysis, and death. It is estimated that more than 10,000 people died from wood alcohol poisoning over the 1920 to 1933 period (McWilliams, 1996), and in the early 1930s, perhaps as many as 50,000 people were permanently paralyzed as a result of consuming an adulterated ginger extract known as Jake (Sullum, 1998). And while saloons that had previously served drinkers were officially closed as a result of the Volstead Act, many went underground and became speakeasies. Estimates suggest that in the 1920s, there were between 30,000 and 100,000 speakeasies in New York City alone (McWilliams, 1996).

> Under [President] Harding, visitors came in two categories: run of the mill guests who were kept downstairs, and served fruit juice.... The President's cronies and other privileged guests, who were invited upstairs, where liquor flowed like water.... Part of the Senate library had been curtained off, and had become "the best bar in town," well-stocked thanks to regular visits from ingratiatingly subservient customs officials bringing with them confiscated liquor. (Behr, 1997, p. 118)

While it has been widely documented that violations of the Volstead Act were common, it is perhaps less well known that such violations were committed by the highest government officials. Walton (2002) suggests that "under [President] Harding, the White House itself was awash with bootleg hootch" during the prohibition era (p. 191).

Although there is some research suggesting that prohibition actually led to a reduction in alcohol consumption and deaths from cirrhosis of the liver in the United States, Miron and Zweibel (1991) indicate that prohibition had no such effects. Thornton (1991a) goes further, noting that while alcohol consumption decreased in the early years of prohibition, it increased dramatically in the ensuing years. Thornton also asserts that the lowering of death rates due to alcoholism and cirrhosis in the United States began before the enactment of prohibition. He further notes that the death rate for alcoholism also declined in countries such as Denmark, Ireland, and Britain during World War I, but in those countries, which did not have alcohol prohibition policies, rates of death from those conditions continued to decline during the 1920s when rates in the United States were either increasing or stable.

While it is thus difficult to uncover positive outcomes associated with alcohol prohibition in the United States, it is far less difficult to identify the numerous problems associated with this legislation. In 1929, the Volstead Act was criticized by Mabel Willebrandt, who in 1928 had resigned from her position as Deputy Attorney General with the responsibility for enforcing prohibition laws. In her book titled *The Inside of Prohibition*, Willebrandt asserted that the enforcement system was in widespread disarray and that the general public did not support the law (Walton, 2002). As the famous scientist Albert Einstein commented,

> The prestige of the government has undoubtedly been lowered considerably by the Prohibition law. For nothing is more destructive of respect for the government and the law of the land than passing laws which cannot be enforced. It is an open secret that the dangerous increase in crime in this country is closely connected with this. (as quoted in Gray, 2001, p. 77)

Among its other negative consequences, prohibition created widespread disrespect for the law (because such a large percentage of the American public violated the law), corrupted law enforcement, and led to increases in violent crime. The act also gave birth to modern organized crime because suppliers of alcohol used violence to settle disputes, enforce contracts, and defend their market shares. The U.S. homicide rate increased from approximately 6 per 100,000 in 1920 to close to 10 per 100,000 in 1933, a trend that was reversed by the repeal of prohibition in that year (Thornton, 1991a). And although supporters of prohibition, such as Billy Sunday, had predicted that the law would "turn [our] prisons into factories and our jails into storehouses and corncribs" (as cited in Thornton, 1991b), in reality, the opposite occurred. In 1920, there were approximately 3,000 inmates in federal prisons in the United States, but by 1932, the federal prison population had increased to 12,000, with two-thirds of the inmates incarcerated for violations of the Volstead Act or Harrison Narcotics Control Act (Gray, 2001). As McWilliams (1996) concludes, the results of the

"Noble Experiment" of prohibition were "innocent people suffered; organized crime grew into an empire; the police, courts, and politicians became increasingly corrupt; disrespect for the law grew; and the per capita consumption of the prohibited substance—alcohol—increased dramatically, year by year" (p. 61).

While recognition of the numerous negative consequences associated with prohibition contributed to its repeal, its demise was also related to the fact that during the Depression era, the government sorely missed the taxes it had previously collected from alcohol sales (Walton, 2002). When the Volstead Act was repealed by the Twenty-First Amendment to the Constitution in 1933 (the only time in the history of the United States that a constitutional amendment has been repealed), alcohol prohibition no longer existed at the national level. However, the amendment allowed individual states to choose for themselves whether they would continue with prohibition policies, and Kansas remained dry until 1948, Oklahoma until 1957, and Mississippi until 1966 (McWilliams, 1996). But although many states remained dry or continued to restrict sales of alcohol, in the first postrepeal year, the federal government collected more than $258 million in alcohol taxes, comprising nearly 9% of total federal revenue in that year (Okrent, 2010).

Alcohol Regulation in the Current Era

Similar to what occurs with respect to the enforcement of laws regulating illegal drugs, it appears as though laws regulating alcohol consumption are not universally applied. For example, in New York City, which has laws banning alcohol consumption in parks and at beaches, several individuals were arrested on July 4, 2003, for drinking beer at a memorial for the victims of the World Trade Center bombings. A few days after these arrests, thousands of people consumed wine in Central Park while listening to a concert by the New York Philharmonic Orchestra. However, police did not issue a single citation. (T. Williams, 2003)

In the current era, there is wide variation across states and local jurisdictions with respect to the regulation of alcohol. States such as Nevada and Louisiana allocate decisions regarding the regulation of alcohol to local governments, with the result that in many cities and counties in these states, an individual can purchase and drink alcohol virtually anywhere, and do so 24 hours a day (Loftin, 2001). In several cities in Louisiana, consumers can purchase daiquiris at drive-through windows (Martell, 2003). Alaska, Louisiana, Tennessee, and Wyoming have partial bans on open containers in vehicles, while Arkansas, Connecticut, Delaware, Mississippi, Missouri, Virginia, and West Virginia allow passengers in vehicles to consume alcoholic beverages (Opencontainerlaws.com). In Montana, which banned open containers in 2003, "there are still people who measure distances in six packs. Bozeman to Billings is a six-pack drive, Bozeman to Butte is a two six-pack trip. Crossing the state would be a whole case" (Tizon, 2003).

In contrast, more than half of all states have dry cities or counties, and nationally, one in nine counties is dry. Forty-two of the 75 counties in Arkansas are dry, as are 37 of 77 in Oklahoma (Hampson, 2010). In Kentucky, a state known worldwide for its production of bourbon, one-third of the counties are dry (Hanson, n.d.). Even Moore County, Tennessee, where the well-known Jack Daniels whiskey is produced, bans the sale and consumption of alcohol (Bonwich, 2003).

Among the most interesting laws regulating alcohol in the United States are those in Utah. Strongly influenced by the Church of Jesus Christ of Latter-Day Saints, which prohibits alcohol consumption by its members, until 2009 (Hampson, 2011), legislation in Utah required that any establishment serving mixed alcoholic drinks without food had to be a private club, and these establishments had to be located at a minimum distance from schools, churches, and other institutions. An individual wishing to consume alcohol had to either purchase an annual membership at one of these clubs, typically at a cost of $12, or a 2-week membership, costing $5, or be sponsored by a member of a club (Loftin, 2001). Taverns in Utah can only serve beer, the maximum alcohol content of which is 3.2%. In addition, when ordering a mixed drink, a person can only get 1 ounce of "primary liquor," which means that a martini (containing 2 ounces of vodka or gin) is illegal, while a Long Island iced tea (which consists of 1 ounce each of tequila, rum, vodka, and gin) is legal (Loftin, 2001).

Similar to other laws regulating drugs, laws such as those in Utah and regulations prohibiting alcohol purchases and consumption in particular jurisdictions may have unintended negative consequences. For example, while a 1993 study of motor vehicle accidents in Kentucky found that dry counties had lower rates of alcohol-related fatalities and alcohol-related nonfatal accidents (Winn & Giaocopassi,1993), a 2003 study in the same state found that a higher proportion of residents from dry counties were involved in such accidents. The obvious reason for the latter finding is that individuals from dry counties have to travel farther from their homes to consume alcohol, thereby increasing the probability of driving while impaired by alcohol.

Additional evidence regarding the effect of alcohol prohibition in certain jurisdictions comes from Indian reservations in the United States. Although somewhat dated and focused on only a limited number of reservations, a 1976 study of seven reservations in Montana and Wyoming found that reservations that had legalized alcohol sales had a 20% lower mortality rate from cirrhosis of the liver, 47% fewer suicides, 18% fewer homicides, and 11% fewer motor vehicle accidents (May, 1976, as cited in Newhouse, 1999). A more recent study of the effects of banning alcohol on Indian reservations in the state of Montana compared two reservations where alcohol was sold to two in which it was not and found no significant differences with respect to alcohol-related traffic deaths (Newhouse, 1999). The banning of alcohol on Indian reservations can also lead individuals—especially young people—to turn to other, often more dangerous substances to satisfy their desires to alter their consciousness. This is manifested in the incredibly high rates of glue and gasoline sniffing among young people in remote Indian reservations in Canada (Gillis, 2012; Moore, 2003) and some reservations in the United States (NIDA, 2000). More generally, studies have found that "dry" jurisdictions have more alcohol-related accidents than those that do not ban alcohol, largely because drinkers drive elsewhere to consume alcohol and then drive home (Hennessy-Fiske, 2012).

Minimum Legal Drinking Age

> I knew my teenagers were out drinking [that Saturday night]. Unlike most American kids, though, my daughters were drinking safely, legally, and under close adult supervision—in the friendly neighborhood pub two blocks from our London home. (T. Reid, 2003)

After the repeal of prohibition in 1933, most states set their minimum legal drinking age at 21 (although some allowed for the purchase of beer at 18). But in the 1960s and 1970s, faced with inconsistencies associated with the fact that young people could be drafted to serve in the military at age 18 but could not drink alcohol until they were 21, 29 states lowered their drinking age to 18. In 1983, a commission appointed by President Reagan to examine drunk driving noted high rates of alcohol-related traffic fatalities among young people and recommended that the federal government require all states to increase their minimum legal drinking age to 21. In 1984, the federal government passed the Uniform Drinking Age Act, which provided for the withholding of federal highway funds to states that did not increase the minimum drinking age; as a result, by 1988 (Wyoming was the last state to raise its legal drinking age to 21), the minimum legal drinking age was 21 in all states (American Medical Association, 2004).

Individuals charged under minimum drinking age statutes face relatively severe penalties in a number of states. In the state of Washington, for instance, violators can face up to 90 days in jail, a $1,000 fine, and can also lose their driving privileges for up to 2 years (Washington State, 2004). In Texas, a minor in possession of alcohol can be penalized with a 30-day driver's license suspension, up to a $500 fine, 8 to 12 hours of community service, and mandatory attendance in alcohol awareness classes (Texas State, 2003). Penalties for supplying alcohol to minors are also severe: In Minnesota, for example, anyone (including parents) who provides alcohol to a minor can be charged with a gross misdemeanor, be sent to jail for up to 1 year, and be fined up to $3,000 (Washington County, 2004).

Supporters of the increase in the minimum drinking age have argued that these laws have led to a significant reduction in traffic fatalities involving 18- to 20-year-old drivers. One study suggested that the laws had reduced traffic fatalities involving 18- to 20-year-old drivers by an estimated 13% between 1975 and 2000 (American Medical Association, 2004). While the increase in minimum drinking age may have been partially responsible for the decline in traffic fatalities, most research on this issue has been unable to disentangle the effects of other factors that might have contributed to this decrease. Over the same period, social norms changed significantly such that drinking and driving became far less socially acceptable, and drinking and driving laws were enforced much more aggressively (Kluger, 2001). The more aggressive enforcement of DUI laws, along with the fact that the penalties for those convicted of drinking and driving offenses became far more severe (see below), likely served to deter a significant number of younger (and older) people from driving after consuming alcohol. Other factors potentially contributing to the decline in traffic fatalities include higher percentages of individuals wearing seat belts and improved safety features (such as airbags) in vehicles.

372 Drugs and Drugs Policy

Research has also questioned whether increasing the minimum drinking age to 21 has actually been effective with respect to its apparent intention—that is, reducing alcohol consumption among young people. While it is true that the proportion of the American population who drink alcohol has declined in the past few decades, this trend began in 1980, well before all states increased their drinking ages. As discussed in Chapter 6, despite these minimum drinking age laws, youth in the United States continue to consume alcohol, and at fairly high rates. By the time they are high school seniors, more than 80% of young people have used alcohol, and more than 60% report that they have been drunk at least once (NIDA, 2001). In addition, the average age at which teenagers start drinking declined from approximately 18 in the mid-1960s to about 16 in the mid-1990s ("Drinking Among Teens," 2001). A meta-analysis of 48 studies that assessed the effects of changes in the drinking age on alcohol consumption found that less than half (45%) of all analyses indicated that a higher legal drinking age was associated with reduced alcohol consumption among youth (Wagenaar & Toomey, 2002). Another study, based on a quota sample of 56 colleges in the United States and including 3,375 students, concluded "it appears that raising the minimum legal purchase age did not reduce underage drinking. In fact, the legislation may actually have contributed to increased drinking among underage students" (Engs & Hanson, 1989, p. 1085). And at least partially as a result of the minimum-age policy for alcohol consumption, much of the drinking that young people engage in is heavy binge drinking that frequently occurs in unsafe contexts (Ross, 1992).

> Because a significant number of young people participate in "power hour"—consuming several drinks on the date of their 21st birthday—the state of Minnesota passed legislation prohibiting bars from serving alcohol to 21-year-olds until 8 a.m. on the day after their birthday. (Gegax, 2005)

Although it ultimately did not lead to change in the minimum drinking age, in the summer of 2008, led by former Middlebury College President John McCordell, a group of college presidents signed what was known as the (now defunct) Amethyst Initiative (http://www.amethystinitiatve.org/statement), which stated that the 21-year-old drinking age was "not working," and that it had led to a "culture of dangerous, clandestine binge drinking"—often taking place in off-campus locations. The initiative called upon elected officials to "support an informed and dispassionate public debate over the effects of the 21-year-old drinking age." More than 100 college presidents signed the initiative, including presidents of private universities such as Duke, Dartmouth, and Johns Hopkins, and large public universities including the Ohio State University and the University of Maryland.

Research has also suggested that one unintended consequence of increasing the minimum drinking age has been to increase marijuana consumption among young people. A longitudinal study using data from the National Household Survey on Drug Use found that while higher minimum drinking age laws slightly reduced the prevalence of alcohol use, they were also accompanied by a slight increase in the prevalence of marijuana use (DiNardo & Lemieux, 2001).

Critics of the United States' minimum-age drinking laws have also pointed out that they are yet another example of American exceptionalism in the drug policy arena. Several countries (including China, Portugal, Sweden, and Thailand) have no minimum drinking age, while individuals have to be at least 14 to drink in Switzerland and 16 in countries such as Austria, Belgium, France, Germany, Greece, Italy, the Netherlands, Norway, Poland, Spain, and Turkey. Most national governments impose a drinking age of 18; countries in this category include Australia, Brazil, Denmark, Finland, Hungary, Ireland, Mexico, Russia, South Africa, and Venezuela. In Canada, the provinces of Alberta, Manitoba, and Quebec have minimum drinking ages of 18, while in all other provinces, the minimum age is 19. Although there is some dispute over this issue, comparisons between the United States and countries with more liberal policies on youth alcohol consumption indicate that the drinking-related behaviors among youth in those countries are similar (Alberta Alcohol and Drug Abuse Commission, 2003).

In considering the minimum age drinking law more generally, there is a clear paradox inherent in the fact that while individuals under the age of 21 are seen as being sufficiently mature to be allowed to vote, to serve in the military, to sign contracts, and to be subject to capital punishment in a number of states, they are not deemed to be sufficiently responsible to consume alcohol. As the statistics on youth drinking presented in Chapter 6 indicate, a significant number of young people in the United States violate the minimum drinking age laws, and many others use false identification to obtain access to alcohol. Such practices may lead to a more general erosion in the respect for the law among young people.

While minimum-age drinking laws can be criticized on a number of grounds, other laws related to age restrictions on alcohol are arguably even more problematic. In Naperville, Illinois, for example, a law passed in 1997, known as the "presence restriction ordinance," allowed nondrinkers under the age of 21 to be issued tickets if they were knowingly in the company of other underage people who were consuming alcohol. Individuals cited under this law are subject to a $75 minimum fine and must appear in court. Between January and June of 2004, law enforcement officials in Naperville issued 68 tickets for violations of this law. The Naperville city prosecutor defended the law on the grounds that the community had an obligation to keep young people "out of the company of those who commit crime" (Rybarczyk, 2004). But in addition to the fact that on its surface this law would appear to violate the constitutional rights of young people, it may also lead to especially problematic outcomes because it discourages young people from acting responsibly. One 19-year-old female received two citations from the police for violating this law after picking up underage friends who had consumed alcohol at a party. Would Naperville city officials rather have the potentially intoxicated youth drive themselves home?

Another example of laws allegedly intended to reduce underage drinking that may be counterproductive are "social host" laws that make parents criminally responsible for underage drinking that occurs in their homes. Several jurisdictions in the United States have passed such laws (Taylor, 2005; Rosenthal, 2011); for example, although it was eventually ruled unconstitutional, a law in San Diego County made it a misdemeanor to hold drinking parties, with penalties including a fine of up to $1,000 and up to 6 months in jail (Saillant, 2005). A law passed by the city council in Chicago specified fines of between $50 and $200 for adults for each underage person found at a party where drinking occurs. In addition, adults in violation of the law could be sent to jail for 3 days to 6 months ("The Spring Drinking," 2006). In Illinois, a woman's homeowner's insurance paid $2.5 million to a 19-year-old male who, after drinking beer in the bedroom of the woman's daughter, drove home, lost control of his car, was involved in a collision, and became paralyzed. In this case, the woman did not purchase the alcohol for the male, nor was she aware he was drinking in her home (Achenbaum, 2009). As Marsha Rosenbaum (2004a) notes in a critique of these laws,

> The parents do not condone or promote drinking. Nor do they provide alcohol at parties. But they understand that underage drinking will occur, whether or not they approve. Ultimately they believe their teens are safer at home where they can be supervised, than on the road.

Regulating Drinking on College Campuses

It may be that young undergrads arriving on campus here have a lot to learn about drinking as well as other things. Learning about life has always been an important part of university education. When students learn about life, they sometimes go too far and engage in activities that they may regret later. And it is precisely experiences like getting drunk and feeling lonely and depressed that force students to learn about themselves.... Moralistic campaigns about safe drinking insulate students from experiences that eventually turn them into mature adults. (Furedi, 1998)

The minimum drinking age of 21 has been especially problematic for colleges in the United States; in fact, college presidents view excessive alcohol consumption as the most serious social problem on their campuses (Christie et al., 2001). In response to alleged increases in binge drinking and more general problems associated with alcohol consumption by students, colleges have implemented a number of policies, including alcohol-free dormitories, and, in some cases, even banning alcohol consumption from campus property altogether.

But do these policies achieve their stated goal of reducing young people's drinking and the harms associated with drinking? Making campuses dry and thereby moving alcohol consumption to other contexts can in fact be counterproductive, and by forcing students (underage or otherwise) who wish to consume alcohol to go off campus, greater harms may result. As one commentator noted, at least partially in response to alcohol prohibition on campuses, "the typical partygoers' schedule" was to "drive off campus or hide in the woods (often alone) and guzzle a pint of bourbon, eat a box of breath mints, and then stumble into the sorority party serenely blotto" (Hitt, 1999). At Washington State University, which experienced an alcohol-fueled student riot in 1998 resulting in restrictions being imposed on campus drinking, the Director of Residences indicated he felt hamstrung by an approach that officially insists that students younger than age 21 not drink: "Prohibition is a non-functional approach. All you do is move [student drinking] somewhere else." He compared efforts at controlling drinking on campuses to the "whack-a-mole" game seen at fairs and carnivals, in which players hammer a plastic rodent into a hole only to have another pop up somewhere else (McDonough, 1999). As David Hanson (cited in Honan, 1995) notes,

> Moving [the Greeks] off campus could be the worst solution of all. As long as drinking is on campus, the school has some control over it. It would lose that control if the students had to go off campus and other places which are not desirable.

In addition to displacing college students' drinking to off-campus venues, the prohibition of alcohol on college campuses has also contributed to the displacement of drinking even further afield. Advertisements for spring break vacations to Mexico, many of them produced in conjunction with American beer and liquor companies, frequently emphasize that the drinking age in Mexico is just 18 and is rarely enforced. One company's advertisement promised "50 hours of free drinking" over 7 days and, while commenting on the beauty of Cancun, added, "Most students just care about the abundance of alcohol. . . . your yearly intake [of alcohol] could happen in one small week in Cancun, Mexico, on spring break" (as quoted in Leinwand, 2003b). In such contexts, problematic drinking is even more likely to occur, and the risks to young people are even greater. As an editorial in the *Wall Street Journal* argued,

> Zero-tolerance for college drinking sounds great on paper, but it reinforces the mystique of intoxication. Indeed, the time may have come to discuss lowering the drinking age from 21 to say, 19, when most students are out of high school. Wouldn't it be better if guys and girls learned the difference between a barrel of beer and a vat of rum from their parents and not the provost or police? ("Binge Drinking," 1997)

Similarly, McCardell (2004) suggests,

> The 21-year-old drinking age is bad social policy and terrible law. It is astonishing that college students have thus far acquiesced in so egregious an abridgment of the age of majority. . . . Would we expect a student who has been denied access to oil paint to graduate with an ability to paint a portrait in oil? Colleges should be given the chance to educate students, who in all other respects are adults, in the appropriate use of alcohol, within campus boundaries and out in the open.

While several colleges have attempted to regulate drinking through the promotion of dry campus policies, another program that has been widely implemented to reduce drinking in recent years is known as "social norms marketing"; these programs have been adopted in close to half of all 4-year residential colleges and universities in the United States (Wechsler et al., 2003), and government agencies have spent several million dollars subsidizing them since the mid-1990s (Trounson, 2003). Based on the theory that college students overestimate the alcohol consumption of their peers, social norms marketing attempts to provide them with "accurate" information on consumption. When students are provided with information that their peers actually drink less than they believed, this theory suggests, they will reduce their own consumption to these lower levels. As Perkins and Wecshler (1996) summarize the basic tenets of social norms marketing,

> when the norm on a specific campus is perceived by a student as quite permissive, he or she is more likely to abuse alcohol. . . . If students' misperceptions that exaggerate their peer norms are exposed and replaced with a more accurate perception of peer expectations and practices, their own drinking behavior is likely to become less problematic. (p. 965)

While supporters of social norms marketing programs have argued that they are effective in reducing alcohol consumption on college campuses, critics have pointed out that most of the studies cited in support of their effectiveness have focused more on student perceptions and attitudes as opposed to their actual drinking behavior. Unfortunately for supporters of the social norms program, most of the studies that examine actual alcohol consumption have failed to demonstrate the effectiveness of the program. A study of college students living in a residence hall at a large public university found that while social norms marketing successfully corrected students' misperceptions of drinking norms, it had no effect and even counterintuitive effects (i.e., it led to an increase in consumption) on drinking behaviors (Clapp et al., 2003). Similarly, a longitudinal study of more than 100 colleges found that these programs are not correlated with a decrease in alcohol consumption among students on campuses where they were implemented. Even more problematically, the programs actually increased alcohol consumption among light to moderate drinkers (Wechsler et al., 2003). Such increases in consumption among light to moderate drinkers should not be surprising in light of the theoretical basis of the social norms model: the light and moderate drinkers are altering their consumption to what they have been informed are "acceptable" levels on their campuses. Wechsler (2000) found that 47% of students *under*estimate the rate of binge drinking on their campuses, while only 29% overestimate it. Although those latter students might benefit from realizing their miscalculation, what about the far greater numbers who underestimate binge drinking? Would they feel compelled to drink more?

Given the above discussion of the problems associated with minimum drinking age laws and more specific policies to reduce underage drinking, it would seem that a more rational approach would focus on teaching moderation rather than promoting abstinence, stressing responsible drinking—not drinking itself—as a sign of maturity (Strand, 2002). As Walton (2002) suggests, "to deny intoxication, even in private contexts, to those under the licensing age is to refuse an essential learning experience, and has no greater chance of success than any other prohibition" (p. 8). In the context of reducing problematic drinking among college students, Weitzman and colleagues (2003) suggest that efforts should be directed toward minimizing access to low-cost alcohol and ensuring that outlets selling and serving alcohol in college towns are doing so in compliance with the law. As noted above, the Amethyst Initiative is indication that at least some colleges and universities feel it is necessary to reconsider the 21 minimum drinking age in the United States.

Drunk Driving Laws

More recent proposals from MADD have recommended lowering the acceptable BAC limit to .06, .04, or even to zero (Balko, 2002). In light of such proposals, Candace Lightner, the founder of MADD, suggested that MADD has turned into a "neoprohibitionist" organization. (Vartabedian, 2002)

The first drunk driving policies in the United States were enacted in the state of New York in 1910; California enacted similar legislation in 1911, and other states soon followed. These early laws merely prohibited driving while intoxicated, with no clear definition of what level of intoxication would result in sanctions. These laws were not vigorously enforced and violators were generally not subject to severe penalties. However, prompted in part by pressure from groups such as Mothers Against Drunk Driving (MADD) and the recommendations of the previously mentioned Commission Against Drunk Driving appointed by President Reagan in 1982, most states strengthened their DUI laws and increased the penalties associated with the violation of these laws in the 1980s and 1990s (National Commission Against Drunk Driving [NCADD], n.d.).

Among other things, the Presidential Commission Against Drunk Driving recommended more aggressive enforcement of drunk driving laws through the use of roadblocks and mandatory minimum sentences for all individuals convicted of driving while impaired (NCADD, n.d.). Drunk driving laws became even more severe in the late 1990s, when Congress passed legislation ordering states to lower the acceptable blood alcohol content (BAC) level to .08 or lose federal highway funds.

In some jurisdictions outside the United States, law enforcement officials have been given even wider latitude in their attempts to apprehend drunk drivers. In Vancouver, British Columbia, for instance, a new strategy introduced in 2002 involved police officers posing as "squeegee kids" and pedestrians in order to catch impaired drivers. Officers also began going undercover into bars and even fast-food drive-throughs where drinking drivers often stop after drinking establishments close. (Cherneki, 2002)

As of February 2004, 47 states, along with the District of Columbia, had adopted .08 BAC "per se" laws as the legal level of intoxication for drivers (National Conference of State Legislatures, 2004). Under these "per se" laws, an individual is considered to be guilty of impaired driving merely as a result of having a blood alcohol content of .08 or higher; no proof of actual impairment is required for charges to be laid. In Washington, D.C., drivers have been arrested as a result of having as little as .01 BAC; one police officer in this jurisdiction commented, "If you get behind the wheel of a car with any measurable amount of alcohol, you will be dealt with in D.C. We have zero tolerance" (as quoted in Schulte, 2005). In 2004, 321 people were arrested in Washington, D.C., with BAC levels below .08; in 2003, 409 were arrested with below .08 BAC.

Drivers are considered to be impaired if they register a BAC at or above the legal limit in every state except Massachusetts. In that state, prosecutors are required to prove that drivers were operating their vehicles while under the influence of alcohol. As a result of these provisions, juries in Massachusetts can find drivers not guilty of driving under the influence of alcohol, even if their blood alcohol level was above the legal limit. In addition, refusing to submit to a blood test or breath analysis cannot be admitted as evidence in drunk-driving cases in Massachusetts, and the minimum penalty for refusing to take these tests is considerably less severe than the penalty associated with failing the test. (Abelson, 2002)

Forty-four states also have policies of zero tolerance (i.e., no alcohol in the bloodstream) for drivers under the age of 21 (Schuman, 2004).

Many drunk driving statutes implicitly define those who are over the legal limit as alcoholics, and as such, at least 27 states require mandatory drug treatment for first-time DUI offenders, and almost all states require treatment for subsequent DUI offenses (National Conference of State Legislatures, 2004). Also, under a procedure known as administrative license suspensions, driver's licenses are rescinded even before the individual has been convicted of the offense when the driver fails or refuses to take a test measuring his or her blood alcohol content; 42 states and the District of Columbia have such laws. Forty-three states require that those convicted of DUI offenses drive only if their vehicles have been equipped with ignition interlock devices that analyze a driver's breath and disable the vehicle if the driver has been drinking (O'Donnell, 2006). In 2004, legislation proposed in New Mexico would have required every new vehicle sold in the state to be equipped with an ignition interlock device by 2008, and every used car by 2009 (Schuman, 2004). Although this legislation was not passed, in 2005, New Mexico became the first state to require ignition interlock devices for first-time DUI offenders, and drivers with four or more DUI convictions are required to drive with interlocks for the rest of their lives (El Nasser, 2005). As of 2009, 11 states had passed laws requiring all individuals convicted of driving while impaired to install ignition interlock devices on their vehicles (Copeland, 2009).

In France, where the legal limit for BAC is 0.05, as of July 1, 2012, all drivers were required to have a "personal breathalyzer" installed in their vehicles. The individual who persuaded the French parliament to pass this law was a part-time employee (making $3,600 per month) of Contralco, the only company in France that manufactures certified breath testing machines. (Barton, 2012; Lauter, 2012)

In 29 states, repeat offenders may be required to forfeit their vehicles if convicted of impaired driving (OHS Health and Safety Services, 2004) and three states (Georgia, Minnesota, and Ohio) require convicted drunk drivers to have special numbers or colors on their license plates that identify them as drunk drivers (National Conference of State Legislatures, 2004).

There were 1,412,333 arrests for impaired driving in the United States in 2010 (second only to "drug abuse violations"; FBI, 2011), and as the discussion above indicates, the consequences for violators of these laws are quite severe. Although the costs vary considerably across states, the total estimated cost of a DUI conviction in Washington State ranged from $3,465 to $24,825 (including $500 to $1,500 for a jury trial; fines and court fees of $685 to $8,125; ignition interlock device installation and operation $730 to $2,800; treatment from $1,200 to $10,000; at least a doubling in insurance rates; and towing fees of $50 to $150; MADD, 2004). Local jurisdictions can also add to the costs of a DUI conviction. In Clark County, Washington, for example, legislation passed in 2003 required defendants convicted of a DUI to pay a $200 "emergency response fee." Individuals prosecuted in the city of Vancouver, Washington, can be required to pay reimbursement of law enforcement costs associated with their arrest of up to $164 per hour and emergency services at a rate of $394 per hour to a maximum penalty of $1,000 (Rice, 2003).

One of the most prominent Washington residents sentenced under the deferred prosecution provision was State Supreme Court Justice Bobbe M. Bridge, who was apprehended by police after she hit a parked car and attempted to drive away from the scene. The justice was allowed deferred prosecution on the DUI charge and the hit-and-run charge was dismissed. Although it was claimed that deferred prosecution for a first-time DUI offender in Washington State was "standard," it is notable that Justice Bridge's BAC level was .22, close to three times the legal limit. (Clarridge, 2003)

While the recent DUI laws are obviously quite severe in terms of the penalties associated with their violation, a number of states have created specialized drunk driving courts and/or allowed for diversion of first-time DUI offenders. In Washington State, under "deferred prosecution" provisions, first-time DUI offenders who are diagnosed with an alcohol addiction and who fully accept the need for treatment are allowed to participate in a 2-year treatment program. Upon successful completion of the program, the original DUI charge will be dismissed, 3 years after completion of the treatment program but not sooner than 5 years from the entry of the deferred prosecution. This deferred prosecution program also requires compliance with other conditions that might be imposed by the sentencing judge, including attendance at Alcoholics Anonymous meetings and the installation of an ignition interlock device on the offender's vehicle. There is no doubt that this program offers potential advantages for DUI offenders; they are spared paying higher insurance premiums, avoid being fined, and also are not subject to administrative license suspensions. However, it is important to note that the 2-year treatment program is quite rigorous and the consequences of noncompliance are quite severe for the offender. Revocation of a deferred prosecution results in conviction on the original DUI charge, and the subsequent penalties may be more severe than if the defendant had simply pled guilty to the original charge. In addition, a deferred prosecution counts as a prior offense if the individual is convicted for a subsequent DUI within 7 years of the DUI for which he or she received the deferred prosecution (The Cowan Smith Kirk Gaston Law Firm, 2002).

A Critical Examination of Drunk Driving Policies

Stringent DUI laws have been justified on the basis of their effectiveness in reducing traffic fatalities. Although other factors, such as improved safety features on vehicles and the increased use of seat belts, have likely contributed to the decline in traffic fatalities over time, there is little doubt that more stringent drunk driving laws and aggressive enforcement of these laws have contributed to a reduction in alcohol-related traffic fatalities in the United States. In 1982, there were 26,173 alcohol-related traffic fatalities in the United States, comprising 60% of all traffic fatalities in that year. In 2009, there were 10,839 (NHTSA, 2010). While these declines in alcohol-related traffic fatalities should certainly be viewed as a positive development, as we have done in other areas of drug policy, we need to critically examine drunk driving policies with respect to their intent, effectiveness, and unintended consequences. We begin with a discussion of the definition of "alcohol-related traffic fatalities."

The Definition of "Alcohol-Related Traffic Fatalities"

In his introduction to the 1983 *Final Report of the Presidential Commission on Drunk Driving*, which launched more stringent drunk driving policies in the United States, President Reagan asserted, "Over the past 10 years, over 250,000 Americans have died in accidents caused by drunk driving, and millions have been maimed or crippled" (cited in NCADD, n.d.). This statement and similar statements made by certain legislators, representatives from groups such as MADD, and media reporters are simply not true. The problem is related to the fact that such statements have equated the term *related* to *caused*; however, it is by no means the case that all of these alcohol-related traffic fatalities are *caused* by alcohol. The National Highway Traffic Safety Administration (NHTSA) defines an alcohol-related accident as any one in which a driver, passenger, cyclist, or pedestrian had *any* measurable alcohol in his or her system. Using the NHTSA data, it is not possible to distinguish between drivers who have merely been drinking and those whose driving has actually been impaired by alcohol (Walker, 2001). In addition, in compiling these figures, the NHTSA does not consider the actual cause of the accident. For example, a chain-reaction crash involving 10 vehicles caused by black ice that results in the death of five people would be considered alcohol-related even if only one of the drivers had taken cough syrup medication (which contains traces of alcohol) prior to being involved in the accident (Wishnick, 1999). More specifically, of the 17,448 traffic deaths attributed to alcohol in 2001, between 2,500 and 3,500 involved deaths in which no driver was legally drunk, but in which some alcohol was detected. Another 1,770 deaths involved pedestrians who had been drinking and 8,000 involved only a single vehicle, leaving a figure of approximately 5,000 sober victims who were killed by drivers who were legally drunk (Vartabedian, 2002; see also NHTSA, 2002).

Harper's magazine presented similar data in a slightly different fashion in its index of statistics: "Percentage of pedestrian fatalities on U.S. roadways last year in which the driver was drunk: (18). Percentage in which the pedestrian was [drunk] (37)" ("Harper's Index," 2003). While this number of deaths is certainly disturbing, it is clearly far lower than the alarmist figures that are commonly invoked to justify the continued strict approach to drunk driving.

The Determination of "Impairment" by Law Enforcement Officers

In order to determine whether drivers are impaired, law enforcement officials typically use two methods: field sobriety tests and analysis of breath and/or blood for alcohol content. Field sobriety tests involve police officers requiring individuals they suspect of being impaired to undergo a number of mental and physical tests, including finger counting (1, 2, 3, 4, 4, 3, 2, 1) and reciting the alphabet backward. Of these and several other tests used to detect impairment, the only three that have been found to have any reliability in predicting whether an individual is above the legal limit of alcohol are the "horizontal gaze nystagmus" test, the "walk and turn" test, and the "one-leg stand" test.

In the horizontal gaze nystagmus test, the officer observes the eyes of an individual as the individual follows a slowly moving object horizontally with his or her eyes. The officer looks for three indicators of impairment in each eye: "if the eye cannot follow a moving object smoothly; if jerking is distinct when the eye is at maximum deviation, and if the angle of onset of jerking is within 45 degrees of center" (NHTSA, 2001). In the walk and turn test, the "subject is directed to take nine steps, heel-to-toe, along a straight line. After taking the steps, the suspect must turn on one foot and return in the same manner in the opposite direction." With this test, officers look for eight possible indicators of impairment: "if the suspect cannot keep balance while listening to the instructions, begins before the instructions are finished, stops while walking to regain balance, does not touch heel to toe, steps off the line, uses arms to balance, makes an improper turn, or takes an incorrect number of steps." In the one-leg stand test, the "suspect is instructed to stand approximately six inches off the ground and count aloud by thousand (one thousand one, one thousand two, etc.) until told to put the foot down. The officer times the subject for 30 seconds. The officer looks for four indicators of impairment, including swaying while balancing, using arms to balance, hopping to maintain balance, and putting the foot down" (NHTSA, 2001).

> The fact that [field sobriety] tests require unfamiliar and unpracticed motor sequences may put an individual at a disadvantage when performing them. . . . The reliance on field sobriety tests by law enforcement officers in their decision to arrest or not and by juries in their decision whether to convict a person of driving under the influence underscores the need to examine field sobriety tests critically. (Cole & Nowaczyk, 1994, p. 103)

Critics have noted that field sobriety tests are "failure designed tests" and are not reliable with respect to their ability to determine impairment. In addition to the fact that few police officers ask the individuals they are testing whether they have any physical disabilities that might affect their performance on these tests, a report by Burns and Moskowitz (1977) found that 47% of the subjects who would have been arrested based on field sobriety test performance actually had a BAC lower than .10 (the decision level used in most states at that time). A later report by Tharp, Burns, and Moskowitz (1981), also using the horizontal gaze nystagmus, walk and turn, and one-leg stand tests, found that 32% of the participants judged to have BACs greater than .10 actually had lower BACS. And in 1994, Cole and Nowaczyk conducted a study in which police officers were asked to rate the performance of subjects who had been videotaped while performing field sobriety tests. Despite the fact that the individuals performing these tests had consumed no alcohol or drugs and were therefore completely sober, 46% of the officers indicated that the subjects performing the tests had had "too much to drink."

Even the NHTSA has acknowledged that under optimal testing conditions, 35% of people who are not above the legal alcohol limit will be inaccurately identified as impaired on the one-leg stand test, 32% on the walk and turn test, and 23% on the horizontal gaze nystagmus test (Head, 2001).

While BAC tests may seem to be a more objective and reliable method of determining impairment than field sobriety tests, there are problems with these as well. Breath analysis machines estimate BAC indirectly, assuming a 2,100-to-1 ratio in converting alcohol detected in the breath to alcohol in the blood. This assumption in itself can lead to false BAC readings due to the fact that the actual ratio varies from 1,900- to 2,400-to-1 among people and also within a particular person over time (Hanson, 2000). One study found that breath readings vary at least 15% from actual blood alcohol concentrations and that more than 20% of individuals tested will have breath readings higher than their actual blood alcohol levels (Simpson, 1987, cited in Taylor, 1999). Another problem with breath-analysis machines is that in addition to detecting the ethyl alcohol contained in alcoholic beverages, they also identify compounds with chemical structures that are similar to alcohol. One study indicated that individuals who have not consumed *any* alcohol can generate readings as high as .05 after consuming certain bread products (Hanson, 2000). Individuals may also fail a breath test as a result of consuming products such as Listerine, which contains 26.9% alcohol ("Listerine Drinker," 2005), and studies have suggested that having diabetes or even following the Atkins diet can result in a falsely high reading for alcohol. An attorney in Washington State conducted an experiment on her own breath-test machine and claimed she once registered a BAC of 0.08 after eating a banana (T. Johnson, 2005).

An interesting issue is that of breathalyzer tests on individuals who have pierced tongues, especially given that most state laws prohibit tests being conducted on individuals who have foreign objects in their mouth. An Indiana Court of Appeals ruled that the results of an alcohol breath test administered to a woman wearing a stainless steel stud in her tongue were not admissible in court. (Hanson, 2004)

Although not a common occurrence in DUI cases in the United States, the New Jersey Supreme Court reversed four DUI convictions on the grounds that breath tests are unreliable in measuring impairment.

Breath testing, as currently used, is a very inaccurate method for measuring BAC. Even if the breath testing instrument is working perfectly, physiological variables prevent early reasonable accuracy. . . . Breath testing for alcohol using a single test instrument should not be used for scientific, medical, or legal purposes where accuracy is important. (Hlatsula, 1985, cited in Taylor, 1999)

DUI Laws in the Context of Other Dangerous Driving-Related Behaviors

It is also necessary to consider these stringent drunk driving laws in the context of other activities that cause traffic accidents, and hence injury and death. A study of 699 drivers in Toronto, Ontario, who had cellular telephones and were involved in traffic accidents concluded that the relative risk of a collision when using a cell phone was four times higher than when they were not used. "The relative risk [of being involved in an accident] is similar to the hazards associated with driving above the legal limit [of alcohol]" (Redelmeier & Tisbshrani, 1997, p. 457). Interestingly, these researchers did not find any safety advantages associated with the use of hands-free cell phones, thus suggesting that accidents result from problems related to drivers being mentally distracted as a result of talking on a cell phone, as opposed to problems associated with physical dexterity (see also Richtel, 2009; K. Thomas, 2005). Another study conducted by the California Highway Patrol found that 11% of all traffic accidents in that state could be attributed exclusively to the distractions associated with cellular phone use (Connelly, 2003). More recent studies using computerized driving simulators and closed driving tracks similarly found diminished driving performances for individuals using cell phones. Problems included less eye movement and reduced scanning of road conditions and, when using a hand-held phone, worse steering. In these studies, cell phone users drove more slowly than other drivers, missed twice as many traffic signals, and exhibited slower braking than drivers without phones and drivers who were legally drunk (Dizon, 2004). Another study comparing the driving skills of those using cell phones and those with a BAC level of .08 concluded, "when controlling for driving conditions and time on task, cell phone drivers exhibited greater impairment than intoxicated drivers" (Strayer, Crouch, & Drews, 2004). Similarly, a study conducted for the NHTSA equipped 100 vehicles with cameras to record the activities of drivers. This study found that dialing a cell phone increased the risk of an accident or near accident by a factor of three (ElBoghdady & Ginsburg, 2006). Finally, a study using the Fatal Analysis Reporting System (for traffic deaths) estimated that 5,870 distracted-driving–related traffic fatalities (a large proportion of which were related to cell phone use) occurred in 2008 (Wilson & Stimpson, 2011; see also Goldberg, 2012). This study also estimated that drivers distracted by talking or texting on cell phones killed an estimated 16,000 people in the United States between 2001 and 2007.

Despite the fact that the risk associated with motorists' use of cell phones is apparently comparable to the risks associated with being impaired by alcohol, and despite calls by the National Safety Council (an advocacy group that has supported seat belt laws and impaired driving awareness) for a complete ban on the use of cell phones (including the use of hands-free devices) while driving (Parker-Pope, 2009), there have not been any concerted campaigns to create legislation to prohibit the use of cell phones in vehicles. While (as of the summer of 2012) 39 states ban texting while driving and 10 states prohibit hand cell phone use while behind the wheel (Goldberg, 2012), the penalties for violations of these laws are not generally severe and in many states constitute a secondary offense (meaning that law enforcement cannot stop an individual for cell phone use alone). And, somewhat ironically, while several states have banned text messaging while driving, as of 2009, 25 states provided traffic updates through twitter messages ("Harper's Index," 2009).

More than 45 countries have banned the use of cell phones while one's vehicle is in motion, and there have been some indications that such bans are effective in reducing traffic accidents. For example, in November of 1999, Japan passed legislation prohibiting the use of cell phones and navigational systems in vehicles. One month after this law was passed, the Japanese police agency reported that the number of traffic accidents resulting in fatalities or injuries caused by drivers using cell phones declined by approximately 75% (from 244 to 62). (Jackson, 2004)

In addition to studies documenting the hazards associated with using a cell phone while operating an automobile, the NHTSA estimates that simple fatigue results in more than 100,000 accidents per year, and it is also known that a significant number of accidents are associated with drivers using antihistamine drugs (Sullum, 2003a).

Similarly, a study by researchers in Australia found that people who drive after having less than 6 hours of sleep have the same risk of being involved in accidents as individuals who drive under the influence of alcohol ("Tiredness," 2004). Another study of medical interns found that they were more than twice as likely to be involved in an accident while driving home after working 24 hours or longer, with the increased accident risk corresponding to impairment of a driver with a BAC level of between 0.06 and 0.09 (L. Johnson, 2005). A 2001 American Automobile Association study found that eating, fumbling with a car stereo, or disciplining children while driving are even more dangerous than cell phone use (Balko, 2002). More generally, a study by the National Highway Traffic and Safety Administration indicated that 5,870 people had died and approximately 515,000 were injured in 2008 in accidents attributed to distracted driving (Halsey, 2009).

Somewhat ironically, the ignition interlock devices being used in several jurisdictions to ensure that drivers do not consume alcohol before or while driving may themselves contribute to more accidents. In addition to requiring drivers to blow into the device to start their vehicles, the systems require drivers to provide breath samples at random intervals while the engine is running. Once the driver is signaled to provide a sample (usually through a beeping noise), he or she has approximately 3 minutes to provide the sample (McGran, 2002). If the sample is not provided or if alcohol is detected on the driver's breath, the ignition interlock device issues a warning, records the event, and activates flashing lights and the vehicle's horn until the vehicle is turned off. Although the instructions issued by manufacturers of these devices recommend that drivers pull over to the side of the road for these "rolling tests," it is questionable whether many will have the opportunity to do so, especially in congested traffic situations. As such, these devices may create additional traffic hazards and accidents.

Unintended Consequences of DUI Laws

There are also several unintended negative consequences associated with stringent drunk driving laws. In California, for example, it was argued that a "dramatic" increase in the number of hit-and-run accidents was at least partially a result of the state's strict drunk driving laws. "With stiff penalties for motorists driving under the influence, including possible loss of driving privileges, some inebriated drivers may be spurred to take off after an accident" (Cabanatuan & McCormick, 2003). And although data from the United States are not available, in Canada, a study by MADD found that thousands of drivers convicted of DUI offenses in the province of Ontario were opting to drive illegally and without insurance rather than have their licenses reinstated. The study found that more than half of the 16,000 drivers in that province who lose their license each year as a result of DUI convictions do not have their licenses renewed ("Thousands Driving," 2004). A later study, based on Ontario Ministry of Transportation statistics, found that between 50% and 90% of convicted drunk drivers in the province failed to register for a course on the dangers of drinking and driving, which was required for them to reacquire their driver's license (Brennan, 2004). In addition, of the drivers required to have ignition interlock devices installed on their vehicles, only about 7% had them installed.

DUI Laws: Conclusion

Under current DUI legislation in most states, an individual who has consumed a relatively moderate amount of alcohol can be incarcerated, fined several thousands of dollars, pay thousands of dollars in attorney fees, lose his or her driver's license and vehicle, be subject to significant increases in the amount paid for automobile insurance, and, in some cases, even lose his or her job (Wishnick, 1999). DUI laws are thus different from most other criminal and traffic laws in the United States in the sense that individuals are essentially punished for what they *might have done* (i.e., become involved in a fatal collision). However, given the fact that multimillion-dollar industries, organizations, and bureaucracies are dependent on maintaining the aura of a drunk-driving epidemic in the United States (Wishnick, 1999), DUI laws are likely to become more, rather than less, severe in the future.[1]

Alternative approaches to reducing drunk driving might instead focus on reducing the opportunities for individuals to drive. It is obvious, but worth stating, that drunk driving would be less frequent in the United States if individuals were less reliant on private automobiles for transportation. H. L. Ross (1992) suggests that it might be useful to consider policies that encourage more dense residential patterns and more extensive local services, including venues where customers can purchase and consume alcohol. He notes that although New York City contains approximately 40% of the population of the state of New York, it typically has only about 3% of the drunk driving convictions in that state in any given year, largely due to the fact that a high percentage of people who live in New York City do not drive. While difficult to implement, policies that encourage higher residential density will lead to reductions in impaired driving.

An additional policy based on reducing the opportunities for individuals to drive would focus on subsidized alternative transportation. H. L. Ross (1992) notes that when Indiana's drinking age was higher than in the adjacent state of Michigan, officials at Notre Dame University (in Indiana) recognized that large numbers of students were driving across the state line to consume alcohol. In order to reduce the incidence of impaired driving and subsequent injuries and deaths, the university provided buses to transport students to and from the state line. More generally, jurisdictions could enact policies providing for more mass transit for recreational travel to reduce the incidence of impaired driving. While policies designed to increase residential density and/or improve access to public transportation obviously require a considerable amount of planning and the commitment of significant financial resources, if the goal of drunk driving policy is to reduce injuries and deaths, such policies should be given consideration.

CONCLUSION

This chapter focused on policies designed to regulate the marketing and consumption of tobacco and alcohol. Given the substantial harm associated with the use of

---

[1]Among those who benefit from current DUI laws are law enforcement agencies, tow truck companies, defense attorneys, prosecutors, companies manufacturing ignition interlock devices, insurance companies, and drug treatment agencies.

these drugs, it is important to recognize the pronounced lack of regulation for these substances as compared to illegal drugs. Policies designed to regulate legal drugs are fundamentally different than those aimed at illegal drugs. As opposed to illegal drug policies, which advocate total abstinence, legal drug policies generally attempt to control the access to drugs (e.g., through zoning, age restrictions, taxation) and, in some cases, to limit the harmful consequences associated with the use of these drugs (e.g., DUI legislation). A fundamental difference between legal and illegal drug regulation is that the companies that produce legal drugs have tremendous political and economic power, which is used to influence the ways in which these substances are regulated.

Attempts to regulate the consumption of tobacco include bans on public smoking, restrictions on the advertising and marketing of tobacco products, and taxes imposed on the sale of tobacco. Bans on smoking in public places have proliferated in recent years. Advocates justify these policies on the basis of their protective effect for the health of individuals who would otherwise be exposed to secondhand smoke in the belief that the policies will reduce smoking by making it more inconvenient for smokers to light up. Although these policies may achieve some success in meeting these goals, a number of unintended consequences accompany smoking bans. Those living in areas with restaurants and bars affected by smoking bans report increased noise complaints, air pollution, and litter problems resulting from smokers being forced outside of the establishments. Business owners complain that the bans reduce their patronage and profits and that those who do not want to be exposed to secondhand smoke can choose not to come to their establishments.

Taxes imposed on the sale of tobacco are another means by which regulators attempt to control tobacco consumption. Research indicates that increasing the price of cigarettes through taxation substantially reduces tobacco consumption, but that the effect varies, being strongest among lower-income people (who can least afford the price hike). The primary justification for imposing a tax on tobacco sales is that the tax will offset the increased health care costs associated with caring for sick and dying smokers. Although it is clear that smoking is associated with several serious health consequences, there is no evidence that society incurs greater health care costs as a result of smoking. Because smokers tend to die earlier than nonsmokers, they may cost society less in terms of health care costs, Social Security, and pension funds (Sullum, 1998; see also Zorn, 2005).

As with tobacco, the use of alcohol is extremely widespread, and it is associated with a great deal of harm in society. The harm associated with consumption of this drug has prompted several temperance and prohibition movements in American history, the most well known coming with the Eighteenth Amendment to the Constitution and the passage of the Volstead Act in 1920, which made purchase and sale of alcohol illegal. Initially, prohibition decreased the consumption of alcohol in the United States, but the policy was far less effective near its end in 1933. Additionally, there were myriad negative consequences associated with the prohibition of alcohol. The most significant problems resulted from the widespread production, transportation, and sale of alcohol through black-market vendors. Prohibition had little effect on the appetite for alcohol, and organized crime flourished as the primary provider of this lucrative banned commodity. Criminal suppliers of alcohol settled disputes and protected their market share through violence, and as a consequence the U.S. homicide rate soared. Corruption increased at all levels of government, and prohibition bred contempt for the law because the policy was widely ignored and virtually unenforceable. At the time of its repeal in 1933, prohibition was believed by the vast majority of Americans to have been a complete failure.

Currently, there is tremendous variation in the regulation of alcohol across municipalities and states. In some American cities, an individual can purchase and drink alcohol virtually anywhere and at any time of the day, while hundreds of other cities are completely dry.

Modern alcohol policies have been enacted with the laudable goal of reducing alcohol-related harm. In practice, some alcohol regulation policies are more effective than others, some are totally ineffective, and some exacerbate alcohol-related problems. In this chapter, we have provided a discussion of age-based alcohol restrictions, alcohol interventions targeted at college populations, and policies designed to limit drunk driving.

Supporters of setting the minimum age for legal drinking at 21 have argued that these laws reduce traffic fatalities and alcohol-related harm, particularly among the young. These policies have likely contributed to the reduced number of traffic fatalities among young adults over the last 25 years, but a number of other factors are also likely to have contributed to this decline. DUI enforcement and penalties have been substantially increased over this period. Partially as a consequence of these increasingly punitive laws, social norms have grown increasingly critical about driving under the influence, deterring people from driving while intoxicated. Additionally, seat belt laws and improved vehicle safety standards have contributed to the reduction in alcohol-related fatalities among young people.

An additional issue is whether increasing the minimum drinking age has reduced alcohol consumption among young people. Drinking among all populations has decreased in the last 30 years, but this trend began in 1980, well before many states increased their minimum drinking age. Many European countries allow drinking in moderation at young ages and experience fewer alcohol-related problems. This suggests that a high minimum drinking age may prompt youth and young adults to drink in ways (i.e., binge and heavy drinking) and in places (e.g., public parks, cars, house parties) that are particularly unsafe (H. L. Ross, 1992).

A number of policies have been adopted with the intent of minimizing alcohol-related harm among college students. Interventions have included dry areas such as alcohol-free dormitories or alcohol-free campuses. While these policies are well intentioned, the question is whether they reduce levels of drinking and alcohol-related harm among students. Dry campuses or college towns may provide some benefits, but there will be a substantial number of students who still want to drink. This causes problems because drinkers are forced to travel greater distances to obtain and consume alcohol, resulting in a higher incidence of automobile accidents and fatalities. Research suggests that the best way to minimize alcohol-related harm among college students is to limit the ability of drinking establishments to promote heavy drinking through happy hours, cheap drink specials, drink promotions, theme nights, and the like, and to ensure that bars and alcohol outlets sell alcohol in compliance with the law.

Drunk driving laws have grown increasingly stringent over the last 30 years. The most significant revision of the DUI policy came in the late 1990s, when Congress passed legislation mandating that states lower the legal BAC level to 0.08 or lose federal highway funds.

DUI laws are based on the assumption that they reduce the number of automobile-related fatalities, and along with the factors discussed above (increased drinking age, seat belt laws, improved vehicle safety standards), these laws have clearly contributed to a reduction in alcohol-related traffic fatalities in the United States. However, as we have done in other areas of drug policy, we need to critically examine drunk driving policies with respect to their intent, effectiveness, and unintended consequences.

One concern with these laws regards the ability of DUI tests to reliably distinguish drivers who are above the legal BAC level from those who are not. There are many field sobriety tests employed by police officers, and only three have been found to be reasonably reliable for predicting legal intoxication: the "horizontal gaze nystagmus" test, the "walk and turn" test, and the "one-leg stand" test. Even these methods have significant false positive rates. The NHTSA notes that even under optimal testing conditions, 35% of people who are not above the legal alcohol limit will be inaccurately identified as impaired on the one-leg stand test, 32% on the walk and turn test, and 27% on the horizontal gaze nystagmus test (Head, 2001).

We have considered stringent drunk driving laws in the context of other activities that cause traffic accidents, and hence injury and death. This includes the use of cell phones. The use of a cell phone while driving significantly increases the risk of a motor vehicle accident because, like alcohol, it distracts drivers from the task of driving. Similarly, the NHTSA estimates that fatigue results in more than 100,000 accidents per year, and ingesting antihistamines in the form of cold and allergy medicine also contributes to a significant number of accidents (Sullum, 2003a).

With respect to these issues and the difficulty of reliably determining impairment associated with low levels of alcohol consumption, some question whether driving under the influence is overregulated. There is no question that some restrictions on driving under the influence are appropriate and contribute to public safety. However, under existing laws in most states, an individual who has consumed a relatively moderate amount of alcohol and is charged with DUI can be incarcerated, fined several thousands of dollars, pay significant amounts of money in lawyers' fees, lose his/her driver's license and vehicle, be subject to significant increases in the amount paid for vehicle insurance, and, in some cases even lose his/her job.

REVIEW QUESTIONS

1. What are the key differences in the United States' policies to regulate legal versus illegal drugs?

2. What unintended consequences have emerged as a result of the imposition of high taxes on tobacco?

3. In what ways did people circumvent the laws prohibiting the manufacture and sale of alcohol during the prohibition era? How are the unintended consequences of the Volstead Act similar to the unintended consequences of current policies on illegal drugs?

4. What are the unintended consequences of minimum drinking age laws in the United States?

5. In addition to alcohol consumption, what other behaviors increase the risk of traffic collisions? Why have there been comparatively fewer attempts to regulate these behaviors?

6. Is alcohol consumption a major problem on your campus? Conduct research on your campus's drinking policies, and suggest possible changes to the policies.

INTERNET EXERCISE

Go to the National Highway Traffic and Safety Administration website (http://www.nhtsa.gov) and access information on "alcohol-related traffic fatalities." Compare the number of fatalities in your state to those in other states. Why might your state have a higher (or lower) rate of alcohol-related traffic fatalities?

CHAPTER 10

Policies Regulating Legal Drugs

Part II: Prescription and Performance-Enhancing Drugs and Herbal Supplements

Similar to the regulation of tobacco and alcohol, policies regulating prescription and performance-enhancing drugs and herbal supplements, many of which cause significant harm to individuals and society, are in stark contrast to those regulating currently illegal drugs. While it is certainly true that tens of millions of people have realized positive health benefits from the products manufactured by pharmaceutical companies, as is discussed in more detail below, in recent years the motivation of these companies to increase their profits appears to have precedence over more general public health concerns. Several unsafe products have been aggressively marketed by these companies and used by consumers, resulting in significant numbers of injuries and deaths. Perhaps more disturbingly, pharmaceutical companies have used their considerable political and monetary power to influence the Food and Drug Administration (FDA) and to shape legislation regulating their products. In fact, events related to the approval of drugs such as Vioxx led one former FDA official to suggest that "the FDA cannot be trusted to protect the public or reform itself" (Graham, as quoted in Kaufman, 2005a). Our discussion of the regulation of pharmaceutical products examines policies related to the approval and advertising of drugs; the criminal and ethically questionable practices of these companies; the ability of pharmaceutical companies to influence politicians, regulators, and doctors, resulting in positive financial outcomes for these companies; and future directions in the regulation of these products.

The regulation of performance-enhancing drugs presents a different although equally interesting set of issues. We first explore the rationale for the regulation of performance-enhancing drugs and note that while many of these products are illegal in the United States, until fairly recently, federal and state governments allowed various sports organizations to create their own policies to regulate these drugs. Our discussion of the regulation of performance-enhancing drugs examines these policies in a number of sports and also addresses controversies surrounding the policies, particularly with respect to major league baseball.

Finally (and more briefly) this chapter addresses the regulation of dietary/herbal supplements. Although these substances are associated with tens of thousands of adverse health outcomes among users in any given year, the regulation of dietary/ herbal supplements is even more lax than the regulation of pharmaceutical products. Our discussion of these policies also emphasizes the ability of companies that manufacture these products to influence regulatory legislation.

> For better and for worse, this enormous and hugely profitable enterprise [the pharmaceutical industry] has become a dominating presence in American life. It uses its great wealth and influence to ensure favorable government policies. It has also, with the acquiescence of a medical profession addicted to company largesses, assumed a role in directing medical treatment, clinical research, and physician education that is totally inappropriate for a profit-driven industry. (Reiman & Angell, 2002)

REGULATION OF PHARMACEUTICAL PRODUCTS

Early Legislation

The first federal law regulating "pharmaceutical products" in the United States came into effect in 1848. This law banned the importation of adulterated drugs, which at the time were causing major health problems in the (U.S. Food and Drug Administration, 1981).

However, given its focus on drugs imported from other countries, the law did not have any impact on domestically produced substances, many of which were adulterated with drugs that are now included under federal drug control statutes. As discussed in Chapter 3, in the late 1800s through the early 1900s, thousands of "medicines" were produced that contained significant amounts of drugs such as opium, heroin, morphine, and cocaine, and these were commonly sold over the counter. The labels on these products did not indicate the substances they contained, and much of the advertising for the products claimed that they were cures for a wide variety of ailments (U.S. Food and Drug Administration, 1981). In fact, prior to 1907, all drugs could be bought and sold in the same way as any other consumer product; manufacturers did not have to disclose the contents of these products.

Prompted in part by Upton Sinclair's 1906 description of the unsanitary conditions in meat packing plants in Chicago, documented in his book *The Jungle*, and Samuel Hopkins Adams's Great American Fraud series (published in *Collier's* magazine), which exposed the dangers associated with patent medicines (cited in Musto, 1999), Congress passed the Pure Food and Drug Act in 1906. This law prohibited interstate and foreign commerce in adulterated and misbranded food and drug products and required manufacturers to list the ingredients, including the quantity of alcohol and other drugs, in their products (U.S. Food and Drug Administration, 1981). However, the law did not attempt to regulate the purchase of drugs or the quantity of drug that could be contained in a particular product (Lester, Andreozzi, & Appiah, 2004).

Fried (1999) notes that the Pure Food and Drug Act of 1906 failed due to its basic philosophy: The law did not require manufacturers of drugs to prove their products were safe before they marketed them; instead, it required the *government* to prove that product was *not* safe before removing it from the market. A number of examples are indicative of the law's inability to protect consumers from the harms associated with certain products. Banbar was a worthless cure for diabetes that was not prohibited under the Act; Lash-Lure was an eyelash dye used by women that caused blindness in significant numbers of those who used it; and Radithor, a tonic containing radium, resulted in the death of several of its users (U.S. Food and Drug Administration, 1981). The Food and Drug Act was eventually revised in 1938, largely in response to a "wonder drug" known as Elixir Sulfanilamide, the use of which resulted in the deaths of more than 100 people, many of them children. Thus, when a new Food, Drugs, and Cosmetics Act was passed in 1938, drug manufacturers were required to demonstrate that their products were safe before marketing them. When the act was revised again in 1962, prompted by the disasters associated with the drug Thalidomide (see below), new stipulations required the manufacturers of pharmaceutical products to demonstrate the effectiveness of their products as well as their safety.

FDA Approval of Pharmaceutical Products

Most people who use pharmaceutical products have limited, if any, knowledge of how these drugs are approved and regulated by the FDA. In order to ensure that consumers are protected from harm, an ideal process for approval of these substances would be for the FDA to conduct its own independent studies of drugs. However, as Breggin and Breggin (1995) note, and in contrast to most popular belief on the issue, all FDA drug approval studies are constructed, supervised, and paid for by pharmaceutical companies themselves. "It seems obvious, but should be underscored, that the pharmaceutical companies will do everything they can to make their studies turn out right" (p. 36).

Instructive in this regard is Breggin and Breggin's (1995) account of how the widely used antidepressant drug Prozac (manufactured by Eli Lilly) was approved. First, the FDA allowed Eli Lilly to use what is known as a "placebo washout" experiment in testing Prozac. Under this method, all participants in the experiment were given a placebo for approximately 1 week, and those patients who demonstrated improvement in their symptoms of depression were removed from the study. The trials were conducted again with a placebo and a drug group, but as Breggin and Breggin point out, this placebo washout method can make a substance appear to be more effective in treating a condition than it really is. They note that some of the patients who were eliminated from the study after showing positive effects from the placebo may have not reacted positively to Prozac if they had received the drug in the second part of the trial: "The placebo washout purposely produces an unnatural pool of patients. It is unscientific" (p. 38). In addition, in conducting the trials for Prozac, Eli Lilly excluded any individuals with suicidal tendencies, children, and elderly adults from participation. However, it is clear that physicians and psychiatrists frequently, and apparently increasingly, prescribe Prozac (and other antidepressant drugs) to individuals from these categories. Perhaps most disturbingly, the total number of patients who completed the (up to 6-week) trials that were used as the FDA's basis for approval of Prozac was 286. "In effect, anyone now taking Prozac for more than a few weeks is part of a giant ongoing experiment on its longer term effects" (Breggin & Breggin, 1995, p. 41).

Drug companies' funding buys them the right to set the research agenda. The results of commercial sponsorship is that medical knowledge grows in the direction that maximizes corporate profits, in much the same way that plants grow towards sunlight. (Abramson, 2004, p. 96)

The process used in the approval of Prozac is very similar to the approval process for other pharmaceutical products. Trials typically focus on the short-term effects of these drugs, and companies are not required to test their products against other substances already used to treat medical conditions; they are only required to test the drugs against the effects of placebos. The current procedures for testing and approving prescription drugs are largely the result of the 1992 Prescription Drug User Fee Act (PDUFA), under which drug companies agreed to pay a $300,000 fee for each new drug approval application; in return, the FDA's Center for Drug Evaluation and Research (CDER) agreed to speed up the drug approval process. By 1997, these "user fees" were adding $87.5 million annually to the FDA's budget, and by 2006, industry money sent to the FDA was expected to reach $382 million (Henderson & Rowland, 2005). As Abramson (2004) comments, "how unbiased can the CDER be when half its budget comes from the drug companies themselves?" (p. 86).

As noted, drug companies usually do not conduct clinical trials of their substances with children and the elderly, but the drugs are commonly prescribed to individuals from both groups. For example, nearly two-thirds of cancer patients are 65 years of age or older, but only one-quarter of all people involved in cancer drug studies have reached the age of 65 (Abramson, 2004). The drug companies are understandably reluctant to test their products on the elderly, even if older people will be the primary users of the substance. As Jeffrey Avorn, a Harvard University physician who has conducted extensive research on drug marketing, comments, "the elderly are messier to do clinical studies on. They tend to be taking other drugs, and they have a distressing tendency to drop dead" (as quoted in Fried, 1999, p. 232).

One of the most controversial recent issues with respect to the regulation of prescription drugs is the use of antidepressant drugs by children and adolescents. In 2003, drug regulators in Britain recommended against the use of all but one antidepressant drug for individuals under the age of 19 due to the fact that these drugs may increase suicidal tendencies in youth. While the British drug regulators concluded that the use of Prozac by youth was acceptable, they recommended that Paxil (manufactured by GlaxoSmithKline), Zoloft (manufactured by Pfizer), Effexor (Wyeth), Celexa and Lexapro (both from Forest Laboratories), and Luvox (Solvay) not be used by children and adolescents (Goode, 2003). In the United States, a study conducted by FDA official Dr. Andrew Mosholder reviewed data from 20 clinical trials involving more than 4,100 children who were taking SSRIs; the study similarly concluded that there was an increased risk of suicidal behavior among children being treated with these drugs. However, in a further example of the government's suppression of information on drugs, a senior FDA official prevented the study from being presented because it had not been "finalized." Later, a panel of American scientists concluded that antidepressant drugs did not increase the risk of suicide in children. Interestingly, 9 of the 10 scientists on this panel had significant ties to the pharmaceutical industry (Harris, 2004b).

> It is estimated that more than half of the experts employed to advise the FDA on the safety and efficacy of pharmaceutical products have financial relationships, including ownership of stocks, consulting fees, or research grants, with the very companies whose products they are supposed to be evaluating. (Cauchon, 2000)

In light of the evidence from Britain and their own study, the FDA eventually recommended that antidepressant drugs include "black box" warnings on their labels indicating that consumption of these substances can worsen depression and/or lead to suicidal thoughts among young people (Neergaard, 2004). In making this recommendation, however, the FDA indicated that it was not entirely clear whether the drugs themselves led to suicidal thoughts or whether an underlying mental illness was responsible. A similar sentiment was expressed by an Eli Lilly spokesperson in response to at least five documented suicides among patients using antidepressant drugs: "Just because this happens while someone is taking the drug doesn't mean the drug caused it" (as quoted in Harris, 2004e). Such caveats are worth considering in the context of governmental and media pronouncements regarding illegal drugs such as marijuana and methamphetamine (see Chapter 1), where it is almost always claimed that the drug itself, not underlying mental or other conditions, is the cause of negative behaviors and/or outcomes.

Not only are there problems associated with the use of prescription drugs by individuals in demographic categories for which they have not been tested, but drugs do not have to be completely risk free in order to be approved by the FDA. For example, the acne drug Acutane, which appeared on the market in 1982, was found to be associated with birth defects in children whose mothers used it during pregnancy. In the mid-1980s, researchers found that women using this drug had a 35% chance of giving birth to children with multiple deformities. When the FDA considered approval of Acutane, it was fully aware of this dangerous side effect, but the drug was approved because it was considered to be a unique treatment for individuals whose faces were affected by "modular cystic acne" (Rafshoon, 2003).

It is also notable how political issues can affect the approval and nonapproval of drugs for use in certain age groups. Morning-after contraception products have been widely available in several European countries for more than 20 years (Shorto, 2006), but in 2004, overruling the recommendation of a panel of scientists, the FDA rejected an application by Barr Laboratories, manufacturer of a morning-after birth control pill known as Plan B, to make the product available without a prescription. In a letter to the company, the FDA asserted that Barr had not proven that females younger than age 16 could safely use the product without the guidance of their doctor. James Trussell, one of the 23 (out of 27) members of the FDA panel of scientists who voted to approve over-the-counter sales of Plan B, noted, "Unfortunately, for the first time in history, the FDA is not acting as an independent agency and is acting as a tool for the White House. And it's a really sad day when politicians start making medical decisions" (as quoted in Kemper, 2004).

Evidence uncovered by *Washington Post* reporter Marc Kaufman (2005c) indicated that David Hager, an obstetrician/gynecologist from Kentucky who apparently wrote the minority report arguing that over-the-counter sales of Plan B should be rejected, had commented (on a videotape), "I argued from a scientific perspective, and God took that information, and he used it through his minority report to influence the decision. Once again, what Satan meant for evil, God turned into good." Dr. Hager had earlier written a book in which he advised women to read the Bible in order to alleviate premenstrual syndrome (Mooney, 2004). As a *New York Times* editorial in response to this situation noted, "The Bush administration has shown a propensity to elevate its ideology and perceived political needs over scientific research, especially when it comes to matters touching on women's health and education" ("Science or Politics," 2004). We must also consider the FDA decision on the morning-after pill in the context of the agency's approval of several other prescription drugs for use in pediatric populations, despite their demonstrated harms (Wood, Drazen, & Greene, 2005).

> I want you out there every day selling Neurontin...Neurontin is more profitable than Acupril so we need to focus on Neurontin....Pain management, now that's money. Monotherapy, that's money. We don't want to share these patients with everybody, we want them on Neurontin only. We want their whole drug budget—not a quarter, not half—the whole thing. We can't wait for them to ask, we need to get out there and tell them up front. That's where we need to be, holding their hand and whispering in their ear: Neurontin for pain, Neurontin for everything. I don't want to see a single patient coming off Neurontin before they've been up to at least 4,800 mg a day. I don't want to hear that safety crap either. (Memo from senior marketing executive of Warner-Lambert, cited in "Big Brother's," 2003)

In August 2005, Susan Wood, then director of the FDA's Office of Women's Health, announced her resignation in response to the FDA's delay in approving over-the-counter sales of Plan B. In an email message to her colleagues, she said,

I can no longer serve as staff when scientific and clinical evidence, fully evaluated and recommended for approval by the professional staff here, has been overruled. The recent decision announced by the Commissioner about emergency contraception, which continues to limit women's access to a product that would reduce unintended pregnancies and reduce abortions, is contrary to my core commitment to improving and advancing women's health. (as quoted in "FDA Aide Quits," 2005)

Echoing Dr. Wood's concerns, in November 2005, the Government Accounting Office concluded that the FDA had relied on ideology and politics rather than scientific evidence in its rejection of over-the-counter sales of Plan B (Rosenbaum, 2005).

Another important issue with respect to approval of drugs by the FDA is "off-label" use of substances. Once a drug has been approved by the FDA, it can be prescribed for *any* condition, whether that condition is officially indicated on the label or not (Fried, 1999). For example, Provigil, a drug produced by Cephalon that is alleged to increase mental alertness, is approved by the FDA only for treatment of narcolepsy, but most of the nearly $200 million in sales of this drug in 2002 were for sleepiness linked to other conditions. Similarly, more than 90% of the $119 million in sales of Thalidomide, manufactured by Celgene, were for cancer, not for its approved use, leprosy. Perhaps one of the best examples of pharmaceutical companies increasing their profits through off-label uses of drugs is that of Neurontin, produced by Warner-Lambert (acquired by Pfizer in 2000) and approved by the FDA for treatment of epilepsy. Warner-Lambert paid several doctors thousands of dollars each to convince other doctors to prescribe Neurontin for uses that had not been approved by the FDA. One doctor received more than $300,000 from Warner-Lambert for speeches he gave between 1994 and 1997, and six others received more than $100,000 each (Petersen, 2003c). Notably, more than 80% of the approximately $2.3 billion in sales of Neurontin were for uses other than epilepsy (Pollack, 2003). More generally, one study estimated that more than one in seven prescriptions for common drugs are for off-label uses (Bradley, Finkelstein, & Stafford, 2006).

Even with such lax standards with respect to approval of drugs by the FDA, there have also been numerous cases in which drug companies have manipulated the results of clinical trials of drugs or deliberately withheld data on the negative side effects of the drugs being tested. One of the best-known examples of such practices concerns the drug Thalidomide, a sedative introduced in the 1950s that was used by some pregnant women to treat morning sickness. When marketed in Britain and Germany, Thalidomide was packaged with labels containing warnings that it could cause "tingling of the nerves," thus indicating that the manufacturers of the drug (William S. Merrell Company) knew about the potential problems associated with it (Fried, 1999). The drug was not approved for use in the United States because the FDA concluded that there was insufficient proof of its safety for humans. However, Thalidomide was used by thousands of women in European countries and Canada, and more than 10,000 children worldwide were born with birth defects (including having seal-like flippers instead of arms and legs) as a result of their mothers' consumption of this drug (Fried, 1999).

There are also several more recent examples of pharmaceutical companies deliberately concealing evidence regarding the harmful effects of their products. A number of nonprescription decongestant and diet drugs contained the substance phenylpropanolamine (PPA), which was linked to thousands of cases of hemorrhagic stroke. The companies producing these drugs were aware of this hazard but launched a campaign to conceal the results until, in 2000, the FDA finally declared the substance unsafe and asked the drug companies to stop selling products containing PPA (Sack & Mundy, 2004). A similar situation occurred with the diabetes drug Rezulin. When Warner-Lambert applied to have this drug approved in 1996, a senior FDA official recommended it not be approved. However, the decision to approve the drug was apparently influenced by officials at the National Institutes of Health. Dr. Eastman, who was in charge of diabetes research at the National Institutes of Health, received $78,455 from Warner-Lambert, and at least 12 of the 22 researchers who were overseeing the $150 million government-sponsored diabetes study were receiving fees or research grants from the company (Abramson, 2004). In addition, executives from Warner-Lambert deliberately concealed from federal regulators data indicating that the substance could cause liver damage (Willman, 2002). By the time this drug was withdrawn from the market in 2000, $1.8 billion worth of it had been sold (Abramson, 2004), and it had been implicated as the cause of 391 deaths and 400 cases of liver failure (Willman, 2001).

One of the most egregious contemporary examples of pharmaceutical companies concealing the negative side effects of drugs involves the anticholesterol drug Baycol, manufactured by Bayer. Well before the company pulled this product from the market, senior executives of Bayer were aware that Baycol was linked to the muscle disorder rhabdomyolysis that caused approximately 100 deaths and 1,600 injuries worldwide ("Bayer Corporation Faces First Trial," 2002). Although Bayer eventually pulled this product from the market in 2001, the company had strong indications of its dangers 3 months after it was introduced in 1998 (Zarembo, 2004). Internal documents also revealed that Bayer officials decided to sell stronger versions of Baycol than had been approved by the FDA, despite their knowledge that the drug had negative side effects that increased at higher doses (Petersen, 2003b).

In August of 2012 (some 50 years after the adverse effects of Thalidomide were first revealed), the Gruenenthal Group (makers of the drug) apologized to the victims and their mothers. The company's chief executive officer stated, "On behalf of Gruenenthal . . . I would like to take the opportunity . . . to express our sincere regrets about the consequences of Thalidomide and our deep sympathy for all those affected, their mothers and their families" (as quoted in Quinn, 2012). However, the apology was rejected as unsatisfactory by the Thalidomide Agency UK, which represents people in Britain who were affected by the drug. A consultant for this group asserted that Gruenenthal was apologizing because of an impending court case initiated by victims of the drug in Australia, and urged the company to "put their money where their mouth is." (as quoted in Quinn, 2012)

In a similar case, after being warned by the FDA that its medicine for heartburn, Propulsid, might have to be banned for children or withdrawn altogether due to its link with heart attacks and death, Johnson & Johnson continued to aggressively market the drug. Several studies sponsored by Johnson & Johnson had identified these concerns; however, they were never published. The company eventually pulled the drug from the market after agreeing to pay $90 million in lawsuits resulting from claims that 300 people died and up to 16,000 were injured as a result of taking Propulsid (Harris & Koli, 2005).

A series of incidents in late 2004 and early 2005 led to further criticism of pharmaceutical companies' practice of concealing negative information about their products. Vioxx (Rofecoxib), a pain relief and arthritis drug manufactured by Merck, was marketed in more than 80 countries and had worldwide sales of more than $2.5 billion in 2003 (Rubin, 2004); more than 25 million Americans took this drug between 1999 and 2004. However, as early as 2001, and by some estimates, 1996 ("An Ailing," 2004), Merck officials had evidence based on their own research that Vioxx could increase the risk of heart attacks or strokes (Meier, 2004c). An article published in the *Journal of the American Medical Association* determined that Vioxx increased the risk of cardiovascular events (Topol, Mukherjee, & Nissen, 2001), as did a study by FDA employee Dr. David Graham. Graham's study, based on analysis of 1.4 million Kaiser Permanente members, linked Vioxx to more than 27,000 heart attacks or sudden cardiac arrests from 1999 to 2003 (Rubin, 2004). Merck also deliberately left out data on the negative effects of Vioxx in an article published in the *Journal of the American Medical Association*. Dr. Graham, who had earlier warned the FDA about the dangers associated with Vioxx, referred to the approval of Vioxx by the FDA as "the single greatest drug safety catastrophe in the history of this country and the history of the world" (as quoted in Lenzer, 2004a) and estimated that between 88,000 and 139,000 Americans had experienced heart attacks or strokes as a result of taking the drug (Graham et al., 2005).

Even in light of emerging evidence regarding the dangers associated with Vioxx, Merck continued to defend the drug, issuing a press release in March of 2001 titled "Merck Confirms Cardiovascular Safety Profile of Vioxx." A FDA warning letter to Merck referred to this press release as "simply incomprehensible" and went on to note that "[Merck's] misrepresentation of the safety profile for Vioxx is particularly troublesome because we have previously, in an untitled letter, objected to promotional materials that also misrepresented Vioxx's safety profile" (cited in Abramson, 2004, p. 36). According to documents released at a Congressional hearing in 2005, Merck ordered its sales representatives not to discuss the side effects of Vioxx with doctors (Alonso-Zaldivar, 2005b). Merck eventually pulled Vioxx from the market in late 2004, but as a *Los Angeles Times* editorial noted, "the recall of the drug may have less to do with the side effects outweighing the benefits than with the legal liabilities outweighing profits" ("A Symptom of FDA," 2004). Richard Hanson, editor of the British medical journal *The Lancet*, commented, "With Vioxx, Merck and the FDA acted out of ruthless, short-sighted, and irresponsible self-interest" (as quoted in Harris, 2004f).

A short time after the problems associated with Vioxx were revealed, the rival company Pfizer attempted to take advantage by running advertisements for one of its Cox-2 inhibitor drugs (Celebrex) in *Newsweek* and other media sources:

Celebrex has been making people with pain and arthritis feel better for years now. And we want to ease your mind too. You've probably heard that Vioxx, a Cox-2 drug for arthritis and pain, has been withdrawn from the market because it increased the risk of heart attacks and stroke. But the information below should make you feel better about Celebrex, which is also a Cox-2 drug. Celebrex is in the same general medication class as Vioxx, but it's NOT the same medicine.

However, Pfizer had evidence from a 1999 clinical trial that elderly patients taking Celebrex suffered heart attacks at a rate of four times those taking a placebo (Berenson & Harris, 2005). Also, in February 2001, the FDA had sent a warning letter to the chief executive officer of Pharmacia (the company that at the time manufactured Celebrex):

Your promotional activities [described above] raise significant health and safety concerns in that they minimize crucial risk information and promote Celebrex for unapproved uses. In two previous untitled letters dated October 6, 1999, and April 6, 2000, we objected to your dissemination of promotional materials for Celebrex that . . . contained unsubstantiated comparative claims, and lacked fair balance. Based upon your written assurances that this violative promotion of Celebrex had been stopped, we considered these matters closed. Despite our prior written notification, and notwithstanding your assurances, Pharmacia has continued to engage in false or misleading promotion of Celebrex. (cited in Abramson, 2004, p. 32)

Given the examples discussed above, consumers should be legitimately concerned about how pharmaceutical products are approved by the FDA. In addition, it is important to note that even though adverse reactions to medicines cause an estimated 100,000 deaths per year (Alonso-Zaldivar, 2005a), the FDA's surveillance of drug safety after products have been approved is "shockingly weak" ("Looking for Adverse," 2004). The system currently in place relies on doctors or other health officials to voluntarily report adverse side effects to drug companies, with the companies being responsible for collecting and evaluating these data. It is estimated that this system captures only 1 to 10% of drug-related side effects and deaths (Elias, 2006). These procedures are in stark contrast to the situation in Europe, where drug approvals are systematically reviewed every 5 years (Pstay et al., 2004). It is also notable that while more than 1,000 people work in the FDA's office of new drugs, there are only slightly more than 110 employed in the office that evaluates the safety of drugs once they are on the market (Graham & James, 2005). Dr. Janet Woodcock, Deputy Commissioner of Operations at the FDA, also emphasized problems in the agency's safety system, commenting that many drug safety problems were preventable because "most adverse events are from known side effects [of drugs]" (as quoted in Harris, 2005a). In addition to the fact that the U.S. system results in significant underreporting of adverse drug effects, as a *New York Times* editorial noted with respect to companies' responsibility for collecting and evaluating data on the safety of their products, "it defies belief that any company whose fortunes are riding on a blockbuster drug will be hard nosed when assessing the unexpected consequences" ("Looking for Adverse," 2004).

REGULATING THE SALE AND ADVERTISING OF PRESCRIPTION DRUGS

Restricting the Sale of Canadian Pharmaceutical Products

> Here's how it works. I can go to Europe and buy their wine for less or go to Asia and buy their clothes for less; American corporations buy their raw materials for less from overseas, or they can move their operations abroad in order to hire cheap labor or management. But in a mind-boggling reversal of the American principle of supply and demand, I cannot purchase cheaper drugs and bring them home. (Whitty, 2004)

The United States has one of the highest costs of prescription drugs of any country in the world, and with the aging population and aggressive marketing of these products by pharmaceutical companies, an increasing number of individuals are using these substances. As drug costs increased in the 1990s and into the 2000s, an increasing number of Americans began to purchase prescription products through companies in Canada; many of these companies operated via the Internet, while others set up storefronts in U.S. cities (Doughton, 2003). Prescription drugs are considerably cheaper in Canada, primarily because the Canadian government regulates the prices of these products. The Congressional Budget Office estimated that U.S. consumers could save as much as $40 billion per year by purchasing prescription drugs from Canada (Harper, 2003), and a number of cities in the United States created programs to allow their employees and retirees to purchase drugs from Canada. In addition, in the early 2000s, a number of states, including California, Illinois, Iowa, Michigan, Minnesota, New Hampshire, and Wisconsin, were either pursuing or studying plans to make it easier for consumers to purchase drugs from Canada.

While federal law prohibits the importation of drugs from foreign countries, the FDA did little to regulate the Canadian companies selling pharmaceutical products until it was pressured by large U.S.–based pharmaceutical companies who were obviously sacrificing considerable profits as a result of the estimated $1 billion American consumers spent on Canadian pharmaceutical products in 2003 (Doughton, 2003). As Stolberg (2003) comments, the FDA's reaction to the importation of Canadian drugs suggests that "The FDA has been co-opted by the very industry it is supposed to regulate."

In response to the increasing sales of Canadian prescription drugs, a number of the large pharmaceutical companies, such as Pfizer and GlaxoSmithKline, cut off supplies of their products to Canadian mail-order pharmacies (Connolly, 2004). The pharmaceutical companies and, later, FDA officials alleged that their concern in calling for the cessation of purchases of drugs from Canadian companies was to ensure an adequate supply of drugs for Canadian customers and to protect American consumers from drugs that did not meet U.S. standards. A flyer produced by the FDA included a picture of a roulette wheel with a skull and crossbones in the center and a headline stating, "it's [buying Canadian pharmaceutical products] a gamble you can't afford to take" (Buchanan, 2004). Further, in response to a proposed Senate bill to ease restrictions on the importation of Canadian pharmaceutical products, GlaxoSmithKline took out a full-page advertisement in *Newsweek* magazine, with the text of the ad stating,

> Drug importation is a game where no one wins. . . . The FDA has said that if Congress opens the floodgates to importation, even the entire U.S. army would not be big enough to carry out the inspections and take the other steps necessary to protect the public against drugs that are not safe or not effective. (GlaxoSmithKline advertisement, 2004)

Another ad paid for by GlaxoSmithKline and appearing in *Atlantic Monthly* and other magazines featured an altered map in which Canadian provinces were depicted as countries such as China, South Africa, Vietnam, India, and the Czech Republic, with the caption "Are you buying your medicine from north of the border or east of the border?" The pharmaceutical industry even went so far as to fund a study explaining how Internet pharmacies in Canada were conducting their business; the study asserted that Internet pharmacies posed a "terrorism threat" (Smith, 2004). Similarly, in a debate with presidential candidate John Kerry in October of 2004, President Bush expressed concern about the importation of Canadian pharmaceutical products:

> When a drug comes from Canada, I want to make sure it cures you and doesn't kill you. What my worry is that, it looks like it's from Canada and it might be from a third-world country. (as quoted in Mills, 2004)

As a reporter for the *Toronto Star* noted in response to this rationale, "It may come as a shock, but Canadians are apparently putting their lives at risk each time they use prescription drugs approved by Ottawa" (Harper, 2003).

While the FDA implied that drugs imported from Canada were not safe, the agency was not able to identify a single case in which a consumer had been harmed by these products (Whitty, 2004). A spokesperson for Health Canada commented, "To our knowledge, nobody has died from taking medications sold in Canada. We don't have any reports of that" (as quoted in Mills, 2004). The FDA admitted that Health Canada, the government agency that regulates drugs in that country, is just as rigorous as the FDA (Harris & Davey, 2004). In fact, a large proportion of the drugs sold in Canada (and reimported into the United States) are actually manufactured in the United States, and there is no evidence to suggest that pharmaceutical

❊{?}❊

Are you buying medicine from north of the border or east of the border?

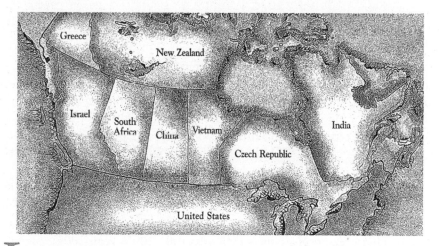

I *f you think you're getting your medicines from our friends to the north, you may be surprised to know that the medications might be coming from much more distant places. Some Internet sites holding themselves out as "Canadian" actually arrange for U.S. customers to receive drugs that never pass through Canada or receive approval from the U.S. Food and Drug Administration (FDA) or its counterpart in Canada. You need to learn more about importation bills before Congress. Because importing drugs is not a safe solution.*

Today's medicines finance tomorrow's miracles.  **GlaxoSmithKline**

Sources: U.S. Senate Judiciary Committee Hearing. "Drug Importation." 108th Congress, 2nd Session. July 14, 2004; Information available at www.canadarx.com/canadaRXorderform. Accessed September 9, 2004. U.S. Senate. Hearing before the Committee on Health, Education, Labor & Pensions. "Importation of Prescription Drugs," 108th Congress, 2nd Session, May 20, 2004. "Prescription Trips." Newsday. September 19, 2004.

companies have questioned the safety of the drugs they sell in Canada (Stark, 2004). Critics of the pharmaceutical companies' and the FDA's response to this situation have also noted that by restricting the importation of pharmaceutical products from Canada, the major drug companies and the FDA may be creating a more serious threat to U.S. consumers by forcing the online pharmaceutical companies to relocate to Eastern European, South American, and African countries. Concerns about the quality and safety of pharmaceutical products from these countries, where regulatory standards are more lax, would be considerably greater (Teather, 2003). Perhaps even more ironically, as pointed out in a *New York Times* editorial, "while the drug industry has been railing against the dangers of foreign imports, it has increasingly transferred its own production to foreign factories to save on labor costs" (cited in Abramson, 2004, p. 161). In fact, then, the biggest importer of foreign drugs is the American pharmaceutical industry itself. Peter Rost (2004), a physician and marketing executive from Pfizer, in an editorial supporting the reimportation of drugs from Canada, commented, "Americans are dying without appropriate drugs because my industry and Congress are more concerned about protecting astronomical profits than they are about protecting the health of Americans."

Advertising Pharmaceutical Products

As noted above, pharmaceutical companies generate considerable profits through sales of their products, and they are clearly motivated to increase these sales and profits. As in other industries, one method of increasing the sales of products is to advertise them. In 2008, pharmaceutical companies spent $4.7 billion on direct-to-consumer advertising of their products (Congressional Budget Office, 2009), and in 2011, they spent $2.4 billion on television advertising alone (Jaspen, 2012).

Pharmaceutical companies in the United States have a unique advantage in advertising their products, given that the United States is now the only country that allows companies to market their drugs directly to consumers (DTC advertising). Studies have indicated that DTC advertising has a significant impact on the purchase and consumption of pharmaceutical products (Mintzes et al., 2003; Pear, 2000); one study found that at least one in eight Americans had asked for and received a prescription drug from his or her doctor as a result of seeing a drug advertisement on television (Landers, 2001). Recognizing the potential profits associated with DTC advertising, the pharmaceutical companies increased their spending on such advertising from approximately $60 million in 1991 (Fried, 1999) to close to $2.5 billion in 2000 (Mello, Rosenthal, & Neumann, 2003) and $4.1 billion in 2004 (Lenzer, 2005a). There are indications that this advertising is successful: As noted in the *Journal of the American Medical Association*, retail sales of the 50 most heavily advertised drugs increased by 32% from 1990 to 2000, compared with 13.6% for all other drugs combined (Hollon, 2005). Similarly, a study conducted by the Kaiser Foundation revealed that for every dollar drug companies spend on DTC advertising, they realize an additional $4.20 in sales (Wilkie, 2005). In addition to direct-to-consumer advertising, more recently, pharmaceutical companies have engaged in the practice of offering free coupons, free trials, and merchandise to consumers who purchase particular products; for instance, GlaxoSmithKline sends free pillowcases to consumers who purchase Flonase allergy spray (Rowland, 2005b).

> Once upon a time, the drug companies promoted drugs to treat diseases. Now it is often the opposite. They promote diseases to fit their drugs. (Angell, 2004, p. 86)

Much of this DTC advertising involves the medicalization of normal human conditions that can allegedly be "treated" with pharmaceutical products, and evidence suggests that pharmaceutical companies are effective in enticing consumers to purchase such products. For example, in the Netherlands there were dramatic increases in doctor consultations for "toenail fungus" after a 3-month media campaign describing this condition. Similarly, in the United States, at least partially as the result of a 1998 media campaign for the hair-restoring drug Propecia, visits to doctors by men concerned about baldness increased by 79% compared with 1997 (Mintzes, 2002). In another example of this, GlaxoSmithKline promoted its drug Ropinirole to treat a condition known as "restless legs syndrome," which the company claimed affected 10% to 15% of adults ("Drug Firms Accused," 2006). There is also a condition known as "eyelash hypotrichosis," which, in an advertisement for the drug Latisse (marketed by Allergan), Brooke Shields described as "inadequate or not enough eyelashes" (Walker, 2009). The pervasiveness of these advertising campaigns is revealed in a market research study that estimated that in 1999, Americans viewed an average of nine prescription drug advertisements on television per day. "To an unprecedented degree, [the advertisements] portrayed the educational message of a pill for every ill—and, increasingly, an ill for every pill" (Mintzes, 2002, p. 909).

More specific examples of the effectiveness of DTC advertising campaigns include the pharmaceutical company Schering-Plough, which spent $185 million advertising their allergy drug Claritin in 1998, with sales of the product doubling over the previous year to more than $21 billion. In 1999, Pfizer spent $57 million to promote its drug Zytec and saw sales of the product increase by 32%; in the same year, Aventia spent $43 million to advertise Allegra, with a resulting 50% increase in sales (Belkin, 2001). In 2001, pharmaceutical companies began advertising ADHD drugs such as Metadate and Ritalin on cable television and in women's magazines (Thomas, 2001; Zernike & Petersen, 2001), breaking with long-standing voluntary restrictions on advertising these highly addictive drugs.

One reason for the tremendous increase in DTC advertising of pharmaceutical products, particularly on television, is a change in FDA regulations on advertising that occurred in 1997. Prior to that time, pharmaceutical companies were required to disclose so many side effects of drugs in their advertisements that it was difficult, if not impossible, to use television advertising. However, the new FDA rules allowed companies to make assertions about the benefits of their drugs with very few restrictions, as long as they provided a website or referenced a publication in which consumers could find out more details regarding the products (Swidey, 2002).

Over the same period in which there was a tremendous increase in the number of DTC advertisements for pharmaceutical products both on television and in print media, the FDA has reduced its monitoring of these ads. In 1998, the FDA sent 158 letters to companies regarding ads the agency believed were false or misleading, compared to only 26 in 2002. Further, over the 1999 to 2001 period, the FDA sent one warning letter to pharmaceutical companies for every 2.8 complaints regarding false advertising, but in the first 6 months of 2002, it sent one letter for every 13.5 complaints (Petersen, 2003d). In 2011, approximately 30 warning letters were sent to pharmaceutical companies by the FDA's Office of Prescription Drug Promotion (U.S. Food and Drug Administration, 2012). At least part of this laxity in monitoring and regulating drug advertisements is related to the fact that in 2001, the FDA had only 30 employees who were responsible for reviewing approximately 34,000 advertisements (Angell, 2004). But even in the context of such apparently low levels of enforcement of restrictions on misleading advertising, some pharmaceutical companies have repeatedly produced misleading advertising for drugs after being cited by the FDA for violations (Pear, 2002a). For example, between 1997 and 2003, manufacturers of the allergy drug Claritin were informed 10 times by the FDA that they had to change their advertisements in order to correct misleading information. The manufacturers of two other drugs—Flonase and Flovent—had been cited 12 times by the FDA for misleading commercials and other sales materials (Judd, 2001). Further evidence of the laxity of the FDA in pursuing actions against pharmaceutical companies is revealed in the case of Prevacid, marketed by TAP pharmaceuticals. In 2002, FDA regulators determined that a television commercial promoting this drug was misleading consumers by failing to clarify that the drug was to be used for serious heartburn problems and not for occasional indigestion. However, a letter written to TAP pharmaceuticals apparently sat in FDA offices for more than 2 months, while millions of consumers were exposed to the misleading information in the advertisement.

In the spring of 2005, the FDA ordered Bayer and GlaxoSmithKline to discontinue an advertisement for their erectile dysfunction drug Levitra. The FDA claimed that the commercial did not adequately inform consumers of the drug's side effects and misleadingly implied that the drug was superior to its competitors. Similarly, in November of 2004, the FDA required Pfizer to discontinue an ad for Viagra that featured an actor growing blue horns the same color as the pill and portrayed him as becoming more sexually interested in his female partner. The FDA expressed concern that this advertisement did not state that the drug was for men and also failed to mention side effects. (Ahrens, 2005)

A change initiated by the Bush administration in 2002 further adversely affected the FDA's ability to reduce misleading advertisements by substantially increasing the amount of time required to issue notices to companies that they were in violation of restrictions. The new regulations resulted in FDA enforcement actions being delayed from 2 to 11 weeks. A potentially more problematic consequence of this change is that due to the fact that a substantial proportion of drug advertisements are on television only for a short period of time (approximately one-fifth of all prescription drug ads run for 1 month, while approximately one-third run for 2 months or less), misleading advertisements can complete their "broadcast cycle" before the FDA warns the manufacturer of problems (Pear, 2002b). Gallagher and Oransky (2005) propose that FDA warning letters for pharmaceutical companies' advertising be replaced by substantial fines: "Otherwise, what is the incentive not to continue misleading ads? The upside of such ads is so tremendous, given the ads' efficacy, that the absence of fines is preposterous."

Even in light of such lax regulation of advertising, pharmaceutical companies have been openly critical of the FDA. In a letter to the FDA from Pfizer, it was asserted that the rules on prescription drug promotion

lead to a regime where manufacturers are precluded from advertising for its intended purpose. . . . One only has to watch a laundry detergent ad to realize that the vendor does not have to disclose the stains that the detergent cannot remove in addition to the ones it can. (cited in Petersen, 2003d)

As in other areas of drug regulation, the federal government has also presented misleading information with respect to DTC advertising. In a Food and Drug Administration "Talk Paper," dated January 13, 2003, it was alleged that the results of a survey of 500 doctors "confirm that direct-to-consumer advertising, when done correctly, can serve positive health functions." The paper noted, "most [physicians] agree that, because their patients viewed a direct-to-consumer ad, he or she asked more thoughtful questions during the visit." A House of Representatives report that reviewed this FDA paper noted that the positive commentary on DTC advertising was based on a question in which doctors were asked to recall their last interaction with a patient regarding a DTC advertisement. In reality, 59% of the physicians surveyed had answered that the interaction had *no* beneficial effects, and only 4% felt that the advertisements had served to inform or educate patients. As the House of Representatives report concluded, "the FDA turned a balanced study into an endorsement of direct-to-consumer advertisements" (U.S. House of Representatives, 2003, p. 28).

A report on DTC advertising of pharmaceutical products in New Zealand recommended that the practice be banned. The report, prepared by academic staff at all four of New Zealand's medical schools, concluded that such advertising did not provide accurate information on the risks and benefits of pharmaceutical products. The report also concluded that at least partially as a result of DTC advertising, patients frequently asked their physicians for drugs that were not appropriate for them. As Mansfield and colleagues (2005) note, while proponents of DTC advertising assert that it increases public knowledge, this can only be true if such advertising provides reliable and balanced information. "Its purpose, as with all advertising, is to persuade rather than to inform. Direct-to-consumer advertising leaves many people with exaggerated perceptions of the benefits of drugs" (p. 6).

The Criminal Practices of Pharmaceutical Companies

With respect to pharmaceutical companies' involvement in criminal activities, the roster of cases is lengthy, and the penalties imposed in such cases need to be considered in comparison to the penalties imposed on traffickers in illegal drugs. While, as described below, the monetary fines imposed on pharmaceutical companies for violations of the law are substantial, we have been unable to document a single case in which a pharmaceutical company executive has been incarcerated for the commission of criminal acts related to his or her business.

- In June of 2003, the pharmaceutical company AstraZeneca signed an agreement to pay a $353 million fine in response to a criminal charge of conspiring with doctors to charge government insurers for free samples of its prostate cancer drug, Zoladex. This settlement occurred 2 years after AstraZeneca's main rival, TAP Pharmaceuticals Inc., was convicted on a similar charge involving its prostate cancer drug (Lupron) and agreed to pay $875 million in criminal and civil penalties. In both of these cases, company employees instructed doctors how to bill Medicare for free samples of drugs and offered doctors inducements to do so, including free trips, fees to give speeches, and "educational grants" (Jaspen, 2003; Sherrid, 2002).

- GlaxoSmithKline was required to pay $87.6 million for overcharging the Medicaid program for the antidepressant drug Paxil and Flonase, an allergy spray (Petersen, 2003a). In 2011, Glaxo paid $3 billion to settle government civil and criminal investigations into its sales and marketing practices for numerous drugs (Wilson, 2011). In commenting on this settlement, the chief executive officer of GlaxoSmithKline commented, "This is a significant step toward resolving difficult, long-standing matters which do not reflect the company we are today. . . . In recent years, we have fundamentally changed our procedures for compliance, marketing and selling in the U.S. to ensure that we operate with a high standard of integrity and that we conduct our business openly and transparently" (as quoted in Wilson, 2011).

- Bayer was required to pay a $257 million fine as a result of a scheme through which the company overcharged for the antibiotic drug Cipro. Similar to the cases cited above, this involved the company selling Cipro to the Kaiser-Permanente health care company at prices lower than the company was charging Medicaid, thereby violating the federal law requiring drug manufacturers to give the Medicaid program the lowest price available to any customer (Petersen, 2003a).

- Similarly, Schering-Plough agreed to pay $350 million in fines for defrauding the Medicaid program. The company pled guilty to charges that it sold products to private health care providers for less than it sold the same products to Medicaid (Harris, 2004c).

- Schering-Plough, manufacturer of the allergy medications Claritin and Clarinex, was accused of using imported, comparatively inexpensive ingredients that were not approved for use in the United States in manufacturing these products. In 2002, the company agreed to pay a $500 million penalty for its failure to remedy problems in manufacturing drugs in four of its factories in New Jersey and Puerto Rico (Petersen, 2002a).

• Purdue Pharma agreed to pay $10 million over a 4-year period to fund drug abuse and drug education programs in West Virginia after admitting it had inappropriately marketed OxyContin to residents of the state. The suit accused the company of purposely concealing from doctors the extent to which the drug could lead to addiction (Thomas, 2004).

• Forest Laboratories was fined $313 million for illegally promoting the drug Celexa for use in children (Singer, 2010).

• In 2009, Eli Lilly agreed to pay $1.4 billion for criminal and civil charges related to its illegal marketing of the antipsychotic drug Zyprexa for unauthorized use in elderly and youth populations (Harris & Berenson, 2009).

• Pfizer agreed to pay approximately $430 million to settle criminal and civil charges that its Warner-Lambert division had marketed Neurontin for unapproved uses. As mentioned above, the drug had been approved by the FDA to treat epilepsy and shingles, but the company aggressively promoted it to treat a variety of psychiatric and other disorders, even though studies demonstrated Neurontin was not effective in treating these conditions. The company had provided kickbacks and free trips to the Olympics and Florida to encourage doctors to prescribe the drug for unapproved uses (Mayer, 2004). While the $430 million fine may appear to be substantial, it needs to be considered in the context of the fact that sales of Neurontin were $2.2 billion in the United States and $2.7 billion worldwide in 2003. And although Pfizer agreed it would stop promoting drugs for unauthorized purposes as part of this settlement, in 2009, another Pfizer unit (Pharmacia and Upjohn) pled guilty to promoting its drug Bextra (approved only for the relief of arthritis and menstrual discomfort) for treatment of all types of acute pain (Evans, 2010). Does this fine serve as a sufficient deterrent to Pfizer (and other pharmaceutical companies more generally) to desist from such practices? The answer seems to be no. The total of $2.75 billion that Pfizer paid in off-label penalties between 2004 and 2008 is only slightly more than 1% of its total revenue of $245 billion over the same period (Evans, 2010).

The ethically questionable and, in many cases, criminal practices of pharmaceutical companies are not restricted to the United States, of course. In Italy, tax regulators asserted that GlaxoSmithKline should be held responsible for corporate crime for offering some 4,000 doctors a variety of incentives, including "medical tours" to the Caribbean and "cultural retreats" at ski resorts, to persuade them to use GlaxoSmithKline products (Popham, 2004). Similar investigations of approximately 4,000 doctors who allegedly accepted bribes from GlaxoSmithKline also occurred in Germany in June of 2004. (Burgermeister, 2004)

THE POLITICAL ECONOMY OF
THE PHARMACEUTICAL BUSINESS

The pharmaceutical business is one of the most profitable industries in the world: The combined profits for the 10 drug companies listed in the Fortune 500 index in 2002 ($35.9 billion) were more than the profits for the other 490 businesses combined ($33.7 billion; Angell, 2004). In contrast to traffickers in illicit drugs, major pharmaceutical companies have at their disposal the ability to contribute to political campaigns and to lobby politicians, and this can have a significant impact on how their products are regulated. From 1997 to 2002, the pharmaceutical industry spent close to $500 million in lobbying activities, and in the 2002 Congressional elections alone, the companies spent more than $30 million in campaign contributions (Pear & Oppel, 2002). In the 2004 elections, drug companies and their officials contributed $17 million to federal candidates, including nearly $1 million to President George W. Bush and $500,000 to Democratic presidential candidate John Kerry (Drinkard, 2005). More recently, spending on lobbying by the pharmaceutical and health products industry totaled more than $241 million in 2011 (Open Secrets, 2012).

Just one example of how such contributions can pay dividends for pharmaceutical companies is evidenced in the case of a domestic security bill in 2002 that limited the legal liability of vaccine manufacturers. Eli Lilly manufactured a vaccine that had as one of its ingredients a preservative known as Thimerosal; lawsuits initiated by thousands of parents claimed that the mercury contained in this preservative had poisoned their children, causing autism and neurological problems (Stolberg, 2002). However, under the provisions inserted into the domestic security bill, these lawsuits would be heard in a special "vaccine court," with the result that many of them would be dismissed. Interestingly, during the 2002 election cycle, Eli Lilly contributed more money to political candidates—$1.6 million—than any other pharmaceutical company, with 79% of the money going to Republicans. It is also notable that the first President Bush sat on the board of Eli Lilly during the 1970s, the White House budget director under George W. Bush (Mitchell E. Daniels Jr.) was a former Eli Lilly executive, and the company's chief executive officer (Sidney Taurel) was appointed to a presidential advisory council on domestic security by President George W. Bush (Stolberg, 2002).

In addition to devoting financial resources to lobbying and political campaigns, as alluded to above, pharmaceutical companies spend considerable sums of money convincing doctors to prescribe their products to patients. One such strategy is to send sales representatives to doctors' offices to promote their company's product; as of 2004, there was at least one sales representative for every seven practicing physicians in the United States, and pharmaceutical companies spent more than $7 billion in the same year for these representatives, according to IMS health (Jaspen, 2005). According to Verispan (a company that monitors promotional spending by pharmaceutical companies), the amount that pharmaceutical companies spend on meetings and events for doctors reached $2.1 billion in 2001 (Kowalczyk, 2002). In addition, Studdert, Mello, and Brennan (2004) suggest that pharmaceutical companies spend approximately $6 billion per year on gifts and payments to physicians, and there is evidence to suggest that even minor gratuities have an effect on the prescribing behavior of doctors. Although more recent data on the specific amounts spent on gifts and payments to doctors are not available, more generally, it is estimated that pharmaceutical companies spend 19 times more on self-promotion than basic research (Eichler, 2012; Light & Lexchin, 2012). While the companies assert that these events are intended to educate doctors about pharmaceutical products, an examination of how the money is spent calls this claim into question. In one example, a doctor from New York State was given an all-expenses-paid trip to a resort in Florida, dinner cruises, hockey game tickets, a ski trip for his family, a day at a spa, and free computer equipment, with a combined worth of approximately $10,000 (Ross & Scott, 2002). In other cases, drug company sales representatives have given their doctors free stethoscopes, taken them to Broadway shows, and even treated them to free stops at service stations in what is referred to as a "gas and go" (Barnard, 2002). In 2004, it was revealed that Schering-Plough was sending $10,000 checks to some doctors for "consulting agreements" that required nothing other than the doctors' commitment to prescribe their products (Harris, 2004a). One surgeon from Wisconsin was paid $400,000 for a consulting contract for which he worked just 8 days (Harris, 2006). In the state of Texas alone, at least 25,000 physicians and researchers received (at least) a combined $57 million in cash payments, research money, free meals, and other benefits (Ramshaw & Murphy, 2011). Further, a survey of medical students found that on average, they receive one gift from or attend one activity sponsored by a pharmaceutical company every week (Guterman, 2005). It is also notable that many of the drug companies' sales representatives are young women, many of whom are "recruited from the cheerleading ranks." Some critics of the pharmaceutical industry, noting that most doctors are men, "view wholesomely sexy drug reps as a variation on seductive inducements like dinners, golf outings, and speaking fees that pharmaceutical companies have dangled to sway doctors to their brands" (Saul, 2005).

Given the apparent reluctance of the federal government to regulate such practices, some states have enacted their own legislation. In 2002, Vermont became the first state to require pharmaceutical companies to disclose the gifts and cash payments they make to doctors, hospitals, and other health care providers (Petersen, 2002b). Under this legislation, pharmaceutical companies can be fined up to $10,000 for each gift over $25 that they fail to report (Barnard, 2002). In May 2002, the state of Hawaii passed a similar law requiring pharmaceutical companies to report how much they were spending on marketing campaigns (Petersen, 2002b).

While pharmaceutical companies' attempts to influence legislators and physicians should be of considerable concern, perhaps even more problematic are financial ties between pharmaceutical companies and government agencies such as the National Institutes of Health (NIH). Willman (2004) reports that at least 530 government scientists employed at the NIH had taken fees, stocks, or stock options from biomedical and/or pharmaceutical companies in the previous 5 years. More specifically,

Dr. Bryan H. Brewer, an employee at NIH, wrote articles recommending the use of the cholesterol medication Crestor; he had received $31,000 from the manufacturer of this drug. Similarly, Dr. P. Trey Sutherland III of NIH received more than $50,000 in fees and related income from Pfizer while collaborating with the company on research on Alzheimer's disease. Although Sutherland did not acknowledge his affiliation with Pfizer, he publicly endorsed use of the company's Alzheimer's drug (Willman, 2004). Daniel Troy, a former advocate for the pharmaceutical industry, was appointed Chief Counsel for the FDA. Troy apparently invited drug companies to inform him of potential lawsuits against them so that he could assist in their defense. Since being appointed to this position, Troy had filed briefs defending four drug companies (Lenzer, 2004b). Similarly, in response to FDA hearings regarding the problems with Cox-2 inhibitor drugs discussed above, it was revealed that 10 of the 32 government advisors who supported the continued marketing of Celebrex, Bextra, and Vioxx had recently consulted with the companies who made these drugs (Harris & Berenson, 2005). More generally, a study published in the *Journal of the American Medical Association* in 2002 found that four out of five experts who participated in the formulation of clinical practice guidelines had financial relationships with the drug companies. As Abramson (2004) comments, "this would be the equivalent of a judge's having an ongoing financial relationship with one of the litigants in a case he was hearing, or a stockbroker's recommending his uncle's IPO" (p. 128).

THE FUTURE OF PRESCRIPTION DRUG REGULATION?

It is outrageous that any company should have the power to mislead doctors and their patients by stressing only positive results and hiding negative findings. . . . Drug companies should be forced to make public the results of all their clinical trials the moment they are completed, and the findings should be disseminated to doctors in an easy-to-understand format. Only then will patients be confident that their doctors have enough information to prescribe medicines wisely. ("When Drug Companies," 2004. Copyright 2006 by the New York Times Co. Reprinted with permission.)

It is estimated that more than 125,000 Americans die from drug reactions and mistakes each year, making pharmaceutical drugs the fourth leading cause of death after heart disease, cancer, and stroke (Donn, 2005). However, testifying before a Congressional committee in 2005 in response to the problems with Vioxx discussed above, Dr. David Graham commented, "The FDA, as currently configured, is incapable of protecting America against another Vioxx. We are virtually defenseless" (as quoted in Scherer, 2005).

In response to GlaxoSmithKline concealing negative information about their antidepressant drug Paxil, the Attorney General of New York State (Elliott Spitzer) initiated a lawsuit in 2004. The suit alleged that GlaxoSmithKline had engaged in persistent fraud by neglecting to inform doctors that some studies of Paxil indicated that the drug was not effective in treating adolescents and could also lead to suicidal thoughts (Harris, 2004d).

There were indications that Spitzer's lawsuit would lead to changes in the practices of pharmaceutical companies. Not long after the action was initiated, GlaxoSmithKline announced that it would create a website publicly listing all clinical trials of its drugs (Meier, 2004b), and Forest Laboratories announced that its antidepressant drug Lexaprol was not effective in treating depressed children and adolescents (Meier, 2004a). However, 6 months after the pharmaceutical industry indicated that the results of clinical trials would be publicly available on the (now defunct) website http://www.clinicalstudyresults.org, drug companies had posted unpublished study results for only five drugs, out of a total of more than 10,800 prescription medications and dosages sold in the United States (Rowland, 2005a). While the pharmaceutical company Eli Lilly subsequently reported several more studies on the National Institutes of Health website, http://www.clinicaltrials.gov (Berenson, 2005), what the *New York Times* referred to as "the big three obfuscators" (Merck, GlaxoSmithKline, and Pfizer) were subverting the requirement of posting their trials by not providing names of the drugs they were testing ("Hiding the Data," 2005). However, developments with respect to the reporting of these studies had improved considerably by 2012, with more than 132,000 studies being listed on the clinical trials website as of September 2012 (U.S. Food and Drug Administration, 2012).

In 2004, the Food and Drug Administration had a budget of $1.4 billion and a staff of approximately 10,000 to regulate pharmaceutical drugs, which are estimated to cause more than 125,000 deaths per year in the United States. The rules created and enforced by the FDA affect nearly 10,000 businesses, which collectively produce more than $1 trillion worth of goods per year, representing about one-quarter of the entire U.S. economy (Harris, 2004c). (As of October 1, 2009, the FDA had a total staff of 11,516, with 2,889 working in the Center for Drug Evaluation and Research, and 3,895 in the Office of Regulatory Affairs; FDA, n.d.) In contrast, federal, state, and local governments spend between $30 and $40 billion annually in order to combat illegal drugs, which produce, at most, between 8,000 and 10,000 deaths per year (Winslow, 2003). The practices of pharmaceutical companies and the lax regulation of these companies and their practices by the FDA contribute to significantly higher costs of prescription drugs for U.S. residents and do little to protect consumers' health and safety.

Given all the problems with the regulation of pharmaceutical products discussed above, there have been calls by organizations such as the *Journal of the American Medical Association* for a new board, independent of the Food and Drug Administration, that would track the safety of drugs and medical devices (Alonso-Zaldivar, 2004). Such changes are worth considering in light of the fact that in 2005, there were approximately 2,300 FDA employees involved in the drug approval process while only 109 studied the safety of drugs after they are released (Scherer, 2005). And in 2005, legislation introduced by Congressman Maurice Hinchey (Democrat of New York) titled the Food and Drug Administration Improvement Act recommended a number of significant changes in the FDA. The legislation included several provisions that would end financial conflicts of interest between FDA officials and pharmaceutical companies; for instance, scientists with financial conflicts of interest would be prohibited from serving on FDA advisory panels. The bill also would have resulted in the establishment of a separate branch of the FDA to monitor the safety of drugs once they were marketed and, in recognition of the fact that almost 50% of the FDA budget is funded by the drug industry, would redirect the fees that drug companies pay the FDA for approval of their drugs to the U.S. Treasury. Finally, the legislation would have imposed penalties of up to $50 million on companies that were in violation of FDA regulations (Lenzer, 2005b).

A more recent scandal related to conflicts of interest and the FDA involved the appointment of three individuals to a drug safety advisory committee without disclosing that these individuals had conflicts of interest with the company—Bayer, whose birth control pills were being reviewed. The review committee recommended that Bayer be allowed to keep these birth control pills (marketed as Yaz and Yasmin) on the market, even though several deaths had been associated with the products. In addition to the fact that three of those serving on the review board had financial ties to Bayer (which the FDA knew about but did not disclose), the FDA excluded Dr. Sydney Wolfe of Public Citizen (the committee's usual consumer representative) from service because he had previously recommended that the drugs be banned. (Goozner, 2012)

This proposed legislation did not pass, and despite such proposals, the prospects of significant and positive change in the regulation of prescription drugs in the United States are not promising. President George W. Bush's nominee for head of the FDA in 2005, Dr. Lester M. Crawford, opposed the creation of an independent body to monitor drug safety. In 1985, when Crawford was director of the FDA's Center for Veterinary Medicine, he was accused of deferring to the interests of the livestock industry and jeopardizing public health. A committee report on Crawford's actions found that he had actually fostered the illegal marketing of unapproved drugs, failed to discourage the illegal use of drugs that tainted the milk supply, failed to remove drugs from the market that had been proven unsafe, and approved drugs that his staff members suspected were carcinogenic (as quoted in Harris, 2005b).

Despite Crawford's opposition, the FDA Drug Safety Board was formally established in June of 2005. However, 11 of the 15 positions on the board were filled by senior managers of the FDA's Center for Drug Evaluation and Research, which potentially compromises the goal of making the drug safety review process separate from the new drug review process (Kaufman, 2005a). In response to this development, Dr. David Graham asserted that efforts to improve the safety of drugs would be set back. He concluded that the panel was "severely biased in favor of the pharmaceutical industry" and that "the FDA cannot be trusted to protect the public or reform itself" (as quoted in Kaufman, 2005a).

The FDA mission statement reads as follows:

> The FDA is responsible for protecting the public health by assuring the safety, efficacy, and security of human and veterinary drugs, medical devices, and our nation's food supply, cosmetics, and products that emit radiation. The FDA is also responsible for advancing the public health by helping to speed innovations that make medicines and foods more effective, safer, and more affordable; and helping the public to get the accurate, science-based information they need to use medicines and foods to improve their health. (U.S. Food and Drug Administration, 2004)

In light of the issues addressed above, we must seriously question whether the FDA is fulfilling its obligation to the public. As one commentator notes, "as politicians have become beholden to drug makers' money, the FDA increasingly has promoted sales over science, serving as the de facto subsidiary of the very industry it is supposed to oversee" (Mundy, 2004).

THE REGULATION OF PERFORMANCE-ENHANCING DRUGS

The Rationale for Regulation

Making clear distinctions with respect to what constitutes a performance-enhancing product is difficult. Corked bats and "doctored" baseballs are banned in baseball, and "skuffed" or soft footballs are prohibited in the National Football League because such balls can be kicked farther or more accurately. Conversely, modified racecars, ultralight racing bicycles, full body suits designed to reduce drag for swimmers and skiers, and high-tech tennis rackets and golf clubs and balls are all accepted in their respective sports. In the same realm, it is also worth considering Lasik surgery and other "vision enhancements which allow almost any athlete the visual acuity that helped make Ted Williams a nonpareil hitter and judge of the strike zone" are permitted (Salerno, 2006). Similarly, does "Tommy John" surgery, which involves grafting a new tendon in a pitcher's arm, constitute performance enhancement? (Hiltzick, 2009a)

As noted in Chapter 4, the use of substances to enhance athletic performance dates back nearly as far as athletic competition itself. However, it has only been in the last century or so that attempts have been made to regulate the use of performance-enhancing substances in sport. One of the first "doping" tests was conducted by the Austrian Jockey Club in 1910, which employed a chemist to test the saliva of race horses for the presence of alkaloids (Ferstle, 2000). Tests of human urine began in the 1930s when the Italian cycling and soccer federations required their respective members to be tested for stimulants (Ferstle, 2000). However, as is the case in other areas of drug regulation, there is considerable inconsistency and often hypocrisy in the regulation of performance-enhancing drugs. Some would argue that anything that "unnaturally" enhances athletic performance should be banned in sports because it perverts the integrity of competition. However, based on this logic, widely accepted supplements such as Creatine, amino acids, and even vitamins and aspirins should be banned, as these substances may also assist athletes (Yesalis, 2000).

> I was training my guts out every day, exhausting myself, risking injury and being beaten again and again by guys I knew were on drugs. It's the way a lot of us get involved [in using drugs], seeing the cheats win, knowing they got away with it. (Werner Reitarer, as quoted in "The 2000 Olympics," 2002)

One argument for the regulation of performance-enhancing drugs in sports is that many athletes may be forced to choose between using these drugs and succeeding or staying clean and becoming uncompetitive against athletes who are using such substances. The case of Werner Reiterer, an Australian discus thrower, illustrates this conflict. Reiterer was considered to be one of Australia's best chances to win a medal at the 2000 Sydney Olympics because he had recently thrown a discus 69.69 meters in competition, an achievement that would have been sufficient to secure an Olympic gold medal. However, while preparing to take a mandatory urinalysis test prior to the games, Reiterer confessed, "By the way, I'm presently full of drugs." He had been taking eight banned substances, including steroids, human growth hormone (hgh), and insulin growth factor. Despite this polydrug use, Reiterer's urinalysis came back clean. Reiterer chose to follow his conscience, ignored the clean drug test, and retired and subsequently wrote a book titled *Positive*, documenting his sports-related drug use (see box). In fact, this belief or knowledge that the "other guy" may be using performance-enhancing drugs may be the most compelling motivation for athletes to use, and presents many athletes with a serious dilemma. As noted by Kees Kooman, editor of the Dutch edition of *Runner's World* magazine, "all athletes someday have to choose. Do I want to compete at a world-class level and take drugs, or do I want to compete at a club level and be clean?" (as quoted in Bamberger & Yeager, 1997). It is also notable that in their book documenting the use of performance-enhancing drugs by prominent San Francisco Giants outfielder Barry Bonds, Fainaru-Wada and Williams (2006) asserted that one of the primary reasons Bonds used steroids was that he believed that other major league baseball players (including Mark McGwire) were also using steroids. In order to remain competitive and to attract the media attention he apparently craved, Bonds initiated the use of several performance-enhancing substances after the 1998 baseball season.

An extraordinary level of self-damage is already regarded as acceptable in sport. Notoriously, boxing is organized brain damage, with a few grudging managerial procedures in place to protect the cerebral cortex. Formula One racing is a mechanism for paralyzing or slaughtering young men. So why, in the context of such sponsored and televised homicide, should a runner not be allowed to risk liver damage, atrophied gonads, and premature senility chasing a medal? (Lawson, 2003)

Many also argue that policy governing performance-enhancing drugs in sport is necessary to protect the health of athletes. Although it is true that substances such as steroids and peptide hormones, like all drugs, do present some health risks, much research indicates that these risks have, to some degree, been exaggerated and that they can be managed (see Friedl, 2000, for a review). For example, studies on the use of steroids for strength and muscle gain—as well as hormone replacement in aging males and as a male contraceptive—have found that these substances can be used safely, at least in the short term (Bhasin et al., 1996; Yesalis, 2000). Although we are certainly not advocating the use of performance-enhancing drugs in sport, it is important to recognize that participation in sport always involves some level of physical risk. Competition in sports such as boxing, football, hockey, and many forms of racing involves a very real risk of serious injury and even death. As such, it is somewhat paradoxical that one of the primary rationales for banning performance-enhancing drugs in sport is to protect the health of athletes. As Yesalis (2000) notes, "based on current knowledge, one could argue, epidemiologically, that the rate of violent death or permanent disability in 'violent' sports including boxing, football, and auto racing far exceeds that observed among steroid users" (p. 7).

Despite these inconsistences in the rationale for regulating performance-enhancing drug use, use of such substances in sport is regulated, in some form, by most athletic governing bodies. The policies for different sports organizations differ substantially, and as is the case with other areas of drug regulation, there is a considerable amount of hypocrisy present in such policies.

National Collegiate Athletic Association

The National Collegiate Athletic Association (NCAA) began its drug-testing program in 1986; the rationale for creation of the program was "so that no one participant might have an artificially induced advantage, so that no one participant might be pressured to use chemical substance in order to remain competitive, and to safeguard the health and safety of participants" (NCAA, 2002). The current NCAA policy bans anabolic steroids; street drugs such as heroin, cocaine, and marijuana; stimulants such as ephedrine; and analogous nonsteroidal performance-enhancing substance such as hgh. Under the NCAA policy, athletes from all team and individual sports are subject to testing, with athletes from Division I and

II schools being subject to tests year round and at all championships and football bowl games, while Division III athletes are tested at postseason championships.

The NCAA drug-testing program is administered by the National Center for Drug-Free Sport, and representatives from this organization inform the particular institution 48 hours in advance that some of its athletes will be tested. Between 18 and 26 players on a football team will be tested for drugs, with both teams and players being randomly selected (Farrey, 2000). Each year, more than 10,000 athletes are tested in the year-round program, with approximately 1,500 more being tested at bowls and championship games (Biertempfel, 2005). The NCAA does not publish the names of those who test positive for drugs. However, the sanction for a first positive test is loss of eligibility for competition for 1 year; a second positive test for steroids (but not street drugs) results in a lifetime ban from competition, representing the most severe sanctions at any level of sports (Biertempfel, 2005).

Approximately 2,500 student athletes annually are screened at championship events, and approximately 11,000 Division I and II student athletes in all sports are tested under the NCAA's year-round testing program (NCAA.org, n.d.).

In addition, several NCAA institutions and some conferences conduct their own testing programs. In the September 1, 2009, to December 31, 2009, period, 5,732 athletes were tested by the NCAA, and there were 68 positive tests (1.2%; Drug-Free Sport, 2010). However, the head of the National Center for Drug-Free Sport, Frank Uryasz, estimated that when substances that are used to mask steroids, as well as players who are ruled ineligible because they refuse to submit to the tests, are taken into account, the figure for steroid use among college athletes would be closer to 2% (Farrey, 2000).

Commentators have pointed out that the NCAA program is "more effective at catching cheaters because it is random" (Farrey, 2000); however, it is important to note that some steroid use by student athletes may not be uncovered because the NCAA does not conduct tests in the summer months. It is also notable that, as in other areas of drug regulation, there is a certain amount of hypocrisy with respect to regulating substance use by college athletes. For example, a number of college athletic departments have endorsement arrangements with companies producing dietary supplements; MET-Rx, a leading supplement manufacturer, has deals with several universities, including the University of Arizona, Florida State University, Syracuse University, and UCLA. MET-Rx also sponsored ABC's college football pregame show (Wertheim, 2003). One college coach commented, "When I was at the University of Texas, we had a $200,000 budget for supplements. If I can get free supplements for my kids [in exchange] for making a few appearances a year, that's really helping my budget" (as quoted in Wertheim, 2003).

International Olympic Committee

Among Olympic athletes, the temptation to use banned performance-enhancing drugs is significant. Although the U.S. Olympic Committee pays athletes $25,000 for winning gold medals, $15,000 for silver, and $10,000 for bronze (Riley, 2012), more substantial financial rewards are associated with the endorsements that typically accompany some level of success. It was estimated that winning a gold medal in Olympic women's figure skating could bring as much as $10 million in endorsements and earnings (McCarthy, 2002). Even before winning his 19th medal at the 2012 London Summer Olympic games, American swimmer Michael Phelps was earning an estimated $5 million annually from corporate endorsements (Rosewater, 2008), and Olympic skier Picabo Street was earning more than a million dollars annually from sponsors such as Chapstick (McCarthy, 2002).

Partly because of the substantial financial rewards that accompany success, some have argued that the use of performance-enhancing drugs by athletes reflects a "win at all costs" attitude that is pervasive in many Western societies, but particularly in competitive athletics. An oft-cited survey of Olympic athletes by Bob Goldman provides an illustration of this attitude. Goldman surveyed 198 Olympic athletes and provided them with the following two scenarios: You are offered a performance-enhancing drug (a "magic pill") and guaranteed two things; first, you will not be caught, and second, you will win. Of the 198 athletes in Goldman's study, 195 said they would take the drug under these circumstances. The second scenario also guaranteed the athlete would not be caught and would win every competition for the next 5 years, but that he or she would die from the side effects of the drug at the end of the 5-year period. Given this scenario, 52% of the athletes still said they would take the drug (Goldman & Klatz, 1997).

Although the use of steroids and other performance-enhancing drugs in Olympic competition has been prevalent for decades, this fact remained relatively obscure to the general public until the 1988 Seoul Olympics. At those games, Canadian sprinter Ben Johnson won the 100-meter dash and set a new world record in the process. When a subsequent drug test revealed that Johnson was on steroids, he was stripped of the gold medal.

> Although Ben Johnson was stripped of the gold medal, the athlete who was ultimately awarded the gold medal in the 100-meter race, American Carl Lewis, had a questionable drug history himself. At the 1988 Olympic trials, Lewis tested positive for small amounts of pseudoephedrine, ephedrine, and phenylpropanolamine. Although the United States Olympic Committee initially disqualified Lewis from competing in the 1988 Olympics, he was eventually allowed to compete, based on his claim that the positive tests were the result of "inadvertent use." (Layden & Yeager, 2003)

Gladwell (2001) asserts that Johnson was a "walking pharmacy," ingesting several performance-enhancing substances before competing in the 1988 Olympics, but ironically, none of the drugs that were part of his normal "pharmaceutical protocol" were responsible for his failed drug test. Many have also questioned the accuracy and rigor of drug testing in the 1988 Olympic games, given that Johnson was the only prominent athlete to test positive. Gladwell (2001) suggests that it is difficult to believe that American female sprinter Florence Griffith-Joyner was not using drugs prior to the games, given that before 1988, her best times in the 100- and 200-meter races were 10.96 and 21.96 seconds.

> In 1988, a suddenly huskier FloJo ran 10.49 and 21.34, times that no [female] runner since has ever come close to equaling. In other words, at the age of 28, when most athletes are beginning their decline, Griffith-Joyner transformed herself in one season from a career-long better-than-average sprinter to the fastest female in history. (Gladwell, 2001)

Attention to the issue of performance-enhancing drugs reached its nadir at the 2000 summer Olympics in Sydney. Sullivan and Song (2000) commented prior to the start of these games, "As you watch the events on the tube, you will have no way of knowing if you are seeing a clean or dirty event, a real athletic competition or a duel between pharmacists." At those Olympics, a female Romanian gymnast was stripped of her medal as a result of testing positive for drugs, and International Olympic Committee (IOC) officials accused the United States of being in denial about the use of performance-enhancing drugs by American athletes ("Steroids Panel," 2005).

The American shot putter C. J. Hunter tested positive for nandrolone in 2000, and there were also questions about his wife, the elite sprinter Marion Jones (Perkins, 2000). When Hunter alleged that his positive test result was due to his ingestion of tainted iron supplements, then-IOC vice president Dick Pound commented, "He would be a very rusty person if that's all it was" (as quoted in "Steroids Panel," 2000). And although Jones initially denied using performance-enhancing drugs, she later admitted such use and pleaded guilty to lying to federal investigators who investigated the Bay Area Laboratory Cooperative ("Jones Pleads Guilty," 2007; see also below). Following the Sydney Olympics, in the summer of 2003, the World Anti-Doping Agency also called for the United States men's 1600-meter relay team at the Sydney Olympics to be stripped of its gold medal because sprinter Jerome Young tested positive for nandrolone in 1999 (Abrahamson, 2003).

During the 2012 Summer Olympic Games in London, at least 13 athletes tested positive for banned substances, and an additional 107 had been sanctioned for doping offenses in the 6 months prior to the games (Grohmann, 2012).

The development of the current drug testing policy of the IOC, which bans more than 100 substances, can be traced to 1961. In that year, prompted by concerns about the use of performance-enhancing drugs, the IOC established a commission to assess the extent of substance use in Olympic sports. In 1962, the IOC passed its first resolution condemning the practice of doping, although the 1964 Olympics in Tokyo was the first attempt by the IOC to initiate control over the use of performance-enhancing substances. The first Olympic games in which relatively comprehensive testing was administered for all sports were the 1972 games in Munich, Germany. At those games, athletes were tested for stimulant drugs such as amphetamines and ephedrine and narcotic drugs such as heroin and morphine (National Center on Addiction and Substance Abuse, 2000). Although at this time it was fairly well known that athletes had shifted from using stimulants to anabolic steroids, a reliable test for steroids had yet to be developed. As Yesalis, Courson, and Wright (2000) comment, "during the 1968 Olympic Games in Mexico City, athletes and coaches did not debate the morality or propriety of taking drugs; the only debate was over which drugs were more effective" (p. 55).

Tests for several of the substances in the steroids class were eventually developed, and these drugs were screened for in the 1976 summer Olympic games in Montreal. Testosterone and caffeine were added to the list of substances banned by the IOC in the early 1980s, beta-blockers and blood doping were banned in 1984, diuretics in 1987, and peptide hormones (e.g., hgh) in 1990 (National Center on Addiction and Substance Abuse, 2000). However, the growing pharmacological sophistication of screened substances presents problems because in addition to costing as much as $1,000 per test, some substances are more difficult to detect than others. The validity of tests also varies by substance (Ferstle, 2000). An additional problem is that even when the technology becomes available to identify particular substances, and when athletes are caught using them, sanctions cannot be applied unless the drugs are included on established lists of banned drugs. As one example of this problem, the IOC attempted to sanction several Russian athletes at the 1996 Atlanta games for the use of Bromatan, a stimulant and masking agent that is very similar to the banned substance Mesocarb. However, the athletes' ban from competition was overturned in an IOC arbitration hearing because Bromatan had not been included on the list of banned substances (Ferstle, 2000).

Under current IOC drug testing policies, for sports involving individual athletes (as opposed to teams), all top five finishers in the competition, plus two other athletes selected at random, are tested (International Olympic Committee, 2012). Individuals who are found in violation of the antidoping rules in Olympic competition can have their results disqualified; those who are found in violation of the rules before Olympic competitions can be declared ineligible to compete. Under IOC policies, individuals who test positive for performance-enhancing drugs for the first time are suspended from competition for 2 years, while a second positive test results in a lifetime ban. In addition, under a policy that went into effect on January 1, 2009, Olympic athletes must provide the IOC with their daily schedules for 3-month periods at least 12 months before the start of Olympic competition and must provide their precise whereabouts for 60 minutes each day. If an agent from the USADA or WADA visits the athlete unannounced during that 60-minute period and the athlete is not present, it counts as a missed drug test and hence a violation of the policy (Thomas, 2009).

Although on the surface it would appear that the IOC attempts to control the use of performance-enhancing substances by athletes, there are some indications that the regulations are not vigorously enforced. An article in the *Tampa Bay Tribune* alleged that prior to the 1984 Olympics, a coordinator of the U.S. Olympic Committee's instructional program provided information on how to beat drug tests to U.S. shot put, discus, javelin, and hammer athletes (cited in Yesalis, Courson, Wright, 2000). There is also evidence that at the 1980 Moscow, 1984 Los Angeles, and 1996 Atlanta summer Olympic games, the IOC did not act on a series of positive drug tests for banned substances among a number of medal winners (Ferstle,

2000; National Center on Addiction and Substance Abuse, 2000). This lack of vigor in enforcing the regulations is perhaps not surprising given that governing bodies face something of a conflict of interest. The IOC depends on corporate sponsors and broadcast rights for approximately 75% to 80% of its income. U.S. broadcasting corporations paid $793 million for the Sydney Olympic games (National Center on Addiction and Substance Abuse, 2000); NBC paid $2.2 billion for the 2010 and 2012 Olympics, and the same network won the rights to broadcast the 2014, 2016, and 2018 Olympics with a bid of more than $4 billion ("NBC Wins Broadcast Rights," 2011). It is probably not in the IOC's best interests to jeopardize such funding (see box).

> Allowing national governing bodies, international federations, and national Olympic committees such as the United States Olympic Committee to govern the testing process to ensure fair play in sport is terribly ineffective. In a sense, it is like having the fox guard the henhouse. There is simply too much money involved in international sports today ... athletes and officials realize this, so they're willing to do whatever it takes to win. And sometimes, that means turning their backs on the drug problem. (Dr. Robert Voy, former director of drug testing for the U.S. Olympic Committee, cited in Ferstle, 2000)

A more recent development in the regulation of performance-enhancing drugs at the international level is related to the establishment of the World Anti-Doping Agency (WADA), which was formed following a conference convened by the IOC in 1999 (WADA, 2005). Although WADA currently has no effective power to test and sanction athletes, the organization has been instrumental in developing and revising the list of prohibited substances for Olympic Athletes. In deciding which substances to prohibit, WADA considers the following issues: (1) Is the substance performance enhancing? (2) Does it represent a risk to the health of the athlete? (3) Is it against the spirit of the sport? If any two of these three criteria are met, WADA considers the drug for inclusion on the list of banned substances (WADA, 2009).

> It's not that U.S. athletes are suddenly dirty. They've always been as dirty as anyone else. It's just that the U.S. Olympic Committee hid positive tests left and right. But American television money runs the Olympics, if it doesn't own them outright, and rather than face up to realities, U.S. officials chose the big lie, covering up drug tests galore. Moreover, in the particular American way, they continued to lecture the world on its drug failings. (Perkins, 2000)

In addition to IOC tests of Olympic athletes, individual countries also conduct drug tests. However, the policies regulating such tests across these countries vary widely. Depending on the particular event, sport, and country in question, athletes may undergo either in-competition or out-of-competition testing, and with or without receiving advanced notice that they will be tested. In addition to these contingencies, the selection criteria for those chosen to be tested ranges from being completely random to selecting the top finishers in a competition or those who are suspected of using drugs. There are also several differences with respect to allowable cutoff levels for certain substances and the penalties involved for testing positive across countries (National Center on Addiction and Substance Abuse, 2000). Another problem is that countries are often quite lax in testing and/or punishing their own athletes, perhaps believing that the problem is pervasive and that rigorous testing at the national level would put them at a disadvantage. The United States is certainly no exception to this. Dr. Wade Exum, director of the United States Olympic Committee's (USOC) drug-control administration from 1999 to 2001, claimed that the USOC ran an ineffective drug testing program and actually may have encouraged the use of performance-enhancing drugs by failing to punish athletes who tested positive for banned substances (Layden & Yeager, 2003). Exum provided documentation indicating that more than 100 U.S. Olympic athletes tested positive for banned substances over the 1998 to 2000 period, and in a significant number of these cases, the offending athletes were not prevented from competing.

In the current period, the number of Olympians (as well as college and professional athletes) who test positive for performance-enhancing drugs is modest, although there is substantial skepticism about the validity of these results. In addition to the apparent laxity in enforcing the regulations, many commentators have noted that it is fairly easy to avoid detection by drug tests. Emil Vrjman, director of the Netherlands' doping-control center, commented, "To be caught is not easy; it only happens when an athlete is either incredibly sloppy, incredibly stupid, or both" (as quoted in Bamberger & Yeager, 1997). Although the rigor of tests has increased somewhat in recent years, one reason that drug tests are often ineffective is that they can only identify recognized drugs, and changing the chemical structure of a substance only slightly (which is relatively easy to do) makes the substance much more difficult to detect (Bamberger Yeager, 1997). Further, some performance-enhancing drugs are either undetectable or, as is the case with most steroids, become undetectable very quickly after their use. Many athletes who use banned performance-enhancing drugs also have become quite savvy about their use, particularly in those sports in which drug tests are more frequently conducted (which includes Olympic sports). In part due to the expansion and increasing sophistication of drug testing, some athletes employ specialists who design performance-enhancing drug programs and monitor the athlete's use, blood, and urine (often at a price of $3,000 a month or more). Awareness of drug testing procedures means that many athletes know exactly how they should use these substances in order to maximize their efficiency while minimizing their chances of detection. As Weiner and Pulitzer (2006) comment, "Despite progress against drugs in sport by the World Anti-Doping Agency and the International Olympic Committee, the remaining loopholes are large enough for athletes to ski, sled, and skate right through."

Let's say I have a deal with a lab under which I can send your urine to test your [steroid] levels. I know exactly when to get you off to fall below the [drug-testing] radar. If I can get you off nine days before your event, we've got it made, because chances are you're not going to lose any of your [strength and endurance] gains in that period. It's simple biochemistry" (Dr. Robert Voy, as quoted in Bamberger & Yeager, 1997).

Testing for performance-enhancing drugs has recently been extended to other activities that would only marginally qualify as sports. For example, the U.S. Chess Federation, in its quest to have chess recognized as an Olympic sport, allowed its players to be tested for a variety of performance-enhancing drugs. According to Stephen Press, vice chairman of the Federation Internationale des Echecs (World Chess Federation), several performance-enhancing drugs, such as caffeine, amphetamines, and Ritalin, could provide users with an unfair advantage in chess. Press even sees testing for steroids and similar drug in chess players as reasonable, noting that such substances might provide "an unfair endurance advantage during a grueling match" ("Drug Testing Part of Quest," 2004).

Similarly, the World Federation of Bridge has attempted to have the card game recognized as an Olympic sport, and as a consequence, the same rules regarding doping are applied. When the silver medalist at the 2002 bridge championship refused to submit to a drug test, she had to forfeit her prize ("Bridge Medalist Refuses," 2002).

Perhaps drug testing of poker players is also on the horizon. One poker player commented, "I can count on more than one hand the guys who did speed and went from average players to making million-dollar bankrolls." (as quoted in Conley, 2005)

Further evidence of this "cat and mouse" game in the use of performance-enhancing drugs can be seen in the scandal involving THG and BALCO Laboratories of San Francisco. THG is a "designer" steroid that was unknown to the public and unidentifiable in drug tests until it was discovered by Dr. Don Catlin at the UCLA Olympic Drug Testing Center. THG resembles two known synthetic steroids, trenbalone and gestrinone. Trenbalone is a veterinary anabolic steroid approved by the Food and Drug Administration to improve weight gain or feed efficiency in beef cattle, while gestrinone is a relatively weak anabolic steroid that becomes much more effective when carbon atoms are added to its chemical structure. By combining these two steroids, the chemical structure of THG became sufficiently different from its constituent parts, rendering it undetectable in existing drug tests (Kaufman & Shipley, 2003). However, once Catlin identified THG, he informed the U.S. Anti-Doping Agency (USADA), which recommended that other agencies test for the substance. Subsequently, several top athletes tested positive for THG, including British sprinter Dwaine Chambers (R. Williams, 2003); Regina Jacobs, the top female middle-distance runner in the United States; and Kevin Toth, the U.S. shot put champion, as well as a number of professional athletes (Longman, 2003).

In comparison to regulations placed on Olympic athletes by the IOC and national sports organizations, policies regulating the use of performance-enhancing drugs by professional athletes are much more lenient. Below, we discuss these policies in a selected number of professional sports. We devote comparatively more attention to baseball, the sport whose relatively lax drug testing policies have been the subject of considerable controversy and discussion in recent times.

Professional Sports

Tennis

Professional tennis has one of the most rigorous drug testing programs in professional sports, with players being required to inform testing authorities regarding their locations 365 days a year, and with random tests being conducted at any time and any place (Robson, 2009). In the past few decades, several tennis players have tested positive for performance-enhancing drugs, including Peter Korda, the 1998 Australian Open champion, who tested positive for nandrolone at the 1998 Wimbledon championships (5 months after winning the Australian Open) and was subsequently banned from competition for a year. Britain's Greg Rusedski and several other professional tennis players also tested positive for nandrolone in the early 2000s but were later cleared of these charges because trainers had been distributing possibly tainted nutritional supplements to players ("Agassi Says," 2004). Prominent tennis player Andre Agassi commented that he believed tennis's policy was nearly infallible, noting how frequently he, Swiss player Roger Federer, and U.S. star Andy Roddick were tested:

> You can use drugs to cheat, but our system—we test so often—I got tested 20 times last year, Federer 23 times, Andy 20 times—we test so extensively that we have absolutely removed the possibility of somebody taking drugs to obtain a strategic advantage. ("Agassi Says," 2004)

Others, however, disagree. During the 2002 French Open, France's Nicholas Escude noted, "To say that tennis today is clean, you have to be living in a dream world" (as quoted in Garber, 2003).

Cycling

As noted in Chapter 4, the greatest current concern in endurance sports such as cycling, running, and cross-country skiing is the use of **erythropoietin** (EPO) for "blood doping." The most common test for EPO, including the one used in cycling's most prominent event, the Tour de France, is a hemocrit test. Hemocrit tests assess the portion of the blood that is composed of red blood cells (and thus the oxygen-carrying capacity of the blood). Normal hemocrit is approximately 42 (meaning that 42% of the blood is red blood cells), and riders are stopped from competing if their hemocrit is 50 or more. Random tests are conducted throughout the Tour de France, but despite these tests, many believe that blood doping continues in cycling. Professor of Pharmacy Michael Audran commented, "Nowadays, EPO is easy to find but still the performances are getting better. Either athletes are employing a new masking process for EPO or they've found a new substance" (as quoted in "The Tour Drug-Free," 2003).

Allegations of widespread performance-enhancing drug use by cyclists, including Lance Armstrong, who won the Tour de France seven times, have plagued the sport for some time. In 2010, in an article in the *Wall Street Journal*, Armstrong's former teammate Floyd Landis, who had been stripped of his Tour de France title after tests showed elevated levels of testosterone, revealed that he had used performance-enhancing drugs with Armstrong (Albergotti & O'Connell, 2010; Macur & Schmidt, 2010); similar allegations were made by another of Armstrong's team-mates, Tyler Hamilton.

Armstrong was eventually stripped of his Tour de France titles by the USADA (Murphy, 2012), which produced an extensive report, relying on testimony of several of Armstrong's former U.S. Postal Service teammates, who confirmed that Armstrong had used several performance-enhancing drugs (Wolff & Epstein, 2012). In addition to using EPO, testosterone, corticosteroids, and transfused blood, Armstrong also pressured other teammates to use banned substances (Shipley, 2012). In two interviews with Oprah Winfrey in January of 2013, Armstrong confessed to using performance-enhancing substances (including EPO, blood doping, and testosterone) but also claimed that he did not believe that his actions constituted cheating, because many of his competitors were also using drugs (Walker, 2013).

Of course, Armstrong and his teammates are by no means the only cyclists who have used performance-enhancing drugs—in fact, every cyclist but one who shared the podium in the Tour de France with Armstrong between 1999 and 2005 was eventually directly implicated in the use of such drugs (Wolff & Epstein, 2012). Further, in 2010, Spaniard Alberto Contador, three-time winner of the Tour de France, tested positive for clenbuterol, a weight-loss and muscle-building drug (Langley, 2012; Macur, 2010). As Specter (2012) comments,

> A cyclist once told me that if you don't use drugs during a race like the Tour de France it's like you are observing a 65 mph speed limit on a highway—while everyone else is doing 80. The time has come for professional cycling to acknowledge reality: cyclists use drugs. Perhaps the best approach is simply to let them. That way everyone can, for the first time in years, compete at the same level.

Hockey

Although Olympic athletes who are caught using performance-enhancing substances face a 2-year ban from competition for a first offense, prior to 2005, some professional sports leagues such as the National Hockey League (NHL) did not test for performance-enhancing substances. According to Ted Saskin, then senior director of the NHL Players Association, the absence of tests for performance-enhancing drugs was due to the fact that "we are fortunate not to have a problem with steroid use in our sport" (as quoted in Wilstein, 2004). Despite such claims, it would be surprising if this were the case, given that hockey is similar to football in terms of requiring players to possess a rare combination of speed, size, and strength. There have also been reports of widespread steroid use by NHL players (Campbell, 2005; Westhead, 2005), and Dick Pound, president of the WADA, suggested that as many as one-third of the NHL's 700 players take some form of performance-enhancing substance (Feschuk, 2009; "Pound Blasts," 2005). Similarly, a book published in 2011 by former National Hockey League player (and "enforcer") Dave Morissette claimed that steroid use was widespread in the league, including use by some of the top performers (Blair, 2011).

At least partially as a result of the U.S. Congress urging professional sports leagues to regulate steroids, the 2005 collective bargaining agreement between the NHL and its players' association included provisions for random tests for performance-enhancing drugs. Under this policy, players are subject to a minimum of two drug tests per year without warning. First-time violators of the policy receive a 20-game suspension; a second offense results in a 60-game suspension, while a third offense results in a permanent ban from the league ("Pound Blasts," 2005). It is important to note, however, that the NHL's policy does not require testing of players in the summer months.

In January 2006, Columbus Blue Jackets defenseman Bryan Berard tested positive for 19-nonandrosterone in a pre-Olympic drug test and received a 2-year suspension from international competition (Allen, 2006). However, he was not suspended from playing in the NHL because it was an international test. Dick Pound commented,

> Here's this guy who has tested for steroids and the NHL is happy to have him play. Oh well, even though our policy was you can't take steroids, we haven't started our testing yet so therefore, you're ok to play with us even though, in international hockey, you're toast for two years. Welcome to the NHL. (as quoted in Ryan, 2006)

Basketball

Under the National Basketball Association's (NBA) early- to mid-2000s drug testing policies, first-year players were tested for steroid (and other drug) use once during training camp, and three times during the regular season; veteran players were tested once during training camp. If a player tested positive for amphetamines, cocaine, LSD, or opiates, he was dismissed and disqualified from the NBA. Positive tests for marijuana resulted in the player being forced to enter a drug treatment program after a first violation; the second violation resulted in a $15,000 fine, while a third violation resulted in a five-game suspension. For steroids, under a policy adopted in 1999, a first positive test resulted in a five-game suspension and mandatory treatment; a second positive tests resulted in a 10-game suspension; third and subsequent positive tests resulted in a 25-game suspension (NBA, 2000). Over the 1999 to 2005 period, of the approximately 400 NBA rookies randomly tested for steroid use, not one was found to be in violation ("Steroids Panel," 2005).

At the 2005 Congressional hearings into steroid use and policies in professional sports, it was noted that the "NBA [steroid] testing program has some 'Shaq-sized' holes in it" (Congress, 2005). The policy was ultimately amended, such that all players could be tested up to twice during the off-season, with the majority not tested more than four times throughout the entire year; however, no tests could occur during the day/night of a game ("Players Agree," 2011). The penalty for a first offense under the policy was increased to a 10-game suspension (Brill, 2012). Although positive tests for performance-enhancing drugs by NBA players have been quite rare (in recent years, OJ Mayo, Rashard Lewis, and Darius Miles had tested positive), similar to what we discussed above with respect to the National Hockey League, there are allegations that use of these substances is much more common among NBA players. For example, although he later denied it, the Chicago Bulls' Derrick Rose was asked (by ESPN) "If one equals 'what are PEDs?' and 10 equals 'Everybody's Juicing,' how big of an issue is illegal enhancing in your sport?'—Rose reportedly answered 'Seven. It's huge'" (as quoted in Lawrence, 2011).

Football

Given steroids' ability to enhance strength and explosive power, use of these substances by professional football players has been alleged to be rampant. The San Diego Chargers hired former U.S. Olympic weightlifting coach Alvin Roy as the first strength conditioning coach in the NFL in 1963, and it has been reported that he introduced Charger players to the steroid Dianabol (Yesalis, Courson, & Wright, 2000). Interviews with former players revealed that they were not informed that the "little pink pills" given to them at the training table were steroids but were told it would be in their interest to take them and that they would be fined if they refused (Yesalis, Courson, & Wright, 2000). Through the 1970s and 1980s, steroid use appears to have been very prevalent in the NFL, particularly at positions that place a premium on strength and size, such as offensive and defensive line. Fox sports analyst and Hall of Fame defensive end Howie Long commented in 1986 that steroid use in the NFL was engaged in by "at least 50% of the big guys. The offensive lines, 75%, defensive line, 40%, plus 35% of the linebackers" (Zimmerman, 1986, cited in Yesalis et al., 1993). Similarly, Joe Klecko, another defensive lineman who played for the New York Jets, admitted to using steroids and estimated that between 65% and 75% of NFL players were on steroids in the late 1980s (Klecko & Fields, 1989). Perhaps the most intense scrutiny directed at steroid use in the NFL came when former player Lyle Alzado, who admitted using steroids throughout his college and 15-season NFL career, developed a rare and fatal form of brain cancer. In an interview with *Sports Illustrated* just prior to his death in 1992, Alzado indicated that he believed his cancer resulted from his use of steroids and accused NFL management and coaches of turning a blind eye to steroids, which he claimed were rampant in the league throughout the 1980s.

In an interview in 1991 (which, perhaps notably, was shortly after the implementation of the NFL steroid policy in 1987), an unnamed NFL player told *Sports Illustrated* "the problem is enforcement. Some clubs have a guy who enforces the testing. Our guy is like one of the boys. He sits in the weight room eating a sandwich. Say it's your turn to be tested. You say 'Pete my urine's a little weak today, let me come back tomorrow,' or you get the trainer to piss in the bottle for you and give Pete that one. It's a joke." (as cited in Ferstle, 2000)

Although it appears to have been extensive in the past, the use of steroids (at least the most commonly known ones) appears to have decreased significantly in the NFL over time. In part, this is due to the fact that the NFL maintains one of the more rigorous testing programs in professional sports, although the policy is still less punitive than that of the IOC. In the NFL, players can be tested as many as nine times during the football season and are also subject to testing in the off-season, and all players are tested at least once per year (NFL Players Association, 2010). The NFL also bans a wide range of substances, including ephedra, androstenedione, DHEA, pseudoephedrine, diuretics and other masking agents, and all steroids, peptide hormones, and illegal recreational drugs. Players testing positive are subject to a four-game suspension (without pay) for their first offense, eight games for a second offense, and after a third positive test, the player is suspended for 1 year and must apply to the league for reinstatement. While on the surface this policy appears to be stringent, it is by no means infallible. As noted above, tests can only identify known drugs, and in 2004, four members of the Oakland Raiders were found to have been using THG once the substance became identifiable. Some have also indicated that personnel assigned to NFL teams to conduct drug testing have undermined the process (see box). It has also been alleged that NFL players circumvent drug tests by using detoxifying products that are available over the Internet. Perkins (2005) comments,

> Can it really be that the NFL, with more than 300 players who weigh more than 300 pounds each, really has no drug problem? . . . There are 320-pound linemen now who are faster than running backs were in the 1970s. How is that possible without artificial help?

Finally, while the NFL changed its rules in 2005 to allow for players to undergo a maximum of six tests in the off-season (from the previous two; Battista, 2011), NFL players are tested only once a year during training camp for amphetamines (Coile, 2005a). They are not tested at all on game days, which gives players a period of at least 24 hours to use fast-acting performance-enhancing drugs without being caught (Macur, 2011). It has also been alleged that as many as 30% of NFL players use HGH (Florio, 2011)—other estimates, including by former quarterback Boomer Esiason, claimed that 60 to 70% of players used hgh (Epstein, 2012), but the league does not currently test for this substance (Florio, 2011).

Baseball

Despite the long history of steroid use in football, it is professional baseball that has received the most scrutiny in recent years over steroids and other performance-enhancing drugs—baseball players have been known to use performance-enhancing (and other) drugs since at least 1889, when Hall of Fame pitcher Pud Galvin used monkey testosterone (Chafets, 2009). Responding to public criticism that the game was "juiced," Major League Baseball (MLB) administered drug tests to players in its 2003 pre-season in order to obtain an estimate of the extent of the problem. Results of the drug tests indicated that 5% to 7% of MLB players were currently using steroids, although limitations inherent in the drug-testing process suggest that the figure was likely higher. In an interview with *Sports Illustrated* and in a book he later published, Jose Canseco admitted to using steroids himself and estimated that 85% of major league baseball players were steroid users (Verducci, 2002). Similarly, in an interview with *Sports Illustrated* in 2002, former National League Most Valuable Player Ken Caminiti admitted to using steroids and claimed that at least half of major league baseball players also used steroids. Noting that he would not discourage other players from using steroids, Caminiti commented,

> Look at the money in the game. A kid got $252 million. So I can't say "Don't do it," not when a guy next to you is as big as a house and he's going to take your job and make the money. ("Caminiti Comes Clean," 2002)

Also, in reference to steroid use in baseball, pitcher Curt Schilling said, "Guys out there look like Mr. Potato Head, with a head and arms and six or seven body parts that just don't look right" (as quoted in Verducci, 2002).

Similar to analyses documenting the rapid improvement in the lifts of Soviet weightlifters in the early 1950s (Yesalis, Courson, & Wright, 2000), several commentators have focused on recent baseball statistics and suggested that they are indicative of pervasive steroid use. For example, between 1994 and 2003, 10 MLB players hit 50 or more home runs in a season, compared to 11 during the previous 118 years. The 70-home-run plateau, which had never been broken in 122 years of major league baseball, was reached twice—by Mark McGwire in 1998 and Barry Bonds in 2001 (Fainaru-Wada & Heath, 2003). Bonds had never hit more than 46 home runs until the 2000 season, and in most years of his career his total was in the 30s. However, at age 35, when most professional baseball players are on the downside of their production, Bonds hit 49 home runs and "the following season turned into Superman" by hitting 73 home runs (Sokolove, 2004). Commenting on Bonds' physique, one writer noted, "[He] has an upper torso that looks six times larger than the one he had just a few years ago. The bulging veins in his biceps look like fat worms. Even his shaved scalp seems to ripple with muscles" (Wilstein, 2002). While Bonds claimed that he developed his impressive physique through vigorous workouts, his connection to the Bay Area Laboratories Company (BALCO) scandal as well as revelations in a book by *San Francisco*

Chronicle reporters Mark Fainaru-Wada and Lance Williams (2006; see below) raises questions.

The increased home run totals of Sammy Sosa also raise questions. In Sosa's first eight major league seasons, he averaged 22 home runs. However, in the 1998 season he hit 66 home runs, and 63 in 1999, followed by seasons of 50, 64, and 49, representing the highest 5-year total in the history of major league baseball. Although some have claimed that the year-long training, strength coaches, and weight rooms now common in professional sports may explain these performances, it is notable that the 2003 baseball season was the first since 1993 in which no player hit 50 home runs. Perhaps coincidentally, this was also the first year in which major league baseball players were tested for steroid use (Fainaru-Wada & Heath, 2003). Verducci (2012) further notes that in the nine seasons before baseball began testing for steroids, 18 players hit 50 or more home runs, while six hit 60 or more. However, in the nine seasons with steroid testing, there were only six 50-home run seasons, and no player had hit 60.

Prior to 2005, the performance-enhancing drug testing program maintained by MLB was among the most lax of any professional sport. Due to the fact (as noted above) that drug tests of 1,438 players in spring training found between 5% and 7% positive for steroids in 2003, a more widespread program was to be implemented in the 2004 and 2005 seasons. However, Dr. Gary Wadler, a member of WADA's medical research committee, referred to baseball's drug testing program as "worse than terrible . . . it's more of an IQ test than a steroid test because you have to be really dumb to fail it" (as quoted in Freeman & Onley, 2003). Because under MLB's policy players knew when they would be tested, they could avoid detection of steroids by timing their use of the substances.

Critics of MLB's steroid testing policy also emphasized that it did not serve to deter players from using steroids because the penalties were not sufficiently severe: one author referred to the policy as "Five Strikes and You're Out" (Powers, 2003). Under the (pre–2005) policy, a first positive test for steroids resulted in the player being forced to undergo treatment; a second violation resulted in a 15-day suspension or a $10,000 fine; a third violation led to a 25-day suspension; a fourth 50 days; and a fifth, 1 year. In response to the MLB policy, Dick Pound, chairman of WADA, commented, "It's an insult to the fight against doping in sport. It's a complete and utter joke. You can test positive for steroids five times, then they think of booting you out for a year? Give me a break" (as quoted in Antonen, 2003). In response to this criticism, Rob Manfred, vice president of labor relations for MLB, retorted, "We don't criticize the Olympics movement and we would ask them to mind their own business" (as quoted in Antonen, 2003).

Perhaps even more problematically, MLB's (pre–2005) policy did not involve tests for amphetamines, the use of which is purported to be rampant among MLB players. Many major league teams actually provided amphetamines to players in the 1950s, and although the practice was discontinued in the 1960s, of approximately 570 major league players surveyed in the spring of 2005, 87.2% reported that amphetamine use existed in MLB, and 35.3% said that at least half the players used amphetamines (Hohler, 2005). As Dr. Charles Yesalis, an expert on steroids, commented,

> On a danger scale, amphetamines are a hell of a lot higher than steroids. If I held a gun to your head and gave you a choice between ingesting a bottle of amphetamines or a bottle of steroids, you damn well better choose steroids. If you choose the amphetamines, you'd be just as dead as if I put a bullet in your head. (as quoted in Hohler, 2005)

> Why does baseball green light greenies? They've been a fixture in the sport's culture for about half a century, and too many players use them to expect the rank and file to stand against them. Last year one American League base runner nearly ran himself into a serious injury when he mistakenly broke for home with a batter swinging. The runner privately blamed his reckless exuberance on an especially strong greenie (Verducci, 2005).
>
> Tom House, a former major league pitcher, discussing the widespread use of amphetamines in baseball during the 1960s and 1970s, commented that he would deal with losses of games by saying "we didn't get beat, we got out-milligrammed" (as quoted in Longman, 2005).
>
> Former Boston Red Sox, Montreal Expo, and Texas Rangers pitcher Dennis ("Oil Can") Boyd wrote in his autobiography that he was under the influence of cocaine drugs for approximately two-thirds of the games he pitched in the major leagues. Boyd claimed that he "wasn't doing anything that hundreds of other ballplayers weren't doing at the time." (as quoted in "Admitted," 2012)

In his 2004 testimony before a federal grand jury examining BALCO, which was alleged to have provided steroids to several amateur and professional athletes, professional baseball player Jason Giambi admitted that he had injected himself with hgh during the 2003 season and said he had been using steroids at least 2 years prior to this (Fainaru-Wada & Williams, 2004). In addition, Gary Anderson, Barry Bonds's personal trainer, told the same grand jury that he had "given steroids to several professional baseball players" (as quoted in Williams & Fainaru-Wada, 2004). As noted above, some months later, former professional baseball player Jose Canseco wrote a book in which he claimed there was widespread use of steroids by baseball players. In response to these events and a Congressional committee on steroid use, in the spring of 2005, MLB Commissioner Bud Selig proposed a new drug testing policy. Under this policy, players who tested positive for the first time would face a 50-game suspension, a second positive test would result in a 100-game suspension, while those testing positive a third time would be banished from Major League Baseball (Bissinger, 2005). The policy also prohibited amphetamines (Curry, 2005); however, the penalties for amphetamine use were not as severe as those for steroids. Players who tested positive for amphetamines would be subject to mandatory evaluation and follow-up testing after a first offense, with a second offense resulting in a 25-game suspension and a third leading to an 80-game suspension (Curry, 2006).

While the new MLB policy was certainly more stringent than the previous policy, legislation proposed by the federal government in 2005, which would apply to all professional sports, mandated a 2-year suspension for a first positive drug test for performance-enhancing drugs and a lifetime ban for a second offense. This bill also would have required random testing of professional athletes at least once per year, would have mandated tests for amphetamines, and punished sports leagues that failed to comply with an initial $5 million fine as well as penalties of $1 million per day for each day the league failed to comply (Coile, 2005a).

In 2007, Major League Baseball released the 409-page Mitchell Report (Mitchell, 2007), which identified 89 former and current MLB players (including prominent players such as Roger Clemens, Andy Pettite, and Miguel Tejada) as users of performance-enhancing drugs. In addition, Mark McGwire, who had pleaded the Fifth Amendment when testifying before the Congressional Committee on Steroids, eventually admitted to using performance-enhancing drugs but claimed that this was to help him recover from injuries (Kepner, 2010). It was also revealed that Alex Rodriguez, star third baseman for the New York Yankees, was among the 104 players who tested positive for steroids in 2003 (Zirin, 2009), and Manny Ramirez was revealed to have used human chorionic gonadotropin (which can be used to lower testosterone levels, thereby masking the use of other drugs; Hiltzick, 2009b). Although baseball commissioner Bud Selig commented, "The use of steroids and amphetamines among today's players has greatly subsided and is virtually non-existent, as our testing results have shown" (as quoted in Kepner, 2010), given general weaknesses in the MLB drug testing policy, given the "cat and mouse" game described above, and given the continuing potential financial benefits associated with use, such a conclusion would seem to be premature.

In the 2012 MLB season, San Francisco Giants outfielder Melky Cabrera tested positive for performance-enhancing drugs. In another example of the cat-and-mouse game between athletes using such drugs and those testing for them, Cabrera attempted to evade the penalty associated with the positive drug test by having an associate purchase a website and create a fake product to make it appear as though Cabrera had ingested a tainted supplement. (Epstein, 2012)

In 2010 and 2011, a total of four MLB players were suspended for violations of the league's drug policy, while five were suspended in 2012. In 2011, National League Most Valuable Player Ryan Braun tested positive for performance-enhancing drugs, although this test was later overturned due to violations related to the collection procedure. And in 2011, Major League Baseball became the first professional sports league in North America to implement blood testing for human growth hormone, with the original policy providing for year-round tests of players in the minor leagues; this was later expanded to test players on MLB rosters only in spring training and the off-season (Epstein, 2012). Mike Jacobs (a former major league player who was rehabilitating in the minor leagues) became the first U.S. athlete to be suspended (for 50 games) as the result of a positive test for hgh in any professional sports league (Borelli, 2011).

Federal Government Regulation of Herbal and Dietary Supplements

> The Dietary Supplement Health and Education Act (also known as the Hatch-Harkin law) was sponsored by Republican Senator Orrin Hatch of Utah. It is perhaps not surprising that Senator Hatch sponsored this legislation that provides clear benefits to the herbal supplements industry, given that he received $137,000 in campaign contributions from the industry between 1993 and 2002. In addition, the supplements industry paid almost $2 million in lobbying fees to companies that employ Senator Hatch's son (Neubauer, Pasternak, & Cooper, 2003). Senator Hatch was also influential in allowing for the dietary supplement DHEA, a substance banned by the World Anti-Doping Agency, the NCAA, NFL, and NBA, to be sold over the counter in the United States. (Kornblut & Wilson, 2005)

Dietary supplements are consumed by an estimated 33.5 million Americans annually (Epstein & Dohrmann, 2009)—people in the United States spent more than $5 billion on these products in 2009 (Thompson, 2010)—and regulation of dietary supplements in the United States also stands in stark contrast to the policies regulating illegal drugs discussed in Chapter 11. According to the American Association of Poison Control Centers, reports of adverse reactions to dietary supplements more than tripled, from 6,914 in 1998 to 22,928 in 2002. Over the same period, cases requiring treatment in a hospital as a result of dietary supplement use increased more than six-fold, to 8,931 in 2002 (Hurley, 2004). However, dietary supplements are regulated under the 1994 Dietary Supplement Health and Education Act (DSHEA), which requires that products derived from herbs and natural sources be classified as foods and not drugs. As such, regulation of these products is even more lax than regulation of pharmaceutical products, allowing companies to market these products without submitting proof of their safety or effectiveness to the FDA (Denham, 2011). This is in contrast to countries such as Germany, where companies manufacturing and marketing these products are required to adhere to strict standards for ingredients and manufacturing processes (Greenwald, 1998).

Under the DSHEA, manufacturers of dietary supplements can make statements that their products improve nutrition without subjecting the products to regulation as drugs. However, if the manufacturer claims the substance can "diagnose, treat, cure, or prevent disease," then the substance is subject to the same regulations as drugs (DSHEA, 1994). The law still allows manufacturers of these products to make a wide range of vague and general claims that their products contribute to health. And in contrast to the manufacturers of prescription drugs, these companies do not have to report adverse events related to the use of their products to the FDA (Mooney, 2003). As just one example of the potential problems associated with these provisions, the manufacturer of MetaboLife, an herbal remedy used by approximately 2.5 million Americans for weight loss that contains a potent combination of ephedra and caffeine, was not required to reveal the more than 14,000 reports of adverse reactions by users of the substance that had been revealed over several years (Grollman, 2003).

A report by the U.S. Department of Health and Human Services (2001) that examined data from 1994 to 1999 found that the FDA was not able to determine the ingredients of close to one-third (1,153 of 3,547) of the products mentioned in adverse events involving supplements. In addition, the FDA did not have product labels for 77% of the substances mentioned in these adverse event reports and was not able to determine the location for 71% of the manufacturers of these products. The report also noted that the FDA had taken only 32 safety actions as a result of adverse event reports related to supplements between January 1994 and June 2000, a period in which more than 100 million people in the United States were consumers of dietary supplements. Commenting on this lax regulation of potentially dangerous dietary supplements, Sidney Wolfe, Director of Public Citizen's Health Research group, noted, "The remedy for all this is to stop dangerously pretending that the pharmacologically active substances called dietary supplements should be treated completely different from pharmacologically active substances called drugs" (as quoted in Specter, 2004).

A Congressional investigation into dietary supplements in 2010 found that nearly all of the 40 products tested contained trace amounts of lead and other contaminants and that at least nine of them made illegal health claims (Harris, 2010). In response to these and other problems with supplements, legislation proposed in February 2010, sponsored by Senators John McCain and Byron Dorgan, would have required supplement manufacturers to register with the FDA and to disclose the ingredients of all their products. This legislation also would have given the FDA authority to recall products. However, the legislation was never passed, when, "with the support of industry lobbies," Senators Hatch and Tom Harkin persuaded the sponsors of this bill to drop it (Denham, 2011).

CONCLUSION

Consumption of psychoactive pharmaceutical products results in considerably more injuries and deaths than does the consumption of currently illegal drugs. While these drugs have certainly produced health benefits for millions of people, pharmaceutical companies aggressively market and advertise these products to consumers, often presenting misleading information regarding the benefits of these drugs. The companies also frequently conceal the known negative side effects associated with these substances and have engaged in criminal practices in attempts to increase their sales. Despite this, current regulation of these products in the United States is incredibly lax, at least partially due to the fact that pharmaceutical companies exert considerable influence on legislators and Food and Drug Administration officials.

Some of the risks associated with prescription drugs could be eliminated with a more rigorous drug oversight and approval process. Although it is not commonly known, and despite recent developments to make the process somewhat more transparent, the FDA approval of a drug is granted on the basis of studies that are designed, supervised, and funded by the pharmaceutical companies that manufacture the drugs. Given the massive financial stakes involved in the sale of a popular pharmaceutical drug, the companies have adopted a number of strategies—including providing substantial financial incentives to doctors and regulators—designed to influence the probability that these drugs will obtain FDA approval. In many instances, this process has resulted in the needs of the companies being placed above the protection of the consumer.

FDA approval of drugs, once granted, is very difficult to revoke. These oversight procedures are in stark contrast to pharmaceutical regulations in European countries, where drug approvals are systematically reviewed every 5 years (Pstay et al., 2004). Additionally, once a drug is approved for use by the FDA, it can be prescribed for *any* condition, whether that condition is officially indicated on the label or not. Drugs that are approved for a relatively obscure condition (e.g., narcolepsy) may be used on a very wide scale when doctors prescribe and people take them for another condition (e.g., "wakefulness").

There are regulations placed on the sale and advertising of prescription drugs, but these regulations typically work to the benefit of the pharmaceutical companies. Partially because of this, the cost of prescription medications in the United States is exceptionally high in comparison to most other Westernized countries. As drug costs increased in the 1990s and into the 2000s, many Americans began to purchase cheaper prescription drug products from Canada, often over the Internet (Doughton, 2003). The FDA responded by restricting the importation of Canadian pharmaceuticals. In effect, this left American consumers with the option of paying for more expensive American pharmaceuticals or purchasing drugs from online companies in foreign countries where drug regulatory standards are more lax, placing the individuals at a higher risk of consuming an adulterated or mislabeled product.

The United States is currently the only country that allows direct-to-consumer (DTC) advertising of prescription medications, a strategy that has been shown to be remarkably effective for increasing drug consumption and sales. DTC advertising of pharmaceuticals has also employed the tactic of "medicalizing" normal human conditions, sometimes leading people to request unnecessary medicines from their physician.

Given the failures of the FDA with respect to regulating drugs and protecting consumers, organizations such as the American Medical Association have questioned whether a new organization should be formed and empowered to track the safety of drugs and medical devices. Recent legislation has also recommended a number of significant changes in the FDA, including the removal of scientists with financial conflicts of interest from FDA advisory panels and the establishment of a separate branch of the FDA to monitory the safety of drugs once approved. Perhaps most important are proposed revisions that would redirect the fees that drug companies pay for approval of their drugs to the U.S. treasury and allow for penalties up to $50 million to be imposed on companies that are in violation of FDA regulations (Lenzer, 2005b).

Until recently, the regulation of performance-enhancing drugs has largely been left to various sports organizations. The use of substances to enhance performance in sports dates far back in history, but it is only during the last century, and particularly in the last 30 years, that there have been meaningful attempts to regulate drug use in sports.

As is the case in other areas of drug regulation, there is considerable inconsistency and often hypocrisy in the regulation of performance-enhancing drugs. It is commonly thought that in athletic competition, anything that "unnaturally" enhances athletic performance should be banned because it perverts the integrity of competition. While this principle seems very reasonable, it is difficult to determine where the line should be drawn between acceptable and unacceptable substances. Based on this logic, widely accepted supplements such as Creatine, amino acids, and even vitamins and aspirins should be banned because all these substances may also assist athletes and enhance their performance (Yesalis, 2000).

Another argument for the regulation of performance-enhancing drugs in sports is that many athletes may be forced to choose between using performance-enhancing drugs and succeeding or staying clean and becoming uncompetitive against athletes who are using such substances. The use of any drug carries some level of risk, and while we are certainly not advocating the use of performance-enhancing drugs in sport, it is important to note that the risk associated with many of these substances has been somewhat exaggerated, at least in terms of the effects of short-term use (Bhasin et al., 1996; Yesalis, 2000). Additionally, participation in sport *always* involves some level of physical risk. Violent sports such as boxing, football, hockey, and many forms of racing place the competitors at risk of serious injury and even death. The violent nature of these sports is intimately tied to their popularity, so it is somewhat paradoxical that one of the primary rationales for banning performance-enhancing drugs in sport is to protect the health of athletes.

We have reviewed the regulation of performance-enhancing drug use by the National Collegiate Athletic Association (NCAA), International Olympic Committee (IOC), and the governing bodies of professional tennis, cycling, hockey, basketball, football, and baseball. What is apparent is that there is no common standard for regulating the use of performance-enhancing drugs in sport. The use of such drugs is much more prevalent in some sports than in others, and the differences are at least partially explained by the rigor of drug testing procedures adopted by each athletic governing body.

The regulation of dietary/herbal supplements is extremely lax in the United States despite the fact that these substances are associated with tens of thousands of adverse health outcomes among users in any given year. Substances considered to be dietary supplements are regulated under the 1994 Dietary Supplement Health and Education Act (DSHEA), which requires that products derived from herbs and natural sources be classified as foods and not drugs. Provided that a manufacturer of these products does not claim that a substance can "diagnose, treat, cure, or prevent diseases," the substance is not subject to the same regulations as scheduled drugs (DSHEA, 1994). Because of this, manufacturers of dietary supplements are able to make a wide range of vague and general claims that their products contribute to health without any evidence that this is the case.

In contrast to producers of prescription drugs, producers of dietary supplements are not required to report "adverse events" related to the use of their products to the FDA. Many performance-enhancing substances have initially been classified as dietary supplements and thus have been legal and widely used in sports before being reclassified as Schedule III controlled substances when substantial evidence of their potential harm accumulates (e.g., GHB, androstenedione).

REVIEW QUESTIONS

1. Why was the Pure Food and Drug Act largely ineffective at preventing unsafe products from entering the marketplace? How is this analogous to the FDA's regulation of drugs today?

2. Why are prescription/pharmaceutical drugs not subject to the same levels of regulation as currently illegal drugs?

3. Who conducts research on the safety and efficacy of drugs that the FDA evaluates when considering approval of a drug for public use?

4. Why are drug company executives not subject to imprisonment for violating laws regulating their products?

5. What does "off-label" approval of a drug mean?

6. Should consumers be concerned about how pharmaceutical products are regulated by the FDA? If so, why?

7. In what ways might political campaign contributions by pharmaceutical companies have an influence on the regulation of prescription drugs?

8. In what ways might gifts to doctors increase profits for pharmaceutical companies?

9. Identify things other than drugs that might be considered performance enhancers in sports.

10. Compare and contrast the performance-enhancing drug policies of at least one professional sports league with the policies of the International Olympic Committee.

11. In what sense can the regulation of performance-enhancing drugs be seen as a cat-and-mouse game?

12. Why are herbal/dietary supplements subject to lax regulation?

INTERNET AND MEDIA EXERCISES

1. Go to the website http://www.clinicaltrials.gov and select one drug (you might try Vioxx or Viagra). Follow the steps and review the results of at least one of the studies, focusing on the purported positive and negative effects of the drug.

2. Retrieve two prescription drug advertisements from a popular magazine such as *Time, Newsweek,* or *Sports Illustrated.* According to the ads, what conditions are the drugs for? What claims are made for the drugs' effectiveness? What are the listed side effects of the drugs (be sure to look at the back of the page when examining side effects)?

3. Use the Internet to find the performance-enhancing drug testing policies of two professional sports leagues (e.g., Major League Baseball, National Football League). Compare and contrast these policies with respect to the substances tested for and penalties for violation of the policy.

CHAPTER 11

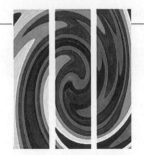

Policies Regulating
Illegal Drugs

As compared to other Western countries, the United States places a great deal of emphasis on criminal justice responses to drug use. With the most recent War on Drugs that began in the mid-1980s, the criminal justice system emphasis became even more pronounced: arrests for drug offenses increased, the sentences for drug offenses were lengthened significantly, and the number of people incarcerated for the commission of drug crimes similarly increased. These policies were apparently implemented with the goal of preventing drug use and drug-related harm, but after 30 years and billions of dollars in criminal justice system expenditures, it is clear that these policies have failed to achieve these goals.

In this chapter, we critically examine these policies, focusing on their effectiveness (or more appropriately, the lack thereof), their economic and social costs, and several unintended consequences that have resulted from them. We begin by addressing trends in arrests and incarcerations for drug offenses and discuss social class and racial inequality in the application of drug laws. We proceed to a discussion of mandatory minimum sentencing policies, which have had a disproportionately negative impact on the poor and members of minority groups. We also discuss ancillary policies such as the denial of welfare and student aid to individuals who are convicted of drug offenses; these policies have similarly had a negative impact on the poor and members of minority groups. The next section of the chapter addresses asset forfeiture and drug tax laws, the RAVE Act, and legislation from the 2000s dealing with methamphetamine, with a focus on the unintended consequences of these policies. We then discuss restrictions on hemp production and medical marijuana legislation, with an emphasis on how the U.S. federal government has actively intervened in states that have passed medical marijuana legislation. The chapter concludes with a discussion of recent changes in drug laws at the state level and interesting developments surrounding marijuana legalization initiatives.

TRENDS IN ARRESTS AND INCARCERATION

With the passage of the Harrison Narcotics Control Act in 1914, the United States launched a policy of arresting and incarcerating increasingly large numbers of users of and traffickers in illicit drugs (Brecher, 1972; Musto, 1999; Zimring & Hawkins, 1992). Historically, this legislation has disproportionately impacted members of minority groups and the poor. Contemporary policies toward illegal drugs in the United States are consistent with principles established early in the 20th century, with a particular focus on a law enforcement approach to the drug problem and stringent penalties attached to violations of drug laws. As Table 11.1 shows, in 2010, there were 1,638,846 arrests for "drug abuse violations" (note that the term *drug abuse violations* is a misnomer, in that an arrest for a drug offense by no means necessarily constitutes drug abuse) comprising more than 12% of the total arrests in that year, and constituting about the same number of arrests as for murder, rape, robbery, burglary, and theft combined (Bureau of Justice Statistics, 2011). And despite the rhetoric on the part of government and law enforcement officials that the War on Drugs is focused on those who traffic in these substances, arrests for possession of drugs were about four times greater than those for trafficking. Despite the additional rhetoric that the War on Drugs is focused on "hard drugs," in 2010, 853,838 individuals were arrested for marijuana offenses, constituting 52% of all drug arrests in that year (Bureau of Justice Statistics, 2011). Between 2000 and 2010, nearly eight million people in the United States were arrested on marijuana charges (Smith, 2011).

Table 11.1   Arrests in the United States—2010

Offense Category	Number of Arrests
Total	13,120,847
Drug abuse violations	1,638,846
Driving under the influence	1,412,223
Simple assaults	1,292,449
Larceny-theft	1,271,410
Disorderly conduct	615,172
Drunkenness	560,718
Liquor laws	512,790

SOURCE: Federal Bureau of Investigation, 2011.

NOTE: Arrests totals are based on all reporting law enforcement agencies and estimates for unreported areas.

Figure 11.1   Drug Arrests by Type, 1982–2007

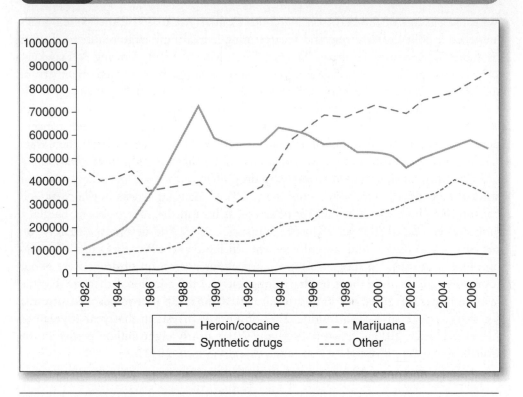

SOURCE: http://bjs.ojp.usdoj.gov/content/dcf/enforce.cfm

Additionally, and as illustrated in Figure 11.1, arrests for marijuana offenses generally increased over the 1982 to 2007 period, despite the fact that self-report surveys and other measures of drug use indicate that use of marijuana remained relatively constant over this period. Since the 1980s, arrests for cocaine and heroin have declined significantly, suggesting that it is possible that the increased focus on marijuana has come at the expense of enforcing laws against hard drugs such as cocaine, heroin, and methamphetamine.

Given the tremendous number of arrests for drug offenses and the severe penalties that result from convictions for such offenses, the drug war has also contributed to unprecedented levels of imprisonment in the United States (Austin & Irwin, 2012). At the end of 2009, there were 2,284,913 individuals incarcerated in the United States, translating to an incarceration rate of 743 per 100,000 population. As of April 2010, approximately 108,000 of the total 211,455 individuals incarcerated in federal prisons were there for drug-related crimes, and about 20% of inmates in state prisons had been convicted of drug-related crimes. As of the mid-2000s, the United States had 100,000 more people incarcerated for drug offenses than the European Union had for all offenses combined, despite the fact that the European Union had 100 million more inhabitants (Wood et al., 2003).

While these data thus indicate that millions of Americans have been incarcerated for violations of drug legislation in the last few decades and that hundreds of thousands have served lengthy prison sentences for such offenses, one of the defining characteristics of U.S. drug laws is that they are applied unequally.

Forty-four-year-old Michael Carpenter spent a total of 3 hours helping to unload hashish from a truck and was sentenced to 12 years in prison (Steinberg, 1994). If offenders such as Carpenter, convicted under federal drug laws, had instead been convicted of robbing a bank, or even rape or murder, their average sentences would be significantly lower than what they receive for what are often very minor drug offenses.

It is also not well known that possession of a single marijuana cigarette can result in deportation. The federal government maintains that, for deportation purposes, two convictions for drug possession are the equivalent of drug trafficking, an "aggravated felony," that requires expulsion and prohibits immigration courts from granting exceptions based on individual life circumstances. In *Carachuri-Rosendo v. Holder*, a long-time legal resident of Texas was deported to Mexico based on convictions for the possession of marijuana and a tablet of Xanax. (Bernstein, 2010, although this decision was eventually overturned by the Supreme Court)

Much of this chapter addresses racial/ethnic disparities in the application of drug laws, but it is also worth considering how an individual's social status can influence how he or she is treated when in violation of drug laws. Given that crime and incarceration statistics do not include information on the social class of offenders, it is worth considering a number of individual cases. Individuals found guilty of cultivating more than 50 marijuana plants are frequently prosecuted at the federal level, where the penalties are significantly more severe than for state-level prosecutions. In 1992, the nephew of Missouri Governor and future Attorney General John Ashcroft received the relatively lenient penalty of probation following a felony conviction for growing 60 marijuana plants with intent to distribute. Ashcroft's nephew tested positive for drugs during his first test after being placed on probation, but unlike many others in similar situations, was not sentenced to prison as a result of the positive test. Although direct evidence implicating then-governor Ashcroft's involvement in the case was not uncovered, Alex Ashcroft's connection to the governor was apparently widely known (Forbes, 2001).

In 1982, the son of President Reagan's Chief of Staff (James Baker) was arrested for selling one quarter of an ounce of marijuana to an undercover agent in Texas. Under Texas law, he could have faced a prison term of between 2 and 20 years; however, he was charged with a misdemeanor and fined $2,000 (Schlosser, 2003).

In 1990, Congressman Dan Burton introduced legislation requiring the death penalty for traffickers in illegal drugs. Four years later, his son was arrested for transporting approximately 8 pounds of marijuana from Texas to Indiana. While awaiting trial on charges stemming from this incident, he was arrested again for growing 30 marijuana plants in an apartment in Indianapolis. Federal charges were not filed in either of these cases, and Burton's son received a term of community service, probation, and house arrest (Schlosser, 2003).

When the son of Richard Riley (former governor of South Carolina who later became President Clinton's Secretary of Education) was charged with conspiracy to sell cocaine and marijuana, he faced 10 years to life imprisonment and a possible $4 million fine. Instead, he was sentenced to 6 months of house arrest.

Inequality in the application of drug laws was perhaps most clearly manifested in the case of Noelle Bush, the daughter of Florida governor Jeb Bush and niece of President George W. Bush. In July 2002, Noelle Bush, who had previously been convicted of prescription drug fraud after attempting to obtain Xanax from a drive-through pharmacy, stole prescription pills from a medicine cabinet at the drug treatment center she was attending. As a result of the offense, Judge Reginald Whitehead sentenced her to 3 days in jail (Canedy, 2002). Some 3 months after this incident, she was found in possession of 0.2 grams of crack cocaine and once again appeared before Judge Whitehead. The judge informed Noelle Bush that he was disappointed with her and sentenced her to 10 days in jail but also allowed her to remain in the drug treatment program ("Gov. Bush's Daughter," 2002).

In response to his daughter being convicted of a drug offense for the third time, Jeb Bush was quoted as saying, "This is a very serious problem. . . . Unfortunately, substance abuse is an issue confronting many families across the nation. We ask the public and media to respect our family's privacy during this difficult time so that we can help our daughter" (as quoted in Nadelmann, 2002a). While Bush's compassionate stance is admirable, it is worth noting that his daughter could have received up to 5 years in prison and a $5,000 fine for this offense. It is also worth contrasting this case with that of hundreds of thousands of others in the United States who are less wealthy and less politically connected who, if convicted for drug offenses, are denied welfare benefits for life. Further, as Williams (2002) notes (and as will be discussed further below),

In a case recently before the Supreme Court, an elderly woman whose retarded granddaughter smoked a joint three blocks from her house was evicted from public housing based on her "relation" to drug use or sale. If such rules were applied across the socio-economic spectrum, we'd have to ask Jeb Bush to give up the governor's mansion. It is, after all, public housing.

To take Williams' argument one step further, it is worth repeating that George W. Bush is Noelle Bush's uncle and that the White House is also public housing.

The daughter of former Chairman of the House of Representatives Ways and Means Committee, Dan Rostenkowski, was charged with possession of 29 grams of cocaine with intent to deliver in June of 1990. Although she was facing up to 15 years in prison, she pled guilty to a lesser charge and received a sentence of 3 years probation, 20 hours of public service, a fine of $2,800, and forfeited the car in which the cocaine was found. Three years later, she was found in possession of 1 gram of cocaine, a violation for which she could have been sentenced to 3 years in prison. However, the charge was dismissed by a judge (Bovard, 1999).

Cindy McCain, wife of former presidential candidate and current Senator John McCain, admitted stealing Percocet and Vicodin (Schedule II drugs) and faced monetary fines and up to 1 year in prison. However, she was allowed to enter a pretrial diversion program and did not face formal prosecution (Bovard, 1999).

Susan Gallo, daughter of former Representative Dean Gallo, was charged with five counts of cocaine possession, five counts of intent to distribute, five counts of distribution, and five counts of conspiracy to distribute cocaine. Facing 5 to 10 years in prison for each charge, she pled guilty to one count of distribution and one count of conspiracy to distribute and was sentenced to 5 years probation (Bovard, 1999).

Talk show host Rush Limbaugh, who in October 1995 stated, "Drug use, some might say, is destroying the country . . . and so if people are violating the law by doing drugs . . . they ought to be convicted and they ought to be sent up" (as quoted in Verhovek, 2006), agreed to enter into drug treatment some 3 years after being charged for receiving approximately 2,000 painkillers prescribed by four doctors in 6 months. Limbaugh's charge, referred to as "doctor shopping," was a felony offense that could have resulted in a sentence of 5 years imprisonment. (Skoloff, 2006)

In presenting the examples above, we are not suggesting that only individuals with political ties and/or financial resources receive lenient treatment when they violate drug laws. However, such examples do cause us to question whether these laws are applied equitably. As is discussed in detail below, among the most glaring and consistent disparities in the application of drug laws is their disproportional impact on members of racial and ethnic minority groups.

RACIAL AND ETHNIC INEQUALITY IN THE
APPLICATION OF DRUG LAWS

> Drug policy has from the beginning been driven, in part, by a deep-seated nativist fear about the moral, political, social, and economic implications of an ever larger, polyglot, urban mass of people whose skin color or ethnic heritage differs from that of the dominant group. (Ryan, 1998, p. 228)

Despite the fact that George W. Bush's drug czar John Walters asserted that racial disparities in the criminal justice system are an "urban myth" (as quoted in Drug Policy Alliance, 2003r), an examination of illegal drug policies and their application leaves little doubt that both historically and in the contemporary period, they have had a disproportionately negative impact on members of minority groups in the United States. In fact, some have referred to the War on Drugs as the "New Jim Crow" (Alexander, 2010; Boyd, 2001).

> Racial disparities in the application of drug laws have also been at least partially responsible for the widespread disenfranchisement of African Americans (Fellner & Mauer, 1998; see also Uggen & Manza, 2002). As of 2010, 12 states had disenfranchisement statutes disqualifying those convicted of drug felonies from voting even after completing their sentences—four states disqualify felons from voting for the rest of their lives (Sentencing Project, 2010). Estimates suggest that as many as 1.4 million African American males (13% of the total population of African American males) are disenfranchised. Alexander (2010) notes that no other country in the world disenfranchises people who are released from prison in a manner even remotely resembling the United States.

It is estimated that approximately 14% of all users of illegal drugs in the United States are African American (SAMHSA, 2011a). However, in 2010, they represented 34% of all drug arrestees (FBI, 2011). More generally, from the mid-1990s to the early 2000s, African Americans comprised 38% of all drug arrests, 59% of prosecutions for drug offenses, and 75% of those incarcerated for such offenses (Harkavy, 2005). It is important to stress that the higher arrest rates for blacks are not the result of higher rates of illegal drug use by blacks; as noted above and as was discussed in more detail in Chapter 5, African Americans use illegal drugs in approximately the same proportion as whites. Instead, these higher arrest rates for African Americans are at least partially the result of law enforcement's emphasis on inner-city areas where illegal drug use and trafficking are more likely to take place in the open, and where African Americans are disproportionately concentrated.

More recent data on incarceration for drug offenses underscore the continued racial disparities in the application of drug laws. In 2010, African Americans comprised 49% of all those incarcerated for drug offenses but only 13% of the population (a rate of 429/100,000 population that is 11 times greater than the rate at which whites are incarcerated for drug offenses (Guerino et al., 2011). Counties with high proportions of African Americans imprison people for drug offenses more frequently, and blacks are disproportionately incarcerated for drug offenses in 97% of the 198 largest counties in the United States (Beatty et al., 2007) and are at least twice as likely as whites to be imprisoned on drug charges in every state (Human Rights Watch, 2010). This disproportionality also applies to African American youth, who are less likely to use drugs than Caucasians (see Chapter 5) and represent only 17% of the population but comprised 48% of those sentenced to detention facilities for drug offenses in 2001 (Snyder, 2003).

Some would argue that these racial disparities in the application of drug laws are the result of a focus on harder drugs such as crack. However, racial disparities also apply to soft drugs such as marijuana. Although more recent data are not available, while blacks and Hispanics represented approximately 20% of the users of marijuana, they comprised 58% of marijuana offenders sentenced under federal drug legislation in 1995 (Zimmer & Morgan, 1997).

Examination of incarceration statistics for selected states from the mid-1990s and early 2000s (the height of the War on Drugs) provides further evidence of racial inequality in the application of drug laws. As of January 1, 2002, there were 19,164 drug offenders incarcerated in New York State. And while blacks and Hispanics constituted 31% of the state's population, they comprised 94% of felony drug offenders sentenced to prison. In New York State, black males are incarcerated for the commission of drug offenses at approximately 11 times the rate of white males ("New York Drug Laws," 2002).

In California, as of December 31, 2002, 33,548 males were incarcerated for drug offenses. Latinos comprised 32.2% of males in the 18 to 59 age group in that state but represented 36.1% of all drug offenders in state prisons. The overrepresentation of blacks imprisoned in California is even more striking. While black males accounted for 6.2% of males ages 18 to 59 in the state, they comprised 31.8% of all male drug offenders in state prisons. Black women accounted for 6.6% of the female population in California but constituted 29.6% of female drug offenders in California state prisons in 2002 (Drug Policy Alliance, 2003e).

In Maryland, as of 2002, 9 out of every 10 people incarcerated for drug crimes were black, despite the fact that African Americans comprised only 28% of the state's population (Whitlock, 2003). From 1986 to 1999 in Maryland, the increase in the number of African Americans sentenced to prison for drug crimes—from 652 to 4,633—was approximately 18 times the increase for whites (from 309 to 534; Whitlock, 2003).

In Georgia, the rates for illicit drug use were estimated to be approximately 20% higher for blacks compared to whites. However, blacks were incarcerated for drug possession at a rate that was 500% greater than that of whites (Fellner, 1996). In the same state, there is a provision in the laws allowing for life imprisonment for conviction on a second drug offense. As of 1995, district attorneys in Georgia had used this clause against only 1% of whites who had a second drug conviction, compared to more than 16% of blacks. At least partially as a result of the provision of this state law and the exercise of prosecutorial discretion, in 1995, 98.4% of those serving life sentences for drug offenses in Georgia were African American (Cole, 1999). Similarly, in Connecticut, while half of those arrested on drug charges were white, 9 out of 10 people in jails or prisons for the commission of drug offenses as of the year 2001 were black or Hispanic (Butterfield, 2001b).

Although Mauer (2009) notes that as of the mid-2000s racial disparities in incarceration for drug offenses were declining, he concludes "While these trends are welcome as a possible indication of a change in policy and practice, they need to be tempered by an assessment of the overall scale of incarceration and punishment" (p. 19). Mauer also speculated that because so many African Americans have already been incarcerated, there are fewer on the street to be arrested (Fears, 2009).

Studies at the local level from the same (1990s–mid-2000s) period also reveal striking differences in the application of drug laws. In the city of Baltimore, Maryland, in 1980, 18 white juveniles and 86 black juveniles were arrested for selling drugs. In 1990, however, the number of white juveniles arrested on drug trafficking charges had decreased to 13, while the number of black juveniles arrested on the same charge had increased to 1,304 (Cole, 1999). In Columbus, Ohio, black males comprised 11% of the population but accounted for 90% of drug arrests. And in Jacksonville, Florida, black males constituted 12% of the population but represented 87% of drug arrests (Cole, 1999).

In the late 1980s, a strategy employed by the Los Angeles Police Department to apprehend drug users and traffickers known as Operation Hammer resulted in the arrest of more than 1,000 people on one weekend alone in October of 1989, all of whom were either black or Hispanic (Walker, Spohn, & DeLone, 1996). A 1993 study by the California State Assembly's Commission on the Status of African American males reported that 92% of the black males arrested by the police on drug charges were subsequently released for lack of evidence or inadmissible evidence (American Civil Liberties Union, 2000b).

In analysis of data from Seattle, Washington, for the years 1999 through 2001, Katherine Beckett found that of those arrested for selling heroin, cocaine, methamphetamine, and ecstasy, 63% were black, 19% were white, and 14% were Hispanic (Beckett et al., 2005). However, data derived from observations of drug markets in Seattle revealed that the majority of actual drug dealers were white. Beckett concluded that black heroin dealers were 22 times more likely to be arrested than white heroin dealers, while black methamphetamine traffickers were 31 times more likely to be arrested than white methamphetamine traffickers (Beckett et al., 2005).

The city of Portland, Oregon, also provides an instructive example of racial inequality in the application of drug laws. In 1992, the city passed a civil law designating a portion of the downtown area as a drug-free zone; this legislation allowed police to banish suspected drug criminals from the area for a 90-day period. Under the provisions of this law, police officers were not required to present evidence before judges in order to issue exclusion orders, and an investigation of these cases found that police routinely excluded individuals where there was insufficient evidence to prosecute them (Franzen, 2001). The investigation also found that, of the 3,700 exclusions issued by the Portland police in 1999, blacks, who constituted approximately 8% of the city's population, represented 45% of the exclusion orders issued by law enforcement. When the constitutionality of these zones was questioned, they were eliminated in 2007 (Hottle, 2011) but were re-created in 2011 and relabeled drug impact areas (DIAs). The law was changed such that judges, as opposed to police, would determine who would be excluded from the DIAs. And although racial disparity apparently decreased under the new law, a report on the first 6 months of the operation of this law by the Multnomah County District Attorney's Office found that 37% of those excluded from the zones were African American (Theriault, 2012).

Another example of racial disparities in the application of drug laws comes from the Texas panhandle town of Tulia, where 46 people, 39 of them black (representing 10% of the town's black population) were arrested and eventually prosecuted on drug trafficking charges in 1999. The local newspaper, the *Tulia Sentinel,* celebrated the arrests, announcing "We do not like these scumbags in our town. [They are] a cancer in our community, it's time to give them a major dose of chemotherapy behind bars." A later headline in the same newspaper in reference to the case stated, "Tulia's Streets Cleared of Garbage" (as cited in Mangold, 2003). All of these individuals were arrested on the uncorroborated, unsubstantiated testimony of Deputy Tom Coleman, who was given the Texas Lawman of the Year award for his efforts in these arrests. However, Coleman had a history of "throwing evidence into the garbage, scrawling important investigative information on his arms and legs, changing testimony from trial to trial, making false statements while under oath, and referring to black people as 'niggers'" (Herbert, 2002).

Subsequent investigations into the Tulia arrests revealed that several of the individuals who Coleman claimed had been dealing cocaine were not in the place he indicated at the time the alleged transactions took place. In addition, when the bags of cocaine Coleman used as evidence were tested for their cocaine content, they ranged from a high of 11.8% cocaine to a low of 2.9%. Most cocaine sold on the street has a purity of 85% to 90% (Mangold, 2003). Eventually, 12 of the defendants in this case, 11 of them African American, were released after spending 4 years in prison (and were given $12,000 in compensation). Despite the fact that these individuals were not involved in drug use and trafficking, the judge admonished them to "make better choices" (as quoted in Hockstader, 2003). Coleman eventually received 10 months probation after being found guilty of perjury for his testimony in the case (Blakeslee, 2005). Contrasting Coleman's sentence to the ones received by the Tulia defendants, Blakeslee commented, "I think some would question whether or not 10 months probation is an adequate sentence after some of the people he accused did four years in prison before they were exonerated" (as quoted in Shemkus, 2005). Sullum (2006), noting the similarity between the events in Tulia and a scandal involving 24 Mexican immigrants in Dallas who were convicted on drug charges after police informants planted bags of ground up billiard chalk on them, noted,

Tulia demands our attention not because the events were so unusual but because they dramatically illustrate the injustices routinely inflicted by the War on Drugs, which results in 1.7 million arrests a year and keeps half a million Americans behind bars for failing to comply with an arbitrary set of pharmacological preferences.

And while the racism associated with the Tulia arrests is relatively well known and has been covered in several media sources, there are many other instances of such injustice. For example, a Drug Enforcement Administration operation in the northern district of Ohio that targeted alleged African American drug dealers disparagingly referred to these individuals as "niggers with rims" (English, 2009).

> From the outset, the drug war could have been waged primarily in overwhelmingly white suburbs or on college campuses. SWAT teams could have rappelled from helicopters in gated suburban communities and raided the homes of high school lacrosse players known for hosting coke and ecstasy parties after their games. The police could have seized televisions, furniture, and cash from fraternity houses based on an anonymous tip that a few joints or a stash of cash could be found hidden in someone's dresser drawer. . . . All of this could have happened as a matter of routine in white communities, but it did not. (Alexander, 2010, p. 121)

Thus, both state and local statistics indicate that drug laws have been applied disproportionately against members of minority groups, in particular, African Americans. In the following sections, we examine specific policies that have contributed to these racial disproportions.

"Crack Babies"

In partial response to the alleged crack cocaine "epidemic" in the late 1980s, a number of states instituted the practice of prosecuting women for using drugs while pregnant, under offense categories including criminal child abuse, neglect, manslaughter, and delivering substances to a minor. While in some cases these laws were applied to mothers who used methamphetamine (Talvi, 2003a), the overwhelming majority of women charged were black, poor, and users of crack cocaine.

The Common Sense for Drug Policy advertisement shown here addresses some of the consequences of the "crack baby" legislation, which involves prosecuting expectant or young mothers with infants who use drugs for the supposed effects of drug use on the child. Although these policies have ostensibly been enacted with the goal of protecting unborn and newborn children, there is no scientific evidence of their effectiveness, and it appears as though they may actually be counterproductive in a number of ways.

One of the first of these cases occurred in 1989 in South Carolina, when Jennifer Johnson, a poor African American woman who allegedly used crack cocaine, was

Is It Sound Policy To Jail Expectant Mothers For Substance Abuse And Take Away Their Babies?

"Marry professional health care and child welfare organizations have banded together against criminalization on the basis that it is antithetical to the best interests of both the mother and the child"

" . . . criminalization has no proven effect on improving infant health or deterring substance abuse by pregnant women."

"In fact, criminalization may deter the pregnant woman from seeking out necessary prenatal care for fear of losing their children or being arrested."

"A drug-exposed infant should be removed from the custody of his/her parent(s) only if the parent(s) are unable to protect and care for the infant and other support services are not sufficient to manage this risk, or the parent(s) have refused such services."

If removal is good policy, shouldn't we also place infants in foster care if the mother smokes, imbibes or is obese? We could build orphanages as well as prisons!

Common Sense for Drug Policy

www.CommonSenseDrugPolicy.org — www.DrugWar-acts.org
www.ManagingChronicPain.org — www.MedicalMJ.org
www.TreatingDrugAddiction.org
info@csdp.org

'Substance Use During Pregnancy: Time for Policy to Catch Up with Research. by Barry M Lester, PhD, Lynne Andreozzi, And Lindsey Appiah, Harm Reduction Journal, published April 20, 2004, on the web at http://www.harmreductionjournal.com/content/1/1/5

convicted of delivery of a controlled substance to a minor; she received a 15-year sentence (14 years of which was probation; Logan, 1999). In another South Carolina case in 2001, a woman who was 8 months pregnant and delivered a stillborn baby was sentenced to 12 years in prison for killing the baby by smoking crack cocaine (Firestone, 2001), despite the fact that there is absolutely no scientific evidence linking cocaine use to stillbirth (Talvi, 2003a).

More generally, at least 24 states laid criminal charges against women for using illicit drugs while pregnant, and at one point, at least 13 states required that public hospitals drug test women suspected of abusing drugs and to report those who tested positive to social service agencies and/or the police (Logan, 1999). As of 2003, at least 100 women in South Carolina and 275 nationally had faced criminal charges as a result of using drugs while pregnant (Talvi, 2003a).

Although, as discussed in Chapter 5, the use of illegal drugs crosses all income levels and racial/ethnic groups, women from minority and lower-class groups were disproportionately targeted by these policies. In a 1989 study conducted in Florida, 380 women in public clinics and 335 in private care were drug tested; the rate of positive drug tests was 15.4% for white women and 14.1% for black women. Despite the lower rates of positive drug tests for black women, they were approximately 10 times more likely to be reported to authorities for substance use (Siegel, 1997). Similarly, an analysis of data from one hospital in South Carolina found that of 30 pregnant women who were arrested for drug use, 29 were African American. The one white woman who was arrested was married to a black man, a fact that had been noted on her medical record (American Civil Liberties Union, 2000a). And the fact that most drug testing of women is conducted at public hospitals that generally service low-income communities results in women of color being disproportionately likely to be the subject of such testing and to subsequently be reported to social service agencies and/or arrested.

While authorities have arrested and prosecuted drug-using pregnant women with the admirable goal of deterring drug use in this population and thereby protecting newborn children, as is the case with several other strategies, this approach is lacking in scientific foundation and may, in fact, be counterproductive. Studies have indicated that there is no specific "crack baby syndrome" that is equivalent to fetal alcohol syndrome. One meta-analysis of studies on the crack baby syndrome found that "there was no consistent negative association between prenatal cocaine exposure and physical growth, developmental test scores, or receptive or expressive language" (Frank et al., 2001). Early reports of the impact of crack cocaine on fetal and childhood development failed to take into account the fact that women who use crack are also more likely to smoke cigarettes, drink alcohol, use other drugs, be malnourished, and live in poverty (Logan, 1999). Each of these factors has been demonstrated to negatively affect fetal and early childhood development even in the absence of cocaine use (Davenport-Hines, 2001; Emmett, 1998; Frank et al., 2001). It is also important to note that policies targeting pregnant women may be counterproductive because the threat of drug testing and possible arrest may deter women from seeking prenatal care. As L. Siegel (1997) concludes with respect to these policies, "mothers who use crack were convenient scapegoats for conservative administrations to blame in order to divert the public's attention from declining social and economic conditions affecting increasing numbers of Americans" (p. 257).

"C.R.A.C.K."

Although it is not officially sanctioned by the federal or state-level governments, another program that has targeted drug-using women is C.R.A.C.K. (Children Requiring a Caring Kommunity [*sic*]; subsequently renamed "Project Prevention"). This program, initiated by Barbara Harris of Orange County, California, has chapters in several states in the United States and pays drug users (including "alcoholics") $200 to submit to birth control or to be permanently sterilized. The program received a $10,000 donation from popular radio talk show host Laura Schlesinger and had received more than $2 million in donations as of 2003 (Roe, 2003). Under this program, prospective clients call a toll-free number and supply their name and address: C.R.A.C.K. then mails them forms to take to their parole officer or drug treatment provider, who documents their history of substance use. The clients then take the completed forms to a clinic, where health care providers verify that they have received an intrauterine contraceptive device, the birth control drug Depo-Provera, a tubal ligation for females, or a vasectomy for males. The use of birth control pills does not qualify for the $200 payment because, according to founder Barbara Harris, "we don't trust them to take a pill every day" (as quoted in Roe, 2003). In addition, the C.R.A.C.K. literature states, "Don't let a pregnancy get in the way of your habit" (as cited in Cox, 2006).

Critics of the C.R.A.C.K. program have noted that clients may simply use the $200 payment to purchase drugs, thereby further contributing to their addiction. However, Harris is apparently not overly concerned how the clients spend the money: "If they choose to use the money to buy drugs, that's their business" (as quoted in Yeoman, 2001). Critics have further charged that this program is reminiscent of earlier eugenics programs in the United States because it targets poor and minority women (see also Paltrow, 2006). Although Harris has rejected this claim, it is notable that data on the racial/ethnic characteristics of those who have participated in the program indicate a substantial overrepresentation of Hispanics and blacks. Of the 4,097 clients who had participated in this program as of May 2012, 53% were white, 24% African American, 12% Hispanic, and 10% were of other ethnic backgrounds (see http://www.projectprevention.org).

MANDATORY MINIMUM SENTENCES

Judges are confronted with the following scenario. A young African American appears for sentencing on a conviction for selling two-tenths of a gram of crack cocaine within 1,000 feet of a school bus stop. The defendant trades his service as a middleman in the deal for a small quantity of cocaine for his own use. Although he made no significant economic gain by facilitating the sale, his standard-range sentence for this first-time drug offense is 45 to 51 months. Contrast that case with that of a Caucasian robber who takes property by threat of force. Even though the defendant already has an identical prior offense, he would face a sentence of only 12 months and a day to 14 months. (Murphy, 2003)

Mandatory minimum sentences have been part of criminal laws in the United States since 1790 (Schulhofer, 1993) but have had arguably their greatest impact in the last three decades. Interestingly, in the 1970 Comprehensive Drug Abuse and Control Act, Congress concluded that mandatory minimum sentences had not served their intended purpose of deterring drug offenders, and virtually all mandatory minimum sentences were repealed at that time. However, prompted at least partially by the "crack cocaine epidemic" discussed in Chapter 1, the federal and several state governments enacted mandatory minimum penalties for drug offenses in the 1980s (some states, such as New York, with its Rockefeller drug laws, enacted such statutes in the 1970s). As of 2012, there were 171 mandatory minimum sentencing statutes at the federal and state levels, about 80% of which were for drug law violations (Tabichnick, 2012).

In 1987, the Minnesota legislature passed a law designating different threshold amounts and different penalty structures for crack and powder cocaine, such that possession of 3 grams of the former would result in a mandatory minimum sentence of 48 months in prison, while possession of 10 grams of powder cocaine would result in a 12-month sentence (Blumstein, 1993). In *State v. Russell* (1991), the Minnesota Supreme Court declared that this differential treatment of powder and crack cocaine was in violation of the state's constitution. The ruling held that the distinction between the two substances was racially discriminatory in its impact: In 1988, 100% of those sentenced for crack cocaine violations in Minnesota were black, while 66% of those sentenced under the powder cocaine statute were white (Blumstein, 1993). The court ruled that because of the disparate impact of this law on African Americans, there had to be a compelling rationale for the differential treatment (Minnesota Sentencing Guidelines Commission, 2004).

At the federal level, the 1986 Anti-Drug Abuse Act reinstated mandatory minimum penalties for drug offenses, with the most important change being a distinction between crack and powder cocaine. Under this legislation, a first-time offender convicted of possession of 5.01 grams of crack cocaine was subject to a mandatory minimum penalty of 5 years of imprisonment. If the offender possessed only 5.0 grams of crack cocaine or less, he or she would be subject to a maximum sentence of 1 year imprisonment (Wilkins, Newton, & Steer, 1993). For powder cocaine, however, the 5-year mandatory minimum sentence did not apply until an individual possessed more than 500 grams of the substance. In passing this legislation, Congress conveniently ignored the fact that crack and powder cocaine are essentially the same drugs pharmacologically and have the same effects and consequences (Hatsukami & Fischman, 1996). Congress also failed to offer any rationale for the selection of the 100 to 1 ratio in amounts of powder cocaine versus crack cocaine that would trigger the mandatory minimum penalties (Sklansky, 1995). As Schlosser (2003) argued, the process of selecting the quantities of drugs to trigger the mandatory minimum sentences was like "pulling numbers out of thin air."

Before addressing some of the more general problems with this and other mandatory minimum sentencing policies, it is important to note that African Americans were far more likely to be arrested and prosecuted under federal crack cocaine statutes than were whites. A study conducted by the United States Sentencing

Commission in 1992 found that in 16 states, including populous ones such as Connecticut, New Jersey, and Illinois, not a *single* white person had been prosecuted under federal crack laws (Gelacak, 1997). Another Sentencing Commission study found that in 1994, blacks accounted for more than 90% of federal prosecutions for crack offenses and whites for less than 1%. The Sentencing Commission also found that in the central district of California, the federal trial court that includes Los Angeles, the first charge against a white defendant under federal crack cocaine laws came in 1995, some 9 years after the crack/powder cocaine distinction was created. In 1993, 88.3% of those sentenced under federal crack statutes were black and 95.4% were nonwhite (Gelacak, 1997).

These racial disparities in prosecutions and sentencing must be placed in the context of data on racial differences in the use of drugs in general, and crack cocaine in particular. Although it is certainly true that hardcore drug use and its consequences may be more severe in inner-city areas where minorities are more likely to be concentrated, overall drug use figures for 1990 reported by the National Institute on Drug Abuse (NIDA) show that whites comprised 77% of the estimated 1.3 million users of illegal drugs, while blacks comprised 15%. Despite the apparent ubiquity of America's drug problem, economically disadvantaged racial minority groups provide the bulk of the raw material for the drug war (Gaines & Kraska, 1997). A defense attorney quoted in Sklansky (1995) noted, "Maybe I'm cynical, but I think that if you saw a lot of young white males getting 5- and 10-year minimums for dealing powder cocaine, you'd have a lot more reaction" (p. 1308).

The U.S. Sentencing Commission itself recognized the racial disparities in sentencing that resulted from the crack/powder cocaine distinction, and while not willing to concede that the law was racially discriminatory in its intent, the Commission noted,

> If the impact of the law is discriminatory, the problem is no less regardless of the intent. The problem is particularly acute because the disparate impact arises from a penalty structure for two different forms of the same substance. It is a little like punishing vehicular homicide while under the influence of alcohol more severely if the defendant had become intoxicated by ingesting cheap wine rather than scotch or whiskey. (Gelacak, 1997, p. 2)

In 1995, the Sentencing Commission unanimously recommended to Congress that the 100-to-1 quantity ratio between powder and crack cocaine be reduced to 1 to 1. However, these recommendations were rejected by Congress and President Clinton (Gelacak, 1997). In 1997, the Sentencing Commission changed its recommendation, suggesting that the quantity to trigger a mandatory sentence for powder cocaine should be between 125 and 175 grams, and for crack, between 25 and 75 grams (Musto, 1999). As will be discussed in more detail below, the ratios were finally altered with the passage of the 2010 Fair Sentencing Act.

In addition to its disproportionately negative impact on African Americans, this law creating a distinction between crack and powder cocaine resulted in a number of other apparently unintended but rather perverse outcomes as a result of the establishment of "cliffs" (Heaney, 1991). Musto (1999) notes that in 1991, 59% of federal crack cases qualified for a mandatory minimum sentence (due to the 5.01-gram cutoff); however, if the powder cocaine cutoff of 500 grams had been applied to these cases, only 3% would have qualified. In the same year, only 27% of powder cocaine cases qualified for the mandatory minimum sentence, but this would have increased to 76% if the 5-gram crack standard had applied. As a result of these distinctions, an individual who sells a 1-pound (454-gram) lot of powder cocaine, from which he could supply 64 others with enough cocaine to produce a 7-gram unit of crack, would not be subject to the mandatory minimum penalties under federal legislation. However, somewhat perversely, each of the 64 individuals he supplied with cocaine to produce crack would be subject to the mandatory minimum penalty. To put it in monetary terms, under this legislation, an individual convicted of trafficking 400 grams of powder cocaine, which had an approximate street value of $40,000 in 1998, would end up serving a shorter sentence than a user he supplied with crack, valued at $500 (Mauer, 1999).

These "cliffs" can also result in questionable and counterproductive law enforcement practices. Due to the fact that the length of a drug offender's sentence is at least partially dependent on the quantity of drugs he participated in purchasing or selling, it appears as though some law enforcement officials attempt to convince suspects to purchase or sell drugs in quantities large enough to trigger the mandatory minimum penalties (Heaney, 1991). In other cases, police officers have postponed the arrest of suspects until they have bought or sold cumulative amounts of drugs sufficient to result in the application of the mandatory minimum sentence. Heaney (1991) notes that one of the counterproductive outcomes related to such practices is that the entire purpose of apprehending drug traffickers is defeated because such individuals will actually be on the streets selling drugs for longer periods of time. Even aside from this issue, it is notable how the very practices law enforcement officers engage in with respect to apprehending drug traffickers—instigating the very crimes for which they later arrest individuals—are not consistent with other law enforcement practices. As Sullum (2006) comments, "police do not commit murder to prevent murder; they do not steal to prevent theft; but they do buy drugs to prevent people from buying drugs, a situation that puts them above the law and encourages corner cutting."

In the case of *United States v. Brigham*, a relatively low-level drug dealer received a sentence of 120 months incarceration while the leader of the organization received only 84 months because he had provided "substantial assistance" to the prosecutor. Commenting on the absurdity of this outcome, the sentencing judge noted, "Mandatory minimum penalties, combined with the power to grant exemptions, create a prospect of inverted sentencing. The more serious the defendant's crimes, the lower the sentence, because the greater his wrongs, the more information and assistance he has to offer to a prosecutor" (as quoted in Schulhofer, 1993, p. 212). In a more recent case from Pensacola, Florida, a 87-year-old African American woman was sentenced to 19 months in prison for selling a $20 rock of crack cocaine to an undercover police officer. She died (in jail) a few months later. ("Never Too Old," 2010)

An additional problem with mandatory minimum sentencing laws for drugs more generally is that they transfer discretion in the criminal justice system from judges to police, probation officers, and, especially, prosecutors (Heaney, 1991). As a result, there is the possibility of even more sentencing disparity due to the fact that the application of guidelines depends on low-visibility prosecutorial decisions, which are typically not reviewable (Schulhofer, 1993), as compared to judicial decisions, which can be appealed.

A provision within the federal mandatory minimum sentencing guidelines for drug offenses allows defendants who provide "substantial assistance" (information on other drug transactions and dealers) to prosecutors to receive "downward departures" (reductions) in their sentences. But as Schulhofer (1993) suggests, this provision frequently results in the unintended consequence of more minor participants in drug trafficking operations receiving more severe sentences than those who are more central to such operations because the latter usually have more information to provide. The United States Sentencing Commission itself has noted that "the value of a mandatory minimum sentence lies not in its imposition, but in its value as a bargaining chip to be given away in return for the resource-saving plea from the defendant to a more leniently sanctioned charge" (as quoted in Alexander, 2010, p. 87).

Recall that the apparent goal of these laws is to deter drug traffickers and thereby reduce the supply of illegal drugs. If, as a result of the application of these laws, low-level drug traffickers end up being punished more severely than the leaders of drug trafficking organizations, has this goal been accomplished?

Apparently, these substantial assistance provisions have also had a negative impact on African Americans. Schulhofer (1993) found that of defendants eligible to receive a mandatory minimum sentence under federal drug laws, 25% of whites, compared with 18% of blacks, received a shorter sentence as a result of providing substantial assistance to the prosecutor. Overall, Schulhofer (1993) found that almost half of whites were sentenced below the mandatory level, while less than one-third of blacks experienced similar leniency.

As we have already documented, given the numerous problems with these mandatory minimum sentencing laws, an increasing number of judges have expressed their displeasure at being forced to invoke them. In addition to the comments of Judge Murphy at the start of this section and the concerns of the sentencing judge in the *United States v Brigham* case, Donald Lay, the former Chief Judge of the Court of Appeals for the 8th Circuit in St. Paul, Minnesota, argued,

> They have set such atrocious and unfair statutory minimum sentences that the result is there is often no relationship between the sentence received and the crime involved. The hysteria over the control of drugs has led us to the point where I think we've broken down many civil rights. (as quoted in Wilkinson, 1993)

California Superior Court Judge James Gray expressed similar sentiments in commenting that mandatory minimum sentencing policies are at least partially responsible for the fact that "our system has arrested, imprisoned, and eliminated from the [drug] market the stupid, unorganized, and less violent drug traffickers and smugglers, thus leaving behind the phenomenally lucrative market open to offenders who are smarter, better organized, and more violent" (Gray, 2001, p. 31). More generally, a survey of federal judges released by the Federal Judicial Center in 1994 found that 59% of circuit court judges and 69% of district court judges were strongly or moderately opposed to the retention of mandatory minimum sentencing laws (as cited in Pratt, 1999).

More objective evidence that a high proportion of judges are dissatisfied with these mandatory minimum penalty structures is provided through an examination of data on departures from the guidelines. Although not specific to drug offenses, in 2001, close to 36% of federal defendants received downward departures (reductions) in their sentences, while fewer than 1% received upward departures (Bowman, 2003). Looking at drug offenses only, a General Accounting Office report focusing on federal drug-related offenses for the 1999 to 2001 period found that more than half of the sentences fell below the mandatory minimum (U.S. General Accounting Office [GAO], 2003). However, the federal government has not reacted favorably to the apparently increasing number of judges who grant downward departures. In July 2003, Attorney General John Ashcroft required all United States Attorneys' offices to report to the Justice Department all instances in which federal judges imposed sentences below the range specified in the federal guidelines against the wishes of the prosecutor (Bowman, 2003).

"SCHOOL ZONE" POLICIES

The federal Anti-Drug Abuse Act of 1988 also provided enhanced mandatory penalties for individuals convicted of dealing drugs within 1,000 feet of playgrounds, youth centers, swimming pools, and video arcades (Gray, 2001). On the surface, these laws also have the laudable goal of preventing the distribution of illegal drugs to young people. At one point, more than 30 states had similar laws; for example, individuals in the state of Alabama who were convicted of selling illegal drugs within a 3-mile radius of *any* educational institution, including colleges and universities, were subject to an additional 5 years of imprisonment.

In Massachusetts, legislation provided for a 2-year mandatory minimum sentence for selling drugs within 1,000 feet of a primary, secondary, or vocational school. An analysis of the application of this law in the city of New Bedford, Massachusetts, found that fully 84% of all drug trafficking cases within the city limits occurred within school zones. However, a detailed review of case files revealed that only 1 of 443 transactions involved the actual sale of drugs to children, and more than 70% of the cases occurred when school was not in session. The authors of this study concluded that the outcome of the legislation was not better protection for children, but instead, a general escalation of the severity of penalties for drug offenses (Brownsberger & Aromaa, 2003). More generally, in the state of Massachusetts, while 43% of those arrested for drug offenses are white, 80% of those sentenced under drug-free-zone statutes were members of racial and ethnic minority groups (Greene, Pranis, & Ziedenberg, 2006).

A similar study focusing on the application of school zone laws in New Jersey found that African Americans and Hispanics, who comprised 27% of the state's population, constituted 96% of all inmates in the state whose most serious offense was a school-zone violation (New Jersey Commission to Review Criminal Sentencing, 2005). Of 90 reported school-zone cases studied in detail by the Commission, not a single one involved selling drugs to minors, and only two of the cases actually occurred on school property. The Commission concluded,

> Essentially what the current law does is add about three years of mandatory prison time to sentences of individuals whose offenses occur in urban areas. Basically New Jersey has two different punishments for the same crime, with the severity of punishment being based on geography and race.

In light of these findings, the Commission recommended altering the definition of school zones from 1,000 to 200 feet and increasing the criminal penalty in the 200-foot zone from a third- to a second-degree offense, thereby targeting the "few people who sell drugs at or near schools" ("Drugs and Racial," 2006). In 2010, New Jersey eliminated mandatory minimum sentencing for individuals convicted of selling drugs in school zones.

PUBLIC HOUSING EVICTIONS

Under the 1998 Anti-Drug Abuse Act, public housing agencies were required to evict tenants if the tenant, a member of his or her own family, or guests were involved in drug-related crimes—these laws potentially affect the more than three million residents of federally funded housing in the United States. The precursors of the federal legislation were law enforcement campaigns in individual cities whereby police would lock all exits to public housing buildings and conduct unannounced, warrantless drug searches of tenants and their guests. In 1989 in Washington, D.C., alone, 209 individuals were evicted from public housing as a result of such police activities (Zeese, 1989).

While these provisions were apparently enacted with the goal of helping communities to reduce drug use and trafficking and the problems associated with the drug trade, it is once again instructive to examine how they have been applied. Here, we refer to four cases from the city of Oakland, which were eventually heard by the United States Supreme Court. In the first case, a 79-year-old disabled male was evicted from public housing because authorities discovered that his full-time caretaker had hidden pipes for smoking crack in his apartment. In a second case, a 63-year-old woman was given an eviction notice when her mentally disabled daughter was arrested three blocks from their residence on charges of possessing cocaine. In two other cases, elderly women were ordered out of their homes when their grandchildren were found smoking marijuana in the parking lot of their public housing complex (Lithwick, 2002). It is important to stress that in none of these cases was the person evicted found personally using or possessing an illegal drug, nor did he or she have knowledge about the accusations.

These four individuals initiated a civil lawsuit, arguing that the evictions were unconstitutional because they had no knowledge of the drug use of their relatives or acquaintances. After a lower court and the 9th U.S. Circuit Court of Appeals in California supported the tenants' claim that the evictions were unconstitutional, the Oakland Public Housing Authority and the federal government appealed the decision to the U.S. Supreme Court (Lithwick, 2002). In an 8-0 decision in 2002, the U.S. Supreme Court upheld the evictions and the law. In the Court's decision, Chief Justice William Rehnquist wrote, "There is an obvious reason why Congress would have permitted local public-housing authorities to conduct no-fault evictions. Regardless of knowledge, a tenant who cannot control drug crime by a household member . . . is a threat to other residents" (as quoted in Richey, 2002). As a San Francisco lawyer remarked, "Our argument has always been that if you read the statute literally, you can evict a grandmother who lives in Oakland if their granddaughter is smoking pot in New York" (as quoted in Nieves, 2002). It is necessary to question whether punishing individuals for the drug uses of their relatives and/or acquaintances serves the objective of reducing drug use and trafficking activities in public housing projects, and like several other drug policies, these laws clearly have a disproportionally negative impact on minorities and the poor. In addition, such policies exacerbate the negative impact of drug convictions on women (Radosh, 2008).

DENIAL OF WELFARE

Under a provision of the 1996 Federal Welfare Reform Act that was apparently debated in Congress for approximately 2 minutes, any individual convicted of a felony drug offense can be denied federal welfare benefits, including food stamps and temporary aid to needy families, for life (Schwartz, 2002). As of 2002, more than 92,000 women had been denied access to welfare as a result of felony drug convictions (Kirkorian, 2002). There is little doubt that the individuals most affected by this particular policy are, once again, the poor and members of minority groups because they are obviously the ones most likely to be welfare recipients. It is by no means clear how the denial of welfare would be a deterrent for those who traffic in illegal drugs, and drug users who are convicted of felony drug offenses and denied welfare may find it more difficult to stop using drugs. Perhaps amazingly, although certainly consistent with much of drug policy in the United States, individuals can commit murder, rape, and other serious crimes without being denied access to federal welfare assistance.

It is somewhat encouraging to note that several states have recognized the potential problems associated with this policy and used their option of not enforcing this provision of the Welfare Reform Act. As of March 2003, 21 states still denied welfare to those convicted of felony drug offenses, while 11 states and the District of Columbia did not enforce the provision. An additional 18 states had modified this provision, either by allowing individuals to receive welfare benefits on the condition of participating in drug treatment, denying benefits only to individuals convicted of drug trafficking offenses, or reducing the restrictions from a lifetime ban on receiving benefits to shorter time periods (Drug Policy Alliance, 2003a). However, the fact that these laws are still in place at the federal level and that close to half the states continue to impose and enforce them is cause for concern.

DENIAL OF STUDENT AID

Under provisions of the Higher Education Act, passed in 1998, individuals applying for federal financial aid are required to answer a question regarding their prior drug convictions. If applicants indicate they have a conviction for a drug offense, or if they refuse to answer the question, they are sent a follow-up questionnaire that asks them to provide more information about the type and number of drug convictions they have, as well as when the convictions occurred (Students for Sensible Drug Policy, 2006). Individuals convicted of drug offenses, including possession of marijuana, or who refuse to answer the question can be denied student aid. For a first drug offense, individuals are ineligible for financial assistance for a period of 1 year, while a second conviction results in a 2-year period of ineligibility. Subsequent convictions can result in permanent denial of student aid. Similar to the welfare restrictions discussed above, this is another provision that is unique to drug offenses: No other class of offenders, including those convicted of rape or murder, is disqualified from receiving student aid.

Students for Sensible Drug Policy (2006) determined that since the drug conviction question was added to federal student aid applications during the 2001 to 2002 school year, 189,065 individuals (approximately 1 in every 400 applicants) had their requests for aid denied because of their answers to the question, and it is notable that a study by the Government Accountability Office found no evidence that this provision helped to deter drug use (U.S. Government Accountability Office, 2005b). Noting that this law, similar to other drug legislation, has a disproportionately negative impact on the poor and members of minority groups, who are more likely to have drug convictions while at the same time requiring student aid to participate in higher education, Davenport-Hines (2001) referred to it as a "blunder of crashing stupidity" (p. 358). The denial of student aid to those with drug convictions "reinforce[s] the discriminatory effect of U.S. drug policy on African Americans. Its cruel and irrational punishment typifies the U.S. drug enforcement mentality. By perpetuating the disadvantages of the ghetto, it perpetuates the conditions that foster addiction." A *New York Times* editorial similarly noted,

> By narrowing access to affordable education, the federal government further diminishes the prospects of young people who are already at risk of becoming lifetime burdens to society. . . . It doesn't take a genius to see that barring young offenders from college leads to more crime, not less. Student aid was never intended for use as a law enforcement weapon. Any attempt to employ it that way will inevitably yield perverse and unfair results. ("Cutting College Aid," 2005)

In response to these policies, some postsecondary institutions, including Yale University, Hampshire College in Massachusetts, and Swarthmore College in Pennsylvania, reimburse students who have been denied federal aid as a result of drug convictions (Rubin, 2003).

ASSET FORFEITURE

The law enforcement agenda that targets assets rather than crime, the 80% of seizures that are unaccompanied by any criminal investigation, the plea bargains that favor drug kingpins and penalize the "mules" without assets to trade, the reverse stings that target drug buyers rather than sellers, the overkill in agencies involved in even minor arrests, the massive shift in resources towards federal jurisdiction over local law enforcement—is largely the unplanned byproduct of this economic incentive structure. (Blumenson & Nilsen, 1998)

Another disturbing development in recent U.S. drug policies is related to provisions allowing for the forfeiture of assets of individuals allegedly involved in drug transactions. Such laws have a long history in the United States: Following the ratification of the Constitution, Congress enacted forfeiture statutes in order to assist in the collection of customs duties and taxes (Shaw, 1998). The more direct precursor to current asset forfeiture laws as they are applied in drug cases was their use in violations of alcohol prohibition laws in the 1920s; several cases in that era involved forfeiture of automobiles that were used to transport liquor. The civil forfeiture of assets related to illegal drug transactions began with the Comprehensive Drug Abuse and Control Act of 1970 and was extended in 1978. In that year, Congress passed legislation that allowed for the forfeiture of

all monies, negotiable instruments, securities, or other things of value furnished or intended to be furnished by a person in exchange for a controlled substance in violation of this [subchapter], all proceeds traceable to an exchange, and all monies, negotiable instruments, and securities used or intended to be used to facilitate any violation of this subchapter. (Jensen & Gerber, 1996, p. 43)

The apparent goal of this legislation was to "take the profit out of crime, paralyze drug operations, eradicate the criminal infiltration of legitimate businesses and labor organizations, and end criminal tactics in business and trade unions" (cited in Shaw, 1998). In addition to federal legislation allowing for asset forfeiture, by 1990, 49 states and the District of Columbia had enacted similar laws. From 1989 to 2010, an estimated $26 billion in assets of "drug traffickers" were seized by U.S. attorneys (Maguire, 2010).

It is important to note that under criminal law in the United States, an individual is generally presumed to be innocent until proven guilty. However, under these civil asset forfeiture provisions, the burden of proof falls on the individual to demonstrate that his or her property is not connected to any involvement in illegal drug activity. Another unique feature of these laws is that the property itself is presumed guilty— known in legal terms as *in rem* jurisdiction—and its owner must either prove its innocence by a preponderance of evidence or lose it altogether (Shaw, 1998).

Examples of the questionable use of these asset forfeiture laws are legion. In April 1988, the Coast Guard boarded and seized a yacht, valued at $2.5 million, because 10 marijuana seeds and two stems were found on board. In the same year, another yacht was impounded for a week because cocaine dust rolled up in a dollar bill was found on board. In a third case, an oceanographic research ship valued at $80 million was seized when the Coast Guard found one-tenth of an ounce of marijuana in a crewman's shaving kit (Wisotsky, 1992). In another case, a man flying to Las Vegas was stopped by Customs officials due to suspicions arising from his purchase of a one-way ticket. When drug-sniffing dogs detected drugs on the money he had in his possession, $9,600 was seized from him (Gray, 2001). In yet another case, government lawyers actually tried to have the gold caps from the teeth of two accused drug dealers removed as part of asset forfeiture ("Gold Diggers," 2006).

There have also been numerous cases of individuals having their homes and/or property seized as a result of the drug-related activities of their children or individuals staying in their homes (Gray, 2001) and cases involving drug-dealing husbands and uninvolved wives. In the latter cases, the courts have generally ruled that a wife who may have had some knowledge of her husband's involvement in drug trafficking but did not act reasonably to stop it will lose her interest in their home under the forfeiture statutes (Shaw, 1998). There have also been instances in which individuals who are only marginally—if at all—connected to the drug trade have been victimized by these laws. For example, a man who operated an airline charter service flew a client he had not previously known from Arkansas to California. It turned out that the passenger was a convicted drug trafficker, and when a search of his luggage resulted in the discovery of $2.8 million in his suitcase, the passenger and the aircraft operator were arrested. The operator also had his $500,000 airplane seized, based on the suspicion that it was connected to a drug transaction (Fitzgerald, 2000).

> In a case that further underlines social class inequities in the application of drug laws, Leslie C. Ohta, a federal prosecutor in Connecticut, seized the house of a couple who were in their 80s when their 22-year-old son was arrested for selling marijuana. Subsequent to this, Ohta's 18-year-old son was arrested for selling LSD from Ohta's vehicle. It was also believed that he had previously sold marijuana from her home. Ohta did not have her vehicle or home seized, although she was eventually transferred out of the United States Attorney's forfeiture unit. (Schlosser, 2003)

In 1984, Congress altered these laws under the Department of Justice Assets Forfeiture Fund, which allowed most of the proceeds from asset forfeiture cases to be retained by local law enforcement agencies. This provision led to widespread misuse of forfeiture laws and considerable corruption; Jensen and Gerber (1996) have referred to these laws as resulting in "policing for profit—due to their dependence on raising revenue, [criminal justice system officials] become the beneficiaries of the illegal drug trade" (p. 430). Similarly, the president of the National Association of Criminal Defense Attorneys argued, "civil forfeiture is essentially government thievery" (as quoted in Shaw, 1998).

A number of examples suggest that the above characterizations of asset forfeiture laws are accurate. In St. Francis County, Arkansas, the sheriff was privately selling cars he had seized to himself and others at prices at or well below their appraised values (Fitzgerald, 2000). In New Jersey, a prosecutor known as the "forfeiture king" assisted a colleague in his purchase of land seized in a marijuana case at a fraction of its actual value (Schlosser, 1997). In California, state and federal agents raided a ranch based on the belief that it contained a marijuana-growing operation. In the course of the raid, the owner of the ranch was killed by a deputy sheriff; however, no marijuana was found and a subsequent investigation revealed that law enforcement officials had been at least partially motivated by a desire to seize the $5 million ranch. In fact, they had obtained an appraisal of the property a few weeks before they conducted the raid (Schlosser, 1997).

In Spokane, Washington, seizures resulting from the discovery of a marijuana-growing operation resulted in a $400,000 bounty for the local police department, including a 1997 BMW 740il sedan, which was subsequently being driven to work by one of the police officers. A Seattle attorney commented, "It's routine for my clients to see their vehicles being driven by police officers. They are like malicious children without supervision. These forfeiture laws give them the toys to play with" (as quoted in Clouse, 2003). In another city, after receiving $1.5 million in forfeiture funds, the police department spent $1,235 on the chief's Christmas party, $208 on an aquarium, $2,100 on a buffet for police officers who worked on Labor Day, $720 on amusement park tickets, and $32,375 on banquets (Shaw, 1998).

The apparent goal of civil forfeiture laws is to deprive major drug traffickers of the property and assets utilized to further their criminal activity. But at least partially as a result of the fact that criminal justice system agencies are allowed to keep significant proportions of the assets seized, they may be led to pursue cases that are not necessarily the most serious ones. Thus, a senior Customs official stated that if police had "a guy with a ton of marijuana and no assets versus a guy with two joints and a Lear jet, I guarantee you they will bust the guy with the Lear jet" (as quoted in Shaw, 1998). And as James Gray (2001) notes, individuals who believe they have been subject to an inappropriate forfeiture action are required to appeal to their local district attorney. However, given that the legislation provides that the district attorney retains 13.5 cents out of every dollar forfeited, it is unlikely that he or she will be motivated to overturn the forfeiture.

An additional problematic aspect of asset forfeiture laws is related to the use of informants, who can receive up to 25% of the amount forfeited in these cases (Gray, 2001). In 1991, at least 24 informants made between $100,000 and $250,000, and at least eight made more than $250,000—one individual received $780,000 (Shaw, 1998). The identity of informants remains unknown in forfeiture proceedings, and consequently, there is no way for the owner of the property being seized to address the truthfulness of the information provided. As Shaw (1998) notes, "paying informants such large sums of money, with little to no requirements for who can be an informant, simply corrupts the world of civil forfeiture more than it otherwise is."

Civil asset forfeiture laws were further revised in 2000, with one of the most important changes being that the government must now prove, by a preponderance of evidence, that the property allegedly connected to drug-related offenses should be forfeited. Alexander (2010) further notes that merely shifting the burden of proof to the government under the revised law did not serve to remove the profit motive in drug law enforcement.

Asset forfeiture laws were enacted with the apparent purpose of deterring trafficking in illegal drugs and hampering the efforts of drug traffickers to continue
their operations. There is little evidence to suggest that asset forfeiture laws have
achieved these goals, and, similar to other drug policies, these laws have resulted in
a number of negative outcomes, particularly with respect to corruption in law
enforcement and an erosion in civil rights. It is also important to recall that, as
mentioned in the quote introducing this section, in approximately 80% of the asset
forfeiture cases, no individual is charged with an actual crime.

ECSTASY AND THE RAVE ACT

As mentioned in Chapter 1, one of the media- and government-constructed drug
"epidemics" of the late 1990s and early 2000s was related to ecstasy (MDMA). In
the early 1980s, ecstasy was actually a legal substance in the United States, but in
1984, sale and possession of the substance was made illegal. And despite a judicial
recommendation that MDMA be placed in Schedule III of the Controlled Substances
Act, the Drug Enforcement Administration insisted that it be placed in Schedule I
(Davenport-Hines, 2001).

In order to stem the ecstasy epidemic that was allegedly occurring in the United
States in the late 1990s and early 2000s, the RAVE (Reducing America's Vulnerability
to Ecstasy) Act was introduced in 2002 and eventually passed into law in 2003. This
legislation was essentially a revision of the federal crack house law that had been
passed in 1986, which made it illegal to maintain a building for the purposes of drug
consumption. Under the RAVE Act, 20 years imprisonment, up to $250,000 in civil
penalties, and $500,000 in criminal fines could be applied to anyone who

> managed or controlled any place, whether temporarily or permanently, either
> as an owner, lessee, agent, employee, occupant, or mortgagee, and knowingly
> and intentionally rent, lease, profit from or make available for use, with or
> without compensation, the place for the purpose of unlawfully manufacturing,
> storing, distributing, or using a controlled substance. (Kopel & Reynolds,
> 2002)

It is important to note that under this legislation, the government is not required
to demonstrate that the owners of the property were actually involved in selling
drugs (Cloud, 2001).

Prior to the passage of this formal federal legislation, owners of a company in
New Orleans that promoted musical events where ecstasy was consumed were
charged with violating the federal crack house law, fined $100,000, and placed on
probation for 5 years. Law enforcement officials justified the arrest of the company's owners by claiming that staff had encouraged consumption of ecstasy by selling
items such as glow sticks and pacifiers, which they alleged were drug related because
glow sticks can stimulate the dilated pupils that can result from ecstasy use, while
pacifiers can relieve the teeth grinding associated with use of the drug (Cloud,

2001). As part of the agreement in this case, the company was also required to ban glow sticks, vapor rub, pacifiers, dust masks, and other legal items and to eliminate air-conditioned "chill-out" rooms from future events (Drug Policy Alliance, 2003d).

The apparent goal of the RAVE Act was to make promoters of musical and other events where ecstasy consumption allegedly occurs liable for the consumption of their patrons. But as Sullum (2003b) argues, it appears highly unlikely that this law will deter individuals from using ecstasy, especially since the penalties are imposed against event organizers and club owners, as opposed to users of the drug. And similar to much of the legislation we have discussed in this chapter, the RAVE Act could also be counterproductive and result in more harm due to the fact that it could serve to push raves underground and discourage some of the safety measures that have been implemented by club owners. For instance, in order to address one of the serious short-term risks associated with ecstasy use—that users "overheat"—many of those involved in organizing raves and other events at which ecstasy consumption occurs have provided bottles of water and access to chill-out rooms. However, under the provisions of the RAVE Act, providing water and chill-out rooms could be used as evidence that owners knew those attending their events would be using drugs (Sullum, 2003b). The legislation could also deter organizers from allowing DANCE-SAFE, an organization that offers testing of ecstasy tablets to ensure that they do not include additional dangerous additives, to attend events where ecstasy may be consumed (Drug Policy Alliance, 2003g).

Critics of the RAVE Act have noted that, applied literally, the provisions of the act could be used to prosecute homeowners whose teenagers are found smoking marijuana on their property (Kopel & Reynolds, 2002) or concert promoters who book reggae artists and sell marijuana-themed t-shirts (Boucher, 2002). And, in consideration of the fact that marijuana and opium are grown on federally owned land in the United States, Bill Piper, Associate Director of National Affairs for the Drug Policy Alliance noted,

> It's a good thing for the federal government that it's not subject to the same laws as the rest of us are. If it was, it would have to indict itself under the RAVE Act, which punishes innocent property owners who fail to stop drug offenses on their property. ("Chronic Hypocrisy" n.d.)

In addition to the RAVE Act, the federal government passed legislation in 2001 that increased the penalties for importing or selling ecstasy to the point that they were more severe than those associated with trafficking in powder cocaine. Under this legislation, the penalty for selling 200 grams (approximately 800 pills) of ecstasy was increased from 15 months to 5 years imprisonment, while the penalty for sale of 8,000 pills was increased from 41 to 120 months (Slevin, 2001). Individual states have proposed, and in some cases passed, even more stringent legislation to deal with ecstasy. For example, legislation passed in Illinois in 2001 provided for mandatory minimum penalties of 6 to 20 years for those selling more than 15 grams of ecstasy (Zeleny & Biesk, 2001). These increased penalties for trafficking in ecstasy could also prove to be counterproductive as a result of the fact that they could lead to the manufacture of counterfeit substances being sold as ecstasy. It is important to note that, as discussed in Chapter 1, most of the problems attributed to ecstasy are not, in fact, related to the drug itself, but rather to the effects of adulterants and counterfeit substances sold to users. The Federation of American Scientists criticized the increased penalties provided for ecstasy in the 2001 legislation, noting that they had "no justification, either pharmacologically or in policy terms" (Lindesmith Center, 2001a).

METHAMPHETAMINE LEGISLATION

In Chapter 1, we discussed the United States' alleged "methamphetamine epidemic" in some detail. As a result of this alleged epidemic, several states enacted legislation to control use of methamphetamine, with most of these laws focusing on restricting access to products containing pseudoephedrine, which is used in manufacturing the drug and is contained in widely used cold and allergy medicines. Following the murder of a state trooper in 2003, Oklahoma became the first state to enact such a law, confining sales of pseudoephedrine products to licensed pharmacies and requiring consumers to sign a logbook when purchasing such products (Suo, 2005c). As of early 2006, 39 other states had passed similar laws (Webley, 2006), with the state of Oregon, under a law passed in 2005, going as far as to require a doctor's prescription for individuals purchasing cold- and allergy-relief medicines (Cain, 2005).

As is the case with other drug legislation, however, the laws restricting access to pseudoephedrine products have led to a number of unintended consequences. For example, 7 months after the state of Iowa passed legislation restricting pseudoephedrine sales, seizures of methamphetamine laboratories in the state declined from 120 per month to 20 per month. While this law apparently achieved its purpose in restricting the manufacture of methamphetamine within the state of Iowa, it was accompanied by a "new flood of crystal methamphetamine coming from Mexico" (Zernike, 2006). The imported Mexican methamphetamine has higher levels of purity and as such is more highly addictive than domestically produced methamphetamine, thus leading to a higher probability of users overdosing. In addition, because the imported methamphetamine is more costly ($800 for 1 ounce) than locally produced methamphetamine ($50 per ounce), some police officers in Iowa indicated that thefts were increasing as people who once cooked the drug at home had to purchase it instead (Zernike, 2006). An additional indicator of the ineffectiveness of this legislation is revealed in data on the reason children are under state protection in Iowa. In southeastern Iowa, 4 months after the law took effect, 49% of children under state protection were taken as a result of their parents using methamphetamine—the same percentage as 2 years earlier (Zernike, 2006).

A similar situation occurred in Oklahoma. Following the passage of its law restricting sales of pseudoephedrine products, lab seizures in the state decreased from 90 per month in 2003 to 9 in the month of June 2005 (Suo, 2005a). However, this led to an influx of methamphetamine from "superlabs" in Mexico that was estimated to have 75% purity; seizures of smokeable Mexican methamphetamine in

Oklahoma increased from 384 cases in the 15 months before the law was passed to 1,875 since (Kurt, 2005). Tom Cunningham, the Task Force Coordinator for the Oklahoma District Attorney's Council, commented, "We took away their production. That didn't do anything for their addiction" (as quoted in Suo, 2005a). Similar comments were made by David Nahmias, U.S. Attorney for the Northern District of Georgia, whose state was also experiencing problems with methamphetamine and had passed legislation restricting the sale of pseudoephedrine products:

> We had problems with the mom and pop labs, but 50 mom and pop labs aren't half of one of these shipments we're seeing here. Mexican cartels will replace meth supplied with local labs with double the volume, double the purity, double the quality. (as quoted in Suo, 2005b)

As of 2012, it was estimated that Mexican methamphetamine (which is as much as 90% pure) accounted for as much as 80% of the substance sold in the United States. The amount of methamphetamine seized on the Southwest border of the United States increased from approximately 4,000 pounds in 2007 to more than 16,000 pounds in 2011. (Salter, 2012)

While it thus appears that laws restricting the sale of pseudoephedrine products are simply displacing the methamphetamine problem, and possibly even exacerbating it, perhaps even more problematic is a law passed in the state of Tennessee in March of 2005. This law, modeled on sex offender notification laws, requires individuals convicted of methamphetamine-related crimes to register with law enforcement officials ("Tennessee Starts," 2006). Individuals in Tennessee can search an online database for the name, alias, birthdate, and location of methamphetamine offenders, with the name of the offender remaining in the database for 8 years (Childress, 2006a). On the surface, such laws seem to violate the civil rights of individuals. Even more problematic, and as has happened in some jurisdictions with sex offender notification laws, it is possible that individuals will access the information from the database to personally harass or inflict harm on individuals they believe to be methamphetamine users.

In considering legislation addressing the methamphetamine problem, it is also notable how, in comparison to the crack cocaine problem in the mid-1980s, the federal government has been relatively inactive. Recall that in the context of the alleged crack epidemic in the 1980s, the federal government moved quickly to establish mandatory sentencing for crack cocaine, creating a 100-to-1 sentencing disparity for crack versus powder cocaine. However, until the summer of 2005, the Drug Enforcement Administration essentially denied that methamphetamine constituted a serious national problem (Suo, 2005d), and the federal government was especially reluctant to consider national legislation that would impose restrictions on the sales of pseudoephedrine products. Considerable pressure exerted by legislators from states that were most affected by methamphetamine eventually led the federal government to pass the Combat Methamphetamine Act in 2006. This law imposed controls over cold remedies containing pseudoephedrine, providing that consumers in every state would be limited to purchasing 3.6 grams of pseudoephedrine per day and 9 grams per month (the equivalent of approximately 300 pills). In addition, by October 2006, all retailers were required to keep cold medicines behind the counter and to record the name and address of all customers who purchased the products (Suo & Barnett, 2006). While this legislation may result in a reduction in the local production of methamphetamine, similar to other federal drug policies, the law is particularly inadequate for addressing the demand for methamphetamine. Notably, out of a total of $12.4 billion drug control budget for 2006, the federal legislation included only $16.2 million in new money for the treatment of methamphetamine users (Friedman, 2005).

MARIJUANA LAWS

Hemp

Although the potential benefits associated with hemp are extensive, and although it has been reintroduced as a cash crop in a number of countries, including Great Britain, Germany, Australia, and Canada, the United States federal government continues to ban hemp and to mislead the public about this product. As Green (2004) notes, the fiber volume supplied by trees that take up to 30 years to grow can be harvested from hemp plants only 3 to 4 months after the seeds are planted, and on one-half the amount of land. Hemp crops are also environmentally friendly, in that they do not require herbicides and require little or no pesticide, and unlike most other crops, hemp actually enriches instead of depletes soil. Hemp is useful as a textile and a building material and in food products.

> In July 2003, the United States 9th Circuit Court of Appeals ruled that it was legal for consumers to purchase granola, energy bars, salad dressings, and other food products that contain the seeds or oil from hemp. The market for hemp products in the United States at that time was estimated to be more than $10 million per year (Kelly, 2003).

Although 28 states have considered legislation to liberalize their laws towards industrial hemp (Kolosov 2009), production of the substance has apparently not taken place in those states due to the federal government's opposition. Similar to other federal stances with respect to drugs, this ban on hemp has been produced through the dissemination of sometimes misleading and other times blatantly false information. For example, Ada Hutchinson, former head of the Drug Enforcement Administration, asserted "many Americans do not know that hemp and marijuana are both parts of the same plant and cannot be produced without producing marijuana" (as quoted in Green, 2004). As Green (2004) points out, however, the reason most people do not know this is because it is simply not true; hemp and marijuana are completely different plants. The Drug Enforcement Administration further justifies its prohibition of hemp through claims that hemp crops provide camouflage for illegal marijuana growers. This contention is similarly nonsensical, given that hemp and marijuana plants are distinguishable from one another and marijuana growers would be reluctant to follow such a strategy because cross-pollination of the plants would ultimately reduce the THC content of marijuana (Green, 2004).

Medical Marijuana

As discussed in Chapter 4, marijuana has been used for medicinal purposes for at least 300 years, and more than 100 articles on the therapeutic uses of the substance were published in professional journals between 1840 and 1900. Cannabis was listed in the *U.S. Pharmacopeia* as a recognized medicine from 1850 until 1942, and it could be purchased in local pharmacies in Texas until 1919 and in Louisiana until 1924 (Davenport-Hines, 2001). And while there is by no means scientific consensus on the medical utility of marijuana, despite the claims of former drug czar John Walters and other government officials, a number of prominent organizations and individuals support use of the substance for medical purposes. Reports by the National Institutes of Health and the Institute of Medicine claimed that cannabis and its constituents may have some clinical utility (National Institutes of Health [NIH], 1997). Similarly, in a publication from the National Academy Press, it was noted that "accumulated data indicate a therapeutic potential for cannabinoid drugs, particularly for symptoms such as pain relief, control of nausea, and vomiting, and appetite stimulation" (Joy, Watson, & Benson, 1999, p. 3). This report also pointed out that with the exception of the harms associated with smoking, the adverse effects of marijuana "are within the range of effects tolerated for other medications" (p. 4). Other organizations in favor of allowing the use of medical marijuana include the American Public Health Association, the Federation of American Scientists, the Physicians' Association for AIDS Care, the Lymphoma Association of America, and the National Association of Prosecutors and Criminal Defense Attorneys (Zimmer & Morgan, 1997). The *New England Journal of Medicine* and the *Journal of the American Medical Association* have also taken stances in favor of medical marijuana.

Georgia Congressman Bob Barr wrote an editorial in 1999 that was syndicated in a number of newspapers across the United States. Referring to scientific studies proving that marijuana had beneficial medicinal properties, Barr (1999) wrote, "What kind of message does this send to our kids? It tells our children that government scientists have concluded that marijuana might be good for them. In other words, it puts mind-altering drugs on the same level as vitamins or healthy breakfast cereal."

In 1988, Francis L. Young, the Chief Administrative Law Judge of the Drug Enforcement Administration, recommended that marijuana be removed from Schedule I of the Controlled Substances Act so that it could be used for medical purposes. Young asserted that cannabis fulfilled the legal requirement of currently accepted medical use in treatment and noted that it was "one of the safest therapeutically active substances known to man" (as quoted in Grinspoon & Bakalar, 1995, p. 1875). However, the DEA ignored this recommendation, and since then, DEA agents and other government officials have actively engaged in a campaign of pursuing medical marijuana users and providers in states where medical marijuana legislation has been passed.

> Although it is not widely known, there was also a federal government program that supplied marijuana to certain individuals. The "compassionate care" program began in 1976 when Robert Randall, who suffered from glaucoma, convinced a court that marijuana was a medical necessity to improve his condition. Fourteen other patients were subsequently enrolled in this program, but enrollment was closed in 1992, and as of 2003, only seven patients remained (Craig, 2003). These individuals received 300 marijuana cigarettes from the government each month, and heavy security requirements meant that keeping them supplied with the substance costs some $285,000 per year. ("Where There's Smoke," 1999)

As of January 2013, 18 states and the District of Columbia had passed medical marijuana legislation, and at least seven other states were considering it (Cohen 2013). Although there is wide variation across states in the specifics of these laws, the most common type protects doctors, pharmacies, and patients involved in federally approved research on the medicinal value of marijuana from prosecution. In most states where marijuana is legal for medicinal purposes, laws protect doctors who prescribe marijuana or discuss its medicinal value with patients, while some states have removed marijuana from Schedule I to a lower schedule in recognition of its medicinal value (Drug Policy Alliance, 2003i). While it would appear on the surface that these state laws allow for the provision of medical marijuana, they are in conflict with federal legislation, which continues to list marijuana as a Schedule I drug, and with Article IV of the Constitution, which holds that the federal law shall be the "law of the land" and hence prevail over state laws.

In states where medical marijuana legislation has passed, businesses catering to consumers have proliferated. For example, as of 2010, Colorado (where a constitutional amendment legalizing medical marijuana passed in 2000; Segal, 2010) had 113,000 residents registered as medical marijuana patients, and an estimated 1,218 marijuana farms and 808 dispensaries (Simon, 2010); the city of Denver alone had at least 250 dispensaries (Reuteman, 2010). In California, an estimated 400,000 individuals had medical marijuana cards—in that state, sales of medical marijuana topped $1.3 billion in 2010 (Harkinson, 2011). Although perhaps overstated, one reporter noted that "in parts of California, licensed medical marijuana dispensaries have become as common as In-N-Out burger stands" (Hendrix, 2009), another commented that [in the state of California] "storefront purveyors (of medical marijuana) are nearly as easy to find as a taco stand" (Welch, 2009).

In response to medical marijuana initiatives passed in Arizona and California in the 1980s, President Clinton's drug czar, Barry McCaffrey, threatened to arrest any doctor who merely *mentioned* to a patient that marijuana might help him or her (Boyd & Hitt, 2002), and at one point referred to medical marijuana as "Cheech and Chong medicine" (as quoted in Forbes, 2000). McCaffrey and other government officials have justified their stance against medical marijuana by, among other things, arguing that there is no need for it because the same beneficial effects can be achieved through the use of Marinol (synthetic THC). However, as Zimmer and Morgan (1997) note, smoking marijuana is more effective than consuming Marinol because smoking delivers THC to the bloodstream more quickly than swallowing Marinol. A further and related disadvantage of Marinol is that because it is swallowed, it must be processed through the body, and a significant portion of the THC is transformed into other chemicals. Smoked marijuana, on the other hand, delivers most of the THC that is inhaled. There is also some evidence to suggest that the psychoactive effects of Marinol are more severe than for smoked marijuana (Zimmer & Morgan, 1997). Conant (1997) further asserts that an indirect indicator of the superiority of marijuana over Marinol is that even though many health insurance plans in the United States will pay for Marinol, a significant percentage of patients spend their own money to purchase marijuana, even at risk of criminal prosecution. And despite the federal government's contention that Marinol is more effective than smoked marijuana, it is notable that the Drug Enforcement Administration and the National Institute on Drug Abuse have actively prevented attempts by scientists to conduct research in order to compare the effectiveness of the two substances. Dr. Donald Abrams, a researcher at the University of California, San Francisco, received approval from the Food and Drug Administration for a comparative study of marijuana and Marinol in 1993, but the DEA and NIDA refused to provide him with access to the marijuana he required to conduct the study (Pollan, 1997).

President George W. Bush's drug czar John Walters was even more stringent in his opposition to medical marijuana laws, at one point referring to medical marijuana as "medicinal crack" (as quoted in Drug Policy Alliance, 2003b). In what some have argued was a violation of the 1939 Hatch Act, which prevents federal government officials from using their authority to affect the outcome of an election, Walters campaigned against a marijuana decriminalization ballot initiative in the state of Nevada in 2000, publicly claiming, among other things, that passage of the law would make Nevada a "vacation spot for drug traffickers" (as quoted in Janofsky, 2002). The proposed Nevada legislation was eventually defeated by a vote of 61% to 39%, and critics also noted that Walters had not reported his activities in campaigning against it to the state of Nevada, as required by the state's campaign laws (Drug Policy Alliance, 2002b). Walters also campaigned against a medical marijuana law in Maryland, urging the state's governor to "see through the con" and not sign

the bill and arguing that the notion that marijuana was a "proven efficacious medicine" made no more sense than "an argument for medicinal crack" (as quoted in
Montgomery & Whitlock, 2003). Maryland Governor Robert Ehrlich eventually
approved the state's medical marijuana legislation, marking the first time a
Republican governor had done so (Drug Policy Alliance, 2003b).

Proposed legislation to allow marijuana for medical purposes was also blocked
in Washington, D.C. In September 2002, a federal appeals court overturned, without
providing any rationale, a previous court ruling that had cleared the way for a
medical marijuana initiative to be considered by voters in an election in D.C.
(Santana, 2002). Interestingly, this was the second time that the measure had been
blocked in D.C.—in 1998, voters approved a medical marijuana initiative by a vote
of 69% to 31%, but Congress prevented the law from going into effect.

In addition to efforts to block medical marijuana legislation, the federal government has initiated a number of campaigns against medical marijuana users
and providers, particularly in California. One such case involved Ed Rosenthal,
a medical marijuana advocate and provider who was convicted of trafficking in
the substance in California. In this case, Judge Charles Breyer prohibited the jury
from hearing Rosenthal's medical marijuana defense. When jurors discovered
this after the trial, several of them wrote to Judge Breyer, expressing concern that
they had convicted Rosenthal without having access to all the evidence in the
case and recommending that the judge not sentence him to prison ("Federal
Persecution," 2003). In commenting on the Rosenthal case, a *New York Times*
editorial referred to the federal government's pursuit of medical marijuana as
"mean-spirited and unconstitutional. . . . Medical marijuana can be a legitimate
treatment for cancer patients who are nauseated by chemotherapy, AIDS patients
who have lost their appetites, and other seriously ill people" ("Medical
Marijuana," 2002). Judge Breyer eventually heeded the jury members' wishes
and sentenced Rosenthal to only one day in prison. However, federal authorities
vowed to continue the fight against marijuana. A spokesman for the Office of
National Drug Control Policy commented,

> It would be unfortunate if anyone misread this ruling to mean that the federal
> government is not going to enforce our laws against drug trafficking. Marijuana
> is a dangerous drug. . . . It would be even more unfortunate if the ruling misled
> sick people who are truly suffering and steered them away from the best medi-
> cine and practices. (as quoted in R. Sanchez, 2003)

While medical marijuana laws remain in a state of flux, a decision by an appellate
court in San Francisco in 2003 held that while doctors could be prosecuted for
assisting their patients in acquiring illegal drugs, they could not be prosecuted for
merely giving patients medical advice indicating that marijuana might be useful in
dealing with their particular medical conditions. The chief judge in this case ruled
that the federal policy was inconsistent with both free speech protections under the
First Amendment to the Constitution and states' traditional authority over the

practice of medicine (Egelko, 2003). However, this court decision did not really result in further clarity for doctors, since it stated,

> If, in making recommendations, the physician intends for the patient to use it as a means for obtaining marijuana, as a prescription is used as a means for a patient to obtain a controlled substance, then the physician would be guilty of aiding and abetting the violation of the federal law. (as quoted in Tuller, 2003)

In another case eventually decided by the U.S. Supreme Court, in response to Drug Enforcement Administration officials' destruction of their medical marijuana plants, two patients and two marijuana providers from the state of California sued the federal government. They argued that applying the Controlled Substances Act to a situation in which marijuana was being grown locally, not in violation of state law, and for no remuneration exceeded Congress's authority under the commerce clause (Eddy, 2006). In 2003, the Ninth Circuit Court of Appeals in San Francisco held that states were free to adopt medical marijuana laws as long as the substance was not sold, transported across state lines, or use for nonmedicinal purposes. However, the federal government appealed this decision, and in June 2005, the Supreme Court, in a six-to-three decision, ruled that Congress's power to regulate commerce extended to local activities that are "part of an economic class of activities that have a substantial effect on interstate commerce" (*Gonzales v. Raich* cited in Eddy, 2006). While the Supreme Court's decision in this case does not overturn state medical marijuana laws, it does allow the Drug Enforcement Administration to continue to enforce the Controlled Substances Act against medical marijuana patients and those who supply them with the drug.

In addition to arresting and prosecuting medical marijuana providers and physicians who recommend marijuana to their patients, the federal government has used crack house statutes to charge individuals who operate medical marijuana clinics and has enacted legislation penalizing states that pass medical marijuana legislation by denying them funds from the Office of National Drug Control Policy (Durbin, 2003b).

The federal government's aggressive pursuit of doctors and medical marijuana providers has led a number of smaller jurisdictions, particularly in California, to pass local ordinances to protect providers. In July 2002, for example, voters in San Francisco approved a local bylaw that would require officials to examine the possibility of the city itself growing and distributing medical marijuana (Drug Policy Alliance, 2002c). Also in California, in response to a DEA raid on a medical marijuana distribution cooperative in Santa Cruz, the city council allowed members of the cooperative to hand out marijuana publicly to its patients at city hall (Ritter, 2002). Later, the same city deputized two members of the "Wo/men's Alliance for Medical Marijuana," thereby providing them with the legal authority to cultivate, distribute, and possess medical marijuana because as deputies, they were, in effect, enforcing drug laws (Watercutter, 2002).

The Recent War on Medical Marijuana

As Norm Stamper (former Seattle police chief) commented, "It wasn't hard to put together a report showing how the Obama administration continues to wage the failed 'war on drugs' even while pretending to end it. Although President Obama has talked about respecting states' rights to enact medical marijuana laws, his DEA [Drug Enforcement Administration] has raided state-legal medical marijuana providers at a higher rate than the Bush administration. Similarly, this president has continued a Bush-era budget ratio that heavily favors spending on punishment over providing resources for treatment, even though he has said drug addiction should be handled as a health issue." (as quoted in Friedersdorf, 2011)

As a presidential candidate, and after taking office, President Obama indicated that his administration would take a hands-off approach to medical marijuana (Egelko, 2011; Yardley, 2011). This stance was reflected in a 2009 statement by federal Justice Department officials that indicated that, as a general rule, prosecutors should not focus their resources on "individuals whose actions are in clear and unambiguous compliance with existing state laws providing for the medical use of marijuana" (as cited in Baker, 2011). However, in an interesting switch in focus, a 2011 Justice Department memo stated, "we maintain the authority to enforce [federal law] vigorously against individuals and organizations that participate in unlawful manufacturing and distribution activity involving marijuana, even if such activities are permitted under state law" (as cited in Baker, 2011). In addition, the 2011 National Drug Control Strategy claimed that marijuana was "addictive and unsafe," and devoted five pages to attacking marijuana legalization and medical marijuana. As Gutwillig and Piper (2011) note,

> The administration's disconnect from science is shocking. A federally commissioned study by the Institute of Medicine more than a decade ago determined that nausea, appetite loss, pain and anxiety can all be mitigated by marijuana. The esteemed medical journal *Lancet Neurology* reports that marijuana's active components "inhibit pain in virtually every experimental pain paradigm." The National Cancer Institute, part of the U.S. Department of Health and Human Services, notes that marijuana may help with nausea, loss of appetite, and insomnia.

Under the Obama administration, there have been at least 200 raids and 70 indictments against medical marijuana providers in six states (Martin, 2012e). While perhaps overstated, Rob Kampia (Director of the Marijuana Policy Project) referred to Obama as "the worst president in history when it comes to medical marijuana" (2012, p. 55). Although some of these raids focused on dispensaries that were located close to schools, one legislator from Washington State (which had recently allowed for the sale of liquor in grocery stores) questioned why marijuana dispensaries were more dangerous to young people than grocers (Martin, 2012e).

> Rob Kampia (Director of the Marijuana Policy Project) asserts that the targeting of medical marijuana providers and consumers is the result of pressures on Drug Enforcement Administration officers to "bust as many people as possible while not getting shot in the process." He notes that it is easier to target a medical marijuana business (many of which advertise in newspapers) than it is to investigate a group selling cocaine, [so] "the DEA guys started targeting people who dispense medical marijuana." (2012, p. 56)

As Ethan Nadelmann, Director of the Drug Policy Alliance, pointed out in a *New York Times* editorial (Nadelmann, 2011), in addition to the hundreds of raids of medical marijuana dispensaries that have been conducted by the Drug Enforcement Administration, pressures are also being exerted on medical marijuana businesses by other federal government agencies (see also Eckholm, 2011). Nadelmann notes, for example, that the Treasury Department has forced banks to close the accounts of medical marijuana businesses that are in fact operating legally under state laws, that the Internal Revenue Service has required dispensary owners to pay punitive taxes that are not imposed on other businesses, and that the Bureau of Alcohol, Tobacco, and Firearms ruled that medical marijuana patients cannot legally purchase firearms. Importantly, Nadelmann argues that these federal crackdowns will not be successful in stopping the trade in marijuana but will instead serve to push it back underground, with potentially higher levels of violence and other social harms resulting.

In light of the scientific evidence demonstrating the medical uses of marijuana and support for medical marijuana laws by several prominent organizations, the federal government's actions with respect to the substance seem terribly misguided. The government's stance on marijuana in general, and medical marijuana in particular, also seems inconsistent with public sentiment toward the substance. A *CBS News* poll conducted in the fall of 2011 found that 77% of Americans thought medical marijuana should be allowed (Backus, 2011). However, some federal government officials apparently view the passage of medical marijuana legislation and the relaxation of penalties for cannabis use as a potential threat to the larger War on Drugs and have deemed it necessary to exercise their hegemony with respect to drug legislation.

Marijuana Legalization Measures

Despite the federal government's stance toward marijuana, in recent years, some states have included marijuana legalization measures on voters' ballots. Rivas (2010) argues that three factors seem to be driving the momentum behind these measures: (1) baby boomers who consumed marijuana in their youth do not share previous generations' fear of the substance; (2) economic crises have reduced the budgets of law enforcement (and state governments more generally), forcing states to seek alternative revenue sources; and (3) the level of drug-related violence in Mexico (see also Chapter 12) "shows what happens when a rhetorical war turns all too real" (Rivas, 2010).

In the fall of 2010, a marijuana legalization measure, Proposition 19 (the "Regulate, Control, and Tax Cannabis Act") was included on the ballot in the state of California

(McKinley, 2010). Likely in reaction to some polls indicating the measure had a reasonably good chance of passing, in an interesting pre-emptive move, Governor Arnold Schwarzenegger signed a law just prior to the vote that made the penalty for marijuana possession in the state of California equivalent to a traffic ticket: a $100 fine and no provision for jail time. This strategy was important, since one of the main arguments of proponents of Proposition 19 was that the state's marijuana laws cost too much to enforce and prosecute (Lagos, 2010). In opposition to this law, there were typical (misguided) pronouncements by law enforcement officials, such as the police chief in Pleasant Hill, California, who claimed, "If the price drops, more people are going to buy it. Low-income people are going to buy marijuana instead of buying food, which happens with substance abusers." He added that passage of Proposition 19 would make the state of California "a laughingstock" (as quoted in Wohlsen, 2010). Interestingly, one of the largest contributors to the campaign against marijuana legalization in California was the state's beer and beverage distributors—"having branded their products with nearly every major American ritual, Big Alcohol does not want marijuana to get a piece of that large pie of money spent to distract ourselves from ourselves" (Egan, 2010). Although Proposition 19 was ultimately defeated by a margin of 56.5% opposed versus 43.5% in favor, younger voters were much more likely to support it, and 65% of voters in San Francisco approved the measure ("Prop. 19," 2010).

In the summer of 2012, Chicago Mayor Rahm Emanuel (former Chief of Staff for President Obama) proposed an ordinance that would allow police officers in that city to issue tickets with fines ranging from $100 to $500 for individuals caught in possession of 15 grams or less of marijuana. Chicago Police Superintendent Garry McCarthy, whose officers made more than 18,000 arrests for marijuana possession in 2011, supported the proposal because, he argued, it would free up police time: "I am pleased that Mayor Emanuel has taken this step to address this important issue.... Passing this ordinance will be a major victory in promoting safe neighborhoods and reducing crime." (as quoted in Mack, 2012)

Three states—Colorado, Oregon, and Washington—had marijuana legalization measures on the fall 2012 ballot. Colorado's measure, known as Amendment 64, would permit retail stores to sell marijuana and would tax and regulate marijuana in a fashion similar to alcohol. Among the backers of the Colorado legislation was Bruce Madison, former associate medical director at the University of Colorado School of Medicine, who commented,

As physicians, we have a professional obligation to do no harm. But the truth is that the Colorado marijuana laws do just that, by wasting millions of dollars in a failed war on marijuana, by ruining thousands of lives by unnecessary arrest and incarceration, and by causing the deaths of hundreds of people killed in black market criminal activities. (as quoted in Horowitz, 2012)

The state of Washington had considered the legalization of marijuana as early as 1971, when a bill was introduced to the legislature but ultimately did not pass. Prior to the inclusion of the marijuana legalization measure on the 2012 ballot, Washington Governor Christine Gregoire (as well as Rhode Island Governor Lincoln Chafee) had petitioned the Drug Enforcement Administration to reclassify marijuana as a Schedule II drug, thereby recognizing its therapeutic value (Martin, 2011). Washington's measure I-502 would make it legal for individuals 21 years of age and older to possess up to 1 ounce of marijuana (or up to 1 pound of marijuana-containing baked goods). It was estimated that if the measure passed, the state of Washington would receive approximately $500 million in taxes and licensing fees per year (Carson, 2012) and that there would be about 328 state marijuana stores serving more than 350,000 customers (Martin, 2012b).

Among the supporters of the Washington legislation were several prominent politicians in the state, former federal prosecutor John McKay, Seattle City Attorney Pete Holmes, Seattle's mayor and city council (Garber & Miletich, 2011; Martin, 2012a), international travel guide Rick Steves, the National Association for the Advancement of Colored People, the Children's Alliance (a statewide advocacy group for children's interests), the American Civil Liberties Union of Western Washington, and the national Drug Policy Alliance, which contributed at least $715,000 to the pro–Initiative 502 campaign (Carson, 2012). In addition, the pro–I-502 campaign received $1.5 million in contributions from Progressive Insurance founder Peter Lewis (Martin, 2012c). King County Sheriff Steve Strachan, a former D.A.R.E. officer, also supported the legalization campaign, noting, "with alcohol being highly regulated, we're able to have a more reasonable discussion about it" (as quoted in Westneat, 2012). However, Sheriff Strachan was apparently rare among his law enforcement counterparts, as among those groups and individuals opposed to the legislation were included the Washington Association of Sheriffs and Police Chiefs. The two candidates for Washington governor (former state Attorney General), Republican Rob McKenna and Democrat Jay Inslee, were also opposed to the measure (O'Neill, 2012).

Interestingly (and as had happened with the 2010 marijuana legalization measure in California), many medical marijuana providers and activists in the state of Washington were opposed to the legislation, partly because of their contention that the legislation did "not go far enough" because it did not allow for legal home growing of marijuana except by medical marijuana patients (Hefter, 2012). This group was also concerned about a clause in the proposed legislation that addressed driving under the influence of marijuana. Under the proposed policy, impairment was assumed at 5 nanograms of THC per milliliter of blood (Johnson, 2011), which, the medical marijuana providers suggested, would result in significant numbers of medical marijuana patients being charged with driving under the influence.

The 2012 Washington State voters' pamphlet listed arguments for and against Initiative 502 (Clark County, 2012). Among the arguments in support of the legislation were included the fact that the initiative would provide "billions in new revenue" for the state and that "almost all marijuana law enforcement is handled by state and local police—it's time for Washingtonians to decide Washington's laws, not the federal government." Among the arguments opposed, it was noted that legalizing marijuana "will greatly increase its availability and lead to more use, abuse, and addiction among adults and youth. . . . Marijuana recently surpassed alcohol as the number one reason youth enter substance abuse treatment." As noted in Chapter 1 and elsewhere in this book, there is little scientific evidence to indicate that the increased availability of marijuana will necessarily lead to long-term increases in use. And, as noted in Chapter 8, the increasing proportion of youth entering treatment for marijuana use is largely the result of criminal and juvenile justice system referrals of youth arrested for using marijuana.

Although the marijuana legalization measure in the state of Oregon did not pass, legalization measures passed in both Colorado (with approximately 55% of voters in favor; "Amendment 64," 2013) and Washington State (with approximately 56% of voters in favor ("Marijuana Legalization," 2012). In an interview with Barbara Walters of *ABC News*, President Obama indicated that recreational marijuana users in Colorado and Washington would not be targeted by federal law enforcement officials: "We've got bigger fish to fry . . . It would not make sense for us to see a top priority as going after recreational users in states that have determined it's [marijuana] legal" (as quoted in Dwyer, 2012). However, if the federal government's actions with respect to medical marijuana are any indication, it is unlikely that the federal agencies will not react. It has been speculated that the federal government might file an injunction to block the bill's passage and/or block federal grant money to the state of Washington (O'Neill, 2012). In fact, when asked a question regarding how the federal government would respond if I-502 passed, in an interview on *60 Minutes*, the deputy U.S. attorney general commented, "We're going to take a look at whether or not there are dangers to the community from the sale of marijuana and we're going to go after those dangers" (as quoted in Hopperstad, 2012).

SIGNS OF CHANGE? RECENT CHANGES IN STATE DRUG LAWS AND DEVELOPMENTS AT THE FEDERAL LEVEL

I don't favor decriminalization, I favor legalization, not just of pot, but of all drugs, including heroin, cocaine, methamphetamine, psychotropics, mushrooms, and LSD. . . . It's not a stretch to conclude that our draconian approach to drug use is the most injurious policy since slavery. (Stamper, 2005b)

A study by the National Center on Addiction and Substance Abuse (2009) estimated that in 2005, federal, state, and local governments spent at least $467.7 billion (combined) as a result of substance abuse and addiction, representing 10.7% of their $4.4 trillion budgets. The study also estimated that of every dollar federal and state governments spent on substance abuse and addiction in 2005, only 1.9 cents was spent on prevention and treatment, 1.4 cents on taxation and regulation, 0.7 cents on interdiction, and 0.4 cents on research. The remaining funds were spent on "shoveling up the wreckage"—with health care costs totaling $207.2 billion and $47 billion on criminal justice system expenditures. The report noted that "the federal government spends more than 30 times as much to cope with the health consequences of addiction as it spends on prevention, treatment, and research."

Bruce Alexander (1990) has argued that one of the primary reasons drug policies have been ineffective, and in many cases counterproductive, is that they are typically determined by national law. He asserts that one possible path to more rational and progressive drug regulations is for them to be "as local as possible" (p. 293). The medical marijuana policies of individual states and localities discussed above are examples of this principle, and recent developments in several states suggest that many of them are rethinking their severe policies toward drugs. While part of the impetus for these changes has been related to a growing realization that drug treatment can be effective (see Chapter 8), a number of states have moved to relax their policies as a result of the costs associated with incarcerating large numbers of drug offenders.

In 2002, the state of Washington passed legislation that reduced by 6 months the 21- to 27-month minimum sentence for first-time convictions for trafficking in heroin and cocaine and also eliminated the "triple-scoring" sentences for nonviolent drug offenders (Thomas, 2002). This law was projected to save Washington State $45 million per year, with the money saved as a result of reductions in the length of sentences being devoted to funding drug courts in the state.

Also in Washington State, a 2003 ballot initiative in the city of Seattle required police to make marijuana possession their lowest enforcement priority. Given his opposition to laws that could potentially reduce the severity of penalties imposed on drug offenders, drug czar John Walters referred to this initiative as a "con" and a "silly and irresponsible game." But there were also indications that at least some law enforcement officials in Washington State were re-evaluating their approach to drugs. Then Seattle Police Chief (current drug czar in the Obama administration) Gil Kerlikowske, in reaction to an announcement that drug czar John Walters would travel to that city to discuss drug issues, noted that while he would be willing to talk to Walters,

> The one thing that is pretty clear here is that there's a strong recognition that the drug issues and the drug problem are not just a law enforcement or criminal justice problem. . . . Just arresting the same people, putting handcuffs on the same people, makes no sense. (as quoted in Pope, 2003)

In March 2003, legislation in Michigan came into effect that repealed that state's mandatory minimum sentences for drug offenses and resulted in the release of several first-time nonviolent drug offenders from prison. This law reformed Michigan's 1978 legislation that required judges to impose lengthy mandatory minimum penalties that were based on the quantity of drugs in given cases. With this particular change, judges in Michigan could use sentencing guidelines to impose sentences based on a range of factors in each case instead of relying strictly on the weight of the drug (Drug Policy Alliance, 2003h).

In 1973, the state of New York enacted legislation (known as the Rockefeller drug laws) that created mandatory minimum sentences of 15 years to life for possession of 4 ounces of drugs (equivalent to the penalty for second-degree murder). Similar to the federal drug legislation discussed above, these laws were disproportionately applied to African Americans (and, to a lesser extent, Hispanics) and led to high levels of incarceration in the state of New York. After considerable criticism of these laws in the late 1990s and 2000s, in 2009, New York Governor David Paterson stated, "I can't think of a criminal justice strategy that has been more unsuccessful than the Rockefeller drug laws" (as quoted in Liu, 2009) and revised the laws. Under the revisions, mandatory minimum sentences for drug laws violations were removed, allowing judges to sentence offenders to shorter prison sentences and also to order substance abusers to enter addiction treatment programs in lieu of prison (Davis, 2012). Importantly, the changes to the legislation were retroactive, allowing more than 1,000 offenders in prison to apply to be resentenced (Canfield, 2009). It was estimated that repeal of the Rockefeller drug laws would save the state of New York approximately $250 million per year (Hastings, 2009).

The state of California, which passed Proposition 215 (the Compassionate Use Act) allowing for the use of medical marijuana in 1996, also passed Proposition 36 (the Substance Abuse and Crime Prevention Act) in 2000. This legislation allowed individuals convicted of their first and second nonviolent drug possession offenses the option of participating in drug treatment in lieu of incarceration. It also allowed offenders on probation or parole for certain offenses to receive treatment instead of incarceration after violations of drug-related conditions of their probation or parole (Uelmen et al., 2002). Individuals convicted of drug trafficking or other felony offenses were not eligible for the program. Although there have been some negative consequences associated with this legislation that were discussed in Chapter 8, in its first year of operation, Proposition 36 was estimated to have saved the state of California $275 million (Haake, 2003).

While these and other drug policy developments at the state level are encouraging, it is clear that the federal government feels such policies represent a threat to its hegemony in the drug policy arena. One example of this is the situation in Arizona. In 1996, voters in that state approved Proposition 200 (by a margin of two to one), which had as its basic premise "drug abuse is a public health problem." The initiative called for the release from prison of all nonviolent drug offenders who had been convicted of drug possession and recommended drug treatment, education, and community service, as opposed to incarceration, for minor drug offenders. The proposition also allowed doctors to prescribe not just marijuana but any Schedule I drug to a patient if medical research supported the effectiveness of using the drug and if a second doctor concurred with the decision. However, the Clinton administration criticized this proposition, with Drug Czar Barry McCaffrey referring to it as "part of a national strategy to legalize drugs" (Schlosser, 1997) and threatened to revoke the licenses of physicians who prescribed marijuana. A Drug Enforcement Administration press release in response to this legislation noted that it was "in conflict with public safety and the physical well-being of innocent citizens" (cited in U.S. Department of Justice, 1996).

An Arizona Supreme Court report on the effectiveness of Proposition 200 estimated that it had saved the state $2.6 billion in 1 year and that 77.5% of those who had been placed on probation for drug possession offenses under the provisions of the Act tested negative for drug use, thus indicating that the law had resulted in several benefits (Arizona Supreme Court, 1999). However, perhaps in response to the above-mentioned pressure from the federal government, the Arizona legislature overturned several of the more progressive aspects of this legislation in 1997.

Other states that have recently softened their drug laws include South Carolina, where in 2010, a law that eliminated mandatory minimum sentencing for some drug offenses and reduced sentences for some repeat drug offenders was passed (The Leadership Conference, 2010).

It is important to note that not all states are moving in the direction of more progressive drug policies. In 2012, Governor Rick Scott of Florida vetoed legislation that would have diverted some nonviolent drug offenders into treatment ("Rick Scott Vetoes," 2012). And, as was discussed in Chapter 7, Florida is among the states that have aggressively promoted drug-testing of public assistance recipients and state employees.

Finally, at the level of the federal government, there was the passage of the Fair Sentencing Act in 2010, which narrowed the gap between crack and powder cocaine sentencing from 100 to 1 to 18 to 1 (Douglas, 2010). Presaging the passage of this legislation, former Republican Congressman J. C. Watts and former Congressman and former head of the Drug Enforcement Administration Asa Hutchinson wrote an editorial in the *Washington Post* calling for the Attorney General (who had earlier implied that changing the federal crack cocaine law would flood the streets of the United States with violent felons) to change the law:

> The truth is that for years our legal system has enforced an unfair approach to sentencing federal crack offenders. . . . It makes no sense that somebody arrested for a crack cocaine offense should receive a substantially longer prison term than somebody who is convicted of a powder cocaine offense. (Watts & Hutchinson, 2008)

In defending the eventual change in this legislation and acknowledging the damage the previous legislation had done, Attorney General Eric Holder essentially concurred with Watts and Hutchison and commented, "There is simply no logical reason why their [crack cocaine users/traffickers] sentences should be more severe than those of other cocaine offenders" (as quoted in Serrano, Savage, & Williams, 2011). Under this change, an estimated 12,000 federal prisoners would be eligible for sentence reductions, with an average reduction of approximately 3 years (Schwartz, 2011). While this change should certainly be viewed as a positive development, a federal appeals court judge in Chicago, noting that the disparity between crack and powder had not been completely eliminated, commented that the act was misnamed, suggesting that it instead should have been called "the not quite as fair as it could be sentencing act" (as quoted in Liptak, 2011). And, as Alexander (2010) comments, "merely reducing sentence length, by itself, does not disturb the basic architecture of the new Jim Crow" (p. 14).

A 1997 ONDCP publication asserted "the foremost objective of the Office of National Drug Control Policy is to create a national drug control strategy based on science rather than ideology (p. 1)—a similar sentiment was echoed in the 2012 National Drug Control Policy statement, which notes that the administration's strategy to reduce drug use and its consequences would be based on a "collaborative, balanced, and science-based approach" (ONDCP, 2012, p. 1). In light of the policies and activities of the federal government reviewed above, this assertion needs to be called into question.

Nevil Franklin, a former Baltimore narcotics police officer and Executive Director of Law Enforcement against prohibition, commented, "President Obama needs to think about where he would be right now had he been caught with drugs as a young black man. It's probably not in the Oval Office, so why does he insist on ramping up a drug war that needlessly churns other young black men through the criminal justice system?" (as quoted in Saunders, 2011)

And despite some optimism that drug policies would change under the Obama administration, this has not been the case. As Alexander (2010) notes, Obama chose Joe Biden, "one of the senate's most strident drug warriors," as his vice president (p. 238). Obama also chose Rahm Emanuel, a "major proponent of the drug war and slashing of welfare rolls during the Clinton administration," as his chief of staff. More generally, Alexander (2010) notes that President Obama's budget for law enforcement was actually worse than that of the Bush administration in terms of the ratio of funds devoted to drug prevention and treatment as opposed to law enforcement.

CONCLUSION

While many Western countries address drug use and dependence primarily as public health issues (see Chapter 12), the United States has a long history of dealing with drug problems through the criminal justice system. Criminal justice responses to drug use tend to do little or nothing to reduce drug use in the general population while simultaneously creating a number of social and economic problems. The most problematic consequences of these policies is that they substantially increase prison populations and justice system expenditures and that they disproportionately impact members of minority groups and the lower social classes.

Drug offenses are among the most severely penalized crimes in the United States. Individuals arrested for drug offenses are among the most likely to be sent to prison for long periods of time, with drug crimes generally being punished more severely than the violent crimes of assault, robbery, and rape. The tremendous number of arrests for drug offenses and the severe penalties that result from a drug conviction have contributed to unprecedented levels of imprisonment in the United States.

As noted, there are substantial disparities in the application of drug laws across social class and race. As discussed in Chapter 5, the use of illegal drugs crosses all income levels and racial/ethnic groups, and African Americans and Hispanics use illegal drugs less frequently or in approximately the same proportion as whites. Despite this, members of minority groups and the lower class have been disproportionately targeted and affected by drug enforcement policies. Members of minority groups are more likely to be poor, and the poor are least able to afford a private attorney, making them less successful at defending themselves from drug charges. Additionally, higher drug arrest rates for African Americans result from the concentration of law enforcement in inner-city areas where illegal drug use and trafficking are more likely to take place in the open and where African Americans are disproportionately concentrated.

Racial- and class-based disparities in the application of drug laws result from a number of specific policies. These include "crack baby" legislation, public housing eviction policies, denying welfare benefits to people convicted of drug offenses, and mandatory minimum sentences for drug offenses, among others. While these policies may have been enacted with the goal of reducing drug use, they have contributed to massive growth in the United States' prison population and have disproportionately affected the poor and racial minorities.

Another disturbing development in recent U.S. drug policies is asset seizure laws that allow for the confiscation of assets of individuals allegedly involved in drug transactions.

The apparent goal of civil forfeiture laws is to deprive drug traffickers of the proceeds and assets that have been produced by their criminal activity and may be used to further it, but there is no evidence to suggest that these laws have reduced drug trafficking and use. Because criminal justice agencies are allowed to keep significant proportions of the assets seized, drug enforcement officials may pursue cases that involve the most lucrative seizures even if those cases do not involve the most serious offenses. These laws also encourage corruption in law enforcement and represent a violation of the civil rights protections guaranteed under the Constitution to individuals charged with crimes.

Both the RAVE Act and legislation intended to control domestic methamphetamine production represent policies implemented hastily in order to "do something" about perceived drug epidemics. In the case of the RAVE Act, policy makers created legislation penalizing rave organizers and club owners for maintaining an environment where ecstasy use is believed to be more likely to occur. As users can consume ecstasy in virtually any setting, the RAVE Act is unlikely to significantly reduce use of the drug, but it may contribute to drug-related harm. This policy discourages safety measures (e.g., chill-out rooms) implemented by club owners because these measures could be used as evidence that club owners are aware that ecstasy use is occurring in their establishment.

Similarly, in an attempt to prevent the production of methamphetamine in light of a socially constructed methamphetamine "epidemic," legislation in the mid-2000s restricted public access to products containing pseudoephedrine. Those laws were partially successful in limiting the domestic manufacture of methamphetamine, but they did not reduce availability of the substance, never mind demand for the drug. The reduction in domestic methamphetamine production resulting from this legislation opened the market for international smugglers, and imported methamphetamine, largely from Mexico, quickly met the demand. Mexican methamphetamine generally has higher levels of purity and thus increases the risk of overdose; in addition, Mexican-produced methamphetamine may be more addictive than domestically manufactured methamphetamine.

A great deal of controversy surrounds the regulation of marijuana in the United States. With respect to the medical use of this product, organizations such as the American Public Health Association, the Federation of American Scientists, and the National Association of Prosecutors and Criminal Defense Attorneys favor policy allowing the use of medical marijuana, but critics of such policies argue that they are just a "disguised step" toward drug legalization. While the federal government resolutely opposes any policy that relaxes the penalties for marijuana, several states have adopted decriminalization policies, treating marijuana possession as an infraction punishable by a fine rather than incarceration.

More generally, an increasing number of legislators at the state level are rethinking the rationality of severe policies toward illegal drugs. In part, this shift in thinking comes from a realization that drug treatment can be effective (see Chapter 8) and that treatment may provide a cost-effective alternative to the exceptionally expensive practice of incarcerating large numbers of nonviolent drug offenders. While these developments at the state level are encouraging, it is clear that the United States federal government feels that such policies represent a threat to federal hegemony in the drug policy arena.

REVIEW QUESTIONS

1. In terms of total numbers, how do drug arrests compare to arrests for violent crime in the United States?

2. What percentage of the drug-using population is African American? What percentage of those arrested, prosecuted, and incarcerated for drug offenses are African American? How do we explain these discrepancies?

3. What has research concluded regarding the scientific validity of the crack baby syndrome?

4. What is the "100 to 1" rule for crack and powder cocaine sentencing? Why can this law be seen as discriminatory against poor and minority groups?

5. Why do drug laws related to public housing, welfare, and student loans have a disproportional impact on the poor and members of minority groups?

6. Laws regulating access to pseudoephedrine have been enacted to limit the production of methamphetamine. What unintended consequences are associated with these laws?

7. Which medical and legal organizations have issued statements in support of medical marijuana? Given the support of these organizations, what explains the opposition of federal government officials and agencies to the passage of medical marijuana legislation?

INTERNET EXERCISES

1. The Bureau of Justice Statistics provides data on the number of people incarcerated in the United States. Access the most recent report on correctional populations in the United States (http://www.ojp.usdoj.gov). Of those incarcerated in the United States, how many people and what proportion of all prisoners are serving time for drug offenses? How many people and what percentage of all prisoners are incarcerated for committing violent crimes? Be sure to examine both state and federal prison populations.

2. Access the website of the National Organization for the Reform of Marijuana Laws (http://www.norml.org) and compare the marijuana policies of your state (with respect to the penalties for possession and sales of marijuana and whether there is a medical marijuana policy) with those of at least one other state. How do you explain the similarities and differences in the policies?

CHAPTER 12

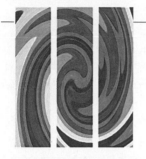

Drug Policies in Other Countries and United States Influence

In a 2002 editorial in the *Washington Post*, Asa Hutchinson, former director of the Drug Enforcement Administration, commented, "Maybe it's time [Europeans] looked to America's drug policy as their model. Our approach—tough drug laws coupled with effective education programs and compassionate treatment—is having success" (Hutchinson, 2002). While the discussion of the failure of U.S. drug policies in previous chapters of this book would certainly lead us to question Hutchinson's suggestion, it is important to place U.S. drug policies in the context of the policies of other countries. Thus, in this chapter, we compare and contrast the drug policies of a sample of other countries with those of the United States and critically examine the U.S. government's efforts to influence drug policies in some of these countries, particularly in Canada and Latin America. It is important to make such comparisons because drug markets are increasingly global, and there are many lessons to be learned in examining alternative approaches to the regulation of consciousness-altering substances that have been adopted. For instance, while many are aware of the fact that the Netherlands has among the most lenient drug policies of Western countries, most will not be aware that the Netherlands has the lowest estimated rate of problem drug users and the lowest level of drug-related mortality. The fact that the Netherlands has 0.1 drug-related deaths per 100,000 population aged 15 to 64—compared to 11.3 per 100,000 in the United States (Degenhardt, Hallam, & Bewley-Taylor, 2009)—suggests that more severe drug policies may not result in a reduction in drug-related harms.

Our discussion here is not intended to be exhaustive; we address policies primarily in Western developed countries. We provide considerably more detail on Britain and Canada because both countries are culturally similar to the United States, and the latter shares a common border with the United States. Before considering illegal drug policies in specific countries, however, it is important to examine the role of international treaties and the International Narcotics Board in influencing drug policies, followed by a discussion of the recently released report of the Global Commission on Drug Policy (2011).

INTERNATIONAL TREATIES

> Beginning in an era of morally tainted racism and colonial trade wars, prohibition-based drug control grew to international proportions at the insistence of the United States. America and the colonial powers were confronted with the effects of drug addiction and abuse at home, but rather than address both demand—the socio-medical nature of such problems—and supply, they focused exclusively on the latter and attempted to stem the flow of drugs into their territories. (Sinha, 2001)

The current system of global drug control is regulated by three international conventions: the 1961 Single Convention on Narcotic Drugs, the 1971 Convention on Psychotropic Substances, and the 1988 Convention Against Illicit Traffic in Narcotics and Psychotropic Substances; these represent the consolidation of nine international drug control treaties negotiated between 1912 and 1953 (Sinha, 2001). These conventions can serve as major barriers to the introduction of progressive and pragmatic drug control policies in individual countries (Bewley-Taylor, 2003), and they tend to promote unrealistic goals, including the eradication of all illegal drug use in the world. For example, one of the stated objectives of the 1961 United Nations Convention on Narcotic Drugs was to eliminate the chewing of the coca leaf and the use of cannabis for other than scientific and medicinal purposes within 25 years and the nonmedical use of opium within 15 years. Needless to say, none of these objectives were achieved. However, more than 40 years after the 1961 Convention, the more general slogan of the United Nations was "a drug free world, we can do it" (Toynbee, 2002), and the head of the United Nations Office on Drugs and Crime, Antonio Maria Costa, echoed a similar goal of eliminating all use of (illegal) drugs globally by 2008. Costa's naïve (if not ridiculous) suggestion led one observer to comment, "presumably his job has given him access to some great reality-excluding dope" (Engel, 2003).

The United Nations conventions have also focused disproportionately on reducing the supplies of illegal drugs, primarily through efforts in developing countries. The very title of the 1988 Treaty, with the words "Against Illicit Traffic," is reflective of this focus. But given that there is considerable demand in Western countries for the illegal drugs grown in these developing countries, and given that some citizens in these countries are dependent on producing these substances for their income, it will continue to be exceedingly difficult to completely eradicate drugs.

> Poor countries cannot and should not be expected to bear the brunt of rich countries' internal social failures. Colombia and growing numbers of other countries are being politically destabilized and destroyed as crime takes over, due to the impossible Western market that both demands drugs and outlaws them. (Toynbee, 2002)

International bodies have also suppressed the publication of reports on drugs that are not consistent with stringent prohibitionist policies. For example, in 1995, the World Health Organization and the United Nations Interregional Institute completed one of the most extensive global studies of cocaine use ever undertaken. However, publication of the study was prevented by the World Health Assembly due to the fact that it "failed to reinforce proven drug control approaches," and had recommended investigation of "the therapeutic benefits of the coca leaf" (as cited in "World Health Organization," 2006).

In recognition of the fact that the United Nations was devoting insufficient attention to the importance of demand for drugs, after the 1988 convention, there was pressure from a number of countries to hold a conference focused on strategies emphasizing demand reduction. These countries, led by Mexico, suggested that while they were constantly being subjected to criticism and pressure for being producers of illegal drugs, the main market for drugs was in Western countries, in particular the United States. However, the call for a conference on demand reduction was resisted by the United States and Britain, whose representatives argued that demand reduction was essentially a domestic issue and hence not within the purview of international agencies (Fazey, 2003).

> It is also interesting to note how the various United Nations conventions on drugs have paid little attention to prescription drugs. Reinarman (2003) notes, "As for pharmaceuticals, the question was never how to prevent use but how to make sure all markets were open, as might be expected when pharmaceutical industry reps helped negotiate the conventions." (p. 207)

While the international conventions discussed above are thus important to consider in the context of policies on illegal drugs in individual countries, it is important to realize that there are no provisions in any of the conventions requiring countries to enforce their drug legislation (MacCoun & Reuter, 2001; G. Smith, 2002). In addition, the International Narcotics Control Board, the administrative body responsible for overseeing these conventions, has no formal power to issue sanctions for noncompliance with the conventions (Bewley-Taylor, 2003). As a result, signatory nations have a certain amount of freedom with respect to their drug policies; this is why there is considerable variation in policies across these countries, including the de facto legalization of marijuana possession in a number of countries.

> Considered in their totality and in comparison to policies in other Western industrialized nations, drug policies in the United States are unique, placing far more emphasis on criminalization of drugs as opposed to harm reduction, which refers to "policies and programs designed to reduce drug-related harm, and aims to improve health, social, and economic outcomes for both the community and the individual" (Miller & Draper, 2001).

Harm-reduction policies are based on the assumption that "a world without drugs will never exist" (Blickman & Jelsma, 2009, p. 3) and have become increasingly popular in other countries. For instance, in 2003, the European Council of Ministers adopted harm reduction as the common position of the European Union toward drugs. As will be discussed in more detail below, Portugal has decriminalized all drug use, Spain and Luxembourg have decriminalized possession and use of most drugs, and several other countries have effectively done the same thing by choosing not to impose criminal sanctions on drug users who are not involved in trafficking. (Reid, 2002)

Harm-reduction programs have also been implemented in the Latin American countries of Brazil, Argentina, and Uruguay. In 2009, the Argentina Supreme Court declared it unconstitutional to prohibit possession of marijuana for personal use, and Ecuador implemented a policy of pardoning small-time drug traffickers (Ross, 2010). Even China, a country with very strict drug laws (including capital punishment for certain drug criminals) has needle-exchange programs for intravenous drug users and, in 2006, began opening methadone clinics for heroin addicts (Blickman & Jelsma, 2009), choosing not to impose criminal sanctions on drug users who are not involved in trafficking. (Reid, 2002)

Given the stringency of U.S. domestic drug policies, it is not surprising that U.S. officials have been critical of the softening of drug policies in other nations. In the National Drug Control Strategy of 2003 (ONDCP, 2003a), it was noted that "the United States is now watching closely as the debate in several European countries increasingly frames the drug issue as a public health rather than a law enforcement problem" (p. 40). Consistent with the distortion of science with respect to drugs that is characteristic of the ONDCP and the U.S. government more generally, the report further criticized these trends in suggesting "decriminalization policies are being promoted as precisely what they are not—a public health response to the drug problem. No policy can seriously be considered in the public good if it advances the contagion of drug use. Yet that is precisely the effect of harm-reduction actions such as marijuana decriminalization. As the drug becomes more available, acceptable, and cheap, it draws in greater numbers of vulnerable youth." (p. 40)

COUNTRIES WITH SEVERE DRUG POLICIES

Before examining the policies in other Western developed nations, it is useful to briefly discuss drug policies in countries that have legislation that is very severe in its treatment of drug users and traffickers, even in comparison to the United States.

Russia

Estimates of the number of drug addicts in Russia range between one and four million, and the country is reported to have a "serious and rapidly growing drug problem" (Glasser, 2004; see also Elovich & Drucker, 2008). In Russia, following the passage of legislation allowing for harsher penalties for drug possession and trafficking, the number of individuals imprisoned for drug offenses increased five-fold between 1997 and 2000 (Wolfe & Malinowska-Sempruch, 2004), and as of 2004, there were an estimated 200,000 to 300,000 individuals incarcerated for drug offenses in that country (The Drug Reform Coordination Network, 2004). More recent estimates suggest that Russia may have more intravenous drug users than any other nation, and there were an estimated 60,000 new HIV cases in 2009 (Schwirtz, 2011), yet opiate substitution therapy and needle exchange programs remain illegal in that country (Elovich & Drucker, 2008). In 2003, Russia created a drug enforcement agency with 40,000 members, four times larger than the United States Drug Enforcement Administration (Glasser, 2004). Under Russian law, possession of even one marijuana cigarette can result in a 3-year prison sentence (The Drug Reform Coordination Network, 2004), and in the oblast (province) of Ekaterinburg, the governor initiated a campaign to mandate the death penalty for drug users. In the same oblast, one of the drug treatment facilities engaged in the practice of stripping alleged drug dealers, jabbing them in the buttocks with syringes, and parading them through the streets for residents to spit on (Wolfe & Malinowska-Sempruch, 2004).

Asian and Middle Eastern Countries

Despite the widespread harm-minimization movement, a number of nations remain committed to prohibition and harsh punishment for the commission of drug offenses. The strictest policies are most commonly found in Middle Eastern and East Asian countries, and there are currently 32 nations that allow the death penalty for drug law violations (Gallahue, 2011).

China initiated a "people's war" against drugs in 1990, and thousands of Chinese attend trials of drug traffickers, which are held in stadiums and other public venues. These trials frequently include antidrug speeches by government officials, the burning of confiscated drugs, and the pronouncement of death sentences for drug traffickers. While execution figures are not released by the Chinese government, some estimates suggest that thousands of individuals are put to death annually for drug crimes (Dui Hua Foundation, 2010). And in 2011, more than 12,000 suspects were arrested for purchasing drugs through online chat rooms ("China Arrests," 2011).

Malaysia, a country that has the goal of being a "drug-free society" by 2015, also has very stringent drug policies. The Malaysian president has referred to drug users as "not human" and "already dead," and in that country, possession of any illegal drug, including cannabis, carries a minimum penalty of 5 years of imprisonment and whipping. Possession of 5 grams of heroin can result in a life sentence, and possession of more than 15 grams of the substance is defined as trafficking and results in a mandatory death sentence (Wolfe & Malinowska-Sempruch, 2004). These severe policies also apply to drugs that are legal in many countries—in 2009, a man who drank alcohol in public was sentenced to 1 year in prison and to be whipped six times. Earlier the same judge had sentenced a 32-year-old woman caught drinking beer in a nightclub to be caned (Zappei, 2009).

Similarly severe drug policies are found in Vietnam, where police are allowed to detain individuals who they find in possession of drugs and, without trial, commit these individuals to compulsory rehabilitation centers for up to 5 years. Over the

2007 to 2010 period, Vietnam sentenced more than 130 people to death for drug crimes (Gallahue, 2011), and most of the over 400 people executed in Singapore since 1991 have been drug offenders. In 2011, more than half of Indonesia's death row population consisted of drug offenders (mostly visiting foreigners; Gelling, 2008), and in that country a 27-year-old Australian woman who was apprehended for smuggling 9 pounds of marijuana into the country was sentenced to 20 years of imprisonment ("Monitoring Quotes," 2005).

Although it has recently allowed for methadone maintenance programs for addicts, drug policy in Iran is more generally quite draconian. In 2011, an estimated 488 people were executed for drug crimes in Iran (Amnesty International, 2011) and many of the 160 juveniles on death row in that country have been convicted of drug offenses (Gallahue, 2011). Similarly, Saudi Arabia put at least 64 people to death for the commission of drug crimes between 2007 and 2010 (Gallahue, 2011).

One positive change, however, has been a reduction in the number of nations permitting capital punishment for drug crimes during the last decade. Since 2000, the Philippines, Uzbekistan, Tajikistan, Jordan, and the Kyrgyz Republic have eliminated the death penalty as a possible penalty for drug crimes (Gallahue, 2011). A 2011 ruling by the Bombay High Court struck down mandatory drug-related death sentences in India, deeming these penalties to be unconstitutional (Barrett, 2011).

DRUG POLICIES IN WESTERN COUNTRIES

Australia

Australia's National Drug Strategy, initiated in 1985, had as its aim "to achieve a balance between demand-reduction and supply-reduction measures to minimize the harmful effects of drugs in Australian society" (Miller & Draper, 2001). Drug policies in Australia are thus generally informed by the principles of harm reduction and include the decriminalization of cannabis in some jurisdictions, the widespread use of methadone maintenance programs for heroin addicts, and safe injection sites.

In contrast to the United States, where the federal government is primarily responsible for creating drug legislation, one of the unique features of the Australian system is that state and territorial governments are responsible for setting drug policies (Bammer et al., 2002). In 1979, the South Australian Royal Commission into the Nonmedical Use of Drugs recommended that cannabis use not be treated as a criminal offense. Although it took several years before this recommendation was translated into law, under legislation subsequently introduced in the state of South Australia in 1987, police issue what is known as an "expiation notice" for possession of up to 100 grams of cannabis, possession of 20 grams of cannabis resin, possession of equipment used to consume cannabis products, or cultivation of up to three cannabis plants. If offenders pay the expiation fee (which ranges from $50 to $150 Australian) within 30 to 60 days, no criminal proceedings are initiated against them, and there is no official record of an offense (Fischer et al., 2003). Similar cannabis legislation also exists in the Australian Capital Territory (enacted in 1992) and the Northern Territory (enacted in 1997; Bammer et al., 2002).

Similar to the situation in the Netherlands (see below), studies indicate that the relaxed penalties for cannabis use and possession have not resulted in increases in use of the substance in South Australia (Bammer et al., 2003). The legislation did result in increases in the number of cannabis offenses recorded by police in South Australia, from approximately 6,000 in 1987 to 1988 to approximately 17,000 in 1994 (although the number of arrests had decreased to 2,518 in 2009–2010; Australian Crime Commission, 2010). Bammer and colleagues suggest that the increase was not due to changes in the prevalence of cannabis use but rather to the ease with which police can issue expiation notices to marijuana users. One negative outcome associated with South Australia's cannabis laws was an increase in the number of individuals incarcerated for possession of the substance, primarily due to the fact that some of those charged are unable to pay the fine (Larsen, 2002; MacCoun & Reuter, 2001) and are subsequently imprisoned.

In addition to its comparatively lenient policies on cannabis, the harm-reduction emphasis in Australian drug policy has resulted in an extensive network of needle exchange programs in that country. In 1994 to 1995, approximately 700 such programs distributed more than six million syringes in Australia, with an additional four million distributed through pharmacies (The Drug Reform Coordination Network, 2002). An evaluation of these programs conducted in 2004 found that needle and syringe exchange programs had been at least partially responsible for 25,000 fewer cases of HIV in Australia and had saved the country up to $7 billion (Ritter, Wodak, & Curtis, 2004). Some Australian jurisdictions, such as Sydney, have also established supervised heroin injection rooms that have proven to be successful as harm-reduction approaches (Nicholls, 2010). As a result of these and other policies, including methadone maintenance programs for heroin users, there is a comparatively low prevalence of HIV infection among intravenous drug users in Australia. More generally, it was estimated that every dollar invested in drug treatment returned savings of up to $12 and that [Australian drug policy's] "harm-reduction components, like the needle exchange and methadone maintenance programs, have saved lives, reduced crime, and decreased the social costs of drugs" (MacIntosh, 2006).

While Australia's drug policies are considerably more lenient than those of the United States, it is important to note that the country was one of the first (in 2004) to implement compulsory roadside blood tests for all drivers involved in fatal accidents (Nicholls, 2004). Interestingly, although two of the first three drivers who tested positive for drugs in roadside tests in the Australian jurisdiction of Victoria were later cleared after laboratory analysis of their samples, several Australian jurisdictions indicated they would continue with the roadside tests (Phillips, 2004). In addition, and similar to the United States, Canada, and Britain (see below), Australian law enforcement continues to focus on cannabis users, with 67% of drug-related arrests in 2009 to 2010 being for cannabis, and 86% of the cannabis arrests consisting of possession (referred to as "consumers") offenses (Australian Crime Commission, 2010).

In 2012, Australian Finance Minister Bob Carr and former Chief of the Australian federal police Mick Palmer issued a statement that police efforts in the war on drugs had "made only a marginal, if any difference" (as cited in Metherell, 2012) and called for a serious discussion of drug law reform in that country. In the same year, reflecting larger global movements with respect to drugs, a group known as Australia 21 issued a report titled *The Prohibition of Illicit Drugs Is Killing and Criminalizing Our Children* (Australia 21, 2012), which similarly called for drug law reform. Support for decriminalization of drugs in Australia was also supported by the former premier of Western Australia (Geoff Gallop), who commented "there are better ways of looking at it [the drug problem] and decriminalising use, I think, would be a very good step forward, and then properly regulating supplying and distribution with a view toward harm minimisation" (as quoted in Kwek, 2012).

Sweden

Drug policy in Sweden in the late 1960s was fairly liberal, reflecting a harm-reduction approach. Currently, however, Sweden is the European country that arguably comes closest to the United States in terms of the stringency of its policies on illegal drugs. Lenke and Olsson (2002) report that by the end of the 1970s, Sweden had moved from a treatment-based approach to drugs to a "police-oriented strategy whose objective was to clear the streets of drug pushers. These were to be placed in compulsory treatment to stop this 'contagious disease,' which is how drug use is portrayed to the public" (p. 69). Swedish drug policies became even more severe in 1992 with the election of a non–Social Democratic government, which, among other things, passed legislation allowing for the imposition of a maximum penalty of 6 months of imprisonment for drug users (including cannabis) convicted of what Swedish legislation refers to as "minor offenses" (Chatwin, 2003). However, under this legislation, the prison sentence can be suspended if the offender agrees to undergo treatment (Drug Prevention Network of the Americas, 2002). The new Swedish legislation also provided the police with increased powers to secure evidence in drug cases, including the ability to impose compulsory urine and blood tests on suspected drug users (Lenke & Olsson, 2002).

Germany

The attempt to eliminate both the supply and the consumption of drugs in our society has failed.... The demand for drugs has not decreased, the physical suffering and social misery of addicts is increasing, more and more addicts are affected by the HI-virus, more and more addicts die, illegal drug trafficking is expanding and making larger profits, the fear of city dwellers in the face of drug trafficking and criminality is rising. (Frankfurt Resolution, cited in Fischer, 1995, p. 396)

In general, drug laws in Germany are far less severe than in the United States, with harm reduction being one of the four "pillars" of the country's national drug strategy ("Country Profiles," 2004). The Frankfurt Resolution, signed by several European cities in 1990, forms the basis of current drug policy in Germany (see box). Provisions in Germany also allow local law enforcement and prosecutorial officials to exercise a considerable amount of discretion in enforcing laws and charging individuals with drug offenses. Prosecutors are given the option to decline prosecution of drug offenders if they believe that the individual's guilt is minor or if there is no compelling public interest in continuing the prosecution (Drug Policy Alliance, 2003f).

Although cannabis is technically an illegal substance in Germany, in 1994, the German Constitutional Court ruled that criminal sentences could not be imposed for possession of cannabis products for "occasional private use if there is no danger to third parties" (MacCoun & Reuter, 2001). With respect to harder drugs such as heroin and cocaine, Fischer (1995) reports that in the mid-1990s, police in the cities of Hamburg and Frankfurt essentially refrained from enforcing the laws against individuals possessing these substances in amounts not larger than for personal consumption. Although allowing considerable discretion for criminal justice system officials in enforcing and prosecuting drug offenses can result in less severe treatment of drug offenders, such discretion also leads to wide variation in the application of drug laws in Germany. For example, Bollinger (1997) found that individuals caught with 6 grams of marijuana in Bavaria would often receive a prison term, while the police in other areas of Germany will not arrest individuals who possess up to 30 grams of the substance. Similarly, German law enforcement definitions of "small amounts" of heroin range from 0.5 to 6.0 grams (The Drug Reform Coordination Network, 2002). Fischer (1995) more generally notes that in Germany, there is harsh criminalization of small amounts of illegal drugs in the southern states but a much higher tolerance by law enforcement officials in the northern states (see also Chatwin, 2003).

Germany also has extensive needle exchange programs for intravenous drug users; sterile syringes can be purchased for a relatively low price in pharmacies, and if drug users do not have the money to purchase these, the pharmacy is obliged to provide them with free syringes. In addition, some German cities have mobile needle exchange programs for intravenous drug users (The Drug Reform Coordination Network, 2002). Germany has also implemented methadone maintenance programs for drug users (Fischer, 1995), and in Frankfurt, approximately 600 clients are allowed to inject their own street-purchased heroin or cocaine in safe injection rooms (Frank, 2002). A study of the effectiveness of this program found that drug overdoses in Frankfurt decreased from 147 in 1991 to 26 in 1997, at least partially due to the existence of these safe injection sites (D. Brown, 2003). More recent data from Germany indicate that there were 986 drug-related deaths in 2011, a 20% decline from 2010 and the lowest total since 1988 (Fuchs, 2012).

Portugal

While it is commonly believed that the Netherlands has the most liberal drug laws of any Western industrialized nation, Portugal's drug laws are even more lenient.

496 Drugs and Drugs Policy

Prior to July 2001, drug use and/or possession was treated as a criminal offense with penalties of up to 3 months of imprisonment or a fine (EMCDDA, 2009). In 1999, Portugal had the highest rate of drug-related deaths in the European Union, and approximately 100,000 people (nearly 1% of the population) were heroin addicts (Specter, 2011). However, in 2001, Portugal became the first European country to officially remove all criminal penalties for possession of drugs, including marijuana, cocaine, heroin, and methamphetamine. Under the 2001 legislation, the use and possession of drugs do not constitute criminal offenses, but instead are treated as "administrative offenses" (van het Loo, van Beusekom, & Kahan, 2002). In Portugal, individuals found guilty of possessing small quantities of drugs and who the police believe are not involved in more serious offenses such as trafficking appear before a panel consisting of a doctor, social worker, and lawyer. While these commissions can impose sanctions on users, the main objective is to "explore the need for treatment and to promote healthy recovery" ("Country Profiles," 2004). Van het Loo and colleagues (2002) note,

> [The Portuguese] generally do not believe that decriminalization will result in an increase in the total number of drug users [and] there is consensus that decriminalization, by destigmatizing drug use, will bring a higher proportion of users into treatment. (p. 69)

Treatment and prevention methods became the priorities of drug policy in Portugal, expanding and incorporating evidence-based practices. In addition, safe injection facilities and needle exchanges were established in many problem areas, methadone substitution therapy became the norm for those with opiate addiction, doctors and pharmacies began providing safe access to methadone and heroin maintenance doses, and healthcare professionals were employed to make regular visits to disenfranchised areas where drug use was common.

Evaluations of the Portuguese approach have generally been positive, indicating that the country has experienced reductions in drug use (problematic and otherwise), crime, and drug-related deaths. For example, in 2001, Portugal experienced close to 400 drug-related deaths, the majority of these from opiate overdoses (Hughes & Stevens, 2012). However, in 2009, there were only 54 drug-related deaths in the country (EMCDDA, 2011). In addition, the rate of hepatitis C among intravenous drug users was 29% in 2009, among the lowest rates in all of Europe (UNODC, 2011), the number of new HIV cases dropped from nearly 1,400 in 2000 to fewer than 400 in 2006 (Greenwald, 2009), and the number of people seeking drug treatment more than doubled (Szalavitz, 2009).

Perhaps most importantly, several studies of the Portuguese approach have found that, despite predictions to the contrary, drug use actually decreased, particularly among young people (Greenwald, 2009; Hughes & Stevens, 2012). Only 16% of Portuguese students reported lifetime use of marijuana in a 2007 survey (ESPAD, 2011), and lifetime use of heroin declined from 2.6% to 1.8% between 2001 and 2006 (Hughes & Stevens, 2012). Perhaps somewhat surprisingly, given its generally conservative nature, the UNODC (2009) commended the "Portuguese experiment."

Spain

Among European countries, Spain was originally quite slow to move toward a harm-minimization drug control strategy, largely due to the influence of the Catholic Church. However, with increasing rates of HIV/AIDS transmission among intravenous drug users in the country in the early 1990s, Spain altered its approach and now has some of the most progressive drug policies among European countries. Spain has maintained a decriminalization policy toward possession of all illicit drugs since 1992, with citations for such offenses resulting in fines and administrative references for counseling and treatment. Opiate substitution therapy has become highly accessible in Spain, with thousands of pharmacies providing needles, methadone, and even heroin to chronic users in an effort to monitor safety and minimize associated crime (UNAIDS, 2008). Spain has also become a leader in implementation of safe injection facilities, and also offers such facilities and methadone therapy at every prison (Marlatt & Witkiewitz, 2010).

As a result of these harm-minimization measures, the drug-related mortality and HIV transmission rates have declined considerably in Spain since 2000, and the country is among the leaders in providing HIV-positive intravenous drug users with access to health care (UNAIDS, 2008). While Spain's drug use rates are not low, they have also not increased substantially during the decriminalization era, and the rate of drug-induced deaths declined after the implementation of these approaches before leveling off in recent years (UNODCP, 2011).

In 2010, Spain's former Prime Minister, Felipe Gonzalez, came out in support of drug legalization, as did former Czarina Araceli Manjon-Cabez, when she referred to drug prohibition as "insanity" and a "savage and inefficient instrument that is not the 'solution' but instead a big part of the problem" (as quoted in Hidalgo, 2010). In accordance with this view, Spain has also recently relaxed restrictions on marijuana in order to avoid wasting resources on what they believe to be a relatively innocuous substance. For instance, in early 2012, the Basque region passed legislation completely legalizing marijuana, entirely removing criminal penalties for consumption or cultivation of up to four marijuana plants. While penalties for public consumption of marijuana have been retained, Basque officials have asserted that prohibition only leads to "clandestine action, delinquency, and the black market" (as quoted in Elliott, 2011).

The Netherlands

There is no drug war in the Netherlands. What's the point of making war on a part of your own country? Drugs are here and they're always going to be. This is a social problem, not a criminal one, and the whole of society has to tackle it—not leave it to the police on their own. (Machel Vewer, Senior Police Detective, as quoted in Rose, 2002)

Consistent with policies that are applied to the regulation of a whole range of social issues—including homosexuality, abortion, euthanasia, and the age of sexual consent—the Netherlands has among the most progressive drug policies of any country in the world (Baker, 2002). The Dutch legislation is based on the principle of the separation of markets for soft (cannabis) and hard (heroin, cocaine, etc.) drugs in order to prevent users from entering the criminal underworld (EMCDDA, 2009).

While the Netherlands enacted laws criminalizing the possession of opium and cocaine in 1928 in order to comply with the requirements of the Geneva Convention on Drugs, law enforcement officials in the country generally did not focus on users of these substances and even tolerated small-scale drug dealing (Davenport-Hines, 2001). In 1976, the Dutch adopted a policy of nonenforcement for violations involving the possession of marijuana, but it is important to note that technically, individuals in the Netherlands can still be sent to jail for as long as 1 month for marijuana possession[1] (Smith, 2002). However, under Dutch law, individuals are allowed to buy and sell amounts of marijuana for personal use, and the cultivation of up to five plants per person for personal use is also tolerated (Blickman & Jelsma, 2009). Thus, as MacCoun and Reuter (2001) note, while Dutch policy toward marijuana has been referred to as legalization, it is more appropriate to call it de facto legalization.

As of the early 2000s, estimates suggested that there were between 1,200 and 1,500 coffee shops (about 1 per 1,200 inhabitants) in the Netherlands that sold cannabis products. Most of these establishments offer a variety of marijuana and hashish with varying potency levels, and the typical coffee shop menu lists from 5 to 20 different varieties of cannabis, as well as coffees, teas, and baked goods that contain the substance (T. R. Reid, 2002). Contrary to the view promoted by American drug enforcement officials, coffee houses selling marijuana in the Netherlands are tightly controlled. Consumers can purchase cannabis in these coffee shops, provided that these establishments meet the following criteria: (1) no overt advertising of cannabis products; (2) no sales or consumption of hard drugs (such as heroin or cocaine); (3) no nuisance or disturbance; (4) no customers under the age of 18; (5) each customer can purchase only up to 5 grams of cannabis per day (Chatwin, 2003). There is something of a paradox in the Dutch policy of de facto legalization of marijuana, however. Although the coffee shops themselves are legal, they are reliant on an illegal market to supply them with cannabis.

Despite the open sale and easy access to cannabis, the rates of consumption of the drug in the Netherlands are comparable to those of adjacent countries such as Belgium and Germany and are considerably lower than in Britain, France, and Spain (Blickman & Jelsma, 2009). It is important to note, however, that despite perceptions that they are ubiquitous in the Netherlands, the number of coffee shops selling cannabis has steadily declined from a peak of approximately 1,500 in the mid-1990s to 702 in 2007 (Blickman & Jelsma, 2009). And in December 2008 (and despite the fact that 80% of Dutch citizens were opposed; Treble, 2008), Dutch officials announced that at least one-fifth of the remaining marijuana cafes in the country would be

---

[1]In response to domestic and international pressure (much of the latter from the United States), the 30-gram threshold was lowered to 5 grams in 1995 (MacCoun & Reuter, 2001).

forced to close. The legislation forced the coffee shops to become members-only clubs and to close those that were located near schools (Pignal, 2010).

While certainly known for their liberal policies on marijuana, the Dutch have also adopted harm-reduction approaches for other substances. They have offered support and assistance to heroin users in the country, with the result that the average age of heroin users increased from approximately 25 in the late 1970s to 36 in the late 1990s (Gray, 1999). Over the same period, the average age of heroin users in the United States declined from 25 to 19 (Gray, 1999). The Dutch have also taken steps to reduce the harms associated with ecstasy use. Although the substance is illegal and is classified as a hard drug, ecstasy users can take their pills to drug treatment centers to have the chemical contents analyzed (Richburg, 2001). This program provides users with information regarding the effects they can expect from consuming the substance and has the additional benefit of providing public health officials with current information on what types of ecstasy are on the market and a profile of users (Cumming, 2004).

Britain

Britain has the highest rate of dependent drug use and among the highest rates of recreational drug use in Europe (Reuter & Stevens, 2007) and has among the most stringent drug policies of any European country. At the same time, the country has a long history of harm-reduction policies. In 1924, the Rolleston Committee recommended that doctors be allowed to prescribe heroin and morphine to opiate addicts (Brecher, 1972), emphasizing the belief that prevention and control of addiction should primarily be the responsibility of the medical profession (Davenport-Hines, 2001) as opposed to the criminal justice system. However, when U.S. officials viewed the success of British heroin maintenance programs as a threat to U.S. policies, the programs were criticized by American officials and severely curtailed when Britain passed its Misuse of Drugs Act in 1971. Among other things, American officials claimed that British reports on the number of heroin addicts were false and that there was still a significant black market for heroin in Britain. They also argued that even if the British heroin maintenance system was successful, it was only because Britain was an island nation, or because the British were more likely to be law-abiding citizens than Americans (Brecher, 1972).

An important difference between drug policies in the United States and Britain is related to drug scheduling. In the United States, drug scheduling is based on the assumption that drugs that are available for physicians to prescribe (such as morphine, amphetamines, and cocaine) should have less severe penalties attached to them than substances that are believed to have no medical uses (Walton, 2002). In contrast, the British system of drug scheduling ranks substances according to their level of toxicity, regardless of their medical uses. Thus under the current British Misuse of Drugs Act, Class A drugs (LSD, ecstasy, heroin, methadone, cocaine, psilocybin mushrooms, methylamphetamine, and amphetamines for injection) have the most severe penalties attached to them (maximum 7 years of imprisonment for possession and maximum life imprisonment for supplying/trafficking); Class B drugs (amphetamines, barbiturates, codeine, and cannabis, which was recently reclassified from Class C, see below) can result in a maximum 5 years imprisonment for possession and 14 years for trafficking; while Class C drugs (benzodiazepines, less potent stimulant drugs, and analgesics) are subject to a maximum of 2 years imprisonment for possession and 14 years for trafficking.

Similar to the situation in the United States (see Chapter 11), Australia, and Canada (see below), the pursuit of cannabis users occupied a considerable amount of police officers' time in Britain in the 1990s: The number of arrests involving cannabis increased from 40,194 in 1990 to 86,034 in 1997 ("Reclassifying Cannabis," 2001). More recently, it was estimated that approximately 160,000 individuals in England and Wales are issued cannabis "warnings" in any given year (UK Drug Policy Commission, 2012). In partial recognition of the fact that law enforcement resources should be devoted to more serious offenses, in 2002, cannabis was downgraded from a Class B to a Class C drug in Britain, resulting in a significant reduction in the penalties associated with possession of the drug, from a maximum of 5 years of imprisonment to 2 years of imprisonment.

> It does great damage to the credibility of messages we give to young people about the dangers of drug misuse if we try to pretend that cannabis is as harmful as drugs such as heroin and cocaine. It quite clearly is not, and if we do not acknowledge that by ensuring our drug laws accurately reflect the relative harms of drugs, young people will not listen to our messages about the drugs which do the greatest harm. (British Parliamentary Undersecretary of State, as quoted in Drug Policy Alliance, 2003m)

The formal change in British cannabis legislation was preceded by a policy of de facto decriminalization of marijuana in the South London neighborhood of Lambeth: In 2001, the local police commissioner adopted a policy whereby officers would not arrest marijuana smokers. Under this policy, officers gave marijuana smokers written warnings and required them to sign a receipt for the marijuana seized. If the individual refused to accept the warning and sign for the seized marijuana, he or she would be arrested (The Drug Reform Coordination Network, 2001). An assessment of this program found that during the first 6 months of its operation, police officers issued 450 warnings for cannabis possession, which freed up at least 1,350 hours of police officers' time that otherwise would have been spent on custody procedures and interviewing suspects (Consultancy Group, 2002). The policy also "removed a major source of friction between the police and the community" (T. Reid, 2002), and it was claimed that the number of robberies in the community declined by almost 50% after its implementation (Roberts & Fisher, 2002). However, reviews of the outcomes associated with this policy were not universally positive. Some police officers in Lambeth claimed that drug dealers were selling crack and other drugs in the area and that children as young as 10 years old were using marijuana (Thompson, 2002).

Based on concerns that cannabis use was linked to mental health problems, there were calls in late 2005 and early 2006 to restore the substance to its previous Class B status under the British drug schedule. The British Advisory Committee on the Misuse of Drugs concluded that such a change was not justified, given that "The current evidence suggests, at worst, that using cannabis increases the lifetime risk of developing schizophrenia by one percent" (cited in Travis, 2006) and also noted that despite the relaxed penalties for cannabis possession, use of the substance among 16- to 24-year olds in Britain had declined from 28% in 1998 to 24% in 2005. Despite the recommendations of the Advisory Committee, in 2008, marijuana was returned to Class B status, apparently due to the previous concerns regarding the mental health effects on users, and also due to related concerns regarding the impact of stronger marijuana (known in Britain as "skunk") (Allenye, 2009).

Despite the relative severity of British drug policies, there have been several recent calls for change. A report on Britain's drug laws by the House of Commons Home Affairs Committee, published in 2002, suggested that, for most young people, drug use was a "passing phase" that "rarely results in long term harm," and recommended that only drug traffickers, as opposed to users, should be subject to criminal punishment (Travis, 2002). Similarly, an editorial in the London *Guardian*, written by Britain's former deputy drug czar, noted that globally, there are at least 200 million users of prohibited drugs and that the illegal market for drugs generates more than $300 billion for organized crime groups—"evidence of the failure of drug policy is overwhelming" (Trace, 2009). Richard Brunstom, Chief Constable of North Wales, argued in a report published in 2007 that all drugs should be legalized:

> If policy on drugs in the future is to be pragmatic and not moralistic, driven by ethics not dogma, then the current prohibitionist stance will have to be swept away as both unworkable and immoral, to be replaced with an evidence-based unified system, aimed at minimization of harms to society. (as quoted in Brown & Langton, 2007)

Further evidence of pressures to reform Britain's stringent drug policies was provided in a 2009 report by the Transform Drug Policy Foundation. This report noted that there were numerous harms associated with drug prohibition, including the destabilization of drug-producing and transit countries, an increase in organized crime and large volumes of low-level acquisitive property crime, the use of dirty needles by drug addicts that leads to increases in HIV infection, and the existence of contaminated drug products of unknown strength and purity being consumed by drug users (Transform Drug Policy Foundation, 2009). The report concluded, "despite the billions spent each year on proactive and reactive drug law enforcement, the punitive prohibitionist approach has consistently delivered the opposite of its stated goals" (p. 3). Even the conservative British *Economist* magazine concluded, "Prohibition [of drugs] has failed; legalization is the best solution" ("How to Stop," 2009).

More recently, the United Kingdom Drug Policy Commission (an independent charity; 2012) produced a report emphasizing that drug problems need to be addressed within their wider social and economic contexts and that most drug users do not experience significant problems. The report recommended that drug policy be considered in terms of two higher-level challenges: (1) a consideration of how "society can enable and support individuals to behave responsibly, tackling the underlying causes of drug use"; and (2) focusing on "how society and government can enable and promote recovery from entrenched drug problems" (p. 11).

Although the previous section thus provides evidence that there is an active and ongoing discussion in Britain regarding a softening of drug laws, it is important to emphasize that the country's current drug policies are similar to those of the United States in a number of ways.

One such similarity is the tendency in both countries to attribute drug problems to minority groups. For example, in an article discussing "drug gangs" in Britain, a police official asserted "The Jamaican [criminals] are entrepreneurs. They will go anywhere there is a ready market. Then there is the potential for conflict and shootings. The threat is we are going to see it all over the place. It is spreading" (as quoted in Hopkins, 2003). The article further noted that a specific police operation focusing on cocaine trafficking had identified more than 500 criminals, 40% of whom were alleged to be Jamaicans. "The rest . . . are British-born criminals, most of whom are black" (Hopkins, 2003). Similarly, in describing the ecstasy market in Britain, Goodchild and Johnson (2004) note, "[the] increase in competition means that [dealers] have been overtaken or replaced by a multitude of traffickers, including Kurds and Albanians."

Britain is also one of the few countries that maintains asset forfeiture laws similar to those of the United States. Under the 1995 British Drug Trafficking Act, it is assumed that all assets, including any owned in the previous 6 years by an individual convicted of a drug trafficking offense, are related to the individual's drug trafficking activity. Unless the offender can prove that such assets were not the result of drug trafficking activity, the court may seize the assets (Drug Prevention Network of the Americas, 2002). Legislation passed in 2004 in Britain even allows police to drug test individuals arrested for minor crimes and to prosecute users for possession even if the only illegal drugs are found in the bloodstream (McSmith & Elliott, 2004). This legislation also allows police to x-ray suspects who are believed to have swallowed illegal drugs in order to evade detection by police, and judges can remand such individuals into police custody for up to 8 days (Blackman, 2004).

An additional similarity between the United States and Britain concerns policies related to ecstasy. In an attempt to punish ecstasy users, who typically consume the substance at raves, Britain's Criminal Justice and Public Order Act of 1994 defined a rave as 100 people playing amplified music "characterized by the emission of a succession of repetitive beats" (Davenport-Hines, 2001). The legislation allowed any law enforcement officer who "reasonably believed" that people were assembling for a rave to order them to disperse. Individuals who refused to comply with such an order could be subject to 3 months of imprisonment and/or a fine of up to $2,500 pounds (Davenport-Hines, 2001). And similar to the U.S. RAVE Act, in 1997, Britain passed the Public Entertainments (Drug Misuse) Act. This legislation allows licensing authorities to revoke the licenses of clubs and other entertainment venues that fail to prevent drug use on their premises (Davenport-Hines, 2001).

In summary, while Britain's drug policies are generally less severe than those of the United States, it is apparent that of all European countries, Britain's policies come closest to those of the United States. Former Home Secretary David Blunkett (2004) summed up the British philosophy and approach to drugs, stating,

> Drugs are one of the scourges of our world. To tackle them we need tough enforcement by the police and effective treatment to get the criminals away from their addictions. . . . But I'm not soft on drugs. We'll help those who want help, both for their sake and that of their families and the communities they destroy, but we must come down like a ton of bricks on those who refuse help or peddle drugs.

Canada

Similar to the United States, Canada has a long history of stringent drug policies with a criminal justice system focus. In fact, Canada's first drug legislation, the Opium and Narcotic Drug Act, was passed in 1908, predating the U.S. Harrision Narcotics Act by 6 years (Mosher, 1999). Similarly, although federal legislation addressing marijuana was not passed in the United States until 1937, Canada added cannabis to its Narcotic Control Act in 1923.

Canada's 1961 revised Narcotic Control Act allowed for a maximum of 7 years of imprisonment for possession of certain drugs, including marijuana, and life imprisonment for most trafficking offenses (Fischer et al., 2003). While recommendations to decriminalize marijuana were made by the LeDain Commission in 1973 (Government of Canada, 1973), the Canadian laws addressing marijuana remained substantially unchanged until 1996. Under the Controlled Drugs and Substances Act passed in that year, individuals found in possession of 30 grams of marijuana or 1 gram of hashish or less were subject to maximum penalties of a $1,000 fine and 6 months of imprisonment for first offenses, with double these penalties for repeat offenders (Fischer et al., 2003).

In 2007, there were more than 100,000 "drug incidents" reported by police in Canada, translating to a rate of 305 per 100,000 population, the highest rate in Canada in 30 years (Dauvergne, 2009). Earlier (in 2003), the rate of drug offenses in Canada declined by 7%, largely due to reductions in the number of arrests for cannabis possession offenses. At that time, legislation to decriminalize possession of small amounts of marijuana was introduced in the House of Commons and the constitutionality of marijuana laws was challenged in a number of court decisions. While the proposed decriminalization legislation did not pass, Dauvergne (2009) suggests that the decrease in marijuana arrests may have been related to the lack of clarity surrounding the legal status of cannabis at that time.

Similar to the situation in the United States, Australia, and Britain, the majority (62%) of drug arrests in Canada involve cannabis, and of those, three quarters were for possession offenses (Dauvergne, 2009). In fact, the per-capita arrest rate for marijuana offenses in Canada is actually higher than in the United States (Fischer et al., 2003). In addition, offenses related to the production/growing of cannabis were eight times higher in 2007 compared to 30 years earlier (Dauvergne, 2009). The second-largest category of drug offenses in Canada involves cocaine, at approximately 25% of all police-reported drug incidents, with roughly half of those cases involving possession and the rest trafficking.

A key difference between Canada and the United States in responding to drug offenses is manifested in sentencing practices. While, as noted in Chapter 11, sentences for drug offenses in the United States are quite severe, in Canada in 2007, 43% of all drug-related adult court cases and 51% of all drug-related juvenile cases were stayed, withdrawn, or dismissed (Dauvergne, 2009). Fifty-five percent of adult cases and 48% of youth cases resulted in a finding of guilt—44% of adults convicted of drug offenses received fines, while 28% received sentences of probation. Also for adults, just over half of those convicted of drug trafficking were sentenced to jail/prison, with an average sentence of 278 days. For adults convicted of possession, 16% were sentenced to prison/jail, with an average length of 19 days (Dauvergne, 2009). Clearly, at the level of sentencing, the United States is much more severe in its response to drug offenders.

Something of a moral panic emerged in the early 2000s over what is reported to be a massive problem with marijuana growing operations in Canada. Law enforcement officials in the country seized an average of 1.4 million marijuana plants annually from 1999 to 2002, representing a six-fold increase from 1993. Based on the size of these seizures and the average yield of marijuana plants, a Royal Canadian Mounted Police (RCMP) report estimated that annual marijuana production in Canada was approximately 800 tons (Humphreys & Bell, 2003). In 2007, it was estimated that the value of marijuana production in the province of British Columbia alone was $7 billion, and *Forbes* magazine referred to marijuana as "Canada's most valuable agricultural product" (as quoted in Sabbag, 2005). Violent crime and murder are attributed to these marijuana-growing operations, and similar to the United States, where trafficking in drugs has been attributed to minority groups (see Chapters 1 and 11), a RCMP report noted,

> Outlaw motorcycle gangs used to enjoy a virtual monopoly over marijuana growing operations, but now they have to contend with an increasing Asian organized crime presence in some parts of the country. . . . It is now a particular favorite of Vietnamese gangs. (Humphreys & Bell, 2003)

Echoing a similar theme, one newspaper reporter noted, "Vietnamese organized crime gangs began muscling in on Vancouver's marijuana networks in the mid-1990s, after realizing the huge potential of hydroponic production. The gangs recruit recently immigrated families from Vietnam to live in rented houses and tend the marijuana" (Howard, 2000).

A Move Toward Harm-Reduction Drug Policies in Canada

In the early 2000s, there were indications that Canada was moving toward drug policies based on harm-reduction principles. In 2002, for example, a special committee of the Canadian Senate recommended the legalization of cannabis possession and use (Government of Canada, 2002). Under the model proposed by the Senate committee, cannabis would have been treated similarly to alcohol, with use and access to supply regulated and only specific situations of harm—for example, driving under the influence of marijuana—being subject to criminal penalties. The Senate committee also recommended expunging the criminal records for the roughly 600,000 (at that time) Canadians previously convicted of marijuana possession.

While not accepting the Senate committee's recommendation to legalize marijuana, the Canadian federal government proposed legislation in 2003 that mandated a maximum $400 fine for adults and $250 for individuals under the age of 18 for possession of 15 grams or less of marijuana (Russo, 2004). In reference to the proposed changes in cannabis laws, then Prime Minister Jean Chretien told a reporter from the *Winnipeg Free Press*, "I don't know what is [sic] marijuana. Perhaps I will try it when it will no longer be criminal. I will have my money in one hand and a joint in the other hand" (as quoted in Drug Policy Alliance, 2003b). Although the proposed law was not passed before Chretien resigned from the leadership of the Liberal Party, incoming Prime Minister Paul Martin indicated his intention to change the marijuana laws when he commented that it achieves "absolutely nothing to give a criminal record to young people caught with small amounts [of marijuana]" (as quoted in J. Brown, 2003). Dana Hanson, president of the Canadian Medical Association, similarly agreed that individuals caught with marijuana should not be subject to sentences of incarceration or criminal records (Smith, 2002). And in a case that overturned a lower-court conviction for a marijuana-growing operation, British Columbia Court of Appeal Justice Mary Southin commented, "In my years on the bench, I have sat on over 40 cases which had something to do with this substance [marijuana] which appears to be of no greater danger to society than alcohol." She further noted that marijuana laws made "criminals of those who are no better or worse, morally or physically, than people who like a martini" (as quoted in Hall, 2003). Even the conservative *National Post* newspaper recommended the "full legalization" of marijuana in Canada:

> It makes little sense to criminalize otherwise law-abiding Canadians simply because they indulge in a substance that is less dangerous or addictive than either alcohol or tobacco. The idea that smoking marijuana should be the subject of social opprobrium has become a joke. ("Ending Reefer Madness," 2004)

Also in the mid-2000s, a report published by the conservative Fraser Institute (Easton, 2004) examining marijuana-growing operations in British Columbia recommended the legalization of marijuana. Going further, a report by the British Columbia Progress Board, examining crime and the operations of the criminal justice system in British Columbia, recommended that the province "Lobby the federal government to legalize the drug trade, perhaps limiting access to the products to adults in the same way that tobacco and alcohol is limited, and in the same vein, treating drug addictions as health rather than criminal justice problems" (Gordon & Kinney, 2006).

With respect to the related issue of medical marijuana, regulations that came into effect in Canada in 2001 allowed certain individuals with chronic or terminal illnesses to apply for federal government permission to use the substance. Included in the list of those allowed to apply for medical marijuana permits were people who were determined by medical authorities to have less than 1 year to live and those suffering from AIDS, cancer, multiple sclerosis, spinal cord injuries, and severe arthritis or epilepsy, among other conditions (Kennedy, 2002). In addition, in March 2002, the Canadian government announced plans to make government-certified medical marijuana available in pharmacies ("Canada Plans," 2004), making Canada only the second country in the world (after the Netherlands) to enact such legislation. Canada also followed a number of European countries in the late 1990s in legalizing hemp production, allowing approximately 250 farmers to grow close to 6,000 acres of the substance. Despite the fact that hemp has a very low THC content and, as an agricultural economist from North Dakota commented, "you'd croak from inhalation before you'd get high on hemp" (as quoted in Cauchon, 1998), then U.S. drug czar Barry McCaffrey asserted that the move to grow hemp in Canada was a "subterfuge" for attempts to legalize marijuana.

There were also indications in the early 2000s that in some jurisdictions, at least, marijuana had been de facto decriminalized in Canada. For example, between 2002 and 2005, the city of Vancouver was home to three marijuana cafes, including establishments named Blount Brothers and New Amsterdam (Mackie, 2003), both of which were located in the downtown core of the city. Although the proprietors of these establishments claimed that they only sold marijuana seeds (as opposed to prepared marijuana), the Da Kine Smoke and Beverage Shop apparently was filling gram bags of marijuana from "football-sized bags of marijuana" and doing "about $30,000 [in marijuana sales] a day" (Hainsworth, 2004). And in 2004, Vancouver achieved what some might see as a dubious distinction when it was chosen by *High Times* magazine as the best place in the world for marijuana smokers to visit, surpassing even Amsterdam (Matas, 2002a). Similarly, in the city of Winnipeg, Manitoba, a "cannabis church café" was opened in 2002 in one of the busiest sections of the city. The purpose of this establishment was to "worship" cannabis—individuals who frequented it would be allowed to smoke marijuana as a religious sacrament (Foss, 2002a). And, as a result of Canada's comparative tolerance of marijuana, the country also attracted a number of "pot refugees" from the United States—by some counts, there were more than 100 expatriate U.S. citizens who sought asylum in Canada from their own country's war on drugs (Campbell, 2002).

Although perhaps overstated, the *New York Times* noted, "pot smoking is pervasive in Canada, especially in British Columbia.... Marijuana is so prevalent in Vancouver that the city has been compared to Amsterdam as a pot smoker's paradise." ("There's a Funny Smell," 2002)

In addition to the developments with marijuana, some Canadian jurisdictions have adopted harm-reduction policies in order to address problems related to intravenous drug use. In the early 2000s, the city of Vancouver had an estimated 12,000 intravenous drug users in a population of 1.3 million, and more than 4,500 of these lived in a 12-block section of the city known as the Downtown Eastside. This area had a drug overdose rate that was five times higher than any other Canadian city and the highest HIV infection rate of any jurisdiction in the Western world. More than 1,000 drug users died in this area over the course of a decade, with 416 overdose deaths in 1998 alone (Glionna, 2003). In response to this situation, beginning with Mayor Philip Owen in the 1990s and continuing with Mayor Larry Campbell, a former Royal Canadian Mounted Police drug squad officer, Vancouver implemented a "four pillars" approach to drug issues—focusing on treatment, prevention, enforcement, and harm reduction—and established a safe injection facility (known as Insite) for intravenous drug users (Mulgrew, 2007).

An evaluation of this facility's first year of operation found that there were approximately 600 visits a day, and although there were more than 1,000 overdose cases, none were fatal. This study found that the site led to reductions in the number of people injecting drugs in public in the downtown eastside of Vancouver, as well as fewer discarded syringes and less injection-related litter in the area (British Columbia Center for Excellence in HIV/AIDS, 2004; see also Wood et al., 2007). Participation in Vancouver's safe injection facility was also associated with a 30% increase of entry into drug detoxification programs (Strathdee & Pollini, 2007), and a study published in the *Canadian Medical Association Journal* (Bayoumi & Zaric, 2008) estimated that Insite would save the province of British Columbia $14 million and prevent 1,000 HIV infections over a 10-year period. Several other more recent evaluations of Insite have reported similarly positive results (Beyrer, 2011; Marshall et al., 2011; Pinkerton, 2010).

In addition to the Vancouver safe injection site, a special Canadian House of Commons committee on drug issues supported the creation of federally approved safe injection sites for hardcore users of heroin or cocaine, the expansion of methadone maintenance programs, and needle exchange programs (MacCharles, 2002). In response to the recommendations of this House of Commons report, Canada initiated a heroin maintenance study in 2003, the first to be implemented in North America. Under this program (known as SALOME—Study to Assess Longer-Term Opioid Medication Effectiveness), which was launched in the major metropolitan cities of Vancouver, Toronto, and Montreal, 80 heroin addicts in each city received free heroin and were able to inject the drug up to three times per day at a treatment center. Addicts also received counseling at the end of the first year and were to be weaned off heroin or offered methadone withdrawal and counseling for an additional year (E. Carey, 2003). Evaluations of this program found that addicts who participated experienced improved physical and mental health and committed fewer crimes ("New Heroin Maintenance Program," 2009). In another example of harm-reduction policies in Canada, in 2011, the city of Vancouver began distributing pipes to crack cocaine smokers (the Canadian cities of Calgary and Winnipeg also distribute crack pipes) with the goal of reducing the transmission of diseases such as hepatitis C and HIV (Sinoski, 2011).

While the policies described above thus signal a move toward harm-reduction policies, it is important to note that there was by no means a consensus in Canada with respect to these policies. The head of the Canadian Police Association referred to the Canadian Senate Committee's report recommending the legalization of marijuana as a "back to school gift for drug pushers" (as quoted in Lunman, 2002), and the Canadian Council of Chief Executives, representing 150 multinational companies, expressed concern that marijuana decriminalization would increase on-the-job injuries, absenteeism, and lead to poor job performance (Fife, 2004). Similarly, Randy White, a member of the (now defunct) right-wing Canadian Alliance Party, who served on the House of Commons committee on drug issues, referred to that committee's harm-reduction proposals as "harm extension" (MacCharles, 2002). More specifically, White, who was part of the committee that visited drug injection facilities in European cities, commented, "There was no checking of the quality of the drugs used. Surrounding the facilities, I saw human carnage for blocks, as well as a substantial gathering of addicts and pushers in areas where trafficking and using were reluctantly permitted" (as quoted in Benzie & Hume, 2002).

United States' Reaction to Canadian Drug Policy Developments

While internal dissent over Canada's recent drug policies is to be expected, an arguably more concerning development has been evidenced in numerous commentaries by U.S. government officials regarding these polices. Historically speaking, Canada and the United States have agreed more than they have disagreed on drug-related policies—as Giffin and colleagues (1991, as cited in Thomas, 2003) comment, "Close cooperation between Canada and the United States on drug control is necessitated to some degree by their long border, but there is also evidence that their relationship on this issue is as much on political objectives as on financial necessity."

But in recent years, there have been direct attempts on the part of U.S. officials to influence Canadian drug policies. Of particular concern on the part of these U.S. officials has been the alleged increased exports of Canadian marijuana, including BC Bud, Quebec Gold, and Winnipeg Wheelchair (the latter so-named because of its reported debilitating effects on users) to the United States. Referring to the (unsubstantiated) U.S. Drug Enforcement Administration's estimates indicating that BC Bud had 25% THC content, drug czar Walters asserted, "Canada is exporting to us the crack of marijuana" (as quoted in Bergman et al., 2004). In an interview on the *Canada AM* morning news program, Walters reiterated many of the myths (see Zimmer & Morgan, 1997) in criticizing Canada's marijuana policies:

> There is no question that marijuana is a dependency-producing substance today. Some people seem to be living with the view of the reefer madness '70s. The issue of the U.S. is that Canada has become a major supplier of certain drugs. We're worried about the common health of our citizens. . . . We have major supply coming in from Canada that's growing and we need to get on top of it. (as quoted in Lunman & McCarthy, 2002)

Similarly, in a visit to Vancouver, Walters claimed that marijuana posed a greater danger to the United States than heroin, cocaine, or amphetamines, and argued that allowing the use of marijuana for medical purposes was not supported by science (Matas, 2002b). He also asserted, "We know that marijuana is a harmful drug, particularly for young people. We also know that if you make more available, you'll get more use. More use leads to more addictions and more problems" (as quoted in D. Brown, 2003). In reference to the proposals to reduce penalties for marijuana possession, Walters claimed (without providing any support evidence), "No country anywhere in the world has reduced drug penalties without getting more drug addictions and trafficking and the consequences of all that" (as quoted in Kraus, 2003). Going further, although he had earlier emphasized that "Canada is a sovereign nation, of course" (as quoted in D. Brown, 2002), in reference to the previously mentioned "marijuana refugees" who had moved to Canada from the United States, Walters said "If Canada wants to become the locus of that kind of activity, they're likely to pay a price" (as quoted in Bailey, 2003). In addition to Walters's threats, the chairman of the United States Congressional Drug Policy Committee warned that decriminalization of marijuana in Canada would lead the United States to tighten border controls, thereby disrupting trade between the two countries (Clark, 2002). Similarly, the U.S. Ambassador to Canada, Paul Celluci, cautioned that young people trying to enter the U.S. from Canada would become the targets of increased scrutiny by border officials if the country did not dispel the perception that it was relaxing the penalties for drug use (Russo, 2004).

Shortly after the Canadian Senate committee issued its discussion paper on cannabis, one of the top U.S. advisors on drug policy, Colonel Robert Maginnis, interviewed by a Canadian reporter, commented that the United States was planning

[t]o antagonize government leaders and grass roots leaders [in Canada] because you insist on having a radical drug policy that we will not ignore in the long term, then it is going to have adverse consequences and I hope we would be able to rectify it before it comes to blows. (as quoted in Thomas, 2003)

Not to be outdone, in a 2007 interview on MSNBC's *Tucker Carlson Show*, Congressman Mark Souder, the ranking Republican on the House of Representatives subcommittee responsible for federal drug policy, claimed that smoking marijuana was not much different from smoking crack cocaine. When asked by Carlson why the U.S. federal government was directing its efforts toward marijuana rather than more dangerous drugs, Souder responded:

The content of BC Bud, Quebec Gold and this marijuana that's currently on the streets isn't like the Cheech and Chong marijuana. It's more like cocaine. In other words, the THC of the ditchweed and what was happening when I was in college in the late '60s and early '70s had a THC content of four to eight percent, maybe as high as 12. Now we're looking at 20, 30, 40 percent. And the kick of the addiction you get, the destruction in your brain cells, is more like coke or crack than it is like the old time marijuana. (as quoted in Piper, 2007)

In the same interview, Souder also asserted that most marijuana users were poly-drug users and that there were several thousand deaths associated with marijuana use in any given year, both of which are gross distortions of the truth.

Walters's and others' claims regarding Canadian marijuana being imported to the United States must be considered in light of actual data—it is notable that estimates suggest that no more than 5% of the marijuana consumed in the United States is produced in Canada (Sabbag, 2005). In 2002, the U.S. Customs Service seized more than 867,000 pounds of marijuana entering the country from Mexico. In the same year, approximately 22,000 pounds of marijuana entering the country from Canada were seized. While it is certainly true that differences in enforcement emphasis and the relative success of customs officials in seizing drugs on the two borders must be taken into account, it seems unlikely that these factors alone would explain the 40:1 ratio of Mexican to Canadian marijuana intercepted at the respective borders.

In the international arena, in addition to continuing concerns regarding the cultivation of marijuana in large-scale growing operations and the importation of marijuana to the United States, there are also allegations that Canada has become a major transshipment location for synthetic drugs such as ecstasy and methamphetamine. The 2009 United Nations Drug Report claimed, "Canada has grown to be the most important producer of MDMA [ecstasy] for North America, and since 2006, all ecstasy laboratories reported have been large capacity facilities operated principally by Asian organized crime groups." This prompted the Canadian newsmagazine *Maclean's* to refer to Canada as Columbia North and to report that "Canada is steadily transforming from being primarily a customer country into a producer nation" (Kirby & MacDonald, 2009). Earlier, in reference to the production of synthetic drugs and marijuana in Canada, the *Economist* published an article with the title "British Columbia or Colombia?" (2009).

Walters was also apparently less concerned about the widespread cultivation of marijuana in states such as California, where cannabis was estimated to be the state's most lucrative cash crop with a value of $1.4 billion in the early 1990s—almost twice the value of the next most lucrative crop, cotton (Pollan, 1997). Richard Cowan, the editor and publisher of marijuananews.com, commented, "They grow more pot in California than in all of Canada" (as quoted in Sabbag, 2005). Walters's musings about Canada's proposed relaxed penalties for marijuana possession also seem rather curious in light of the fact that 11 states in the United States had virtually eliminated all criminal penalties associated with possession and use of the substance (MacCoun & Reuter, 2001).

In the summer of 2005, Walters was influential in the arrest (and request for extradition to the United States) of Marc Emery, who operated a marijuana seed and shipping business (and the previously mentioned Blount Brothers café) in Vancouver. Emery, who listed his occupation as "marijuana seed vendor" and also broadcast *Pot TV* on the Internet, had been arrested at least 21 times for marijuana-related offenses in Canada but was usually punished with small fines of short jail sentences

(Struck, 2006). However, Emery and two of his employees were eventually indicted by a Seattle-based grand jury on drug and money-laundering charges. There were indications that Walters's actions might have been motivated by a previous interaction with Emery—while delivering a speech in Vancouver criticizing Canada's drug laws, Walters was subjected to taunts and heckling from Emery and other marijuana activists. Emery noted, "He [Walters] just had a total slow burn. . . . I'm sure I've never been forgiven for that" (as quoted in Lewis, 2005). However, Karen Tandy of the U.S. Drug Enforcement Administration emphasized larger goals in commenting on Emory's arrest:

> Today's arrest of Marc Scott Emery, publisher of *Cannabis Culture* magazine and the founder of a marijuana legalization group, is a significant blow not only to the marijuana trafficking trade in the U.S. and Canada, but also to the marijuana legalization movement . . . hundreds of thousands of Emery's illicit products are known to have been channeled to marijuana legalization groups active in the U.S. and Canada. (as quoted in Lewis, 2005)

One Canadian commentator claimed that the Emery case "mocks our independence as a country . . . Canadian police grew so frustrated that neither prosecutors nor the courts would lock up Emery and throw away the key, they urged their U.S. counterparts to do the dirty work" (Mulgrew, 2008). The same commentator added, "If Emery has been breaking the law and must be jailed, our Justice Department should charge him and prosecute him in Canada. It's time for [Justice Minister] Rob Nicholson to step up and say, sorry Uncle Sam, not today, not ever." The U.S. Attorney who prosecuted the Emery case claimed that Emery was "adding fuel to the fire of the growing problem of violence surrounding marijuana growing [operations]" (as quoted in Inwood, 2010), and Emery was eventually sentenced to 5 years in prison by Seattle District Court judge Ricardo Martinez.

In addition to criticizing Canada's proposed marijuana policies and blaming the country for importation of marijuana to the United States., Walters also referred to the abovementioned safe injection site for IV drug users in Vancouver as "state-sponsored suicide."

> The very name is a lie. There are no safe injection sites. It is reprehensible to allow people and encourage people to continue suffering. That is why we [the United States] don't make this choice and I don't believe we ever will. (as quoted in D. Brown, 2003)

Walters's comments prompted then Vancouver Mayor Larry Campbell to retort:

> I think all you have to do is look at your [United States] prison system and your law enforcement to see if the drug war is being won in the States. It's an unmitigated disaster and they know it, but they can't back out of it. (as quoted in Novack, 2003)

Walters and the U.S. government have also criticized Canada for being a primary source of ephedrine, used to manufacture methamphetamine. A 2003 U.S. report listed Canada and the Netherlands among a group of countries identified as "offenders" in the international drug trade, the former largely for failing to control its exports of pseudoephedrine (Koring & Sallot, 2003). While it is certainly true that ephedrine has been imported to the United States from Canada, this criticism seems to be somewhat misplaced. A former agent in the Canadian Security Intelligence Service commented:

> The U.S. has been trying to make us a scapegoat for a long time. As far as I'm concerned, it's just a big political game. They're trying to pass the buck, but the fact is, it stops with them. Now it's drugs. Before they accused us of harboring terrorists. And that was bogus too. The September 11 hijackers didn't come through Canada. They came through the front door. (as quoted in Koring & Sallot, 2003)

Recent Developments in Canadian Drug Legislation Under the Harper Government

Stephen Harper's federal Conservative party obtained a minority victory in the 2006 Canadian federal election and was re-elected with a strong majority in 2008. Harper, a former member of the right-wing Canadian Reform Party and former president of the National Citizens' Coalition, an organization that one commentator referred to as "the most virulently right-wing and anti-government organization in the country" (Dobbin, 2006), has taken a hard line on crime policies in general and drug policies in particular. An article in *The Economist* ("How to Stop," 2009) noted that one-third of the bills introduced in the Canadian House of Commons in 2009 dealt with some aspect of the criminal justice system; a later article in *Maclean's* titled "Jailhouse Nation" (MacQueen, 2010) outlined the changes in Canadian crime policies under Harper. In 2008, the Tackling Violent Crime bill came into effect, which, among other things, mandated longer sentences for gun-related crimes and an increased use of indefinite sentences for repeat violent or sexual offenders; the Truth in Sentencing Act eliminated a provision whereby prisoners received a two-for-one credit for time they served prior to being convicted.

With respect to drug policies, Bill C-26 imposed mandatory minimum sentences for growing marijuana and included "aggravating factors" such as if the offense was committed at or near a school, that would increase sentences for drug-related crimes (Mulgrew, 2007). The bill also reduced funding for the previously mentioned harm-reduction programs. With respect to the supervised injection site, Prime Minister Harper stated, "If you remain a drug addict, I don't care how much harm you reduce, you are going to have a short and miserable life" (as quoted in "PM Wants," 2007). Former Federal Health Minister Tony Clement hinted that the government would discontinue the site altogether, asking the question:

Do safe injection sites contribute to lowering drug abuse and fighting addiction? Right now the only thing the research to data has proven conclusively is that drug addicts need more help to get off drugs. . . . given the need for more facts, I am unable to approve the current request to extend the Vancouver site for another three and a half years. (as quoted in Garmaise, 2006)

> A 2011 (unanimous) Canadian Supreme Court decision required the federal Minister of Health to grant immediate exemption to allow Insite to operate. In justifying this decision, Chief Justice McLachlin noted: "Insite saves lives. The benefits have been proven. There are no discernible negative impacts on the public safety and health objectives of Canada during its eight years of operation." ("Vancouver's Insite Drug Injection Clinic Will Stay Open," 2011)

But as Garmaise (2006) pointed out, the primary purpose of the safe injection facility was never to get people to stop using drugs—instead, it was designed to reduce the harms from injection drug use by reducing public disorder, overdoses, deaths, emergency room visits, and needle sharing. The research reviewed above suggests that Insite has been fairly successful with respect to these measures.

In November 2007, the Harper government proposed changes to the Controlled Substances Act that would (1) allow for a 5-year mandatory minimum sentence for drug trafficking if a weapon or violence was involved; (2) provide a 2-year mandatory minimum sentence for dealing hard drugs (cocaine, heroin, or methamphetamines) near a school or in other areas frequented by young people; (3) enact a 2-year mandatory minimum penalty for marijuana-growing operations of more than 500 plants; and (4) increase the maximum penalty for marijuana cultivation from 7 to 14 years (Fitzpatrick & Foot, 2007). If these policies seem familiar, they should—they are of course reminiscent of several of the failed U.S. policies addressed in Chapter 11.

After a "Senate and Commons tug of war" in 2010, the Senate finally passed a drug sentencing bill that provided mandatory 6-month terms of incarceration for growing five or more marijuana plants with intent to sell and 1-year sentences if marijuana trafficking was linked to organized crime or weapons (Tibbetts, 2010). This theme of getting tougher on drug crimes was further emphasized in the Harper government's 2010 National Drug Strategy (Canada, 2010), which potentially provided close to an additional $170 million over a 5-year period for law enforcement efforts to "help locate, investigate, and shut down organizations involved in the production and distribution of illicit drugs." In comparison, the strategy would devote only $30 million in new funding to drug prevention efforts and $100 million for drug treatment over the same 5-year period. The policies enacted and the attitudes toward drug problems expressed by the Harper government signal a retreat from the harm-reduction principles established in the early 2000s.

These "get tough on drug" strategies on the part of the Harper government need to be considered in the context of attitudes of the Canadian public toward drug issues. While the government's stance on mandatory sentences for large-scale drug dealers was supported by the majority surveyed, 57% of Canadians believed it would be wrong to eliminate harm-reduction programs (the percentage opposed to the elimination of harm-reduction programs was 64% in British Columbia), and 53% supported legalization of marijuana (AngusReidStrategies, 2008). In addition, at a fall 2012 conference, the Union of British Columbia Municipalities passed a resolution calling for the decriminalization of marijuana (Sinoski, 2012). This measure was supported by the former Attorney General of British Columbia (Geoff Plant), who commented that British Columbia municipalities "all govern and live with this disastrous failure of public policy" (as quoted in Sinoski, 2012).

AMERICAN INFLUENCE AND INTERVENTION IN DRUG-PRODUCING COUNTRIES

The message this country is really sending the rest of the world is that we in the U.S. are simply unable to stop our people from using these drugs, so the rest of the world must stop their people from producing them. (Gray, 2001, pp. 82–83)

In 20th-century drug wars, one of the prominent themes of the United States government has been to place much of the blame for its domestic drug problems on countries that are the sources of these drugs. For instance, in the 1940s, the head of the Federal Bureau of Narcotics, Harry Anslinger, argued, "Today, it is the communists of Red China who are exploiting the opium poppy who are financing and fostering aggressive warfare through depravity and human misery" (as quoted in Davenport-Hines, 2001, p. 284). More recently, the attribution of blame for drug problems is especially evident in the case of cocaine. But in discussing drug issues and policies in drug-producing countries, it is important to emphasize that, without the demand for consciousness-altering substances that exists in the United States and other highly populated Western industrialized countries, there would be little need for drugs to be produced and transported in/from countries such as Colombia, Mexico, and Afghanistan.

In early 2009, the Latin American Commission on Drugs and Democracy, led by former Brazilian president Fernando Henrique Cardoso (and including former presidents Ernesto Zedillo of Mexico and Cesar Gaviria of Colombia), published a report which referred to the U.S.–led drug war as a "failed war" and recommended that governments consider alternatives, including the decriminalization of marijuana (Tierney, 2009). The report noted that the antidrug strategy was "corrupting judicial systems, governments, the political system, and especially the police forces."

Cardoso, Zedillo, and Gaviria also published an editorial in the *Wall Street Journal* (February 23, 2009) in which they argued:

> In order to drastically reduce the harm caused by narcotics, the long-term solution is to reduce demand for drugs in the main consumer countries. . . . We must start by changing the status of addicts from drug buyers in the illegal market to patients cared for by the public health system. . . . By treating consumption as a matter of public health, we will enable police to focus their efforts on the critical issue: the fight against organized crime.

Similarly, in 2012, the presidents of Guatemala, Honduras, El Salvador, and Costa Rica, whose countries had among the highest homicide rates in the world, at least partially related to drug transit, publicly questioned the efficacy of continuing the prohibition of drugs. Otto Perez Molina, president of Guatemala, noted that the United States' inability to reduce drug consumption left his country with no option but to consider legalizing drugs (Dettner, 2012). While generally failing to acknowledge that demand for drugs is a major problem, the U.S. government has spent considerable sums of money attempting to disrupt (in particular) the cocaine trade in South American (and increasingly Central American) countries. One aspect of this strategy has been to provide funding for law enforcement and military operations to apprehend drug traffickers in these countries, a policy that has led to increasing levels of violence in countries such as Colombia (Gray, 2001) and Mexico (see below). U.S. policies have also authorized the shooting down (by U.S. military planes) of aircraft believed to be involved in the transportation of illegal drugs. As a result of opposition to this policy by some officials in Peru, the United States altered its practices: U.S. planes fly surveillance missions but carry "fly-along" officers from the local countries who are the individuals authorizing the shootings. In 2001, this policy was indirectly responsible for the shooting down of a plane suspected of being used for drug trafficking in Peru but that turned out to have only civilian occupants (Vann, 2001).

In addition to support for military operations in source countries, the U.S. government has allocated considerable financial resources to the eradication of cocaine crops (and opium crops; see below) through chemical spraying. While U.S.–financed eradication programs have led to reductions in coca growing in some areas of Colombia, production simply shifts to other regions (in what has been referred to as the "balloon effect"; Rouse & Arce, 2006; M. Sanchez, 2003)—for example, the Choco region of western Colombia had a 32% increase in the cultivation of coca in 2007 (Romero, 2009a) largely as the result of crop spraying in other areas of Colombia. Spraying of crops and military operations has also led to the displacement of coca production to other South American countries such as Peru and Venezuela. In Peru, coca cultivation increased by 4% in 2007 to a total of 290 tons, making that country second only to Colombia in cocaine production (Romero, 2009b, 2010). In addition, the amount of cocaine flowing into Venezuela from Colombia increased from an estimated 60 metric tons in 2004 to 260 tons in 2007

(Forero, 2009), and it was estimated that Venezuela accounted for 41% of all cocaine shipments to Europe (Hawley, 2010; see also Neuman, 2012). More generally, despite the fact that the U.S. government spent more than $4 billion on antidrug programs in the Andean region of South America, the size of the coca crop increased by 18% over the 2003 to 2008 period to an estimated total of 1,100 tons (Forero, 2008).

Coca leaves have deep cultural and religious value in South American countries such as Colombia and Bolivia—coca can mitigate altitude sickness, aids in digestion, and suppresses hunger and fatigue. Evo Morales, president of Bolivia (an Aymara Indian and former leader of the coca growers union in Bolivia), questioned, "How can it be possible that the coca leaf, which represents our identity, which is ancestral, be penalized?" Bolivia proposed an amendment to the Single Convention on Narcotic Drugs, which required signatories to prohibit the chewing of coca leaves, arguing that the language was discriminatory (Bajak, 2011) and violated the UN Declaration of the Rights of Indigenous Peoples, which guarantees the right to maintain and control traditional culture. (Reiss, 2010)

These data suggest that the crop-eradication programs have generally been unsuccessful, and at least part of the reason for this lack of success is that insufficient resources have been devoted to promoting alternative crops for poor farmers in these countries. While the United States has devoted some resources to promoting alternative crops such as bananas and coffee, the depressed markets for such crops mean that farmers can earn as little as one-tenth of their potential earnings from coca, a crop that can be harvested three to four times in a single year (Padgett, 2002). As one farmer in Bolivia who planned to double the size of his cocaine crop commented, "The prices of oranges, mandarins, coffee and other products are too low, and they do not give you enough to survive. . . . So we are obligated to plant coca" (as quoted in Forero, 2008). T. C. Miller (2003) notes that the spraying of coca crops has "ruined the lives of thousands of people in South Colombia, where migrants are dirt-poor farmers who seized on cocaine as a steady, if illegal, source of income." At one point, the former minister of Peru actually recommended that, instead of crop eradication programs, the United States purchase the illegal cocaine crops (Lusane, 1991).

In addition to the financial hardships these programs impose on farmers, there is considerable evidence to suggest that, due to the toxic chemicals used to eradicate crops, residents of these South American countries have experienced significant health problems. Although U.S. officials claim that the herbicide used to spray cocaine crops in South American countries is safe for humans, the warning labels on the chemical employed in spraying explicitly urge caution in using it near people and note that it can cause vomiting and other medical problems (Forero, 2002). T. C. Miller (2003) notes that many coca farmers in Colombia report that the repeated spraying of crops has led to sickness among themselves, their children, and animals. In response to claims by the U.S. State Department's Anti-Narcotics Bureau that the spraying of crops posed no risk to humans, Senator Patrick J. Leahy commented, "There are reports of health problems and food crops destroyed from fumigation. Spraying a toxic chemical over large areas, including where people and livestock graze, would not be tolerated in our country. We should not be spraying first and asking questions later" (as quoted in Marquis, 2002).

In a more general commentary on the wisdom of the policy of spraying coca crops, Allman (2002) notes, "from the official U.S. perspective, raining down chemical defoliants on these people and their crops has something to do with trying to stop Americans from snuffing coke in distant U.S. suburbs and cities" (p. 6).

Clearly, these policies conveniently neglect the fact that the United States represents the single largest market for illegal drugs in the world, accounting for approximately one-eighth of the total demand ("Stumbling in the Dark," 2001). The policies also neglect the fact that lower-income citizens in drug-producing countries become involved in the production of illicit drugs because they have few alternatives. In Colombia, for example, per-capita income was $1,700 per year in the mid-2000s, which drives a substantial number of rural peasants to grow coca (Deans, 2004). As Lusane (1991) noted in a statement that still applies, "to stop the importation of illegal drugs into the United States, egalitarian economic development, social opportunity, and political reform must be created in the Third World" (p. 201).

Certification Policies

The United States government also exerts considerable control over drug-producing countries through its policies of certification. Under the Foreign Assistance Act of 1961 (amended in 1986), the president must submit to Congress a list of "major illicit drug-producing countries" and "major drug transit countries." The president must then decide whether governments of major drug-producing countries and/or drug-transit countries are fully cooperating with the United States in attempting to eradicate illegal drugs (M. Jones, 2002). If countries are assessed as uncooperative, they will be decertified, resulting in the withdrawal of all U.S. financial aid (with the exception of funds for humanitarian and antidrug programs), possible trade sanctions, and the withholding of the United States's vote from international funding agencies such as the International Monetary Fund. However, as is the case in other areas of U.S. drug policy, decertification decisions reflect glaring contradictions. For example, while Colombia was subject to decertification in 1996 and 1997 (Youngers, 1998), Mexico, which is the main transshipment point for marijuana, heroin, and cocaine entering the United States and which has consistently failed to meet the antidrug targets set by the United States, has never been subject to decertification by the U.S. government. James Gray (2001), quoting from the *Orange County Register* (March 2, 1998), noted,

> President Clinton announced [on Friday] that he will participate in the annual game of "let's pretend." The President will pretend that Mexico is a cooperating partner in the war on drugs, the U.S. will continue to send Mexico aid that it and the Mexican government will pretend will help to win the war, and citizens pretend that it is all helping the cause. (p. 82)

It is also notable that Canada, the alleged source of considerable quantities of marijuana and ephedrine entering the United States (see discussion above), has never been subject to decertification. The obvious reason for these contradictions is that Canada and Mexico have far closer economic and political ties to the United States than do countries such as Colombia.

More recently (in 2009), President Obama listed Bolivia as one of three nations not upholding international drug conventions. While Bolivia is certainly the source of a considerable proportion of cocaine entering the United States, this decertification also appears to be politically motivated. The country's failure to renew USAID contracts on the grounds that they were providing opportunities for interference by Drug Enforcement Administration agents and concerns regarding the country's decriminalization of drugs seem to be the reason for its decertification (Reiss, 2010). Similarly, the South American country of Venezuela was also subject to decertification, likely due to the ongoing criticism of U.S. policies (drug-related and others) by Venezuela's president, Hugo Chavez.

We conclude this chapter with a discussion of developments in two prominent drug-producing/transshipment countries, Mexico and Afghanistan.

Mexico and Other Central American Countries

Mexico has historically been a major transshipment country for illicit drugs eventually imported to the United States, and at least partially as a result of U.S. "success" in reducing drug production in Colombia in recent years, Mexico has become even more prominent as a transshipment and drug-producing country. The drug trade and U.S. interventions in Mexico as part of the Merida Initiative (which began during the administration of George W. Bush and has continued under the Obama administration) has led to a wave of violence in that country, with more than 50,000 deaths related to the drug trade between 2006 and 2011 (Keefe, 2012), and widespread corruption, with drug cartels making payments to federal, state, and municipal authorities (including law enforcement officials). This corruption has spread to high levels of the Mexican government—even President Felipe Calderon's own drug czar was charged in 2008 with accepting $450,000 in bribes each month from drug cartels (Keefe, 2012). The wave of violence connected to the drug trade in Mexico has also spread into the United States, in particular to states that border Mexico such as Arizona. U.S. officials identified 230 (U.S.) cities where Mexican drug cartels and their associates "maintain drug distribution networks or supply drugs to distributors" (Archibold, 2009).

A study published in October 2012 by the Mexican Competitiveness Institute, titled "If Our Neighbors Legalize," claimed that proposals to legalize marijuana in Colorado, Oregon, and Washington (see discussion in Chapter 11) could reduce the profits of Mexican drug cartels by as much as 30% (Castillo & Wyatt, 2012). The study assumed that legalization in a state would allow growers in such a state to produce marijuana cheaply and would create a flow of marijuana into other states, thereby reducing the involvement of Mexican cartels in the marijuana trade.

At least partially in response to the drug-related violence in Mexico, legislation approved by the country's Congress in the spring of 2006 removed criminal charges for possession of up to 25 milligrams of heroin, 5 grams of marijuana, and half a gram of cocaine. The legislation stipulated that "no charges will be brought against . . . addicts or consumers who are found in possession of any narcotic for personal use" (as quoted in "Mexico May Permit," 2006). However, under pressure from the Bush administration, which alleged that the proposed law would encourage Americans to visit Mexico as "drug tourists" (Chapman, 2006), Mexican President Vicente Fox decided not to ratify the legislation. Continuing internal pressure to change the drug laws finally led to decriminalization of most illicit drugs, including cocaine, heroin, and marijuana in 2009 (Grillo, 2009).

In an editorial printed in several newspapers in Mexico, President Calderon directly blamed the United States for the drug-related violence in his country: "The origin of our violence problem begins with the fact that Mexico is located next to the country with the highest levels of drug consumption in the world. It is as if our neighbor were the biggest drug addict in the world" (as quoted in Booth, 2010). At a hearing of the U.S. Senate Judiciary Committee on Crime and Drugs and the Senate Caucus on Drug Control in 2009, it was acknowledged that demand for drugs in the United States and the government's failure to stop the stream of weapons and laundered money into Mexico has fueled the drug trade and resulting violence. At the hearing, Senator Richard Durbin of Illinois stated, "the insatiable demand for illegal drugs in the United States keeps the Mexican cartels in business" (as quoted in Meyer, 2009). This was also acknowledged by Secretary of State Hillary Clinton, who commented,

We know very well that the drug traffickers are motivated by the demand for illegal drugs in the United States, that they are armed by the transport of weapons from the United States to Mexico. . . . Clearly, what we have been doing has not worked and it is unfair for our incapacity . . . to be creating a situation where people are holding the Mexican government and people responsible. (as quoted in Ellingwood, 2009a)

Despite such pronouncements, it is notable that in 2009, the Obama administration planned to devote $700 million to "enhance Mexican law enforcement and judicial capacity"—an amount that is double the budget for research for the National Institute on Drug Abuse (Miloy, 2009). It is also important to note that major U.S. banks, including Wachovia (which was bought out by Wells Fargo), have been complicit in laundering money for Mexican drug traffickers (Smith, 2010).

As Mexican authorities (with U.S. assistance) have focused on drug trafficking and production in that country, the problems have migrated to other Central American countries such as Guatemala, with Mexican traffickers relocating to that country to store and repackage drugs and to stockpile weapons (Ellingwood, 2009b). Further evidence of displacement was revealed in the summer of 2009, when it was reported that close to 10 million pseudoephedrine pills (recall that pseudoephedrine is the key ingredient in methamphetamine) were seized from a shipping container in Guatemala—drug cartels were increasingly smuggling pseudoephedrine through other Central American countries such as El Salvador (Miroff & Booth, 2010) to circumvent the Mexican ban on imports of the product. Earlier, there were indications that the pseudoephedrine trade was shifting to Argentina, which, although not a manufacturer of ephedrine, saw its imports of the substance increase from 2.9 tons in 2004 to 19.1 tons in 2007 (McDonnell, 2008).

Clearly, as has been emphasized throughout this chapter, the global traffic in illicit drugs will not subside until the demand for these substances is reduced.

Afghanistan

Since the United States invaded Afghanistan in response to the terrorist attacks of September 11, 2001, opium production in that country has soared to unprecedented levels—Afghanistan supplies 90% of the world's opium, and the crop comprises one-third of the country's gross domestic product (Dilanian, 2009). It was estimated that more than 365,000 Afghan farm households cultivate opium, and the average annual cash income of such households was 53% higher than that of non–opium poppy-growing households (DeYoung, 2009; see also Moreau & Yousafzai, 2006). The high production of opium and its relatively cheap price (a "hit" of opium sells for as little as 20 cents, while a dose of heroin sells for 60 cents) has also led to an increase in opiate addicts in Afghanistan (Vogt, 2010). A 2005 United Nations survey revealed that there were more than 200,000 opium addicts in the country, which has a population of approximately 35 million (Filkins, 2009)—a later estimate put the number of heroin or opium addicts at one million (Zucchino, 2009).

The initial strategy of President Obama to address the opium problem was to continue destroying poppy fields in Afghanistan. However, even members of Obama's administration questioned this approach. Richard Holbrooke, the administration's coordinator of Afghanistan policy, noted that eradicating the poppy fields was "wasteful and ineffective" and had resulted in "pushing farmers into the Taliban's hands because it destroys farmers' livelihoods and leaves them with few alternatives" (as quoted in Dilanian, 2009). Thus, in the summer of 2009, the United States and Britain announced a plan to sell wheat seeds and fruit saplings to farmers at low prices and to pay farm workers to work on roads and irrigation ditches. Given that switching to farming alternative products would result in significantly lower levels of income for farmers (DeYoung, 2009), it is unlikely that this shift in policy will be effective in encouraging them to abandon poppy production.

> Afghan's finance minister criticized the war on drugs, noting, "Today, many Afghans believe that it is not drugs, but an ill-conceived war on drugs that threatens their economy and nascent democracy.... Destroying [the opium trade] without offering our farmers a genuine alternative livelihood has the potential to undo the embryonic gains of the past three years." (as quoted in Hitchens, 2004)

According to the United Nations Office on Drugs and Crime, the value of the Afghan opium crop increased from $29 per pound in 2009 to $77 per pound in 2010. Although the amount of land devoted to growing poppies in Afghanistan was estimated to have remained the same over this period (approximately 304,000 acres), the number of families growing poppies had increased, with more than 1.5 million Afghanis dependent on the sale of opium for the livelihood (Constable, 2011).

CONCLUSION

> Billions have been spent by governments in Western Europe and North America fighting the drug dealers. But the war is being lost. Heroin, cocaine, methamphetamine, and other illegal drugs are cheaper, purer, and easier to get a hold of than ever; and in the U.S. alone half a million people are behind bars on drug charges—more than the entire prison population of Europe. (Wynne-Jones, 2004)

Policy approaches for controlling drug use and drug-related problems vary considerably across nations. Although there are countries that have adopted very severe penalties for the use, sale, and production of drugs (e.g., Russia, China, and Indonesia), the United States possesses one of the most punitive drug policies of all Western developed nations. Canada, Australia, and several Western European countries have shifted from strategies based exclusively on drug criminalization and enforcement to drug control strategies that place more emphasis on the principles of harm minimization or harm reduction.

We began this chapter with a quote from Asa Hutchinson, former head of the United States Drug Enforcement Administration, who urged other countries to adopt America's strategies on illicit drug use as their model. It is apparent, however, that a number of countries are moving in a direction opposite to that of the United States. In a 2004 report by the European Parliament, the "failure" of drug policies in European countries was emphasized (Europarl, 2004). The report noted that "a national drugs policy must be based on scientific knowledge concerning each type of drug, not an emotional response," and suggested that priority must be given to "protecting the lives and health of users of illicit substances, improving their well-being by means of a balanced and integrated approach to the problem." The report also lamented the marginalization of drug users that current policies have created and suggested that "rather than implementing repressive strategies which verge on and have frequently led to violations of human rights, set up rehabilitation programs for offenders/users as alternatives to prison." The former chief of Interpol (the international police agency) similarly declared the war on drugs to be lost, claiming that enforcement policies had not served the purpose of protecting the world from drugs and calling for harm reduction instead of "obsolete international conventions" (as cited in Toynbee, 2004).

More recently, the 2011 Global Commission on Drug Policy, whose members included the former presidents of Mexico, Brazil, and Colombia, the Prime Minister of Greece, former United Nations Secretary General Kofi Annan, former U.S. Secretary of State George Schultz, and British billionaire Richard Branson, among others, called for radical changes in drug policy. The commission noted that its starting point was the recognition that the global drug problem is "a set of interlinked health and social problems to be managed, rather than a war to be won" (2011, p. 4). The principles that should guide drug policy as listed by the Commission were (1) that drug policies should be based on solid empirical and scientific evidence, and (2) that drug policies must be based on human rights and public health principles (2011, p. 5). In contrast to the United Nations principles outlined earlier in this chapter, the Commission recommended that national governments should have the freedom to experiment with drug policies that are more suited to their particular circumstances. The Commission report was particularly critical of the United States' policies, but the U.S. Office of National Drug Control Policy responded to this criticism by alleging that the report was "misguided" ("War on Drugs a Failure," 2011).

For many countries, the shift to a drug policy based on harm-reduction principles transpired in recognition of the substantial challenges and costs, both human and financial, that accompany drug criminalization and the rigorous enforcement of drug laws. Throughout this chapter, we have emphasized the challenges facing countries that have adopted such policies. Conversely, harm-reduction advocates emphasize policies that consider and attempt to balance the damage done by the *response* to drug use against the harms of drugs per se. As an analogy, Hunt (2005) urges us to consider the regulation of automobile use. He notes that although there are many hazards associated with driving—including considerable environmental damage, injuries, and deaths—elimination of driving is clearly not seen as realistic. Instead, societies have implemented laws on speed limits, the control of emissions, and seat belt and other safety devices as harm-reduction strategies to reduce the risks associated with automobile use. Harm-reduction policies set similar goals for drug use.

It is clear that drug policies that are disproportionately based on criminalization and enforcement fail because they create a vast array of problems while doing little or nothing to reduce the demand for drugs. Criminalization policies are least defensible when they target "soft" drugs such as marijuana because they incur considerable costs and do a great deal of harm to users in their attempt to prevent the use of a drug (marijuana) that, in many cases, is certainly no worse than available legal drugs. Harm-reduction efforts aimed at "hard" drug use are more controversial. Some, such as needle exchange programs, have nothing to do with the legal status of a drug and simply attempt to minimize the consequences associated with heroin and other drug use. Thus, programs such as these are typically criticized on purely moral grounds. Other harm-reduction programs, such as the experimental heroin maintenance programs and safe injection facilities discussed above, are even more controversial because they provide users with illegal drugs. Advocates of these programs remind us that they in no way "approve" of heroin use; they are simply designed to deal with severe drug problems (e.g., high rates of overdose and HIV infection) that have not been effectively managed in any other way. Critics of such programs claim that they "only make the problem worse." But empirical research, not emotion, should be relied upon to determine the efficacy of these programs for managing drug use and drug-related problems and harm.

In addition to domestic policy interventions, some countries, and the United States in particular, have attempted to prevent domestic drug use by eliminating the production of drugs in other countries. These efforts face many challenges and are often misguided. Because there is considerable demand for consciousness-altering substances in Western developed countries, the impoverished residents of underdeveloped countries have a strong incentive to produce illegal drugs. Combined with high international demand for substances is the fact that drugs can be grown or produced nearly anywhere. Efforts to eliminate drugs "at the source" through programs such as crop eradication only create further hardships for impoverished people and tend to fail due to the "balloon" or displacement effect; drug production is not eliminated but simply relocated to some other areas.

Future policy should consider the empirical evidence on the harms posed by particular drugs and enact laws that do more good than harm. The shift of most developed countries to a drug control approach that is at least partially based on harm minimization and the lack of substantial increases in drug use following these policy changes suggest that the United States should consider a more balanced approach aimed at reducing the harms associated with drug use.

REVIEW QUESTIONS

1. Define harm reduction/minimization. Provide some examples of drug policies/programs that are consistent with this philosophy. Recall our discussion of methadone maintenance in Chapter 8; how is this form of treatment consistent with a harm-minimization approach to drug problems?

2. How do rates of illegal drug use in countries with more progressive drug policies compare to rates of illegal drug use in the United States? What does this suggest about the effect of more progressive drug control policies on drug use?

3. What regulations are placed on coffee houses that sell marijuana in the Netherlands? In what ways are these regulations analogous to regulations on bars in the United States?

4. What conditions motivated the establishment of a safe injection site in Vancouver, Canada? What outcomes were associated with this program?

5. What are displacement effects in drug production? How has displacement contributed to the failure of policy aimed at eliminating foreign drug production through crop eradication?

6. Why has the United States taken such an active role in attempting to influence the drug policies of other countries? Is it legitimate for the United States to take such a role?

INTERNET EXERCISE

Access the European Legal Database on Drugs website (http://emcdda.europa .eu), click on "country profiles," and access information on drug laws and drug use for any two European countries. Compare the legislation and drug use data to legislation and drug use data for the United States.

Glossary

Acculturation The adoption of new cultural information and social skills by an immigrant group, which often replace traditional cultural beliefs, practices, and interaction patterns to some degree. Acculturation is typically measured with indicators such as language use and preference, ethnic identification, and nativity of both the respondent and the respondent's parents.

Acute toxicity Negative health consequences that occur immediately or very quickly, as in the case of a drug overdose.

Addiction In the context of substance use, addiction refers to a person's inability to stop using a drug when it is causing him or her problems. The term is very loosely used in society, and many health professionals now avoid using the term *addiction*. In part, this is because *addiction* is commonly used to refer to many behaviors that have nothing to do with drugs or anything able to generate physical dependence (e.g., sex, gambling, exercise, TV, shopping). See also *Physical dependence, Psychological dependence, Tolerance, Withdrawal.*

Amotivational syndrome A persistent apathy or unwillingness to participate in normal social activities. Some have claimed that marijuana use causes amotivational syndrome, but others claim that heavy marijuana use is likely a symptom of amotivation rather than the cause.

Androstenedione A steroid with androgenic properties that is sometimes used by athletes to build muscle.

BAC Blood alcohol content. The concentration of alcohol in blood. It is measured either as a percentage by mass or by mass per volume. For example, a BAC of 0.20% means 1 gram of alcohol per 500 grams of blood.

Bath salts The shorthand term used to describe a broad range of synthetic drugs that have garnered media attention in recent years after being marketed legally as a variety of household products until 2012. Usually referring to a broad range of substances with a variety of effects, this term became widely applied despite its imprecision after widespread media attention followed a small number of overdoses involving substances marketed as "bath salts," which usually had the stimulant mephedrone as an active ingredient.

Behavioral toxicity An adverse change in a person's functioning as a result of using drugs. For example, a person under the influence of a drug may intentionally or accidentally hurt others or damage property.

Blood doping A process in which athletes remove a unit of blood weeks prior to an event and then transfuse the blood back into their body just prior to a competition. As the body will naturally replace a unit of blood in approximately 3 weeks, blood doping gives an athlete an extra unit of blood (and that many more red blood cells), which increases his or her oxygen-carrying capacity.

Bufotenine The form of DMT contained in the venom secreted by many species of *Bufo* toads. See also *DMT, Toad licking, Toad smoking.*

Central nervous system The mass of nerve tissue that controls and coordinates the activities of an animal. In vertebrates, it consists of the brain and the spinal cord.

Chronic toxicity Negative health consequences that result from long-term exposure to a drug, such as emphysema associated with smoking or cirrhosis caused by alcohol consumption.

Controlled Substances Act Title II of the U.S. Comprehensive Drug Abuse Prevention and Control Act, passed in 1970. It classifies drugs into five legal "schedules." The legal classification of a drug is allegedly based on (1) the potential for abuse of the drug, (2) whether the drug has medical applications, and (3) the potential of the drug to generate psychological and physical dependence. See also *Schedule I controlled substances, Schedule II controlled substances.*

Coverage error A research error that occurs when all members of the population do not have an equal (or known) probability of being included in a survey sample. It is a major concern in survey research on substance use because some of the people who are most likely to use and abuse illegal drugs are also among the most difficult to contact. This can hamper the ability of a survey to yield findings that are generalizable to the entire population.

Crack cocaine Crack cocaine is made by dissolving cocaine hydrochloride in water and adding baking soda to make a solution that is then boiled or put in a microwave and finally cooled, often in ice or a freezer. The result is a yellowish-white substance that looks like soap, and small chunks (often called "rocks") are broken off and smoked, making "cracking" sounds when burned—hence the name "crack."

Creatine An amino acid that helps to supply energy to muscle cells. It is often taken as a supplement by bodybuilders or others who wish to build muscle.

D.A.R.E. (Drug Abuse Resistance Education) A nonprofit police officer–led school-based drug education program. D.A.R.E. was founded in 1983 in Los Angeles and was eventually implemented in more than 43 countries, though little evidence has been found to indicate program success.

DAWN See *Drug Abuse Warning Network.*

DMT A hallucinogenic compound similar to psilocybin and LSD that has been used by indigenous peoples of Central and South America for centuries. DMT will have no effect if orally ingested because it is broken down quickly by stomach acid, but if injected or smoked, DMT has a powerful hallucinogenic effect. First synthesized in 1931, DMT is naturally present in numerous plant and animal species, including toads, moth larvae, grubs, fish, mushrooms, trees, vines, and grasses. See also *Bufotenine, Toad licking, Toad smoking.*

Dopamine A chemical naturally produced in the body. In the brain, dopamine functions as a neurotransmitter, activating dopamine receptors. Dopamine is also a neurohormone released by the hypothalamus. Its main function as a hormone is to inhibit the release of prolactin from the anterior lobe of the pituitary. See also *Neurotransmitters.*

Drug Abuse Warning Network (DAWN) An agency of the U.S. Department of Health and Human Services that collects data on drug-related visits to hospital emergency departments and drug-related deaths investigated by medical examiners and coroners.

DTC advertising Direct-to-consumer advertising. The United States is one of only two countries (the other being New Zealand) that allow pharmaceutical companies to market their drugs directly to consumers. Studies have indicated that DTC advertising has a significant impact on the consumption of pharmaceutical products.

DUI Driving under the influence. The criminal offense of operating a motor vehicle after consuming alcohol or other drugs to the degree that mental and motor skills are impaired.

DXM Dextromethorphan, a cough suppressant that can produce hallucinations if it is taken in concentrated form.

Ecstasy The street name of the drug MDMA. See also *MDMA.*

Enactogens Substances thought to have the ability to help mental patients to access painful and heavily guarded emotions.

Ephedrine An alkaloid naturally found in several species of the ephedra plant, which is a leafless bush that grows in arid regions throughout the world. Ephedrine together with adrenaline is used to create the amphetamines.

FAS Fetal alcohol syndrome. See also *Fetal alcohol syndrome.*

FDA United States Food and Drug Administration. The federal agency responsible for ensuring that foods are safe, wholesome, and sanitary; human and veterinary drugs, biological products, and medical devices are safe and effective; cosmetics are safe; and electronic products that emit radiation are safe.

Fetal alcohol syndrome A condition in which some babies born to alcoholic mothers display neurological problems, low birth weight, mental retardation, and facial malformations.

Gateway drug A substance claimed to cause its users to go on to harder drugs such as cocaine and heroin.

Hashish A psychoactive drug derived from the leaves and flowers of the *Cannabis indica* plant.

hCG Human chorionic gonadotropin. A nonsteroidal hormone that stimulates the production of testosterone in the body.

hGH Human growth hormone. A nonsteroidal hormone secreted by the pituitary gland that promotes growth during childhood and adolescence.

Hyperavailability Excessive access and exposure to drugs and alcohol.

IGF-1 Insulin-like growth factor. A nonsteroidal hormone that stimulates the production of testosterone in the body.

MDMA Methylenedioxymethamphetamine, also known as ecstasy. A drug invented by German psychiatrists in 1912. It was tested as a "truth drug" by the United States Central Intelligence Agency in the 1940s and has also been used to facilitate psychotherapy. It stimulates the brain to produce serotonin, which causes perceptual and mood effects. See also *Serotonin*.

Methadone maintenance The use of the synthetic narcotic methadone to treat heroin addiction. Methadone is thought to be less addicting than heroin because it is administered orally and because the euphoric effects last much longer than heroin.

Methamphetamine The most potent and fast-acting of the amphetamines; it is a powder that is snorted, smoked, or injected, which intensifies its effects. Street names include meth, crank, speed, ice, glass, crystal, and crystal meth. As with other amphetamines, both the rush and the high associated with methamphetamine result from the release of dopamine into the areas of the brain that regulate pleasure.

Minnesota Model A multimodal therapeutic approach to treating alcohol and drug addiction based on the philosophy of Alcoholics Anonymous.

Monitoring the Future Study An ongoing, annual study of the behaviors, attitudes, and values of U.S. secondary school students, college students, and young adults. It is one of the most widely used sources of information on substance use and abuse.

Native American Church A religious organization that combines traditional Native American beliefs with some elements of Christianity. The teachings of the church, known as "the Peyote Road," view peyote as a holy sacrament able to connect the user to God and to help cure physical and spiritual disease.

Neurotransmitters Messenger chemicals that carry messages within the brain and from the brain to the rest of the body. Commonly known neurotransmitters include serotonin, dopamine, and adrenaline.

NIDA-5 The five most commonly used illegal drugs as identified by the National Institute of Drug Abuse: marijuana, cocaine, methamphetamine, opiates, and phencyclidine (PCP).

Pharmacotherapy The use of drugs and medications in the treatment of substance abuse and dependency. Substances in this form of treatment are typically used in one of two ways: on a temporary basis as the individual attempts to quit the use of another drug or on a permanent or long-term basis in the belief that taking the new drug will reduce or eliminate the use of a more problematic drug.

Physical dependence The potential of a drug to generate a withdrawal syndrome. Drugs that are not accompanied by a withdrawal syndrome when long-term or heavy use is stopped are not regarded as physically addicting. Physical dependence can occur because the body has come to depend on the presence of some amount of the drug in the system. Also known as physiological dependence. See also *Addiction, Psychological dependence, Tolerance, Withdrawal.*

Pseudoephedrine A main precursor substance used in the manufacture of methamphetamine. See also *Methamphetamine.*

Psychoactive substances Chemical substances that act primarily upon the central nervous system and alter brain function, resulting in temporary changes in perception, mood, consciousness, and behavior.

Psychological dependence A desire (i.e., "craving") to repeatedly use a drug. A drug that cannot cause a user to become physically dependent may still be able to produce psychological dependence. Also known as behavioral dependence. See also *Addiction, Physical dependence, Tolerance, Withdrawal.*

Psychotherapeutic drugs The broad class of prescription drugs used to treat psychological disorders that includes antidepressants, antipsychotics, anxiolytics, sedatives and hypnotics, and central nervous system stimulants.

Schedule I controlled substance A substance deemed under the U.S. Controlled Substances Act to have a high potential for abuse, no medical use in the United States, and a lack of accepted safety for use under medical supervision.

Schedule II controlled substance A substance deemed under the U.S. Controlled Substances Act to have a high potential for abuse that may lead to severe psychological or physical dependence but has a currently accepted medical use in the United States. Schedule II substances can be prescribed by a doctor.

Selective serotonin reuptake inhibitors (SSRIs) Psychoactive substances that block the reuptake (or removal) of one specific neurotransmitter, serotonin, and thus prolong the improved mood states associated with the release of serotonin. They are prescribed to treat depression, anxiety disorders, and some personality disorders. See also *Neurotransmitters, Psychoactive substances, Serotonin.*

Serotonin A neurotransmitter produced in the central nervous system that plays an important role in regulating mood, sleep, and appetite. See also *Neurotransmitters.*

Sinsemilla The product of removing male cannabis plants from the growing environment before they have a chance to fertilize the females. The resultant cannabis contains more psychoactive compounds in comparison to cannabis that has been grown in a pollinated environment.

Social desirability The tendency of survey respondents to reply to sensitive questions in ways that are believed to be more socially appropriate, for example, to fail to report illegal behavior.

SSRIs See *Selective serotonin reuptake inhibitors*.

THC Delta 9-tetrahydrocannabinol, the primary psychoactive agent in cannabis, which is concentrated in the plant's resin.

Therapeutic ratio The ratio between the amount of drug needed to get a desired or therapeutic effect and the amount that is dangerous or even lethal to the user. If the therapeutic ratio is narrow, the amount needed to get the desired effect is close to the amount that is dangerous to the user. A wide therapeutic ratio means death by overdose is much less likely.

Toad licking The practice of licking the venomous slime from the skin of a *Bufo marinus* toad, which contains DMT, in an attempt to get high. The method is ineffective because orally consumed DMT is not psychoactive. See also *DMT, Toad smoking*.

Toad smoking The practice of smoking the venomous slime from the skin of a *Bufo alvarius* toad, which contains DMT. Smoking the toad venom provides an intense hallucinogenic high. See also *DMT, Toad licking*.

Tolerance A need for increased amounts of a drug to achieve the desired effect or a markedly diminished effect with continued use of the same amount of the substance. Tolerance develops because the body has adapted to repeated drug use so that the same dose of a drug produces less of the desired effect.

Toxicity The negative health consequences associated with ingesting a drug. See also *Acute toxicity, Chronic toxicity*.

Tylenol 3 Tablets containing acetaminophen and codeine.

Underreporting The tendency of survey respondents to lie, minimize, or fail to answer questions that are perceived to be threatening to the respondent.

Withdrawal A predictable set of symptoms that affect the user when the use of a drug is discontinued after some period of use. See also *Physical dependence*.

Bibliography

Abbott, P. (2009). A review of the community reinforcement approach in the treatment of opioid dependence. *Journal of Psychoactive Drugs, 41,* 379–385.

Abelson, J. (2002, December 1). DUI laws cost state millions in funds. *Boston Globe.* Retrieved December 1, 2002, from http://www.boston.com

Abrahamson, A. (2003, August 28). Pound wants U.S. to forfeit medals. *Los Angeles Times.* Retrieved August 28, 2003, from http://www.latimes.com

Abramson, J. (2004). *Overdosed America: The broken promise of American medicine.* New York: HarperCollins.

Achenbaum, E. (2009, February 12). Young man paralyzed after drinking party wins lawsuit against Lake Forest homeowner. *Chicago Tribune.* Retrieved February 12, 2009, from http://www.chicagotribune.com

Adam, D. (2005, February 2). Treating agony with ecstasy. *Guardian.* Retrieved February 17, 2005, from http://www.guardian.co.uk

Adams, W., Zhong, Y., Barboriak, J., & Rim, A. (1993). Alcohol-related hospitalizations of elderly people: Prevalence and geographic variation in the United States. *Journal of the American Medical Association, 270,* 1222–1225.

Adams, W. L., Barry, K. L., & Fleming, M. F. (1996). Screening for problem drinking in older primary care patients. *Journal of the American Medical Association, 276*(24), 1964–1967.

Adamson, S. J., & Sellman, J. D. (2001). Drinking goal selection and treatment outcome in out-patients with mild-moderate alcohol dependence. *Drug and Alcohol Review, 20*(4), 351–359. doi:10.1080/09595230120092670

Addicts blamed for old-growth thefts. (2001, November 26). *Longview Daily News,* p. 1.

Adler, P. T., & Lotecka, L. (1973). Drug use among high school students: Patterns and correlates. *International Journal of the Addictions, 8,* 537–548.

Admitted. (2012, February 20). *Sports Illustrated,* p. 20.

Ads show reality of "heroin chic." (1996, June 18). *Knight-Ridder.* Retrieved June 18, 1996, from http://www.knight-ridder.com

Advancement Project. (2000). *Opportunities suspended.* Retrieved July 10, 2009, from http://civilrightsproject.ucla.edu/research/k-12-education/school-discipline/opportunities-suspended-the-devastating-consequences-of-zero-tolerance-and-school-discipline-policies

Advisory Council on the Misuse of Drugs. (2002). Retrieved November 3, 2003, from http://www.drugs.gov.uk/drugs-laws/acmd/

Agassi says tennis is the cleanest. (2004, March 25). *BBC Sports.* Retrieved March 25, 2004, from http://news.bbc

.co.uk/go/pr/fr/-/sport1/hi/tennis/3570009
.stm

Agnew, R. (1992). Foundation for a general theory of crime and delinquency. *Criminology, 30,* 47–87.

Aguirre, B. (2003, June 25). Some students see sly pitch to teens in Salem cigarette ad. *Seattle Times.* Retrieved June 25, 2003, from http://www.seattletimes.com

Aguirre-Molina, M., & Caetano, R. (1994). Alcohol use and alcohol-related issues. In C. Molina & M. Aguirre-Molina (Eds.), *Latino health in the United States: A growing challenge* (pp. 393–424). Washington, DC: American Public Health Association.

Ahrens, F. (2005, April 16). FDA orders Levitra ad off the air. *Washington Post.* Retrieved April 16, 2005, from http://www.washingtonpost.com

Akers, R. (1973). *Deviant behavior: A social learning approach.* Belmont, CA: Wadsworth.

Akers, R. (1992). *Drugs, alcohol and society.* Belmont, CA: Wadsworth.

Akers, R. (1998). *Social learning and social structure: A general theory of crime and deviance.* Boston: Northeastern University Press.

Akers, R., Krohn, M., Lanza-Kaduce, L., & Radosevich, M. (1979). Social learning and deviant behavior. *American Sociological Review, 44,* 636–655.

Akers, R., & Lee, G. (1996). A longitudinal test of social learning theory: Adolescent smoking. *Journal of Drug Issues, 26,* 317–343.

Akers, R., & Sellers, C. (2009). *Criminological theories* (5th ed.). New York: Oxford University Press.

Akins, S., Cline, S., Lanfear, C., & Mosher, C. (2012). *Revisiting patterns of American Indians' substance use.* Unpublished manuscript.

Akins, S., Mosher, C., Rotolo, T., & Griffin, R. (2003). Patterns and correlates of substance use among American Indians in Washington State. *Journal of Drug Issues, 33,* 45–74.

Akins, S., Mosher, C., Smith, C., & Gauthier, J. (2008). The effect of acculturation on patterns of Hispanic substance use in Washington State. *Journal of Drug Issues, 38,* 103–118.

Alaniz, L. (1998). Alcohol availability and targeted advertising in racial/ethnic minority communities. *Alcohol Health and Research World, 22,* 286–289.

Albaugh, B., & Anderson, P. (1974). Peyote in the treatment of alcoholism among American Indians. *American Journal of Psychiatry, 131,* 1247–1250.

Albergotti, R., & O'Connell, V. (2010, July 2). Blood brothers. *Wall Street Journal.* Retrieved September 27, 2012, from http://online.wsj.com

Alberta Alcohol and Drug Abuse Commission. (2003). *Position on the legal drinking age.* Edmonton, AB: Author.

Albrecht, S., Amery, C., & Miller, M. (1996). Patterns of substance abuse among rural black adolescents. *Journal of Drug Issues, 26,* 751–781.

Alcoholics Anonymous. (2005). *Alcoholics Anonymous: The big book.* New York: Author.

Alexander, B. (1990). *Peaceful measures: Canada's way out of the war on drugs.* Toronto: University of Toronto Press.

Alexander, M. (2010). The new Jim Crow—Mass incarceration in the age of color-blindness. New York: The New Press.

Alford, J., Hibbing, C., & Funk, J. (2005). Are political orientations genetically transmitted? *American Political Science Review, 99,* 153–167.

Allen, K. (2006, January 20). Jackets' Berard tests positive for steroid. *USA Today.* Retrieved January 20, 2006, from http://www.usatoday.com

Allentuck, S., & Bowman, K. (1942). The psychiatric aspects of marijuana intoxication. *American Journal of Psychiatry, 99,* 248–250.

Alleyne, R. (2009, December 1). Skunk linked to huge increase in risk of psychotic disease. *The Telegraph*. Retrieved December 2, 2009, from http://www.telegraph.co.uk

Allman, T. D. (2002). Blow-back. In M. Gray (Ed.), *Busted* (pp. 3–16). New York: Thunder's Mouth Press/Nation Books.

Alonso-Zaldivar, R. (2004, November 26). When drugs go wrong: Role of the FDA debated. *Los Angeles Times*. Retrieved November 26, 2004, from http://www.latimes.com

Alonso-Zaldivar, R. (2005a, June 9). FDA's acting chief is cleared of affair charges. *Los Angeles Times*. Retrieved June 9, 2005, from http://www.latimes.com

Alonso-Zaldivar, R. (2005b, May 6). Sales pitch dodged Vioxx perils, notes show. *Los Angeles Times*. Retrieved May 6, 2005, from http://www.latimes.com

Alphonso, C. (2000, June 3). Police got math wrong: Record-breaking seizure of ecstasy not so big after all. *Globe and Mail*. Retrieved June 3, 2000, from http://www.theglobeandmail.com

Alvarez, L. (2003, August 11). Antitobacco trend has reached Europe. *New York Times*. Retrieved August 11, 2003, from http://www.nytimes.com

Amendment 64—Legalize Marijuana Election Results. (2013, January 30). *Denver Post*. Retrieved January 30, 2013, from http://data.denverpost.com

American Association of Poison Control Centers (AAPC). (2012, April 16). *Synthetic marijuana data updated*. Retrieved from https://aapcc.s3.amazonaws.com/files/library/Synthetic_Marijuana_Data_for_Website_1.09.2013.pdf

American Civil Liberties Union. (1999). Report calls employee testing a bad investment. Retrieved July 15, 2005, from http://www.aclu.org/workplacerights/drugtesting/13413prs19991215.html

American Civil Liberties Union. (2000a, November 1). *Ferguson v. City of Charleston: Social and legal contexts*. Retrieved May 30, 2005, from http://www.aclu.org/reproductiverights/lowincome/12511res20001101.html

American Civil Liberties Union. (2000b, March 23). *Testimony of Barry Steinhardt on CODIS before the House Judiciary Subcommittee on Crime*. Retrieved June 10, 2005, from http://www.aclu.org/privacy/medical/14850leg20000323.html

American Civil Liberties Union. (2003, December 15). *South Carolina students were terrorized by police raids with guns and drug dogs, ACLU lawsuit charges*. Retrieved December 15, 2003, from http://www.aclu.org/drug policy/youth/index.html

American Gastroenterological Association. (2004). *Many take more pain relievers than recommended*. Retrieved July 15, 2004, from http://alcoholism.about.com/od/prescription/a/blaga040522p.htm

American Heart Association. (2004). *Atherosclerosis*. Retrieved June 10, 2005, from http://www.americanheart.org/presenter.jhtml?identifier=4440

American Indian Religious Freedom Act Amendments of 1994, Pub. L. No. 103–344, 108 Stat. 3124 (1994).

American Medical Association. (2004). *Addressing the minimum legal drinking age (MLDA) in college communities*. Retrieved December 10, 2004, from http://www.alcoholpolicymd.com/alcohol_and_health/study_legal_age.htm

American Psychiatric Association. (2000). *Diagnostic and statistical manual of mental disorders* (4th ed., Text rev.). Washington, DC: Author.

Amaro, H., Whitaker, R., Coffman, G., & Heeren, T. (1990). Acculturation and marijuana and cocaine use: Findings from HHANES 1982–84. *American

Journal of Public Health, 80(S), 54–60.

Amnesty International. (2011). *Addicted to death: Drug offenses in Iran.* London: Amnesty International. Retrieved August 7, 2012, from http://www.amnesty.org

Amodeo, M., Robb, N., Peou, S., & Tran, H. (1997). Alcohol and other drug problems among Southeast Asians: Patterns of use and approaches to assessment and intervention. *Alcoholism Treatment Quarterly, 15,* 63–77.

An ailing, failing, FDA. (2004, November 23). *Los Angeles Times.* Retrieved November 23, 2004, from http://www.latimes.com

Anderson, E. (1990). *Streetwise: Race, class and change in an urban community.* Chicago: University of Chicago Press.

Anderson, E. (1999). *Code of the street.* New York: W. W. Norton and Company.

Anderson, L. (1980). Leaf variation among cannabis species from a controlled garden. *Harvard University Botanical Museum Leaflets, 28,* 61–69.

Andrews, D. A., Zinger, I., Hoge, R. D., Bonta, J., Gendreau, P., & Cullen, F. T. (1990). Does correctional treatment work? A clinically relevant and psychologically informed meta-analysis. *Criminology, 28*(3), 369–404.

Andrews, M. (2012, January 16). Anti-smoking efforts often fall short. *Los Angeles Times.* Retrieved January 16, 2012, from http://www.latimes.com

Angell, M. (2004). *The truth about drug companies.* New York: Random House.

Anglin, M. D., Longshore, D., & Turner, S. (1999). Treatment alternatives to street crime: An evaluation of five programs. *Criminal Justice and Behavior, 26,* 168–195.

AngusReidStrategies. (2008, May 12). *Canadians want federal government to retain harm reduction programs.* Retrieved December 18, 2010, from http://www.angus-reid.com

Anslinger, H. (1943). The psychiatric aspects of marihuana intoxication. *Journal of the American Medical Association, 121,* 212–213.

Anti-drug pitch goes wide. (2003, September 22). *Los Angeles Times.* Retrieved September 22, 2003, from http://www.latimes.com

Antonen, M. (2003, November 16). Baseball defends steroids policy. *USA Today.* Retrieved November 16, 2003, from http://www.usatoday.com

Appel, J., Backes, G., & Robbins, J. (2005). California's Proposition 36: A success ripe for refinement and replication. *Criminology and Public Policy, 3,* 585–592.

Aquilino, W., & LoSciuto, L. (1990). Interview mode effects in drug use surveys. *Public Opinion Quarterly, 54,* 362–395.

Archibold, R. (2009, March 23). Mexican drug cartel violence spills over, alarming U.S. *New York Times.* Retrieved March 23, 2009, from http://www.nytimes.com

Arria, A., & O'Brien, M. (2011). The "high" risk of energy drinks. *Journal of the American Medical Association, 305,* 600–601.

Arizona Supreme Court. (1999, March). *Drug treatment and education fund legislative report: Fiscal year 1997–1998.* Retrieved May 10, 2005, from http://www.csdp.org/research/dteftoday.pdf

Armor, D., Polich, J., & Stambul, H. (1976). *Alcoholism and treatment.* Santa Monica, CA: Rand.

Arnett, J. (1998). Risk behavior and family role transitions during the twenties. *Journal of Youth and Adolescence, 27,* 301–320.

Arrestee Drug Abuse Monitoring. (2002). *IADAM in eight countries: Approaches and challenges.* Washington, DC: National Institute of Justice.

Arrestee Drug Abuse Monitoring. (2003). Preliminary report on drug use and related matters among adult arrestees and juvenile detainees. Washington, DC: National Institute of Justice.

Arrestee Drug Abuse Monitoring. (2012). *ADAM-II 2011 annual report.* Washington, DC: Office of National Drug Control Policy.

Arria, A. M., & O'Brien, M. C. (2011). The "high" risk of energy drinks. *JAMA: The journal of the American Medical Association, 305,* 600–601.

Ashley, R. (1975). *Cocaine: Its history, use, and effects.* New York: St. Martin's Press.

Askwith, R. (1998, September 13). How aspirin turned hero. *Sunday Times.* Retrieved April 10, 2005, from http://www.timesonline.co.uk

Assael, S. (2012, August 24). Is Olympic HGH test ready for NFL? *ESPN.* Retrieved October 2, 2012, from http://espn.go.com

A symptom of FDA laxity. (2004, October 1). *Los Angeles Times.* Retrieved October 1, 2004, from http://www.latimes.com

Atwood-Lawrence, E. (2004). *Sun dance.* Retrieved June 15, 2005, from http://www.crystalinks.com/sundance.html

Auriacombe, M., Franques, P., & Tignol, J. (2001). Deaths attributable to methadone vs. buprenorphine in France. *Journal of the American Medical Association, 285,* 45.

Austin, J., & Irwin, J. (2012). *It's about time—America's imprisonment binge.* Independence, KY: Cengage.

Australia 21. (2012). *The prohibition of illicit drugs is killing and criminalising our children.* Weston, ACT. Author. Retrieved September 9, 2012, from http://www.australia21.org.au

Australian Crime Commission. (2010). *Annual report.* Retrieved August 17, 2012, from http://www.crimecommission.gov.au

Bachman, J., Wallace, J., O'Malley, P., Johnston, L., Kurth, C., & Neighbors, H. (1991). Racial/ethnic differences in smoking, drinking, and illicit drug use among American high school seniors, 1976–1989. *American Journal of Public Health, 81,* 372–377.

Backus, F. (2011, November 18). Poll: Public supports medical marijuana, but not full pot legalization. *CBS News.* Retrieved June 8, 2012, from http://www.cbsnews.com

Baggott, M. J., Erowid, E., Erowid, F., Galloway, G. P., & Mendelson, J. (2010). Use patterns and self-reported effects of Salvia divinorum: An Internet-based survey. *Drug & Alcohol Dependence, 111,* 250–256.

Bahr, S., Masters, A., & Taylor, B. (2012). An evaluation of a short-term drug treatment for jail inmates. *International Journal of Offender Therapy and Comparative Criminology 92* (2), 155–174.

Bahrke, M. (2000). Psychological effects of endogenous testosterone and anabolic-androgenic steroids. In C. Yesalis (Ed.), *Anabolic steroids in sport and exercise* (2nd ed., pp. 247–278). Champaign, IL: Human Kinetics.

Bahrke, M., Yesalis, C., & Wright, J. (1996). Psychological and behavioral effects of endogenous testosterone and anabolic-androgenic steroids: An update. *Sports Medicine, 22,* 367–390.

Bai, M. (1997, March 31). White storm warning. *Newsweek.* Retrieved February 12, 2003, from http://www.msnbc.msn.com

Bailey, E. (2003, February 2). The drug war refugees. *Los Angeles Times.* Retrieved February 2, 2003, from http://www.latimes.com

Bajak, F. (2011, January 18). U.S. objects to Bolivia bid for licit cocaine chewing. *Washington Post.* Retrieved January 18, 2011, from http://www.washingtonpost.com

Baker, M. (2011, May 3). States reassess marijuana laws after federal warning. *Associated Press.* Retrieved May 3, 2011, from http://www.ap.org

Baker, R. (2002). George Soros's long strange trip. In M. Gray (Ed.), *Busted* (pp. 51–61). New York: Thunder's Mouth Press.

Balko, R. (2002, December 9). Targeting social drinkers is just MADD. *Los Angeles Times.* Retrieved December 9, 2002, from http://www.latimes.com

Bamberger, M., & Yeager, D. (1997). Over the edge. *Sports Illustrated, 86*(15), 60–70.

Bammer, G., Hall, W., Hamilton, M., & Ali, R. (2002). Harm minimization in a prohibition context: Australia. *Annals, 582,* 80–93.

Bandura, A. (1973). *Aggression: A social learning analysis.* Englewood Cliffs, NJ: Prentice-Hall.

Bandura, A. (1977). *Social learning theory.* Englewood Cliffs, NJ: Prentice-Hall.

Barma, M., Patel, R., & Patel, M. (2008). Female sexual dysfunction: From causality to cure. *U.S. Pharmacist.* Retrieved August 29, 2012, from http://www.uspharmacist.com

Barnard, A. (2002, June 30). Drug industry freebies. *Boston Globe.* Retrieved June 30, 2002, from http://www.boston.com

Barnes, G. (1990). Impact of family on adolescent drinking patterns. In R. Collins, K. Leonard, & J. Searles (Eds.), *Alcohol and the family: Research and clinical perspectives* (pp. 137–161). New York: Guilford Press.

Barnes, G., Welte, J., & Hoffman, J. (2002). Relationship of alcohol use to delinquency and illicit drug use in adolescents: Gender, age and racial/ethnic differences. *Journal of Drug Issues, 32,* 153–178.

Barnes, J. (2000, August 21–27). The hardest test. *New Yorker.* Retrieved August 21, 2000, from http://www.newyorker.com

Barr, B. (1999, March 28). Medical debacle. *Columbian.* Retrieved March 28, 1999, from http://www.columbian.com

Barr, K., Farrell, M., Barnes, G., & Welte, J. (1993). Race, class and gender differences in substance abuse: Evidence of a middle-class/underclass polarization among black males. *Social Problems, 40,* 314–327.

Barry, E. (2003, January 1). Testosterone tested as mood drug. *Boston Globe.* Retrieved January 1, 2003, from http://www.boston.com

Barrett, D. (2011, June 17). Indian court overturns mandatory death penalty for drug offences. *International Center on Human Rights and Drug Policy.* Retrieved September 2, 2012, from http://www.humanrightsanddrugs.org

Barton, A. (2012, March 5). France says "oui" to mandatory breathalyzers in cars. *Globe and Mail.* Retrieved March 5, 2012, from http://www.theglobeand mail.com

Bath salts ban could curb some use of legal drugs linked to violent behavior, but not all. (2012, August 25). *Associated Press.* Retrieved August 25, 2012, from http://www.ap.org

Battista, J. (2011, May 8). NFL considers forcing new testing standards. *New York Times.* Retrieved May 8, 2011, from http://www.nytimes.com

Bauman, K., & Graf, N. (2003). *Educational attainment: 2000. Census 2000 brief.* Washington, DC: U.S. Department of the Census.

Bayer corporation faces first trial in Baycol drug litigation. (2002, July 3). *U.S. Newswire.* Retrieved July 3, 2002, from http://www.usnewswire.com

Bayoumi, A., & Zaric, G. (2008). The cost-effectiveness of Vancouver's supervised injection facility. *Canadian Medical Association Journal, 179,* 1143–1151.

Bazelon, L. (2003, July). Testing, testing, everywhere. *Legal Affairs.* Retrieved July 15, 2003, from http://www.legalaffairs. org

Beatty, P., Petteruti, A., & Ziedenberg, J. (2007). *The vortex: The concentrated racial impact of drug imprisonment and the characteristics of punitive counties.* Washington DC: Justice Policy Institute, December.

Beauvais, F. (1998). American Indians and alcohol. *Alcohol Health and Research World, 22,* 253–259.

Beauvais, F., & LaBoueff, S. (1985). Drug and alcohol abuse intervention in American Indian communities. *International Journal of the Addictions, 2,* 139–171.

Beauvais, F., Oetting, E., & Edwards, R. (1985). Trends in drug use of Indian adolescents living on reservations. *American Journal of Drug and Alcohol Abuse, 11,* 209–229.

Bebow, J. (2004, January 30). Flood of heroin ravaging city. *Chicago Tribune.* Retrieved January 30, 2004, from http://www.chicagotribune.com

Becker, H. (1963). *Outsiders: Studies in the sociology of deviance.* New York: Free Press.

Beckett, K., Nyrop, K., Pfingst, L., & Bowen, M. (2005). Drug use, drug possession arrests and the question of race: Lessons from Seattle. *Social Problems, 52,* 419–441.

Behr, E. (1997). *Prohibition: Thirteen years that changed America.* London: BBC Books, Penguin.

Beiser, V. (2000, September/October). Patchy justice: Is a new drug test too error prone? *Mother Jones.* Retrieved September 10, 2000, from http://www.motherjones.com

Belenko, S. (2001). *Research on drug courts: A critical review, 2001 update.* New York: Columbia University, National Center on Addiction and Substance Abuse.

Belkin, L. (2001, March/April). Prime time pushers. *Mother Jones.* Retrieved March 2, 2001, from http://www.motherjones.com

Bendavid, N. (2002, March 24). Critics defy ads linking drugs, terror. *Chicago Tribune.* Retrieved March 24, 2002, from http://www.chicagotribune.com

Bennett, W. (2001, March 5). Advice for the next drug czar. *Miami Herald.* Retrieved March 5, 2001, from http://www.miami.com

Benshoff, B., Harrawood, L., & Koch, D. (2003). Substance abuse and the elderly: Unique issues and concerns. *Journal of Rehabilitation, 69,* 43–48.

Benzie, R., & Hume, M. (2002, December 10). Clement vows to block drug injection sites. *National Post.* Retrieved December 10, 2002, from http://www.canada.com/nationalpost

Berenson, A. (2005, May 31). Despite vow, drug makers still withhold data. *New York Times.* Retrieved May 31, 2005, from http://www.nytimes.com

Berenson, A., & Harris, G. (2005, February 1). Pfizer says 1999 trials revealed risks with Celebrex. *New York Times.* Retrieved February 1, 2005, from http://www.nytimes.com

Bergman, B., et al. (2004, August 23). This bud's for the U.S. *Time.* Retrieved August 25, 2004, from http://www.time.com

Bernstein, N. (2010, March 30). How one marijuana cigarette may lead to deportation. *New York Times.* Retrieved March 30, 2010, from http://www.nytimes.com

Bewley-Taylor, D. (2003). Challenging the U.N. drug control conventions: Problems and possibilities. *International Journal of Drug Policy, 14,* 171–179.

Beyrer, C. (2011). Safe injection facilities save lives. *Lancet, 377,* 1385–1386.

Bhasin, S., Storer, T., Berman, N., Callegari, C., Clevenger, B., Phillip, J., et al. (1996). The effects of supraphysiologic doses of testosterone on muscle size and strength in normal men. *New England Journal of Medicine, 335,* 1–7.

Biertempfel, R. (2005, May 22). NCAA drug-testing system gets results. *Pittsburgh Tribune-Review.* Retrieved June 1, 2005, from http://www.pittsburghlive.com

Big brother's little helper. (2003, March). *Harper's.* Retrieved March 10, 2003, from http://www.harpers.org

Bilger, B. (2009, November 24). A better brew. *New Yorker.* Retrieved November 24, 2008, from http://www.newyorker.com

Biskupic, J. (2009, April 16). Strip search review tests limits of school drug policy. *USA Today*. Retrieved April 16, 2009, from http://www.usatoday.com

Binge drinking. (1997, September 5). *Wall Street Journal*. Retrieved September 5, 1997, from http://www.wsj.com

Bissinger, B. (2005, May 5). Home runs wanted, no questions asked. *New York Times*. Retrieved May 5, 2005, from http://www.nytimes.com

Black, S., & Markides, K. (1993). Acculturation and alcohol consumption in Puerto Rican, Cuban-American and Mexican-American women in the United States. *American Journal of Public Health, 83*, 890–893.

Blackman, O. (2004, December 18). Scanner blitz on gulping druggies. *London Daily Mirror*. Retrieved December 18, 2004, from http://mirror.co.uk

Blair, J. (2011, November 6). Will Georges Laraque's claims about hockey and steroids fall on deaf ears? *Globe and Mail*. Retrieved November 6, 2011, from http://www.theglobeandmail.com

Blake, S., Ledesky, R., Goodenow, C., Sawyer, R., Lohrmann, D., & Windsor, R. (2003). Condom availability programs in Massachusetts high schools: Relationships with condom use and sexual behavior. *American Journal of Public Health, 93*, 955–962.

Blakeslee, N. (2005). *Tulia: Race, cocaine, and corruption in a small Texas town*. New York: Public Affairs.

Blendon, R., & Young, J. (1998). The public and the war on illicit drugs. *Journal of the American Medical Association, 279*, 827–832.

Blickman, T., & Jelsma, M. (2009). *Drug policy reform in practice*. Amsterdam: Transnational Institute.

Block, L., Morwitz, V. G., Putsis, B., & Sen, S. (2002). Assessing the impact of anti-drug advertising on adolescent drug consumption: Results from a behavioral economic model. *American Journal of Public Health, 92*, 1346–1351.

Blocker, K. (2001a, October 28). Meth cases jam justice system. *Spokesman-Review*. Retrieved October 28, 2001, from http://www.spokesmanreview.com

Blocker, K. (2001b, October 11). Range of meth problems is staggering. *Spokesman-Review*. Retrieved October 11, 2001, from http://www.spokesman-review.com

Bloy, M. (n.d.). *The Irish famine, 1845–9*. Retrieved June 15, 2005, from http://www.victorianweb.org/history/famine.html

Blum, J. (2011, March 6). Fake pot comes with real risks. *Portland Press Herald*. Retrieved March 6, 2011, from http://www.portlandpressherald.com

Blum, K., Futterman, S., & Pascarosa, P. (1977). Peyote, a potential ethnopharmacologic agent for alcoholism and other drug dependencies: Possible biochemical rationale. *Clinical Toxicology, 11*, 459–472.

Blumenson, E., & Nilsen, E. (1998). Policing for profit: The drug war's hidden economic agenda. *University of Chicago Law Review, 65*, 35–114.

Blumstein, A. (1993). Making rationality relevant—The American Society of Criminology 1992 presidential address. *Criminology, 31*, 1–16.

Blunkett, D. (2004, November 25). Home secretary: My law clampdown. *London Daily Mirror*. Retrieved November 25, 2004, from http://www.mirror.co.uk

Board of Education et al. v. Earls et al., 536 U.S. 822 (2002).

Boardman, J., Finch, B., Ellison, C., Williams, D., & Jackson, J. (2001). Neighborhood disadvantage, stress, and drug use among adults. *Journal of Health and Social Behavior, 42*, 151–165.

Bogenschutz, M. P., Tonigan, J. S., & Miller, W. R. (2006). Examining the effects of alcoholism typology and AA attendance on self-efficacy as a mechanism of change. *Journal of Studies on Alcohol, 67*(4), 562–567.

Bollinger, L. (1997). *German drug law in action: The evolution of cannabis science: From prohibition to human right.* Berlin: Peter Lang.

Bond, J., Kaskutas, L., & Weisner, C. (2003). The persistent influence of social networks and alcoholics anonymous on abstinence. *Journal of Studies on Alcohol, 64,* 579–588.

Bonwich, J. (2003, September 10). Splash of Tennessee spirit jacks up the flavor of food. *St. Louis Post-Dispatch.* Retrieved September 10, 2003, from http://www.stltoday.com

Booth, W. (2010, June 16). Mexico's drug violence claims hundreds of lives in past 5 days. *Washington Post.* Retrieved June 16, 2010, from http://www.washingtonpost.com

Borelli, S. (2011, August 18). Mike Jacobs' positive HGH test first in pro sports. *USA Today.* Retrieved August 18, 2011, from http://www.usatoday.com

Borio, G. (2003). *Tobacco timeline.* Retrieved June 10, 2004, from http://www.tobacco.org/resources/history/Tobacco_History17.html

Boseley, S. (2002, September 2). Ecstasy not dangerous, say scientists. *Guardian.* Retrieved September 2, 2002, from http://www.guardian.co.uk

Bostwick, J. (2012). Blurred boundaries: The therapeutics and politics of medical marijuana. *Mayo Clinical Proceedings, 87,* 172–186.

Boucher, G. (2002, August 3). Police targeting ecstasy of raves. *Los Angeles Times.* Retrieved August 3, 2002, from http://www.latimes.com

Bouffard, J., Richardson, K., & Franklin, T. (2010). Drug courts for DWI offenders? The effectiveness of two hybrid drug courts on DWI offenders. *Journal of Criminal Justice, 38,* 25–33.

Bouncer fatally stabbed over NYC smoking ban. (2003, April 14). *USA Today.* Retrieved April 14, 2003, from http://www.usatoday.com

Bovard, J. (1999, July). Prison sentences of the politically connected. *Playboy.* Retrieved July 15, 2003, from http://www.playboy.com

Bowles, D., O'Bryant, C., Camidge, D., & Jimeno, A. (2012). The intersection between cannabis and cancer in the United States. *Clinical Reviews in Oncology/Hematology, 83,* 1–10.

Bowman, F. (2003, August 15). When sentences don't make sense. *National Association of Criminal Defense Lawyers.* Retrieved April 10, 2005, from http://www.nacdl.org/public.nsf/legislation/ci_03_36? OpenDocument

Bowers, J. (2008). Contraindicated drug courts. *UCLA L. Rev., 55,* 783–1971.

Boyadjev, N., Georgieva, R., Massaldjivea, S., & Gueorguiev, S. (2000). Reversible hypogonadism and azoospermia as a result of anabolic-androgenic steroid use in a bodybuilder with personality disorder: A case report. *Journal of Sports Medicine and Physical Fitness, 40,* 271–274.

Boyce, P., & Judd, F. (1999). The place for the tricyclic antidepressants in the treatment of depression. *Australia and New Zealand Journal of Psychiatry, 33,* 323–327.

Boyd, G. (2001, July 31). The drug war is the new Jim Crow. *American Civil Liberties Union.* Retrieved August 1, 2001, from http://www.aclu.org/drugpolicyracialjustice/10830pub20010731.html

Boyd, G., & Hitt, J. (2002). This is your Bill of Rights. In M. Gray (Ed.), *Busted* (pp. 149–154). New York: Thunder's Mouth Press/Nation Books.

Bradley, D., Finkelstein, S., & Stafford, R. (2006). Off-label prescribing among office-based physicians. *Archives of Internal Medicine, 166,* 1021–1026.

Braiker, B. (2003, April 15). "Just say know": An advocate of drug law reform says DARE is a 20-year-old failure. *Newsweek.* Retrieved April 15, 2003, from http://www.msnbc.msn.com

Bandon, K. (2001, June 10). Metham-phetamine sparks worry for babies. *Chicago Tribune*. Retrieved June 10, 2001, from http://www.chicagotribune.com

Brave Heart, M., Chase, J., Elkins, J., & Altschul, D. (2011). Historical trauma among indigenous peoples of the Americas: Concepts, research, and clinical considerations. *Journal of Psychoactive Drugs, 43*, 282–290.

Brecher, E. (1972). *Licit and illicit drugs*. Boston: Little, Brown.

Breggin, P., & Breggin, G. (1995). *Talking back to Prozac*. New York: St. Martin's Press.

Brennan, R. (2004, December 22). Province ignoring report, MADD charges. *Toronto Star*. Retrieved December 22, 2004, from http://www.thestar.com

Brezina, T. (1996). Adapting to strain: An examination of delinquent coping responses. *Criminology, 34*, 39–60.

Brick, M. (2003, April 30). Stiff fines accompany city's smoking ban. *New York Times*. Retrieved April 30, 2003, from http://www.nytimes.com

Bridge medalist refuses drug test, loses prize. (2002, September 4). *Globe and Mail*. Retrieved September 4, 2002, from http://www.theglobeandmail.com

Briffa, J. (2004, February 1). Brew romance. *Observer*. Retrieved February 1, 2004, from http://www.observer.co.uk

Brill, J. (2012, September 12). Why the NBA has never had a major doping scandal. *Huffington Post*. Retrieved September 12, 2012, from http://www.huffingtonpost.com

British Columbia Center for Excellence in HIV/AIDS. (2004). *Evaluation of the supervised injection site: One-year summary*. Vancouver, BC: Author. Retrieved October 5, 2004, from http://www.vandu.org/pdfs/sisyear report.pdf

British Columbia or Colombia? (2009, May 28). *Economist*. Retrieved September 22, 2009, from http://www.economist.com

Broadwater, T. (2004, December 3). Anti-tobacco programs underfunded. *Spokesman-Review*. Retrieved December 3, 2004, from http://www.spokesmanreview.com

Brodsky, A., & Peele, S. (1991, November). AA abuse. *Reason*, 34–39.

Browder, K. (2001). Anabolic steroids. In R. Carson-DeWitt (Ed.), *Encyclopedia of drugs, alcohol and addictive behavior* (pp. 122–128). New York: MacMillan Reference.

Browder, K., Blow, F., Young, J., & Hill, E. (1991). Symptoms and correlates of anabolic androgenic steroids dependence. *British Journal of Addiction, 86*, 759–768.

Brown, D. (2002, September 5). Canadian panel backs legalizing marijuana. *Washington Post*. Retrieved September 5, 2002, from http://www.washingtonpost.com

Brown, D. (2003, August 2). With injection sites, Canadian drug policy seeks a fix. *Washington Post*. Retrieved August 2, 2003, from http://www.washingtonpost.com

Brown, J. (2003, December 18). Martin to roll out his own pot bill. *Canadian Press*. Retrieved December 18, 2003, from http://www.cp.org

Brown, J., & Langton, D. (2007, October 15). Legalise all drugs: Chief constable demands end to "immoral laws." *Independent*. Retrieved October 15, 2007, from http://www.independent.co.uk

Brown, R. (2010). Associations with substance abuse treatment completion rates among drug court participants. *Substance Use and Misuse, 45*, 1874–1891.

Brown, R. (2012, July 20). Atlanta curbs smoking, part of southern wave of bans. *New York Times*. Retrieved July 20, 2012, from http://www.nytimes.com

Brown, R., Zuelsdorff, M., & Gassman, M. (2009). Treatment retention among

African-Americans in Dane County drug treatment court. *Journal of Offender Rehabilitation, 48,* 336–349.

Brownsberger, W., & Aromaa, S. (2003). Prohibition of drug dealing in school zones. *FAS Drug Policy Analysis Bulletin, 9.*

Brownstein, H. (1996). *The rise and fall of a violent crime wave: Crack cocaine and the social construction of a crime problem.* New York: Guilderland.

Brunel, P., Lovett, L., & Sport, P. (1996). *Intimate portrait of the Tour de France: Masters and slaves of the road* (2nd ed.). Denver, CO: Buonpane.

Buchanan, D., & Wallack, L. (1998). This is the partnership for a drug free America: Any questions? *Journal of Drug Issues, 28,* 329–356.

Buchanan, W. (2004, April 15). Online drugs raise warning. *Seattle Post-Intelligencer.* Retrieved April 15, 2004, from http://seattlepi.nwsource.com

Buchen, L. (2010, April 16). Party drug could ease trauma long term: Pilot studies demonstrate effectiveness of MDMA for post-traumatic stress disorder. *Nature News.* Retrieved August 15, 2012, from http://www.nature.com/news

Buck, H. (2005, November 22). Clark College banishes tobacco. *Columbian.* Retrieved November 22, 2005, from http://www.columbian.com

Buckley, W. F., Nadelmann, E. A., Schmoke, K., McNamara, J. D., Sweet, R. W., Szasz, T., et al. (1996, February 12). The war on drugs is lost. *National Review.* Retrieved May 8, 2005, from http://www.nationalreview.com

Buckley, W., Yesalis, C., Friedl, K., Anderson, W., Streit, A., & Wright, J. (1988). Estimated prevalence of anabolic steroid use among high school seniors. *Journal of the American Medical Association, 260,* 3441–3445.

Bureau of Justice Statistics. (2003). *Prisoners in 2002.* Washington, DC: U.S. Department of Justice.

Bureau of Justice Statistics. (2011). *Prisoners in 2010.* Washington, DC: U.S. Department of Justice.

Burgermeister, J. (2004). German prosecutors probe again into bribes by drug companies. *British Medical Journal, 328,* 1333.

Burgess, R., & Akers, R. (1968). A differential association-reinforcement theory of criminal behavior. *Social Problems, 14,* 128–147.

Burkett, S., & Warren, B. (1987). Religiosity, peer associations, and adolescent marijuana use: A panel study of underlying causal factors. *Criminology, 25,* 109–131.

Burns, M., & Moskowitz, H. (1977). *Psychophysical tests for DWI arrest [DOT-HS-5-01241].* Washington, DC: U.S. Department of Transportation, National Highway Traffic Safety Administration.

Busch, S. (2005, June 3). Elegy for a habit. *Guardian.* Retrieved June 3, 2005, from http://www.guardian.co.uk

Bushman, B., & Cooper, H. (1990). Effects of alcohol on human aggression: An integrative literature review. *Psychological Bulletin, 107,* 341–354.

Busse, P. (2003, June 26). Your rights: Up in smoke. *Portland Mercury,* p. 3.

Butterfield, F. (2001a, September 29). New drug offender program draws unexpected clients. *New York Times.* Retrieved September 29, 2001, from http://www.nytimes.com

Butterfield, F. (2001b, September 2). States easing stringent laws on prison time. *New York Times.* Retrieved September 2, 2001, from http://www.nytimes.com

Butzin, C. A., Martin, S. S., & Inciardi, J. A. (2005). Treatment during transition from prison to community and subsequent illicit drug use. *Journal of Substance Abuse Treatment, 28*(4), 351–358. doi:10.1016/j.jsat.2005.02.009

Byrd, S. (2011, January 22). Official: "Bath salts" are growing drug problem. *San*

Francisco Chronicle. Retrieved January 22, 2011, from http://www.sfgate.com

Cabanatuan, M., & McCormick, E. (2003, July 27). California's hit and run crisis: More flee fatal accidents here than any other state. *San Francisco Chronicle.* Retrieved July 27, 2003, from http://www.sfgate.com

Cadoret, R. (1995). Adoption studies. *Alcohol Health and Research World, 19,* 195–201.

Cadrain, D. (2003, January). Are your employee drug tests accurate? *HR Magazine.* Retrieved May 15, 2004, from http://www.shrm.org/hrmagazine

Caetano, R. (1984). Ethnicity and drinking in northern California: A comparison among whites, blacks, and Hispanics. *Alcohol and Alcoholism, 19,* 31–44.

Caetano, R. (1988). Alcohol use among Hispanic groups in the United States. *American Journal of Drug and Alcohol Abuse, 14,* 293–308.

Caetano, R., & Clark, C. (1998). Trends in drinking patterns among whites, blacks, and Hispanics: 1984–1995. *Journal of Studies on Alcohol, 59,* 659–668.

Caetano, R., Clark, C., & Tam, T. (1998). Alcohol consumption among racial/ethnic minorities. *Alcohol Health and Research World, 22,* 233–241.

Caetano, R., & Kaskutas, L. (1995). Changes in drinking patterns among whites, blacks, and Hispanics, 1984–1992. *Journal of Studies on Alcohol, 56,* 558–565.

Caetano, R., & Medina-Mora, M. (1989). Acculturation and drinking among people of Mexican descent in Mexico and the United States. *Journal of Studies on Alcohol, 49,* 462–470.

Cahalan, D. Cisin, I. H., & Crossley, H. M. (1969). *American drinking practices: A national study of drinking behavior.* New Brunswick, NJ: Rutgers Center of Alcohol Studies.

Cain, B. (2005, July 31). Oregon bill targets meth labs. *Associated Press.* Retrieved July 31, 2005, from http://www.ap.org

Cambanis, T. (2003, October 9). Heroin influx spurs N.E. drug epidemic. *Boston Globe.* Retrieved October 9, 2003, from http://www.boston.com

Caminiti comes clean: Ex-MVP says he won award while using steroids. (2002, May 28). *Sports Illustrated.* Retrieved May 28, 2002, from http://www.sportsillustrated.cnn.com

Campaign for Tobacco-Free Kids. (2009, December). *A broken promise to our children.* Washington, DC: Author.

Campaign for Tobacco-Free Kids. (2012). *Broken promises to our children.* Retrieved June 15, 2012, from http://www.tobaccofreekids.org

Campbell, D. (2002, July 20). U.S. cannabis refugees cross border. *Guardian.* Retrieved July 20, 2002, from http://www.guardian.co.uk

Campbell, I. (2003). Nicotine replacement therapy in smoking cessation. *Thorax, 58,* 464–465.

Campbell, M. (2005, March 26). Users only see the big picture. *Toronto Star.* Retrieved March 26, 2005, from http://www.thestar.com

Cami, J., & Farre, M. (2003). Drug addiction. *New England Journal of Medicine, 349,* 975–986.

Canada plans to offer medical marijuana in B.C. pharmacies, but move won't heal government pot program's woes, activist says. (2004, March 26). *Drug War Chronicle.* Retrieved March 26, 2004, from http://stopthedrug war.org/chronicle/330/healthcanada.shtml

Canedy, D. (2002, July 18). Daughter of Governor Bush is sent to jail in a drug case. *New York Times.* Retrieved July 18, 2002, from http://www.nytimes.com

Canfield, D. (2009, October 8). Drug law reforms in place. *Huffington Post.* Retrieved June 6, 2012, from http://www.huffingtonpost.com

Canetto, S. S. (1991). Gender roles, suicide attempts and substance abuse. *Journal of Psychology, 125,* 605–620.

Cardoso, F., Gaviria, C., & Zedillo, E. (2009, February 23). The war on drugs is a failure. *Wall Street Journal.* Retrieved February 23, 2009, from http://online.wsj.com

Carey, B. (2003, May 26). Searching for the next Prozac. *Los Angeles Times.* Retrieved May 26, 2003, from http://www.latimes.com

Carey, E. (1998, February 15). Cannabis conundrum. *Toronto Star.* Retrieved February 15, 1998, from http://www.thestar.com

Carey, E. (2003, October 22). Heroin addicts to get drug for free. *Toronto Star.* Retrieved October 22, 2003, from http://www.thestar.com

Carhart-Harris, R., Leech, R., Williams, T., Erritzoe, D., Abbassi, N., Barglotas, T., Hobden, P., Sharp, D., Evans, J., Fielding, A., Wise, R., & Nutt, D. (2012a). Implications for psyche-delic-assisted psychotherapy: Functional magnetic resonance imaging with psilocybin. *British Journal of Psychiatry, 200,* 238–244.

Carhart-Harris, R., Carhart-Harris, R. L., Erritzoe, D., Williams, T., Stone, J. M., Reed, L. J., Colasanti, A., Tyacke, R. J., Leech, R., Malizia, A. L., Murphy, K., Hobden, P., Evans, J., Feilding, A., Wise, R. G., & Nutt, D. J. (2012b). Neural correlates of the psychedelic state as determined by fMRI studies with psilocybin. *Proceedings of the National Academy of Sciences of the United States of America, 109,* 2138–2143.

Carillo, C. (1990, January 31). Toads take a licking from desperate druggies. *New York Post.* Retrieved April 11, 2004, from http://www.nypost.com

Carroll, L. (2003, November 4). Fetal brains suffer badly from effects of alcohol. *New York Times.* Retrieved November 4, 2003, from http://www.nytimes.com

Carson, R. (2012, September 30). Washington's marijuana legalization measure creates strange bedfellows among foes, backers. *Tacoma News-Tribune.* Retrieved September 30, 2012, from http://www.thenewstribune.com

Carter, W., & Barker, R. (2011). Does completion of juvenile drug court deter adult criminality? *Journal of Social Work Practice in the Addictions, 11,* 181–193.

Carvel, J. (2003, May 24). Friendly advice replaces "just say no" drug message. *Guardian.* Retrieved May 24, 2003, from http://www.guardian.co.uk

Castle, K. (2010, October 2). Concern over K2 growing as poison control groups see calls multiply. *Times News.* Retrieved October 3, 2010, from http://www.timesnews.net

Castillo, E., & Wyatt, K. (2012, October 31). Mexico study: US legalization cuts cartel profits. *Associated Press.* Retrieved October 31, 2012, from http://www.ap.org

Castro, F., Proescholdbell, R. J., Abeita, L., & Rodriguez, D. (1999). Ethnic and cultural minority groups. In B. McCrady & E. Epstein (Eds.), *Addictions: A guide for professionals* (pp. 499–526). New York: Oxford.

Catalano, R., & Hawkins, J. D. (1996). The social development model: A theory of antisocial behavior. In J. D. Hawkins (Ed.), *Delinquency and crime: Current theories* (pp. 149–197). New York: Cambridge University Press.

Catalano, R., Oesterle, S., Fleming, C., & Hawkins, D. (2009). The importance of bonding to school for healthy development: Findings from the Social Development Group. *Journal of School Health, 74,* 252–261.

Cauchon, D. (1998, October 7). Canadian hemp isn't going to pot. *USA Today.* Retrieved October 7, 1998, from http://www.usatoday.com

Cauchon, D. (1999, April 13). Zero tolerance policy lacks flexibility. *USA Today.* Retrieved April 13, 1999, from http://www.usatoday.com

Cauchon, D. (2000, September 25). FDA advisers tied to industry. *USA Today.* Retrieved September 25, 2000, from http://www.usatoday.com

Cave, D. (2009, January 14). Budget woes expose rifts over tobacco money. *New York Times.* Retrieved January 14, 2009, from http://www.nytimes.com

Censored. (1996, May/June). *Mother Jones.* Retrieved June 1, 1996, from http://www.motherjones.com

Center for Cognitive Liberty and Ethics. (2004). *Threats to cognitive liberty: Pharmacotherapy and the future of the drug war.* Davis, CA: Author. Retrieved March 15, 2005, from http://www.cognitiveliberty.org

Centers for Disease Control and Prevention. (2007). *School health policies and programs study.* Atlanta, GA: Author.

Centers for Disease Control and Prevention. (2008). Smoking-attributable mortality, years of potential life lost, and productivity losses—United States, 2000–2004. *Morbidity and Mortality Weekly Report, 57,* 1226–1228.

Centers for Disease Control and Prevention. (2010). Vital signs: Binge drinking, frequency, and intensity among adults—United States, 2010. *Morbidity and Mortality Weekly Report, 61,* 14.

Centers for Disease Control and Prevention. (2011a). *Tobacco-related mortality.* Retrieved July 10, 2012, from http://www.cdc.gov

Centers for Disease Control and Prevention. (2011b). Vital signs: Overdoses of prescription opioid pain relievers—United States, 1999–2008. *Morbidity and Mortality Weekly Report, 60*(43), 1487. Retrieved from http://www.cdc.gov/mmwr/pdf/wk/mm6043.pdf

Centers for Disease Control and Prevention. (2012a). *Poisoning in the United States: Fact sheet.* Atlanta, GA: U.S. Department of Health and Human Services, Centers for Disease Control. Retrieved from http://www.cdc.gov/homeandrecreationalsafety/poisoning/poisoning-factsheet.htm

Centers for Disease Control and Prevention. (2012b). Vital signs: Binge drinking prevalence, frequency, and intensity among adults—United States, 2010. *Morbidity and Mortality Weekly Report, 61,* 14.

Chafets, Z. (2009, February 12). A-Rod, get back on the 'roids. *Los Angeles Times.* Retrieved February 12, 2009, from http://www.latimes.com

Chammas, L. (2011, June 15). E-cigs gain celebrity status. *Washington Post.* Retrieved June 15, 2011, from http://www.washingtonpost.com

Chambliss, W. (1969). *Crime and the legal process.* New York: McGraw-Hill.

Chambliss, W. (1994). Policing the ghetto underclass: The politics of law and law enforcement. *Social Problems, 41,* 177–194.

Chandler, R., Fletcher, B., & Volkow, N. (2009). Treating drug abuse and addiction in the criminal justice system: Improving public health and safety. *Journal of the American Medical Association, 301,* 183–190.

Chapman, S. (2005, December 10.). Matter of smoke and hire. *Sydney Morning Herald.* Retrieved December 10, 2005, from http://www.smh.com.au

Chapman, S. (2006, May 18). The false threat of liberal drug laws. *Chicago Tribune.* Retrieved May 18, 2006, from http://www.chicagotribune.com

Chase, J. (2005, August 22). State taxes burn smokers. *Chicago Tribune.* Retrieved August 22, 2005, from http://www.chicagotribune.com

Chatwin, C. (2003). Drug policy developments within the European Union. *British Journal of Criminology, 43,* 567–582.

Cheever, S. (2004). *"My name is Bill Wilson"—His life and the creation of Alcoholics Anonymous.* New York: Simon and Schuster.

Cherneki, T. (2002, December 6). Police crack down on drunk drivers. *Vancouver Sun.* Retrieved December 6, 2002, from http://www.canada.com

Chilcoat, H., Dishion, T., & Anthony, J. (1995). Parent monitoring and the incidence of drug sampling in urban elementary school children. *American Journal of Epidemiology, 1,* 25–31.

Childress, S. (2006a, January 30). Meth epidemic: Tennessee's registry. *Newsweek.* Retrieved January 30, 2006, from http://www.msnbc.msn.com

China arrests 12,000 in online narcotics crackdown. (2011, October 29). *Associated Press.* Retrieved October 29, 2011, from http://www.ap.org

Christie, J., Fisher, D., Kozup, J., Smith, S., Burton, S., & Creyer, E. (2001). The effects of bar-sponsored alcohol beverage promotions across binge and non-binge drinkers. *Journal of Public Policy and Marketing, 20,* 240–254.

Chronic hypocrisy. (n.d.). Retrieved August 10, 2005, from http://djmixed.com/djmixed/newsandfeatures/article.cfm?Article_ID=2911

Cicero, T., Ellis, M., & Surratt, H. (2012). Effect of abuse-deterrent formulation of OxyContin. *New England Journal of Medicine, 367,* 187.

Cigarette marketing increased 85 percent in four years after 1998 tobacco settlement. (2004, October 22). *U.S. Newswire.* Retrieved October 22, 2004, from http://www.usnewswire.com

Clapp, J., Lange, J., Russell, C., Shillington, A., & Voas, R. (2003). A failed social norms marketing campaign. *Journal of Studies on Alcohol, 64,* 409–414.

Clark, C. (2002, October 2). U.S. warns against liberalizing laws on pot. *Globe and Mail.* Retrieved October 2, 2002, from http://www.theglobeandmail.com

Clark County. (2012). *State of Washington and Clark County voters' pamphlet.* Retrieved October 1, 2012, from http://www.clark.wa.gov

Clark County PREVENT! (2012). *Rx take back a huge success.* Accessed online October 12, 2012, at www.preventclarkcounty.org/rx_take_back

Clark, M. (1999, March 19). Her life with "one big brother." *San Jose Mercury News.* Retrieved September 12, 2003, from http://www.mercurynews.com

Clarridge, C. (2003, March 27). Bridge accepts treatment: DUI prosecution deferred. *Seattle Post-Intelligencer.* Retrieved March 27, 2003, from http://seattlepi.nwsource.com

Clausing, J. (2011, December 1). Suit filed after NM teen cuffed for burp in class. *Associated Press.* Retrieved December 1, 2011, from http://www.ap.org

Cloninger, C., Bohman, M., & Sigvardsson, S. (1981). Inheritance of alcohol abuse: Cross-fostering analysis of adopted men. *Archives of General Psychiatry, 36,* 861–868.

Cloud, J. (2000, June 5). The lure of ecstasy. *Time.* Retrieved June 10, 2000, from http://www.time.com

Cloud, J. (2001, April 9). Ecstasy crackdown. *Time.* Retrieved April 12, 2001, from http://www.time.com

Clouse, T. (2003, June 29). Cars seized in drug busts add flash to cops' fleet. *Spokesman-Review.* Retrieved June 29, 2003, from http://www.spokesmanreview.com

Cloward, R. A., & Ohlin, L. E. (1960). *Delinquency and opportunity: A theory of delinquent gangs.* New York: Free Press.

CNN. (2001, August 26). Report: Minorities lack proper mental health care. (2001). *CNN Health.* Retrieved from http://www.cnn.com/2001/HEALTH/08/26/mental.health/

CNN. (2012). Dump those prescription drugs. *The Chart.* Accessed October 12,

2012, at http://thechart.blogs.cnn.com/2012/09/28/dump-those-prescription-drugs/?hpt=he_c2

Cochran, J., & Akers, R. (1989). Beyond hellfire: Exploration of the variable effects of religiosity on adolescent marijuana and alcohol use. *Journal of Research in Crime and Delinquency, 26,* 198–225.

Coghlan, A. (2002, June 23). Vaccines may prevent tobacco addiction. *Toronto Star.* Retrieved June 23, 2002, from http://www.thestar.com

Cohen, A. (1955). *Delinquent boys.* Glencoe, IL: Free Press.

Cohen, A. (2013, January 28). Will states lead the way to legalizing marijuana nationwide? *Time.* Retrieved January 30, 2013, from http://www.time.com

Cohen, A. (2011, August 29). Drug testing the poor: Bad policy, even worse law. *Time.* Retrieved August 29, 2011, from http://www.time.com

Cohen, E., Feinn, R., Arias, A., & Kranzler, H. (2007). Alcohol treatment utilization: Findings from the National Epidemiologic Survey on alcohol and related conditions. *Drug and Alcohol Dependence, 86,* 214–221.

Cohen, J., Noakes, T., & Benande, A. (1988). Hyperchloesteremia in male powerlifters using anabolic-androgenic steroids. *The Physician and Sports Medicine, 16,* 49–56.

Coben, J. H., Davis, S. D., Furbee, P. M., Sikora, R. D., Tillotson, R. D., & Bossarte, R. M. (2010). Hospitalizations for poisoning by prescription opioids, sedatives, and tranquilizers. *American Journal of Preventive Medicine, 38,* 517–524.

Cohen, J., Morrison, S., Greenberg, J., & Saidinejad, M. (2012). Clinical presentation of intoxication due to synthetic cannabinoids. *Pediatrics, 129*(4), 1064–1067.

Coile, Z. (2005a, April 27). Bill seeks to toughen drug testing in pro sports. *San Francisco Chronicle.* Retrieved April 27, 2005, from http://www.sfate.com

Cole, D. (1999). *No equal justice: Race and class in the American criminal justice system.* New York: The New Press.

Cole, J. (2005). *End prohibition now!* Retrieved January 15, 2006, from http://www.leap.cc/publications/endprohnow.htm

Cole, S., & Nowaczyk, R. (1994). Field sobriety tests: Are they designed for failure? *Perceptual and Motor Skills, 79,* 99–104.

Coleman, J. (2002, June 26). Senate committee approves bill to raise minimum age to buy tobacco to 21. *San Francisco Chronicle.* Retrieved June 26, 2002, from http://www.sfgate.com

Collins, D., Abadi, M. H., Johnson, K., Shamblen, S., & Thompson, K. (2011). Non-medical use of prescription drugs among youth in an Appalachian population: Prevalence, predictors, and implications for prevention. *Journal of Drug Education, 41,* 309–326.

Collins, J. (2011, August 17). Tobacco companies sue the federal government over graphic warning labels, say they're unfair. *Chicago Tribune.* Retrieved August 17, 2011, from http://www.chicagotribune.com

Colliver, V. (2011, June 25). Armed robberies of pharmacies on the rise. *San Francisco Chronicle.* Retrieved June 25, 2011, from http://www.sfgate.com

Comer, S., Collins, E., Kleber, H., Nuwayser, E., Kerrigan, J., & Fischman, M. (2002). Depot Naltrexone: Long-lasting antagonism of the effect of heroin in humans. *Psychopharmacology, 159,* 351–360.

Conant, M. (1997, February 3). This is smart medicine. *Newsweek.* Retrieved October 12, 2003, from http://www.msnbc.msn.com

Condelli, W., & Hubbard, R. (1994). Client outcomes from therapeutic communities. In F. M. Tims, G. De Leon, & N. Jainchill (Eds.), *Therapeutic* community: *Advances in research and application. NIDA research monograph 144* (pp. 80–98). Rockville, MD: National Institute on Drug Abuse.

Congressional Budget Office. (2009). *Promotional spending for prescription drugs.* Washington, DC: Author.

Congress. (2005). Congressional Hearing on Steroids.

Conley, K. (2005, July 11–18). The players. *New Yorker.* Retrieved July 12, 2005, from http://www.newyorker.com

Conlon, C. (2003). Urineschool: A study of the impact of the Earls decision on high school random drug testing policies. *Journal of Law and Education, 32,* 297–319.

Connelly, J. (2003, July 16). Cellular phones: They can distract you to death. *Seattle Post-Intelligencer.* Retrieved July 16, 2003, from http://www.seattlepi.nw source.com

Connolly, C. (2004, July 15). Drug reimportation plan saves city $2.5 million. *Washington Post.* Retrieved July 15, 2004, from http://www.washington post.com

Connolly, J., Cracy, J., McGoon, M., Hensrud, D., Edwards, B., & Schaff, H. (1997). Valvular heart disease associated with fenfluramine-phentermine. *New England Journal of Medicine, 337,* 581–588.

Constable, P. (2011, January 14). As opium prices soar and allies focus on Taliban, Afghan drug war stumbles. *Washington Post.* Retrieved January 14, 2011, from http://www.washingtonpost.com

Constitutional literacy. (2001, May 7). *The Nation.* Retrieved May 7, 2001, from http://www.thenation.com

Consultancy Group. (2002, June). *Evaluation of Lambeth's pilot of warnings for possession of cannabis.* Retrieved July 10, 2002, from http://bbsnews.net/research/uk-cannabis-report-summary.pdf

Cooper, M. (2011, November 30). 2 governors asking U.S. to ease rules on marijuana to allow for its medical use. *New York Times.* Retrieved from http://www.nytimes.com/2011/12/01/us/federal-marijuana-classification-should-change-gregoire-and-chafee-say.html

Copeland, J., Peters, R., & Dillon, P. (2000). Anabolic-androgenic steroid use disorders in a sample of Australian competitive and recreational users. *Drug and Alcohol Dependence, 60,* 91–96.

Copeland, L. (2009, July 30). U.S. may require anti-DWI locks on vehicles. *USA Today.* Retrieved July 30, 2009, from http://www.usatoday.com

Costello, D. (2005, February 7). Their drug of choice: Teens are turning to Vicodin, Ritalin, and other easily obtained prescription pills. *Los Angeles Times.* Retrieved February 7, 2005, from http://www.latimes.com

Cotts, C. (2002, March 9). The partnership: Hard sell in the drug war. *The Nation.* Retrieved March 10, 2002, from http://www.thenation.com

Country profiles. (2004). *European legal database on drugs.* Retrieved December 12, 2004, from http://eldd.emcdda.europa.eu/

Cowan, R. (1986, December 5). How the narcs created crack. *National Review.* Retrieved November 10, 2002, from http://www.nationalreview.com

The Cowan Smith Kirk Gaston Law Firm. (2002). *DUI information.* Retrieved April 10, 2004, from http://dui.cowan lawfirm.com

Cox, A. (2006). *Cracked lenses: The visual exploitation of crack mothers.* Retrieved April 10, 2006, from http://www.wom enandprison.org

Craig, J. (2003, February 17). Hazy guidelines make pot tough to prescribe. *Spokesman-Review.* Retrieved February 17, 2003, from http://www.spokesman review.com

Crister, G. (2004, January 25). Truth: A bitter pill for drug makers. *Los Angeles Times.* Retrieved January 25, 2004, from http://www.latimes.com

Cronk, C., & Sarvela, P. (1997). Alcohol, tobacco, and other drug use among rural/small town and urban youth: A secondary analysis of the monitoring the future data set. *American Journal of Public Health, 87,* 760–764.

Cronkite, W. (2006, February 23). Why I support DPA, and so should you. *Drug Policy Alliance.* Retrieved February 23, 2006, from http://www.drugpolicy.org

Cronley, C., White, H., Mun, E., Lee, C., Finlay, A., & Loeber, R. (2012). Exploring the intersection of neighborhood racial and economic composition and individual race on substance use among male adolescents. *Journal of Ethnicity in Substance Abuse, 11,* 52–74.

Cross, G., Morgan, C., Mooney, A., Martin, C., & Rafter, J. (1990). Alcoholism treatment: A ten-year follow-up study. *Alcoholism: Clinical and Experimental Research, 14,* 169–173.

Crum, R., Helzer, J., & Anthony, J. (1993). Level of education and alcohol abuse in adulthood: A further inquiry. *American Journal of Public Health, 83,* 830–837.

Csete, J., & Grob, P. (2012). Switzerland, HIV and the power of pragmatism: Lessons for drug policy development. *International Journal of Drug Policy, 23,* 82–86.

Cumming, A. (2004, November 7). Ecstasy testing rejected. *Sydney Morning Herald.* Retrieved November 7, 2004, from http://www.smh.com.au

Curry, J. (2005, May 1). Selig orders harder line on drugs in baseball. *New York Times.* Retrieved May 1, 2005, from http://www.nytimes.com

Curry, J. (2006, April 1). With greenies banned, up for a cup of coffee? *New York Times.* Retrieved April 1, 2006, from http://www.nytimes.com

Curtis, W. (2012, January-February). My nutmeg bender. *Atlantic.* P. 30.

Cutting college aid, and fostering crime. (2005, July 20). *New York Times.* Retrieved July 20, 2005, from http://www.nytimes.com

Dakof, G. A., Cohen, J. B., Henderson, C. E., Duarte, E., Boustani, M. Blackburn, A., Venzer, E., & Hawes, S. (2010). A randomized pilot study of the Engaging Moms program for family drug court. *Journal of Substance Abuse Treatment, 38,* 263–274.

Daneman, M. (2012, September 10). More college campuses ban smoking. *USA Today.* Retrieved September 10, 2012, from http://www.usatoday.com

Danger. (1938, April). *Survey Graphic,* 221.

D.A.R.E. (1996). *Curriculum.* Retrieved June 10, 1997, from http://www.charltonpd.org/dare.htm

D.A.R.E. (2009). *National D.A.R.E. Day.* Retrieved June 6, 2011, from http://www.dare.com

Dauvergne, M. (2009). *Trends in police-reported drug offences in Canada.* Ottawa: Statistics Canada.

Davenport, P. (2010, June 25). Ariz. Gov: Most illegal immigrants smuggling drugs. *Associated Press.* Retrieved June 25, 2010, from http://www.ap.org

Davenport-Hines, R. (2001). *The pursuit of oblivion: A global history of narcotics.* London: Weidenfeld and Nicolson.

Davies, D. L. (1962). Normal drinking in recovered alcohol addicts. *Quarterly Journal of Studies on Alcohol, 24,* 730–733.

Davies, S. (n.d.). *New techniques and technologies of surveillance in the workplace.* Retrieved March 9, 2004, from http://www.amicustheunion.org/pdf/surveillencetechniques.pdf

Davis, C. (2012, April 27). New York drug laws. *Drug Rehab.* Retrieved June 5, 2012, from http://www.edrugrehab.com

Davis, R. (1995, September 7). Meth use in the 90s: A growing epidemic. *USA Today.* Retrieved October 10, 2002, from http://www.usatoday.com

Dawson, D., Goldstein, R., & Grant, B. (2007). Rates and correlates of relapse among individuals in remission from *DSM-IV* alcohol dependence: A 3-year-follow-up. *Alcoholism: Clinical and Experimental Research, 31*, 2036–2045.

Dawson, D., Grant, B., & Stinson, F., et al. (2005). Recovery from *DSM-IV* alcohol dependence: United States, 2001–2002. *Addiction, 100*, 281–292.

Daynard, R., Parmet, W., Kelder, G., & Davidson, P. (2001). Implications for tobacco control of multi-state tobacco settlement. *American Journal of Public Health, 91*, 1967–1970.

de Jong, B. C., Prentiss, D., McFarland, W., Machekano, R., & Israelski, D. M. (2005). Marijuana use and its association with adherence to antiretroviral therapy among HIV-infected persons with moderate to severe nausea. *Journal of Acquired Immune Deficiency Syndromes, 38*, 1, 43–46.

de Miranda, J. (2011). Non-12-step addiction treatment. *Alcoholism and Drug Abuse Weekly, 23*, 5.

Deans, B. (2004, November 23). Colombia winning drug war, Bush says. *Seattle Post-Intelligencer*. Retrieved November 23, 2004, from http://www.seattlep.nwsource.com

Deas, D., & Clark, A. (2009). Current state of treatment for alcohol and other drug use disorders in adolescents. *Alcohol Research and Health, 32*, 76–82.

Degenhardt, L., Hallam, C., & Bewley-Taylor, D. (2009). *Comparing the drug situation across countries: Problems, pitfalls, possibilities*. London: Beckley Foundation.

Delaney, A. (2012, February 27). Drug testing bill targets Florida state workers, lawmakers. *Huffington Post*. Retrieved February 27, 2012, from http://www.huffingtonpost.com

Delate, T., Simmons, V., & Motheral, B. (2004). Patterns of use of Sildenafil among commercially insured adults in the United States: 1998–2002. *International Journal of Impotence Research, 16*, 313–318.

DeLeon, G. (1994). The therapeutic community: Toward a general theory and model. In F. Tims, G. DeLeon, & N. Jainchill (Eds.), *Therapeutic community: Advances in research and application. NIDA research monograph 144* (pp. 16–48). Rockville, MD: U.S. Department of Health and Human Services.

DeLeon, G. (1995). Residential therapeutic communities in the mainstream: Diversity and issues. *Journal of Psychoactive Drugs, 27*, 3–15.

Delgado, M. (1995). Hispanic natural support systems and alcohol and other drug services: Challenges and rewards for practice. *Alcohol Treatment Quarterly, 12*, 17–31.

DeMillo, A. (2012, September 3). Medical marijuana backers seek inroads in south. *Seattle Times*. Retrieved September 3, 2012, from http://www.seattletimes.com

Denham, B. (2011, July 5). Dietary supplements: Regulatory issues and implications for public health. *Journal of the American Medical Association (Online)*, PP. E1–E2.

Dennis, T. (2011, June 25). Tobacco labels—A model for potato chip labels? *Los Angeles Times*. Retrieved June 25, 2011, from http://www.latimes.com

De Quincey, T. (1971). *Confessions of an English opium eater*. New York: Viking Press. (Original work published 1821)

Des Jarlais, D. C., Sloboda, Z., Friedman, S. R., Tempalski, B., McKnight, C., & Braine, N. (2006). Diffusion of the D.A.R.E. and syringe exchange programs. *American Journal of Public Health, 96*, 1354–1358.

Detrick, P. (2012). Reason TV replay: Why the Feds banned Four Loko (And is your favorite drink next?). *Reason TV*. Retrieved from http://reason.com/

blog/2012/11/18/reason-tv-replay-why-the-feds-banned-fou

Dettner, J. (2012, April 23). An end to the war on drugs? *MacLean's*. Retrieved April 23, 2012, from http://www .macleans.ca

Devereaux, B. (2012a, April 6). New drugs: Lawmakers in a race against chemists for control of synthetic substances. *MLive.com*. Retrieved from http:// www.mlive.com/news/saginaw/index .ssf/2012/04/new_drugs_lawmakers_ in_a_race.html

deVise, D. (2011, February 28). Fake pot reportedly used at Air Force academy. *Washington Post*. Retrieved February 28, 2011, from http://www.washington post.com

DeVoe, J., & Darling-Churchill, K. (2008). *Status and trends in the education of American Indians and Alaska Natives*. Washington, DC: National Center for Education Statistics, U.S. Department of Education.

DeWit, D., Offord, D., & Wong, M. (1997). Patterns of onset and cessation of drug use over the early part of the life course. *Health Education and Behavior, 24*, 746–758.

DeYoung, K. (2009, August 8). U.S. and Britain target Afghan poppies. *Washington Post*. Retrieved August 8, 2009, from http://www.washington post.com

Díaz-Anzaldúa, A., Díaz-Martínez, A., & Díaz-Martínez, L. R. (2011). The complex interplay of genetics, epigenetics, and environment in the predisposition to alcohol dependence. *Salud Mental, 34*(2), 157–166.

Dick, D., Edenberg, H., Xuei, X., Goate, A., Kuperman, A., Schuckit, M., et al. (2004). Association of GABRG3 with alcohol dependence. *Alcoholism: Clinical and Experimental Research, 28*, 4–9.

Dietary Supplement Health and Education Act of 1994, Pub. L. No. 103-417 (1994).

Dilanian, K. (2006, January 14). Dutch pot laws under a cloud. *Seattle Times*. Retrieved January 14, 2006, from http://www.seattletimes.com

Dilanian, K. (2009, March 31). Afghanistan's poppies pose dilemma. *USA Today*. Retrieved March 31, 2009, from http:// www.usatoday.com

Diller, L. (1998). *Running on Ritalin*. New York: Bantam Books.

Dillman, D. (2000). *Mail and Internet surveys: The tailored design method* (2nd ed.). New York: John Wiley.

Dillworth, T. (2005). Reasons for drinking, drinking goals, belief about alcoholism, and sexual identity as predictors for alcohol treatment preferences in a community sample. Paper presented at the University of Washington Department of Psychology, Seattle, WA.

DiNardo, J., & Lemieux, T. (2001). Alcohol, marijuana, and American youth: The unintended consequences of government regulation. *Journal of Health Economics, 20*, 991–1010.

Dineen, T. (2001, February 19). When it comes to drug abuse programs, "just say no" to time-wasters like DARE. *Report Magazine*. Retrieved February 19, 2001, from http://www.mapinc.org/ drugnews/v01.n657.a02.html

Disheau, D., & Perrone, M. (2012, October 22). FDA investigates Monster drink in 5 deaths. *Seattle Times*. Retrieved October 22, 2012, from http://www .seattletimes.com

Discipline decided in student inhaler incident. (2003, October 10). Retrieved October 10, 2003, from http://www .click2houston.com/news/2547143/ detail.html

Ditore, L. (2003, June 22). The last hurrah for tobacco-sponsored sports. *Tacoma News Tribune*. Retrieved June 22, 2003, from http://www.thenewstribune .com

Dizon, K. (2004, November 16). So you can phone and drive? Think again. *Seattle*

Times. Retrieved November 16, 2004, from http://www.seattletimes.com

Dobbin, M. (2006). *Will the real Stephen Harper please stand up?* Retrieved October 17, 2006, from http://www.canadians.org

Doblin, R. (2003). Exaggerating MDMA's risks to justify a prohibitionist policy. *Multidisciplinary Association for Psychedelic Studies*. Retrieved November 20, 2003, from http://www.maps.org/mdma/rd011604.html

Donkin, K. (2012, June 25). Bath salts: Nicknamed drug causes confusion for Toronto beauty retailers. *Toronto Star*. Retrieved June 25, 2012, from http://www.thestar.com

Donn, J. (2005, April 17). Americans buy much more medicine than people in any other country. *Associated Press*. Retrieved April 17, 2005, from http://www.ap.org

Donovan, J. E. (1996). Problem behavior theory and the explanation of adolescent marijuana use. *Journal of Drug Issues, 21*, 379–404.

Dorsman, J. (1996). Improving alcoholism treatment: An overview. *Behavioral Health Management, 16*, 26–29.

Dougherty, J. (1996, October 10). Children of Synanon. *Phoenix New Times*. Retrieved October 7, 2003, from http://www.phoenixnewtimes.com

Doughton, S. (2003, May 26). Buying drugs via Canada gets tougher. *Seattle Times*. Retrieved May 26, 2003, from http://www.seattletimes.com

Douglas, W. (2010, July 28). Congress narrows gap in cocaine sentences. *Washington Post*. Retrieved July 28, 2010, from http://www.washingtonpost.com

Doweiko, H. (1999). *Concepts of chemical dependency* (4th ed.). Pacific Grove, CA: Brooks/Cole.

Downey, P., & Roman, J. (2010). *A Bayesian meta-analysis of drug court cost-effectiveness*. Washington, DC: Urban Institute.

Doyle, M. (2009, June 26). Court rules strip search illegal. *Seattle Times*. Retrieved June 26, 2009, from http://www.seattletimes.com

Drake, E., Aos, S., & Miller, M. (2009). *Evidence-based public policy options to reduce crime and criminal justice costs: Implications in Washington State*. Olympia, WA: Washington State Institute for Public Policy.

Drinkard, J. (2005, April 26). Drugmakers go furthest to sway congress. *USA Today*. Retrieved April 26, 2005, from http://www.usatoday.com

Drinking among teens widespread despite laws. (2001, July 6). *USA Today*. Retrieved July 6, 2001, from http://www.usatoday.com

Drug Courts Program Office, U.S. Department of Justice. (1997). *Defining drug courts: The key components*. Washington, DC: U.S. Department of Justice.

Drug Enforcement Administration (DEA). (2011). *Drug fact sheet: 4-Iodo-2,5-Dimethoxyphenethylamine (Street Names: 2C-I, i)*. Retrieved from http://www.deadiversion.usdoj.gov/drugs_concern/2c_i.pdf

Drug firms accused of turning healthy people into patients. (2006, April 11). *Guardian*. Retrieved April 11, 2006, from http://www.guardian.co.uk

Drug-Free Sport. (2010). *NCAA drug testing*. Retrieved August 10, 2012, from http://www.drugfreesport.com

Drug Policy Alliance. (2002a, February 28). Bush administration's controversial new anti-drug campaign to be target of upcoming roll call ad by drug policy alliance. Retrieved February 28, 2002, from http://www.drug policy.org

Drug Policy Alliance. (2002b, December 5). *MPP declares war on drug czar's illegal campaigning*. Retrieved December 5, 2002, from http://www.drugpolicy.org

Drug Policy Alliance. (2002c, July 11). *San Francisco to consider growing medical marijuana.* Retrieved July 11, 2002, from http://www.drugpolicy.org

Drug Policy Alliance. (2002d, September 26). *Scientists criticize conclusions of new MDMA (ecstasy) report.* Retrieved September 26, 2002, from http://www.drugpolicy.org

Drug Policy Alliance. (2003a, April). *Barriers to re-entry for convicted drug offenders.* Retrieved April 28, 2003, from http://www.drugpolicy.org

Drug Policy Alliance. (2003b, October 3). *Chretien waiting to inhale.* Retrieved October 3, 2003, from http://www.drugpolicy.org

Drug Policy Alliance. (2003c, May 15). *Congress debates drug war ads.* Retrieved May 15, 2003, from http://www.drugpolicy.org

Drug Policy Alliance. (2003d, June 26). *Court: Government can ban glow sticks.* Retrieved June 26, 2003, from http://www.drugpolicy.org

Drug Policy Alliance. (2003e). *Drug war impact on Latinos in California.* Retrieved June 6, 2004, from http://www.drugpolicy.org/docUploads/archive/latino_fact_sheet.pdf

Drug Policy Alliance. (2003f, December 11). *German court permits medical marijuana use.* Retrieved December 11, 2003, from http://www.drugpolicy.org

Drug Policy Alliance. (2003g, January 9). *Harm reduction banned at rave, "club drugs" blamed for deaths.* Retrieved January 9, 2003, from http://www.drugpolicy.org

Drug Policy Alliance. (2003h, February 6). *Michigan to release drug prisoners.* Retrieved February 6, 2003, from http://www.drugpolicy.org

Drug Policy Alliance. (2003i, July 10). *More than half U.S. states have medical marijuana laws.* Retrieved July 10, 2003, from http://www.drugpolicy.org

Drug Policy Alliance. (2003j, April 3). *ONDCP to end drug terror ads, cancel evaluation.* Retrieved April 3, 2003, from http://www.drugpolicy.org

Drug Policy Alliance. (2003k, December 11). *Penn supreme court finds random student drug testing unconstitutional.* Retrieved December 11, 2003, from http://www.drugpolicy.org

Drug Policy Alliance. (2003l, June 27). *Study shows pot causes no permanent brain damage.* Retrieved June 27, 2003, from http://www.drugpolicy.org

Drug Policy Alliance. (2003m, March 27). *U.K. government refutes INCB nonsense.* Retrieved March 27, 2003, from http://www.drugpolicy.org

Drug Policy Alliance. (2006, February 9). *The right response to the war on drugs.* Retrieved February 9, 2006, from http://www.drugpolicy.org

Drug Policy Alliance. (2011). *Drug courts are not the answer: Toward a health-centered approach to drug use.* Washington, DC: Author.

Drug Prevention Network of the Americas. (2002, April). *The changing face of European drug policy.* Retrieved April 6, 2003, from http://www.dpna.org/resources/trends/changingface.htm

The Drug Reform Coordination Network. (2001, June 22). Creeping cannabis normalization in London. *Drug War Chronicle.* Retrieved June 22, 2001, from http://stopthedrugwar.org/chronicle/191/londoncannabis.shtml

The Drug Reform Coordination Network. (2002). *Comparing drug policies of various nations and the U.S.* Retrieved March 27, 2002, from http://www.stopthedrugwar.org

The Drug Reform Coordination Network. (2004, May 14). Russia enacts sweeping reforms in drug laws. *Drug War Chronicle.* Retrieved May 14, 2004, from http://www.stopthedrugwar.org

Drugs and racial discrimination. (2006, January 12). *New York Times.* Retrieved January 12, 2006, from http://www.nytimes.com

Drug testing part of quest for Olympic status. (2004, August 12). *Associated*

Press. Retrieved August 12, 2004, from http://www.ap.org

Drug treatments for alcohol. (2002, April). *Harvard Mental Health Letter, 10,* 4–7.

Duan, L., Chou, C., Andreeva, V., & Pentz, M. (2009). Trajectories of peer social influences and long-term predictors of drug use from early through late adolescence. *Journal of Youth and Adolescence, 74,* 454–465.

Duckert, F. (1995). The impact of the controlled drinking debate in Norway. *Addiction, 90,* 1167–1169.

Dui Hua Foundation. (2010). Dialogue: Reducing death penalty crimes in China more symbol than substance. *Dui Hua Foundation, 41,* 6.

Duncan, M. J., Smith, M., Cook, K., & James, R. S. (2011). The acute effect of caffeine containing energy drink on mood state, readiness to invest effort and resistance exercise to failure. *Journal of Strength & Conditioning Research.* [Advance online publication.] Retrieved from http://www.ncbi.nlm.nih.gov/pubmed/22124354

Durbin, K. (2003a, June 5). Drug unit may lose dollars under bill. *Columbian.* Retrieved June 5, 2003, from http://www.columbian.com

Durbin, K. (2003b, June 22). The menace of meth: Clark County's illegal drug of choice tightens its grip. *Columbian.* Retrieved June 22, 2003, from http://www.columbian.com

Dworkin, A. (2010, June 15). Finding fake urine a real challenge for drug-testing labs. *Oregonian.* Retrieved June 15, 2010, from http://www.oregonlive.com

Dwyer, D. (2012, December 14). *ABC News.* Retrieved December 16, 2012, from http://abcnews.go.com

Earleywine, M. (2002). *Understanding marijuana: A new look at the scientific evidence.* New York: Oxford University Press.

Earleywine, M. (2003, April 23). *Gateway belief wrecks drug abuse prevention.* Retrieved April 23, 2003, from http://www.drugpolicy.org

Earleywine, M., & Barnwel, S. S. (2007). Decreased respiratory symptoms in cannabis users who vaporize. *Harm Reduction Journal, 4*(11), 172–186.

Easton, S. (2004). *Marijuana growth in B.C.* Fraser Institute. Retrieved August 15, 2004, from http://www.fraserinstitute.org

Eaton, J. (2004, March 1). Parents make home drug tests big business online. *USA Today.* Retrieved March 1, 2004, from http://www.usatoday.com

Eckholm, E. (2011, November 23). Medical marijuana industry is unnerved by a U.S. crackdown. *New York Times.* Retrieved November 23, 2011, from http://www.nytimes.com

Eddy, M. (2006). *Medical marijuana: Review and analysis of federal and state policies.* Washington, DC: Congressional Research Service.

Editorial. (1894). *Journal of Mental Science, 40,* 107–108.

Editorial: Tobacco imperialism. (1992, January/February). *Multinational Monitor, 14.* Retrieved May 27, 2003, from http://www.multinationalmonitor.org

Egan, T. (2010, September 29). Reefer gladness. *New York Times.* Retrieved September 29, 2010, from http://www.nytimes.com

Egelko, B. (2002, July 14). Government mind games. *San Francisco Chronicle.* Retrieved July 14, 2002, from http://www.sfgate.com

Egelko, B. (2003, July 11). Bush escalates marijuana war. *San Francisco Chronicle.* Retrieved July 11, 2003, from http://www.sfgate.com

Egelko, B. (2011, July 5). Is Obama changing his tune on marijuana? *San Francisco Chronicle.* Retrieved July 5, 2011, from http://www.sfgate.com

Ehrenreich, B. (2000, March). Your urine, please. *Progressive.* Retrieved March 10, 2000, from http://www.progressive.org

Ehrenreich, B. (2001). *Nickel and dimed.* New York: Henry Holt and Company.

Ehrman, M. (2003, March 3). The heretical Dr. X. *Los Angeles Times.* Retrieved March 3, 2003, from http://www.latimes.com

Eichler, A. (2012, August 9). Pharmaceutical companies spent 19 times more on self-promotion than basic research. *Huffington Post.* Retrieved September 5, 2012, from http://www.huffingtonpost.com

Eisler, P., & Leinwand, D. (2002, September 1). Canada top source for drug chemical. *USA Today.* Retrieved September 1, 2002, from http://www.usatoday.com

Eisner, B. (1993). *Ecstasy: The MDMA story* (2nd ed.). Berkeley, CA: Ronin.

Eisner, R. (2001, March 22). Medical hallucinogens? Researchers studying possible medical use of LSD, peyote, psilocybin. *ABC News.* Retrieved March 22, 2001, from http://www.abcnews.com

Ettner, S., Huang, D., Evans, E., Ash, D. R., Hardy, M., Jourabchi, M., & Hser, YI. (2006). Benefit-cost in the California treatment outcome project: Does substance abuse treatment "pay for itself"? *Health Services Research, 41,* 192–213.

ElBoghdady, D., & Ginsburg, S. (2006, April 21). Drowsy, distracted, and driving. *Washington Post.* Retrieved April 21, 2006, from http://www.washingtonpost.com

Elias, M. (2006, May 2). New anti-psychotic drugs carry risks for children. *USA Today.* Retrieved May 2, 2006, from http://www.usatoday.com

Elder, G. (1985). Perspective on the life-course. In G. Elder (ed.), *Life course dynamics* (pp. 23–49). Ithaca, NY: Cornell University Press.

Eligon, J. (2011, March 17). 31 are accused of conspiracy to traffic in oxycodone. *New York Times.* Retrieved March 17, 2011, from http://www.nytimes.com

Ellingwood, K. (2009a, March 26). U.S. shares blame for Mexico drug violence, Clinton says. *Los Angeles Times.* Retrieved March 26, 2009, from http://www.latimes.com

Ellingwood, K. (2009b, June 4). Drug violence spilling into Guatemala. *Los Angeles Times.* Retrieved June 4, 2009, from http://www.latimes.com

Elliott, D., Huizinga, D., & Ageton, S. (1985). *Explaining delinquency and drug use.* Beverly Hills, CA: Sage.

Elliott, S. (2011, December 13). Spanish Basque country legalizing marijuana in 2012. *Toke of the Town.* Retrieved August 10, 2012, from http://www.tokeofthetown.com

Ellis, M. (2004, January 12). Smokers might not qualify for jobs with Spokane County. *Columbian.* Retrieved January 12, 2004, from http://www.columbian.com

Ellison, J. (2006, January 27). The smoking ban: No ifs or ands...but plenty of butts. *Seattle Post-Intelligencer.* Retrieved January 27, 2006, from http://www.seattlepi.nwsource.com

Ellis, J., & Wechsler, P. (2011, July 4). Employers getting tougher with smokers. *San Francisco Chronicle.* Retrieved July 4, 2011, from http://www.sfgate.com

El Nasser, H. (2005, June 24). States turn on to idea of ignition interlocks. *USA Today.* Retrieved June 24, 2005, from http://www.usatoday.com

Elovich, R., & Drucker, E. (2008). On drug treatment and social control: Russian narcology's great leap backwards. *Harm Reduction Journal, 5,* 23.

ElSohly, M., Ross, S., Mehmedic, Z., Arafat, R., Yi, B., & Banahan, B. (2000). Potency trends of Delta 9-THC and other cannabinoids in confiscated marijuana from 1980–1997. *Journal of Forensic Sciences, 45*(1). Retrieved November 11, 2002, from http://journalsip.astm.org/JOURNALS/FORENSIC/jofs_home.html

Emmett, G. (1998). What happened to "Crack Babies"? *FAS Drug Policy Analysis Bulletin, 4.*

Ending reefer madness. (2004, August 23). *National Post.* Retrieved August 23, 2004, from http://www.canada.com/nationalpost

Eng, M., Luczak, S., & Wall, T. (2007). ALD2, ADH1B, and ADH1C genotypes in Asians: A literature review. *Alcohol Research & Health, 30,* 22–27.

Engel, M. (2003, April 29). Prohibition, mark two. *Guardian.* Retrieved April 29, 2003, from http://www.guardian.co.uk

English, T. J. (2009, December). Dope. *Playboy.* Retrieved December 12, 2009, from http://www.playboy.com

Engs, R., & Hanson, D. (1989). Reactance theory: A test with collegiate drinking. *Psychological Reports, 64,* 1083–1086.

Engs, R., Hanson, D., & Diebold, A. (1996). The drinking patterns and problems of a national sample of college students, 1994. *Journal of Alcohol and Drug Education, 41,* 13–33.

Ensminger, M., & Everett, J. (2001). Vulnerability as a cause of substance abuse: Gender. In R. Carson-DeWitt (Ed.), *Encyclopedia of drugs, alcohol, and addictive behavior* (pp. 1319–1322). New York: MacMillan.

Enstrom, J., & Kabat, G. (2003). Environmental tobacco smoke and tobacco-related mortality in a prospective study of Californians, 1960–1968. *British Medical Journal, 326,* 1057–1061.

Epstein, D., & Dohrmann, G. (2009, May 18). What you don't know might kill you. *Sports Illustrated.* Retrieved May 20, 2009, from http://www.si.com

Epstein, D. (2012, October 29). Moving the needle. *Sports Illustrated,* pp. 17–18.

Erlanger, S. (2010, February 24). French ad shocks, but will it stop young smokers? *New York Times.* Retrieved February 24, 2010, from http://www.nytimes.com

Eskenazi, S. (2005, December 23). Two weeks into smoking ban, some fuming but few cited. *Seattle Times.* Retrieved December 23, 2005, from http://www.seattletimes.com

ESPAD. (2011). *The 2011 ESPAD report.* Retrieved June 5, 2012, from http://www.espad.org

Estaban, M. (2011, April 19). State places emergency ban on bath salts. *Komo News.* Retrieved April 19, 2011, from http://www.komonews.com

Esterl, M., & Corbett-Dooren, J. (2011, November 8). Judge temporarily blocks graphic cigarette labels. *Wall Street Journal.* Retrieved November 8, 2011, from http://online.wsj.com

Esteve, H. (2003, December 4). Kulongoski says new task force will battle growing meth threat. *Oregonian.* Retrieved December 4, 2003, from http://www.oregonian.com

Ettner, S. L., Huang, D., Evans, E., Rose Ash, D., Hardy, M., Jourabchi, M., & Hser, Y. I. (2005). Benefit-cost in the California Treatment Outcome Project: Does substance abuse treatment "pay for itself"? *Health Services Research, 41*(1), 192–213.

Evans, D. (2010, March 21). When drug makers' profits outweigh penalties. *Washington Post.* Retrieved March 21, 2010, from http://www.washingtonpost.com

Europarl. (2004, December 15). *European parliament recommendation to the council and the European council on the EU drugs strategy.* Retrieved January 11, 2005, from http://europa.eu.int/europarl/europarl.htm

European Monitoring Centre for Drugs and Drug Addiction. (1997, December). *Improving the comparability of general population surveys on drug use in the European Union.* Lisbon: Author.

European Monitoring Centre for Drugs and Drug Addiction. (2002a). *Report to the EMCDDA by the Reitox Focal Point.*

The Netherlands drug situation 2002. Retrieved March 15, 2005, from http://www.emcdda.europa.eu/?nnodeid=435

European Monitoring Centre for Drugs and Drug Addiction. (2002b). Technical implementation and update of the European Union databank on national population surveys on drug use and carrying out a joint analysis of data collected. Lisbon: Author.

European Monitoring Centre for Drugs and Drug Addiction (EMCDDA). (2009). *Annual report*. Retrieved May 15, 2012, from http://www.emcdda.europa.eu

European Monitoring Centre for Drugs and Drug Addiction (EMCDDA). (2011). *Annual report 2011: The state of the drugs problem in Europe*. Retrieved from http://www.emcdda.europa.eu/online/annual-report/2011

European Monitoring Centre for Drugs and Drug Addiction. (2012). *Country profiles*. Retrieved from http://eldd.emcdda.europa.eu/

Eyle, A. (2002). Mayor Rocky Anderson talks about what it's like to...drop the DARE program. In M. Gray (Ed.), *Busted* (pp. 77–80). New York: Thunder's Mouth Press/Nation Books.

Fackelmann, K. (2002, June 24). Inhalants hold hidden threat for families. *USA Today*. Retrieved June 24, 2002, from http://www.usatoday.com

Facts and fancies about marihuana. (1936, October 24). *Literary Digest*.

Fagan, K. (2010, March 16). "Pharma parties" a troubling trend among youths. *San Francisco Chronicle*. Retrieved March 16, 2010, from http://www.sfgate.com

Fainaru, S., & Heath, T. (2003, November 16). Baseball faces major league scrutiny over steroid finding. *Washington Post*. Retrieved November 16, 2003, from http://www.washingtonpost.com

Fainaru-Wada, M., & Williams, L. (2004, December 2). Giambi admitted taking steroids. *San Francisco Chronicle*. Retrieved December 2, 2004, from http://www.sfgate.com

Fainaru-Wada, M., & Williams, L. (2006). *Game of shadows: Barry Bonds, Balco, and the steroids scandal that rocked professional sports*. New York: Gotham Books.

Farabee, D., Hser, Y. I., Anglin, M. D., & Huang, D. (2005). Recidivism among an early cohort of California's Proposition 36 offenders. *Criminology and Public Policy, 3*, 563–584.

Farley, M. (2005, January 17). New York orders online cigarette buyers to cough up taxes. *New York Times*. Retrieved January 17, 2005, from http://www.nytimes.com

Farrey, T. (2000, December 20). NCAA drug testing program. *espn.com*. Retrieved July 10, 2004, from http://www.espn.com

Fauber, J. (2012, October 2). Many injured workers remain on opioids, study finds. *Journal Sentinel*. Retrieved October 10, 2012, from http://wwwjsonline.com

Faupel, C. (1991). *Shooting dope*. Gainesville: University of Florida Press.

Faupel, C., Horowitz, A., & Weaver, G. (2004). *The sociology of American drug use*. New York: McGraw-Hill.

Fazey, C. (2003). The Commission on Narcotic Drugs and the United Nations International Drug Control Programme: Politics, policies, and prospects for change. *International Journal of Drug Policy, 14*, 155–169.

FDA aide quits in protest of morning after pill decision. (2005, August 31). *Associated Press*. Retrieved August 31, 2005, from http://www.ap.org

FDA. (2012). *Clinical trials*. Retrieved August 20, 2012, from http://www.clinicaltrials.gov

Fears, D. (2009, April 15). State prisons see drop in blacks held for drugs. *Washington Post*. Retrieved April 15, 2009, from http://www.nytimes.com

Fed panel says value of workplace drug testing unproven. (1995). *Forensic Drug Abuse Advisor, 7,* 6.

Federal Bureau of Investigation. (2011). *Crime in the United States.* Washington, DC: Author.

Felberbaum, M. (2011, April 25). FDA to regulate e-cigs as tobacco products. *Associated Press.* Retrieved April 25, 2011, from http://www.ap.org

Fellner, J. (1996). Stark racial disparities found in Georgia drug law enforcement. *Overcrowded Times, 7,* 8–13.

Fellner, J., & Mauer, M. (1998). *Losing the vote: The impact of felony disenfranchisement laws in the United States.* Washington, DC: The Sentencing Project, Human Rights Watch.

Fenna, D., Mix, L., Schaefer, O., & Gilbert, J. (1971). Ethanol metabolism in various racial groups. *Canadian Medical Association Journal, 105,* 472–475.

Fendrich, M., & Vaughn, C. (1994). Diminished lifetime substance use over time: An inquiry into differential underreporting. *Public Opinion Quarterly 58,* 96–123.

Fen-phen maker agrees to $3.75 billion settlement. (1999, October 8). *CNN.com.* Retrieved October 9, 1999, from http://www.cnn.com/HEALTH/diet.fitness/9910/08/fen.phen/index.html?eref=sitesearch

Ferdinand, P. (2003, February 7). Drug is making deadly inroads in New England. *Washington Post.* Retrieved February 7, 2003, from http://www.washington post.com

Fernández-Balsells, M. M., Murad, M. H., Lane, M., Lampropulos, J. F., Albuquerque, F., Mullan, R. J., Agrwal, N., et al. (2010). Adverse effects of testosterone therapy in adult men: A systematic review and meta-analysis. *Journal of Clinical Endocrinology & Metabolism, 95*(6), 2560–2575. doi:10.1210/jc.2009-2575

Ferri, M., Amato, L., & Davoli, M. (2006). Alcoholics Anonymous and other 12-step programmes for alcohol dependence. *Cochrane Database of Systematic Reviews, 3*(2), 1–25.

Ferstle, J. (2000). Evolution and politics of drug testing. In C. Yesalis (Ed.), *Anabolic steroids in sport and exercise* (2nd ed., pp. 363–413). Champaign, IL: Human Kinetics.

Feschuk, D. (2009, May 28). NHL must get serious about steroids. *Toronto Star.* Retrieved May 28, 2009, from http://www.thestar.com

Fields, S. (1999). Deadly heroin makes a comeback. *Insight on the News.* Retrieved March 15, 2002, from http://www.findarticles.com/p/articles/mi_m1571/is_37_15/ai_56184212

Fife, R. (2004, November 22). CEOs fear reefer madness. *National Post.* Retrieved November 22, 2004, from http://www.canada.com/nationalpost

Filkins, D. (2009, May 6). Drugs hollow out Afghan lives in cultural center. *Washington Post.* Retrieved May 6, 2009, from http://www.washingtonpost.com

Fillmore, K., Bacon, S. D., & Hyman, M. (1979). *The 27-year longitudinal panel study of drinking by students in college, 1947–76* (Final report, No. C-22). Berkeley, CA: Social Research Group.

Fingarette, H. (1990). Why we should reject the disease concept of alcoholism. In R. Engs (Ed.), *Controversies in the addiction field* (pp. 48–55). Dubuque, IA: Kendall Hunt.

Finn, P. (2005, October 2). Russia's 1-step program: Scaring alcoholics dry. *Washington Post.* Retrieved October 2, 2005, from http://www.washington-post.com

Fiorentine, R. (1997). Does increasing the opportunity for counseling increase the effectiveness of outpatient drug treatment? *American Journal of Drug and Alcohol Abuse, 25,* 369–382.

Firestone, D. (2001, May 18). Woman is convicted of killing her fetus by smoking cocaine. *New York Times*. Retrieved May 18, 2001, from http://www.nytimes.com

Firoz, S., & Carlson, G. (2004). Characteristics and treatment outcome of older methadone-maintenance programs. *American Journal of Geriatric Psychiatry, 12,* 539–541.

Fischer, B. (1995). Drugs, communities, and "harm reduction" in Germany: The new relevance of "public health" principles in local responses. *Journal of Public Health Policy, 16,* 389–411.

Fischer, B., Ala-Leppilampi, K., Single, E., & Robins, A. (2003). Cannabis law reform in Canada: Is the saga of promise, hesitation, and retreat coming to an end? *Canadian Journal of Criminology and Criminal Justice, 45,* 265–297.

Fischer, R. (2012, August 13). Bath salts in the wound. *Vice.com*. Retrieved August 13, 2012, from http://www.vice.com

Fishbein, M., Hall-Jamieson, K., Zimmer, E., von Haeften, I., & Nabi, R. (2002). Avoiding the boomerang: Testing the relative effectiveness of antidrug public service announcements before a national campaign. *American Journal of Public Health, 92,* 238–245.

Fitzgerald, R. (2000, March 1). Guilty until proven innocent. *Reader's Digest*. Retrieved March 3, 2000, from http://www.rd.org

Fitzpatrick, M., & Foot, R. (2007, November 20). New legislation would impose minimum sentences for drug crimes. *Vancouver Sun*. Retrieved November 20, 2007, from http://www.canada.com

Florio, M. (2011, September 30). Fujita estimates low percentage of HGH users in NFL. *NBC Sports*. Retrieved September 15, 2012, from http://www.nbcsports.com

Floyd, D. (1996, March 22). Drug search was lesson in tyranny. *Spokesman-Review*. Retrieved March 22, 1996, from http://www.spokesmanreview.com

Flynn, K. (2001, May 19). Violent crimes undercut marijuana's mellow image. *New York Times*. Retrieved May 19, 2001, from http://www.nytimes.com

Flynn, P., Porto, J., Rounds-Bryant, J., & Kristiansen, P. (2003). Costs and benefits of methadone treatment in DATOS, Part 2: Gender differences for discharged and continuing patients. *Journal of Maintenance in the Addictions, 2,* 151–169.

Foldvary, F. (n.d.). The zero tolerance lemon policy. *Progress Report*. Retrieved July 6, 2004, from http://www.progress.org/fold184.htm

Forbes, D. (2000, July 27). *Fighting "Cheech and Chong" medicine*. Retrieved July 27, 2000, from http://www.salon.com

Forbes, D. (2001, January 12). *Ashcroft's nephew got probation after major pot bust*. Retrieved January 12, 2001, from http://www.salon.com

Forbes, D. (2002, November 19). *The myth of potent pot*. Retrieved November 22, 2002, from http://www.msn.com.

Forero, J. (2002, September 4). U.S. is stepping up drive to destroy coca in Colombia. *New York Times*. Retrieved September 4, 2002, from http://www.nytimes.com

Forero, J. (2008, September 3). Despite U.S. aid, coca cultivation on rise in Andes. *Washington Post*. Retrieved September 3, 2008, from http://www.washingtonpost.com

Forero, J. (2009, July 19). Report: Venezuela a major drug player. *Washington Post*. Retrieved July 19, 2009, from http://www.washingtonpost.com

Forgione, M. (2011, February 23). New York City gets its own public-smoking ban. Who's next? *Chicago Tribune*. Retrieved February 23, 2011, from http://www.chicagotribune.com

43,000 students with drug convictions face denial of student aid. (2001, December

29). *New York Times*. Retrieved December 29, 2001, from http://www.nytimes.com

Fortier, J. (2011). Above the influence: Examining the impact of unintentional normative messages in fear appeal based anti-marijuana public service announcements. Proquest Dissertations.

Foss, K. (2002a, March 30). Holy smoke: Cannabis church cafE9 set to open. *Globe and Mail*. Retrieved March 20, 2002, from http://www.theglobeandmail.com

Foss, K. (2002b, November 2). Manitoba school embarking on testing for drugs. *Globe and Mail*. Retrieved November 2, 2002, from http://www.theglobeandmail.com

Four guilty in GHB death. (2000, March 14). *Detroit News*. Retrieved March 14, 2000, from http://www.detnews.com

Fox, A., & Rodriguez, N. (2010). Using a criminally involved population to examine the relationship between race/ethnicity, structural disadvantage, and methamphetamine use. *Crime and Delinquency*. Advance online publication. doi:10.1177/0011128710364825

Franceschina, P. (2005, December 21). South Florida judge uses anklets to keep tabs on problem drinkers. *South Florida Sun-Sentinel*. Retrieved December 21, 2005, from http://www.sun-sentinel.com

Frank, D., Augustyn, M., Grant Knight, W., Pell, T., & Zuckerman, B. (2001). Growth, development, and behavior in early childhood following prenatal cocaine exposure: A systematic review. *Journal of the American Medical Association, 285*, 1613–1625.

Frank, M. (2002). BYO heroin. In M. Gray (Ed.), *Busted* (pp. 67–69). New York: Thunder's Mouth Press/Nation Books.

Franklin, T., Franklin, T. R., Harper, D., Kampman, K., Kildea-McCrea, S., Jens, W., Lynch, K. G., O'Brien, C. P., &Childress, A. R. (2009). The GABA B agonist baclofen reduces cigarette consumption in a preliminary double-blind placebo-controlled smoking reduction study. *Drug and Alcohol Dependence, 103*, 30–36.

Franzen, R. (2001, February 23). Federal magistrate tosses out lawsuit on drug-free zone. *Oregonian*. Retrieved February 23, 2001, from http://www.oregonian.com

Frary, C. D., Johnson, R. K., & Wang, M. Q. (2005). Food sources and intakes of caffeine in the diets of persons in the United States. *Journal of the American Dietetic Association, 105*, 110–113.

Freeman, M., & Onley, B. (2003, April 22). New drug tests in baseball stir debate among players. *New York Times*. Retrieved April 22, 2003, from http://www.nytimes.com

French Monitoring Center for Drugs and Drug Addiction. (2004). *Substitution treatments in France: Recent results 2004*. Retrieved August 6, 2005, from http://www.drogues.gouv.fr/IMG/pdf/tend37.pdf

Freudenheim, M. (2002, March 29). Spending on prescription drugs rises sharply. *New York Times*. Retrieved March 29, 2002, from http://www.nytimes.com

Fried, S. (1999). *Bitter pills: Inside the hazardous world of legal drugs*. New York: Bantam Books.

Friedersdorf, C. (2011, June 15). The war on drugs turns 40. *Atlantic*. Retrieved June 16, 2011, from http://www.theatlantic.com

Friedl, K. (2000). Effects of anabolic steroids on physical health. In C. Yesalis (Ed.), *Anabolic steroids in sport and exercise* (2nd ed., pp. 175–224). Champaign, IL: Human Kinetics.

Friedman, L. (2005, August 19). Nationwide anti-meth strategy criticized. *San Gabriel Valley Tribune*. Retrieved August 19, 2005, from http://www.sgvtribune.com

Frith, M. (2005, December 3). Anger as world health body bans smokers. *Independent*. Retrieved December 3, 2005, from http://www.independent.co.uk

Frood, A. (2006, September 13). Dropping acid may help headaches. Cluster headache sufferers say LSD can abort attacks. *Nature News*. Retrieved from http://www.nature.com/news/2006/060911/full/ news060911-05.html

Frosch, D. L., Kruger, P. M., Hornik, R. C., Cronholm, P. F., & Barg, F. K. (2007). Creating demand for prescription drugs: A content analysis of television direct-to-consumer advertising. *Annals of Family Medicine, 5*, 6–13.

Fuller, R., & Hiller-Sturmhofel, S. (1999). Alcoholism treatment in the United States. *Alcohol Research and Health, 23*, 69–77.

Fuchs, R. (2012, March 28). Drug related deaths down in Germany. *Deutchewelle.com*. Retrieved August 8, 2012, from http://www.deutsche-welle.com

Furedi, F. (1998, January 22). Students and drink: Have Puritans taken over the bar? *Independent*. Retrieved January 22, 1998, from http://www.independent.co.uk

Gahlinger, P. (2001). *Illegal drugs: A complete guide to their history, chemistry, use and abuse*. Salt Lake City, UT: Sagebrush Press.

Gaines, L., & Kraska, P. (Eds.). (1997). *Drugs, crime, and justice*. Prospect Heights, IL: Waveland.

Gale, K. (2009). Surprised? Black market steroids usually mislabeled. *Reuters*. Retrieved from http://www.reuters.com/article/2009/12/08/us-steroids-mislabeled-idUSTRE5B64GT20091208

Gallagher, R., & Oransky, I. (2005, May 23). How to fix drug ads. *The Scientist*. Retrieved May 23, 2005, from http://www.the-scientist.com

Gallahue, P. (2011). The death penalty for drug offenses, global overview, 2011: Shared responsibility and shared consequences. London: International Harm Reduction Association.

Gandhi, A. G., Murphy-Graham, E., Petrosino, A., Chrismer, S. S., & Weiss, C. H. (2007). The devil is in the details—Examining the evidence for "proven" school-based drug abuse prevention programs. *Evaluation Review, 31*, 43–74.

Garber, A., & Miletich, S. (2011, June 21). Former U.S. attorney McKay backs effort to legalize pot in Washington. *Seattle Times*. Retrieved June 11, 2011, from http://www.seattletimes.com

Garber, G. (2003, July 18). ITF doing EPO testing for first season. *ESPN*. Retrieved July 18, 2003, from http://www.espn.com

Garcia-Andrade, C., Wall, T. L., & Ehlers, C. L. (1997). The firewater myth and response to alcohol in mission Indians. *American Journal of Psychiatry, 154*, 983–988.

Gardiner, C. (2008). From inception to implementation: How SACPA has affected the case processing and sentencing of drug offenders in one California county. University of California, Irvine. Retrieved June 10, 2012, from https://www.ncjrs.gov/pdffiles1/nij/grants/223468.pdf

Garfield, S. (2003, July 27). Hugs not drugs. *Observer*. Retrieved July 27, 2003, from http://www.observer.co.uk

Garmaise, D. (2006). Supervised injection facility granted limited-time extension. *HIV/AIDS Policy Law Review, 11*, 21–23.

Garnier, H. E., & Stein, J. A. (2002). An 18-year model of family and peer effects on adolescent drug use and delinquency. *Journal of Youth and Adolescent Psychiatry, 31*, 45–56.

Gastfriend, D., Garbutt, J., Pettinati, H., & Forman, R. (2007). Reduction in heavy drinking as a treatment outcome in alcohol dependence. *Journal of Substance Abuse Treatment, 33*, 71–80.

Gay, M. (2010, July 12). States start to crack down as more smoke synthetic pot. *New York Times*. Retrieved July 12, 2010, from http://www.nytimes.com

Gegax, T. (2005, June 6). An end to "power hour." *Newsweek*. Retrieved June 6, 2005, from http://www.msnbc.msn.com

Gelacak, M. (1997). *Cocaine and federal sentencing policy*. Washington, DC: United States Sentencing Commission.

Gelling, P. (2008, July 13). Executions for drug crimes are resumed in India. *New York Times*. Retrieved July 13, 2008, from http://www.nytimes.com

Genberg, B. L., Gange, S. J., Go, V. F., Celentano, D. D., Kirk, G. D., Latkin, C. A., & Mehta, S. H. (2011). The effect of neighborhood deprivation and residential relocation on long-term injection cessation among injection drug users (IDUs) in Baltimore, Maryland. *Addiction, 106*, 1966–1974.

Geranios, N. (2009, May 6). Teed off: Golf course smoking ban angers golfers. *Associated Press*. Retrieved May 6, 2009, from http://www.ap.org

Gerra, G., Fantoma, A., & Zaimovic, A. (2006). Naltrexone and buprenorphine combination in the treatment of opioid dependence. *Journal of Psychopharmacology, 20*(6), 806–814. doi:10.1177/0269881106060835.

Gettman, J. (2009). Marijuana arrests in the United States. *Bulletin of Cannabis Reform, 7*. Retrieved June 8, 2012, from http://www.drugscience.org/

Gilbert, M., & Cervantes, R. (1986). Patterns and practices of alcohol use among Mexican-Americans: A comprehensive review. *Hispanic Journal of Behavioral Sciences, 8*, 1–60.

Gill, J. R., Hayes, J. A., deSouza, I. S., Marker, E., & Stajic, M. (2002). Ecstasy (MDMA) deaths in New York City. *Journal of Forensic Sciences, 47*, 121–126. Retrieved March 12, 2003, from http://mdma.net/toxicity/new-york.html

Gillespie, N. (2005, October 26). *Meth still driving people nuts*. Retrieved October 26, 2005, from http://www.reasononline.com

Gillis, C. (2012, April 23). The end of the dry run. *MacLean's*. Retrieved May 1, 2012, from http://www.macleans.ca

Giordano, P., Cernkovich, S., & DeMaris, A. (1993). The family and peer relations of black adolescents. *Journal of Marriage and the Family, 55*, 277–298.

Girion, L., & Levin, M. (2002, June 7). R. J. Reynolds fined for ads aimed at teens. *Los Angeles Times*. Retrieved June 7, 2002, from http://www.latimes.com

Gladwell, M. (2001, September 10). Drugstore athlete. *New Yorker*. Retrieved September 10, 2001, from http://www.newyorker.com

Glass, S. (1997, March 3). Don't you dare. *The New Republic*. Retrieved June 5, 2002, from http://www.tnr.org

Glasser, S. (2004, September 22). Russian drug unit criticized over dubious tactics, priorities. *Washington Post*. Retrieved September 22, 2004, from http://www.washingtonpost.com

GlaxoSmithKline advertisement. (2004, December 20). *Newsweek*, 17.

Gleiberman, L., Harburg, E., Di Franceisco, W., & Schork, A. (1991). Familial transmission of alcohol use: IV. A seventeen-year follow-up on the relationships between parent and adult offspring alcohol use; Tecumseh, Michigan. *International Journal of Epidemiology, 20*, 441–447.

Glionna, J. (2003, June 1). Light and darkness in Canada. *Los Angeles Times*. Retrieved June 1, 2003, from http://www.latimes.com

Global Commission on Drug Policy. (2011). *Report of the Global Commission on Drug Policy*. Retrieved June 5, 2012, from http://www.globalcommissionondrugs.org/

Gold diggers. (2006, June). *The Progressive*, p. 11.

Goldberg, C. (2003, November 12). Nicotine studied as treatment for brain disorders. *Boston Globe*. Retrieved November 12, 2003, from http://www.boston.com

Goldberg, J. (2012, June 8). Distracted driving: California gets $1.5 million to keep eyes on road. *Los Angeles Times*. Retrieved June 8, 2012, from http://www.latimes.com

Goldman, B., & Klatz, R. (1997). *Death in the locker room II: Drugs and sports*. Chicago: Elite Sports Medicine.

Gomart, E. (2002). Towards generous constraint: Freedom and coercion in a French addiction treatment. *Sociology of Health and Illness, 24,* 517–549.

Goodchild, S., & Johnson, A. (2004, November 28). Cheaper, easier to get, harder to police: Britain's drug problem. *Independent*. Retrieved November 28, 2004, from http://www.independent.co.uk

Goode, E. (1970). *The marijuana smokers*. New York: Basic Books.

Goode, E. (1999). *Drugs in American society* (5th ed.). New York: McGraw-Hill College.

Goode, E. (2003, December 11). Most antidepressants risky for young, British warn. *New York Times*. Retrieved December 11, 2003, from http://www.nytimes.com

Goodnough, A. (2010, September 23). A wave of addiction and crime, with the medicine cabinet to blame. *New York Times*. Retrieved September 23, 2010, from http://www.nytimes.com

Goodnough, A., & Zezima, K. (2011a, April 9). Newly born, and withdrawing from painkillers. *New York Times*. Retrieved April 9, 2011, from http://www.nytimes.com

Goodnough, A., & Zezima, K. (2011b, July 16). An alarming new stimulant, legal in many states. *New York Times*. Retrieved July 16, 2011, from http://www.nytimes.com

Goodwin, D., Schulsinger, F., Hermansen, L., Guze, S., & Winokur, G. (1973). Alcohol problems in adoptees raised apart from alcoholic biologic relatives. *Archives of General Psychiatry, 38,* 965–969.

Goozner, M. (2012, January 12). Conflict of interest scandal rocks FDA. *The Fiscal Times*. Retrieved January 12, 2012, from http://www.thefiscaltimes.com

Gordon, R., & Kinney, J. (2006). *Reducing crime and improving criminal justice in British Columbia: Recommendations for change*. BC Progress Board. Retrieved January 15, 2007, from http://www.bcprogressboard.com

Gossop, M., Stewart, D., & Marsden, J. (2008). Attendance at Narcotics Anonymous and Alcoholics Anonymous meetings, frequency of attendance and substance use outcomes after residential treatment for drug dependence: A 5-year follow-up study. *Addiction, 103,* 119–125.

Gottfredson, D. C., Najaka, S. S., & Kearly, B. (2003). Effectiveness of drug treatment courts: Evidence from a randomized trial. *Criminology and Public Policy, 2,* 171–196.

Gov. Bush's daughter sent to jail. (2002, October 18). *Washington Post*. Retrieved October 18, 2002, from http://www.washingtonpost.com

Government launches frank drugs campaign. (2003, May 23). *Guardian*. Retrieved May 23, 2003, from http://www.guardian.co.uk

Government of Canada. (1973). *Commission of inquiry into the non-medical use of drugs*. Final report. Ottawa: Queen's Printer.

Government of Canada. (2002). *Report of the senate special committee on illegal drugs*. Ottawa: Queen's Printer. Retrieved June 2, 2003, from http://www.cfdp.ca/sen2000.htm

Graham, D., Campen, D., Hui, R., Spence, M., Cheetham, C., Levey, G., et al.

(2005). Risk of acute myocardial infarction and sudden cardiac deaths in patients treated with cyclo-oxygenase 2 selective and non-selective non-steroidal anti-inflammatory drugs: Nested case control study. *The Lancet, 365,* 475–481.

Graham, J., & James, F. (2005, February 20). Flaws in drug agency put consumers at risk. *Chicago Tribune.* Retrieved February 20, 2005, from http://www.chicagotribune.com

Graman, K. (2006, January 27). Bars say business gone with smoke. *Spokesman-Review.* Retrieved January 27, 2006, from http://www.spokesmanreview.com

Graves, L. (2012, April 2). Lawmakers in 5 states tell feds to back off medical marijuana. *Huffington Post.* Retrieved from http://www.huffingtonpost.com/2012/04/02/lawmakers-in-5-states-tell-feds-medical-marijuana_n_1397811.html

Gray, J. (2001). *Why our drug laws have failed and what we can do about it.* Philadelphia: Temple University Press.

Gray, M. (1999, September 20). The perils of prohibition. *The Nation.* Retrieved September 20, 1999, from http://www.thenation.com

Green, L. (2004, January 18). The demonized seed. *Los Angeles Times.* Retrieved January 18, 2004, from http://www.latimes.com

Green, T., et al. (2009). Women who abuse prescription opioids: Findings from the addiction severity index-multimedia version. *Drug and Alcohol Dependence, 103,* 65.

Greenberg, G. (2003, November/December). Is it Prozac? Or placebo? *Mother Jones.* Retrieved December 15, 2003, from http://www.motherjones.com

Greene, J., Pranis, K., & Ziedenberg, J. (2006). *Disparity by design.* Washington, DC: Justice Policy Institute.

Greenwald, G. (2009). *Drug decriminalization in Portugal: Lessons for creating fair and successful drug policies.* Washington, DC: Cato Institute.

Greenwald, J. (1998, November 23). Herbal healing. *Time.* Retrieved November 23, 1998, from http://www.time.com

Gregory, S. (2002, July 1). This tobacco money may be hazardous to your health. *Time.* Retrieved July 1, 2002, from http://www.time.com

Griffiths, R. R., Johnson, M. W., Richards, W. A., Richards, B. D., McCann U., & Jesse R. (2011). Psilocybin occasioned mystical-type experiences: Immediate and persisting dose-related effects. *Psychopharmacology, 218,* 649–665.

Griffiths, R. R., Richards, W. A., McCann, U., & Jesse, R. (2006). Psilocybin can occasion mystical-type experiences having substantial and sustained personal meaning and spiritual significance. *Psychopharmacology, 187*(3), 268–283.

Grillo, I. (2009, August 26). Mexico's new drug law may set example. *Time.* Retrieved August 26, 2009, from http://www.time.com

Grim, R. (2007, February 7). Bush wants funding jump for anti-drug ads rated as useless. *Politico.* Retrieved February 7, 2007, from http://www.politico.com/news/stories/0207/2673.html

Grinspoon, L., & Bakalar, J. (1979). *Psychedelic drugs reconsidered.* New York: Basic Books.

Grinspoon, L., & Bakalar, J. (1995). Marijuana as medicine: A plea for reconsideration. *Journal of the American Medical Association, 273,* 1875–1876.

Grohmann, K. (2012, August 11). Update 1—Olympics—Doping—Syrian hurdler expelled after positive test. *Reuters.* Retrieved August 15, 2012, from http://www.reuters.com

Grollman, A. (2003, February 23). Regulation of dietary drugs is long overdue. *New York Times.* Retrieved

February 23, 2003, from http://www.nytimes.com

Groopman, J. (2002, July 29). Hormones for men. *New Yorker*. Retrieved August 1, 2002, from http://www.newyorker.com

Gross, C., Sofer, B., Bach, P., Rajkumar, R., & Forman, H. (2002). State expenditures for tobacco control programs and the tobacco settlement. *New England Journal of Medicine, 347,* 1080–1086.

Grotenhermen, F., & Müller-Vahl, K. (2012). The therapeutic potential of cannabis and cannabinoids. *Deutsch Arzteblatt International, 109*(29–30), 495–501. PubMed PMID: 23008748

Gruber, V. A., Delucchi, K. L., Kielstein, A., & Batki, S. L. (2008). A randomized trial of 6-month methadone maintenance with standard or minimal counseling versus 21-day methadone detoxification. *Drug and Alcohol Dependence, 94,* 199–206.

Gual, A., Bravo, F., Lligona, A., & Colom, J. (2009). Treatment for alcohol dependence in Catalonia: Health outcomes and stability of drinking patterns over 20 years in 850 patients. *Alcohol and Alcoholism, 44,* 409–415.

Guastafero, W. (2012). Using the level of service inventory-revised to improve assessment and treatment in drug court. *International Journal of Offender Therapy and Comparative Criminology, 56*(5), 769–789.

Guerino, P., Harrison, P., & Sabol, W. (2011). *Prisoners in 2010.* Washington, DC: U.S. Department of Justice, Bureau of Justice Statistics.

Gullo, K. (2001, March 21). Guidelines stiffened for selling ecstasy. *Associated Press*. Retrieved March 21, 2001, from http://www.ap.org

Gunja, F., Cox, A., Rosenbaum, M., & Appel, J. (2003). *Making sense of student drug testing: Why educators are saying no.* New York: American Civil Liberties Union and Drug Policy Alliance.

Gupta, S. (2003, August 25). Move over, Viagra. *Time*. Retrieved August 25, 2003, from http://www.time.com

Gusfield, J. (2003). Constructing the ownership of social problems: Fun and profit in the welfare state. In J. Orcutt & D. Rudy (Eds.), *Drugs, alcohol and social problems* (pp. 7–18). New York: Rowan and Littlefield.

Guterman, L. (2005, September 7). Medical students are bombarded by drug company blandishments, survey finds. *Chronicle of Higher Education*. Retrieved September 7, 2005, from http://chronicle.com/

Gutwillig, S., & Piper, B. (2011, July 14). Medical marijuana: A science-free zone at the White House. *Los Angeles Times*. Retrieved July 14, 2011, from http://www.latimes.com

Haake, J. (2003, July 21). UCLA study: Drug rehab has financial benefits over incarceration. *Daily Bruin*. Retrieved July 21, 2003, from http://www.dailybruin.ucla.edu

Hagan, J. (1991). Destiny and drift: Subcultural preferences, status attainments, and the risks and rewards of youth. *American Sociological Review, 56,* 567–582.

Haggin, P. (2012, July 10). Obama signs federal ban on "bath salt" drugs. *Time Newsfeed*. Retrieved from http://newsfeed.time.com/2012/07/10/obama-signs-federal-ban-on-bath-salt-drugs/

Hainsworth, J. (2004, September 10). CafE9 continues to sell pot after raid. *Vancouver Sun*. Retrieved September 10, 2004, from http://www.canada.com

Hall, N. (2003, June 21). Pot growers no worse than martini drinkers, judge says. *Vancouver Sun*. Retrieved June 21, 2003, from http://www.vancouversun.com

Hall, N. (2011, March 21). Proposal to criminalize herb used by Miley Cyrus opposed by BCCLA. *Vancouver Sun*. Retrieved March 21, 2011, from http://www.canada.com

Halladay, J. (2011, February 11). States race to ban risky "bath salts" drug. *USA Today*. Retrieved February 11, 2011, from http://www.usatoday.com

Halpern, J., & Pope, H. (2003). Hallucinogen persisting perception disorder: What do we know after 50 years? *Drug and Alcohol Dependence, 69*, 109–119.

Halpern, J., Sherwood, A. R., Hudson, J. I., Gruber, S., Kozin, D., & Pope Jr., H. G. (2011). Residual neurocognitive features of long-term ecstasy users with minimal exposure to other drugs. *Addiction, 106*, 777–786.

Halsey, A. (2009, November 17). U.S. teens report "frightening" levels of texting while driving. *Washington Post*. Retrieved November 17, 2009, from http://www.washingtonpost.com

Hamilton, J. (2012, January 30). Could a club drug offer "immediate relief" from depression? *NPR Morning Edition*. Ret

Hammann, J. (2002, June 18). Young adults line up for free smokes. *Chicago Tribune*. Retrieved June 18, 2002, from http://www.chicagotribune.com

Hampson, R. (2003, March 11). States squander chance to fight smoking. *USA Today*. Retrieved March 11, 2003, from http://www.usatoday.com

Han, B., Gfroerer, J. C., Colliver, J. D., & Penne, M. A. (2008). Substance use disorder among older adults in the United States in 2020. *Addiction, 104*(1), 88–96.

Haney, M., Gunderson, E. W., Jiang, H., Collins, E. D., & Foltin, R. W. (2010). Cocaine-specific antibodies blunt the subjective effects of smoked cocaine in humans. *Biological Psychiatry, 67*, 59–65.

Hanson, D. (2000). *Drinking and driving*. Retrieved August 6, 2004, from http://www2.potsdam.edu/hansondj/DrinkingAndDriving.html

Hanson, D. (n.d.). Dry counties. Retrieved August 10, 2004, from http://www2.potsdam.edu/hansondj/Controversies/1140551076.html

Harburg, E., DiFranceisco, W., Webster, D., Gleiberman, L., & Schork, A. (1990). Familial transmission of alcohol use: II. Imitation of and aversion to parent drinking (1960) by adult offspring (1977)—Tecumseh, Michigan. *Journal of Studies on Alcohol, 51*, 245–256.

Harkavy, W. (2005, January 4). The numbers beyond the bling. *Village Voice*. Retrieved January 4, 2005, from http://www.villagevoice.com

Harkinson, J. (2011, January–February). Joint ventures. *Mother Jones*. Retrieved January 15, 2011, from http://www.motherjones.com

Harmer, P. A. (2010). Anabolic-androgenic steroid use among young male and female athletes: Is the game to blame? *British Journal of Sports Medicine, 44*(1), 26–31.

Harper, T. (2003, October 26). "Buy Canada" drug plan sweeping U.S. *Toronto Star*. Retrieved October 26, 2003, from http://www.thestar.com

Harper's Index. (2003, August). *Harper's*. Retrieved August 5, 2003, from http://www.harpers.org

Harper's index. (2009, December). *Harper's*. Retrieved December 10, 2009, from http://www.harpers.org

Harris, G. (2004a, June 27). A doctor writes prescription, drug company writes a check. *New York Times*. Retrieved June 27, 2004, from http://www.nytimes.com

Harris, G. (2004b, December 6). At FDA, strong drug ties and less monitoring. *New York Times*. Retrieved December 6, 2004, from http://www.nytimes.com

Harris, G. (2004c, July 16). Guilty plea seen for drug maker. *New York Times*. Retrieved July 16, 2004, from http://www.nytimes.com

Harris, G. (2004d, June 3). N.Y. state official sues drug maker over test data.

New York Times. Retrieved June 3, 2004, from http://www.nytimes.com

Harris, G. (2004e, February 12). Student, 19, in trial of antidepressant commits suicide. *New York Times.* Retrieved February 12, 2004, from http://www.nytimes.com

Harris, G. (2004f, November 5). Study says drug's dangers were apparent years ago. *New York Times.* Retrieved November 5, 2004, from http://www.nytimes.com

Harris, G. (2005a, June 9). Drug safety system is broken, a top FDA official says. *New York Times.* Retrieved June 9, 2005, from http://www.nytimes.com

Harris, G. (2005b, March 17). FDA nominee may face scrutiny of tough year and tough post. *New York Times.* Retrieved March 17, 2005, from http://www.nytimes.com

Harris, G. (2006, January 25). In article, doctors back ban on gifts from drug makers. *New York Times.* Retrieved January 25, 2006, from http://www.nytimes.com

Harris, G. (2010, May 25). Study finds supplements contain contaminants. *New York Times.* Retrieved May 25, 2010, from http://www.nytimes.com

Harris, G., & Berenson, A. (2005, February 25). FDA panelists have ties to drug makers. *New York Times.* Retrieved February 25, 2005, from http://www.nytimes.com

Harris, G., & Berenson, A. (2009, January 15). Lilly said to be near $1.4 billion settlement. *New York Times.* Retrieved January 15, 2009, from http://www.nytimes.com

Harris, G., & Davey, M. (2004, January 24). FDA begins push to end drug imports. *New York Times.* Retrieved January 24, 2004, from http://www.nytimes.com

Harris, G., & Koli, E. (2005, June 10). Dozens died, but drug was still kept on the market. *New York Times.* Retrieved June 10, 2005, from http://www.nytimes.com

Hart, C. L., & Ksir, C. (2013). *Drugs, society, and human behavior* (15th ed.). New York: McGraw-Hill.

Harvard University Press Herbaria. (2002). *R. Gordon Wasson (1898–1986) archives.* Retrieved April 25, 2003, from http://www.huh.harvard.edu/libraries/wasson.html

Hashibe, M., Morgenstern, H., Cui, Y., Tashkin, D. P., Zhang, Z.-F., Cozen, W., Mack, T. M., et al. (2006). Marijuana use and the risk of lung and upper aerodigestive tract cancers: Results of a population-based case-control study. *Cancer Epidemiology Biomarkers & Prevention, 15*(10), 1829–1834. doi:10.1158/1055-9965.EPI-06-0330

Hastings, D. (2009, April 4). States pull back after decades of get-tough laws. *Associated Press.* Retrieved April 4, 2009, from http://www.ap.org

Hatsukami, D., & Fischman, M. (1996). Crack cocaine and cocaine hydrochloride: Are the differences myth or reality? *Journal of the American Medical Association, 276,* 1580–1588.

Haupt, H., & Rovere, G. (1984). Anabolic steroids: A review of the literature. *American Journal of Sports Medicine, 12,* 469–484.

Havrelly, W. (2010, October 15). Oregon bans synthetic marijuana. *KGW News.* Retrieved October 15, 2010, from http://www.kgw.com/news

Hawken, A., & Kleiman, M. (2009). *Managing drug-involved probationers with swift and certain sanctions: Evaluating Hawaii's HOPE.* Washington, DC: U.S. Department of Justice.

Hawkins, D. (2002, August 12). Tests on trial: Jobs and reputations ride on unproven drug screens. *US News and World Report.* Retrieved August 12, 2002, from http://www.usnews.com

Hawkins, D., Jenson, J., Catalano, R., & Lishner, D. (1988). Delinquency and drug use: Implications for social services. *Social Service Review, 62,* 258–284.

Hawkins, J., Lishner, D., & Catalano, R. (1990). Childhood predictors and prevention of adolescent substance abuse. In *NIDA monograph 56, etiology of drug abuse* (p. 93). Rockville, MD: NIDA.

Hawley, C. (2010, July 21). Venezuela drug trade booms. *USA Today*. Retrieved July 21, 2010, from http://www.usatoday.com

Hayashi, K., Wood, E., Wiebe, L., Qi, J., & Kerr, T. (2010). An external evaluation of a peer-run outreach-based syringe exchange in Vancouver, Canada. *International Journal of Drug Policy*, 21(5), 418–421.

Hays, T. (2000, April 3). Drug seizures suggest ecstasy flow becoming epidemic. *Associated Press*. Retrieved April 3, 2000, from http://www.ap.org

Hazckamp, A., & Grotenhermen, F. (2010). Review on clinical studies with cannabis and cannabinoids 2005–2009. *Cannabinoids*, 5, 1–21.

Head, W. (2001). *Field sobriety testing information*. Retrieved May 7, 2003, from http://www.drunkdrivingdefense.com

Healton, C. (2001). Who's afraid of the truth? *American Journal of Public Health*, 91, 554–558.

Healy, M. (2012, March 28). Teens' cinnamon challenge: Dangerous, not innocent. *Los Angeles Times*. Retrieved March 28, 2012, from http://www.latimes.com

Heaney, G. (1991). The reality of guidelines sentencing: No end to disparity. *American Criminal Law Review*, 28, 161–232.

Heather, N., Adamson, S. J., Raistrick, D., & Slegg, G. P. (2010). Initial preference for drinking goal in the treatment of alcohol problems: I. Baseline differences between abstinence and non-abstinence groups. *Alcohol and Alcoholism*, 45(2), 128–135.

Hebdige, D. (1979). *Subculture: The meaning of style*. New York: Methuen.

Hedrich, D., Pirona, A., & Wiessing, L. (2008). From margin to mainstream: The evolution of harm reduction responses to problem drug use in Europe. *Drugs: Education, Prevention, and Policy*, 15, 503–517.

Hefter, E. (2012, August 16). Even at Hempfest, no consensus on legalizing pot in Washington. *Seattle Times*. Retrieved August 16, 2012, from http://www.seattletimes.com

Heimann, R. K. (1960). *Tobacco and Americans*. New York: McGraw-Hill.

Henderson, C. (2004, February 24). Pantani death raises questions. *BBC*. Retrieved February 24, 2004, from http://www.bbc.co.uk

Henderson, D., & Rowland, C. (2005, April 10). Once "too slow," FDA approvals called "too fast." *Boston Globe*. Retrieved April 10, 2005, from http://www.boston.com

Henderson, G., Harkey, M., & Jones, A. (1990). Rapid screening of fentanyl (China white) powder samples by solid-phase radioimmunoassay. *Journal of Analytical Toxicology*, 14, 172–175.

Henderson, L., & Glass, W. (1994). Introduction. In L. Henderson & W. Glass (Eds.), *LSD: Still with us after all these years* (pp. 1–8). Lanham, MD: Lexington Books.

Hendrix, S. (2009, November 16). Boomers see views relaxing on marijuana. *Washington Post*. Retrieved November 16, 2009, from http://www.washingtonpost.com

Hennessy-Fiske, M. (2012, February 23). Alcohol sales fuel spirited debates in East Texas. *Los Angeles Times*. Retrieved February 23, 2012, from http://www.latimes.com

Henry, J. A., Oldfield, W. L., & Kon, O. M. (2003). Comparing cannabis with tobacco. *British Medical Journal*, 327, 942–943.

Hepburn, J. R., & Albonetti, C. A. (1994). Recidivism among drug offenders: A survival analysis of the effects of offender characteristics, type of offense, and two types of intervention. *Journal of Quantitative Criminology, 10*(2), 159–179.

Hepburn, J., & Harvey, A. (2007). The effect of the threat of legal sanction on program retention and completion: Is that why they stay in drug court? *Crime and Delinquency, 53*, 255–280.

Herbert, B. (2002, December 26). The latest from Tulia. *New York Times*. Retrieved December 26, 2002, from http://www.nytimes.com

Herd, D. (1994). The effects of parental influences and respondents' norms and attitudes on black and white adult drinking patterns. *Journal of Substance Abuse, 6*, 137–154.

Hernandez, R. (2000, August 2). In new drug battle, use of ecstasy among young soars. *New York Times*. Retrieved August 2, 2000, from http://www.nytimes.com

Herper, M. (2011, May 11). America's most popular drugs. *Forbes, Pharmaceuticals*. Retrieved from http://www.forbes.com/2010/05/11/narcotic-painkiller-vicodin-business-healthcare-popular-drugs.html

Hersey, B. (2001). *The controlled drinking debates: A review of four decades of acrimony*. Retrieved July 23, 2003, from http://www.doctordeluca.com/library/abstinencehr/fourdecadesacrimony.htm

Hertzberg, H. (2002, September 9). Bloomberg butts in. *New Yorker*. Retrieved September 9, 2002, from http://www.newyorker.com

Herz, D. (2000). *Drugs in the heartland: Methamphetamine use in rural Nebraska* [Research brief]. Washington, DC: National Institute of Justice.

Hester, R., Delaney, H., & Campbell, W. (2011). Moderatedrinking.com and moderation management: Outcomes of a randomized clinical trial with non-dependent problem drinkers. *Journal of*

Consulting and Clinical Psychology, 79, 215–224.

Hibell, B., Guttormsson, U., Ahlstrom, S., Balakireva, O., Bjarnason, T., Kokkevi, A., & Kraus, L. (2012). *The 2011 ESPAD report: Substance use among students in 36 European countries*. Stockholm: The Swedish Council for Information on Alcohol and Other Drugs (CAN); EMCDDA.

Hickman, M., Vickerman, P., Macleod, J., Lewis, G., Zammit, S., Kirkbride, J., & Jones, P. (2009). If cannabis caused schizophrenia—how many cannabis users may need to be prevented in order to prevent one case of schizophrenia? England and Wales calculations. *Addiction, 104*, 1856–1861. doi: 10.1111/j.1360-0443.2009.02736.x

Hidalgo, J. (2010, September 22). Spain's former drug czarina endorses legalization. *Cato Institute*. Retrieved April 27, 2012, from http://www.cato-at-liberty.org

Hiding the data on drug trials. (2005, June 1). *New York Times*. Retrieved June 1, 2005, from http://www.nytimes.com

Hilts, P. J. (1994, August 2). Is nicotine addictive? It depends on whose criteria you use. *New York Times*. Retrieved from http://www.nytimes.com

Hiltzick, M. (2009a, March 2). Athletes, steroids, and public hysteria. *Los Angeles Times*. Retrieved March 2, 2009, from http://www.latimes.com

Hitltzick, M. (2009b, May 8). Baseball's anti-doping program faces renewed scrutiny in light of Ramirez case. *Los Angeles Times*. Retrieved May 8, 2009, from http://www.latimes.com

Himmelstein, J. (1983). *The strange career of marijuana*. Westport, CT: Greenwood Press.

Hirschi, T. (1969). *Causes of delinquency*. Berkeley: University of California Press.

Hitchens, C. (2004, December 13). Let the Afghan poppies bloom. *Vanity Fair*. Retrieved December 13, 2004, from http://www.vanityfair.com

Hitt, J. (1999, October 24). The battle of the binge. *New York Times Magazine.* Retrieved October 24, 1999, from http://www.nytimes.com

Hoberman, J. (1992). *Mortal engines: The science of performance and the dehumanization of sport.* New York: The Free Press.

Hockstader, L. (2003, June 17). For Tulia 12 "it feels so good." *Washington Post.* Retrieved June 17, 2003, from http://www.washingtonpost.com

Hoeffel, E. M., Rastogi, S., Kim, M. O., & Shahid, H. (2012). *The Asian population: 2010; 2010 Census briefs.* Retrieved from http://www.census.gov/prod/cen2010/briefs/c2010br-11.pdf

Hoeffel, J. (2009, July 2). Justice Department shoots down commercial marijuana cultivation. *LA Times.* Retrieved from http://articles.latimes.com/2011/jul/02/local/la-me-medical-marijuana-20110702

Hoeffel, J. (2011, July 9). U.S. decrees that marijuana has no accepted medical use. *LA Times.* Retrieved from http://articles.latimes.com/2011/jul/09/local/la-me-marijuana-20110709

Hoffman, J. (1994). Investigating the age effects of family structure on adolescent marijuana use. *Journal of Youth and Adolescence, 23,* 215–232.

Hoffman, M. B. (1999). The drug court scandal. *NCL Rev., 78,* 1437.

Hofmann, A. (1970). The discovery of LSD and subsequent investigations on naturally occurring hallucinogens. In F. Ayd, Jr. & B. Blackwell (Eds.), *Discoveries in biological psychiatry* (pp. 91–106). Philadelphia: J. B. Lippincott.

Hohler, B. (2005, April 27). Baseball slow to act on use of "speed." *Boston Globe.* Retrieved April 27, 2005, from http://www.boston.com

Hollon, M. (2005). Direct to consumer advertising. *Journal of the American Medical Association, 293,* 2030–2033.

Holloway, K., Bennett, T., & Farrington, D. (2005). The effectiveness of criminal justice and treatment programmes in reducing drug-related crime: A systematic review. *Home Office On-line Research Report, 26*(05).

Holmes, D. (2012). Prescription drug addiction: The treatment challenge. *Lancet, 379,* 17–18.

Home Office. (2001). *Drug misuse declared in 2000: Results from the British crime survey.* London: Author.

Honan, W. (1995, December 6). Study ties binge drinking to fraternity house life. *New York Times.* Retrieved December 6, 1995, from http://www.nytimes.com

Hooker, J. M., Xu, Y., Schiffer, W., Shea, C., Carter, P., & Fowler, J. S. (2008). Pharmacokinetics of the potent hallucinogen, salvinorin A in primates parallels the rapid onset and short duration of effects in humans. *Neuroimage, 41,* 1044–1050.

Hopkins, N. (2003, June 14). Drug gang warning by police. *Guardian.* Retrieved June 14, 2003, from http://www.guardian.co.uk

Hopperstad, J. (2012, October 24). If voters legalize marijuana in state, will the Feds step in to stop it? *Q13 Fox News.* Retrieved October 24, 2012, from http://www.q13fox.com/news

Horgan, J. (1990). Bufo abuse: A toxic toad gets licked, boiled, tee'd up and tanned. *Scientific American, 263,* 26–27.

Hornik, R., Maklan, D., Cadell, D., Prado, A., Barmada, C., Jacobsohn, L., et al. (2002). *Evaluation of the national youth anti-drug media campaign, fourth semi-annual report of findings.* Rockville, MD: Westat.

Horowitz, S. (2012, October 11). Marijuana legalization on ballot in three states, but Justice Department remains silent. *Washington Post.* Retrieved October 11, 2012, from http://www.washingtonpost.com

Hottle, M. (2011, March 30). Old town businesses, residents ask help from city to deal with drug problems. *Oregonian.* Retrieved March 30, 2011, from http://www.oregonlive.com

Houston, M. (2004). Commissioner denies plans for a Europe-wide smoking ban. *British Medical Journal, 328,* 544.

How a habit forced Bob onto the street [Advertisement]. (1998, September 15). *New York Times,* p. 35.

How to stop the drug wars. (2009, March 5). *The Economist.* Retrieved September 5, 2009, from http://www.economist.com

Howard, G. (1918). Alcohol and crime: A study in social causation. *American Journal of Sociology, 24,* 61–80.

Howard, R. (2000, April 3). A children's garden of dope: Vietnamese gangs make cultivating marijuana a family affair. *Maclean's.* Retrieved April 3, 2000, from http://www.macleans.ca

Howard, T. (2003, August 25). Expect an ad-stravaganza as Viagra gets competition. *USA Today.* Retrieved August 25, 2003, from http://www.usatoday.com

Hubbard, R., Craddock, S. G., & Anderson, J. (2003). Overview of 5-year follow-up outcomes in the drug abuse treatment outcome studies (DATOS). *Journal of Substance Abuse Treatment, 25,* 125–134.

Hubbard, R., Marsden, M., Rachal, J., Harwood, H., Cavanagh, E., & Ginzburg, H. (1989). *Drug abuse treatment: A national study of effectiveness.* Chapel Hill: University of North Carolina Press.

Huestis, M., Gorelick, D., Heishman, S., Preston, K., Nelson, R., Moolchan, E., et al. (2001). Blockade of effects of smoked marijuana by the CB1-selective cannabinoid receptor antagonist SR141716. *Archives of General Psychiatry, 58,* 322–328.

Huffington, A. (2000, October 20). *Bye, bye, Barry McCaffrey.* Retrieved October 20, 2000, from http://www.salon.com

Hughes, C., & Stephens, A. (2012). A resounding success or a disastrous failure? Re-examining the interpretation of evidence on the Portuguese decriminalisation of illicit drugs. *Drug and Alcohol Review, 31,* 101–113.

Hughes, J., Goldstein, M., Hurt, R., & Shiffman, S. (1999). Recent advances in the pharmacotherapy of smoking. *Journal of the American Medical Association, 28,* 72–76.

Hull, J., & Bond, C. (1986). Social and behavioral consequences of alcohol consumption and expectancy: A meta-analysis. *Psychological Bulletin, 99,* 347–360.

Human Rights Watch. (2010). *Drug policy and human rights.* Author. Retrieved June 15, 2011, from http://www.hrw.org

Humensky, J. L. (2010). Are adolescents with high socioeconomic status more likely to engage in alcohol and illicit drug use in early adulthood? *Substance Abuse Treatment, Prevention, and Policy, 5*(1), 19.

Humphreys, A., & Bell, S. (2003, October 29). Violence grows as marijuana profits rise. *National Post.* Retrieved October 29, 2003, from http://www.canada.com/nationalpost

Hunt, N. (2005). *A review of the evidence-base for harm reduction approaches to drug use.* Retrieved December 12, 2005, from http://www.forward-thinking-on-drugs.org/review2-print.html

Hurley, D. (2004, April 11). As Ephedra ban nears, a race to sell the last supplies. *New York Times.* Retrieved April 11, 2004, from http://www.nytimes.com

Hussong, A., & Hicks, R. (2003). Affect and peer context interactively impact adolescent substance use. *Journal of Abnormal Child Psychology, 31,* 413–426.

Hutchinson, A. (2002, October 9). Drug legalization doesn't work. *Washington Post.* Retrieved October 9, 2002, from http://www.washingtonpost.com

Ilgen, M., Wilbourne, P., Moos, B., & Moos, R. (2008). Problem-free drinking over 16 years among individuals with alcohol use disorders. *Drug and Alcohol Dependence, 92,* 116–122.

IMS Institute for Healthcare Informatics. (2011). *The use of medicines in the United States: Review of 2010.* Parsippany, NJ: IMS Healthcare Informatics. Retrieved from http://www.imshealth.com/imshealth/Global/Content/IMS%20Institute/Documents/IHII_UseOfMed_report%20.pdf

Inciardi, J. (1993). Kingrats, chicken heads, slow necks, freaks, and blood suckers: A glimpse at the Miami sex-for-crack trade. In M. Ratner (Ed.), *Crack pipe as pimp* (pp. 37–67). New York: Lexington Books.

Indian Health Service. (2001). *Facts on Indian health.* Washington, DC: Author.

Indian Hemp Drugs Commission. (1893–1894). Sixmal, India: Author.

Institute of Medicine. (2004). *Testosterone and aging: Clinical research directions.* Washington, DC: National Academies Press.

International Olympic Committee. (2012). *Drug-testing policy.* Retrieved August 7, 2012, from http://www.olympic.org

Introduction. (1996, February 12). *National Review.* Retrieved March 12, 2006, from http://www.nationalreview.com

Inwood, D. (2010, September 12). From prince of pot to prince of prison. *The Province.* Retrieved September 12, 2010, from http://www2.canada.com/theprovince

Irwin, J., & Austin, J. (1997). *It's about time: America's imprisonment binge.* Belmont, CA: Wadsworth.

It's school, not prison. (2002, April 14). *Los Angeles Times.* Retrieved April 14, 2002, from http://www.latimes.com

Iversen, L. (2003). Cannabis and the brain. *Brain, 126,* 1252–1270. Retrieved July 23, 2004, from http://brain.oxfordjournals.org/cgi/content/abstract/126/6/1252

Ivy, J. L., Kammer, L., Ding, Z., Wang, B., Bernard, J. R., Liao, Y. H., & Hwang, J. (2009). Improved cycling time-trial performance after ingestion of a caffeine energy drink. *International Journal of Sport Nutrition and Exercise Metabolism, 19*(1), 61–78.

Jacobson, N., Ensminger, M. E., & Ohlenroth, P. (2001). Poverty and drug use. In R. Carson-DeWitt (Ed.), *Encyclopedia of drugs, alcohol and addictive behavior* (Vol. 1, pp. 35–37). Toronto, ON: Macmillan Reference USA.

Jackson, D. (2004, April 26). Cell phones just one of many lethal distractions for drivers. *Seattle Post-Intelligencer.* Retrieved April 26, 2004, from http://www.seattlepi.nwsource.com

James, D., Adams, R. D., Spears, R., et al. (2010). Clinical characteristics of mephedrone toxicity reported to the UK National Poisons Information Service. *Emerging Medicine Journal, 28,* 686–689.

Jang, S., & Johnson, B. (2001). Religiosity and adolescent use of illicit drugs: A test of multilevel hypotheses. *Criminology, 39,* 109–141.

Janofsky, M. (2002). Nevadans weigh proposal to make marijuana legal. *New York Times.* Retrieved August 2, 2002, from http://www.nytimes.com

Jardine-Tweedie, L., & Wright, P. (1998). Workplace drug testing: Avoiding the test addiction. *Journal of Managerial Psychology, 13,* 534–543.

Jaspen, B. (2003, June 21). Drug giant guilty in Medicare sales fraud. *Chicago Tribune.* Retrieved June 21, 2003, from http://www.chicagotribune.com

Jaspen, B. (2005, May 8). Drug sales calls wear on doctors. *Chicago Tribune.* Retrieved May 8, 2005, from http://www.chicagotribune.com

Jaspen, B. (2012, February 2). Drug makers dial down. *New York Times.* Retrieved June 6, 2012, from http://www.nytimes.com

Jefferson, D. (2005, August 8). America's most dangerous drug. *Newsweek.*

Retrieved August 8, 2005, from http://msnbc.msn.com

Jellinek, E. M. (1960). *The disease conception of alcoholism.* New Brunswick, NJ: Hillhouse.

Jelsma, M. (2003). Drugs in the U.N. system: The unwritten history of the 1998 United Nations general assembly special session on drugs. *International Journal of Drug Policy, 14,* 181–195.

Jensen, E., & Gerber, J. (1996). The civil forfeiture of assets and the war on drugs: Expanding criminal sanctions while reducing due process protections. *Crime and Delinquency, 42,* 421–434.

Jensen, E., & Mosher, C. (2006). Adult drug courts: The judicial origins, evaluations of effectiveness, and expansions of the model. *Idaho Law Review, 42,* 443–470.

Jessor, R., Graves, T., Hanson, R., & Jessor, S. (1968). *Society, personality, and deviant behavior: Study of a tri-ethnic community.* New York: Holt, Rinehart, & Winston.

Jessor, R., & Jessor, S. (1975). Adolescent development and the onset of drinking: A longitudinal study. *Journal of Studies on Alcohol, 36,* 27–51.

Jessor, R., & Jessor, S. (1977). *Problem behavior and psychosocial development: A longitudinal study of youth.* New York: Academic Press.

Jessor, R., & Jessor, S. (1980). A social-psychological framework for studying drug use. In D. Lettieri (Ed.), *Theories on drug abuse* (pp. 54–71). Rockville, MD: National Institute on Drug Abuse.

Johnson, B. A., Rosenthal, N., Capece, J. A., Wiegand, F., Mao, L., Beyers, K., & Swift, R. M. (2007). Topiramate for treating alcohol dependence. *JAMA: Journal of the American Medical Association,* 298(14), 1641–1651.

Johnson, C., & Sudermann, H. (2002, November 5). Tobacco giveaways on the rise. *Spokesman-Review.* Retrieved November 5, 2002, from http://www.spokesmanreview.com

Johnson, D. (1996, February 22). Good people go bad in Iowa, and a drug is blamed. *New York Times.* Retrieved February 22, 1996, from http://www.nytimes.com

Johnson, G. (2011, November 20). State's effort to legalize pot faces legal pitfalls. *Associated Press.* Retrieved November 20, 2011, from http://www.ap.org

Johnson, J., & Leff, M. (1999). Children of substance abusers: Overview of research findings. *Pediatrics, 103*(S), 1085–1099.

Johnson, L. (2005, January 13). Study: Sleep-deprived doctors a danger to other drivers as well as patients. *Boston Globe.* Retrieved January 13, 2005, from http://www.boston.com

Johnson, M. W., MacLean, K. A., Reissig, C. R., Prisinzano, T. E., & Griffiths, R. R. (2011). Human psychopharmacology and dose-effects of salvinorin A, a kappa-opioid agonist hallucinogen present in the plant Salvia divinorum. *Drug and Alcohol Dependence, 115,* 150–155.

Johnson, R., Marcos, A., & Bahr, S. (1987). The role of peers in the complex etiology of adolescent drug use. *Criminology, 25,* 323–340.

Johnson, T. (2005, August 5). New DUI law tossed out by judges across state. *Seattle Post-Intelligencer.* Retrieved August 5, 2005, from http://www.seattlepi.com

Johnston, L., O'Malley, P., & Bachman, J. (2003a). *Monitoring the future national survey results on drug use, 1975–2002, volume I: Secondary school students.* Bethesda, MD: National Institute on Drug Abuse.

Johnston, L., O'Malley, P., & Bachman, J. (2003b). *Monitoring the future national survey results on drug use, 1975–2002, volume II: College students and adults ages 19–40.* Bethesda, MD: National Institute on Drug Abuse.

Johnston, L. D., O'Malley, P. M., Bachman, J. G., & Schulenberg, J. E. (2011).

Monitoring the Future national results on adolescent drug use: Overview of key findings, 2010. Ann Arbor: Institute for Social Research, University of Michigan.

Johnston, L. D., O'Malley, P. M., Bachman, J. G., & Schulenberg, J. E. (2012a). *Monitoring the Future national results on adolescent drug use: Overview of key findings, 2011.* Ann Arbor: Institute for Social Research, University of Michigan, p. 78.

Johnston, L., O'Malley, P., Bachman J., & Schulenberg. J., (2012b). *Monitoring the Future national survey results on drug use, 1975–2011. Volume I: Secondary school students.* Ann Arbor: Institute for Social Research, University of Michigan, p. 751.

Johnston, L. D., O'Malley, P. M., Bachman, J. G., & Schulenberg, J. E. (2012c). *Monitoring the Future national survey results on drug use, 1975–2011. Volume II: College students and adults ages 19–50.* Ann Arbor: Institute for Social Research, University of Michigan, p. 314.

Jones, C. (2003, July 2). Ban ignites smoking wars in NYC. *USA Today.* Retrieved July 2, 2003, from http://www.usato day.com

Jones, M. (2002). Policy paradox: Implications of U.S. drug control policy for Jamaica. *Annals, 582,* 117–133.

Jones pleads guilty, admits lying about steroids. (2007, October 15). *Associated Press.* Retrieved August 20, 2012, from http://www.ap.org

Jones-Webb, R. (1998). Drinking patterns among African-Americans: Recent findings. *Alcohol Health and Research World, 22,* 260–265.

Jones-Webb, R., Hsiao, C., & Hannan, P. (1995). Relationships between socioeconomic status and drinking problems among black and white men. *Alcoholism: Clinical and Experimental Research, 19,* 623–627.

Jones-Webb, R., Snowden, L., Herd, D., Short, B., & Hannan, P. (1997).

Alcohol-related problems among black, Hispanic, and white men: The contribution of neighborhood poverty. *Journal of Studies on Alcohol, 57,* 539–545.

Josefson, D. (2003). Arkansas bans selling of clean urine to beat drug testing. *British Medical Journal, 326,* 300.

Joy, J., Watson, S., & Benson, J. (Eds.). (1999). *Marijuana and medicine: Assessing the science base.* Washington, DC: National Academy Press.

Judd, J. (2001, January 4). *Truth in advertising?* Retrieved January 4, 2001, from http://www.abcnews.com

Jung, J. (2001). *Psychology of alcohol and other drugs: A research perspective.* Thousand Oaks, CA: Sage.

Justice Policy Institute. (2011). *Addicted to courts: How a growing dependence on drug courts impacts people and communities.* Washington, DC: Author.

Kaiser Family Foundation. (2011). *Prescription drug trends.* Retrieved September 5, 2012, from http://www.kff.org

Kandel, D. (1974). Inter-generational and intra-generational influences on adolescent marijuana use. *Journal of Social Issues, 30,* 108–135.

Kandel, D. (1980). Drug and drinking behavior among youth. *Annual Review of Sociology, 6,* 235–285.

Kandel, D. (2003). Does marijuana cause the use of other drugs? *Journal of the American Medical Association, 289,* 482–483.

Kandel, D., & Davies, M. (1991). Friendship networks, intimacy, and illicit drug use in young adulthood: A comparison of two competing theories. *Criminology, 29,* 441–467.

Kandel, D., & Yamaguchi, K. (1987). Job mobility and drug use: An event history analysis. *American Journal of Sociology, 92,* 836–878.

Kang, Y., Cappella, J., & Fishbein, M. (2009). The effect of marijuana scenes in anti-marijuana public service announcements on adolescents" evaluation of ad effectiveness. *Health Communication, 24,* 483–493.

Kaplan, H. (1975). *Self attitudes and deviant behavior.* Pacific Palisades, CA: Goodyear.

Kaplan, H. (1980). Self-esteem and self-derogation theory of drug abuse. In D. Lettieri et al. (Eds.), *Theories on drug abuse* (pp. 128–131). Rockville, MD: National Institute on Drug Abuse.

Kaplan, H., Tolle, G., & Yoshida, T. (2001). Substance use-induced diminution of violence: A countervailing effect in longitudinal perspective. *Criminology, 39,* 205–224.

Kaplan, S. (1996, May/June). Tobacco dole. *Mother Jones.* Retrieved June 1, 1996, from http://www.motherjones.com

Karriker-Jaffe, K. J., Zemore, S. E., Mulia, N., Jones-Webb, R., Bond, J., & Greenfield, T. K. (2012). Neighborhood disadvantage and adult alcohol outcomes: Differential risk by race and gender. *Journal of Studies on Alcohol, 73,* 865–873.

Kast, E. (1966). Pain and LSD-25: A theory of attenuation of anticipation. In D. Solomon (Ed.), *LSD: The consciousness-expanding drug* (pp. 239–254). New York: Putnam.

Kastelic, A., Dubajic, G., & Strbad, E. (2008). Slow-release oral morphine for maintenance treatment of opioid addicts intolerant to methadone or with inadequate withdrawal suppression. *Addiction, 103,* 1837–1846.

Katz, C. M., Fox, A. M., & White, M. D. (2011). Assessing the relationship between immigration status and drug use. *Justice Quarterly, 28*(4), 541–575.

Kauffman, S., Silver, P., & Poulin, J. (1997). Gender differences in attitudes about alcohol, tobacco, and other drugs. *Social Work, 42,* 231–243.

Kaufman, M. (1999, August 3). Study fails to find value in DARE program. *Washington Post.* Retrieved August 3, 1999, from http://www.washington post.com

Kaufman, M. (2003, June 3). FDA may receive tobacco authority. *Washington Post.* Retrieved June 3, 2003, from http://www.washingtonpost.com

Kaufman, M. (2005a, June 8). Drug safety board biased, official says. *Washington Post.* Retrieved June 8, 2005, from http://www.washingtonpost.com

Kaufman, M. (2005b, July 19). Impotence drugs will get blindness warning. *Washington Post.* Retrieved July 19, 2005, from http://www.washington post.com

Kaufman, M. (2005c, May 12). Memo may have swayed plan B ruling. *Washington Post.* Retrieved May 12, 2005, from http://www.washingtonpost.com

Kaufman, M., & Shipley, A. (2003, October 29). FDA bans steroid at center of scandal. *Washington Post.* Retrieved October 29, 2003, from http://www .washingtonpost.com

Keefe, P. (2012, June 15). Cocaine incorporated. *New York Times.* Retrieved June 15, 2012, from http://www.nytimes .com

Kelly, E. (2003, July 1). Still can't smoke it, but court says you can eat it. *Los Angeles Times.* Retrieved July 1, 2003, from http://www.latimes.com

Kelly, J., & White, W. (2012). Broadening the base of addiction mutual-help organizations. *Journal of Groups in Addiction and Recovery, 7,* 2–4.

Kemper, V. (2004, May 7). FDA: Doctor must still OK "morning after" pill. *Los Angeles Times.* Retrieved May 7, 2004, from http://www.latimes.com

Kendler, K., Heath, A., Neale, M., Kessler, R., & Eaves, L. (1992). A population-based twin study of alcoholism in women. *Journal of the American Medical Association, 268,* 1877–1882.

Kenna, G. A., Nielsen, D. M., Mello, P., Schiesl, A., & Swift, R. M. (2007). Pharmacotherapy of dual substance abuse and dependence. *CNS drugs, 21*(3), 213–237.

Kennedy, M. (2002, May 8). Medical marijuana is bad weed. *Saskatoon Star Phoenix*. Retrieved May 8, 2002, from http://www.canada.com/saskatoonstar phoenix

Kepner, T. (2010, January 12). McGwire admits that he used steroids. *New York Times*. Retrieved January 12, 2010, from http://www.nytimes.com

Kerlikowske, G. (2012, May 19). *Prescription drug abuse: The national perspective*. Presented at the National Association Boards of Pharmacy Annual Meeting.

Kerr, R. (1982). *The practical use of anabolic steroids with athletes*. San Gabriel, CA: Kerr.

Kessler, D. (2001). *A question of intent: A great American battle with a deadly industry*. New York: Public Affairs.

Khantzian, E. (1985). The self-medication hypothesis of addictive disorders: Focus on heroin and cocaine dependence. *American Journal of Psychiatry, 142*, 1259–1264.

Killeen, T. K., McRae-Clark, A. L., Waldrop, A. E., Upadhyaya, H., & Brady, K. T. (2012). Contingency management in community programs treating adolescent substance abuse: A feasibility study. *Journal of Child and Adolescent Psychiatric Nursing, 25*(1), 33–41.

King, R. (2006). The next big thing? *Methamphetamine in the United States*. Washington, DC: The Sentencing Project. Retrieved June 10, 2006, from http://www.sentencingproject.org/pdfs/methamphetamine_report.pdf

Kingston, A. (2003, November 22). Viagra has lessons to teach us. *National Post*. Retrieved November 22, 2003, from http://www.canada.com/nationalpost

Kirby, J., & MacDonald, N. (2009, August 24). Canada is Colombia North. *MacLean's*, 16–18.

Kirkorian, G. (2002, February 28). Welfare ban for drug felons harms children, study says. *Los Angeles Times*. Retrieved February 28, 2002, from http://www.latimes.com

Kirsch, I., Moore, T., Scobaria, A., & Nicholls, S. (2002). The emperor's new drugs: An analysis of antidepressant medication data submitted to the U.S. Food and Drug Administration. *Prevention and Treatment, 5*, 23–33.

Klecko, J., & Fields, J. (1989). *Nose to nose: Survival in the trenches in the NFL*. New York: Morrow.

Kleiman, M., & Satel, S. (1996, May 1). Meth is back and we're not ready. *Los Angeles Times*. Retrieved May 1, 1996, from http://www.latimes.com

Klingemann, H., & Rosenberg, H. (2009). Acceptance and therapeutic practice of controlled drinking as an outcome goal by Swiss alcohol treatment programmes. *European Addiction Research, 15*, 121–127.

Kluger, J. (2001, June 18). How to manage teenage drinking (the smart way). *Time*. Retrieved June 18, 2001, from http://www.time.com

Knight, J., & Levy, S. (2007). The national debate on drug testing in schools. *Journal of Adolescent Health, 41*, 419–420.

Knight, K. (2012). Endocannabinoids motivated exercise evolution. *Journal of Experimental Biology, 215*(8), i–ii.

Knight, K., Simpson, D., & Hiller, M. (1999). Three-year incarceration outcomes for in-prison therapeutic community treatment in Texas. *Prison Journal, 79*, 337–351.

Knox, D. (2012, April 24). Poison control responds to hand sanitizer abuse. *Wish TV*. Retrieved April 25, 2012, from http://www.wishtv.com

Koch, W. (2012, August 17). E-cigarettes: No smoke but fiery debate. *USA Today*. Retrieved August 17, 2012, from http://www.usatoday.com

Kolansky, H., & Moore, W. (1971). Effects of marijuana on adolescents and young adults. *Journal of the American Medical Association, 216,* 486–492.

Kopel, D., & Reynolds, G. (2002, January 30). Feel like dancing? Be aware of Tom Daschle. *National Review.* Retrieved January 30, 2002, from http://www.nationalreview.com

Korf, D., & Benschop, A. (2002). Drug use and the narrowing of the gender gap. In *Technical implementation and update of the European Union databank on national population surveys on drug use and carrying out a joint analysis of data collected* (pp. 29–47). Lisbon: EMCDDA.

Koring, P., & Sallott, J. (2003, January 31). U.S. faults Canada for letting drugs across border. *Globe and Mail.* Retrieved January 21, 2003, from http://www.theglobeandmail.com

Korn, M. (2011, May 24). Anheuser-Busch to cut alcohol in tilt. *Wall Street Journal.* Retrieved May 24, 2011, from online.wsj.com

Kornblut, A., & Wilson, D. (2005, April 17). How one pill escaped a place on list of controlled steroids. *New York Times.* Retrieved April 17, 2005, from http://www.nytimes.com

Kolosov, C. (2009). Evaluating the public interest: Regulation of industrial hemp under the Controlled Substances Act. *UCLA Law Review, 57,* 237.

Kosten, T., & Gorelick, D. (2002). The Lexington narcotic farm. *American Journal of Psychiatry, 159,* 22.

Kotaluk, R. (2002, October 21). Addiction fears rise about Xanax. *Chicago Tribune.* Retrieved October 21, 2002, from http://www.chicagotribune.com

Kowalczyk, L. (2002, December 15). Drug firms and doctors: The offers pour in. *Boston Globe.* Retrieved December 15, 2002, from http://www.boston.com

Kposowa, A. J., Adams, M. A., & Tsunokai, G. T. (2010). Citizenship status and arrest patterns in the United States: Evidence from the arrestee drug abuse monitoring program. *Crime, Law and Social Change, 53*(2), 159–181.

Kraus, C. (2003, May 18). Canada parts with U.S. on drugs policies. *New York Times.* Retrieved May 18, 2003, from http://www.nytimes.com

Kraus, L., & Augustin, R. (2002). Analysis of age of first cannabis use in Germany, Greece and Spain. In *Technical implementation and update of the European Union databank on national populations surveys on drug use and carrying out a joint analysis of data collected* (pp. 20–38). Lisbon: EMCDDA.

Krebs, C. P., Lindquist, C. H., Koetse, W., & Lattimore, P. K. (2007). Assessing the long-term impact of drug court participation on recidivism with generalized estimating equations. *Drug and Alcohol Dependence, 91*(1), 57–68. doi:10.1016/j.drugalcdep.2007.05.011

Krebs, T. S., & Johansen, P. O. (2012). Lysergic acid diethylamide (LSD) for alcoholism: Meta-analysis of randomized controlled trials. *Journal of Psychopharmacology* [Epub ahead of print]. Retrieved from http://jop.sagepub.com/content/26/7/994.short

Kumpfer, K. (1999). Outcome measures of interventions in the study of children of substance-abusing parents. *Pediatrics, 103*(S), 1128–1144.

Kunitz, D. (2001, October). On drugs: Gateways to gnosis, or bags of glue? *Harper's.* Retrieved October 6, 2001, from http://www.harpers.org

Kurtz, E. (2002). Alcoholics Anonymous and the disease concept of alcoholism. *Alcoholism Treatment Quarterly, 20,* 5–39.

Kuo, M., Wechsler, H., Greenberg, P., & Lee, H. (2003). The marketing of alcohol to college students: The role of low prices and special promotions. *American Journal of Preventive Medicine, 25,* 204–211.

Kurt, K. (2005, August 18). Oklahoma meth users importing. *Seattle Times.*

Retrieved August 18, 2005, from http://www.seattletimes.com

Kwek, G. (2012, January 24). War on drugs a failure, decriminalize now: Branson. *Sydney Morning Herald*. Retrieved January 25, 2012, from http://www.smh.com.au

Lagos, M. (2010, October 2). State downgrades pot possession. *San Francisco Chronicle*. Retrieved October 2, 2010, from http://www.sfgate.com

Lake, H. (2011, August 10). Scott Co. Sheriff: Connection between prayer and meth lab busts. *WBIR*. Retrieved August 12, 2011, from http:www.wbir.com

Landers, S. (2001, December 24). *Studies show pharmaceutical ads piquing patient interest*. Retrieved January 2, 2002, from http://www.amednews.com

Langley, W. (2012, August 26). The wheels come off in a tour de farce. *London Telegraph*. Retrieved August 27, 2012, from http://www.telegraph.co.uk

Lapham, L. (2003, July). Social hygiene. *Harper's*. Retrieved July 2, 2003, from http://www.harpers.org

Larney, S. (2010). Does opioid substitution treatment in prisons reduce injecting-related HIV risk behaviors? A systematic review. *Addiction, 105*, 216–223.

Larsen, D. (2002, January 18). Decriminalization is dangerous. *Cannabis Culture Magazine*. Retrieved January 20, 2002, from http://www.cannabisculture.com

Latour, F. (2002, June 22). Drug test for hub officers stirs bias fear. *Boston Globe*. Retrieved June 22, 2002, from http://www.boston.com

Lauman, E., Paik, A., & Rosen, R. (1999). Sexual dysfunction in the United States: Prevalence and predictors. *Journal of the American Medical Association, 281*, 537–544.

Laurance, J. (2010, March 19). Glaxo funded backers of "danger" drug. *Independent*. Retrieved March 19, 2010, from http://www.independent.co.uk

Lauter, D. (2012, August 25). A new Breathalyzer law drives anger in France. *Los Angeles Times*. Retrieved August 25, 2012, from http://www.latimes.com

Lavelle, M. (2000, February 7). Teen tobacco wars. *US News and World Report*. Retrieved February 10, 2000, from http://www.usnews.com

Law Enforcement Against Prohibition. (n.d.). *Mission statement*. Retrieved February 10, 2006, from http://www.leap.cc/mission.htm

Lawrence, M. (2011, May 22). Chicago Bulls MVP Derrick Rose backs off steroids statement. *New York Daily News*. Retrieved September 20, 2012, from http://www.nydn.com

Lawson, M. (2003, June 7). Blood on the tracks. *Guardian*. Retrieved June 7, 2003, from http://www.guardian.co.uk

Layden, T., & Yeager, D. (2003, April 14). Playing favorites? *Sports Illustrated*. Retrieved April 15, 2003, from http://sportsillustrated.cnn.com

The Leadership Conference. (2010). *South Carolina eliminates crack/powder sentencing disparity and mandatory minimums*. Retrieved August 17, 2012, from http://www.civilrights.org

Lee, C., Mun, E. Y., White, H. R., & Simon, P. (2010). Substance use trajectories of black and white young men from adolescence to emerging adulthood: A two-part growth curve analysis. *Journal of Ethnicity in Substance Abuse, 9*(4), 301–319.

Lee, J. (2011, November 22). South Korea pulls plug on late-night adolescent online gamers. *CNN*. Retrieved October 28, 2012, from http://www.cnn.com

Lee, N., & Rawson, R. (2008). A systematic review of cognitive and behavioral therapies for methamphetamine dependence. *Drug and Alcohol Review, 27*, 309–317.

LeFoll, B., & Goldberg, S. (2005). Cannabinoid CB1 receptor antagonists as promising new medications for drug dependence. *Journal of Pharmacology and Experimental Therapeutics, 312,* 825–833.

Leinwand, D. (2002, September 22). Ecstasy-Viagra mix alarms doctors. *USA Today.* Retrieved September 22, 2002, from http://www.usatoday.com

Leinwand, D. (2006a, May 5). Heroin mix tied to dozens of deaths. *USA Today.* Retrieved May 5, 2006, from http://www.usatoday.com

Leinwand, D. (2006b, August 29). Anti-drug advertising campaign a failure, GAO report says. *USA Today.* Retrieved August 29, 2006, from http://www.usatoday.com

Leinwand, D. (2010, May 24). Places race to outlaw K2 "spice" drug. *USA Today.* Retrieved May 24, 2010, from http://www.usatoday.com

Leinwand-Leger, D. (2011, November 14). Surge in babies addicted to drugs. *USA Today.* Retrieved November 14, 2011, from http://www.usatoday.com

Leinwand, D., & Fields, G. (2000, April 19). Feds crack down on ecstasy pills. *USA Today.* Retrieved April 19, 2000, from http://www.usatoday.com

Leipzig, R., Cumming, R., & Tinetti, M. (1999). Drugs and falls in older people: A systematic review and meta-analysis. *Journal of the American Geriatric Society, 1,* 30–39.

Leland, J. (1976). *Firewater myths: North American Indian drinking and alcohol addiction.* New Brunswick, NJ: Rutgers Center for Alcohol Studies.

Lemanski, M. (1999). *A history of addiction treatment in the United States.* Tucson, AZ: Sharp Press.

Lembke, A., & Humphreys, K. (2012). Moderation management: A mutual-help organization for problem drinkers who are not alcohol-dependent. *Journal of Groups in Addiction & Recovery,* 7(2–4), 130–141. doi:10.1080/1556035X.2012.705657

Lemle, R., & Mishkind, M. (1989). Alcohol and masculinity. *Journal of Substance Abuse Treatment, 6,* 213–222.

Lenke, L., & Olsson, B. (2002). Swedish drug policy in the 21st century: A policy model going astray. *Annals, 582,* 64–79.

Lenzer, J. (2004a). FDA is incapable of protecting us against another Vioxx. *British Medical Journal, 329,* 1253.

Lenzer, J. (2004b). FDA's counsel accused of being too close to drug industry. *British Medical Journal, 329,* 189.

Lenzer, J. (2005a). FDA investigates direct to consumer adverts. *British Medical Journal, 331,* 1102.

Lenzer, J. (2005b). New law aims to distance the FDA from the drug industry. *British Medical Journal, 330,* 1106.

Leshner, A. (1999). Science-based views of drug addiction and its treatment. *Journal of the American Medical Association, 282,* 1314–1316.

Lester, B., Andreozzi, L., & Appiah, L. (2004). Substance use during pregnancy: Time for policy to catch up with research. *Harm Reduction Journal, 1,* 1–44.

Levin, M. (2002, November 10). Cigarettes, greed and betrayal: An insider's saga. *Los Angeles Times.* Retrieved November 10, 2002, from http://www.latimes.com

Levin, M. (2003, March 1). Big tobacco in Canadian fraud case. *Los Angeles Times.* Retrieved March 1, 2003, from http://www.latimes.com

Levin, M. (2004, December 19). Philip Morris image a tough sell. *Los Angeles Times.* Retrieved December 19, 2004, from http://www.latimes.com

Levin, S. M., & Kruger, J. (Eds.). (2000). *Substance abuse among older adults: A guide for social service providers.* Rockville, MD: Substance Abuse and Mental Health Services Administration.

Levine, H. (2001). *The secret of world-wide drug prohibition.* Retrieved June 10, 2002, from http://www.cedro-uva.org/lib/levine.secret.html

Levine, S. B., & Coupey, S. M. (2009). Nonmedical use of prescription medications: An emerging risk behavior among rural adolescents. *Journal of Adolescent Health, 44,* 407–409.

Levy, S., Van Hook, S., & Knight, J. (2004). A review of Internet-based home drug-testing products for parents. *Pediatrics, 113,* 720–726.

Lewin, T. (2002, September 29). With court nod, parents debate school drug tests. *New York Times.* Retrieved September 29, 2002, from http://www.nytimes.com

Lewis, D. (2005). *Meth science not stigma: Open letter to the media.* Retrieved February 2, 2006, from http://www.jointogether.org/sa/files/pdf/Meth_Letter.pdf

Lewis, K. (1992, January/February). Addicting the young *Multinational Monitor.* Retrieved October 3, 2003, from http://www.multinationalmonitor.org

Lewis, R., & Irwanto, M. (2001). Families and drug use. In R. Carson-DeWitt (Ed.), *Encyclopedia of drugs, alcohol, and addictive behavior* (pp. 515–521). New York: MacMillan.

Libertarian Party. (2001, February 21). *Lemon drop drugs and paper guns: Zero-tolerance laws get bizarre [Press release].* Retrieved June 18, 2003, from http://www.datow.com/poli1.htm

Light, D., & Lexchin, J. (2012). Pharmaceutical research and development: What do we get for all that money? *British Medical Journal.* Retrieved September 4, 2012, from http://www.bmj.com

Lillie-Blanton, M., Anthony, J., & Schuster, C. (1993). Probing the meaning of racial/ethnic group comparisons in crack cocaine smoking. *Journal of the American Medical Association, 269,* 993–997.

Lindesmith Center. (2001a, May 7). *Harsh new penalties for ecstasy take effect.* Retrieved May 7, 2001, from http://www.drugpolicy.org

Lindesmith Center. (2001b, April 13). *Reefer madness science.* Retrieved April 13, 2001, from http://www.drug policy.org

Lindsay, R. (2010). Cannabis and schizophrenia is probably a minimal relationship. *Beyond Highbrow—Robert Lindsay.* [Web log comment]. Retrieved from https://robertlindsay.wordpress.com/2010/03/23/cannabis-and-schizophrenia-is-probably-a-minimal-relationship/

Lingford-Hughes, A. R., Welch, S., Peters, L., & Nutt, D. J. (2012). *Journal of Psychopharmacology, 26*(7), 899–952.

Liptak, A. (2009, March 24). Strip search of girl tests limits of school policy. *New York Times.* Retrieved March 24, 2009, from http://www.nytimes.com

Liptak, A. (2011, April 18). Judges see sentencing injustice. *New York Times.* Retrieved April 18, 2011, from http://www.nytimes.com

Lipton, D. (1995). *The effectiveness of treatment of drug abusers under criminal justice supervision.* Washington, DC: National Institute on Drug Abuse.

Liska, K. (2000). *Drugs and the human body* (6th ed.). New York: MacMillan.

Listerine drinker arrested for DUI. (2005, January 17). *Associated Press.* Retrieved January 17, 2005, from http://www.ap.org

Lithwick, D. (2002, February 19). Too old to narc. *Slate.* Retrieved February 20, 2002, from http://www.slate.com/id/2062274/

Litt, M. D., Kadden, R. M., Kabela-Cormier, E., & Petry, N. (2007). Changing network support for drinking: Initial findings from the network support project. *Journal of Consulting and Clinical Psychology, 75,* 542–555.

Liu, I. (2009, January 9). Paterson once arrested over Rockefeller drug law. *Albany Times Union*. Retrieved June 5, 2012, from http://www.timesunion .com

Loftin, J. (2001, October 28). *Controlling Utah liquor laws*. Retrieved May 27, 2003, from http://www.Desertnews .com

Logan, E. (1999). The wrong race, committing crime, doing drugs, and maladjusted for motherhood: The nation's fury over "crack babies." *Social Justice, 26*, 115–138.

Longman, J. (2003, October 24). Steroid is reportedly found in top runner's urine test. *New York Times*. Retrieved October 24, 2003, from http://www .nytimes.com

Longman, J. (2004, January 26). East German steroids toll: They killed Heidi. *New York Times*. Retrieved January 26, 2004, from http://www.nytimes.com

Longman, J. (2005, May 18). Steroid-assisted fastballs? Pitchers face new spotlight. *New York Times*. Retrieved May 18, 2005, from http://www .nytimes.com

Longman, J. (2008, November 28). High schools take on doping with no consensus on strategy. *New York Times*. Retrieved November 28, 2008, from http://www.nytimes.com

Longshore, D., Urada, D., Evans, E., Hser, Y., Prendergast, M., Hawken, A., et al. (2004). *Evaluation of the Substance Abuse and Crime Prevention Act 2003 report*. Los Angeles, CA: UCLA Integrated Substance Abuse Program.

Looking for adverse drug effects. (2004, November 27). *New York Times*. Retrieved November 27, 2004, from http://www.nytimes.com

Lopez, W. D., Krueger, P. M., & Walters, S. T. (2010). High-risk drug use and sexual behaviors among out-of-treatment drug users: An aging and life course perspective. *Addictive Behaviors, 35*(5),

432–437. doi:10.1016/j.addbeh.2009 .12.010

Lucas, P. (2012). Cannabis as an adjunct to or substitute for opiates in the treatment of chronic pain. *Journal of Psychoactive Drugs, 44*, 125–133.

Luebbe, A. M., & Bell, D. J. (2009). Mountain Dew® or Mountain Don't? A pilot investigation of caffeine use parameters and relations to depression and anxiety symptoms in 5th- and 10th-grade students. *Journal of School Health, 79*, 380–387.

Luna, C. (2002, November 10). Excuse for teens to forgo drugs. *Los Angeles Times*. Retrieved November 10, 2002, from http://www.latimes.com

Lunman, K. (2002, September 5). Senators want pot legalized. *Globe and Mail*. Retrieved September 5, 2002, from http://www.theglobeandmail.com

Lunman, K., & McCarthy, S. (2002, December 12). Drug czar talks about tightening border. *Globe and Mail*. Retrieved December 12, 2002, from http://www.theglobeandmail.com

Lusane, C. (1991). *Pipe dream blues*. Boston: South End Press.

Lynskey, M., Heath, A., Bucholz, K., Slutskie, W., Madden, P., Nelson, E., et al. (2003). Escalation of drug use in early onset cannabis users vs. co-twin controls. *Journal of the American Medical Association, 289*, 427–433.

MacCharles, T. (2002, December 9). Safe sites urged for hard drug users. *Toronto Star*. Retrieved December 9, 2002, from http://www.thestar.com

MacCoun, R., & Reuter, P. (2001). *Drug war heresies*. Cambridge, UK: Cambridge University Press.

MacIntosh, A. (2006, March 13). Tougher drug laws only scratch the surface of the problem. *Sydney Morning Herald*. Retrieved March 13, 2006, from http:// www.smh.com.au

Mack, K. (2012, June 15). Emanuel backs decriminalizing small amounts of marijuana. *Chicago Tribune*. Retrieved June 15, 2012, from http://www.chicagotribune.com

Mackie, J. (2003, January 21). B.C.—A pot friendly, pot-profitable province. *Vancouver Sun*. Retrieved January 21, 2003, from http://www.canada.com

Macur, J. (2010, October 4). 2nd failed test puts heat on Contador. *New York Times*. Retrieved October 4, 2010, from http://www.nytimes.com

Macur, J. (2011, August 5). NFL falls short of a leap on high. *New York Times*. Retrieved August 5, 2011, from http://www.nytimes.com

Macur, J., & Schmidt, M. (2010, May 20). Landis, admitting doping, accuses top U.S. cyclists. *New York Times*. Retrieved May 20, 2010, from http://www.nytimes.com

MacQueen, K. (2010, September 7). Jailhouse nation. *MacLean's*. Retrieved October 15, 2010, from http://www2.macleans.ca

MADD (Washington). (2004). *Costs of driving under the influence in Washington*. Retrieved July 17, 2004, from http://www.maddwashington.org/dui_cost.htm

Maguire, K. (2010). *Sourcebook of criminal justice statistics*. Washington, DC: U.S. Department of Justice.

Mail, P., & Johnson, S. (1993). Boozing, sniffing, and toking: An overview of the past, present, and future of substance abuse by American Indians. *American Indian and Alaska Native Mental Health Research, 5*, 1–33.

Majer, J. M., Jason, L. A., Ferrari, J. R., & Miller, S. A. (2011). 12-Step involvement among a U.S. national sample of Oxford House residents. *Journal of Substance Abuse Treatment, 41*(1), 37–44. doi:10.1016/j.jsat.2011.01.010

Makimoto, K. (1998). Drinking patterns and drinking problems among Asian-Americans and Pacific Islanders. *Alcohol Health and Research World, 22*, 270–275.

Malarek, V. (2003, July 12). Tobacco companies had Natives smuggle. *Globe and Mail*. Retrieved July 12, 2003, from http://www.theglobeandmail.com

Malinauskas, B. M., Aeby, V. G., Overton, R. F., Carpenter-Aeby, T., & Barber-Heidal, K. (2007). A survey of energy drink consumption patterns among college students. *Nutrition Journal, 6*(35), 1–7.

Mammen, K., & Bell, J. (2009). The clinical efficacy and abuse potential of combination buprenorphine–naloxone in the treatment of opioid dependence. *Expert Opinion on Pharmacotherapy, 10*(15), 2537–2544. doi:10.1517/14656560903213405

Manchikanti, L., Fellows, B., Ailinani, H., & Pampati, V. (2010). Therapeutic use, abuse, and nonmedical use of opioids: A ten-year perspective. *Pain Physician, 13*, 401–435.

Manderson, D. (1999). Formalism and narrative in law and medicine: The debate over medical marijuana use. *Journal of Drug Issues, 29*, 121–134.

Mangold, T. (2003, March 3). The rogue cop of Tulia, Texas. *The Age*. Retrieved January 20, 2006, from http://www.theage.com.au/articles/2003/03/02/1046540066770.html

Mann, K., & Hermann, D. (2010). Individualised treatment in alcohol-dependent patients. *European Archives of Psychiatry and Clinical Neuroscience, 260*, 116–120.

Manrique-Garcia, E., Zammit, S., Dalman, C., Hemmingsson, T., & Andreasson, S. (2012). Cannabis, schizophrenia and other non-affective psychoses: 35 years of follow-up of a population-based cohort. *Psychological Medicine, 42*(6), 1321–1328.

Mansfield, P., Mintzes, B., Richards, D., & Toop, L. (2005). Direct-to-consumer advertising. *British Medical Journal, 330*, 5–6.

Manski, C. F., Pepper, J. V., & Petrie, C. V. (Eds.). (2001). *Informing America's policy on illegal drugs: What we don't know keeps hurting us.* Washington, DC: National Academy Press.

Marczinski, C. A., Fillmore, M. T., Bardgett, M. E., & Howard, M. A. (2011). Effects of energy drinks mixed with alcohol on behavioral control: Risks for college students consuming trendy cocktails. *Alcoholism: Clinical and Experimental Research, 35,* 1282–1292.

Marijuana: A conversation with NIDA's Robert L. Dupont. (1976, May 14). *Science,* 647–649.

Marijuana legalization on the ballot. (2012, November 7). *Huffington Post.* Retrieved November 11, 2012, from http://www.huffingtonpost.com

Marijuana menaces youth. (1936, March). *Scientific American,* 150–151.

Marijuana: Millions of turned on users. (1967, July 7). *Life,* 16–23.

Marijuana more dangerous than heroin or cocaine. (1938, May). *Scientific American,* 293.

Markel, H. (2005, August 22). Burning money. *New York Times.* Retrieved August 22, 2005, from http://www.nytimes.com

Marlatt, G. A. (1983). The controlled drinking controversy: A commentary. *American Psychologist, 38,* 1097–1110.

Marlatt, G. A., Larimer, M., Baer, J., & Quigley, L. (1993). Harm reduction for alcohol problems: Moving beyond the controlled drinking controversy. *Behavior Therapy, 24,* 461–504.

Marlatt, A., & Witkiewicz, K. (2010). Update on harm-reduction policy and intervention research. In NolenHoeksema, T., Cannon, D., & Widiger, T. (Eds.), *Annual review of clinical psychology 6* (pp. 591–606). Palo Alto, CA: Annual Reviews.

Marlowe, D. B., Festinger, D. S., Dugosh, K. L., Arabia, P. L., & Kirby, K. C. (2008). An effectiveness trial of contingency management in a felony preadjudication drug court. *Journal of Applied Behavior Analysis, 41*(4), 565.

Marquis, C. (2002, September 6). Coca spraying poses no risk to Colombians, U.S. declares. *New York Times.* Retrieved September 6, 2002, from http://www.nytimes.com

Marsch, L. (1998). The efficacy of methadone maintenance interventions in reducing illicit opiate use, HIV risk behavior and criminality: A meta-analysis. *Addiction, 93,* 515–532.

Marshall, B., Milloy, M., Wood, E., Montaner, J., & Kerr, T. (2011). Reduction in overdose mortality after the opening of North America's first medically supervised injecting facility: A retrospective population-based study. *Lancet, 377,* 1429–1437.

Martell, B. (2003, September 30). Louisiana finally drops level for DUI. *Houston Chronicle.* Retrieved September 30, 2003, from http://www.chron.com

Martin, C., & Gale, C. (2003). Tobacco, coffee, and Parkinson's disease. *British Medical Journal, 326,* 561–562.

Martin, J. (2002, April 24). New drug, new crime. *Spokesman-Review.* Retrieved April 24, 2002, from http://www.spokesmanreview.com

Martin, J. (2011, December 1). Gregoire to DEA: Make marijuana a legal drug. *Seattle Times.* Retrieved December 1, 2011, from http://www.seattletimes.com

Martin, J. (2012a, September 10). Children's alliance backs pot measure on ballot. *Seattle Times.* Retrieved September 10, 2012, from http://www.seattletimes.com

Martin, J. (2012b, September 23). State could be test case in marijuana legalization. *Seattle Times.* Retrieved September 23, 2012, from http://www.nwsource.com

Martin, J. (2012c, October 1). $1 million more for marijuana legalization campaign—and support from King County sheriff. *Seattle Times.* Retrieved October 1, 2012, from http://www.seattletimes.com

Martin, J. (2012d, October 21). Marijuana Initiative 502 a tough sell in Eastern Washington. *Seattle Times*. Retrieved October 21, 2012, from http://www.seattletimes.com

Martin, J. (2012e, September 21). Medical-pot allies tell DEA: "Get off our back." *Seattle Times*. Retrieved September 21, 2012, from http://www.seattletimes.com

Martin, J., Roarke, M., & Gaddy, A. (2002, February 14). Toxic high poisons region. *Spokesman-Review*. Retrieved February 14, 2002, from http://www.spokesmanreview.com

Martinez, M. (2012, June 27). *Tests in cannibalism case: Zombie-like attacker used pot, not "bath salts."* CNN. Retrieved June 27, 2012, from http://www.cnn.com

Massey, D., & Denton, N. (1993). *American apartheid: Segregation and the making of the underclass*. Cambridge, MA: Harvard University Press.

Matas, R. (2002a, June 29). Magazine picks Vancouver as pot lover's paradise. *Globe and Mail*. Retrieved June 29, 2002, from http://www.theglobeandmail.com

Matas, R. (2002b, September 30). Pot factory to be first in Canada. *Globe and Mail*. Retrieved September 30, 2002, from http://www.theglobeandmail.com

Mauer, M. (1999, February 9). Crack sentences and unwise punishment. *Seattle Post-Intelligencer*. Retrieved February 9, 1999, from http://www.seattlepi.com.nwsource

Mauer, M. (2009). *The changing racial dynamics of the war on drugs*. Washington, DC: The Sentencing Project.

May, P. (1982). Substance abuse and American Indians: Prevalence and susceptibility. *International Journal of the Addictions, 17*, 1185–1209.

Mayer, C. (2004, May 14). Fraud sold drug, Pfizer admits. *Washington Post*. Retrieved May 14, 2004, from http://www.washingtonpost.com

Mayo Clinic. (2012). *Human growth hormone (HGH): Does it slow aging?* Retrieved from http://www.mayoclinic.com/health/growth-hormone/HA00030

McCabe, S. E., Morales, M., Cranford, J. A., Delva, J., McPherson, M. D., & Boyd, C. J. (2007). Race/ethnicity and gender differences in drug use and abuse among college students. *Journal of Ethnicity in Substance Abuse, 6*(2), 75–95.

McCann, S. (2004, November 17). Meth ravages lives in northern counties. *Minneapolis Star Tribune*. Retrieved November 17, 2004, from http://www.startribune.com

McCardell, J. (2004, September 13). What your college president didn't tell you. *New York Times*. Retrieved September 13, 2004, from http://www.nytimes.com

McCarthy, M. (2002, February 24). Expect to see new Olympic smiles in ads soon. *USA Today*. Retrieved February 24, 2002, from http://www.usatoday.com

McCarthy, N. (1995, August 27). Meth: The new epidemic. *Oregonian*. Retrieved August 27, 1995, from http://www.oregonian.com

McCaughan, J. A., Carlson, R. G., Falck, R. S., & Harvey A. S. (2005). From "candy kids" to "chemi-kids": A typology of young adults who attend raves in the midwestern United States. *Substance Use & Misuse, 40*(9–10), 1503–1523. doi: 10.1081/JA-200066830

McCaul, M., & Furst, J. (1994). Alcoholism treatment in the United States. *Alcohol Health and Research World, 18*, 253–260.

McClellan, A., Lewis, D., O'Brien, C., & Kleber, H. (2000). Drug dependence, a chronic medical illness: Implications for treatment, insurance, and outcomes. *Journal of the American Medical Association, 284*, 1689–1695.

McColl, W. (2001, March 19). *Appropriate sentencing guidelines for MDMA.* Testimony Before U.S. Sentencing Commission. Washington, DC.

McCollister, K. E., & French, M. T. (2002). The economic cost of substance abuse treatment in criminal justice settings. In C. G. Leukefeld, F. Tims, & D. Farabee (Eds.), *Treatment of drug offenders: Policies and issues* (pp. 22–37). New York: Springer.

McDonnell, P. (2008, October 13). Argentina a new hub for meth traffickers. *Los Angeles Times.* Retrieved October 13, 2008, from http://www.latimes.com

McDonough, T. (1999, August 26). Dry idea given wet welcome at Washington State. *Moscow-Pullman Daily News,* p. 3.

McGran, K. (2002, December 24). Device won't let drinkers start car. *Toronto Star.* Retrieved December 24, 2002, from http://www.thestar.com

McKean, J., & Warren-Gordon, K. (2011). Racial differences in graduation rates from adult drug treatment courts. *Journal of Ethnicity in Criminal Justice, 9,* 41–55.

McKinley, J. (2010, March 25). Legal-marijuana advocates focus on a new green. *New York Times.* Retrieved March 25, 2010, from http://www.nytimes.com

McMurran, M. (2009). Motivational interviewing with offenders: A systematic review. *Legal and Criminological Psychology, 14*(1), 83–100. doi:10.1348/135532508X278326

McNeil, D. (2003, September 6). Report of ecstasy drug's great risks is retracted. *New York Times.* Retrieved September 6, 2003, from http://www.nytimes.com

McReal, C. (2012, January 9). The U.S. schools with their own police. *Guardian.* Retrieved January 10, 2012, from http://www.guardian.co.uk

McSmith, A., & Elliott, F. (2004, November 21). PM makes war on drugs the election battleground. *Independent.* Retrieved November 21, 2004, from http://www.independent.co.uk

McWilliams, P. (1996). *Ain't nobody's business if you do.* Los Angeles: Prelude Press.

Medical marijuana in court. (2002, May 25). *New York Times.* Retrieved May 25, 2002, from http://www.nytimes.com

Meier, B. (2004a, June 26). Drug maker acknowledges some negative test results. *New York Times.* Retrieved June 26, 2004, from http://www.nytimes.com

Meier, B. (2004b, June 19). Glaxo plans public listing of drug trials on website. *New York Times.* Retrieved June 19, 2004, from http://www.nytimes.com

Meier, B. (2004c, November 24). Questions are seen on Merck's stance on pain drugs use. *New York Times.* Retrieved November 24, 2004, from http://www.nytimes.com

Mello, M., Rosenthal, M., & Neumann, P. (2003). Direct to consumer advertising and shared liability for pharmaceutical manufacturers. *Journal of the American Medical Association, 289,* 477–481.

Menard, S., Elliott, D., & Wofford, S. (1993). Social control theories in developmental perspective. *Studies in Crime and Crime Prevention, 2,* 69–87.

Mendoza, N. S., Walitzer, K. S., & Connors, G. J. (2012). Use of treatment strategies in a moderated drinking program for women. *Addictive Behaviors, 37*(9), 1054–1057.

Menke, R., & Flynn, H. (2009). Relationships between stigma, depression, and treatment in white and African American primary care patients. *Journal of Nervous and Mental Disease, 197*(6), 407–411.

Mensch, B., & Kandel, D. (1988). Underreporting of substance use in a national longitudinal youth cohort: Individual and interviewer effects. *Public Opinion Quarterly, 52,* 100–124.

Merlin, M. (2003). Archaeological evidence for the tradition of psychoactive plant use in the old world. *Economic Botany, 57,* 295–323.

Merline, A., O'Malley, P., Schulenberg, J., Bachman, J., & Johnston, L. (2004). Substance use among adults 35 years of age: Prevalence, adulthood predictors, and impact of adolescent substance use. *American Journal of Public Health, 94,* 96–102.

Merton, R. K. (1938). Social structure and anomie. *American Sociological Review, 3,* 672–682.

Merton, R. K. (1957). *Social theory and social structure.* New York: Free Press.

Meth threatens Hawaii's way of life. (2003, September 15). *Associated Press.* Retrieved September 15, 2003, from http://www.ap.org

Metherell, M. (2012, April 3). Gillard and Carr divided over decriminalization of drugs. *Sydney Morning Herald.* Retrieved April 3, 2012, from http://www.smh.com.au

Mexico may permit some drug use to help its fight against traffickers. (2006, April 29). *Seattle Times.* Retrieved April 29, 2006, from http://www.seattletimes.com

Meyer, E. (2003, May 26). Gavel falls on S.M.D. legacy. *Washington Post.* Retrieved May 26, 2003, from http://www.washingtonpost.com

Meyer, J. (2009, March 18). U.S. shares blame in Mexico drug violence, senators say. *Washington Post.* Retrieved March 18, 2009, from http://www.washingtonpost.com

Miller, M. (2010, June 18). FDA nixes "female Viagra" flibanserin. *CBS News.* Retrieved from http://www.cbsnews.com/2100-18563_162-6596444.html

Miller, M., & Draper, G. (2001). *Statistics on drug use in Australia 2000* (Drug statistics series 8). Canberra: Australian Institute of Health and Welfare. Retrieved July 13, 2003, from http://www.aihw.gov.au/publications/phe/sdua00/sdua00.pdf

Miller, T. C. (2003, June 8). Major cocaine source wanes. *Los Angeles Times.* Retrieved June 8, 2003, from http://www.latimes.com

Miller, W. (1958). Lower class culture as a generating milieu of gang delinquency. *Journal of Social Issues, 14,* 5–19.

Miller, W. (1986). Haunted by the zeitgeist: Reflections on contrasting treatment goals and concepts of alcoholism in Europe and the United States. *Annals of the New York Academy of Sciences, 472,* 110–129.

Mills, A. (2004, October 10). Canadian drug safety no concern: U.S. seniors. *Toronto Star.* Retrieved October 10, 2004, from http://www.thestar.com

Miloy, C. (2009, May 20). Time for drug treatment to rattle its saber. *Washington Post.* Retrieved May 20, 2009, from http://www.washingtonpost.com

Minnesota Sentencing Guidelines Commission. (2004). *Report on 2002 departure data.* Retrieved June 8, 2003, from http://caliber.ucpress.net/doi/abs/10.1525/fsr.2004.16.4.285

Minozzi, S., Amato, L., Vecchi, S., Davoli, M., Kirchmayer, U., & Verster, A. (2006). Oral naltrexone maintenance treatment for opioid dependence. *Cochrane Database Syst Rev, 1,* 1–43.

Mintzes, B. (2002). Direct to consumer advertising is medicalising normal human experience. *British Medical Journal, 324,* 908–909.

Mintzes, B., Barer, M., Kravitz, R., Kazanjian, A., Basset, K., Joel Lexchin, et al. (2003). Influence of direct to consumer pharmaceutical advertising and patients requests on prescribing decisions: Two site cross-sectional survey. *British Medical Journal, 324,* 278–279.

Miroff, N., & Booth, W. (2010, July 27). Mexican drug cartels bring violence with them in move to Central America. *Washington Post.* Retrieved July 27, 2010, from http://www.washingtonpost.com

Miron, J. A., & Zwiebel, J. (1991). Alcohol consumption during prohibition. *American Economic Review, 81*(2), 242–247.

Mishori, R. (2009, August 4). Packing a heavier warning. *Washington Post.* Retrieved August 4, 2009, from http://www.washingtonpost.com

Mitchell, G. (2007). *Report to the Commissioner of Baseball of an independent investigation into the illegal use of steroids and other performance-enhancing substances by players in Major League Baseball.* Retrieved July 5, 2012, from http://mlb.mlb.com

Mitchell, O., Wilson, D. B., Eggers, A., & MacKenzie, D. L. (2012). Assessing the effectiveness of drug courts on recidivism: A meta-analytic review of traditional and non-traditional drug courts. *Journal of Criminal Justice, 40*(1), 60–71. doi:10.1016/j.jcrimjus.2011.11.009

Mithofer, M., Jerome, L., & Doblin, R. (2003). MDMA ("ecstasy") and neurotoxicity. *Science, 300,* 1504.

Mitka, M. (2003). Office-based primary care physicians called on to treat the "new" addict. *Journal of the American Medical Association, 290,* 735–736.

Mohl, B. (2004, February 17). Internet cigarette retailers targeted. *Boston Globe.* Retrieved February 17, 2004, from http://www.boston.com

Moilanen, R. (2004, January). Just say no again. *Reasononline.* Retrieved May 10, 2004, from http://www.reason.com/0401/fe.rm.just.shtml

Moir, D., Rickert, W. S., Levasseur, G., Larose, Y., Maertens, R., White, P., & Desjardins, S. (2007). A comparison of mainstream and sidestream marijuana and tobacco cigarette smoke produced under two machine smoking conditions. *Chemical Research in Toxicology, 21*(2), 494–502. doi:10.1021/tx700275p

Mokdad, A., Marks, J. S., Stroup, D. F., & Gerberding, J. L. (2004). Actual causes of death in the United States, 2000. *Journal of the American Medical Association, 291,* 1238–1249.

Molina, P., et al. (2011). Cannabinoid administration attenuates the progression of Simian immunodeficiency virus. *Aids Research and Human Retroviruses, 27, 585–592.*

Monaghan, L. (2001). *Bodybuilding, drugs and risk.* London: Routledge.

Monitoring quotes from Australian press. (2005, December 8). *BBC News.* Retrieved April 15, 2006, from http://www.bbc.co.uk

Montgomery, L., & Whitlock, C. (2003, March 27). Medical marijuana bill passes. *Washington Post.* Retrieved March 27, 2003, from http://www.washingtonpost.com

Mooney, C. (2003, May/June). Teen herbicide. *Mother Jones.* Retrieved June 2, 2003, from http://www.mother jones.com

Moore, D. (2003, December 3). Reserve status renews debate over booze ban for relocated Labrador Innu. *Vancouver Sun.* Retrieved December 3, 2003, from http://www.canada.com

Moore, D., Aveyard, P., Connock, M., Wang, D., Fry-Smith, A., & Barton, P. (2009). Effectiveness and safety of nicotine replacement therapy assisted reduction to stop smoking: Systematic review and meta-analysis. *BMJ: British Medical Journal, 338,* 867–871.

Moore, J. (2001). Hispanics and drug use in the United States. In R. Carson De-Witt (Ed.), *Encyclopedia of drugs, alcohol, and addictive behavior* (pp. 610–613). New York: Macmillan.

Moore, S. (2006, March 23). Cooking up a meth epidemic. *Portland Mercury,* p. 3.

Moos, R., & Moos, B. (2006). Rates and predictors of relapse after natural and treated remission from alcohol use disorders. *Addiction, 101,* 212–222.

Moreau, R., & Yousafzai, S. (2006, January 9). A harvest of treachery. *Newsweek*. Retrieved January 9, 2006, from http://www.msnbc.msn.com

Morlin, B. (2003, June 19). DEA says large drug-smuggling ring busted. *Spokesman-Review*. Retrieved June 19, 2003, from http://www.spokesmanreview.com

Morral, A., McCaffrey, D., & Paddock, S. (2002). Reassessing the marijuana gateway effect. *Addiction, 97,* 1493–1504.

Mosher, C. (1985). *The twentieth century marihuana phenomenon in Canada*. Unpublished master's thesis, Simon Fraser University, Burnaby, British Columbia, Canada.

Mosher, C. (1999). Imperialism, irrationality, and illegality: The first 90 years of Canadian drug policy. *New Scholars, New Visions, 3,* 1–40.

Mosher, C. (2001). Predicting drug arrest rates: Conflict and social disorganization perspectives. *Crime and Delinquency, 47,* 84–104.

Mosher, C., & Phillips, D. (2006). The dynamics of a prison-based therapeutic community for women offenders: Retention, completion, and outcomes. *Prison Journal, 86,* 6–31.

Mottram, D., & George, A. (2000). Anabolic steroids. *Balliere's Clinical Endocrinology and Metabolism, 14,* 55–69.

Move over, tobacco. (2005, January 15). *Los Angeles Times*. Retrieved January 15, 2005, from http://www.latimes.com

Mundy, A. (2004, September). Risk management. *Harper's*. Retrieved September 3, 2004, from http://www.harpers.org

Mulgrew, I. (2007, October 10). City drug policy at odds with Harper's announced plans. *Vancouver Sun*. Retrieved October 10, 2007, from http://www.canada.com

Mulgrew, I. (2008, January 14). Marc Emery agrees to five years in Canadian prison. *Vancouver Sun*. Retrieved January 14, 2008, from http://www.canada.com

Munro, C. (2006, March 5). The drug that's transforming normal people into monsters. *Sydney Morning Herald*. Retrieved March 5, 2006, from http://www.smh.com.au

Munro, G. (1998). *Drugs and schooling: Braving a new world*. Melbourne: Australian Drug Foundation, Center for Youth Drug Studies. Retrieved February 12, 2003, from http://www.cyds.adf.org.au/

Murphy, A. (2012, September 3). Finished. *Sports Illustrated*. pp. 14–15.

Murphy, J. (2003, February 17). Sentencing disparities an injustice. *Spokesman-Review*. Retrieved February 17, 2003, from http://www.spokesmanreview.com

Murphy, J. (2011). Drug court as both a legal and medical authority. *Deviant Behavior, 32*(3), 257–291. doi:10.1080/01639621003771979

Murphy, S. L., Xu, J., & Kochanek, K. D. (2012). Deaths: Preliminary data for 2010. *Division of Vital Statistics, National Vital Statistics Reports, 60*(4). Retrieved September 12, 2012, from http://www.cdc.gov/nchs/data/nvsr/nvsr61/nvsr61_06.pdf

Musto, D. (1999). *The American disease*. New Haven, CT: Yale University Press.

My mistress methamphetamine. (2006, August 30–September 5). *Bohemian*. Retrieved July 7, 2010, from http://www.bohemian.com

Nadelmann, E. (1996). Doing methadone right. *Public Interest, 123,* 83–93.

Nadelmann, E. (2002a, February 10). A sound basis for drug policy. *Denver Post*. Retrieved February 10, 2002, from http://www.denverpost.com

Nadelmann, E. (2002b). Commonsense drug policy. In M. Gray (Ed.), *Busted* (pp. 173–186). New York: Thunder's Mouth Press/Nation Books.

Nadelmann, E. (2011, November 6). Reefer madness. *New York Times*. Retrieved November 6, 2011, from http://www.nytimes.com

Nano, S. (2011, November 1). Deaths from painkiller overdoses triple in decade. *New York Times*. Retrieved November 1, 2011, from http://www.nytimes.com

Nastech Pharmaceutical Company. (2012, June 4). *Nastech initiates phase II intranasal apomorphine trial for male erectile dysfunction*. Press release. Retrieved from http://investor.nastech.com/phoenix.zhtml?c=83674&p=irol-newsArticle&ID=418933&highlight=

National Academy of Sciences. (1999). *Marijuana and medicine: Assessing the science base*. Retrieved August 6, 2002, from http://newton.nap.edu/html/marimed/

National Association of Criminal Defense Lawyers. (2009). *America's problem-solving courts: The criminal costs of treatment and the case for reform*. Washington, DC: Author.

National Basketball Association. (2000). *NBA and NBPA anti-drug program*. Retrieved June 15, 2003, from http://news.findlaw.com/legalnews/sports/drugs/policy/basketball/index.html

National Center for Education Statistics. (2003). *Suspensions and expulsions of public elementary and secondary school students, 2000*. Retrieved June 3, 2004, from http://nces.ed.gov/programs/digest/d03/tables/dt147.asp

National Center on Addiction and Substance Abuse. (2000). *Winning at any cost: Doping in Olympic sports*. New York: Author.

National Center on Addiction and Substance Abuse. (2004). *CASA 2003 teen survey: High stress, frequent boredom, too much spending money: Triple threat that hikes risk of teen substance abuse*. Retrieved June 18, 2004, from http://www.casacolumbia.org/absolutenm/templates/PressReleases.asp?articleid-348&zoneid-46

National Center on Addiction and Substance Abuse. (2005). *Under the counter: Diversion and abuse of prescription medication in the U.S.* New York: National Center on Addiction and Substance Abuse. Retrieved from http://www.casacolumbia.org/absolutenm/articlefiles/380-under_the_counter_-_diversion.pdf

National Center on Addiction and Substance Abuse. (2009). *Shoveling up II: The impact of substance abuse on federal, state, and local budgets*. New York: Columbia University.

National Collegiate Athletic Association. (2002). *NCAA drug testing program*. Retrieved July 15, 2004, from http://www.ncaa.org

National Collegiate Athletic Association. (n.d.) *Drug testing*. Retrieved July 12, 2012, from http://www.ncaa.org

National Commission Against Drunk Driving. (n.d.). *Presidential commission against drunk driving*. Retrieved April 14, 2003, from http://www.ncadd.com/pc_recommendations.cfm

National Conference of State Legislatures. (2004). *State drunk driving laws*. Retrieved November 3, 2004, from http://www.ncsl.org/programs/lis/dui/dui-home.htm

National Highway Traffic and Safety Administration. (2001). *Detection and standardized field sobriety testing, student manual*. Washington, DC: Author.

National Highway Traffic and Safety Administration. (2002). *Development of a standardized field sobriety test*. Retrieved May 27, 2005, from http://www.nhtsa.dot.gov

National Highway Traffic and Safety Administration. (2010). *Fatal analysis reporting system*. Retrieved July 13, 2012, from http://www.nhtsa.dot.gov

National Institute of Mental Health. (2000). *Depression*. Retrieved January 26, 2003, from http://www.nimh.nih.gov/publicat/depression.cfm

National Institute on Alcohol Abuse and Alcoholism. (1998). *Alcohol alert #40*. Bethesda, MD: Author.

National Institute on Alcohol Abuse and Alcoholism. (2000). *Alcohol alert #40.* Bethesda, MD: Author.

National Institute on Drug Abuse. (1999). *Principles of drug addiction treatment: A research-based guide* (NIH Publication #99-4180). Retrieved October 6, 2003, from http://www.drugabuse.gov/pdf/podat/podat.pdf

National Institute on Drug Abuse. (2000). *Research report series: Inhalant abuse.* Retrieved January 23, 2002, from http://www.nida.nih.gov/ResearchReports/Inhalants/Inhalants.html

National Institute on Drug Abuse. (2001). *Monitoring the future: National survey results on drug use, 1975–2000.* Retrieved March 15, 2002, from http://www.monitoringthefuture.org/pubs.html

National Institute on Drug Abuse. (2005). *Prescription drugs: Abuse and addiction.* Washington, DC: U.S. Department of Health and Human Services.

National Institute on Drug Abuse. (2011, November). *DrugFacts: Understanding Drug Abuse and Addiction.* Publications: DrugFacts. Retrieved from http://www.drugabuse.gov/publications/drugfacts/understanding-drug-abuse-addiction

National Institute on Drug Abuse (NIDA). (2012). *DrugFacts: Spice (synthetic marijuana).* NIH Publications. Retrieved from http://www.drugabuse.gov/publications/drugfacts/spice-synthetic-marijuana

National Institutes of Health. (1997). *Workshop on the medical utility of marijuana.* Retrieved February 2, 2003, from http://www.nih.gov/news/med-marijuana/MedicalMarijuana.htm

National Institutes of Health. (1998). Effective medical treatment of opiate addiction: National consensus development panel on effective medical treatment of opiate addiction. *Journal of the American Medical Association 280,* 1936–1943.

National Institutes of Health. (2012). *Substance use disorders in the U.S. armed forces.* The National Academies. Retrieved from http://www.nap.edu/catalog.php?record_id=13441

National Organization for the Reform of Marijuana Laws. (2002). *Your government is lying to you (again) about marijuana.* Retrieved April 2, 2003, from http://www.norml.org

National Public Radio. (2012). Synthetic "bath salts" an evolving problem for DEA. *NPR online.* Accessed online September 1, 2012, from http://www.npr.org/2012/06/30/156048262/synthetic-bath-salts-an-evolving-problem-for-dea

NBC wins broadcast rights for Olympics from 2014 to 2020. (2011, June 7). *New York Post.* Retrieved August 15, 2012, from http://www.nypost.com

Neary, B., & Moreno, I. (2012, February 24). Drug tests for welfare recipients gaining momentum. *Time.* Retrieved February 25, 2012, from http://www.time.com

Neergaard, L. (2004, March 23). FDA warns of antidepressants-suicide link. *Associated Press.* Retrieved March 23, 2004, from http://www.ap.org

Neubauer, C., Pasternak, J., & Cooper, R. T. (2003, March 3). Senator, his son get boost from makers of ephedra. *Los Angeles Times.* Retrieved March 3, 2003, from http://www.latimes.com

Neuman, W. (2012, July 26). Cocaine's flow is unchecked in Venezuela. *New York Times.* Retrieved July 26, 2012, from http://www.nytimes.com

Never too old. (2010, November 15). *MacLean's,* p. 65.

New heroin maintenance program to get underway later this year. (2009). *Drug War Chronicle.* Retrieved June 11, 2012, from http://www.stopthedrugwar.org/chronicle

Newcomb, M., & Bentler, P. (1988). *Consequences of adolescent drug use:*

Impact on the lives of young adults. Thousand Oaks, CA: Sage.

Newhouse, E. (1999, August 23). Making reservation "dry" is no guarantee. *Great Falls Tribune*. Retrieved April 22, 2003, from http://www.greatfallstribune.com

New Jersey Commission to Review Criminal Sentencing. (2005). *Report on New Jersey's drug free zone crimes and proposal for reform*. Trenton, NJ: Author.

New views on pot. (1971, May 31). *Time*, p. 65.

New York drug laws: Who goes to prison? (2002, June 22). *Human Rights Watch*. Retrieved June 22, 2002, from http://www.hrw.org/campaigns/drugs/ny-drugs.htm

NFL Players Association. (2010). *Policy on anabolic steroids and related substances*. Retrieved September 19, 2012, from http://www.nflpa.com

Nicholls, S. (2010, September 15). Supervised injecting centre. *Sydney Morning Herald*. Retrieved September 16, 2010, from http://www.smh.com.au

Niedzwiecki, M., & Duong, T. (2004). *Southeast Asian-American statistical profile*. Washington, DC: Southeast Asia Action Resource Center.

Nieves, E. (2001, May 13). Drug labs in valley hideouts feed nation's habit. *New York Times*. Retrieved May 13, 2001, from http://www.nytimes.com

Nieves, E. (2002, March 28). Drug ruling worries some in public housing. *New York Times*. Retrieved March 28, 2002, from http://www.nytimes.com

Nightline. (2001, January 29). Distribution of antidote may save addicts. *ABC News*. Retrieved from http://abcnews.go.com/Nightline/story?id=128918&page=1

Novack, K. (2003, July 7). Shooting up legally up north. *Time*. Retrieved July 8, 2003, from http://www.time.com

Nutt, D., King, L. A., Saulsbury, W., & Blakemore, C. (2007). Development of a rational scale to assess the harm of drugs of potential misuse. *Lancet, 369*, 1047–1053.

O'Brien, C. (1997). A range of research-based pharmacotherapies for addiction. *Science, 278*, 66–70.

O'Brien, M. C., McCoy, T. P., Rhodes, S. D., Wagoner, A., & Wolfson, M. (2008). Caffeinated cocktails: Energy drink consumption, high-risk drinking, and alcohol-related consequences among college students. *Academy of Emerging Medicine, 15*(5), 453–460.

O'Connor, A. (2004, August 3). New ways to loosen addiction's grip. *New York Times*. Retrieved August 3, 2004, from http://www.nytimes.com

O'Donnell, J. (2006, April 27). Car alcohol detectors weighed. *USA Today*. Retrieved April 27, 2006, from http://www.usatoday.com

O'Grady, M. (2010, March 22). The war on drugs is doomed. *Wall Street Journal*. Retrieved March 22, 2010, from http://online.wsj.com

Oetting, E., Edwards, R., Goldstein, G., & Garcia-Mason, V. (1980). Drug use among five southwestern Native American tribes. *International Journal of the Addictions, 15*, 439–445.

Office of National Drug Control Policy. (1997, August 4). *ONDCP statement on medical marijuana*. Washington, DC: Author.

Office of National Drug Control Policy. (2002a). *Drug descriptions: Marijuana*. Retrieved February 2, 2003, from http://www.dea.gov/concern/marijuana.html

Office of National Drug Control Policy. (2002b). *Fact sheet: MDMA*. Retrieved February 3, 2003, from http://www.whitehousedrugpolicy.gov/publications/pdf/ncj201387.pdf

Office of National Drug Control Policy. (2002c, February). *National youth anti-drug campaign links drugs and terror*. Retrieved March 2, 2002, from http://

www.whitehousedrugpolicy.gov/ NEWS/press02/020302.html

Office of National Drug Control Policy. (2003a). *National drug control strategy.* Washington, DC: U.S. Government Printing Office.

Office of National Drug Control Policy. (2003b). *What Americans need to know about marijuana.* Washington, DC: Author.

Office of National Drug Control Policy. (2003c). *What you need to know about drug testing in schools.* Retrieved July 8, 2004, from http://www.whitehousedrugpolicy.gov/publications/pdf/mj_rev.pdf

Office of National Drug Control Policy. (2010). *President Obama releases national strategy to reduce drug use and its consequences.* Washington, DC: Office of National Drug Control Policy. Retrieved from http://www.whitehouse.gov/the-press-office/president-obama-releases-national-strategy-reduce-drug-use-and-its-consequences

Office of National Drug Control Policy. (2011, June). *Advancing a new approach to drug policy: Key accomplishments.* Washington, DC: The White House. Retrieved from http://www.whitehouse.gov/ondcp/national-drug-control-strategy-introduction

Office of National Drug Control Policy. (2012). *National drug control strategy.* Washington, DC: U.S. Government Printing Office.

Office of National Statistics. (2011, August 23). *Deaths related to drug poisoning in England and Wales, 2010.* Statistical Bulletin, Mortality Analysis Team, Health and Life Events Division. Retrieved May 12, 2012, from http://www.ons.gov.uk/ons/rel/subnational-health3/deaths-related-to-drug-poisoning/2010/stb-deaths-related-to-drug-poisoning-2010.html

Ofshe, R. (1980). The social development of the Synanon cult: The managerial strategy of organizational transformation. *Sociological Analysis, 41,* 109–127.

OHS Health and Safety Services. (2004). *DUI/DWI laws as of March, 2004.* Retrieved August 28, 2005, from http://www.ohsinc.com/drunk_driving_laws_blood_breath%20_alcohol_limits_CHART.htm

Okrent, D. (2010). *The rise and fall of Prohibition.* New York: Scribner.

Olfson, M., & Marcus, S. C. (2009). National patterns in antidepressant medication treatment. *Archives of General Psychiatry, 66*(8), 848.

Olsen, K. (2001, November 21). Tipplers do well, health survey finds. *Columbian.* Retrieved November 21, 2001, from http://www.columbian.com

Olsen, K. (2002, February 14). A health peril for all of us. *Spokesman-Review.* Retrieved February 14, 2002, from http://www.spokesmanreview.com

Olsen, K. (2003, January 26). Anti-tobacco campaigns: Working, or just going up in smoke? *Columbian.* Retrieved January 26, 2003, from http://www.columbian.com

O'Neill, B. (2012, October 14). I-502 discussion important—and entertaining. *Tacoma News Tribune.* Retrieved October 15, 2012, from http://www.thenewstribune.com

Open Secrets. (2012). *Pharmaceuticals/ health products lobbying.* Retrieved June 10, 2012, from http://www.opensecrets.org

Orr, J., & Goswami, N. (2005, November 6). River of cocaine. London: *The Telegraph.* Retrieved from http://www.telegraph.co.uk/news/uknews/1502321/River-of-cocaine.html

Ortiz, F. (1995, August 27). Mexican crime groups make meth. *Oregonian.* Retrieved August 27, 1995, from http://www.oregonian.com

Oxford, M., Harachi, T., Catalano, R., & Abbott, R. (2001). Preadolescent predictors of substance initiation: A test of both the direct and mediated effect of family social control factors on deviant peer associations and substance initiation. *American Journal of Drug and Alcohol Abuse, 27,* 599–616.

Padgett, T. (2002, August 5). Taking the side of the coca farmer. *Time.* Retrieved August 5, 2002, from http://www.time.com

Pagano, M., Friend, K., Tonigan, J., & Stout, R. (2004). Helping other alcoholics in Alcoholics Anonymous and drinking outcomes: Findings from project MATCH. *Journal of Studies on Alcohol, 65,* 766–773.

Paltrow, L. (2006). Why caring communities must oppose C.R.A.C.K./Project Prevention: How C.R.A.C.K. promotes dangerous propaganda and undermines the health and well-being of children and families. *Journal of Law in Society, 5,* 11–117.

Pappas, S. (2012). Latest designer drug called "Smiles" linked to teen deaths. *Live Science.* Retrieved from http://www.livescience.com/23388-designer-drug-smiles-teen-deaths.html

Parhar, K., Wormith, J., Derkzen, D., & Beauregard, A. (2008). Offender coercion in treatment: A meta-analysis of effectiveness. *Criminal Justice and Behavior, 35,* 1109–1135.

Parker-Pope, T. (2009, January 13). A problem of the brain, not the hands: Group urges phone ban for drivers. *New York Times.* Retrieved January 13, 2009, from http://www.nytimes.com

Parolaro, D., & Massi, P. (2008). Cannabinoids as potential new therapy for the treatment of gliomas. *Expert Review of Neurotherapeutics, 8*(1), 37–49.

Partanen, J., Bruun, K., & Markkanen, T. (1996). *Inheritance of drinking behavior.* Helsinki: Finnish Council for Alcohol Studies.

Partnership for a Drug-Free America. (2000). *Partnership attitudes tracking survey: Spring 2000, teens in grades 7 through 12.* Retrieved December 12, 2005, from http://italy.usembassy.gov/pdf/other/pats2000full.pdf

Partnership for a Drug-Free America. (2005a). *Generation Rx: National study reveals new category for substance abuse emerging.* Retrieved December 12, 2005, from http://www.drugfree.org

Partnership for a Drug-Free America. (2005b). *Partnership attitude tracking study.* Retrieved December 14, 2005, from http://www.drugfree.org

Partnership for a Drug-Free America/ONDCP [Advertisement]. (2003, March 24). *The Nation,* p. 7.

Past pandemics that ravaged Europe. (2005, November 7). *BBC News.* Retrieved November 10, 2005, from http://www.bbc.co.uk

Patrick, S., Schumacher, R., Benneyworth, B., Krans, E., McAllister, J., & Davis, M. (2012). Neonatal abstinence syndrome and associated health care expenditures 2000–2009. *Journal of the American Medical Association, 307,* 1934–1940.

Patterson, T., Lacro, J., & Jeste, D. (1999). Abuse and misuse of medications in the elderly. *Psychiatric Times, 16,* 54–57.

Patton, G., Coffey, C., Carlin, J., Degenhardt, L., Lynskey, M., & Hall, W. (2002). Cannabis use and mental health in young people: Cohort study. *British Medical Journal, 325,* 1195–1198.

Pear, R. (2000, September 20). Marketing tied to increase in prescription drug sales. *New York Times.* Retrieved September 20, 2000, from http://www.nytimes.com

Pear, R. (2002a, December 4). Investigators find repeated deception in ads for drugs. *New York Times.* Retrieved December 4, 2002, from http://www.nytimes.com

Pear, R. (2002b, July 30). Patent law change urged to speed generic drugs. *New York*

Times. Retrieved July 30, 2002, from http://www.nytimes.com

Pear, R., & Oppel, R. (2002, November 21). Drug industry seeks ways to capitalize on election success. *New York Times*. Retrieved November 21, 2002, from http://www.nytimes.com

Pearson, J., Richardson A., Niaura R., Vallone D., & Abrams D. (2012). E-cigarette awareness, use, and harm perceptions in U.S. adults. *American Journal of Public Health, 102*, 1758–1766.

Peele, S. (1983). Through a glass darkly. *Psychology Today, 17*, 38–42.

Peele, S. (1989). *Diseasing of America: Addiction treatment out of control.* Lexington, MA: Lexington Books.

Peele, S. (1998, March/April). All wet. *The Sciences*, 17–21.

Pena, M. (2001, May 13). Deadly solvent abuse up. *San Francisco Chronicle*. Retrieved May 13, 2001, from http://www.sfgate.com

Penberthy, J. K., Ait-Daoud, N., Vaughan, M., & Fanning, T. (2010). Review of treatment for cocaine dependence. *Curr Drug Abuse Rev, 3*, 49–62.

Pennell, S., Ellett, J., Rienick, C., & Grimes, J. (1999). *Meth matters: Report on methamphetamine users in 5 western cities.* Washington, DC: National Institute of Justice.

Perez-Pena, R. (2004, May 12). A city of quitters?: In strict N.Y. city, 11% fewer smokers. *New York Times*. Retrieved May 12, 2004, from http://www.nytimes.com

Perkins, D. (2000, September 26). Hunter fall guy in IOC's drug war. *Toronto Star*. Retrieved September 26, 2000, from http://www.thestar.com

Perkins, D. (2005, August 23). NFL drug pitch a scam. *Toronto Star*. Retrieved August 23, 2005, from http://www.thestar.com

Perkins, H. W., & Wechsler, H. (1996). Variation in perceived college drinking norms and its impact on alcohol abuse: A nationwide study. *Journal of Drug Issues, 26*, 961–974.

Perrone, M. (2010, March 18). Prescription-drug heists on the rise. *Seattle Post-Intelligencer*. Retrieved March 18, 2010, from http://www.seattlepi.com

Petersen, M. (2002a, June 20). U.S. is investigating Schering on ingredients used in drug. *New York Times*. Retrieved June 20, 2002, from http://www.nytimes.com

Petersen, M. (2002b, June 13). Vermont to require drug makers to disclose payments to doctors. *New York Times*. Retrieved June 13, 2002, from http://www.nytimes.com

Petersen, M. (2003a, April 17). Bayer agrees to pay U.S. $257 million in drug fraud. *New York Times*. Retrieved April 17, 2003, from http://www.nytimes.com

Petersen, M. (2003b, March 19). Bayer cleared of liability in a lawsuit over drug. *New York Times*. Retrieved March 19, 2003, from http://www.nytimes.com

Petersen, M. (2003c, May 30). Court papers suggest scale of drug's use. *New York Times*. Retrieved May 30, 2003, from http://www.nytimes.com

Petersen, M. (2003d, June 29). Who's minding the drugstore? *New York Times*. Retrieved June 29, 2003, from http://www.nytimes.com

Petersen, R., & Goldberg, L. (1996). Adverse effects of anabolic steroids. *Journal of the American Medical Association, 276*, 257.

Peterson, K. (2001, March 21). Till Viagra do us part? *USA Today*. Retrieved March 21, 2001, from http://www.usatoday.com

Peterson, R., Krivo, L., & Harris, M. (2000). Disadvantage and neighborhood violent crime: Do local institutions matter? *Journal of Research in Crime and Delinquency, 37*, 31–63.

Petry, N. M., Alessi, S. M., & Ledgerwood, D. M. (2012). Contingency management delivered by community therapists in outpatient settings. *Drug and Alcohol Dependence, 122*(1–2), 86–92. doi:10.1016/j.drugalcdep.2011.09.015

Phillips, M. (2004, December 24). Drug bus on its way, despite glitches. *Sydney Morning Herald*. Retrieved December 24, 2004, from http://www.smh.com.au

Pickens, R., Svikis, D., McGure, M., Lykken, D., Heston, L., & Clayton, P. (1991). Heterogeneity in the inheritance of alcoholism. *Archives of General Psychiatry, 48*, 19–28.

Pierce, J., Messker, K., James, L., White, M., Kealey, S., Vallone, D., & Healton, C. (2010). Camel No. 9 cigarette-marketing campaign targeted young teenage girls. *Pediatrics, 125*, 619–626.

Pierre, R. (2003, June 17). In Missouri, an uphill battle against "meth." *Washington Post*. Retrieved June 17, 2003, from http://www.washingtonpost.com

Pignal, S. (2010, October 8). Amsterdam's cannabis-selling coffee shops face crackdown. *Washington Post*. Retrieved October 8, 2010, from http://www .washingtonpost.com

Pilon, M. (2012, September 22). Middle schools add a team rule: Get a drug test. *New York Times*. Retrieved September 22, 2012, from http://www .nytimes.com

Pinkerton, S. (2010). Is Vancouver, Canada's supervised injection facility cost-saving? *Addiction, 105*, 1429–1436.

Piper, B. (2007, February 12). What is Congressman Souder smoking? *Huffington Post*. Retrieved February 12, 2007, from http://www.huffington post.com

Plataforma, SINC. (2012, March 8). Cannabinoid 2 receptors regulate impulsive behavior. *Science Daily*. Retrieved July 11, 2012, from http:// www.sciencedaily.com

Players agree to summer PED tests. (2011, December 17). *Associated Press*. Retrieved August 15, 2012, from http:// www.ap.org

Plunkett, M., & Mitchell, C. (2000). Substance use rates among American Indian adolescents: Regional comparisons with monitoring the future high school seniors. *Journal of Drug Issues, 30*, 575–592.

PM wants mandatory sentences for "serious" drug crimes. (2007, October 4). *CBC News*. Retrieved October 10, 2010, from http://www.cbc.ca/news

Pollack, A. (2003, April 27). Taking up a drug for this (and that). *New York Times*. Retrieved April 27, 2003, from http://www.nytimes.com

Pollan, M. (1997, July 20). Living with medical marijuana. *New York Times Magazine*. Retrieved July 20, 1997, from http://www.nytimes.com

Pollan, M. (1999, September 12). A very fine line. *New York Times Magazine*. Retrieved September 12, 1999, from http://www.nytimes.com

Pollan, M. (2001). *The botany of desire*. New York: Random House.

Pope, C. (2003, June 27). White house to tap Seattle in drug war. *Seattle Post-Intelligencer*. Retrieved June 27, 2003, from http://www.seattlepi.nwsource.com

Pope, H., Kouri, E., & Hudson, J. (2000). Effects of supraphysiologic doses of testosterone on mood and aggression in normal men: A randomized controlled trial. *Archives of General Psychiatry, 57*, 133–140.

Popham, P. (2004, May 28). Thousands of Italian doctors named by police in Glaxo corruption case. *Independent*. Retrieved May 28, 2004, from http:// www.independent.co.uk

Porter, E. (2004, September 26). Indian sales of tobacco face new pressure. *New York Times*. Retrieved September 26, 2004, from http://www.nytimes.com

Porterfield, A. (1946). *Youth in trouble*. Fort Worth, TX: Leo Potishman Foundation.

Poulin, C. (2001). Medical and nonmedical stimulant use among adolescents: From sanctioned to unsanctioned use. *Canadian Medical Association Journal, 165,* 1039–1046.

Pound blasts NHL drug use. (2005, November 25). *Canadian Press.* Retrieved November 25, 2005, from http://www.cp.org

Powers, J. (2003, November 14). Usage more than growing problem. *Boston Globe.* Retrieved November 14, 2003, from http://www.boston.com

Powers, M., Vedel, E., & Emmelkamp, P. (2008). Behavioral couples therapy (BCT) for alcohol and drug use disorders: A meta-analysis. *Clinical Psychology Review, 28,* 952–962.

Pratt, R. (1999, January 10). Senseless sentencing: A federal judge speaks out. *Des Moines Register.* Retrieved January 10, 1999, from http://www.desmoinesregister.com

Prescott, C. A., & Kendler, K. S. (1995). Twin study design. *Alcohol Health and Research World, 19,* 200–205.

Price, S. R., Hilchey, C. A., Darredeau, C., Fulton, H. G., & Barrett, S. P. (2010). Energy drink coadministration is associated with increased reported alcohol ingestion. *Drug & Alcohol Review, 29,* 331–333.

Principal plants drugs in student's locker. (2004, February 2). *WNDU News Center.* Retrieved February 10, 2004, from http://www.wndu.com/news/022004/news_24227.php

Prittie, J. (2000, May 30). Many questions left unanswered. *National Post.* Retrieved May 30, 2000, from http://www.canada.com/nationalpost

Prop. 19—Marijuana initiative drew strongest support in Bay area but failed in "Emerald Triangle." (2010, November 3). *Los Angeles Times.* Retrieved November 10, 2010, from http://www.latimes.com

Pstay, B., Furberg, C., Ray, W., & Weiss, N. (2004). Potential for conflict of interest in the evaluation of suspected adverse drug reactions: Use of Cerivastatin and Rhabdomyolysis. *Journal of the American Medical Association, 292,* 2622–2631.

Putting a match to the marijuana myth. (1980, September). *Saturday Evening Post,* pp. 12, 18, 19.

Queensland Department of Natural Resources. (2004). *The cane toad:* Bufo marinus. Queensland Government: Natural Resources, Mines and Energy.

Quenqua, D. (2011, May 30). Putting a crimp in the hookah. *New York Times.* Retrieved May 30, 2011, from http://www.nytimes.com

Quinn, B. (2012, August 31). Thalidomide victims get apology from makers after half a century. *Guardian.* Retrieved August 31, 2012, from http://www.guardian.co.uk

Radosh, P. (2008). War on drugs: Gender and race inequities in crime control strategies. *Criminal Justice Studies, 21,* 167–178.

Rafshoon, E. (2003, April 27). What price beauty? *Boston Globe.* Retrieved April 27, 2003, from http://www.boston.com

Ragels, L. A. (2000). *Is Alcoholics Anonymous a cult? An old question revisited.* Retrieved August 8, 2004, from http://www.aadeprogramming.com/oldquestion.html

Ragge, K. (1992). *More revealed: A critical analysis of Alcoholics Anonymous and the 12 steps.* Henderson, NV: Alert! Publishing.

Ramsay, M., & Partridge, S. (1999). *Drug misuse declared in 1998: Results from the British crime survey.* London: Home Office.

Ramshaw, E., & Murphy, R. (2011, November 24). Payments to doctors by pharmaceutical companies raises issues of conflicts. *New York Times.* Retrieved November 24, 2011, from http://www.nytimes.com

Randall, T. (1992). Cocaine, alcohol mix in body to form even longer-lasting, more lethal drug. *Journal of the American Medical Association, 267,* 1043–1044.

Randolf, W., Stroup-Benham, C., Black, S., & Markides, K. (1998). Alcohol use among Cuban-Americans, Mexican-Americans and Puerto-Ricans. *Alcohol Health and Research World, 22,* 265–269.

Rashbaum, W. (2000, February 26). Drug experts report a boom in ecstasy use. *New York Times.* Retrieved February 26, 2000, from http://www.nytimes.com

Ray, O., & Ksir, C. (2004). *Drugs, society and human behavior* (10th ed.). New York: McGraw-Hill.

Reclassifying cannabis. (2001, October 25). *Guardian.* Retrieved October 25, 2001, from http://www.guardian.co.uk

Redelmeier, D., & Tibshrani, R. (1997). Association between cellular telephone calls and motor vehicle collisions. *New England Journal of Medicine, 336,* 453–459.

Reece, A. (2007). Psychosocial and treatment correlates of opiate free success in a clinical review of a naltrexone implant program. *Substance Abuse Treatment, Prevention, and Policy, 2,* 35.

Reefers on KPFA. (1954, May 10). *Newsweek,* 17.

Reid, T. R. (2002, May 3). Europe moves drug war from prisons to cities. *Washington Post.* Retrieved May 3, 2002, from http://www.washingtonpost.com

Reid, T. R. (2003, May 11). U.S. underage drinking laws flawed. *Columbian.* Retrieved May 11, 2003, from http://www.columbian.com

Reid, T. (2005). Caffeine. *National Geographic, 207,* 2–32.

Reinarman, C. (2002). Why Dutch drug policy threatens the U.S. In M. Gray (Ed.), *Busted* (pp. 127–133). New York: Thunder's Mouth Press/Nation Books.

Reinarman, C. (2003). Geo-political and cultural constraints on international drug control treaties. *International Journal of Drug Control Policy, 14,* 205–208.

Reinarman, C. (2004). Between genes and determinism: A critique of genetic determinism. *Drugs and Alcohol Today, 4,* 32–34.

Reinarman, C., & Levine, H. G. (1997). Crack in context: America's latest demon drug. In C. Reinarman & H. G. Levine (Eds.), *Crack in America: Demon drugs and social justice* (pp. 1–17). Berkeley: University of California Press.

Reiss, S. (2010). *Beyond supply and demand: Obama's drug wars in Latin America.* North American Congress on Latin America, Report on the Americas (January/February). Retrieved July 10, 2011, from https://nacla.org/node/6429

Reiman, A., & Angell, M. (2002, December 16). America's other drug problem. *New Republic.* Retrieved January 3, 2003, from http://www.tnr.com

Renfroe, C., & Messinger, T. (1985). Street drug analysis: An eleven-year perspective on illicit drug alteration. *Seminar in Adolescent Medicine, 1,* 247–258.

Retracted ecstasy paper "an outrageous scandal." (2003, September 16). *The Scientist.* Retrieved September 16, 2003, from http://www.the-scientist.com/

Reuteman, R. (2010, April 20). Medical marijuana business is on fire. *USA Today.* Retrieved April 20, 2010, from http://www.usatoday.com

Reuter, P., & Stevens, A. (2007). *An analysis of UK drug policy.* London: UK Drug Policy Commission.

Revill, J., Doward, J., & Hinsliff, G. (2005, December 18). Smoking ban would shift risk to children at home. *Observer.* Retrieved December 18, 2005, from http://www.observer.co.uk

Rey, J. (2002). Cannabis and mental health. *British Medical Journal, 325,* 1183–1184.

Ribisil, K., Williams, R., & Kim, A. (2003). Internet sales of cigarettes to minors.

Journal of the American Medical Association, 290, 1356–1359.

Ricaurte, G., Yuan, J., Hatzidimitriou, G., Cord, B., & McCann, U. (2002). Severe dopaminergic neurotoxicity in primates after a common recreational dose regimen of MDMA ("ecstasy"). *Science, 97,* 2260–2263.

Rice, H. (2005, August 16). "Syrup" abuse rising in Houston. *Houston Chronicle.* Retrieved August 16, 2005, from http://www.chron.com

Rice, S. (2003, August 11). DUI now more expensive. *Columbian.* Retrieved August 11, 2003, from http://www.columbian.com

Richards, B. (1994, March 7). Toad-smoking gains on toad-licking among drug users: Toxic, hallucinogenic venom, squeezed, dried, and puffed has others turned off. *Wall Street Journal.* Retrieved July 17, 2003, from http://www.wsj.com

Richburg, K. (2001, April 15). Pragmatic Dutch tolerate ecstasy use. *Washington Post.* Retrieved April 15, 2001, from http://www.washingtonpost.com

Richey, W. (2002, March 27). Public housing evictions over drugs upheld. *Christian Science Monitor.* Retrieved June 2, 2003, from http://www.csmonitor.com

Richtel, M. (2009, July 18). Drivers and legislators dismiss cell phone risks. *New York Times.* Retrieved July 18, 2009, from http://www.nytimes.com

Rick Scott vetoes bill sending non-violent drug offenders to rehab after serving half sentence in jail. (2012, April 4). *Huffington Post.* Retrieved April 5, 2012, from http://www.huffingtonpost.com

Riley, C. (2012, July 10). Olympians face financial hardship. *CNN Money.* Retrieved September 19, 2012, from http://money.cnn.com

Ringwalt, C., Ringwalt, C., Vincus, A., Hanley, S., Ennett, S., Bowling, J., &

Rohrbach, L. (2009). The prevalence of evidence-based drug use prevention curricula in U.S. middle schools in 2005. *Prevention Science, 10,* 33–40.

Ritter, A., Wodak, A., & Crofts, J. N. (2004). Reducing drug-related harm: Australia leads the way. *Medical Journal of Australia, 181,* 242–243.

Ritter, J. (2002, September 17). Pot raid angers state, patients. *USA Today.* Retrieved September 17, 2002, from http://www.usatoday.com

Rivas, O. (2010, August 8). War on drugs: Why the U.S. and Latin America could be ready to end a fruitless 40-year struggle. *Reuters.* Retrieved August 8, 2010, from http://www.guardian.co.uk

Roan, S. (2003, February 24). Steeped in science. *Los Angeles Times.* Retrieved February 24, 2003, from http://www.latimes.com

Robbins, C. (1989). Sex differences in psychosocial consequences of alcohol and drug abuse. *Journal of Health and Social Behavior, 30,* 117–130.

Robert, J. (1949). *The story of tobacco.* Chapel Hill: University of North Carolina Press.

Roberts, B., & Fisher, L. (2002, May 30). Right again: Paddick vindicated as street crime halved. *Daily Mirror.* Retrieved May 30, 2002, from http://www.mirror.co.uk

Robinson, T., & Berridge, K. (1993). The neural basis of drug craving: An incentive-sensitization theory of addiction. *Brain Research Reviews, 18,* 247–291.

Robinson, T., & Berridge, K. (2001). Incentive-sensitization and addiction. *Addiction, 96,* 103–114.

Robson, D. (2009, January 26). Players try to adjust to new drug testing policy. *USA Today.* Retrieved January 26, 2009, from http://www.usatoday.com

Roe, A. (2003, January 29). The fix. *Willamette Week.* Retrieved January 29, 2003, from http://www.wweek.com

Roebuck, M., French, M., & McClellan, M. (2003). DATStats: Results from 85 studies using the drug abuse treatment cost analysis program. *Journal of Substance Abuse Treatment, 25,* 51–57.

Roesler, R. (2005, August 1). State goes after smokers who buy cigarettes on web. *Spokesman-Review.* Retrieved August 1, 2005, from http://www.spokesman review.com

Romero, S. (2009a, April 22). Wider drug war threatens Colombian Indians. *New York Times.* Retrieved April 22, 2009, from http://www.nytimes.com

Romero, S. (2009b, March 18). Cocaine trade helps reignite war in Peru. *New York Times.* Retrieved March 18, 2009, from http://www.nytimes.com

Romero, S. (2010, June 13). Coca production makes comeback in Peru. *New York Times.* Retrieved June 13, 2010, from http://www.nytimes.com

Roozen, H. G., de Waart, R., & van der Kroft, P. (2010). Community reinforcement and family training: An effective option to engage treatment-resistant substance-abusing individuals in treatment. *Addiction, 105*(10), 1729–1738. doi:10.1111/j.1360-0443.2010 .03016.x

Rorvig, L. (2004, February 1). Students find dialogue more effective than drug testing. *USA Today.* Retrieved February 1, 2004, from http://www.usatoday.com

Rose, D. (2002, February 24). Two countries took the drug test. Who passed? *Observer.* Retrieved February 24, 2002, from http://www.observer.co.uk

Rosenbaum, D. (2005, November 20). Politics as usual and then some. *New York Times.* Retrieved November 20, 2005, from http://www.nytimes.com

Rosenbaum, D., & Hanson, G. (1998). Assessing the effects of school-based drug education: A six-year multilevel analysis of project DARE. *Journal of Research in Crime and Delinquency, 35,* 381–412.

Rosenbaum, M. (2002). *Safety first: A reality-based approach to teens, drugs, and drug education.* San Francisco: Drug Policy Alliance. Retrieved March 12, 2003, from http://www.drugpolicy.org

Rosenbaum, M. (2003, December 8). Stop pointing guns at our kids. *Alternet.* Retrieved December 10, 2003, from http://www.alternet.org

Rosenbaum, M. (2004a, December 29). Keep teenagers safe: Zero tolerance for alcohol may increase drinking and driving. *San Jose Mercury News.* Retrieved December 29, 2004, from http://www .mercurynews.com

Rosenbaum, M. (2004b, January 28). No silver bullet. *Drug Policy Alliance.* Retrieved January 28, 2004, from http://www.drugpolicy.org

Rosenthal, B. (2011, December 24). New city underage drinking law targets parents. *Seattle Times.* Retrieved December 24, 2011, from http://www.seattletimes .com

Rosewater, A. (2008, August 19). Agent: Phelps could earn $100 million over lifetime. *ESPN.* Retrieved September 19, 2012, from http://espn.go.com

Ross, B., & Scott, D. (2002, March 23). How pharmaceutical companies use enticement to "educate" physicians. *abcnews.com.* Retrieved March 23, 2002, from http://www.abcnews.com

Ross, E. (2002, January 25). Drink or three a day deters dementia, study concludes. *Associated Press.* Retrieved January 25, 2002, from http://www.ap.org

Ross, H. L. (1992). *Controlling drunk driving.* New Haven, CT: Yale University Press.

Ross, O. (2010, May 22). Why decriminalizing drugs is the only fix for Mexico's "murder city." *Toronto Star.* Retrieved May 22, 2010, from http://www.thestar.com

Rost, P. (2004, October 30). Medicines without borders. *New York Times.* Retrieved October 30, 2004, from http://www.nytimes.com

Rothenberg, S., Schottenfeld, S., Meyer, R., Krauss, B., & Gross, K. (1977). Performance differences between addicts and non-addicts. *Psychopharmacology, 52,* 299–306.

Rounsaville, B., & Kosten, T. (2000). Treatment for opioid dependence: Quality and access. *Journal of the American Medical Association, 283,* 1337–1339.

Rouse, S., & Arce, M. (2006). The drug-laden balloon: U.S. military assistance and coca production in the Central Andes. *Social Science Quarterly, 87,* 540–557.

Roux, P., Villes, V., Blanche, J., Bry, D., Spire, B., Feroni, I., & Carrieri, M. P. (2008). Buprenorphine in primary care: Risk factors for treatment injection and implications for clinical management. *Drug and Alcohol Dependence, 97*(1), 105–113.

Rowan, J. (2001). A guide to humanistic psychology: Encounter. *Association for Humanistic Psychology.* Retrieved June 7, 2003, from http://www.ahpweb.org/rowan_bibliography/chapter8.html

Rowland, C. (2005a, January 9). Drug firms lagging on openness. *Boston Globe.* Retrieved January 9, 2005, from http://www.boston.com

Rowland, C. (2005b, January 17). Drug firms seek profit in giveaways. *Boston Globe.* Retrieved January 17, 2005, from http://www.boston.com

Rowley, B. (2001, September). No bull: Canned energy—Men's fitness takes Red Bull to the lab and discovers the heat behind the hype. *Men's Fitness.* Retrieved March 3, 2003, from http://www.findarticles.com/p/articles/mi_m1608/is_9_17/ai_80309795

Rubin, B. (2003, January 11). Fight brews over policy denying tuition aid based on drug conviction. *Seattle Times.* Retrieved January 11, 2003, from http://www.seattletimes.com

Rubin, R. (2004, December 12). Can Americans trust their medicine? *USA Today.* Retrieved December 12, 2004, from http://www.usatoday.com

Rubinow, D., & Schmidt, P. (1996). Androgens, brain, and behavior. *American Journal of Psychiatry, 153,* 974–984.

Russo, R. (2004, January 21). Tougher pot bill penalties might prevent increased border scrutiny: Cellucci. *Vancouver Sun.* Retrieved January 21, 2004, from http://www.canada.com

Ryan, A. (2006, January 23). NHL drug policy "flawed." *Toronto Star.* Retrieved January 23, 2006, from http://www.thestar.com

Ryan, K. (1998). Clinging to failure: The rise and continued life of U.S. drug policy. *Law and Society Review, 32,* 221–242.

Rybarczyk, T. (2004, June 11). Young non-drinkers decry Naperville law. *Chicago Tribune.* Retrieved June 11, 2004, from http://www.chicagotribune.com

Sabbag, R. (2005, July). High in the Canadian Rockies. *Playboy.* Retrieved July 15, 2005, from http://www.playboy.com

Sack, C., & McDonald, B. (2008, September 9). Salvia's popularity may thwart medical use. *New York Times.* Retrieved September 9, 2008, from http://www.nytimes.com

Sack, K., & Mundy, A. (2004, March 29). How drug linked to strokes remained on market. *Seattle Times.* Retrieved March 29, 2004, from http://www.seattletimes.com

Saillant, C. (2005, December 24). Putting a cork in teen parties. *Los Angeles Times.* Retrieved December 24, 2005, from http://www.latimes.com

Salazar, C. (2011, February 20). Has NYC gone too far by banning smoking in parks? *Associated Press.* Retrieved February 20, 2011, from http://www.ap.org

Salazar-Martinez, E., Willett, W., Ascherio, A., Manson, J., Leitzmann, M., Stampfer, M., et al. (2004). Coffee consumption and risk for type-2 diabetes mellitus. *Annals of Internal Medicine, 140,* 1–8.

Salerno, S. (2006, March 16). Let Barry be. *Los Angeles Times.* Retrieved March 16, 2006, from http://www.latimes.com

Salter, J. (2012, October 11). Mexican cartels flood U.S. with cheap meth. *Associated Press.* Retrieved October 11, 2012, from http://www.ap.or

Salter, J., & Suhr, J. (2011, April 6). Synthetic drugs send thousands to ER. *Associated Press.* Retrieved April 6, 2011, from http://www.ap.org

Sampson, R., & Laub, J. (2003). *Crime in the making: Pathways and turning points through life.* Cambridge, MA: Harvard University Press.

Sanchez, M. (2003, May 16). When the war on drugs is too narrow. *Washington Post.* Retrieved May 16, 2003, from http://www.washingtonpost.com

Sanchez, R. (2003, June 5). One jail day for marijuana felony. *Washington Post.* Retrieved June 5, 2003, from http://www.washingtonpost.com

Santana, A. (2002, September 20). Court blocks D.C. vote on medical use of marijuana. *Washington Post.* Retrieved September 20, 2002, from http://www.washingtonpost.com

Saul, S. (2005, November 28). Gimme an RX! Cheerleaders pep up drug sales. *New York Times.* Retrieved November 28, 2005, from http://www.nytimes.com

Saunders, D. (2011, June 12). At least four good reasons to end the war on drugs. *San Francisco Chronicle.* Retrieved June 12, 2011, from http://www.sfgate.com

Savage, M. (2010, July 10). The growing buzz on "spice"—the marijuana alternative. *Washington Post.* Retrieved July 10, 2010, from http://www.washingtonpost.com

Saw-toothed. (1951, August 11). *New Yorker,* 18–19.

Shafer Commission. (1973). *History of alcohol prohibition.* Retrieved May 6, 2002, from http://www.druglibrary.org/Schaffer/LIBRARY/studies/nc/nc2a.htm

Shaffer, D. K. (2011). Looking inside the black box of drug courts: A meta-analytic review. *Justice Quarterly, 28*(3), 493–521. doi:10.1080/07418825.2010.525222

Shannon, L. M., Havens, J. R., Oser, C., Crosby, R., & Leukefeld, C. (2011). Examining gender differences in substance use and age of first use among rural Appalachian drug users in Kentucky. *American Journal of Drug and Alcohol Abuse, 37*(2), 98–104.

Scheft, B. (2003, November 24). The show. *Sports Illustrated.* Retrieved November 24, 2003, from http://www.sportsillustrated.cnn.com

Scherer, M. (2002, November/December). Up in smoke. *Mother Jones.* Retrieved December 3, 2002, from http://www.motherjones.com

Scherer, M. (2005, May/June). The side effects of truth. *Mother Jones.* Retrieved June 3, 2005, from http://www.motherjones.com

Schilit, R., & Lisansky-Gomberg, E. (1991). *Drugs and behavior.* Thousand Oaks, CA: Sage.

Schlosser, E. (1997, April). More reefer madness. *Atlantic Monthly.* Retrieved April 15, 1997, from http://www.theatlantic.com

Schlosser, E. (2003). *Reefer madness.* Boston: Houghton Mifflin.

Schuckit, M. (1985). Genetics and the risk for alcoholism. *Journal of the American Medical Association, 245,* 2614–2617.

Schuckit, M. (1995). A long-term study on sons of alcoholics. *Alcohol Health and Research World, 19,* 172–175.

Schulenberg, J., O'Malley, P., Bachman, J., Johnson, L., & Laetz, V. (2004). *How social role transitions from adolescence to adulthood relate to trajectories of wellbeing and substance use* (Monitoring the Future Occasional Paper No. 56). Ann Arbor, MI: Institute for Social Research.

Schulhofer, S. (1993). Rethinking mandatory minimums. *Wake Forest Law Review, 28,* 199–222.

Schulte, B. (2005, October 12). Single glass of wine immerses D.C. driver in legal battle. *Washington Post.* Retrieved October 12, 2005, from http://www.washingtonpost.com

Schultes, R., Hofmann, A., & Ratsch, C. (2001). *Plants of the gods: Their sacred, healing and hallucinogenic powers* (2nd ed.). Rochester, VT: Healing Art Press.

Schultes, R., Klein, W., Plowman, T., & Lockwood, T. E. (1974). Cannabis: An example of taxonomic neglect. *Harvard University Botanical Museum Leaflets, 23,* 337–367.

Schultz, G. (1989, October 27). Schultz on drug legalization. *Wall Street Journal.* Retrieved February 19, 2006, from http://www.wsj.com

Schulz, P., & Macher, J. (2002). The clinical pharmacology of depressive states. *Dialogues in Clinical Neuroscience, 4,* 47–56.

Schuman, S. (2004, May 25). Drinking and driving tolerance. *Oregonian.* Retrieved May 25, 2004, from http://www.oregonian.com

Schwartz, A., & Schwartz, R. (1993). *Depression, theories and treatment: Psychological, biological and social perspectives.* New York: Columbia University Press.

Schwartz, H. (2002, March 21). Out of jail and out of food. *New York Times.* Retrieved March 21, 2002, from http://www.nytimes.com

Schwartz, J. (2011, June 30). Thousands of prison terms in crack cocaine cases could be erased. *New York Times.* Retrieved June 30, 2011, from http://www.nytimes.com

Schwenk, C. R., & Rhodes, S. L. (1999). *Marijuana and the workplace: Interpreting research on complex social issues.* Westport, CT: Quorum Books.

Schwirtz, M. (2011, January 16). Inadequate fight against drugs hampers Russia's ability to curb HIV. *New York Times.* Retrieved January 16, 2011, from http://www.nytimes.com

Science News. (2010). Symptoms of "male menopause" unzipped. *Science Daily.* Retrieved from http://www.science-daily.com/releases/2010/06/10061617 1639.htm

Science or politics at the FDA? (2004, February 24). *New York Times.* Retrieved February 24, 2004, from http://www.nytimes.com

Scoffield, H. (2002, July 11). Rights watchdog bans workplace drug tests. *Globe and Mail.* Retrieved July 11, 2002, from http://www.theglobeandmail.com

Secular Organizations for Sobriety. (2003). *An overview of SOS: A self-empowerment approach to recovery.* Retrieved June 17, 2003, from http://www.secular sobriety.org/

Seelye, K. (2011, December 17). Increasingly, smoking indoors is forbidden at public housing. *New York Times.* Retrieved December 17, 2011, from http://www.nytimes.com

Segal, D. (2010, June 25). When capitalism meets cannabis. *New York Times.* Retrieved June 25, 2010, from http://www.nytimes.com

Seltz, J. (2000, October 15). Blowing smoke: There is an easy answer to why children are ignoring schools' anti-drug efforts. *Boston Globe.* Retrieved October 15, 2000, from http://www.boston.com

Selvin, M., & Hoffman, C. (2005, December 14). Cigarette maker pours it on strong in promo. *Los Angeles Times.* Retrieved December 14, 2005, from http://www.latimes.com

Sentencing Project. (2010). *Federal crack cocaine sentencing.* Retrieved October 15, 2010, from http://www.sentencing project.org

Serrano, R., Savage, D., & Williams, C. (2011, June 1). Early release proposed for crack cocaine offenders. *Los Angeles Times*. Retrieved June 1, 2011, from http://www.nytimes.com

Shafer, J. (2005, August 9). The meth-mouth myth. *Slate*. Retrieved September 20, 2005, from http://www.slate.com

Shafer, J. (2006, January 19). This is your county on meth. *slate.com*. Retrieved January 19, 2006, from http://www.slate.com

Shafer, J. (2010, December 14). Stupid drug story of the week—the nutmeg scare. *Slate*. Retrieved September 10, 2012, from http://www.slate.com

Shah, S. (2001, October). The orgasm industry: Drug companies search for a female Viagra. *Progressive*. Retrieved October 5, 2001, from http://www.progressive.org

Shahandeh, B., & Caborn, J. (2003). Ethical issues in workplace drug testing in Europe. Retrieved January 10, 2003, from http://www.ilo.org/public/english/protection/safework/drug/wdt.pdf

Shapiro, S. (2003, November/December). Jails for Jesus. *Mother Jones*. Retrieved December 5, 2003, from http://www.motherjones.com

Shaw, R. (1998). *Losing one's livelihood to the grasp of fiction: The law of civil forfeiture in the United States*. Retrieved May 17, 2003, from http://www.qualitylegalcounsel.com/CivilForfeiture.pdf

Shedler, J. S., & Block, J. (1990). Adolescent drug use and psychological health. *American Psychologist, 45*, 612–630.

Shemkus, S. (2005, December 14). Justice, Texas style. *American Prospect*. Retrieved December 14, 2005, from http://www.prospect.org

Shen, X., & Kosten, T. (2011). Immunotherapy for drug abuse. *CNS & neurological disorders drug targets, 10*(8), 876–879.

Shenk, J. (1999, May). America's altered states. *Harper's*. Retrieved May 15, 1999, from http://www.harpers.org

Shenk, J. (2003, May/June). Think different. *Mother Jones*. Retrieved June 12, 2003, from http://www.mother jones.com

Shepard, E. (2001). *The economic costs of DARE* (Research Paper #22). Syracuse, NY: Le Moyne College, Institute of Industrial Relations.

Shepard, E., & Clifton, T. (1998, November/December). Drug testing: Does it really improve labor productivity? *Working USA, 76*.

Sher, K. (1991). *Children of alcoholics*. Chicago: University of Chicago Press.

Sher, K., & Levenson, R. (1982). Risk for alcoholism and individual differences in the stress-response-dampening effect of alcohol. *Journal of Abnormal Psychology, 91*, 350–368.

Sherman, K. (2011, May 5). Tacoma-Pierce county health officials take hard look at electronic cigarettes. *Tacoma News-Tribune*. Retrieved May 5, 2011, from http://www.thenewstribune.com

Sherrid, P. (2002, June 17). Fewer doc freebies. *U.S. News and World Report*. Retrieved June 17, 2002, from http://www.usnews.com

Shipley, A. (2012, June 13). *U.S. anti-doping agency brings new doping charges against Lance Armstrong*. Retrieved June 13, 2012, from http://www.washingtonpost.com

Short, J. (1968). *Gang delinquency and delinquent subcultures*. New York: Harper and Row.

Short, J. F., & Nye, I. (1957). Reported behavior as a criterion of deviant behavior. *Social Problems, 5*, 207–213.

Shorto, R. (2006, May 7). Contra-contraception. *New York Times Magazine*. Retrieved May 7, 2006, from http://www.nytimes.com

Shrine, B. (2000). Nicotine vaccine moves towards clinical trials. *NIDA Notes, 15*, 5. Retrieved May 5, 2002, from http://www.nida.nih.gov/NIDA_Notes/NNVol15N5/Vaccine.html

Shute, N. (1997, September 8). What A.A. won't tell you. *US News and World Report*. Retrieved September 8, 1997, from http://www.usnews.com

Sidney, S. (2003). Comparing cannabis with tobacco—Again. *British Medical Journal, 327,* 635–636.

Siebert, D. J. (1994). Salvia divinorum and salvinorin A: New pharmacologic findings. *Journal of Ethnopharmacology, 43,* 53–56.

Siegel, L. (1997). The pregnancy police fight the war on drugs. In C. Reinarman & H. Levine (Eds.), *Crack in America: Demon drugs and social justice* (pp. 249–259). Berkeley: University of California Press.

Siegel, M., Tanwar, K., & Wood, K. (2011). Electronic cigarettes as a smoking cessation tool—results from an online survey. *American Journal of Preventive Medicine, 40,* 472–475.

Siegel, R. (1989). *Intoxication: Life in pursuit of artificial paradise.* New York: EP Dutton.

Sigmon, S. C., Herning, R. I., Better, W., Cadet, J. L., & Griffiths, R. R. (2009). Caffeine withdrawal, acute effects, tolerance, and absence of net beneficial effects of chronic administration: Cerebral blood flow velocity, quantitative EEG, and subjective effects. *Psychopharmacology, 204*(4), 573–585.

Silverman, J. (2002, December 20). Study finds random drug testing effective at school. *Houston Chronicle.* Retrieved December 20, 2002, from http://www.chron.com

Simmons, D. (2010, January 29). State siphons tobacco-settlement funds. *Chicago Tribune.* Retrieved January 29, 2010, from http://www.chicagotribune.com

Simon, C. (1921, November 21). From opium to hasheesh: Startling facts regarding the narcotic evil and its many ramifications throughout the world. *Scientific American, 125A,* 14–15.

Simon, M., & Mosher, J. (2007). *Alcohol, energy drinks and youth: A dangerous mix.* Marin Institute: Alcohol Industry Watchdog. Retrieved from http://health.state.ga.us/pdfs/prevention/summit/energy_drink_report-marin_institute.pdf

Simon, S. (2010, March 19). In mile high city, weed sparks up a counterculture clash. *Wall Street Journal.* Retrieved March 19, 2010, from http://online.wsj.com

Singer, N. (2010, September 15). Forest, maker of Celexa, to pay more than $313 million to settle marketing case. *New York Times.* Retrieved September 15, 2010, from http://www.nytimes.com

Sinha, J. (2001). *The history and development of the leading international drug control conventions.* Ottawa: Senate Special Committee on Illegal Drugs.

Sinoski, K. (2011, August 2). Vancouver Coastal Health to hand out $50,000 worth of crack pipes. *Vancouver Sun.* Retrieved August 2, 2011, from http://www.vancouversun.com

Sinoski, K. (2012, September 27). B.C. mayors vote to decriminalize pot. *Vancouver Sun.* Retrieved September 27, 2012, from http://www.vancouversun.com

Sitamariah, G. (1996, June 16). Meth turning kids into monsters. *Spokesman-Review.* Retrieved June 16, 1996, from http://www.spokesmanreview.com

Sivagnanam, G. (2011). A vaccine against cocaine abuse. *Journal of Pharmacology & Pharmacotherapeutics, 2*(2), 143–144.

Skager, R. (2001). On reinventing drug education, especially for adolescents. *Reconsider Quarterly, 1,* 14–18.

Skiba, R., & Peterson, R. (1999). The dark side of zero tolerance. *Phi Delta Kappan, 80,* 372–378.

Skiba, R., & Rausch, M. (2006). Zero tolerance, suspension, and expulsion. Questions of equity and effectiveness. In C., Everston, & C. Weinstein, (Eds.), *Handbook of classroom management* (pp. 1063–1089). Mahwah, NJ: Lawrence Erlbaum Associates.

Skinner, B. F. (1953). *Science and human behavior*. New York: MacMillan.

Sklansky, D. (1995). Cocaine, race, and equal protection. *Stanford Law Review, 47*, 1283–1322.

Skoloff, B. (2006, April 30). Limbaugh drug case: Both sides win. *Associated Press*. Retrieved April 30, 2006, from http://www.ap.org

Slevin, P. (2001, March 21). Sentencing guidelines toughened for ecstasy. *Washington Post*. Retrieved March 21, 2001, from http://www.washingtonpost.org

Smith, G. (2002, December 11). Many other countries try decriminalization. *Globe and Mail*. Retrieved December 11, 2002, from http://www.theglobeandmail.com

Smith, G. (2004, October 25). Was big pharma caught in its own web of spin? *Globe and Mail*. Retrieved October 25, 2004, from http://www.theglobeandmail.com

Smith, M. (2010, June 30). U.S. banks' role in Mexican drug trade. *San Francisco Chronicle*. Retrieved June 30, 2010, from http://www.sfgate.com

Smith, P. (2011, September 20). A drug arrest every 19 seconds. *Stop the drug war*. Retrieved May 18, 2012, from http://www.stopthedrugwar.org

Smyer, M., Gatz, M., Simi, N., & Pedersen, N. (1998). Childhood adoption: Long-term effects in adulthood. *Psychiatry, 61*, 191–205.

Smyth, J. (2003, November 15). Divorce lawyers see a new marriage killer—Viagra. *National Post*. Retrieved November 15, 2003, from http://www.canada.com/nationalpost

Snyder, N. (2003). *Juvenile arrests*. Washington, DC: U.S. Department of Justice.

Sobell, M. B., & Sobell, L. C. (1973). Alcoholics treated by individualized behavior therapy: One year treatment outcomes. *Behavior Research and Therapy, 11*, 599–618.

Sobell, M. B., & Sobell, L. C. (1978). *Behavioral treatment of alcohol problems: Individualized therapy and controlled drinking*. New York: Plenum Press.

Sobell, M. B., & Sobell, L. C. (1995). Controlled drinking after 25 years: How important was the great debate? *Addiction, 90*, 1149–1153.

Sobell, M. B., & Sobell, L. C. (2011). It is time for low-risk drinking goals to come out of the closet. *Addiction, 106*(10), 1715–1717.

Socreds told smoking pot makes you gay. (1979, November 3). *Vancouver Sun*, p. 7.

Soeffing, J. M., Martin, L. D., Fingerhood, M. I., Jasinski, D. R., & Rastegar, D. A. (2009). Buprenorphine maintenance treatment in a primary care setting: Outcomes at 1 year. *Journal of substance abuse treatment, 37*(4), 426–430.

Sokolove, M. (2004, January 18). The lab animal. *New York Times*. Retrieved January 18, 2004, from http://www.nytimes.com

Solotaroff, P. (2003, January 23). Plague in the heartland. *Rolling Stone*. Retrieved January 23, 2003, from http://www.rollingstone.com

Solowij, N., Stephens, R., Roffman, R., Babor, T., Kadden, R., Miller, M., et al. (2002). Cognitive functioning of long-term heavy cannabis users seeking treatment. *Journal of the American Medical Association, 287*, 1123–1133.

Specter, M. (2004, February 2). Miracle in a bottle. *New Yorker*. Retrieved February 5, 2004, from http://www.newyorker.com

Specter, M. (2011, October 17). Getting a fix. *New Yorker*, pp. 36–45.

Specter, M. (2012, October 12). It's not about the bike. *New Yorker*. Retrieved October 12, 2012, from http://www.newyorker.com

Spiesel, S. (2006, April 24). The FDA's statement on medical marijuana isn't about science. *Slate.com*. Retrieved from http://www.slate.com/articles/health_and_science/medical_examiner/2006/04/all_smoke.html

The Spring Drinking Season. (2006, May 8). *Chicago Tribune.* Retrieved May 8, 2006, from http://www.chicagotribune.com

St. George, D. (2011, December 28). In Washington area, African-American students suspended and expelled two to five times as often as whites. *Washington Post.* Retrieved December 28, 2011, from http://www.washingtonpost.com

Stafford, L. (2012, June 14). Pure ecstasy can be "safe" if consumed responsibly: B.C. health officer. *Globe and Mail.* Retrieved June 14, 2012, from http://www.theglobeandmail.com

Stamper, N. (2005a). *Breaking rank.* New York: Nation Books.

Stamper, N. (2005b, October 16). Let those dopers be. *Seattle Times.* Retrieved October 16, 2005, from http://www.seattletimes.com

Stark, P. (2004, December 11). Fears over drug imports baseless. *Knight-Ridder.* Retrieved December 11, 2004, from http://www.kri.com

State of the Union: President's State of the Union message to Congress and the nation. (2004, January 21). *New York Times.* Retrieved January 21, 2004, from http://www.nytimes.com

State v. Russell, 477 NW2d 886 (Minn. 1991).

Staudenmeier, W. (1989). Urine testing: The battle for privatized social control during the 1986 war on drugs. In J. Best (Ed.), *Images of issues: Typifying contemporary social problems.* New York: Aldine de Gruyter.

Stein, J. (2002, November 4). The new politics of pot. *Time.* Retrieved November 6, 2002, from http://www.time.com

Steinberg, J. (1999, July 18). ACLU to sue Oklahoma school district over student drug testing. *New York Times.* Retrieved July 18, 1999, from http://www.nytimes.com

Steinberg, N. (1994, May 5). The law of unintended consequences. *Rolling Stone.* Retrieved June 6, 2001, from http://www.rollingstone.com

Steroid use by teens soaring. (2003, May 8). *CBS News.* Retrieved May 8, 2003, from http://www.cbsnews.com/stories/2003/05/07/eveningnews/main552790.shtml

Steroids panel calls on NBA's Dixon. (2005, May 18). *Toronto Star.* Retrieved May 18, 2005, from http://www.thestar.com

Stockdale, S. E., Wells, K. B., Tang, L., Belin, T. R., Zhang, L., & Sherbourne, C. D. (2007). The importance of social context: Neighborhood stressors, stress-buffering mechanisms, and alcohol, drug, and mental health disorders. *Social Science & Medicine, 65*(9), 1867–1881.

Stolberg, S. (2002 November 29). A Capitol Hill mystery: Who aided drug maker? *New York Times.* Retrieved November 29, 2002, from http://www.nytimes.com

Stone, M., Laughren, T., Jones, M. L., Levenson, M., Holland, P. C., Hughes, A., Hammad, T. A., Temple, R., & Rochester, G. (2009). Risk of suicidality in clinical trials of antidepressants in adults: Analysis of proprietary data submitted to U.S. Food and Drug Administration. *British Medical Journal, 339,* 2880.

Strand, K. (2002, December). Sociological approaches hold promise to curb campus drinking. *ASA Footnotes, 5.*

Straus, R., & Bacon, S. (1953). *Drinking in college.* New Haven, CT: Yale University Press.

Strathdee, S., & Pollini, R. (2007). A 21st century Lazarus: The role of safer injection sites in harm reduction and recovery. *Addiction, 102,* 848–849.

Strauss, R., & Yesalis, C. (1993). Additional effects of anabolic steroids on women. In C. Yesalis (Ed.), *Anabolic steroids in sports and exercise* (pp. 151–160). Champaign, IL: Human Kinetics.

Strayer, D., Crouch, D., & Drews, F. (2004). *A comparison of the cell phone driver and the drunk driver* (Working Paper No. 04–13). Washington, DC: AEI-Brookings Joint Center.

Stroup, K., & Armentano, P. (2002). The problem is pot prohibition. In M. Gray (Ed.), *Busted* (pp. 223–224). New York: Thunder's Mouth Press/Nation Books.

Struck, D. (2006, March 18). High crimes, or a tokin' figure? *Washington Post.* Retrieved March 18, 2006, from http://www.washingtonpost.com

Studdert, D., Mello, M., & Brennan, T. (2004). Financial conflicts of interest in physicians' relationships with the pharmaceutical industry: Self-regulation in the shadow of federal prosecution. *New England Journal of Medicine, 351,* 1891–1900.

Students for Sensible Drug Policy. (2006, April 17). *Harmful drug law hits home.* Retrieved April 18, 2006, from http://www.ssdp.org.

Stumbling in the dark. (2001, July 26). *Economist.* Retrieved July 26, 2001, from http://www.economist.com

Substance Abuse and Mental Health Services Administration. (1997). *National Institute on Drug Abuse, National Institutes of Health, Center for Substance Abuse Prevention and Treatment: National conference on marijuana use.* Arlington, VA: Author.

Substance Abuse and Mental Health Services Administration. (2001). *Development of computer-assisted interviewing procedures for the national household survey on drug abuse.* Rockville, MD: Office of Applied Studies.

Substance Abuse and Mental Health Services Administration. (2003). *Emergency department trends from the Drug Abuse Warning Network: Final estimates, 1995–2002.* Rockville, MD: Office of Applied Studies.

Substance Abuse and Mental Health Services Administration. (2004). *The 2003 national survey on drug use and health.* Rockville, MD: Office of Applied Studies.

Substance Abuse and Mental Health Services Administration. (2005a). *About buprenorphine therapy.* Retrieved October 10, 2005, from http://buprenorphine.samhsa.gov/about.html

Substance Abuse and Mental Health Services Administration. (2005b). *New DAWN: Why it cannot be compared with old DAWN.* Rockville, MD: Office of Applied Studies.

Substance Abuse and Mental Health Services Administration [SAMHSA]. (2009). *The TEDS Report: Substance Abuse Treatment Admissions Referred by the Criminal Justice System.* Rockville, MD: Office of Applied Studies, 2009. Retrieved June 2, 2012, from http://oas.samhsa.gov/2k9/211/211CJadmits2k9.pdf

Substance Abuse and Mental Health Services Administration (SAMHSA). (2010a). *Highlights of the 2009 Drug Abuse Warning Network (DAWN) findings on drug-related emergency department visits. The DAWN Report.* Rockville, MD: Substance Abuse and Mental Health Services Administration, Office of Applied Studies.

Substance Abuse and Mental Health Services Administration (SAMHSA). (2010b). *The NSDUH report: Substance use among Asian adults.* Rockville, MD: Substance Abuse and Mental Health Services Administration, Office of Applied Studies.

Substance Abuse and Mental Health Services Administration (SAMHSA). (2010c, May 20). *The NSDUH report: Substance use among Asian adults.* Rockville, MD: Substance Abuse and Mental Health Services Administration, Office of Applied Studies.

Substance Abuse and Mental Health Services Administration. (2011a). *Results from the 2010 NSDUH.* Retrieved June 15, 2012, from http://www.samhsa.gov

Substance Abuse and Mental Health Services Administration (SAMHSA). (2011b). *Results from the 2010 National Survey on Drug Use and Health: Summary of national findings*. Rockville, MD: Substance Abuse and Mental Health Services Administration, NSDUH Series H-41 (HHS Publication No. SMA-11-4658).

Substance Abuse and Mental Health Services Administration (SAMHSA). (2011c). *Drug Abuse Warning Network, 2009: National estimates of drug-related emergency department visits*. HHS Publication No. (SMA) 11-4659, DAWN Series D-35. Rockville, MD: Substance Abuse and Mental Health Services Administration.

Substance Abuse and Mental Health Services Administration. (2011e, September 1). *The NSDUH report: Illicit drug Use among older adults*. Rockville, MD: Center for Behavioral Health Statistics and Quality.

Substance Abuse and Mental Health Services Administration (SAMHSA). (2012a). *State estimates of substance use and mental disorders from the 2009–2010 National Surveys on Drug Use and Health*, NSDUH Series H-43, HHS Publication No. (SMA) 12-4703. Rockville, MD: Substance Abuse and Mental Health Services.

Substance Abuse and Mental Health Services Administration (SAMHSA). (2012b). *DAWN emergency department Excel files—national tables*. Rockville, MD: SAMHSA. Retrieved from http://www.samhsa.gov/data/DAWN.aspx#DAWN%202010%20ED%20Excel%20Files%20-%20National%20Tables

Sullivan, J. (2010, December 17). Police say driver smoked synthetic marijuana before Pike Place crash. *Seattle Times*. Retrieved December 17, 2010, from http://www.seattletimes.com

Sullivan, R., & Song, S. (2000, September 11). Are drugs winning the games? *Time*. Retrieved September 15, 2000, from http://www.time.com

Sullum, J. (1998). *For your own good: The anti-smoking crusade and the tyranny of public health*. New York: The Free Press.

Sullum, J. (2002, February 8). Terror tactic. *Reason.com*. Retrieved February 10, 2002, from http://www.reason.com/sullum/020802.shtml

Sullum, J. (2003a). *Saying yes*. New York: Jeremy P. Tarcher/Putnam.

Sullum, J. (2003b, May 30). When holding a party is a crime. *New York Times*. Retrieved May 30, 2003, from http://www.nytimes.com

Sullum, J. (2005, September 2). Is meth a plague, or the next Katrina? Or is it a million times more horrible than all of them combined? *Reasononline.com*. Retrieved September 3, 2005, from http://www.reasononline.com

Sullum, J. (2006, May). Blow for injustice. *Reasononline.com*. Retrieved May 25, 2006, from http://www.reasononline.com

Sulzberger, A., & Medina. J. (2011, January 17). Arizona shooting suspect was known to have smoked hallucinogen. *New York Times*. Retrieved January 17, 2011, from http://www.nytimes.com

Sun, L. (2011, December 12). Teens swapping cigarettes for flavored mini cigars. *Washington Post*. Retrieved December 12, 2011, from http://www.washingtonpost.com

Sutter, J. (2012, August 6). 5 warning signs of game addiction. *CNN*. Retrieved October 29, 2012, from http://www.cnn.com

Suo, S. (2005a, September 25). As laws dry up home meth labs, Mexican cartels flood U.S. market. *Oregonian*. Retrieved September 25, 2005, from http://www.oregonian.com

608 Drugs and Drugs Policy

Suo, S. (2005b, June 5). Huge increases in imports by Mexico of the key chemical in meth signal a switch in strategy by drug cartels to move labs south of the border. *Oregonian*. Retrieved June 5, 2005, from http://www.oregonian.com

Suo, S. (2005c, December 25). Meth's local curse grows into U.S. cause. *Oregonian*. Retrieved December 25, 2005, from http://www.oregonian.com

Suo, S. (2005d, September 25). More potent meth wipes out success against home labs. *Oregonian*. Retrieved September 25, 2005, from http://www.oregonian.com

Suo, S., & Barnett, J. (2006, March 3). Congress oks landmark restrictions to fight meth. *Oregonian*. Retrieved March 3, 2006, from http://www.oregonian.com

Sutherland, A., Fasick, K., & Fermino, J. (2010, July 3). Smokers huff and puff over new cigarette tax. *New York Post*. Retrieved July 3, 2010, from http://www.nypost.com

Sutherland, E. (1939). *Principles of criminology*. Philadelphia: Lippincott.

Swetlow, K. (2003). *Children at clandestine methamphetamine labs: Helping meth's youngest victims*. Washington, DC: U.S. Department of Justice. Retrieved December 2, 2003, from http://www.ojp.usdoj.gov/ovc/publications/bulletins/children/welcome.html

Swidey, N. (2002, November 17). The costly case of the purple pill. *Boston Globe*. Retrieved November 17, 2002, from http://www.boston.com

Szabo, L. (2010, March 15). Study: Camel No. 9 cigarette ads appeal to teen girls. *USA Today*. Retrieved March 15, 2010, from http://www.usatoday.com

Szalavitz, M. (2009, April 26). Drugs in Portugal: Did decriminalization work? *Time*. Retrieved June 15, 2009, from http://www.time.com

Szalavitz, M. (2010, July 21). The link between marijuana and schizophrenia. *Time*. Retrieved from http://www.time.com/time/health/article/0,8599,2005559-2,00.html

Szalavitz, M. (2012, May 14). *DSM-5* could categorize 40% of college students as alcoholics. *Time*. Retrieved October 26, 2012, from http://www.time.com

Tabichnick, C. (2012, September 25). Straight talk from a judge. *The Crime Report*. Retrieved September 25, 2012, from http://www.crimereport.org

Tai, B., & Blaine, J. (1997). *Naltrexone: An antagonist therapy for heroin addiction*. Washington, DC: National Institute on Drug Abuse.

Talvi, S. (2003a, December 3). Criminalizing motherhood. *The Nation*. Retrieved December 5, 2003, from http://www.thenation.com

Talvi, S. (2003b, April 9). Reefer madness redux. *The Nation*. Retrieved April 15, 2003, from http://www.the nation.com

Tamam, L., & Ozpoyraz, N. (2002). Selective serotonin reuptake inhibitor discontinuation syndrome: A review. *Advances in Therapy*, *19*(1), 17–26.

Task force on narcotics and drug abuse, 1967. (2002). In D. Musto (Ed.), *Drugs in America: A documentary history* (pp. 287–305). New York: New York University Press.

Tate, C. (2003, June 22). Puffin' pariahs: America's relentless war against smokers. *Seattle Times*. Retrieved June 22, 2003, from http://www.seattletimes.com

Taxman, F. (2008). *Findings from a national survey of correctional agencies on substance abuse treatment and health services: Who can get served?* Washington, DC: National Institute on Drug Abuse.

Taylor, B., & Bennett, T. (1999). *Comparing drug use rates of detained arrestees in the United States and England*. Washington, DC: Department of Justice.

Taylor, J. (2005, July 18). Parents get word on teen drinking. *Chicago Tribune.* Retrieved July 18, 2005, from http://www.chicagotribune.com

Taylor, L. (1999). *Drunk driving defense.* New York: Aspen Law and Business.

Teather, D. (2003, June 20). No smoke without ire. *Guardian.* Retrieved June 20, 2003, from http://www.guardian.co.uk

Teenagers "bagging" mothballs to get high. (2008, July 27). *Reuters.* Retrieved July 27, 2008, from http://www.reuters.com

Tennessee starts meth crime registry. (2006, January 19). *NPR Morning Edition.* Retrieved January 19, 2006, from http://www.npr.org

Terra, M., Barros, H., Stein, A., Figueira, I., Palermo, L., Athayde, L., & da Silveira, D. (2008). Do Alcoholics Anonymous groups really work? Factors of adherence in a Brazilian sample of hospitalized alcohol dependents. *American Journal on Addictions, 17*(1), 48–53. doi:10.1080/10550490701756393

Terry-McElrath, Y. M., & McBride, D. C. (2004). Local implementation of drug policy and access to treatment services for juveniles. *Crime & Delinquency, 50*(1), 60–87.

Teruya, C., & Hser, Y. (2010). Turning points in the life course: Current findings and future directions in drug use research. *Current Drug Abuse Reviews, 3,* 189.

Tetrault, J. M., Desai, R. A., Becker, W. C., Fiellin, D. A., Concato, J., & Sullivan, L. E. (2007). Gender and non-medical use of prescription opioids: Results from a national U.S. survey. *Addiction, 103*(2), 258–268.

Texas State. (2003). *Save lives on Texas roads.* Retrieved July 23, 2003, from http://www.window.state.tx.us/etexas2003/gg25.html

Tharp, V., Burns, M., & Moskowitz, H. (1981). *Development and field test of psychophysical test for DUI arrests* (DOT-HS-805,864). Washington, DC: U.S. Department of Transportation.

There's a funny smell in the air. (2002, July 21). *New York Times.* Retrieved July 21, 2002, from http://www.nytimes.com

Theriault, D. (2012, January 26). New and improved? *Portland Mercury.* Retrieved January 26, 2012, from http://www.portlandmercury.com

Thomas, C. (1999, June 7). Marijuana arrests and incarceration in the United States. *FAS Drug Policy Alliance Bulletin.* Retrieved May 5, 2003, from http://www.mpp.org/site/c.glKZLeMQIsG/b.1086497/k.BF78/Home.htm

Thomas, G. (2003). Balance in theory but not in practice: Exploring the continued emphasis on supply reduction in Canada's national drug control strategy. In John Howard Society, *Perspectives on Canadian drug policy, volume II* (pp. 26–41). Kingston, ONT: John Howard Society.

Thomas, G., Farrell, M., & Barnes, G. (1996). The effects of single-mother families and nonresident fathers on delinquency and substance abuse in black and white adolescents. *Journal of Marriage and the Family, 58,* 884–894.

Thomas, K. (2001, August 28). Back to school for ADHD drugs. *USA Today.* Retrieved August 28, 2001, from http://www.usatoday.com

Thomas, K. (2005, July 12). Driving, cell phone use don't mix, study shows. *Associated Press.* Retrieved July 17, 2005, from http://www.ap.org

Thomas, L. (2004, November 6). Maker of OxyContin reaches settlement with West Virginia. *New York Times.* Retrieved November 6, 2004, from http://www.nytimes.com

Thomas, P. (2009, January 20). For snowboarders, drug testing can be a real bummer. *Los Angeles Times.* Retrieved January 20, 2009, from http://www.latimes.com

Thomas, R. (2002, January 22). Maleng seeks more treatment, less jail time for drug offenders. *Seattle Times*. Retrieved January 22, 2002, from http://www.seattletimes.com

Thombs, D. L., O'Mara, R. J., Tsukamoto, M., Rossheim, M. E., Weiler, R. M., Merves, M. L., & Goldberger, B. A. (2010). Event-level analyses of energy drink consumption and alcohol intoxication in bar patrons. *Addictive Behaviors, 35*(4), 325–330.

Thompson, D. (2010, December 18). U.S. spending millions to see if herbs really work. *USA Today*. Retrieved December 18, 2010, from http://www.usatoday.com

Thompson, T. (2002, June 23). Brixton? Right now it's a 24-hour crack supermarket. *Guardian*. Retrieved June 23, 2002, from http://www.guardian.co.uk

Thornberry, T. (1987). Towards an interactional theory of delinquency. *Criminology, 25*, 601–637.

Thornton, M. (1991a). Alcohol prohibition was a failure. *Cato Policy Analysis,* 157. Retrieved June 17, 2003, from http://www.cato.org/pubs/pas/pa-157.html

Thornton, M. (1991b). *The economics of prohibition.* Salt Lake City: University of Utah Press.

Thoumi, F. (2005). The numbers game: Let's all guess the size of the illegal drug industry. *Journal of Drug Issues, 22*, 185–200.

Thousands driving illegally: Study. (2004, May 19). *Canadian Press*. Retrieved May 19, 2004, from http://www.cp.org

Tibbetts, J. (2010, November 26). Senate passes bill with mandatory minimum for growing five pot plants. *Vancouver Sun*. Retrieved November 26, 2010, from http://www.canada.com

Tierney, J. (2009, February 23). Latin Americans decry U.S. drug war. *New York Times*. Retrieved February 23, 2009, from http://www.nytimes.com

Tierney, J. (2011, November 7). A tool to quit smoking has some unlikely critics. *New York Times*. Retrieved November 7, 2011, from http://www.nytimes.com

Tims, F., Jainchill, N., & De Leon, G. (1994). Therapeutic communities and treatment research. In F. Tims, G. De Leon, & N. Jainchill (Eds.), *Therapeutic community: Advances in research and application* (pp. 1–16). Rockville, MD: Department of Health and Human Services.

Tiredness as dangerous as drink on roads: Study. (2004, May 27). *Sydney Morning Herald*. Retrieved May 27, 2004, from http://www.smh.com.au

Tittle, C., Villimez, W., & Smith, D. (1978). The myth of social class and criminality: An empirical assessment of the empirical evidence. *American Sociological Review, 43,* 643–656.

Tizon, T. (2003, May 7). Open containers for open roads: That's Montana. *Los Angeles Times*. Retrieved May 7, 2003, from http://www.latimes.com

Tobacco advertisement. (1995, October 17). *New York Times*, p. 23.

Tomlinson, S. (2012, April 5). Cheap, easy to get heroin leads to spike in Oregon overdose deaths. *Oregonian*. Retrieved April 5, 2012, from http://www.oregonlive.com

Tonry, M. (1995). *Malign neglect.* New York: Oxford University Press.

Topol, E., Mukherjee, D., & Nissen, S. (2001). Risk of cardiovascular events associated with selective cox-2 inhibitors. *Journal of the American Medical Association, 286*, 954–1000.

Torpedoing a tobacco suit. (2005, June 10). *New York Times*. Retrieved June 10, 2005, from http://www.nytimes.com

Tough, P. (2001, August 29). The alchemy of OxyContin: From pain relief to drug addiction. *New York Times*. Retrieved August 29, 2001, from http://www.nytimes.com

The tour drug-free in '03: The experts doubt it. (2003, July 5). *Velo News*. Retrieved July 7, 2003, from http://www

.velonews.com/tour2003/news/articles/4355.0.html

Townsend, L., Gearing, R. E., & Polyanskaya, O. (2012). Influence of health beliefs and stigma on choosing Internet support groups over formal mental health services. *Psychiatric Services*, *63*(4), 370–376.

Toynbee, P. (2002, April 12). As long as drugs are illegal, the problem won't go away. *Guardian*. Retrieved April 12, 2002, from http://www.guardian.co.uk

Toynbee, P. (2004, November 3). In the war on drugs, Europe must make a separate peace. *Guardian*. Retrieved November 3, 2004, from http://www.guardian.co.uk

Trace, M. (2009, March 11). The global drug charade. *Guardian*. Retrieved March 11, 2009, from http://www.guardian.co.uk

Transform Drug Policy Foundation. (2009). *A comparison of the cost effectiveness of the prohibition and regulation of drugs*. Retrieved April 20, 2009, from http://www.tdpf.org.uk

Travis, A. (2002, May 22). MPs signal new era in drugs war. *Guardian*. Retrieved May 22, 2002, from http://www.guardian.co.uk

Travis, A. (2006, January 20). Clarke to overhaul drug classifications. *Guardian*. Retrieved January 20, 2006, from http://www.guardian.co.uk

Travis, A., & Weaver, M. (2010, March 18). Ministers to receive advice on whether to ban mephedrone by end of month. *Guardian*. Retrieved March 18, 2010, from http://www.guardian.co.uk

Trebach, A. (1988, September 29). *Drug policies for a democratic nation*. Testimony Before Select Committee on Narcotics Abuse and Control. Washington, DC.

Treble, P. (2008, December 8). Amsterdam orders pot cafes to close. *MacLean's*. Retrieved January 20, 2009, from http://www.macleans.ca

Trice, H., & Staudenmeier, W. (1989). A sociocultural history of Alcoholics Anonymous. In M. Galanter (Ed.), *Recent developments in alcoholism vol. 7: Treatment research* (pp. 11–35). New York: Plenum Press.

Trinh, N. H. T., LaRocca, R., Regan, S., Chang, T. E., & Gilman, S. E. (2011). Using the electronic medical record to examine racial and ethnic differences in depression diagnosis and treatment in a primary care population. *Primary Health Care: Open Access*, *1*(106), 2.

Trounson, R. (2003, July 24). Study casts doubt on popular strategy to curb campus drinking. *Los Angeles Times*. Retrieved July 24, 2003, from http://www.latimes.com

Troyer, R., & Markle, G. (1983). *Cigarettes: The battle over smoking*. New Brunswick, NJ: Rutgers University Press.

Tuller, D. (2003, October 28). Doctors tread a thin line on marijuana advice. *New York Times*. Retrieved October 28, 2003, from http://www.nytimes.com

Turner, S., Longshore, D., Wenzel, S., Deschenes, E., Greenwood, P., Fain, T., et al. (2002). A decade of drug treatment court research. *Substance Use and Misuse, 37*, 1489–1527.

The 2000 Olympics: Games of the drugs? (2002, January 31). *CBS News*. Retrieved January 31, 2002, from http://www.cbsnews.com

Tyndall, M. W., Kerr, T., Zhang, R., King, E., Montaner, J. G., & Wood, E. (2006). Attendance, drug use patterns, and referrals made from North America's first supervised injection facility. *Drug and alcohol dependence, 83*(3), 193–198.

Uelmen, G., Abrahamson, D., Appel, J., Cox, A., & Taylor, W. (2002). *Substance abuse and crime prevention act of 2000*. Sacramento, CA: Drug Policy Alliance.

Uggen, C., & Manza, J. (2002). Democratic contraction? Political consequences of felon disenfranchisement in the United States. *American Sociological Review, 67,* 777–803.

UK Drug Policy Commission. (2012). *Report.* Retrieved October 15, 2012, from http://www.ukdpc.org

Ungar, L. (2012, August 27). Kentucky sees surge in addicted infants. *Louisville Kentucky Courier Journal.* Retrieved August 30, 2012, from http://www.courier-journal.com

UNAIDS. (2008). Progress on implementing the Dublin Declaration on Partnership to Fight HIV/AIDS in Europe and Central Asia. Copenhagen: World Health Organization.

United Nations. (2007). *World drug report.* Retrieved October 15, 2011, from http://www.unodc.org

United Nations. (2011). *World Aids Day report.* Retrieved September 3, 2011, from http://www.unaids.org

United Nations Office on Drugs and Crime. (2003). *Investing in drug abuse treatment: A discussion paper for policy makers.* New York: United Nations International Drug Control Program.

United Nations Office on Drugs and Crime. (2009). *World drug report.* Retrieved August 5, 2011, from http://www.unodc.org

United Nations Office on Drugs and Crime. (2011). *World drug report.* Retrieved September 3, 2012, from http://www.unodc.org

United Nations Office on Drugs and Crime (UNODC). (2012). *World drug report 2012.* Vienna: United Nations Publications. Retrieved from http://www.unodc.org/unodc/en/data-and-analysis/WDR-2012.html

Urbina, I. (2009, October 12). It's a fork, it's a spoon, it's a...weapon? *New York Times.* Retrieved October 12, 2009, from http://www.nytimes.com

Urbina, I. (2012, May 11). Addiction diagnoses may rise under guideline changes. *New York Times.* Retrieved May 11, 2012, from http://www.nytimes.com

U.S. Census Bureau. (2002). *The Asian population: 2000.* Washington, DC: Author.

U.S. Census Bureau. (2004). *Current population survey, 2004.* Washington, DC: Author.

U.S. Department of Health and Human Services. (2001). *Inspector general's study of adverse event reporting for dietary supplements.* Washington, DC: Author.

U.S. Department of Health and Human Services. (2003a). *Drug use among racial/ethnic minorities.* Washington, DC: Author.

U.S. Department of Health and Human Services. (2003b). *Youth risk behavior surveillance system: 2003 high school survey.* Atlanta, GA: Centers for Disease Control and Prevention.

U.S. Department of Health and Human Services, Centers for Disease Control and Prevention. (2002). *Methadone maintenance treatment.* Retrieved June 15, 2004, from http://www.cdc.gov

U.S. Department of Health and Human Services, Centers for Disease Control and Prevention. (2003a). *About the youth risk behavior surveillance system.* Retrieved May 15, 2004, from http://www.cdc.gov/HealthyYouth/yrbs/index.htm

U.S. Department of Health and Human Services, Centers for Disease Control and Prevention. (2003b). *Youth risk behavior surveillance system: 2003 high school survey.* Atlanta, GA: Author.

U.S. Department of Justice. (1996, November 6). *Arizona proposition 200 and California proposition 215* [Press release]. Retrieved July 15, 2004, from http://www.ojp.usdoj.gov

U.S. Department of Justice. (2003). *Meth production site: Not really a laboratory.* Retrieved April 6, 2004, from http://

www.ojp.usdoj.gov/ovc/publications/ bulletins/children/pg2.html

U.S. Department of Justice. (2005). *Drugs of abuse.* Retrieved December 10, 2005, from http://www.usdoj.gov/dea/pubs/ abuse/doa-p.pdf.

U.S. Drug Enforcement Administration (1988, Sept. 6). *In the matter of marijuana rescheduling petition* [Docket #86-22]. Washington, DC: Department of Justice.

U.S. Drug Enforcement Administration. (1994). *Report of the international conference on abuse and trafficking of anabolic steroids.* Washington, DC: Office of Diversion Control, United States Drug Enforcement Agency.

U.S. Drug Enforcement Administration. (2003). *Drug trafficking in the United States.* Washington, DC: Author.

U.S. Food and Drug Administration. (1981, June). History of the FDA. *FDA Consumer.* Retrieved March 5, 2005, from http://www.fda.gov

U.S. Food and Drug Administration. (2004). FDA's mission statement. Retrieved March 5, 2005, from http://www.fda. gov/opacom/morechoices/mission.html

U.S. Food & Drug Administration. (2006). *Inter-agency advisory regarding claims that smoked marijuana is a medicine.* Silver Spring, MD: Author. Retrieved from http://www.fda.gov/bbs/topics/ NEWS/2006/NEW01362.html

U.S. Food and Drug Administration. (2012). *Warning letters, 2011.* Retrieved June 8, 2012, from http://www.fda.gov

U.S. General Accounting Office. (2003). *Federal drug offenses: Departures from sentencing guidelines and mandatory minimum sentences, fiscal years 1999– 2001.* Retrieved November 1, 2003, from http://www.gao.gov/cgi-bin/ getrpt?GAO-04-105

U.S. Government. (2012, May 21). *Statement of the government of the United States of America World Federation Against Drugs 3rd World Forum,* Stockholm, Sweden. Retrieved from http://www.whitehouse.gov/ondcp/ news-releases-remarks/principles-of- modern-drug-policy-directors-remarks- at-the-world-federation-against-drugs

U.S. Government Accountability Office. (2005a, March). *Anti-drug media campaign.* Washington, DC: Author.

U.S. Government Accountability Office. (2005b, September 26). *Drug offenders: Various factors may limit the impacts of federal laws that provide for denial of selected benefits.* Retrieved September 27, 2005, from http://www. gao.gov/cgi-bin/getrpt?GAO-05-238

Government Accountability Office. (2005c). *Adult drug courts: Evidence indicates recidivism reductions and mixed results for other outcomes* (GAO-05-219). Washington, DC: General Accounting Office.

U.S. Government Accountability Office. (2006, August). *ONDCP media campaign.* Washington, DC: Author.

U.S. Government Accountability Office. (2011). *Studies show courts reduce recidivism, but DOJ could enhance future performance measure revision efforts.* Washington, DC: Author.

U.S. House of Representatives. (2003, August). *Politics and science in the Bush administration.* Retrieved September 2, 2003, from http://www .reform.house/gov/min

Uchtenhagen, A. (2011). Heroin maintenance treatment: From idea to research to practice. *Drug and Alcohol Review, 30,* 130–137.

Vakili, S., Currie, S., & el-Guebaly, N. (2009). Evaluating the utility of drug testing in an outpatient addiction program. *Addictive Disorders & Their Treatment, 8*(1), 22–32. doi: 10.1097/ ADT.0b013e318166efc4

Valdez, A. (2006, March 22). Meth madness. *Willamette Week.* Retrieved March 25, 2006, from http://www .wweek.com

Valentine, G. (2002). MDMA and ecstasy. *Psychiatric Times, XIX*(2). Retrieved June 10, 2003, from http://www.psychiatrictimes.com/p020246.html

Vallely, P. (2005, December 10). Christmas appeal: Taking the drugs fight to school. *Independent.* Retrieved December 10, 2005, from http://www.independent.co.uk

Vallely, P. (2006, March 2). Drug that spans the ages: The history of cocaine. *Independent.* Retrieved March 2, 2006, from http://www.independent.co.uk

Vallis, M. (2002, May 7). Antidepressant puts newborns at risk. *National Post.* Retrieved May 7, 2002, from http://www.canada.com/nationalpost

van Amsterdam, J., Opperhuizen, A., Koeter, M., & van den Brink, W. (2010). Ranking the harm of alcohol, tobacco and illicit drugs for the individual and the population. *European Addiction Research, 10,* 202–207.

Vancouver's Insite drug injection clinic will stay open. (2011, September 30). *CBC News.* Retrieved October 1, 2011, from http://www.cbc.ca.news

van den Brink, W., Hendriks, V., Blanken, P., Koeter, M., van Zwieten, B., & van Ree, J. (2003). Medical prescription of heroin to treatment resistant heroin addicts: Two randomised control trials. *British Medical Journal, 327,* 310–312.

van het Loo, M., van Beusekom, I., & Kahan, J. (2002). Decriminalization of drug use in Portugal: The development of a policy. *Annals, 582,* 49–63.

Vann, B. (2001, April 24). Missionary plane shot down in Peru: Collateral damage in US "drug war." *World Socialist Web Site.* Retrieved June 5, 2006, from http://www.wsws.org

Vartabedian, R. (2002, December 30). A spirited debate over DUI laws. *Los Angeles Times.* Retrieved December 30, 2002, from http://www.latimes.com

Vastag, B. (2001). Pay attention: Ritalin acts much like cocaine. *Journal of the American Medical Association, 286,* 905–906.

Vastag, B. (2003). In-office opiate treatment: "Not a panacea": Physicians slow to embrace therapeutic option. *Journal of the American Medical Association, 290,* 731–735.

Vedantam, S. (2003, May 16). Epilepsy drug may help alcoholics give up drinking. *Washington Post.* Retrieved May 16, 2003, from http://www.washingtonpost.com

Vedantam, S. (2004, September 15). Child antidepressant warning is urged. *Washington Post.* Retrieved September 15, 2004, from http://www.washingtonpost.com

Vega, W., Alderete, E., Kolody, B., & Aguilar-Gaxiola, S. (1998). Illicit drug use among Mexicans and Mexican-Americans in California: The effects of gender and acculturation. *Addiction, 93,* 1839–1851.

Vega, W., & Gil, A. (1998). Acculturative stress and drug use among immigrant and U.S.-born Latino adolescents: Toward an integrated model. *Drugs and Society, 14,* 55–71.

Vega, W., Gil, A., & Wagner, E. (1998). Cultural adjustment and Hispanic adolescent drug use. In W. Vega & A. Gil (Eds.), *Drug use and ethnicity in early adolescence* (pp. 125–149). New York: Plenum Press.

Veilleux, J. C., Colvin, P. J., Anderson, J., York, C., & Heinz, A. J. (2010). A review of opioid dependence treatment: Pharmacological and psychosocial interventions to treat opioid addiction. *Clinical Psychology Review, 30*(2), 155–166.

Verducci, T. (2002, June 3). Totally juiced. *Sports Illustrated.* Retrieved June 10, 2002, from http://www.sports illustrated.cnn.com

Verducci, T. (2004, March 2). SI flashback: Totally juiced. *Sports Illustrated.* Retrieved from http://sportsillustrated

.cnn.com/2004/magazine/03/02/flash-back_juiced/index.html

Verducci, T. (2005, January 24). Semi-tough. *Sports Illustrated*. Retrieved January 24, 2005, from http://www.sportsillus-trated.cnn.com

Verducci, T. (2012, June 4). To cheat or not to cheat. *Sports Illustrated*. Retrieved June 4, 2012, from http://www.sportsil lustrated.com

Verhovek, S. (2006, April 29). Rush Limbaugh booked on drug charges, gets deal for treatment. *Los Angeles Times*. Retrieved April 29, 2006, from http://www.latimes.com

Vernonia School District 47J v. Acton, 515 U.S. 646 (1995).

Vogel, K. (2005, August 28). Lose the cigs? Or the job? *News Tribune*. Retrieved August 28, 2005, from http://www.thenewstribune.com

Vogt, H. (2010, June 22). Afghan opiate use doubles in 5 years, U.N. says. *Associated Press*. Retrieved June 22, 2010, from http://www.ap.org

von Zielbauer, P. (2003a, November 9). Court treatment system is found to help drug offenders stay clean. *New York Times*. Retrieved November 9, 2003, from http://www.nytimes.com

von Zielbauer, P. (2003b, July 23). If misery loves company, city smokers should like state's law. *New York Times*. Retrieved July 23, 2003, from http://www.nytimes.com

Wagenaar, A., & Toomey, T. (2002). Effects of minimum drinking age laws: Review and analysis of the literature from 1960 to 2000. *Journal of Studies on Alcohol, Supplement No. 14*, 206–225.

Wagner-Etchegaray, F., Schultz, C., Chilcoat, H., & Anthony, J. (1994). Degree of acculturation and the rise of crack-cocaine smoking among Hispanic-Americans. *American Journal of Public Health, 84*, 1825–1827.

Waldorf, D. (1973). *Careers in dope*. Englewood Cliffs, NJ: Prentice-Hall.

Walgate, R. (2003, September 16). Retracted ecstasy paper "an outrageous scandal." *The Scientist*. Retrieved November 6, 2003, from http://www.maps.org/mdma/retraction/scientist091603.html

Walker, R. (2009, August 2). Eyelash of the beholder. *New York Times*. Retrieved August 2, 2009, from http://www.nytimes.com

Walker, S. (2001). *Sense and nonsense about crime and drugs*. Belmont, CA: Wadsworth.

Walker, S. (2011, June 22). Krokodile: The drug that eats junkies. *The Independent*. Retrieved June 22, 2011, from http://www.independent.co.uk

Walker, S., Spohn, C., & DeLone, M. (1996). *The color of justice*. Belmont, CA: Wadsworth.

Walker, T. (2013, January 18). Lance Armstrong confesses to Oprah Winfrey: My mythic story would have been impossible without doping. *Independent*. Retrieved January 18, 2013, from http://www.independent.co.uk

Wallace, J. (1999a). Explaining race differences in adolescent and young adult drug use: The role of racialized social systems. *Drugs and Society, 14*, 21–33.

Wallace, J. (1999b). The social ecology of addiction: Race, risk and resilience. *Pediatrics, 103*, 1122–1127.

Wallace, J., & Bachman, J. (1991). Explaining racial/ethnic differences in adolescent drug use: The impact of background and lifestyle. *Social Problems, 38*, 333–357.

Wallace, J., Bachman, J., O'Malley, P., Schulenberg, J., Cooper, S., & Johnston, L. (2003). Gender and ethnic differences in smoking, drinking, and illicit drug use among American 8th, 10th, and 12th grade students, 1976–2000. *Addiction, 98*, 225–234.

Walsh, J. T. (1894). Hemp drugs and insanity. *Journal of Mental Science, 40*, 21–36.

Walters, J. (2002, May 1). The myth of "harmless" marijuana. *Washington Post*. Retrieved May 1, 2002, from http://www.washingtonpost.com

Walters, M., Ayers, R., & Brown, D. (1990). Analysis of illegally distributed steroid products by liquid chromatography with identity confirmation by mass spectrometry or infrared spectrophotometry. *Journal of the Association of Analytical Chemistry, 73,* 904–926.

Walton, S. (2002). *Out of it: A cultural history of intoxication.* New York: Harmony Books.

Wanjek, C. (2002, June 4). The real dope. *Washington Post.* Retrieved June 4, 2002, from http://www.washington post.com

Wang, T., Collet, J. P., Shapiro, S., & Ware, M. A. (2008). Adverse effects of medical cannabinoids: a systematic review. *Canadian Medical Association Journal, 178*(13), 1669–1678.

War on drugs a failure. (2011, June 2). *Reuters.* Retrieved June 2, 2011, from http://www.reuters.com

Warheit, G., Vega, W., Khoury, E., Gil, A., & Elfenbein, P. (1996). A comparative analysis of cigarette, alcohol, and illicit drug use among an ethnically diverse sample of Hispanic, African-American, and non–Hispanic white adolescents. *Journal of Drug Issues, 26,* 901–922.

Warner, B., & Leukfeld, K. (2001). Rural–urban differences in substance use and treatment utilization among prisoners. *American Journal of Drug and Alcohol Abuse, 27,* 265–280.

Warner, M., Chen, L. H., Makuc, D. M., Anderson, R. N., & Miniño, A. M. (2010). *Drug poisoning deaths in the United States, 1980–2008.* NCHS data brief, no 81. Hyattsville, MD: National Center for Health Statistics.

Warr, M. (1993). Parents, peers and delinquency. *Social Forces, 72,* 247–264.

Warr, M. (1996). Organization and instigation in delinquent groups. *Criminology, 34,* 11–37.

Warr, M. (2002). *Companions in crime: The social aspects of criminal conduct.* New York: Cambridge University Press.

Warr, M., & Stafford, M. (1991). The influence of delinquent peers: What they think or what they do? *Criminology, 29,* 851–866.

Wartell, J., & LaVigne, N. (2004). *Prescription fraud.* Washington, DC: U.S. Department of Justice, Office of Community Oriented Policing Services.

Warthan, M., Uchida, T., & Wagner, R. (2005). UV light tanning as a type of substance-related disorder. *Archives of Dermatology, 141,* 963–966.

Washington County (Minnesota). (2004). *Consequences of supplying alcohol to minors.* Retrieved June 10, 2005, from http://www.co.washington.mn.us/info_for_residents/public_health/

Washington State. (2004). *DUI laws.* Retrieved August 15, 2004, from http://www.wa.gov/wtsc/drunk_driving_issues.html

Washington State Department of Social and Health Services. (2003). *Treatment of stimulant addiction including addiction to methamphetamine results in lower health care costs and reduced arrests and convictions.* Retrieved July 10, 2004, from http://www1.dshs.wa.gov/RDA/research/11/114.shtm

Washington State Institute for Public Policy. (2002, March). *Washington State's drug courts for adult defendants: Outcome evaluation and cost-benefit analysis.* Seattle, WA: Author.

Wasson, R., Hofman, A., & Ruck, C. (2008). *The road to Eleusis: Unveiling the secret of the mysteries.* New York: North Atlantic Books.

Watercutter, A. (2002, December 11). Santa Cruz council votes to deputize medical marijuana growers. *San Francisco Chronicle.* Retrieved December 11, 2002, from http://www.sfgate.com

Watts, J., & Hutchinson, A. (2008, February 12). Reforming crack-cocaine law. *Washington Post*. Retrieved May 5, 2008, from http://www.washingtonpost.com

Webley, K. (2006, January 22). Washington wants tougher meth laws. *Oregonian*. Retrieved January 22, 2006, from http://www.oregonian.com

Webster, D. W., Harburg, E., Gleiberman, L., Schork, A., & DiFranceisco, W. (1989). Familial transmission of alcohol use I: Parent and adult offspring alcohol use over 17 years—Tecumseh, Michigan. *Journal of Studies on Alcohol, 50*, 557–566.

Wechsler, H. (2000, October 20). Binge drinking: Should we attack the name or the problem? *Chronicle of Higher Education*. Retrieved October 20, 2000, from http://www.chronicle.com

Wechsler, H., Davenport, A., Dowdall, G., Moeykens, B., & Castillo, S. (1994). Health and behavioral consequences of binge drinking in college. *JAMA: The Journal of the American Medical Association, 272*(21), 1672–1677.

Wechsler, H., Lee, J., Kuo, M., Seibring, M., Nelson, I., & Lee, H. (2002). Trends in college binge drinking during a period of increased prevention efforts: Findings from four Harvard School of Public Health college alcohol study surveys: 1993–2001. *Journal of American College Health, 50*, 203–222.

Wechsler, H., Nelson, T., Lee, J. E., Seibring, M., Lewis, C., & Keeling, R. P. (2003). Perception and reality: A national evaluation of social norms marketing interventions to reduce college students' heavy alcohol use. *Journal of Studies on Alcohol, 64*, 484–494.

Wedge, D. (2000, March 5). *Ecstasy subs heighten drug danger*. Retrieved May 2, 2001, from http://www.boston herald.com

Weeks, C. (2012, August 15). Australia's "plain packaging" cigarette ruling: Bold leadership or draconian? *Globe and Mail*. Retrieved August 15, 2012, from http://www.theglobeandmail.com

"Welcome to Provigil.com." (2012). *Provigil homepage*. Retrieved from Provigil .com.

Weil, A. (1986). *The natural mind: A new way of looking at drugs and the higher consciousness*. Boston: Houghton Mifflin.

Weil, A., & Rosen, W. (1998). *From chocolate to morphine*. Boston: Houghton Mifflin.

Weiner, R., & Pulitzer, C. (2006, February 10). Loopholes in Olympic drug policy big enough to ski through. *Seattle Post-Intelligencer*. Retrieved February 10, 2006, from http://www.seattlepi.com. nwsource

Weinstein, H., & Levin, M. (2002, October 31). EU alleges mob ties to tobacco. *Los Angeles Times*. Retrieved October 31, 2002, from http://www.latimes.com

Weitzman, E., Folkman, A., Folkman, K., & Wechsler, H. (2003). The relationships of alcohol outlet density to heavy and frequent drinking and drinking-related problems among college students at eight universities. *Health and Place, 9*, 1–6.

Weitzman, E., Nelson, T., Lee, H., & Wechsler, H. (2004). Reducing drinking and drinking-related harms in college: Evaluation of the "A Matter of Degree" program. *American Journal of Preventive Medicine, 27*, 187–196.

Welch, W. (2009, September 30). Booming medical pot sales concern officials. *Washington Post*. Retrieved September 30, 2009, from http://www.washingtonpost.com

Welsh, W. N. (2010). Inmate responses to prison-based drug treatment: A repeated measures analysis. *Drug and Alcohol Dependence, 109*(1), 37–44.

Werner, C. (1922). *Tobacco land*. New York: Tobacco Leaf.

Wertheim, J. (2003, April 7). Jolt of reality. *Sports Illustrated*. Retrieved April 10,

2003, from http://www.sportsillus
trated.cnn.com

Westhead, R. (2005, July 28). NHL drug
tests attacked. *Toronto Star*. Retrieved
July 28, 2005, from http://www.thestar
.com

Westneat, D. (2012, October 2). King
County sheriff makes case for pot.
Seattle Times. Retrieved October 2,
2012, from http://www.seattletimes
.com

Wexler, H., Falkin, G., Lipton, D., &
Rosenbaum, A. (1992). Outcome evalu-
ation of a prison therapeutic commu-
nity for substance abuse treatment. In
C. G. Leukefeld & F. M. Tims (Eds.),
*Drug abuse treatment in prisons and
jails. NIDA Research Monograph 118*
(pp. 156–175). Washington, DC: U.S.
Department of Health and Human
Services.

Wexler, H., Melnick, G., Lowe, L., & Peters,
J. (1999). Three-year incarceration outcomes for amity in-prison therapeutic
community and aftercare in California.
The Prison Journal, 79, 321–336.

Wexler, H., & Williams, R. (1986). The
stay'n out therapeutic community:
Prison treatment for substance abusers.
Journal of Psychoactive Drugs, 18,
221–230.

When drug companies hide data. (2004,
June 6). *New York Times*. Retrieved
June 6, 2004, from http://www.nytimes
.com

Where there's smoke, there's medicine.
(1999, December 4). *Economist*.
Retrieved December 4, 1999, from
http://www.economist.com

White, A. M., Hingson, R. W., Pan, I., & Yi,
H. (2011). Hospitalizations for alcohol
and drug overdoses in young adults
ages 18–24 in the United States, 1999–
2008: Results from the Nationwide
Inpatient Sample. *Journal of Studies on
Alcohol and Drugs, 72*(5), 774–785.

White, W. (2000a). Addiction as a disease.
Counselor Magazine, 1, 46–51.

Retrieved March 20, 2003, from http://
www.counselormagazine.com/display_
article.asp?aid=addictoin_as_a_disease
.asp

White, W. (2000b). The rebirth of the disease concept of alcoholism in the 20th
century. *Counselor Magazine, 1,* 62–66.
Retrieved March 20, 2003, from http://
www.counselormagazine.com/display_
article.asp?aid=rebirth_disease_
concept_alcohol.asp

White, W., & Kurtz, E. (2006). *Linking
addiction treatment and communities
of recovery: A primer for addiction
counselors and recovery coaches.*
Pittsburgh, PA: IRETA/NeATTC.

The White House. (1989). *National drug
control strategy.* Washington, DC:
Author. Available online at http://www
.whitehouse.gov

The White House. (2006). *National drug
control strategy.* Retrieved February 2,
2006, from http://www.white house-
drugpolicy.gov/publications/policy/
ndcs05/ndcs05.pdf

Whitlock, C. (2003, October 24). Study cites
race disparity in Maryland drug incarcerations. *Washington Post*. Retrieved
October 24, 2003, from http://www
.washingtonpost.com

Whitty, J. (2004, March/April). Smuggling
hope. *Mother Jones*. Retrieved April 2,
2004, from http://www.moth erjones
.com

Wichstrom, L., & Pedersen, W. (2001). Use
of anabolic-androgenic steroids in adolescence: Looking good or being bad?
Journal of Studies on Alcohol, 62, 5–13.

Wiechelt, S. A., Gryczynski, J., Johnson,
J. L., & Caldwell, D. (2012). Historical
trauma among urban American Indians:
Impact on substance abuse and family
cohesion. *Journal of Loss and Trauma,
17*(4), 319–336.

Wilkie, D. (2005, May 23). Patient empow-
erment or Pandora's box? *The Scientist*.
Retrieved May 23, 2005, from http://
www.the-scientist.com/

Wilkins, W., Newton, P., & Steer, J. (1993). Competing sentencing policies in a "war on drugs" era. *Wake Forest Law Review, 28,* 305–327.

Wilkinson, F. (1993, June 10). Can Janet Reno bust the war on drugs? *Rolling Stone.* Retrieved June 26, 2002, from http://www.rollingstone.com

Will, G. (2005, December 19). 2005's kind of progress. *Newsweek.* Retrieved December 19, 2005, from http://www.msnbc.msn.com

Williams, D., & Collins, C. (1995). U.S. socioeconomic and racial differences in health: Patterns and explanations. *Annual Review of Sociology, 21,* 349–386.

Williams, L., & Fainaru-Wada, M. (2004, February 18). Steroid affidavits implicate trainer. *San Francisco Chronicle.* Retrieved February 18, 2004, from http://www.sfgate.com

Williams, P. (2002, March 25). Virtual reality. *The Nation.* Retrieved March 25, 2002, from http://www.the nation.com

Williams, R. (2003, September 1). White test casts a cloud over Paris. *Guardian.* Retrieved September 1, 2003, from http://www.guardian.co.uk

Williams, T. (2003, July 12). N.Y. city mayor sparks debate on beer, wine. *Associated Press.* Retrieved July 12, 2003, from http://www.ap.org

Willman, D. (2001, March 11). Risk was known as FDA ok'd fatal drug. *Los Angeles Times.* Retrieved March 11, 2001, from http://www.latimes.com

Willman, D. (2002, June 30). Hidden risks, lethal truths. *Los Angeles Times.* Retrieved June 30, 2002, from http://www.latimes.com

Willman, D. (2004, December 22). The National Institutes of Health: Public servant or private marketer? *Los Angeles Times.* Retrieved December 22, 2004, from http://www.latimes.com

Wills, T. A., & Shiffman, S. (1985). Coping and substance use: A conceptual framework. In S. Shiffman & T. A. Wills (Eds.), *Coping and substance use* (pp. 3–24). Orlando, FL: Academic Press.

Wilson, D. (2009, June 16). Tobacco regulation is expected to face a free-speech challenge. *New York Times.* Retrieved June 16, 2009, from http://www.nytimes.com

Wilson, D. (2010a, February 19). Coded to obey law, lights become Marlboro Gold. *New York Times.* Retrieved February 19, 2010, from http://www.nytimes.com

Wilson, D. (2010b, April 18). Flavored tobacco pellets are denounced as lure to young users. *New York Times.* Retrieved April 18, 2010, from http://www.nytimes.com

Wilson, D. (2011, November 3). Glaxo settles case for $3 billion. *New York Times.* Retrieved November 3, 2011, from http://www.nytimes.com

Wilson, D. M., Varvel, S. A., Harloe, J. P., Martin, B. R., & Lichtman, A. H. (2006). SR 141716 (Rimonabant) precipitates withdrawal in marijuana-dependent mice. *Pharmacology Biochemistry and Behavior, 85*(1), 105–113. doi:10.1016/j.pbb.2006.07.018

Wilson, F., & Stimpson, J. (2011). Trends in fatalities from distracted driving in the United States, 1999 to 2008. *American Journal of Public Health, 100,* 2213–2219.

Wilson, T. (2011, May 12). Illinois lawmakers target bath salts. *Chicago Tribune.* Retrieved May 12, 2011, from http://www.chicagotribune.com

Wilson, W. J. (1987). *The truly disadvantaged: The inner city, the underclass and public policy.* Chicago: University of Chicago Press.

Wilson, W. J. (1996). *When work disappears: The world of the new urban poor.* New York: Knopf.

Wilstein, S. (2002, May 20). Bonds shrugs off worries about steroids. *San*

Francisco Chronicle. Retrieved May 20, 2002, from http://www.sfgate.com

Wilstein, S. (2004, March 20). NHL can't afford to be aloof about drug testing. *Associated Press.* Retrieved March 20, 2004, from http://www.ap.org

Winerman, L. (2005). Helping men to help themselves: Research aims to understand why men are less likely than women to seek mental health help, and what psychologists can do to change that. *Monitor on Psychology, 36,* 57. Retrieved November 12, 2005, from http://www.apa.org/monitor/jun05/helping.html

Winfree, L. T., & Bernat, F. (1998). Social learning, self-control, and substance abuse by eighth-grade students: A tale of two cities. *Journal of Drug Issues, 28,* 539–558.

Winn, R., & Giaocopassi, D. (1993). Effects of county-level alcohol prohibition on motor vehicle accidents. *Social Science Quarterly, 74,* 783–792.

Winslow, G. (2003). Capital crimes. In T. Herivel & P. Wright (Eds.), *Prison nation: The warehousing of America's poor* (pp. 41–56). New York: Routledge Press.

Winstanley, E. L., Steinwachs, D. M., Ensminger, M. E., Latkin, C. A., Stitzer, M. L., & Olsen, Y. (2008). The association of self-reported neighborhood disorganization and social capital with adolescent alcohol and drug use, dependence, and access to treatment. *Drug and alcohol dependence, 92*(1), 173–182.

Wisborg, K., Hedegaard, M., & Brink Henriksen, T. (2003). Consumption of coffee during pregnancy. *British Medical Journal, 326,* 1269.

Wishnick, S. (1999). *Sheldon's speech.* Retrieved March 15, 2003, from http://www.motorists.com/issues/dwi/questions.html

Wisotsky, S. (1992). A society of suspects: The war on drugs and civil liberties. *Cato Policy Analysis.* Retrieved February 12, 2002, from http://www.cato.org/pubs/pas/pa-180es.html

Wohlsen, M. (2010, September 26). California measure shows state's conflicted link to pot. *Associated Press.* Retrieved September 26, 2010, from http://www.ap.org

Wolfe, D., & Malinowska-Sempruch, K. (2004). *Illicit drug policies and the global HIV epidemic.* New York: Open Society Institute.

Wolff, A., & Epstein, D. (2012, October 27). A massive fraud now more fully exposed. *Sports Illustrated*, pp. 40–48.

Wood, A., Drazen, J., & Greene, M. (2005). A sad day for science at the FDA. *New England Journal of Medicine, 353,* 1197–1199.

Wood, D. M., Davies, S., Puchnarewicz, M., et al. (2010). Recreational use of 4-methylmethcathinone (4-MMC) with associated sympathomimetic toxicity. *Journal of Medical Toxicology, 6,* 327–330.

Wood, E., Kerr, T., Spittal, P., Tyndall, M., O'Shaugnessy, M., & Schechter, M. (2003). The health care and fiscal costs of the illicit drug use epidemic: The impact of conventional drug control strategies, and the potential of a comprehensive approach. *B.C. Medical Journal, 45*(3), 128–134.

Wood, E., Tyndall, M. W., Stoltz, J. A., Small, W., Zhang, R., O'Connell, J., & Kerr, T. (2005). Safer injecting education for HIV prevention within a medically supervised safer injecting facility. *International Journal of Drug Policy, 16*(4), 281–284.

Wood, E., Tyndall, M. W., Montaner, J. S., & Kerr, T. (2006). Summary of findings from the evaluation of a pilot medically supervised safer injecting facility. *Canadian Medical Association Journal, 175*(11), 1399–1404. doi:10.1503/cmaj.060863

Wood, E., Tyndall, M., Zhang, R., Montaner, J., & Kerr, T. (2007). Rate of detoxification service use and its impact among a cohort of supervised injection facility users. *Addiction, 102*, 916–919.

Wood, S. (2005, May 11). R. B. Smith's "whizzinator" prompts NFL inquiry. *USA Today.* Retrieved May 11, 2005, from http://www.usatoday.com

Woodman, S. (2002, September 2). The women's Enron. *The Nation.* Retrieved September 5, 2002, from http://www.thenation.com

World Anti-Doping Agency. (2005). *The year of the code.* Retrieved February 3, 2006, from http://www.wada-ama.org/rtecontent/document/WADAAnnualReport 2003.pdf

World Anti-Doping Agency. (2009). *The world anti-doping code.* Retrieved August 17, 2012, from http://www.wada-ama.org/en/World-Anti-Doping-Program/Sports-and-Anti-Doping-Organizations/The-Code/

World Health Organization. (2006). *Drug policy news.* Retrieved January 26, 2006, from http://www.drug policy.org

World Health Organization. (2011). *Global status report on alcohol and health, 2011.* Geneva: Department of Mental Health and Substance Dependence, Noncommunicable Diseases and Mental Health Cluster, World Health Organization.

World Health Organization. (2012). *Tobacco fact sheet.* Geneva: Department of Mental Health and Substance Dependence, Noncommunicable Diseases and Mental Health Cluster, World Health Organization. Retrieved from http://www.who.int/mediacentre/factsheets/fs339/en/index.html

Wormer, K., & Persson, L. (2010). Drug treatment within the U.S. federal prison system: Are treatment needs being met? *Journal of Offender Rehabilitation, 49*, 363–375.

Wright, J. (1982). *Anabolic steroids and sport II.* Natick, MA: Sports Science Consultants.

Wright, K. (2001, March 15). DARE rethinks drug prevention. *Seattle Post-Intelligencer.* Retrieved March 15, 2001, from http://www.seattlepi.com.nwsource

Wright, N., & Tompkins, C. (2004). Supervised injecting centres. *British Medical Journal, 328*, 100–102.

Wu, F. C. W., Tajar, A., Beynon, J. M., Pye, S. R., Silman, A. J., Finn, J. D., O'Neill, T. W., et al. (2010). Identification of late-onset hypogonadism in middle-aged and elderly men. *New England Journal of Medicine, 363*(2), 123–135. doi:10.1056/NEJMoa0911101

Wu, L., & Blazer, D. (2011). Illicit and non-medical drug use among older adults: A review. *Journal of Ageing and Health, 23*, 481–504.

Wynne-Jones, R. (2004, November 22). World of drugs. *London Daily Mirror.* Retrieved November 22, 2004, from http://www.mirror.co.uk

Wysong, E., Aniskiewicz, R., & Wright, D. (1994). Truth and DARE: Tracking drug education to graduation and as symbolic politics. *Social Problems, 41*, 448–472.

Wysong, E., Aniskiewicz, R., & Wright, D. (2003). Truth and DARE. In J. Orcutt & D. Rudy (Eds.), *Drugs, alcohol, and social problems* (pp. 93–119). New York: Rowan and Littlefield.

Xenova. (2004). *TA-CD.* Retrieved June 15, 2005, from http://www.cantab.co.uk/dc_ta_cd.html

Yamaguchi, R., Johnston, L., & O'Malley, P. (2003). Relationship between student illicit drug use and school drug-testing policies. *Journal of School Health, 73*, 159–164.

Yardley, W. (2011, May 7). New federal crackdown confounds states that allow medical marijuana. *New York Times.* Retrieved May 7, 2011, from http://www.nytimes.com

Yates, W. (2000). Testosterone in psychiatry: Risks and benefits. *Archives of Psychiatry, 57*, 155–156.

Yeoman, B. (2001, November/December). Surgical strike. *Mother Jones*. Retrieved December 1, 2001, from http://www.motherjones.com

Yeoman, B. (2003, March/April). Secondhand diplomacy. *Mother Jones*. Retrieved April 2, 2003, from http://www.motherjones.com

Yesalis, C. (2000). Introduction. In C. Yesalis (Ed.), *Anabolic steroids in sport and exercise* (2nd ed., pp. 1–13). Champaign, IL: Human Kinetics.

Yesalis, C., Bahrke, M., Kopstein, A., & Barsukiewicz, C. (2000). Incident of anabolic steroid use: A discussion of methodological issues. In C. Yesalis (Ed.), *Anabolic steroids in sport and exercise* (2nd ed., pp. 73–115). Champaign, IL: Human Kinetics.

Yesalis, C., Courson, S., & Wright, J. (1993). History of anabolic steroid use in sport and exercise. In C. Yesalis (Ed.), *Anabolic steroids in sport and exercise* (pp. 35–47). Champaign, IL: Human Kinetics.

Yesalis, C., Courson, S., & Wright, J. (2000). History of anabolic steroid use in sport and exercise. In C. Yesalis (Ed.), *Anabolic steroids in sport and exercise* (2nd ed., pp. 35–47). Champaign, IL: Human Kinetics.

Yin, X.-H. (2000, October 9). The two sides of America's "model minority." *Los Angeles Times*. Retrieved October 9, 2000, from http://www.latimes.com

Young, L. (2010). *Barbiturates*. International Substance Abuse Library. Retrieved from http://www.drugtext.org/Recreational-Drugs/barbiturates.html

Young, T. (1988). Substance use and abuse among Native Americans. *Clinical Psychology Review, 8*, 125–138.

Youngers, C. (1998). *Waging war: U.S. policy toward Colombia*. Retrieved July 17, 2005, from http://136.142.158.105/LASA98/Youngers.pdf

Zagier, A. (2010, September 15). Bans on fake pot do little to deter business. *Associated Press*. Retrieved September 15, 2010, from http://www.ap.org

Zappei, J. (2009, July 21). Beer-drinking Muslim model Kartika Sari Dewi Skukarno, sentenced to public flogging in Malaysia. *Huffington Post*. Retrieved July 21, 2009, from http://www.huffingtonpost.com

Zarembo, A. (2004, November 23). Report: Bayer held back on drug dangers. *Los Angeles Times*. Retrieved November 23, 2004, from http://www.latimes.com

Zayas, L., Rojas, M., & Malgady, R. (1998). Alcohol and drug use and depression among Hispanic men in early adulthood. *American Journal of Community Psychology, 26*, 425–438.

Zeese, K. (1989). Housing: The new battleground in the war on drugs. *Drug Policy Letter, 1*, 6.

Zeleny, J. (2009, June 23). Occasional smoker, 47, signs tobacco bill. *New York Times*. Retrieved June 23, 2009, from http://www.nytimes.com

Zeleny, J., & Biesk, J. (2001, May 11). State lawmakers OK ecstasy, DUI bills. *Chicago Tribune*. Retrieved May 11, 2001, from http://www.chicagotribune.com

Zemore, S., Kaskutas, L., & Ammon, L. (2004). In 12-step groups, helping helps the helper. *Addiction, 99*, 1015–1023.

Zernike, K. (2006, January 23). Potent Mexican meth floods in as states curb domestic variety. *New York Times*. Retrieved January 23, 2006, from http://www.nytimes.com

Zernike, K., & Petersen, M. (2001, August 19). Schools' backing of behavior drug comes under fire. *New York Times*. Retrieved August 19, 2001, from http://www.nytimes.com

Zernike, K. (2006, January 23). Potent Mexican meth floods in as states curb domestic variety. *New York Times*. Retrieved from http://www.nytimes.com

Zezima, K., & Goodnough, A. (2010, October 25). Drug testing poses quandary for employers. *New York Times*. Retrieved October 25, 2010, from http://www.nytimes.com

Zickler, P. (2001). NIDA scientific panel reports on prescription drug misuse and abuse. *NIDA Notes, 16*(3). Retrieved July 10, 2002, from http://www.drugabuse.gov/NIDA_notes/NNVol16N3/Scientific.html

Zimmer, L., & Morgan, J. (1997). *Marijuana myths, marijuana facts.* New York: The Lindesmith Center.

Zimring, F., & Hawkins, G. (1992). *The search for rational drug control.* Cambridge, NY: Cambridge University Press.

Zirin, D. (2009, February 9). A-Rod, anabolic agonist. *The Nation.* Retrieved February 10, 2009, from http://www.thenation.com

Zorn, E. (2005, December 22). Thank you, sir—cough—may we pay more taxes? *Chicago Tribune.* Retrieved December 22, 2005, from http://www.chicagotribune.com

Zucato, E., Chiabrando, C., Castiglioni, S., Calamari, D., Bagnati, R., Schiarea, S., et al. (2005). Cocaine in surface waters: A new evidence-based tool to monitor community drug abuse. *Environmental Health: A Global Access Science Source, 4,* 14–21. Retrieved December 12, 2005, from http://www.ehjournal.net

Zucchino, D. (2009, July 31). Afghanistan faces growing addiction problem. *Los Angeles Times.* Retrieved July 21, 2009, from http://www.latimes.com

Zuger, A. (2002, December 31). The case for drinking (All together now: In moderation!). *New York Times.* Retrieved December 31, 2002, from http://www.nytimes.com

Index

A.A. *See* Alcoholics Anonymous
AAPCC (American Association of Poison Control Centers), 156, 434
Abrams, D., 473
Abramson, J., 394, 412
Abstinence
  Alcoholics Anonymous and, xx, 52, 333, 334, 335, 341, 342
  assumptions about, xvi, 76
  drug education and, 298
  drug treatment and, 319, 321, 336, 337, 346
  from alcohol, 314, 315, 334, 335, 336, 337–338, 377–378
  from tobacco, 305
  in therapeutic communities, 323
  minorities and, 205, 247
  reasons for, 243, 246
  temperance movements and, 266, 365, 366
Acamprosate, 314, 336
Acculturation
  alcohol use and, 249
  definition of, 525
  illegal drug use and, 213–214
  legal drug use and, 249
Acetaminophen, 128, 130, 131
Acton, J., 287–288
Acton, Vernonia School District v., 287–288
Acutane, 395
Acute toxicity, 82–83, 152, 159, 174, 232, 525
ADAM. *See* Arrestee Drug Abuse Monitoring
Adams, S. H., 392
Adamson, S. J., 336
ADD (Attention deficit disorder), 97, 108
Adda, J., 355
Adderall, 109
Addiction
  definition of, 525
  disease theory of, xvi, 51–55
  misinformation about, 33–34

  overview of, 85
  to benzodiazepines, 118
  to cocaine, 102–103
  to heroin, 63–64
  to methadone, 307
  to opiates, 123
  to pain killers, 130
  to stimulants, 33–34
  to tanning, 55
  to tobacco, 97, 315
  to video gaming, 53
  See also Dependence; Drug treatment
Addiction Severity Index, 202–203
ADHD (Attention deficit hyperactivity disorder), 103, 108, 405
Administrative license suspension, 378, 380
Adolescents
  African Americans' illegal drug use, 206, 208
  alcohol, minimum legal age, 371–374, 388
  American Indians' illegal drug use, 215
  antidrug advertising and, 276–283
  API's illegal drug use, 216
  drug testing policies, 286–291
  energy drinks and, 92, 93
  Hispanic illegal drug use, 210–212 (table)
  Hispanic legal drug use, 247, 249
  illegal drug use and age, 177, 195, 228, 231 (figure)
  illegal drug use and race/ethnicity, 210–213, 212 (table)
  illegal drug use by gender, 200 (figure)–201, 202
  legal drug use by age, 225–232, 226 (figure), 227 (figure), 229 (table), 230 (table), 231 (table), 234
  legal drug use by gender, 237, 238 (table), 239–240
  legal drug use by location, 258 (table)

legal drug use by social class,
    218, 219–220 (figure), 257
MTF survey of drug use, 181 (table)–183
salvia and, 144, 228, 232–234
surveys of drug use, 183–185
tobacco advertising and, 357
tobacco purchases over Internet by, 360
tobacco taxes and, 360
zero tolerance policies and, xviii–xix,
    283–286
See also Students; Youths
Adoption, alcoholism and, 49–51
Adrenaline, 82, 103, 106, 110
Adulterants, 31, 392–393
Adults
    adult illegal drug use offenders, 188–194
    African American illegal drug use, 204, 206,
        208–209
    American Indian illegal drug use, 204, 215
    API illegal drug use, 204, 216
    Hispanic illegal drug use, 204,
        211–212 (table)
    illegal drug use, surveys on, 185–187
    illegal drug use by location, 221 (table)
    legal drug use by gender, 240 (table)
    legal drug use by location, 258–259 (table)
    legal drug use patterns by age,
        225–227 (figure), 226 (figure)
    legal drug use patterns by race,
        243–244 (table), 252
    legal drug use patterns of elderly,
        234, 236–237
    MTF survey of drug use, 182
    white illegal drug use, 204
Advancement Project, 284, 285
Advertising
    alcohol products, 247
    antidrug advertising campaigns, xviii,
        276–283
    pharmaceutical products, 236, 404–408
    prescription drugs, regulation of, 404–408
    tobacco products, 356–357
Advil, 295
Aerosols, 119–120
Afghanistan, 520–521
African Americans
    crack baby legislation and, 450–452
    crack cocaine linked with, 24–25
    crack cocaine use by, 75
    illegal drug use by, 203–204, 205–210
    inequality in drug laws, 74, 446–449
    legal drug use by, 245–247
    mandatory minimum sentences and,
        453–455.456
    parent-adolescent relationship, 208, 247

school zone policies and, 459
social conflict theory and, 74
strain theory and, 71–72
AGA (American Gastroenterological
    Association), 131
Agassi, A., 425
Age
    illegal drug use and, 177, 194–199,
        195 (figure), 196 (table), 197 (table)
    legal drug use and, 225–237, 226 (figure),
        227 (figure), 229 (table), 230 (table),
        231 (table), 234, 256 (figure)
    minimum legal drinking age, 371–374
    tobacco restrictions, 352
Age-graded theory, 68–69, 70 (figure), 77
Aggression, 81, 168–169
Agnew, R., 71
AIDS/HIV, xv, 5, 14, 167, 172, 187, 307, 491,
    493, 497, 501, 507
Akers, R., 59, 60, 77, 292
Alabama, 40, 289, 296, 458
Alaska, 215, 369
Alcohol
    African Americans' use of, 242, 243 (table),
        244 (table), 245–246
    American Indians' use of, 215, 242, 243,
        249–250
    animals and, 2
    API's use of, 244 (table), 251, 252
    Asian Americans' use of, 242
    Asians/Pacific Islanders' use of, 252
    barbiturates and, 117
    cocaine ingestion with, 102
    deaths from, 2, 84, 113–114, 368
    drinking and social learning theory, 61–62
    drug testing of workers, 297
    effects of, 81, 112–115
    energy drinks combined with, 94
    Hispanic's use of, 213–214, 242, 243 (table),
        244 (table), 248–249
    pharmacological treatment of, 313, 314
    regulation of, xxi
    scare tactics for, 266
    sedatives and, 118
    use by age, 225–228, 226 (figure),
        227 (figure), 229 (figure), 230 (table),
        256 (figure)
    use by elderly, 198–199, 236–237
    use by gender, 237–238 (table), 248
    use by population size,
        258 (table)–259 (figure)
    use by race/ethnicity, 71–72, 242–245,
        243 (table), 244 (table), 245–246 (table),
        248–249, 253 (table)
    use by rural/urban location, 222

Bath salts, 41–42, 107–108, 525
Baume Commission, 24
Bay Area Laboratories Company (BALCO), 420, 430–431
Baycol, 398
Bayer Laboratories
    Baycol of, 398
    criminal activities of, 408
    heroin marketed by, 124
    Levitra of, 161, 406
BCS. *See* British Crime Survey
BD (1,4-butanediol), 119
Beauvais, F., 143
Becker, H., 59, 151
Beckett, K., 448
Behavioral toxicity, 82, 86, 526
Belgium, 373, 498
Belief (social bonding theory), 65
Bender drinking, 213, 215
Bennett, W., 26
Benshoff, B., 236
Bentler, P., 270
Benzedrine, 103, 108
Benzodiazepines, 117–118, 236
Berard, B., 427
Bextra, 409, 412
Biden, J., 484
Billboard advertising, 356
Binge drinking
    by age, 226 (figure), 246 (figure)
    by race/ethnicity, 213, 242, 246 (figure), 248, 253 (figure)
    by state, 260 (figure)
    college campus drinking regulations and, 374–375, 376
    definition of, 325
Birth defects, 395, 397, 398
Bizarre behavior, 3–4, 6, 13, 35–36, 40, 41–42, 43
Blacks. *See* African Americans
Blakemore, C., 29
Blakeslee, N., 449
Blindness, 162
Block, J., 270
Blood Alcohol Concentration (BAC)
    breath analysis machines, 382–383
    definition of, 525
    drunk driving laws, 377–378
    field sobriety tests and, 381–383
Blood doping, 172–173, 425–426, 526
Blunkett, D., 503
Board of Education v. Earls et al., 288
Bogenschutz, M. P., 341
Boje, O., 166–167
Bolivia, 416, 516, 518

Bollinger, L., 495
Bond, C., 113
Bonding, xvii, 56, 65–67, 77
Bonds, B., 416, 430–431
Bonnette, R., 25
Boredom, 195
Boston Medical and Surgical Journal, 125
Bowman, K., 11
Brain
    alcohol's effects on, 114
    barbiturates and, 116
    ecstasy and, 28–30
    marijuana use and, 21–22, 151
    methamphetamine and, 33
    tobacco and, 95, 97
    See also Central nervous system
Brandon, K., 33
Branson, R., 522
Braun, R., 433
Brazil, 342, 373, 490, 522
Breast cancer, 92, 163, 167
Breath analysis, 379, 382–383
Brecher, E., 5, 6, 31, 123, 306–307
Breggin, G., 393
Breggin, P., 393
Brennan, T., 411
Brewer, B. H., 412
Breyer, C., 474
Bridge, B. B., 379
Brigham, United States v., 456
Bristol-Meyers-Squibb, 276
Britain
    cannabis use in, 187
    death rate from alcoholism, 368
    drug education in, 275
    drug policies of, 499–503
    drug-related deaths in, 84 (figure)
    drug testing in, 297
    drug treatment in, 311, 345
    ecstasy in, 27, 111
    heroin maintenance for addicts, 311, 499
    marijuana studies in, 24
    Thalidomide and, 398
    See also British Crime Survey (BCS)
British Advisory Council on the Misuse of Drugs, 501
British American Tobacco Company, 360, 361
British Association of Pharmacology (BAP), 311, 313, 315, 345
British Crime Survey (BCS)
    data on adult drug use, 185–186
    on drug use, 178
    poverty and illegal drug use, 219
    validity of survey findings, 180

British Drug Trafficking Act, 502
British Journal of Addiction, 116
British Medical Journal, 22, 123
Brodsky, A, 339
Bromatan, 421
Bromberg, W., 9, 11
Brown, D., 172
Brown-Seguard, C., 166
Brunstom, Richard, 501
Buckley, W. F., Jr., xiv
Bufotenine, 145–146, 526
Bulletin of the Health Organization of the League of Nations, 166
Buprenorphine (Subutex), 309–311, 315
Bureau of Justice Statistics, 23, 74
Burke, J., 276
Burns, M., 382
Burroughs, W., 116
Burton, D., 444
Bush, G. W.
  antidrug advertising and, 282
  campaign contributions and, 410
  cigarette advertising and, 362–363
  connections with pharmaceutical companies, 410
  drug treatment and, 346–347
  emergency contraception and, 396
  importation of Canadian pharmaceuticals and, 402
  prescription drug advertising and, 407
  prescription drug regulation and, 402
  school drug testing and, 286, 290
Bush, J., 444, 445
Bush, N., 444, 445
Butyl nitrite, 120

Cabanatuan, M.
Cabrera, M., 433
Caetano, R., 244–245
Caffeine
  deaths from, 91
  effects of, 90–92, 93, 94, 435
  health benefits of, 92
  Olympics ban on, 421
Cahalan, D., 61
California
  asset forfeiture in, 465
  bath salts use in, 41
  Canadian prescription drugs and, 401
  compulsory treatment programs in, 326, 330–331
  drug law changes in, 482
  drunk driving laws in, 377, 385
  inequality in drug laws, 447, 455
  marijuana cultivation in, 475

  marijuana offenders in, 23
  marijuana sentences in, 23
  medical marijuana laws and, 472–473, 474–475
  minimum drinking age and, 374
  Proposition 19, 477–478
  Proposition 36, 330–331, 482
  Proposition 215, 482
  public housing evictions in, 460
  second-hand smoke study in, 354
California Department of Alcohol and Drug Programs, 34, 326
California Department of Education, 268–269
California Highway Patrol, 383
Cambanis, T., 26
Cambodians, 217, 218
Camels (cigarettes), 357
Caminiti, K., 171, 430
Campbell, L., 507, 511
Canada
  alcohol prohibition in, 366
  alcohol treatment programs in, 337
  certification policies and, 518
  drug approvals in, 397
  drug marijuana as gateway drug, 21
  drug policies of, 503–508
  drug policies of, U.S. reaction to, 508–512
  drug testing in, 297
  drunk driving laws in, 385
  ecstasy "epidemic' in, 27
  Internet drug sales and, 401–402, 436
  legislation under Harper government, 512–514
  minimum-age drinking laws in, 373
  pharmaceutical sales, restriction of, 401–404
  supervised injection facilities in, 312
  tobacco taxes in, 360
Canadian Council of Chief Executives, 508
Canadian Human Rights Commission, 297
Canadian LeDain Commission Report, 24
Canadian Medical Association Journal, 507
Canadian Police Association, 508
Canadian Senate Committee Report, 21
Cancer
  breast cancer, 92, 163, 167
  corporate crime and, 408
  ecstasy and, 110
  green tea and, 92
  hormone therapy and, 163
  LSD for terminal cancer, 136
  lung cancer, 23, 92, 152–153, 354
  marijuana and, 22–23, 152–153
  off-label sales and, 397
  performance-enhancing drugs and, 170
  steroids for, 167

Cannabis, synthetic, 40–41. *See also* Marijuana

Cannabis plant
  drug policy and, 492–493
  effects of, 7–8
  history of, 7, 151
  parts of, 149–150
  pollination and, 17, 529
  species of, 149
  See also Hemp

Canseco, J., 430

Carcinogenic effects, of marijuana, 22

Cardiovascular disease, 170–171

Carmona, R., 363

Carpenter, M., 443

Carr, Bob, 494

Carter, J., xv

The Case Against the Little White Slaver
  (Ford), 352

Castro, F., 210

Catalano, R., 66

Catlin, D., 424

CDER (Center for Drug Regulation and
  Reform), 394

Celebrex, 400, 412

Celexa, 158, 395, 409

Celgene, 397

Celluci, P., 509

Cellular telephones, 383–384, 389

Center for Cognitive Liberty and Ethics, 317

Center for Cognitive Neuroscience, 105

Center for Drug Evaluation and Research, 414

Center for Drug Regulation and Reform
  (CDER), 394

Center for Human Toxicology, 296

Center on Addiction and Substance Abuse,
  18–19

Centers for Disease Control and Prevention
  on binge drinking, 113
  on inaccuracy of drug testing, 294
  on methadone, 127, 308
  on tobacco smoking, 362
  on tobacco taxes, 358
  YRBS survey, 183

Central Intelligence Agency (CIA), 26, 136

Central nervous system
  amphetamines and, 104
  definition of, 526
  depressants and, 112, 114, 116
  heroin and, 125
  nicotine and, 96
  opiates and, 122, 125

Cephalon, 397

Certification policies, 517–518

Chafetz, M., 115

Chaffee, L., 155, 479

Chambers, D., 424

Chambliss, W., 74

Chapman, S., 355

Charles II (England), 90–91

Chavez, H., 518

Chemical spraying, 515, 516–517

Chemical weapons, 136

Chicago, IL
  drop in cocaine use in, 189
  marijuana policy in, 478
  minimum drinking age and, 374
  youth drug use in, 72

The Chicago Medical Review, 52

Chicago Tribune, 26

Children
  antidepressant drugs and, 394–395, 409
  illegal drugs as threat to, 26
  methamphetamine and, 36–37
  school zone policies, 458–459
  See also Adolescents; Babies; Youths

Children Requiring a Caring Kommunity
  (C.R.A.C.K.), 453

Children's Alliance, 479

Chile, 98, 190

China
  anti-tobacco legislation in, 352
  black market cigarettes and, 361
  caffeine in historical, 91
  drug treatment in, 490
  minimum-age drinking laws and, 373
  severe penalties in, 491
  World Drug Report and, 187

Chinese, 216, 217, 218

Chinese-Americans, 252

Cholesterol, 171

Chretien, J., 505

Christopher, J., 343

Chronic toxicity, 82, 84, 174, 526

CIA (Central Intelligence Agency), 26, 136

Cialis, 161, 162

Ciba, 108

Cinnamon, misuse of, 39

Cipro, 408

Cirrhosis, 82, 114, 174, 193, 368, 370

Cisin, I. H., 61

Clarinex, 408–409

Claritin, 405, 406, 408–409

Clark, C., 244–245

Clement, Tony, 512–513

Clenbuterol, 426

Cliffs, 456

Clinton, B., xiii, 25, 31, 363, 455, 482, 518

Cloward, R. A., 69

Cluster headaches, 140

Coca-Cola, 99–100

Cocaethylene, 102
Cocaine
    administration routes, 101, 103
    arrests for, 442, 448
    declining use of, 182, 189
    drug antagonist for, 316–317
    drug-producing countries, U.S. and,
        515–516
    effects of, 82, 97–103
    in THC study with monkeys, 24
    marijuana and, 19, 24
    racial differences in usage, 206
    treatment for, 316–317
    use in Italy, 185
    See also Crack cocaine
Coca leaves, 97–98
Codeine, 121, 122, 127–128
Coffee, 90–92
Coffee shops, 498–499
Cognitive behavioral therapy (CBT), 345
Cognitive functioning, 21–22
Cole, J., xiii, xv
Cole, S., 382
Coleman, T., 449
College
    alcohol consumption in, 257
    drinking regulations on campus, 374–377
    NCAA drug-testing program, 417–418
Colombia
    antidrug advertising and, 279
    cocaine trade in, 515–516
    crime in, 488
    crop spraying in, 515, 516–517
    decertification by U.S., 517
    drug policy and, 522
    terrorist organizations in, 279
Colorado, 353, 472, 478, 480
Columbus, C., 94
Columbus, OH, 448
Combat Methamphetamine Epidemic Act, 470
Commitment (social bonding theory), 65
Common Sense for Drug Policy (CSDP),
    xii–xiii, 450–451
Community-based drug treatment, 325–330.
    See also Outpatient drug treatment
Community Reinforcement and Family
    Training (CRFT), 340
Community Reinforcement Approach (CRA),
    331–332
Compassionate care program, 472
Compassionate Use Act, 482
Comprehensive Drug Abuse and Control Act,
    454, 463
Comprehensive Drug Abuse Prevention and
    Control Act, 87–88

Compulsory treatment programs, xix,
    322–332
    community-based programs, 325–330
    definition of, 301
    economic benefits of, 322, 323
    history of, 322
    prison-based programs, 323
Conant, M., 473
Condelli, W., 321
Confessions of an English Opium Eater
    (De Quincey), 122
Conflict perspective, xvii, 73–76
Confrontation therapy, 320
Congressional Budget Office, 401
Connecticut, 366, 369, 464
Connors, G. J., 336
Consciousness alteration, 46–47, 80
Constipation, 123, 159
Contador, A., 426
Contingency management (CM), 345–346
Contraception regulation, 396–397, 453
Contraceptive products, 417
Controlled drinking, 334–335, 336–337
Controlled Drug and Substances Act, 503
Controlled Substances Act, 87–88, 89, 107,
    156, 466, 513, 526
Controversies. See Drug controversies/
    demonization
Convention Against Illicit Traffic in Narcotic
    Drugs and Psychotropic Substances,
    1988, 488
Convention on Psychotropic Substances, 488
Cooper, J., 36
Correlates, of illegal drug use, 194–222
Cosmetic effects, 169
Cost
    of drug treatment programs, 303, 320–321
    of DUI conviction, 379
    of prescription drugs, 401, 436
Costa, A. M., 488
Cotts, C., 276
Cough syrup, 31, 128, 148, 231
"A Counterblast to Tobacco" (James I), 95
Courson, S., 421
Coverage error, 179, 526
Cowan, R., 367, 510
CRA (Community Reinforcement Approach),
    331–332
C.R.A.C.K. (Children Requiring a Caring
    Kommunity), 453
Crack cocaine
    controversies/demonization of, 24–25
    crack baby legislation, 450–452
    description of, 101, 526
    effects of, 101, 102–103

mandatory minimum sentences for, 454–456
popularity of, 182
race/ethnicity and, 75
See also Cocaine
Crawford, L. M., 414
Creatine, 228, 238, 239, 416, 437, 526
Crestor, 412
CRFT (Community Reinforcement and Family
Training), 340
Crime(s)
heroin users and, 63–64
in Colombia, 488
methamphetamine and, 34–35
of pharmaceutical companies, 408–409
pharmaceutical company robberies,
129–130
property, 3, 34–35, 307, 501
Criminal Justice and Public Order Act, 502
Criminal justice system
arrests/incarcerations for drug offenses, 2,
441–445
assets forfeiture, 462–466
compulsory treatment programs, 323
demonization of illegal drugs, 3, 4, 40
illegal drug policies, 441–445
mandatory minimum sentences, 453–458
marijuana incarcerations, 23, 447
marijuana laws, xxiii, 470–480, 485
PCP and, 148
Prohibition and, 365–369, 387–388
public housing evictions, 459–460
social conflict theory and, 74
state drug law changes, 480–484, 485
Cronkite, W., xiv
Crop eradication programs, 516, 520–521, 523
Crossley, H. M., 61
Crum, R., 254–255
Cryer, B., 131
Crystal methamphetamine, 182, 468
CSDP (Common Sense for Drug Policy),
xii–xiii, 450–451
Cults, 319, 339–340
Cunningham, T., 469
Cycling, 167, 425–426
Cyrus, Miley, 39
Czeisler, C., 92

Da Kine Smoke and Beverage Shop
(Canada), 506
DANCE-SAFE, 467
Daniels, M. E., 410
D.A.R.E. *See* Drug Abuse Resistance Education
(D.A.R.E.)
Davel, Charlie, 40
Davenport-Hines, R., 461

Davies, D. L., 333
Davis, W., 146
DAWN. *See* Drug Abuse Warning Network
Dawson, D., 336
DEA. *See* Drug Enforcement Administration
Death penalty, 491, 492
Deaths
DAWN statistics on, 191–192
ecstasy and, 27
from 2C-L, 111
from alcohol, 2, 84, 113–114, 368
from antidepressants, 159
from barbiturates, 116–117
from bath salts, 107
from benzodiazepines, 117
from caffeine, 91
from dangerous driving, 384
from drunk driving, 381
from energy drinks, 94
from GHB, 119
from glue-sniffing, 6
from heroin, 43, 125, 211
from inhalants, 121
from methadone, 311
from methamphetamine, 33
from oxycodone, 129
from pharmaceutical products, 128
from prescription drugs, xi, 42, 83 (table),
398, 412
from substance use and age, 198
from tobacco, 2, 22, 84, 97
Decertification, 518
Dederich, C., 318, 319
Deferred prosecution, 379–380
de Jerez, Rodrigo, 94
Delaware, 39, 63, 366, 369
DeLeon, G., 319, 320
Delinquency, 62
Delirium tremens, 114
Dementia, 115, 237
de Miranda, J., 341
Demonization. *See* Drug controversies/
demonization
Denmark, 311, 368, 373
Department of Education, U.S., 179, 284
Department of Health and
Human Services, 435
Department of Housing and Urban
Development, 353
Department of Justice (DOJ), 326, 345,
362, 464
Dependence
abuse *vs.*, 87
on cocaine, 102
on heroin, 126

on illicit drugs, 85, 86, 174–175, 233 (figure)
on opiates, 122–123, 232, 314–315
on steroids, 171
overview of, 85
See also Addiction; Physical dependence; Psychological dependence
Deportation, 443
Depressants, effects of, 112–121
    alcohol, 81, 112–115
    barbiturates, 115–117
    benzodiazepines, 117–118
    GHB, 118–119
    inhalants, 119–121
    nonopiate analgesics, 130–131
    opiates, 82–83 (table), 121–123
Depression
    amphetamines and, 104
    ecstasy and, 30
    energy drinks and, 93
    ketamine and, 149
    LSD and, 136
    marijuana and, 13, 22
De Quincey, T., 122
De Sahagún, B., 142
Des Jarlais, D. C., 168
Detoxification therapy, 304
Development theories. *See* Lifecourse/ age-graded theory
Deviance, 67–68
Dexedrine, 103, 109
Dextromethorphan (DXM), 31, 148, 527
DHEA, 429, 434
Diabetes, 92, 383, 393, 398
Diagnostic and Statistical Manual of Mental Disorders (DSM-IV-TR), 53, 55, 85, 87, 138
Dianabol, 428
Dietary/herbal supplements, xxi, 106, 392, 434–435, 437–438
Dietary Supplement Health and Education Act (DSHEA), 434–435, 438
Diet pills, 239
Differential association theory, 77
DiMaggio, J., 356
Direct-to-consumer (DTC) advertising, 404–405, 406, 407–408, 436, 527
Dirtcheapcig.com, 359
Discontinuation syndrome, 159–160
The Disease Concept of Alcoholism (Jellinek), 54
Disease model
    as basis for A.A., 52–54, 333
    of substance use, xvi, 51–55
    summary of, 76

Distillation, 112
Disulfiram (Antabuse), 313
DMT, 145–146, 527
Doblin, R., 30
Doctors, 408, 410–411
Doctor shopping, 443
Dopamine, 28, 30, 82, 105, 110, 158, 527
"Doping" (Boje), 166–167
Dorgan, B., 435
Dou-hyun, Han, 53
Dovzhenko Method, 305
DPA (Drug Police Alliance), xii–xiii
DPA (Drug Policy Alliance), xii–xiii, 279, 326, 477, 479
Drinking. *See* Alcohol; Alcoholism; Binge drinking
Driving under the influence (DUI)
    cost of conviction, 379
    definition of, 527
    drug courts and, 327
    drunk driving laws, 377–386
    enforcement of laws, 371, 388
    number of arrests for, 379
Dropouts
    alcohol use by, 179
    illegal drug use by race/ethnicity, 205, 210
    self-report surveys and, 179
Drug Abuse Resistance Education (D.A.R.E.), 266–273
    costs of, 267
    definition of, 526
    evaluations of, 268
    evaluations of, officials' reaction to, 268–273
    evidence-based practices and, 273
    ineffectiveness of, xviii, 268–269, 270–271, 298
    popularity of, 272
    scare tactics of, 266
    specialized sub-programs, 272–273
Drug Abuse Warning Network (DAWN)
    age and illegal drug use, 198
    definition of, 178, 527
    illegal drug use statistics, 190–194
    marijuana in emergency room admissions, 16–17
    on ecstasy, 26, 27
    race/ethnicity and emergency room visits, 216
Drug agonists, 304, 305–312
Drug and Alcohol Services Information System, 16
Drug antagonists, 304–305, 312–317
Drug controversies/demonization
    bath salts, 41–42
    conclusions about, 43–44

crack cocaine, 24–25
drug epidemics of 2000s/2010s, 39
drug use statistics, 1–2
ecstasy, 26–31
glue-sniffing, 5–7
heroin, 3, 25–26
marijuana, 7–24
methamphetamine, 31–38
overview of, xvi
prescription drugs (synthetic opiates), 42–43
salvia divinorum, 39–40
spice/K2, 40–41
strategies for, 3–4
tobacco, 352
Drug courts, 325–330, 345–346, 347–348
Drug czars, xiii, 14, 15, 17, 25, 26
Drug education programs, xviii
    alternative programs, 273–275, 298
    Drug Abuse Resistance Education,
        266–273, 298
Drug Enforcement Administration (DEA)
    bath salts and, 107
    buprenorphine and, 310
    ecstasy classification and, 466
    marijuana classification and, 17, 154, 155,
        472, 479
    medical marijuana laws and, 154, 472, 473,
        475–476, 477
    methamphetamine and, 34, 469
    on drugs from foreigners, 4, 27
    racism and, 450
    seizure of assets, 465
    state drug law changes and, 482
    synthetic drugs and, 108
Drug epidemics
    crack cocaine, 24–25
    ecstasy, 26–31
    glue-sniffing, 5–7
    heroin, 25–26
    methamphetamine, 31–38
    of 2000s and 2010s, 39–43
    social construction of, 4–5
Drug episodes, 191, 193
Drug Medicalization, Prevention and Control
    Act, 332
Drug mentions, 191
Drug Police Alliance (DPA), xii–xiii
Drug policies, xi–xii
    Controlled Substances Act, 87–88, 89, 107,
        156, 466, 513, 526
    drug testing policies, 286–297
    for legal/illegal drugs, xxi–xxii
    in U.S./other countries, xxii–xxiii
    reform, need for, xiv–xv
    social conflict theory and, 73–76

zero tolerance policies, xviii–xix, 283–286
    See also Drug policies, illegal drugs; Drug
        policies, legal drugs; International drug
        policies; Tobacco policies
Drug policies, illegal drugs
    arrests/incarcerations, 441–445
    asset forfeiture, 462–466
    conclusions about, 484–485
    C.R.A.C.K. program, 453
    drug tax laws, 463, 477
    ecstasy/RAVE Act, 466–468
    legal drug policies vs., 480–484
    mandatory minimum sentences, 453–458
    marijuana laws, 470–480
    methamphetamine legislation, 468–470
    overview of, 440
    public housing evictions, 459–460
    racial/class-based inequality, 446–453
    school zone policies, 458–459
    state drug laws, recent changes in,
        480–484, 485
    student aid, denial of, 461–462
    welfare, denial of, 460–461
Drug policies, international vs. U.S.
    conclusions about, 521–523
    international treaties, 488–490
    in Western countries, 492–514
    severe drug policies, countries with,
        490–492
    U.S. influence/intervention in drug-
        producing countries, 514–521
Drug policies, legal drugs
    alcohol, 365–386, 387–388
    conclusions about, 386–389, 435–438
    issues of, 350–351
    overview of, 350–351
    performance-enhancing drugs, 415–435
    pharmaceutical business, political economy
        of, 410–312
    pharmaceutical products, 392–401
    prescription drug regulation, future of,
        412–415
    prescription drugs, sale/advertising of,
        401–409
    tobacco, 351–365, 387
Drug Policy Alliance (DPA), xii–xiii, 279, 326,
    477, 479
Drug Policy Commission, 501–502
Drug prevention programs
    antidrug advertising campaigns, xviii,
        276–283
    conclusions about, 297–299
    drug education programs, xviii, 265–283
    drug testing policies, 286–297
    zero tolerance policies, xviii–xix, 283–286

Drug-producing countries, 514–521
Drugs, effects of
  ADD prescription drugs, 108–109
  alcohol, 81, 112–115
  amphetamines, 82, 103–106
  antidepressant drugs, 80–81, 157–169
  aphrodisiacs/erectile dysfunction drugs, 81,
    160–164
  barbiturates, 115–117
  bath salts, 107–108
  benzodiazepines, 117–118
  caffeine, 90–92, 93, 94, 435
  cocaine, 82, 97–103
  codeine, 127–128
  conclusions about, 173–175
  depressants, 112–121
  ecstasy, 109–111
  energy drinks, 92–94
  GHB, 118–119
  hallucinogens/psychedelics, 133–146
  heroin, 124–127
  inhalants, 119–121
  marijuana, 151–154
  morphine, 123
  non-opiate analgesics, 130–131
  opiates, 82–83 (table), 121–123
  overview of, xvii, 80–88
  oxycodone, 128–130
  risks of, 86, 94, 134 (figure), 197, 198, 199
  routes of transmission of, 86
  steroids/performance-enhancing drugs, 81,
    165–173
  stimulants, 90–111
  tobacco, 95–97
  U.S. legal drug schedules, 89
Drug safety, 414–415, 436–437
Drug Safety Board, 414–415
Drug "take-back" programs, 129
Drug tax laws, 463, 477
Drug testing policies
  drug testing of workers, xix, 291–297, 299
  in schools, xix, 286–291
Drug trade
  Canadian prescription drugs, 401–404
  drug-producing countries, U.S. influence/
    intervention in, 514–521
  hyper-availability of drugs, 206, 208
  mandatory minimum sentences and, 456,
    457–458
  social conflict theory and, 75–76
  See also Trafficking
Drug treatment
  Alcoholics Anonymous, 332–343
  compulsory treatment programs, xix,
    322–332

  conclusions about, 346–348
  costs of, 303, 320–321
  effectiveness of, 324 (table)
  faith-based substance abuse programs, 347
  issues about, 301–303
  medical marijuana laws, 471–477
  methamphetamine users, 34
  outpatient drug treatment, 343–346
  overview of, xix–xx, 301–303
  pharmacological treatment approaches,
    303–317
  race/ethnicity and, 210
  residential drug treatment programs,
    317–321
  rural areas and, 222
Drug Use Among Racial/Ethnic Minorities
  (National Institute on Drug Abuse), 248
Drug Use Forecasting (DUF) program, 32, 188
Drug use prevention, xviii–xix
Drug use theories
  conclusions about, 76–78
  disease theory, xvi, 46, 51–55
  genetic/biological theories, xvi, 45–46,
    47–51
  nature theories, xvi, 45, 46–47
  overview of, xvi–xvii, 45–46
  psychological theories, xvi–xvii, 46, 56–58
  sociological theories, xvii, 46, 58–76
Drug War propaganda, xii
Drunk driving laws, 377–380
  alcohol-related traffic fatalities, 380–381
  conclusions about, 386, 389
  consequences of, 385
  critical examination of, 380
  dangerous driving-related behaviors,
    383–385
  impairment, determination of, 381–383
DSHEA (Dietary Supplement Health and
  Education Act), 434–435
D:side Project, 275
DTC (Direct-to-consumer) advertising,
  404–405, 406, 407–408, 436, 527
DUF (Drug Use Forecasting) program, 32, 188
Dupont, R., 287
Dupont, R. L., 12
Durbin, K., 33
DXM (Dextromethorphan), 31, 148, 527
Dyer, J. E., 7

Earle, C. W., 52
Earls, L., 288
Earls et al., Board of Education v., 288
Eastman, Dr., 398
E-cigarette, 365
The Economist, 512

Ecstasy (MDMA)
  Britain's drug policies and, 27, 111
  Canada's drug policies and, 27, 510
  definition of, 527, 528
  drug controversies/demonization, 26–31
  effects of, 109–111, 157
  Netherlands' drug policies, 499
  popularity of, 182
  RAVE Act, 466–468
  study using monkeys, 28–30
Ecstasy/RAVE Act, 466–468
Ecuador, 98, 490
ED (erectile dysfunction) drugs, 160–164
Edison, T., 95, 98
Education, drug. See Drug education programs
Educational attainment
  illegal drug use and, 208–209, 216, 218–219
  legal drug use and, 248
Effects. See Drugs, effects of
Effexor, 158, 395
Egypt, ancient, 121, 166
Ehrenreich, B., 293
Ehrlich, R., 474
Eighteenth Amendment, 52, 366, 387
Einstein, A., 368
Elderly persons
  legal drug use patterns of, 234, 236–237
  substance use among, 198–199
Eli Lilly
  Cialis of, 161–162
  criminal activities of, 409
  lawsuits, 410
  LSD and, 136
  politics and, 395
  posting of drug studies, 413
  production of ephedrine, 106
  Prozac approval, 393–394
  thefts of products of, 42–43
Emanuel, Rahm, 478, 484
EMCDDA (European Monitoring Center for
    Drugs and Drug Addiction), 186–187
Emergency contraception, 396–397
Emergency department visits
  antidepressants and, 159
  bath salts and, 41
  DAWN statistics on drug-related visits,
      16–17, 26, 27, 190–193,
      192 (figure), 198
  geriatric patients, 236–237
  marijuana and, 16–17
  NSAIDs and, 131
  pain relievers and, 191
  prescription drugs and, 42, 117,
      129, 232
  race/ethnicity and

Emery, M., 510–511
Employees
  drug testing of, 291–297
  smoking restrictions for, 352, 355
Employment Division of Oregon v. Smith, 143
Enactogens, 110, 527
Energy drinks, 92–94
Engaging Moms Program, 331
England. See Britain
Engs, R., 256
Enoch, ? [this person is not in references], 250
Entorphine, 126
Ephedra, 80, 435
Ephedrine, 103, 106, 512, 527
Epidemics. See Drug epidemics
Epinephrine, 82
EPO (erythropoietin), 172, 425–426
Erectile dysfunction (ED) drugs, 160–164
Ergot, 135
Erythropoietin (EPO), 172, 425–426
Escapism, 75
Escude, N., 425
Esiason, B., 429
ESPAD (European School Survey Project on
    Alcohol and Drugs), 178, 183–184
Estrogen, 14, 166, 169, 171
Estrogen replacement therapy, 163
Ether, 105, 120
Ethics, 64, 322, 501
Ethnicity. See Race/ethnicity
Ethnographic data, 178
Europe
  alcohol treatment programs in, 337
  anti-tobacco legislation in, 352–353
  drug approvals in, 397, 400
  drug policies in, 494–503
  drug testing in, 297, 423
  drug treatment in, 314
  heroin maintenance for addicts,
      311, 492, 499
  supervised injection facilities in, 312
  See also European Union (EU)
European Council of Ministers, 490
European Journal of Pharmacology, 29
European Model Questionnaire (EMQ),
    186–187
European Monitoring Center for Drugs and
    Drug Addiction (EMCDDA), 186–187
European Parliament, 522
European School Survey Project on Alcohol
    and Drugs (ESPAD), 178, 183–184
European Union (EU)
  black market cigarette sales in, 361
  drug-related deaths in, 496
  EMCDDA and, 186–187

harm reduction and, 490
incarceration level in, 2, 442–443
methadone maintenance in, 307
Evictions, 459–460
Evidence-based practices (EBP), 347
Exceptionalism, American, 297, 337, 373
Executive Order 12564, 291–292
Experimental Therapeutics, 29
Exum, W., 423

Failure rates, 322, 342
Fainaru-Wada, M., 416, 431
Fair Sentencing Act, 455, 483
Faith-based drug treatment programs, 347
Fall-off effect, 61
Family. *See* Parents
Family Smoking Prevention and Tobacco
    Control Act, 364
Farah, Dr., 105
Farrell, M., 208
FAS (fetal alcohol syndrome), 114–115, 527
Fatal Analysis Reporting System, 384
Fatal overdose, 18, 82, 152
Faupel, C., 63–64, 322
FBI (Federal Bureau of Investigation), 6
FBN. *See* Federal Bureau of Narcotics
FDA. *See* Food and Drug Administration
Federal Bureau of Narcotics (FBN), 8, 11
Federal Welfare Reform Act, 460
Federation of American Scientists, 468, 471
Federer, R., 425
Females. *See* Gender; Women
Female sexual dysfunction (FSD), 162–163
Fen-phen, 104
Feodorovich, M., 351–352
Fetal alcohol syndrome (FAS), 114–115, 527
Fields, G., 27
Field sobriety tests, 381–383
Filipino-Americans, 252
Filipinos, 216, 217
Fillmore, K., 61
Film, marijuana portrayal in, 9–10, 11
*Final Report of the Presidential Commission
    on Drunk Driving,* 380
Financial aid, student, 461–462
Fingarette, H., 50, 54–55
Finland, 115, 373
First Amendment, 143, 340, 364, 474–475
Fischer, B., 495
Flashbacks, 138
Flavored malt beverages, 113
Flibanserin, 163
Flonase, 405, 406, 408
Florida
    bath salts use in, 42

drug courts in, 327
drug regulation and race in, 448, 452, 456
illegal drug use of Hispanics, 213, 249
increase in venereal disease in, 162
school drug testing in, 289
workplace drug testing in, 294
Flovent, 406
Flushing response, 48, 252
Food, Drug, and Cosmetics Act, 393
Food and Drug Administration (FDA)
    antidepressant drug warning, 160
    approval of pharmaceutical products,
        393–401
    buprenorphine (Subutex) and, 309
    Canadian prescription drugs and, 401–402
    description of, 527
    dietary supplements and, 435
    energy drinks and, 94
    home drug testing kits and, 291
    mission statement of, 415
    pharmaceutical companies and,
        163, 391, 397
    politics and, 396–397
    prescription drug advertising and, 405–407
    prescription drug approval, 108, 436
    prescription drug regulation, future of,
        413–414
    regulation of legal drugs, 395, 398, 424
    ties with pharmaceutical companies,
        399–404, 412
    tobacco regulation and, 363, 364, 365
Food and Drug Administration Improvement
    Act, 414
Football, 428–429
Forbes, 504
Forbes, D., 17
Ford, G., 136
Ford, H., 352
Ford Motor Company, 352
Foreign Assistance Act of 1961, 517
Foreign traffickers
    antidrug advertising campaigns and, 277,
        278–279
    drug "epidemic" attributed to, 4
    of ecstasy, 27
    of heroin, 26
    of methamphetamine, 38
Forest Laboratories, 395, 409, 413
Forfeiture laws, 462–466
Forman, H., 337–338
Forman, R., 337–338
Formication, 105
Fortier, J., 282
Four Loko, 94
Four pillars approach, 495, 507

Fourteenth Amendment, 142, 287
Fourth Amendment, 284, 287, 288
France
    antismoking advertising in, 364
    drug testing in, 297
    drug treatment in, 310
    drunk driving laws in, 379
    minimum-age drinking laws in, 373
Frankfurt Resolution, 494, 495
Franklin, B., 122
Franklin, N., 483
Franz, Ward, 40
Free speech, 364
Freud, S., 100–101
Fried, S., 393
Friedman, M., xiv
Frosch, D. L., 236

GABA (gammaaminobutyric acid), 306
Gahlinger, P., 82, 98, 144, 146
Galanter, M., 339
Gale, C., 172
Galen, 121
Gallagher, R., 407
Gallo, S., 445
Galvin, P., 430
Gama-butrolactone (GBI), 119
Gammaaminobutyric acid (GABA), 306
Gamma-hydroxybutyric acid (GHB), 118–119
Gandhi, A. G., 274
GAO (Government Accountability Office),
    282, 362, 397, 461
Garbott, J. [spelling Garbutt in references],
    337–338
Garmaise, D., 513
Gases (inhalants), 120, 121
Gastfriend, D., 337–338
Gateway drug
    coffee as, 91
    definition of, 528
    lack of evidence for marijuana as,
        12, 20, 266
    marijuana as, research on, 18–19
    marijuana's portrayal as, 11–12, 152
    tobacco as, 97
Gatz, M., 51
GBI (gama-butrolactone), 119
Gender
    drug treatment and, 327
    drug use and, xviii
    illegal drug use and, 177, 199–203
    legal drug use and, 237–241,
        238 (table), 248
General Accounting Office, 458
General strain theory, 71–73

Genetic/biological theories, xvi, 47–51, 76
Genetic markers, 315
Geneva Convention on Drugs, 498
Geography and rural/urban location
    illegal drug use and, 220–222, 221 (table)
    legal drug use and, 258–262
Georgia, 40, 447–448, 469
Gerber, J., 464
Geriatric population. See Elderly
Germany
    drug policies of, 494–495
    drug treatment in, 311
    GlaxoSmithKline and, 409
    herbal and dietary supplement regulation
        in, 434
    minimum-age drinking laws in, 373
    use of cannabis in, 186
Gestrinone, 424
GHB (gamma-hydroxybutyric acid),
    118–119
Gil, A., 214
Gillespie, N., 32, 33
Ginsberg, A., 145
Gladwell, M., 419–420
Glass, S., 269
GlaxoSmithKline
    antidepressant drugs and suicidality, 395
    Canadian prescription drugs and, 402
    criminal activities of, 408
    Levitra of, 161, 406
    Paxil fraud by, 412–413
    posting of drug studies, 413
    prescription drug advertising, 402, 403
    product merchandise, 405
    Ropinirole of, 405
Global Commission on Drug Policy, xv, 522
Glue-sniffing, 5–7, 370
Goldman, B., 419
Gonzales v. Raich, 475
Goode, E., 58, 64–65
Gossop, M., 342
Government
    crack cocaine, demonization of, 24, 25
    demonization of illegal drugs, 3, 4, 24
    ecstasy, portrayal of, 26–27, 28
    heroin, demonization of, 25–26
    marijuana, portrayal of, 11, 13
    methamphetamine, demonization of,
        31–32, 36
    on glue-sniffing, 6
    pharmaceutical company ties, 399–404,
        411–412
    regulation of steroids/dietary
        supplements, 435
    Spice/K2, demonization of, 40–41

Government Accountability Office (GAO),
    282, 362, 397, 461
Graham, D., 399, 412, 414–415
Grant, C., 137
Grant, U. S., 98
Gray, J., 367, 457–458, 465
"Great American Fraud" (Adams), 392
Great Britain. See Britain
Greece
    ancient, 121, 166
    modern, 186, 187, 373, 522
Green, L., 470–471
Green tea, 92
Gregoire, C., 155, 362, 479
Griffin, R., 508
Griffith-Joyner, F., 419–420
Grinspoon, L., 135
Gruenenthal Group, 398
Gullo, K., 26–27
Gumm, E., 36
Gun Free Schools Act, 283
Gusfield, J., 343
Gutwillig, S., 476
Gynecomastia, 169, 172

Hagan, J., 257
Hager, D., 396
Hair tests, 296–297
Halcion, 118
Hallucinogen persisting perceptual disorder
    (HPPD), 138
Hallucinogens/psychedelics, effects of
    description of, 133, 135
    DMT, bufotenine, 145–146
    LSD, 1345–139
    PCP, ketamine, 147–149
    peyote, mescaline, 141–144
    psilocybin, 139–141
    salvia divinorum, 39–40, 144–145
Halstead, W. S., 98
Hamilton, T., 426
Hand sanitizer, misuse of, 39
Hannan, P., 72
Hanson, D., 375, 505
Hanson, R., 399
Harding, W. G., 367–368
Harkin, T., 435
Harm reduction
    in Australia, 493
    in Britain, 499
    in Canada, 504–508, 513–514
    in Germany, 495
    in Netherlands, 499
    in Sweden, 494
    in U.S., 365

move toward, 522–523
    policies for drugs, xxii–xxiii, 490
    principle of, xxii–xxiii
Harper, S., 512–514
Harper's Magazine, 381
Harris, B., 453
Harrison Narcotics Act, 304, 322, 368
Hashibe, M., 153
Hasish, 150, 528
Hatch, O., 434, 435
Hatch Act, 473
Hatch-Harkin law, 434
Hawaii, 40, 411–412
Hawaii Opportunity Probation and
    Enforcement (Project HOPE), 331
Hawkins, G., 4
Hawkins, J., 66
Hays, T., 26
HCG (human chorionic gonadotropin),
    172, 528
HDL (high-density lipoprotein cholesterol), 171
Headaches
    caffeine and, 91, 92, 93
    cluster, 140
    codeine and, 128
    marijuana and, 154
    NSAIDs and, 131
    Ritalin and, 109
Health and Human Services, Department
    of, 435
Health benefits
    of alcohol, 115
    of caffeine, 92
    of tobacco, 97
Health Canada, 402
Health care
    access to, 215, 497
    criminal justice system expenditures, 480
    in Netherlands, 20
    in Spain, 497
    obesity and costs of, 364
    smokers and costs of, 355, 356, 359, 387
Heart attacks, 94, 115, 163, 171, 173,
    399, 400
Heart disease
    alcohol consumption and, 114, 115
    caffeine and, 91
    diet drugs and, 104
    green tea and, 92
    hormone therapy and, 163
    performance-enhancing drugs and, 170, 171
    prescription drugs and, 412
    tobacco and, 354
Heffter, A., 143
Helzer, J., 254–255

Hemocrit test, 425
Hemp
    history of, 7–8
    laws, 470–471
    reintroduced as cash crop, 470
    uses of, 150
Herbal supplements. *See* Dietary/herbal
    supplements
Herbicide, 470, 516
Herd, D., 71
Heredity. *See* Genetic/biological theories
Heroin
    arrests for, 442, 448
    Chinese treatment, 490
    crime and, 3, 63–64
    deaths from, 43, 125, 211
    declining use of, 182
    demonization of, 3, 25–26
    dependence on, 126
    drug antagonists for, 314, 315
    drug controversies/demonization, 25–26
    effects of, 121, 124–127
    heroin maintenance therapy, 311, 499
    methadone maintenance, 127, 304,
        306–309, 492, 493, 528
    supervised injection facilities for, 311–312
HGH (human growth hormone), 172, 173,
    429–430, 528
Hickman, M., 153
High-density lipoprotein cholesterol
    (HDL), 171
Higher Education Act, 461
High Times, 506
Himmelstein, J., 12
Hinchey, M., 414
Hippocrates, 121
Hirschi, T., 65
Hispanics
    crack cocaine use by, 75
    dropout rates, 179, 205, 210
    illegal drug use by, 151, 210–214,
        212 (table)
    incarceration for drug offenses, 447
    inequality in drug laws, 74, 447, 448,
        449–450
    legal drug use patterns of, 247–249
    school zone policies and, 459
    strain theory and, 72
Hitler, A., 35
HIV/AIDS, xv, 5, 14, 167, 172, 187, 307, 491,
    493, 497, 501, 507
Hmong, 217, 218
Hockey, 426–427
Hoffman, A., 135, 139, 140
Hoffman, J., 40

Hoffman-LaRoche pharmaceutical company,
    117, 118
Holder, E., 483
Holland. *See* Netherlands
Holmes, P., 479
Home drug testing kit, 291
Homeless, 184
Homicide, 114, 368, 388
Homosexuality, marijuana use and, 13–14
Hookah bars, 353
Horizontal gaze nystagmus test, 381, 382, 389
Hormonal side effects, 171
Hormone replacement therapy (HRT),
    163, 417
Hospital. *See* Emergency department visits
Hospital for Sick Children, 159
House, forfeiture of, 464
The House I Live In (Women's Christian
    Temperance Union), 266
Housing, evictions from public, 459–460
Howard, G., 114
HPPD (hallucinogen persisting perceptual
    disorder), 138
HRT (hormone replacement therapy),
    163, 417
Hsiao, C., 72
Hubbard, R., 321, 344
Hull, J., 113
Human chorionic gonadotropin (HCG),
    172, 528
Human growth hormone (hGH),
    172, 429–430, 433–434, 528
Hungary, minimum-age drinking laws in, 373
Hunt, N., 522
Hunter, C. J., 420
Hutchinson, A., 470, 483, 521–522
Hydrocodone, 128
Hyman, M., 61
Hyperavailability
    definition of, 528
    of alcohol on college campus, 257
    of drugs in black communities,
        206, 208, 247
Hypersensitization, 48

I-ADAM (International Arrestee Drug Abuse
    Monitoring), 190
Ibuprofen, 130, 131, 295
Idaho, 286, 296, 352
Ignition interlock devices, 378, 380, 385
Illegal drugs
    deaths from, 2, 83 (table)
    driving under the influence of, 479, 505
    legal drugs vs., xii, xvii
    need for drug law reform, xiv–xv

regulation of, xx
use statistics, 1–2, 20 (table)
See also Drug policies, illegal drugs
Illegal drug use, patterns of
   adult offenders, data on substance use by,
      188–194
   age and, 194–199, 227 (figure)
   conclusions about, 223
   Drug Abuse Warning Network statistics,
      190–194
   gender/sex and, 177, 199–203
   international, 178, 185–188, 190
   overview of, 177–178
   race/ethnicity and, 203–218
   rural/urban location and, 220–222,
      221 (table)
   self-report surveys, 178–185
   social class and, 75–76, 177, 218–220
   surveys on adolescent drug use, 26,
      181 (table)–185
   surveys on adult drug use, 185–186
   validity of survey findings, 180
Illegal immigrants, illegal drug use by, 214
Illinois
   ban on Spice in, 40
   Canadian prescription drugs and, 401
   drug testing of school athletes in, 289
   ecstasy trafficking in, 467
   minimum-age drinking laws in, 373
   minimum drinking age and, 374
   tobacco taxes in, 359–360
Imitation, 46, 59
Immigrants, inequality in drug laws, 449–450
Impairment, 381–383
Imperial Tobacco, 360
Incarceration
   compulsory treatment programs, xix,
      322, 323
   drug laws and, xi, 446–448
   for drug offenses, 442–443
   for marijuana offenses, 23, 447
   number in prison on drug charges, 2
   racial/class-based inequality in drug laws,
      xxii, 74, 446–448
Incas, 98
India, 2, 7, 150, 215, 402, 492
Indiana
   alcohol breath test, 383
   bath salts in, 41
   D.A.R.E. in, 268, 269, 271
   drug testing of welfare recipients in, 294
   minimum drinking age in, 386
   prohibition in, 366
Indian Health Service, 214–215
Indian Hemp Drugs Commission, 7

Indolence, 13, 14
Inequality in drug laws, racial/class-based, xxii,
      74, 446–453
Infants. *See* Babies
Informants, 449, 465
Inhalants
   effects of, 119–121
   use by age, 228
   use by race/ethnicity, 243
   use by rural/urban location, 221–222
Injection sites, 311, 492, 495, 507, 511,
      512–513
Inner Change program, 347
Innocent VIII (Pope), 150
*An Inquiry Into the Effects of Ardent
      Spirits Upon the Human Body and Mind*
      (Rush), 52
The Inside of Prohibition (Willebrandt), 368
Inslee, J., 479
Institute of Medicine, 229, 293, 471
Insulinlike growth factor (IGF-1), 172, 528
Interactional theory, 66–67 (figure), 68–69, 77
Internal Revenue Service, 477
International Arrestee Drug Abuse Monitoring
      (I-ADAM), 190
International drug policies
   Afghanistan, 520–521
   certification policies, 517–518
   conclusions about, 521–523
   international treaties, 488–490
   in Western countries, 492–514
   Mexico and other Central American
      countries, 518–520
   minimum legal drinking age, 373
   overview of, 487
   severe drug policies, countries with,
      490–492
   tobacco legislation, 362–363
   U.S. influence/intervention in drug-
      producing countries, 514–521
*International Journal of Impotence
      Research,* 161
International Narcotics Control Board,
      487, 489
International Olympic Committee (IOC),
      418–425, 437
International tobacco legislation, 362–363
International treaties, 362–363, 488–490
Internet
   Canadian prescription drugs on,
      401–402, 436
   products designed to beat drug tests, 295
   tobacco purchases over, 359–360
Interpol, 27, 187, 522
Inuit, 81

Involvement (social bonding theory), 65
IOC (International Olympic Committee), 418–425
Iowa, 40, 357, 366, 401, 468
Iproniazid, 158
Iran, 492
Ireland, 352, 368, 373
Isobutyl nitrite, 120
Isolation
    linguistic isolation, 218
    physical, 222
    social, 72, 75, 199, 213, 218, 219, 222, 247
Isoniazid, 158
Israel, ecstasy trafficking and, 27
Italy
    cocaine use in, 185
    corporate crime in, 409
    GlaxoSmithKline and, 409
    minimum-age drinking laws in, 373
Iversenf, L., 22, 29, 30

Jacksonville, FL, 448
Jacobs, M., 434
Jacobs, R., 424
James, D., 288
James I (England), 94–95
Japan, dangerous driving legislation in, 384
Japanese, 217, 218
Japanese Americans, 252
Jardine-Tweedie, L., 293
Jazz, 11, 151
Jellinek, E., 54
Jenkins Act, 359
Jensen, E., 464
Jerome, L., 30
Johnson, B., 419
Johnson, G., 211
Johnson, J., 450, 452
Johnson & Johnson, 399
Johnston, L., 269, 272
Jones, M., 420
Jones-Webb, R., 72
Jordan, 492
Jorgenson, ? [this person is not in the reference list], 313
Journal of Ethnopharmacology, 146
Journal of Forensic Sciences, 17
Journal of Mental Science, 7–8
Journal of Pharmacology, 29
Journal of the American Medical Association
    on cocaine, 102
    on crack cocaine, 25
    on drug safety, 413
    on government/pharmaceutical companies, 399, 412

on marijuana, 11, 13, 471
on methadone maintenance, 308
on prescription drug advertising, 404
on Ritalin, 109
Jung, J., 54
The Jungle (Sinclair), 392
Justice Department, 476
Justice Policy Institute, 326
"Just Say No To Drugs" message, 267, 268, 270, 271, 272, 275, 276
Juveniles, 32, 283, 285, 328–329, 338, 492, 504. See also Adolescents; Children; Youth

Kaiser Foundation, 404–405
Kaiser Permanente Health Care, 115, 408
Kampia, R., 476, 477
Kandel, D., 18, 205
Kang, Y., 282
Kansas, 40, 369
Kaplan, H., 56, 71
Kaplan, S., 363
Kaufman, M., 363, 396
Kennedy, A. M., 288
Kentucky, 40, 42, 370
Kerlikowske, G., 42, 347, 481
Kerry, J., 402, 410
Ketamine, 147, 148–149
"Kingrats, Chicken Heads, Slow Necks, Freaks, and Blood Suckers: A Glimpse at the Miami Sex-for-Crack Trade" (Inciardi), 64
Kirsch, I., 159
Klecko, J., 428
Kleiman, M., 38
Knight, J., 291
Kolansky, H., 13–14
Kooman, K., 416
Korda, P., 425
Korean Americans, 252
Koreans, 216
Krieger, H., 170
Ksir, C., 125, 147, 148, 343–344
Kubacki, R., 291
Kyrgyz Republic, 492

Labeling theory, 57
The Lancet, 399
Lancet Neurology, 476
Laotians, 217, 218
Larimer, M., 336
Latisse, 405
Laudanum, 122
Law Enforcement Against Prohibition (LEAP), xv

Laws. *See* Drug policies
Lay, D., 457
LEAF (Long Term Economic Advancement
    Foundation), 361
LEAP (Law Enforcement Against
    Prohibition), xv
Learning process, 59–60, 62–63, 273, 275
Leary, T., 137
LeDain Commission Report, 24, 503
Ledger, H., 42
Lee, C., 204
Legal classification of drugs, 87–89
Legal drinking age, minimum, 371–374, 388
Legal drugs
    illegal drugs vs., xii, xvii
    regulation of, xx–xxi
    use statistics, 1
U.S. legal drug schedules, 89. *See also* Drug
    policies, legal drugs
Legal drug use, patterns of
    age and, 225–237
    conclusions about, 262–263
    gender/sex and, 237–241
    race/ethnicity and, 242–253
    rural/urban location and, 258–262
    social class and, 253–257
Legalization
    of drugs, xiv–xv, 347, 485, 497, 501
    of marijuana, 477–480, 498, 505, 508,
        511, 514, 519
Leinwand, D., 27, 282
Lenke, L., 494
Leo XIII (Pope), 98
Leshner, A., 28
Leukfeld, K., 222
Levant, G., 269
Levine, H., 24
Levitra, 161, 162, 406
Levy, S., 291
Lewis, C., 419
Lewis, D. C., 106
Lewis, P., 479
Lewis, R., 428
Lexapro, 395
Lexaprol, 411
Libertarian Party, 284
Librium, 117
Lifecourse/age-graded theory, 67–69, 77, 237
Life magazine, 14
Lillie-Blanton, M., 75, 206
Limbaugh, R., 445
Lindesmith Center, 24
Linguistic isolation, 218
Liver
    alcohol treatment and, 313

cirrhosis of, 82, 114, 174, 193,
    368, 370
diabetes treatment and, 398
nonopiate analgesics and, 131
steroids' effects on, 166, 170, 172
London Olympics, 419, 420
Long, H., 428
Long Term Economic Advancement
    Foundation (LEAF), 361
Long-term residential drug treatment, xix,
    317–322
Lorillard, 364
Los Angeles, CA, methamphetamine deaths
    in, 33
Los Angeles Times
    on drug recalls, 399
    on methamphetamine, 38
    on need for drug law reform, xiv–xv
    on smoking ban, 354
Loughner, Jared, 39–40
Louisiana, 40, 296, 369, 466–467
LSD (lysergic acid diethylamide), 135–139
    route of administration, 86, 137
Luce, H., 137
Lung cancer, 23, 92, 152–153, 354
Luprex (Lupron), 408
Lusane, C., 296
Luvox (Solvay), 395
Luxembourg, 490
Lynskey, M., 19
Lysergic acid diethylamide. *See* LSD

MacCoun, R., 271, 498
MADD (Mothers Against Drunk Driving),
    377, 385
Madison, B., 478
Maginnis, R., 509
Maine, 25, 353, 366
Maintenance therapy, 304
Majer, J. M., 342
Major League Baseball (MLB), 430–434
Malaysia, 491
Male contraception, 167, 417
Male menopause, 163–164
Males. *See* Gender; Men
Malta, 352–353
Maltzman, I., 334
Manco Capac (Incan Emperor), 98
Mandatory minimum sentences, 303, 377,
    453–458
Manfred, R., 431
Manjon-Cabez, A., 497
Mansfield, P., 407
MAO (monoamine oxidase) inhibitors, 158
Mariani, A., 98

Marijuana
    antidrug advertising campaigns and, 8
    arrests for marijuana offenses, 15, 442
    as gateway drug, 11–12, 18–19, 152
    asset forfeiture and, 464
    Australia's drug policies, 493–494
    Britain's drug policies on, 16, 500–501
    Canada's drug policies on, 16, 503–504
    Canadian, export of, 508–510
    classification of, 17, 154, 155, 472, 479
    drug antagonist for, 316, 317
    drug driving laws, 505
    drug laws, inequality in application of, 447
    drug testing and, xix
    drug testing of students, 289
    drug testing of workers, 293, 294–295, 299
    effects of, 151–154
    Germany's drug policies on, 494–495
    Hispanics' use of, 151
    increase in use of, 182–183
    laws, xxiii, 470–480, 485
    legalization of, 477–480, 498, 505, 508,
        511, 514, 519
    medicinal use of, 7, 150, 154, 471–477
    minimum legal drinking age and, 372–373
    misinformation in D.A.R.E. program, 270
    misinformation in DAWN data, 16–17
    misinformation on, 13–14
    Netherlands' drug policies, 496, 498–499
    overdose potential, 2
    portrayal of, 1800's to 1960, 7–12
    portrayal of, 1960s to 1980s, 12–15
    portrayal of, 1980 and beyond, 15–24
    social learning theory and, 59, 63
    Spain's drug policies, 497
    state drug law changes, 154–155
    synthetic, 40–41, 155–157 (table)
    treatment for, 316, 317, 328–329
    use by age, 227 (figure)
    use by elderly, 199
    use by gender, 199–201 (figure),
        200 (figure)
    use by high school students, xiii
    use by social class, 219
    vaporized delivery of, 150
Marijuana Policy Project (MPP), xii–xiii
The Marijuana Smokers (Goode), 63
Marinol (synthetic THC), 473
Marketing, 356–357. See also Advertising
Marlatt, A., 340
Marlatt, G. A., 334, 335, 336
Martin, P., 505
Maryland, 447, 448, 473–474
Massachusetts
    anti-tobacco legislation in, 351

    drunk driving laws in, 378
    heroin "epidemic" in, 26
    prohibition in, 366
    school zone policies, 458
    tobacco taxes in, 359
Masters, A., 315
Mauer, M., 448
Mayo, OJ, 428
Mayo Clinic, 104
MBD (minimal brain dysfunction), 103
McCaffrey, B., xiii, 25, 31, 32, 473, 482, 506
McCaffrey, D., 19
McCain, C., 445
McCain, J., 435
McCardell, J., 375
McCarthy, G., 478
McCordell, J., 372
McGwire, M., 430, 433
McKay, J., 479
McKenna, R., 479
McKinley, W., 100
McNamara, J., xiv
McWilliams, P., 368–369
MDMA. See Ecstasy (MDMA)
MDPV, 107, 108
Media
    demonization of bath salts, 41–42
    demonization of illegal drugs, 3, 4, 24
    on bath salts, 107–108
    on crack cocaine, 24–25
    on ecstasy, 27, 28–30
    on glue sniffing, 6
    on heroin, 25–26
    on marijuana, 8–11, 12–13, 14–15
    on methamphetamine, 31, 32–36,
        37–38, 106
    on methadone maintenance, 309
    on salvia divinorum, 39–40
Medicaid, 408
Medical marijuana
    laws, 154, 471–477, 472, 473,
        475–476, 477
    legalization measures, 477–480, 485
    recent war on, 476–477
Medicinal alcohol, 329
Mello, M., 411
Memory, 21–22, 136
Men
    alcohol-related problems by race/
        ethnicity, 248
    andropause, 163–164
    aphrodisiacs/"erectile dysfunction" drugs,
        160–164
    illegal drug use, 177, 199–203
    legal drug use, 237–241, 238 (table), 248

male contraceptives, 417
See also Gender
Mendoza, N. S., 336
Menninger, K., 144
Menopause, 163, 167
Mensch, B., 205
Mental health, 241
Mental illness, 22, 135, 141, 153–154
Merck pharmaceutical company, 101, 399
Mercury, 410
Merton, R., 69
Mescaline, 136, 141, 143–144
Mescocarb, 421
Mesh-tightening, 328–329
Metabolife, 435
Metadate, 405
Meth-addicted baby, 106
Methadone clinics, 490
Methadone maintenance, 127, 304, 306–309,
    492, 493, 528
Methamphetamine
    ADAM data on, 189, 222
    crime and, 34–35
    definition of, 528
    drug controversies/demonization, 31–38
    effects of, 103, 105–106
    in ecstasy study, 28–29
    legislation, 468–470, 485
"Meth is Death" website, 34
Methylphenidate, 108–109
MET-Rx, 418
Metzner, R., 109
Mexicans, psilocybin use by, 139
Mexico
    alcohol/drug use in, 213
    drug policy and, 522
    drug-related killings/violence in, 518–519
    drug war and, 514–515
    heroin imported from, 211
    marijuana imported from, 510
    methamphetamine imported from,
        38, 468–469
    minimum-age drinking laws in, 373, 375
    steroids imported from, 289
    U.S. certification of, 518
Mexico City Olympic Games, 421
Meyers, A., 343
Michigan, 23, 366, 401, 481
Middle Eastern countries, drug policies of, 492
Miles, D., 428
Military. *See* U.S. military
Miller, W., 334
Miller, W. R., 341
Minimal brain dysfunction (MBD), 103
Minimum legal drinking age, 371–374, 388

Minimum legal smoking age, 352
Minneapolis Star Tribune, 37
Minnesota
    Canadian prescription drugs and, 401
    mandatory minimum sentences, 454
    methamphetamine in, 33
    minimum legal drinking age in, 371, 372
    prohibition in, 366
Minnesota Model, 317, 528
Minorities
    and abstinence, 205, 247
    Britain's drug policies and, 502
    crack baby legislation and, 450–452
    drug testing of workers and, 296–297
    marijuana and, 8
    social conflict theory and, 74
    strain theory and, 71–72
    trafficking of methamphetamine, 38
    underreporting by, 179, 180, 205
    See also African Americans; American
        Indians; Asians and Pacific Islanders
        (APIs); Hispanics
Miron, J. A., 368
Misinformation
    in antidrug advertising campaigns,
        276–279
    in D.A.R.E. program, 266, 271, 273
    on addiction, 33–34
    sources of information on drugs, xi–xiii,
        12, 23–24
    See also Drug controversies/demonization
Mississippi, 40, 42, 369
Missouri, 32, 34, 40, 289, 369
Misuse of Drugs Act, 499–500
Mitchell Report, 433
Mithoefer, M., 30
MK-ULTRA research program, 136
MLB (Major League Baseball), 430–434
Modafinil, 104
Moilanen, R., 266
Monitoring the Future (MTF) study
    Adderall use, 109
    definition of, 528
    description of, 177–178, 528
    drug misinformation and, xiii
    drug use information from, 177–178
    illegal drug use by gender,
        200 (figure)–201 (figure), 218
    illegal drug use by race/ethnicity, 210–211
    illegal drug use by social class, 218,
        220 (figure)
    legal drug use by age, 228, 229 (figure)
    legal drug use by gender, 237–238 (table)
    legal drug use by location,
        220–221 (table), 222

legal drug use by race/ethnicity,
    203, 204 (figure), 242, 248
salvia use, 144
surveys of illegal drug use, 18, 156,
    180–183, 181 (figure)
validity of survey findings, 180
Monoamine oxidase (MAO) inhibitors, 158
Monster energy drink, 94
Montana, 369, 370
Mood disorders, 241
Mooney, J., 142
Moore, S., 35
Moore, W., 13
Moral judgment, 330
Moral model, 51, 52
Morgan, J., 17, 19, 23, 473
Morissette, Dave, 427
Mormon tea, 106
Morning-after contraception products,
    396–397
Morphine
    drug antagonists for, 314
    effects of, 121
    heroin vs., 127
Morral, A., 19
Moscherosch, J. M., 95
Mosher, C., 8, 74
Moskowitz, H., 382
Mothball bags, misuse of, 39
Mothers Against Drunk Driving (MADD),
    377, 385
Motivation, 301–302, 321, 323, 342
MPP (Marijuana Policy Project), xii–xiii
MTF study. See Monitoring the Future (MTF)
    study
Multi-disciplinary Association for Psychedelic
    Studies, 31
Munro, G., 274
Musculoskeletal effects, 171
Mushrooms, 139–141
Muslims, 90
"The Myth of Harmless Marijuana"
    (Walters), 15

NAACP (National Association for the
    Advancement of Colored People), 479
NAC (Native American Church), 142–143, 528
NADCP (National Association of Drug Court
    Professionals), 327
Nadelmann, E., 279, 477
Nahmias, D., 469
The Naked Lunch (Burroughs), 116
Naltrexone, 314–315
Nandrolone, 420, 425
Naperville, IL, 373

Narcolepsy, 103, 104, 397
Narcotic Control Act, 503
Narcotic Drug Act, 503
Narcotics Anonymous (N.A.), 341
Narcotics hospitals, 322
Nasal spray, 162
Nastech, 162
National Academy of Sciences, 21
National Academy of Sciences Institute of
    Medicine, 23
National Academy Press, 471
National Association for the Advancement of
    Colored People (NAACP), 479
National Association of Counties, 33
National Association of Criminal Defense
    Lawyer, 326
National Association of Drug Court
    Professionals (NADCP), 327
National Basketball Association (NBA),
    427–428
National Center for Drug-Free Sport, 418
National Center for Education Statistics, 285
National Center on Addiction and Substance
    Abuse, 195, 480
National Centers for Health Statistics
    (NCHS), 191
National Collegiate Athletic Association
    (NCAA), 417–418, 437
National Commission Against Drunk Driving
    (NCADD), 377
National Commission on Marijuana and Drug
    Abuse, 138–139
National Community Pharmacists
    Association, 129
National Council on Alcoholism, 334
National Drug Control Strategy of 2003
    (ONDCP), 476, 490
National Drug Control Strategy of 2112
    (ONDCP), 483
National Drug Strategy, Australia, 492–494
National Drug Strategy, Canada, 513
National Drug Strategy, U.S., 287, 292
National Football League (NFL), 173
National Highway Traffic and Safety
    Administration (NHTSA)
    alcohol-related traffic fatalities and,
        380–381
    distracted driving and, 384
    field sobriety tests and, 382, 389
National Hockey League (NHL), 426–427
National Household Survey on Drug Abuse,
    19, 20, 32, 207 (table), 372–373
National Institute of Justice
    ADAM program, 188–190
    on methamphetamine, 32, 33

National Institute on Alcohol Abuse and
    Alcoholism, 337
National Institute on Drug Abuse (NIDA)
    antidrug advertising campaigns and, 280
    definition of drug abuse, 325
    ecstasy study and, 28
    heroin survey, 25
    legal drug use by gender, 240
    mandatory minimum sentences and, 455
    marijuana misinformation of, 12, 23–24
    medical marijuana laws and, 473
    NIDA-5, 189
    on Hispanics' drug use, 248
    on inaccuracy of drug tests, 296
    on nicotine vaccine, 315
National Institutes of Health (NIH),
    308, 411–412, 413, 471
National Organization for the Reform of
    Marijuana Laws (NORML)
    information drawn from, xii–xiii
    marijuana as gateway drug and, 21
    on adolescent marijuana treatment
        admissions, 16
National Post, 505
National Research Council, 293
National Review, xiv
National Safety Council, 384
National Survey on Drug Use and Health
    (NSDUH)
    drug use information from, 177, 178
    illegal drug use by Hispanics,
        211–212 (table)
    illegal drug use by race/ethnicity, 204, 206,
        211–212 (table)
    legal drug use by gender, 240
    surveys of illegal drug use, 184–185
Native American Church (NAC), 142–143, 528
Native Americans. *See* American Indians
Nature perspective, xvi, 46–47, 76
NBA (National Basketball Association),
    427–428
NBC, 422
NCAA (National Collegiate Athletic
    Association), 417–418, 437
NCADD (National Commission Against
    Drunk Driving), 377
NCHS (National Centers for Health
    Statistics), 191
Nebraska, 32, 206, 222, 296, 366
Needle-exchange programs, 490, 493, 495, 497
Neighborhood disadvantage, 209–210
Nervous system. *See* Central nervous system
Netherlands
    anti-tobacco legislation in, 352–353
    drug education in, 275

drug policies of, 21, 497–499
drug testing in, 297, 423
drug treatment in, 311
heroin maintenance for addicts, 311
illegal drug use over lifetime, 20 (table)
marijuana studies in, 24
minimum-age drinking laws in, 373
prescription drug advertising in, 405
U.S. drug czar on drugs in, xiii
Net-widening, 328
Neurons, 81–82
Neurotonin, 396, 397, 409
Neurotransmitters, 81–82, 95, 158, 528
Nevada, 369, 473–474
Newcomb, M., 270
New England Journal of Medicine, 471
New Hampshire, 366, 401
New Jersey, 289, 459, 464–465
New Life Partners, 341
New Mexico, 35, 211, 378
Newsweek
    glue-sniffing article in, 6
    marijuana article in, 11
    methamphetamine articles in, 32–33
    pharmaceutical advertising in, 400, 402
New York
    drug law changes in, 481–482
    drug treatment in, 326
    drunk driving laws in, 377
    marijuana offenders in, 23
    prohibition in, 366
    tobacco settlement money, 361
    tobacco taxes in, 358
New York, NY
    alcohol regulation in, 369
    anti-tobacco legislation in, 353, 354
    drop in cocaine use in, 189
    marijuana sentences in, 23
    tobacco taxes in, 358, 359
New Yorker, 11, 51
New York Times
    antidrug advertising campaigns, 277
    on amphetamines, 104
    on denial of student aid, 461
    on Ed Rosenthal case, 474
    on glue-sniffing, 6
    on marijuana in Canada, 506
    on need for drug law reform, xiv, xv
    on nicotine replacement therapy, 306
    on salvia divinorum, 39–40
    on pharmaceutical companies,
        401, 413
    on Plan B, 396
    on tobacco settlement, 362
    tobacco advertisement, 363

New Zealand, 312, 407
NFL (National Football League), 173
NHL (National Hockey League), 426–427
Nichols, D., 141
Nicholson, R., 511
Nicorette, 306
Nicotine, 95–96. *See also* Tobacco
Nicotine replacement therapy (NRT),
    86, 305–306
Nicotine vaccine, 315
NIDA. *See* National Institute on Drug Abuse
NIDA-5, 189, 528
Nitrites (inhalants), 120, 121
Nitrous oxide (laughing gas), 120
Nixon, R., 3
Nonopiate analgesics, 130–131
Nonsteroidal anti-inflammatory drugs
    (NSAIDs), 131
Nonsteroidal hormones, 172
NORML. *See* National Organization for the
    Reform of Marijuana Laws
North Carolina, 296, 351, 358, 361
North Dakota, 33, 36, 40, 362
Norway, 297, 337, 352–353, 373
NRT (nicotine replacement therapy),
    86, 305–306
NSAID (nonsteroidal anti-inflammatory
    drugs), 131
NSDUH. *See* National Survey on Drug Use
    and Health
Nuprin, 295
Nutmeg, misuse of, 39
Nutt, David, 39, 111

Oakland, CA, 459–460
Obama, B., and administration
    D.A.R.E. program and, 273
    drug policy and, 484
    drug treatment and, 303, 326, 347
    international drug policy and, 518–519,
        520–521
    legalization of marijuana and, 480
    medical marijuana and, 155, 476
    opium eradication and, 520–521
    supervised injection facilities and,
        311–312
    war on drugs and, 476
Office of Management and Budget, 281
Office of National Drug Control Policy
    (ONDCP)
    antidrug advertising campaigns, 276–283
    drug misinformation from, xiii
    faith-based substance abuse programs, 347
    marijuana report of, 15–17, 18, 21–22
    medical marijuana laws and, 474

National Drug Control Strategy of 2003
    on drug courts, 326
    on ecstasy, 27, 111
    on global drug policies, 522
    on marijuana and mental illness, 22
    on methadone, 308
    on student drug testing, 290
    state drug law changes and, 483
Office of Prescription Drug Promotion, 406
Off-label use, 397
O'Grady, M., 3
Ohio, 283, 284, 289, 290, 379, 448, 450
Ohlin, L. E., 69
Ohta, L. C., 464
Oklahoma, 23, 288, 369, 370, 468–469
Olsen, K., 361
Olson, F., 136
Olsson, B., 494
Olympic Games, 53, 173, 416, 418–425,
    419, 437
"On Coca" (Freud), 100–101
ONDCP. *See* Office of National Drug Control
    Policy
One-leg stand test, 381–382, 389
Operant conditioning, 59
Operation Hammer, 448
Opiates
    dependence on, 122–123, 232, 314–315
    drug antagonists for, 314–315
    effects of, 82–83 (table), 121–123
    heroin maintenance for addicts,
        311, 492, 499
    increase in use of, 234
    methadone maintenance, 127, 304,
        306–309, 492, 493, 528
    pharmacological treatment options
Opioids, 121
Opium
    decline in global cultivation of, 187
    history of, 121–122
    in Afghanistan, 279, 520–521
    RAVE Act and, 467
Opium and Narcotic Drug Act, 503
Oral naloxone, 310
Oransky, I., 407
Oregon
    drug test fraud and, 296
    drug testing in schools, 287–288, 289
    heroin in, 43
    legalization of marijuana and, 478, 480
    methamphetamine in, 35
    prohibition in, 366
    property crime in, 35
Oregonian (newspaper), 35
Osborne, T., 32

Ostapchuk, Nadzeya, 173
Outpatient drug treatment, 343–346
    cognitive behavioral therapy, 345
    definition of, 301
    effectiveness of, 344–345
Outsiders (Becker), 59, 151
Overdose
    marijuana and, 2
    of alcohol, 114
    of GHB, 119
    of heroin, 125, 211
    of methadone, 127
    of opiate-based analgesics, 82, 83 (table),
        130 (figure)
    of PCP, 147
    of prescription drugs, 192
Oversampling, 182
Owen, Philip, 507
Oxycodone, 128–130
OxyContin
    adolescents' use of, 258, 259 (figure)
    effects of, 128–129
    marketing of, 409

Pacific Islanders, 81
Paddock, S., 19
Pain, 123, 125, 128, 129, 130–131, 135
Palmer, A., 356
Palmer, M., 494
Panic attacks, 138
Paracelsus, 122
Parents
    crack baby legislation, 450–452
    illegal drug use by black youths and,
        208, 247
    social bonding theory and, 67
    social learning theory and, 60–62
Parke-Davis, 98, 147
Partnership for a Drug-Free America (PFDFA),
        25, 26, 276–283
Paterson, D., 481–482
Patterson, T., 236
Paxil, 157, 158, 159–160, 395, 408
PDUFA (Prescription Drug User Fee Act), 394
PED, 173, 238–239
Pedersen, N., 51
Peele, S., 55, 339
Peers
    drug use and, 65
    self-derogation model and, 56–57
    social bonding theory and, 66–67
    social learning theory and, 62, 69
Pendery, M., 334
Pennsylvania, 288–289, 296
Peptide hormones, 417

Percocet, 128, 445
Percodan, 128
Performance-enhancing drugs
    effects of, 119
    use by age, 228
    use by gender, 238–239
Performance-enhancing drugs, regulation of,
        391, 415–435, 437
    herbal/dietary supplements, 434–435
    International Olympic Committee, 418–425
    NCAA program, 417–418
    overview of, xxi
    professional sports, 425–434
    rationale for, 415–417
Perkins, D., 429
Perkins, H. W., 376
Peru, 515, 516
Pesticides, 470
Pettinati, H., 337–338
Peyote, 141–144
PFDFA. *See* Partnership for a Drug-Free
        America
Pfizer
    Celebrex of, 400
    criminal activities of, 409
    prescription drug advertising, 405, 406, 407
    ties with government agencies, 400,
        404, 412
    Viagra of, xii, 161, 162, 406
    Zoloft of, 395
Pharmaceutical companies
    advertising of, 404–408
    Canadian prescription drugs and, 401–404
    clinical trial/side effects manipulation by,
        397–400
    criminal practices of, 408–409
    drug regulations and, 410–412
    FDA approval of products, 393–401
    lawsuits, 412–413
    off-label use and, 397
    political economy of business, 410–412
Pharmaceutical products, regulation of,
        392–401
    Canadian products, restriction of sales of,
        401–404
    early legislation, 392–393
    FDA approval of, 393–401
    future of, 412–415
Pharmachem, 296
Pharmacia, 400, 409
Pharmacological drug treatment, 303–317
    definition of, 301
    description of, xix–xxi
Pharmacological treatment options
    Dovzhenko Method, 305

drug agonists, 305–312
drug antagonists, 312–317
history of, 304
Pharmacotherapy, 303–304, 336, 529
Pharming, 228
Phelps, Michael, 419
Phenobarbital, 116
Phenylpropanolamine (PPA), 398
Philip Morris, 363, 364
Philippines, 492
Physical dependence
definition of, 529
on drugs, 85, 86, 174, 175
on opiates, 122–123
Physician-prescribed alcohol, 366–367
Piper, B., 467, 476
Placebos, 393
Plan B, 396–397
Poison Control Centers, 39, 40, 41, 42
Poland, minimum-age drinking laws in, 373
Police
asset forfeiture and, 465
impairment determination by, 381–383
See also Drug Abuse Resistance Education
(D.A.R.E.)
Policies. See Drug policies
Political economy, of pharmaceutical business,
410–412
Political views, 49
Pollan, M., xi–xii, 151
Polyphenols, 92
Pope, H., 144, 239
Portland, OR, 448–449
Portugal, 187, 373, 490, 495–496
Positive (Reiterer), 416
Posttraumatic stress disorder, 110–111
Pound, D., 420, 427, 431
Poverty
American Indians and, 250–251
illegal drug use and, 208, 217, 219
legal drug use and, 247
social conflict theory and, 75
strain theory and, 72
Power, xvii
Power differentials, 73, 78
PPA (phenylpropanolamine), 398
Pregnancy
antidepressant drugs and, 159
crack baby legislation, 450–452
fetal alcohol syndrome, 114–115, 527
Prempro, 163
Prescription drugs
addiction to pain killers, 130
advertising, 401–409
amphetamines, effects of, 82, 103–106

costs of, 401, 436
deaths from, xi, 42, 83 (table), 398, 412
drug testing and, 294–295
emergency room visits for, 42
"epidemic," 42–43
international policies and, 489
stimulants and select opiates, 235 (figure)
use by elderly, 198–199
use by elderly persons, 234, 236
use by gender, 240–241
use by location, 258, 260
use by race/ethnicity, 243
use by rural/urban location, 221–222
use by social class, 254, 255 (figure)
use patterns by age, 42
use statistics, 1
Prescription drugs, regulation of
advertising, 404–408
Canadian products, sale of, 401–404
early legislation, 392–393
FDA approval of, 393–401
future of, 412–415
overview of, xxi
Prescription Drug User Fee Act (PDUFA), 394
Presence restriction ordinance, 373
Presidential Commission on
Drunk Driving, 377
Press, S., 424
Prevacid, 406
Prevention. See Drug prevention programs;
Drug use prevention
Priestly, J., 120
Prison
compulsory treatment programs in, 323
increase in population of, xxi
See also Incarceration
Prisoners in 2010 (Bureau of Justice
Statistics), 74
Problem behavior theory, xvii, 46, 57–58, 77
Productivity, 292
Professional sports, 425–434
Prohibition, 365–369, 387–388
Project HOPE (Hawaii Opportunity Probation
and Enforcement), 331
Propaganda, xii, xiv, See also Drug
controversies/demonization;
Misinformation
Propecia, 405
Property crime, 3, 34–35, 307, 501
Proposition 19 (CA), 477–478
Proposition 36 (CA), 330–331
Proposition 200 (AZ), 332, 492
Proposition 215 (CA), 482
Propulsid, 399
Provigil, 104, 397

Prozac, 157, 158, 160, 393–394, 395
Pseudoephedrine
    attributed to foreigners, 38
    definition of, 529
    in cold medications, 106
    methamphetamine legislation and, 468, 470
Psilocybin, 139–141
Psychedelics, definition of, 135. *See also*
        Hallucinogens/psychedelics, effects of
Psychiatry, 135–136
Psychmedics, 291
Psychoactive effects, 80, 174
    drug antagonists block, 313–315
Psychoactive substances
    definition of, 529
    drug policies, xviii
    effects of, xvii, 80–82
    use of, reasons for, xvi–xvii
Psychological dependence
    definition of, 529
    drug antagonists for, 315–316
    on drugs, 85, 86, 174–175
    on heroin, 126
Psychological theories
    on substance use, xvi–xvii, 56–58
    problem behavior theory, 46, 57–58
    self-derogation model, 56
    summary of, 76–77
Psychosocial therapy, 345
Psychotherapeutic drugs, 529
Public housing evictions, 459–460
Public places, bans on smoking in, 352–355
Puck Technology, 205
Pulitzer, C., 423
Punishment, 59, 60, 74
Purdue Pharma, 128, 129, 409
Pure Food and Drug Act, 363, 392–393
Purple jelly, 231

Quaalude, 117
Quest Diagnostics, 295
Quigley, L., 336

Race/ethnicity
    adolescent illegal drug use, 210–213,
        212 (table)
    alcohol advertising and, 247
    alcohol use by, 71–72, 242–245, 243 (table),
        244 (table), 245–246 (table), 248–249
    antidepressant use by, 245
    arrests for drug offenses and, xxii
    binge drinking by, 242, 246 (figure),
        253 (figure)
    crack cocaine and, 25
    CRACK program and, 453

drug policies and, 446–453
drug testing and, 296–297
drug treatment and, 310, 328
drug use and, xvii, xviii
illegal drug use by, 177, 203–218
legal drug use and, 242–253
legal drug use patterns, 243–244 (table), 252
mandatory minimum sentences and,
        453–458
racial/class-based inequality in drug laws,
        74, 446–453, 484
school zone policies and, 458–459
social class/alcohol use and, 72, 246–247
social class/illegal drug use and, 218, 219
social conflict theory and, 74–75
strain theory of drug use and, 71–72, 77–78
zero tolerance policies and, 285
Racism, 74, 209, 245, 248, 450, 488
Ragge, K., 340–341
Raich, Gonzales v., 475
Ramirez, Manny, 433
Rand Corporation, 333–335
Rape drug, 118, 119
Rausch, M., 284
RAVE Act, 466–467, 485, 502
Raves, 26
Ray, O., 125, 147, 343–344
RCMP (Royal Canadian Mounted Police), 27,
        31, 504
RCPA (Research Council on Problems of
        Alcohol), 53–54
Reagan, R., and administration, 14, 25,
        291–292, 362, 371, 377, 380
Reasoner, H., 334
Red Bull, 92
Redding, S., 284
Reefer Madness (film), 10, 11
Reform, xiii, xiv–xv
Rehnquist, W., 460
Reinarman, C., 24, 51, 489
Reinforcement, 59, 69
Reisser, O., 165
Reiterer, W., 416
Religion
    faith-based substance abuse programs, 437
    peyote use by NAC, 143–144
    twelve steps of A.A. and, 339–341
Research Council on Problems of Alcohol
        (RCPA), 53–54
Reservations, Indian, 370
Residence, drug use and, 177
    illegal drug use and, 220–222, 221 (table)
    legal drug use and, 258–262
Residential drug treatment programs, 317–321
    definition of, 301

effectiveness of, 321
models of, 317
therapeutic communities, xix, 318–321
Resocialization, 317, 320, 321
Restorative justice, 325
Restoril, 118
Reuter, P., 271, 498
Rey, J., 22
Rezulin, 398
Rhabdomyolysis, 398
Rhode Island, prohibition in, 366
Ricaurte, G., 28–30
Riley, R., 444
Ringwalt, C., 274
Rio Arriba County, NM, 211
Risks, of drug use, 86, 94, 134 (figure),
    174, 184
Risk-taking, 16, 46, 47, 58, 77, 201
Ritalin, 108–109, 234, 405, 424
Rivas, O., 177
RJ Reynolds, 357, 360–361, 362, 364
Robitussin, 148, 231
Robo-dosing, 148
Rockefeller drug laws, 481–482
Roddick, A., 425
Rodriguez, D., 433
Rohypnol (flunitrazepam), 118, 119
Rolleston Committee, 499
Rome, ancient, 166
Ropinirole, 405
Rose, D., 428
Rosen, W., 14–15, 90, 126, 137, 147, 148, 271
Rosenbaum, D., 268
Rosenbaum, M., 270, 271, 275, 290, 374
Rosenthal, E., 474
Ross, H. L., 115, 386
Rost, P., 404
Rostenkowski, D., 445
Roux, P., 310
Roy, A., 428
Royal Canadian Mounted Police (RCMP), 27,
    31, 504
Rozga, David, 40
Rubin, B., 356
Rural/urban location
    illegal drug use and, 220–222, 221 (table)
    legal drug use and, 258–262
Rusedski, G., 425
Rush, B., 52, 97
Russell, State v., 454
Russia, 305, 351–352, 373, 490–491
Ryan, M., 42

Sacramento, CA, 189
Safe and Drug-Free Schools Act, 283

Safe injection sites, 311, 492, 495, 507, 511,
    512–513
Safety First: A Reality Based Approach to
    Teens, Drugs, and Drug Education
    (Rosenbaum), 275
Salazar, W., 211
Salvia divinorum, 39–40, 144–145
SAMHSA (Substance Abuse and Mental
    Health Services Administration), 1, 191
Sandoz Laboratories, 135–136, 140
San Francisco, CA
    Bay Area Laboratories Company, 420, 424
    drug courts in, 474–475
    marijuana legalization and, 478
San Francisco Chronicle, 430–431
Santa Cruz, CA, 475
Saskin, T., 426
Satcher, D., 215
Satel, S., 38
Saudi Arabia, 492
SBIRT (screening, brief interventions, referral
    to treatment), 193
Scalia, J., 287–288
Schedule I drug, 40, 89, 110, 111, 138–139,
    155, 156, 472, 529
Schedule II drug, 89, 109, 155, 445, 529
Schedule III drug, 89, 438
Schedule IV drug, 89
Schedule V drug, 89
Schering-Plough, 405, 408, 411
Schilling, C., 430
Schizophrenia, 135–136, 153–154
Schlesinger, L., 453
Schlosser, E., 23, 454
Schmoke, K., xiv
Schneider, J., 310
Schools
    drug testing policies, 286–291
    school zone policies, 458–459
    zero tolerance policies, xviii–xix,
        283–286, 298
    See also Students
Schulhofer, S., 457
Schultz, G., 522
Schultz, H., 91
Schumer, Chuck, 94
Schuster, C., 75, 206
Schwarzenegger, Arnold, 478
Science, 28, 29, 30, 334
Scientific American, 8, 11
Scotland, 115, 190
Scott, R., 483
Screening, brief interventions, referral to
    treatment (SBIRT), 193
Screw, D. J., 231

Seattle, WA
    antismoking legislation in, 354–355
    drug law changes in, 481
    racial/class-based inequality in drug laws, 448
    use of K2 in, 40
Seconal, 116
Secondhand smoke, 352, 353, 354
Secular Organizations for Sobriety, 343
Securitization, 362
Seizures, 465, 484–485
Selective interaction/socialization model, 64–65
Selective serotonin reuptake inhibitors (SSRIs),
    158, 395, 529, 530
Self-derogation model, xvi–xvii, 46, 56–57,
    76–77
Self-efficacy, 340–341, 342
Self-esteem, 248, 251, 267. See also Self-
    derogation model
Self-inflicted pain, 47
Self-Management And Recovery Training
    (SMART), 343
Self-report surveys, 54
    of illegal drug use, 178–185, 181 (table)
    underreporting in, 179–180
Selig, B., 432, 433
Sellman, J. D., 336
Semeron, 180
Senate Appropriations Committee, 281
Sensitization theory, 48
Sentences
    drug treatment programs and, 329, 330
    for marijuana offenses, 23
    in Asian countries, 491–492
    in Canada, 503, 504
    in Europe, 494, 496, 498, 499–500
    in Russia, 491
    lengthening for drug offenses, 440
    mandatory minimum sentences, 377, 453–458
    race/ethnicity and, 74
Seoul Olympics, 53, 416, 419, 420, 422
Sernyl, 147
Sernylan, 147
Serotonin, 82, 110, 149, 157, 158, 529
Seroxat, 160
Serturner, F., 123
Serzone, 158
Sex education, 274
Sexual activities
    aphrodisiacs/"erectile dysfunction" drugs, 81
    glue-sniffing and, 6
    marijuana use and, 9, 11, 13–14
    teenage sex and protection, 268
Sexual side effects, 171
Shafer Commission Report, 24
Shaffer, D. K., 327, 329, 332, 346
Shapiro, S., 347

Shedler, J. S., 270
Shenk, J., 276
Shepard, E., 267
Shepard, R., 146
Sher, Brian, 40
Shields, B., 405
Shultes, R., 149
Sidney, S., 23
Siegel, R., 35
Sight, 121, 162
Simi, N., 51
Sinclair, U., 392
Single Convention on Narcotic Drugs, 488
Sinsemilla, 17, 529
60 Minutes, 334
Skager, R., 275
Skiba, R., 284
Sklansky, D., 455
Slang, 64
Slow-release oral morphine (SROM), 309
SMART (Self-Management And Recovery
    Training), 343
Smiles (2C-L), 111
Smith, E., 35
Smith, Employment Division of Oregon v., 143
Smith, O., 295
Smith, R., 52–53, 54
Smuggling, cigarette, 360–361
Smyer, M., 51
Sobell, L. C., 334, 335, 337
Sobell, M., 334, 335, 337
Social class
    alcohol use by, 75, 254 (table)–257,
        255 (table)
    alcohol use by race/ethnicity and,
        72, 246–247
    consequences of alcohol use and, 257
    drug policies and, 443–445
    drug treatment and, 327
    drug use and, xvii, xviii
    illegal drug use and, 75–76, 177, 218–220
    inequality in drug laws and, xxii, 74–75,
        446–453
    legal drug use and, 218, 219–220 (figure),
        253–257
    tobacco tax and, 358
    tobacco use and, 254, 358
    zero tolerance policies and, 285
Social conflict theory, 73–76
Social control, 329
Social control/bonding theories, xvii, 65–67, 77
Social desirability, 180, 530
Social development model, 66
Social host laws, 373
Social isolation, 72, 75, 199, 213, 218, 219,
    222, 247

Social learning theory
    differential association theory and, 59, 60
    self-derogation model and, 57
    substance use and, xvii, 46, 59–62
    summary of, 77
Social norms marketing, 376
Socioeconomic status
    illegal drug use by race/ethnicity and, 215
    of American Indians, 215
    of Asians, 216–217
Sociological theories
    anomie/strain theories, xvii, 69, 71–73
    differential association theory, 58–59
    lifecourse/age-graded theory, 67–69
    on substance use, xvii, 58–76
    social conflict theory, 73–76
    social control/bonding theory, xvii,
        65–67, 77
    social learning theory, 58, 59–62
    subcultural theories, 62–65
    summary of, 77
Soeffing, J. M., 310
Solowij, N., 21–22
Solvay, 395
Solvents, 7, 119, 121
Song, S., 420
Sosa, S., 431
Souder, M., 509–510
Souter, D., 284
South Africa, minimum-age drinking laws in, 373
South Australian Royal Commission, 492
South Carolina, 354, 450–451, 482
Southeast Asians, 217, 252
Southin, M., 505
Spain, 186, 373, 490, 497
Speakeasies, 367
Specter, M., 426
Spending
    on drug testing of workers, 292, 293
    on lobbying by pharmaceutical companies, 410
    on marketing by pharmaceutical companies,
        410–411
    on prescription drug advertising, 404–405
    on rights to broadcast Olympics, 422
    on tobacco advertising, 356–357
Spice/K2, 40–41, 155–157 (table)
Spirituality
    faith-based substance abuse programs, 347
    peyote use by NAC, 142–143
    twelve steps of AA, 338–341
Spitzer, E., 412
Spokesman-Review, 32
Sports. See Performance-enhancing drugs;
    Performance-enhancing drugs, regulation
    of; Steroids
Sports Illustrated, 171, 428–429, 430

Spraying, chemical, 515, 516–517
SR141716 drug antagonist, 316, 317
SROM (slow-release oral morphine), 309
SSRIs (selective serotonin reuptake inhibitors),
        158, 395, 529, 530
Stamper, N., xiv–xv, 476
Starbucks, 91
Star Scientific, 362
States
    alcohol use by state, 260 (figure), 261 (figure)
    drug law changes, 154–155, 480–484, 485
    Internet tobacco sales and, 359–360
State v. Russell, 454
Stay'N Out program, 323
Stephenson, R. L., 98
Stereotypes, 214, 218
Steroids
    administration routes, 166
    baseball players and, 430–431
    basketball players and, 427–428
    demonization of, 417
    dosages, 168
    drug testing of students, 289
    effects of, 81, 165–173
    football players and, 428–429
    hockey players and, 427
    medical use of, 167
    Olympic athletes and, 419, 420–421, 423
    regulation of, 418, 435
    THG, 424, 429
    use by gender, 170
Stevens, Calvin, 148
Steves, R., 479
Stillbirth, 91
Stimulants, effects of, 90–111
    amphetamines, 82, 103–106
    caffeine, 90–92
    cocaine, 82, 97–103
    tobacco, 95–97
St. Louis Dispatch, 8
Stolberg, S., 401
Stone, M., 160
Strachan, S., 479
Strain theories, xvii, 69, 71–73
Street, P., 419
Strokes, 399
Studdert, D., 411
Student aid, denial of, 461–462
Students
    alcohol and tobacco use by, 229 (figure)
    cigarette giveaways and, 357
    college campus drinking, 374–377, 388
    D.A.R.E. program and, xviii, 266–273
    denial of financial aid, 461–462
    drug testing policies, 286–291, 298
    illegal drug use by gender, 200 (figure)

illegal drug use by race/ethnicity,
    203–204 (figure), 211, 212 (table)
illegal drug use students outside U.S., 183–184
legal drug use by gender, 239 (table)–241
legal drug use by location, 259 (figure)
legal drug use by social class,
    254 (table)–257, 255 (table)
minimum drinking age and, 372
MTF survey of drug use, 181 (table)–183
prescription drug use by, 228, 232
steroid use by, 418
zero tolerance policies and, xviii–xix,
    283–286, 375
See also Adolescents; Youths
Students for Sensible Drug Policy, 461
Subcultural theories, 56, 62–65
Subculture
    definition of, 63
    self-derogation model and, 56
    slang in, 64
Substance abuse, substance dependence vs., 87
Substance Abuse and Crime Prevention Act
    (SACPA), 330–331
Substance Abuse and Mental Health Services
    Administration (SAMHSA), 1, 191,
    273–274, 310
Success rates, of treatment, 302–303, 311, 316,
    322–323, 337, 340
Suicidality, 160, 394–395
Suicide, 11, 91, 114, 117
Sullivan, R., 420
Sullum, J., 3, 19, 32, 97, 112–113, 277,
    449–450, 456, 467
Sun Dance ceremony, 47
Sunday, B., 368
Supervised injection facilities (SIF), 311–312
Supreme Court. See U.S. Supreme Court
Surgeon General, 356
Survey Graphic (magazine), 8, 10
Surveys
    adolescent illegal drug use, 183–184
    limitations of, 179–180
    on adult drug use, 185–186
    on illegal drug use, 177–178
    self-report surveys of illegal drug use, 178–180
    validity of, 180
Suspensions
    administrative license, 378, 380
    school, 284, 285
Sutherland, P. T, III, 412
Sweat patch tests, 296, 297
Sweden, 297, 373, 494
Swetlow, K., 36–37
Switzerland, 110, 311, 337, 373
Sydenham, T., 122
Sydney Olympics, 416, 420, 422

Synanon drug treatment program, 318–319
Synesthesia, 137
Synthetic Drug Abuse Act, 108

TA-CD drug, 315–317
Tactile hallucination, 105
Tajikistan, 492
Tam, T., 244–245
Tampa Bay Tribune, 421
Tandy, K., 511
Tanning, addiction to, 55
TAP Pharmaceuticals, Inc., 406, 408
Taurel, S., 410
Tax Equity and Fiscal Responsibility Act, 358
Taxes
    drug tax laws, 463, 477
    on tobacco, 96, 357–361, 387
Taylor, B., 315
TCs (therapeutic communities), xix, 318–321
Tea, 91, 92
Teenagers. See Adolescents; Youths
Teen Challenge program, 347
Telephones, cellular, 383–384, 389
Television advertising, 356
Temperance movements, alcohol, 365
Tennessee, 34, 38, 40, 369, 469
Tennis, 425
Terminal cancer patients, 136
Terra, M., 342
Terrorism, antidrug advertising and,
    278–279, 280
Testing, 286–297
Testosterone
    andropause and, 163–164
    baseball and, 430, 433
    deficiency of, 167
    depression and, 157–158
    effects of, 170
    Olympics and, 421, 426
Texas
    compulsory treatment in, 322
    corporate gift-giving in, 411
    drug testing of school athletes in, 289
    kickbacks to doctors, 411
    marijuana offenders in, 23, 443
    minimum legal drinking age in, 371
    race and application of drug laws, 449–450
    school-based drug policy in, 283–286
    school drug testing, 289, 290
Thailand, minimum drinking age and, 373
Thalidomide, 393, 397
Tharp, V., 382
THC
    anandamide and, 151
    brain and, 151
    definition of, 530

levels of marijuana, 17–18
   of cannabis plant, 149–150
   study using monkeys, 24
   synthetic, 473
Theory, 45. *See also* Drug use theories
Therapeutic communities (TCs), xix, 318–321
Therapeutic jurisdiction, 325
Therapeutic ratio, 117, 530
The Strange Case of Dr. Jekyll and Mr. Hyde
      (Stephenson), 98
THG (steroid), 424, 429
Thimerosal, 410
Thomas, G., 508
Thombs, D. L., 94
Thornberry, T., 66, 77
Thornton, M., 368
Thoumi, F., 188
Time magazine, 14
Toad licking, 145, 146, 530
Toad smoking, 145, 146, 530
Tobacco
   benefits of, 97
   carcinogens from, 95
   deaths from, 2, 22, 84, 97
   demonization of, 352
   drug antagonists and, 315
   effects of, 95–97
   history of, 94–95
   Internet purchases of, 359–360
   nicotine replacement therapy, 86, 305–306
   propaganda about, 266
   regulation history, 94–95, 351–352
   regulation of, xxi, 363, 364, 365
   use by age, 228, 352
   use by Asians/Pacific Islanders, 252
   use by gender, 239–240 (figure)
   use by location, 258, 262
   use by race/ethnicity, 243, 252
   use by social class, 254, 358
   use statistics, 1, 96 (figure)
Tobacco companies
   cigarette smuggling by, 360–361
   lawsuits, 356, 360–361
   promotional spending by, 356–357
   tobacco settlement of 1998 and, 361–362
Tobacco policies, x, 351–365, 387
   advertising/marketing restrictions, 356–357
   ban on smoking in public places, 352–355
   future of, 363–365
   history of tobacco regulation, 351–352
   international tobacco legislation, 362–363
   taxes on tobacco products, 96, 357–361, 387
   tobacco settlement of 1998, 361–362
Tobacco settlement of 1998, 361–362
Tolerance, 85, 87, 530
Tompkins, C., 312

Tonigan, J. S., 341
Topirimate, 314
Toronto Star, 402
Toth, K., 424
Tour de France, 167, 425–426
Toxicity, 174, 530
Tracking Violent Crime bill, 512
Traffic fatalities/accidents
   alcohol-related traffic fatalities, 114, 380–381
   dangerous driving-related behaviors, 383–385
   drunk driving policies and, 380–381
   minimum legal drinking age and, 371
Trafficking
   drug-producing countries, U.S. influence/
      intervention in, 514–521
   drug tax laws, 462–466
   mandatory minimum sentences for, 456,
      457–458
   of cocaine, 448
   of ecstasy, 448
   of heroin, 26, 448
   of methamphetamine, 448
   RAVE Act and, 466–467, 485, 502
   state drug laws, recent changes in, 481
   terrorism and, 278–279, 280
   See also Drug trade
Trajectory, 68
Transitions, 68
Treasury Department, 477
Treatment. *See* Drug treatment
Trenbalone, 424
Tricyclics, 158
Truly disadvantaged, 209
Trussell, J., 397
Truth drug, 26, 109
Truth in Sentencing Act, 512
Tulia, Texas, 290, 449–450
Turkey, minimum-age drinking laws in, 373
Turner, C., 14
Twelve-step facilities (TSF), 342
   See also Alcoholics Anonymous
Twenty-First Amendment, 369
Twin studies, 49
Tylenol, 276, 284
Tylenol #3, 128, 530

Underreporting
   by minorities, 179, 180, 205
   definition of, 530
   in self-report surveys, 179–180
   in survey research on drug use, 184, 185
Unemployment, 215, 219, 251
Uniform Drinking Age Act, 371
United Kingdom (UK). *See* Britain
United Nations Convention on Narcotic
      Drugs, 488

United Nations Drug Report, 510
United Nations drug use survey, 187
United Nations Interregional Institute, 489
United Nations Office on Drugs and Crime
    (UNODC), 1–2, 488, 496
United States (U.S.)
    alcohol use by state, 260 (figure), 261 (figure)
    drug law reform, need for, xiv–xv
    drug use statistics, 1
    illegal drug use over lifetime, 20 (table)
    prescription narcotic consumption in global
        context, 235
    reaction to Canadian drug policy, 508–512
United States Naval Research Laboratory, 296
United States Sentencing Commission, 454–455
United States v. Brigham, 456
University of Pennsylvania, 280, 281
UNODC (United Nations Office on Drugs and
    Crime), 1–2, 488, 496
Upjohn, 409
Urinalysis
    ADAM data, 189
    drug courts and, 326, 328, 329, 346
    drug testing in schools, 287, 288, 289
    drug testing of workers, 292
    for performance-enhancing drugs, 287, 416
    fraud and, 295–296
Uruguay, 490
U.S. Anti-Doping Agency (USADA),
    421, 424, 426
USA Today, 33, 35
U.S. Census Bureau, 34
U.S. Chess Federation, 424
U.S. Coast Guard, 463–464
U.S. Customs Service, 26, 27
U.S. House of Representatives, 407, 445,
    509–510
U.S. military
    drug testing in, 291
    LSD and, 136
    morphine and, 123
    substance abuse in, 229
U.S. National Commission on Marijuana and
    Drug Abuse, 138–139
U.S. National Household Survey on Drug
    Abuse, 19, 20, 32, 207 (table), 372–373
U.S. National Institute on Alcohol Abuse and
    Alcoholism, 337
U.S. Olympic Committee, 418–419
U.S. Shafer Commission Report, 24
U.S. Supreme Court
    drug testing in schools and, 287–288
    illegal searches and, 284
    medical marijuana laws and, 475
    on public housing evictions, 459–460
U.S. Surgeon General, 114, 215, 268, 356, 363

Utah, 260, 352, 370
"UV Light Tanning as a Type of Substance-
    Related Disorder" (Warthan, Uchida, &
    Wagner), 55
Uzbekistan, 492

Vaillant, G. G., 339
Valium (diazepam)
    barbiturates and, 116–117
    effects of, 117, 118
    gender and use of, 117
Vancouver, BC, 377
Van Hook, S., 291
Vaugh, W., 95
Vega, W., 214
Veilleux, J. C., 307–308
Venereal disease, 162
Venezuela, 373, 515–516, 518
Verducci, T., 431
Verispan, 410
Vermont, 366, 411
Vernonia School District v. Acton, 287
Veterinary anesthetic, 147
Viagra, xii, 161, 162, 406
Vicodin, 128, 258, 445
Victimless crimes, 74
Victoria (England), 7, 100
Video gaming, 53
Vietnam, 491–492
Vietnamese, 216, 217, 218
Vietnamese-Americans, 252
Vine-Go, 366
Violence
    drug-related killings in Mexico, 518–519
    drug trade and, 75–76,
    marijuana and, 15–16
    PCP and, 148
Vioxx (Rofecoxib), 391, 399–400, 412
Virginia
    alcohol regulation and, 369
    school class searches, 286
    school drug testing, 289
    school suspensions in, 284, 285
    tobacco regulation and, 351, 354, 358
    tobacco settlement funds and, 361–362
Viropause, 163
Volatile solvents, 7, 119, 121
Volkow, Nora, 41
Volstead Act, 366–369, 387
Vomiting, 114, 122, 144
Voodoo pharmacy, 3
Vrjman, E., 423

WADA (World Anti-Doping Agency), 289,
    420, 421, 423, 427, 431
Wadler, G., 289, 431

Wagner, E., 214
Wales, 91, 186, 187, 500, 501
Walitzer, K. S., 336
Walk and turn test, 381, 382, 389
Wallace, J., 205, 206, 208, 215, 248
Wall Street Journal, 375, 426
Walsh, J. T., 7–8
Walters, J., xiii, 15, 17, 21, 23, 279, 281–282, 287, 347, 446, 471, 473–474, 481, 508–509, 510–512
Walters, M., 172
Walton, S., 358–359, 368, 376–377
Warheit, G., 213
Warner, B., 222
Warner-Lambert, 397, 398, 409
War on Drugs/war on drugs
    arrests/incarcerations for drug offenses, 441
    as war on marijuana, 15, 279, 477
    drug treatment and, 317, 323
    ending of, 348, 476
    international drug policies, 279, 494, 506, 518, 521, 522
    justice system and, 440, 441
    justification of, 3
    need for drug law reform, xiv–xv
    racial/class-based inequality in drug laws, 446, 447, 450
    refugees in Canada, 506
Washington, D.C., 358, 378, 459, 460, 463, 472
Washington, G., 7
Washington Post, 15, 21, 24, 396
Washington state
    anti-tobacco legislation in, 353
    asset seizure in, 465
    bath salts use in, 42
    cigarette giveaways and, 357
    drug law changes in, 481
    drug treatment in, 327
    DUI offenders in, 379–380
    legalization of marijuana and, 478–480
    medical marijuana and, 476
    methamphetamine in, 32, 33, 34–35, 36
    minimum legal drinking age in, 371, 375
    smoking ban in, 354–355
    smoking restrictions for workers, 355
    spending on tobacco prevention programs, 361
    tobacco advertising in, 361
    tobacco taxes in, 359
Washington State Institute for Public Policy, 327
Washington State University, 375
Wasson, G., 139–140
Watts, J. C., 483
WCTU (Women's Christian Temperance Union), 266, 366

Weapons, 23, 36–37, 283, 286, 513, 519, 520
Wechsler, H., 376
Weight loss, 104
Weil, A., 2, 14–15, 46–47, 90, 126, 137, 146, 147, 148, 151, 269, 271
Weiner, R., 423
Welfare
    denial of, 460–461
    drug testing recipients, 294
Welte, J., 208
West, ? [This person is not in the reference list], 334
West Virginia, 289, 369, 409
White, R., 508
White, W., 341
Whites
    crack baby legislation and, 452
    crack cocaine use by, 75
    illegal drug use by, 177, 204
    legal drug use by, 243–244, 245
    mandatory minimum sentences and, 455
    racial/class-based inequality in drug laws, 74
    school zone policies and, 458
    social class and illegal drug use, 218
    social class and legal drug use, 251–257
    social conflict theory and, 74
    strain theory and, 71–72, 78
Whizzinator product, 295
WHO. *See* World Health Organization
Willebrandt, M., 368
Williams, L., 416, 431
Williams, P., 444
Williams, T., 354, 356
William S. Merrell Company, 397
Willman, D., 411–412
Wilson, B., 52–53, 54, 332, 333, 339
Wilson, J. (Big Moon), 142
Wilson, W., 366
Wilson, W. J., 72, 209
Wine
    coca leaves and, 18
    consumption of, 18
    effects of, 112–113
    health benefits of, 115
    historical use of, 112
    label warnings and, 114
    prohibition and, 366, 367
    regulation of, 369
    sacramental, 367
Winfrey, O., 426
Winstanley, E. L., 219–220
Winter, T., 41
Wisconsin, 401, 411
Withdrawal
    antidepressants and, 158–159
    buprenorphine treatment and, 309–311

definition of, 87, 530
depressants and, 112, 114, 174, 314
from antidepressant drugs, 159
from benzodiazepine, 118
from caffeine, 91
from cocaine, 24, 102
from ecstasy, 111
from heroin, 126, 127
from opiates, 123, 304, 306, 307, 309
from video gaming, 53
marijuana and, 316
misinformation about, 33
Wolfe, S., 435
Women
abuse of pharmaceuticals by, 203
contraception regulation and, 396–397, 453
crack baby legislation, 450–452
C.R.A.C.K. program and, 453
illegal drug use, 177, 199–203
legal drug use, 237–241, 238 (table), 248
masculinizing effect of steroids on, 170
morphine use by, 123
prescription sex drugs for, 162–163
smoking ban and, 352
social stigma against drug use and, 201
See also Gender
Wo/men's Alliance for Medical Marijuana, 475
Women's Christian Temperance Union
(WCTU), 266, 366
Wood, A., 123
Wood, S., 396–397
Wood alcohol poisoning, 367
Woodcock, J., 400–401
Workers
drug testing of, xix, 291–297, 299
smoking restrictions for, 352, 355
World Anti-Doping Agency (WADA), 289, 420,
421, 423, 427, 431
World Chess Federation, 424
World Drug Report, 187–188
World Federation Against Drugs, 347
World Federation of Bridge, 424
World Health Organization (WHO)
cocaine study, 102, 489
on tobacco-related deaths, 97
smoking restrictions for workers, 355
World Health Organization (WHO) Program
on Substance Abuse, 24, 102
World War II, 103, 306
Wright, J., 421
Wright, N., 312
Wright, P., 293
Wu, F. C. W., 163
Wyeth, 163, 395
Wyoming, 369, 370, 371
Wysong, E., 268, 269, 271

Xanax (alprazolam), 118
Xenova, 3

Yamaguchi, R., 289, 290
Yesalis, C., 417, 421, 432
Young, F., 155
Young, F. L., 472
Young, J., 420
Young adults. See Students; Youth
Youth Risk Behavior Survey (YRBS), 183
Youths
alcohol, minimum legal drinking age, 372
antidepressant drugs and suicidality, 160
antidrug advertising campaigns and, 276–283
college campus drinking regulations,
374–377
D.A.R.E. program and, 266–273
drug use prevention and, xviii–xix
ecstasy use of, 26–27
energy drinks and, 92
glue-sniffing by, 5–6
illegal drug use and age, 177, 196–197
inhalants used by, 120–121
legal drug use and race, 245, 251
marijuana and drug treatment, 16
marijuana as gateway drug and, 11–12,
18–19, 152
methamphetamine use by, 34
problem behavior theory and, xvii, 46,
57–58, 77
Ritalin, effects of, 108–109, 234, 424
salvia and, 144
school zone policies, 458–459
self-derogation model and, xvi–xvii, 76–77
self-report surveys of illegal drug use,
181 (table)–185
social bonding theory and, xvii, 77
spice use by, 156
surveys on drug use, 26, 183–184
tobacco advertising and, 356, 357
tobacco and, 243 (table)
tobacco taxes and, 358
zero tolerance policies and, xviii–xix,
283–286
See also Adolescents; Children

Zayas, L., 213
Zero-tolerance policies, xviii–xix, 283–286,
375, 378
Zimmer, L., 17, 19, 23, 473
Zimring, F., 3–4
Zoladex, 408
Zoloft, 157, 158, 395
Zweibel, J. [spelled Zwiebel in references], 368
Zyprexa, 409
Zytec, 405

About the Authors

Clayton Mosher received his Ph.D. in Sociology from the University of Toronto, and is currently a Professor in the Department of Sociology at Washington State University Vancouver. He is the author of several books and articles in the areas of inequality in criminal justice system processing, drugs and drug policies, and the impact of prison construction on employment. Besides co-authoring the Second Edition of *Drugs and Drug Policy*, he co-authored the Second Edition of *The Mismeasure of Crime* (SAGE, 2012) with Terance Miethe and Timothy Hart. In 2013, he was the recipient of Washington State University's Sahlin Award for Faculty Excellence in Outreach and Engagement.

Scott Akins received his Ph.D. in Sociology from Washington State University, and is currently Associate Professor of Sociology in the School of Public Policy at Oregon State University. His research interests include drug use and policy; immigration/acculturation, drug use and deviance; and the intersection of disadvantage, ethnicity, and crime. His recent work has been published in *Sociological Perspectives*, *Journal of Drug Issues*, and *Homicide Studies*.

$SAGE researchmethods

The essential online tool for researchers from the world's leading methods publisher

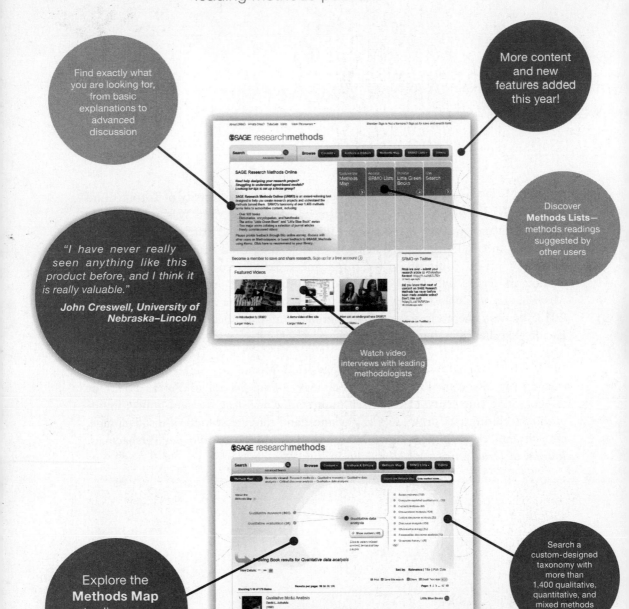

Find exactly what you are looking for, from basic explanations to advanced discussion

More content and new features added this year!

Discover **Methods Lists**—methods readings suggested by other users

"I have never really seen anything like this product before, and I think it is really valuable."

John Creswell, University of Nebraska–Lincoln

Watch video interviews with leading methodologists

Explore the **Methods Map** to discover links between methods

Search a custom-designed taxonomy with more than 1,400 qualitative, quantitative, and mixed methods terms

Uncover more than 120,000 pages of book, journal, and reference content to support your learning

Find out more at
www.sageresearchmethods.com